Handbook on Evolution and Society

HANDBOOK ON EVOLUTION AND SOCIETY

Toward an Evolutionary Social Science

Edited by

Jonathan H. Turner
Richard Machalek
Alexandra Maryanski

Paradigm Publishers
Boulder • London

All rights reserved. No part of the publication may be transmitted or reproduced in any media or form, including electronic, mechanical, photocopy, recording, or informational storage and retrieval systems, without the express written consent of the publisher.

Copyright © 2015 by Paradigm Publishers

Published in the United States by Paradigm Publishers, 5589 Arapahoe Avenue, Boulder, CO 80303 USA.

Paradigm Publishers is the trade name of Birkenkamp & Company, LLC,
Dean Birkenkamp, President and Publisher.

Library of Congress Cataloging-in-Publication Data

Handbook on evolution and society : toward an evolutionary social science / edited by Jonathan H. Turner, Richard Machalek, Alexandra Maryanski.
    pages cm. — (Paradigm handbooks)
  Includes bibliographical references and index.
  ISBN 978-1-61205-814-6 (hardcover : alk. paper) — ISBN 978-1-61205-815-3 (library ebook)
  1. Historical sociology. 2. Social sciences. I. Turner, Jonathan H., editor. II. Machalek, Richard, 1946– editor. III. Maryanski, Alexandra, editor.
  HM487.H354 2014
  300—dc23
                                                                              2014027717

Printed and bound in the United States of America on acid-free paper that meets the standards of the American National Standard for Permanence of Paper for Printed Library Materials.

Contents

List of Figures and Tables — viii
Editors' Introduction — xi

Part One: General Issues in Evolutionary Analysis in the Social Sciences

1. Neo-Darwinian Evolutionary Theory and Sociology: Throwing a New Light on an Old Path — 2
   Richard Machalek and Michael W. Martin
2. The Biological Character of Social Theory — 31
   Alexander Rosenberg
3. Modes of Variation and Their Implications for an Extended Evolutionary Synthesis — 59
   Marion Blute
4. Evolutionary Transitions in Individuality and Selection in Societal Evolution — 76
   Matthew B. Dunn
5. The Prospects and Limitations of Evolutionary Theorizing in the Social Sciences — 92
   Jonathan H. Turner and Alexandra Maryanski

Part Two: Sociobiology and Evolutionary Psychology

6. Yanomamö: The Sociobiology People — 114
   Napoleon A. Chagnon and Shane J. Macfarlan
7. Sociobiology at Work in Modern Populations — 122
   Rosemary L. Hopcroft
8. Evolutionary Psychology and Its Relevance to the Social Sciences — 136
   Satoshi Kanazawa
9. Where Do We Stand with Respect to Evolutionary Studies of Human Behavior? — 157
   John Alcock
10. The Evolution of the Social Mind: The Limitations of Evolutionary Psychology — 177
    Jonathan H. Turner

Part Three: Evolutionary Sociology

11. Evolutionary Sociology — 194
    W. G. Runciman

12	Spencer's Conception of Evolution and Its Application to the Political Development of Societies *Robert L. Carneiro*	215
13	Darwinian Conflict Theory: A Unified Evolutionary Research Program *Stephen K. Sanderson*	228
14	The Sociocultural Evolution of World-Systems *Christopher Chase-Dunn*	267
15	The Evolution of the Human Brain *David D. Franks*	285
16	The Human Behavioral Ecology of Foragers *Robert L. Kelly*	295
17	Evolving Communities: Evolutionary Analysis in Classical and Neoclassical Human Ecology *Michael D. Irwin*	316
18	Organizational Ecology: Darwinian and Non-Darwinian Dynamics *Jonathan H. Turner*	333

Part Four: Sex, Gender, and Mating

19	Marry In or Die Out: Optimal Inbreeding and the Meaning of Mediogamy *Robin Fox*	350
20	On the Origins of Gender Inequality *Joan Huber*	383
21	The Evolution of Tenuous Pair Bonding in Humans: A Plausible Pathway and Indicators of Design *Timothy Crippen*	402

Part Five: Cooperation, Hierarchy, and Social Control

22	The Evolution of Social Control *Christopher Boehm*	424
23	Human Cooperation: Evolutionary Approaches to a Complex Phenomenon *Lee Cronk*	441
24	When and Why Power Corrupts: An Evolutionary Perspective *Charleen R. Case and Jon K. Maner*	460
25	Biosociology of Dominance and Deference *Allan Mazur*	474
26	Intergroup Threat and Extralegal Police Aggression: An Evolutionary Interpretation *Malcolm D. Holmes*	493

Part Six: From Primate Legacies to Future Directions

27	A Salience Theory of Learning and Behavior and Rights of Apes *Duane M. Rumbaugh*	514
28	Language Use among Apes: Audio-Visual Archival Documentaries for Ape Language and Cognition *Ken Schweller*	537

29 Evolutionary Sociology: A Cross-Species Strategy for Discovering
    Human Nature
        Jonathan H. Turner and Alexandra Maryanski   546
30 Evolved Human Sociality and Literature
        Joseph Carroll   572
31 Contrast Effects in Social Evolution and Schumpeter's Creative Destruction
        Michael Hammond   609

Index   629
About the Contributors   649

Figures and Tables

Figures

5.1	Levels of social reality	101
5.2	Sociocultural embedding as survivor machines	105
7.1	Predicted number of biological children by sex and income, United States (1994)	126
7.2	Predicted number of offspring by sex, income, and education, Sweden	127
7.3	Predicted number of children by sex, education, and income, from OLS regression, United Kingdom	127
7.4	Predicted lifetime reproductive success by sex, income, and education, all Europeans	128
8.1	Basic theoretical structure of evolutionary psychology	141
8.2	The Coleman Boat (micro-macro model)	147
8.3	Reproductive motives behind suicide bombing	149
8.4	Determinants of marriage institution	152
14.1	The iteration model of sociocultural evolution of world-systems	271
14.2	Waves of colonization and decolonization since 1400, number of colonies established and number of decolonizations	274
14.3	Trade globalization, 1820–2012 imports/GDP	276
16.1	A graphic representation of how a hypothetical diet changes with decreases in high-ranked resources	299
16.2	Graphic representation of the marginal value theorem	300
16.3	Ideal-free distribution	302
16.4	A model of technological change, showing a hypothetical relationship between spear and gill net fishing return rates	303
16.5	The economic defensibility model	306
16.6	The Winterhalder model of sharing relations between individual foragers translated into relations between groups of foragers	307
16.7	Relationship between foraging-group size and per capita return rate	308
16.8	One potential utility function describing the relationship between the utility of resources and amounts of that resource	312
18.1	The basic Darwinian dynamic in organizational ecology	334
18.2	The elaborated Darwinian dynamic in organizational ecology	337
18.3	McPherson's ecological model of organizational ecology in Blau-space	340

18.4	Layers of embedding of generic sociocultural formations and the changing nature of selection processes operating	344
19.1	The kinship atom	356
19.2	Sister exchange and double cross-cousin marriage	357
19.3	Father's brother's daughter (FBD) marriage	358
19.4	Kinship and fertility of human couples in Iceland, 1888–1965	367
19.5	Simplified genealogy of the Ptolomies	368
19.6	Fruit fly population rise and fall over two years	369
19.7	Curves of the relationship between fertility (pgr) and population growth (N) in 1,400 species	370
19.8	Long House Valley population, 800–1300 AD	371
19.9	Related sperm combine to compete in deer mice ovarian tract	372
19.10	TraA mediated cell-cell interactions and myxobacteria social behavior	374
19.11	Idealized Ayllu kinship charter	377
19.12	Schematic illustration of moiety fission in the Ayllu	377
19.13	Declining world fertility	378
25.1	Cartoon expressions of dominance and deference	477
25.2	Men of varying facial dominance who became high-ranked generals, shown as cadets and in late career	478
25.3	Each morphed portrait combines seven cadet portraits. Which one looks more like a leader?	479
25.4	Waveform of a male student during about twenty-five minutes of casual conversation with a previously unknown professor	488
25.5	Waveform of a male student during about forty seconds	490
26.1	Predicted number of sustained citizen complaints by black dissimilarity quintile	507
27.1	Salience theory embraces instinct, respondent and operant conditioning, and emergent behaviors	515
27.2	A rhesus trained to use his foot uses his hand instead when given a choice	519
27.3	A lowland gorilla strikes a significant emergent gait	520
27.4	Gabby using her rope in innovative, emergent ways	522
27.5	By holding both ends of her rope, Gabby is able to swing in a wide, graceful arc	523
27.6	A gibbon brachiates from one tree to another	523
27.7	Article in *Time* magazine about Lana's language accomplishments	527
27.8	Lana at her keyboard	528
27.9	Lana and her second infant Mercury	528
27.10	The effects of early rearing on cognitive competencies	530
27.11	Kanzi has become a skilled flint knapper	531
27.12	After a hard day of play and fun, Kanzi walks bipedally as though on his way home	535
28.1	Recursive sentence produced by Lana	539
28.2	Lana keyboard simulator	540

28.3	A close-up of one of the first panels on which Lana worked	540
28.4	Online simulation of Lana's lab	541
28.5	NuMath	541
28.6	Sherman and Austin	542
28.7	Current lexigram keyboard, panel 1	543
28.8	Lexigram keyboard in an online virtual environment	543
28.9	New lexigram keyboard	544
28.10	Lexigram keyboard for mobile apps	544
28.11	Bonobo facility at the Ape Cognition and Conservation Initiative	545

Tables

7.1	Studies showing a positive relationship between male status and number of surviving offspring	124
9.1	A summary of the major criticisms leveled against EHB, followed by rebuttals to these criticisms	169
14.1	Similarities and differences between sociocultural and biological evolution	270
21.1	Select aspects of the socioecology and mating strategies of the lesser and great apes	405
22.1	Capital punishment in fifty LPA foraging societies	430
22.2	Methods of social suppression	432
22.3	Social predators	434
29.1	Strength of social ties among extant species of great apes	548
29.2	Relative size of brain components of apes and humans, compared with *Tenrecinae*	560
29.3	Variants of primary emotions	562
29.4	Combinations of primary emotions	563
29.5	The structure of shame and guilt	563

Editors' Introduction

Jonathan Turner, Richard Machalek, and Alexandra Maryanski

Evolutionary thinking boasts an old pedigree in the social sciences. A number of historians of evolutionary thought have noted, for example, that Darwin acknowledged an indebtedness to the social philosopher and sociologist Herbert Spencer for the very expression "the survival of the fittest." However, early evolutionary thought in the social sciences suffered serious scientific deficiencies by contemporary standards, and it also often was sullied by ideological agendas, most famously, social Darwinism. Thus, by the first third or so of the twentieth century, evolutionary theory waned in the social sciences and was replaced by one or another strain of cultural determinism.

This trend underwent a reversal, however, during the second half of the twentieth century, especially after 1975 when the evolutionary biologist Edward O. Wilson published his massive volume, *Sociobiology: The New Synthesis*. Wilson's book, and sociobiology in general, was met with an alarmist response by many social and behavioral scientists, and charges of biological reductionism, genetic determinism, and ideological agendas were leveled at Wilson and others who were interested in and receptive to his "new synthesis." Now, almost four decades after Wilson published his opus, things have begun to change. Many of the concerns, both analytical and ideological, of critics of applying evolutionary thinking to the study of human social behavior have been allayed, and evolutionary thinking has gained traction and momentum in a number of the behavioral and social sciences, including psychology, anthropology, political science, economics, and sociology. Even within sociology, perhaps the social science that raised the most strident objections to Wilson's work, evolutionary analysis has gained a new foothold. In fact, recently, a small (but enthusiastic!) group of sociologists established a section called "Evolution, Biology, and Society" within the American Sociological Association (ASA), which sponsors sessions at the ASA meetings, a newsletter, and awards for outstanding papers and books featuring biological approaches to human social behavior. Evolutionary analysis has proliferated even more rapidly in anthropology and psychology, and inroads have also been established in economics and political science. In fact, as the readers of this volume will learn, evolutionary ideas have even been adopted in some analyses by scholars in the humanities, such as literary analysis.

The three editors converged on an interest in evolutionary thinking by different pathways. It was perhaps inevitable that Turner, a general sociological theorist with wide-ranging interests, would eventually have investigated and assessed the reemergence of evolutionary thinking in the social and behavioral sciences. It is not surprising that evolutionary theory in general and a realization of the value of cladistic analysis for shedding light on human social origins would have inspired Maryanski, a student of both human social behavior and primatology, to help found and establish what is now known as "evolutionary sociology." And a fascination with biology that predated his college years persisted and eventually prompted Machalek to find a way to incorporate his interests in nonhuman social species into his work as a sociologist. After deciding that the time was right to invite a broad range of scientists and scholars to contribute to a volume in which each would provide an example of how he or she has used evolutionary thinking in his or her own work, Turner and Maryanski invited Machalek to join them as a coeditor in this venture, and he enthusiastically agreed.

The chapters in this volume are all original contributions that we solicited from our peer evolutionary social and behavioral thinkers. The volume is organized on the basis of six parts. Part One, "General Issues in Evolutionary Analysis in the Social Sciences," provides a broad introduction to efforts to bring biology in general and evolutionary theory in particular to bear on analyses of human social behavior and society. It provides an orientation to what is entailed by using evolutionary biology to study *Homo sapiens*, a general assessment of the potential inherent in such a venture, and pitfalls that confront anybody engaged in trying to add a biological dimension to social science analyses. It also addresses the important processes of variation and selection in the evolution of human societies, issues that are central to evolutionary analysis.

Part Two, "Sociobiology and Evolutionary Psychology," contains a chapter about some of the earliest work that entailed applying sociobiology to an empirical study of humans, the Yanomamö, an indigenous population in South America. Part Two also contains a chapter on how sociobiology can be applied to studying modern human populations as well. The evolution of the human mind has become a thriving enterprise in evolutionary psychology and the social sciences, and Part Two provides an overview and assessment of what is entailed in trying to explain the role of the human mind in social behavior, as well as limitations that inhere in such efforts.

As sociologists, we are pleased to report that evolutionary thinking has established itself to the extent that it is now surprisingly easy to find a growing number of our peer sociologists engaged in evolutionary studies of human society and social behavior. Part Three, "Evolutionary Sociology," begins with a chapter that provides an overview of issues involved in integrating an evolutionary perspective into sociology. The following chapter reviews the work of Herbert Spencer, an early pioneer of evolutionary thinking in sociology, a novel integration of conflict theory in sociology with Darwinian evolutionary theory. There is also a chapter on the evolution of world systems, or intersocietal systems, which has grown as a subfield in sociology and the social sciences more generally. Returning to an old theme but with a Darwinian approach, there is a sociological analysis of the evolution of the human brain and how it contributes to the production of human social behavior. Reflecting sociology's long-standing tradition of developing ecological analyses of human societies and social behavior, Part Three contains chapters on the value of new strains of ecological thinking for social analysis. A chapter on how behavioral ecology enhances anthropological analyses of foraging peoples and another that reviews the history of evolutionary analysis in classical and neoclassical human ecology illustrate how social science has been reinvigorated by ecological approaches.

The biology of human reproduction and mating systems is central to any evolutionary approach to human social behavior, and Part Four, "Sex, Gender, and Mating," provides examples of how social scientists are now using insights derived from what has been called the "second Darwinian revolution" to advance our understanding of these topics. One chapter provides a highly original perspective on the topic of the respective costs and benefits of selecting a mate to whom one is very closely biologically related versus choosing a mate from among individuals to whom one is distantly related. The conclusion of this chapter will almost certainly come as something of a surprise to many social and behavioral scientists. A second chapter traces the origins and development of gender inequality among humans to a basic fact about the biology of reproduction among humans: females lactate, and males don't. Finally, Part Four concludes with an analysis of pair bonding in humans, a phenomenon that is often taken as a given by many social and behavioral scientist but, in fact, has evolved by means of a much more complex pathway than has been commonly recognized.

Part Five, "Cooperation, Hierarchy, and Social Control," addresses topics that are fundamental not only to evolutionary social science but to the social sciences in general. What has long been characterized as the "problem of order" in the social sciences can be recast as the "problem of cooperation" by adopting an evolutionary perspective. Research on the evolution of cooperation makes up a significant part of the new evolutionary social science literature, and this section contains a chapter that reviews and evaluates a significant part of that literature. Cooperation and social order often depend on the existence and exercise of mechanisms of social control for regulating conflict and deviance, and one chapter in this section uses an evolutionary approach to analyze conflict and aggression between police officers and putative offenders. Another social science concept that is indispensable in any discussions of social order and conflict is power. Two chapters in this section address the issues of power and hierarchy directly. One employs an evolutionary psychological perspective to account for the apparent ubiquity of the tendency of power to corrupt, and the second examines relations of dominance and deference among both human and nonhuman social species. All of the chapters in Part Five shed new light on the evolutionary origins and dynamics of cooperation, social hierarchy, and social control.

Part Six, "From Primate Legacies to Future Directions," opens with three chapters emphasizing how important the study of primates is to understanding hominin ancestors of humans. The behavioral capacities of apes—from their facility with language to a wide range of behavior propensities for reading gestures, imitating emotions, empathy and role taking, rhythmic synchronization of communication, weak-tie formations, low-level group formation, collective emotional effervescence, reciprocity, calculations of fairness and justice in exchanges, seeing themselves as objects, and concerns with relative status—give us clues to biological dispositions of the ancestors of human and, hence, humans today.

By studying extant great apes, as well as other primates, we have a distant mirror to see what our primate ancestors were like. Two chapters in this section are devoted to language acquisition and use in great apes and to outlining an extended bibliography on studies of language in apes that can be used in evolutionary analysis. These chapters are followed by a cladistic analysis of extant apes, coupled with an ecological analysis of their evolution and the implications of comparative anatomy on the brains of humans and apes. The final two chapters in Part Six demonstrate new and future directions for evolutionary analysis not only in the social sciences but in the humanities as well.

Finally, as broad as the coverage is in these chapters, we should emphasize that this volume does not examine all of the new evolutionary approaches in the social sciences. We began with commitments from important scholars in these areas not covered, but as is inevitable in a project this large and involving over thirty people from diverse fields, we lost some along the way, and, hence, their potential contribution to expanding the coverage was not included in this volume. If there is a volume 2 of this project, we will be sure to capture authors to fill in what we could not cover here, such as chapters on coevolution, agent-based modeling, contemporary stage models of societal evolution, more neurology, and several other evolutionary approaches in the social sciences.

Jonathan Turner
Richard Machalek
Alexandra Maryanski

ONE
GENERAL ISSUES IN EVOLUTIONARY ANALYSIS IN THE SOCIAL SCIENCES

Chapter One
Neo-Darwinian Evolutionary Theory and Sociology
Throwing New Light on an Old Path
Richard Machalek and Michael W. Martin

> After decades during which sociology largely ignored biology, the publication of Wilson's *Sociobiology: The New Synthesis* (1975) prompted a small, but now growing, number of sociologists to explore the possible value of incorporating contemporary evolutionary thinking into sociology. The result was the emergence of a new *evolutionary sociology* built on the platform of neo-Darwinian evolutionary theory. Rejecting the tabula rasa assumption about the human mind, evolutionary social and behavioral scientists, including sociologists, are attempting to reconstruct the phylogeny of the human brain and mind in an effort to identify evolved adaptations that may influence human social behavior. Their work addresses several areas of human social life, including the bases and origins of gender inequality, the manner in which the human mind works in both archaic and novel social environments, and the interaction between biological and sociocultural factors in shaping human behavior. Additional topics of investigation include efforts to integrate neurological research into the study of human social behavior, the use of cladistics to reconstruct human nature, and the study of the distribution and functioning of generic forms of sociality across species lines. A promising area of future inquiry involves sociological reconstructions of elementary and archaic social forms that could have constituted selection forces that gave rise to evolved adaptations for coping with human social life.

Much light will be thrown on the origin of man and his history.
Charles Darwin

In the conclusion of *The Origin of Species*, Darwin predicts that the theory of evolution by natural selection will strengthen the foundation of psychology, which had been "already well laid by Mr. Herbert Spencer" (n.d.: 373). Spencer (1885), of course, helped lay a foundation not only for psychology but for a field with which he is now even more closely associated, sociology. However, despite Darwin's optimism, it was not until the last quarter of the twentieth century that the theory of evolution by natural selection began to illuminate a new, promising path of inquiry that would soon be followed by an emerging cadre of social and behavioral scientists. The new science that began to throw light on that path was *sociobiology*, the "systematic study of the biological basis of all social behavior" (Wilson 1975: 4).

Specifically, sociobiology entails using explanatory principles and empirical findings derived from evolutionary biology to describe and explain social behavior among animals, including humans. It also draws on and incorporates thinking and research in ecology, especially behavioral ecology. The contributions of biologists such as R. A. Fisher, W. D. Hamilton, Robert Trivers, and George Williams were foundational for the development and emergence of sociobiology, and that emergence culminated with the publication of *Sociobiology: The Modern Synthesis* by Edward O. Wilson in 1975. This chapter explores the impact of sociobiology on theory and research in sociology during the nearly four decades since the publication of Wilson's opus.

Wilson's book is a tome, stretching to twenty-seven chapters and 697 pages of text. Had it not been for the fact that the title and subject of Chapter 27 was "Man: From Sociobiology to Sociology," it might have been recorded in the annals of science as a magisterial synthesis of much of what was then known about the evolution of social behavior in animals, but its influence may not have extended much beyond a few other fields such as biological anthropology or comparative psychology. But by expanding the scope of his analysis to include humans, Wilson provoked one of the great intellectual and scientific debates of the late twentieth century and helped stimulate the development of entirely new programs of research in the social and behavioral sciences.

Today, much of the heat and shrillness of the "sociobiology debate" of the late 1970s and early 1980s has subsided, and the fears of critics that it would lead to a resurrection of social Darwinism or new strains of biological reductionism and genetic determinism have failed to materialize. Instead, the basic logic and the fundamental explanatory principles of sociobiology have contributed to the rise of new types of inquiry in the social and behavioral sciences, inquiries that are informed by contemporary thinking in evolutionary biology. The behavioral and social science literature now features both theoretical articles and empirical studies produced by scientists and scholars who call themselves Darwinian (or evolutionary) anthropologists, evolutionary psychologists, evolutionary economists, and even evolutionary sociologists.

Evolutionary biologists use the expression "the Modern Synthesis" to describe the integration of Darwinian evolutionary theory with Mendelian genetics. In the first few pages of *Sociobiology*, Wilson speculates about the possibility that sociology and the other social sciences as well as the humanities might eventually be included as part of the Modern Synthesis and thus become "truly biologicized" (1975: 4). Not surprisingly, these statements smacked of intellectual imperialism to some readers in the social sciences and humanities and caused them to view the emergence of sociobiology with suspicion and distrust (Segerstråle 2000). However, nearly four decades have passed since the publication of *Sociobiology*, and neither the social sciences nor the humanities have become cannibalized and absorbed by the Modern Synthesis. Rather, the incorporation of thinking stimulated by the Modern Synthesis has inspired new kinds of intellectual questions and prompted new types of inquiry within many of these fields. Central to these new types of biologically informed inquiries is the question of "human nature." For most of the twentieth century, the social sciences, sociology included, developed largely absent any conception of an evolved human nature. As "social constructionist" thinking gained ground in sociology with the popularization of the work of sociologists such as Berger and Luckmann (1967), any effort to incorporate systematic thinking about an evolved human nature into sociological analysis increasingly became viewed by most sociologists as ill-fated and doomed from the outset. In fact, to the extent that serious discussions about human nature appeared at all in the sociological literature, they were often dismissive in tone. Consider, for example, Berger and Luckmann's (1967) declaration that humans are born "biologically unfinished" and that anything resembling a human nature exists only as a social construction. Accordingly, sociologists came to regard the concept of human nature as largely vacuous in its relation to sociological analysis.

Recently, however, the notion that humans possess an evolved, universal, species-typical psychological nature has gained considerable traction among behavioral and social scientists whose work is informed by neo-Darwinian evolutionary theory. In fact, the search for an evolved human nature has become the foundation of the discipline that now calls itself "evolutionary psychology" (Buss 2012; Daly and Wilson 1988). Similarly, the human brain and mind has also become the subject of an expanding literature produced by a growing number of sociologists whose work has been influenced by evolutionary theory (Franks 2010; Kalkhoff, Thye, and Lawler 2012; Turner 2000; Turner and Maryanski 2008). This chapter introduces and discusses key issues addressed in recent efforts by sociologists, and some other social and behavioral scientists as well, to incorporate a conception of an evolved human nature into their analyses of human society and social behavior.

THE DEMISE OF TABULA RASA

During the late nineteenth and early twentieth centuries, certain strains of social thought such as social Darwinism propagated a crude and excessive *over*-"biologicization" of explanations of human society and social behavior. However, during the first half of the twentieth century, biological explanations of human social behavior came under relentless assault, and by the 1940s or so, the concept of culture had triumphed as the pivotal notion for explaining human society and social behavior (Degler 1991). At that point, most social scientists had rejected scientifically fraudulent biological explanations, many of which had been developed in an ill-fated effort to explain racial differences in social behavior, and had embraced, instead, a tabula rasa view of the human mind. As a result, they adopted an explanatory approach that attributed virtually all human social behavior to culture and individual learning, and most biological approaches to the study of human social behavior became exiled from the social sciences, including sociology. By the early 1960s, however, a "growing number of social scientists" had become willing to "take a hard second look at earlier decisions to extirpate biology and heredity from explanations for human behavior" (Degler 1991: 216). Then, just over a decade later, the publication of *Sociobiology* (1975) triggered alarm among many social and behavioral scientists who became concerned about the possibility of a resurgent, reductionist, biological determinist account of human social behavior and the possible loss of hard-earned explanatory ground based on the view of the human mind as nearly infinitely malleable (Pinker 2002). The idea of the human brain as a powerful information processing machine that is virtually devoid of any innate content that specifies social behaviors has dominated social and behavioral science thought for decades. In this way of thinking, cultures are often thought of as scripts, and the members of societies as actors who will execute whatever cultural script to which they are exposed. Sociologists will recognize this kind of thinking as characteristic of the dramaturgical school of sociological theory (Goffman 1959). From this point of view, any information that prescribes and generates human social behavior must be extra-somatic in origin, since the brain is thought to be empty of any content specifying social behavior. Thus, it was the explanatory centrality of individual learning and cultural transmission in most social scientists' outlooks to which the emergence of sociobiology posed the greatest threat.

In the early 1990s, this orthodoxy was summarized and codified by Tooby and Cosmides (1992) into what has become widely known as the Standard Social Science Model, or SSSM. The key tenets of the SSSM include objections that sociobiology neglects the role of the environment in shaping human behavior, is incapable of accounting for the extraordinary variation within and among social and cultural systems the world over, neglects the role of learning in human behavior, misrepresents human behavior as the direct product of genes, generally misattributes human social behavior to specific genes instead of culture and learning, and fails to acknowledge that the human mind is essentially a tabula rasa information processor that is devoid of any content that could prescribe overt social behaviors (Machalek and Martin 2004: 458; Tooby and Cosmides 1992). The SSSM has dominated the social sciences for most of the twentieth century and, in fact, still flourishes (Wilson 1998: 311).

Rejecting the tabula rasa, SSSM view of the human brain and mind, Tooby and Cosmides (1992) proposed that it be replaced with an alternative model based on evolutionary theory and research, which they came to call the "adapted mind." The evolutionary psychological notion of the adapted mind, preceded by and largely derived from sociobiology (Lumsden and Wilson 1981), was founded on the assumption that humans possess an array of behavioral "predispositions" that have evolved by natural selection and represent adaptations to life in ancestral human environments, now commonly called the "environment of evolutionary adaptedness," or the EEA (Bowlby 1969; Tooby and Cosmides 1990). These predispositions have been identified and labeled with various terms including "epigenetic rules" (Lumsden and Wilson 1981; Wilson 1998, 2012), "cognitive algorithms" (Tooby and Cosmides 1992), "behavioral propensities" (Turner 2015), and "behavioral predispositions" (Lopreato 1984; Lopreato and Crippen 1999). A casual, though potentially misleading, way of thinking about such predispositions to social behavior would be to call them "social instincts," the sum total of which are said to compose the adapted *social* mind. Those who subscribe to the SSSM effectively exempt themselves from having to consider the human brain as anything but a general, all-purpose information processing machine that mediates the influence of culture on human conduct and, thus, specifies and produces social behavior. However, social scientists receptive to the idea that humans are in possession of an *adapted* mind that is the product of organic evolution by natural selection find themselves having to address and come to grips with an array of new questions, two of which are foremost: (1) how is learning relevant to human social behavior, and (2) exactly how are evolved adaptations for social behavior instantiated in the human brain and manifested in human social behavior?

PREPARED LEARNING

The extent to which a heritable trait can vary under a range of environmental conditions and experiences is called the "norm of reaction," an important concept in evolutionary theory that acknowledges the dual contribution of genes and environments in producing phenotypes (Wilson 1998: 307). Some epigenetic rules manifest a narrow norm of reaction, which means that their expression will be minimally influenced by environmental variation. An example is what Pinker (1994) calls "the language instinct." Rooted in the work of Chomsky (1957) and his notion of a universal grammar, the language instinct implies that, save a limited number of very extreme conditions such as near-total social isolation, all humans will develop the ability to speak a language, a capability indicative of a trait that is subjected to a very narrow norm of reaction. The actual language that they learn (e.g., Spanish, Farsi, Greek), however, is not specified by their genotype, meaning that it develops under a very broad norm of reaction and is determined by the sociocultural environment to which they are exposed.

The operation of the norm of reaction is evident in the phenomenon that psychologists call "biased," or "prepared," or "directed" learning (Garcia and Koelling 1966; Rachman and Seligman 1976; Seligman 1971, 1993; Seligman and Hager 1972). Recall that, in the SSSM view, the human brain is a general, equipotential, all-purpose, information processing machine (Tooby and Cosmides 1992). That is, the brain is not predisposed to learn and retain certain contents over others. Rather, it is equally well equipped to develop, for example, a love or a fear of bunny rabbits or snakes, depending on the vagaries of individual experience or the particularities of cultural content and subsequent socialization. By way of contrast, the notion of prepared learning contends that the human brain is likely to be equipped with strong learning biases that reflect our ancestors' experiences of both threats and opportunities that were present in the EEA and were highly salient to their fitness outcomes (survival and reproductive chances). For example, venomous snakes have posed a serious threat to humans for millennia. Consequently, Wilson (1984, 1998: 79) contends that the human mind is probably well prepared to learn a fear of snakes. An indifference or inattentiveness to serpentine forms encountered in nature would have been fatal to many humans living in the EEA; accordingly, it is possible that humans evolved a cognitive algorithm that makes them highly alert to the presence of snakes and averse to close encounters with them. The natural fear of snakes can attain phobic proportions, and when it does, it is called "ophidiophobia" (Wilson 1998:79). Though fear of and aversion to snakes may not compose a totally unlearned behavioral predisposition, thereby qualifying for status as a true "instinct" in the traditional sense of the term, they likely represent a strong learning bias, meaning that through instruction, personal experience, or both, humans have a highly evolved "aptitude" for developing and retaining a strong fear of snakes. It is interesting to note that humans tend to develop phobias about natural threats (snakes, water, height, etc.) more easily than phobias about other, often more common and lethal threats encountered in the modern world, such as phobias about fast-moving vehicles, firearms, or electricity. Thus, ophidiophobia may be an extreme manifestation of an evolved cognitive algorithm (or epigenetic rule) that represents a learning bias that was highly adaptive for many ancestral humans in the EEA. However interesting the development of phobias about natural phenomena such as snakes, predators, heights, water, and so on, these forms of prepared learning and the behavioral predispositions to which they give rise are unlikely to be very relevant to most sociological analyses. Rather, sociobiological notions such as prepared learning, learning biases, behavioral predispositions, cognitive algorithms, and epigenetic rules are more likely to have sociological relevance when they are considered in relation to social interaction and social structure.

The Adapted Social Mind

Having abandoned a tabula rasa model of the human mind, social scientists whose thinking has become influenced by the evolutionary life sciences posit that the human mind is likely to be equipped with evolved adaptations for social life. That is, they are receptive to the idea that it is reasonable to expect that humans do not depend on culture alone in order to navigate group life successfully. Rather, they have become willing to entertain the possibility that built into the design of the human brain are sets of processes that were selected for because of the advantages they confer for coping with group life. These neural processes are the product of selection forces to which hominins have been subjected for millennia (Turner 2000, 2015). And though, as we shall see, evolutionary-minded social and behavioral scientists are not of one mind about how the social brain is organized and functions to produce social behavior, they all share the premise that careful, rigorous research will continue to reveal how the phylogeny of *Homo sapiens* provides clues about how the forces of natural selection produced a mind that is not totally devoid of innate content that generates social behavior, but rather a mind that has been equipped with evolved propensities for coping successfully with archaic, enduring, and fitness-relevant challenges posed by group living. We will review two approaches developed by social and behavioral scientists for framing inquiry into the evolution of the adapted human mind. The first, developed and advocated by two evolutionary psychologists, places primary emphasis on human *cognition* and pursues a research program designed to reveal how humans reason about various aspects of social life (Cosmides and Tooby 1992). The second, developed and advocated by two evolutionary sociologists, places primary emphasis on human *emotions* and pursues a research program designed to reveal how the evolution of social relationships among humans produced powerful emotional capabilities, the absence of which would have severely limited the evolution of human social behavior and society itself (Turner 2000; Turner and Maryanski 2005, 2008).

The Modular Brain Hypothesis

The study of reciprocity and exchange enjoys a long and venerable history in the social sciences in general, and in sociology in particular (Ekeh 1974; Lévi-Strauss 1969; Lopreato 2001; Smith [1776] 1805). The ability of members of a group to exchange resources is one of the most valuable and powerful forms of cooperation found in human social systems. However, processes of reciprocity and exchange are not limited to humans alone (Clutton-Brock 2009; Trivers 1971). When systems of reciprocity and exchange are *contractual* in nature, participants are subjected to an expectation, often in the form of a norm (or, in the case of nonhuman species, some other type of mechanism) that requires the recipient of a resource to repay his or her benefactor either simultaneously or in the future. The failure to reciprocate poses a threat to the stability of such a system, and it would be profoundly maladaptive for a benefactor to continue providing resources indefinitely to a recipient absent reciprocity by the recipient. In fact, when one organism successfully usurps resources (labor, material resources, information) from another organism without repaying its benefactor, evolutionary biologists describe the beneficiary as a social parasite and the benefactor as a host (Clutton-Brock 2009; Wilson 1975). The systematic and persistent failure to reciprocate in systems of social exchange can be conceptualized as an expression of social parasitism, and it can pose a serious threat to social order.

Viewed in evolutionary terms, exchange systems, including social contracts, present both potential opportunities and threats to their participants. By entering into an exchange relationship, an actor can gain access to resources that she or he might otherwise be denied. However, benefactors who provide resources to beneficiaries who fail to repay them are at risk of being exploited in precisely the same manner as that by means of which a parasite exploits a host. Thus, systems of cooperation based on reciprocity or exchange exhibit a dual nature: on the one hand, they can be extremely productive for all of their participants, but on the other hand, they can pose serious, even debilitating or lethal, threats to participants who are "cheated" by their putative exchange partners (Axelrod 1984). The failure of reciprocity, then, can constitute a selection force, because it poses a threat to resource donors who are not paid back, a threat that, in evolutionary terms, can be no less significant than predation, competition, or disease.

If anthropological accounts of ancestral human societies are accurate, systems of reciprocity and exchange appear to be diagnostic of foraging (hunting-gathering) societies (Kelly 1995: 164–181). Often, anthropologists emphasize the extent to which "sharing" is normative in such societies. A closer view of sharing in such societies typically reveals that sharing actually entails patterns of reciprocity, often delayed reciprocity. Among sociological exchange theorists, these types of behaviors are conceptualized with a variety of terms including indirect reciprocity, reciprocal exchange, univocal reciprocity, directional reciprocity, and generalized exchange (Ekeh 1974; Lévi-Strauss 1969; Lawler, Thye, and Yoon 2007; Molm, Collett, and Schaefer 2007). To the extent that the participants in such systems depend on the reliability of exchange partners from whom they receive resources that are vital for their survival and general well-being, it is critical that they not permit themselves to be systematically exploited by recurring incidents of nonreciprocity, or cheating. Systems of reciprocity and exchange acquire evolutionary significance when it can be said that they pose "adaptive challenges" to their participants, and, over time, natural selection can produce *adaptations* for coping with those challenges. An adaptive challenge can take two forms: it can present itself as either a threat or an opportunity. If an organism possesses a heritable phenotypic trait that evolved as a response for protecting the organism from a threat or enabling the organism to capitalize on an opportunity, then that trait may very well be an adaptation. Adaptations are identified by exhibiting specialized design features that solve an adaptive challenge, are unlikely to have arisen by chance alone, and are not mere by-products of other traits that evolved to solve some other adaptive problem (Tooby and Cosmides 1992: 55–63; Williams 1966).

Guided by convictions that exchange and reciprocity have been ubiquitous in human societies, that the consequences of exchange and reciprocity have long been significant for humans' chances of survival and reproductive success (fitness), that systems of exchange and reciprocity present both opportunities and threats to humans, and that the elementary components of social exchange are generic and universal to the human species, the evolutionary psychologists Cosmides and Tooby (1992) hypothesized that the human brain might feature an evolved cognitive algorithm (mental rule) for *detecting instances in which reciprocity is not forthcoming*. Using the conceptual framework of game theory and the prisoner's dilemma problem, they conceptualized nonreciprocity as a type of defection, to which they attached the more casual term "cheating" (1992). By adapting an experimental scenario called the "Wason selection task," Cosmides and Tooby designed an experiment to try to determine whether humans have an innate propensity to be skilled at detecting situations in which the terms of a social contract may be violated by a failure to reciprocate. To their satisfaction, their research yielded evidence in support of the existence of a "cheating detection mechanism" in the human mind, and that this mechanism constitutes an evolved adaptation, shared by all humans, to the threat of nonreciprocity in social relations of exchange. Specifically, Cosmides and Tooby (1992) see the cheating detection mechanism as a specialized cognitive algorithm, modular in nature, that evolved by natural selection in response to the selection forces comprising situations of social exchange. Furthermore, they argue that the human mind consists of a great many (actual numerical estimates not provided) such specialized, evolved modules that are mental adaptations to fitness challenges with which humans have been confronted since the EEA, including challenges presented by group living itself.

Thus, in rejecting the SSSM view of the human mind as an all-purpose, general information processing machine, Cosmides and Tooby propose instead a view of the mind as a complex information processing machine that is generously supplied with an extensive array of specialized mental adaptations for coping with many of the survival and reproductive challenges that humans have confronted since the EEA. In order to emphasize the image of the mind as an assemblage of many "special purpose tools" rather than as a monolithic instrument, they often compare the mind to a Swiss Army knife, which contains far more than a cutting blade. It contains an entire "toolbox" of *specialized instruments*, such as screwdrivers with different tips, files, scissors, pliers, awls, and so on.

What is most relevant about the Cosmides-Tooby view of the human mind for our purposes here is its putative *modularity*. The modules themselves are interpreted as specialized, functional capabilities of the human mind that evolved in response to specific selection pressures to which humans have been subjected since the EEA. The SSSM image of the human mind emphasizes its *adaptability*, which is to say its *lack of specialization* in terms of prescribing behaviors, including social behaviors. The SSSM emphasizes the mind's malleability, and thus its ability to improvise and construct ad hoc solutions to any situation that humans encounter. The *adapted* mind imagery proffered by Cosmides and Tooby stands in sharp contrast. As Tooby and Cosmides (1992) put it, the adapted mind contains information about coping with situations that the individual has yet to experience. That is, it "knows" about the aspects of environments that the individual has yet to encounter. For example, prior to an individual's actual experience of social exchange relations, the adapted mind "knows" that the individual will encounter and be engaged in exchange relations his or her entire life, and that virtually all of these exchange relations will exhibit certain universal and generic opportunities and threats, including the threat of nonreciprocity. Accordingly, it should come as no surprise that the human mind contains an evolved adaptation that increases the chances that the individual will be able to detect the threat of cheating and behave defensively against it.

Cosmides and Tooby's image of the adapted mind has gained considerable traction in evolutionary psychology and even in other behavioral and social science quarters. Our purpose here is not to argue in support of or in opposition to their reasoning. Rather, it is to introduce one, rather influential, approach by means of which evolutionary thinkers have tried to replace the SSSM view of the human brain and mind with a model that is more consistent with evolutionary theory and research.

A Sociological Critique of the Modular Mind Hypothesis and an Alternative Proposal

In this volume and elsewhere, Turner (2000, 2015) and Turner and Maryanski (2008) provide an alternative to the modular mind hypothesis as an explanation of the evolution of sociality among humans. Challenging the imagery of the human mind as consisting of "discrete, functional modules," Turner contends that the neural systems that produce social behavior comprise "rather diffuse and complex sub-assemblages across large expanses of the neocortex and subcortex" (2015: 177). Turner also contends that rather than having evolved among humans during the Pleistocene era alone, "bioprogrammers for group living" among humans evolved "through directional selection *on existing mosaics of brain structures* ... during the Eligocene, Eocene, and Miocene" (2015: 177). In a manner reminiscent of those critical of the "one gene, one behavior" fallacy sometimes found in unsophisticated versions of evolutionary thinking (see Wilson 1998: 125–163 for a critique of this fallacy), Turner calls into question what could be termed the "one module, one behavior" imagery of how the brain produces adaptations for group living. Although Turner views the human brain and mind as highly adapted for group life, he rejects what he sees as an erroneous view of the adapted mind as a Swiss Army knife–like ensemble of specialized modules, each of which generates a specific, adaptive behavior. Instead, Turner (2000, 2015) carefully and painstakingly attempts to reconstruct the phylogeny of the human brain and specify the neural process by means of which it produces behaviors, including social behaviors. He is especially critical of any attempt to "localize" morphological structures within the human brain, characterize them as "modules," and attribute to them specialized functions for producing adaptive social behaviors. Rather, he is careful to identify evolved mental adaptations as based in very complex "sub-assemblages" of "neuronets" that operate as "bioprogrammers" that, in turn, contribute to the generation of social behaviors.

Turner's image of the adapted mind also differs from that advanced by many evolutionary psychologists in terms of his focus on human emotions rather than human cognition (reasoning). While evolutionary psychologists like Cosmides and Tooby focus their inquiry on evolved cognitive algorithms that guide how humans reason, Turner (2000, 2015) and Turner and Maryanski (2008) emphasize how the evolution of human emotional capacities has supported the evolution of human social life and societies. Although sociologists are fond of declaring that humans are "social by nature," the phylogeny (evolutionary history) of human sociality is rarely a topic of discussion among most sociologists. In contrast, Maryanski (1992) and Maryanski and Turner (1992) have conducted detailed phylogenetic analyses and have concluded that, despite conventional sociological thinking, the earliest humans were probably surprisingly *asocial*, and only as a result of ecological changes to which archaic humans were subjected did *Homo sapiens* evolve into a highly social species whose group members were conjoined by strong social ties. Based on a cladistics analysis of primates, Maryanski concluded that the "last common ancestor" (LCA) of chimpanzees and hominins was probably a primate whose social organization was based on weak, even ephemeral, social ties (1992, 1993; Maryanski and Turner 1992). In fact, Maryanski and Turner contend that weak social ties among human primate ancestors were probably adaptive. While living in arboreal habitats, these primates were relegated to the margins of that niche, and the terminal areas of trees composing forest canopies simply could not have supported permanent, large groups (Turner and Maryanski 2008; Turner 2015). Accordingly, weak social ties that permitted relatively small social groups to form and dissolve on the basis of food availability were probably adaptive for these arboreal primates. However, as the climate changed and cooling set in, the arboreal forests shrank, and apes were forced to relocate into open-country, savanna habitats (Turner and Maryanski 2008; Turner 2015).

The ecological changes that compelled apes to relocate from forests onto savannas exposed them to new selection forces, one of which was an increased risk of predation. The ability of these apes to organize themselves into larger, highly cohesive groups would have been adaptive in that it would have performed the function of providing protection against predation for members of those groups. Accordingly, Turner (2000, 2015) and Turner and Maryanski (2008) contend that selection favored a "re-wiring" of the hominin brain to enhance its emotional capabilities, especially capabilities that could contribute to the formation and maintenance of strong social ties. In their view, it was the evolution of an expanded "palette" of emotions that accelerated the evolution of sociality among early hominins. Eventually, *Homo sapiens* became more "social by nature" than other apes (and more like monkeys), but this did not occur until selection for enhanced emotionality was well under way.

To a much greater extent than is the case in most evolutionary psychological explanations of the evolution of human sociality, Turner attempts to reconstruct the phylogeny of the human brain and the way in which this reconstruction, or "rewiring" as he often calls it, was responsible for eventually making humans, as opposed to other apes, highly "social by nature." But like evolutionary psychologists, Turner challenges the SSSM view of the human brain as a tabula rasa machine. In fact, Turner identifies a number of "hard-wired behavioral propensities" that are present in many apes and, presumably, were present in hominins as well, thereby providing a platform on which selection could operate and eventually enhance human sociality. The following are a few examples of such propensities as identified by Turner: following the gaze and eye movements of others, very young infants' abilities to imitate orofacial movements of caretakers, monitoring the faces of conspecifics for emotional content, using nonverbal signals to communicate meanings and coordinate actions, using imitation to learn signals and behaviors, engaging in reciprocity in social interaction, and experiencing empathy with conspecifics (2015). According to Turner, the evolution of these and other propensities long precedes the Pleistocene era, during which evolutionary psychologists say the human-adapted mind evolved.

The role of emotions in facilitating human social behavior is not limited to supporting the evolution of strong social ties. As first argued by Darwin (1872) in his classic statement on the evolution of emotions in animals and humans, emotions evolved to enable and guide social interaction. Similarly and more recently, Turner (2000) also contends that complex patterns of social interaction are under the guidance and control of specialized emotions. For example, in his original sociobiological treatment of reciprocal altruism, Trivers (1971) introduced the notion of "moralistic aggression" and explained its importance in systems of reciprocity and exchange. As discussed earlier, the threat of cheating (defection) in situations where parties to an exchange are obligated to reciprocate benefits they have received from each other may have occasioned the evolution of a cheating detection mechanism in the human mind (Cosmides and Tooby 1992). However, once cheating has been detected, the problem is far from solved. In fact, unless the victim can respond effectively, cheating can become iterated, thereby indefinitely imposing serious costs on the victim. Realizing this, Trivers (1971) suggested that humans had evolved a suite of emotions that, in turn, evoked a pattern of behavior for punishing and deterring cheaters, and he called the behavior "moralistic aggression." The concept of moralistic aggression is intended to capture the feeling of indignation and outrage that one can experience when having suffered an injustice, and the violation of a social contract formed and executed in good faith can certainly stimulate a sense of injustice and outrage. Trivers went on to explain that this emotion is functional (adaptive), because it helps solve a problem created by social living, that is, the threat of nonreciprocity. But why would an intense emotion be required to sanction the violation of a social contract? Why would not *retaliation*, as it is labeled by game theorists, be executed automatically by the victim of nonreciprocity?

Retaliation is not a risk- or cost-free behavioral strategy. The target of retaliation can counter-retaliate, thereby imposing injury or cost on the aggrieved victim, thus leading to even greater losses than those incurred by the cheating alone. However, if the victim fails to take action in response to having been cheated, either his or her exploiter or others may observe the failure to sanction and attempt to exploit the victim further. Even then, the victim may come to a "rational" decision that attempting to retaliate may not be worth the risk, or the victim may settle for the psychological reward of regarding himself or herself as virtuous, even forgiving, and not succumb to the base temptation of seeking vengeance. This, of course, can further embolden the cheater to continue exploiting his or her victim. The solution to this problem, in Trivers's view, is the emotional and behavioral complex of moralistic aggression. Even if the slight suffered by the victim is minimal, failing to retaliate can have the effect of eliciting subsequent, and more costly, incidents of nonreciprocity. Accordingly, if a victim experiences sufficient moral outrage and anger, she or he may retaliate aggressively, discounting the risks or costs such aggression might precipitate. This provides an example of what the evolutionary economist Frank (1988) described as "passions within reason," the process by which emotions can "protect us from ourselves," motivating us to behave in a manner that we otherwise might avoid if we based a decision entirely on dispassionate cost-benefit analysis. Thus, moralistic aggression represents a solution, enabled by emotions, to a Darwinian social problem, the threat of being repeatedly victimized by nonreciprocity in relations of social exchange.

Emotions enable and mediate complex social behaviors among humans in other ways as well. In a discussion of how emotions can have moral effects and thereby mediate social interactions among people and support the establishment of social order, Stets and Turner report that shame, guilt, sympathy, and empathy are commonly regarded as the "moral emotions" (2007: 544). Stets and Turner contend, however, that the list of moral emotions that mediate social life among humans should be much longer, including, for example, gratitude, elation, concern, grief, contempt, anger, disgust, love, and hate, among others (2007). In fact, many human emotions are unintelligible in other than a social context. For example, Stets and Turner distinguish among "self-critical moral emotions" (shame and guilt), "other-critical moral emotions" (contempt, anger, and disgust), "other-suffering moral emotions" (empathy and sympathy), and "other-praising moral emotions" (gratitude and elevation) (2007: 550–556).

The experience of such emotions is unlikely to confer survival advantage in coping with aspects of environments that are nonsocial. For example, fear can protect potential victims from both nonsocial threats (heights) and social threats (powerful adversaries), but contempt, though a powerful instrument of social sanctioning and control, is unlikely to be of much use in coping with nonsocial environmental threats, such as electrical storms. Similarly, one might feel relief by not having been injured by a falling rock, but the same situation is unlikely to elicit gratitude unless that good fortune can be attributed to someone's intervention, perhaps a shove from an altruist who, at some risk to himself or herself, removes the potential victim from the path of danger. In short, an inventory of human emotions makes evident the fact that many are likely to have evolved only to enable humans to navigate the complexities of social life. Consequently, sociologists could benefit by using the strategy of "reverse engineering" to pursue a phylogenetic understanding of human emotions. In this approach, an emotion is identified as a candidate adaptation for solving a yet unspecified adaptive problem. For example, the feeling of suspicion can alert a potential victim to an impending social threat. It could act as an "alert system" that identifies potential threats posed by a social scenario and thus reduces the likelihood that an individual will actually fall victim to a social threat such as betrayal, an archaic and universal threat to stable patterns of cooperation. Although a general feeling of unease can alert one to nonsocial threats (such as an impending flash flood), suspicion is better interpreted as a more specialized emotion that protects actors from social threats. Thus, as scientific research continues to expand our knowledge about the full complement of emotions experienced by humans, valuable opportunities will emerge for analyzing those human emotions as possible adaptations for navigating the complexities of group life.

Although Darwin (1872) himself recognized the evolutionary significance of the "expression of emotions in man and animals," until recently, most sociologists have failed to follow suit and make emotions a topic of sociological inquiry (Stets and Turner 2007). However, an expanding literature on the sociology of emotions, some of it framed in evolutionary terms, has shed new light on how natural selection is likely to have instantiated the human mind with adaptive emotional capabilities that are designed specifically for social life, and, as it continues to develop, this line of inquiry will continue to drive nails into the coffin of tabula rasa (Davis 2007; Hammond 2003, 2007; Massey 2002, 2005; Stets and Turner 2007; Turner 1999, 2000; Turner and Stets 2005).

Applying Evolutionary Thinking to Sociological Analysis

Even before Wilson published *Sociobiology* in 1975, two anthropologists were calling for the development of a "zoological anthropology" (Tiger and Fox 1966, 1971), and at least one sociologist was promoting the idea of "bringing beasts back in" to sociology (van den Berghe 1974). In less than a decade, a few biologically minded sociologists began exploring the possibility of reframing sociological analyses in terms of sociobiological theory. For example, Lopreato (1984) conducted a comprehensive analysis of human cultural universals in order to discern the existence of possible behavioral predispositions that had evolved by natural selection. More recently, a growing number of sociologists have applied evolutionary theory, including sociobiology and behavioral ecology, to the study of specific topics in sociological inquiry. We will identify and briefly discuss a few examples of such analyses in order to provide a sense of the various ways in which contemporary sociologists are incorporating evolutionary perspectives, including sociobiology, into their work.

Evolutionary Perspectives on Gender Inequality

In order to introduce an evolutionary dimension to a long-standing sociological convention that characterizes humans as social "actors," Hopcroft (2009b) has posited that several innate psychological predispositions are implicated in various types of human social behavior, including patterns of marriage and family relations and social stratification dynamics. In that effort, she has recast the traditional sociological notion of the social "actor" as an "evolved actor" (Hopcroft 2009b). In her view, humans almost certainly possess a range of evolved, innate behavioral predispositions, including a propensity to learn social norms above other kinds of rules, a predisposition to be concerned with fairness and the expression of altruism when interacting with non-kin, a predisposition toward religious sentiments, a predisposition to form status hierarchies, a predisposition to express loyalty preferentially to kin groups (i.e., tribes or ethnic groups), and gender differences in predispositions to engage in risky behavior (2009b). Hopcroft (2002, 2006, 2009a, 2009b) has used sociobiological theory to develop a theoretical explanation of gender inequality, and she has adduced empirical evidence to evaluate these explanations.

In sociobiological theory, males are seen as confronting a problem of paternity uncertainty, which, in turn, promotes male sexual jealousy and a preoccupation with controlling female sexuality, a key component of promoting patriarchy and male dominance (Hopcroft 2009a: 1849). Paternity uncertainty is said to contribute to the development of mate-guarding strategies adopted by males in an effort to reduce the likelihood of cuckoldry. Sociobiologists interpret paternity uncertainty and the behaviors it occasions in terms of Darwin's theory of sexual selection and male-female differences in traits preferred in mates. For example, females are said to have preferences for high status in males, because status signifies access to resources from which a female and her offspring can benefit, and males are said to prefer traits in females that indicate high fertility (i.e., youth) and high fidelity, thereby reducing paternity anxiety.

Drawing on these evolutionary ideas, Hopcroft hypothesizes that paternity uncertainty and male-female differences in mate preference characteristics may be implicated in the origin of gender inequality. Specifically, Hopcroft (2002, 2006, 2009a, 2009b) hypothesizes that males can be expected to favor female traits that indicate their "controllability," and thus a reduced likelihood that they will confront their mates with the threat of paternity uncertainty. Hopcroft further contends that females might signal their "controllability," and therefore provide assurance to prospective mates of their fidelity, by expressing deference to males (but not to other females). Female controllability can also signal the promise of enhanced effectiveness by males in their efforts to employ mate-guarding strategies (Buss 2002; Thornhill and Palmer 2000: 43, 61–62). Furthermore, Hopcroft predicts that female expressions of deference to males should be age-specific. That is, females should be most likely to express deference to males during their prime reproductive years, but such expressions of deference should decline, if not disappear, later in their lives, especially after menopause (Hopcroft 2009a). Hopcroft (2002: 46) contends that an empirical pattern that entails a cognitive bias toward low task-related self-esteem in young women when comparing themselves with males may be a manifestation of young women's predisposition to defer to males as a signal of controllability and fidelity. In addition, she hypothesizes that as women live beyond their reproductive years, the propensity to defer to males should disappear, and that their social status should be more likely to increase during this stage in their life cycle (Hopcroft 2006). Hopcroft surmises that status attainment by young females can pose a threat to males, because it may signify female independence that, in turn, can elevate male anxiety about the controllability of females and paternity confidence. However, when females reach post-reproductive years, their status attainment is less likely to pose a threat to males, and thus both status attainment and self-esteem among females can be expected to increase after menopause (Hopcroft 2009a: 1858).

Hopcroft reports data that support her argument about the evolutionary origins of gender inequality in social interaction among men and women. For example, she reports that the gender gap between males and females in self-esteem is greatest between ages fifteen and eighteen, an age during which, ironically, and by objective measure, girls are achieving more than are boys (e.g., are exhibiting fewer behavior problems, are earning better grades, and are more likely to go to college). To the extent that low female self-esteem is related to female deference toward males, Hopcroft believes this pattern can be explained in terms of an evolved behavioral predisposition produced by sexual selection in an environmental context in which males are confronted by the threat of paternity uncertainty. However, as women age, Hopcroft (2009a: 1859) reports that both their self-esteem and social status increase, because neither female assertiveness nor status attainment continues to threaten their mating and reproductive prospects. More specifically, Hopcroft (2006: 368) reports that the pattern of female deference toward males vanishes by the time women become fifty years old.

Another biologically minded sociologist proposes an alternative explanation of the origins of gender inequality among humans. Although she exhorts sociologists to incorporate "biodata" into their analyses of human social behavior, Huber (2007) does not invoke possible differences in the evolved psychology of males and females in order to explain the origins and near-universality of patriarchy and male dominance. She does not attribute male dominance to any sort of evolved behavioral predispositions among females that would enable them to be more easily controlled and dominated by males. Instead, Huber looks to male-female differences in the division of reproductive labor to provide an explanation of the emergence and pervasiveness of patriarchy. Specifically, Huber rests her argument on what economists call "opportunity costs," the inability to "invest" in one opportunity because of a prior allocation of resources to another opportunity. Thus, Huber (2007: 117) contends that, in most societies, women have not been able to take advantage of opportunities to participate and excel in various arenas of societal life, especially military and political activity, because their resources, of biological necessity, had to be allocated to a more immediate and pressing responsibility, nursing their offspring.

Huber explains that, until recently, the only way to meet the nutritional requirements of infants and very young (less than four years old) children was by nursing them. And because only female humans lactate, human biology necessitated that women with young children were inextricably bound to their offspring by the frequent nursing schedules that are species-typical for humans. Huber (2007: 93) carefully and thoroughly documents the near-total dependency of human babies on their mother's milk, and the highly restrictive demands that frequent nursing imposes on mothers' time and energy. Until about the 1950s, when infant formula began to replace human milk in the Western world, and became readily available and affordable, it was not possible for most human mothers (with the exception of those who could benefit from the services of a nursemaid) to delegate the responsibility of feeding pre-weaned offspring to others, including the children's fathers (Huber 2007: 78). Consequently, women with young children were precluded from pursuing opportunities to participate and succeed in ventures such as business, political involvement, and military activity, all of which have long been important avenues of status attainment in human societies (Huber 2007: 117). In short, for most of human history, lactation and nursing imposed opportunity costs on mothers that inhibited their chances of attaining positions of power, influence, and privilege in stratification systems. In that sense, it could be said that the division of reproductive labor based on biological differences between human males and females virtually ordained the rise of patriarchy and the near-universal subordination of women to men. It was not until recently that the development of infant formula and bottle-feeding made possible, but hardly mandated, greater equality between men and women in the expenditure of parental investment that is required of members of a highly altricial species like humans.

Another biologically minded sociologist has examined androgen levels in both males and females as proximate causal influences on patterns of gender socialization (Udry 2000; Udry, Morris, and Kovenock 1995). Essentially, Udry (2000) contends that efforts to socialize either females or males into traditional "feminine" patterns of behavior are inhibited by elevated androgen levels. By employing an integrated "biosocial model" of gendered behavior, Udry concludes that high prenatal androgen levels in females will produce "masculinized" behavioral predispositions at later developmental stages in life. High androgen levels will also inhibit "feminizing" socialization processes (Udry 2000: 452). Furthermore, since prenatal androgen levels among males are much higher (up to ten times) than those of females, Udry infers that males are much more resistant to "feminizing" socialization processes. Although few biosociologists typically extend their analyses to address policy implications of their research, Udry speculated about prospects for reducing gender inequality based on his findings regarding androgen levels and gendered behavior. Though not advocating a biologically based program to achieve gender equality, Udry (2000: 452–453) contends that any efforts to reduce, if not eradicate, gender differences in behavior will be more likely to succeed if they entail socialization practices designed to produce more "masculine" traits in females than alternative practices designed to socialize males to become more "feminine." Despite disavowals that he was advocating such policies, Udry's statements drew intense criticism from other sociologists (Miller and Costello 2001; Risman 2001). Not surprisingly, some of these criticisms derived from uncritical adoption of the SSSM and misunderstandings of and misattributions about evolutionary theory; consequently, they were misdirected. Currently, evolutionary sociologists rarely venture policy suggestions based on their work. Rather, most devote themselves primarily, if not exclusively, to efforts designed to use evolutionary theory and research to try to understand the origins of human social behaviors and apply that understanding to enhance sociological explanations of contemporary patterns of human social behavior.

As is evident in the work of Hopcroft, Huber, and Udry, adopting an evolutionary approach to the study of the origins and persistence of gender inequality does not mean that sociologists must embrace monolithic explanations of human social behavior. Rather, sociologists can be assured that framing an analysis in terms of evolutionary theory in general, or sociobiology in particular, permits the development of alternative, and often competing, accounts of the influence of natural (and sexual) selection on human society and social behavior, accounts whose credibility will be adjudicated ultimately by the power of reason and the weight of empirical evidence.

How Evolved Mental Adaptations Are Expressed in Contemporary Societies

The work of sociologist and evolutionary psychologist Kanazawa and his colleagues provides an interesting example of the implications of analyzing contemporary social phenomena in light of a view of human nature as comprising a social mind consisting of archaic, evolved algorithms. Like Cosmides and Tooby (1992), Kanazawa subscribes to the view that the human mind comprises specialized, domain-specific mental adaptations for coping with specific survival and fitness challenges. However, he also acknowledges that the human mind exhibits "general intelligence" that is measured by instruments such as IQ tests (Kanazawa 2010a: 281). Thus, Kanazawa views the human mind as comprising *both* specialized, evolved mental adaptations for coping with some adaptive problems and general, global thinking and reasoning abilities for coping with other problems. Kanazawa integrates these two positions in an interesting way that he labels the "Savanna-IQ Interaction Hypothesis" (2010a: 279–280). Humans confront some problems that are adaptively salient, recurrent, and probably universal, such as having to recognize instances of nonreciprocity in social contracts. But they also confront other challenges that are adaptively salient yet evolutionarily novel. In Kanazawa's view, the human mind possesses specialized, evolved cognitive algorithms for coping with adaptive challenges that were common in the EEA, as well as general intelligence (IQ) for enabling humans to think and reason creatively about problems that are evolutionarily novel and for which specialized mental modules do not exist.

All humans possess general intelligence; it is an adaptation featuring zero heritability, but precise IQ levels vary among individuals. Kanazawa contends that individuals with higher IQs should be better at developing solutions for evolutionarily novel challenges that they encounter. Conversely, there should be less variation among individuals in terms of solving evolutionarily familiar problems that have confronted humans since the EEA. Kanazawa's position is shared by Wilson himself, who observes that over the millions of years during which humans have evolved, they have acquired a nature that features an "unprecedented intelligence yet (is) still guided by complex inherited emotions and biased channels of learning" (2006: 1481). And alluding to a mind that comprises an evolved, universal human nature, Wilson goes on to observe that human nature "is the commonality of the hereditary responses and propensities that define our species," and it arose "during the far simpler conditions in which humanity lived during more than 99 percent of its existence," thus constituting "what Darwin called the indelible stamp of our lowly origin" (2006: 1482).

Kanazawa's Savanna Principle enables him to offer new insights about human behavior in contemporary societal environments, insights that otherwise would be unavailable to social scientists studying social phenomena in contemporary settings. For example, Kanazawa (2004: 41) notes that predictions derived from microeconomic theories such as decision theory and game theory often fail. He attributes these failures to the fact that the assumptions and scope conditions required by these theories were often not met in the ancestral social environments composing the EEA. For example, Kanazawa reports that prisoner's dilemma models in game theory predict that a rational actor will defect, but often he or she does not. The model also predicts that "cheap talk" (unenforceable threats and promises) will not influence actors' choices, but it does (Kanazawa 2004: 41). However, laboratory experiments show that about half the subjects playing prisoner's dilemma games cooperate and that cheap talk increases the rate of participation in games (Kanazawa 2004: 41). Why do these predictions fail? According to Kanazawa, the game theory model presumes that actors are anonymous to each other and that the game is not iterated. However, in the social environments composing the EEA, actors knew each other personally and interacted repeatedly, so a predisposition to cooperate was not as risky as the single-shot (non-iterated) episode model implies.

Similarly, public choice theory makes assumptions that are inconsistent with the features of the EEA. Specifically, free riding was probably much less of a threat in the EEA than in the social circumstances posited by public choice theory. For example, in contrast to public choice theory, Kanazawa (2004: 46) suggests that individuals in the EEA were probably well informed about the choices made by others, and that the contributions of actors to the public good were often significant, not negligible as assumed by public choice theory. Under such social conditions, free riding was less likely to have posed a threat of the significance as that posited by public choice theory. On the other hand, the assumptions on which social network theory is based more closely approximate the empirical realities of social interaction in the EEA, and accordingly, network models about the role of power and dependency in relations of social exchange better predict and explain social relations than do other theories whose assumptions are at odds with the empirical realities of the EEA.

Kanazawa uses the Savanna-IQ Interaction hypothesis to offer explanations about other aspects of social behavior in contemporary social contexts. For example, he reports that people with higher IQs are better able to distinguish television characters as imaginary, and thus evolutionarily novel. Accordingly, viewers with higher IQs are less likely to report being satisfied with their friendships as a function of watching more television (Kanazawa 2010a: 286). Similarly, Kanazawa (2010b) and Kanazawa and Hellberg (2010) report that liberalism, atheism, experimentation with regulated or banned drugs, and the practice of sexual exclusivity by males are evolutionarily novel phenomena, and that this may explain the higher incidence of these behaviors among individuals with higher IQ scores.

Finally, Kanazawa and Still (2000) explain that some empirical patterns of social behavior in the contemporary world are tractable to evolutionary explanation without having to posit a "mismatch" between the social environments of the EEA and contemporary societies. One such pattern is the disproportionate representation of young males among those who commit violent crimes and property crimes (Kanazawa and Still 2000). Sexual selection theory suggests that male reproductive opportunities are strongly influenced by a male's social status (including the resources at his disposal), and that intense competition among young males for both resources and mates is often associated with both violence and property crime. Furthermore, as males mate successfully and produce one or more offspring, they incur greater risk by competing violently and committing property crimes, and the resources they do accumulate are better directed toward parental investment in their offspring rather than continued intra-sexual competition for additional reproductive opportunity. Accordingly, Kanazawa and Still (2000: 444) propose that this can help explain the "aging out of crime" effect documented by criminologists. Thus, intra-sexual selection produced an evolved psychology among young males to compete intensely for both mates and resources. Consequently, a phylogeny of intense male-male competition is likely to have contributed significantly to the elevated incidence of both violent crimes and property crimes among contemporary males.

INTERACTION BETWEEN BIOLOGICAL AND SOCIOCULTURAL FACTORS IN SOCIAL BEHAVIOR

When sociobiology first emerged in the late 1900s as a possible new way to explain aspects of social behavior among humans, a common concern among many of its critics was the fear that it advocated biological reductionism, even genetic determinism, at the expense of acknowledging cultural and social structural determinants of human social behavior (see Machalek and Martin 2004, 2010; Segestråle 2000). Subsequently, and contrary to this concern, sociologists who framed their work in evolutionary terms typically reaffirmed the necessity of considering how biological and sociocultural factors commonly *interact* to produce social behavior among humans (Lopreato and Crippen 1999: 59, 111).

Recent genetic research supports the position that interaction between genes and environments, including social environments, influences the incidence of various behaviors (Simons, Beach, and Barr 2012). Criticizing behavioral genetics, Simons, Beach, and Barr (2012: 145–147) find greater support for an epigenetic approach for explaining how genes can influence social behavior. Unlike behavioral genetics, epigenetics places emphasis on how the expression of genes is shaped by their environments to produce phenotypic variation. Simons, Beach, and Barr (2012) review and evaluate several "gene by environment" models and conclude that a "differential susceptibility" model is the most promising for explaining how genes interact with their social environments to influence behavior. Specifically, Simons, Beach, and Barr (2012: 150–151) report genetic research that documents the existence of "risk alleles," also conceptualized as "plasticity" or "sensitivity" alleles in 40–50 percent of the population studied. The more of these alleles that a person possesses, the more sensitive he or she will be to environmental influences. It is especially interesting that sensitivity alleles amplify the effects of both adverse and favorable environments on the behaviors of those who carry them. For example, an individual who carries two copies of a risk (sensitivity) allele is *more likely* to exhibit delinquent behavior when subjected to adverse social environments, but also *less likely* to exhibit delinquent behavior when subjected to favorable environments (Simons, Beach, and Barr 2012: 149–157). Thus, this research supports the conventional sociological claim that social environments are important determinants of behaviors such as delinquency, but it qualifies this position by adducing evidence that genetic factors will determine how "susceptible" different individuals are to social environmental variation.

Examples of the interaction between biological and social factors are provided by the work of Mazur and his colleagues, who have studied the relationship between the androgenic hormone testosterone and social behaviors, especially aggression and dominance, among humans (Booth, Mazur, and Kivlighan 2006; Mazur 2005, 2006), and the work of Udry and his colleagues (Udry 2000; Udry, Morris, and Kovenock 1995), who studied the effects of androgen on the development of gendered behavior. Another example of how biology and sociocultural factors can interact to produce complex social behaviors is provided by the work of Machalek and Martin (2012) on how emotions and culture (religious ideology) interact to help explain the rapid growth of a highly successful social movement, early Christianity. We will briefly discuss each of these areas of inquiry in turn.

Belief in a putative link between testosterone levels in males and aggressive, even violent, behavior has become prevalent in popular culture. For example, in an article in *Ms. Magazine* published in 1975, the actor Alan Alda introduced the expression "testosterone poisoning," which eventually became common in popular culture and was even quoted in *A Feminist Dictionary* (Kramarae and Teichler 1985). However, the work of Mazur and his colleagues calls into question the hypothesized link between testosterone and aggressiveness. Specifically, research fails to document a direct relationship between testosterone levels and aggressiveness (Booth, Mazur, and Kivlighan 2006: 167; Mazur 2005). Instead, research has shown that testosterone levels are related to both social conditions encountered in dominance contests and rank in dominance orders, and that these relationships are complex and bidirectional. In these studies, aggression is defined as the intent to inflict injury on another, and dominance refers to the intent to gain or maintain status in a hierarchy (Mazur 2005, 2006). The social contexts in which such dominance contests occur include, for example, sporting events, street confrontations among young men, and military settings (Booth, Mazur, and Kivlighan 2006; Mazur 2005, 2006). The relationship between testosterone levels and dominance behaviors is mediated by social factors such as the anticipation of a contest, the outcome of a contest, parent-child relations, relations among other family members and peers, marital relations, and the presence of honor cultures (Booth, Mazur, and Kivlighan 2006; Mazur 2006).

For example, male testosterone levels become elevated both in anticipation of and during dominance contests, and they remain higher among contest winners than among losers after the competition is over. Similarly, male testosterone levels are sensitive to the perceived strength of opponents and the perceived importance of the contest. In fact, if winners believe that their victory is attributable to luck rather than skill and effort, they experience little, if any, post-contest elevation in their testosterone levels (Booth, Mazur, and Kivlighan 2006: 174). Further evidence of interactions between testosterone levels and social factors has been found in parent-child relations for both sons and daughters. Specifically, among sons who experience poor relations with their parents, high levels of testosterone are associated with increased antisocial behavior, and low levels are associated with depression. Daughters with elevated testosterone levels who have poor relations with their mothers are more likely to engage in risky and antisocial behaviors, while daughters with low testosterone levels who have poor relations with their fathers are more likely to experience depression (Booth, Mazur, and Kivlighan 2006: 177). Peer relations also mediate the correlation between testosterone levels and behavior. For example, boys with high testosterone levels who have positive relations with their peers are more likely to exhibit assertive and dominance behaviors that are associated with leadership, but those who have poor relations with their peers and high testosterone levels are more likely to exhibit nonaggressive character disorders (Booth, Mazur, and Kivlighan 2006: 179). Finally, boys with elevated testosterone levels who have positive relations with their mothers or sisters are more likely to perceive their relations with their peers in a favorable light (Booth, Mazur, and Kivlighan 2006: 179).

The interactive dynamism that can transpire between biological and social factors is vividly evident in the short-term variability in testosterone levels and stages of dominance contests. As noted earlier, testosterone levels among males become elevated in anticipation of a dominance contest, and among winners, remain elevated after the contest is concluded (Mazur 2006). As a result, young males who live in social environments where they must remain continuously vigilant to the threat of status challenges are more likely to experience elevated testosterone levels than males who live in less confrontational social environments (Mazur 2006: 27). Environments in which males consistently confront status challenges are often the product of "honor cultures" that require males, especially young males, to be constantly prepared to defend their reputations against affronts committed by other young males (Nisbett and Cohen 1996). Mazur suggests that honor cultures are common not only in certain regions such as the American South, but also in social contexts such as those experienced by many inner-city African American males, contexts that can amplify male concern with reputation and status, thereby creating a persistent expectation of having to engage in dominance contests. Both the anticipation of such contests and the outcomes of those contests contribute to elevated testosterone levels among their participants, especially the winners. Thus, Mazur (2006: 28) concludes that a "culture of honor," the dominance contests to which it gives rise, and the outcomes of those contests all can contribute to vicious cycles of violence, some of which are lethal for the participants. Although Mazur expresses criticism of both sociobiology and evolutionary psychology, the interaction dynamics between biology and social structure that he reports are consistent with the explanatory principles of the norm of reaction (Wilson 1998) and the interaction principle (Lopreato 1984) used by sociobiologists to discuss the reciprocal influences of biology and social structure in shaping human social behavior.

Another example of interaction between evolved psychological traits, in this case, emotions, and sociocultural factors is provided by an analysis of "serial reciprocity" in early Christianity (Machalek and Martin 2012). Using multiple sources of evidence and guided by several theoretical perspectives in sociology, Stark (1996) analyzed the factors that contributed to the rise of Christianity as a successful social movement. Among the range of factors to which Stark attributes Christianity's success, the early Christians' response to epidemics that swept the Greco-Roman world in 165 and 251 CE is, perhaps, one of the most interesting. The epidemics themselves, probably smallpox and measles, were responded to differently by pagans versus Christians. Available evidence suggests that people in that era had an awareness of the threat of contagion. In response, pagans assiduously avoided people who became ill, but Christians often provided care for the stricken. Stark explains that an otherwise healthy person who falls victim to either disease has a reasonable chance of surviving it if he or she is provided fairly simple nursing care such as simple nutrition and hydration. Using epidemiological data, Stark (1996: 88–91) estimates that victims who were the recipients of nursing may have experienced a survival rate of 90 percent in contrast to a 70 percent survival rate among those denied such assistance.

Stark (1996: 90–91) avows that patients who survived their illness would have become immune and therefore could have constituted a "whole force" of potential nurses and caregivers who would have been available to tend to the needs of others who became ill. To observers of the time, this cadre of caregivers is likely to have been perceived as a body of "miracle workers" (Stark 1996: 91). In his analysis of Christian versus pagan responses to the plagues, Stark focuses primarily on the role of cognitive culture, specifically, on new theological meanings introduced by Christianity about the nature of God and God's relationship to humanity. Specifically, and in stark contrast to pagans' conceptions of their deities, Christians were taught that theirs is a loving God who cares deeply for all of humanity and *expects humans to care deeply for each other and to support each other*. In Stark's view, this new religious meaning system supported the development of strong, novel, pro-social norms that would have required Christians to render aid to those who needed it, including plague victims. In fact, Stark cites documentary evidence that such norms existed and Christians acted on them. For example, the emperor Julian observed the caregiving that Christians provided to other Christians, lamented the absence of such caregiving by pagans, and sought to establish "pagan charities in an effort to match the Christians" (Stark 1996: 83).

Stark's analysis is persuasive, and in our view, it invites extension and further development guided by evolutionary theory (Machalek and Martin 2012). Stark's reasoning is that Christian victims who survived their illness due, in part, to caregiving they received from other Christians were likely to become caregivers themselves. Stark avows that this process was likely to have become autocatalytic, thereby contributing to the growth and expansion of caregiving among members of the Christian population, which, in turn, helps explain Christianity's rapid and disproportionate growth during the first three to four centuries of its existence. However, Stark's analysis raises additional questions that we believe can best be addressed by adopting an evolutionary sociological framework of analysis. Specifically, we contend that the power of Christian ideology promoted caregiving by activating *evolved social emotions*, which, in and of themselves, were insufficient to cause altruistic caregiving at the scale reported by Stark. Conversely, absent the evolved social emotions of sympathy, empathy, and gratitude, it is unlikely that the pro-social ideology of Christianity would have succeeded in producing caregiving that required significant, sometimes fatal, sacrificial and altruistic behavior by the caregivers. In short, Christianity introduced a new religious meaning system and ideology that exhorted its believers to help those in need by feeding the hungry, providing drink to the thirsty, clothing the naked, visiting the imprisoned, and *caring for the sick* (Matthew 25:40 Red Letter Testament). While Stark may very well be correct in his conclusion that victims who survived the plagues due to the caregiving they received from Christian "nurses" went on to become caregivers themselves, his analysis gains strength and plausibility if it is enhanced by reasoning and insights derived from evolutionary sociology.

It is possible to reconstruct the factors that may have given rise to an ever-expanding cadre of Christian nurses if we integrate ideas and research findings from several areas of inquiry, including sociological exchange theory, the sociology of emotions, and evolutionary sociology, which, itself, owes its recent emergence to the rise of sociobiology. Specifically, the notion of *serial reciprocity* provides a pivotal concept in terms of which such an integration can be achieved (Boulding 1981; Machalek and Martin 2012; Moody 2008). In serial reciprocity, an individual, A, provides a benefit (resource, service, etc.) to another individual, B, who thereby incurs a debt to A. However, B is relieved of his debt not by repaying A but by providing a benefit to a third party, C. C, in turn, repays her debt by providing a benefit to D, and so on. In popular culture, this process has come to be known as "paying it forward."

According to Moody (2008), this process can be conceptualized as a form of reciprocity despite the fact that no benefactor is ever repaid by any beneficiary. Instead, beneficiaries "repay" their benefactors by transmitting a benefit to a third party. According to Moody (2008: 136), this process can be regarded as true reciprocity, because subjectively, each beneficiary regards his or her act of beneficence to others (third parties) as a form of repayment to his or her benefactor. Thus, plague victims who survived their illnesses due to the benefits they received from caregivers and, in turn, became caregivers of other victims were "serial reciprocators." Although the logic of serial reciprocity is implicit in Stark's explanatory account, he does not specify the sociological and psychological mechanisms by means of which serial reciprocity is likely to have occurred in early Christianity, but this can be accomplished by employing an evolutionary sociological framework.

The activation of serial reciprocity entails three components: sacrifice, gratitude, and obligation, and both cultural meanings and evolved emotions are implicated in this process (Machalek and Martin 2012: 50–65). In the context of epidemics during early Christianity, sacrifice operated at two levels. First, caregivers incurred sacrifices in nursing the plague victims, and their sacrifices were sometimes lethal in that they contracted and succumbed to the illnesses they were treating. Second, the theological salience of sacrifice was central to the meaning system of Christianity in that God's love of humanity motivated him to permit his son to be sacrificed in order to redeem humanity. Stark

(1996: 86) explains that pagan deities were viewed as incapable of love for human beings and thus indifferent to human well-being. Therefore, the notion of a God who cared about, loved, and would sacrifice for humanity was a novel theological innovation in the Greco-Roman world (Stark 1996: 86). Observing the suffering of plague victims can lead to the experience of both sympathy and empathy, which, in turn, can cause altruistic behavior (Stets and Turner 2007: 554–555). As "other suffering" emotions, the ability to feel both empathy and sympathy with the plight of victims can motivate actors to provide assistance, even at significant personal costs to themselves. Of course, all normal humans experience the evolved emotions of empathy and sympathy, but as Stark explained, these emotional capabilities were probably activated more strongly among Christians than pagans, because Christians, not pagans, worked as caregivers to victims of the plagues. This illustrates the interaction between evolved human psychological attributes and cultural meanings that can either activate or suppress them.

Sacrifice for a benefit provided to a victim is likely to evoke what Stets and Turner call the "other praising" emotion of gratitude (2007: 555–556). The intensity of the gratitude felt is a function of cost incurred by the benefactor, the value of the benefit to the beneficiary, the intention of the benefactor, and the degree to which the act of beneficence is voluntary (Machalek and Martin 2012: 56–57; McCullough, Kimeldorf, and Cohen 2008: 281). In the case of early Christianity, God's sacrifice of his son represents a loss that is almost certain to resonate with any parent, thereby helping explain the motivational power of Christianity (Machalek and Martin 2012: 57–58). Similarly, the actual costs incurred by those Christians who provided caregiving for plague victims were vividly apparent, because they sometimes resulted in the caregiver's contraction of the disease. In the eyes of Christian believers, the value of the benefit they received from God's sacrifice of his son was redemption, the promise of eternal life. The value of nursing provided to the ill by Christian caregivers included psychological comfort, physical nourishment, and an increased likelihood of survival, all of which were unambiguous both to those suffering from disease and to observers. In the minds of believers, it would be difficult to attribute the intention of God in permitting his son to be sacrificed for humanity to anything other than altruism. A being characterized as omnipotent in the Christian cosmology can hardly be expected to be acting on behalf of his own self-interest by permitting such a sacrifice. And if and when Christian caregivers provided caregiving indiscriminately to all victims suffering from the plagues, their intentions were likely to have been viewed as altruistic as well, especially since those who had not yet been infected could also contract the disease and die. Finally, God's tolerance of his son's sacrifice would hardly have been interpreted as involuntary by Christian believers. How could an omnipotent being be compelled to do *anything* involuntarily? The most compelling alternative explanation is that God was motivated exclusively by his love of humanity, and he acted on a strictly voluntary basis.

Considering the motivations of Christians who provided nursing for plague victims, it is at least possible that their behavior was propelled by some sort of "ulterior," self-aggrandizing motive. If they provided care for a plague victim, then they might expect comparable services if they, or members of their families, for example, ever fell victim to the epidemics. Similarly, they might enjoy status gains and the approbation of others for sacrificing their own well-being to care for the stricken. However, Stark (1996: 81–82) reports accounts that describe early Christians as having "welcomed the great epidemic" and having greeted it with "unimaginable joy," because it provided an opportunity to test and affirm their faith. Within the limits of information that is available about the motivations of the early Christian caregivers, it is plausible that their altruism was voluntary rather than coerced or the product of utilitarian exchange motives. Thus, examining the circumstances under which Christian caregivers provided assistance to victims of the epidemics that ravaged the Greco-Roman world, it is plausible to infer that beneficiaries of caregiving, and possibly their family members, other relatives, and friends, experienced intense gratitude.

The emotion of intense gratitude is likely to contribute to the development of a cognition of indebtedness and a sense of obligation to repay the debt (Machalek and Martin 2012: 60–65; Stets and Turner 2007: 556). This sense of obligation can be supported by another evolved "self-critical" moral emotion, guilt, which can create an uncomfortable level of anxiety by not taking action to discharge the obligation to repay the debt (Stets and Turner 2007: 550–553). Although it is common to associate guilt with having committed a behavior that one later regrets, guilt can also be activated by an awareness that one *failed* to take a course of action when it was called for. As Stets and Turner (2007: 555–556) explain, however, gratitude is an emotion that typically is experienced as pleasant, and it may be associated with feelings of elevation. Gratitude, then, is likely to motivate the beneficiary of an altruist's sacrifice to search for a potential beneficiary (a third party) toward whom he or she can behave benevolently. In this regard, gratitude is probably the most powerful psychological force that drives serial reciprocity.

Victims of the plagues of 165 CE and 251 CE who enjoyed the benefits provided by Christian nurses were very likely to have experienced gratitude that was made especially intense by virtue of two factors: (1) as an evolved moral emotion, gratitude is instantiated in the evolved psychology of humans because it promotes pro-social behavior (Stets and Turner 2007: 556), and (2) the evolved emotional psychology that makes gratitude an emotion that is available for promoting pro-social behavior was activated by the cognitive power of the theme of God's sacrifice in the Christian worldview, and the tangible evidence of the altruism of Christian caregivers who risked their own lives to care for the plague victims. In that sense, it can be said that biology and culture colluded and constituted a powerful "dual-force" that was likely to have activated a stream of serial reciprocity that, in turn, contributed significantly to the expansion of Christian culture in the West and the increasing proportion of Christians in Europe and eventually the world (Machalek and Martin 2012).

In our view, this type of analysis provides an example of how conventional sociological reasoning can be integrated with evolutionary thinking to yield new and potentially enhanced accounts of sociological phenomena such as the rise of what eventually became a world-successful social movement. At first blush, it is unlikely that many historical sociologists would think to turn to sociobiology, evolutionary psychology, or evolutionary sociology to gain purchase in their efforts to explain historical phenomena. The adoption of the concept of serial reciprocity in conjunction with ideas derived from sociological exchange theory, the sociology of emotions, and evolutionary sociology demonstrates, to our satisfaction, the possible value of just such an approach.

Suntne Angeli?

Schneider (1975: 93–94) relates a story, very likely apocryphal, about architectural plans for a Catholic school that were sent to the Vatican. They were returned with the question, "Suntne angeli?" which means, "Are they angels?" The plans for the school had failed to include toilet facilities. Until recently, it would be plausible to infer that the plans could have been drawn up by sociologists. Sociology's long-standing disinterest in human biology and its influence on social behavior has, on occasion, developed into an overt aversion that has been labeled "biophobia" (Daly and Wilson 1988: 152–156). However, the publication of *Sociobiology: The New Synthesis* (Wilson 1975) prompted the development of a renewed discussion about biology and social behavior, the results of which have led to the emergence of new fields like "evolutionary sociology" (Maryanski 1998).

We have reviewed a variety of sociological studies, some of which have been influenced by neo-Darwinian evolutionary theory in general, others by sociobiology in particular. However, these types of studies do not exhaust the range of inquiries about biology and social behavior in which sociologists are now engaged. For example, a recently published book on "neurosociology" examines the relationship between neuroscience and social psychology (Franks 2010). Following this new approach for linking biology to sociology, other researchers have begun integrating recent findings from the neurosciences with sociological analysis in efforts to cast new light on human social behavior (e.g., Firat and Hitlin 2012; Franks and Davis 2012; Leveto and Kalkhoff 2012). Research such as this proceeds on the assumption that the human brain is not simply a global, cultural information processor. Rather, it explores the possibility that the human brain's role in producing behavior reflects its evolutionary history and may play a complex role in producing social behavior by means other than simply executing cultural "programs" that are installed by socialization. Thus, the work of neurosociologists will almost certainly continue to erode the tabula rasa view of the human mind and the SSSM of which it is a part.

Another type of sociological analysis that sociobiology has helped inspire involves comparisons among multiple social species, including humans. One variant of this approach is Maryanski's (1992) use of cladistics analysis to reconstruct the likely behavioral characteristics of the "last common ancestor" of humans and other primates. By focusing on comparisons between humans and other primates, Maryanski uses evolutionary reasoning to try to shed new light on the selection forces that, over vast stretches of time, constructed what is commonly viewed as "human nature" (Maryanski and Turner 1992).

Another variant of cross-species analysis shifts attention from evolved human nature to fundamental forms of social organization that are often distributed across species lines (Machalek 1992). Extending the logic of Simmel's "formal sociology" to include the study of sociality among both human and nonhuman social species, Machalek (1992) has analyzed the evolutionary forces that have made possible the evolution of "macrosocieties" among social species that are phylogenetically far removed from each other, the eusocial insects (especially ants) and humans. For example, despite the fact that ants possess brains that are only about the size of a grain of salt, and the human brain weighs, on average, about 3.5 pounds, both ants and humans have converged in assembling societies with very large populations (hundreds to millions of individuals) whose members are organized into a complex division of labor that is executed by social categories (castes among ants, occupational groups among humans) comprising anonymous individuals engaged in impersonal patterns of cooperation (Machalek 1992). Similarly, what Durkheim called "social facts," emergent properties of populations and groups, are not unique to human societies. Rather, social systems with emergent characteristics are found among a range of both vertebrate and invertebrate social species, including eusocial insects, the ants, bees, wasps, and termites (Machalek 1999). And although the mechanisms by means of which emergence operates in ant versus human societies vary considerably due to vast differences in the biology that produces ant and human behavior, ant societies exhibit complex, emergent forms of social structure such as "adaptive demography" in ant colonies (Wilson 1971), "dense heterarchies" that regulate social behaviors in ant colonies, series-parallel and parallel-series operations in the division of labor, and homeostatic mechanisms that restore equilibrium in ant colonies that have been subjected to perturbations (Machalek 1999: 54–60).

Finally, behaviors that sociologists characterize as "property crime" or "social exploitation" and biologists classify as "social parasitism" are attributable, in part, to structures and processes of social organization and interaction that enable such social behaviors (Cohen and Machalek 1988; Machalek 1995, 1996). For example, Cohen and Machalek (1988) demonstrated that the logic of "routine activities theory," an influential theory of expropriative crime, represents a manifestation of a broader, more comprehensive explanation of "social parasitism" that has been developed and applied in both sociobiology and behavioral ecology. Subsequently, Machalek (1996) expanded and generalized elements of both routine activities theory in criminology and the theory of social parasitism in behavioral ecology to construct a general theory of social exploitation that focuses on how various "production strategies" enable the development of "exploitation strategies" among a range of social species. Again, the focus of this approach is not the evolved "psychology" of a species but rather forms of social organization that develop among its members. In this case, Machalek has shown how certain forms of socially organized production invite invasion by behavioral strategies that usurp goods and services from those who have produced them. This type of cross-species comparison can be thought of as an extension of Simmel's call for a "formal sociology" (Wolff 1950), because it focuses attention on underlying forms of sociation rather than specific contents. And in this case, formal sociology transgresses species lines and does not restrict itself to a preoccupation with *Homo sapiens* alone.

To the extent that sociology becomes increasingly "biologized," to use Wilson's slightly inelegant, yet straightforward characterization, we should expect even more innovation for integrating sociological and biological thinking. For example, in their respective searches for evolved features of the human social mind (and despite differences in their approaches), the work of Cosmides and Tooby on the one hand and Turner and Maryanski on the other points the way to at least one new type of sociological analysis that is waiting to be identified, formalized, and fully developed. The notion of a social mind that features evolved adaptations for coping with social life in all of its variety and complexity, waiting to be explored and described in detailed analysis, creates an opportunity for the traditional sociologist to contribute to such a project. Whether comprising a suite of specialized, modular, evolved "cognitive algorithms" of the sort described by Cosmides and Tooby (1992) versus sets of neural systems that take the form of "rather diffuse and complex sub-assemblages" that produce social behavior (Turner 2015), both approaches seek to specify the evolutionary processes by means of which humans have come to be equipped with an evolved social mind that is instantiated with *some sort of evolved neural adaptations* for coping with the challenges and opportunities associated with social living. How, then, can we identify those adaptations, and how can we determine what specific social "problems" they evolved to solve?

In response to these questions, consider two additional questions: (1) What requirements must be met for a group to develop and persist? (2) What must individuals be able to do in order to become members of, participate in, and derive benefits from a group?

The first question immediately brings to mind the tradition of sociological theory known as "functionalism" or "structural-functionalism," and especially the notion of the "functional requirements" or "functional prerequisites" of society (Parsons and Smelser 1956). The second question, however, has not received as much attention in mainstream sociology, because for many sociologists, the answer is a forgone conclusion: people must be "socialized" to become members of groups and to be able to participate effectively in group life. The notion of an evolved social mind, however, implies that the process of socialization itself *may be enabled and guided by evolved mental adaptations with which all humans are endowed.* In the view of Cosmides and Tooby (1992), the putative "cheating detection mechanism" is one such adaptation, and in the view of Turner (2000, 2015) and Turner and Maryanski (2008), a palette of emotions that facilitate human social behavior represents another set of such adaptations. In both cases, an interesting sociological question becomes relevant to any effort to discover the evolved properties of the social mind: Considering the nature and scale of the collectivities in which ancestral humans lived during the time period in which the human social mind evolved, what were the *specific aspects of social organization and interaction that posed adaptive challenges* to our hominin (and in Turner's view, even pre-hominin) ancestors? That is, in order to achieve and maintain membership in something like a hunter-gatherer group, what social capabilities would an individual had to have possessed?

This is a slightly different question than one that asks, "What conditions must be realized in order for a group to come into being and survive/persist?" This is the basic question posed by traditional sociological functionalists. The question we pose, however, can be stated as follows: As with any other environment, social environments exhibit features that constitute adaptive challenges (both opportunities and threats) to those occupying those environments. Many of those challenges derive from the social structural features of small-scale foraging groups of which humans, and their hominin ancestors, have been members for millennia. Accordingly, can social scientists reconstruct the characteristics of those groups, characteristics that could have acted as *selection forces* that, in turn, favored *evolved mental adaptations for coping with those forces*?

Cosmides and Tooby (1992) on the one hand, and Turner (2000, 2015) and Turner and Maryanski (2008) on the other have taken explanatory steps in precisely that direction. Specifically, in that reciprocity is a universal feature of small-scale foraging groups, if not all human groups, the threat of non-reciprocity (cheating, or defection in game-theoretic terms) has long posed an adaptive threat to humans and their ancestors. Accordingly, Cosmides and Tooby (1992: 170–179) hypothesized that it is reasonable to expect an evolved mental adaptation in the human mind for coping with that challenge. Similarly, Turner (2000) hypothesizes that selection would have favored the evolution of highly cohesive groups when early hominins migrated to open savanna habitats, because cohesive groups provide protection against predation. In order to achieve and maintain membership in such groups, ancestral hominins would have to have had the capacity to form strong, emotionally based social ties, a capability that is more characteristic of monkeys than apes. Thus, Turner (2000) and Turner and Maryanski (2008) hypothesize that humans evolved an enhanced "palette of emotions" out of which strong social ties could have been forged. In their view, humans are not simply "socialized" from a tabula rasa behavioral platform into the ability to form strong social ties; rather, they are equipped by natural selection with neurological and hormonal machinery that creates a system that is an adaptation for forming close ties to others, thereby enabling them to achieve and maintain "membership in good standing" in highly cohesive, small-scale groups.

Being able to detect cheating and to form close emotional attachments to others are by no means sufficient to equip individuals for meeting all of the adaptive challenges posed by small-scale social life. Rather, the structures and processes that compose such groups pose additional adaptive challenges to candidate members, and most of these adaptive problems have yet to be identified. For example, simply being able to detect cheating does not mean that one will cope successfully with it. One must find ways of reacting against cheating so as not to be victimized by it in the future. This is precisely the adaptive challenge to which Trivers (1971) posited the emotional and behavioral complex that he called "moralistic aggression" as a possible adaptation.

We contend that this sort of thinking creates an opportunity for mainstream, conventional sociologists to identify precisely those features of small-group life (including, perhaps, some of those features that constitute "primary groups") that, in turn, pose adaptive challenges to anyone living in such groups. For example, besides birth, how does one gain entrée to and become a member of such groups? What sorts of behaviors must one exhibit consistently to maintain membership in such groups? How must one behave so as to engender trust by other members of the group? What sorts of interactive skills must one possess in order to gain access to the resources that such groups mobilize and store? These and related questions provide opportunities for sociologists to try to reconstruct the sorts of groups of which humans have been members for millennia, and to which the human social mind is likely to be adapted. For example, if the elementary structures and processes that constitute "primary groups" are universal to the human condition, then sociologists might be able to identify those structures and processes that may have acted as selection forces in response to which an adapted social mind could have evolved. We would think, for example, that this is exactly the sort of analysis in which social network theorists, exchange theorists, small-group specialists, ethnomethodologists, and many other sociologists who work at the micro-level of analysis could become productively engaged. In short, what game theory and the prisoner's dilemma model did for the identification of the "cheating detection mechanism," other variants of sociological theory and models could do on behalf of efforts to identify *additional* evolved features of the adapted social mind.

As we reported in the introduction to this chapter, Wilson ruminated about the extent to which sociology, the other social sciences, and the humanities might become integrated into the Modern Synthesis and thus become "truly biologicized" (1975: 4). And, as we have tried to explain, becoming "truly biologicized" does not mean that sociologists must surrender themselves to any version of biological reductionism, including genetic determinism, and abandon those explanatory frameworks on the basis of which their discipline has developed. Instead, evolutionary thinking in general, and sociobiology in particular, can complement mainstream, well-established modes of thinking and analysis that have helped sociology, along with anthropology, economics, and political science, become established, in Wilson's view, as one of the four fundamental social sciences (1998: 181). And if sociology were to become included in the Modern Synthesis and thus part of the "Second Darwinian Revolution," it might come closer to realizing its full explanatory power as a social science (Machalek and Martin 2004; Wilson 1975).

References

Axelrod, R. 1984. *The Evolution of Cooperation*. New York: Basic Books.
Berger, P. L., and T. Luckmann. 1967. *The Social Construction of Reality: A Treatise in the Sociology of Knowledge*. Garden City, NY: Anchor.
Booth, A., A. Mazur, and K. Kivlighan. 2006. "Testosterone and Social Behavior." *Social Forces* 85: 167–191.
Boulding, K. E. 1981. *A Preface to Grants Economics: The Economy of Love and Fear*. Westport, CT: Praeger Publishers.
Bowlby, J. 1969. *Attachment and Loss*. Vol. 1, *Attachment*. New York: Basic Books.
Buss, D. M. 2002. "Human Mate Guarding." *Neuroendocrinology Letters* 23 (Suppl. 4): 23–29.
———. 2012. *Evolutionary Psychology: The New Science of the Mind*. Boston: Pearson Allyn and Bacon.
Chomsky, N. 1957. *Syntactic Structures*. The Hague: Mouton and Company.
Clutton-Brock, T. 2009. "Cooperation between Non-kin in Animal Societies." *Nature* 462: 51–57.
Cohen, L. E., and R. Machalek. 1988. "A General Theory of Expropriative Crime: An Evolutionary Ecological Approach." *American Journal of Sociology* 94: 465–501.

Cosmides, L., and J. Tooby. 1992. "Cognitive Adaptations for Social Exchange." In *The Adapted Mind: Evolutionary Psychology and the Generation of Culture*, edited by J. H. Barkow, L. Cosmides, and J. Tooby, 163–228. New York: Oxford University Press.

Daly, M., and M. Wilson. 1988. *Homicide*. Hawthorne, NY: Aldine de Gruyter.

Darwin, C. 1872. *The Expression of the Emotions in Man and Animals*. London: Oxford.

———. n.d. *The Origin of Species by Means of Natural Selection or the Preservation of Favored Races in the Struggle for Life and the Descent of Man and Selection in Relation to Sex*. New York: Modern Library.

Davis, M. H. 2007. "Empathy." In *Handbook of the Sociology of Emotions*, edited by J. E. Stets and J. H. Turner, 443–466. New York: Springer.

Degler, C. N. 1991. *In Search of Human Nature: The Decline and Revival of Darwinism in American Social Thought*. New York: Oxford University Press.

Ekeh, P. P. 1974. *Social Exchange Theory: The Two Traditions*. Cambridge, MA: Harvard University Press.

Firat, R., and S. Hitlin. 2012. "Morally Bonded and Bounded: A Sociological Introduction to Neurology." In *Advances in Group Processes: Biosociology and Neurosociology*, edited by W. Kalkhoff, S. Thye, and E. Lawler, 165–199. Bingley, UK: Emerald.

Frank, R. H. 1988. *Passions within Reason: The Strategic Role of Emotions*. New York: Norton.

Franks, D. D. 2010. *Neurosociology: The Nexus between Neuroscience and Social Psychology*. New York: Springer.

Franks, D. D., and J. Davis. 2012. "Critique and Refinement of the Neurosociology of Mirror Neurons." In *Advances in Group Processes: Biosociology and Neurosociology*, edited by W. Kalkhoff, S. Thye, and E. Lawler, 77–117. Bingley, UK: Emerald.

Garcia, J., and R. Koelling. 1966. "Relation of Cue to Consequence in Avoidance Learning." *Psychonomic Science* 4: 123–124.

Goffman, E. 1959. *The Presentation of Self in Everyday Life*. Norwell, MA: Anchor.

Hammond, M. 2003. "The Enhancement Imperative: The Evolutionary Neurophysiology of Durkheimian Solidarity." *Sociological Theory* 21: 359–374.

———. 2007. "Evolutionary Theory and Emotions." In *Handbook of the Sociology of Emotions*, edited by J. E. Stets and J. H. Turner, 368–385. New York: Springer.

Hopcroft, R. 2002. "The Evolution of Sex Discrimination." *Psychology, Evolution & Gender* 4 (1): 43–67.

———. 2006. "Status Characteristics among Older Individuals: The Diminished Significance of Gender." *The Sociological Quarterly* 47: 361–374.

———. 2009a. "Gender Inequality in Interaction—An Evolutionary Account." *Social Forces* 87 (4): 1845–1872.

———. 2009b. "The Evolved Actor in Sociology." *Sociological Theory* 27 (4): 390–406.

Huber, J. 2007. *On the Origins of Gender Inequality*. Boulder, CO: Paradigm Publishers.

Kalkhoff, W., S. R. Thye, and E. J. Lawler, eds. 2012. *Advances in Group Processes: Biosociology and Neurosociology*. Bingley, UK: Emerald.

Kanazawa, S. 2004. "The Savanna Principle." *Managerial and Decision Economics* 25: 41–54.

———. 2010a. "Evolutionary Psychology and Intelligence Research." *American Psychologist* 65 (4): 279–289.

———. 2010b. "Why Liberals and Atheists Are More Intelligent." *Social Psychology Quarterly* 73 (1): 33–37.

Kanazawa, S., and J. Hellberg. 2010. "Intelligence and Substance Use." *Review of General Psychology* 14 (4): 382–396.

Kanazawa, S., and M. Still. 2000. "Why Men Commit Crimes (and Why They Desist)." *Sociological Theory* 18 (3): 434–447.

Kelly, R. L. 1995. *The Foraging Spectrum: Diversity in Hunter-Gatherer Lifeways*. Washington, DC: Smithsonian Institution Press.

Kramarae, C., and P. A. Teichler. 1985. *A Feminist Dictionary*. Boston: Pandora Press.

Lawler, E. J., S. R. Thye, and J. Yoon. 2007. "Social Exchange and Micro Social Order." *American Sociological Review* 73: 519–542.

Leveto, J. A., and W. Kalkhoff. 2012. "Biosocial Interaction Rituals of Autism Spectrum Disorders: A Research Agenda for Neurosociology." In *Advances in Group Processes: Biosociology and Neurosociology*, edited by W. Kalkhoff, S. Thye, and E. Lawler, 119–138. Bingley, UK: Emerald.

Lévi-Strauss, C. 1969. *The Elementary Structures of Kinship*. Rev. ed. Boston: Beacon.

Lopreato, J. 1984. *Human Nature and Biocultural Evolution*. Winchester, MA: Allen and Unwin.

———. 2001. "Sociobiological Theorizing: Evolutionary Sociology." In *Handbook of Sociological Theory*, edited by J. H. Turner. New York: Kluwer Academic/Plenum Publishers.

Lopreato, J., and T. Crippen. 1999. *Crisis in Sociology: The Need for Darwin*. London: Transaction.

Lumsden, C. J., and E. O. Wilson. 1981. *Genes, Mind and Culture: The Coevolutionary Process*. Cambridge, MA: Harvard University Press.

Machalek, R. 1992. "The Evolution of Macrosociety: Why Are Large Societies Rare?" *Advances in Human Ecology* 1: 33–64.

———. 1995. "Basic Dimensions and Forms of Social Exploitation: A Comparative Analysis." *Advances in Human Ecology* 4: 35–68.
———. 1996. "The Evolution of Social Exploitation." *Advances in Human Ecology* 5: 1–32.
———. 1999. "Elementary Social Facts: Emergence in Nonhuman Societies." *Advances in Human Ecology* 8: 33–64.
Machalek, R., and M. W. Martin. 2004. "Sociology and the Second Darwinian Revolution: A Metatheoretical Analysis." *Sociological Theory* 22: 455–476.
———. 2010. "Evolution, Biology, and Society: A Conversation for the 21st Century Classroom." *Teaching Sociology* 38 (1): 33–45.
———. 2012. "Sacrifice, Gratitude, and Obligation: Serial Reciprocity in Early Christianity." In *Advances in Group Processes: Biosociology and Neurosociology*, edited by W. Kalkhoff, S. Thye, and E. Lawler, 39–75. Bingley, UK: Emerald.
Maryanski, A. 1992. "The Last Ancestor: An Ecological-Network Model on the Origins of Human Sociality." *Advances in Human Ecology* 2: 1–32.
———. 1993. "The Elementary Forms of the First Proto-Human Society: An Ecological/Social Network Approach." *Advances in Human Evolution* 2: 215–241.
———. 1998. "Evolutionary Sociology." *Advances in Human Ecology* 7: 1–56.
Maryanski, A., and J. H. Turner. 1992. *The Social Cage: Human Nature and the Evolution of Society*. Stanford, CA: Stanford University Press.
Massey, D. S. 2002. "A Brief History of Human Society: The Origin and Role of Emotion in Social Life." *American Sociological Review* 67: 1–29.
———. 2005. *Strangers in a Strange Land: Humans in an Urbanizing World*. New York: W. W. Norton and Company.
Mazur, A. 2005. *Biosociology of Dominance and Deference*. New York: Rowman and Littlefield.
———. 2006. "The Role of Testosterone in Male Dominance Contests that Turn Violent." *Social Biology* 53 (1–2): 24–29.
McCullough, M. E., M. B. Kimeldorf, and A. D. Cohen. 2008. "An Adaptation for Altruism: The Social Causes, Social Effects, and Social Evolution of Gratitude." *Current Directions in Psychological Science* 17: 281–285.
Miller, E., and C. J. Costello. 2001. "The Limits of Biological Determinism." *American Sociological Review* 66: 592–598.
Molm, L. D., J. L. Collett, and D. R. Schaefer. 2007. "Building Solidarity through Generalized Exchange: A Theory of Reciprocity." *American Journal of Sociology* 113: 205–242.
Moody, M. 2008. "Serial Reciprocity: A Preliminary Statement." *Sociological Theory* 26: 130–151.
Nisbett, R. E., and D. Cohen. 1996. *Culture of Honor: The Psychology of Violence in the South*. Boulder, CO: Westview.
Parsons, T., and N. J. Smelser. 1956. *Economy and Society*. New York: Free Press.
Pinker, S. 1994. *The Language Instinct: How the Mind Creates Language*. New York: Harper Collins.
———. 2002. *Blank Slate: The Modern Denial of Human Nature*. New York: Penguin.
Rachman, S. J., and M.E.P. Seligman. 1976. "Unprepared Phobias: Be Prepared." *Behaviour Research and Therapy* 14: 333–338.
Risman, B. 2001. "Calling the Bluff of Value-Free Science." *American Sociological Review* 66: 605–611.
Schneider, L. 1975. *The Sociological Way of Looking at the World*. New York: McGraw-Hill.
Segerstråle, U. 2000. *Defenders of the Truth: The Battle for Science in the Sociobiology Debate and Beyond*. Oxford: Oxford University Press.
Seligman, M.E.P. 1971. "Preparedness and Phobias." *Behavior Therapy* 2: 307–320.
———. 1993. *What You Can Change and What You Can't*. New York: Fawcett Columbine.
Seligman, M.E.P., and J. L. Hager. 1972. *Biological Boundaries of Learning*. New York: Meredith.
Simons, R. L., S.R.H. Beach, and A. B. Barr. 2012. "Differential Susceptibility to Context: A Promising Model of the Interplay of Genes and the Social Environment." In *Advances in Group Processes: Biosociology and Neurosociology*, edited by W. Kalkhoff, S. Thye, and E. Lawler, 139–163. Bingley, UK: Emerald.
Smith, A. (1776) 1805. *An Inquiry into the Nature and Causes of the Wealth of Nations*. London: Davis.
Spencer, H. 1885. *The Principles of Sociology*. New York: Appleton-Century-Crofts.
Stark, R. 1996. *The Rise of Christianity: A Sociologist Reconsiders History*. Princeton, NJ: Princeton University Press.
Stets, J. E., and J. H. Turner, eds. 2007. *Handbook of the Sociology of Emotions*. New York: Springer.
Thornhill, R., and G. T. Palmer. 2000. *A Natural History of Rape: Biological Bases of Sexual Coercion*. Cambridge, MA: MIT Press.
Tiger, L., and R. Fox. 1966. "The Zoological Perspective in Social Science." *Man* 1: 75–81.
———. 1971. *The Imperial Animal*. New York: Holt, Rinehart and Winston.
Tooby, J., and L. Cosmides. 1990. "The Past Explains the Present: Emotional Adaptations and the Structure of Ancestral Environments." *Ethology and Sociobiology* 11: 375–424.

———. 1992. "The Psychological Foundations of Culture." In *The Adapted Mind: Evolutionary Psychology and the Generation of Culture*, edited by J. H. Barkow, L. Cosmides, and J. Tooby, 19–136. New York: Oxford University Press.
Trivers, R. L. 1971. "The Evolution of Reciprocal Altruism." *Quarterly Review of Biology* 46: 35–57.
Turner, J. H. 1999. "Toward a General Sociological Theory of Emotions." *Journal for the Theory of Social Behavior* 29: 133–162.
———. 2000. *On the Origins of Human Emotions: A Sociological Inquiry into the Evolution of Human Affect*. Stanford, CA: Stanford University Press.
———. 2015. "The Evolution of the Social Mind: The Limitations of Evolutionary Psychology." In *Handbook on Evolution and Society: Toward an Evolutionary Social Science*, edited by J. H. Turner, R. Machalek, and A. Maryanski, 177–191. Boulder, CO: Paradigm.
Turner, J., and A. Maryanski. 2005. *Incest: Origins of the Taboo*. Boulder, CO: Paradigm Publishers.
———. 2008. *On the Origin of the Societies by Natural Selection*. Boulder, CO: Paradigm Publishers.
Turner, J. H., and J. E. Stets. 2005. *The Sociology of Emotions*. New York: Cambridge University Press.
———. 2007. "Moral Emotions." In *Handbook of the Sociology of Emotions*, edited by J. E. Stets and J. H. Turner, 544–566. New York: Springer.
Udry, J. R. 2000. "Biological Limits of Gender Construction." *American Sociological Review* 65 (June): 443–457.
Udry, J. R., N. M. Morris, and J. Kovenock. 1995. "Androgen Effects on Women's Gendered Behaviour." *Journal of Biosocial Science* 27: 359–368.
van den Berghe, P. 1974. "Bringing Beasts Back In: Toward a Biosocial Theory of Aggression." *American Sociological Review* 39: 777–788.
Williams, G. C. 1966. *Adaptation and Natural Selection*. Princeton, NJ: Princeton University Press.
Wilson, E. O. 1971. *The Insect Societies*. Cambridge, MA: Belknap Press of Harvard University Press.
———. 1975. *Sociobiology: The New Synthesis*. Cambridge, MA: Belknap Press of Harvard University Press.
———. 1984. *Biophilia*. Cambridge, MA: Harvard University Press.
———. 1998. *Consilience: The Unity of Knowledge*. New York: Alfred A. Knopf.
———, ed. 2006. *From So Simple a Beginning: The Four Great Books of Charles Darwin*. New York: W. W. Norton and Company.
———. 2012. *The Social Conquest of Earth*. London: Liveright.
Wolff, K. H. 1950. *The Sociology of Georg Simmel*. New York: Free Press.

CHAPTER TWO
THE BIOLOGICAL CHARACTER OF SOCIAL THEORY
Alexander Rosenberg

> This chapter argues that all social sciences need to take seriously their status as divisions of biology, and that, as such, they need to recognize the central role of Darwinian processes in all the phenomena they seek to explain. The argument is formulated in terms of a small number of relatively precise premises that focus on the nature of the kinds and taxonomies of all the social sciences. The analytical taxonomy of the social sciences is shown to require a Darwinian approach to human affairs, though not a nativist or genetically driven framework. The fundamental role of Darwinian processes in human cultural evolution establishes limitations on the explanatory aspirations of alternative theories in the social sciences, including especially rational choice theory, the currently most fashionable explanatory approach in several social and behavioral sciences. An apparently widespread objection to a biological approach to human affairs proceeds from the denial that there are "replicators," and in particular "memes," in human affairs. This objection is shown to be misdirected. The chapter goes on to expound a general account of how Darwinian processes operate in human affairs by selecting for strategies and sets of strategies humans employ. The last section shows how a great deal of social science can be organized in accordance with Tinbergen's approach to biological inquiry, an approach required by the fact that the social sciences are all divisions of biology, and in particular the studies of one particular biological species.

INTRODUCTION

Homo sapiens is a biological species. That should be enough of a basis on which to argue that the social sciences are biological sciences, must proceed in accordance with the explanatory and evidential strictures of biology, and cannot be expected to transcend whatever limits biology faces as a domain of scientific inquiry.[1] It should be enough of a basis for this conclusion, but it never yet has been.

The first two sections of this chapter offer another reason why the social sciences must be biological that may be more compelling and that provides more guidance about how they should proceed than the anodyne observation that human beings are biological creatures. In particular, the argument underwrites a Darwinian approach to human affairs, but not a nativist, innatist, or genetically driven framework. In the third section we see how the argument establishes limitations on the explanatory aspirations of alternative theories, including especially rational choice theory, the currently most fashionable explanatory approach in several social and behavioral sciences. In the fourth section one equally fashionable objection to a biological approach to human affairs is disposed of. The fifth section develops a positive though still relatively general account of how Darwinian processes operate in human affairs. The last section explores how a research program about human affairs driven by a Darwinian approach should proceed and how much of current, conventional social science can be expected to "recover."

The Taxonomies and the Regularities of the Social Sciences Must Be Biological

There is a fairly direct argument for the claim that the taxonomies of the social sciences and the spatiotemporally restricted regularities, *ceteris paribus* laws, a priori mathematical models, and for that matter historical narratives they invoke to explain phenomena in their domains identify biological categories and causal relations among biological categories.

1. Almost all significant features of human affairs—historical actions, events, processes, norms, organizations, institutions—have functions.
2. Functions are all adaptations,[2] and the only sources of adaptation in nature—including human affairs—are Darwinian processes of blind variation and environmental filtration.[3]

Therefore,

3. All regularities about the character and relationships among adaptations (or their direct results) are local evolutionary equilibria, which are eventually broken up by "arms races."[4] All biological regularities are "restricted," limited in their spatiotemporal domains, and draw their explanatory power from underlying unrestricted Darwinian regularities.

Therefore,

4. All restricted regularities about human affairs are local equilibria (or their consequences) and are eventually broken up by arms races.
5. Regularities about human affairs have explanatory power because they are underwritten by unrestricted Darwinian regularities.
6. A social science in the business of explaining human behavior and human affairs should proceed by explicitly Darwinian research strategies—identifying adaptations and the processes that determine their emergence, proliferation, persistence, and extinction.

The two premises are controversial. The rest of the argument reflects fairly well established conclusions in the philosophy of biology about the nature of biological laws, models, theories, and explanations more generally. This section begins the process of justifying them. The task is not completed until the end of the next section.

Premise 1 may seem dubious at first blush. How could almost everything in human affairs have a function and so be an adaptation? That sounds like an idea worthy of Pollyanna or Voltaire's Dr. Pangloss. Even in biology, not everything turns out to be an adaptation. Much of evolution is a matter of drift—the play of chance on small and sometimes even large populations that leads to changes in the distribution of adaptations, and even to the persistence of nonadaptive and maladaptive traits. Moreover, important biological traits either are the result of physical constraints or were acquired as adaptations early enough in evolutionary processes to remain fixed long after they ceased to be adaptations. Surely all the same must be said of the course of human affairs. Indeed, for obvious reasons, there may well be a greater role for drift and constraint in human affairs than in biological processes.

Of course, premise 1 needs to be understood as qualified by the reality of drift and constraint in human affairs. In fact, the plausibility of the claim that premise 1 makes about the adaptedness of most features of human affairs relies a great deal on the qualification "significant." There will be many features of human affairs that are the result of drift, and yet little of what interests social scientists about human affairs is the result of random drift alone or even mainly. Similarly, social scientists will recognize constraints of many kinds as forcing subsequent features of human affairs to adapt to them. But few social scientists accord such constraints the fixed character that constraints—especially physical ones—have in biological evolution. In fact, the most revolutionary social changes break down the oldest, firmest, and most pervasive constraints. The real issue is whether such change is the result of blind variation and environmental filtration—cultural selection.

A little reoriented reflection on human affairs does suggest that, even more than in biology, significant features of social life are largely or even wholly functionally beneficial—for someone, or some group, or some practice.

The notion that all, most, many, or at least some human social institutions have functions is not a new one. The idea goes back to Durkheim, and forward beyond Parsons. These nineteenth- and twentieth-century functionalists were right about the functional character of almost all social institutions. But a serious oversight in their analysis condemned it to implausibility, and it went into eclipse long ago. The simple error that functionalists made, which made their view sound so implausible, was to misidentify the *beneficiaries* of the functions that institutions, practices, and organizations fulfilled. They assumed, quite myopically and wrongly, that the function of institutions, practices, and organizations was to fulfill the needs of people, of human beings. But it was obvious that many institutions, practices, and organizations are in fact harmful to people and confer no net advantage or benefit on them, for instance, most religions, Chinese foot binding, or tobacco smoking. This Panglossianism about all social institutions made functionalism a laughing stock when it was not pilloried as an invitation to complacence and conservatism: if almost all human institutions fulfilled functions for us, then it is tempting to reason that we should not change them lest we deprive ourselves of the benefits they confer on us. Whence the charge of complaisance and conservativism.

Only in the late twentieth century did it become apparent that in these and other cases, a change in perspective—a *Gestalt switch*—would enable us to see what was not previously apparent: the relevant beneficiaries of those features of institutions, practices, and organizations harmful to people were the institutions, practices, and organizational structures themselves. Institutions, organizations, and practices prey on, parasitize people, treat people as niches, environments to be exploited. To vindicate functionalism we need to begin to think of people as the environment and think of types of institutions, practices, and organizations as the things that survive, replicate, and spread or recede and become extinct owing to the degree their features *exploit* human characteristics. Institutions, practices, and organizations emerge, persist, and spread owing to how well their features *function* to encourage people to participate in them. Viewed this way the functionalist perspective becomes more difficult to resist: many socially significant institutions, practices, organizations confer huge net benefits on people—money, the firm, the market price system. Many others confer huge net harms on people, but in so doing ensure their own persistence—think again of foot binding or tobacco smoking or heroin addiction. Other institutions confer benefits on some people and harms on others—slavery, for example. Most institutions—religions, for example—confer a mixture of harms and benefits on different mixtures of persons over time.

One way to effect the *Gestalt switch* necessary to accept thoroughgoing functionalism about human affairs is to employ the game theorist's notion of a "strategy." A "strategy" is simply a rule, norm, or procedure of the form "Under condition X, do Y." Strategies may be reflexive or voluntary, moral or ritual, matters of fashion or style, short-lived or not, obligatory or optional, complex or simple, consciously followed or not, beneficial to the agent employing them or harmful to him or her. People's behaviors are determined by and express reveal, manifest the strategies they internalize. These strategies are traits, like left-handedness, or speaking French, or wearing miniskirts, that can come and go. They are acquired by social learning, by imitation or enforcement, by unconscious classical and operant conditioning and transmitted from person to person. Individuals' strategies interact with other strategies, cooperating with them, competing with them, subordinated to them, or subordinating them. Human social institutions, from a book club to feudalism, are nested sets of coordinated strategies. Think of practices like patrilateral cross-cousin marriage or purdah or the incest taboo. Think of organizations like the free masons or the parish council. Human affairs are a matter of nested institutions, organizations, and practices, all composed of the strategies individuals employ. Then there are the strategies each individual employs to navigate through these institutions, organizations, practices—these packages of strategies. The institutions, organizations, and practices have functions. They thrive or perish depending on how well the strategies they impose on people enable the institutions, organizations, and practices to fulfill these functions for their beneficiaries—often themselves.

Focusing on the strategies instead of the humans whose behavior is described (and perhaps directed by them) enables us to embrace the thoroughgoing functionalism of theorists like Durkheim and Parsons without the Panglossian implausibility that daunted their approach. Think of strategies as symbionts, or parasites, or sometimes combinations of both, living on human life, and changing it for the better or for the worse, but always adapting to ensure their own survival. (Much more on this approach below.)

It's difficult to think of tobacco smoking or heroin addiction as having functions, because they are harmful. Their functions are not functions for us, but for themselves. To see this we first need to see how smoking or foot binding functions in an environment composed of humans. They are harmful to humans, but they are practices with features that function to ensure their persistence and spread through human history, at least until their environments change and their effects start to be selected against. Chinese foot binding is a clear example of how this works. Foot binding persisted for about 1000 years in China. It got started because women with bound feet were more attractive as wives. Bound feet were a signal of wealth, since only rich families could afford the luxury of preventing daughters from working. Girls with bound feet were easier to keep track of and so likelier to be virgins. So, at first, when the practice arose, foot-bound girls had more suitors. Pretty soon every family that could afford it was binding daughters' feet to ensure they'd get married. Result: when every girl's feet were bound, foot binding no longer provided an advantage in the marriage market, and all foot-bound girls were worse off because they couldn't walk and suffered other health effects. Foot binding starts out as an adaptation for some girls, and for some families, but by the time it becomes really widespread and fixed, it is actually a physical maladaptation that lowered every foot-bound girl's fitness. But once everyone was doing it, no one could get off the foot-binding merry-go-round. Anyone who stopped binding daughters' feet condemns them to spinsterhood. Here we have a tradition, a norm—Bind daughters' feet!—that by the time it was widely adopted ceased to convey any benefit on the people whose behavior it governs. Why did it persist despite its maladaptive effects on foot-bound girls? For whom or for what were its features adaptations? For itself, for the practice, norm, institution of foot binding! The practice persists, like any parasite, because of those of its features that functioned to exploit the "weaknesses" of humans and their institutions—marriage, the desire for virgin brides and large dowries, the desire to control women before and after marriage.[5]

Once we widen the range of the possible beneficiaries of a function, the claim that almost everything of interest to social scientists in human affairs has functions becomes far less Panglossian. But can it be correct? Here is another deep reason to suppose that the taxonomies of all the social sciences individuate functionally: the vocabularies of all ordinary languages do so predominantly. That is, almost every common noun in all languages is defined in terms of the causes and effects, especially the effects. Few things are defined in ordinary language even partly in terms of their material composition. The same goes for all the sciences, especially at their inceptions. There is not really any alternative, given that the goal of many sciences is to identify the structures that produce effects of interest. That's why they start with taxonomy of kinds characterized by effects. When it comes to biological, the effects we notice first and hit upon to define them are the ones that appear to be functions—to confer benefits and advantages, to meet needs, and so on. In fact, as biologists have been reminded (Gould and Lewontin 1979), the tendency to taxonomize this way needs to be tempered by careful study of traits of interest to establish whether they really are functions, and if so what their functions are. Mere observation is often misleading about what functions are served and for which beneficiaries. This caution, however, does nothing to undermine the indispensability in biology of starting off with hypotheses about functions.

The same considerations enforce functional taxonomies in the social sciences, even among social scientists innocent of a biological agenda. It's hard to begin a research program in any other way than by describing the phenomena of interest in terms of effects of interest to the human scientist.

Moreover, the predictive and ameliorative goals that the human sciences impose on their research programs assume that most of the significant features of human affairs have functions for some individuals and groups and are dysfunctional for other groups. Though each of the social sciences may be neutral on the functional significance of the actions, events, norms, practices, and institutions in the domains of the other social and behavioral sciences, it will not be agnostic about those within its proprietary domain. This will be true so long as a discipline has ameliorative ambitions for social processes in its domain. The remodeling and redesign of political, legal, economic, social, or cultural institutions, rules, norms, and practices would be impossible if these items did not function to benefit or harm individuals and groups of various sizes and compositions.

So much for premise 1 in the argument above. What of the second premise?

Premise 2 asserts that all functions are Darwinian adaptations, brought into existence, maintained, and shaped by Darwinian processes, not biological but social.[6] The reasons have only to be stated to be seen as obvious. Once premise 1 is accepted, a serious problem confronts the social scientist. It cannot be a mere coincidence that almost everything of interest to social science has functions. Science doesn't tolerate coincidences on this scale. Either having functions is part of the causal process that brings socially significant features into existence, or their existence and their functions have a common cause. Of course, the explanation could be selection bias: the social scientist's interests are myopically focused on only those features of human affairs with functions. Even if selection bias does explain the fact and even if, implausibly, much that is significant in shaping human affairs has no function, it is going to turn out that the only plausible causal process that brought into existence all those features of human affairs that do have functions is a Darwinian one.

Once we rule out accident or drift, there are only a limited number of possible causal processes that can bring about something that has a function: conscious design and fabrication, purposive future causation, immanent teleology, a benevolent deity, or Darwinian natural selection. It requires no more than a sentence or two to rule out three of these alternatives. Everything we know about the physical and biological sciences prohibits the existence of and causal role of future purposes. It's not just that events in the future cannot bring events that precede them, the special theory of relativity even rules out simultaneous causation. Aristotelian immanent causation ("entelechies") is equally untenable on evidential considerations, if not also grounds of intelligibility, and inferences from the functionality of human institutions to the existence of a divine deity who planned and implemented them are excluded on similar grounds. This leaves only human intentional design and human contrivance to explain the character of social institutions, practices, and organizations, or some process of blind variation and cultural selection.

The grip of human intentionality on the explanatory strategies of the social sciences has always been strong and has strengthened in recent decades owing to the intellectual imperialism of economics and the attendant prestige of rational choice theory. There is a widely held but mistaken view that economics has achieved some sort of "takeoff" as a science more completely than other disciplines. Combined with the mathematical tractability of aggregating individual constrained preference maximization as an account of human affairs, the mistake has encouraged the notion that social institutions, practices, and organizations have "microfoundations" in rational choice theory's formalization of intentional human choices. The unsatisfactory character of such approaches to explaining the functions of social institutions needs to be clearly established. Once this has been accomplished, the inevitability of a biological—a Darwinian approach to human affairs will be evident.

The Limits of Intentional Design and Rational Choice in Human Affairs

In general, social scientists overestimate the role of intentional human design in human affairs. This is especially true among economists and political scientists who employ the rational choice models economists have developed over the last century or so.[7]

To see most clearly the limits on intentional human design and rational choice approaches to the nature of human affairs, it is best to focus on a number of important examples from the home base of such approaches: economics. So, let us consider how to explain the emergence of three central economic facts: the ubiquity of markets, the emergence of money, and the existence of firms. Each of these institutions fulfills an important *need* individuals have. None emerged from a rational choice process. It was the Nobel Prize–winning economist Friedrich Hayek (1945) who first and most clearly recognized the problem facing economic theory of explaining the emergence of economic institutions. He called it the problem of "spontaneous order." But that is just to label the problem, as we'll see.

In the case of the firm, the human need is to solve a transaction cost problem, as Ronald Coase (1937) first noticed only in 1937. Without a solution to this problem, the division of labor must come to a standstill and with it almost all the productivity increases humans have contrived since the Middle Ages. No rational agent recognized what the problem was that everyone faced; no one decided to invent the firm in order to solve this problem. It emerged "spontaneously" to "order" exchanges between individuals in ways that solved a transaction-cost problem. The firm is an example of "spontaneous order." If the firm was not a conscious contrivance, nor the gift of a benevolent deity, its emergence demands an explanation.

Money solves the biggest problem of barter: what the economists call the double coincidence of wants. Without money, if I want oranges and have only bananas, I need to find someone who wants bananas and has oranges. What's more, since we can't divide and store bananas and oranges, I'll need to find someone who wants to trade in exact whole numbers of bananas and oranges that match up with the amounts I am prepared to trade. This is a problem that becomes intractable very early in human exchange. How does it get solved? Several times in distant cultures the same solution was hit upon: the emergence of a commodity with the common features of portability, divisibility, durability, utility or widespread desirability, and short-term limits on its quantity. When money emerged, no one consciously recognized that it would have to have these features. No one intentionally or rationally chose to adopt some commodity owing to its having the features that solved the problem of the double coincidence of wants.

The emergence of money requires that agents solve another problem, one of coordination. Sooner or later they must all converge on the same commodity to serve as money. People must solve a "common knowledge" problem. Somehow each agent must be willing to adopt a certain commodity as money and must come to believe that everyone else will adopt the same commodity, and must believe that everyone else will be confident that every other agent has adopted the same commodity. You can see that this is a set of problems that can't be solved by individual rational choice, that were not solved by some explicit social contract. The institution of money is another example of order emerging without anyone intending it or taking steps to bring it about. Of course, to say money emerged spontaneously is simply to label the problem. To model the acceptance among large numbers of rational individuals of a commodity as the numeraire, as the optimal solution to a cooperative game is not to solve this problem but to structure it in a way that cries out for a Darwinian approach to its solution: once the optimal outcome is retrospectively recognized, we can set about identifying forces that will select for variations in human behavior that approach and eventually realize it. It's clear that this process will not involve conscious calculation by individuals of the sort that monetary economists recognize.

The third example—Hayek's example, the system of market prices—is the most important but the most difficult to understand of these problems of spontaneous order. The unsolvable problem of socialist central planning is informational. Central planning faces the mathematical problem of converting a list of available inputs and a list of desired outputs into a list of production orders, and then continually updating this list as input availability changes and desired outputs change. Central planning faces the further problem of sending information about each of the changes in inputs and outputs only to those who need to have this information in order to change their production plans. The central planner can't send the changes to everyone: we'd have to spend the better part of every day just trying to find the information we need from a daily massive data dump. But the central planner can no more figure out to whom exactly to send the updated information than he or she can figure out the initial production order. Updating this order as circumstances change is still another challenge beyond the powers of rational, intentional choice and planning implementation. These are all what mathematicians call NP-hard problems (nondeterministic polynomial-time hard problems). There is no known algorithmic, computerizable solution to such problems, and a good chance that none exists. This is the fundamental reason the soviet economies collapsed. Even a society composed exclusively of exemplars of New Socialist Man would not be able to solve the relevant NP-hard problem.

Yet the problem is solved all day, every day, instantaneously by the system of market prices. The market price system is an information storage, retrieval, and calculation system—a vast virtual computer—that provides the closest approximation to mathematically correct solutions to the central planners' calculation problems and at no cost whatever.

The market price system performs a function indispensable not just to modern life but to all human life beyond the Pleistocene. It meets a need that cannot have been foreseen by humans, no matter how rational. It is a solution to that need that no human or coalition of humans could have filled by intentional design and contrivance. Indeed it is a solution that rational choice would have led individuals to try to undermine or subvert in their own interests. But the solution to the problem people face is so ingenious it automatically and successfully responds to such subversion attempts. Even the strongest exponents of rational choice theory have recognized this feature of markets: their prescription for the elimination of monopoly, externalities, insider trading, and other "market failures" is to leave them alone. The excess "rents" these failures produce send price signals to the rest of the rational agents in the economy that will change their behavior and compete away the rents and the market failures.

The market price system operates continually to meet a need that no human or set of humans could fulfill by intentional and deliberate action. The function served by the market price system cannot be met by people, no matter how rational they are, and no matter how powerful and inexpensive their information storage, retrieval, and computational resources are. And the market price system emerged, like money, spontaneously, independently, repeatedly, and without malice of human forethought throughout human affairs, across the globe.

These three examples of spontaneous order highlight the economist's version of a problem facing all social sciences. If rational choice theory is incapable of dealing with the problem in its home base, it has few prospects of dealing with it elsewhere in human affairs. But the problem of spontaneous order is pervasive.

Of course, rational choice theory is but a formalization of the commonsense folk psychology. This theory is at work, especially in narrative history, to explain how many human institutions, organizations, and practices were intentionally designed and implemented in order to function in foreseen ways. And it is undeniable that such institutions exist. But institutions, practices, and organizations that result from conscious human contrivance—the US Constitution, the UN Charter, various diplomatic treaties—are a minority, probably a small minority of human norms, practices, and institutions.[8] They don't last as long, don't spring up repeatedly and independently, and have far more limited impact on the character of everyday human affairs.

Once we have excluded divine benevolence, future teleology, Aristotelian entelechies, and random chance, the only well-established, available mechanism that explains the emergence, persistence, spread, and recession and extinction of things with functions is a Darwinian process of blind variation and environmental filtration. The "only" problem that faces the social scientist is to identify the details of this process. Let us see how far we can get in doing so.

Regularities in Human Affairs Are All Local Equilibria

Premise 3 in the argument tells us that all "laws," regularities, generalizations, explanatory models, and theories about human affairs will be, at most, descriptions of "local equilibria" waiting to be broken up by arms races among the adapted institutions, practices, and organizations they describe. Why is this?

If human affairs are mostly the emergence, persistence, and improvement of adaptations by Darwinian processes, then we can expect only a limited number of different kinds of regularities about the relationships between them, regularities of the sort already familiar in biology and exemplified in the original argument set out above. To begin with, in human affairs individual adaptations will emerge, and then there will be pairs or larger sets of adaptations, each of which constitutes selective components of one another's environment; they will either accommodate to one another, or cooperate with one another, over long periods, or will compete with one another over such periods. In either of the first two cases, any variations that can exploit to its selective advantage the accommodation or the cooperation will do so. The result will eventually be the emergence of exploitation or a competition somewhere. The exploitation or competition may persist in a local equilibrium. But it must eventually break down into an extinction or an arms race as further variants of each adaptation emerge. The results of the emergence of adaptations and of the persistence of these alternative relations between adaptations are the regularities we recognize in the social sciences.

First, there are regularities about the (real, often latent) function of a behavior or norm or practice or institution: "Firms (function to) solve the transaction cost problem." Then there will be regularities about the co-occurrence of adaptations in the same individuals or lineages of them, regularities about the co-occurrence of adaptations in two or more distinct individuals or lineages—cases of coevolution or mutualism, or parasitism (the most famous example of a regularity of coevolution or mutualism in political science is given below). These regularities will in effect record local equilibria among adaptations, ones that last as long as the historically contingent circumstances that brought them about obtain.

But, as in biology, each individual's or group's adaptation sets a design problem for the individuals and groups with which it finds itself in local equilibrium. The existence of these mutual design problems together with the persistent but blind variation among adaptations means that the prospects for arms races are ever present. Beneath every local equilibrium there is a seething rumble of blind variations continually being tested by and testing the local equilibrium. The latter must always eventually be broken up by one of these variants that precipitate an arms race. Whence the restricted character of every explanatory regularity and all the models in social science.

Examples of these restricted regularities and models are easy to identify. Consider perhaps the most robust regularity in international relations, perhaps even in the whole of political science: arguably, no two democracies have ever gone to war with one another. There is apparently not a single exception to this regularity since democracies emerged at the end of the eighteenth century, even though the number of pairs of countries that could have gone to war with each other since 1776 is literally in the several thousands.[9] Apparently, the trait of being a democracy and the trait of not going to war with a democracy are for the moment at least coadapted to each other. This probably helps explain several things, like why democracies do better economically than even market-economy dictatorships (they engage in fewer wars), and why the number of democracies seems to be increasing. It has also guided foreign policy—the US and European encouragement of new democracies to ensure stability and peace.

But, nothing is forever. We can be confident that somewhere or somewhen, some democracy is going to find a way to exploit this regularity by attacking some completely unsuspecting fellow democracy, lulled into a false sense of the permanence of peace among democracies. How can we be so confident? Just as Mother Nature searches through biological design space for variations on that trait that can take advantage of the environment of other adaptations the variation faces, so too will it search for variations in the human social design space. And the rate of variation will be vastly accelerated in comparison with biological evolution. For human evolution doesn't have to wait a twenty-year generation for a genetic variation to change a trait the way that biological evolution must.

One more example, this time of a mathematical model that is explanatory over a restricted domain, but whose explanatory power is destroyed by an arms race breaking up a local equilibrium. Consider again what was for a long time the most influential model in economics, and perhaps even all of social science—the LM/IS graphs and equations of Keynesian macroeconomics. This set of graphs enabled economists of the third quarter of the twentieth century to successfully model the stable relationship between sets of macroeconomic variables, including investment and savings, consumption and gross national income, the interest rate and the money supply, and with one another.

The stagflation of the '70s put an end to the model's general acceptance and resulted in its replacement by newer ones, including the rational expectations model. This model explained why the superseded model was no longer a basis for effective intervention. The analysis of why the Keynesian model ceased to work, if it ever worked at all, was roughly that the coadaptations it identified were broken up by an arms race. The model's widespread dissemination, or at least the fact that economic agents had become acquainted with the governmental interventions it guided, resulted in a change in their choices, one that rendered Keynesian fine-tuning ineffective.

The beautiful and temporarily powerful model of the capitalist economy that John Maynard Keynes (1936) inspired ceased to work because the relationships it described broke down once some of the institutions, groups, and individuals the model included began to exploit the fact that other institutions were guided by it, to frustrate the policies the model guided. The result was that ten or fifteen years after it became widely known, the Keynesian model became the victim of an arms race.

Examples are not arguments even though they can be proliferated ad infinitum. But there is a simple argument that they buttress and that explains them. It shows exactly why restricted regularities and mathematical models are explanatory and why they are the best we can hope for in the explanation of human affairs.

It is widely recognized among philosophers of biology that there are no completely invariant regularities, no laws, in biology except for those reported in the Darwinian theory of natural selection. A variety of arguments have been offered for this consensus view, of which perhaps the most influential is John Beatty's (1995) "evolutionary contingency thesis": all other regularities in biology—from the most invariant to the least—obtain only as a result of the operation of natural selection on initial conditions that have obtained in the history of the Earth, and are subject to abrogation by the operation of natural selection on later conditions.

The general argument is obvious, and it has immediate implications for biological arms races. Since nature builds adaptations by a process of environmental filtration of random variations, when environments change, adaptations can become maladaptations and vice versa; variations neutral in fitness in one environment can become adaptive or maladaptive in another one. But nothing is forever: even the most stable environmental conditions will sometimes change, and sometimes even quickly. Consider how the asteroid impact at the Cretaceous-Tertiary boundary 65 million years ago changed the environment and killed off all dinosaurs within a few years. Thus, no regularity thrown up by the process of natural selection is immune to breakdown as a result of environmental change.

Once the evolutionary environment comes to include creatures and their effects on one another, the lifetimes of regularities about creatures' adapted traits are reduced from the scale of billions of years (archebacteria—whose environment has not changed for 3 billion years), to multiple geological epochs (oxygen respirators), to hundreds of millions of years (vertebrates), to weeks and months in the case of others (the AIDS virus). Owing to the role of environmental change, even the most established and long-lasting regularities in biology are not as invariant as any well-established regularity of physical science.[10]

Given the slowness of most environmental changes, regularities about individual species can remain invariant over geologically long periods. Changes such as the shift to an oxygen-rich atmosphere, continental drift, or the onset of ice ages will break up some invariances and create new ones. Other, more rapidly occurring species-making or species-changing processes such as earthquakes or major droughts will have similar results. But the invariances produced will be hard to break down for the same reason that massive and long-lasting environmental change was required to put them in place.

However, matters begin to change quite radically once members of any species become part of the selective environment of members of another species. In these circumstances, regularities about the latter species become comparatively shorter lived, more temporary, and more spatially restricted as well. The reason, of course, is that species become part of one another's selective environments when they compete, or one predates upon or parasitizes the other, or both are predated by a third species, or both predate a third species, or both cooperate for that matter. Under all these circumstances, nature is persistently searching through design space seeking variations in both species that will provide them with a selective advantage over the other. Until it finds one, the two species are locked into a local equilibrium, one that may be noticed by the naturalists and be reported in a temporarily invariant regularity. The theory of natural selection, however, assures us that, if it can, natural selection will break up these local equilibria along with the regularities that describe them and *their consequences*.[11]

When traits are genetically coded, the arms race process will be relatively slow, though much faster than non–arms race adaptational change. Since favorable mutations are rare, biological invariances between genetically encoded traits will often be locked in as the result of some relatively long-term stable equilibrium in the arms race. Besides interspecific competition, there is also a great deal of intraspecific competition, arms races between lineages within a single species, which also makes and breaks invariances at an even faster rate than intraspecific competition does.

The upshot is that all invariances among genetically encoded traits are restricted. During the periods that they obtain, they are vulnerable to being undermined by random variations that break up coadaptational equilibria. As the rate of variation increases, the life span of an invariant regularity decreases, as will the spatial range over which it obtains. In the case of competition between very fast breeding species—say, between parasites and their host targets (e.g., phage and bacteria or bacteria and humans)—regularities may remain invariant only for a few years, months, or even weeks. (Consider the lifetimes of antibiotic effectiveness.)

In biology, restricted regularities are explanatory and its mathematical models applicable, because they reflect local equilibria underwritten by unrestricted regularities—laws of nature—that Darwin discovered.[12] These regularities are restricted owing to the inevitability of arms races ordained by the unrestricted regularities Darwin discovered. Insofar as the social sciences individuate their descriptive taxonomies functionally and seek regularities that obtain between instances of their taxonomic categories, all of their regularities and models will have to be similarly restricted, as open to exceptions, *ceteris paribus* hedges, and as predictively imprecise as those of biology. After all, social science is a branch of biology.

We now have a well-grounded explanation for why no social science has succeeded in uncovering real laws in its domain, why at best the quantitative models advanced in the most self-consciously mathematical (parts of each of the) disciplines have limited application and unimprovable precision, and are overtaken by events. But the payoff is not purely negative. We now have the theoretical framework for a research program in the social sciences that expect the kinds of successes in explanation and application that evolutionary biology has secured: identify the functions that manifest themselves in individual and aggregated behavior, and account for them as adaptations by identifying the selective forces that bring them about, shape their changes, and determine their trajectories of persistence, spread, and extinction. Before sketching the shape of this research program, one widely discussed objection to the approach must be disposed of.

Disposing of the No-Memes Objection to Darwinism about Human Affairs

The argument given at the outset of this chapter will be accused of invoking Darwinian processes without showing that their necessary conditions obtain, and it will be argued that a crucial one among those necessary conditions cannot obtain in human affairs.

The objection is simple: Darwinian processes require replicators and interactors. In particular they require high-fidelity replicators to store and transmit traits faithfully enough and long enough for environmental filtration to shape them into adaptations and to maintain them as adaptations. In the biological domain these replicators are the genes. There are no equivalent replicators in human affairs, or at least there are not enough of them for Darwinian processes to explain human affairs. Darwinism of the sort evinced in the argument given at the outset requires cultural replicators—*memes*. But there are no memes.[13] No memes, ergo no Darwinian processes. (Cf. Sperber 2000 for the origin of this widely mooted argument.)

The issue is serious for Darwinian social science. That natural selection is an attractive metaphor in the description of human affairs is both unexceptional and uninteresting. The issue is whether it is more than a metaphor. Are all social processes literally, actually, really matters of blind variation and environmental filtration? That is the issue. If a real Darwinian process requires actual replicators, then the no-memes critique must be addressed. It can be.

Darwinian social scientists should respond to this objection in several ways. To begin with, it is obvious that the literal application of Darwinian theory to a domain does not require that the domain contain gene-like replicators. Biological replicators—genes—did not predate Darwinian processes. Natural selection presumably got its start prior to the emergence of these replicators, and for that matter, prior to the emergence of any recognizable very high-fidelity informationally rich replicators. Moreover, natural selection is likely to produce replicators of the sort that the genes constitute only when environments change slowly, when evolution is extremely gradual, cumulative, and atomistic in its shaping of individual traits, one by one, for adaptations. When one or more of these conditions do not obtain, adaptive evolution may employ replicators and processes of replication quite unlike genes (cf. note 9).

Following Richerson and Boyd (2006), defenders of Darwinian approaches to culture have also argued that cultural replicators need not have the high-fidelity features of genes, since there are a variety of practices, norms, and institutions in human culture that have emerged as adaptations precisely because they preserve the adaptive informational content of replicators even under conditions of low-copy fidelity (cf. Driscoll 2008 for a useful recent discussion).

It may be granted that Darwinism about human affairs does require cultural replicators, probably a variety of quite different kinds of replicators, and some of them may be gene-like. But the memes Darwinism about human affairs requires will be huge in number, short in life spans, and extremely difficult to individuate, for the very same reason regularities in the human sciences are restricted: because of the ubiquity of arms races. So, it will be no surprise that few obvious examples of memes can be provided now, or perhaps ever.

To see the real problem with the argument from no memes to no Darwinian processes in human affairs, consider its first premise: memes have to be like genes, because natural selection only works in culture when there are gene-like replicators. But, the argument continues, there are no such gene-like replicators in human affairs. Ergo, no Darwinian processes in human affairs. The trouble with this argument is that it rests on an idea of what genes are and how they work that was obsolete about a hundred years ago. This is the one trait–one gene idea, the notion that most or many significant observed inherited traits are controlled by a single gene.

There is only a small number of such traits in any mammal, and in humans only about seven such traits are known—for example, tongue rolling or the widow's peak. All other inherited traits in humans, like eye color and skin color, even sexual characteristics, are the result of the inheritance of many and in some cases a huge number of genes. In fact, genes don't really transmit or control the appearance of any of the biological traits that common sense and folk biology think they do. Each gene controls the production of a protein or other large molecule. There are 25,000 of these genes, switched on and off in every cell of our bodies. It's the protein molecules they code for, and the order in which the proteins are produced by the genes that build and operate biological machinery. Many different traits that don't have anything to do with each other are built or controlled by the same gene; many traits that look absolutely the same to us across individuals—say, eye color—are the result of different sets of different genes in different people. And when we actually locate the genes inside the nucleus of our somatic cells, and in the sperm and egg that develop into our bodies when they combine, these genes can differ from one another substantially without that difference making any difference for the proteins they produce.

The moral for memes is obvious: if memes are like genes, then any single meme will by itself almost never control the appearance of a behavior or action or anything else that common sense or even sophisticated social science is interested in. It will take many, many memes working together to produce anything of interest to the human sciences, and we will never be able to detect or identify memes by doing anything like garden-variety sociology, economics, anthropology, or even psychology. Whatever memes are, they are going to be as complicated and hard to identify as genes are, or even more so!

If memes are anything like genes, it is going to be very hard to identify them, isolate or individuate them, and learn the details of how they work. Doing any of these things for "memetics" will be orders of magnitude more difficult than what a century of molecular biology has done for genetics. And the reason for all three of these difficulties will in large measure be the ubiquity of arms races cutting short the lifetime of any regularity about a particular package of memes. The shorter this lifetime, the more difficult it will be for any social or behavioral scientist to design a method for identifying these packages, still less identifying their component memes. To figure out the mechanism of transmission of some package of memes that controls a socially interesting adapted behavior will require, first, a long enough lived regularity about that adapted behavior and, second, another long enough lived regularity about how the particular package of memes that codes for the behavior and transmits it does each of these things. Since in a social environment of accelerating change these packages of memes and the memes themselves will be transmitted faster and faster, and their modes of transmission and control interfered with more and more effectively, as arms races accelerate, the chances of identifying and locating memes become lower and lower as culture change accelerates.

This is not an argument for the existence of memes. At most it is a well-grounded explanation for why social and behavioral scientists are unlikely to find them, an excuse erected on the criticism of a bad argument against the very possibility of memes. If there are memes, regularities about their transmission, mode of action, and realizations in the brain will be complex, short-lived, and completely beyond the reach of any hypothesis testing in the social sciences. So, if we can't identify them, why suppose that there are any memes?

The real argument for memes is the two premises of the original argument. If these premises are reasonable and support the conclusion that human affairs must be Darwinian in nature, then that's the argument for memes, or whatever replicators are required by Darwinian processes in human affairs.

Should the human sciences cease work until neuroscience or some even more molecular subdiscipline has established the existence or nonexistence of memes? Did the rest of biology stop working while geneticists did the century of research that was required first to establish the existence of genes and then to identify their location, composition, and model of action? Of course not. The same goes for the human sciences.

THE SMALLEST UNITS OF DARWINIAN CULTURAL SELECTION

The task of identifying the memes that transmit and encode matters of interest to the social scientist can be left, for the foreseeable future, to cognitive neuroscience. Meanwhile, the Darwinian social scientist needs to get on with the tasks of identifying the regularities reflecting local equilibria in human affairs, tracking the incipient and inevitable arms races that break them up, and employing this knowledge to ameliorate human life and perhaps even design human institutions that move us to preferred equilibria and protect us from the harms so often precipitated by arms races. How should the Darwinian social scientist proceed to do this? Here the obvious source of guidance is that part of Darwinian biology that has succeeded while remaining agnostic about the underlying molecular genetics that drives the emergence and breakup of local equilibria: Darwinian population biology as it figures in agriculture, in some aspects of medicine, and increasingly in human behavioral ecology and evolutionary anthropology. This approach begins with biologically significant traits—hypothesized adaptations. It tests hypotheses about whether they are and what they are adaptations for (i.e., what their functions are or have been in the past). Then it goes on to the rest of the questions Tinbergen identified as on the research agenda of an evolutionary discipline: questions about ontogenic development, evolutionary origin, and mechanism of operation. But where to start? What are the traits to be subjected to evolutionary analysis? We need to identify some broad class, category, kind of aspect, unit, or feature of human affairs whose instances recur regularly enough and share enough in common so that some interesting generalizations can be framed about them, or so that we can apply to them some models already effective in systematizing biological phenomena. The rest of this chapter is devoted to arguing for the adoption of a single such "unit" among all subdivisions of a Darwinian approach to human affairs: a reconfiguration of the concept of a "strategy" introduced in the first section.

Recall its suggestion above that we treat human institutions, groups, and practices as packages of *strategies* employed by people. The features, characteristics, and traits of institutions, organizations, and practices are composed of these packages of strategies.

At the basement level of individual agents, the strategies they employ are their own individual adaptations—traits that have payoffs for them or for someone else that result in these strategies persisting—being used over and over, and spreading—by imitation or instruction, reinforcement or coercion, or receding by operant punishment, or legal sanction, and so on. Individual strategies are traits of individual people. Their cognitive equipment is what passes them on, modifies them.

The word "strategy" is not quite right to describe the full range of patterns of individual behavior it has to include to do the work required by a Darwinian approach. A strategy will be everything from scratching itches, speaking with an accent, signing one's name, walking around and not under ladders, crossing one's self before takeoff, using a compass, employing corporal punishment, practicing polygamy, employing the 1662 Book of Common Prayer, saving for retirement, voting, all the way to choosing a spouse or ordering in the Old Guard at Waterloo. It may well include every repeatable (but not necessarily repeated) bit of action or behavior that isn't genetically encoded (such as responding to operant reinforcement or classical conditioning). There is also an ambiguity in the word "strategy" between describing the behavior and describing the "rule" that "governs" the behavior. "Governed" in quotes because there should be no suggestion that behaviors reflecting strategies need be intentional or strategies that the agent in all cases is conscious of acting upon. In the sense of rule, "strategies" have a normative flavor: "If (or when) in circumstance C, then do B!" A strategy is often expressed in a norm—categorical or instrumental. But agents need not be conscious of their obligatory force. So, think about a strategy(-type) as a repeatable pattern or instance of behavior (a strategy token) people can repeatedly perform.

Now, as noted in the first section, the key "Gestalt switch" Darwinian social science requires us to make is to shift focus from the selection of agents who behave in accordance with strategies to thinking about the selection among behaviors or strategies that describe them. Darwinian evolutionary theory is a theory about trait fitness and trait frequencies, not individual fitness. Counting individuals' offspring numbers is a matter of bookkeeping, not the causal process that results in their changes. Similarly, cultural evolution is not a matter of more adapted individuals having more offspring, but of more adapted strategies having more offspring strategies, copies of themselves. It's a matter of completion and coadaptation of copies among strategies being played more frequently, by more people, over a longer time. (Some evolutionary game theorists have been self-consciously doing this for quite a while. See Skyrms 2010.) If memetics were simple, we could dispense with the behaviors that token strategies and just count the instances of a certain neural pattern that encodes a strategy spreading from brain to brain. Watching their demographic expansion and contraction over time would enable us to measure the memes' relative fitness via their effects on behavioral strategies. Alas, not even genetics is that simple. So, in both cases the scientist must track the traits that interact directly with environments—phenotypes in the biological case, behaviors in the social case—and eventually perhaps infer the character of the molecularly encoded genes and the neurally encoded memes. Long before they can do so, much important biological and social science will have built up.

The easiest way to expound the approach to Darwinian cultural evolution as carried by strategies is by a genealogical illustration, starting at the hunter-gatherer origin of social institutions. This route to recognizing that strategies are the basic explanatory unit in human affairs is not the only one. But it is a natural one.

Well before *Homo sapiens*, humans were employing strategies first to survive and then to thrive, moving up the food chain on the African savanna by cooperating with one another. In particular the domestic division of labor involves already having distributed roles in accordance with gender-based strategies in child rearing, gathering, hunting, fire preservation, and so on. These social strategies are formed by a familiar process of operant learning and transmitted by a combination of learning (imitate the most successful strategy, the most frequent strategy, and eventually the most prestigious strategy—once social institutions have become established). Even prior to the strategies that combine to constitute the domestic division of labor, the environment had been operating to select for packages of cooperative strategies that constitute symbolic communication—speech—out of gestures, eye movements, and the theory of mind our ancestors shared with primates. But we may take some Darwinian account of the emergence of language as given for present purposes. The initial emergence of distinct behavioral strategies between male and female in the domestic division of labor well before the appearance of *Homo sapiens*, indeed prior to the appearance of *Homo*, or primates for that matter, has significant productivity effects that increase longevity and population size, which in turn provides further opportunities for the division of labor, for the appearance and selection for still more distinct strategies, whether in the fabrication of tools, specialization in targets of predation, food preparation, even trade. Over time individual strategies get "packaged" together into rudimentary social practices, institutions, and organizations. The time scale required even for the precipitation of the earliest of these packages will have been great, and the selection pressures that shaped them must have been varying in force or even intermittent until population densities increased much beyond nuclear families. Throughout this and subsequent periods, new strategies were continually emerging through blind variation, and mostly being extinguished by selection against them, or drift. For example, the strategy of combining a hand ax and a shaft into a compound tool surely appeared more than once in the million years between the emergence of the former and the eventual proliferation of the latter. But the variant was not copied with sufficient frequency to withstand drift until populations grew large enough.

Strategies played by more than one individual may conflict or synergize. When they do the latter, there will be selection for the packages that combine them. When they synergize, enhancing one another's fitness, the result is a local equilibrium. Such equilibria may be very short lasting or quite long lasting. The local equilibria among strategies may be harmful or beneficial to all, some, or none of the individuals or groups that employ them. Long-lasting packages of such strategies in local equilibrium will typically be recognizable as historically venerable institutions—feudalism, the Roman Catholic Church, chattel slavery. When strategies make individuals or groups compete, they may survive even as individuals or groups playing them become extinct. The result may be extinction of the strategies as well. Or the conflict between players may also eventuate in a local equilibrium in strategies. Packages of strategies in local equilibria will themselves become environmental settings, niches that structure the replication and transmission of lower-level strategies that make up the packages among lineages playing the individual strategies. Since transmission of strategies is not genetic, but by learning, imitation, enforcement, and the lineages of these strategies will spread and shrink (when they become maladaptive) through populations of genetically unrelated individuals.

But as in other processes of natural selection, local equilibria are perpetually threatened by random variations that may be selected for owing to their ability to exploit and break up local equilibria. The history of evolution is a history of arms races breaking out, putting an end to local equilibria, and eventually settling into new local equilibria. Sometimes this process proceeds with glacial slowness (e.g., consider camouflage and camouflage detection between predator and prey); sometimes it moves with great speed (e.g., consider the response of the AIDS virus to antiretrovirals). The rate of breakup of local equilibria in cultural selection will run the gamut from the time scale of cultural epochs to faster than arms races in the bacterial cases. The brevity and fragility of most local equilibria between strategies make it difficult to identify them and impossible to exploit them. But the few long-lasting ones are usually of far greater significance for human life. Consider the local equilibrium that characterized church/state relations in Europe from 1500 to the Thirty Years' War.

Packages of strategies, all the way from the smallest (those of the domestic division of labor) to the largest (the ultra social complex state), are built from this smallest package by a Darwinian process of selection operating to package together those smallest packages that synergize, and to select for variants in smaller packages that enhance synergies. As the process of blind variation and environmental filtration of packages proceeds, new environments are created that have selective effects on the smaller packages of strategies that operate within the niches created by larger ones, selecting for variations among the strategies played within these smaller packages.

The natural and cultural environments that constitute the original packages of strategies are sufficiently similar across the locations where human social evolution proceeded to independents produce a good deal of convergent cultural evolution. Consider some of the major cultural universals: marriage rules and other sexual mores, religion, inequality and hierarchy precipitated by the transition from hunter-gatherer modes to agriculture. And of course, differences in local circumstances will select for quite different packages of strategies as well, thus producing the diversity and complexity of institutions, practices, and organizations that characterize human culture.

It is crucial to emphasize that the unit of adaptation in this approach is not the individual person or group of people who adopt a strategy that confers some benefit on him, her, or them. The unit of adaptation is the strategy itself, or its token instance played by individuals or groups of them (consciously, unconsciously, willingly, under coercion, incentivized, etc.). People are the environments in which strategies are selected for, owing to whether their effects on people who play them and on whom they are played by others affect the probability or frequency with which they are copied or not copied. It is open to memeticists to hold that strategies are "represented" in memes in minds, and that a bit of strategic behavior is the meme's "phenotypic" effect. But as we have seen, this is not a commitment Darwinian cultural evolution need embrace, or having embraced, need actually confirm at this stage of social scientific research. At this stage, a Darwinian social science need commit itself to nothing more than the evolution of strategies.

It will be objected that strategies, even adapted ones, do not proliferate, "reproduce" over time, but may be played by a roughly constant number of people at a roughly constant rate, and so cannot count as replicators whose fitness increase is a matter of offspring size. No reproductive increase, no replicators, no replicators, no Darwinian process. This critique reflects oversight about important evolutionary processes.

As a Darwinian process, cultural evolution repeatedly results in "major transitions," as Maynard Smith and Szathmáry (1995) called them: occasions in which individual strategies enter into packages that persist and in which the individual strategies cease to reproduce independently and competitively. In purely biological evolution there have been several such transitions: from independent replicators to chromosomes, from prokaryotes to eukaryotes, from asexual to sexual reproducers, from single cell creatures to metazoans, from individual organisms to colonies with nonreproductive castes and the division of labor (e.g., the social insects). In each case, individuals have surrendered their independent replication strategy (but not their other strategies) to the ensemble of which they are members. The mystery is why selection for reproductive fitness should result in the surrender of independent reproduction in favor of controlled reproduction as part of a larger individual. This is a crucial question on the research agenda of evolutionary biology, and tentative answers are increasingly available. The answers will probably differ for each of the major transitions. But the important fact to bear in mind is that major transitions that shut down or control the replication of particular packages of strategies will occur in the case of Darwinian cultural evolution at least as frequently as they occur in purely biological evolution. This means that uncontrolled replication will be surrendered for controlled reproduction.

Godfrey-Smith (2009) has aptly called this state of affairs "de-Darwinization."[14] The simplest and clearest cases of de-Darwinization occur when free-living single cell organisms combine into a single multicellular organism. Many of the strategies that characterize the individual cells persist because they synergize with other copies of themselves and with other quite different strategies into a package that enables the hitherto free-living cells to persist over longer periods. But the packaging requires the suppression of one strategy: in constrained independent reproduction. Multicellular creatures persist only when they successfully suppress individual unconstrained fitness maximization by their component cells, when they suppress a strategy that had been selected for when cells were individual free-living units. When multicellular individuals fail to do this, the result is cancer—the unconstrained multiplication of individual cells at the expense of the rest of the component cells and the strategies they are "playing." According to Maynard Smith and Szathmáry (1995), major transitions have occurred some seven times in biological evolution, each time involving the suppression of reproductive strategies of the component individual units. Once larger packages of coordinated strategies are selected for, these component strategies are de-Darwinized, in Godfrey-Smith's useful term. That is, the component packages of strategies surrender their reproductive strategies while continuing to play their other ones to mutual advantage. Along with de-Darwinization, the transition to multicellularity will select for division of labor, including the specialization of some cells to engage in reproduction on behalf of the entire ensemble of cells composing the multicellular individual—the sequestration of the germ line, as Weismann put it. At this point, survival of the fittest will be one of survival of the fattest ... the individual package of strategies played by the multicellular organism persists for a long time as it enforces controlled replication among the strategies played by component packages and individual strategies. Multicellular individuals do reproduce, though at much slower rates than the individual cells from which they are composed used to do before combining. This slows down rates of adaptive evolution to the generation times of the multicellular individuals. In some cases, reproduction ceases almost altogether. Consider the quaking aspen. A grove of these trees is just one organism, all the trees being ramets of one genet.[15]

Of course, multicellular individuals need to reproduce, and before the emergence of sexual reproduction they did not by and large reproduce via sequestration of germ line and genetic recombination. Mostly they reproduced by various sorts of fission, in which they either lost a few cells that eventually grew as a colony of the original multicellular individual, or disaggregated into individual component cells that later regrouped into new individuals after asexual reproduction.

As noted, there is a major mystery about the major transitions in which successive individuals surrender their selfish genetic strategy of maximizing their own representation in offspring generations in exchange for membership in larger individuals. Why did free-living mitochondria and nuclear cells join to provide the eukaryotic cell? Why did eukaryotic cells join to make multicellular organisms? Why did multicellular organisms such as the social insects surrender their reproductive strategies to a single queen or to classes of reproducers? These are important questions on the agenda of biological Darwinian evolution. They are the problems of the major transitions, in which lower-level packages of strategies give up their reproductive autonomy.

The packaging of individual strategies into sets and their de-Darwinization is a crucial process in the emergence, persistence, adaptation, and succession of human institutions, practices, and organizations. Individual strategies will coadapt to one another tightly enough to ensure the package's integrity even under circumstances that would challenge the individual strategies severely. In many cases there will be selection for strategies of enforcement of the coadaptations, and strategies that encourage or even control the deployment and reproduction of other strategies. If they are relatively weak, they may be expressed in preferences of participants. If stronger, these strategies will look to participants and to us like norms. In fact, they will constitute norms. Norming strategies will enforce the conformity of new instances of strategies to the form of their predecessors, thus ensuring a copy-fidelity that preserves the package of strategies over time. But de-Darwinization ensures that few strategies will spread like wildfire in a culture, or certainly not in a traditional one, narrowly constrained by natural circumstances and larger packages of strategies that include strong enforcement strategies among their repertoires. This means that in Darwinian cultural evolution we should not expect to find a large number of individual strategies engaged in a great deal of replication, recombination, or variation. They will too often be constrained by the iterated hierarchy of packages of packages of packages of strategies in which they figure to behave like the strategies of free-living individuals engaged in unconstrained rapid asexual reproduction of the sort that genes engage in. Insofar as individual strategies are memes or behaviors under the control of memes, then memes will turn out to be very different from germ line genes and much more like somatic genes in de-Darwinized populations of memes.

TINBERGEN'S FOUR QUESTIONS AND THE FUTURE OF SOCIAL SCIENCE

Niko Tinbergen (1963) famously organized the agenda of behavioral biology, and all of biology for that matter, around four questions: What is the trait's current function? By what particular Darwinian trajectory did it emerge? How does it develop in the individual? What is the mechanism whereby it delivers its function?

It was long supposed that in biology, answers to all four of these questions required appeal to the operation of genes—germline and somatic. We now recognize that in their home base of biology, for many species the answers to all four questions increasingly include Darwinian cultural processes. This is just as we would expect given the continuities between *Homo sapiens* and other species. Darwinian cultural evolution is not confined to humans. Human cultural evolution is a subcategory, not an extension of, still less a metaphorical application of Darwinian evolution. The analysis of human affairs fits neatly into preestablished components of biology.

Tinbergen's first question, "What is it for, what is its function?" has preoccupied this chapter. Biologists have come to see answers to this question nuanced in at least three respects we should also expect in human affairs. First, identifying a trait's function is a highly fallible matter requiring clever experimentation and observation. Some traits of some organisms are actually imposed on them by other organisms: they are adaptations for the imposing organisms. What is more, functions change over time. As environments change, traits with one function can be shaped, pruned, combined by natural selection to take on quite different functions. Gould and Vrba (1982) called such traits exaptations. Feathers are a prime example: evolved for warmth, then selected for flight. Exaptations will be common among human practices. Second, selection operates at many different levels—the individual lineage, the family and local interbreeding population, indeed perhaps even the species. Strategies are traits. In the biological domain, selection for packages of strategies (e.g., among the caste-organized social insects) is not uncommon. Third, as noted above, cultural selection operates in the biological domain as well as genetic selection (we return to this important matter below). Other species besides ours have culture, and their cultures evolve by Darwinian processes. Human Darwinian cultural evolution is of a piece with that of other organisms.

The second question on the agenda of the biologist is clearly inseparable from the first: "What is the particular sequence of events that resulted in the emergence of the functional trait?" Since identifying current function is largely based on identifying what current and past "design problems" the trait's environment posed, answering the functional question requires us to address the phylogenetic question. Of course, the role of drift, small population numbers, and physical constraint operate to channel Darwinian natural selection. But as the previous paragraph noted, biologists are increasingly appreciating the role of developmental plasticity, social learning, long-term niche construction, historical contingencies (founder effects), and other apparently cultural factors in filtering variations to generate the actual trajectory whereby a biological trait emerged and to identify its function. The details of natural history, insofar as they can be recovered, answer this question. Human history needs to be examined to identify the "design problems" and the Darwinian processes that solved them. The traditional explanations offered in human history and even data about their *explanantia*, however, may not be of much use in this inquiry.

Tinbergen's third question is, "How does the trait work, how does it accomplish the function that the process of adaptive evolution conferred upon it?" Lessons from the study of behaviors such as bird song reveal that a variety of top-down and bottom-up strategies can elucidate mechanisms at several different finenesses of grain, including somatic gene expression, neural processing, sensory stimulation and deprivation, hormonal changes, and seasonal factors, for that matter (Bateson and Laland 2013). There are obvious and severe limitations on the application of experimental methods to learn about equivalent processes that enable traits to accomplish their functions for humans and on humans, but these are not in principle obstacles to biological social science. In the case of individual behavioral strategies, these are tasks for cognitive neuroscientists. In the case of packages of strategies selected for their adaptational functions, answering the "how does it work" question, the role of sociologists, political scientists, and economists is obvious. There may even be room for some "thick description" of the sort cultural anthropologists are eager to provide. But in most cases the answers are unlikely to involve much appeal to human design and intentional maintenance.

The fourth question is the developmental or ontogenetic one: "How does the trait emerge, develop, and appear among the organisms that bear it?" Tinbergen was particularly interested in nongenetic determinants of the development of animal behaviors, dispositions, and capacities (including social learning in birds, rodents, cetaceans, and insects) that operate on genetic inheritance to shape predation, feeding, nesting, communication, and so on. This is just the sort of cultural learning long supposed to be limited to humans. Behavioral biologists have shown that these learned traits are faithfully transmitted over many generations by niche construction and other epigenetic processes. The nature/nurture distinction has pretty much lost whatever role it had in biology.

In areas of biology that have developed greatly since Tinbergen proposed the quadripartite division of biological inquiry, answers to each of his four questions have had important spillover implications for answers to others (Bateson and Laland 2013). There are now entire subdisciplines that intersect two or more of his questions: "evo-devo," the study of how developmental patterns are selected and how these patterns channel or constrain evolutionary trajectories. But such combinations are built on separate first draft answers to each of the questions, and especially to the first and second of them: What is it for? By what process of variation and selection did it emerge? Testing hypotheses about answers to each of these two questions is the only way to proceed in answering the other, and both need at least a well-supported answer before we go on to address questions 3 and 4.

The proprietary taxonomy of biology was functional long before Darwin. No one had to argue that it had to be, and once Darwin's theory emerged, evidence-based answers to the first two questions organized the rest of the discipline. The same assumption that traits are individuated in terms of their function is equally strong in the human sciences. It is this assumption that forces social science to be Darwinian. But this step in turn raises at least three questions: What will a properly biological division of the social sciences into manageable research programs look like? How much of social science will Darwinian cultural evolutionary theory "recover" or "preserve"? What will the payoff to such research programs be?

One obvious way of assigning tasks to distinct research programs starts by making distinctions between traits, that is, between strategies. The current division of the social science can be construed as implausibly dividing these into psychological, sociological, political, economic, or some such taxonomy of kinds. This taxonomy is probably mistaken. Two reasons for this are evident. It has not eventuated in much significant explanatory agreement and cumulative predictive improvement. It reflects commonsense taxonomies we have excellent reasons to suspect from the wrongness of such taxonomies in physics, chemistry, and biology.

These considerations suggest that the principal subdivisions of a Darwinian science of human affairs will look quite different from the current set of social sciences. There are several possibilities, some of which "recover" more of current social science than others, some of which proliferate subdisciplines, and some of which make separate sciences—even inexact ones—impossible, because they reflect the operation of multiple and inseparable causes for every *explanandum* of interest. Which alternative is right is a vast empirical question. But some Darwinian social scientists have already taken sides on various possibilities that are worth illustrating.

Runciman (2009) has argued that Darwinian processes operate among humans in three different ways: biological selection, social selection, and cultural selection:

> At three different levels of natural cultural and social selection, there are three different types of behavior: *evoked* behavior, where the agent is responding directly and instinctively to some feature of the environment; acquired behavior, where the agent is imitating or has learned from some other agent, whether directly or indirectly; and *imposed* behavior, where the agent is performing a social role underwritten by institutional inducements and sanctions. (8)

Like a long tradition of sociologists, going back at least as far as Durkheim, Runciman insists that imposed behavior is not reducible to learned behavior, so that there are two distinct levels of Darwinian selection operating in human affairs:

> The difference is not that social, as opposed to cultural, *rules* have to be followed....
> The difference is that information encoded in institutional practices make society roles what they are independently of how successive incumbents have come to learn to perform them or what their individual motives are for doing so....
>
> The ... differences between one society and another are just as much the outcome of a process of heritable variation and competitive selection irreducible to cultural evolution as the beliefs and attitudes which distinguish one culture from another are the outcomes of a process of heritable variation and competitive selection irreducible to biological evolution. (39)

Runciman treats selection of individual strategies as historically prior to the selection of social institutions—what I have called packages of strategies: "[O]nce material resources began to be accumulated and stored and families of households to settle in designated locations..., the necessary conditions for the transition from acquired [culturally selected, learned behavior] to [socially] imposed behavior are in place" (2009: 41). Runciman treats the shift as a major transition in the Maynard Smith/Szathmáry (1995) sense: "The culture-to-society transition...was a revolutionary transformation of interpersonal relationships and consequential behavior patterns without precedent in the earlier history of the human species" (42).

If the shift from hunter-gatherers to sedentary groups produced a qualitatively different unit of variation/selection from the individual strategies that characterize the biological and domestic division of labor, then there will be scope for an autonomous Darwinian sociology. The difference between small packages that characterize biological/domestic divisions and larger ones may of course be only a matter of degree. Selection for group strategies may already have kicked in among the primates, enabling *Homo* to succeed on the African savanna. The difference between group selection and correlated individual selection is either semantic or also a matter of degree. Whether there is full-blooded group selection (a Maynard Smith/Szathmáry major transition [1995]) or only a complicated set of pairwise correlated individual strategies, there will still be scope for a scientific division of labor between the study of institutions, organizations, and practices on the one hand and individual behavioral ones on the other. In effect, a Darwinian approach "recovers" a recognizable distinction between *social* science (the study of packages of strategies) and *behavioral* science (the study of individual ones), with social psychology somewhere in between.

Nelson and Winter (1982) long ago argued for an evolutionary theory of economic change to supplant the mainstream approach with its heavy reliance on (global) equilibrium thinking. In particular, they introduced the business "routine" as the unit of selection and used it to offer an analysis of firms, industries, and markets. "Routines" are pretty obviously strategies as elaborated here.

> Our general term for all regularities and predictable behavior patterns of firms is "routine."... In our evolutionary theory, these routines play the role that genes play in biological evolutionary theory. They are persistent features of the organism and determine its possible behavior...; they are heritable in the sense that tomorrow's organisms generated from today's (for example by building a new plant) have many of the same characteristics, and they are selectable in the sense that organisms with the same routines may do better than others, and if so, their relative importance in the population (the industry) is augmented over time. (14)

Two notions that Nelson and Winter needed to more fully articulate the parallel between strategies and genes were the parallel between routines and *somatic* (non-germline) genes in controlling repeated behavior within the same individual (organism or firm), and the importance of de-Darwinization of replicators that are parts of larger individuals. De-Darwinized but highly adapted routines, like highly adapted genes, will increase the economic strength and size of the individual firms they figure in, but may not increase the number of such firms—this is selection of the fattest, not fittest, as in the growth of Aspen ramets.

Two questions arising from their proposal are obvious: First, why has it met with such resistance in a discipline that should be much more concerned with change and local equilibria than with stasis and general equilibria? Second, why has the approach not generated a research program fruitful enough to displace the ruling paradigm in economics? Answers to the first question would take us far afield. They would largely reflect the assumptions economists since Walras have made to attain mathematical tractability of their theory at the expense of relevance—for example, constant returns to scale, probabilistic risk instead of radical uncertainty, maximizing of measurable objective functions. Seeking answers to the second question is more important here and will have a sobering impact on what we should demand of all the research programs of Darwinian social science.

The most significant problem facing a Darwinian approach to human affairs—whether in economics or elsewhere—is the mismatch between what a Darwinian theory can provide and what social scientists, policy makers, and other consumers of social science want from theories in the human sciences.

Darwinian biological science faces significant limits on application and prediction. On the one hand, generation time between replication and development is often so long that great patience, lots of resources, and a research protocol whose lifetime exceeds that of individual scientists are required to conduct experiments. Moreover, there are more variables that matter in Darwinian evolution than we can identify or control, and quasi experiments exploiting experimental controls imposed by nature are few and far between. Add in the random character of mutation and recombination and the importance of statistical drift and it becomes obvious why great predictive expectations of Darwinian theory in biology are unreasonable. Even in laboratory contexts, where many of these problems can be mitigated, precise quantitative predictions are impossible, owing to the fact that rates of random variation increase radically as generation time drops and population size increases. What is more, inferences from laboratory results to predictions about natural setting are fraught to say the least. This is the problem well known in social science of "external validity." The best we can do in Darwinian biological science is the development of models—Hardy-Weinberg equilibrium, Lotka-Volterra predator/prey equations, Turing's pattern formation models, Fisher sex-ratio result, game theory model such as iterated prisoner's dilemma or Hawk/Dove, and so on. These models explain post facto, but no one can employ them in reliable prediction since we can't establish the values of their independent variables reliably enough, nor control for exogenous factors, nor otherwise establish whether their application conditions obtain. These limitations have in part motivated the focus of molecular biologists on domains in which such problems do not arise or can be mitigated with resultant predictive payoffs in medical and agricultural biotechnology.

The problems a Darwinian approach to human affairs faces must be far greater than those that Darwinian approaches face in the biological realm. In considering them it has to be rigorously borne in mind that there is no alternative approach that does not face these and other more serious problems. Darwinian social science is the only game in town. The first and most serious obstacle to predictive testing and technological application of Darwinian theories in any social domain is the very opposite of the first problem identified above for Darwinian biological science: instead of the length of experiments having to be vastly beyond the lifetimes of even many generations of investigators, in the social realm, the pace of change is so fast that there is not enough time to construct and carry out experiments that will have much relevance to social phenomena even a few days later than the dates of the experiments. Consider the limitation on market research. The number and values of the independent variables in any Darwinian model we might seek to apply in the social domain will be too great and too difficult to measure, and they will change too rapidly for replication. Then there is the arms race phenomenon that in the biological domain eventually unpredictably unravels all local equilibria, even ones that last geological epochs. In human affairs the rates of variation are so great that many local equilibria that policy designers may wish to exploit last at most for weeks, days, or even just hours.

It is fair to say, therefore, that Darwinian approaches to domains treated by more traditional theories will not do much better than they have done by way of explanations that can be confirmed via their predictive consequences. Consider the widespread disensus in political science regarding alternative theories about international relations, the behavior of states, and transnational actors. There are at least a dozen competing theories (realism, neorealism, liberalism and post-liberalism, rational choice theory, constructivism, Marxian theory, and others) employed to explain and predict the behavior of nations and especially the likelihood of conflict and cooperation between them. In this domain, retrospective explanations are plentiful, but no theory has a track record of increasing (or even regular) predictive success. A Darwinian theory that focuses on variation and selection for strategies—ones played by states, or ministries, or individual political agents, and so on—is not going to do any better than these theories. So why should it be preferred to them?

To begin with, we can already be confident that a Darwinian approach to human affairs is right and that any incompatibility with other theories must be resolved in its favor. That is because humans are biological creatures, and we have conclusive evidence that such creatures must be shaped by Darwinian processes. Furthermore, Darwinian processes are the only way the functional kinds identified in all the social sciences could have arisen. This means that the Darwinian approach can provide a non–ad hoc explanation of its own predictive limitations and those of competing theories. We know from the original domain of application what the difficulties are, and we can see how they arise in the human domain even more forcefully. A good deal of the explanation for particular explanatory failures, predictive disconfirmation, and general fruitlessness of many research programs in the human sciences turns on the facts about their target subject matter that inhibit general theory—local equilibrium, arms races, and frequency-dependent and other reflexive forms of strategy selection. Thus, for example, the problems facing explanation and prediction in economics are well understood from a Darwinian perspective on human affairs.

But since the Darwinian theory of human cultural evolution is a derived special case of the more general Darwinian theory, it secures substantial indirect empirical confirmation, including predictive vindication, from the successes of the theory in the purely biological domain. This will, of course, be cold comfort to those who seek to apply the theory to predictions in the human domain, but it will mitigate criticism that explanations exploiting Darwinian cultural evolutionary theory can't satisfy even modest demands for indirect predictive improvements. Every Darwinian prediction vindicated in domains such as agriculture, medicine, genomics, or molecular biology provides such indirect support for Darwinian cultural evolutionary theory. Moreover, the relationship between models and data in the purely biological domain provides good guidance for what we should expect by way of successful application of the theory in the human domain. Fisher's sex-ratio theory can't explain why all sexually reproducing species have a 1:1 sex ratio, because they don't! But Darwinian theory can explain why many species have such a ratio, why *Homo sapiens* have a 1:1.05 ratio, why some paper wasps have a 7:1 ratio. Similarly, a Darwinian approach will provide guidance about developing/applying models in human affairs and also guide our identification of factors that falsify the models in some domains, obstruct their improvement in others, and explain away their exceptions in non–ad hoc ways. (A good example of this sort of guidance is how Darwinian theory helps us evaluate the significance of findings such as Henrich et al. 2004.)

The upshot is that, first of all, a Darwinian approach is unlikely to recover or vindicate a good deal of received social theory (as opposed to making some good use of at least some of the data it has mounted up); second, it may not enhance our ability to predict, control, or even fine-tune human affairs. But this is not something a scientifically sophisticated approach to human affairs should find troubling. Third, what a sophisticated science of human affairs should do is obvious: identify the functions—almost certainly latent, unnoticed—of social events, states, and processes and then build models that explain (and even modestly predict) their emergence, persistence, spread, and recession as the result of multilevel processes of environmental filtration, a.k.a. natural selection. How good we can get at achieving these explanations and predictions will depend on the ratio of the rate at which we can acquire and organize data and the rate at which the local equilibria we seek to identify are overtaken by arms races of various sorts.

Acknowledgments

I am indebted to Sir Patrick Bateson for comments on an earlier draft. No agreement on his part with the views here expressed should be assumed.

Notes

1. Arguments to the contrary must start from premises much more controversial than the claim that humans are biological creatures—for instance, some tendentious claim about the role of free will or cognition or consciousness in exempting us from the natural order. Claims to the effect that the sort of knowledge or understanding or wisdom the social sciences should seek differs from that which natural science in general or biology in particular can provide are of a piece with the former sort of tendentious claim, and in fact rest on such claims when they rest on anything at all.
2. There is a vast literature on these two notions. To a first approximation, and for present purposes, a function can be defined as the behavior of a system's component that meets a need, confers a benefit, or provides an advantage to the system, and whose occurrence or presence is contingent on its doing so. An adaptation is a "selected effect," a trait that has emerged through a process of Darwinian (but not necessarily genetic) selection owing to its enhancing the fitness of systems that bear it. The factual thesis that all functions are adaptations is uncontroversial in biology. That function should be defined in terms of selected effects is a somewhat controversial claim in the philosophy of biology. See Rosenberg and McShea (2008) for an introduction.
3. Variation is usually qualified as random, not blind. But its blindness to need or benefit is crucial. Darwin described the process he discovered as natural selection. A better label is "environmental filtration." It emphasizes the crucially passive character of the process Darwin misleadingly called "selection." I use "environmental filtration" hereafter as a terminological variant on "natural selection" to emphasize this point.
4. This notion is further explained below. Competing (and for that matter cooperating) adaptations will affect one another's fitness and eventually find themselves in a local equilibrium. Owing to the persistence of random variation among all traits, including adaptations, there is a constant threat

that one or the other will change perhaps only slightly but enough to exploit the other adaptation. This breaks up the local equilibrium and precipitates an "arms race" in which variations in the second adaptation that can respond to the first one's new variant will be selected for. Thus is provoked an "arms race."

5. See Mackie (1996) for an introduction to Chinese foot binding in a game-theoretical framework. I am indebted here to Andres Luco.
6. As becomes clear below, "Darwinian processes" are construed somewhat broadly to include operant learning, which is only Darwinian selection operating ontogenetically, and other means of producing non-hardwired environmentally appropriate behavior put in place by Darwinian selection. The argument of this chapter is certainly not that human institutions and behaviors are the result of selection operating on genes. Quite the contrary, Darwinian cultural selection is mainly social and only in a few early but important cases is it a matter of dual genetic/cultural coevolutionary processes, for example, lactose tolerance and pastoralism.
7. Recognizing the limitations on rational choice theory or intentional human design to be identified here does not, however, relegate mathematical models that employ it, or experimental and evolutionary economic results that employ it to explanatory and predictive irrelevance. Just as biological processes appear to approach optima of various sorts well modeled by attributing "design" to Mother Nature, the same kind of instrumental approach in the social sciences can sometimes make use of rational choice models. More on the role of models below.
8. There is further reason to suppose that the processes of human conscious intentional creation are themselves Darwinian ones carried out within the brain(s) of those who intend them. For the explanation of the apparently purposive creations of human intention faces the same problems as the explanation of other biological adaptations: once we have ruled out future causation, immanent teleologies, or vital/spiritual forces and disembodied minds, there seems no alternative to treating brain processes that eventuate in individual actions as Darwinian ones as well. Pursuing this argument would take us into the intricacies of neuroscience. But see Dennett (1995) and Campbell (1965).
9. See Maoz and Russett (1993). Rare dissenters from this view have invoked the US Civil War and the belligerency of Kaiser Wilhelm's Germany as counterexamples (Layne 1994), since both parties to the Civil War considered themselves democracies, and Germany had an elected (if largely powerless) Reichstag. Suffice it to say that these counterexamples are controversial and have been rejected on a variety of counts. If accepted, they would not undermine the argument advanced here.
10. Consider what was until recently thought to be the most invariant of biological regularities: all genes are composed of DNA. For a long time this regularity was subject to no exception. But because it remained invariant over a very long period, its operation provided an environment that would allow for the selection for any new biological system that could take advantage of the fact that all genes are composed of DNA. Such a system eventually came into existence—the RNA viruses, whose genes are made of RNA and parasitize the machinery of DNA replication (HIV is the most notable example of these viruses). Thus, the regularity that all genes are made of DNA gives way to the regularity that they are all made of nucleic acids (either RNA or DNA). But we can be sure that the arms race of evolutionary competition will eventually undermine this new invariant regularity, by producing an alternative means of genetic transmission that exploits the regularity (unless it already has done so, by bringing about the prion protein that transmits Mad Cow disease). The same arms race between DNA and RNA and prions also disposes of another invariance of molecular biology, the so-called Central Dogma (in its strong form) that the flow of genetic information is always from DNA to RNA to proteins.
11. Natural selection even produces locally invariant regularities between traits that are not adapted at all but are correlated as the *by-products* of traits mutually selected for. For example, consider a remarkable discovery of Darwin's: in all mammalian species subject to domestication, at least some examples are "piebald"—that is, have spots, usually white on dark—and this trait is heritable. Darwin's observation has since been widely confirmed, even in "natural experiments," in domestication of hitherto wild and non-piebald species such as the mink. Presumably, being piebald is not an adaptation, and in general animal breeders do not select for it. The relationship between being domesticated and being piebald is nevertheless invariant, or has been hitherto. However, we pretty

much know why. Domestication has always proceeded by allowing the tamest, least aggressive young to reproduce with one another. Tameness is a hereditary trait. At least some of the genes involved in tameness behavior are probably located close together on the same chromosomes as recessive genes that control for variegated coat color. Repeated interbreeding always brings out the recessive trait of piebald coat in at least some descendants. So long as those chromosomes are not broken in meiosis at points between the herd genes and the piebald genes, the regularity that domestic species have some piebald members will be invariant. But of course this generalization is evolutionarily contingent. There are several obvious circumstances—human and natural interventions—that can and someday probably will break it down. Besides a suite of mutations, a founder effect recombination that breaks the chromosomal link, or (equivalently) a persistent program of artificial selection to breed non-piebald domestic animals, there is the possibility of a new move in some arms race we have not noticed breaking the invariance. Being piebald may become an adaptational disadvantage owing to the conspicuousness or other fitness-lowering effect of such marks in an evolutionary arms race with predators or parasites.

12. R. A. Fisher's model of the sex ratio is a particularly powerful illustration of the restricted character of generalizations and mathematical models in biology. It is a regularity that in almost all vertebrate species—indeed, in almost all sexually reproducing species—the sex ratio is 1:1 (50 percent males, 50 percent females). That there is almost always almost exactly the same number of men as women was long treated as strong evidence of the benevolence of God. Fisher developed a mathematical model to show that the 1:1 sex ratio generalization is an adaptationally advantageous stable equilibrium that results from a Darwinian process of blind variation and passive environmental filtration. Women have varying hereditary predispositions to give birth to males or to females. Whenever the sex ratio departs from 1:1 in favor of more females, those mothers who disproportionately bare male children will have more and fitter grandchildren, since their sons are scarcer relative to females and can be choosier. More grandchildren carrying genes that favor having boys results in more boys and so moves the sex ratio back to 1:1. When the ratio begins to favor males over females, the same process in reverse shifts it back to 50 percent of each. Whence the stable sex ratio equilibrium. But of course the model gives false results for a number of species, including us. In humans the long-run equilibrium sex ratio at birth is 1.05:1, slightly favoring male births. Why? Because boys' mortality rates are higher than girls' mortality rates, or at least were higher in the environment that selected for *Homo sapiens*. Darwinian natural selection had to fine-tune the sex ratio to make it 1:1 at sexual maturity. Doing that required more boys at birth than girls. So, the model needs to be revised: what is equalized is not the sex ratio, but the amount of parental investment in males and females. Additionally, there are several species of insects in which the sex ratio is heavily biased toward females.

13. I employ the term "meme" here to identify whatever it is that is the replicator in Darwinian cultural evolution. At about the same time Dawkins coined the term, E. O. Wilson and Lumsden (1981) introduced the word "culturgen" to name whatever fills the replicator role in culture. Had things turned out differently, Wilson's term would have become the meme for "memes" instead.

14. In biological cases, "de-Darwinization" frequently occasions and in fact is required for reproduction and thus selection at higher levels. This will be not be invariable in cases of social and cultural de-Darwinization.

15. The aspen trees in a grove are all parts of a single organism—ramets of a genet. They are genetic clones, the offshoots of a spreading root system, which persists and grows new buds even as its older buds, the trees, grow up and die off. The single individual may survive thousands of years. But it remains the unit exposed to the vicissitudes of a Darwinian process. Many human institutions—packages of strategies—will be like the aspen.

References

Bateson, P., and K. Laland. 2013. "Tinbergen's Four Questions: An Appreciation and an Update." *Trends in Ecology and Evolution* 28 (12): 712–718.

Beatty, J. 1995. "The Evolutionary Contingency Thesis." In *Concepts, Theories, and Rationality in the Biological Sciences*, edited by G. Wolters and J. Lennox. Pittsburgh, PA: University of Pittsburgh Press.

Campbell, D. T. 1965. "Variation and Selective Retention in Socio-cultural Evolution." In *Social Change in Developing Areas: A Reinterpretation of Evolutionary Theory*, edited by H. R. Barringer, G. I. Blanksten, and R. W. Mack, 19–49. Cambridge, MA: Schenkman.
Coase, R. H. 1937. "The Nature of the Firm." *Economica* 4: 386–405.
Dennett, D. 1995. *Darwin's Dangerous Idea*. New York: Simon and Schuster.
Driscoll, C. 2008. "The Problem of Adaptive Individual Choice in Cultural Evolution." *Biology and Philosophy* 23: 101–113.
Godfrey-Smith, P. 2009. *Darwinian Populations*. New York: Oxford University Press.
Gould, S. J., and R. C. Lewontin. 1979. "The Spandrels of San Marco and the Panglossian Paradigm: A Critique of the Adaptationist Programme." *Proceedings of the Royal Society B* 205: 581–598.
Gould, S. J., and E. S. Vrba. 1982. "Exaptation—a Missing Term in the Science of Form." *Paleobiology* 8: 4–15.
Hayek, F. 1945. "The Uses of Knowledge in Society." *American Economic Review* 35: 519–530.
Henrich, J., R. Boyd, S. Bowles, C. Camerer, E. Fehr, and H. Gintis. 2004. *Foundations of Human Sociality: Economic Experiments and Ethnographic Evidence from Fifteen Small-Scale Societies*. New York: Oxford University Press.
Keynes, J. M. 1936. *The General Theory of Employment, Interest and Money*. London: Macmillan.
Layne, C. 1994. "Kant or Cant: The Myth of the Democratic Peace." *International Security* 19: 5–49.
Mackie, G. 1996. "Ending Footbinding and Infibulation: A Convention Account." *American Sociological Review* 61: 999–1017.
Maoz, Z., and B. Russett. 1993. "Normative and Structural Causes of Democratic Peace, 1946–1986." *American Political Science Review* 87: 624–638.
Maynard Smith, J., and E. Szathmáry. 1995. *The Major Transitions in Evolution*. Oxford and New York: W. H. Freeman and Company.
Nelson, R., and S. Winter. 1982. *An Evolutionary Theory of Economic Change*. Cambridge, MA: Belknap Press of Harvard University Press.
Richerson, P., and R. Boyd. 2006. *Not by Genes Alone*. Chicago: University of Chicago Press.
Rosenberg, A., and D. McShea. 2008. *Philosophy of Biology*. London: Routledge.
Runciman, W. G. 2009. *The Theory of Cultural and Social Selection*. Cambridge: Cambridge University Press.
Skyrms, B. 2010. *Signals: Evolution, Learning, and Information*. New York: Oxford University Press.
Sperber, F. 2000. "An Objection to the Memetic Approach to Culture." In *Darwinizing Culture: The Status of Memetics as a Science*, edited by R. Aunger, 163–173. Oxford: Oxford University Press.
Tinbergen, N. 1963. "On the Aims of Ethology." *Zeitschrift fur Tierpsychologie* 20: 410–433.
Wilson, E. O., and C. Lumsden. 1981. *Genes, Mind and Culture*. Cambridge, MA: Harvard University Press.

Chapter Three

Modes of Variation and Their Implications for an Extended Evolutionary Synthesis

Marion Blute

> This chapter synthesizes modes or principles of variation in evolution. This is not usually done and is important because it is often assumed that evolutionary theory has little to say about variation beyond the idea that it is "random," that is, "non-prescient" (Campbell 1956), and hence, among other things, there is nothing to generalize from to a sociocultural context. But there are such principles—at least some. These include basic logical sets of kinds of variations; modularity; major transitions; evo-devo; von Baer's laws; nongenetic inheritance including culture, origins, and rates of innovation; and forms of introgressive or reticulate evolution (i.e., evolutionary nets). Moreover, most of these modes or principles of variation have implications for subsequent evolution and are currently under active theorizing and research—a large part of the effort under way to achieve an extended evolutionary synthesis.

Basic Kinds of Variation

There is a basic set of kinds of variation—mutations (as they are called in biological evolution) or innovations or inventions (as they are commonly called in sociocultural evolution—including here for convenience linguistic, economic, and scientific and technological evolution). These are adding, subtracting, substituting, and rearranging elements. The meaning of adding and subtracting is self-evident, but substituting implies a combination of adding and subtracting, of roughly the same amounts in the same location. The first car I drove had a heater, but since then air conditioning has been added, running boards have been removed, front-wheel drive has replaced rear-wheel drive, and the controls have been extensively rearranged. Moreover, all four of these can take place at a variety of scales in both realms. A biological mutation may involve anything from a single genetic element (in structural terms a base pair, or in functional terms a three-base pair codon) all the way through a whole chromosome or even a whole set of chromosomes. Socioculturally, an innovation may affect a single idea or norm or value—all the way through an entire role or status, organization, or even an entire institution such as a kinship or a religious, political, or economic system (Abrutyn 2014). Developmental biologists as opposed to evolutionary biologists prefer a different classification suggested by phenotypes (observable characteristics) rather than genotypes—heterotopy (change in location), heterochrony (change in time), heterometry (change in amount), and heterotypy (change in kind) (Arthur 2011). In either case, the four basic types or modes of innovation are simply logically possible categories and, by themselves, have no particular evolutionary implications. What follows utilizes the first classification. The section on modularity and origins is about adding; the section on major transitions is about whether something is substituted or added. Sections on evo-devo, von Baer's laws, nongenetic inheritance, and whether innovation rates are selectable apply to all four kinds of innovations. Finally, the section on evolutionary nets is about whether something is added or subtracted.

Modularity: Parts Give Rise to More Parts

In the 1960s Susumu Ohno (1970) made an important discovery and elaborated an important principle—"evolution by gene duplication." He discovered that additions to genomes come from overduplication of existing genomic sequences. These duplications can range from a single base pair all the way to an entire genome (called polyploidy). His view was that duplication of (usually part of) an existing genome had the effect that the redundant copy was free to gradually evolve to take on some new function, enabling the evolution of complexity. Common descent originating internally in this way is termed "paralogy" or "serial homology" by analogy with the more familiar external "homology." Since Ohno's time, important new observations and ideas have been added. For example, not only can redundant copies of genes take on new functions, but the old and the new can specialize in different aspects of the old function, or the new can take on control functions—genes acting to flexibly control the activities of other genes.

Evolution by endoduplication takes place not only genetically but at a whole host of levels of biological organization—the whole phenomenon coming to be known as "modularity" (for an overview see Raff 1996 and the articles in Callebaut and Rasskin-Gutman 2005). Modules differentiated by function are explicable, the principle being that specialists (in this case specialist parts) are commonly more efficient in what they specialize in than are generalists in that part. But what of unspecialized or repetitive modularity? Insect abdomens typically have eleven or twelve segments, the first seven or so of which are typically undifferentiated from each other. The structure of vascular plants is divided into roots and shoots (the latter composed of stems and leaves), but branches of both give rise to branches that themselves give rise to branches, and so on, yielding a fractal pattern (one that is self-similar on more than one scale). So are such phenomena simply indicative of a principle of variation, of origins by overduplication, or do they also have evolutionary implications in the sense that there is also some general reason why they have been selected? Many think they do and there is. In particular, by functioning semiautonomously, even such undifferentiated modules can enhance overall performance while at the same time minimizing connection costs (Clune, Mouret, and Lipson 2013), ultimately increasing "evolvability" (for a review see Arenas and Cooper 2013).

Socioculturally, enterprises are known to do this as well—employing loosely coupled departments or divisions, creating semiautonomous profit centers (for an overview see Baldwin and Clark 2000). If endoduplication is one of the most important modes of variation by which complexity is increased, major transitions or additions are the other.

Major Transitions: Wholes Give Rise to More Wholes

Major Transitions

With modularity, parts give rise to more parts, but in major transitions, wholes give rise to more wholes. In their book *The Major Transitions in Evolution*, Maynard Smith and

Szathmáry (1995) initiated a significant new stream of theory and research in evolution that continues to this day. "Major transitions" was not meant in the broad sense of key innovations such as the invention of photosynthesis, movement, or warm-bloodedness (Calcott and Sterelny 2011: 4; Lane 2009). Rather, it was meant in a narrower sense that "entities that were capable of independent replication before the transition can replicate only as part of a larger whole after it" (Maynard Smith and Szathmáry 1995: 4). They included a long list of such hypothesized transitions in their survey—"the origin of life, of the genetic code, of cells, of sex, of multicellular organisms, of societies, and of language" (xiii). Later researchers have tended to focus on paradigmatic cases such as the evolution of eukaryotic cells (which include organelles that were once free-living prokaryotic cells), the evolution of multicellularity from unicellularity, and the evolution of eusocial colonies from multicellularity (e.g., Michod 1999 on cells and multicellularity). As Bouchard and Huneman (2013) later put it, in major transitions evolution has gone "from groups to individuals." While some prefer the term "organisms" (see some of the essays in the former collection) or even "mergers and clubs" (Bapteste et al. 2012), most have continued to talk about the evolution of new kinds of collective or aggregate "individuals." Godfrey-Smith (2009) described "Darwinian populations" and "Darwinian individuals" and major transitions as "the appearance of new entities that can enter into Darwinian processes in their own right" (122). In many cases (including the eukaryotic cell and multicellularity) this involves "changes to the status of collective entities" in which, as the new collectives gradually become "Darwinized," the old gradually become "de-Darwinized" (122–128), although he is somewhat ambivalent about the latter, as was Michod (1999) to some degree.[1]

Bourke (2011) argued that such transitions take place in three stages, which he called social group formation, social group maintenance, and social group transformation. For multicellularity, such stages might be described as follows:

1. A metapopulation of evolving cells in a population of multicellular organisms (i.e., before the transition only the cells are evolving)
2. A metapopulation of evolving cells in a population of evolving multicellular organisms (i.e., during the transition both are evolving)
3. A metapopulation of cells in a population of evolving multicellular organisms (i.e., after the transition only the multicellular organisms are evolving). In Godfrey-Smith's (2013) terms, in the last stage the cells have finally been "de-Darwinized."

MAJOR ADDITIONS

The alternative to this "replacement" view of transitions is that the second stage never disappears; that is, there is always a metapopulation of evolving prokaryotic cells in a population of evolving eukaryotic cells, a metapopulation of evolving cells in a population of evolving multicellular organisms, and a metapopulation of evolving multicellular individuals in a population of evolving eusocial colonies. On this view, evolution on the original level has not been replaced. Instead, it has become "encapsulated" (Blute 1977, 2010: 193) or "nested" (Nachtomy, Shavit, and Smith 2002) as it becomes the mechanism of development of individuals in the newly added evolving population. Such a view was traditionally defended by Buss (1987) and more recently by Kupiec (2009), who emphasized the stochastic nature of gene expression, and by Clarke (2011) for root and shoot meristems in plants.

A hierarchical "fate map" of a multicellular animal such as *C. elegans* is a tree. Unlike familiar evolutionary trees, however, these developmental trees are repeated and constricted enough in time and space to be experimented on. Stimulated by Weismann's original view of the segregation of determinants in development and eventually the difference of opinion between embryologists Roux and Driesch, generations of classical embryologists did innumerable transplantation experiments on a variety of model animals (but most commonly amphibians) to test whether development was "mosaic" or autonomous (ancestry matters) versus "regulative" or dependent (the local environment matters). If you transplant part of an embryo replacing a part somewhere else, does it become what it would have become in its original location (i.e., ancestry matters), or is it regulated by the new environment to become what would have developed there from what was removed (i.e., the local environment matters)? The answers found varied by group and by the part of the embryo involved. The most general finding was that the earlier the stage of development, the more regulative, while the later the stage, the more mosaic (i.e., heritable changes in cell groups, their lineages, and cells themselves eventually come into existence in development; see any traditional text in developmental biology). Add to this the facts that cell death ("apoptosis") and differences in cell proliferation rates are also parts of normal animal development. Hence, to argue that this is *not* evolution among cells one would have to argue that, even so, the heritable differences as opposed to the nonheritable ones among cells make no difference to what cells survive and proliferate and what ones do not—an argument that would surely be special pleading. So there is variation (called differentiation) in development, inheritance, and differences in fitness—this is evolution by definition. The existence of cancer is only the most obvious manifestation of the fact that the evolution of multicellularity is an addition and not a replacement.

A simple model of a mechanism of transition by addition may make this clear. It has been suggested that the condition necessary for a major transition is a minimum of two alternative strategies, each of which, as a by-product, constructs the ecological conditions that favor the other. Gradually, those conditions come to induce (or the conditions predicting them come to induce) the other strategy such that a new aggregate developmental life cycle (i.e., one capable of repeating itself) emerges (Blute 2010: 191). Assume that in a patchy environment we begin with a metapopulation of cells in a population of many small cell groups (whether originating "fraternally" [i.e., by descendants "staying together"] or by "egalitarian" means [i.e., by the unrelated "coming together"]—see Queller 1997; Tarnita, Taubes, and Nowak 2013). Cells in groups on patches with plentiful resources grow and multiply, while those in groups on patches with scarce resources die off, creating a population of fewer, larger groups. At that point, selection favors groups dividing and dispersing into patches that previously had few resources but now have had an opportunity to recover. This creates a population of more numerous smaller groups again. Why disperse in subgroups rather than as a whole? That is easy—because subgroups can disperse in more directions. But then at the opposite extreme, why not disperse as single cells rather than as cell groups? Surface area increases less than linearly with volume. As a consequence, all other things being equal, groups encounter proportionately less resistance than do single cells in moving. Moreover, while the small (single cells) are better adapted to consume (eat and excrete), the large (cell groups) are better adapted to digest (break down and build up). Hence subgroups are better able than single cells to move and sustain themselves as they move until they arrive where resources are plentiful again.

Such a mechanism can be realized in the simplest case in a haploid asexual population in which two alternative alleles expressed in cells and in groups of them are competing, going respectively from a +− relationship to − + and back again. In Okasha's (2006) terms, causal, cross-level by-products obtain in both directions between "particles" and "collectives," but here changing directions cyclically. In Michod's (1999) terms, covariances between traits and fitness obtain for both lower- and higher-level entities, but here changing signs cyclically. As cycles repeat, selection will also favor these alleles or genotypes evolving to anticipate the conditions that favor them or even using signals that predict those conditions to behave appropriately. By such means the cell growth and multiplication phase becomes the somatic growth phase, and the cell group division phase becomes the reproductive phase (between which there is a trade-off in the allocation of resources) of the new, additional, multicellular kinds of individuals reproducing by multicellular propagules.[2] This simple case is a semelparous life cycle (big bang reproduction all at the end of the life cycle). Possibilities other than switches between growth and motility/maintenance in a patchy environment include the same in a colonizable environment (on the general importance of the latter see Waters, Ceridvven, and Hewitt 2013) or between growth and mutability in one patchy in niche (there is likely to be sampling error and therefore novelty introduced when fewer large groups divide).

SOME COMPARISONS

Okasha (2006) emphasized that Maynard Smith and Szathmáry turned the old problem of units of selection into a dynamical historical one about the evolutionary emergence of new ones. But understanding transitions as innovations, not by replacement but by addition, particularly with the kind of model described above, makes them dynamical in a second sense as well—a developmental one; together they compose an evo-devo dynamic. While providing a fundamental theoretical rationale for the existence of multiple levels of selection at all, they also limit the latter. Where an addition by such a means has taken place and a new aggregate life cycle has emerged, multiple levels of selection exist; but where it has not, they do not.

Multiple levels of selection characterize the sociocultural world as much as they do the biological—the world of information or ideas manifested in behavior and artifacts (Mesoudi, Whiten, and Laland 2004, 2006), norms and values governing a variety of these depending on circumstances, social roles or status, organizations, institutions, and even whole cultures and societies. Moreover, a developmental process characterizes at least some sociocultural entities as much as it does the biological. "No act or artifact is an instantaneous event but grows and develops over however shorter or longer a period of time. Whether it is a task being carried out, a sentence uttered, a social role maturing, a hand axe being napped, or a car being built on an assembly line—all have a shorter or longer period of somatic growth and development" (Blute 2013: 111). However, an additions view of transitions with evolution among the old becoming the mechanism of development of the new does place limits on how far these extend. Certainly culturally transmitted ideas, behaviors, and social roles have a life cycle that is reproduced. However, for most organizations, let alone institutions such as kinship and religious, political, or economic institutions consisting of multiple roles and even organizations, let alone whole cultures and societies, that life cycle is at best singular (i.e., evolution among them is only viability rather than reproductively based). Hence, they constitute units of selection only in that very limited sense.

An "additions" as opposed to a "replacement" view of major transitions should not be taken to mean that there are no differences between evolution on lower and higher levels—among cells as the developmental mechanism of multicellular individuals, for example, and conventional evolution. Despite the fact that multicellular organisms including humans are increasingly being shown to be genetic mosaics (for an overview see Lupski 2013), it is likely that most of the heritable differences in cell groups, their lineages, and cells themselves in multicellular development are epigenetic rather than genetic. Even so, it can be experimentally shown that competition among cells takes place (e.g., Claveria et al. 2013). It also seems likely that much of the heritable change of whatever type comes to be internally "directed" in development in a way that it is not in evolution. Overall, a somewhat analogous case is the relationship between individual learning and social learning and sociocultural evolution. While we can consider the two selection processes separately (whether viewed as analogous or as two tokens of the same general type, selection processes), it is unlikely that one would want to argue that individual learning ceases once social learning and cultural evolution have been added. To extend a metaphor that has been used, an additions point of view is neither "deflationary," recognizing evolution on the lower level only, nor "inflationary," recognizing it on the higher level only, but both simultaneously.

As emphasized in the titles of this and the previous section, in the introduction of a new module, parts give rise to more parts, while in a major transition, wholes give rise to more wholes. However, they are similar in that they are probably the two most interesting modes of variation in evolution because they are the most important means by which complexity is added. It is not that increases in complexity are inevitable or even usual in evolution. Most prokaryotes have remained prokaryotes, most unicells have remained unicells, and most multicellular individuals are not part of eusocial colonies, for example. Similarly, most lineages have not become clans, most clans tribes, most tribes nations, or most nations empires. So while such increases in complexity have not in fact tended to prevail in evolution, we still seem to find them the most interesting. Why that is so is puzzling, but it does perhaps suggest that the pre-Darwinian concept of evolution rooted in the medieval "great chain of being" (Lovejoy 1936) still echoes down through the ages. Even Bourke's use of the term "stages" rather than "states" for evolutionary transitions, like that of traditional "evolutionary" social science (for a history see Sanderson 2007), carries an echo of this as if movement through such a sequence in phylogeny is inevitable in the same way that movement through such a sequence in ontogeny is more or less once established.

Evo-Devo: Genes as Followers as Well as Leaders?

Dobzhansky famously defined evolution as the "gradual change of gene frequencies within populations" that "serves, by extension, as an adequate model for all evolutionary events" (1937: xxiv). But the "by extension" simply glosses over too much. In particular, as has often been pointed out, the definition recognizes the role of heredity in evolution but ignores those of development and of ecology.

Consider two of the ways in which evolutionary innovations can be initiated (both simultaneously are conceivable, but far less likely). In the one "inductive-type"[3] pathway of old genes or gene combinations in a new environment, phenotypes lead and genes follow. If a new food source becomes available that the carrier of some preexisting genetic alternative but not others is able to make use of, the former is ecologically induced by the new diet to grow more, live longer, or have more or better offspring, ultimately resulting in an evolutionary-genetical change in allele frequencies in the population. This has long been known as a pre-adaptation or exaptation (Gould and Vrba 1982). In the other "constructive-type" pathway of new genes or gene combinations in an old environment, genes lead and phenotypes follow. If a new genetic mutation or recombination enables its carrier but not others to "construct" (Odling-Smee, Laland, and Feldman 1996) its ecological niche differently, to use a preexisting but unutilized resource, for example, the carrier's development is altered similarly, resulting in an evolutionary-genetical change.

To recognize the role of development and ecology in evolution and to include exaptations by formally acknowledging the existence of both of these pathways (as well as other things—microevolution does not in itself incorporate a theory of speciation, and there can be nongenetic as well as genetic inheritance), taking a lead from Van Valen's definition "evolution is the control of development by ecology" (1973), the following definition has been suggested:

> Microevolution by natural selection is any change in the inductive control of development (whether morphological, physiological or behavioral) by ecology and/or in the construction of the latter by the former which alters the relative frequencies of (genetic or other) hereditary elements in a population beyond those expected of randomly chosen variants. (Blute 2008: 4, 2010: 168)

Ingeniously, Schwander and Leimar (2011: 149) used ancestral state reconstruction methods to determine how commonly switches and losses have taken place between genetic polymorphisms and polyphenisms and found "no clear tendency for genes to be followers or leaders overall," which underlines the importance of a more inclusive definition. In short, recognizing that genes are as likely to be followers as leaders in evolution by employing a more inclusive definition of evolution by natural selection is long overdue.

Such a recognition fits within the definition of the subject matter of evolutionary developmental biology (evo-devo) by the author of its first textbook, Brian K. Hall, who defined it as "how development (proximate causation) impinges on evolution (ultimate causation) to effect evolutionary change and how development itself has evolved" (1992: 2). It might not satisfy those content with the traditional definition or even those to whom evo-devo is primarily the comparative molecular genetics of development—particularly of "tool kit" genes, which regulate the level, location, or timing of the expression of other genes (e.g., see Carroll 2005). At the opposite extreme, it might also not satisfy more radical revisionists who would see interaction between environments and phenotypes as necessarily adaptive, that is, who would revert to a pre-Darwinian teleology (readers can decide for themselves how far in that direction works such as those of West-Eberhard 2003, Jablonka and Lamb 2005, and some of the essays in Sansom and Brandon 2007, Gissis and Jablonka 2011, and Hallgrímsson and Hall 2011 go). While phenotypes can be plastic to be sure, can evolve to bet hedge under uncertainty, or can be adaptively plastic under uncertainty with reliable cues (Roff 2002), *novel* environmental influences on phenotypes are more likely to have maladaptive than adaptive effects, just as novel genes do. Robertson, Rehage, and Sih (2013) well reviewed the former fact under the rubric of "evolutionary traps." The fact that inductive-type innovations are similar to constructive-type ones in that sense does not in any way diminish their evolutionary importance.

The same two modes of innovation should be possible in sociocultural as well as biological evolution—an inductive-type pathway in which a new environment induces an old idea to be manifested in behavior or artifacts differently and a constructive-type pathway involving a new idea in an old environment, with selection then in either case resulting in a statistical change in the composition of a population of ideas. Of course, just as with the biological, there is no evidence that sociocultural innovations are biased *statistically* in the direction required for them to spread successfully. This holds most famously for stock picking and market timing but also for any field one chooses to look at—papers being cited, patents utilized, new businesses succeeding, or new products being successfully marketed (Blute 1979).

Von Baer's Laws: Variation Biased toward Later Developmental Stages?

In the nineteenth century the great German embryologist Karl Ernst von Baer proposed laws of embryological development—general characteristics and structural relations develop before special ones; the form of an embryo does not converge on that of others but diverges from them; and the embryo of an animal never resembles the adult of another animal but only its embryo. In modern language, embryological development is a process of differentiation in the sense that parts of an embryo become differentiated from each other and that members of different but related groups become more different from each other. Although von Baer was not an evolutionist, Darwin thought that the early similarity of members of different groups was the best evidence for his theory of common descent. As he wrote in the *Origin*, "Community in embryonic structure reveals community of descent" (Darwin [1859] 1958: 417).

Is this pattern of change in development—less change earlier, more later—a principle of variation? Does it mean, for example, that variations in the form of mutations that affect development are more likely to occur later rather than earlier? The consensus view is no, rather than biased mutation, the pattern is most readily explained by constraints. A genetic mutation or recombination that affected the earliest stage of development would have more side effects down the road than would one that first acted later, and many of these would likely be maladaptive. So it is not so much that innovations affecting the later stage occur preferentially as it is that those affecting the earlier stage are selected out preferentially. Analogous phenomena are found in other selection processes. For example, a rat learning a maze with a series of choice points reinforced at the end eliminates mistakes in a backward direction (i.e., change takes place more readily in the later than in the earlier stages of the entire sequence). Undoubtedly it obtains socioculturally as well—in the plans for assembling a new model of car beginning with those for the previous model, for example. The philosopher of biology, William C. Wimsatt, called the constraint principle in the evolution of development "generative entrenchment" (Wimsatt and Schank 1988).

In the 1990s, however, it turned out that the empirical generalization "more evolutionary change has taken place later than earlier in development" does not quite hold—rather, the difference between members of different but related groups resembles an hourglass or an egg timer (e.g., Duboule 1994). Groups differ more in the very earliest phase of development, converge to become more similar (the hourglass narrows to what is called the phylotypic stage, or in animals, the zootype; for a historic overview see Slack 2003), and then diverge again quite a bit for the bulk of the rest of development. Kalinka et al. (2010) confirmed this hourglass pattern for gene transcription involved in key developmental processes by comparing six species of *Drosophila*.

The constraints logic might be taken to imply that the in-between phylotypic stage of minimal change/differences between groups, rather than reduced selection pressures there which has been widely suggested, might represent the actual historical origin of the taxa involved (Blute 2010: 146–148). This interpretation was borne out by Domazet-Lošo and Tautz (2010). Using "phylostratigraphic" methods they had previously pioneered, they found from the transcriptome (all RNA molecules present) that the genes expressed in zebra fish in the equivalent of the animal phylotypic stage are indeed older than those in any other, including the earliest phase. They also confirmed this for some other groups using data from the literature.

But another question remains. Again, if the constraints logic is valid, how has so much evolutionary change in the earliest phase of development been possible? I have argued that it is because what appears to be the earliest phase of development is, in actuality, a later phase. Such would be the case if it were largely a maternal effect (i.e., a later phase of the mother's development). Intriguingly Domazet-Lošo and Tautz (2010) did find significant differences between the age of genes expressed in the late juvenile and adult phases of males and females in zebra fish with more new genes in females than in males. They suggested this may be related to recent sexual selection (although it should be noted that zebra fish are not notably sexually dimorphic and that there is little evidence that female choice is more significant than male-male competition among them—if anything, the reverse may be the case). However, the sex difference is not really a test of the maternal effect hypothesis anyway. While maternally inherited RNAs would show up in the transcriptome, what would not necessarily show up would be if they were maternally inherited, or transcribed from maternally imprinted genes, or expressed as a consequence of maternally inherited protein transcription factors, for example. Hence, I eagerly await whether the maternal effects hypothesis of "too much" change early in development can and will be tested. If confirmed, von Baer's law would in a sense be restored. I doubt, however, that there is a basis for such "maternal effects" psychologically or socioculturally, although that remains to be seen.

Nongenetic Inheritance and Cultural Evolution: Lamarckian?

We now know that in a wide range of cases, environmentally induced phenotypic changes can indeed be inherited by a variety of mechanisms, so that is another means by which variation is introduced into a population. The many known examples of nongenetic inheritance have variously been classified into epigenetic, behavioral, and symbolic by Jablonka and Lamb (2005) and into epigenetic, parental effects, ecological, and cultural inheritance by Danchin et al. (2011). One example I like to use is a simple one. Imagine a parental cell that doubles in size and divides once. Then the material included in the two offspring cells (including one strand of each DNA molecule for that matter) was *acquired* by the parental cell rather than *inherited* by it, that is, in this simplest of all cases, the inheritance of acquired characteristics is 50 percent (Blute 2010: 205). We now know that vast genomic hierarchies and networks exist—genes that control the expression of other genes that control the expression of other genes, and so on, at every stage from transcription to post-translation (for an overview see Gilbert 2014, Chapter 2). And the more complex and differentiated the biochemistry is in this way, the more potential targets there are for environmental influences on development as well as for the effects of these influences to be inherited nongenetically. Because a lot more than DNA (which constitutes a very small proportion of a cell by dry weight) is inherited, critics are surely wrong when they make claims such as "the level of the gene is where the conceptual buck stops. More precisely, it is at the level of the genes that the *first* effect of a system that can organize environmental inputs and respond to them, by building more complex systems, begins" (Dickins and Rahman 2012: 2917; italics added).

Critics, however, complain, among other things, that those who emphasize such "Lamarckian" phenomena have not produced a new general theory of heredity, let alone of evolution, to rival Mendel's theory of heredity and the population genetics-based theory of the traditional synthetic theory of evolution (e.g., Dickins and Rahman 2012: 2917). But to be fair, they have generally not claimed to. Rather, Danchin et al. (2011) have called for the development of an "inclusive" theory of inheritance, Jablonka and Lamb (2005) for an evolutionary theory that "acknowledges Darwinian, Lamarckian and saltational processes" (quoted in Dickins and Rahman 2012: 2913), and Pigliucci and Müller (2010) for an "extended" evolutionary synthesis.

On the other hand, it is certainly important to distinguish between Lamarckian inheritance and Lamarckian evolution because the latter carries a lot of baggage in addition to the former. Lamarck thought that there was an inherent tendency to perfection that, as Lovejoy (1936) described it, would drive organisms up the medieval great chain of being. The need to adapt to the environment pushes some off that path, creating a tree. Trees grow taller, giraffes stretch their necks to reach food, and those lengthened necks are inherited by their offspring, he thought. However, it is important to distinguish between inductive environmental influences on phenotypes that organisms have evolved to "expect" (as described in the section on major additions, for example), subsequently inherited nongenetically or not, and those that are novel. Again, novel environmental influences are as (and probably more) likely to induce subsequently nongenetically inherited maladaptations as adaptations. They are no different than subsequently inherited genetic mutations or recombinations in that respect.

It is sometimes thought that this is different when the environmental influences are those controlling learning or involving cultural transmission. It is certainly the case that biological evolution can and often does program the behavior of organisms to be reinforced by, and therefore to learn individually, things that are biologically adaptive—witness the commonness of the reinforcing effects of acquiring food or opportunities for sexual activity in many species. However, because chance is as common psychologically as it is biologically, not all individual learning is biologically adaptive as demonstrated by Skinner's (1948) famous "superstition" experiments, for example. Moreover, organisms can be programmed to learn by culture as well as by genes. Mesoudi et al. (2013: 189) are certainly correct in claiming that the presence of culture "can create new genetic equilibria that would not exist in the absence of non-genetic inheritance" (e.g., see Boyd and Richerson 1985; Durham 1991; Richerson and Boyd 2005). With cultural transmission and gene-culture coevolution, the direction of inheritance is critically important for understanding its likely biological effects. With vertical cultural transmission (parents to offspring or closely related kin), the relationship between genes and culture is likely to be mutualistic (+ +), not only because genetic evolution will favor the cultural transmission of biologically adaptive traits, but also because cultural evolution will favor the genetic transmission of culturally adaptive traits. With horizontal transmission the relationship is apt to be selfish (+ –), most obviously when sects, cults, and churches appeal to pseudo-kinship to spread themselves at the expense of recruits' genes, for example. With oblique transmission it is likely to be competitive (– –)—if your biological offspring were to become my cultural offspring and vice versa, then genes and culture would be in competition with each other (Blute 2006a). In conclusion, Lamarckian inheritance, while important, should not be equated with (necessarily biologically adaptive) Lamarckian evolution.

Origins: Singular or Plural? Innovation Rates Selectable?

The ultimate variations, of course, are origins themselves—whether of life, that is, of the biological from the physio-chemical, the psychological from the biological, or the socio-cultural from the psychological—which unfortunately remain among the most poorly understood evolutionary innovations of all. The traditional issue with respect to the origin of life is which one or which combination came first—compartments (membranes), metabolism (protein enzymes), replication (nucleic acid, specifically RNA), or autocatalytic and therefore replicating cycles of protein or RNA enzymes (for an overview see Maynard Smith and Szathmáry 1995). Another approach can be taken from an evo-devo perspective. If life began as small, simple "juveniles," then it would seem that development came first and evolution must have developed, but if it began as large, complex "adults," then it would seem that evolution came first and development must have evolved. While the "small and simple" starting point would seem most logical, if origins were multiple, then viability selection and hence evolution in the form of "competitive development" would have obtained as well (Blute 2006b) with reproduction and ultimately heredity somehow emerging subsequently (e.g., Blute 2007; Salazar-Ciudad 2013). While the near universality of the genetic code might be taken to imply a single origin of life, it actually does not imply that, but only that all forms of life today are descendants of only one of those origins. That is the typical situation in evolutionary processes. As Cavalli-Sforza (2000: 79) made clear, because there was a Y chromosomal-Adam or a mitochondrial-Eve in the human species, for example, does not mean that only one male or one female lived at the appropriate times in Africa. Similarly, even if it were true that all human language families (as opposed to the languages within each family) share a common ancestry, that would not imply that only one group of humans began to talk, but rather that extant language families are the descendants of only one of those that did. So while origins are typically plural rather than singular, descent from one or a small number of these can still be, and often is, the norm.

A related issue is whether *rates* of variation in existing lineages are themselves selectable, a phenomenon sometimes called "adaptive mutation." The weight of opinion is that they are (Freeman and Herron 2004: 117–118). Mutation rates are thought to be selected for under conditions of stress, a fact particularly well documented in prokaryotes (for an empirical overview and formal proofs see Ram and Hadany 2012). Socioculturally, it is not surprising that since the onset of the recent recession stimulated by the financial crisis, governments everywhere have been seeking more means of increasing scientific, technological, and economic innovation rates and that the Global Innovation Index (sponsored by Cornell University, Insead, and the World Intellectual Property Organization [a UN agency], ranking 142 economies on 84 indicators; see http://www.globalinnovationindex.org/content.aspx?page=GII-Home) is being given more attention than it might command in better times.

Introgressive, Anastomizing, Reticulate, or Compositional Evolution: Nets Rather Than Trees?

In a letter to J. D. Hooker in 1858, Darwin ([1859] 1958) called his "Principle of Divergence" the "key-stone" of his book, and he also discussed this in the latter part of Chapter 4 of the *Origin*. As Kohn (2009) has made beautifully clear, that was because it linked the other two great principles of his theory, natural selection and common descent (see also Sober 2011: 32–36). Under Malthusian population pressure and ecological interactions, it was natural selection *for* divergence—because that way "*the greatest amount of life can be supported*"—which, along with extinction, gives rise to the branching tree of the history of life (Darwin [1859] 1958: 113, italics added). Moreover, contexts make clear that he viewed this principle of divergence as applying at all levels—among individuals no less than among varieties, species, genera, orders, and so forth (although he sometimes used the term "variety" both for what we would call individual variation and for varieties—the contemporary term "variant" not being in use at the time). In his famous diagram and discussion of it, Darwin showed divergence emerging among individuals within a variety and from that the (two) most distinct varieties and eventually species emerging:

> Let (A) be a common, widely-diffused and varying species.... Only those variations which are in some way profitable will be preserved or naturally selected. And here the importance of the principle of benefit being derived from divergence of character comes in; for this will generally lead to the most different or divergent variations (represented by the outer dotted lines) being preserved and accumulated by natural selection. When a dotted line reaches one of the horizontal lines, and is there marked by a small numbered letter, a sufficient amount of variation is supposed to have been accumulated to form it into a fairly well-marked variety, such as would be thought worthy of record in a systematic work. ([1859] 1958: 116)

In short, in modern terms, Darwin thought that because it supports more life, disruptive natural selection has thus been responsible for creating the tree of life. However, since all of half a niche is not necessarily better than half of all a niche, that way of "supporting more life" in fact requires a specific condition—namely, that *specialists be commonly more efficient in the range of a niche that they specialize in than are generalists in that range*. And why might that be? It would have to be because they possess some comparative advantage as the economists call it in what they specialize in. Note that all other things being equal, two kinds of specialists would have to be slightly more than twice as efficient, three kinds slightly more than three times as efficient, and so on, which becomes increasingly less likely as the numbers rise. That shows the wisdom of Darwin's diagram in that while he shows diversity among individuals, in each case he shows only the two most distinct varieties eventually branching off from them, two species from them, and so on—in anticipation of the cladistic understanding that evolution normally takes place by bivariate branching. But his "principle of divergence" explains a lot more than the emphasis on bivariate branching about Darwin's thinking. That emphasis on the relentless pressure toward divergent specialization explains why he thought species had no more special status than the members of other levels in the taxonomic hierarchy; why he emphasized what we call homology (tree thinking) over homoplasy (parallel and convergent evolution); why he emphasized speciation by ecological rather than by geographic or sexual selection means; and of particular interest here, why he emphasized branching over introgressive, anastomizing, reticulate, or compositional evolution (e.g., Watson 2006).

However, we now know that anastomizing as well as branching processes do indeed take place in evolution—ones including horizontal gene transfer, hybridization, and symbiosis, which, if they prevailed, would make evolution more netlike than treelike. We know that horizontal gene transfer is more common than was once thought, particularly early in the history of life, and still today in prokaryotes, viruses, and other mobile genetic elements. In a few, very rare cases, even cells of multicellular organisms can be horizontally transmitted, like the famous Tasmanian devil facial tumor disease. We know that quite a few plant species are hybrids. We know that the most spectacular example of symbiosis claimed by Margulis (1971; Margulis and Sagan 2003)—that of mitochondria in animals and plastids and mitochondria in plants—is indeed the case. Similar phenomena occur socioculturally. In science, for example, facts, theories, or methods from one discipline are sometimes applied to a problem in another (analogous to horizontal gene transfer); whole disciplines or segments of them sometimes merge, creating a new discipline (analogous to hybridization); and teams of individuals from different disciplines can work together on a problem (analogous to symbiosis) (Blute and Armstrong 2011: 408).

On the other hand, how common horizontal gene transfer is in eukaryotes remains in doubt, and cancers transmissible clonally rather than by viruses are extremely rare; animal hybrids, when formed at all, tend to be sterile; and the other spectacular example of symbiosis proposed by Williamson (1992, 2003)—that of larval stages in life histories—has been pretty much discredited. As a consequence, most biological evolutionists (but not all—see, for example, Bapteste et al. 2012) still think of the tree rather than the net of life, albeit perhaps a tree with some "cobwebs" (source of this metaphor unknown to me). In the social sciences, I recall at the Cold Spring Harbor Centennial Symposium organized by James Watson in 1990 on "Evolution: From Molecules to Culture," some of the world's most prominent historical linguists literally pounding the table at the naivete of some biologists who thought that perhaps languages sometimes merge. Pigeons and creoles notwithstanding, it has never happened, the linguists assured us. That is because a language (as opposed to a dialect) in linguistics corresponds to a species (as opposed to a variety) in biology by definition—that within which individuals are able to exchange communications/genes respectively but not outside of it.

Applications of "tree-thinking" (Baum and Smith 2013), phylogenetic methods borrowed from biology, have become very well developed in the last couple of decades in some social science disciplines, including linguistics, archaeology, cultural anthropology, and even, albeit rarely, for political organization (e.g., Currie et al. 2010), but unfortunately not so far in sociology or economics (for an overview see Blute 2010, Chapter 2; for some recent examples see Buckley 2012, Walker et al. 2012, and Altschuler et al. 2013). Variants of these methods can moreover be used to detect anastomizing processes where they do exist—see, for example, the treatment by Tehrani (2013) of the East Asian "tiger grandmother" folk tale as a probable hybrid of "little red riding hood" and "the wolf and the kids" tales, the latter popular throughout Europe and the Middle East. However, on this issue I think we should give the last word (for now) to David Hull, probably the most prominent philosopher of biology at the time of his death in 2010. In an interview conducted the year before, he said on this point:

> Splitting is difficult; merger is even more difficult. The question is why. Splitting is not as common as we thought it was, merger turns out to be more common than we thought it was... Now how different and how common is merger in all these areas whether it's biology or science studies? We have to do empirical research because there's no a priori answer to that question. (quoted in Blute and Armstrong 2011: 419)

CONCLUSION: TOWARD AN EXTENDED EVOLUTIONARY SYNTHESIS

Population genetics, uniting Darwin's theory of evolution with Mendel's theory of heredity forged in the 1920s and '30s primarily by Ronald Fisher, J.B.S. Haldane, and Sewall Wright, which banished the Lamarckianism, orthogenesis, and saltationism that had created such confusion in the immediate post-Darwinian period, was a major intellectual achievement. So too was its application in a variety of fields in the synthetic theory of evolution by Dobzhansky, Mayr, Huxley, Simpson, Stebbins, and Rensch in subsequent decades and since. However, evolutionary theory is not static; it continues and will continue to change. Concepts and theories in science vary, are transmitted, and evolve (Toulmin 1972; Hull 1988; Blute and Armstrong 2011). Because of the variety and importance of new ideas and results, there have been calls in recent years for a "new" synthesis or at least for an "extended" one (e.g., Pigliucci 2009 and the articles in Pigliucci and Müller 2010). Not surprisingly, however, there are differences of opinion about what is most important to be included and few claims about what this new or extended theory will look like overall, if indeed it is achieved. I have chosen here to focus on the theme of modes of variation beyond logically basic sets—including modularity, major transitions, evo-devo, the distribution of variations across the life cycle, nongenetic inheritance including culture, origins and rates of innovation, and compositional or reticulate variation as well as their evolutionary implications.

The call has perhaps been strongest for the need to more explicitly address development in an "evo-devo" theory. Toward that end, and as potential contributions to an extended synthesis, I have emphasized an additions rather than a replacement theory of transitions, a revised definition of evolution by natural selection that incorporates development and ecology, and a historical origins and maternal effects theory of the developmental hourglass. In all of these cases, however, it remains that Darwin was essentially correct. Adaptation is achieved in both the biological and sociocultural realms, not because it is what is sought, but because selection controls what evolves.

Notes

1. In his later essay, Godfrey-Smith (2013) seems to be somewhat ambivalent about whether the new kind of Darwinian individuals are added to or replace the old. "As one Darwinian population evolves, it can give rise to new kinds of Darwinian individuals," which sounds like an addition (i.e., both are evolving). But then he adds, "Darwinian individuals can also go out of focus—lose their Darwinian characteristics," which sounds like a replacement (i.e., only the new are evolving) or perhaps it is suggesting that some cases are additions and others are replacements. But then he seems to settle on the view that all cases are partly one and partly the other, "The evolution of new individuals *partly* 'de-Darwinizes' the old ones that make them up" (24–25; italics added). Finally, the "partly" is modified even further by "tend to": "collectives *tend to partly* de-Darwinize their constituent parts" (26; italics added). Similarly, Michod (1999) tells us that, on the one hand, in a transition lower-level units go from being selfish to being cooperative, but also that "the tension between lower and higher level units is never completely resolved in any evolutionary transition" so units are "nested but partially decoupled" (4).
2. Later, at least in the case originating by "staying together," distinct germ line cells could emerge, perhaps by Bourke's (2011) "virtual dominant" mechanism. Nascent germ cells might emerge from those cell lineages with a lower division and hence a lower mutation rate so that nascent somatic cells would be more related to the former than to each other and hence the former could come to "virtually dominate" the latter.
3. "Induction" has been the traditional term used in embryology for processes in which a part of an embryo causes another part to develop in a particular direction by contact or local diffusion and has sometimes been extended to the influence of the external environment on development. Recently a group of mainly philosophers adopted a metaphor of "scaffolding" to incorporate environmental influences on development, whether biological or sociocultural, and possibly much else as well. The scaffolding metaphor originated in cognitive psychology with respect to learning to build three-dimensional structures (Wood, Bruner, and Ross 1976) and language learning (Ninio and Bruner 1978), both in children, and eventually spread more widely in the educational literature to refer to various ways of supporting the learning of students. At least to some extent, this adoption was attractive to educators because it avoided (rather than solved) debates over behavioral versus cognitive theories of learning, of classical versus operant learning processes, of individual versus social learning, and of social learning by observation versus by verbal instruction. Unfortunately, a full set of statements of this usage with respect to development understood broadly, which is in Caporael, Griesemer, and Wimsatt (2014), was not yet available at the time of this writing. Hence, I have, for now at least, retained the more traditional concept of induction.

References

Abrutyn, S. 2014. *Revisiting Institutionalism in Sociology: Putting the "Institution" Back in Institutional Analysis*. New York: Routledge, Taylor & Francis Group.

Altschuler, E. L., A. S. Calude, A. Meade, and M. Pagel. 2013. "Linguistic Evidence Supports Date for Homeric Epic." *Bioessays* 35 (5): 417–420.
Arenas, C. D., and T. F. Cooper. 2013. "Mechanisms and Selection of Evolvability: Experimental Evidence." *Federation of European Microbiological Societies* 37: 572–582.
Arthur, W. 2011. *Evolution: A Developmental Approach*. Oxford: John Wiley & Sons.
Baldwin, C. Y., and K. B. Clark. 2000. *Design Rules*. Vol. 1, *The Power of Modularity*. Cambridge, MA: MIT Press.
Bapteste, E., P. Lopez, F. Bouchard, F. Baquero, J. O. McInerney, and R. M. Burian. 2012. "Evolutionary Analyses of Non-genealogical Bonds Produced by Introgressive Descent." *Proceedings of the National Academy of Sciences* 109: 18266–18272.
Baum, D. A., and S. D. Smith. 2013. *Tree Thinking: An Introduction to Phylogenetic Biology*. Greenwood Village, CO: Roberts and Company Publishers.
Blute, M. 1977. "Darwinian Analogues and the Naturalistic Explanation of Purposivism in Biology, Psychology and the Sociocultural Sciences." PhD diss., University of Toronto.
———. 1979. "Sociocultural Evolutionism: An Untried Theory." *Behavioral Science* 24: 46–59.
———. 2006a. "Gene-Culture Coevolutionary Games." *Social Forces* 85: 151–166.
———. 2006b. "Origins and the Ecoevodevo Problem." *Biological Theory* 1: 116–118.
———. 2007. "The Evolution of Replication." *Biological Theory* 2: 10–22.
———. 2008. "Is It Time for an Updated 'Eco-Evo-Devo' Definition of Evolution by Natural Selection?" *Spontaneous Generations: A Journal for the History and Philosophy of Science* 1: 1–5.
———. 2010. *Darwinian Sociocultural Evolution: Solutions to Dilemmas in Cultural and Social Theory*. Cambridge: Cambridge University Press.
———. 2013. "'Variation and Selective Retention' as an Evolutionary Epistemology: Were Donald Campbell's Life Histories Sufficient?" *Israel Journal of Ecology & Evolution* 59 (2): 109–116.
Blute, M., and P. Armstrong. 2011. "The Reinvention of Grand Theories of the Scientific/Scholarly Process." *Perspectives on Science* 19: 391–425.
Bouchard, F., and P. Huneman, eds. 2013. *From Groups to Individuals: Evolution and Emerging Individuality*. Cambridge, MA: MIT Press.
Bourke, A.F.G. 2011. *Principles of Social Evolution*. Oxford and New York: Oxford University Press.
Boyd, R., and P. J. Richerson. 1985. *Culture and the Evolutionary Process*. Chicago: University of Chicago Press.
Buckley, C. D. 2012. "Investigating Cultural Evolution Using Phylogenetic Analysis: The Origin and Descent of the Southeast Asian Tradition of Warp Ikat Weaving." *PLoS ONE* 7: e52064.
Buss, L. W. 1987. *The Evolution of Individuality*. Princeton, NJ: Princeton University Press.
Calcott, B., and K. Sterelny, eds. 2011. *The Major Transitions in Evolution Revisited*. Cambridge, MA: MIT Press.
Callebaut, W., and D. Rasskin-Gutman, eds. 2005. *Modularity: Understanding the Development and Evolution of Natural Complex Systems*. Cambridge, MA: MIT Press.
Campbell, D. 1956. "Perception as Trial and Error." *Psychological Review* 63: 330–342.
Caporael, L. R., J. R. Griesemer, and W. C. Wimsatt, eds. 2014. *Developing Scaffolds in Evolution, Culture and Cognition*. Cambridge, MA: MIT Press.
Carroll, S. B. 2005. *Endless Forms Most Beautiful: The New Science of Evo Devo and the Making of the Animal Kingdom*. New York: W. W. Norton & Company.
Cavalli-Sforza, L. L. 2000. *Genes, Peoples, and Languages*. New York: Farrar, Straus and Giroux.
Clarke, E. 2011. "Plant Individuality and Multilevel Selection Theory." In *The Major Transitions in Evolution Revisited*, edited by B. Calcott and K. Sterelny, 227–250. Cambridge, MA: MIT Press.
Claveria, C., G. Giovinazzo, R. Sierra, and M. Torres. 2013. "Myc-driven Endogenous Cell Competition in the Early Mammalian Embryo." *Nature* 500: 39–44.
Clune, J., J. Mouret, and H. Lipson. 2013. "The Evolutionary Origins of Modularity." *Proceedings of the Royal Society B* 280: 20122863.
Currie, T. E., S. J. Greenhill, R. D. Gray, T. Hasegawa, and R. Mace. 2010. "Rise and Fall of Political Complexity in Island South-East Asia and the Pacific." *Nature* 467: 801–804.
Danchin, É., A. Charmantier, F. A. Champagne, A. Mesoudi, B. Pujol, and S. Blanchet. 2011. "Beyond DNA: Integrating Inclusive Inheritance into an Extended Evolutionary Synthesis." *Nature Reviews Genetics* 12: 475–486.
Darwin, C. (1859) 1958. *The Origin of Species*. Introduction by Sir Julian Huxley. New York: New American Library/Mentor.
Dickins, T. E., and Q. Rahman. 2012. "The Extended Evolutionary Synthesis and the Role of Soft Inheritance in Evolution." *Proceedings of the Royal Society B* 279: 2913–2921.
Dobzhansky, T. 1937. *Genetics and the Origin of Species*. New York: Columbia University Press.
Domazet-Lošo, T., and D. Tautz. 2010. "A Phylogenetically Based Transcriptome Age Index Mirrors Ontogenetic Divergence Patterns." *Nature* 468: 815–818.

Duboule, D. 1994. "Temporal Colinearity and the Phylotypic Progression: A Basis for the Stability of a Vertebrate Bauplan and the Evolution of Morphologies through Heterochrony." *Development* (Supplement) 120: 135–142.
Durham, W. H. 1991. *Coevolution: Genes, Culture and Human Diversity.* Stanford, CA: Stanford University Press.
Freeman, S., and J. C. Herron. 2004. *Evolutionary Analysis.* 3rd ed. Upper Saddle River, NJ: Pearson Prentice Hall.
Gilbert, S. F. 2014. *Developmental Biology.* 10th ed. Sunderland, MA: Sinauer Associates.
Gissis, S. B., and E. Jablonka, eds. 2011. *Transformations of Lamarckism: From Subtle Fluids to Molecular Biology.* Cambridge, MA: MIT Press.
Godfrey-Smith, P. 2009. *Darwinian Populations and Natural Selection.* Oxford and New York: Oxford University Press.
———. 2013. "Darwinian Individuals." In *From Groups to Individuals: Evolution and Emerging Individuality,* edited by F. Bouchard and P. Huneman, 17–36. Cambridge, MA: MIT Press.
Gould, S. J., and E. S. Vrba. 1982. "Exaptation—A Missing Term in the Science of Form." *Paleobiology* 8: 4–15.
Hall, B. K. 1992. *Evolutionary Developmental Biology.* London: Chapman & Hall.
Hallgrímsson, B., and B. K. Hall, eds. 2011. *Epigenetics: Linking Genotype and Phenotype in Development and Evolution.* Berkeley and Los Angeles: University of California Press.
Hull, D. L. 1988. *Science as a Process: An Evolutionary Account of the Social and Conceptual Development of Science.* Chicago: University of Chicago Press.
Jablonka, E., and M. J. Lamb. 2005. *Evolution in Four Dimensions: Genetic, Epigenetic, Behavioral and Symbolic Variation in the History of Life.* Cambridge, MA: MIT Press.
Kalinka, A. T., K. M. Varga, D. T. Gerrard, S. Preibisch, D. L. Corcoran, J. Jarrells, U. Ohler, C. M. Bergman, and P. Tomancak. 2010. "Gene Expression Divergence Recapitulates the Developmental Hourglass Model." *Nature* 468: 811–814.
Kohn, D. 2009. "Darwin's Keystone: The Principle of Divergence." In *The Cambridge Companion to the Origin of Species,* edited by M. Ruse and R. Richards, 87–108. Cambridge: Cambridge University Press.
Kupiec, J. 2009. *The Origin of Individuals.* Singapore; Hackensack, NJ: World Scientific Publishing.
Lane, N. 2009. *Life Ascending: The Ten Great Inventions of Evolution.* New York: W. W. Norton.
Lovejoy, A. O. 1936. *The Great Chain of Being: A Study of the History of an Idea.* Cambridge, MA: Harvard University Press.
Lupski, J. R. 2013. "Genetic Mosaicism: One Human, Multiple Genomes." *Science* 341: 358–359.
Margulis, L. M. 1971. *Origin of Eukaryotic Cells.* New Haven, CT: Yale University Press.
Margulis, L. M., and D. Sagan. 2003. *Acquiring Genomes: A Theory of the Origin of Species.* New York: Basic Books.
Maynard Smith, J., and E. Szathmáry. 1995. *The Major Transitions in Evolution.* Oxford and New York: W. H. Freeman and Company.
Mesoudi, A., S. Bianchet, A. Charmantier, É. Danchin, L. Fogarty, E. Jablonka, K. N. Laland, T.J.H. Morgan, G. B. Müller, F. J. Odling-Smee, and B. Pujol. 2013. "Is Non-genetic Inheritance Just a Proximate Mechanism: A Corroboration of the Extended Evolutionary Synthesis." *Biological Theory* 7: 189–195.
Mesoudi, A., A. Whiten, and K. L. Laland. 2004. "Is Human Cultural Evolution Darwinian? Evidence Reviewed from the Perspective of the Origin of Species." *Evolution* 58: 1–11.
———. 2006. "Towards a Unified Science of Cultural Evolution." *Behavioral and Brain Sciences* 29: 329–383.
Michod, R. E. 1999. *Darwinian Dynamics: Evolutionary Transitions in Fitness and Individuality.* Princeton, NJ: Princeton University Press.
Nachtomy, O., A. Shavit, and J. Smith. 2002. "Leiznizian Organisms, Nested Individuals, and Units of Selection." *Theory in Biosciences* 121: 205–230.
Ninio, A., and J. Bruner. 1978. "The Achievement and Antecedents of Labelling." *Journal of Child Language* 5: 1–15.
Odling-Smee, F. J., K. N. Laland, and M. W. Feldman. 1996. "Niche Construction." *American Naturalist* 146: 641–648.
Ohno, S. 1970. *Evolution by Gene Duplication.* Berlin: Springer-Verlag.
Okasha, S. 2006. *Evolution and the Levels of Selection.* Oxford: Oxford University Press.
Pigliucci, M. 2009. "An Extended Synthesis for Evolutionary Biology." *Annals of the New York Academy of Sciences* 1168: 218–228.
Pigliucci, M., and G. B. Müller. 2010. *Evolution—The Extended Synthesis.* Cambridge, MA: MIT Press.
Queller, D. C. 1997. "Cooperators since Life Began." *Quarterly Review of Biology* 72: 184–188.
Raff, R. A. 1996. *The Shape of Life: Genes, Development and the Evolution of Animal Form.* Chicago: University of Chicago Press.
Ram, Y., and L. Hadany. 2012. "The Evolution of Stress-Induced Hypermutation in Asexual Populations." *Evolution* 66: 2315–2328.
Richerson, P. J., and R. Boyd. 2005. *Not by Genes Alone: How Culture Transformed Human Evolution.* Chicago: University of Chicago Press.

Robertson, B. A., J. S. Rehage, and A. Sih. 2013. "Ecological Novelty and the Emergence of Evolutionary Traps." *Trends in Ecology and Evolution* 28: 552–560.

Roff, D. A. 2002. *Life History Evolution.* Sunderland, MA: Sinauer Associates.

Salazar-Ciudad, I. 2013. "Evolution in Biological and Non-Biological Systems: The Origins of Life." *Biological Theory* 7: 26–37.

Sanderson, S. K. 2007. *Evolutionism and Its Critics: Deconstructing and Reconstructing an Evolutionary Interpretation of Human Society.* Boulder, CO: Paradigm Publishers.

Sansom, R., and R. N. Brandon, eds. 2007. *Integrating Evolution and Development: From Theory to Practice.* Cambridge, MA: MIT Press.

Schwander, T., and O. Leimar. 2011. "Genes as Leaders and Followers in Evolution." *Trends in Ecology and Evolution* 26: 143–151.

Skinner, B. F. 1948. "'Superstition' in the Pigeon." *Journal of Experimental Psychology* 38: 168–172.

Slack, J.M.W. 2003. "Phylotype and Zootype." In *Keywords & Concepts in Evolutionary Developmental Biology,* edited by B. K. Hall and W. M. Olsom, 309–318. Cambridge, MA: Harvard University Press.

Sober, E. 2011. *Did Darwin Write the Origin Backwards?* Amherst, NY: Prometheus Books.

Tarnita, C. E., C. H. Taubes, and M. A. Nowak. 2013. "Evolutionary Construction by Staying Together and Coming Together." *Journal of Theoretical Biology* 320: 10–22.

Tehrani, J. J. 2013. "The Phylogeny of Little Red Riding Hood." *PLoS ONE* 8: e78871.

Toulmin, S. E. 1972. *Human Understanding: The Collective Use and Understanding of Concepts.* Princeton, NJ: Princeton University Press.

Van Valen, L. 1973. "Fetschrift." *Science* 180: 488.

Walker, R. S., S. Wichmann, T. Mailund, and C. J. Atkisson. 2012. "Cultural Phylogenetics of the Tupi Language Family in Lowland South America." *PLoS ONE* 7: e35025.

Waters, J. M., I. F. Ceridvven, and G. M. Hewitt. 2013. "Founder Takes All: Density-Dependent Processes Structure Biodiversity." *Trends in Ecology and Evolution* 28: 78–85.

Watson, R. A. 2006. *Compositional Evolution: The Impact of Sex, Symbiosis, and Modularity on the Gradualist Framework of Evolution.* Cambridge, MA: MIT Press.

West-Eberhard, M. J. 2003. *Developmental Plasticity and Evolution.* New York: Oxford University Press.

Williamson, D. I. 1992. *Larvae and Evolution: Towards a New Zoology.* New York: Chapman and Hall.

———. 2003. *The Origins of Larvae.* Norwell, MA: Kluwer Academic Publications.

Wimsatt, W. C., and C. Schank. 1988. "Two Constraints on the Evolution of Complex Adaptations and the Means for Their Avoidance." In *Evolutionary Progress,* edited by M. H. Nitecki, 231–273. Chicago: University of Chicago Press.

Wood, D., J. S. Bruner, and G. Ross. 1976. "The Role of Tutoring and Problem Solving." *Journal of Child Psychology and Psychiatry, and Allied Disciplines* 17: 89–100.

Chapter Four
Evolutionary Transitions in Individuality and Selection in Societal Evolution

Matthew B. Dunn

> This chapter presents a theory of societal evolution where selection operates on corporate units. In presenting such a theory of societal evolution the chapter makes three broad claims. First, it outlines the group selection debate in both evolutionary biology and evolutionary sociology, concluding that evolutionary sociologists should take a pluralistic approach to selection and move beyond the group selection debate. Second, it applies the logic of evolutionary transitions in individuality to human society, arguing that while societies do not meet the conditions required to qualify as evolutionary individuals, the corporate units within societies do meet these conditions, thus holding the status of evolutionary individuals. As evolutionary individuals are the units targeted by selection, corporate units are the units targeted by selection in societal evolution. Finally, it outlines Godfrey-Smith's (2009) five criteria that populations of interacting entities must meet to experience Darwinian selection processes. These five criteria are then applied to populations of corporate units, concluding that populations of corporate units do meet the criteria required for evolution via Darwinian selection.

Charles Darwin's discovery of natural selection as the primary driver of evolution revolutionized the field of biology. Thirty-four years after Darwin published his revolutionary insights in *On the Origin of Species*, Émile Durkheim applied the logic of Darwin's natural selection to human societies. In *The Division of Labor in Society*, Durkheim ([1893] 1963) argues that population growth increases the density of a population and this increase in density leads to competition for resources in society. Such competition leads to increased functional specialization in the division of labor. Turner (1995, 2010) has elaborated Durkheim's insights about selection, combining them with insights from Herbert Spencer to create a general theory of selection in society.

As populations grow, either through an increase in the reproductive rate or through incorporating members from other populations, it causes selection pressures for solutions to what Turner (1995, 2010) terms first-order logistical loads. An increase in the size of a population means more mouths to feed. More mouths to feed means that more calories must be harvested from the environment, converted into consumable materials, and distributed to the population. This intensification of production and distribution requires an intensification of the regulatory apparatus of the population. If societies are not able to expand production, consolidate regulatory power, and intensify distribution systems, they are not able to respond to the first-order logistical loads caused by population growth, and they will face the specter of Malthusian correction or dissolution (Turner 1995, 2010).

To meet first-order logistical loads, populations of individuals band together, forming corporate units,[1] which enables the elaboration of production, distribution, and regulation. When populations group together into corporate units, they face the problems associated with what Turner (1995, 2010) terms second-order logistical loads. Second-order logistical loads involve problems of coordination and control of the numerous societal units that have arisen as the result of selection pressures for dealing with first-order logistical loads (Turner 1995, 2010). The process of populations experiencing selection pressures in response to mounting first-order and second-order logistical loads leads to elaboration and change in the corporate and categoric units of a society, in the institutional structures, and in the stratification systems of that society. Together these interlocked processes of institutional change, change in stratification systems, and change in corporate and categoric units in response to the selection pressures caused by the operation of macrodynamic forces are societal evolution.

Selective processes play an important role in shaping the structure of the social world. Thus, in order to understand why the social world is the way that it is, it is necessary to have theories of societal selection. As selection is a key topic in evolutionary biology, insights about selection from evolutionary biology can be applied to the social world to further sociological theorizing, which some theorists have already begun to do (Runciman 2009; Blute 2010; Turner and Maryanski 2008; Turner 2010; Sanderson 2014). While it is important to apply insights from evolutionary biology to sociology in order to understand how selection operates at a societal level, it is also important for evolutionary sociologists not to get bogged down in the many debates regarding selection that have persisted in evolutionary biology. Perhaps the most onerous of these debates in biology is the group selection debate, which asks whether Darwinian natural selection can act on groups, just as it can on individuals.

Recently, evolutionary theorists have been providing clarity to the group selection debate by using both individual and group selection approaches to understand evolutionary transitions in individuality (see Buss 1987; Maynard Smith and Szathmáry 1995; Michod 2000; Okasha 2006; Godfrey-Smith 2009; Bourke 2011). Work on evolutionary transitions in individuality highlights the hierarchical nature of the biological world and how this hierarchy is itself the product of evolution; genes occur in chromosomes, chromosomes occur in cells, cells occur in multicellular organisms, and multicellular organisms can occur in societies (Maynard Smith and Szathmáry 1995). When the entities at one level of the hierarchy come together to form a group and this group takes on the properties of a cohesive, indivisible whole, a major transition in evolution has taken place, and the cohesive group, which was once a collection of separate individuals, represents a new evolutionary individual. This new evolutionary individual, who exists as an indivisible grouping of lower-level entities, is the unit of selection in evolution; selection occurs at the level of evolutionary individuals (Michod 2000, 2005, 2007). What counts as an individual depends on the level of the biological hierarchy being investigated.

In order to provide clarity to the group selection debate for evolutionary sociologists and to address the nature of the selective processes that operate in societal evolution, this chapter will summarize the group selection debate in evolutionary biology and evolutionary sociology. After summarizing this debate, the evolutionary transitions in individuality will be outlined and the evolution of human society will be analyzed, in order to demonstrate that when humans came together to form corporate units, these corporate units took on the characteristics of evolutionary individuals. The formation of corporate units represents a major transition in evolution. The chapter will conclude by analyzing the nature of selection among corporate units, arguing that selection of corporate units within a resource niche can represent Darwinian natural selection and not some other type of selective process (Price 1995).

Group Selection in Biology and Sociology

The controversy surrounding the level at which natural selection operates has a long history in evolutionary biology, dating back to the work of Charles Darwin and his struggles to explain the apparently altruistic behaviors of two different types of organisms: insects with sterile worker castes and humans (Okasha 2006; Costa 2013). Why should natural selection favor cooperative behaviors, behaviors that benefit other individuals, when these behaviors are costly to the individuals performing them? Darwin asked himself this question in *On the Origin of Species*, when he puzzled over worker sterility in insect castes, concluding that worker sterility was unlikely to evolve via individual selection processes but could potentially evolve via selection processes acting at the level of the colony (Okasha 2006; Costa 2013).

Darwin again addressed this question in *The Descent of Man*, when he sought to explain the existence of altruistic traits in humans (Okasha 2006; Costa 2013; Godfrey-Smith 2014). Darwin reasoned that altruistic tendencies could be selected for in humans by a form of group selection due to competition between tribes: "A tribe including many members who, from possessing in a high degree the spirit of patriotism, fidelity, obedience, courage, and sympathy, were always ready to aid one another, and to sacrifice themselves for the common good, would be victorious over most other tribes; and this would be natural selection" (1871: 160). In explaining both human altruism and the existence of sterile worker castes in certain insect species, Darwin made recourse to group-level selection (Okasha 2006; Costa 2013; Godfrey-Smith 2014).

Other early biologists were more skeptical than Darwin of using group selection arguments to explain cooperative behaviors. Prominent architects of the neo-Darwinian synthesis such as R. A. Fisher and J.B.S. Haldane published criticisms of group selection, each biologist instead seeing selection as a process that operated on individuals (Okasha 2006). Despite the skepticism of biologists such as Fisher and Haldane, by the 1950s group selectionist reasoning had gained prominence in evolutionary analyses of animal behavior, where the cooperative behaviors of individual animals were explained by reference to the group benefits that such behaviors conferred. These early group selection arguments reached their pinnacle in 1962, when V. C. Wynne-Edwards (1962) published *Animal Dispersion in Relation to Social Behaviour*, which argues that group selection led to the presence of numerous group beneficial behaviors in a variety of animal species.

The prominence of such group selection approaches was short-lived (Okasha 2006). In 1966, George C. Williams published *Adaptation and Natural Selection*, which argues that group selection may be theoretically possible, but it is empirically unlikely. For this reason, an explanation positing selection between individuals should be favored over explanations positing selection between groups. According to Williams (1966), the group beneficial behaviors that were used to support the existence of group selection were more parsimoniously explained as the statistical by-products of selection acting at the individual level. To illustrate this point, Williams (1966) wrote that when a deer escapes predation by a bear, the deer's escape can be attributed to selection on individual deer for fleetness. When a herd of deer escape predation by a bear, the herd escaping is not due to selection for a fleet herd; rather, it is due to selection of fleet deer. When fleet deer group together, they form a fleet herd, but the herd's fleetness is a product of selection acting at the level of the individual deer rather than selection acting at the level of the herd. The fleetness of the herd is a by-product of the fleetness of the deer, which compose the herd. As this example demonstrates, behaviors that appear to have group-level benefits can be explained as the result of individual selection. Williams's influential criticism of group selection was popularized by Richard Dawkins in his 1976 book *The Selfish Gene*. As a result of mounting critiques of group selection, a consensus arose in biological circles: group selection does not occur. This consensus remains in many biological circles today; however, a group of biologists has been working to demonstrate that the rejection of group selection was a mistake (Okasha 2006).

In 1975, D. S. Wilson published an article redefining the idea of group selection. Prior conceptions of group selection, such as that of Wynne-Edwards, used the appearance of group beneficial behaviors to argue for the existence of group-level selection. Wilson (1975) abandoned such a focus on group beneficial behaviors and instead argued that if a population was structured so that individuals lived and reproduced in groups, selection could act among individuals within each group, but it could also operate between groups as well. According to Wilson's model, selection can be partitioned into two parts: selection acting on individuals within groups and selection acting on individuals between groups. Selection acting within groups is individual-level selection, whereas selection acting between groups is group-level selection. This approach, pioneered by D. S. Wilson and his colleagues (Wilson 1975; Wilson and Sober 1989; Sober and Wilson 1998; Wilson and Wilson 2007), is known as the multilevel selection approach as it specifies that selection can act on multiple levels—the individual level (selection occurring within the group) and the group level (selection occurring between groups). Although many biologists are still skeptical of the operation of group selection in the real world (see West, Mouden, and Gardner 2011 for an overview of such skepticism), multilevel selection approaches have reinvigorated debates regarding group-level selection in evolutionary biology.

As the concept of selection has been imported from evolutionary biology into sociology, the controversy regarding group selection has been imported into sociology as well. Some evolutionary sociologists, especially those influenced by sociobiology, are skeptical of group selection, favoring individual selection as an explanation for the evolution of cooperative behaviors. Perhaps the clearest statement in advocacy of individual selection within evolutionary sociology comes from Sanderson (2008). Writing about the influence of Darwinism on sociology, Sanderson says, "Cooperative social relations exist because they are the relations that will best promote each individual's self-interests, not because they promote the well-being of the group or society as a whole. The selection of cooperative social forms happens at the level of the individual, not the group or society" (2008: 20). Group selection arguments are also rejected by Nielsen (1994), who in his review of sociobiology and its potential relationship with sociology writes that sociobiologists have rejected explanations for cooperative behavior based on group selection, instead favoring explanations that rely on kin selection and reciprocity. Nielsen (1994) further adds that the rejection of group selection in favor of individual selection by sociobiologists is similar to the rejection of functionalism in favor of methodological individualism by sociologists.

Lopreato and Crippen (1999) reject group selection explanations for cooperative behaviors, leaving any discussion of group selection absent from *Crisis in Sociology*. Instead, they argue that kin selection and reciprocity account for the substantial amounts of cooperation found in human societies. In his outline of potential nomological principles of neo-Darwinian sociology, Crippen (1994) argues that group selection is unlikely to explain the behavioral predispositions of humankind as the conditions that are required for group selection to be operative are unlikely to be met by any human populations. Lastly, Machalek (2010), in his outline of sociobiology and sociology, favors explanations of cooperation based on individual-level selection, explaining human cooperative behavior as the result of kin selection and reciprocity, omitting any mention of group selection.

Despite the skepticism of some evolutionary sociologists toward group selection, others are open to the possibility of group-level selection. Blute (2010) takes a pluralistic perspective when explaining the evolution of cooperation in *Darwinian Sociocultural Evolution*. Blute (2010) argues that a variety of mechanisms account for the evolution of cooperative behaviors, including kin selection, reciprocal altruism, signaling (Blute uses the example of greenbeards), by-product mutualism, and group selection. In discussing group selection, Blute (2010) emphasizes how contemporary group selection arguments take the form of multilevel selection models.

Lenski (2005) doesn't explicitly enter into the group selection debate in his book *Ecological-Evolutionary Theory*; however, he presents a theory in which societal evolution happens via both intrasocietal and intersocietal selection processes. Within societies individuals experience selection pressures while they compete with other members of their society to meet their various needs; this is intrasocietal selection. Intersocietal selection occurs when societies compete with each other over access to resources; in these competitions the more technologically advanced societies have had a greater probability of success. This dynamic creates intersocietal selection for greater levels of technological development. While Lenski (2005) does not directly address the group selection debate, his distinction between intrasocietal and intersocietal selection is similar to the distinction made by multilevel selection models of within-group and between-group selection. Thus, Lenski's (2005) theory supports the operation of a type of selection in the sociocultural universe that is similar to the type of selection modeled in multilevel selection models.

Runciman (2009) adds clarity to the nature of the group selection debate in evolutionary sociology in his *Theory of Cultural and Social Selection*, noting that selection happens at three levels: the biological level, the cultural level, and the social level. In discussing both biological and cultural selection, Runciman accepts the existence of group selection, arguing that it would be a mistake for sociologists to reject group selection as a significant force in biological evolution and that the problems associated with many biological models of group selection do not apply when culture is the information source being acted on by selection. In further support of group selection, Runciman notes that societal selection is a matter of group selection by definition as societal selection involves the selection of institutional practices, which requires the interaction of the multiple individuals who perform the different roles that make up the institutional practice. Lastly, Turner (2010), in *Theoretical Principles of Sociology*, makes an argument similar to the application of evolutionary transitions in individuality to social structure by noting that a type of "group selection" operates on social structures, but that this "group selection" is fundamentally different from the type of group selection represented in the group selection debate in evolutionary biology.

Given the debate over the existence of group selection in evolutionary biology and evolutionary sociology, should evolutionary sociologists accept group-level selection or instead see selection as a process acting solely on individuals? Evolutionary sociologists should take a pluralistic approach, as it turns out that selection can act at both an individual and a group level. Although some adherents on each side of the debate will argue that group selection and individual selection are fundamentally different phenomena, individual and group selection approaches are mathematically equivalent, as has been demonstrated in a multitude of ways (Hamilton 1975; Grafen 1984; Queller 1992; Frank 1998; Kerr and Godfrey-Smith 2002). Both approaches are correct because they both focus on maximization of the same quantities; they just use different notation to represent this focus. Both individual and group selection models focus on the process of inclusive fitness maximization, where inclusive fitness is the sum of an individual's direct fitness (the number of offspring an individual produces) and indirect fitness (the effect of an individual's behavior on the offspring production of others weighted by the individual's relatedness to these others) (Bourke 2011). Individual and group selection approaches are simply different ways of keeping the books on the maximization of the quantities underlying inclusive fitness.

As individual and group selection models are mathematically equivalent, Okasha (2006) calls for a pluralistic explanatory strategy when it comes to the level of selection question, likening the mathematical equivalence of individual and group selection approaches in biology to the equivalence of the Heisenberg and Schrödinger formulations of quantum mechanics in physics. Queller (2012) compares the situation to speaking English versus speaking Russian. Neither language is right or wrong; they just use different sets of symbols for transmitting the same information. As group selection and individual selection models are mathematically equivalent, further debate on whether selection is an individual or group process seems a waste of time. Selection can be seen to occur at the level of groups or at the level of individuals, depending on how one models selection. Due to this fact, evolutionary sociologists need to move beyond the group selection debate when conceiving of societal selection processes.

Evolutionary Transitions in Individuality

A second reason why sociologists should move beyond the group selection debate revolves around the major transitions in evolution, which are also referred to as evolutionary transitions in individuality. Evolutionary transitions in individuality shift the focus from the level at which selection is acting to the unit upon which selection is acting.

The structure of the living world is hierarchically ordered. At the low end of the hierarchy are genes, which are ordered into chromosomes, which are packed into cells. Cells in turn make up multicellular organisms, which group together to make their own colonies and societies (Maynard Smith and Szathmáry 1995; Okasha 2006, 2009; Godfrey-Smith 2009; Bourke 2011). This hierarchy did not appear ex nihilo; it evolved over the history of life on earth just as the properties of organisms have evolved over time. Each new addition to this biological hierarchy represented a major transition in evolution as in each transition a new evolutionary individual was formed[2] (Okasha 2006). Maynard Smith and Szathmáry (1995) argue that fewer than ten major transitions in evolution have occurred during the history of life on earth. Some of these transitions include the origin of chromosomes, the origin of eukaryotes, the origin of sexual reproduction, the origin of multicellular organisms, and the origin of social groups. Evolutionary transitions occur as selection pressures favor high levels of cooperation among a group of entities. These selection pressures lead to both the evolution of mechanisms for encouraging cooperation, such as reciprocal relations and assorted population structures, and the evolution of mechanisms for punishing selfish behavior, such as division of labor and policing. Over time, as within-group cooperation increases, the group of once-separate entities transforms into a cohesive, inseparable unit. This transformation represents a transition in evolutionary individuality (Michod 2000; Godfrey-Smith 2009; Bourke 2011).

Evolutionary transitions in individuality are important for understanding selection processes because when an evolutionary transition in individuality takes place, the entity at the new level of the biological hierarchy, the new evolutionary individual, becomes the unit of selection. This is because when a transition in individuality occurs, "entities that were capable of independent replication before the transition can replicate only as part of the larger whole after it" (Maynard Smith and Szathmáry 1995: 6). Selection acts on the level of the reproducing entity (Gould and Lloyd 1999; Godfrey-Smith 2009, 2014), which after an evolutionary transition is the new evolutionary individual, not the entities that conjoined to create this individual. An example can be used to clarify this abstract process. Consider the transition from unicellular to multicellular organisms. Ecological pressures shaped the interaction of unicellular organisms, encouraging cooperation between these organisms. As these pressures increased, unicellular organisms evolved mechanisms to promote cooperation and suppress competition within groups of unicellular organisms. As these mechanisms fostered increasing amounts of cooperation among the entities of one level (unicellular organisms), these one-time separate entities came to form a cohesive collective (a multicellular organism). Although selection may have originally been operating on the level of unicellular organisms, when cells came together to form a multicellular organism, it is best to see selection as acting on this new evolutionary individual, the multicellular organism. Applying this logic to human societies, it is clear that if human societies represent an evolutionary transition in individuality, arguments regarding the primacy of individual- versus group-level selection are misplaced. The new evolutionary individual is the target of selection, even though this unit might be composed of numerous lower-level entities.

Before applying the logic of evolutionary transitions in individuality to human society, it is necessary to outline what criteria must be met to consider a conglomeration of entities an evolutionary individual. Maynard Smith and Szathmáry (1995) argue that evolutionary transitions in individuality involve the creation of divisions of labor and the creation of new ways of transmitting information. Michod and colleagues add further specificity to what must occur for an evolutionary transition to take place, arguing that evolutionary transitions of individuality require a reorganization of fitness. When evolutionary transitions in individuality occur, the fitness of the lower-level entities is exported to the higher-level collective (Michod and Nedelcu 2003; Michod 2005, 2007; Michod et al. 2006). When this happens, the fitness[3] of the collective becomes decoupled from the fitness of the entities that make up that collective. This means that the collective exhibits fitness, but the fitness of the individual entities that make up the collective is null (Michod and Nedelcu 2003; Michod 2005, 2007; Michod et al. 2006); the welfare of the collective becomes disconnected from the welfare of any of the individual entities that make up the collective (Okasha 2009). Once this decoupling of individual fitness from collective fitness has occurred, the collective can be viewed as a new evolutionary individual.

This abstract process can be clarified using an example from the human body. The human body is made up of trillions of cells (Bianconi et al. 2013). Whereas it makes sense to talk about the fitness of human individuals, it does not make sense to talk about the fitness of their specific cells. That's because as unicellular organisms grouped together to form multicellular organisms, the individual cells of these multicellular organisms have been organized into a reproductive division of labor. The cells of the human body are specialized into either somatic cells or gametes. Gametes are specialized sex cells; this means they have high fecundity but zero viability. As fitness is the product of viability and fecundity (Michod et al. 2006), the fitness of individual gametic cells is zero. Somatic cells are the cells that build and maintain human bodies. They have high viability but no fecundity; thus, the fitness of somatic cells is also zero. It is only the collective of gametic cells and somatic cells, the human individual, who has fitness. As individual cells have no fitness but the human body has fitness, the transition between unicellular organisms and multicellular bodies involved a reorganization of fitness, signaling that an evolutionary transition in individuality has taken place.

Bourke (2011) proposes the size-complexity hypothesis to explain why transitions in individuality occur. The size-complexity hypothesis argues that evolutionary transitions in individuality happen when evolutionary and ecological factors favor increases in group size and such increases in group size lead to the evolution of both reproductive and nonreproductive divisions of labor. Once such divisions of labor are in place, they have a positive feedback effect on group size, leading to further increases in the size of the group (Bourke 2011). Simple groups, exhibiting low levels of evolutionary individuality, are transformed into complex groups with high levels of evolutionary individuality due to this positive feedback relationship between group size and complexity. Evolutionary transitions in individuality are the result of a positive feedback relationship between group size and complexity (Bourke 2011). For an evolutionary transition in individuality to occur, not only must fitness be exported from the lower-level entities to the higher-level collective, but a positive feedback relationship between group size and complexity must also exist.

In order to assess whether human societies represent an evolutionary transition in individuality, Bourke's (2011) size-complexity hypothesis and Michod's (2005, 2007) criteria of fitness of reorganization can be applied to human social groups. If increases in group size lead to more complex divisions of labor, which have positive feedback effects on group size, and if the fitness of human groups is decoupled from the fitness of the individuals within these groups, human societies represent an evolutionary transition in individuality.

Human Society and Evolutionary Transitions in Individuality

Stearns (2007) argues that humans are stalled partway through an evolutionary transition. Human society was on its way toward evolving all of the features of an evolutionary individual, but this process was disrupted by sociocultural developments, which have kept society from attaining the status of an evolutionary individual and becoming the unit of selection. Stearns (2007) argues that early humans living in hunting and gathering groups faced pressures that favored in-group cooperation and out-group aggression. These pressures started to quell the individualistic nature of humans, producing both biological and cultural mechanisms for enticing group-oriented behavior in a formerly self-oriented primate. For instance, selection pressures caused by group living worked on human biology to produce emotions such as shame and guilt, which orient individuals to the needs of others. These pressures also worked on human culture, creating fairness norms and other ethical codes, which promoted a group orientation. The evolution of such traits moved human society toward the status of an evolutionary individual. With the dawn of agriculture, this movement came to a halt, due to changes in social life brought about by the new changes in subsistence technology.

Stearns (2007) argues that as food surpluses facilitated a drastic increase in population size, intergroup conflicts became increasingly intense until different groups began to band together into city-states in the service of self-defense. Over time these city-states evolved into complex empires. Stearns (2007) notes that complex empires were highly differentiated societies and that in these differentiated societies individuals belonged to many different social groups. Although membership in many groups facilitated interaction among different segments of the population, it also led to divided loyalties as members of one's in-group in one domain may be members of one's out-group in another domain. As the distinction between in-group and out-group became increasingly unclear, the evolution of both biological and cultural mechanisms enforcing a group orientation stalled, stalling the transition of human society from a collection of individuals to an evolutionary individual in its own right (Stearns 2007).

Stearns (2007) makes a convincing case that human society has yet to evolve into an evolutionary individual, but this conclusion applies only to his specific level of sociological analysis. Sociologists recognize that the social world exists at three different levels: the micro, the meso, and the macro. The micro realm consists of the dynamics of face-to-face interactions, the meso realm consists of the dynamics of corporate and categoric units, and the macro realm consists of the dynamics of institutions, stratification systems, societies, and intersocietal systems (Turner 2010). Stearns (2007) uses a macro level of analysis when applying the logic of evolutionary transitions in individuality to human society as a whole. When applying this logic to the macro level, it appears as Stearns (2007) argues; the transition of human society to an evolutionary individual is incomplete. However, the logic of evolutionary transitions can be applied to the meso level as well as the macro level; more specifically it can be applied to corporate units. When this is done, it appears that human society has undergone an evolutionary transition; corporate units within different societies are evolutionary individuals. In order for corporate units to qualify as evolutionary individuals, thus qualifying as the unit of selection, corporate units must satisfy Bourke's size-complexity hypothesis and Michod's criteria of fitness reorganization.

Corporate units are the outcome of dynamic processes occurring at both the macro and micro levels of society (Turner 2010). At the macro level, the operation of five forces—population, production, distribution, regulation, reproduction—lead to first-order logistical loads, or survival problems, that must be met in order for a society to survive. As population size increases, it necessitates the intensification of the productive, distributive, regulatory, and reproductive apparatuses of society. This intensification creates logistical loads, or survival problems, that must be met by members of the society in order to survive. Increasing logistical loads creates selection pressures for actors to find ways to mitigate these survival problems. Such selection pressures lead individuals to band together into corporate units in order to meet survival problems. Corporate units are collectives of individuals that have divisions of labor for realizing various goals (Turner 2010) and are "functionally differentiated and symbiotically integrated" (Hawley 1986: 68). When corporate units successfully meet the challenges posed by first-order logistical loads, it allows for continued societal growth. Societal growth in turn leads to increased logistical loads, which creates selection pressures for more complex corporate units. Bourke's (2011) size-complexity hypothesis states that a feedback relationship between size and group complexity must exist for a transformation in individuality to take place. As increasing population size creates selection pressures for increasingly complex corporate units, which allows for continued increase in population size, corporate units meet this criterion for an evolutionary transition in individuality.

As humans deal with the survival problems posed by first- and second-order logical loads, new corporate units are formed. When a new corporate unit is formed that utilizes the same template of functional differentiation and symbiotic integration as an already existing corporate unit, the creation of this new corporate unit can be seen as an act of reproduction.[4] As the reproduction of a corporate unit involves the creation of a completely new corporate unit, the fitness of a corporate unit is decoupled from the fitness of the individuals within that unit. Corporate units, by definition, exhibit divisions of labor.

When a corporate unit is reproduced, this division of labor must be reproduced. The division of labor within a corporate unit requires the functional coordination of numerous individuals; therefore, no individual can reproduce a corporate unit by himself or herself. Reproducing a corporate unit requires the coordination of many individuals, at least as many individuals as there are roles in the corporate unit.

In terms of societal evolution, the individuals within a corporate unit have no fitness, as no solitary individual can reproduce a corporate unit. In fact, in societal evolution, it does not make much sense to talk about the fitness of the individual within the corporate unit, just as in biological evolution it does not make much sense to talk about the fitness of an individual cell within a multicellular organism. Only a collective of individuals, who as a collective have the ability to produce the same form of functional differentiation and symbiotic integration, can reproduce a corporate unit. Just as only a collection of cells, no individual cell is able to reproduce a multicellular organism. For this reason, the fitness of the corporate unit should be conceptualized at the level of the corporate unit and not at the level of the individuals composing the corporate unit. Okasha (2009), elaborating on Michod's criteria of fitness reorganization, argues that when a reorganization in fitness occurs, the welfare of the collective becomes disconnected from the welfare of the individuals within the collective. This appears to be the case in corporate units, as the success of the corporate unit becomes disconnected from the success of the particular individuals in the corporate unit. According to Michod (2005, 2007), the decoupling of individual fitness from collective fitness is a necessary and sufficient condition for an evolutionary transition in individuality. Corporate units exhibit such a decoupling of individual and collective fitness; thus it is justified to treat corporate units as evolutionary individuals. As selection acts on evolutionary individuals (Lewontin 1970; Michod 2000; Godfrey-Smith 2009, 2014), evolutionary sociologists are justified in conceptualizing selection in societal evolution as a process that acts on corporate units, bypassing the individual versus group selection debate entirely.

Darwinian Selection of Corporate Units

Now that the level of selection question in sociology has been addressed, it is possible to address the extent to which the selection processes acting on corporate units are Darwinian; to what extent is selection among corporate units natural selection compared with some other type of selection process, such as subset selection (Price 1995)? To answer this question it is necessary to first put forward a list of criteria that must be met for Darwinian selection to take place, and then assess the extent to which selection of corporate units meets these criteria. Evolutionary biologist Richard Lewontin put forward three criteria that have been largely accepted as necessary for Darwinian selection to occur.[5] Lewontin's summary states that Darwinian selection will result when three conditions are met: first, "different individuals in a population have different morphologies, physiologies and behaviors (phenotypic variation)"; second, "different phenotypes have different rates of survival and reproduction in different environments (differential fitness)"; and third, "there is a correlation between parents and offspring in the contribution of each to future generations (fitness is heritable)" (Lewontin 1970: 1). According to this summary, natural selection will occur whenever a population exhibits heritable variations in fitness.

Despite the success of Lewontin's summary as an abstract representation of Darwinian selection, it is not without problems. Godfrey-Smith (2009) notes that there can be situations where a population exhibits heritable variations in fitness, yet no evolutionary change occurs. This situation violates Lewontin's summary of Darwinian selection.

Such a situation can happen because heritability need not involve direct replication of a trait from parent to offspring; a nonrandom statistical relationship between parent and offspring in a population of individuals also illustrates heritability (Godfrey-Smith 2009). According to Godfrey-Smith (2009), the type of heritability that a population exhibits will determine how the population responds to fitness differences within the population. This creates the potential for situations where the inheritance system can cancel out the role of fitness differences, leading to no evolutionary change even when the conditions of Lewontin's summary are met. To rectify this inconsistency, Godfrey-Smith (2009) provides an elaboration of the conditions that must be met for Darwinian selection to take place.

Godfrey-Smith (2009) expands the three criteria put forth by Lewontin into a list of five criteria that must be met for Darwinian selection to operate. When these criteria are met, a paradigm Darwinian population exists; when some criteria are met but not others, a marginal Darwinian population exists. Marginal Darwinian populations appear to change via processes of Darwinian selection, but these selection processes are not actually true cases of Darwinian selection; they represent a fundamentally different type of selective process, such as the subset selection outlined by Price (1995). For true Darwinian selection to occur, a population must meet Godfrey-Smith's (2009) criteria of Darwinian populations.

The first criterion outlined by Godfrey-Smith (2009) is the fidelity of heredity. If inheritance is too noisy the products of evolution will be lost, disrupting the cumulative nature of change in Darwinian selection. On the other hand, if inheritance is perfect, new variation will never be introduced into a population, minimizing the operation of selection. Thus, the first criterion for Darwinian selection to occur is that the fidelity of heredity in a population must be not only reliable but also slightly imperfect (Godfrey-Smith 2009). The second criterion is that there must be an abundance of variation. Some variation in a population is not enough; depending on the nature of this variation, it may not be targeted by natural selection. For instance, if it represents an extreme region in phenotypic space, or if all variation is biased toward a certain location in phenotypic space, it will not be targeted by natural selection. Because selection requires variation on which to act, an abundance of variation in a population is required for paradigm Darwinian selection (Godfrey-Smith 2009).

The third criterion put forth by Godfrey-Smith (2009) regards the level of competition. As the level of competition between individuals in a population increases, it becomes more likely that Darwinian selection will be operative, as such competition heightens the struggle for survival and reproduction. Paradigm Darwinian populations have high levels of competition between individuals (Godfrey-Smith 2009). The fourth criterion is that differences in fitness are due to the intrinsic characters of individuals in a population and not extrinsic factors. Intrinsic characters are features of the individual itself, whereas extrinsic characters are features that are external to the individual. For instance, if a corporate unit is able to successfully reproduce because a property of its structural organization allows it to outcompete other corporate units in its resource niche, this success is due to an intrinsic character of the corporate unit. If a corporate unit is successful because of its geographic location, this success is due to an extrinsic factor. Paradigm Darwinian populations require fitness differences in a population to be due to the intrinsic characters of individuals in the population (Godfrey-Smith 2009).

The final criterion, which paradigm Darwinian populations must exhibit, is continuity. A population has continuity when small changes in the character of an individual result in small changes in fitness. If small changes in the character of an individual lead to variable changes in fitness, a population does not have continuity. Applying the notion of continuity to Sewall Wright's metaphor of the adaptive landscape, when the landscape is smooth, a population has high continuity; when the landscape is rugged, a population has low continuity. Paradigm Darwinian populations have high levels of continuity (Godfrey-Smith 2009). In summary, according to Godfrey-Smith (2009), for a population to experience Darwinian selection, it must be a paradigm Darwinian population. Paradigm Darwinian populations have reliable but not too reliable systems of inheritance, an abundance of variation, and high levels of competition. Fitness differences in these populations depend on intrinsic characters, and the relationship between these characters and fitness exhibits continuity (Godfrey-Smith 2009). Now that the criteria, which must be met for the occurrence of Darwinian selection, have been outlined, it is possible to apply these criteria to populations of corporate units responding to the selection pressures of sociocultural evolution in order to determine whether selection on corporate units is Darwinian.

Turner (1995, 2010) distinguishes between two types of selection, Durkheimian selection and Spencerian selection, which operate on corporate units. Spencerian selection is selection for completely new types of corporate units; Durkheimian selection is selection among corporate units competing in a niche (Turner 1995, 2010). Durkheimian selection in societal evolution is analogous to Darwinian selection in biological evolution. Thus, when applying Godfrey-Smith's (2009) criteria of paradigm Darwinian populations to selection processes on corporate units, sociologists are talking about what could be called "paradigm Durkheimian populations."

Applying Godfrey-Smith's (2009) criteria to corporate units makes the case that corporate units do exist in Darwinian populations, thus experiencing Darwinian selection. First, corporate units can exhibit reliable heredity. If a new corporate unit is created that utilizes a similar, but not exact, template of functional differentiation and symbiotic integration, this is reliable, but imperfect, heredity. Godfrey-Smith's first criterion is met. With regard to variation, there need not be an abundance of variation in a niche, but there certainly can be. Corporate units within a niche may all be uniform in their structural organization, but they may also be remarkably different. The degree of variation within a niche of corporate units is an empirical question for each niche. Thus, the second criterion, an abundance of variation, can be met. Also, as Spencerian selection leads to the creation of new forms of corporate units, it introduces variation into a population of corporate units. High levels of Spencerian selection should increase the amount of variation in a population of corporate units. Thus, the operation of Spencerian selection facilitates the operation of Darwinian selection on corporate units by introducing novel variation into populations of corporate units.

The third criterion that must be met for selection on corporate units to qualify as Darwinian selection is that a high level of competition must exist between corporate units in a population. A resource niche need not have high levels of competition, but high levels of competition between corporate units certainly can and does happen. Thus, the third criterion can be met in many empirical circumstances. The fourth criterion that must be met is that the fitness of a corporate unit depends on intrinsic factors. While extrinsic factors play a role in the success of any corporate unit, if the likelihood that a corporate unit will reproduce creating more corporate units with the same structural form depends on qualities of the corporate unit that are related to its functional differentiation, then fitness differences are due to intrinsic characteristics and the fourth criterion is met. Finally, the fifth criterion regards the continuity in relationship between individual characteristics and fitness differences. As with most of the criteria put forth by Godfrey-Smith (2009), the level of continuity that traits in a population of corporate units exhibit is an empirical question; however, it certainly stands to reason that populations of organizations can exhibit high levels of continuity in the relationship between their structural organization and their fitness. Thus, Godfrey-Smith's (2009) fifth criterion can be met by populations of corporate units.

Although the specific extent to which a population of corporate units will meet Godfrey-Smith's (2009) five criteria of paradigm Darwinian populations is an empirical question that must be empirically assessed for different real-world populations of corporate units, at a theoretical level, populations of corporate units locked in a struggle of Durkheimian selection exhibit the characteristics of paradigm Darwinian populations. This means that it is philosophically justifiable to refer to selection processes acting on corporate units as processes of Darwinian natural selection. Populations of corporate units form Darwinian populations; thus, corporate units are subject to Darwinian selection.

Conclusion

Societal evolution takes place as increasing population size sets in motion series of logistical loads, or survival problems, that individuals must collectively meet in order to ensure their survival. To meet such survival problems, individuals group together, forming corporate units, whereby their individual efforts are functionally organized into collective responses, allowing individuals to mitigate the survival problems caused by societal growth. When ecological and evolutionary pressures led to the formation of the first of these societal groups, a major transition in evolution had taken place, signaling the evolution of a new evolutionary individual. Just as ecological and evolutionary pressures drove independently replicating molecules to form chromosomes, and just as these pressures drove unicellular organisms to join together in the formation of multicellular organisms, ecological and evolutionary pressures drove individually oriented humans to group together, forming corporate units.

The implications of such reasoning are manifold. First, by linking the formation of corporate units to other transitions in evolutionary individuality, the process of societal evolution is connected at a fundamental level to the process of biological evolution. A significant challenge in the study of evolutionary transitions in individuality is uncovering the extent to which common principles explain the multiple evolutionary transitions. Bourke (2011) proposes the size-complexity hypothesis as a general principle, explaining the transformation from a collection of separate individuals to a unified social group. In support of the size-complexity hypothesis, Bourke (2011) presents evidence from the transition of unicellular to multicellular organisms and the transition to eusocial insect societies. This chapter used Turner's (1995, 2010) societal dynamics to argue that the positive feedback dynamic outlined by the size-complexity hypothesis operates on corporate units. The size-complexity hypothesis outlines a relationship between size and complexity that operates on corporate units just as it does on multicellular organisms and eusocial societies. This serves as additional evidence supporting the size-complexity hypothesis as a general principle of evolutionary transitions in individuality.

A second implication of seeing corporate units as evolutionary individuals is that it negates any need for evolutionary sociologists to debate whether selection takes place at the level of the individual or the group when discussing societal evolution. Selection acts on evolutionary individuals, as corporate units are evolutionary individuals in societal evolution, selection processes act on corporate units. Moreover, evolutionary biologists have demonstrated the mathematical equivalence of individual and contemporary group selection approaches (Hamilton 1975; Grafen 1984; Queller 1992; Frank 1998; Kerr and Godfrey-Smith 2002). Given their mathematical equivalence, evolutionary sociologists should recognize that both individual and contemporary group selection approaches can explain the evolution of cooperative behaviors, as both approaches focus on the maximization of inclusive fitness. Whether a group or an individual selection approach should be used to explain the evolution of a particular behavior depends on the specific behavior under investigation and how the researchers intend to model the evolution of such behavior.

A final implication of identifying corporate units as evolutionary individuals is that it facilitates the application of concepts from biological evolution to societal evolution. This chapter began such application by applying Godfrey-Smith's (2009) five criteria of Darwinian populations to populations of corporate units, in order to demonstrate that selection on corporate units in a resource niche can happen via processes of Darwinian selection. Other concepts from biological evolution can be applied to corporate units in the same manner. Various authors focus on the importance of reproduction (Gould and Lloyd 1999; Godfrey-Smith 2009), fitness (Michod 2000; Orr 2009; Costa 2013), and adaptation (Dawkins 1982; Godfrey-Smith 2014) in biological evolution. Given the importance of these concepts in biological evolution, the details of corporate unit reproduction, fitness, and adaptation can be elaborated in order to create a more complete picture of societal evolution.

Notes

1. Corporate units are societal units that have a division of labor for realizing goals. Corporate units exist in three forms: groups, organizations, and communities (Turner 2010).
2. The major transitions in individuality have been analyzed using both Hamilton's rule (see Bourke 2011) and multilevel selection models (see Buss 1987); this provides further support to the argument that individual and group selection approaches are equivalent explanatory approaches.
3. Michod (2005, 2007) defines fitness as the product of viability and fecundity.
4. An example of corporate unit reproduction is franchising (Turner 2010).
5. An alternative way of representing evolution by natural selection is the replicator and vehicle/interactor distinction put forth by Dawkins (1982) and Hull (1980). The summary of natural selection put forth by Lewontin (1970) and its elaboration by Godfrey-Smith (2009) is preferred to the replicator/vehicle summary of Darwinian selection for a number of reasons, which are presented at length in Jablonka and Lamb (2006), Okasha (2006), and Godfrey-Smith (2009). For the purposes of this chapter, it is sufficient to say the replicator-vehicle approach represents a special case of Lewontin's summary, which is a more general recipe for Darwinian selection.

References

Bianconi, E., A. Piovesan, F. Facchin, A. Beraudi, R. Casadei, F. Frabetti, L. Vitale, M. Chiara Pelleri, S. Tassani, F. Piva, S. Perez-Amodio, P. Strippoli, and S. Canaider. 2013. "An Estimation of the Number of Cells in the Human Body." *Annals of Human Biology* 40 (6): 463–471.
Blute, M. 2010. *Darwinian Sociocultural Evolution*. New York: Cambridge University Press.
Bourke, A.F.G. 2011. *Principles of Social Evolution*. New York: Oxford University Press.
Buss, L. W. 1987. *The Evolution of Individuality*. Princeton, NJ: Princeton University Press.
Costa, J. T. 2013. "Hamiltonian Inclusive Fitness: A Fitter Fitness Concept." *Biology Letters* 9: 1–5.
Crippen, T. 1994. "Toward a Neo-Darwinian Sociology: Its Nomological Principles and Some Illustrative Applications." *Sociological Perspectives* 37 (3): 309–335.
Darwin, C. 1871. *The Descent of Man, and Selection in Relations to Sex*. New York: D. Appleton and Company.
Dawkins, R. 1976. *The Selfish Gene*. Oxford: Oxford University Press.
———. 1982. *The Extended Phenotype*. Oxford: Oxford University Press.

Durkheim, É. (1893) 1963. *The Division of Labor in Society.* New York: Free Press.
Frank, Steven A. 1998. *Foundations of Social Evolution.* Princeton, NJ: Princeton University Press.
Godfrey-Smith, P. 2009. *Darwinian Populations and Natural Selection.* New York: Oxford University Press.
———. 2014. *Philosophy of Biology.* Princeton, NJ: Princeton University Press.
Gould, S. J., and E. A. Lloyd. 1999. "Individuality and Adaptation across Levels of Selection: How Shall We Name and Generalize the Units of Darwinism?" *Proceedings of the National Academy of Sciences* 96 (21): 11904–11909.
Grafen, A. 1984. "Natural Selection, Kin Selection and Group Selection." In *Behavioural Ecology,* 2nd ed., edited by J. R. Krebs and N. B. Davies, 62–84. Oxford: Blackwell Scientific Publishing.
Hamilton, W. D. 1975. "Innate Social Aptitudes of Man: An Approach from Evolutionary Genetics." In *Biosocial Anthropology,* edited by R. Fox, 133–153. London: Malaby Press.
Hawley, A. H. 1986. *Human Ecology—A Theoretical Essay.* Chicago: University of Chicago Press.
Hull, D. L. 1980. "Individuality and Selection." *Annual Review of Ecology and Systematics* 11: 311–332.
Jablonka, E., and M. J. Lamb. 2006. *Evolution in Four Dimensions—Genetic, Epigenetic, Behavioral, and Symbolic Variation in the History of Life.* Cambridge, MA: MIT Press.
Kerr, B., and P. Godfrey-Smith. 2002. "Individualist and Multi-level Perspectives on Selection in Structured Populations." *Biology and Philosophy* 17: 477–517.
Lenski, G. 2005. *Ecological-Evolutionary Theory.* Boulder, CO: Paradigm Publishers.
Lewontin, R. C. 1970. "The Units of Selection." *Annual Review of Ecology and Systematics* 1: 1–18.
Lopreato, J., and T. Crippen. 1999. *Crisis in Sociology: The Need for Darwin.* New Brunswick, NJ: Transaction Publishers.
Machalek, R. S. 2010. "Sociobiology and Sociology." In *Historical Developments and Theoretical Approaches in Sociology/Social Theory,* edited by C. Crothers, 1–31. Oxford: UNESCO-EOLSS.
Maynard Smith, J., and E. Szathmáry. 1995. *The Major Transitions in Evolution.* Oxford: W. H. Freeman and Company.
Michod, R. E. 2000. *Darwinian Dynamics—Evolutionary Transitions in Fitness and Individuality.* Princeton, NJ: Princeton University Press.
———. 2005. "On the Transfer of Fitness from the Cell to the Multicellular Organism." *Biology and Philosophy* 20 (5): 967–987.
———. 2007. "Evolution of Individuality during the Transition from Unicellular to Multicellular Life." *Proceedings of the National Academy of Sciences* 104 (1): 8613–8618.
Michod, R. E., and A. M. Nedelcu. 2003. "On the Reorganization of Fitness During Evolutionary Transitions in Individuality." *Integrative and Comparative Biology* 43: 64–73.
Michod, R. E., Y. Viossat, C. A. Solari, M. Hurand, and A. M. Nedelcu. 2006. "Life-History Evolution and the Origin of Multicellularity." *Journal of Theoretical Biology* 239: 257–272.
Nielsen, F. 1994. "Sociobiology and Sociology." *Annual Review of Sociology* 20: 267–303.
Okasha, S. 2006. *Evolution and the Levels of Selection.* Oxford: Oxford University Press.
———. 2009. "Individuals, Groups, Fitness and Utility: Multi-level Selection Meets Social Choice Theory." *Biology and Philosophy* 24: 561–584.
Orr, H. A. 2009. "Fitness and Its Role in Evolutionary Genetics." *Nature Reviews Genetics* 10: 531–539.
Price, G. R. 1995. "The Nature of Selection." *Journal of Theoretical Biology* 175 (3): 389–396.
Queller, D. C. 1992. "Quantitative Genetics, Inclusive Fitness, and Group Selection." *American Naturalist* 139 (3): 540–558.
———. 2012. "Two Languages, One Reality." Edge.org. Accessed February 18, 2014. http://edge.org/conversation/the-false-allure-of-group-selection#22467.
Runciman, W. G. 2009. *The Theory of Cultural and Social Selection.* New York: Cambridge University Press.
Sanderson, S. K. 2008. "The Impact of Darwinism on Sociology." In *The New Evolutionary Social Science,* edited by H.-J. Niedenzu, T. Meleghy, and P. Meyer, 9–25. Boulder, CO: Paradigm Publishers.
———. 2014. *Human Nature and the Evolution of Society.* Boulder, CO: Westview Press.
Sober, E., and D. S. Wilson. 1998. *Unto Others: The Evolution and Psychology of Unselfish Behavior.* Cambridge, MA: Harvard University Press.
Stearns, S. C. 2007. "Are We Stalled Part Way through a Major Evolutionary Transition from Individual to Group?" *Evolution* 61 (10): 2275–2280.
Turner, J. H. 1995. *Macrodynamics—Toward a Theory on the Organization of Human Populations.* New Brunswick, NJ: Rutgers University Press.
———. 2010. *Theoretical Principles of Sociology.* Vol. 1, *Macrodynamics.* New York: Springer.
Turner, J. H., and A. Maryanski. 2008. *On the Origin of Societies by Natural Selection.* Boulder, CO: Paradigm Publishers.

West, S. A., C. E. Mouden, and A. Gardner. 2011. "Sixteen Common Misconceptions about the Evolution of Cooperation in Humans." *Evolution and Human Behavior* 32: 231–262.

Williams, G. C. 1966. *Adaptation and Natural Selection*. Princeton, NJ: Princeton University Press.

Wilson, D. S. 1975. "A Theory of Group Selection." *Proceedings of the National Academy of Sciences* 72: 143–146.

Wilson, D. S., and E. O. Wilson. 2007. "Rethinking the Theoretical Foundation of Sociobiology." *Quarterly Review of Biology* 82 (4): 327–348.

Wilson, D. S., and E. Sober. 1989. "Reviving the Superorganism." *Journal of Theoretical Biology* 136: 337–356.

Wynne-Edwards, V. C. 1962. *Animal Dispersion in Relation to Social Behaviour*. Edinburgh, UK: Oliver & Boyd.

Chapter Five

The Prospects and Limitations of Evolutionary Theorizing in the Social Sciences

Jonathan H. Turner and Alexandra Maryanski

This chapter outlines some of the limits on the uses of biological theorizing in the social sciences. The adoption of biological ideas by social scientists can significantly expand many explanations about the operative dynamics of the social universe, but we nonetheless must remain attuned to the limitations of biological theory when incorporated into social science theorizing. Biological theories cannot replace social science theories, but they can make social science explanations more robust. The limitations of biological theorizing become evident when we ask the following: What does it mean to say that sociocultural systems evolve? What dimensions of the sociocultural universe evolve? What are the units of selection in sociocultural evolution? What is the nature of selection in the sociocultural universe? By answering these questions, it becomes clear that biological concepts become less useful in understanding complex, multilayered sociocultural formations than recent efforts at modeling on the evolution of social systems would suggest. Biological theoretical ideas can be very useful, but they cannot explain a good portion of the properties and dynamics of the social world. The enthusiasm with which many trumpet the coming of biology in the social sciences is, at the very least, overdrawn and, at most, harmful to the social sciences. Hence, it is essential that social scientists recognize the limitations in using biological theorizing for explaining the social universe.

and yet you are the editors of this volume

Introduction

Herbert Spencer's (1851) famous phrase—"survival of the fittest"—uttered eight years before Darwin published *On the Origin of Species* indicates that early nineteenth-century social philosophy was thinking about the evolution of social systems by means of natural selection. In his notion of "survival of the fittest" as applied to sociology, Spencer ([1874–1896] 1898) argued that the evolution of societies from simple to complex forms is driven by conflict and warfare between societies, with the larger, more technologically advanced, and better-organized society being more fit and, hence, more likely to win wars with smaller, less technologically advanced, and less organized societies. As these conquered societies were killed off or, more likely, incorporated into the sociocultural formations of the more fit society, the overall level of organization and complexity of societies would increase. With the evolution of industrial production and free markets for distribution, Spencer felt that warfare had become a hindrance to societal evolution because it led to the concentration of power, increasing inequality, and internal conflict among subpopulations in a society. War, Spencer argued, can be replaced by competition in both domestic and international markets. Competition in markets would reduce the concentration of coercive power in polity, while encouraging the expansion of law to regulate production and distribution; and as new institutional domains evolved, further growth in the scale and complexity of societies would ensue. This rather idealistic view of the future was, of course, destroyed by the violence of World War I, but the basic notion that markets institutionalize competition and cause social "speciation" of new sociocultural forms was basically sound. In 1893, Émile Durkheim more explicitly incorporated Darwin's notion of natural selection in his book *The Division of Labor in Society* ([1893] 1997). The focus of the book was on the growing specialization of activities in evolving societies, with increasing specialization of the divisions of labor in societies being the sociological equivalent of *speciation* in the biotic universe. Durkheim argued that when populations grow and/or become more concentrated in space, both material and moral density increase, setting off competition for resources, with the more fit gaining resources in one niche and the less fit creating or finding new resource niches in which they could survive and reproduce.

The intellectual provenance of these Darwinian ideas in twentieth-century social science is ambiguous, but at both the University of Chicago and the University of North Carolina, Chapel Hill, ecological analysis emerged in the second decade of the twentieth century, just as stage model evolutionary analysis of societies from simple to more complex forms was being abolished from sociology and anthropology because it was seen as ethnocentric, if not racist (in the view that preliterate peoples were "primitive" and that the end state of societal evolution was the industrialism of western European societies). Thus, Darwinian ideas have existed in sociology for well over one hundred years and became institutionalized in programs of human ecology and in sociology as urban ecology (see Chapter 17), and, later, as organizational ecology (see Chapter 18). In urban ecology, individuals, families, or other collective actors like business corporations, schools, and churches compete for urban space, thus causing the division of urban space into various specialized districts, zones, and other geographical formations as a result of competition for land use in markets, especially real estate markets. From this competition over land use, urban areas become differentiated or specialized by distinctive types of activities—whether these are residential activities in neighborhoods of varying levels of wealth, educational activities in various types of schools, industrial activities, business and retail activities, and, of course, governmental activities. And, this mode of analysis is still very prominent today. In the 1970s, organizational ecology emerged in sociology and changed the way that organizations were studied and theorized (Hannan and Freeman 1977). Here, populations of organizations were defined by the resource niches in which they sought resources, with the evolution of populations of organizations determined by the level of density in various niches, the level of competition, and the level of selection on various forms of organizations within a niche. Less fit organizations in a given niche die or move to a new niche where they are able to secure resources and, thereby, become a new type of organization. Organizational ecology explicitly borrowed from evolutionary theory in biology and, unlike other efforts to import ideas from biology, gained wide acceptance in organizational sociology and organizational analysis in business schools. Indeed, organizational ecology seemed to legitimate some aspects of neoliberal ideology of capitalism and market dynamics in a way that did not offend as Social Darwinism had (actually Social Spencerianism) in the early decades of the twentieth century.

Ecological theorizing and research underscored the fact that there are homologies in the evolutionary dynamics of the biotic and sociocultural universes. Yet, at the same time, it was increasingly evident to sociologists that wholesale importation of Darwinian ideas and, more generally, biological models into the social sciences has limitations. The invasion of biological approaches such as sociobiology and evolutionary psychology into traditional social science, especially sociology, was considered reductionist and dangerous to the integrity of the social sciences. This almost hysterical fear was unfounded, but a more reasoned concern increasingly has become evident: overextending biological theorizing in the social sciences. Those who raised this concern were more sympathetic to biology but also aware that the use of biological thinking must be judicious.

In this chapter, we will pursue the limitations of evolutionary theory from biology in developing evolutionary theories in sociology and in the social sciences more generally. Sociocultural systems reveal unique features that require alterations and adjustments of biological theory in the social sciences; moreover, biological ideas often have little explanatory value in the social sciences and, in fact, can be harmful to the further development of the social sciences. The goal of this chapter is to raise these concerns by outlining the problems and limitations of incorporating biological theory into the social sciences.

THE LIMITATIONS OF EVOLUTIONARY ANALYSIS IN BIOLOGY WHEN APPLIED TO THE SOCIAL SCIENCES

WHAT IS EVOLUTION IN SOCIOCULTURAL SYSTEMS?

A Darwinian point of view emphasizes that evolution is "descent with modification"; in the biotic universe, evolution is descent with modifications between *generations* of organisms. In the Modern Synthesis of evolutionary theorizing, modification involves alterations in the phenotypes and underlying genotypes of individual organisms that, in turn, are reflected in distribution of alleles in the gene pool. Existing genotypes are subject to selection and, potentially, genetic drift and gene flow, thereby changing the distribution of phenotypical traits in successive populations and the genotype of the overall population. Mutations provide yet another source of variation on which selection can work to sort out those that facilitate, and those that work against, fitness of organisms and their underlying genotype, with changes in the overall distribution of genes and alleles marking evolution of a population of individual organisms. But, in trying to apply these ideas to superorganisms, problems immediately arise.

First, how do we establish what inheritance is, and what constitutes a generation? If evolution is descent with modification in the organic world, how do we take this idea and apply it to sociocultural systems? If a person is born, we can see a new generation or at least a new phenotype (and underlying genotype) added to the population (and its gene pool). But do all sociocultural formations have offspring in the same regular way? And, more importantly, corporate units (units with divisions of labor) all have the capacity for agency; hence, they can change their structure at any time, which makes their evolution Lamarckian rather than Darwinian. Indeed, modifications in the structure and culture of sociocultural units often come from innovations, as noted, but equally often they come from diffusion and borrowing of traits. And as corporate units borrow new traits (the modification element in Darwin's phrase), does this constitute a new generation? Indeed, while some sociocultural formations evolve through modifications, a great deal of evolution in the social units occurs by segmentation of new units that are very much like existing units. There is descent, often without too much or any modification, but the increase in absolute number of segmented units changes the nature of the more inclusive sociocultural formations within which segmentation is occurring. For example, if a society proliferates urban and suburban areas as its population grows, segmentation of urban structures and cultures absorbs much of this population growth, but at the same time new kinds of structures, such as political and legal structures as well as new types of distributive systems, such as roads, canals, ports, airports, and market systems, are created to coordinate and integrate the segmented units. Moreover, new kinds of productive and perhaps even reproductive structures will be created to manage the maintenance of the larger population and larger set of segmented units organizing members of the population. How can Darwinian ideas manage this kind of modification in the sociocultural realm?

They cannot, because evolution in the social universe involves building up social structures and their attendant cultures in response to selection pressures, thereby making much sociocultural evolution teleological rather than random selection on variants of existing social structures. Moreover, as we will emphasize later, selection as a key process in both the biotic and sociocultural worlds is not always Darwinian because of humans' capacity for agency to create new variants by innovation (Richerson and Boyd 2005).

Second, how is it possible to explain evolution of various types and layers of sociocultural formations in purely Darwinian terms? For example, sociologists and other social scientists often want to address the evolution of various types of social units, such as communities; institutional systems like economy, polity, kinship, religion, or education; populations of organizations of a given type; stratification systems; whole societies; and intersocietal systems. All of these nested and interconnected in layers of sociocultural reality make analyzing descent with modification difficult because, as emphasized above, there are no clear markers of reproduction across generations of phenotypes, nor is there even a clear notion of the relevant phenotype that has evolved. Social units do not have offspring in the same manner as biological organisms, but they do change and are modified as they respond to environmental constraints and exigencies. How, then, would we define fitness if we cannot use the passing of genes to subsequent generations and their survival as a measure of fitness?

In reality, the only definition of fitness for a sociocultural system would be either the length of time that it exists in its environment or its ability to persist in a variety of environments. There is nothing that is the equivalent of a genotype being passed across generations among those phenotypes that prove fit. Moreover, sociocultural phenotypes often remain fit by deliberately changing their structures and cultures and/or moving to new niches, or even creating their own resource niches in which they can remain fit. Evolution of this nature is mostly Lamarckian because the units are using their resources to alter their structure and culture in order to sustain themselves. There is nothing that is the equivalent of genes in sociocultural systems, despite Richard Dawkins's (1976) view of a meme pool to understand culture (Aunger 2000; Blackmore 1999; Distin 2005). Such an idea makes no sense in the sociocultural world because the social universe is not directed by inherited genes but by structures and symbol systems that can be constantly under reconstruction, especially in changing environments. In fact, the notion of a pool of memes underemphasizes organization of cultural symbols into a system connected to structural systems within and across types of social units. For example, values, ideologies, technologies, institutional norms, and other types of cultural systems are not a pool but a system in which counting the distribution of cultural traits robs them of their essential essence *as systems*. Thus, any analogy to the notion of a gene pool or view of culture as a bunch of discrete traits that are distributed with varying frequencies distorts what culture is: a system of symbols operating at many different levels to provide meanings as well as instructions for actors. And, most importantly, these systems of cultural symbols can be reformulated in response to selection pressures, thereby allowing sociocultural formations to modify themselves and remain fit in their environments.

Third, following from the above, humans can remake the very sociocultural formations that allow them to survive—or their "survivor machines" in the colorful terminology of sociobiology. Humans have capacities for agency under selection pressures from their environments, or even just because some actors with power decide to make changes and impose them on the less powerful. These sociocultural formations as survivor machines are evolving, to be sure, but what are the mechanisms driving this evolution? Are they Darwinian? In part they probably are, but other mechanisms not conceptualized by biological theorizing are also driving this evolution. A model of evolution emphasizing that selection works only on individual phenotypes and that populations evolve (by shifts in the distribution of genes) is singularly incapable of explaining all of the types and levels of evolution in sociocultural systems. Even when something like a Darwinian situation exists—say, a set of social units like business firms are competing for resources in a given resource niche—these units can intentionally change themselves and create the very variants that make them more fit under threats from competitors. Like biological evolution, the new structural and cultural elements in a social phenotype will be retained as long as they enhance fitness and allow the organization to secure necessary resources in a given niche, whether this niche be biophysical or sociocultural. Thus, Darwinian selection sorts out the most effective strategies pursued by sociocultural units, but the mechanisms driving innovation and creating necessary variants are much different than those of the biotic universe.

Fourth, as Spencer emphasized, even when sociocultural formations—whole societies, communities, organizations, groups, and so on—find themselves in competition, this competition does not always lead to the "death" of the individuals in these sociocultural formations, nor even the formation itself. For instance, a war between two societies does not always lead to the killing off of members of the weaker society or even the destruction of its institutional systems. The members of the conquered society are incorporated into a larger sociocultural formation, in a variety of potential ways: as colonies, as trading partners (typically under unfavorable terms), and as partially integrated into the more successful society. And, just as individuals are not killed off, neither are the culture and institutional systems of the conquered population. For example, during the expansion of the Soviet Union in the first half of the twentieth century, the culture and institutions of its constituent satellite societies did not disappear under Russian rule. Indeed, despite considerable prosecution, key elements of their indigenous culture and institutional arrangements remained functionally operative, as was all too evident when the empire collapsed in the 1990s and many features of the older institutional arrangements in these satellites became fully operational within a very short period of time. The same is true when business corporations merge, communities annex outlying communities into their fold, regional governments consolidate communities into larger regional formations (such as states in the United States and other types of regional formations within a larger society), school systems merge, societies claim territories of others to now be within their jurisdiction, and other possible forms of consolidation, annexation, and incorporation. To be sure, there is modification of both the constituent formations and the larger formations into which they are incorporated in some manner, but the culture and structure of the constituent formations do not die, any more than the individual members (organisms) die. Perhaps there are analogies to be made about memes and structural elements remaining in a structure and meme pool, but the basic evolutionary processes retaining these elements and their reconstitution are very different in sociocultural systems than in populations of biotic organisms.

At times, of course, corporate units do die, as when a company goes out of business because it cannot compete in a given market niche. But even here many of its "cultural memes" may float and be adopted in modified form by other businesses, along with its employees who carry this culture. While organizational ecology can explain the life and death of organizations in highly Darwinian terms, organizational ecology—like other forms of Darwinian theorizing—cannot fully explain evolutionary processes in which the persons, their structural formations, and their cultures persist within a new type of sociocultural formation. The mechanisms involved in such evolution are not biological, and there is no unambiguous analogue to these processes in evolutionary theory in biology.

A related issue emphasized more by Durkheim than by Spencer is that niche density and high rates of competition for resources do not always lead to the death of persons or, more importantly, corporate units. They can both move to a new resource niche, as when individuals look for work in a different field or when corporate units move to a new, less densely populated resource niche. For example, in studies of community-service organizations in the United States, many of these have responded to increased competition in a shrinking resource niche by moving to a new demographic niche seeking more working-class members as their pool of interested middle-class members has declined (McPherson 1983, 1988). These clubs have evolved in that there is some modification in the demography of their members, but in most cases the basic structure of the club remains unchanged and, often, only minor adjustments in its culture occur. The clubs have evolved and been modified, and so there is a kind of homology with evolution in biology, as would be the case when one species simply migrates away from an existing niche or habitat to avoid competition that cannot be won. By virtue of the migration of early humans "out of Africa," this small population was able to survive—thus ensuring that the human genome would survive (but it was a close call, as is evident in the incredibly low level of diversity in the human genome, compared with other primates and mammals). Still, the homology begins to break down once sociocultural systems become complex and highly differentiated, thereby creating many sociocultural niches. Moreover, as markets evolve in sociocultural systems, they institutionalize competition and sort with much greater speed and efficiency among individuals and corporate units in niches.

Equally significant is that humans as agents alone or organized into corporate units can create new resource niches. Corporate units can innovate and create demand for their innovations in markets, which, in turn, funnel resources to the organization. Moving to a new niche or creating a niche in ways that only dynamic markets can allow enables new corporate units to emerge and for older ones to survive. One of the great accelerators of sociocultural evolution, then, is the creation of free markets that order competition within niches but that also open up opportunities for structural development of new resource niches (or in economic terms "new markets"). Once dynamic markets exist as a sociocultural phenotype, the resource environments in which sociocultural formations survive (and hence their incumbents as well) will expand and change rapidly. Market collapses can, of course, cause rapid Darwinian free fall, but eventually markets recover and set into motion another wave of differentiation (or social speciation) that, in turn, creates new demands for resources and hence resource niches, while enabling actors to create through innovations demands for new types of resources. These dynamics are not easily captured by the central concepts of biological theory, even when we try to describe them with a Darwinian vocabulary. They are an emergent set of evolutionary phenomena that necessitate the formulation of new concepts to describe and explain the mechanisms involved.

> But SB/EP not trying to explain that

In sum, then, once we move to superorganisms organized by culture and social structures, conceptualizing the dynamics of evolution must change. Some superorganisms, such as insect societies, can be explained by evolutionary theory in biology because their organization is still under genetic control. Such is not wholly the case with human societies and their internal sociocultural formations. Culture, social structure, agency, and capacities for innovation are not directly regulated by genes. This fact exposes the fatal flaw of both sociobiology's (Cosmides and Tooby 1992; Trivers 1971; Pinker 2002) and evolutionary psychology's efforts to explain complex sociocultural formations by emphasis on hardwired behavioral propensities—whether kin selection, reciprocal altruism, and other types of behaviors that are seen to have evolved in a purely Darwinian manner. There can be no doubt that humans have behavioral propensities that are hardwired and that have been subject to evolution in the terms described by the Modern Synthesis, but these propensities do not dictate or even circumscribe all behaviors in sociocultural systems, much less the dynamics of structure and culture in these systems. We think that a better way to see the insights of sociobiology and evolutionary psychology is to view behavioral propensities as putting selection pressures on sociocultural evolution to build social structures and to develop systems of culture that allow individuals to behave in ways that are compatible with hardwired behavior propensities. But these can be overridden by the power of social structure and culture, once created, although over the long run sociocultural systems that deny individuals opportunities to express these behavioral propensities will be subject to tension and conflict.

In all societies, individuals use layers of embedded social structures and their cultures as their "survivor machines," which, in essence, provide even more layers of protection beyond the human body. The dynamics of these new kinds of survivor machines become an important part of the conceptualization of evolution and, as a consequence, force us to add new theoretical elements to evolutionary analysis not available in the biological conceptual tool kit. As noted above and explored below, part of this new conceptual tool kit is to conceptualize just what is evolving, above and beyond the phenotypes and underlying genotypes of organisms.

What Is Evolving in Sociocultural Evolution?

Evolutionary theory in biology emphasizes that natural selection and the other forces of evolution (mutations, gene flow, and genetic drift) work on individual organisms, and out of the operation of these forces, the distribution of phenotypes and their underlying genotypes in a population evolves. As we have emphasized above, when these ideas are mechanically applied to human social structure and culture, they lose not only clarity but also explanatory power. For instance, non–social scientists entering sociology from other disciplines often emphasize that many aspects of social structure and culture can be explained by behavioral propensities for kin selection and reciprocal altruism (e.g., Barclay 2004; Hamilton 1964; Marlowe et al. 2011; Skyrms 1996; Williams 1966). Not so surprisingly, economists who have shifted their models drawn from neoclassic economics have also begun with similar foundation assumptions about what drives human behavior and, hence, the building up of social structures and cultures (e.g., Gintis 2000, 2009). These explanations can be made to seem more plausible by running simulations of actors driven by selfishness, kin selection, reciprocal altruism, or any hypothesized behavior propensity to create cooperative structures. Most of this agent-based modeling, which is in many ways borrowed from neoclassic economics (Maynard-Smith 1972), ends up being as flawed as it is in economics (Gintis et al. 2007). One can produce outcomes showing that utility-maximizing actors or those driven by reciprocal altruism can produce, in computer simulations, a state of cooperation, which hardly explains the diversity of the layers of social reality that operate in the real world. These simulations, for all their elegance, do not take account of culture and social structure as they *actually exist*, nor do these simulations explain sociocultural formations in their *most robust forms*. Evolutionary psychology makes much the same mistake by arguing that certain behaviors were needed for cooperation; hence, modules producing these behaviors miraculously evolved in the brain during the Pleistocene, and then a "just so" story is constructed to explain why and how this behavior promotes fitness. In all of this work, it becomes increasingly difficult to specify what is evolving. On the one hand, the distribution of genes regulating the brain modules producing cooperative behaviors is evolving, but so are the neuro-systems in the brain, the patterns of behavior generated by these neuro-systems, and the cooperative patterns of social organization. So, is the survivor machine evolving (i.e., structures of cooperative behavior), or are the genes regulating the behaviors generating this machine? Or is it both? Once the cooperation generated by these behaviors is institutionalized into a pattern of social organization and culture, does it have any power or dynamics of its own that have reverse causal effects on genetically/neurologically generated behavior? Or is it only the brain, underlying genes, and behavioral propensity that are evolving? It would not be unreasonable to say that they are all evolving, but then we need to know how they interact with each other as they are evolving. Constructing what are, in reality, rather simple simulations or convenient "just so" stories does not help us here at all; instead, it just conflates what is evolving while giving the illusion of explaining social reality, especially as social reality becomes complex and layered. To pronounce that one can account for cooperation in a simulation hardly explains the majesty and complexity of how cooperation becomes institutionalized in complex sociocultural formations. The elaboration of cooperative behaviors at various levels of social organization results in the creation of new emergent properties that require a more robust theory to explain them.

If such theorists are willing to admit that sociocultural formations constitute an emergent reality, revealing their distinctive dynamics, then a different kind of theory is required. It is for this reason that accomplished scholars in biology and psychology are almost never willing to admit this, because it makes their favored, rather reductionist explanation woefully incomplete. There is a kind of dogma in much biologically inspired theorizing that selection works on individuals (their phenotype and underlying genotype), but it is a population that evolves, although in recent decades some have begun to break ranks with this dogma (e.g., Sober and Wilson 1998; Boyd and Richerson 1983; Durham 1991). But what if the population involved organizes itself into what Herbert Spencer termed a *superorganism*, or a complex pattern of organization of organisms? The only possible explanation from biology is that behaviors leading to the construction of social structure and the creation of culture are genetically driven and, hence, so are sociocultural formations, even when they become highly elaborated, layered, and complex. Even some sociologists who not only are good sociologists but also well versed in biological theory (e.g., Sanderson 1999, 2001) adhere to this dogma. The result is that most sociologists find that biological explanations are not very useful because they simply refuse to acknowledge the fact that the social universe unfolds at many levels and that with each emergent level new theoretical ideas are necessary to explain what is occurring. To a sociologist, then, it is the sociocultural system or systems that are evolving as they alter their structure and culture over time. It is not that explanations of this evolution in terms of genetically controlled behavioral propensities are wholly wrong, but that such explanations are incomplete. These behavioral propensities, from our point of view, can be seen as a kind of "selection pressure" pushing on individuals to build social structures and codify culture in certain directions compatible with human needs and favored behavioral propensities.

We have made this argument in many places (e.g., Maryanski and Turner 1992; Turner and Maryanski 2005, 2008; and Chapter 29 in this book), but we do not assume that isolating hardwired behavioral propensities and then speculating on their consequences for how social organization is built up comes close to a full explanation when the unit of evolution is a sociocultural formation. Each level of social organization has emergent properties with their own dynamics, which now need to be part of a theory of their evolution. And since these structures are often nested inside each other, they constitute environments that exert selection pressures on each other, which can be partially but not wholly explained in Darwinian terms because the phenomena evolving are not body phenotypes and the underlying genotype but, instead, *super-organic phenotypes* driven by *social* and *cultural* forces that regulate operation of these superorganisms (see Turner 2010a, 2013 for one effort to isolate these forces).

The problem becomes complex because, once societies evolve beyond hunting and gathering (where nuclear kinship and band are the only basic social structures), social reality becomes layered. Evolution thus is operating on different types of sociocultural formations, each revealing somewhat unique dynamics; if we add evolutionary forces from biology as they affect human behavioral propensities, we have yet another layer— the individual's phenotype—of this layering of survivor machines for genes. While still somewhat questionable, the formation of cooperative social arrangements during early human evolution might be the result of selfish genes working to create survivor machines to supplement body phenotypes. This kind of argument is difficult to sustain with any credibility for complex and layered social formations that have evolved over the last twelve thousand years. There may still be constant pressure from these selfish genes, but in reality, social reality drives itself, often at the expense of fitness. One can, of course, make statements that markets are a way to structure and regulate selfish activity so as to sustain survivor machines, and this argument has a kind of surface plausibility. However, it does not explain the dynamics of markets, per se, nor does it even provide a very useful explanation of why markets evolved in the first place. The same can be said for the emergence of systems of technology, power, learning, knowledge-seeking, and other dimensions of complex social formations.

Once institutionalized, new, emergent dynamics begin to drive the operation of these systems, with the consequence that they cannot be explained by the evolution of human phenotypes, gene pools, or gross characterizations of distributions of genes in the population. For as populations become organized by social structural and cultural phenotypes rather than organismic phenotypes, the relevance of theorizing about organismic phenotypes (including their behavioral aspects) and underlying genotypes declines because they are not evolving as much or as fast as the multiple layers of sociocultural survivor machines in which phenotypes are embedded. It is no longer just the population (and distribution of genes among members of this population) that is evolving; the structure and culture *organizing* the population are evolving, and more purely sociological theories are needed to explain the operative dynamics of the forces driving this sociocultural evolution.

In Figure 5.1 we outline one way to visualize the various levels of the human social universe. There are, in reality, just a few basic types of social structures and their corresponding cultures that have been used by humans as their building blocks of the largest and most complex social structures. As the figure emphasizes, social reality has unfolded during societal evolution into three distinctive levels, which can be roughly labeled *micro*,

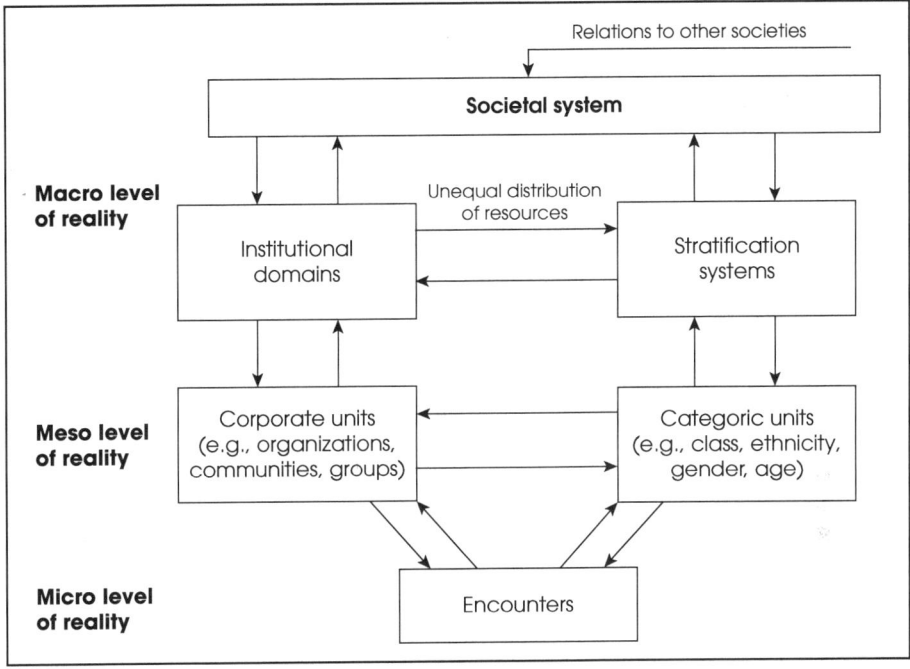

Figure 5.1 Levels of social reality

meso, and *macro*. The social world of humans for 95 percent of their time on earth was clearly more micro, consisting of face-to-face encounters among individuals in two basic types of corporate units: nuclear families (mother, father, offspring) and bands composed of perhaps a dozen nuclear families wandering territories in search of food. There was only one institutional system—kinship—but embedded within kinship and using division of labor among kindred were the first economies (hunting and gathering) and the early rise of religion (typically practiced by individual members of the family, with, at times, a shaman playing non-kin roles). These were the earliest sociocultural survivor machines among humans that supplemented the human body. Stage model theories of evolution in sociology, anthropology, and, to a lesser extent, political science seek to explain the forces driving the growth and increasing differentiation among the micro, meso, and macro levels of reality, as well as internal differentiation of each level, particularly the meso and macro levels. Encounters at the micro level of social organization are strips of face-to-face interaction among individuals; these are almost always embedded in or lodged inside two basic types of meso-level units: (1) *corporate units* that reveal a division of labor for coordinating activities to realize goals, no matter how vaguely defined, and (2) *categoric units* that define salient social categories and place persons in these categories (with age and gender being the only universal categories, but other categoric units revolve around differences in religion, class, ethnicity, national origin, sexual preferences, etc.). Corporate units are the building blocks of *institutional domains* at the macro level of social organization. Thus, distinctive institutional domains have evolved (economy, polity, law, religion, kinship, education, science, medicine, etc.), using distinctive types of corporate units (families, businesses, political parties, courts, schools, churches, clinics, etc.) as the building blocks, with various mechanisms of structural and cultural integration holding these blocks together to sustain a distinctive institutional domain.

For each differentiated institutional domain and, hence, the corporate units from which each is constructed, there are unique cultures (norms, beliefs, ideologies) as well as patterns of structural interdependence among the corporate units of a domain. Stratification systems are created by the unequal distribution of resources in corporate units, creating a system of social-class categoric units, which are often correlated with membership in other categoric units such as gender, age, ethnicity, religious affiliation, and so on. *Societies* are constructed from institutional domains and stratification systems, and *intersocietal systems* are built from relations among societies, particularly their institutional domains (polity, economy, law, and sometimes kinship and religion).

Jonathan Turner (2010a, 2010b, 2013) has theorized about the dynamics of each of these levels, as have many other theorists. The specifics of this kind of theorizing are less important than what such theorizing implies: *each level* of social reality has *distinctive but interconnected dynamics* that, for the most part, cannot be reduced to theoretical ideas from biology or any of the key variants of biological thinking that have made inroads into sociology and other social sciences (e.g., sociobiology and evolutionary psychology). Some of these levels of social reality have been conceptualized with evolutionary theory, as is the case with urban communities (e.g., Hawley 1981) and populations of organizations (e.g., Hannan and Freeman 1977) as two basic types of corporate units and also as has been done with some forms of categoric units like ethnicity (Olzak 1992). For example, organizational ecology is true to its Darwinian roots by emphasizing that it is the population of organizations that evolves, with selection working on individual organizations. The number of organizations in a niche will inevitably increase, especially when markets and the incentives that they generate pull organizations into a given niche. As the number of organizations increases, density also increases, causing competition where the less fit organizations die or potentially transform themselves and move to a new niche.

This kind of explanation is one way that Darwin-inspired theory can be adopted by the social sciences. The basic model, revolving around niches, number of organizations in a niche, density of niche, competition, and selection, is retained, but note that there are larger differences along several fronts: the unit on which selection works is a corporate unit, not an individual organism; the unit has the capacity for agency to change its structure and/or move to new, less dense niches; often the unit does not really die but, instead, is consolidated into more fit organizations through mergers and other mechanisms of consolidation; the equivalent of the underlying genotype in organizations is their culture, which is subject to change in a Lamarckian process. So, considerable insight can be generated using ecological models, derived from early sociology and later evolutionary biology and bioecology, but few in sociology would see these as *the complete explanation* of organizational dynamics. Other dynamics on how corporate units "act" need to be theorized beyond the concern for the life and death of organizations in a population.

There are, then, emergent properties at each level that require additional theories. There is a large literature on the dynamics of organizations, with ecological theorizing being only *one type* of explanation. To understand the evolution of organizations requires that these other theories be part of the explanation. And, what is true of organizations at the meso level is true of units at all three levels of social reality, or all levels together. An ecological dynamic is frequently involved, but it is often a very minor part of the explanation of a unit or units at varying levels of social organization. Theories about the persistence and transformations (evolution) can use some key ideas from biologically based evolutionary theory, but these must be supplemented by concepts and models from more purely sociological theories.

Depending on the focus of evolutionary explanation, theories will vary. Intersocietal evolutionary theories (e.g., Wallerstein 1974; Chase-Dunn 2001) will be different from stage-models of societal-level evolution (e.g., Lenski and Nolan 2014), which, in turn, will be different from evolutionary theories about institutional dynamics (Turner 2003) and the corporate units creating and sustaining institutional domains and evolutionary theories about stratification systems built from evolving institutional domains and their respective categoric units (Turner 2010a). Similarly, while ecological models derived from biology are prominent in the analysis of types of corporate units (e.g., Aldrich and Ruef 2006; Scott 2008; Hannan and Freeman 1989) and categoric units (e.g., Turner 2013; Blalock 1982), there are also other properties and dynamics of these meso-level units that require theories from the social sciences rather than the biological sciences. Even the encounters at the most micro-level unit require their own theories, distinct from those about human behavior (e.g., Collins 2004; Turner 2002, 2010b).

When a society as a whole evolves, almost every other level of organization in the society also evolves in the sense of being modified in significant ways. Conversely, when evolution is occurring at any level, it is likely that this evolution will eventually cause transformations in societies and perhaps even the intersocietal systems linking societies together. From a sociological perspective, Figure 5.1 suggests the various levels where evolution can occur: intersocietal, societal, institutional, stratification systems, corporate units (groups, organizations, and communities), categoric units, and even encounters. *What* is evolving is not a simple thing like populations (and their gene pool), because the structures and cultures organize members of a population at different levels of social reality. Depending on *which* level of reality is being theorized, a somewhat different conceptual tool kit is needed. Thus, there will not be *a general theory* of sociocultural evolution, but a series of theories that may or may not be integrated into a more general theory at some point in the future. Elements in these theories can draw heavily from biological theory, and perhaps be integrated with other theories that are more purely sociological.

As long as evolution is seen as modifications in the distribution of traits (phenotypically and genetically), biological theorizing will be of limited use to social scientists. Populations are *organized* by the structures and the cultures attending these structures that are outlined in Figure 5.1. While one can count traits, such as number of organizations of a given type in a niche, this hardly explains how units subject to selection processes are organized. What, for example, are the mechanisms of cultural and structural integration among organizations in a given niche, or corporate units constituting an institutional domain? These are emergent properties of sociocultural systems, and their dynamics can be explained only with more purely social science theories that bring many non-Darwinian forces into the explanation of evolution.

What Are the Units of Selection?

From a social science viewpoint, superorganisms—whether groups, organizations, or communities at the meso level or institutional domains, whole societies, or intersocietal systems at the macro level—are potential units subject to selection. For example, we might see a world-level pandemic as subjecting individuals (and their immune systems) to intense selection pressures; such pressures would cause evolution in the distribution of genes determining immune systems in the phenotypes of individuals. This would be an appropriate level of analysis that can draw from biological theory. But since individuals in most societies have access to a survivor machine—say, organizations and their integration into the institutional domain of medicine—these organizations or the health system in general could easily be units subject to selection, with the result that we could see selection as working on health systems in a kind of Spencerian struggle to find a way to create new medicines and/or medical delivery systems in order to kill off the pathogens causing the pandemic. The society with a well-developed health system is more likely to retain its population than one without a well-developed medical delivery system, as is evident in the comparative rates of death from AIDS in postindustrial and in third- and fourth-world nations.

Once multilevel selection is viewed as a plausible way to analyze evolution, the controversy over individual versus group selection immediately emerges (Okasha 2006; Pinker 2012; Queller 1992; Runciman 2009; Lewontin 1970; see Chapter 4 in this volume). Some (e.g., Pinker 2012) dogmatically insist that it is still the individual that is subject to selection, but this dogmatism flies in the face of social science literature that most biologists have not read and, hence, do not see as relevant. But for most sociologists, it is so obvious that selection is working on social structures and their cultures organizing individual organisms that it is difficult to see what the controversy is all about in biology. Individuals are incumbent in corporate units within institutional domains, within societies, and, potentially, within an intersocietal system; these are survivor machines that are surely as important to survival as are the human epidermis and immune system. They protect individuals from potentially harmful effects of the environment. Like organismic phenotypes, the sociocultural phenotypes absorb blows from selection, and unlike the body phenotype, these survivor machines can rapidly adjust and adapt (through agency and innovation) to selection pressures far more rapidly than can a body and its immune system and other cybernetic processes that protect its precious cargo: genes. For example, when the American automobile industry went into rapid decline in the first decade of the twenty-first century, it was not automobile workers who were subject to direct selection but the viability of the corporate structures and their cultures that organized workers for production. For a time it looked as if a company such as Toyota was the most fit in the niche created by market demand for automobiles, and if Darwinian selection had been allowed to take its course, there would be fewer (or no) American automobile companies. Most of the workers in these companies would not die; they would move to a new niche, emphasizing that it was not the workers who were the objects of selection but the corporate units organizing those workers. Moreover, the car companies themselves were lodged in a more inclusive survivor machine, the institutional domains of economy and polity, with the latter acting in ways to shield, say, General Motors, from certain death by bankruptcy. So, not only was General Motors subject to selection, so were key institutional domains—economy, polity, and law—and perhaps the entire American society.

To understand the evolutionary processes that have occurred over the last decade in something as seemingly simple as the auto industry requires an emphasis on not only group selection but also multilevel selection on diverse social structures and their cultures. Furthermore, all of these sociocultural formations have the capacity for agency and innovation, allowing them to change their structure and culture within generations; however, we might want to conceptualize "generations" for nonbiological corporate units. That is, superorganisms created by humans can spawn new, fitness-enhancing characteristics rapidly, thereby obviating the process of selecting out sociocultural units. Much more than Darwinian theory is needed, then, to explain this collective response at multiple levels to the selection pressures imposed by a shrinking resource niche—the market for automobiles—that increased the density and competition among car companies.

As we have emphasized, once collective or corporate actors become units of selection, it is difficult to determine what is evolving. In the example above, a Darwinian approach would see the population of car companies as evolving as selection in markets institutionalizing competition selected out the less fit. This analysis would be very useful, and yet it is incomplete from a sociological perspective. For one could make the case that it is the car companies themselves that are evolving because they are "modifying" their structures; or perhaps it is the economy that is evolving as the distribution of manufacturing activities shifts as a result of market forces affecting car companies; or it could be the political and legal systems as they develop new mechanisms for "bailing out" distressed companies; or it could be the world system (intersocietal system) as world-level companies and their geopolitical patrons (e.g., polities, legal systems, and economies) fight each other for market shares.

In Figure 5.2, we present the material from Figure 5.1 in a new way to emphasize that the morphology and culture of different types of social structures are the equivalent of body phenotypes as survivor machines. At the center is the genotype protected by the phenotype that expresses genes; biology stops at this point, but from a sociological perspective, the body is lodged inside of successive layers of sociocultural formations. Encounters are lodged in groups, groups in organizations, organizations in communities. These meso structures—that is, groups, organizations, communities—are embedded in institutional domains, and institutional domains are embedded in societies and intersocietal systems. And, at each level there are structural and cultural mechanisms integrating systems of organizations, communities, and institutional domains in societies and intersocietal systems (see Turner 2010a for an outline of these mechanisms).

In the social universe, as opposed to the biotic universe, *the organization* of individual phenotypes dramatically expands the number of survival machines available to protect genes. Biological theory, then, must take account of these because they surely exist in human populations and, as some are finally beginning to recognize (e.g., D. S. Wilson 1975, 2002; Wilson and Wilson 2007; E. O. Wilson 1998, 2012), in populations of other

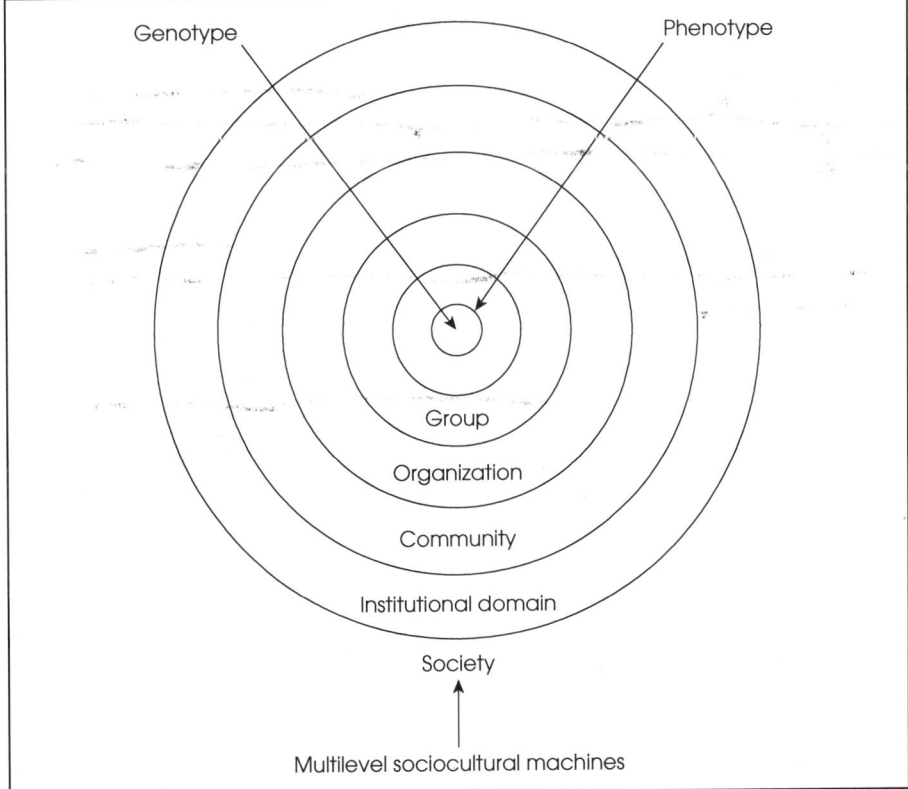

Figure 5.2 Sociocultural embedding as survivor machines

life forms as well. If social science can contribute anything to biology, it is this idea of group selection that breaks the dogma—indeed, the collective mantra—that selection works on individuals but it is the population that evolves (population being defined as the distribution of traits of a given kind among a population). Group selection surely must count for something in this distribution, because herds, pods, flocks, troops, packs, swarms, hives, schools (of fish), prides, troops, and other forms of group-level organization affect the fitness of their incumbents. And so, it would be reasonable to see populations of these grouping systems as what evolves and, hence, to analyze selection on the grouping system rather than the individuals that are incumbent in this system. At the very least, it should be a topic of analysis, if only to determine whether or to what degree the structure of the grouping system promotes fitness of its individual members. And for human organization, it is imperative that this be examined in all evolutionary theory because humans cannot survive biologically without being encased in sociocultural formations.

As superorganisms building up social structures and using culture unfold, they do so by creating multiple levels of successively embedded structures, as illustrated in Figure 5.2. Long-term organismic evolution has done much the same thing in increasing the size and complexity of organisms, and so the evolution of superorganisms (i.e., organization of organisms) is only an extension of what has occurred in organic evolution over the last few billion years—as Herbert Spencer emphasized 150 years ago. Moreover, modes of integration among structures and their cultures can change very rapidly when subject to selection. Thus, evolutionary analysis must examine how these various types and levels of survivor machines evolve, how they are integrated to form larger superorganisms, and how they protect their incumbents' phenotype and underlying genotype. Each level of sociocultural formation, as well as the mechanisms integrating these formations within and between levels of social reality, is subject to selection, and all levels can be evolving in concert in response to these selection pressures. Sociology makes biology more complex, and biologists need to learn some sociology if they are to have more than a marginal impact on how social science explains the dynamics of the social universe.

How Does the Nature of Selection Vary in the Social and Biotic Universes?

Once the units of selection can "acquire new characteristics," the other forces of evolution—mutations, gene flow, and genetic drift—have only metaphoral counterparts in the sociocultural realm. For example, processes such as innovations, diffusion, migration, and subgroup formation can be seen as sociocultural counterparts of mutations, gene flow, and genetic drift, but these are not true homopolies; rather, they are only analogies that have limited explanatory power. Only the notion of selection remains useful, because however units are formed, they are still subject to selection in terms of their fitness in securing resources from their environments, which can no longer be defined in terms of reproduction since generations of producers and reproducers are no longer evident in multilevel superorganisms. Rather, the only criterion for assessing fitness is the extent to which a unit under selection is able to persist over time in an environment, because it has (1) structural and cultural characteristics that allow it to secure a steady flow of resources, (2) agency and capacities to transform itself in ways that increase its access to resources, and/or (3) abilities to migrate to new niches when its existing niche becomes too dense and competitive.

However, selection is not operating in a blind way, because as (2) above emphasizes, sociocultural systems and individuals in them can see and analyze selection pressures emanating from the environment and then develop plans and strategies for responding to these pressures. They may not be successful in these efforts, but they are not passively locked into a genotype and its expression in a phenotype; they can alter the structure of the sociocultural phenotype under selection, sometimes successfully and sometimes not so, as the history of societal failures and successes in war or in sustaining structural and cultural integration document. As a derivative of this point, as we mentioned earlier, there are two basic types of selection in sociocultural systems, only one of which is Darwinian or Durkheimian (in tribute to Durkheim's incorporation of Darwinian ideas in *The Division of Labor in Society*). The other is Spencerian, derived from the implicit assumptions of sociological functionalism. Darwinian or Durkheimian selection involves pressures from the environment on the structure and culture of sociocultural formations in niches with varying levels of resources, density, and competition among units seeking these resources (e.g., as is evident in urban and organizational ecological analysis). If an existing sociocultural formation has the characteristics allowing the formation to secure resources, then its structure and culture are fitness-enhancing. Conversely, if this structure and culture cannot respond to adaptive problems, then the structure is less fit and can fall apart or even die out as a template for organizing individuals. And in extreme cases, the individuals themselves can die if they cannot discover a way to meet selection pressures. Evolution can be very Darwinian because existing variants of sociocultural formations vary in terms of their fitness or, alternatively, the agency of actors to create, when needed, fitness-enhancing variants under conditions of niche density, competition, and selection. This last alternative has implications for an entirely new type of selection that we are terming "Spencerian selection."

Spencerian selection has two forms. One is, as indicated above, the capacity of actors in social units to create a fitness-enhancing variant under conditions of high competition for scarce resources. Most organisms cannot change their structure and genotype within a generation, and thus they are locked into their fate in terms of the degree to which their phenotypes promote fitness; selection will work on variations in individuals' phenotypes (and underlying genotypes) and retain those that promote fitness while causing those that do not to die or migrate, thereby taking their genes out of the population's gene pool. But as functional theorists implicitly argued, individuals and the social units in which they are incumbent can alter structure and culture (generating acquired characteristics) and change their structures, at least some of the time, in ways that increase fitness. This variant is still very Darwinian, and it is what Durkheim implied when he saw new forms of specialization (sociological "speciation") as social units move to alternative sociocultural and biophysical niches or as they create new niches of resources that can be used to sustain themselves.

The other form of Spencerian selection emphasizes that often there is *a complete lack of variants in sociocultural formations that can promote fitness*. Indeed, there may be no formation that is relevant or able to meet selection pressures or, as functionalists phrased the matter, to meet functional needs and survival requisites. In Darwinian selection, all of these social units that cannot meet selection pressures would die, whereas in the history of human evolution, individuals and corporate units organizing their activities can create *entirely new sociocultural formations* by innovation, by diffusion, by conquest, by borrowing, or by trial and error. Many of the selection pressures on human populations during the course of societal evolution have involved Spencerian selection where there is an adaptive problem and no existing variants of structure or culture in a society that can deal with this problem. The adaptive structures had to be created. For example, when populations first began to grow in more settled hunter-gatherer populations, problems of coordination and control escalated, with the result that some populations were able to create viable political structures where there had previously been none. Similarly, horticulture was adapted as the first economic system to meet selection pressures for producing more food for larger, more settled populations and was independently institutionalized all over the globe because hunter-gatherers knew the secret of seeds and planting but did not want to work so hard in producing food; population growth pushed them out of their Garden of Eden into the hard work (performed mostly by women) of gardening for food. As populations also grew, they had to create legal systems and expand religion beyond kin units and shaman. Indeed, the process of institutional differentiation—which is one way to describe the long-term trend of societal evolution—can be viewed mostly as a process of Spencerian selection in which actors in a society have been forced to find fundamentally new types of structures and culture, where previously there had been none. Once variants in these types were created, however, more Darwinian or Durkheimian selection processes could fine-tune the best variants in terms of fitness, although the evolution of power and stratification worked to "select" the variant that increased inequalities that do not maximize fitness; and so, there is nothing like a maximization dynamic operating in Spencerian selection (as is often postulated since the models employed were taken from neoclassic economics; see Maynard-Smith 1972). Rather, as long as variants promote "just enough" adaptation, those variants that favor the rich and powerful tend to be selected, although in the long run inequalities generate internal conflicts and potential societal disintegration and, hence, do not promote fitness over longer stretches of time. Thus, as societies have grown historically, Spencerian selection has been biased as much by pressures from those with power as by pressures from the biophysical environment. In fact, most selection pressures on societies now come from problems of integration among differentiated subunits pursuing their own interests and often diverse agendas or from tensions generated by growing inequalities in the distribution of resources. To be sure, securing sufficient food and other resources from the biophysical environment and protecting a society from incursion by other societies have always existed, but over time, it is the internal environment generated by complexity and inequality that generates intense selection pressures that can be both Darwinian/Durkheimian and Spencerian.

Evolution of larger and more complex superorganisms dramatically expands the environments to which societies as a whole as well as their constituent structural units and attending cultures must adapt. If there are available variants of sociocultural formations to meet adaptive problems, selection will be more Durkheimian, and ecological models from biology can be useful in understanding these dynamics. If, however, there are no viable variants and/or relevant structures at all, then selection will be Spencerian and revolve around a search for new kinds of sociocultural formations. This kind of selection is not easily conceptualized within a biological framework because it is essentially Lamarckian in that actors discover and create "acquired characteristics" that can resolve problems of adaptation by virtue of their capacity for agency.

Thus, evolution in sociocultural systems will be a mix of Darwinian and Lamarckian processes set in motion by Darwinian/Durkheimian and Spencerian selection as they, respectively, select on existing variants or push for the creation of new and needed sociocultural formations that can promote adaptation to the diverse environments of all societies, including the sociocultural environment of the society or some subpart of the society itself.

Conclusion

Many highly sophisticated efforts applying evolutionary theory from biology now exist in sociology and the social sciences more generally (e.g., Lenski 2005; Sanderson 2001;

Runciman 1989, 2009; Turner and Maryanski 2008; Weingart et al. 1997; D. S. Wilson 2002; Bellah 2011; Blute 2010; Boehm 2010). To varying degrees, most of these cannot deal with some of the problems that we have raised in this chapter. The larger and more complex the sociocultural systems that are evolving, the less traction simple borrowing of ideas from biology will have in generating explanations of sociocultural evolution. It is still possible to use evolutionary theory in agent-based models, but these suffer from a lack of ability to model complex social processes because they tend to see just one or two dynamics in play, when in fact there are many. Efforts to find isomorphic forces in biotic and sociocultural universes can be useful, as is the case with ecological approaches in sociology, but it soon becomes evident that the isomorphisms break down because there are no corresponding manifestations in sociocultural systems of key ideas like phenotype, genotype, descent, generations, reproduction, fitness, genetic drift, gene flow, and mutations. Even selection is a more varied and complex process in sociocultural formations. Add to these problems the many levels at which evolution operates and the prevalence of group selection as opposed to selection on individual phenotypes, and it becomes increasingly evident that there are profound limitations on a Darwinian interpretation of the social universe, even an interpretation that is supplemented by ideas of the Modern Synthesis. Much like the first blush of promise in interdisciplinary theorizing and modeling proposed by General Systems Theory in the 1940s, 1950s, 1960s, and even into the present era, the isomorphism across system levels begins to break down and becomes more metaphorical than denotative of real convergence in the operation of diverse types of systems.

The reductionism of sociobiology and evolutionary psychology holds out another promise that cannot be met: explaining emergent phenomena by the dynamics inhering in biological forces. Reductionism is, of course, a goal of all science, but we need to take heed when new emergent phenomena in any universe make such reductionism less useful. All reductionist efforts, at some point, fail in explaining emergent phenomena that arise from *the organization of constituent parts*; nowhere is this more evident than in the differences between organisms and superorganisms. The model for the evolution of populations of organisms can be used when concern is with populations of superorganisms, but once we recognize that evolution of superorganisms themselves is a complex, multilevel process revolving around structures and processes that are not isomorphic with those in biological theory, we must then begin to search for theoretical traction outside of biology proper in the social sciences. It is always a useful exercise to push theories to their explanatory limits and, then, to recognize that limits have been reached and, as a consequence, that new types of theorizing will be necessary. Unfortunately, too much of the effort to bring biology to the social sciences has been pushed by scholars who, for all their brilliance and accomplishment in the biological sciences, remain woefully ignorant of theory and research in the social sciences; and what is more, they are not even apologetic about this fact—such is, we gather, their arrogance.

In our various efforts as sociologists to apply biological ideas to sociology (e.g., Maryanski and Turner 1992; Turner and Maryanski 2005, 2008), we have learned a great deal about evolutionary biology. It would be nice if those entering sociology from other fields would do the same before they announce that they have solved explanatory problems in the social sciences. They have not solved anything but, indeed, have only argued by fiat and dogmatic assertion that biological ideas can explain the complexity of the sociocultural universe. It would be wonderful if such were the case, but it is not possible; moreover, these efforts give biology a bad name in sociology when what we seek is the proper and judicious use of biological ideas to develop more robust explanations of the social universe.

We have outlined in this chapter only some of the problems and limitations in rote applications of biological ideas to sociocultural phenomena; our critique, however, is intended to enlighten and challenge those interested in explaining the dynamics of the sociocultural universe to meet us, as sociologists who are open to biological ideas, halfway with some understanding of how the social universe is conceptualized in the social sciences. At some point the non-isomorphic nature of the sociocultural universe with the biotic universe forces the abandonment of biological models and theoretical constructs in favor of more purely social science constructs and models. Yet, at the same time, it is important to push biological ideas as far as they can go and, when they lose traction, to integrate these biological models and theories into those produced by social scientists. If this is not done, the current wave of interest in using biological ideas in the social sciences will go the way of General Systems Theory—essentially into oblivion, which would be a shame because humans have evolved like all other animals and thus biological ideas are relevant to and understanding of the vast social universe that humans have created. But, as with the physical universe, there was a "big bang" in human evolution when populations settled and started to grow; the social universe began to expand, and *new forces* emerged to drive this expansion. Hence, the goal of biosociology or, to use our term, *evolutionary sociology*, should be to develop a unified theory blending the forces of biological evolution with the forces of sociocultural evolution.

References

Aldrich, H. E., and M. Ruef. 2006. *Organizations Evolving*. Newbury Park, CA: Sage Publications.
Aunger, R., ed. 2000. *Darwinizing Culture: The Status of Memetics as a Science*. New York: Oxford University Press.
Barclay, P. 2004. "Trustworthiness and Competitive Altruism Can Also Solve the 'Tragedy of the Commons.'" *Evolution and Human Behavior* 25: 209–220.
Bellah, R. N. 2011. *Religion in Human Evolution: From the Palaeolithic to the Axial Age*. Cambridge, MA: Harvard University Press.
Blackmore, S. 1999. *The Meme Machine*. Oxford: Oxford University Press.
Blalock, H. 1982. *Toward a Theory of Minority Group Relations*. New York; New Brunswick, NJ: Transaction Books.
Blute, M. 2010. *Darwinian Sociocultural Evolution: Solutions to Dilemmas in Cultural and Social Theory*. New York: Cambridge University Press.
Boehm, C. 2010. *Moral Origins: The Evolution of Virtue, Altruism, and Shame*. New York: Basic Books.
Boyd, R., and P. J. Richerson. 1983. *Culture and the Evolutionary Process*. Chicago: University of Chicago Press.
Chase-Dunn, C. 2001. "World Systems Theory." In *Handbook of Sociological Theory*, edited by J. H. Turner. New York: Springer.
Collins, R. 2004. *Interaction Ritual Chains*. Princeton, NJ: Princeton University Press.
Cosmides, L., and J. Tooby. 1992. "The Psychological Foundations of Culture." In *The Adapted Mind: Evolutionary Psychology and the Generation of Culture*, edited by J. H. Barkow, L. Cosmides, and J. Tooby, 19–136. New York: Oxford University Press.
Dawkins, R. 1976. *The Selfish Gene*. Oxford: Oxford University Press.
Distin, K. 2005. *The Selfish Meme*. Cambridge: Cambridge University Press.
Durham, W. H. 1991. *Coevolution: Genes, Culture, and Human Diversity*. Stanford, CA: Stanford University Press.
Durkheim, É. (1893) 1997. *The Division of Labor in Society*. New York: Free Press.
Gintis, H. 2000. "Strong Reciprocity and Human Sociality." *Journal of Theoretical Biology* 206: 169–179.
———. 2009. *The Bounds of Reason: Game Theory and the Unification of the Behavioral Sciences*. Princeton, NJ: Princeton University Press.
Gintis, H., S. Bowles, R. Boyd, and E. Fehr. 2007. "Explaining Altruistic Behaviour in Humans." In *The Oxford Handbook of Evolutionary Psychology*, edited by R.I.M. Dunbar and L. Barrett, 605–619. Oxford: Oxford University Press.
Hamilton, W. D. 1964. "The Genetical Evolution of Social Behaviour." I and II. *Journal of Theoretical Biology* 7: 1–16, 17–52.
Hannan, M. T., and J. H. Freeman. 1977. "The Population Ecology of Organizations." *American Journal of Sociology* 82: 910–943.

———. 1989. *Organizational Ecology*. Cambridge, MA: Harvard University Press.
Hawley, A. 1981. "Human Ecology: Persistence and Change." *American Behavioral Scientist* 24: 423–444.
Lenski, G. 2005. *Ecological-Evolutionary Theory*. Boulder, CO: Paradigm Publishers.
Lenski, G., and P. Nolan. 2014. *Human Societies*. New York: Oxford University Press.
Lewontin, R. C. 1970. "The Units of Selection." *Annual Review of Ecology and Systematics* 1: 1–18.
Marlowe, F. W., J. C. Bergesque, C. Barrett, A. Bolyanatz, M. Gurven, and D. Tracer. 2011. "The 'Spiteful' Origins of Human Cooperation." *Proceedings of the Royal Society B* 278: 2159–2164.
Maryanski, A., and J. H. Turner. 1992. *The Social Cage: Human Nature and the Evolution of Society*. Stanford, CA: Stanford University Press.
Maynard-Smith, J. 1972. *Evolution and the Theory of Games*. Cambridge: Cambridge University Press.
McPherson, M. 1983. "An Ecology of Affiliation." *American Sociological Review* 48: 519–532.
———. 1988. "A Theory of Voluntary Organization." In *Community Organizations: Studies in Resource Mobilization and Exchange*, edited by C. Milofsky, 42–76. New York: Oxford University Press.
Okasha, S. 2006. *Evolution and Levels of Selection*. Oxford: Oxford University Press.
Olzak, S. 1992. *The Dynamics of Ethnic Competition and Conflict*. Stanford, CA: Stanford University Press.
Pinker, S. 2002. *The Blank Slate: The Modern Denial of Human Nature*. London: Allen Lane Science.
———. 2012. "The False Allure of Group Selection." Edge.org, http://edge.org/conversation/the-false-allure-of-group-selection.
Queller, D. C. 1992. "A General Model of Kin Selection." *Evolution* 46: 376–380.
Richerson, P. J., and R. Boyd. 2005. *Not by Genes Alone: How Culture Transformed Human Evolution*. Chicago: University of Chicago Press.
Runciman, W. G. 1989. *A Treatise on Social Theory*. Vol. 2, *Substantive Social Theory*. Cambridge: Cambridge University Press.
———. 2009. *The Theory of Cultural and Social Selection*. Cambridge: Cambridge University Press.
Sanderson, S. K. 1999. *Social Transformations: A General Theory of Historical Development*. Lanham, MD: Rowman & Littlefield Publishers.
———. 2001. *The Evolution of Human Sociality: A Darwinian Conflict Perspective*. Lanham, MD: Rowman and Littlefield.
Scott, W. R. 2008. *Institutions and Organizations*. Newbury Park, CA: Sage Publications.
Skyrms, B. 1996. *Evolution of the Social Contract*. New York: Cambridge University Press.
Sober, E., and D. S. Wilson. 1998. *Unto Others: The Evolution and Psychology of Unselfish Behavior*. Cambridge, MA: Harvard University Press.
Spencer, H. (1851) 1898. *Social Statics*. New York: Appleton Century.
———. (1874–1896) 1898. *The Principles of Sociology*. 3 vols. New York: Appleton Century.
Trivers, R. L. 1971. "The Evolution of Reciprocal Altruism." *Quarterly Review of Biology* 46: 35–57.
Turner, J. H. 2002. *Face to Face: Toward a Sociological Theory of Interpersonal Behavior*. Stanford, CA: Stanford University Press.
———. 2003. *Human Institutions: A New Evolutionary Theory*. Boulder, CO: Rowman and Littlefield.
———. 2010a. *Theoretical Principles of Sociology*. Vol. 1, *Macrodynamics*. New York: Springer.
———. 2010b. *Theoretical Principles of Sociology*. Vol. 2, *Microdynamics*. New York: Springer.
———. 2013. *Theoretical Principles of Sociology*. Vol. 3, *Mesodynamics*. New York: Springer.
Turner, J. H., and A. Maryanski. 2005. *Incest: Origins of the Taboo*. Boulder, CO: Paradigm Publishers.
———. 2008. *On the Origin of Societies by Natural Selection*. Boulder, CO: Paradigm Publishers.
Wallerstein, E. 1974. *The Modern World System*. Vol. 1. New York: Academic Press.
Weingart, P., P. Richerson, S. D. Mitchell, and S. Maasen. 1997. *Human by Nature: Between Biology and the Social Sciences*. Mahwah, NJ: Erlbaum.
Williams, G. C. 1966. *Adaptation and Natural Selection: A Critique of Some Evolutionary Thought*. Princeton, NJ: Princeton University Press.
Wilson, D. S. 1975. "A Theory of Group Selection." *Proceedings of the National Academy of Sciences* 72: 143–146.
———. 2002. *Darwin's Cathedral: Evolution, Religion, and the Nature of Society*. Chicago: University of Chicago Press.
Wilson, D. S., and E. O. Wilson. 2007. "Rethinking the Theoretical Foundations of Sociobiology." *Quarterly Review of Biology* 82: 327–348.
Wilson, E. O. 1998. *Consilience: The Unity of Knowledge*. London: Little, Brown.
———. 2012. *The Conquest of Earth*. New York: W. W. Norton.

Two
Sociobiology and Evolutionary Psychology

Chapter Six
Yanomamö: The Sociobiology People
Napoleon A. Chagnon and Shane J. Macfarlan

> The subject of cultural anthropology underwent a number of significant changes beginning in the early 1960s. Some of these resulted from breakthroughs in the science of biology, with the development of inclusive fitness theory by William Hamilton (1964a, 1964b), the focus on individuals as the unit of selection by George Williams (1966), the development of an overall theory of life histories by Richard Alexander (1979), and others. This was coupled with the general admission by anthropologists and other social scientists that the behavior of *Homo sapiens* made more sense when they were viewed as just another species when scientists from different fields collaborated in explanations of their behavior. Apart from the remarkable changes in science during this period, it was a period of radical political change in the United States and Western Europe. These political changes, especially the role that the United States and its allies played in the Vietnam War, had marked negative effects on the social sciences such as anthropology, sociology, and political science in the United States.
>
> The lead author began his training in cultural anthropology during this period and was attempting to integrate cultural anthropology more effectively with Darwinian evolutionary theory, as distinct from a cultural evolutionary theory that harked back to and reflected more the thinking of social and political theorists like Émile Durkheim, Herbert Spencer, and Karl Marx. This chapter documents some of the obstacles that seemed to impede the integration of social anthropology with Darwinian evolutionism, an integration that now continues at an increasingly rapid pace.

A major point I[1] want to make is that my long-term field research on the Yanomamö (1964–1997) came at a time when Darwinian and biological views of human social behavior were not only discouraged in the field of cultural anthropology but often greeted with disapproval, sarcasm, and even scorn by senior members of cultural anthropology programs. For example, on learning from my early publications that the Yanomamö fought a great deal over women, a very prominent anthropologist then at the University of Chicago, David Schneider, exclaimed in a letter to me: "Women? Gold and diamonds I can understand, but women? Never!" Another prominent anthropologist at Columbia University, Marvin Harris, told me he interrupted the publication of his influential book, *The Rise of Anthropological Theory*, in order to make a comment on my recent PhD dissertation (Chagnon 1966) as it pertained to the nineteenth-century ethnologist and lawyer

John McLennan's ([1865] 1970) theory of "marriage by capture," with the comment that my dissertation lent "new dignity to [his] more lurid speculations" (Harris 1968: 197).

Yet my widely popular ethnographic monograph, originally published as *Yanomamö: The Fierce People* (1968),[2] was enthusiastically used in large courses in cultural anthropology in most major US universities and in a number of universities in Europe. Though it is now in its sixth revised edition (Chagnon 2012), it is probably the best known and most widely used ethnographic monograph in the history of modern American anthropology, eventually eclipsing Margaret Mead's *Coming of Age in Samoa* (1928).

In the fourth edition (Chagnon 1992), I dropped the subtitle, *The Fierce People*, because I began receiving complaints from cultural anthropologists who claimed they had used the first three editions but might not assign a new edition to their students because the subtitle suggested to them that I had *deliberately* chosen a derogatory phrase that demeaned the Yanomamö and knowingly suggested that they were cruel, barbaric, bloodthirsty, and brutish. Never mind that the Yanomamö themselves would explain to me "Yanomamö täbä waiteri" whenever I asked them why particular men had been killed by raiders as I constructed their group's recent history, fissions, conflicts, and settlement patterns with Yanomamö informants. This Yanomamö phrase translates into English as "Human beings are fierce" because, in their eyes, all humans are ultimately Yanomamö. Latin American anthropologists were especially concerned about my subtitle because their own languages were Romance languages—Spanish, Portuguese, and in a few cases foreign French researchers—and they seem to have chosen the most derogatory meaning of the English word "fierce" when in fact a more appropriate translation would have been "human beings fight valiantly" as in "when our troops were overrun by German troops in the Ardennes they fought valiantly and repelled them." In Spanish, for example, the word *fierra* is a more appropriate translation of the Yanomamö word *waiteri* in the Yanomamö phrase "Yanomamö täbä waiteri," and most of these anthropologists were aware of this more innocent meaning. I had to conclude that they were making a politically correct complaint, possibly motivated by academic jealousy, but my ongoing field research depended in large measure on keeping on good terms with my Venezuelan (and Brazilian) colleagues, so I dropped the original subtitle in the fourth edition.

While my empirical field research interests fell squarely within the traditional subjects of cultural anthropology—topics like kinship organization, alliances based on marriage exchanges between exogamic lineages, feasting, myths, cosmology, political relationships between different and often antagonistic groups—my theoretical interests, by contrast, were affected by my interest in Darwin's theory of evolution by natural selection and how some of the major questions in the history of anthropology could possibly be resolved using more of the tools that were used in the life sciences. For example, understanding kinship systems and kinship organization was so overwhelmingly *the central issue* in the history of anthropology that Elman Service (1985), one of my professors at the University of Michigan, ended his publishing career with a book entitled *A Century of Controversy: Ethnological Issues from 1860 to 1960*. This "century of controversies" revolved around what anthropologists thought about kinship and what it meant in human societies. The general view was, surprisingly, that "whatever kinship is about, it is *not* about biology." Apparently nothing has changed among some prominent anthropologists: in 2012, Marshall Sahlins presented a paper at the annual meetings of the American Anthropological Association entitled "What Kinship Is Not—Biology."[3] But nearly all sensible American cultural anthropologists agreed that kinship organization in human societies had been important in the evolution of culture from the time when hunters and gatherers dominated the world in the Paleolithic era until political states and more elaborate sociopolitical groups like nations and empires emerged. By the middle of the nineteenth century the remaining tribal peoples of the world lived in marginal areas, remote places that were often inhospitable, and generally in regions that were unwanted by people who lived in the industrialized world. By then anthropologists had to go to more remote and hard-to-reach parts of the world in order to study and understand what these great mysteries were about. I was fortunate enough in the middle of the twentieth century to have found one of the last tribes that still retained many of the characteristics of that vanishing world and optimistically believed I could possibly solve some of the "controversies" that Service (1985) discussed in his book by attempting, for example, to quantify variables like kinship relationships between known relatives.

Cultural anthropologists generally agreed that kinship was a central organizing principle in the tribal world and that close kinship was important because anthropologists usually found that tribesmen generally regarded close kin as more reliable and trustworthy than distant kin or non-kin and tended to favor them. Nevertheless, I was astonished that anthropologists never really came up with a procedure to discuss "closeness" and "remoteness" of kinship in a quantitative way, relying instead on anecdotes and the authority of their teachers and mentors.

But by the 1920s, there were well-known ways to measure and quantify kinship relatedness and ways to quantitatively describe and more precisely express how two organisms were genealogically related to each other and demonstrate that they were or were not more closely related than some other pair of genealogically related individuals. This procedure was established by the statistical mathematician and theoretical geneticist, Sewall Wright (1922).

But there was another struggle occurring in the early development of both anthropology and sociology, one that generally impeded the use of certain kinds of quantitative approaches and, thus, the integration of these two social sciences with a Darwinian view of human behavior.

That struggle was being waged by the prominent nineteenth-century French sociologist Émile Durkheim, who was attempting to establish a whole new social science called *sociology*, which was then intimately embedded within the discipline of social psychology. Durkheim's ([1895] 1938) basic argument was that there were certain "facts" regarding human behavior that were purely "social" and could be examined in their own right without reference to biology or how the mind allegedly worked (i.e., social facts had an existence independent of the mind and of human psychology). They deserved to have a special science dedicated to their study. His position, sometimes referred to as Durkheim's dictum, was that "anytime a *social fact* is reduced to and explained in terms of a psychological fact you can be certain the explanation is false" (Durkheim [1895] 1938: 129).

Most anthropologists and sociologists acknowledge Durkheim as one of the important academic founders of *their respective disciplines*. Indeed, a nearly identical struggle occurred in anthropology through the history of the social and cultural interests of Herbert Spencer, Edward Burnett Tylor, and Leslie White, the latter having been one of my professors at the University of Michigan, a man whose theoretical arguments influenced my own early views. White, like Durkheim, wanted to establish a *science of culture* that, like Durkheim's sociology, would be independent of not only psychology but also biology. White (1949) suggested "culturology" for this science. In his view, there were "cultural facts" that were irreducible, just as Durkheim argued for his irreducible "social facts." And this suggested to them that a science of social facts or cultural facts warranted the independent academic disciplines of "culturology" and "sociology." Durkheim's sociology was ultimately established as a field independent of social psychology. White's culturology simply continued in the Americas with the original name—cultural anthropology.

In my attempts to make at least some portion of cultural anthropology more "scientific" than what it appeared to me to be, my first field research trip to the Yanomamö (1964–1966) focused on marriage alliances, kinship, and descent from common ancestors. For the first seventeen months I busied myself collecting genealogies and making detailed censuses of the villages I visited, which, I soon discovered, were "descended" historically from the same earlier population that simply subdivided into smaller groups because of fights that generally occurred over the possession of women. Over time and with population growth, they would again become large and again fission into smaller groups. I also discovered that nearby Yanomamö populations had followed the same pattern of growth and fissioning and the several existing adjacent villages had a different historical origin but arose by this same process.

By then I had discovered the usefulness of Sewall Wright's work on how geneticists and animal breeders used his coefficients of inbreeding and relatedness to keep track of closeness and remoteness of related individuals—the historic anthropological problem Service's book focused on and one I thought I might solve portions of.

I initially zeroed in on a then prominent anthropological debate over kinship and descent and how each contributed to what French and British sociologists and anthropologists referred to as "social solidarity," a kind of mysterious "social glue" that held societies together. I also discovered in this essentially European-based debate that some of the participants (especially the British-trained social anthropologist Meyer Fortes [1969]), unlike their American counterparts, were in principle willing to view kinship relationships in the tribes they studied as in fact having something to do with the biological and genetic meaning of human kinship. The Yanomamö were a nearly perfect ethnographic example in this debate because their villages "fissioned" after they got too large for kinship, descent, and marriage ties to hold them together whenever within-group fighting over "resources" (members of the opposite sex—women) increased.[4] However, in the "Alliance versus Descent" debate, Fortes argued that the "social glue" provided by *closeness of kinship ties* is what held groups together, as contrasted with the majority of other social anthropologists who argued that "descent" from lineage founders provided this glue because wealth and material resources needed to acquire mates tended to be passed through lines of descent and that *lineages*, therefore, were the most important social element in tribal politics. Indeed, the view of the day was that the "domain of politics" was the responsibility of lineages, whereas the "domain of the household and domestic life" was the responsibility of the "kinship" organization.

For me, it was a relief to be able to discuss human kinship in biological terms without being challenged or castigated by my anthropological peers for "violating" Durkheim's dictum.

By the mid-1970s I was reading more works in ecology, ethology, genetics, and theoretical biology—things that most cultural anthropologists would not normally read.

One reason I began reading things in these areas came from my empirical findings on family size. I discovered that some Yanomamö men, because they had so many wives, sired very large families, and this was clearly related to their individual ability to influence the public policies of their group. This biological fact—that a man with five wives could produce more offspring than a woman with five husbands—also explained, in my opinion, why patrilineal descent was more common in the ethnographic record than matrilineal descent. Thus, the variation in reproductive success among males was very large, which was also—and largely the reason—why the incidence of marriage with cross-cousins was so high in some groups.[5] This also appeared to be the reason why villages founded by Shinbone's descendants managed to sustain larger villages (i.e., did not fission as frequently as other villages did, villages in which the incidence of cross-cousin marriage was lower).

High frequencies of cross-cousin marriage seemed to be the mysterious glue that held groups together. It also turned out that larger villages were able to take advantage of smaller villages and forcibly take nubile females away from smaller villages by coercion or by threat of attacks.

In 1975, E. O. Wilson published *Sociobiology: The New Synthesis*, a book that provoked an astonishing and mostly hostile reaction in the social sciences and among a small handful of Marxist but prominent biologists, including Richard Lewontin and Stephen J. Gould, both of whom were Wilson's departmental colleagues at Harvard University. The previous and mostly intermittent skepticism and denigration of biological and psychological "explanations" for social and cultural facts within anthropology came fully into the open as anthropologists took often extreme and antagonistic positions in the ensuing debates.

By then enough of my publications had appeared that were both tolerant of, if not sympathetic to, what Lionel Tiger and Robin Fox (1966) referred to as "the zoological perspective" in social science that I was now considered to be a "member" of what Wilson (1975) defined as the new field of sociobiology. I defended and expanded my pro-biology position in subsequent publications.

THE PARADIGM SHIFT IN THE SOCIAL SCIENCES AND THE GROWTH OF DARWINIAN SOCIAL SCIENCE

I was always uneasy about dropping the original subtitle of my Yanomamö monograph because I felt that I had made a concession to political correctness and to what Paul Gross and Norman Levitt (1997) called the "academic left" (see also Gross 2001). Were I to make that decision today, I would simply change the subtitle such that my widely read ethnographic monograph would be called *Yanomamö: The Sociobiological People*. My argument would be that by 1992, when the fourth edition of Yanomamö appeared, my research and publications were already being discussed by prominent evolutionary biologists and becoming part of the emerging new direction in evolutionary studies of the tribesmen that cultural anthropologists traditionally studied (see Alexander [1979] and Lumsden and Wilson [1981, 1983] for prominent examples).

It would be pretentious to suggest that my Yanomamö field research and publications were the only stimulus in setting into motion new and important threads in the emergence of a more Darwinian cultural anthropology that the growing numbers of "traditional" tribal societies now studied by evolution-minded cultural anthropologists have done during the past twenty or more years. But, I do believe that my research efforts have stimulated the kinds of work many younger researchers now routinely do in several branches of a Darwinian social science and with increasingly sophisticated methods and tools.

With respect to my possible broader impacts on the field of Darwinian and scientific anthropology, researchers routinely now employ the mathematically precise concept of kinship I helped reestablish in anthropology (Chagnon 1975a, 1975b), via Sewall Wright (1922) and W. D. Hamilton (1964a, 1964b), to examine topics as disparate as the evolutionary ecology of cooperation (e.g., Alvard 2003, 2009, 2011; Gurven 2004; Hames and McCabe 2007; Macfarlan and Quinlan 2008; Macfarlan, Remiker, and Quinlan 2012; Macfarlan et al. 2014; Nolin 2010, 2011; Patton 2005; Wiessner 2002; Ziker and Schnegg 2005), demography, health, mating, and reproduction (e.g., Anderson 2005; Quinlan

2001; Quinlan and Flinn 2005; Quinlan and Hagen 2006; Shenk 2004, 2005), and group structure and composition (e.g., Hill et al. 2011; Walker et al. 2013), to name a few. It should be noted that this body of research has not demonstrated that human social behavior is structured by simple genetic relatedness. Rather, this body of research has employed the concept of genetic relatedness in conjunction with a variety of other evolutionarily viable mechanisms to assess quantitatively which, if any, are responsible for explaining variation in human sociality. However, without the firm footing provided by a mathematically precise definition of kinship, such tests of hypothetical mechanisms are unthinkable (and among those anthropologists who eschew or reject this paradigm, such tests are not even possible).

Furthermore, my efforts at promoting an anthropology that was both scientifically rigorous and parsimonious with respect to evolutionary biology spurred the growth of evolutionary anthropology itself. Researchers working within this tradition (many of whom were trained by me directly and many have been trained by those I trained) have created their own section within the American Anthropological Association (i.e., the Evolutionary Anthropology Society), have joined forces with researchers from allied social sciences to create a variety of professional societies inspired by Darwinian evolution (e.g., Human Behavior and Evolution Society, European Human Behavior and Evolution Association), and maintain and publish research in a number of journals that focus on the interface between evolutionary theory and human behavior and cognition (e.g., *Evolutionary Anthropology: Issues, News, and Reviews*; *Evolutionary Psychology*). Two academic journals in particular have a close relationship to the paradigm I helped to establish within the field of anthropology: *Human Nature—An Interdisciplinary and Biosocial Perspective* and *Evolution and Human Behavior*. It's reassuring to know that these journals are themselves high ranking with respect to their own disciplines. According to the 2012 ISI Journal Citation Reports, *Human Nature* ranks 15th out of 83 anthropology journals, and *Evolution and Human Behavior* ranks 39th out of 559 psychology journals (Thomson-Reuters 2014), based on their impact factor (the average number of times that articles from the journal that were published in the two years prior to 2012 have been cited). Indeed, evolutionary anthropology is a healthy subdiscipline of the larger Darwinian enterprise, and I am proud to have had a hand in making this happen along with the many others whose similar work has led to this end.

Lastly, my work among the Yanomamö continues to act as a reference point for discussing social life in pre-state, tribal-level society in general, and humanity writ large. Citations of my research contained in two major evolutionary psychology texts (Buss 2004, 2005) indicate that the Yanomamö have been used to elucidate the nature of human mate preferences, physical attractiveness, and variance in reproductive success; coalition formation, aggression, and warfare; and social status and intra-sexual competition. Furthermore, of the 508 articles published in the journal *Human Nature* from 1990 to 2014, 107 make reference to my Yanomamö research.

I would like to end this chapter with a question that my lifelong friend, colleague, and evolutionist Bill Irons put to me in 2009:

> When you and I were at Penn State and we were both becoming visible as enthusiasts for sociobiology, an influential senior member of the Penn State Department told me that we (you and I) could not win if we continued to pursue sociobiology. If we did this, we would have "both the crowd and the authority figures against us" and with this sort of opposition we could not win. Neither of us heeded this advice, and we did take many hits from both authority figures and crowds over the next thirty plus years. Did we win?

To this question I responded:

> Some of us who stood up for sociobiology paid a substantial price, but the costs inflicted on us allowed others to continue to expand their research goals with less opposition to their work, nudging the study of man back toward the standard scientific methods we all should defend. Did we win? Some of us certainly did. For others like me the victory was Pyrrhic.[6]

Notes

1. The first author will speak in the first person throughout this chapter for reasons of literary intelligibility.
2. The number of citations to this work outnumbers all other citations to my work by a very wide margin.
3. Elman Service left the University of Michigan because Sahlins and other concerned faculty members not only protested the war in Vietnam but began favoring graduate students in anthropology on the basis of their participation in public protests against the United States' involvement in the war.
4. This was also a chronic problem in the evolution of political systems and theories of the origin of the state.
5. See Chagnon's (2013: 330) discussion of the figure described as "all descendants of 'Shinbone' (EGO 1221) . . ." that explains how a highly successful lineage founder can initiate a genealogical structure that makes cross-cousin marriage by his descendants very likely.
6. The price some of us paid is discussed in the last three chapters of my recent book, *Noble Savages: My Life among Two Dangerous Tribes—The Yanomamö and the Anthropologists*.

References

Alexander, R. D. 1979. *Darwinism & Human Affairs*. Seattle: University of Washington Press.
Alvard, M. 2003. "Kinship, Lineage, and an Evolutionary Perspective on Cooperative Hunting Groups in Indonesia." *Human Nature* 14 (2): 129–163.
———. 2009. "Kinship and Cooperation." *Human Nature* 20 (4): 394–416.
———. 2011. "Genetic and Cultural Kinship among the Lamaleran Whale Hunters." *Human Nature* 22 (1–2): 89–107.
Anderson, K. G. 2005. "Relatedness and Investment in Children in South Africa." *Human Nature* 16 (1): 1–31.
Buss, D. M. 2004. *Evolutionary Psychology: The New Science of the Mind*. 2nd ed. Boston: Pearson.
———, ed. 2005. *The Handbook of Evolutionary Psychology*. Hoboken, NJ: John Wiley & Sons.
Chagnon, N. 1966. "Yanomamö Warfare, Social Organization and Marriage Alliances." PhD diss., Department of Anthropology, University of Michigan.
———. 1968. *Yanomamö: The Fierce People*. New York: Holt, Rinehart and Winston.
———. 1975a. *Studying the Yanomamö*. Studies in Anthropological Method. New York: Holt, Rinehart and Winston.
———. 1975b. "Genealogy, Solidarity, and Relatedness: Limits to Local Group Size and Patterns of Fissioning in an Expanding Population." *Yearbook of Physical Anthropology* 19: 95–110.
———. 1992. *Yanomamö*. 4th ed. New York: Harcourt Brace, Jovanovich, College Publishers.
———. 2012. *Yanomamö*. 6th ed. Belmont, CA: Wadsworth Cengage.
———. 2013. *Noble Savages: My Life among Two Dangerous Tribes—The Yanomamö and the Anthropologists*. New York: Simon and Schuster.
Durkheim, É. (1895) 1938. *The Rules of the Sociological Method*. Translated by S. Soloway and J. Mueller. New York: Free Press.
Fortes, M. R. 1969. *Kinship and the Social Order: The Legacy of Lewis Henry Morgan*. Chicago: Aldine Publishing Company.
Gross, P. 2001. "Exorcising Sociobiology." *New Criterion* 19: 24.
Gross, P., and N. Levitt. 1997. *Higher Superstition: The Academic Left and Its Quarrels with Science*. Baltimore: Johns Hopkins University Press.

Gurven, M. 2004. "To Give or Not to Give: The Behavioral Ecology of Food Transfers." *Behavioral and Brain Sciences* 27 (4): 453–559.
Hames, R., and C. McCabe. 2007. "Meal Sharing among the Ye'kwana." *Human Nature* 18 (1): 1–21.
Hamilton, W. D. 1964a. "The Genetical Evolution of Social Behaviour. I." *Journal of Theoretical Biology* 7 (1): 1–16.
———. 1964b. "The Genetical Evolution of Social Behaviour. II." *Journal of Theoretical Biology* 7 (1): 17–52.
Harris, M. 1968. *The Rise of Anthropological Theory*. New York: Thomas Y. Crowell.
Hill, K. R., R. S. Walker, M. Bozicevic, J. Eder, T. Headland, B. Hewlett, A. M. Hurtado, F. Marlowe, P. Wiessner, and B. Wood. 2011. "Co-Residence Patterns in Hunter-Gatherer Societies Show a Unique Human Social Structure." *Science* 331 (6022): 1286–1289.
Lumsden, C. J., and E. O. Wilson. 1981. *Genes, Mind and Culture*. Cambridge, MA: Harvard University Press.
———. 1983. *Promethean Fire*. Cambridge, MA: Harvard University Press.
Macfarlan, S. J., and R. Quinlan. 2008. "Kinship, Family, and Gender Effects in the Ultimatum Game." *Human Nature* 19: 294–309.
Macfarlan, S. J., M. Remiker, and R. J. Quinlan. 2012. "Competitive Altruism Explains Labor Exchange Variation in a Dominican Village." *Current Anthropology* 35 (1): 118–124.
Macfarlan, S. J., R. S. Walker, M. V. Flinn, and N. A. Chagnon. 2014. "Lethal Coalitionary Aggression and Long-Term Alliance Formation among Yanomamö Men." *Proceedings of the National Academy of Sciences of the USA*. doi:10.1073/pnas.1418639111.
McLennan, J. F. (1865) 1970. *Primitive Marriage: An Inquiry into the Origin of the Form of Capture in Marriage Ceremonies*. Chicago: University of Chicago Press.
Mead, M. 1928. *Coming of Age in Samoa*. New York: Morrow.
Nolin, D. 2010. "Food Sharing Networks in Lamalera, Indonesia." *Human Nature* 21 (3): 243–268.
———. 2011. "Kin Preference and Partner Choice." *Human Nature* 22 (1–2): 156–176.
Patton, J. Q. 2005. "Meat Sharing for Coalitional Support." *Evolution and Human Behavior* 26 (2): 137–157.
Quinlan, R. J. 2001. "Effect of Household Structure on Female Reproductive Strategies in a Caribbean Village." *Human Nature* 12 (3): 169–189.
Quinlan, R. J., and M. V. Flinn. 2005. "Kinship, Sex, and Fitness in a Caribbean Community." *Human Nature* 16 (1): 32–57.
Quinlan, R. J., and E. H. Hagen. 2006. "New Genealogy: It's Not Just for Kinship Anymore." *Field Methods* 20 (2): 129–154.
Sahlins, M. D. 2012. "What Kinship Is Not—Biology." American Anthropological Association Annual Meeting. Montreal, Canada.
Service, E. R. 1985. *A Century of Controversy: Ethnological Issues from 1860 to 1960*. New York: Academic Press.
Shenk, M. K. 2004. "Embodied Capital and Heritable Wealth in Complex Cultures: A Class-Based Analysis of Parental Investment in Urban South India." *Research in Economic Anthropology* 23: 307–333.
———. 2005. "Kin Networks in Wage-Labor Economies: Effects on Child and Marriage Market Outcomes." *Human Nature* 16: 81–114.
Thomson-Reuters. 2014. "2012 Journal Citation Reports Social Sciences Edition." Accessed March 1, 2014. http://about.jcr.incites.thomsonreuters.com.
Tiger, L., and R. Fox. 1966. "The Zoological Perspective in Social Science." *Man* 1: 75–81.
Walker, R. S., S. Beckerman, M. V. Flinn, M. Gurven, C. R. Von Rueden, K. L. Kramer, R. D. Greaves, L. Córdoba, D. Villar, E. H. Hagen, J. M. Koster, L. Sugiyama, T. E. Hunter, and K. R. Hill. 2013. "Living with Kin in Lowland Horticultural Societies." *Current Anthropology* 54 (1): 96–103.
White, L. A. 1949. *The Science of Culture*. New York: Grove Press.
Wiessner, P. 2002. "Hunting, Healing, and *hxaro* Exchange: A Long-Term Perspective on !Kung (Ju/'hoansi) Large Game Hunting." *Evolution and Human Behavior* 23 (6): 407–436.
Williams, G. C. 1966. *Adaptation and Natural Selection*. Oxford: Oxford University Press.
Wilson, E. O. 1975. *Sociobiology: The New Synthesis*. Cambridge, MA: Harvard University Press.
Wright, S. 1922. "Coefficients of Inbreeding and Relationship." *American Naturalist* 56: 330–338.
Ziker, J., and M. Schnegg. 2005. "Food Sharing at Meals." *Human Nature* 16 (2): 178–210.

Chapter Seven
Sociobiology at Work in Modern Populations

Rosemary L. Hopcroft

> Sociobiology predicts that high-status, dominant individuals will outreproduce low-status individuals in a population. This prediction has been seemingly contradicted in modern societies, where women in high-income households have fewer children than women in low-income households. Yet if status is measured as personal income, in the United States and a variety of European countries there is a great deal of evidence that high-status males outreproduce low-status males (while the reverse is true for women). In this chapter, I show how these findings are consistent with trends in preindustrial societies. I further review studies of modern societies that support another important sociobiological prediction as given by the Trivers-Willard hypothesis. I suggest that all these results are evidence that sociobiology (and associated evolutionary psychology) are relevant to modern populations.

It has been over two decades since Vining (1986) claimed that data on fertility differentials and the lack of a positive relationship between family socioeconomic status and fertility meant that sociobiology was no longer relevant to populations in advanced industrial societies such as the contemporary United States. More recently he has noted that every year US census data show that women in higher-income households have fewer children than women in lower-income households (Vining 2011; see also Dye 2008). Vining (2011: 366) concludes that "humans in modern societies have stumbled, as they so often do in human history . . . into a situation, i.e., urban civilization, that is self-defeating sociobiologically."

In this chapter, I argue that Vining's conclusion is overstated, and I make the case that sociobiology and its offshoot evolutionary psychology are relevant to modern populations. I begin by noting that in preindustrial societies there is clear evidence of the link between socioeconomic status and offspring for men, while there is evidence of the reverse for women. I also discuss the demographic transition and the fertility decline of the last century or so and its implications for sociobiology. Then I review the recent evidence that shows that in modern societies in Europe and elsewhere men turn some forms of status into offspring, and I describe how this evidence fits with the trends observed in preindustrial societies. Finally, I discuss the evidence for another sociobiological prediction—the Trivers-Willard effect—in modern populations. I argue that these results, contra Vining (1986, 2011), argue for the relevance of both sociobiology and evolutionary psychology in the modern world.

The Relationship between Status and Fitness in Preindustrial Societies

The link between status and reproductive success among humans in preindustrial societies is clear for men (see Table 7.1). In foraging (hunting and gathering, fishing) societies, high-status men often have a few more children than lower-status men. As production intensifies in horticultural and agrarian societies, the difference in reproductive success between high-status men and low-status men increases such that high-status men often have many more children than low-status men. In addition, some men have many more children than the average woman. Particularly in large, complex, stratified agrarian societies, the very highest status men often have thousands of children. Betzig (1986) has chronicled the reproductive feats of emperors, sultans, and other absolute rulers throughout history. In a recent review of all available data, Betzig (2012) shows that ranges and variances of reproductive status are slightly higher for men than women in hunting and gathering societies, but the sex difference increases in more sedentary societies.

The link between status and reproductive success is less clear for women in preindustrial societies and is often reversed. In many societies, elite women are cloistered to protect their value on the marriage market, a market in which they face great competition from lower-status women given hypergynous marriage systems (Dickemann 1979). In such societies some elite women never marry. In preindustrial Europe, many daughters of elite families were sent to convents. In one analysis of the medieval Portuguese elites, by the sixteenth century, approximately 35 percent of noblewomen who reached early adulthood were placed in convents (Boone 1986). As a result, the men in the highest Portuguese nobility outreproduced the women. In China and India, the reproductive success of elite women was curtailed by female infanticide among elites, non-remarriage of widows, and widow suicide (Dickemann 1979). In India, two elite clans—the Jhareja Rajuts and the Bedi Sikhs—went so far as to kill all their daughters at birth, thus effectively bringing female fertility in these high-status clans to zero. Lower-status groups killed only later-born daughters (Hrdy 1999: 326). In Japan, widow remarriage was uncommon among elites, and elite women often entered nunneries (Dickemann 1979). It is probably not a coincidence that the woman who has the distinction of being in the Guinness Book of Records (2013) for having the most children was a peasant woman, not an elite woman.

The Demographic Transition

All preindustrial societies fit the typical pattern of being high-mortality (both infant and adult) and high-fertility societies. Starting in about 1650 in Europe, mortality rates began to fall. Then, by the nineteenth century and at varying times and rates across European countries, fertility rates also began to fall. The dramatic fall in fertility rates did not occur until the twentieth century in the United States. Crude birth rates (the number of births per thousand population per year) in the United States fell from about 30 in 1909 to around 14 today.

For Vining (2011) and other scholars, the demographic transition appears to defy the logic of sociobiology. He writes, "Sociobiology predicts that humans would raise their birth rates when they get richer" (Vining 2011: 364). Yet over the last century or so, as people grew richer in absolute terms, the number of children they had fell. It is a pattern that has been repeated in country after country around the world, notably in East Asia in

Table 7.1 Studies showing a positive relationship between male status and number of surviving offspring

Society	Status measure	Reference(s)
Aché of Paraguay	Hunting ability	Kaplan and Hill 1985; Hill and Hurtado 1996
Aka-Mormons	Political status	Walker and Hewlett 1990
Aka of the Central African Republic	Political status	Hewlett 1988; Walker and Hewlett 1990
Bakkarwal of India	Prestige, wealth	Casimir and Rao 1995
Caribbean farmers	Land ownership	Flinn 1986
Dogon of Mali	Land ownership, income	Strassman 1997
Efe of Zaire	Wealth	Bailey 1991
Gabbra of Kenya	Wealth	Mace 1996a, 1996b
Medieval Europeans	Wealth, power	Betzig 1992, 1993, 1995
Ifaluk	Wealth	Turke and Betzig 1985; Betzig 1988
Kipsigis of Kenya	Land ownership	Borgerhoff Mulder 1987, 1988, 1990, 1995, 2000
Krümmhorn farmers of the eighteenth and nineteenth centuries	Land ownership	Voland 1988, 1990; Voland and Dunbar 1995
!Kung of the Kalahari	Social status	Pennington and Harpending 1993
Lancashire farmers of the eighteenth century	Occupational status	Hughes 1986
Mormons of Utah	Wealth, religious rank	Faux and Miller 1984; Mealey 1985
Mukogodu of Kenya	Wealth, social status	Cronk 1991
Norwegian farmers of the eighteenth to twentieth centuries	Age, wealth	Røskaft, Wara, and Viken 1992
Portuguese elites of the sixteenth to eighteenth centuries	Land ownership	Boone 1986
Qing China	Rank in nobility	Lee and Campbell 1997; Lee, Campbell, and Wang 1993; Wang, Lee, and Campbell 1995
Ancient Romans	Wealth, power	Betzig 1992
Swedish farmers of the nineteenth century	Occupational status, land ownership	Low 1991; Low and Clark 1992
Yanomamö	Political status	Chagnon 1979, 1980, 1988
Yomut Turkmen of Iran	Wealth	Irons 1979, 1980

the years following World War II. Indeed, most countries of the world today are seeing both rising incomes and falling fertility rates, with the exception of some parts of Africa and Asia. Today below-replacement fertility is reported in some countries in Europe as well as in Japan. Overwhelmingly, it appears that people are choosing higher standards of living over more offspring.

But does sociobiology predict that humans will raise their birthrates as they get richer? It is true that sociobiology predicts that dominant, high-status individuals will outreproduce less dominant, lower-status individuals. But sociobiology also predicts that individuals adjust their behavior to their environment. Evolutionary scholars have argued that the demographic transition and fertility decline are a response to the radical environmental change from a rural, agriculture preindustrial environment to a modern, urban, industrial environment. They suggest that the conditions of industrializing societies have created increasing trade-offs between the quality and the quantity of children, as well as the associated trade-offs for women between economic production and reproduction (Kaplan et al. 2002; Lawson and Mace 2010). Children in industrial societies have to be educated in order to be successful in the labor market, and this is an expensive and time-consuming undertaking that takes away from other productive pursuits. The demographer John Caldwell (1976, 2005) has explained it as a change in the role of children—children have gone from being productive assets to being economic liabilities. This can help explain why people began to have fewer and fewer children as societies industrialized. There is evidence that fertility declines when opportunities in the wage economy grow (Rosenzweig 1990). Other factors that have been noted are the growing opportunity costs for mothers, who have to trade off work and education opportunities for fertility opportunities; a decline in contact with kin and the social supports that kin supply (Newson et al. 2005); and cultural changes favoring small families (Richerson and Boyd 2005).

Fertility in Modern Societies

It does seem difficult to reconcile the aggregate evidence of below-replacement fertility in some countries (along with shrinking populations) with an adaptive argument. It is important to remember that it is individuals, not societies, who maximize reproductive success. So are individuals in advanced industrial societies maximizing their reproductive success? I argue here that they are, but conditions are such in modern societies to severely curtail individual fertility.

The environment of modern societies clearly deters fertility among women. Women in the contemporary United States who are aged 40–44 and have likely completed childbearing have about two children, and this varies little by class, region, or ethnic group (Dye 2008). Women in other advanced industrial societies have even fewer children. The total fertility rate, an estimate of the total number of children a woman would have if her fertility was typical of all women in her society, in Japan and Germany is currently 1.4, as compared with 2.1 in the United States (US Census Bureau 2013). Consistent with sociobiology, the variance on fertility for women is low. Lower-class women tend to have more children than higher-class women, but the magnitude of the difference is small. For example, in the contemporary United States women aged 40–44 in high-income households have an average of 1.8 children, versus 2.2 for the lowest-income households (Dye 2008). Currently, evidence suggests that by having fewer children, higher-class women have fewer descendants and therefore less reproductive success than lower-class women (Kaplan et al. 1995; Goodman, Koupil, and Lawson 2012).

Yet the class differential in women's fertility may not be so different from the case in pre-demographic transition societies, as we discussed above. In history, elite women have often had lower fertility than lower-class women. Further, sociobiology notes that male reproductive success is often more variable than female reproductive success. This means that the real variation in reproductive success is likely to be found with male fertility, not female fertility, and the census results described above are based on female fertility. In all societies, including modern societies, male and female fertility are not the same thing. No society has perfect monogamy, and this is certainly true of modern industrial societies that have recently seen increasing rates of single parenthood, divorce, and remarriage (Heuveline, Timberlake, and Furstenberg 2003).

In fact, a growing number of studies of modern societies in Europe and elsewhere illustrate the difference between male and female fertility and show that males (but not females) turn some forms of status into offspring. These studies use sample surveys that ask men and women about their biological children, or the population registers that are used in many Scandinavian countries. Such data sources are better sources of information about male fertility than census reports, which are usually reports of female fertility.

Given that the relevant forms of status for men vary in preindustrial societies (as seen in Table 7.1), we could expect that in the contemporary world the relevant form of status might vary across societies also. Studies show that there is some variation across developed societies in the source of status that is associated with reproductive success for men. In the United States, the source of status for men is income (Hopcroft 2006); in other countries, sources of status for men also include education and job status (Fieder and Huber 2007; Nettle and Pollet 2008; Kaptijn et al. 2010; Goodman and Koupil 2010; Lappegård and Rønsen 2013; Nisén et al. 2013). In the United States, Hopcroft (2006), using data collected by the General Social Survey in a special module fielded in 1994, shows that for men income is positively associated with number of offspring (see Figure 7.1). In Sweden, Fieder and Huber (2007) use representative data from the Total Population Register of the year 2000 to show that income and education are positively associated with offspring count for men only (see Figure 7.2). For the UK, Nettle and Pollet (2008) use data on all the babies born in Britain during the period March 3–9, 1958, and subsequently restudied over time to show that income and education are positively associated for men only (see Figure 7.3). For the Netherlands, Kaptijn et al. (2010) find evidence that for men their greater mate value, as measured by job status, is translated into greater reproductive success, as measured by

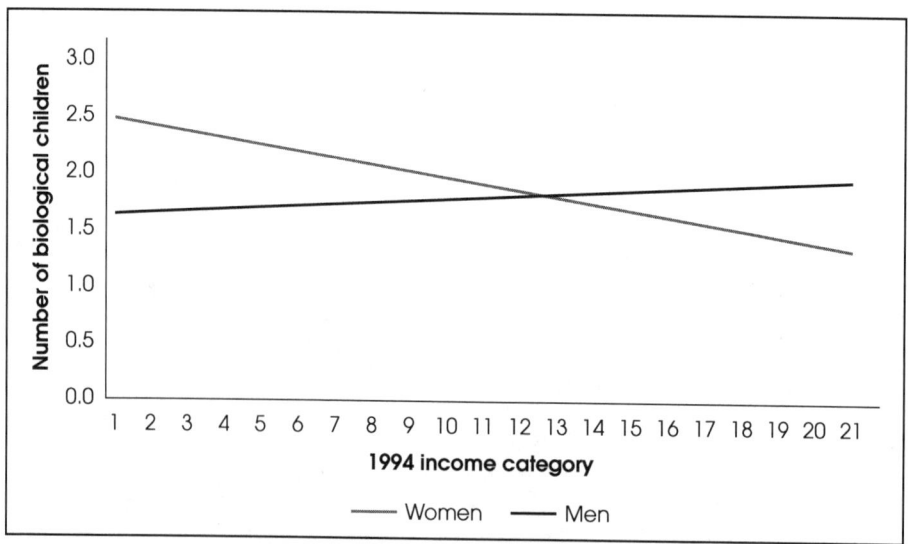

Figure 7.1 Predicted number of biological children by sex and income, United States (1994)

Source: Hopcroft (2006).

the number of grandchildren. In Norway, Lappegård and Rønsen (2013) show that men with high education and income have the highest chances of becoming fathers and are more likely to have additional children with the same partner as well as with later partners.

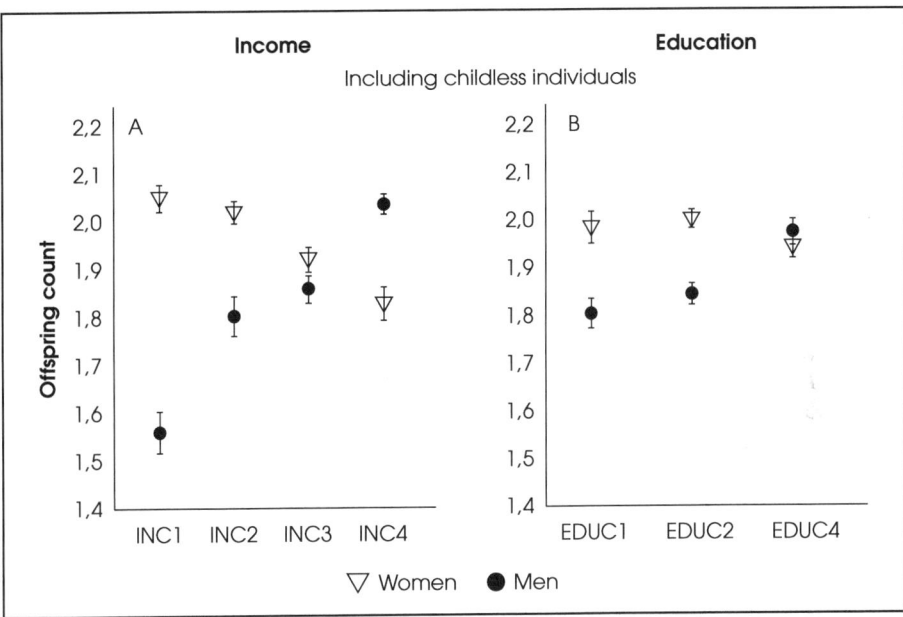

Figure 7.2 Predicted number of offspring by sex, income, and education, Sweden

Source: Representative data from the Total Population Register of the year 2000 obtained from Statistics Sweden (Fieder and Huber 2007).

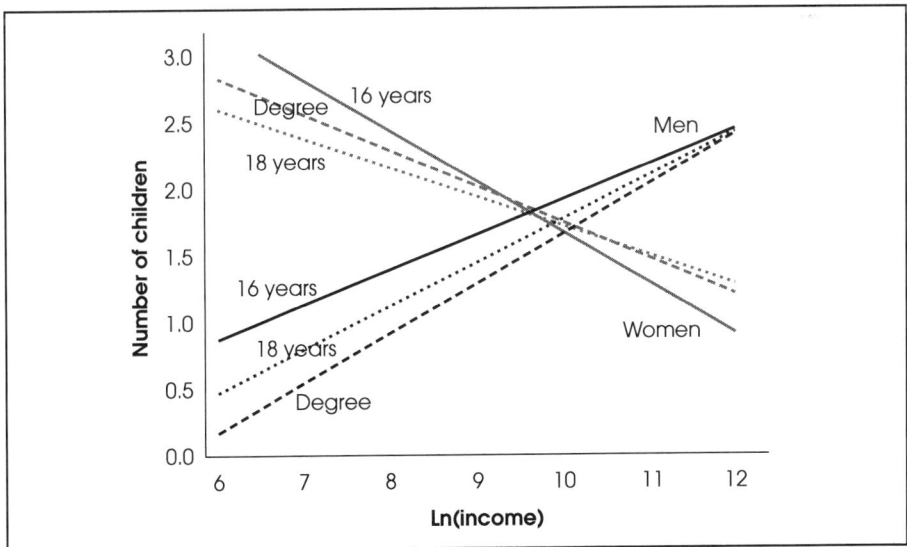

Figure 7.3 Predicted number of children by sex, education, and income, from OLS regression, United Kingdom

Source: Data from all babies born in Britain during the period March 3–9, 1958 (Nettle and Pollet 2008).

In all countries, the positive relationship for men between income and reproductive success holds within educational categories. For example, with a representative sample of modern Europeans, Barthold, Myrskylä, and Jones (2012) find a positive relationship between income and lifetime reproductive success within education categories (Figure 7.4).

Lappegård and Rønsen (2013) show evidence that part of the mechanism for the relationship between status and offspring for men in Norway is multipartner fertility by high-status men (see also Forsberg, Lindqvist, and Tullberg 1995 for Sweden; Bereczkei and Csanaky 1996 for Hungary; and Jokela et al. 2010 for the United States). However, it appears that the primary driver of the relationship between status and reproductive success for men in Europe is the greater likelihood of childlessness among low-status men (Fieder and Huber 2007; Barthold, Myrskylä, and Jones 2012; Goodman, Koupil, and Lawson 2012). In the United States, childlessness also accounts for most of the relationship between male income and number of offspring (Hopcroft, forthcoming). Goodman and Koupil (2010), using Swedish longitudinal data, find that for men only a higher family socioeconomic position is associated with a greater number of descendants.

All of these studies find that the trend is reversed for women. That is, higher education, own income, and job status decrease the number of offspring (and hence descendants) for women. This helps explain the census results showing that higher household income is associated with lower fertility for women. Women who earn a great deal themselves likely have the highest household income, given class homogamy in the United States and other similar societies, as high-income women tend to marry high-income men.

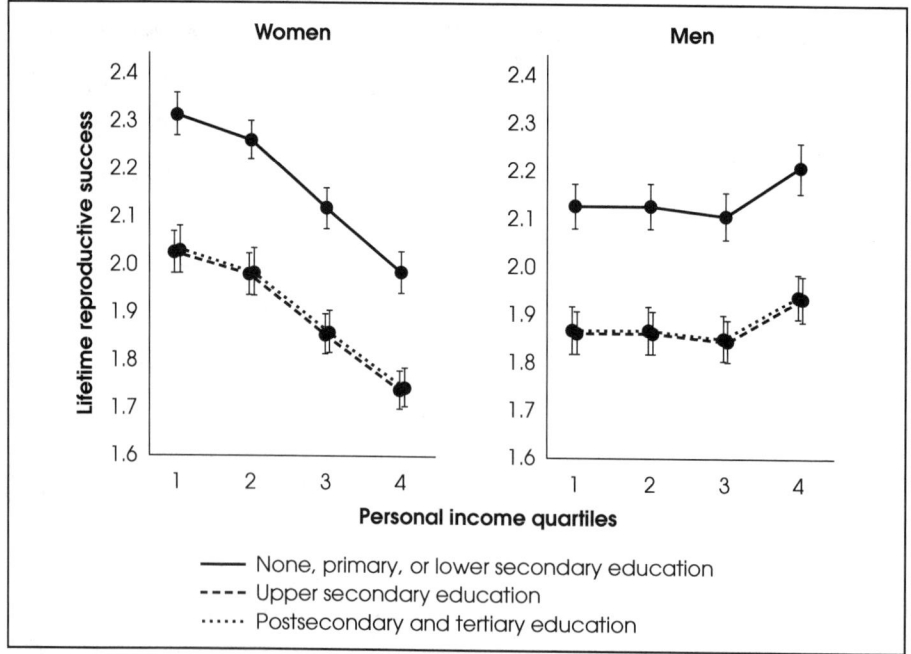

Figure 7.4 Predicted lifetime reproductive success by sex, income, and education, all Europeans

Source: Barthold, Myrskylä, and Jones (2012).

Evolutionary scholars have debated whether there is an optimal number of children that can maximize reproductive success in a modern society (Jones and Bird 2014). Yet empirically no optima have been found, and the relationship between number of children and number of descendants in modern societies appears linear and positive (Kaplan et al. 1995; Mueller 2001). Goodman, Koupil, and Lawson (2012), using Swedish multigenerational data, show that while low fertility increases descendant socioeconomic position it reduces long-term fitness. Jones and Bird (2014) argue that these results are likely because of the great changes in Swedish society over the course of the twentieth century, and that in such cases looking only at number of descendants is not a good measure of fitness. They argue that the timing of births matters for fertility and that if births are properly timed, a low-fertility strategy can have the same fitness as a high-fertility strategy. At present this argument awaits further empirical verification.

These results show that in the contemporary United States and Europe, the individuals with the highest reproductive success are high-income-earning males and low-income-earning females. The same is likely true in many other contemporary societies as well. For example, Fieder, Huber, and Bookstein (2011) show evidence that high-income men are the least likely to be childless and to have not ever married in contemporary Brazil, Mexico, Panama, South Africa, and Venezuela, while the reverse is true for women in all these countries.

Institutions Matter

The results described above show that in some parts of Europe, men's educational attainment, not just men's income, is positively associated with number of offspring (Lappegård and Rønsen 2013; Nisén et al. 2013). In the United States, educational attainment is not positively associated with number of offspring for men. This is likely because of the difference in the nature of educational institutions in Europe and the United States and a lower correlation between education and income in the United States. This is because, first, a larger proportion of people in the United States complete high school and obtain a college degree than in Europe. Second, there is more variation in the quality of schools and colleges across the United States than in Europe, where educational systems are typically centrally organized and funded. This means that measures of educational attainment such as years of education or highest credential that do not take into account the quality of the credential or degree are less reliable predictors of income in the United States than in Europe. Third, in Europe there is often a clearer link between educational credentials at all levels and particular occupations than in the United States (Kerckhoff 1995), so there is a tighter link between educational outcomes and income outcomes for the individual. Finally, greater income inequality in the United States means there is likely more variation in income among men at different levels of education in the United States than in Europe (Smeeding 2005).

Despite some societal differences in appropriate measures of male status, the evidence presented above shows that there is a relationship between status and reproductive success for men in both Europe and the United States and that there is greater variance on reproductive success for men than women, as sociobiology would predict. There is a negative association between social status (as measured by own income, education, and job status) and reproductive success for women. This may seem counter to sociobiological arguments, although it fits with trends from preindustrial societies. This may be because measures such as own income are not the best measures of status for women. However, sociobiology does predict lower variance on reproductive success for women, and this is what the census data show.

TRIVERS-WILLARD EFFECT

Given that status for males pays off in reproductive success in modern societies, it may be expected that the Trivers-Willard effect will also come into play. The Trivers-Willard hypothesis predicts that individuals in good condition will invest more in male offspring, and individuals in poor condition will invest more in female offspring (Trivers 1972; Trivers and Willard 1973). The authors specifically note that "the model can be applied to humans differentiated on a socioeconomic scale, as long as the reproductive success of a male at the upper end of the scale exceeds his sister's, while that of a female at the lower end of the scale exceeds her brother's" (Trivers and Willard 1973: 91). Given that high-status males have greater reproductive success than high-status females in modern societies, we would expect to see evidence of greater investment in boys at the top of the socioeconomic hierarchy, and greater investment in girls at the bottom of the socioeconomic hierarchy.

This investment can be a biological investment by the mother before birth, and it is shown in the sex ratio at birth (for a review of evidence for all societies, see Lazarus 2002). In the United States, Almond and Edlund (2007) found evidence of a Trivers-Willard effect in the sex ratio of births and infant deaths to white mothers between 1983 and 2001. Cameron, Dalerum, and Reby (2009) found an excess of boys among the children of men on the Forbes billionaire list. Hopcroft (2005) and Hopcroft and Martin (2014) found that boys were more likely than girls to have high-status fathers, and high-status fathers were more likely to have boys than girls among their offspring. There is also evidence that the sex ratio is responsive to stresses during gestation, resulting in a lowered sex ratio after major disasters have occurred and in more girls born than boys, and this can be understood as a Trivers-Willard effect (Hansen, Møller, and Olsen 1999; Catalano 2003; Catalano and Bruckner 2005; Khashan et al. 2009; Fukuda et al. 1998; Subbaraman et al. 2010; Torche and Kleinhaus 2012).

Studies measuring nonbiological parental investment using self-reports of specific activities with, or investments in, small children and adolescents in the United States have given null effects (Freese and Powell 1999; Keller, Nesse, and Hofferth 2001). However, Hopcroft (2005) and Hopcroft and Martin (2014) argue that the largest investment parents in the United States make in their offspring and the one that is most consequential for their future is in their children's education. In the United States, educational attainment is positively correlated with economic success, health, family stability, and social connections (Hout 2012), so by investing in their children's education, parents can help ensure their children's future economic, social, and reproductive success. Using the father's socioeconomic status when the respondent was sixteen as the measure of parental status, Hopcroft (2005) and Hopcroft and Martin (2014) find that the sons of higher-status fathers obtain higher degrees and more years of education than the daughters, while the daughters of lower-status fathers obtain higher degrees and more years of education than the sons. This is consistent with the Trivers-Willard hypothesis of differential parental investment.

It is unlikely that this specific finding on educational attainment will be replicated in Europe. This is because of the differing nature of educational institutions in Europe and the United States, as noted above, along with the fact that in the United States the education of children is more in the hands of parents than it is in Europe. College tuition is comparatively high in the United States and is generally paid by the student's family or by the student himself or herself, while this is less true in Europe. In addition, parents have more ability to choose the educational institution for their child in the United States, as there is little early division of students into different types of educational tracks as is often true in European school systems.

The Relevance of Evolutionary Psychology to Modern Populations

The effect of status on reproductive success for men and the Trivers-Willard effect described above entirely conform to predictions from sociobiological theory. Sociobiology is concerned with the ultimate consequences of behavior, namely, the extent to which individuals further their genetic fitness and increase their genetic representation in future generations. The theory is largely silent on the mechanisms by which this occurs, while evolutionary psychology is not. Evolutionary psychology suggests that evolved adaptations (sometimes called modules or psychological mechanisms) in the brain shape individual preferences that guide human behavior, particularly reproductive behavior. These adaptations and the preferences they promote are hypothesized to influence behavior in a context-sensitive manner, so actual behavior will vary from situation to situation. However, given anisogamy and greater investment in offspring by females than males, evolutionary psychologists hypothesize that females will have psychological mechanisms that encourage them to be choosier about mates than males, as well as psychological mechanisms that encourage them to prefer males as mates who are both willing and able to invest in prospective offspring. There is evidence of greater female choosiness, particularly with regard to sexual partners. Men approached by attractive strangers are much more likely to agree to sex than are women (Clark and Hatfield 1989; Guéguen 2011). There is also evidence of greater female preference for financial prospects in a mate (Buss 1989; Buss et. al. 2001; Henry, Helm, and Cruz 2013), along with other sex differences in mate preferences.

While evolutionary psychologists are agnostic as to whether such preferences serve to maximize reproductive success in contemporary settings, preferring to see individuals as "adaptation executors" rather than "fitness maximizers," the results described above suggest that these preferences do have behavioral and hence fitness consequences. If female (and not male) choice determines who fathers children, then it appears that women in the United States, like women in Europe, not only prefer financial prospects in a mate but also disproportionately choose higher-income men as the fathers of their children. That the sex differences in mate preferences documented by evolutionary psychologists have behavioral consequences underlines the importance of studying the preferences themselves, and hence the value of much work within the field of evolutionary psychology.

Conclusion

In this chapter I have reviewed recent studies of modern populations in the United States and Europe that support two major predictions of sociobiology: the relationship between status and reproductive success, and the Trivers-Willard hypothesis of differential parental investment. Specifically, these studies show that for males only, social status as measured by income (and in some countries, education and job status) is associated with greater reproductive success. Further, there is evidence that high-status parents are more likely to invest in boys than in girls along lines predicted by the Trivers-Willard hypothesis. These studies also show that the nature of social status differs by society and is shaped by the institutions of that society, emphasizing that sociobiological processes are as much social processes as they are biological processes. Contra Vining (2011), these studies suggest that sociobiology and its associated discipline, evolutionary psychology, are relevant to modern populations, just as they are relevant to premodern populations.

References

Almond, D., and L. Edlund. 2007. "Trivers–Willard at Birth and One Year: Evidence from U.S. Natality Data 1983–2001." *Proceedings of the Royal Society B* 274: 2491–2496.

Bailey, R. 1991. *The Behavioral Ecology of Efe Pygmy Men in the Ituri Forest, Zaire*. Ann Arbor: University of Michigan Museum of Anthropology.

Barthold, J. A., M. Myrskylä, and O. R. Jones. 2012. "Childlessness Drives the Sex Difference in the Association between Income and Reproductive Success of Modern Europeans." *Evolution and Human Behavior* 33 (6): 628–638.

Bereczkei, T., and A. Csanaky. 1996. "Mate Choice, Marital Success, and Reproduction in a Modern Society." *Ethology and Sociobiology* 17 (1): 17–35.

Betzig, L. 1986. *Despotism and Differential Reproduction: A Darwinian View of History*. New York: Aldine.

———. 1988. "Redistribution: Equity or Exploitation?" In *Human Reproductive Behavior*, edited by L. Betzig, M. Borgerhoff Mulder, and P. Turke, 49–63. Cambridge: Cambridge University Press.

———. 1992. "Roman Polygyny." *Ethology and Sociobiology* 13: 309–349.

———. 1993. "Sex, Succession and Stratification in the First Six Civilizations: How Powerful Men Reproduced, Passed Power on to Their Sons, and Used Power to Defend Their Wealth, Women and Children." In *Social Stratification and Socioeconomic Inequality*. Vol. 1, *A Comparative Biosocial Analysis*, edited by L. Ellis, 37–74. Westport, CT: Praeger.

———. 1995. "Medieval Monogamy." *Journal of Family History* 20: 181–215.

———. 2012. "Means, Variances, and Ranges in Reproductive Success: Comparative Evidence." *Evolution and Human Behavior* 33 (4): 309–317.

Boone, James L. 1986. "Parental Investment and Elite Family Structure in Preindustrial States: A Case Study of Late Medieval-Early Modern Portuguese Genealogies." *American Anthropologist* 88: 859–878.

Borgerhoff Mulder, M. 1987. "Cultural and Reproductive Success: Kipsigis Evidence." *American Anthropologist* 89: 617–634.

———. 1988. "Reproductive Success in Three Kipsigis Cohorts." In *Reproductive Success: Studies of Individual Variation in Contrasting Breeding Systems*, edited by T. H. Clutton-Brock, 419–435. Chicago: University of Chicago Press.

———. 1990. "Kipsigis Women's Preferences for Wealthy Men: Evidence for Female Choice in Mammals?" *Behavioral Ecology and Sociobiology* 27: 255–264.

———. 1995. "Bridewealth and Its Correlates: Quantifying Changes over Time." *Current Anthropology* 36: 573–603.

———. 2000. "Optimizing Offspring: The Quantity-Quality Tradeoff in Agropastoral Kipsigis." *Evolution and Human Behavior* 21 (6): 391–410.

Buss, D. M. 1989. "Sex Differences in Human Mate Preferences: Evolutionary Hypotheses Tested in 37 Cultures." *Behavioral and Brain Sciences* 12: 1–49.

Buss, D. M., T. K. Shackelford, L. A. Kirkpatrick, and R. J. Larsen. 2001. "A Half Century of Mate Preferences: The Cultural Evolution of Values." *Journal of Marriage and Family* 63: 491–503.

Caldwell, J. C. 1976. "Toward a Restatement of Demographic Transition Theory." *Population and Development Review* 2 (3/4): 321–366.

———. 2005. "On Net Intergenerational Wealth Flows: An Update." *Population and Development Review* 31: 721–740.

Cameron, E. Z., F. Dalerum, and D. Reby. 2009. "A Trivers-Willard Effect in Contemporary Humans: Male-Biased Sex Ratios among Billionaires." *PloS ONE* 4 (1). http://www.plosone.org/article/fetchObject.action?uri=info%3Adoi%2F10.1371%2Fjournal.pone.0004195&representation=PDF.

Casimir, M. J., and A. Rao. 1995. "Prestige, Possessions and Progeny: Cultural Goals and Reproductive Success among the Bakkarwal." *Human Nature* 6 (3): 241–272.

Catalano, R. A. 2003. "Sex Ratios in the Two Germanies: A Test of the Economic Stress Hypothesis." *Human Reproduction* 18 (9): 1972–1975.

Catalano, R. A., and T. Bruckner. 2005. "Economic Antecedents of the Swedish Sex Ratio." *Social Science & Medicine* 60: 537–543.

Chagnon, N. A. 1979. "Is Reproductive Success Equal in Egalitarian Societies?" In *Evolutionary Biology and Human Social Behavior: An Anthropological Perspective*, edited by N. A. Chagnon and W. Irons, 374–401. North Scituate, MA: Duxbury Press.

———. 1980. "Kin Selection Theory, Kinship, Marriage and Fitness among the Yanomamö Indians." In *Sociobiology: Beyond Nature/Nurture?*, edited by G. Barlow and I. Silverberg, 545–571. Boulder, CO: Westview Press.

———. 1988. "Life Histories, Blood Revenge, and Warfare in a Tribal Population." *Science* 238: 985–992.

Clark, R. D., and E. Hatfield. 1989. "Gender Differences in Receptivity to Sexual Offers." *Journal of Psychology and Human Sexuality* 2: 39–55.
Cronk, L. 1991. "Wealth, Status and Reproductive Success among the Mukogodo of Kenya." *American Anthropologist* 93 (2): 345–360.
Dickemann, M. 1979. "The Ecology of Mating Systems in Hypergynous Dowry Societies." *Social Science Information* 18: 163–195.
Dye, J. L. 2008. *Fertility of American Women: 2008.* Current Population Reports, P20–563. Washington, DC: U.S. Census Bureau.
Faux, S. F., and H. Miller. 1984. "Evolutionary Speculations on the Oligarchic Development of Mormon Polygyny." *Ethology and Sociobiology* 5: 15–31.
Fieder, M., and S. Huber. 2007. "The Effects of Sex and Childlessness on the Association between Status and Reproductive Output in Modern Society." *Evolution and Human Behavior* 28: 392–398.
Fieder, M., S. Huber, and F. L. Bookstein. 2011. "Socioeconomic Status, Marital Status and Childlessness in Men and Women: An Analysis of Census Data from Six Countries." *Journal of Biosocial Science* 43 (5): 619–635.
Flinn, M. 1986. "Correlates of Reproductive Success in a Caribbean Village." *Human Ecology* 14: 225–243.
Forsberg, A., J. Lindqvist, and B. Tullberg. 1995. "The Relationship between Cumulative Number of Cohabiting Partners and Number of Children for Men and Women in Modern Sweden." *Ethology and Sociobiology* 16 (3): 221–232.
Freese, J., and B. Powell. 1999. "Sociobiology, Status and Parental Investment in Sons and Daughters: Testing the Trivers-Willard Hypothesis." *American Journal of Sociology* 104 (6): 1704–1743.
Fukuda, M., K. Fukuda, T. Shimizu, and H. Møller. 1998. "Decline in Sex Ratio at Birth after Kobe Earthquake." *Human Reproduction* 13 (8): 2321–2322.
Goodman, A., and I. Koupil. 2010. "The Effect of School Performance upon Marriage and Long-Term Reproductive Success in 10,000 Swedish Males and Females Born 1915–1929." *Evolution and Human Behavior* 31 (6): 425–435.
Goodman, A., I. Koupil, and D. W. Lawson. 2012. "Low Fertility Increases Descendant Socioeconomic Position but Reduces Long-Term Fitness in a Modern Post-Industrial Society." *Proceedings of the Royal Society B* 279: 4342–4351. doi: 10.1098/rspb.2012.1415.
Guéguen, N. 2011. "Effects of Solicitor Sex and Attractiveness on Receptivity to Sexual Offers: A Field Study." *Archives of Sexual Behavior* 40 (5): 915–919.
Guinness Book of World Records. 2013. "Most Prolific Mother Ever." Accessed December 19. http://www.guinnessworldrecords.com/world-records/3000/most-prolific-mother-ever.
Hansen, D., H. Møller, and J. Olsen. 1999. "Severe Periconceptional Life Events and the Sex Ratio in Offspring: Follow Up Study Based on Five National Registers." *British Medical Journal* 28 (319): 548–549.
Henry, J., H. W. Helm Jr., and N. Cruz. 2013. "Mate Selection: Gender and Generational Differences." *North American Journal of Psychology* 15: 63–70.
Heuveline, P., J. M. Timberlake, and F. F. Furstenberg. 2003. "Shifting Child Rearing to Single Mothers: Results from 17 Western Nations." *Population and Development Review* 29: 47–71.
Hewlett, B. S. 1988. "Sexual Selection and Paternal Investment among Aka Pygmies." In *Human Reproductive Behavior: A Darwinian Perspective,* edited by L. Betzig et al., 263–276. New York: Cambridge University Press.
Hill, K., and A. M. Hurtado. 1996. *Aché Life History: The Ecology and Demography of a Foraging People.* New York: Aldine de Gruyter.
Hopcroft, R. L. 2005. "Parental Status and Differential Investment in Sons and Daughters: Trivers-Willard Revisited." *Social Forces* 83 (3): 1111–1136.
———. 2006. "Sex, Status and Reproductive Success in the Contemporary U.S." *Evolution and Human Behavior* 27: 104–120.
———. Forthcoming. "Sex Differences in the Relationship between Status and Number of Offspring in the Contemporary U.S." *Evolution and Human Behavior.*
Hopcroft, R. L., and D. O. Martin. 2014. "The Primary Parental Investment in Children in the Contemporary USA. Is Education: Testing the Trivers-Willard Hypothesis of Parental Investment." *Human Nature* 25 (2): 235–250.
Hout, M. 2012. "Social and Economic Returns to College Education in the United States." *Annual Review of Sociology* 38: 379–400.
Hrdy, S. B. 1999. *Mother Nature.* New York: Ballantine Books.
Hughes, A. 1986. "Reproductive Success and Occupational Class in Eighteenth Century Lancashire, England." *Social Biology* 33: 109–115.
Irons, W. 1979. "Cultural and Biological Success." In *Evolutionary Biology and Human Social Behavior: An Anthropological Perspective,* edited by N. A. Chagnon and W. Irons, 257–272. North Scituate, MA: Duxbury Press.
———. 1980. "Is Yomut Social Behavior Adaptive?" In *Sociobiology: Beyond Nature/Nurture?* edited by G. W. Bar-

low and J. Silverberg, 417–473. American Association for the Advancement of Science Series on Science: The State of the Art. Boulder, CO: Westview Press.

Jokela, M., A. Rotkirch, I. J. Rickard, J. Pettay, and V. Lummaa. 2010. "Serial Monogamy Increases Reproductive Success in Men but Not in Women." *Behavioral Ecology* 21: 906–912.

Jones, J. H., and R. B. Bird. 2014. "The Marginal Valuation of Fertility." *Evolution and Human Behavior* 35 (1): 65–71. http://dx.doi.org/10.1016/j.evolhumbehav.2013.10.002.

Kaplan, H., and K. Hill. 1985. "Hunting Ability and Reproductive Success among Male Aché Foragers." *Current Anthropology* 26: 131–133.

Kaplan, H., J. B. Lancaster, S. Johnson, and J. Bock. 1995. "Does Observed Fertility Maximize Fitness among New Mexican Men? A Test of an Optimality Model and a New Theory of Parental Investment in the Embodied Capital of Offspring." *Human Nature* 6 (4): 325–360.

Kaplan, H., J. B. Lancaster, W. T. Tucker, and K. G. Anderson. 2002. "An Evolutionary Approach to Below Replacement Fertility." *American Journal of Human Biology* 14: 233–256.

Kaptijn, R., F. Thomesea, T. G. van Tilburga, A. C. Liefbroerab, and D.J.H. Deega. 2010. "Low Fertility in Contemporary Humans and the Mate Value of Their Children: Sex-Specific Effects on Social Status Indicators." *Evolution and Human Behavior* 31: 59–68.

Keller, M. C., R. M. Nesse, and S. Hofferth. 2001. "The Trivers-Willard Hypothesis of Parental Investment: No Effect in the Contemporary United States." *Evolution and Human Behavior* 22: 343–360.

Kerckhoff, A. C. 1995. "Institutional Arrangements and Stratification Processes in Industrial Societies." *Annual Review of Sociology* 21: 323–347.

Khashan, A. S., P. B. Mortensen, R. McNamee, P. N. Baker, and K. M. Abel. 2009. "Sex Ratio at Birth Following Prenatal Maternal Exposure to Severe Life Events: A Population-Based Cohort Study." *Human Reproduction* 24: 1754–1757.

Lappegård, T., and M. Rønsen. 2013. "Socioeconomic Differences in Multipartner Fertility among Norwegian Men." *Demography* 50: 1135–1153.

Lawson, D. W., and R. Mace. 2010. "Optimizing Modern Family Size." *Human Nature* 21 (1): 39–61.

Lazarus, J. 2002. "Human Sex Ratios: Adaptations and Mechanisms, Problems and Prospects." In *Sex Ratios: Concepts and Research Methods*, edited by I.C.W. Hardy, 287–311. Cambridge: Cambridge University Press.

Lee, J., and C. Campbell. 1997. *Fate and Fortune in Rural China: Social Organization and Population Behavior in Liaoning, 1774–1873*. Cambridge: Cambridge University Press.

Lee, J., C. Campbell, and F. Wang. 1993. "The Last Emperors: An Introduction to the Demography of the Qing Imperial Lineage." In *New and Old Methods in Historical Demography*, edited by D. Rehler and R. Schofield, 361–382. Oxford: Oxford University Press.

Low, B. S. 1991. "Occupational Status, Land Ownership, and Reproductive Behavior in 19th Century Sweden: Tuna Parish." *American Anthropologist* 92: 115–126.

Low, B. S., and A. L. Clark. 1992. "Resources and the Life Course: Patterns through the Demographic Transition." *Ethology and Sociobiology* 13: 463–494.

Mace, R. 1996a. "When to Have Another Baby: A Dynamic Model of Reproductive Decision-Making and Evidence from the Gabbra Pastoralists." *Ethology and Sociobiology* 17: 263–273.

———. 1996b. "Biased Parental Investment and Reproductive Success in Gabbra Pastoralists." *Behavioral Ecology and Sociobiology* 38: 75–81.

Mealey, L. 1985. "The Relationship between Social and Biological Success: A Case Study of the Mormon Religious Hierarchy." *Ethology and Sociobiology* 6: 249–257.

Mueller, U. 2001. "Is There a Stabilizing Selection around Average Fertility in Modern Human Populations?" *Population and Development Review* 27: 469–498.

Nettle, D., and T. V. Pollet. 2008. "Natural Selection on Male Wealth in Humans." *American Naturalist* 172 (5): 658–666.

Newson, L., T. Postmes., S.E.G. Lea, and P. Webley. 2005. "Why Are Modern Families Small? Toward an Evolutionary and Cultural Explanation for the Demographic Transition." *Personality and Social Psychology Review* 9: 360–375.

Nisén, J., P. Martikainen, J. Kaprio, and K. Silventoinen. 2013. "Educational Differences in Completed Fertility: A Behavioral Genetic Study of Finnish Male and Female Twins." *Demography* 50 (4): 1399–1420.

Pennington, R., and H. Harpending. 1993. *The Structure of an African Pastoralist Community: Demography, History and Ecology of the Ngamiland Herero*. New York: Oxford University Press.

Richerson, P. J., and R. Boyd. 2005. *Not by Genes Alone: How Culture Transformed Human Evolution*. Chicago: University of Chicago Press.

Rosenzweig, M. R. 1990. "Population Growth and Human Capital Investments: Theory and Evidence." *Journal of Political Economy* 98 (5): S38–S70.

Røskaft, E., A. Wara, and Å. Viken. 1992. "Human Reproductive Success in Relation to Resource-Access and Parental Age in a Small Norwegian Farming Parish during the Period 1700–1900." *Ethology and Sociobiology* 13: 443–461.

Smeeding, T. 2005. "Public Policy, Economic Inequality, and Poverty: The United States in Comparative Perspective." *Social Science Quarterly* 86: 955–983.

Strassman, B. 1997. "Polygyny Is a Risk Factor for Child Mortality among the Dogon." *Current Anthropology* 38: 688–695.

Subbaraman, M., S. Goldman-Mellor, E. Anderson, K. LeWinn, L. Saxton, and M. Shumway. 2010. "An Exploration of Secondary Sex Ratios among Women Diagnosed with Anxiety Disorders." *Human Reproduction* 25: 2084–2091.

Torche, F., and K. Kleinhaus. 2012. "Prenatal Stress, Gestational Age and Secondary Sex Ratio: The Sex-Specific Effects of Exposure to a Natural Disaster in Early Pregnancy." *Human Reproduction* 27 (2): 558–567.

Trivers, R. L. 1972. "Parental Investment and Sexual Selection." In *Sexual Selection and the Descent of Man, 1871–1971*, edited by B. Campbell, 136–179. Chicago: Aldine.

Trivers, R. L., and D. E. Willard. 1973. "Natural Selection of Parental Ability to Vary the Sex Ratio of Offspring." *Science* 179 (4068): 90–92.

Turke, P., and L. Betzig. 1985. "Those Who Can Do: Wealth, Status and Reproductive Success on Ifaluk." *Ethology and Sociobiology* 6: 79–87.

US Census Bureau. 2013. "International Data Base." Accessed December 13. http://www.census.gov/population/international/data/idb/informationGateway.php.

Vining, D. R., Jr. 1986. "Social versus Reproductive Success: The Central Theoretical Problem of Human Sociobiology." *Behavioral and Brain Sciences* 9 (1): 167–187.

———. 2011. "Sociobiology's Relevance to Modern Society: Commentary on Two Articles Published Here." *Evolution and Human Behavior* 32: 364–367.

Voland, E. 1988. "Differential Infant and Child Mortality in Evolutionary Perspective: Data from the Late 17th to 19th Century Ostfriesland (Germany)." In *Human Reproductive Behavior*, edited by L. Betzig et al., 253–276. Cambridge: Cambridge University Press.

———. 1990. "Differential Reproductive Success within the Krummhörn Population (Germany, 18th and 19th Centuries)." *Behavioural Ecology and Sociobiology* 26: 65–72.

Voland, E., and R.I.M. Dunbar. 1995. "Resource Competition and Reproduction: The Relationship between Economic and Parental Strategies in the Krummhörn Population (1720–1874)." *Human Nature* 6: 33–49.

Walker, P. L., and B. S. Hewlett. 1990. "Dental Health Diet and Social Status among Central African Foragers and Farmers." *American Anthropologist* 92: 383–398.

Wang, F., J. Lee, and C. Campbell. 1995. "Marital Fertility Control among the Qing Nobility: Implications for Two Types of Preventative Checks." *Population Studies* 49: 383–400.

Chapter Eight

Evolutionary Psychology and Its Relevance to the Social Sciences

Satoshi Kanazawa

> This chapter introduces the reader to the emerging science of evolutionary psychology and how it starkly contrasts with the Standard Social Science Model (SSSM), which predominates most of the social sciences today. The chapter explicates some of the fundamental principles of evolutionary psychology and introduces the Savanna Principle, about the evolutionary constraints and limitations of the human brain and how they manifest in everyday behavior. Among other things, the Savanna Principle explains why much of human behavior today is maladaptive and why directional human evolution stopped 10,000 years ago. The chapter illustrates the relevance and utility of evolutionary psychology to the social sciences with a micro example (why most suicide bombers are Muslim) and a macro example (why different societies have varied institutions of marriage like monogamy and polygyny).

Evolutionary psychology is a new, emerging field. It is "the new science of the mind" (Buss 2011). The first landmark studies in evolutionary psychology were published in the late 1980s (Buss 1989; Cosmides 1989; Daly and Wilson 1988), and the birth of modern evolutionary psychology was marked in 1992 with the publication of the tome *The Adapted Mind: Evolutionary Psychology and the Generation of Culture* (Barkow, Cosmides, and Tooby 1992), which is often regarded as the "Bible" of modern evolutionary psychology (Ellis and Bjorklund 2005: x). What was there before then? Before I introduce evolutionary psychology in this chapter, let's pause for a moment to consider what theories and explanations were available to social scientists before its advent.

The Standard Social Science Model (SSSM)

Most social scientists explain human behavior in a more or less typical fashion. The particular school of thought is called "the Standard Social Science Model" (SSSM) (Barkow 2006; Tooby and Cosmides 1992: 24–49). Because social scientists and their theories tend to have a lot of influence on the general public, the same view also characterizes how lay individuals account for human behavior in their everyday lives.

What exactly is the SSSM? A set of related principles characterizes its main tenets:

1. *Humans are exempt from biology.* Social scientists who subscribe to the SSSM know that biology (and its branches like zoology, ornithology, entomology, etc.)

can explain the behavior of all other species in nature. Yet they make an exception for humans as the sole species in nature whose behavior is *not* explained by biological principles and theories. Human exceptionalism is the hallmark of the SSSM. Many social scientists have aversive reactions to biological explanations of human behavior; such aversive reaction is called *biophobia* (Ellis 1996; Daly and Wilson 1988: 152–156; Machalek and Martin 2004). Most social scientists are extremely biophobic. This principle states that humans are exceptions in nature.

2. *Evolution stops at the neck* (Campbell 1999: 243). Social scientists in the SSSM tradition, who are biophobic and do not believe in biological influences on human behavior and cognition, nevertheless acknowledge that human anatomy has been shaped by evolution. They recognize that the human body parts, such as the fingers and the toes, are the way they are because of a long evolutionary process of natural and sexual selection. However, they contend that evolution has had no effect on the contents of the human brain and the human mind. This principle states that the brain is an exception to the human body in that it has *not* been shaped by evolutionary forces.

3. *Human nature is tabula rasa (a blank slate)* (Pinker 2002). As a result of Principle 2 above, social scientists in the SSSM tradition contend that humans are born with a mind like a blank slate. Once again, they recognize that all the other species in nature have innate natures: dogs have an innate dog nature with which they are born and which makes them behave more or less the same no matter where they live or what their individual life experiences have been, and cats have an innate cat nature with which they are born and which similarly makes them behave the same but different from dogs. The same goes for all species in nature, *except for humans*. Humans do not have an innate nature, as they are born with minds that are blank slates. Principle 3, like Principle 1, is again an example of human exceptionalism.

4. *Human behavior is a product almost entirely of the environment and socialization.* According to the SSSM, since humans have no innate human nature that guides their behavior, the contents of human nature must be written after birth. The SSSM contends that this occurs by a lifelong process of socialization (learning via instructions, imitation, copying, etc.) provided by the agents of socialization (parents, older siblings, other family members, teachers, other adults in society, the media, etc.). Humans become the way they are because of socialization; socialization makes them human. In particular, men and women acquire their typical male and female behavior through "gender socialization." This is why another name for the SSSM is *environmentalism*. Most social scientists believe that the environment and life experiences almost entirely shape and determine human behavior.

Admittedly, this is a somewhat simplified version of the SSSM, but it is not far off the mark. Not all social scientists may agree with all four tenets, but most agree with most of them to a large extent, and many agree with all of them (Ellis 1996). A comprehensive survey of introductory textbooks in sociology, for example, reveals very cursory (if at all) and often inaccurate discussion of human evolution and its effects on behavior (Machalek and Martin 2004).

A Brief Introduction to Evolutionary Psychology

I will now present a brief introduction to an evolutionary psychological perspective. Fuller introductions to the field already abound. Academic readers may want to consult

Barkow et al. (1992), Buss (1995, 2011), Cartwright (2008), Daly and Wilson (1988), and Kanazawa (2001). Nonacademic popular introductions to the field include Buss (2003), Miller and Kanazawa (2007), Pincott (2008), Pinker (2002), Ridley (1993), and Wright (1994).

Evolutionary psychology is the study of human nature. While the phrase "human nature" is often bandied about in common discourse to connote something essential but otherwise undefined about being human, it has a very specific meaning in evolutionary psychology. It refers to a collection of components in the brain called *evolved psychological mechanisms* or *psychological adaptations*. (The two terms are roughly synonymous and interchangeable.) Human nature is the sum total of such evolved psychological mechanisms, and evolutionary psychologists aim to discover more and more such psychological adaptations in humans. What, then, is an evolved psychological mechanism?

An adaptation is a product of evolution by natural and sexual selection. Natural selection is the process whereby some individuals live longer than others, and sexual selection is the process whereby some individuals leave more offspring (or copies of their genes) than others. Natural selection is a matter of survival; sexual selection is a matter of reproductive success.[1]

An adaptation allows an organism to solve particular adaptive problems (Williams 1966). Our body is full of adaptations. Our eye is an adaptation; it allows us to see, navigate efficiently and safely, find prey, and avoid predators. Our hand is an adaptation; it allows us to hold and manipulate objects efficiently, collect and eat food, throw objects, and use and manufacture tools. If you can imagine what your life would be like without an eye or a hand, you can begin to see the range of problems that these physical adaptations solve. Problems that adaptations are designed to solve are called *adaptive problems*. Adaptive problems are problems of survival and reproduction. Without solving adaptive problems, we will not be able to live long enough or reproduce successfully.

Psychological adaptations (or evolved psychological mechanisms) are like these physical adaptations in our body, except they are in our brain. They allow us to solve some adaptive problems by predisposing or inclining us to think or feel in certain ways (Kanazawa 2001). Just as we see or manipulate objects without much conscious thought, psychological adaptations often operate behind and beneath our conscious thinking. All adaptations (physical and psychological) are also *domain-specific*; they operate and solve problems only within a narrow area of life. The eye allows us to see but not manipulate objects; the hand allows us to manipulate but not see them. What the eye can do, the hand cannot, and vice versa. This is true for psychological adaptations as well. They operate and solve problems only in a narrow range of life.

Our preference for sweets and fats is an example of an evolved psychological mechanism (Barash 1982: 144–147). Throughout most of human evolutionary history, procuring sufficient calories was a serious problem; malnutrition and starvation were common. In this environment, those who, for reasons of random genetic mutations, had a "taste" for sweets and fats, which are high in calories, and preferentially ate them, were better off physically than those who did not have such a taste and thus eschewed them. Those who had a sweet tooth, therefore, lived longer, led healthier lives, and produced more healthy offspring than those who did not have a sweet tooth. They in turn passed on their (genetically influenced) taste to their offspring, over many thousands of generations. In every generation, those with this taste outreproduced those without it, generation after generation, until most of us living today have a strong preference for sweets and fats.

Male sexual jealousy is another example of an evolved psychological mechanism (Daly, Wilson, and Weghorst 1982). Because gestation in humans and most other mammalian species occurs inside the female body, males of these species (including men) can never be certain that they are the father of their mate's offspring, while females are always certain of their maternity. In other words, the possibility of cuckoldry—unwittingly raising children who are not genetically their own—exists only for men, not for women. A man is cuckolded when his wife has an affair with someone, has a child by the lover, but successfully passes the child off as the husband's. According to one estimate, about 13–20 percent of children in the contemporary United States and 9–17 percent in contemporary Germany are not the genetic offspring of the man whose name appears on the child's birth certificate (Gaulin et al. 1997). Another study shows that about 10–14 percent of children in Mexico have legal fathers different from the genetic fathers (Cerda-Flores et al. 1999). Earlier estimates from the United States, the UK, and France are around 10–30 percent of all children (Baker and Bellis 1995: 200, Box 8.4). As anyone who has ever watched a daytime talk show knows, concerns about biological paternity are far from a remote theoretical possibility. In fact, anywhere from one out of ten to one out of three children are raised by men who are unrelated to them genetically.

In evolutionary terms, men who are cuckolded and invest their limited financial and emotional resources in the offspring of other men end up wasting these resources, as their genes will not be represented in the next generation. For this reason, men have a strong evolutionary reason to be sexually jealous, while women, whose maternity is always certain, do not. The same psychological mechanism of sexual jealousy often leads to men's attempts to guard their mates physically, in order to minimize the possibility of sexual contact with other men, sometimes with tragic consequences (Buss 1988, 2000; Buss and Shackelford 1997).

While men and women are the same in the frequency and intensity of their jealousy in romantic relationships (White 1981; Buunk and Hupka 1987), there are clear sex differences in what triggers jealousy. The evidence from surveys and physiological studies conducted in different cultures indicates that men become jealous of their mates' *sexual infidelity* with other men, underlying their reproductive concern for cuckoldry. In contrast, women become jealous of their mates' *emotional involvement* with other women, because emotional involvement often leads to diversion of their mates' resources from them and their children to their romantic rivals (Buss, Larsen, and Westen 1992; Buss et al. 1999). While critics of evolutionary psychology have questioned these conclusions mostly on methodological grounds (Harris 2003; DeSteno et al. 2002), both strong evolutionary logic and a preponderance of empirical evidence support the clear sex differences in romantic jealousy described above (Del Giudice 2009, 2013; Pietrzak et al. 2002). As one of the deans of modern evolutionary psychology, David M. Buss, notes (Buss, Larsen, and Westen 1996), evolutionary psychologists (Daly, Wilson, and Weghorst 1982; Symons 1979: 226–246) *predicted* the existence of these sex differences in romantic jealousy on the basis of evolutionary logic alone more than a decade before any systematic data existed.

Basic Theoretical Structure of Evolutionary Psychology

Figure 8.1 presents the basic theoretical structure of evolutionary psychology. Some adaptive problem of survival or reproductive success has led to the evolution of psychological mechanisms through natural or sexual selection. Individuals who possess certain genetically encoded psychological mechanisms live longer (because the psychological mechanisms help them survive) or reproduce more successfully (because the psychological mechanisms help them find and keep mates and invest in their children). Those with such psychological mechanisms outreproduce those without them in each generation, and more and more individuals come to possess the psychological mechanisms generation after generation. Eventually, all individuals come to possess them, and they become part of universal (or species-typical) human nature. Evolved psychological mechanisms engender values, preferences, desires, emotions, and other internal states that serve as the proximate causes of behavior (Kanazawa 2001). These internal states produce adaptive behavior that solves the original adaptive problem *in the context of the environment of evolutionary adaptedness (EEA)*. The evolved psychological mechanisms would not have been selected and would not exist if they did not solve the adaptive problems in the EEA efficiently and reliably.

However, the problem arises because we now live in the current environment (postindustrial society in the twenty-first century), which is radically different from the EEA (signified by the two bold wavy lines in Figure 8.1, indicating the significant passage of time since the Pleistocene). The 10,000 years since the end of the Pleistocene Epoch, during which most of our evolved psychological mechanisms emerged, has not been long enough for us to have undergone significant evolutionary changes (see below). That means that, even though we now live in an environment that is radically different from the EEA, our evolved psychological mechanisms in our brain are still essentially the same as they were 10,000 years ago and operate in the same manner. The combination of evolved psychological mechanisms that have remained the same for 10,000 years and the disjuncture between the EEA and the current environment means that both the internal states and the behavior that the evolved psychological mechanisms produce are often maladaptive in the context of the current environment. I will return to this very important observation and its implications later in the chapter. Evolutionary psychology explains both the internal states and behavior as functions of evolved psychological mechanisms expressed in the context of the current environment, which is radically different from the EEA.

Individuals in the current environment are conscious of only the internal states—their values, preferences, desires, and emotions—that incline them to behave in a certain way. They are *not* aware of the evolutionary logic and process (the original adaptive problems and the natural and sexual selection that led to the evolution of the evolved psychological mechanisms that produce the internal states). If you ask individuals, "Why did you do X?" no matter what X may be, the most accurate and honest answer they can give you is "Because I wanted to," in other words, because they had a desire or preference for it. They *are* aware that their internal states led to their behavior. However, if you further ask, "Why did you have a desire to do X?" the individuals are usually unable to answer the question, or any answer that they may come up with is likely to be a post hoc rationalization that is not the true (evolutionary) reason that led to the evolution of the internal states.

If you ask individuals, "Why do you have the desire to eat chocolates?" they may respond, "Because I always eat chocolates on Christmas/Valentine's Day/Easter/Thursdays" or "Because eating Belgian chocolates reminds me of my childhood vacation in Brussels" or "Because they go so well with the espresso that I'm drinking." Few are likely to say, "Because our ancestors who did not prefer to eat sweets like chocolates did not survive long enough to produce many offspring." Similarly, if you ask men, "Why did you get so upset when you thought that your wife may be cheating on you?" they may respond, "Because I love my wife" or "Because the marriage vows we exchanged ought to be sacred" or "It's against our religious values." Few are likely to say, "Because our ancestral men who did not care if their mates cheated on them were likely to be cuckolded and wasted their valuable investment in someone else's genetic children, without leaving many genetic children of their own."

All the "thinking" has been done by evolution, so to speak, and it simply equips the human brain with the appropriate psychological mechanisms, which efficiently and

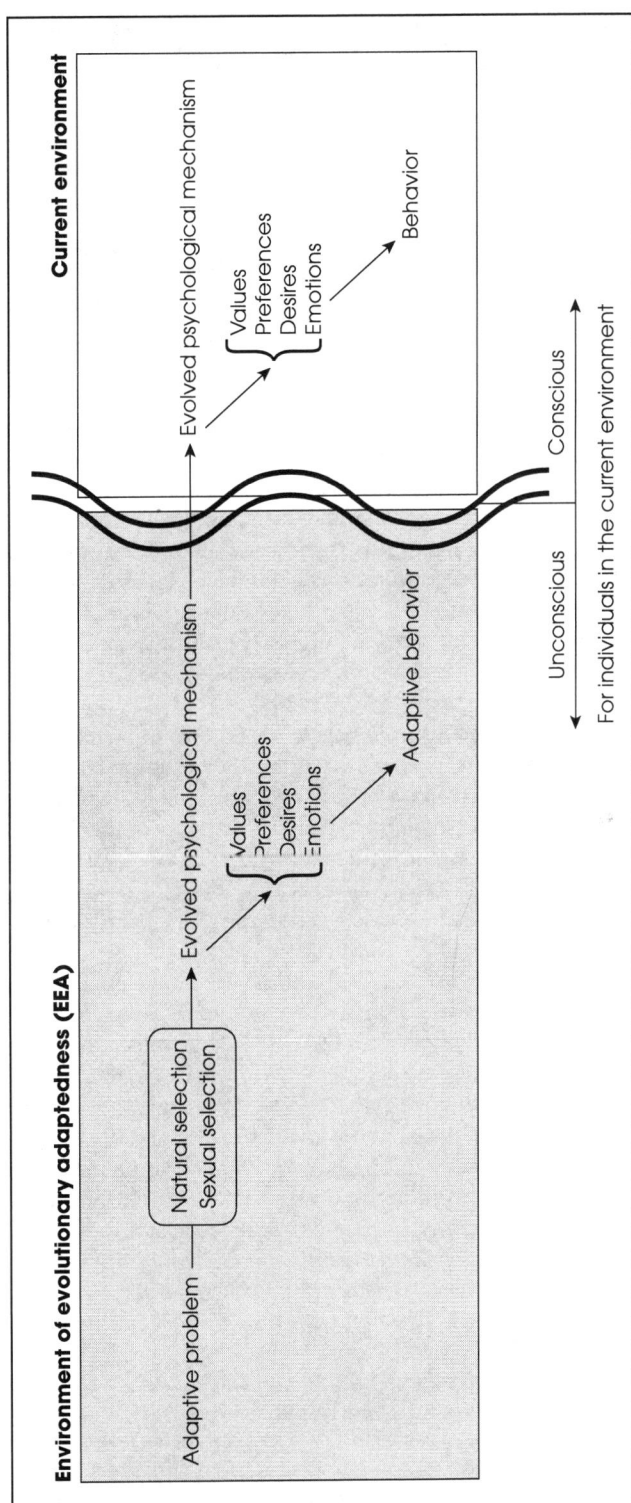

Figure 8.1 Basic theoretical structure of evolutionary psychology

reliably produced solutions to adaptive problems in the context of the EEA. Humans are *not* privy to evolutionary logic; they do not know the true reason that they do what they do. We do not consciously and rationally choose to like sweets and fats or experience sexual jealousy. We simply execute the psychological mechanisms that evolution equips us with.

Principles of Evolutionary Psychology

Evolutionary psychology is characterized by the following four principles, which form very clear contrasts to the four principles of the SSSM discussed above.

1. *People are animals* (Betzig 1997a). The first and most fundamental principle of evolutionary psychology is that there is nothing special about humans. They are just like all the other animal species. Now that does *not* mean that humans are not unique; they are. But then so are all other species. The reason that human beings are a separate species from, say, chimpanzees or bonobos is because no other species have exactly the same set of traits and characteristics that humans do. But the same is true of dogs, cats, giraffes, amebas, and fruit flies. Humans are unique, but no more or less so than fruit flies. Evolutionary psychology recognizes that the same biological laws of evolution apply to humans as they do to all other species. It therefore refutes the human exceptionalism of the SSSM. In the words of the great sociobiologist Pierre van den Berghe, "Certainly we are unique, but we are not unique in being unique. Every species is unique and *evolved* its uniqueness in adaptation to its environment" (1990: 428).
2. *There is nothing special about the human brain.* For evolutionary psychologists, the brain is just another body part, just like the hand or the pancreas. Just as millions of years of evolution have gradually shaped the hand or the pancreas to perform certain functions, so has evolution shaped the human brain to perform its function, which is solving adaptive problems, to help humans survive and reproduce successfully. Evolutionary psychologists apply the same laws of evolution to the human brain as they do to any other part of the human body. Evolution does *not* stop at the neck; it goes all the way up.
3. *Human nature is innate.* Just as dogs are born with innate dog nature, and cats are born with innate cat nature, humans are born with innate human nature. This follows from Principle 1 above. What is true of dogs and cats must also be true of humans, because evolutionary psychology strongly denies human exceptionalism. Socialization and learning are very important for humans, but humans are born with the capacity for cultural learning, which is innate. Culture and learning are part of the evolutionary design for humans. Socialization merely reiterates and reinforces what is already in our brain (like the sense of right and wrong). This principle of evolutionary psychology is in clear contrast to the blank slate ("tabula rasa") assumption of the SSSM. In the memorable words of William D. Hamilton, who is universally regarded as the greatest Darwinian since Darwin, "The *tabula* of human nature was never *rasa* and it is now being read" (endorsement on the cover of Betzig 1997b).
4. *Human behavior is the product of both innate human nature and the environment.* Genes very seldom express themselves in a vacuum. Their expressions—how the genes translate into behavior—often depend on and are guided by the environment. The same genes can express themselves differently depending on the context. In this sense, both innate human nature, which the genes program, and

the environment in which humans grow up are equally important determinants of behavior. Unlike those in the school of the SSSM, evolutionary psychologists do not believe that human behavior is determined 100 percent by either factor.

The Savanna Principle

The second principle of evolutionary psychology discussed in the previous section—that there is nothing special about the human brain as a body part—leads to an important observation, briefly alluded to above. Just as the basic shape and function of the hand or the pancreas have not changed since the end of the Pleistocene Epoch, which ended about 10,000 years ago, the basic functions of the human brain have not changed very much in the last 10,000 years. The human body (including the brain) evolved over millions of years in the African savanna and elsewhere on earth where humans lived during most of this time. This ancestral environment, where humans lived in small bands of 150 or so related individuals as hunter-gatherers, is called the environment of evolutionary adaptedness (EEA) (Bowlby 1969). It is to the EEA for which our entire body (including the brain) is designed and to which it is adapted. Even though we now live in the twenty-first century, we have a stone-age brain (just as we have stone-age hands and a stone-age pancreas).

Our hominid ancestors spent 99.9 percent of their evolutionary history as hunter-gatherers on the African savanna and elsewhere on earth. It was not until about 10,000 years ago when the Agricultural Revolution happened that our ancestors started planting and cultivating their food through agriculture and animal husbandry. Almost everything we see around us today—cities, nation-states, houses, roads, governments, written languages, contraception, TVs, telephones, computers, automobiles, airplanes—emerged in the last 10,000 years. That means that our stone-age brain and body are not necessarily designed for and adapted to the things that came about since the end of the Pleistocene Epoch about 10,000 years ago. Ten thousand years is a very short period of time on the evolutionary time scale; it simply is not enough time for our brain and body to make changes to accommodate the things that came about in the meantime, especially since the environment has been changing too rapidly relative to how slow we mature and reproduce.

Natural and sexual selection can only operate against the backdrop of a stable environment, and the speed of evolution for a species is relative to its rate of maturation (see below). It takes humans fifteen to twenty years to mature and be ready to reproduce. In other words, we still have the same evolved psychological mechanisms that our ancestors possessed more than 10,000 years ago. This observation leads to a new proposition in evolutionary psychology called the Savanna Principle (Kanazawa 2004a), which states:

> The human brain has difficulty comprehending and dealing with entities and situations that did not exist in the ancestral environment.

One example of an entity that did not exist in the ancestral environment is TV or any other realistic images of other humans, such as photographs, videos, or films. The Savanna Principle would therefore predict that the human brain has difficulty comprehending and dealing with images shown on TV. This indeed appears to be the case (Derrick, Gabriel, and Hugenberg 2009; Gardner and Knowles 2008; Kanazawa 2002). Individuals who watch certain types of TV programs are more satisfied with their friendships, as if they had more friends or socialized with them more frequently. According to the Savanna Principle, this is probably because the human brain, designed for and adapted to the ancestral environment, has difficulty distinguishing between our real friends in the flesh and the characters we repeatedly see on TV. In the ancestral environment, any realistic images of other humans *were* other humans, and if you saw them repeatedly and they did not try to kill or harm you in any way, then more than likely they were your friends. Our stone-age brain therefore assumes that the characters we repeatedly encounter on TV, very few of whom try to kill or harm us, are our real friends, and our satisfaction with friendships thereby increases by seeing them more frequently.

Blind Execution of Evolved Psychological Mechanisms in the Current Environment Often Leads to Maladaptive Behavior

Recall the example of our preference for sweets and fats as an evolved psychological mechanism. This psychological mechanism solved the adaptive problem of survival in the ancestral environment by allowing those who possessed it to live longer and stay healthier. Our preferred consumption of sweets and fats was therefore adaptive *in the ancestral environment*. However, we now live in an environment where sweets and fats are abundantly available in every checkout line in every supermarket, in every city, in every industrial society, twenty-four hours a day/seven days a week. In other words, the original adaptive problem (malnutrition and starvation) no longer exists; very few people die of malnutrition in industrial societies. Yet we still possess the same psychological mechanism that compels us to consume sweets and fats. Because our environment is so vastly different from the ancestral environment, we now face a curious situation where those who behave according to the dictates of the evolved psychological mechanism are *worse off* in terms of survival. Obesity and diabetes (to which overconsumption of sweets and fats leads) hinder survival. The Savanna Principle suggests that we continue to have (currently maladaptive) preferences for sweets and fats and as a result become obese and diabetic because our brain cannot really comprehend the supermarkets, abundance of food in general, and indeed agriculture, none of which existed in the ancestral environment. Our brain still assumes that we are hunter-gatherers with very precarious and unpredictable sources of food. If our brain truly comprehended supermarkets, we would not crave sweet and fatty foods.

Similarly, male sexual jealousy is another evolved psychological mechanism that hasn't quite caught up to modern times. It solved the adaptive problem of reproductive success in the ancestral environment by allowing men who possessed it to maximize paternity certainty and minimize the possibility of cuckoldry. Sexual jealousy was therefore adaptive *in the ancestral environment*. However, sex and reproduction are often separated in the current environment; many episodes of sex do not lead to reproduction. There is an abundance of reliable methods of birth control in industrial societies, and many women use the contraceptive pill. For these women, sexual infidelity does not lead to pregnancy and childbirth, and their mates will not have to waste their resources on someone else's children. Even if their mates cheated on them and got pregnant as a result, reliable paternity testing removes any paternity uncertainty. In other words, the original adaptive problem (paternity uncertainty) is much less of a threat to reproductive success of men in the current environment; men today are much less likely unwittingly to invest in someone else's genetic children. Yet men still possess the same psychological mechanism that makes them extremely jealous at even the remotest possibility of their mates' sexual infidelity and compels them to guard their mates to minimize the possibility of such infidelity. *The fact that his adulterous wife was on the pill at the time of her sexual infidelity offers very little consolation to a man.* If men's brain could truly comprehend modern contraception, they should not care at all if their wives on the pill sleep with other men.

Further, once again because our current environment is so vastly different from the ancestral environment, we now face a curious situation where those who behave according to the dictates of the evolved psychological mechanism are often *worse off* in terms of reproductive success. Extreme forms of mate guarding, such as violence against mates or romantic rivals, are crimes in most industrial nations. Incarceration, and consequent physical separation from their mates, does everything to reduce the reproductive success of the men. Yet men continue to exhibit sexual jealousy, and many men engage in extreme forms of mate guarding and vigilance, including violence (Buss 1988, 2000; Buss and Shackelford 1997). The Savanna Principle suggests that this is because their brains cannot truly comprehend effective birth control, written laws, the police, and the courts. If they did, they would not engage in extreme forms of mate guarding (such as violence) or any other criminal behavior for which they would likely go to jail.

Directional Human Evolution Stopped about 10,000 Years Ago

The Savanna Principle points to a couple of very important—but often neglected—observations about human evolution: evolution happens very gradually, and natural and sexual selection require a stable, unchanging environment to which it can respond and against which it can make its selection.

Evolution takes many *generations*, and so the speed of evolution of a species is relative to how long it takes for individuals of the species to mature sexually. Evolution happens faster for fast-maturing species and slower for slow-maturing species. Fruit flies are one of the fastest-maturing species in nature, and humans are one of the slowest. It takes only seven days for fruit flies to mature sexually under ideal conditions, whereas it takes fifteen to twenty years for humans. It means that there can be more than fifty generations of fruit flies in one year, before a human baby can even begin to walk. There are more than a thousand generations of fruit flies in one human generation (twenty years), for which humans need more than 20,000 years. Evolution for fruit flies can happen pretty fast, which is precisely the reason that they are the favorite species for human geneticists to study. Human evolution happens much, much slower. No human scientists can see it in action the way they can observe fruit fly evolution unfold in the lab.

The second point is even more important: natural and sexual selection under most circumstances require a stable, unchanging environment for many, many generations. For example, if the climate is very cold for centuries and millennia, then gradually individuals who have better resistance to cold will be favored by natural selection, and their neighbors who have less resistance to cold (who are more adapted to a hot climate) will die out before they can leave many children. This will happen generation after generation, until one day all humans have great resistance to cold. A new trait—resistance to cold—has now evolved and become part of universal human nature. But this trait could not have evolved if the climate was cold for one century (a mere five human generations, albeit 5,200 fruit fly generations), and then hot for another century, only to be cold again in the third century. Natural selection would not know who (with which traits) to select.

Since the advent of agriculture about 10,000 years ago and the birth of human civilization that followed, humans have not had a stable environment against which natural selection can operate. For example, a mere two centuries (ten generations) ago, the United States and the rest of the Western world were largely agrarian; most people were farmers. In the agrarian society, men achieved higher status by being the best farmers; those who possessed certain traits that made them good farmers had higher status and thus greater reproductive success than others who didn't possess such traits.

Then, only a century later, the United States and Europe were predominantly industrial societies; most men made their living working in factories. Traits that made men good factory workers (or, better yet, factory *owners*) may or may not be the same as the traits that made them good farmers. Traits such as intelligence, diligence, and sociability probably remained important (Kanazawa 2004b), but others, such as a feel for nature, a feel for the soil and animals, and the ability to work outdoors or forecast weather, ceased to be important. Traits such as punctuality, the ability to follow instructions, a feel for machinery, mechanical aptitude, and the ability to work *indoors* suddenly became important.

Now we are in a postindustrial society, where most people work neither in farming nor in the factory but in the service industry. Computers and other electronic devices have become important, and an entirely new set of traits is necessary to be successful. Bill Gates and Sir Richard Branson (and other successful men of today) may not have made particularly successful farmers or factory workers. All of these dramatic changes happened within ten generations. And there is no telling what the next century will bring and what traits will be necessary to be successful in the twenty-second century. We have an unstable, ever-changing environment, and have done so for about 10,000 years.

For hundreds of thousands of years before that, our ancestors lived as hunter-gatherers on the African savanna, in a stable, unchanging environment to which natural and sexual selection could respond. That is why all humans today have traits that would have made them good hunter-gatherers in Africa—men's great spatiovisual skills that allowed them to follow animals on a long hunting trip for days and for miles without a map or a global positioning satellite device and return home safely, and women's great object location memory that allowed them to remember where fruit trees and bushes were and return there every season to harvest, once again without maps or permanent landmarks.

For the last 10,000 years or so, however, our environment has been changing too rapidly for evolution to catch up. Evolution cannot work against moving targets. That's why humans have not evolved in any predictable direction since about 10,000 years ago. Some studies suggest that new alleles may have appeared in the human genome in the last 10,000 years (Evans et al. 2005; Cochran and Harpending 2009). However, with the sole exception of lactose tolerance, these new genes do not appear to have led to the emergence of new evolved physiological or psychological mechanisms in the last 10,000 years. There does not appear to have been any *directional* selection that has produced a new adaptation.

I hasten to add that certain features of our environment have remained more or less constant for the last 10,000 years: we have always had to get along with other humans, and we have always had to find and keep our mates. So certain traits, like sociability or physical attractiveness, have always been favored by natural and sexual selection. But other features of our environment have changed too rapidly relative to our generation time, in a relatively random fashion. (Who could have predicted computers and the Internet a century ago?) So we have not been able to adapt and evolve against the constantly moving target of the environment.

Evolutionary Psychology's Relevance to the Social Sciences

Different branches and fields of the social sciences are roughly divided into two groups. *Micro* social sciences, such as social psychology, political psychology, and microeconomics, mostly explain individual behavior of human actors. *Macro* social sciences, in contrast, such as international relations and macroeconomics, explain the behavior of aggregates of individuals, such as nations, economies, firms, and social groups.

The relevance of evolutionary psychology to micro social sciences is obvious. As it explains human behavior as a function simultaneously of internal states, such as values, preferences, desires, and emotions, produced by evolved psychological mechanisms and of environmental factors, evolutionary psychology offers important theoretical insights to fields like political psychology, such as "Why are some individuals left-wing liberals while others are right-wing conservatives?" (Kanazawa 2010).

However, evolutionary psychology is also relevant to macro social sciences, which seek to explain the behavior of aggregate entities. Because all good science is reductionist (Coleman 1990; Weinberg 1992), all phenomena at a higher level of aggregation must be explained by causal mechanisms operative at a lower level of aggregation in a *micro-macro model* (Hechter 1983; Huber 1991). In social sciences, this typically means that phenomena at the level of collectivities, such as groups, economies, and nations, must be explained by the behavior of the constituent individuals. Every macro social scientific theory of an aggregate phenomenon requires an actor model as its microfoundation (Whitmeyer 1994).

Figure 8.2 presents a micro-macro model of reductionist explanation in social sciences known as the Coleman Boat (Coleman 1990: 1–23). Upper-case letters (X and Y) represent phenomena at the macro level of collectivities, and lower-case letters (x and y) represent phenomena at the micro level of individuals. X/x are the independent variables, and Y/y are the dependent variables. X presents some structural and institutional constraints that individuals within the collectivities face and within which they make their decisions. In a dynamic model, X is usually the macrolevel outcome at an earlier point in time (Y_{t-1}) (Kanazawa 2001: 1131–1134). x represents the causes of individual behavior, which are often the internal states of the individuals (values, preferences, desires, emotions, etc.). X and x together determine the individual behavior y, and y aggregates to the macrolevel explanandum of the model, which, in a reductionist model, emerges as the aggregation of individual choices and actions by a large number of actors.

In the Coleman Boat, x → y represents the microfoundation and the actor model of the macro social scientific theory, which explains how individuals behave. X → x → y → Y represents the reductionist explanation of the macrosocial phenomenon Y in terms of the aggregation of the individual behavior, which in turn is explained in terms of the macrosocial factors X and individual factors x. I now present an example each of the application of evolutionary psychology to the microlevel x → y (or, in this particular example, X → x → y) and the macrolevel X → x → y → Y.

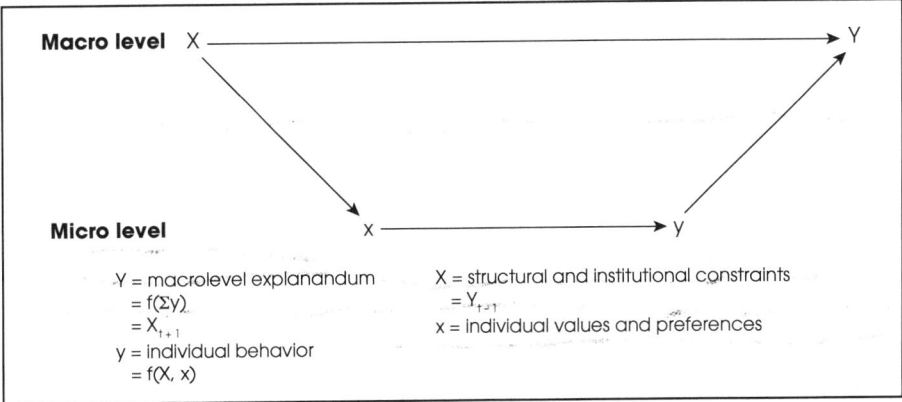

Figure 8.2 The Coleman Boat (micro-macro model)

Micro Illustration: The Hidden Reproductive Motives of Suicide Bombing

According to the Oxford University sociologist Diego Gambetta (2005: 259–263), editor of *Making Sense of Suicide Missions* (a comprehensive history of suicide bombings), while not all suicide missions are religiously motivated, when religion is involved, it is always Islam. No other religion besides Islam ever motivates suicide missions. Indeed, despite varied geography, cultures, languages, and ethnicities, one factor that unites all of our otherwise diverse enemies in the current "War on Terror," from Alqaeda in the Middle East, to Jemaah Islamiyah in Southeast Asia, to the Chechen rebels in Russia, to the Palestinians in Israel, to the Sunni insurgents in Iraq, is Islam. Major Nidal Hassan, Faisal Shahzad, Tamerlan Tsarnev, Dzhokhar Tsarnev, Michael Adebolajo, and Michael Adebowale have very little in common besides Islam.

Why is this? Why is Islam the only religion that motivates its followers to commit suicide missions? Why is Islam a common factor in our otherwise diverse enemies in the current global war? Even though most analysts of suicide bombings assume that the perpetrators' motives are either political or religious, an evolutionary psychological perspective may shed new light on this otherwise puzzling phenomenon. It highlights potential and hidden *reproductive* motives behind suicide bombing.

What distinguishes Islam from other major world religions (Christianity and Judaism) is that it sanctions polygyny. Polygyny, by allowing some men to monopolize women, increases competitive pressure on men, especially young men of low status, who are most likely to be left without reproductive opportunities when older men of higher status and greater resources marry multiple women (Daly and Wilson 1988; Kanazawa 2003; Kanazawa and Still 1999). Polygyny therefore increases the likelihood that young men will resort to violent means to gain access to mates because they have little to lose and much to gain by doing so, compared with men who already have wives. This is why, across all societies, polygyny increases violent crimes, such as murder and rape, even after controlling for such potential confounds as economic development, economic inequality, population density, the level of democracy, and world regions (Kanazawa and Still 2000). So the first unique feature of Islam, which partially contributes to the prevalence of suicide bombings among its followers, is polygyny, which makes young men violent everywhere.

However, polygyny by itself, while it increases violence, is not sufficient to explain suicide bombings. Societies in sub-Saharan Africa and the Caribbean are much more polygynous than the Muslim nations in the Middle East and North Africa; eighteen of the twenty most polygynous nations in the world are in sub-Saharan Africa and the Caribbean (Kanazawa 2007: 11–12, *n*3). Accordingly, nations in these regions have very high levels of violence, and sub-Saharan Africa suffers from a long history of interminable civil wars, *but not suicide bombings*. So polygyny itself is not their sufficient cause.

The other key ingredient is the Koran's promise of seventy-two virgins waiting in heaven for any martyr in Islam. This creates a strong incentive for any young Muslim men who are excluded from reproductive opportunities to commit suicide bombings. Now a vague promise of seventy-two virgins waiting in heaven may not sound so appealing if the Muslim men have even one real mate on earth. However, for young, low-status Muslim men who are excluded from any mating opportunities because of polygyny among older, higher-status men, even such a vague promise in the afterlife begins to be appealing in light of their bleak reproductive prospect on earth.

The Savanna Principle (Kanazawa 2004a), discussed above, is key to understanding the effect of the promise of seventy-two virgins on young Muslim men's motivation to commit suicide bombings. Recall that the Savanna Principle states that the human brain has difficulty comprehending and dealing with entities and situations that did not exist in the ancestral environment. This difficulty, once again, stems from the fact that the human brain, just like any other body part of any other species, is adapted to and designed for the conditions of its evolutionary environment, not necessarily to the current environment (Crawford 1993; Symons 1990; Tooby and Cosmides 1990). (Recall Principle 2 of evolutionary psychology discussed above.) For humans, this means that the human brain implicitly assumes that we still live on the African savanna as hunter-gatherers during the Pleistocene Epoch, roughly 1.6 million to 10,000 years ago.

For example, many young Western men who find themselves chronically dateless resort to pornography for sexual satisfaction. When men see images of sexually receptive women in pornography, they become aroused. This does not make sense, because these men should know that they would never actually meet, let alone copulate with, these sexually receptive women in the movies. So there is no point in getting an erection when they watch pornography, because the only biological function of an erection is to allow men to have sexual intercourse with women. The Savanna Principle suggests, however, that the brain of these men does not really comprehend that they would never copulate with the sexually receptive women they see on the screen, because there were no TV, videos, DVDs, or the Internet in the ancestral environment. All sexually receptive women that our ancestral men ever saw were real, and they were able to have sexual intercourse with them. Adapted to the conditions of the ancestral environment without TV and videos, the brain of young men today cannot really comprehend that they cannot have sex with the porn stars they see on TV. *more nonsense*

Just as the brain of young Western men today is tricked by porn movies, which did not exist in the ancestral environment, the brain of young Muslim men today is tricked by the Koran, which also did not exist in the ancestral environment. Just as the brain of Western men thinks that they can potentially copulate with the sexually receptive women they see in porn movies, the brain of Muslim men thinks that they could copulate with the seventy-two virgins in heaven, *if they die as martyrs*. The behavior of chronically mateless men both in the West and in Muslim nations is partially influenced by their brain's difficulty in comprehending evolutionarily novel entities, such as porn movies or the Koran.

Figure 8.3 presents a partial Coleman Boat (micro-macro model) of suicide bombing from an evolutionary psychological perspective. Just like all living creatures in nature, Muslim men's behavior is largely (albeit mostly unconsciously) motivated by their desire for reproductive success. Unlike other men in other religions and cultures, however, Muslim men make their decisions in the (macrolevel) institutional contexts of polygyny and reproductive reward for martyrdom, both sanctioned by Islam. Muslim men who lack reproductive opportunities on earth and who make their decisions within the institutional constraints of Islam may make the decision to engage in suicide bombing in order to gain access to the seventy-two virgins promised by the Koran.

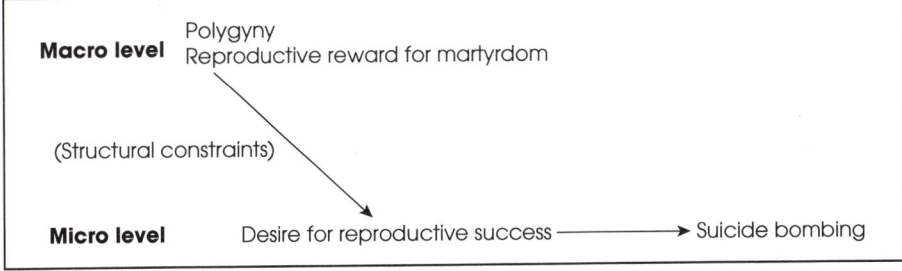

Figure 8.3 Reproductive motives behind suicide bombing

Studies of actual suicide bombers are largely consistent with this view (Kanazawa 2007). Muslim men who join extremist groups like Hezbollah and Hamas tend to be better educated and come from wealthier families than Muslim men who do not join such groups, possibly because such memberships are extremely violent end of political activism and more educated individuals from privileged backgrounds are more likely to participate in politics in general (Krueger and Maleckova 2003). However, once inside the organizations, it is the less educated and poorer members, precisely those with few alternative reproductive opportunities on earth, who often volunteer to become suicide bombers (Berrebi 2003; Krueger and Maleckova 2003). And, during the entire period of the American occupation of Iraq, Iraqi suicide bombers killed *more than sixty times* as many Iraqi civilians as coalition troops (200 coalition troops killed vs. 12,284 Iraqi civilians killed) (Hicks et al. 2011: 910, Table 3). It is as if the Iraqi suicide bombers were trying to eliminate as many of their intrasexual rivals (fellow Iraqi men) as possible, rather than killing coalition troops (the infidels and occupiers) or Iraqi military and police personnel (traitors and collaborators with the enemies).

Among other things, this example illustrates how universal human nature interacts with environmental conditions to produce varied behavior. The evolved psychological mechanism that inclines Muslim men to want to maximize their reproductive success is part of universal human nature, so it is one that Muslim men share with all humans. However, within the macro institutional contexts of polygyny, which increases intrasexual competition among men and reproductive reward for martyrs, it translates into a unique behavior of suicide booming, which is observed in no other religions (Gambetta 2005).

An evolutionary psychological perspective suggests that Muslim suicide bombings may have nothing to do with Islam or the Koran (except for two lines in it, one condoning polygyny, another promising seventy-two virgins to all martyrs). They may have nothing to do with religion, politics, culture, race, ethnicity, language, or region. As is everything else from an evolutionary psychological perspective, they may have everything to do with sex or, in this case, the *absence* of sex.

Macro Illustration: The Institution of Marriage

Why are marriages in some societies monogamous while those in others are polygynous?[2] What accounts for the gradual historical shift from polygyny to monogamy in the course of human civilization? What explains the particular form the institution of marriage takes in a given society or a given time in history? Despite the central importance of marriage and the family in the social sciences, there are few theories of the institution of marriage that address these questions. Kanazawa and Still (1999) provide a macrolevel theory of the emergence of the institution of marriage with a microfoundation of evolutionary psychology.

Among the psychological mechanisms that are most often studied and best documented by evolutionary psychologists are those about mate preferences and selection. There is by now ample evidence that men value youth and physical attractiveness in women and women value wealth and status in men, and that this is largely invariant both historically (Buss and Barnes 1986; Hill 1945; Hudson and Henze 1969; McGinnis 1958) and cross-culturally (Buss 1989, 2003). Men value young and physically attractive women because youth and physical attractiveness were reliable indicators of health and fecundity in the EEA, and women value wealth and status in men because resourceful men of high status can better protect the women and their children and are better able to invest in the children than poor men of low status. Women in the EEA were typically unable to acquire and accumulate valued resources themselves, and men are rare among males in nature in the extent of male parental investment they provide, so women need resourceful men of high status to invest in their children. These evolutionary considerations (such as physical attractiveness and resources) serve as the ultimate causes, of which actors are typically unaware and unconscious (see Figure 8.1). The effects of such ultimate causes on behavior (mate selection) are mediated by proximate causes (love, attraction, desire, and other emotions). Humans believe that they are choosing to mate with the ones they love and desire, not the ones whose characteristics increase their reproductive success. The strength of evolutionary psychology is that it can predict from the ultimate causes whom humans are likely to love and find desirable.

Earlier theories of marriage institution (Alexander 1987; Alexander et al. 1979; Betzig 1986; MacDonald 1990) assume that men's preferences and choices create a particular institution and impose it on women. Kanazawa and Still (1999) first point out that mating is a female choice in every species in which the female makes greater parental investment in the offspring than the male, including humans (Trivers 1972), and then propose a theory that assumes that a particular institution of marriage spontaneously emerges out of thousands or millions of independent choices and decisions made by women.

If women prefer to marry men with greater resources, then, in the absence of any institution of marriage in the form of laws and customs, women should choose to marry polygynously if the resource inequality among men is greater. This is because, under structural conditions where rich men are so much wealthier than poor men, it would be better for women to share a man with greater resources than to have exclusive access to a man with fewer resources. By the same token, women should choose to marry monogamously if the resource inequality among men is less. Under structural conditions where rich men are not that much richer than poor men, women are better off having exclusive access to poor men than sharing rich men.

Further, the effect of resource inequality among men on the marriage institution should be stronger to the extent that women have greater power to decide whom to marry. There should therefore be an interaction effect of resource inequality among men and women's power in society on the marriage institution. Kanazawa and Still (1999) test and support both of these hypotheses with data collected from 127 nations and territories throughout the world. Societies are more likely to have the polygynous institution of marriage when resource inequality among men is greater, and this relationship is stronger to the extent that women have greater power to decide whom to marry.

Figure 8.4 represents Kanazawa and Still's (1999) female choice theory of the marriage institution in a micro-macro model of the Coleman Boat. At the macro level, the society has given levels of resource inequality among men and women's power, both of which are exogenous to the model. These macro structural factors set constraints within which women must make their decisions. Women have the (evolutionarily given) desire to maximize their children's welfare, and choose to marry either monogamously or polygynously, depending on the societal conditions (set by the two macro exogenous factors). Separate and independent individual decisions of thousands or millions of women to marry either monogamously or polygynously will aggregate at the societal level to a particular type of institution of marriage (monogamy or polygyny). Once the institution is in place (Y), it will independently affect and constrain the future marriage choices of women (X_{t+1}). Kanazawa and Still's (1999) theory explains only the original emergence of the marriage institution and its gradual historical change.

Like the micro illustration of suicide bombing discussed above, the macro illustration of the marriage institution also underscores a few important points about the use of evolutionary psychology as a microfoundation for macrosocial theories. First, even though

Figure 8.4 Determinants of marriage institution

the evolved psychological mechanism that produces the desire to maximize the welfare of children is universal among all women (and females of most other species), it interacts with structural constraints (the degree of resource inequality among men and women's power) to produce differential values and preferences (the desire to marry polygynously or monogamously) under different conditions. Second, while women's decision to marry polygynously or monogamously is consciously made, their desire to maximize the welfare of children is not consciously chosen. It derives from a genetically encoded evolved psychological mechanism, and all the thinking behind women's desire to maximize the welfare of children has already been done by evolution. Third, this psychological mechanism (like any other psychological mechanisms) evolved in the EEA and thus only "makes sense" and produces adaptive behavior in the EEA. This is why women's choice of a mate is still largely determined by the men's status and resources in every society even though, at least in the modern Western societies with free capitalist economies, women can choose to acquire resources themselves as well as men can.

Conclusion

Evolutionary psychology is a new, emerging science of the mind, which explains human cognition and behavior as a function of the interaction between species-typical (universal) human nature (or sex-specific male human nature or female human nature) and the environmental factors, such as structural and institutional constraints. It provides a stark contrast to the Standard Social Science Model (SSSM), which pervades most of traditional social sciences. Understanding evolutionary psychology is crucially important for the social sciences for two reasons. First, for micro social scientists who seek to explain human behavior at the individual level, evolutionary psychology currently provides the most ultimate explanation for human behavior, which answers the ultimate, evolutionary question of *why* human beings behave the way they do. Second, for macro social scientists who seek to explain social structures, institutions, and other aggregate outcomes, evolutionary psychology provides the most accurate microfoundation of the Coleman Boat (a micro-macro explanation of social phenomena). Social scientists ignore the biological, genetic, and evolutionary foundations of human behavior and social outcomes only at their own peril.

Notes

1. This is how Darwin originally defined natural and sexual selection, as two separate processes. That is why he wrote two separate books—*On the Origin of Species by Means of Natural Selection* (1859) to explain natural selection, and *The Descent of Man, and Selection in Relation to Sex* (1871) to explain sexual selection. In the 1930s, however, biologists redefined natural selection to subsume sexual selection and began to contend that differential reproductive success was the currency of natural selection. This is now the orthodoxy in all biology textbooks, which claim that sexual selection is but one branch of natural selection (Cronin 1991: 231–243).

    I, however, argue against this orthodoxy. I concur with Geoffrey F. Miller (2000: 8–12), Anne Campbell (2002: 34–35), and others in the current generation of evolutionary psychologists and believe that we should return to Darwin's original definitions and treat natural and sexual selection separately, as two distinct processes. This is still controversial and of the minority opinion, but I firmly believe that the conceptual separation of natural and sexual selection will bring clarity in evolutionary biology and psychology.

2. Because there is a lot of confusion over terminology, I must first clarify different institutions of marriage. *Monogamy* is the marriage of one man to one woman, *polygyny* is the marriage of one man to

more than one woman, *polyandry* is the marriage of one woman to more than one man, and *group marriage* is the marriage of more than one man to more than one woman. *Polygamy*, even though it is often used in common discourse as a synonym for polygyny, refers to polygyny, polyandry, and group marriage simultaneously. It is therefore ambiguous as to what polygamy refers to, and the word should be avoided in any scientific discussion, unless it refers specifically to polygyny, polyandry, and group marriage simultaneously. The reason people use "polygyny" and "polygamy" interchangeably is that there are very few polyandrous societies in the world (polyandry contains the seed of its own extinction), and there are no actual recorded cases of a society that practices group marriage. Thus virtually all polygamous societies are indeed polygynous (Miller and Kanazawa 2007: 81–85).

References

Alexander, R. D. 1987. *The Biology of Moral Systems*. New York: Aldine.
Alexander, R. D., J. L. Hoogland, R. D. Howard, K. M. Noonan, and P. W. Sherman. 1979. "Sexual Dimorphisms and Breeding Systems in Pinnipeds, Ungulates, Primates and Humans." In *Evolutionary Biology and Human Social Behavior: An Anthropological Perspective*, edited by N. A. Chagnon and W. Irons, 402–435. North Scituate, MA: Duxbury Press.
Baker, R. R., and A. Bellis. 1995. *Human Sperm Competition: Copulation, Masturbation and Infidelity*. London: Chapman and Hall.
Barash, D. P. 1982. *Sociobiology and Behavior*. 2nd ed. New York: Elsevier.
Barkow, J. H., ed. 2006. *Missing the Revolution: Darwinism for Social Scientists*. Oxford: Oxford University Press.
Barkow, J. H., L. Cosmides, and J. Tooby, eds. 1992. *The Adapted Mind: Evolutionary Psychology and the Generation of Culture*. New York: Oxford University Press.
Berrebi, C. 2003. "Evidence about the Link between Education, Poverty and Terrorism among Palestinians." Working Paper #477, Industrial Relations Section, Princeton University.
Betzig, L. L. 1986. *Despotism and Differential Reproduction: A Darwinian View of History*. New York: Aldine.
———. 1997a. "People Are Animals." In *Human Nature: A Critical Reader*, edited by L. Betzig, 1–17. New York: Oxford University Press.
———, ed. 1997b. *Human Nature: A Critical Reader*. New York: Oxford University Press.
Bowlby, J. 1969. *Attachment and Loss*. Vol. 1, *Attachment*. New York: Basic Books.
Buss, D. M. 1988. "From Vigilance to Violence: Tactics of Mate Retention." *Ethology and Sociobiology* 9: 291–317.
———. 1989. "Sex Differences in Human Mate Preferences: Evolutionary Hypotheses Tested in 37 Cultures." *Behavioral and Brain Sciences* 12: 1–49.
———. 1995. "Evolutionary Psychology: A New Paradigm for Psychological Science." *Psychological Inquiry* 6: 1–30.
———. 2000. *The Dangerous Passion: Why Jealousy Is as Necessary as Love and Sex*. New York: Free Press.
———. 2003. *The Evolution of Desire: Strategies of Human Mating*. 2nd ed. New York: Basic Books.
———. 2011. *Evolutionary Psychology: The New Science of the Mind*. 4th ed. Boston: Pearson.
Buss, D. M., and M. Barnes. 1986. "Preferences in Human Mate Selection." *Journal of Personality and Social Psychology* 50: 559–570.
Buss, D. M., R. J. Larsen, and D. Westen. 1992. "Sex Differences in Jealousy: Evolution, Physiology, and Psychology." *Psychological Science* 3: 251–255.
———. 1996. "Sex Differences in Jealousy: Not Gone, Not Forgotten, and Not Explained by Alternative Hypotheses." *Psychological Science* 7: 373–375.
Buss, D. M., and T. K. Shackelford. 1997. "From Vigilance to Violence: Mate Retention Tactics in Married Couples." *Journal of Personality and Social Psychology* 72: 346–361.
Buss, D. M., T. K. Shackelford, L. A. Kirkpatrick, J. C. Choe, M. Hasegawa, T. Hasegawa, and K. Bennett. 1999. "Jealousy and the Nature of Beliefs about Infidelity: Tests of Competing Hypotheses about Sex Differences in the United States, Korea, and Japan." *Personal Relationships* 6: 125–150.
Buunk, B., and R. B. Hupka. 1987. "Cross-Cultural Differences in the Elicitation of Sexual Jealousy." *Journal of Sex Research* 23: 12–22.
Campbell, A. 1999. "Staying Alive: Evolution, Culture, and Women's Intrasexual Aggression." *Behavior and Brain Sciences* 22: 203–52.
———. 2002. *A Mind of Her Own: The Evolutionary Psychology of Women*. Oxford: Oxford University Press.
Cartwright, J. 2008. *Evolution and Human Behavior: Darwinian Perspective on Human Nature*. 2nd ed. Basingstoke: Palgrave Macmillan.
Cerda-Flores, R. M., S. A. Barton, L. F. Marty-Gonzalez, F. Rivas, and R. Chakraborty. 1999. "Estimation of Nonpaternity in the Mexican Population of Nuevo Leon: A Validation Study with Blood Group Markers." *American Journal of Physical Anthropology* 109: 281–293.

Cochran, G., and H. Harpending. 2009. *The 10,000 Year Explosion: How Civilization Accelerated Human Evolution*. New York: Basic Books.
Coleman, J. S. 1990. *Foundations of Social Theory*. Cambridge, MA: Harvard University Press.
Cosmides, L. 1989. "The Logic of Social Exchange: Has Natural Selection Shaped How Humans Reason? Studies with the Wason Selection Task." *Cognition* 31: 187–276.
Crawford, C. B. 1993. "The Future of Sociobiology: Counting Babies or Proximate Mechanisms?" *Trends in Ecology and Evolution* 8: 183–186.
Cronin, H. 1991. *The Ant and the Peacock: Altruism and Sexual Selection from Darwin to Today*. Cambridge: Cambridge University Press.
Daly, M., and M. Wilson. 1988. *Homicide*. New York: De Gruyter.
Daly, M., M. Wilson, and S. J. Weghorst. 1982. "Male Sexual Jealousy." *Ethology and Sociobiology* 3: 11–27.
Darwin, C. 1859. *On the Origin of Species by Means of Natural Selection*. London: John Murray.
———. 1871. *The Descent of Man, and Selection in Relation to Sex*. London: John Murray.
Del Giudice, M. 2009. "On the Real Magnitude of Psychological Sex Differences." *Evolutionary Psychology* 7: 264–279.
———. 2013. "Multivariate Misgivings: Is *D* a Valid Measure of Group and Sex Differences?" *Evolutionary Psychology* 11: 1067–1076.
Derrick, J. L., S. Gabriel, and L. Hugenberg. 2009. "Social Surrogacy: How Favored Television Programs Provide the Experience of Belonging." *Journal of Experimental Social Psychology* 45: 352–362.
DeSteno, D., M. Y. Bartlett, J. Braverman, and P. Salovey. 2002. "Sex Differences in Jealousy: Evolutionary Mechanism or Artifact of Measurement?" *Journal of Personality and Social Psychology* 83: 1103–1116.
Ellis, B. J., and D. F. Bjorklund, eds. 2005. *Origins of the Social Mind: Evolutionary Psychology and Child Development*. New York: Guilford.
Ellis, L. 1996. "A Discipline in Peril: Sociology's Future Hinges on Curing Its Biophobia." *American Sociologist* 27: 21–41.
Evans, P. D., S. L. Gilbert, N. Mekel-Bobrov, E. J. Wallender, J. R. Anderson, L. M. Vaez-Azizi, S. A. Tishkoff, R. R. Hudson, and B. T. Lahn. 2005. "*Microcephalin*, a Gene Regulating Brain Size, Continues to Evolve Adaptively in Humans." *Science* 309: 1717–1720.
Gambetta, D. 2005. "Can We Make Sense of Suicide Missions?" In *Making Sense of Suicide Missions*, edited by D. Gambetta, 259–299. Oxford: Oxford University Press.
Gardner, W. L., and M. L. Knowles. 2008. "Love Makes You Real: Favorite Television Characters Are Perceived as 'Real' in a Social Facilitation Paradigm." *Social Cognition* 26: 156–168.
Gaulin, S. J. S., D. H. McBurney, and S. L. Brakeman-Wartell. 1997. "Matrilateral Biases in the Investment of Aunts and Uncles: A Consequence and Measure of Paternity Uncertainty." *Human Nature* 8: 139–151.
Harris, C. R. 2003. "A Review of Sex Differences in Sexual Jealousy, Including Self-Report Data, Psychophysiological Responses, Interpersonal Violence, and Morbid Jealousy." *Personality and Social Psychology Review* 7: 102–128.
Hechter, M., ed. 1983. *The Microfoundations of Macrosociology*. Philadelphia: Temple University Press.
Hicks, M. H., H. Dardagan, P. M. Bagnall, M. Spagat, and J. A. Sloboda. 2011. "Casualties in Civilians and Coalition Soldiers from Suicide Bombings in Iraq, 2003–10: A Descriptive Study." *Lancet* 378: 906–914.
Hill, Reuben. 1945. "Campus Values in Mate Selection." *Journal of Home Economics* 37: 554–558.
Huber, Joan, ed. 1991. *Macro-Micro Linkages in Sociology*. Newbury Park, CA: Sage Publications.
Hudson, J. W., and L. F. Henze. 1969. "Campus Values in Mate Selection: A Replication." *Journal of Marriage and the Family* 31: 772–775.
Kanazawa, S. 2001. "De Gustibus *Est* Disputandum." *Social Forces* 79: 1131–1163.
———. 2002. "Bowling with Our Imaginary Friends." *Evolution and Human Behavior* 23: 167–171.
———. 2003. "Why Productivity Fades with Age: The Crime-Genius Connection." *Journal of Research in Personality* 37: 257–272.
———. 2004a. "The Savanna Principle." *Managerial and Decision Economics* 25: 41–54.
———. 2004b. "General Intelligence as a Domain-Specific Adaptation." *Psychological Review* 111: 512–523.
———. 2007. "The Evolutionary Psychological Imagination: Why You Can't Get a Date on a Saturday Night and Why Most Suicide Bombers Are Muslim." *Journal of Social, Evolutionary, and Cultural Psychology* 1: 7–17.
———. 2010. "Why Liberals and Atheists Are More Intelligent." *Social Psychology Quarterly* 73: 33–57.
Kanazawa, S., and M. C. Still. 1999. "Why Monogamy?" *Social Forces* 78: 25–50.
———. 2000. "Why Men Commit Crimes (and Why They Desist)." *Sociological Theory* 18: 434–447.
Krueger, A. B., and J. Maleckova. 2003. "Education, Poverty and Terrorism: Is There a Causal Connection?" *Journal of Economic Perspectives* 17: 119–144.
MacDonald, K. 1990. "Mechanisms of Sexual Egalitarianism in Western Europe." *Ethology and Sociobiology* 11: 195–238.

Machalek, R., and M. W. Martin. 2004. "Sociology and the Second Darwinian Revolution: A Metatheoretical Analysis." *Sociological Theory* 22: 455–476.

McGinnis, R. 1958. "Campus Values in Mate Selection: A Repeat Study." *Social Forces* 36: 368–373.

Miller, A. S., and S. Kanazawa. 2007. *Why Beautiful People Have More Daughters*. New York: Perigee.

Miller, G. F. 2000. *The Mating Mind: How Sexual Choice Shaped the Evolution of Human Nature*. New York: Doubleday.

Pietrzak, R. H., J. D. Laird, D. A. Stevens, and N. S. Thompson. 2002. "Sex Differences in Human Jealousy: A Coordinated Study of Forced-Choice, Continuous Rating-Scale, and Physiological Responses on the Same Subjects." *Evolution and Human Behavior* 23: 83–94.

Pincott, J. 2008. *Do Gentlemen Really Prefer Blondes? Bodies, Behavior, and Brains—The Science Behind Sex, Love, and Attraction*. New York: Delta.

Pinker, S. 2002. *The Blank Slate: The Modern Denial of Human Nature*. London: Penguin.

Ridley, M. 1993. *The Red Queen: Sex and the Evolution of Human Nature*. New York: Penguin.

Symons, D. 1979. *The Evolution of Human Sexuality*. Oxford: Oxford University Press.

———. 1990. "Adaptiveness and Adaptation." *Ethology and Sociobiology* 11: 427–444.

Tooby, J., and L. Cosmides. 1990. "The Past Explains the Present: Emotional Adaptations and the Structure of Ancestral Environments." *Ethology and Sociobiology* 11: 375–424.

———. 1992. "The Psychological Foundations of Culture." In *The Adapted Mind: Evolutionary Psychology and the Generation of Culture*, edited by J. H. Barkow, L. Cosmides, and J. Tooby, 19–136. New York: Oxford University Press.

Trivers, R. L. 1972. "Parental Investment and Sexual Selection." In *Sexual Selection and the Descent of Man 1871–1971*, edited by B. Campbell, 136–179. Chicago: Aldine.

van den Berghe, P. L. 1990. "From the Popocatepetl to the Limpopo." In *Authors of Their Own Lives: Intellectual Autobiographies by Twenty American Sociologists*, edited by B. M. Berger, 410–431. Berkeley: University of California Press.

Weinberg, S. 1992. *Dreams of a Final Theory*. New York: Pantheon.

White, G. L. 1981. "Some Correlates of Romantic Jealousy." *Journal of Personality* 49: 129–147.

Whitmeyer, J. M. 1994. "Why Actor Models Are Integral to Structural Analysis." *Sociological Theory* 12: 153–165.

Williams, G. C. 1966. *Adaptation and Natural Selection: A Critique of Some Current Evolutionary Thought*. Princeton, NJ: Princeton University Press.

Wright, Robert. 1994. *The Moral Animal: The New Science of Evolutionary Psychology*. New York: Vintage.

Chapter Nine
Where Do We Stand with Respect to Evolutionary Studies of Human Behavior?

John Alcock

> Evolutionary studies of human behavior (EHB), whether conducted by biologists, psychologists, sociologists, or anthropologists, are based on the theory of evolution by natural selection, a powerful and well-tested theory. The theory provides the foundation for explanations, or hypotheses if you will, on the adaptive value of particular behavior traits, hypotheses that must be and have been tested prior to their acceptance. Testing always involves deriving predictions (expected results) from the hypothesis in question and then securing the data, observations, and experimental findings that permit an evaluation of the validity of the predictions and thus of the related hypothesis. The approach of EHB is the same as that employed by scientists in general, and as a result we now know a great deal about the effects of past reproductive competition on the evolution of human behavioral attributes. Despite the scientific nature of EHB, work in this area has been subject to many criticisms, ranging from the assertion that researchers in this field accept wild-eyed speculations about the adaptive basis of human behavior to the claim that EHB provides a foundation for immoral social and political positions. These critiques owe a great deal to Stephen Jay Gould, an influential evolutionary biologist, who wrote many pieces, starting in the 1970s, arguing that EHB was fatally flawed. Here I review these arguments, which have been picked up by a number of modern journalists despite the fact that rebuttals to the standard claims against EHB are legion and have been around for years. Although academics have largely been persuaded by the rebuttals, which are also outlined here, the repetition of outdated and unfounded complaints about EHB continues in the popular press. I consider some possible reasons why criticism of EHB is so persistent in the nonacademic arena and what might be done to bring about general acceptance of the value of an evolutionary approach to human behavior.

I found inspiration for this chapter in an opinion piece published in the *New York Times* by Dan Slater (2013), a journalist and author, who wrote disparagingly of evolutionary psychology and its approach to behavioral differences between men and women. The overwhelming majority of the many persons who commented on this piece agreed enthusiastically with Slater. For Slater and most of his readers, evolutionary psychology is a seriously flawed discipline whose shortcomings have been revealed by social scientists employing a sociocultural alternative to evolutionary thinking. Here I want to examine the nature of the criticisms advanced by Slater and numerous others in order to show that these complaints are woefully outdated and essentially irrelevant for academics using evolutionary theory to study human behavior (Kenrick 1995; Lopreato and Crippen 1999; Alcock 2001; Pinker 2002). Nevertheless, the persistence and apparent attractiveness of these claims for the general public raise important questions for researchers in the various fields linked to an evolutionary approach: why are failed critiques of evolutionary human behavior still prevalent, and how should researchers respond to these attacks? I plan to examine these questions in the latter part of the chapter.

First, however, why might sociologists with an evolutionary interest in human behavior care about a book chapter inspired by a journalist's critique of evolutionary psychology? For one thing, both evolutionary psychology and evolutionary sociology use natural selection theory as a foundation for an analysis of human social behavior (Maryanski 1994; Nielsen 1994; Daly and Wilson 1999). These two disciplines, as well as human sociobiology (Smith, Borgerhoff Mulder, and Hill 2001) and evolutionary anthropology (Cronk 1991), make up what might be called the evolutionary study of human behavior (EHB). Yes, there are ongoing debates about the proper theoretical foundation of the various disciplines exploring human behavior (Symons 1989; Reeve and Sherman 1993; Smith, Borgerhoff Mulder, and Hill 2001; Wilson and Wilson 2007). However, researchers in these four fields of EHB share the conviction that Darwinian evolutionary theory, of which natural selection theory is central, provides a basis for the study of human behavior and the underlying psychological and sociological mechanisms that influence what we do (Mysterud 2004; Durrant and Ward 2011). If a human behavioral ability is the product of natural selection, it is expected to help individuals reproduce successfully or pass on their genes to subsequent generations—to the extent that the present environment matches the one in which the ability evolved. This expectation underlies all the disciplines of EHB, and all other evolutionary disciplines for that matter. Thus, an attack on evolutionary psychology is also an attack on evolutionary sociology. In order to develop an effective response to these criticisms, let us review what some of the major criticisms are and how they have been dealt with in the past.

Complaint #1: EHB Researchers Are Unscientific

Of the many complaints about EHB, perhaps the most severe is that academics in this collection of fields are failed scientists. This charge underlies the freedom with which critics have vilified research and researchers who employ an adaptationist (i.e., selectionist) approach to human behavior. The name-calling began when Stephen Jay Gould and his colleagues denounced sociobiology (Allen et al. 1975; Allen et al. 1976) following publication of a book with that title by Edward O. Wilson (1975). In a multiauthored paper on the supposed failures of this supposedly "new" discipline, Gould and company outline a large number of items before summarizing, "What we are left with then is a particular theory about human nature, which has no scientific support" (Allen et al. 1975: 44). For "particular" you can substitute "idiosyncratic" or "arbitrary."

Subsequently, when Gould turned his attention to evolutionary psychology, which can be thought of as an outgrowth or new form of sociobiology, he amplified his claim that academics in this field were nonscientists. As Steven Pinker (1997) has pointed out, Gould (1997a, b) in articles in the *New York Review* labeled evolutionary psychologists "foolish," "fatuous," "pathetic," "egregiously simplistic," and "fanatical." As evidence for the failure of sociobiologists (and by extension other EHB researchers) to do "real" science, Gould and his colleague Richard Lewontin proclaimed that these academics favored just-so stories (i.e., wildly fanciful speculations à la Rudyard Kipling) that were published without an effort to determine their validity, the very antithesis of proper scientific investigation (Gould and Lewontin 1979). Although Gould rarely identified specific examples of just-so stories, the canard continues to be popular (Ehrlich and Feldman 2003). For a recent example, see the article by Anthony Gottlieb (2012) in the *New Yorker*, in which he tells us that evolutionary psychologists offer worthless speculations about the function of the human mind rather than producing true insights about the relationship between brain and behavior.

The just-so story criticism has irritated many evolutionary biologists and psychologists (Alcock 2001; Andrews, Gangestad, and Matthews 2002). In one of the first responses, Jerram Brown (1982) correctly pointed out that silly speculations of the sort that Gould attributed to sociobiologists and others were not favored by scientists of any sort, whereas sensible speculations were universally used as a critical first step in doing science. This point has been repeated many times because it is a valid rebuttal that gets to the heart of how science is actually done (Barash and Lipton 2010; Kurzban 2012). Scientists must lay out a possible explanation for something they wish to explain before going on to test that hypothesis. By labeling someone else's hypotheses as (silly) just-so stories, the labeler hopes to have readers join him or her in dismissing these explanations out of hand without ever considering how they might be tested (Kurzban 2012). Untested speculations, especially absurd ones, do not get into the scientific literature now—or back in the 1970s.

The just-so story is only one of several variants designed to convince others that EHB researchers fail to meet even the minimum standards of scientific investigation. In Slater's *New York Times* piece, he focuses on how EHB researchers try to explain differences between men and women in their sexual behavior. These researchers, according to Slater (2013), "begin with a hypothesis about how modern humans mate: say, that men think about sex more than women do. Then they gather evidence—from studies, statistics and surveys—to support that assumption. Finally, and here's where the leap occurs, they construct an evolutionary theory to explain why men think about sex more than women." In other words, readers are told that these pseudoscientists start with an assumption about a difference between the sexes that they then support by selective data collection before constructing some sort of wild theory (namely, a just-so story) about the evolutionary basis for what they assumed was true from the beginning.

If Slater had even cursorily examined papers by evolutionary psychologists, he would see that he has things completely backward. EHB types *start* with Darwinian evolutionary theory, which provides a foundation for their hypotheses—and an awfully good foundation it is, I might add—one that has been well tested, long used, and subject to continuous scrutiny since 1859. Here's what really happens when EHB scientists try to explain why (for example) men and women seem to differ in their enthusiasm for casual sex. The basic EHB argument is that male reproductive success could usually be raised by having sex with women whom the gentlemen in question had no intention of supporting down the road (Daly and Wilson 1983; Geary 2010). Sex of this sort might in some cases lead to pregnancy; some pregnancies might result in offspring that the women were able to rear to the age of reproduction without the help of the actual father. If men with inclinations for casual sex really did produce more surviving offspring than individuals who refused opportunities for this kind of sexual activity, then Darwinian natural selection would favor whatever hereditary contribution there was for the development of differences between the two categories of men. Over time, natural selection could produce populations of males almost universally capable of considering casual sex as an option under some circumstances.

Women, on the other hand, can generally be expected to avoid sexual promiscuity because their reproductive success is dependent on the number of offspring they produce that will reach the age of reproduction, something that is rarely increased by indiscriminate sexual activity (Daly and Wilson 1983; Gangestad and Simpson 2000). Pregnancies are costly to childbearing women; the presence of a helpful partner should often help the pregnant woman pay those costs and the others that follow childbirth. If so, natural selection might well have favored women who were less interested in chances to mate with many different partners. Selection of this sort should eliminate genes that predispose women to engage in casual sex.

The point here is that evolutionary theory *precedes* the development of evolutionary hypotheses. Once a hypothesis is in place, then the goal of the researcher is to test his or her explanation—not to seek out supportive evidence that will "prove" that the hypothesis is correct. Biased testing of this sort will rarely, if ever, pass muster when the paper is submitted for review prior to publication. Researchers of all sorts no doubt hope that their tests will show that their ideas are correct, but the point of testing is to accurately determine whether a hypothesis is in fact right or wrong. The elimination of incorrect explanations is acknowledged to be a worthy outcome by all scientists, including those working in the area of EHB, thanks to the philosopher of science Karl Popper (1959).

We might test the proposition that the sexual behavior of men and women reflects past natural selection for different degrees of interest in casual sex by then *predicting* that men today will think more about sexual activity than women. The relevant data could be gathered by surveys of men and women, and they have been (Ellis and Symons 1990). They confirm the prediction that men do indeed think more about sex than women; this result leads to greater confidence in the hypothesis that produced the prediction.

This is of course not the only testable prediction that follows from EHB as applied to differences among men and women in the degree to which they are capable of indiscriminate sexual behavior. Homosexual men *should* (i.e., are predicted to) be more willing to engage in sex with strangers than homosexual women (Symons 1979). If offered a chance to engage in casual sex, men *should* be more likely to say yes than are women (Clark and Hatfield 1989; Gueguen 2011). If asked how many partners they would like to have over a period of time, men *are predicted to* indicate a larger number than are women (Buss and Schmitt 1993). Men *are expected to* have lower standards when asked about the IQ of a casual sexual partner than are women (Kenrick et al. 1990). Men, not women, *should* be willing at times to pay for the opportunity to copulate (Symons 1979). All these tests and many more (Salmon 2012) have been conducted with positive results suggesting that the EHB hypothesis about what causes men and women to differ with respect to indiscriminate sex is correct.

The key is that EHB is a science in which evolutionary theory provides an underpinning for the development of testable hypotheses. The theory comes first, not last. There is a huge scientific literature in the area of animal behavior, not just human behavior, that demonstrates the productivity of this approach. To discard it when trying to understand human behavior would be inane. More importantly, the nature of EHB research shows that the workers in this field use exactly the same scientific procedures as all other evolutionary biologists, and indeed all other scientists.

Complaint #2: The Panadaptationist Charge

Slater (2013) quotes Gould approvingly as the author of the complaint that the field of evolutionary human behavior "had become overrun with 'ultra-Darwinians,'" by which

Gould meant individuals who assumed that every trait was a naturally selected adaptation that by definition helped individuals pass on their genes successfully. Indeed, only researchers who believed in the universality of adaptation would accept willy-nilly the just-so accounts of the adaptive value of the attributes of living things. Gould, in keeping with his eagerness to bad-mouth the groups he had selected as his opponents, sometimes referred to these uncritical individuals as Panglossian Darwinians or pop sociobiologists (Gould and Lewontin 1979). For him, true evolutionary biologists (such as Stephen Jay Gould) were aware of the diversity of mechanisms for evolutionary change and so avoided the (obvious) errors made by unsophisticated believers that natural selection alone was responsible for all the characteristics observed in all living things. Gould (1997b) liked to characterize himself as a pluralist who understood that evolution could be influenced by factors other than natural selection, such as genetic drift, extinction, and so on.

That the charge of single-minded (i.e., foolish) panadaptationism is a gross distortion of the approach of EHB researchers is a point that has been made many times, perhaps most vehemently by John Tooby and Leda Cosmides (1997). They point out that in their own research into the psychological basis of human social behavior, they specifically considered nonadaptationist hypotheses such as the possibility that the traits under investigation arose as by-products of the operation of psychological mechanisms with other adaptive properties (Crespi 2000). Thornhill and Palmer (2000), whose study of rape generated much indignant criticism, also emphasized that the hypothesis that rape was adaptive under some conditions was only one possible explanation for the occurrence of forced copulation in humans. An alternative that received equal attention from them (but not from their critics) is that this capacity is a side effect of other sexual motivating mechanisms, such as ease of sexual arousal, which have adaptive effects distinct from the nonadaptive or maladaptive consequences of rape attempts. In other words, evolutionary scientists of all sorts, not just Stephen Jay Gould and his followers, are aware of the need to consider hypotheses other than the first one that comes to mind about the possible adaptive value of this or that attribute.

Well before Gould began his crusade, George C. Williams (1966) urged caution in assigning the label adaptation to biological traits. Williams was concerned primarily with uncritical attributions of group benefits for characteristics that were more likely to have evolved because of their contribution to individual genetic success. Even so, the fact that his extremely influential book was published in 1966 demonstrates that an awareness of the need to carefully define adaptation preceded Gould by a decade.

Moreover, even when one recognizes that natural selection produces complex traits whose genetic benefits to individuals exceed their costs, one still has to test one or more hypotheses on how the trait in question achieves this unconscious goal. Imagine that there really were Panglossian adaptationists who believed that all traits were adaptations of one sort or another. These persons would still have to rigorously test the putative adaptive function(s) that they ascribed to the trait in order to publish their ideas; fair tests would reveal the error of their ways if they were indeed erroneous.

COMPLAINT #3: THE "NO TIME MACHINE" ARGUMENT

Some EHB researchers, notably Tooby and Cosmides (1992), have made the point that our psychological systems evolved in the distant past. If we could identify what selection pressures were present in the human environment then, we might better understand the evolved properties of our brain. Some critics have argued that there is no reason to think that our brain is largely unchanged given the possibility of rapid genetic evolution in response to altered cultural and environmental conditions. But if one puts forth a hypothesis based on the assumption that a feature of brain operation evolved in the distant past and is wrong, then the test of the hypothesis will force the erroneous EHB researcher to reject his or her idea and consider alternatives. No damage done.

A more common complaint about EHB research based on the kind of approach favored by Tooby and Cosmides is that we cannot go back in a time machine to see what was going on in the environment of the past (the environment of evolutionary adaptedness—Tooby and Cosmides 1992). Therefore, we can only speculate fruitlessly about the adaptive value of assorted human psychological mechanisms and behavioral traits. Dan Slater (2013) puts it this way in his *New York Times* opinion piece: "Of course, no fossilized record can really tell us how people behaved or thought back then, much less *why* they behaved or thought as they did." The point that Slater hopes to make here is that you cannot study the evolution of human behavior in the absence of some record of what people did or thought in the prehistory of our species.

Most persons who raise this complaint never apply it to species other than humans, although Gould (1981, 1982, 1984) did. He tried to attack behavioral ecologists in general for their supposedly excessive interest in adaptations of nonhuman animals, knowing that if the discipline were widely accepted (as it is now), criticisms of a similar evolutionary approach to human behavior would become less effective. Yet despite an absence of time machines, behavioral ecologists routinely test hypotheses about the adaptive value of the traits of ants and zebras and everything in between (Alcock 2013). Let me emphasize that hypotheses about ants and zebras that are wrong with respect to their underlying assumptions about past selection will, if tested properly, be shown to be wrong. The same applies to hypotheses about the adaptive value of human behavioral traits.

Moreover, in the case of humans, it is bizarre to claim that we can know *nothing* about the conditions that applied in our evolutionary past that could have affected behavioral evolution. There are numerous features of the ancestral human environment that we can be reasonably confident applied to persons who were alive then thanks to studies of modern hunter-gatherers as well as studies of our closest relative, the chimpanzee. These traits include such things as the rearing of children primarily by females, greater aggression among males than among females, and so on. As Hagen (2005) points out, the fact that so many features of human behavior have been shown to be *currently* adaptive is evidence that the ancestral environment of humans had many features in common with the current environment—because our behavioral abilities evolved in that ancestral environment, not the current one.

The evolutionary effect of likely features of the past can be examined by testing EHB hypotheses about the adaptive value of particular traits. For example, given that women have for millennia ovulated for only a few days each month, sociobiologists have predicted that men will find ovulating women more sexually attractive than those who are in the nonovulatory phase of their menstrual cycle (Penton-Voak et al. 1999; Singh and Bronstad 2001). Matings with ovulating women are much more likely to result in offspring than matings with women in the other phases of the menstrual cycle. The prediction of a male preference for ovulating women goes against the conclusion of many reproductive biologists prior to the last decade or so that neither women nor men could tell when a woman was fertile (Thornhill and Gangestad 2008). Despite the general view, evolutionary psychologists were willing and able to place the EHB prediction on the table for checking. For example, when men are offered a chance to see two composite images of the same set of women, one set taken during ovulation and the other when the women were in their nonovulatory phase, men find the ovulatory composite significantly more attractive (Jones et al. 2008). The differences between the two images are slight, but the ability to detect those differences could increase the probability that men will seek to copulate with ovulating women (i.e., partners with the ability to become pregnant), in which case the preference will promote the propagation of the males' genes.

The idea that ovulating women might be especially attractive to men has been tested many times. Indeed, one relatively recent paper on changes in the facial attractiveness of women across the menstrual cycle has already been cited over three hundred times (Penton-Voak et al. 1999). A more recent test of the hypothesis that male behavior is affected by female ovulation comes from a study of the tips men supplied to the lap dancers with whom they had interacted (Miller, Tybur, and Jordan 2008). Researchers led by Geoffrey Miller predicted that for lap dancers off the pill, women who were at the ovulatory phase of their menstrual cycle would receive larger tips than women at different stages. In addition, they predicted that women who were on the pill (and thus could not conceive, of course) would receive smaller tips than their ovulating coworkers. The actual data collected from a group of New Mexican lap dancers were consistent with the predictions, leading the researchers to conclude (properly) that their findings supported the EHB hypothesis that ovulation makes women more sexually appealing to men. Incidentally, the paper on this subject received an Ig Nobel Prize in 2008 for irrelevant economics research, but it should have been lauded as an example of testable EHB research. The men presumably could unconsciously detect the ovulatory state of their lap dancer partner by her odor and from her behavior. Here is a novel adaptive ability of humans that has been identified via EHB science. The more general point is that the absence of time machines has not prevented EHB researchers from testing hypotheses about the adaptive value of the attributes of humans any more than behavioral ecologists have been unable to study behavioral adaptations in spotted hyenas and western bluebirds.

Complaint #4: The Charge of Genetic Determinism

Gould and his adherents repeatedly asserted that sociobiologists and the like accept the absurd conclusion that human behavior is genetically determined (Gould 1976; Rose 1997). That this view is indeed absurd is obvious to anyone with even a passing knowledge of cultural diversity, which is to say almost everybody. The differences between Masai warriors and US Marines ought to be enough to convince even the most hardened genetic determinist, if any such person actually exists, that the environment plays a role, in fact an important role, in the development of human behavior. In reality, of course, biologists and others have long known that the development of all organisms is an interactive process in which genetic information by itself can do nothing. Instead, development is well known to require both genetic information and environmental inputs in the form of molecules ingested, or neuronal stimulation, or experiences sensed by the developing organism (Durrant and Ward 2011). This understanding is not recent; in the second edition of my textbook, published in 1979, I had no difficulty finding and reporting on evidence of "the complementary role genes and the environment play in the development of all behavioral abilities" (Alcock 1979: 100).

Another version of the genetic determinist complaint is that EHB research requires that human behavior be "hardwired," a term that is rarely defined but clearly means that the behavior is innate, inflexible, immutable (i.e., genetically determined). When John Horgan (2012) says that we are not natural-born killers but that certain things in our environments, our cultures, and our wartime experiences can create killers, he implies that evolutionary psychologists believe that killing is something we are all hardwired to perform no matter what. For Horgan, killers are "a cultural problem, not a genetic one."

Horgan was writing in response to an article by the columnist David Brooks that Horgan found too sympathetic to evolutionary psychology. But Brooks himself has been critical of the discipline in a piece in which he reviewed the claim that ostentatious materialism is part of an evolved male mating strategy to demonstrate the wealth of the individual, thereby improving a male's attractiveness to females. Brooks wrote, "But individuals aren't formed before they enter society. Individuals are created by social interaction. Our identities are formed by the particular rhythms of maternal attunement, by the shared webs of ideas, symbols and actions that vibrate through us second by second. Shopping isn't merely a way to broadcast permanent, inborn traits. For some people, it's also an activity of trying things on in the never-ending process of creating and discovering who they are" (2009).

Horgan and Brooks evidently believe that the existence of cultural (environmental) effects on human activities eliminates the possibility that our evolutionary history influences which environmental factors have these effects. Brooks's quote provides a classic example of the failure to distinguish between the immediate (proximate) and the historical (evolutionary) causes of behavior (see below). For the purposes of this section, the quote also illustrates the mistaken belief that "inborn traits" are genetic, inflexible, fixed attributes of some sort. As everyone knows, human behavior is highly flexible and culturally diverse; the goal of the genetic determinism criticism is therefore to show that EHB researchers must be totally out of touch with reality. In addition, critics of this sort are claiming that if human behavioral traits are *not* universal but vary from culture to culture, then there can be *no* genetic basis for the traits in question; therefore, these traits cannot be the result of an evolutionary process based on natural selection, which acts on hereditary variation among individuals.

But just a second. Horgan, Brooks, and all others who bandy about the charge of genetic determinism ought to realize that the ability to acquire a language (for example) requires genetic information. Our DNA helps us develop a very special kind of brain, one that underlies our ability to learn the language of our culture. In other words, our crowning distinction, the ability to learn a complex human language as an infant, is both "genetic" (in the sense of being dependent on portions of the brain that are the product of an interaction between genetic information and the environment) and flexible in responding to the various acoustical conditions that an infant experiences (Pinker 1994).

Language is just one example of a trait dependent on an evolved *conditional strategy* (Dawkins 1980), to employ the jargon of behavioral ecology. Behavioral ecologists usually escape abuse from environmental determinists and other critics probably because humans are not among the animals of interest to the vast majority of persons working in this field. But thanks to the studies of behavioral ecologists on species other than *Homo sapiens*, we know that the ability to switch from one behavioral option to another is itself a naturally selected attribute of many species. A male hangingfly that fails to secure a dead cricket or other bit of insect carrion with which to attract a female will often secrete a small dollop of saliva that may do the job instead. If the male is unable to produce or defend an edible salivary gift, he may instead track down a female and try to force her to copulate with him (Thornhill 1981).

In other words, the adult male hangingfly and a human infant being reared by Urdu-speaking parents have more in common than meets the eye. They both have an evolved nervous system that endows them with the adaptive capacity to respond in particular ways to the variable environmental conditions they may encounter. The male hangingfly that cannot acquire a dead cricket is not doomed to reproductive failure but will pick the second-best option, which enables him to do better than he could if he dropped out of the competition for mates altogether. The child of Urdu parents who speak the Dakhni dialect will have no trouble acquiring that dialect; but if the baby is born to parents who speak the Khariboli dialect, the child's brain has properties that make learning that dialect a nonproblem, the better to speak a dialect of a language that fits the cultural world the child is likely to inhabit. The fact that the behavioral flexibility of the human is based on learning does not mean that genetic information is unneeded; quite the contrary, for if the human brain is to learn *adaptively*, the neural subsystems that underlie the learning must be prepared to change in particular ways. This is not an argument in favor of genetic determinism; it is an argument based on the reality of adaptive conditional strategies (Gross 1996; Smith 2011).

Complaint #5: The Charge that EHB Is Reductionist

As Richard Dawkins in conversation with Steven Pinker has pointed out, the claim that research on human behavior is reductionist is not intended as a compliment: "Reductionism is one of those words that makes me want to reach for my revolver. It means nothing. Or rather it means a whole lot of different things, but the only thing anybody knows about it is that it's bad, you're supposed to disapprove of it" (Dawkins and Pinker 1999).

The reason reductionism is supposed to be bad when it comes to human behavior is that the causes of our actions are supposedly far too complex to be "reduced" to a cause linked to evolution by natural selection. It is true that one could conceivably try to analyze the causes of something at a level that was impossibly difficult (for the time being) or one could insist that one's preferred approach was the *only way* to gain an understanding of the trait. So, for example, someone might want to know how the molecules in the nerve cells in our brain interact in ways that provide us with visual sensations. Here we would be *reducing* the search for a cause to the molecular level even though it might be more productive at least initially to try to establish what components of the brain's visual centers were needed to create visual perceptions. Moreover, even if we succeeded in deriving a detailed molecular basis for human vision, we could still profitably explore the causes of vision with other kinds of research, such as how it happened that in our species a particular set of molecules have over time become critically important for vision. The idea that these other levels of analysis were irrelevant provided that we had a complete molecular analysis of vision in hand would be an example of reductionism gone wild.

In reality, behavioral researchers recognize that there are several different but complementary levels of analysis that need to be assembled and intercalated before one can claim to have identified a complete set of causes of any trait of interest (Mayr 1961; Tinbergen 1963). So, for example, in the study of human vision, after one had a better understanding of the operational features of the visual centers in the cerebral cortex, one could (given the necessary technological advances) explore the molecular foundation of the operating rules of the cells in the visual centers. One could also ask how genetic information in concert with particular components of the environment interacted to construct the neural machinery of vision or to change the properties of a visual nerve cell in response to visual experience. Or one could try to trace the history of those mechanisms in the ancestral lineage of beings that gave rise to modern humans as a way of helping us understand why we possess a cerebral cortex with certain modules rather than others. Or rather than outlining the historical sequence of events that occurred over the course of our evolutionary history as a visual creature, we could ask how a process of change based on natural selection was responsible for the evolution of our brain with the mechanisms that make visual perception possible in people today. To argue that we need only figure out how the brain's molecular building blocks work in order to "understand" why we can see things is no more or less foolish than claiming that the study of naturally selected neural adaptations tells us all we need to know about human vision. Bad reductionism is the claim that we can reduce the study of biology to one level (i.e., one discipline) rather than exploring Mendelian and molecular genetics, development, neural and hormonal physiology, ecology, and evolution, which actually are all needed to produce a complete picture, a fuller understanding of the totality of causes of any given behavior or other biological attribute.

Complaint #6: On the Inferiority of Evolutionary Hypotheses Compared with Proximate Ones

The concept of multiple complementary levels of analysis is fundamental to the evaluation of yet another common criticism of EHB, namely, that evolutionary analyses are inferior to those that explore the development and operation of the mechanisms underlying the behavior of interest. This assertion is founded on the failure to understand that the proximate or immediate causes of behavior are neither better than nor a replacement for the ultimate or evolutionary causes of the trait. Yet, Gould regularly placed proximate and ultimate hypotheses in opposition to one another (Gould and Lewontin 1979; Gould 1981, 1996). He claimed that studies of the development and operation of the underlying mechanisms of behavior were all that was needed and that one could dispense with any examination of the possible adaptive value of the behavior. So, for example, Gould (1981) tells us that he and his good friend Francis Crick (codiscoverer of the structure of DNA) agreed that if one figured out how the pseudopenis of the female spotted hyena developed, questions of its adaptive function (if any) became irrelevant. Writing many years later, Anthony Gottlieb, contributor to the *New Yorker*, writes that "you don't have to know about the evolution of an organ in order to understand it" (2012: 86). For Gottlieb as for Gould, the evolutionary bases of the human brain can be ignored if one has information on the immediate factors that make the brain work.

Richard Polt, an academic philosopher, takes a position similar to that of Gottlieb when he writes in the *New York Times*, "I have no beef with entomology or evolution, but I refuse to admit that they teach me much about ethics" (2012). Polt claims that evolutionary explanations of human brains and our behavior cannot deal with the fact that we make choices about how to behave. As Polt puts it, "This is where ethical discourse comes in—not in explaining how we're 'built,' but in deliberating on our own future acts. Should I cheat on this test? Should I give this stranger a ride? Knowing how my selfish and altruistic feelings evolved doesn't help me decide at all." Polt seems not to realize that a decision to cheat or not has proximate causes (such as the kind of feelings the student has when confronted with an opportunity to cheat) and ultimate causes (the evolution of a brain capable of providing us with the sensation of free will or the emotion of guilt).

This sort of argument is ironic given the frequency with which critics of EHB, including Gottlieb and Polt, have tarred opponents with the charge of reductionism. As it turns out, reductionist thought is apparently all right if one looks only to certain proximate causes of behavior and dismisses the ultimate causes. But if you want to know *why* the brain produces certain decisions, not others, knowledge of its evolution is indispensable.

Knowing the adaptive basis of particular brain components does not replace information about how these components were assembled and the way in which their constituent neurons contribute to the operation of the mechanism or how the brain responds to ethical dilemmas; but the evolutionary angle adds another dimension, a different level of analysis (Sherman 1988), to research on the human brain.

Indeed, the conceptual distinction between proximate and ultimate has as one of its major virtues the prevention of unnecessary arguments that occur when someone says that your (proximate) hypothesis is wrong because the alternative (ultimate) hypothesis that I favor is correct. Or vice versa. These arguments are counterproductive because both kinds of hypotheses could be right; certainly if one is right, then the other is not necessarily wrong (Alcock and Sherman 1994).

This point is particularly relevant given the eagerness with which Gould, Slater, and others claim that a sociocultural explanation for human behavior invalidates any evolutionary hypothesis. The typical socioculturalist says that we can explain human behavior in terms of the effects on maturing individuals of exposure to their culture's traditions (Scott-Phillips, Dickens, and West 2011). (There is another kind of sociocultural hypothesis, which looks to the past rather than the cultural effects in the present. This kind of approach can be said to be based on the history that shaped the culture over time so that today people are exposed to stimuli that are the product of cultural evolution, an ultimate explanation [Durrant and Ward 2011] for why we, for example, learn the particular form of English or Urdu that is our patrimony.) But usually cultural conditioning theory concerns itself with the *current* consequences of growing up in a particular society, where a person learns a great deal about how to behave by absorbing the mores and traditions of that society.

Slater (2013) is confident that hypotheses of this sort are true alternatives to evolutionary ones when it comes to explaining human behavior. In this view, he is not alone. Once again, Stephen Jay Gould leads the way. He, for example, claimed that evolutionary explanations for genocide were unnecessary because this unpleasant behavior could be explained as the result of cultural indoctrination with some societies promoting the behavior while others did not (Gould 1996). And yes, cultures do differ in their approval or disapprobation of genocidal violence. Therefore, human behavior differs from place to place. The implication that the socioculturalist often wishes to draw from this fact is that the major differences among people are the random or arbitrary products of human imagination, which in its clearest version takes the form of blank slate theory (Pinker 2002). According to this worldview, the human brain provides us with the capacity to learn all things equally easily. This notion is laughably incorrect (Pinker 2002). No matter what proximate causes are invoked, tested, and verified, left unanswered at this level of analysis would be questions about why we might have evolved the neural mechanisms that make sociocultural learning or other proximate causes possible, questions that need to be answered with *ultimate* hypotheses.

And this is the point, now recognized nearly universally by biologists, which is that the immediate or proximate causes of behavior are critically important for understanding how the trait of interest develops, but equally important are insights into the evolution of the proximate mechanisms that enable immediate causes to have their effects. We learn a language because as infants we begin to decode the sounds made by adults around us; particular regions of the brain facilitate language learning in individuals. But these proximate causes are also dependent on past natural selection that has shaped brain evolution so that almost every human now living possesses functional neural mechanisms that make it relatively easy for us to learn the language of our culture. The underlying mechanisms that make cultural diversity possible are themselves adaptations that bias learning toward adaptive ends in different environments (Pinker 2002; Durrant and Ward 2011). We need to explore both general levels of analysis if we are to construct a complete picture of how and why we or any other animal behave the way we do.

COMPLAINT #7: EHB RESEARCH JUSTIFIES AND EXCUSES IMMORAL HUMAN BEHAVIOR AND UNJUST POLITICAL SYSTEMS

Gould and others claimed that when EHB researchers, such as the sociobiologist E. O. Wilson, identified traits as adaptations they were in effect saying that these evolved characteristics were good in a moral sense. Thus, according to the critics, the EHB "approach allows Wilson to confirm selectively certain contemporary behavior as adaptive and 'natural' and thereby justify the present social order" (Allen et al. 1975: 43; Allen et al. 1976). Because the "present social order" leaves much to be desired, Gould and like-minded individuals were really saying that EHB research provides the basis for concluding that objectionable behavioral traits are morally acceptable. Here is Slater (2013) using the same tactic when he says that "Darwinians have spent the past 40 years trying to explain and justify [gender differences in sexual behavior] on evolutionary grounds." The journalist Sharon Begley (2010) was even more emphatic in her *Newsweek* article originally entitled "Don't Blame the Caveman," in which she claims that the researchers Randy Thornhill and Craig Palmer had provided "a get out of jail free" card for rapists by discussing the possibility that rape was a reproductively advantageous trait for some men under some conditions.

You would think that charges of this sort, of giving aid and comfort to rapists and the like, would have attracted a response particularly since criticisms of this sort have been around ever since Gould and company entered the fray against sociobiology. The critics charged Wilson with providing future fascists and Nazis with scientific cover for their evil policies. And of course Wilson and those EHB researchers who followed him were not rendered speechless by the charge that they were justifying bad behavior. They and many others have pointed out that the goal of science is explanation, not to legitimize or to condemn anything (Pinker 2002). No one accuses parasitologists of approving of the parasites whose adaptations they document; no one says that persons studying infanticide in ground squirrels must think it is *morally* appropriate for female ground squirrels to kill and eat the offspring of others. There is even a name for making the mistake of thinking that a natural or evolved trait is desirable on moral grounds; the title of this mistake is the naturalistic fallacy, a fallacy that Thornhill and Palmer (2000) discuss at length in relation to their explanatory work on rape. They attempt to explain (not justify) rape by testing alternative hypotheses on the causes of a behavior that everyone knows is immoral (Palmer and Thornhill 2003).

ON THE PERSISTENCE OF CRITICISMS OF EHB

We have seen that the long list of criticisms of EHB is matched by an equivalent set of rebuttals (Table 9.1). These responses have evidently proven persuasive in the academic universe because, for example, there has been a dramatic increase in the number of evolutionary psychology articles published in the last several decades. The number of papers appearing over five-year periods starting in 1985 has gone from fewer than 10 to almost 1,000 (Durrant and Ward 2011). Evolutionary sociology has its adherents (Nielsen 1994; Lopreato and Crippen 1999), and growth in interest continues here as well (Machalek and Martin 2010); even evolutionary approaches to political science (Fowler and Schreiber 2008) and medicine (Stearns et al. 2010; Alcock 2012) have blossomed in recent years.

Table 9.1 A summary of the major criticisms leveled against EHB, followed by rebuttals to these criticisms

The criticisms

1. EHB researchers fail to practice rigorous science as illustrated by their creation and acceptance of just-so stories.
2. EHB researchers rely on panadaptationism, the belief that every last trait is an adaptation.
3. EHB researchers cannot construct a persuasive picture of the environment in which human behavior is said to evolve.
4. EHB researchers do not know that human behavior is environmentally influenced.
5. EHB research is unnecessarily reductionist.
6. EHB researchers do not realize that proximate hypotheses are superior to ultimate ones.
7. EHB research provides a justification for immoral behavior and bankrupt political systems.

The rebuttals

1. Just-so stories are hypotheses, which are an essential first step in all scientific investigations.
2. EHB researchers are fully aware that not all traits are adaptations and therefore routinely consider and test alternatives to adaptationist hypotheses, most notably the possibility that some traits are the nonadaptive or maladaptive by-products of the operation of mechanisms that evolved because of their benefits in some other arena.
3. Key elements of the ancestral environment of humans can be accurately described by reference to hunter-gatherer societies, paleontological findings, and comparative studies of our closest primate relatives.
4. All evolutionary biologists know that phenotypes are the developmental product of an interaction between genetic information and the environment.
5. EHB researchers, as is true for all other scientists, choose the level of analysis appropriate to the problem they seek to study. Reducing the focus of work to a manageable level is what all scientists do.
6. Proximate hypotheses are complementary to, not in opposition to, ultimate, evolutionary hypotheses; both are equally important in constructing a complete picture of the causes of a trait.
7. EHB research is explanatory, not justificatory.

Yes, some resistance to EHB continues in psychology, anthropology, and sociology (as illustrated, for example, by the nature of standard sociology textbooks; Leahy 2012). Some of this hostility can be attributed to academic territoriality. For example, when Wilson (1975) wrote the last chapter of *Sociobiology*, he described sociology as an immature discipline that would be reshaped by the incorporation of insights from biology, especially evolutionary human sociobiology. Not surprisingly, many sociologists believed that Wilson was depreciating the field and undermining their careers; they were not amused. However, leaving aside Wilson's intentions, the effect of EHB has been an expansion of psychology, anthropology, and sociology, not the takeover of entire departments by evolutionary biologists. This outcome makes sense given that psychology, anthropology, and sociology have traditionally focused largely or exclusively on the proximate causes of behavior. EHB adds the ultimate dimension, one that complements, rather than replaces, the work of those who study the environmental causes of our behavior. Perhaps because it is now clear that departments of psychology, anthropology, and sociology are not about to disappear, academic resistance to EHB has diminished.

Academic acceptance of EHB, although far from universal, tells you something, namely, that some researchers have been persuaded that the approach is valid, so much so that there is now an abundant supply of academicians willing to stake their futures on the evolutionary study of human behavior. But the growing acceptance of EHB by professional academics, especially in the fields of psychology and biology, has not been matched by a similar response from the public. This despite the fact that many educated individuals are fully prepared to accept that evolution by natural selection is a "fact," by which is meant that the evidence is overwhelming that the characteristics of living things have evolved. Nonetheless, Slater (2013) in his *New York Times* piece feels confident that he can dramatically misrepresent the nature of EHB research and get away with it. Indeed, a lay reader would never guess from Slater's article or those written by other anti-EHB journalists (Angier 1999; Begley 2010; Gottlieb 2012) that the claims they make, which were pioneered by Gould in the 1970s and repeated through the 1990s, had been seen and dismissed by researchers in the relevant fields.

Perhaps one reason for journalistic ignorance about these rebuttals may lie with Gould himself because he rarely acknowledged the replies to his many and varied complaints about EHB and instead continued to reiterate his disapproval right up to the time of his death in 2002 (Barash 2002; Gould 2002). As a result, the various commentators who have passed Gould's charges on to the general public may well be under the impression that EHB researchers failed to comment on the assaults on themselves and their disciplines, even though they have.

In any event, criticisms of EHB have resonated with the general public. Why? Perhaps in part because the general public admires and is eager to be persuaded by familiar science authorities, such as Stephen Jay Gould and Margaret Mead, both of whom were highly lauded during their lifetimes and beyond (Barash 2002). Gould wrote monthly essays that attracted a large readership when they were published in the magazine *Natural History*, which is produced by the Museum of Natural History in New York. He bundled these essays together in the highly popular books *Ever Since Darwin* (Gould 1977) and *Hen's Teeth and Horse's Toes* (Gould 1983). From time to time in these and other essays he launched attacks against sociobiology and evolutionary psychology, in which the targets of his displeasure were characterized in highly unfavorable ways (Gould 1978, 1996, 1997a).

Through his attacks, Gould portrayed himself as a defender of reason battling against pseudoscientists who accepted the flimsiest of stories without question about adaptation in human behavior (and elsewhere) and who amazingly enough were unaware of human cultural variation. He became famous as he spoke out strongly against political reactionaries, tyrants, and social Darwinists, fools and knaves who failed to grasp the most obvious truths. The dragon of right-wing thought apparently needed to be slain by any means possible.

Margaret Mead did not speak out against EHB time and again as Gould did, but she did not have to in light of her long-standing advocacy of a sociocultural theory, believing as she did that the behavioral differences among people arose from differences in their cultural traditions. In her famous book, *Sex and Temperament in Three Primitive Societies*, she claims that a sample of three New Guinean societies revealed that in one society, men were aggressive and dominant; in another society, the sexes enjoyed equivalent status; and in another society, women called the shots (Mead 1935). The clear message: all possible sex roles are equally probable given the extreme flexibility of human behavior.

The bottom line for Mead (1935: 221): "We are forced to conclude that human nature is almost unbelievably malleable, responding accurately and contrastingly to contrasting cultural conditions."

According to Derek Freeman, Mead's work was profoundly flawed, her "data" on the sexual freedoms supposedly operative in Samoa, where she began her anthropological career (Mead 1928), were provided by mischievous informants, her interpretations mistaken, her conclusions determined in advance by her ideological mind-set (Freeman 1983, 1998). In essence, Freeman accused Mead of doing the kind of deplorable "research" that Slater assigns to evolutionary psychologists. According to her fellow anthropologists, Mead "knew" in advance that cultural differences were the arbitrary products of the human imagination; she then collected information strictly to support her views, after which she constructed a grand cultural theory based on cultures whose traditions she had misrepresented and misunderstood. No matter. Freeman's books were dismissed by major figures in cultural anthropology, and Mead continues to be a revered figure in anthropological circles and in the public's mind.

But even though Gould and Mead were and are accepted by many as powerful academic authorities on the causes of human behavior, we can ask why their views, which are no longer predominant in some academic circles, continue to exert such appeal for journalists and the readers of opinion pieces in the *New York Times*. I suggest that the attractiveness of the outdated views of Gould and Mead lies in their match with what the public has always considered obvious about the causes of human behavior.

Let's start with Margaret Mead and the sociocultural perspective on human behavior. Slater (2013) makes it appear that sociocultural position offers a recent and novel response to evolutionary psychology. In reality, the idea that our behavior is purely the product of the cultures in which we live has been around for ages (Pinker 2002). And it's an idea with considerable plausibility given the great cultural differences in mores and traditions that affect the language we speak, the clothes that we wear, the religious practices that we follow, and so on. The concept that we are what we learn, with the brain acting as a blank slate on which is inscribed experience, has had and continues to have huge influence on everyday life in America. The notion that autism is due to childhood vaccines despite much evidence to the contrary (Orenstein et al. 2013), that mental illness in children arises because their parents are hostile to them (Dolnick 1998), that teachers can improve the average performance of their students every year ad infinitum (a tenet of the current administration's educational "race to the top"), and much more have their roots in the environmental determinism inherent in blank slate theory (Pinker 2002).

For persons who believe that environmental differences are central to any differences among humans, evolutionary considerations are not merely secondary but are left out of the equation altogether. Even now, as Slater's article reveals, few people apparently realize that evolutionary hypotheses and those on how the mechanisms that make learning and cultural conditioning possible are not antagonistic but complementary. The relatively recent introduction of evolutionary thinking in explaining human behavior has to overcome both the widespread certainty that only cultural factors are important and the general ignorance about the proximate-ultimate distinction.

The view that we alone of all animals have escaped from evolutionary constraints, a position once strongly supported by cultural anthropology and traditional sociology, has been reinforced by the religious emphasis on human exceptionalism. This emphasis is particularly strong, of course, in fundamentalist Protestantism, with its insistence on the literal truth of the Bible and the value of creation "science." But even in somewhat more enlightened religious circles, the view persists that humans have at least some divinely created properties. Pope John Paul II, while accepting that evolutionary theory was more than a hypothesis, nevertheless specifically ruled out any evolutionary explanation for the human "soul" (Farrell 2010).

Even competent scientists have adopted the religious argument that there are features of human behavior that are inexplicable from a scientific perspective. Francis Collins (2006), head of a team that decoded the human genome and current chief of the National Institutes of Health, writes that he personally is convinced of the hand of God in shaping human behavior because our moral codes cannot be explained through evolutionary science. This assertion tells us that either he has failed to examine the abundant evolutionary literature on human morality (Alexander 1979, 1987; Wright 1994) or he has chosen to ignore what he has read.

Collins, although unusual in being a scientist who supports religious faith, is not at all unusual in American society as a whole, where only about a third of all persons polled by the Pew Research Center say that they agree that living things have evolved by natural processes (Keeter and Horowitz 2009). Against this background, it is probably not surprising that many people find evolutionary hypotheses about human behavior unacceptable, particularly because of the tendency to equate "evolved" with rigid, inflexible, and unchangeable attributes that quite rightly do not jibe with the reality of our behavior.

What to Do about the Persistent Criticisms of EHB

Most of us employed by the academy believe that with the appropriate rational arguments we can persuade others of differing views to change their position. To some considerable extent this has happened in departments of psychology, anthropology, and even in sociology where EHB researchers have carved out a niche for themselves. And yes, even the general public may be more accepting of evolutionary psychology in particular than at one time thanks perhaps to the occasional news magazine reports of the work of evolutionary researchers on such things as the behavioral differences between the sexes (see the list of articles available on archive from *Psychology Today*, http://www.psychologytoday.com/basics/evolutionary-psychology). But the opposition is far from vanquished, as noted above.

The failure of EHB researchers to persuade many a journalist or philosopher of science or educated reader of the *New York Times* of the validity of their research is not for lack of trying. Some of the most brilliant popularizers of science, notably Steven Pinker (1994, 2002) and Richard Dawkins (1977, 1986), have written many books and articles directed at the general public designed to illustrate the intellectual shortcomings of the arguments of Gould and other critics of EHB. Many far less well known scientists have also done their best to educate nonscientists about the beauty and productivity of evolutionary research into human behavior—among them David Barash (Barash 2008, 2009, 2012; Barash and Lipton 2010) and yours truly (Alcock 2000). Even some persons without scientific training have taken it upon themselves to explain what EHB is really all about. Robert Wright's (1994) book *The Moral Animal* is proof that a journalist can get it right.

Then there are those of us who think that we can set university students on the path to evolutionary enlightenment (Machalek and Martin 2010; Stearns 2012). Some of us have written textbooks with chapters that have this goal in mind (Alcock 2013), and this includes textbooks for sociology students (Turner 2013). The problem, then, is not a shortage of educational materials available to the general public. Something else must explain why, despite an abundance of books and articles accessible to all, so many persons remain convinced that EHB is baloney purveyed by academics apparently unaware of the most basic features of human life.

Here I suspect that standard sociology has something important to say at a proximate level, which is that people with formed worldviews (including scientists) do not generally welcome information that conflicts with their established thinking (Margolis 1987). According to this perspective, we have a strong tendency to seek support for previously adopted positions rather than calmly sorting through competing ideas (Mercier and Sperber 2011; Mercier and Landemore 2012). In other words, we are not would-be scientists trying to use dispassionate reason to solve a problem, but would-be lawyers and press secretaries who employ the devices of argumentation to defend our preconceived conclusions (or those of our bosses).

The political divide is an example of this phenomenon. I never, and I mean never, watch Fox News, because I know that it promotes arguments that I do not accept and do not want to hear; my brother-in-law, on the other hand, tells me that the only unbiased source of news in America is supplied by the good folks at Fox News. My brother-in-law and I are examples of the strong tendency of human beings to applaud "information" that supports their position and to ignore or reject arguments to the contrary, a confirmation bias that promotes polarization of views on many issues (Shermer 2011; Strickland, Taber, and Lodge 2011).

The divide between religion and atheism is one such issue. Despite the utterly devastating analyses (as far as I am concerned) of religious belief in books by Sam Harris (2004), Richard Dawkins (2006), Daniel Dennett (2006), and Christopher Hitchens (2007), most Americans, among them Francis Collins, not only profess to believe in God but consider atheists to be the lowest of the low in terms of trustworthiness or suitability for political office (judging from a wealth of surveys available at http://atheism.about.com/od/atheistbigotryprejudice/a/AtheistSurveys.htm).

The divide between evolutionary proponents and opponents would appear to be another issue in which the confirmation bias plays a major role. Think creation science versus Darwinian science. Unattractive though it is for me, I have to at least consider the possibility that my views are as biased and unbalanced as those of Gould and his modern-day acolytes writing in the *New Yorker* and the *New York Times*. I would like to think that researchers using evolutionary theory have established a sufficiently massive and powerful record of discovery to warrant my continuing enthusiasm for research of this sort, including the component attributable to EHB. But even if I am right about the evidence that supports an evolutionary analysis of human behavior, there is also abundant data that repeated recitation of the arguments in favor of EHB has not persuaded the general public to come around. There is much more work to be done on this front, but it is not clear to me how one might convince Dan Slater and others like him to change their minds. My best wishes to all who try to explain what evolutionary studies of human behavior are all about—but it will not be easy.

References

Alcock, J. 1979. *Animal Behavior: An Evolutionary Approach*. 2nd ed. Sunderland, MA: Sinauer Associates.
———. 2000. "Misbehavior: How Stephen Jay Gould Is Wrong about Evolution." *Boston Review* 25: 21–23.
———. 2001. *The Triumph of Sociobiology*. New York: Oxford University Press.
———. 2012. "Emergence of Evolutionary Medicine: Publication Trends from 1991 to 2010." *Journal of Evolutionary Medicine* 1: 1–12. doi:10.4303/jem/235572.
———. 2013. *Animal Behavior: An Evolutionary Approach*. 10th ed. Sunderland, MA: Sinauer Associates.

Alcock, J., and P. W. Sherman. 1994. "On the Utility of the Proximate-Ultimate Dichotomy in Biology." *Ethology* 96: 58–62.

Alexander, R. D. 1979. *Darwinism and Human Affairs*. Seattle: University of Washington Press.

———. 1987. *The Biology of Moral Systems*. Hawthorne, NY: Aldine de Gruyter.

Allen, E., B. Beckwith, J. Beckwith, S. Chorover, D. Culver, N. Daniels, and D. Dorfman. 1975. "Against 'Sociobiology.'" *New York Review of Books* 22 (Nov. 13): 43–44.

Allen, E., B. Beckwith, J. Beckwith, S. Chorover, D. Culver, M. Duncan, and S. J. Gould. 1976. "Sociobiology—Another Biological Determinism." *BioScience* 26: 182–186.

Andrews, P. W., S. W. Gangestad, and D. Matthews. 2002. "Adaptationism, Exaptationism, and Evolutionary Behavioral Science." *Behavioral and Brain Sciences* 25: 534–553.

Angier, N. 1999. "Men, Women, Sex and Darwin." *New York Times Magazine*, February 21, 48–53.

Barash, D. P. 2002. "Grappling with the Ghost of Gould." *Human Nature Review* 2: 283–292.

———. 2008. "How Did Honor Evolve?" *Chronicle Review* 54: B11.

———. 2009. "The Roar of the Crowd." *Chronicle Review* 44: B8.

———. 2012. "The Evolutionary Mystery of Homosexuality." *Chronicle Review*, November 19. http://chronicle.com/article/The-Evolutionary-Mystery-of/135762/.

Barash, D. P., and J. E. Lipton. 2010. "How the Scientist Got His Ideas." *Chronicle Review*, January 3. http://chronicle.com/article/How-the-Scientist-Got-His/63287/.

Begley, S. 2010. "Can We Blame Our Bad Behavior on Stone-Age Genes?" *Newsweek*, March 13. http://www.newsweek.com/can-we-blame-our-bad-behavior-stone-age-genes-80349.

Brooks, D. 2009. "Human Nature Today." *New York Times*, June 25. http://www.nytimes.com/2009/06/26/opinion/26brooks.html?_r=.

Brown, J. L. 1982. "The Adaptationist Program." *Science* 217: 884–886.

Buss, D. M., and D. P. Schmitt. 1993. "Sexual Strategies Theory: An Evolutionary Perspective on Human Mating." *Psychological Review* 100: 204–232.

Clark, R. D., and E. Hatfield. 1989. "Gender Differences in Receptivity to Sexual Offers." *Journal of Psychology and Human Sexuality* 2: 39–55.

Collins, F. S. 2006. *The Language of God*. New York: Simon & Schuster.

Crespi, B. J. 2000. "The Evolution of Maladaptation." *Heredity* 84: 623–629.

Cronk, L. 1991. "Human Behavioral Ecology." *Annual Review of Anthropology* 20: 25–53.

Daly, M., and M. Wilson. 1983. *Sex, Evolution and Behavior*. Boston: Willard Grant Press.

———. 1999. "Human Evolutionary Psychology and Animal Behaviour." *Animal Behaviour* 57: 509–519.

Dawkins, R. 1977. *The Selfish Gene*. New York: Oxford University Press.

———. 1980. "Good Strategy or Evolutionarily Stable Strategy?" In *Sociobiology: Beyond Nature/Nurture?* edited by G. W. Barlow and J. Silverberg, 331–337. Boulder, CO: Westview Press.

———. 1986. *The Blind Watchmaker*. New York: W. W. Norton.

———. 2006. *The God Delusion*. New York: Houghton Mifflin.

Dawkins, R., and S. Pinker. 1999. "Is Science Killing the Soul?" Edge, April 7. http://www.edge.org/documents/archive/edge53.html.

Dennett, D. C. 2006. *Breaking the Spell: Religion as a Natural Phenomenon*. New York: Viking.

Dolnick, E. 1998. *Madness on the Couch*. New York: Simon & Schuster.

Durrant, R., and T. Ward. 2011. "Evolutionary Explanations in the Social and Behavioral Sciences: Introduction and Overview." *Aggression and Violent Behavior* 16: 361–370.

Ehrlich, P., and M. Feldman. 2003. "Genes and Cultures—What Creates Our Behavioral Phenome?" *Current Anthropology* 44: 87–107.

Ellis, B. J., and D. Symons. 1990. "Sex-Differences in Sexual Fantasy: An Evolutionary Psychological Approach." *Journal of Sex Research* 27: 527–555.

Farrell, J. 2010. "Catholics and the Evolving Cosmos." *Wall Street Journal*, updated August 27. http://online.wsj.com/article/SB10001424052748703846604575447493644515142.html.

Fowler, J. H., and D. Schreiber. 2008. "Biology, Politics, and the Emerging Science of Human Nature." *Science* 322: 912–914.

Freeman, D. 1983. *Margaret Mead and Samoa: The Making and Unmaking of an Anthropological Myth*. Cambridge, MA: Harvard University Press.

———. 1998. *The Fateful Hoaxing of Margaret Mead: A Historical Analysis of Her Samoan Research*. Boulder, CO: Westview Press.

Gangestad, S. W., and J. A. Simpson. 2000. "Trade-offs, the Allocation of Reproductive Effort, and the Evolutionary Psychology of Human Mating." *Behavioral and Brain Sciences* 23: 624–644.

Geary, D. C. 2010. *Male, Female: The Evolution of Human Sex Differences*. Washington, DC: American Psychological Association.

Gottlieb, A. 2012. "It Ain't Necessarily So." *New Yorker*, September 17, 84–89.
Gould, S. J. 1976. "Biological Potential vs. Biological Determinism." *Natural History* 85: 12–16.
———. 1977. *Ever Since Darwin*. New York: W. W. Norton.
———. 1978. "Sociobiology: The Art of Storytelling." *New Scientist* 80: 530–533.
———. 1981. "Hyena Myths and Realities." *Natural History* 90: 16–24.
———. 1982. "The Guano Ring." *Natural History* 91: 12 ff.
———. 1983. *Hen's Teeth and Horse's Toes*. New York: W. W. Norton.
———. 1984. "Only His Wings Remained." *Natural History* 93: 10–18.
———. 1996. "The Diet of Worms and the Defenestration of Prague." *Natural History* 105: 18–24.
———. 1997a. "Darwinian Fundamentalism." *New York Review* 44: 34–37.
———. 1997b. "The Pleasures of Pluralism." *New York Review* 44: 47–52.
———. 2002. *The Structure of Evolutionary Theory*. Cambridge, MA: Harvard University Press.
Gould, S. J., and R. C. Lewontin. 1979. "The Spandrels of San Marco and the Panglossian Paradigm: A Critique of the Adaptationist Programme." *Proceedings of the Royal Society of London B* 205: 581–598.
Gross, M. R. 1996. "Alternative Reproductive Strategies and Tactics: Diversity within Species." *Trends in Ecology and Evolution* 11: 92–98.
Gueguen, N. 2011. "Effects of Solicitor Sex and Attractiveness on Receptivity to Sexual Offers: A Field Study." *Archives of Sexual Behavior* 40: 915–919.
Hagen, E. H. 2005. "Controversies Surrounding Evolutionary Psychology." In *The Evolutionary Psychology Handbook*, edited by D. M. Buss, 145–173. Hoboken, NJ: John Wiley & Sons.
Harris, S. 2004. *The End of Faith: Religion, Terror, and the Future of Reason*. New York: W.W. Norton.
Hitchens, C. 2007. *God Is Not Great: How Religion Poisons Everything*. New York: Hachette Book Group.
Horgan, J. 2012. "The Worst Column Ever by *Times* Pundit David Brooks: 'When the Good Do Bad.'" *Scientific American*, May 21. http://blogs.scientificamerican.com/cross-check/2012/05/21/worst-column-ever-by-times-pundit-david-brooks-when-the-good-do-bad/.
Jones, B. C., L. M. DeBruine, D. I. Perrett, A. C. Little, D. R. Feinberg, and M.J.L. Smith. 2008. "Effects of Menstrual Cycle Phase on Face Preferences." *Archives of Sexual Behavior* 37: 78–84.
Keeter, S., and J. Horowitz. 2009. "On Darwin's 200th Birthday, Americans Still Divided about Evolution." Pew Research Center, February 5. http://www.pewresearch.org/2009/02/05/on-darwins-200th-birthday-americans-still-divided-about-evolution/.
Kenrick, D. T. 1995. "Evolutionary Theory versus the Confederacy of Dunces." *Psychological Inquiry* 6: 56–61.
Kenrick, D. T., E. K. Sadalla, G. Groth, and M. R. Trost. 1990. "Evolution, Traits, and the Stages of Human Courtship: Qualifying the Parental Investment Model." *Journal of Personality* 58: 97–116.
Kurzban, R. 2012. "Just So Stories Are (Bad) Explanations. Functions Are Much Better Explanations." *The Evolutionary Psychology Blog*, September 24. http://www.epjournal.net/blog/2012/09/just-so-stories-are-bad-explanations-functions-are-much-better-explanations/.
Leahy, T. 2012. "The Elephant in the Room: Human Nature and the Sociology Textbook." *Current Sociology* 60: 806–823.
Lopreato, J., and T. Crippen. 1999. *Crisis in Sociology: The Need for Darwin*. New Brunswick, NJ: Transaction Publishers.
Machalek, R., and M. W. Martin. 2010. "Evolution, Biology, and Society: A Conversation for the 21st-Century Sociology Classroom." *Teaching Sociology* 38: 35–45.
Margolis, H. 1987. *Patterns, Thinking and Cognition: A Theory of Judgment*. Chicago: University of Chicago Press.
Maryanski, A. 1994. "The Pursuit of Human Nature in Sociobiology and Evolutionary Sociology." *Sociological Perspectives* 37: 375–389.
Mayr, E. 1961. "Cause and Effect in Biology." *Science* 134: 1501–1506.
Mead, M. 1928. *Coming of Age in Samoa*. New York: William Morrow.
———. 1935. *Sex and Temperament in Three Primitive Societies*. New York: William Morrow.
Mercier, H., and H. Landemore. 2012. "Reasoning Is for Arguing: Understanding the Successes and Failures of Deliberation." *Political Psychology* 33: 243–258.
Mercier, H., and D. Sperber. 2011. "Why Do Humans Reason? Arguments for an Argumentative Theory." *Behavioral and Brain Sciences* 34: 57–74.
Miller, G. F., J. Tybur, and B. Jordan. 2008. "Ovulatory Cycle Effects on Tip Earnings by Lap-Dancers: Economic Evidence for Human Estrus?" *Evolution and Human Behavior* 28: 375–381.
Mysterud, I. 2004. "One Name for the Evolutionary Baby? A Preliminary Guide for Everyone Confused by the Chaos of Names." *Social Science Information sur les Sciences Sociales* 43: 95–114.
Nielsen, F. 1994. "Sociobiology and Sociology." *Annual Review of Sociology* 20: 267–303.
Orenstein, W. A., J. A. Paulson, M. T. Brady, L. Z. Cooper, and K. Seib. 2013. "Global Vaccination Recommendations and Thimerosal." *Pediatrics* 131: 149–151.

Palmer, C. T., and R. Thornhill. 2003. "Straw Men and Fairy Tales: Evaluating Reactions to a Natural History of Rape." *Journal of Sex Research* 40: 249–255.
Penton-Voak, I. S., D. I. Perrett, D. L. Castles, T. Kobayashi, D. M. Burt, L. K. Murray, and R. Minamisawa. 1999. "Menstrual Cycle Alters Face Preference." *Nature* 399: 741–742.
Pinker, S. 1994. *The Language Instinct.* New York: W. W. Morrow.
———. 1997. "Evolutionary Psychology: An Exchange." *New York Review of Books,* October 9. http://www.nybooks.com/articles/archives/1997/oct/09/evolutionary-psychology-an-exchange/?pagination=false.
———. 2002. *The Blank Slate: The Modern Denial of Human Nature.* New York: Viking.
Polt, R. 2012. "Anything but Human." *New York Times,* August 5. http://opinionator.blogs.nytimes.com/2012/08/05/anything-but-human/.
Popper, K. R. 1959. *The Logic of Scientific Discovery.* London: Routledge.
Reeve, H. K., and P. W. Sherman. 1993. "Adaptation and the Goals of Evolutionary Research." *Quarterly Review of Biology* 68: 1–32.
Rose, S. 1997. *Lifelines, Biology beyond Determinism.* Oxford, UK: Oxford University Press.
Salmon, C. 2012. "The Pop Culture of Sex: An Evolutionary Window on the Worlds of Pornography and Romance." *Review of General Psychology* 16: 152–160.
Scott-Phillips, T. C., T. E. Dickens, and S. A. West. 2011. "Evolutionary Theory and the Proximate-Ultimate Distinction in the Human Behavioral Sciences." *Perspectives on Psychological Science* 6: 38–47.
Sherman, P. W. 1988. "The Levels of Analysis." *Animal Behaviour* 36: 616–618.
Shermer, M. 2011. *The Believing Brain.* New York: Henry Holt.
Singh, D., and P. M. Bronstad. 2001. "Female Body Odour Is a Potential Cue to Ovulation." *Proceedings of the Royal Society of London B* 268: 797–801.
Slater, D. 2013. "Darwin Was Wrong about Dating." *New York Times,* January 13. http://www.nytimes.com/2013/01/13/opinion/sunday/darwin-was-wrong-about-dating.html?pagewanted=all&_r=0.
Smith, E. A. 2011. "Endless Forms: Human Behavioural Diversity and Evolved Universals." *Philosophical Transactions of the Royal Society B* 366: 325–332.
Smith, E. A., M. Borgerhoff Mulder, and K. Hill. 2001. "Controversies in the Evolutionary Social Sciences: A Guide for the Perplexed." *Trends in Ecology and Evolution* 16: 128–135.
Stearns, S. C. 2012. "Evolutionary Medicine: Its Scope, Interest and Potential." *Proceedings of the Royal Society B* 279: 4305–4321.
Stearns, S. C., R. M. Nesse, D. R. Govindaraju, and P. T. Ellison. 2010. "Evolutionary Perspectives on Health and Medicine." *Proceedings of the National Academy of Sciences U.S.A.* 107: 1691–1695.
Strickland, A. A., C. S. Taber, and M. Lodge. 2011. "Motivated Reasoning and Public Opinion." *Journal of Health Politics, Policy, and Law* 36: 935–944.
Symons, D. 1979. *The Evolution of Human Sexuality.* New York: Oxford University Press.
———. 1989. "A Critique of Darwinian Anthropology." *Ethology and Sociobiology* 10: 131–144.
Thornhill, R. 1981. "*Panorpa* (Mecoptera: Panorpidae) Scorpionflies: Systems for Understanding Resource-Defense Polygyny and Alternative Male Reproductive Efforts." *Annual Review of Ecology and Systematics* 12: 355–386.
Thornhill, R., and S. W. Gangestad. 2008. *The Evolutionary Biology of Human Female Sexuality.* New York: Oxford University Press.
Thornhill, R., and C. T. Palmer. 2000. *A Natural History of Rape: The Biological Bases of Sexual Coercion.* Cambridge, MA: MIT Press.
Tinbergen, N. 1963. "On the Aims and Methods of Ethology." *Zeitschrift für Tierpsychologie* 20: 410–433.
Tooby, J., and L. Cosmides. 1992. "The Psychological Foundations of Culture." In *The Adapted Mind: Evolutionary Psychology and the Generation of Culture,* edited by J. H. Barkow, L. Cosmides, and J. Tooby, 19–136. New York: Oxford University Press.
———. 1997. Letter to the editor. *New York Review of Books,* July 7. http://cogweb.ucla.edu/Debate/CEP_Gould.html.
Turner, J. H. 2013. *Contemporary Sociological Theory.* Thousand Oaks, CA: Sage Publications.
Williams, G. C. 1966. *Adaptation and Natural Selection: A Critique of Some Current Evolutionary Thought.* Princeton, NJ: Princeton University Press.
Wilson, D. S., and E. O. Wilson. 2007. "Rethinking the Theoretical Foundation of Sociobiology." *Quarterly Review of Biology* 82: 327–348.
Wilson, E. O. 1975. *Sociobiology: The New Synthesis.* Cambridge, MA: Harvard University Press.
Wright, R. 1994. *The Moral Animal: Evolutionary Psychology and Everyday Life.* New York: Pantheon.

Chapter Ten

The Evolution of the Social Mind
The Limitations of Evolutionary Psychology

Jonathan H. Turner

> Evolutionary psychology is found deficient in its conception of both how the brain was rewired during hominin evolution and how neurological systems evolve. The modular structure of the brain was in place many epochs before the Pleistocene, with evolution on the hominin line revolving primarily around directional selection on the tail ends of trait distributions and producing rather diffuse and complex sub-assemblages across large expanses of the neocortex and subcortex rather than discrete, functional modules. Most of the behavioral traits characteristic of humans already existed as bioprogrammers in the mammalian and/or primate brain, but were insufficient to increase sociality and group bonding without some enhancement by directional selection on the neurological systems responsible for these behaviors and, more importantly, on the subcortical emotional systems that became the replacement for the typical bioprogrammers for group formation among mammals that had been lost to great apes during their evolution in the arboreal habitat. By engaging in comparative anatomy, using present-day brains of the great apes as a distant mirror on the ancestors of extant apes and humans, differences in the wiring of ape and human brains provide a much better picture of how the hominin and then human brain evolved during the Pleistocene.

Many lines of evolutionary psychology argue that the distinctive behaviors of humans are driven by brain modules, which evolved during the Pleistocene among late hominins and early humans (Cosmides and Tooby 1992). Unfortunately, this line of reasoning does not fit well with the facts of primate evolution, especially the evolution of hominin and then human neuroanatomy, nor does evolutionary psychology fully appreciate the extent to which evolution, and particularly evolution of the brain, modifies biological structures through directional selection *on existing mosaics of brain structures* that originally evolved during the Oligocene, Eocene, and Miocene. Indeed, if the hypothesized modules exist, they are not very discrete but, rather, complex subassemblies of neuronets that are often spread across the brain. Modules can be found for specific functions for olfaction, hormone production, neurotransmitter release, autonomic nervous system, and other brain activities, but much of the brain involves wiring all over the neocortex as well as between the neocortex and subcortical areas of the brain; and these are the wirings most likely to direct behaviors of interest to evolutionary psychologists and to sociologists. Moreover, despite the elaboration and increased connectivity in the human brain, the basic structure of these neuronets was already present in the neuroanatomy of primates *long before* the Pleistocene.

In this chapter, I illustrate this line of argument by tracing the evolution of humans' capacity for those social behaviors that were built on the neuroanatomy of primates in general, and the great apes in particular, during the course of primate evolution. This argument avoids the implicit functionalism of evolutionary psychology that posits a module for needed behaviors.

Some Elementary Considerations

Before tracing the evolution of primates, several basic points about evolution need to be emphasized. First, in Darwin's words, biological evolution is "descent with modification," which means that natural selection and two other forces of evolution (genetic drift and gene flow) modify *existing* biological structures, if these modifications promote fitness. Mutations create new structures, but it must be remembered that most mutations do not promote fitness, and large mutations are especially unlikely to increase the fitness of individual organisms. Moreover, mutations in the brain, whether large or small, are more likely to be harmful than fitness-enhancing. And, in a complex and highly interdependent structure like the brain, these generalizations are even more likely to be true (Fisher 1930). Thus, while mutations can be an important force, evolution is conservative, building more upon the existing phenotypes and underlying genotypes of a species.

Second, selection often operates on spandrels (Gould 2002) and/or preadaptations. For example, as Geschwind (1965a, 1965b, 1985) and Geschwind and Damasio (1984) document, the language capacity of the great apes is a by-product of previous selection millions of years ago that converted arboreal mammals to visual dominance that subordinated other sense modalities to vision (i.e., olfaction, haptic, auditory), but once this preadaptation existed in neocortical and around the inferior parietal lobe (Geschwind 1965a, 1965b, 1985), it would be available for further selection if, in this example, language would enhance fitness of evolving primates. Like the capacity for language, selection on *existing* sub-assemblages in the brain enhanced the linguistic capacities of later hominins and early humans.

Third, evolution is often punctuated and directional (Gould 2002), and most of the time such selection operates on the tail ends of bell curves in the distribution of phenotypical traits (and underlying genomes producing these traits). If the tail end of the bell curve arraying the distribution of a trait promotes fitness, while the rest of the distribution does not, rapid directional evolution will be more likely to occur. Those organisms possessing the trait at the favored tail end of a distribution are more likely to survive and reproduce, while those in the rest of the distribution may be selected out, with the result that a new normal curve is created for new generations, but this time around, the distribution among traits has shifted toward the favored end of the previous distribution. If the tail end of this new distribution promotes fitness over the rest of this new distribution, then selection on the favored tail will push distribution of traits further in this direction, with the result that the gene pool of successive generations of members of a population will continue to shift even further to the favored tail. And if this process is repeated over a number of generations, evolution can be directional and fast, even in the absence of mutations.

Fourth, as Fisher (1930) demonstrated long ago, large mutations are typically harmful to organisms and thus work against fitness—as I noted earlier but bears repeating. Smaller and less dramatic mutations are generally retained because they are more likely to promote fitness. Such is particularly likely to be the case for neurological structures because of their complexity and interdependence; *any* large mutation in the brain will most likely reduce fitness, not only because of the complex interdependencies in neurosystems, but also because these systems are so important for all other body systems (Le Doux 1996). Even smaller mutations are more likely to be harmful at the neuroanatomical level—an empirical fact that argues against evolutionary psychology, which tends to see new modules as constantly emerging (often by mutations) to promote the fitness of Pleistocene hominins. In contrast, for neurological systems in particular, selection on tail ends of a distribution of existing traits promoting fitness is much more likely to operate in the evolution of neurological structures because these traits make organisms for fit in their environments without disrupting other brain functions.

In the case of the evolution of the hominin and later human brain, brain size increased dramatically in a relatively short time frame (less than 2 million years and perhaps more rapidly than that) as *Homo erectus* gave way to *Homo sapiens*. Yet, most of the critical brain systems that drive human behaviors *already existed* in primate brains—thereby giving directional selection something to work on, if the tail end of a distribution of traits would promote fitness. The result was not new, clean, and discrete modules but a more jury-rigged neurological structure spread all over the brain. Selection took what was present and went to work to rewire the human brain so that it revealed *enhanced* capacities among hominins rather than entirely new capacities. This means that selection was working on traits that had evolved earlier across many geological epochs for mammals in general, and across the three epochs preceding the Pleistocene for primates. The reason that evolutionary psychology has not documented many discrete modules is because they do not exist as modular entities. Even structures that look like modules—for example, the amygdala (center for fear and anger in the subcortex) and Broca's area (center for speech production)—*lost* much of their modularity in the evolution of the human brain. The entire region between Broca's area and Wernicke's area (for speech comprehension)—in other words, most of the temporal lobe—is involved in speech production and comprehension, as is the association cortices around the inferior parietal lobe (where the basic capacity for language evolved for reintegration of sense modalities around visual dominance). If the entire area is considered a "module," then the notion of module becomes a gloss that has relatively little meaning by the dictionary definition of what a module is. Moreover, the asymmetry between the left and right temporal lobes in humans already existed in the great apes and, hence, the last common ancestor of humans and extant great apes; and so the basic structures or, if you prefer, modules responsible for language production and comprehension along the left temporal lobe already existed long before the Pleistocene. In essence, existing modules were highjacked and rewired by natural selection to increase language production and comprehension because spoken language enhanced fitness of late hominins and early humans.

The Big Changes in Neuroanatomy

The human brain is, first of all, the result of the evolution of mammals from reptiles. This evolution divided the neocortex into distinctive lobes (frontal, parietal, temporal, and occipital) that were laid over and around older subcortical areas of the brain where olfaction, hormone production, autonomic nervous system responses, emotions, and short-term memory dynamics operate.

Second, this basic mammalian neuroanatomy was significantly altered by the evolution of primates in an arboreal habitat in several ways: the neocortex was expanded because arboreal animals that are smart are better able to navigate a precarious three-dimensional habitat and, thus, less likely to fall from trees; the emotional repertoire was expanded beyond simple fear and defensive aggression, presumably by expansion of subcortical emotion centers; the neocortex and subcortex were rewired to make vision the dominant sense modality and olfaction recessive (the dominant sense modality in most mammals, except for those using echolocation or the auditory modality).

Third, selection also transformed the basic mammalian anatomy and locomotion in ways that facilitated movement through the arboreal habitat. The result was animals with more generalized body plans, grasping hands and sensitive fingertips, strong wrists, and locomotion patterns that served as a preadaptation for bipedalism, tool making, and other features of human behavior and social organization. These changes in anatomy were, much like those for neuroanatomy, more the result of directional selection on tail ends of distribution than mutations, although the latter were no doubt involved.

We have the advantage of being able to compare human anatomy and neuroanatomy with close relatives—the great apes—and, from these comparisons, to make inferences about the changes that natural selection wrought on hominins and eventually humans. Humans share a last common ancestor with all of the great apes and, closer to the present, with common chimpanzees, with whom we share 98.5 percent of the same genetic material (which still produces large differences between chimps and humans, especially since these genes are arrayed across a different number of chromosomes). The habitats of these great apes have not changed dramatically for several million years, whereas the habitat for hominins changed dramatically as our primate ancestors were forced to leave the receding forests for the more open-country habitat of the African savanna. We are thus able, in a very real sense, to use the great apes as a "distant mirror" to see what our common ancestors were like, especially with respect to behaviors that obviously do not fossilize. Thus, comparative anatomy between apes and humans, coupled with cladistic analysis of the behavioral propensities of extant apes and other primates, makes possible a more productive approach to understanding the evolution of the human brain than is evident in much evolutionary psychology. (See Chapter 29, by Turner and Maryanski, for more details.)

By comparing brain structures of humans and the great apes, it is possible to see the handiwork of natural selection on where the brain was altered, without having to assert the presence of a module (typically unspecified) for every universal behavior of humans. And by doing comparative analysis of behavior, it is possible to see the extent to which human behaviors are unique and which are merely extensions of hardwired behavioral propensities already present in the ape clade. And further, by employing cladistic analysis of extant apes, a much better sense for the behaviors and social structures of the last common ancestor to the great apes and humans is possible; and then, by comparing these behavioral propensities of the last common ancestor with current human behavioral and organizational patterns, we can see how natural selection changed not only extant ape behavioral and organizational propensities but also human behavioral and organizational propensities. To be sure, speculation is certainly involved in drawing conclusions from such analysis, but it is speculation based on proven forms of empirical analysis.

The result is an analysis that relies less on assumptions about behaviors being driven by discrete and unspecified modules that met selection pressures during the Pleistocene. Instead, behaviors are seen as outcomes of much more complex and extended networks of neuronets evident in present-day apes and, hence, the common ancestor to apes and humans—neuronets that evolved long before the Pleistocene and that were in place for further selection during the Pleistocene. Evolution was not so much a reworking of the brain to produce new modules but, instead, a more chaotic rewiring of brain structures already present in apes.

A Short and Condensed History of Primate Evolution

Some 64 million years ago, a small rodent-like mammal or mammals climbed into the arboreal habitat to initiate the primate line, which is now divided into three branches: prosimians or pre-monkeys, monkeys, and apes. Current classifications add a fourth branch—*Homo*—and place humans or their direct ancestors into a separate lineage (i.e., the hominin clade), but humans are, in reality, just another great ape. Apes and monkeys were not dramatically different from each other 30 million years ago, except in their life history characteristics (Wolpoff 1999; Falk 2000), and for my purposes here, they coevolved for at least 10 million years, beginning around 33 million years ago. Then, about 23 million years ago, they differentiated in significant ways. Some of this differentiation was the result of monkeys' increased fitness relative to apes in the arboreal habitat. Monkeys began to occupy and dominate the verdant cores of trees, perhaps because they acquired the ability to eat unripe fruit, which is something that apes cannot do to this day (Andrews 1981, 1996). The result was for apes to be pushed to the terminal feeding areas of the arboreal habitat, where there is not enough food or room to support large numbers of individuals permanently. In contrast, monkeys could support larger, more permanent groups in the core areas where food is more plentiful, and so they developed the social structure that we see today among all monkeys—a social structure revolving around generations of female matrilines, male dominance hierarchies, and cohesive troop organization. Females never leave their natal group, and they form dense kin networks within their natal group. In contrast, males migrate at puberty to another group and begin the competition for dominance, while being replaced in their natal troop by males from other troops. Thus, monkey societies are built around well-structured local groups (Maryanski and Turner 1992; Turner and Maryanski 2008).

Apes may have had structures similar to those of monkeys at one time, but their niche in the arboreal habitat precluded large or stable groupings. Selection worked to reduce strong ties so that individuals would not form large, permanent groupings that would put pressure on the limited resources in the terminal feeding areas of the arboreal habitat. Selection favored animals that had weaker ties and that could be mobile as resource levels varied. Thus, for millions of years, selection pushed for weaker ties among apes forced to live in the terminal feeding areas of the arboreal habitat (i.e., the tops of trees and the undersides of branches). The anatomy of apes, including their neuroanatomy, was altered by having to adapt to this set of niches, along a number of fronts: apes developed stronger arms, wrists, and hands than monkeys; apes acquired the capacity to brachiate (rotate their arm 360 degrees, something a monkey cannot do); apes developed somewhat better sensitivity and strength in their fingers; apes became smarter than monkeys; and apes became programmed to form weak rather than strong ties.

Critical to my argument is that beyond morphological changes to ape anatomy was the transformation of their *social morphology* or social structures; and these transformations were, no doubt, partially the result of changes to ape neuroanatomy. Apes became programmed to build structures around weak ties, mobility, individualism, and constant fusion-fission in groupings. If humans' more immediate ancestors had been monkeys, then the assumption that humans are "naturally social" with strong bioprogrammers for group solidarity would be justified. But, humans are evolved apes, and to the extent that we have bioprogrammers from our early ape ancestors, these push humans to be more individualistic, mobile, and community oriented instead of group oriented. Thus, group cohesiveness would have to be achieved by a different route than hardwired bioprogrammers for group formations among the ancestors of humans, once group cohesiveness had selective advantages.

Around 10 million years ago, the forest of Africa began to recede and the great savannas began to expand. Many arboreal primates were forced from this habitat to the floor of the savanna, where predators were common. Monkeys did not have great difficulty making this transition, because baboons and other larger monkeys can live on the savanna today because they are well organized, often in an almost militaristic fashion, when they walk across open-country savanna. Apes, however, are not organized at the group level, and the result was a great extinction of ape species as the forest receded. No ape today, except humans, can live full-time on the savanna. As selection worked on ape phenotypes and underlying genotypes, a number of strategies for survival on the savanna emerged. One was to make apes enormously large (as tall as eight feet) as a response to predation, but the food requirements and the problems of releasing heat from such a large animal eventually doomed apes like *Gigantopithecus* to extinction some 1.6 million years ago (Maryanski and Turner 1992; Turner and Maryanski 2008). Some apes may have become more hierarchical, since gorillas and chimpanzees reveal propensities for hierarchy in the natural habitats; but without the female matrilines to hold the troop together, this was a doomed strategy in an open-county, predator-ridden habitat.

And so, the interesting question becomes this: How did the ancestors of humans beat the odds and survive in open-country savanna, where tight-knit group organization would have a selective advantage in food foraging and defense against predators? Before answering this question—which is at the core of my neurological story—let me firmly establish the fact that apes are indeed weak-tie animals and that the common ancestor that humans have with apes was probably even more weak-tie than present-day apes, except for orangutans, who are virtually solitary.

Most research on primates has a behavioral bias, with emphasis on recording patterns of behavior among individual members. Sociology is the science of social structure, and so emphasis is on the patterns of relationships that emerge and persist among conspecifics. This distinction between behavior and social structure is often lost on psychologists and ethologists, who do most of the research on primates, but it is critical to understanding the social organization of apes. Alexandra Maryanski (1986, 1987, 1992, 1993, 1995) conducted a new kind of study when she recoded all of the existing behavioral data from published studies on primates in terms of the network structure among conspecifics. That is, emphasis was on who formed social relations with whom, and to what degree of intensity and permanence. She created a simple scale: very weak or no ties, moderate ties, and strong ties. Strength of ties was coded by rates and durations of interaction, grooming, and other behaviors signaling a strong, moderate, weak, or null tie. She coded data on all species of apes and representative species of monkeys (since there are so many species of monkeys compared with the handful of ape species). These data have been tabulated and published in a number of places (see above citations, plus Maryanski and Turner 1992; Turner and Maryanski 2005, 2008; Turner 2000), and so I will not reproduce the tabulations here. But the overall pattern is as described earlier. Ape societies reveal very few strong ties, mostly those associated with mother-infant bonding, which is a pattern among all mammals. Virtually all other ties are weak or, at best, moderate, with the exception of gibbon-siamangs, where males and females form a lifetime bond (although these are very small Asian apes, way off the human line). Other exceptions include the following: male chimpanzees sometimes develop a moderate-to-strong bond with their mothers that can exist for a lifetime, as is evidenced by frequent visits (but *no* permanent group formation); lead-silverback male gorillas preside over groups that include harems of females, although these harems are more appearance than reality because females sneak off to have sexual relations with other males and use the silverback as a babysitter, and moreover, the tie is broken once females no longer have offspring; brothers among chimpanzees sometimes form moderate-to-strong bonds or even friendships with non-kin males. Otherwise, great ape societies do not form cohesive groups because:

1. Sexual relations among males and females are promiscuous, with paternity never known, even in gorilla harems, and with nothing like a family present.
2. At puberty, all females leave their natal group and community to be replaced by immigrating females from different communities who remain relative strangers to each other and do not form strong ties.
3. At puberty, all males leave the natal community, except chimpanzee males who remain in their natal community for their lifetime.
4. Adult-male and adult-female relations do not exist beyond promiscuous sexual encounters.

As is evident, then, there is little basis for strong or permanent ties among the great apes, except the harems of gorillas and the ties of chimpanzee males to each other and to their mothers. None of these lead to permanent groups, although the gorilla harem persists for a time but eventually breaks apart as offspring leave the natal group. Male chimpanzees will visit their mother for a time and hang out with brothers or other males, but these are not permanent groups, just prolonged encounters that are iterated but that do not form a cohesive group structure.

After recording the data, Maryanski (1986, 1987) performed a cladistic analysis in order to determine the nature of the social structure organizing the behaviors of the last common ancestor to humans and contemporary great apes. Cladistic analysis involves a reconstruction of a structure based on the frequency of characteristics among related species. If a set of species all have the same characteristics, for example, it can be assumed that the last common ancestor of these species also revealed these characteristics. If a particular species in this related set does not reveal one of these characteristics but still reveals the other, then it can be assumed that this one characteristic evolved in response to particular selection pressures in a new habitat or niche. For example, among all great apes, except for chimpanzee males, both males and females leave their natal communities at puberty. It is reasonable to assume that this one exception is the outcome of selection pressures operating in a particular niche that tied males to their natal community.

Another feature of cladistic analysis is to have a set of sister species as a comparison point to the species of interest. In this case, Maryanski performed a network analysis on representative species of monkeys, which all revealed the general pattern of female matrilines and male transfer at puberty, male dominance hierarchies, and tight-knit group structures. It can be assumed, therefore, that the last common ancestors of these species of monkeys also revealed these structural characteristics, making for tighter-knit groups. Thus, the differences between monkeys and apes are real and are part of the ancestral line of each because they evidence distinctive patterns of network ties typical of their respective lineages.

With these data in place, Maryanski concluded that the last common ancestor of the great apes was probably most like the contemporary orangutan in its social structure, or in this case, the last common ancestor of apes and humans revealed an almost complete lack of social structure. The only strong tie among orangutans is mother-offspring bonding up to puberty, at which point males and females leave their mother's community forever. Otherwise, no strong ties exist among orangutans, a network structure (or lack thereof) that was probably typical of the last common ancestor. Such a weak structure would be highly adaptive in the terminal feeding areas of the arboreal habitat, where food supplies were unpredictable and uneven, with individuals rather than groups moving about to find sufficient resources. But if selection pressures suddenly shifted toward demands for more social organization, such weak-tie animals would be at an enormous disadvantage, and in all likelihood would go extinct.

And so, as the forest on the savanna receded and apes were pushed onto the predator-ridden savanna, they were doomed; they simply did not have bioprogrammers for troop organization compared with monkeys. The result was the mass extinction of apes, except for the handful that exist today. Among the great apes, there are two subspecies of chimpanzees and gorillas, and one species among orangutans and humans. Of the hundreds, perhaps thousands of species of apes that once existed, this small handful is all that is left. There are about the same number of species among gibbons and siamangs, but these are very distant cousins and are not considered great apes.

Implications of Cladistic Analysis for the Evolution of the Human Brain

Pushed to the savanna by the declining forest ecology, apes were under intense selection pressures to get organized *at the group level*, or die. Groups are not natural formations for great apes, and thus it is not surprising that most went extinct. Perhaps this fact is surprising because apes and, in many cases, monkeys as well possess a number of hard-wired behavioral propensities on which natural selection could have worked to produce a more social and group-oriented ape. These include (citations summarize neurological structures, if known, involved in generating these behavioral propensities):

1. Visual dominance over haptic and auditory sense modalities, thereby subordinating other sense modalities to vision (Maryanski and Turner 1992; Ettlinger 1977; Passingham 1982: 51–55) and increasing behavioral propensity to read visual gestures in communication.
2. Behavioral propensity to follow the gaze and eye movements of others (Tomasello and Call 1997; Hare, Call, and Tomasello 2001, 2006; Povinelli and Eddy 1977, 2000; Itakura 1996; Baizer et al. 2007; Tomasello, Hare, and Fogleman 2001; Okamoto et al. 2002), thus increasing propensity to interpret gestures of eyes and face.
3. Ability of infants to imitate orofacial movements of caretakers within weeks of birth (Emde 1962; Ekman 1984; Sherwood et al. 2004).
4. Propensity for face monitoring for signs of action by conspecifics, particularly for emotional content (Leslie, Johnson-Frey, and Grafton 2004; Gazzaniga and Smylie 1990; Parr, Waller, and Fugate 2005), thereby increasing capacity to role-take with other and to read emotional dispositions in conspecifics.
5. Capacity to communicate meanings and coordinate actions through nonverbal signals, especially by eyes and face (Menzel 1971; Turner and Maryanski 2008).
6. Enhanced propensity to use imitation to learn appropriate signals and behaviors (Tomonaga 1999; Subiaul 2007; Horowitz 2003; Gergely and Csibra 2006).
7. Increased cortical control of subcortical areas through projections of axons (Raghanti et al. 2008; Sherwood 2007; Sherwood et al. 2005).
8. Enlarged decision-making prefrontal cortex (Semendeferi et al. 2002; Rilling and Insel 1999).
9. The ability among the great apes to learn and use language at the level of a three-year-old human child (Geschwind 1965a, 1965b; Geschwind and Damasio 1984; Rumbaugh and Savage-Rumbaugh 1990; Savage-Rumbaugh and Lewin 1994;

Savage-Rumbaugh et al. 1993; Savage-Rumbaugh, Sevcik, and Hopkins 1988; Bickerton 2003).
10. The ability to recognize an image in a mirror as a reflection of self as an object in the environment (Gallup 1970, 1979, 1982), thereby creating the necessary preadaptation for the formation of identities and, thus, self-monitoring, control, and evaluation.
11. Rhythmic synchronization, especially of emotions, via mirror neurons (Schütz-Bosbach and Pinz 2007; Rizzolatti et al. 2002), that are a necessary preadaptation for role taking and emotion-generating interactions.
12. Propensities for reciprocity in the give and take of resources (Cosmides 1989; de Waal 1989, 1991, 1996; de Waal and Brosnan 2006).
13. Propensity to compare shares of resources with others in making judgments of fairness and justice (Brosnan and de Waal 2003; Brosnan, Schiff, and de Waal 2005; Bekoff and Pierce 2009; Boehm 2012).
14. Capacity to experience variants among primary emotions, particularly among chimpanzees (Darwin 1872; Turner 2000).
15. Capacity to experience empathy with conspecifics (de Waal 1996, 2009), and especially those with whom they are familiar (Campbell and de Waal 2014), thus facilitating in-depth role-taking for emotions experienced by community members.
16. Capacity to read emotions, which in turn enhances the capacity for empathy (Turner 2000, 2012; Leslie, Johnson-Frey, and Grafton 2004).

By discovering the neurological complexes responsible for these behavioral capacities and propensities of current higher-order primates, we will go a long way to understanding *what brain structures natural selection worked on to produce the more extensive abilities of humans* (Passingham 1973, 1975; Sherwood et al. 2008) to be social. Many of the references cited for the sixteen behavioral capacities listed above document at least some of the brain structures—or modules, if one is still so disposed—involved. Still there is much more detailed work to be done.

Yet, even with these hardwired behavior capacities and propensities, the extinction of so many species of apes, especially compared with monkeys that were already highly organized (by female matrilines and male dominance hierarchies), indicates that selection did not initially grab onto these potential traits, select on the tail ends of distributions, and thereby create a more social and group-oriented animal. Thus, natural selection as a more random process did not make apes more fit on the savanna, despite a number of hardwired neurologically driven behavioral capacities that could potentially enhance sociality and group solidarity *if* subject to further selection. For millions of years, savanna-dwelling apes were going extinct and, then, somehow blind natural selection hit upon a solution to the weak-tie propensities of apes and certainly the last common ancestor to apes and humans (who, as noted earlier, was probably much like the virtually solitary orangutan with no strong ties beyond mother-offspring ties that disappear at puberty when males and females leave, forever).

What was this solution? An answer to this question is speculative, but it will be based on some combination or sequence of already existing neurological wiring for behavioral capacities listed above. The modules—if this is even the appropriate term to use—were already present; they did not evolve in the Pleistocene, but, in fact, they evolved millions of years earlier to solve problems of adaptation among mammals and then primates or as spandrels or preadaptations that were, in essence, "sitting there" waiting to be selected upon.

The evolution of the brain in terms of its size gives us some clues that may help us determine where selection initially went to work to rewire the hominin brain. Since the neocortex did *not grow dramatically* up to the time of arrival of Homo erectus some 2 million years ago, it is reasonable to conclude that all of those existing structures in the brain that required spoken language and culture composed of artificial symbols were not initially responsible for increasing sociality and solidarity in hominin groups. Only with the arrival of *Homo erectus* did the neocortex begin to grow significantly, indicating that selection was now directional and enlarging the neocortex and, it is reasonable to conclude, expanding the neuronets between the neocortex, and particularly between the prefrontal cortex and subcortical areas of the brain where emotions are generated. What, then, was selection doing?

I have argued that selection was working primarily on the subcortical emotion centers of the brain (Turner 2000), and while the growth and rewiring of the subcortex are not as dramatic as was to be the case for the larger neocortex laid over and around these subcortical areas, enhancing emotions could immediately begin to promote stronger social bonds and group-level solidarity, especially in conjunction with existing propensity to read facial gestures and the eyes; to develop empathy; to reciprocate favors; and to determine whether reciprocations are just and fair (at an emotional rather than cultural level). Increasing the emotionality involved in all of these behavior capacities would be the easiest route to making a low-sociality ape more social and group oriented. Moreover, by increasing emotionality, natural selection did not need to work separately on the sixteen behavioral propensities listed earlier. Emotions, once enhanced, would automatically add to the power of these propensities, thereby making hominins more social. And, given that the last common ancestor to apes and hominins could use language, if required to do so (as is the case with modern great apes when exposed to language), this important cognitive capacity made possible by association cortices around the inferior parietal lobe would not have to "wait" for growth in the neocortex and symbolic abilities of hominin. But, these association cortices around the inferior parietal lobe could be used much earlier in evolution to create what I call "the language of emotions" that reveals emotional phonemes and syntax connecting the phonemes to generate emotional meanings, which would make the power of emotions that much greater. Just by watching a movie with the sound turned off, we can see this language of emotions as body and face gestures linked into morphemes and a syntax communicating emotional states of individuals.

If we compare measurements on subcortical areas of the human brain where emotions are generated for apes and humans, key areas of the human subcortex are, on average, twice as large as those in great apes, controlling for effects of body size differences between apes and humans (see data provided by Stephan 1983; Stephan and Andy 1969, 1977; Stephan, Frahm, and Baron 1981; Stephan, Baron, and Frahm 1988; and Eccles 1989). The neocortex of humans is three times the size of that of great apes, specifically chimpanzees; and so while the size differences in subcortical modules are not as dramatic as the differences in the respective neocortex of humans and apes, they are still rather striking at being twice as large. This growth indicates that selection was working earlier on older subcortical structures in hominins over the last 8 million years, long before selection began to increase the size of the neocortex that would allow for culture using linguistic symbols. Thus, as important as neocortical development is, subcortical evolution is perhaps even more important in understanding how hominins and then humans became more social, more oriented to groups, and more fit in open-country savanna conditions. All other apes went extinct, and present-day apes must use the forests as safe havens from the savanna; and this capacity to survive in a more dangerous environment was primarily the result of changes in the subcortex of the hominin and eventually human brain millions of years before spoken language and culture evolved in the hominin line. The evolution of dramatically enhanced emotional capacities is as important in understanding human behavior as are language and culture (Massey 2002; Turner 1996a, 1996b, 1997, 1998, 2000).

Only with *Homo erectus*, it can be hypothesized, did selection begin to add true symbols (artificial signs designating objects and states of being), laying these new symbolic capacities made possible by an expanded neocortex over the more primal language of emotions generated in the subcortex but using the modules around the inferior parietal lobe to create the first and most primal language: the language of emotions using visually ready phonemes and morphemes put together by a syntax to communicate a dramatically expanded palate of more complex and nuanced emotional states. Perhaps a nonverbal gestural sign language began to evolve at some point, or a crude auditory or spoken language began to emerge, alongside the language of emotions, which is primarily a language of body and facial gestures. Yet, data on the key genes among humans responsible for muscles that enable fine-grained capacities to articulate words have been under selection for only 200,000 years (Enard 1978; Enard et al. 2002a, 2002b); and so, truly refined auditory language may be unique only to humans. With culture and language, morality can be articulated, with individuals invoking moral codes to regulate conduct and to evaluate self. Perhaps only with the rapid growth of the neocortex over the last million years of hominin evolution did the capacity to see self as an object of evaluation emerge, although it is equally possible that this key mechanism of social control emerged earlier as individuals developed a language of emotions to role-take, experience empathy, render justice evaluations, and monitor reciprocities. Whenever the ability to possess identities about self emerged, it would dramatically increase social control, especially in conjunction with the evolution of new kinds of emotions. New emotions like *shame* and *guilt* could emerge to evaluate self in relation to the expectations of conspecifics and cultural codes expressed symbolically; with these emotions, individuals would engage in self-evaluations and self-control in order to avoid experiencing such negative emotions and enduring the negative sanctions from conspecifics that produce these emotions.

Were new modules created in this process? The answer depends on what a module is. If it is a discrete area of neuronets devoted to activating specialized behaviors, then Broca's and Wernicke's areas (for downloading mental thought into speech and uploading speech into the brain's way of thinking) might qualify. These areas were usurped by natural selection on the left hemisphere for language production made possible by the association cortices around the inferior parietal lobe (near Wernicke's area) that give apes the capacity for language. But, as noted earlier, long before language, there were asymmetries between the right and left temporal lobes, because these can be seen in the great apes; and so, the module was not new as much as redirected for new behavior capacities.

Thus, what a comparative, cross-species approach gives us is a much better set of tools for understanding how and even when the brain became wired or, more accurately, *re*wired for certain behaviors. Most of these behaviors were not "new"; they had long existed in primates and especially apes long before the Pleistocene. The "modules," if one insists on this terminology, already existed, but most of these were not very discrete but, in fact, congeries of neuronets spread across the brain and between the neocortex and subcortical areas of the brain. Yet, to use the term "modules" to describe what are complex and far-ranging subassemblies of neuronets distorts the meaning of modules, as relatively discrete circuits that have been added to, or plugged into, the existing brain of hominins and humans. The imagery of modules, then, is not very useful, because it fails to denote how the human brain was rewired during hominin evolution. Most of the new elements of the brain are enhanced connections among older areas of the brain rather than a system of discrete modules for specific fitness-enhancing behaviors. The brain is a general-processing machine, if this imagery is correct, and its power is in creating new neuro-networks among existing brain structures that have been part of the primate brain for millions of years, and even longer since many of the distinct areas of the brain are part of the entire mammalian line.

Conclusion

In sum, then, social scientists and biologists should be very skeptical about the claims of evolutionary psychology. We should, however, be grateful for evolutionary psychology because it is correct in its assertion that many fitness-enhancing behaviors evolved through the rewiring of the brain; and once this initial step is taken, it encourages social scientists to learn more about the brain and the forces of evolution that have been working on the brain over millions of years during primate and then hominin evolution. When the latter is undertaken, we can have neurosociology (Franks 2010; Franks and Turner 2012) that sees many brain subassemblies as the result of directional selection on existing brain systems in response to pressures for increased levels of social organization and group solidarity among hominins; and we can have an evolutionary sociology that revolves around comparative analysis between humans and their closest ape relatives. This analysis can be behavioral, cladistic, anatomical, and neuroanatomical; and it can invoke arguments that are closer to those made by evolutionary biologists than evolutionary psychologists. So, once we abandon the misleading arguments of evolutionary psychology about modules and the assertion that these evolved as specialized nodes in the brain during the Pleistocene, we can give evolutionary sociology a sounder empirical and conceptual footing.

References

Andrews, P. 1981. "Species Diversity and Diet in Monkeys and Apes during the Miocene." In *Aspects of Human Evolution*, edited by C. B. Stringer. London: Taylor and Francis.
———. 1996. "Palaeoecology and Hominoid Palaeoenvironments." *Biological Review* 71: 257–300.
Baizer, J. S., J. F. Baker, K. Haas, and R. Lima. 2007. "Neurochemical Organization of the Nucleus *Paramedinaus Dorsalis* in the Human." *Brain Research* 1176: 45–52.
Bekoff, M., and J. Pierce. 2009. *Wild Justice: The Moral Lives of Animals*. Chicago: University of Chicago Press.
Bickerton, D. 2003. "Symbol and Structure: A Comprehensive Framework for Language Evolution." In *Language Evolution: The States of the Art*, edited by M. S. Christiansen and S. Kirby, 77–93. Oxford: Oxford University Press.
Boehm, C. 2012. *Moral Origins: The Evolution of Virtue, Altruism, and Shame*. New York: Basic Books.
Brosnan, S. F., and F.B.M. de Waal. 2003. "Fair Refusal by Capuchin Monkeys." *Nature* 425: 297–299.
Brosnan, S. F., H. C. Schiff, and F.B.M. de Waal. 2005. "Tolerance for Inequity May Increase with Social Closeness in Chimpanzees." *Proceedings of the Royal Society of London* 272: 253–258.
Campbell, M. W., and F.B.M. de Waal. 2014. "Chimpanzees Empathize with Group Mates and Humans, but Not with Baboons or Unfamiliar Chimpanzees." *Proceedings of the Royal British Society: Biological Sciences* 281: 1782.
Cosmides, L. 1989. "The Logic of Social Exchange: Has Natural Selection Shaped How Humans Reason?" *Cognition* 31: 187–276.
Cosmides, L., and J. Tooby. 1992. "Cognitive Adaptations for Social Exchange." In *The Adapted Mind: Evolutionary Psychology and the Generation of Culture*, edited by J. H. Barkow, L. Cosmides, and J. Tooby. New York: Oxford University Press.
Darwin, C. 1872. *The Expression of the Emotions in Man and Animals*. London: John Murray.
de Waal, F.B.M. 1989. "Food Sharing and Reciprocal Obligations among Chimpanzees." *Journal of Human Evolution* 18: 433–459.

———. 1991. "The Chimpanzee's Sense of Social Regularity and Its Relation to the Human Sense of Justice." *American Behavioral Scientist* 34: 335–349.
———. 1996. *Good Natured: The Origins of Right and Wrong in Humans and Other Animals*. Cambridge, MA: Harvard University Press.
———. 2009. *The Age of Empathy: Nature's Lessons for a Kinder Society*. New York: Three Rivers Press.
de Waal, F.B.M., and S. F. Brosnan. 2006. "Simple and Complex Reciprocity in Primates." In *Cooperation in Primates and Humans: Mechanisms and Evolution*, edited by P. Kappeler and C. P. van Schaik, 85–106. Berlin: Springer-Verlag.
Eccles, J. C. 1989. *Evolution of the Brain: Creation of Self*. London: Routledge.
Ekman, P. 1984. "Expression and the Nature of Emotion." In *Approaches to Emotion*, edited by K. Scherer and P. Edman, 319–343. Hillsdale, NJ: Lawrence Erlbaum.
Emde, R. N. 1962. "Level of Meaning for Infant Emotions: A Biosocial View." In *Development of Cognition, Affect and Social Relations*, edited by W. A. Collins Hillsdale, 1–37. Hillsdale, NJ: Lawrence Erlbaum.
Enard, W. M. 1978. "Myths about Hunter-Gatherers." *Ethnology* 17: 439–448.
Enard, W. M., et al. 2002a. "Molecular Evolution of TOXP2, a Gene Involved in Speech and Language." *Nature* 418: 869–872.
———. 2002b. "Intra- and Interspecific Variation in Primate Gene Expression Patterns." *Science* 296: 340–342.
Ettlinger, G. 1977. "Cross-Modal Equivalence in Non-Human Primates." In *Behavioral Primatology, Volume 1*, edited by A. M. Schriver. Hillsdale, NJ: Lawrence Erlbaum.
Falk, D. 2000. *Primate Diversity*. New York: W. W. Norton.
Fisher, R. A. 1930. *The Genetical Theory of Natural Selection*. Oxford: Clarendon.
Franks, D. D. 2010. *Neurosociology: The Nexus between Neuroscience and Social Psychology*. New York: Springer.
Franks, D. D., and J. H. Turner, eds. 2012. *Handbook of Neurosociology*. New York: Springer.
Gallup, G. G., Jr. 1970. "Chimpanzees: Self-Recognition." *Science* 167: 86–87.
———. 1979. *Self-Recognition in Chimpanzees and Man: A Developmental and Comparative Perspective*. New York: Plenum Press.
———. 1982. "Self-Awareness and the Emergence of Mind in Primates." *American Journal of Primatology* 2: 237–248.
Gazzaniga, M. S., and C. S. Smylie. 1990. "Hemisphere Mechanisms Controlling Voluntary and Spontaneous Mechanisms." *Annual Review of Neurology* 13: 536–540.
Gergely, G., and G. Csibra. 2006. "Sylvia's Recipe: The Role of Imitation and Pedagogy in the Transmission of Cultural Knowledge." In *Roots of Human Sociality: Culture, Cognition, and Human Interaction*, edited by N. J. Enfield and S. C. Levenson, 229–255. Oxford: Berg Press.
Geschwind, N. 1965a. "Disconnection Syndromes in Animals and Man, Part I." *Brain* 88: 237–294.
———. 1965b. "Disconnection Syndromes in Animals and Man, Part II." *Brain* 88: 585–644.
———. 1985. "Implications for Evolution, Genetics, and Clinical Syndromes." In *Cerebral Lateralization in Non-Human Species*, edited by S. Glick. New York: Academic.
Geschwind, N., and A. Damasio. 1984. "The Neural Basis of Language." *Annual Review of Neuroscience* 7: 127–147.
Gould, S. J. 2002. *The Structure of Evolutionary Theory*. Cambridge, MA: Harvard University Press.
Hare, B., J. Call, and M. Tomasello. 2001. "Do Chimpanzees Know What Conspecifics Know?" *Animal Behavior* 61: 139–159.
———. 2006. "Chimpanzees Deceive a Human Competitor by Hiding." *Cognition* 101: 495–514.
Horowitz, A. C. 2003. "Do Humans Ape? Or Do Apes Human? Imitation and Intention in Humans (*Homo sapiens*) and Other Animals." *Journal of Comparative Psychology* 117: 325–336.
Itakura, S. 1996. "An Exploratory Study of Gaze-Monitoring in Non-Human Primates." *Japanese Psychological Research* 38: 174–180.
LeDoux, J. E. 1996. *The Emotional Brain: The Mysterious Underpinnings of Emotional Life*. New York: Simon and Schuster.
Leslie, K. R., S. H. Johnson-Frey, and S. T. Grafton. 2004. "Functional Imaging of Face and Hand Imitation: Towards a Motor Theory of Empathy." *NeuroImage* 21: 601–607.
Maryanski, A. 1986. "African Ape Social Structure: A Comparative Analysis." PhD diss., Department of Social Science, University of California, Irvine.
———. 1987. "African Ape Social Structure: Is There Strength in Weak Ties?" *Social Networks* 9: 191–215.
———. 1992. "The Last Ancestor: An Ecological-Network Model on the Origins of Human Sociality." *Advances in Human Ecology* 2: 1–32.
———. 1993. "The Elementary Forms of the First Proto-Human Society: An Ecological/Social Network Approach." *Advances in Human Evolution* 2: 215–241.
———. 1995. "African Ape Social Networks: A Blueprint for Reconstructing Early Hominid Social Structure." In *Archaeology of Human Ancestry*, edited by J. Steele and S. Shennan, 67–90. London: Routledge.

Maryanski, A., and J. H. Turner. 1992. *The Social Cage: Human Nature and the Evolution of Society*. Stanford, CA: Stanford University Press.

Massey, D. 2002. "A Brief History of Human Society: The Origin and Role of Emotion in Social Life." *American Sociological Review* 67: 1–29.

Menzel, E. W. 1971. "Communication about the Environment in a Group of Young Chimpanzees." *Folia Primatologica* 15: 220–232.

Okamoto, S., M. Tomonaga, K. Ishii, N. Kawai, M. Tanaka, and T. Matsuzawa. 2002. "An Infant Chimpanzee (*Pan troglodytes*) Follows Human Gaze." *Animal Cognition* 5: 107–114.

Parr, L. A., B. M. Waller, and J. Fugate. 2005. "Emotional Communication in Primates: Implications for Neurobiology." *Current Opinion in Neurobiology* 15: 716–720.

Passingham, R. E. 1973. "Anatomical Differences between the Neo-cortex of Man and the Other Primates." *Brain Behavioral Evolution* 7: 337–359.

———. 1975. "Changes in the Size and Organisation of the Brain in Man and His Ancestors." *Brain and Behavior Evolution* 11: 73–90.

———. 1982. *The Human Primate*. Oxford: Freeman.

Povinelli, D. J. 2000. *Folk Physics for Apes: The Chimpanzee's Theory of How the World Works*. Oxford: Oxford University Press.

Povinelli, D. J., and T. J. Eddy. 1997. "Specificity of Gaze-Following in Young Chimpanzees." *British Journal of Developmental Psychology* 15: 213–222.

Raghanti, M. A., C. D. Stimpson, J. L. Marchiewicz, et. al. 2008. "Differences in Cortical Serotonergic Innervation among Humans, Chimpanzees, and Macaque Monkeys: A Comparative Study." *Cerebral Cortex* 18: 584–597.

Rilling, J. K., and T. R. Insel. 1999. "The Primate Neocortex in Comparative Perspective Using Magnetic Resonance Imaging." *Journal of Human Evolution* 37: 191–223.

Rizzolatti, G., L. Fadiga, L. Fogassi, and V. Gallese. 2002. "From Mirror Neurons to Imitation: Facts and Speculations." In *The Imitative Mind: Development, Evolution and Brain Bases*, edited by W. Prinz and A. N. Meltzoff, 247–266. Cambridge: Cambridge University Press.

Rumbaugh, D., and S. Savage-Rumbaugh. 1990. "Chimpanzees: Competencies for Language and Numbers." In *Comparative Perception*, Vol. 2, edited by W. Stebbins and M. Berkley. New York: Wiley and Sons.

Savage-Rumbaugh, S., and R. Lewin. 1994. *Kanzi: The Ape at the Brink of the Human Mind*. New York: John Wiley and Sons.

Savage-Rumbaugh, S., J. Murphy, J. Sevcik, K. Brakke, S. L. Williams, and D. Rumbaugh. 1993. "Language Comprehension in the Ape and Child." *Monographs of the Society for Research in Child Development* 58.

Savage-Rumbaugh, S., R. Sevcik, and W. Hopkins. 1988. "Symbolic Cross-Model Transfer in Two Species." *Child Development* 59: 617–625.

Schütz-Bosbach, S., and W. Prinz. 2007. "Perceptual Resonance: Action-Induced Modulation of Perception." *Trends in Cognitive Sciences* 11: 349–355.

Semendeferi, K., A. Lu, N. Schenker, and H. Damasio. 2002. "Humans and Great Apes Share a Large Frontal Cortex." *Nature Neuroscience* 5: 272–276.

Sherwood, C. C. 2007. "The Evolution of Neuron Types and Cortical Histology in Apes and Humans." In *Evolution of Nervous Systems 4: The Evolution of Primate Nervous Systems*, edited by T. M. Preuss and J. H. Kaas, 355–378. Oxford: Academic Press.

Sherwood, C. C., R. L. Holloway, J. M. Erwin, and P. R. Hoff. 2004. "Cortical Orofacial Motor Representation in Old World Monkeys, Great Apes and Humans." *Brain Behavior and Evolution* 63: 82–106.

Sherwood, C. C., R. L. Holloway, K. Semendeferi, and P. R. Hoff. 2005. "Is Prefrontal White Matter Enlargement a Human Evolutionary Specialization?" *Nature Neuroscience* 8: 537–538.

Sherwood, C. C., F. Subiaul, H. Tadeusz, and W. Zawidzki. 2008. "A Natural History of the Human Mind: Tracing Evolutionary Changes in Brain and Cognition." *Journal of Anatomy* 212: 426–454.

Stephan, H. 1983. "Evolutionary Trends in Limbic Structures." *Neuroscience and Biobehavioral Review* 7: 367–374.

Stephan, H., and O. J. Andy. 1969. "Quantitative Comparative Neuroanatomy of Primates: An Attempt at Phylogenetic Interpretation." *Annals of the New York Academy of Science* 167: 370–387.

———. 1977. "Quantitative Comparison of the Amygdala in Insectivores and Primates." *Acta Anatomica* 98: 130–153.

Stephan, H., G. Baron, and H. Frahm. 1988. "Comparative Size of Brains and Brain Components." In *Neurosciences*, Vol. 4, edited by H. Steklis and J. Erwin. New York: Alan Liss.

Stephan, H., H. Frahm, and G. Baron. 1981. "New and Revised Data on Volumes of Brain Structures in Insectivores and Primates." *Folia Primatoligica* 35: 1–29.

Subiaul, F. 2007. "The Imitation Faculty in Monkeys: Evaluating Its Features, Distribution, and Evolution." *Journal of Anthropological Science* 85: 35–62.

Tomasello, M., and J. Call. 1997. *Primate Cognition*. Oxford: Oxford University Press.

Tomasello, M., B. Hare, and T. Fogleman. 2001. "The Ontogeny of Gaze Following in Chimpanzees, *Pan troglodytes*, and Rhesus Macaques, *Macaca mulatta*." *Animal Behavior* 61: 335–343.
Tomonaga, M. 1999. "Attending to the Others' Attention in Macaques' Joint Attention or Not?" *Primate Research* 15: 425.
Turner, J. H. 1996a. "The Evolution of Emotions in Humans: A Darwinian-Durkheimian Analysis." *Journal for the Theory of Social Behaviour* 26: 1–34.
———. 1996b. "Cognition, Emotion, and Interaction in the Big-Brained Primate." In *Social Processes and Interpersonal Relations*, edited by K. M. Kwan. Greenwich, CT: JAI Press.
———. 1997. "The Evolution of Emotions: The Nonverbal Basis of Human Social Organization." In *Nonverbal Communication: Where Nature Meets Culture*, edited by U. Segerstrale and P. Molnar. Mahwah, NJ: Lawrence Erlbaum.
———. 1998. "The Evolution of Moral Systems." *Critical Review* 11: 211–32.
———. 2000. *On the Origins of Human Emotions: A Sociological Inquiry into the Evolution of Human Affect*. Stanford, CA: Stanford University Press.
———. 2012. "The Biology and Neurology of Group Processes." *Advances in Group Processes* 29: 1–38.
Turner, J. H., and A. Maryanski. 2005. *Incest: Origins of the Taboo*. Boulder, CO: Paradigm Press.
———. 2008. *On the Origins of Societies by Natural Selection*. Boulder, CO: Paradigm Press.
Wolpoff, M. H. 1999. *Paleoanthropology*. 2nd ed. New York: McGraw-Hill.

Three
Evolutionary Sociology

Chapter Eleven
Evolutionary Sociology
W. G. Runciman

> Neo-Darwinian evolutionary theory has been increasingly brought to bear on the agenda of comparative sociology since the last quarter of the twentieth century. The protracted controversies provoked by the publication of E. O. Wilson's *Sociobiology* in 1975 have given way to a recognition that sociology is not reducible to biology, but the fundamental Darwinian process of heritable variation and competitive selection applies at the cultural and social no less than at the biological level. Topics central to sociologists' traditional concerns, including the origin of the state, the continuing reproduction and diffusion of religious beliefs and practices, and the maintenance of cooperative social relationships within large populations of unrelated strangers, have been incorporated within the neo-Darwinian paradigm. At the same time, evolutionary game theory has proved increasingly successful in addressing the topic of collective action through field studies, laboratory experiments, and computer simulations. More broadly, teleological explanations of how the human societies in the historical, ethnographic, and archaeological record have evolved into being the kinds of societies that they are are being superseded by explanations in terms of open-ended but path-dependent sequences of interaction between the forces of natural, cultural, and social selection.

Introduction

The idea that human societies and their constitutive institutions evolve in some determinable direction out of one into another kind has a long history in the European intellectual tradition going back through Montesquieu and the historical sociologists of the Scottish Enlightenment to the philosophers of Classical Greece. But by the end of the twentieth century, teleological theories of all and any kinds were being steadily abandoned as it came to be more and more widely accepted that cultural and social, like biological, evolution is a path-dependent but open-ended process of variation and selection out of which mutations emerge and are differentially diffused and reproduced under changing environmental pressures. It is no longer a question of whether Darwin's fundamental insight about what he called "descent with modification" can be applied to the study of human social behavior, but only of how.

The neo-Darwinian approach has, however, been resisted by critics who not only deny the possibility that human behavior patterns can be explained by what they see as misplaced recourse to biology but dismiss the extension of Darwinian methods and concepts to cultural and social evolution as a purely metaphorical restatement in ostensibly more scientific language of questions that it does nothing thereby to resolve. Their objections are motivated in part by the recollection of the misuses of biology in the late nineteenth and early to mid-twentieth century to justify social policies subsequently discredited as both scientifically erroneous and morally reprehensible. But they are motivated also by what is seen as a threat to established academic disciplines in which human beings are taken to be self-conscious decision-makers whose diverse behavior patterns must be explained in their own terms. The result has been a succession of disputes of which those provoked by the publication of E. O. Wilson's *Sociobiology* in 1975 were conducted with a vehemence that calls for sociological explanation in itself (Segerstråle 2000). By the second decade of the twenty-first century, however, a steadily expanding volume of increasingly well-validated findings has tempered the more exaggerated claims of the disputants on both sides, and terminological arguments fueled by mutual accusations of political bias to give way to collaboration in the formulation of questions about the evolution of distinctive human behavior patterns in such a way as to enable rival hypotheses to be tested against one another (Borgerhoff Mulder 2013).

Many of the earlier arguments arose from the difficulty of specifying what exactly it is that the process of variation and selection is to be taken to be selecting and exactly what it means to say that an observed behavior pattern is adaptive, or an adaptation, or maladaptive, or an exaptation (Laland and Brown 2002). But it is now generally recognized that selection operates at different levels and comes to bear in different ways in biological, cultural, and social evolution alike. Information that is acted out in phenotypic behavior can be transmitted by genetic inheritance, by imitation and social learning, or by institutional imposition of binding rules. Biological, cultural, or social variants can be traced through homologous descent in the same population, through lateral or oblique transmission from one population to another, or through convergent evolution where the same selective pressures come to bear on spatially and temporally separate populations. The underlying process is both continuous and irreversible in species, cultures, and societies alike.

By many sociologists, these issues can continue to be disregarded as irrelevant to their own research. On one side are those for whom "social theory" is not a social-scientific so much as a philosophical exercise in presenting and defending personal convictions about the state of the contemporary world or, more generally still, the human condition. On the other are those concerned to frame and test hypotheses that will explain, in accordance with standard quantitative and/or qualitative methods, reported changes over a short time period within one or more of the conventionally demarcated fields of social behavior in one or more chosen societies—occupational structure, voting behavior, crime (or "deviance"), ethnic or gender discrimination, social mobility, industrial relations, and so on. But no sociologist concerned with either long-term societal change or large-scale intersocietal comparison can afford to ignore either the workings of natural selection and its effects on collective human behavior or the analogous and complementary processes of cultural and social selection.

Sociobiology

Despite the controversies that it has generated, the term "sociobiology" can still serve to cover three subdisciplines that have in common the direct application of the theory of natural selection to topics relevant to sociologists' concerns.

Behavior geneticists study differences within rather than between populations in order to establish the heritability of predispositions that cause different individuals to respond differently to their more and less similar environments, and their findings are to that extent of interest more to psychologists than sociologists. The difficulties involved in estimating the proportion of variation to be attributed to inheritance when interaction with the environment is continuous over an extended period from, and even before, birth is as well known to geneticists (Cavalli-Sforza 1995) as to psychologists or sociologists. The idea, which goes back to Galton, that the best approximation to controlled experimentation comes from studying twins was widely publicized in the results of the Minnesota Study, which between 1979 and 1999 examined carefully assembled pairs of identical twins separated soon after birth and brought up in different environments (Segal 2012), and is currently being carried forward in the Twins' Early Development Study based on records of both identical and nonidentical twins born in the United Kingdom between 1994 and 1996 (Oliver and Plomin 2007; Asbury and Plomin 2013). These findings, together with those of behavior geneticists studying antisocial behavior (Ciba Foundation 1996) and mental illness (Plomin et al. 1997, Chapter 10), have called into question assumptions shared among many twentieth-century sociologists about the strength of environmental influences on children and adolescents during the course of their upbringing. But resolution of the outstanding disagreements in this area is likely to have to await further improvements in the techniques for mapping genomes and precise specification of the genes involved.

Behavioral ecologists, by contrast, set out from the assumption to which many sociologists are congenitally resistant: that collective behavior patterns will evolve under environmental pressure to maximize reproductive fitness. Much of their attention has focused on small and relatively simple societies and on such topics as optimal foraging theory or the link between hunting skill and reproductive success, which are of limited interest to sociologists studying the institutions of large and complex present-day societies. It is not in dispute that during the history of *Homo sapiens* since the last common ancestor shared with the chimpanzees, the distribution and quality of the resources available in the environments in which human groups lived influenced the character of those groups and the relationships both among and between males and females (Foley 1995). Human sociality is a product of natural selection, and there is a biologically based inheritance that both directs behavior in certain adaptive directions and constrains the possible range of behavioral variation (Turner and Maryanski 2008). But that range has widened to the point that the direct influence of the ecological environment has been increasingly attenuated. Cultural adaptation has generated well-attested quasi-experimental examples where either groups sharing different cultures respond differently to the same ecological environment or groups sharing the same culture behave in the same way in different environments (Richerson and Boyd 2005). Moreover, human (and not only human) groups behave in ways that modify their environments through an increasingly well-understood process of niche construction (Laland, Odling-Smee, and Feldman 2000).

Evolutionary psychology has a more direct bearing on sociologists' concerns to the extent that its advocates insist that domain-specific psychological mechanisms naturally selected in the ancestral environment dictate human beings' responses to the environment of the present day and thereby undermine the assumptions that they attribute to the majority of anthropologists about the malleability of human behavior patterns under the influence of culture as anthropologists have traditionally defined it (Geertz 1975). They are therefore concerned to overturn once and for all the assumption of what they call the Standard Social Science Model (Tooby and Cosmides 1992)—that the human mind is a "blank slate" (Pinker 2002) on which different cultures inscribe, so to speak, the instructions that the individuals reared in them are to follow. The claims made by "narrow-sense" evolutionary psychology have, however, been strongly criticized (Mameli 2007) and have given rise to numerous unresolved controversies (Confer et al. 2010). For sociologists, the most relevant criticisms are that the ancestral environment of the Pleistocene was far from uniform, that the amount of behavioral variation is too large to be accounted for by the postulated mechanisms for adaptive thinking, that very little of it is directly evoked by interaction with the environment in an unmediated way, and that the evolutionary-psychological model is unable to accommodate the extent of diversity of behavior within populations whose members are experiencing the same environmental conditions.

It is safe to conclude that more of human social behavior can be explained by appeal to evolutionary biology than most twentieth-century sociologists were willing to concede. It is no longer possible to dismiss out of hand the existence of cultural universals (Brown 1991) and a universal human nature (Weingart et al. 1997). But it is also safe to conclude that the relevance of biology to sociology is more in what it allows or excludes than in what it prescribes. The metaphor of a leash is sometimes deployed to suggest this (Lumsden and Wilson 1981). But the leash is too long for the image to be appropriate. More important for sociologists' interests and purposes is that the widely different human cultures documented in the archaeological, ethnographic, and historical record can be shown to be the products of an analogous evolutionary process of heritable variation and competitive selection of units or bundles of information affecting phenotypic behavior transmitted by imitation or social learning from mind to mind.

CULTURAL SELECTION AND DUAL INHERITANCE

The idea that "culture evolves" in both *Homo sapiens* and other species is by now widely accepted across the behavioral sciences (Whiten et al. 2011). But although recent advances in cultural primatology (McGrew 2004; Whiten et al. 2009; Whiten 2011; Boesch 2012) have confirmed Darwin's insights about the intellectual and emotional dispositions and capacities of other animals, it is still only among humans that language and symbolism have made possible a continuous sequence of both rapid and cumulative variation and selection of information affecting phenotypic behavior transmitted vertically, laterally, and obliquely from mind to mind. The evolution of cultural evolution is itself a complex process (Henrich and McElreath 2003). But the diverse beliefs, attitudes, norms, values, fashions, and skills generated by it have been acted out in the prodigious range of cultures and subcultures documented in the archaeological, ethnographic, and historical record. Neo-Darwinian theory has been brought directly to bear on the agenda of social anthropology (Dunbar, Knight, and Power 1999), and the diffusion and reproduction of cultural mutations modeled with the help of methods borrowed from population genetics (Cavalli-Sforza and Feldman 1981; Boyd and Richerson 1983) together with a phylogenetic approach borrowed from evolutionary biology (Mace, Holden, and Shennan 2005) and the techniques of evolutionary game theory (see below).

Natural selection does not, however, cease to act on human populations, however much more slowly it takes effect than does cultural selection. Not only can it favor cultural mutations that enhance reproductive fitness but it can itself be reciprocally influenced by cultural mutations (Durham 1991; Fisher and Ridley 2013). The consequential phenomenon of "coevolution" or "dual inheritance" means that to account for a change from one to another distinctive cultural behavior pattern involves an assessment not only of the relative force of natural and cultural selection independently of each other but of the feedback between them. Moreover, reconstruction of the right "how come?" story that will account for the cultural-evolutionary trajectory observed is complicated by the need to establish whether selection is operating at the level of the individual or of the group. It was at one time more or less axiomatic among theoretical biologists that selection could operate only at the level of the individual organism (Williams 1966). But this was subsequently modified by the recognition that under certain possible conditions, however improbable, it could also operate between groups (Hamilton 1975). Whatever the difficulties in the way of establishing conclusively that it applies in a given case, it seems safe to say that the possibility of cultural group selection is no longer controversial (Sober and Wilson 1998).

A further complication is the lack of agreement about what exactly are the objects that cultural selection selects. By many leading researchers in their particular fields, from evolutionary biology (Pagel 2012) to "Darwinian" archaeology (Shennan 2002), the term "meme" is accepted as a matter of course as denoting whatever units (or complexes or bundles) of information (or instructions) affecting phenotypic behavior are diffused and reproduced within a given population by imitation or social learning. But there are others for whom it is controversial or even unacceptable (Aunger 2000). This in part reflects skepticism about both what are dismissed as exaggerated claims for "memetics" as a science on a par with genetics (Blackmore 1999; Distin 2005) and what is held to be a too close presumptive analogy between memes and genes. But memes do not have to be replicators in the same sense that genes are. Nor does their transmission need to be particulate as is that of genes. It is formally demonstrable that cultural evolution does not require high-fidelity replication of representations at the individual level (Henrich and Boyd 2002). Perhaps surprisingly, Richerson and Boyd (2005) deliberately eschew the use of "meme" (although it appears, and reads entirely naturally, in one passage of their text). But "cultural variant," which they prefer, has the disadvantage of blurring the distinction between the phenotypic effects of cultural mutations and the information transmitted from one to another carrier (or "vehicle") whose behavior is its phenotypic effect (including such extended phenotypic effects as utensils, artworks, grave goods, weaponry, jewels, musical instruments, and so forth, which are part of the stock-in-trade of both anthropologists and archaeologists). It is true that nobody is in a position to say what memes are in the way that can, thanks to the advances made by twentieth-century molecular biologists, be said of genes. But the progress of research ought not to be retarded by definitional arguments over a term of evident convenience, particularly when the widely used term "gene-culture coevolution" is, logically speaking, a category mistake. Those reluctant to follow Friedman and Singh (2004) and others in talking of the coevolution of memes and genes should be talking not of "gene-culture" but of "nature-culture" coevolution.

That said, there are two topics central to sociologists' concerns on which dual-inheritance theory bears directly and which are, moreover, bound up with one another (Henrich et al. 2010): cooperation and religion.

The need to explain how large populations of self-interested strangers can cooperate sufficiently for societies of different kinds to evolve and cohere was during much of the twentieth century formulated and discussed by sociologists as the "problem of order" (Cohen 1968, Chapter 2). But the protracted debates between "structural-functionalists" and "conflict theorists" did little to resolve it. It began to be constructively addressed only when the "problem of order" was displaced by the "problem of altruism." Following the seminal contributions of Hamilton (1964) on inclusive reproductive fitness and Trivers (1971) on reciprocal altruism, increasing attention began to be given to accounting for the evolution of "unconditional" altruism, where individuals behave in ways that confer benefits on others at an unreciprocated cost to themselves. There is by now an extensive literature addressing the question of how cooperation and "prosocial" (Hinde and Groebel 1991) behavior can be sustained between individuals and/or groups through relationships of trust, including the "radius of trust" (Delhey, Newton, and Welzel 2011) and the spread of trust through "competitive" altruism, whereby prestige can be won by a reputation for trustworthiness (Barclay 2004). It has also been shown how cooperation can be enhanced by costly signaling (Gintis, Smith, and Bowles 2001), including the extreme case where an infiltrator into a criminal "family" has to participate in criminal acts in order to be accepted as a member (Gambetta 2009; Campana and Varese 2013). Critical to the spread of cooperation, however, is the willingness of cooperators to punish not only non-cooperating defectors, free riders, bullies, and cheats but also those unwilling to punish them. "Strong reciprocity" (Gintis 2000; Gintis et al. 2007) extends beyond "spiteful" willingness to punish a violator of a norm of cooperation who has harmed the punisher directly (Marlowe et al. 2011) to third-party punishment where punishers punish anonymous violators. There is good reason to suppose both that coordinated punishment can proliferate when rare as the cost of punishment to the punishers declines (Boyd, Gintis, and Bowles 2010) and that the populations of larger societies engage in significantly more third-party punishment than those of smaller societies (Marlowe et al. 2008). Within-group cooperation is strengthened by hostility toward, and stereotyping of, out-groups that are distinguished by ethnic markers (McElreath, Boyd, and Richerson 2003). The frequency of warfare attested in the archaeological record (Keeley 1996) and estimates of deaths in intergroup conflicts between the Late Pleiocene and Holocene hunter-gatherers (Bowles 2009) endorse the importance of organized lethal violence in the evolution of altruism in human populations through natural and cultural group selection (Bowles and Gintis 2011) in accordance with Darwin's own hypothesis in *The Descent of Man* that groups in which a higher proportion are willing to sacrifice themselves will outcompete those with a lower one.

The evolution of altruistic cooperation is at the same time bound up with the evolution of religion—a term still, like so many in the vocabulary of sociology, bedeviled by definitional disputes but in the present context denoting the combination of belief in the existence of one or more quasi-personal supernatural beings capable of observing human behavior with acknowledgment of codes of conduct rewarded or punished by them. Although it is questionable how far the fear of supernatural retribution (Johnson 2005) has ever deterred defectors, free riders, bullies, and cheats, there is no doubt that religious, like ethnic, linguistic, and sartorial markers, promote in-group cooperation and out-group hostility and that costly ritual and signaling behavior both enhance commitment to communities of believers (Sosis and Alcorta 2003) and stabilize cooperative arrangements and the places of individuals within them (Gibbard 1990). Sociologists of religion are unlikely to accept that the evolution of religions and their associated moral codes can be explained by natural selection alone (Broom 2003) or that the diversity of religious experience can be explained by pointing to its neural correlates in the brain (McNamara 2008). But a broadly evolutionary approach is widely shared (Burkert 1996; Rappaport 1999; Whitehouse 2003; Bellah 2011), and it includes explanations of religion in terms of an evolved intuitive ontology (Boyer 2001), the evolved modularities of the human mind (Atran 2002), and cultural group selection on the classic Darwinian model (D. S. Wilson 2002). Sociologists who adhere to the "secularization" thesis (Bruce 2011) maintain that belief in gods (or *a* God) is in long-term decline along with deference to the moral authority of religious leaders and institutions. But if the definition of religion is extended to cover sacralization in all its forms, including adherence to the rituals and norms of nations, parties, communes, sects, and social movements, the reproductive fitness of the same combination of within-group cooperation and hostility to, and stereotyping of, out-groups can be readily documented.

The neo-Darwinian approach is sometimes queried on the grounds that it is unable to allow for cultural stagnation. Whenever and however human beings developed the capacity for spoken language, the frequency of variation and speed of diffusion thereby generated led not only to cumulative changes in shared beliefs, attitudes, norms, values, fashions, and skills but to the runaway effects of crazes and panics familiar from societies all over the world. Frequency-dependent conformity to the behavior of others, imitation of the most prestigious or successful, and the spread of innovations along the familiar S-shaped logistic curve all combine to create memetic lineages analogous to the lineages of natural selection. But evolutionary sociology can equally well explain how in an environment of geographic isolation, no contact with or immigration from other populations, and low population density, successive generations will accept from parents or mentors memes transmitted with consistently high fidelity from one generation to the next and how, as in the extreme but well-documented case of Tasmania, an isolated aboriginal population of hunter-gatherers not only failed to innovate but suffered maladaptive cultural losses in technical expertise (Henrich 2004).

Evolutionary Game Theory

The biologist John Maynard Smith, who is widely regarded as the father of evolutionary game theory, has commented on how the theory of games, although initially conceived (von Neumann and Morgenstern 1944) as offering solutions to problems arising within sociology, was borrowed by biologists such as himself before being reintroduced into sociology later on (Maynard Smith 1982, Chapter 13). Since then, it has been widely applied to the study of both animal and human behavior through formal modeling, computer simulation, laboratory experiments, and field studies in ways that bear directly on the question of how groups, communities, and societies evolve and cohere. In this approach, the objects of selection are the strategies of which the players are the carriers, the measure of success is their respective gains or losses in fitness in accordance with the payoff matrices of repeated encounters, and an "evolutionarily stable strategy" as defined by Maynard Smith is one such that if all the members of a population adopt it, no mutant can invade. Evolutionary game theory has thereby come to be seen as offering an alternative paradigm for the study of cooperation between unrelated strangers to the rational choice theory favored by sociologists (Coleman 1990) as well as economists.

Formal analysis of the replicator dynamics enabling social contracts to evolve and of the conditions under which mutual commitment can be sustained through interpersonal communication within social networks (Skyrms 1996, 2004) has been supplemented by a long succession of ingeniously designed game-theoretic experiments in which players are found to follow strategies other than those dictated by rational self-interest as defined in classical economic theory. Trust games, dictator games, ultimatum games, moonlighting games, snatch games, public goods games, and the celebrated Prisoner's Dilemma have all been used to demonstrate the extent to which experimental subjects do not all behave as rational egoists, with the consequential risk that policies formulated in the belief that they do will crowd out the potential for cooperative solutions. Moreover, players in public goods games who are allowed to punish low-contributing free riders have been shown to do so even where the experiment is designed so as to rule out the possibility of net future gain through strategic punishment (Fehr and Gächter 2000).

Some sociologists may be disposed to doubt whether either computer simulations or laboratory experiments are a reliable guide to cooperative behavior in the real world and to agree with Guala (2012) in querying what exactly it is that punishment experiments do or don't demonstrate. Not only are the participants interacting with others who may in many ways be unlike the people with whom they have dealings in real-life settings of competition and conflict, but they are also aware that they are being observed in an artificial environment designed by the experimenter. But experiments done with real money as payoff are arguably more realistic than questionnaires administered by interviewers in sample surveys of the kind on which sociologists habitually rely (Falk and Heckman 2009). The more telling criticism of the earlier experiments was that the participants were recruited from highly literate university students in developed market societies. But it was effectively answered by a project involving fifteen different small-scale societies (Henrich et al. 2004) that followed on from awareness that participants in ultimatum games drawn from Southeastern Peru (Henrich 2000), and likewise in Southwestern Tanzania (Pacciotti and Hadley 2003), behaved quite differently. Cross-cultural comparison not only undermined the model of rational self-interest as a universal norm of human behavior, but disclosed an extent of variation between the different groups that reflected ascertainable differences in their habitual forms of social interaction and the beliefs and attitudes underlying them. Sociologists and anthropologists might be unsurprised by findings that experimental subjects drawn from societies more closely integrated into market exchange should respond differently from those drawn from societies unfamiliar with the workings of markets, or that those drawn from societies where a gift is interpreted as an attempt to impose an obligation on a presumptively inferior recipient should respond differently from those drawn from societies where it is interpreted as an act of kindness. But the cross-cultural contextualization of game-theoretic experiments has enhanced their contribution to the study of cooperation to the point that "framing effects" and their contingent antecedents are now routinely taken into account (Gerkey 2013).

The results of the multitude of game-theoretic experiments on record bear as much on the traditional concerns of economists, political scientists, and social psychologists as on those of sociologists. But arguably the most important single contribution to the "problem of order" during recent decades has come from the work of Elizabeth Ostrom (1990) on the evolution of institutions for collective action. The logic of what has come to be known as the "tragedy of the commons" (Hardin 1968) was already well understood by Hume in the eighteenth century. But from a game-theoretic perspective, it can be formalized as a standard Prisoner's Dilemma where defection is the better strategy whatever strategy is chosen by the other player. It was for some time widely assumed that the only solution is the coercive imposition by an external authority of rules that compel the players to adopt a different strategy from the one they would choose if left to themselves. But Ostrom and associates showed in the evidence both of field studies and of game-theoretic experiments that it is possible for common-pool resource problems to be solved by self-organized monitoring—that, in other words, there can be "covenants without a sword" (Ostrom, Walker, and Gardner 1992). Taken alongside field research, the number of subjects in carefully controlled experiments who turn out to be trustworthy, are ready to reciprocate trust, and are willing to inflict retribution (Ostrom 2005, Chapter 3) has shown how a game-theoretic approach can be integrated with evolutionary theory in a way that has clear implications for issues by which sociologists have long been exercised.

From Cultural to Social Selection

Evolution through natural selection is frequently contrasted with "sociocultural" evolution (Campbell 1965; Stuart-Fox 1986; Trigger 1998; Rousseau 2006; Blute 2010). But if the mechanisms of "sociocultural" selection are the same as those of cultural selection, the "socio" is redundant, while if they are not then those of "social" selection need to be separately specified—as, for example, in an evolutionary schema for the replacement in Indo-European societies of bridewealth, which all of their religious ideologies of the past two millennia have rejected, by dowry (Testart 2013). A distinction, whether implicit or explicit, between the cultural and the social has generally been taken as given among sociologists, including both Marxists for whom culture is a superstructure whose form and content are determined by an economic base and Weberians for whom culturally transmitted attitudes and beliefs such as those of the celebrated "Protestant Ethic" can influence the evolution of economic institutions no less than the other way around. More broadly, the concern of sociologists with relations of power, or more specifically "social" power (Mann 1986), implies a fundamental, if fluid, contrast between associations held together by informal sanctions and institutions held together by formal ones: conformity to conventional norms acquired by imitation or learning is very obviously different in kind from obedience to laws imposed by a sovereign state on pain of forcible deprivation of liberty.

The difficulty of clearly distinguishing social from cultural selection is unfortunately compounded by differences over the definitions of "social" and "institution." "Social evolution" can be used to advance an explicitly anti-Darwinian thesis (Hallpike 1986), or to argue for an explicitly Darwinian "conflict perspective" (Sanderson 2001), or to cover only "social natural selection" whereby inclusive reproductive fitness is maximized (Frank 1998). "Institution" can be defined to embrace any established customs, usages, norms, and organizational forms (Young 1998), or "rules of the game" by which human interaction is shaped (J. Knight 1990), or learned conventions culturally transmitted (Bowles and Gintis 2011), or any form of constraint shaping human interaction (North 1990). However, the concept that best captures the significance of the transition from cultural to social evolution is that of "role," which has long been recognized as central to sociological theory (Dahrendorf 1968, Chapter 2). The word can also be used in informal interpersonal contexts where, for example, "leaders" are distinguished from "followers" or "enemies" from "friends." But in formal institutional contexts, roles can be occupied and performed by successive incumbents irrespective of the incumbents' personal traits. Individuals come *to* power instead of personally constructing it (Sahlins 1974). "Social mobility" becomes from then on a standard topic on the sociological agenda as individual role incumbents rise or fall between different institutional roles located above or below one another in social space. Such roles may on occasion be left vacant. But the critical difference is that power attaches to the role as such: it may be forfeited by inadequate performance, but it will normally then be filled by a successor, whether by inheritance, appointment, usurpation, election, acclamation, patronage, or assassination. There are always words in the vernacular terminology for the roles constitutive of evolved political, ideological, or economic institutions, as is attested in the ethnographic, literary, and epigraphic record alike, and even where the role structure has to be inferred from archaeological evidence alone, funereal, architectural, and other material remains can license the inference that the transition from cultural to social evolution has been made (Flannery and Marcus 2012).

Thereafter, information affecting phenotypic behavior that is encoded in beliefs, attitudes, norms, values, fashions, and skills transmitted by imitation and learning coevolves alongside information that is encoded in the rule-governed practices by which institutional roles are defined (Runciman 1989, 2009). The individuals who in bands of hunters and foragers are acknowledged as skillful hunters or eloquent speakers or repositories of wisdom and experience turn into chiefs, priests, magistrates, military commanders, controllers of surplus resources, and employers or directors of the labor of unrelated others.

The textbook examples of an intermediate stage in the transition are the much studied "big men" of the horticultural societies of the Pacific Islands (Oliver 1955; Strathern 1971), whose superior position depends on continued manifestation of personal prowess including conspicuous gift-giving. It is formally possible for the division and specialization of labor to give rise by itself to economic inequality between subgroups within a population through cultural learning and the positive valuation of economic success (Henrich and Boyd 2008). But once social as well as cultural selection is under way, it generates the castes, classes, orders, strata, age-grades, estates, and status groups that are sociologists' stock-in-trade, including the extreme case of slavery, where one individual is totally subordinated to another (or, as in the case of temple slaves, to an institution). Slavery involves in all its variants a cultural legitimation of the "social death" of the slave (Patterson 1982), which may simply rest on the slave having been spared from execution after capture in war. But the diffusion and reproduction of enslavement requires power to attach to the role of the master or owner of the slave, which is a matter of much more than imitation and learning, even if subsequently used to free the slave by self-purchase or testamentary disposition or as a reward for performance in battle or however else the master or owner may choose. Practices through which the slave is institutionally subordinated may also be observed in roles such as serfdom, peonage, or indenture, or in roles whose function is in other societies performed by free citizens. But it is always a social as well as cultural construction whose reproductive fitness or, as it may be, extinction has to be explained accordingly.

The transition from cultural to social selection can also be traced in the evolution of systems of kinship. This has been a contentious topic ever since the nineteenth-century research of Lewis H. Morgan, whose pioneering study of matrilinearity provoked successive reactions against the conjectural history of "progress" that he based on it. Such was the volume of inconclusive debate as to lead one twentieth-century anthropologist to wonder whether the whole idea of "family" is not fundamentally misconceived (Leach 1961). But it has since been shown how the study of kinship can be integrated within evolutionary theory (Alvard 2000; Cronk and Gerkey 2007; Allen et al. 2008). Naturally selected relationships of biological parenthood can clearly not be mapped directly onto culturally defined relationships of cousinage, avuncularity, affinity, and so forth. Still less can natural selection explain by itself the form and extent of the institutionalized power exercised by the incumbents of some kinship roles over others, of which the *patria potestas* of the Roman father is the extreme example: the Roman jurists debated only whether fathers had a wholly unconditional legal right to kill their sons. But the variations documented in the ethnographic and historical record can all be analyzed as outcomes of a path-dependent evolutionary sequence of meme-practice coevolution driven by ascertainable selective pressures. Furthermore, relations of kinship can be mapped onto a system of slavery, as with female servitude in pre-Communist China (Watson 1980). Adoption can be used, as in Classical Rome, to give an unrelated adoptee the same rights of succession to a position of power as a natural heir (Crook 1967, Chapter 3), and fictive kinship can bind an unrelated clansman to a Highland Scottish chief who is then empowered to order him into battle or to remove his family and household from one place to another at his unfettered discretion (Smout 1969, Chapter 1).

The convergent evolution of agriculture on different continents at different times following periods of mixed subsistence and nonagricultural sedentism (Kennett and Winterhalder 2006; Killion 2013) is generally taken to be the decisive stage in the transition from mobile bands in which would-be "aggrandizers" (Hayden 1998) are held in check by ostracism, censure, ridicule, and, on occasion, violence to large sedentary populations with accumulated resources, permanent residential structures, and forms of social organization in which some individuals, groups, families, and households come to exercise ongoing power over others (Johnson and Earle 1987). From an evolutionary perspective, the long millennia of dual inheritance during which our ancestors hunted and foraged can then be seen as an interlude between the dominance hierarchies of the chimpanzees and archaic humans and the institutionalized inequalities of the last 10,000 or 15,000 years (Boehm 1999, 2010). Agriculture is not a necessary condition. It has long been known that where aquatic resources are sufficiently abundant, as on the Northwest Pacific coast of the American continent, there can evolve similar structures of roles, including slaves. But the combination of sedentism, storage, population growth, residential concentration, and the domestication of plants and animals that first occurred in the ecological and climatic environment of Southwest Asia (Bar-Yosef 1998) favored the reproduction of practices defining institutionalized political, ideological, and economic roles that brought into being military, religious, and wealth-holding elites who permanently dominated their subordinates, inferiors, and dependents. Thereafter, the ongoing variation and selection of practices expanded, modified, and sometimes destroyed the role structures of the societies within which they emerged under pressure from their changing environments. Populations neither anatomically nor psychologically different from the hunters and foragers from whom they were descended entered a world of armies, markets, priests, merchants, courts (in both senses), landholders (including temples or churches) and tenants, debtors and creditors, rulers and subjects, schoolteachers and pupils, masters and slaves, and employers and employees.

Neither cultural nor social evolution proceeds at a uniform pace. But whatever the chosen criterion of measurement, the rate of change in the forms and functions of the institutions constitutive of human societies during the past few millennia has accelerated, particularly in the last few centuries, to a spectacular degree. In part, this has been due to the increase in material resources available for use in intersocietal conflict through the variation and selection of "techno-memes" (Stankiewicz 2000): the arms races of the human world and concomitant advances in the methods of waging war (McNeill 1983) parallel the "arms races" of the animal world in which natural selection increases the speed and agility of both predators and prey. But it has also been due to a wider sequence of meme-practice coevolution in which the reproductive fitness of mutant beliefs, attitudes, norms, values, fashions, and skills transmitted by imitation and learning enhances and is enhanced by mutant social practices. The reciprocal influence of agriculture and religion (Cauvin 1997) can be traced in the archaeological record well before the invention of writing brought into being the post-foraging but pre-industrial world of the plough, sword, and book (Gellner 1988).

Older and now discarded evolutionary theories generally presupposed a unilinear sequence of stages, whether cultural (from magic to religion to science), social (from slavery to feudalism to capitalism to socialism), or more tendentiously still from "primitive" to "advanced" or "savage" to "civilized." But the coevolving memes and practices that outcompete their rivals follow widely divergent and inherently unpredictable trajectories. Slavery again offers as good an example as any, appearing as it does as soon as it became institutionally feasible and persisting or reappearing long after. It is documented in a historical and ethnographic literature that covers every part of the world and traces the diffusion, reproduction, and extinction of its constituent roles and practices in forms that range from the chattel slavery of the Graeco-Roman world and the Southern United States to the "rights-in-persons" that African societies or, more specifically, their constituent kin groups and lineages acquired and held over purchased, adopted, kidnapped, or captured outsiders (Miers and Kopytoff 1977), and include also at various times and places convicted criminals, deviants, or dissidents. Every example on record from the initial transition from cultural to social selection onward involves a coevolution of practices by which slaves are held in subjection to their individual or corporate masters and memes by which that subjection is legitimated. Moreover, slavery evolves alongside alternative roles such as those of wage-workers, junior kin, pawns, peons, indentured apprentices, corvee laborers, serfs, conscripts, or tenants, whose defining practices may drive to extinction those defining the roles of master and slave.

Evolution of the State

The transition from cultural to social selection does not by itself bring about a transition to statehood. Melanesian big-man societies are by no means the only example. So are nomadic pastoralists and societies of autonomous peasant producers who collaborate voluntarily for the purposes of self-defense or pooling of labor. The ethnographic and historical record is replete with "tribes without rulers" (Middleton and Tait 1958), "paramount" chiefs who are not, or not yet, rulers of states (Brumfiel 1983), "semi-" as well as "proto-states" (Runciman 1982), chiefdoms that may or may not be classified as "state societies" (Kristiansen 1991), "early" and often inchoate states (Claessen and Skalnik 1978), and small polities headed by petty kings or "kinglets" such as the *basileis* of Archaic Greece or the *reguli* of early Anglo-Saxon England. The critical practices that bring about the evolution of statehood are those that empower rulers or ruling groups to exercise coercive control over a subject population and to extract from that population by tax, tribute, extortion, liturgy, levy, render, rents, profits, tithes, or dues resources adequate to support the military and administrative assistants and servants on whom they necessarily depend. Whether the evolution of statehood was inevitable (Claessen 2002) is a question much like the question of whether natural selection was bound to lead to the emergence of a species with the capacity for symbolic, linguistic, and in due course literary culture. In both cases, the answer must be that it was not unconditionally inevitable. But in the absence of climatic or ecological catastrophe, both were—sooner or later—overwhelmingly likely.

Once it had happened, the ongoing variation and selection of practices generated a widening range of political institutions constitutive of increasingly elaborately organized and powerful states. But they fall into no agreed taxonomy, follow no unilinear trend, and share no universal environmental conditions. The number of states in a given geographical area may be expanded either by convergent evolution or by "secondary" state formation under pressure from preexisting states (Price 1978). But it may also be reduced as stronger states absorb or eliminate weaker ones in classic Darwinian fashion. Population growth in regions where adjacent societies are competitors for scarce resources is likely to favor the reproduction and diffusion of the practices that give rise to statehood, but not where, as over most of Africa, the availability of free land made dispersal an option (Goody 1971), or where "interstitial" frontiers (Kopytoff 1987) delimited areas lying between rather than bordering on already settled populations. Chiefdoms that anthropologists were earlier inclined to view as a stage in a linear causal sequence leading from "tribes" to "states" came increasingly to be recognized as both unstable and cyclical and as resting on variable combinations of military, economic, and ideological power (Earle 1989).

Nor does evolution into statehood offer any guarantee of permanence. Societies, like both cultures and species, are frequently driven to extinction. But statehood can also re-evolve out of a previous collapse, as in post-Mycenaean Greece or England after the withdrawal of Rome. From the beginnings of the tradition of European political thought, theorists have looked for trends or cycles that might account for how one form of state either rises and declines on the model of youth, maturity, senescence, and death or gives way to another on the model of monarchy (or "tyranny"), oligarchy, democracy, anarchy, and back to monarchy again. Similarly, Ibn Khaldun saw in Islamic societies cycles of dissolution and revival as decadent rulers are displaced by ascetic rebels who lapse into decadence in their turn. But the explanation of any given case depends on assessing the adaptiveness of the practices that determine the form of the state in question, and this depends on finding quasi-experimental contrasts through which rival hypotheses can be tested against one another. Both early-medieval and early-modern Europe offer examples from which persuasive inferences can be drawn. In the former, the critical practices were those that determined how resources were extracted from subordinate cultivators and deployed in such a way as to overcome structural fragmentation (Wickham 2005). In the latter, competition between patrimonial and bureaucratic practices combined with those differentiating absolutist from constitutional regimes in an environment of near-continuous warfare that proved lethal to patrimonial/constitutional societies such as Poland and Hungary (Ertman 1997). "Failed" states do not then reverse, so to speak, into societies of the kind out of which they emerged. No more can social than either cultural or natural selection run backward in such a way as to re-create the past. But practices initially favored in a previous environment can turn out to be maladaptive in a different one no less than can memes or genes.

By contrast, once past the transition to statehood, some rulers are able to extend the geographical and institutional reach of their power to bring under their control populations that they hold in subordination without admitting them to membership of their own societies. Empires appear in the historical record remarkably soon after states do and sometimes expand with equally remarkable speed. As with states, the critical practices on which they depend are those that facilitate revenue extraction and military mobilization, together with ritual and ceremonial practices that function to legitimate the power of the centers over their subaltern peripheries. The ongoing process of variation and selection generates an increasing diversity of "imperial" institutional forms (Burbank and Cooper 2010) that follow their own distinctive evolutionary trajectories. But all end sooner or later in failure, not so much through inevitable "overstretch" (Kennedy 1987) as because unless the subject populations are either fully incorporated into the role structure of the metropolitan society or else conceded the status of independent allies, any combination of political, ideological, and economic practices defining the roles linking center and periphery will be inherently unstable (Runciman 2011). Those roles are all intermediate by definition. The power attaching to them is delegated from the center, and this carries the inescapable risk of rebellion or secession, whether because the rulers at the center exercise too little control or because, on the contrary, they try to exercise too much. The practices whose diffusion and reproduction make possible the realization of would-be imperialists' ambitions become increasingly likely to prove maladaptive in the longer term. There was at the time no possible way to predict the particular changes in their different environments and contingent events within their own domestic institutions that brought to an end the Mesopotamian, Egyptian, Hittite, Assyrian, Iranian, Hellenistic, Roman, Byzantine, Chinese, Islamic, Aztec, Inca, African, Mongol, Venetian, Javanese, Malaccan, Ottoman, Spanish, Portuguese, Dutch, British, Austro-Hungarian, Nazi German, and Soviet Russian empires. But their disappearance could only be a matter of time.

EVOLUTIONARY MACROSOCIOLOGY

Nothing brings out more clearly the distance by which evolutionary sociology lags behind evolutionary biology than sociology's lack of anything approaching a comprehensive Linnaean taxonomy with an underlying Darwinian rationale. There are well-known data collections within which subsets of societies are compared and contrasted such as the anthropological and archaeological Human Relations Area Files at Yale or Murdock's *Ethnographic Atlas* or the Smithsonian Institution's multivolume *Handbook of North American Indians*. But nowhere is there a scheme of classification in which all the societies in the archaeological, ethnographic, and historical record can in principle be assigned a place. Even within such restricted categories as "authoritarian" societies (Slovik 2012) or "communist" societies—which can be classed as a subtype of authoritarian societies alongside personal autocracies and military dictatorships (Dimitrov 2013)—there is scope for extensive debate about how many there have been (or are) and where the definitional boundaries between them lie. Such is the range of variation and selection of practices and the roles defined by them that systematic institutional comparison is difficult to extend to a more than limited extent in place and time except at the cost of explanatory value. Moreover, there are already significant differences among the hunters and foragers (Kelly 1995), let alone the horticulturalists, nomadic pastoralists, and independent arms-bearing peasant cultivators. Even slave societies are generally compared and contrasted only within geographical and temporal limits such as the Graeco-Roman world (Wiedemann 1981), Africa (Miers and Kopytoff 1977; Lovejoy 1983), or North and South America (Elliott 2006).

Yet sociologists of all theoretical persuasions can usually agree when a chosen society has evolved out of one modal category into another. Where they are more likely to disagree, as evolutionary biologists likewise do, is over the question of whether major changes of kind are driven more by gradual mutations on the classic Darwinian model or by "punctuated equilibrium" giving rise to sudden spurts over short periods of time (Somit and Peterson 1992). In both biology and sociology, the debate has been exacerbated by mutual accusations of political bias, with advocates of punctuated equilibrium accusing their opponents of commitment to market capitalism and advocates of gradualism accusing theirs of commitment to revolutionary socialism. But any survey of macrosociological evolution over the past ten millennia will include well-attested instances of both. Finding the right answer to the "how come?" question depends on separating changes resulting from exogenous disturbance through climate change, epidemic disease, natural disaster, intersocietal competition, warfare, or conquest from changes that are the outcome of endogenous variation and selection.

The complexity of the relation between the two is thoroughly familiar to sociologists of revolution, where an existing institutional equilibrium is punctuated by a violent transfer of power. But it is necessary to distinguish the overthrow of one type of regime and its replacement by another from the replacement of the members of a ruling elite by newcomers drawn from elsewhere. Invaders or usurpers who have demoted, exiled, or killed the previous rulers may leave the society's institutions unchanged, in which case the sequence of events that brought them to power is of no social-evolutionary relevance, however dramatic the story it tells. Moreover, there is also the difficulty of distinguishing revolutions as standardly defined from secessions, civil wars, wars of liberation, coups, or so-called revolutions from above, like the Meiji Restoration in Japan—a difficulty that applies as much to the world of Classical Greece (Lintott 1982) as to the world of the twentieth century CE. Viewed in hindsight from the closing decades of that century, the

French, Russian, and Chinese Revolutions could be singled out as the exemplars with which others should be compared and contrasted (Skocpol 1979). But all three of these, as with the Mexican Revolution (A. Knight 1986), are explicable only as outcomes of unpredictable sequences of improbable concatenations of singular causes and effects that for the purposes of evolutionary sociology have to be accepted as given in order to trace the practices and roles whose reproduction and diffusion were subsequently favored in their changed environment.

The ongoing course of history does, however, throw up from time to time natural experiments from which can be derived otherwise untestable hypotheses about the relative strength of the selective pressures that come to bear on the institutions of postrevolutionary societies. In the decades after 1945, a topic of increasing interest to sociologists (and to economists and political scientists) was the survival, diffusion, and reproduction of market practices within communist societies. Their continued existence in small-scale local enterprises and networks of both legal and illegal exchange was to a varying extent observable in all of them. But the question by which contemporary observers were increasingly exercised, particularly in the cases of the Soviet Union and the People's Republic of China, was what would happen if market practices were to be diffused and reproduced within or alongside those of the centralized command economies of their single-party political regimes. In the event, they weakened the power of the state in Russia in a way that they did not in China. But in China, three practices have been found to be adaptive in preserving institutional stability: non-zero-sum protest bargaining, legal-bureaucratic absorption, and patron-clientelism (Lee and Zhang 2013).

In the opening years of the twentieth century, the macrosociological agenda was largely set by the unmistakable contrast between the institutions of the "Western" societies, which gave them seemingly unchallenged political, ideological, and economic dominance over the rest of the world, and the "Eastern" or "Oriental" societies, which appeared to have forfeited the lead they had once enjoyed. But by the opening years of the twenty-first century, it was evident that from an authentically global perspective the period of Western dominance was no more than part of a long history of shifting relative advantages driven by geographical, climatic, and ecological pressures within local environments where the nature and availability of food, minerals, and other material resources, vulnerability to infectious diseases, and scope for technological exploitation explained as much or more about social evolution than differences of culture (Diamond 1997). In the second half of the twentieth century, when the outcome of World War II appeared to vindicate Tocqueville's prediction that America and Russia would one day divide the world between them, there were commentators on one side who argued that capitalist liberal democracy as it had evolved in the United States was the model to which the rest of the world would increasingly conform, and commentators on the other who argued that the rest of the world would come increasingly to follow the example of the Soviet Union. But by now, it hardly needs saying that both sides were as mistaken as each other.

An alternative macrosociological theory that seeks to preserve the idea of a shared worldwide trend without unduly privileging the history of the "West" is the theory of "modernization" developed and expounded by S. N. Eisenstadt (1973, 2003; Ben-Rafael and Sternberg 2005). From this perspective, the irreversible impact of the major civilizations that have determined the course of human history is seen as having arisen out of a common rejection of traditional conceptions of the cosmic and social order in favor of new and contested cultural and political forms that originated in what Karl Jaspers christened the "Axial Age" (Eisenstadt 1982; Bellah and Joas 2012). Many of the individual histories narrated in terms of "modernization" could be rephrased without loss of meaning in terms of cultural and social variation and selection. But in two respects they conflict.

First, the concept of "modernity" has no function in neo-Darwinian theory: unless it is used as a measure of teleological progress toward a predetermined goal, all new cultural and social forms are "modern" when they first appear, only to become "ancient" in their turn with the passage of time. Second, the allowance that has to be made for "multiple modernities" in order to accommodate the diversity of cultures and societies is such as to diminish the explanatory value of the common denominator. It is true that many societies have in common a self-conscious desire among their members to discard "traditional" beliefs and attitudes as well as practices inherited from the past. But this can be observed in societies whose constitutive institutions range across the whole political, ideological, and economic spectrum: it does not in itself account for the divergent evolutionary trajectories that they subsequently follow.

Any macrosociological theory has to be able to accommodate not only the punctuated equilibria by which the evolutionary trajectory of any society may at any time be driven off course but also "sick" (Edgerton 1992) or "collapsed" (Tainter 1988) societies in which memes and practices previously adaptive lose their reproductive fitness in a changed environment. Some sociologists are more impressed than others by the resilience of human societies under the pressures to which they are subjected (McAnny and Yoffee 2010). But whatever the relative incidence of collapse and resilience across the total of societies on record, maladaptations are, like exaptations, neither unusual nor anomalous in cultural and social evolution any more than in biological evolution. Of the objections leveled against neo-Darwinian evolutionary theory by its critics, one of the least persuasive is that it interprets any and every outcome of heritable variation and competitive selection as a Panglossian best of possible worlds.

Conclusion

Despite the advances made in recent decades in evolutionary sociology and the related behavioral sciences on which it draws, the prospect of a unified theory of human behavior, whether achieved through interdisciplinary synthesis (Sear, Lanson, and Dickins 2007), game theory (Gintis 2009), or a wider process of scientific "consilience" (E. O. Wilson 1998), is still remote. Given that sociologists are seeking to explain as best they can how human groups, communities, institutions, and societies come to be of the different kinds that they are, sociology cannot but be, like biology, a historical science. That does not mean that sociological explanation is never more than anecdotal. But it does mean that sociologists have to look to unpredictable contingencies that from their perspective might as well be random to furnish the quasi-experimental contrasts on which they will continue to depend. There is no contradiction between either the aims or the methods of evolutionary sociologists and narrative historians. But they address different questions: the sequences of unique events and decisions that narrative historians link in relations of cause and effect do not account for their long-term sociological consequences, any more than the sequences of variation and selection of information affecting collective behavior patterns traced by evolutionary sociologists account for the initial mutations that set those sequences in train.

The future of sociology is as unforeseeable as that of any other science for the familiar reason that any sociologist able to foresee it would be practicing it already. But it is not foolishly optimistic to hope that increasingly close collaboration within and between increasingly large and well-resourced research teams will continue to advance the neo-Darwinian agenda that has evolved out of that bequeathed to twentieth-century sociologists by Marx, Weber, and Durkheim.

References

Allen, N. J., H. Callan, R. Dunbar, and W. James. 2008. *Early Human Kinship: From Sex to Social Reproduction*. Oxford: Blackwell.
Alvard, M. 2000. "Kinship, Lineage Identity and an Evolutionary Perspective on the Structure of Cooperative Big Game Hunting Groups in Indonesia." *Human Nature* 14: 129–163.
Asbury, K., and R. Plomin. 2013. *G Is for Genes: The Impact of Genetics on Education and Achievement*. Oxford: Wiley-Blackwell.
Atran, S. 2002. *In Gods We Trust: The Evolutionary Landscape of Religion*. Oxford: Oxford University Press.
Aunger, R., ed. 2000. *Darwinizing Culture: The Status of Memetics as a Science*. Oxford: Oxford University Press.
Barclay, P. 2004. "Trustworthiness and Competitive Altruism Can also Solve the 'Tragedy of the Commons.'" *Evolution and Human Behavior* 25: 209–220.
Bar-Yosef, O. 1998. "The Natufian Culture in the Levant, Threshold to Agriculture." *Evolutionary Anthropology* 6: 159–177.
Bellah, R. N. 2011. *Religion in Human Evolution: From the Palaeolithic to the Axial Age*. Cambridge, MA: Harvard University Press.
Bellah, R. N., and H. Joas, eds. 2012. *The Axial Age and Its Consequences*. Cambridge, MA: Harvard University Press.
Ben-Rafael, E., and J. Sternberg, eds. 2005. *Comparing Modernities: Pluralism versus Homogeneity. Essays in Homage to Shmuel N. Eisenstadt*. Leiden: Brill.
Blackmore, S. 1999. *The Meme Machine*. Oxford: Oxford University Press.
Blute, M. 2010. *Darwinian Sociocultural Evolution: Solutions to Dilemmas in Cultural and Social Theory*. Cambridge: Cambridge University Press.
Boehm, C. 1999. *Hierarchy in the Forest: The Evolution of Egalitarian Behaviour*. Cambridge, MA: Harvard University Press.
———. 2010. *Moral Origins: The Evolution of Virtue, Altruism, and Shame*. New York: Basic Books.
Boesch, C. 2012. *Wild Cultures. A Comparison between Chimpanzee and Human Cultures*. Cambridge: Cambridge University Press.
Borgerhoff Mulder, M. 2013. "Why an Ape with Complex Cumulative Culture Dominates the World: Different Views." *Evolutionary Anthropology* 22: 34–39.
Bowles, S. 2009. "Did Warfare among Ancestral Hunter-Gatherer Groups Affect the Evolution of Human Social Behaviors?" *Science* 324: 1293–1298.
Bowles, S., and H. Gintis. 2011. *A Cooperative Species: Human Reciprocity and Its Evolution*. Princeton, NJ: Princeton University Press.
Boyd, R., H. Gintis, and S. Bowles. 2010. "Coordinated Punishment of Defectors Sustains Cooperation and Can Proliferate When Rare." *Science* 328: 617–620.
Boyd, R., and P. J. Richerson. 1983. *Culture and the Evolutionary Process*. Chicago: University of Chicago Press.
Boyer, P. 2001. *Religion Explained: The Human Instincts that Fashion Gods, Spirits and Ancestors*. London: Heinemann.
Broom, D. M. 2003. *The Evolution of Morality and Religion*. Cambridge: Cambridge University Press.
Brown, D. E. 1991. *Human Universals*. New York: McGraw Hill.
Bruce, S. 2011. *Secularization: In Defence of an Unfashionable Theory*. Oxford: Oxford University Press.
Brumfiel, E. M. 1983. "Aztec State Making: Ecology, Structure, and the Origin of the State." *American Anthropologist* 85: 261–284.
Burbank, J., and F. Cooper. 2010. *Empires and the Politics of Difference in World History*. Princeton, NJ: Princeton University Press.
Burkert, W. 1996. *Creation of the Sacred: Tracks of Biology in Early Religion*. Cambridge, MA: Harvard University Press.
Campana, P., and F. Varese. 2013. "Cooperation in Criminal Organisations: Kinship and Violence as Credible Commitments." *Rationality and Society* 25: 263–289.
Campbell, D. T. 1965. "Variation and Selective Retention in Sociocultural Evolution." In *Social Change in Developing Areas*, edited by H. R. Beringer, G. I. Blanksten, and R. W. Mack, 19–49. Cambridge, MA: Schenkman.
Cauvin, J. 1997. *Naissance des Divinités Naissance de l'Agriculture: La Révolution des Symboles au Néolithique*. Paris: Flammarion.
Cavalli-Sforza, L. L. 1995. "Postscript." In *The Great Human Diasporas: The History of Diversity and Evolution*, edited by L. L. Cavalli-Sforza and F. Cavalli-Sforza, 267–283. New York: Addison-Wesley.
Cavalli-Sforza, L. L., and M. W. Feldman. 1981. *Cultural Transmission and Evolution: A Quantitative Approach*. Princeton, NJ: Princeton University Press.
Ciba Foundation. 1996. *Genetics of Criminal and Antisocial Behaviour*. Chichester, NY: Wiley.

Claessen, H.J.M. 2002. "Was the State Inevitable?" *Social Evolution and History* 1: 101–117.
Claessen, H.J.M., and P. Skalnik, eds. 1978. *The Early State*. The Hague: Mouton.
Cohen, P. S. 1968. *Modern Social Theory*. London: Heinemann.
Coleman, J. S. 1990. *Foundations of Social Theory*. Cambridge, MA: Harvard University Press.
Confer, J. C., J. A. Easton, D. S. Fleischmann, C. O. Goetz, D.M.F.C. Perilloux, and D. M. Buss. 2010. "Evolutionary Psychology: Controversies, Questions, Prospects, and Limitations." *American Psychologist* 65: 110–126.
Cronk, L., and D. Gerkey. 2007. "Kinship and Descent." In *The Oxford Handbook of Evolutionary Psychology*, edited by R.I.M. Dunbar and L. Barrett, 463–478. Oxford: Oxford University Press.
Crook, J. 1967. *Law and Life of Rome*. Ithaca, NY: Cornell University Press.
Dahrendorf, R. 1968. *Essays in the Theory of Society*. Stanford, CA: Stanford University Press.
Delhey, J., K. Newton, and C. Welzel. 2011. "How General Is Trust in 'Most People'? Solving the 'Radius of Trust' Problem." *American Sociological Review* 76: 786–807.
Diamond, J. 1997. *Guns, Germs and Steel: The Fates of Human Societies*. London: Cape.
Dimitrov, M. K. 2013. "Understanding Communist Collapse and Resilience." In *Why Communism Did Not Collapse: Understanding Authoritarian Regime Resilience in Asia and Europe*, edited by M. K. Dimitrov, 3–39. Cambridge: Cambridge University Press.
Distin, K. 2005. *The Selfish Meme*. Cambridge: Cambridge University Press.
Dunbar, R., C. Knight, and C. Power, eds. 1999. *The Evolution of Culture: An Interdisciplinary View*. Edinburgh, UK: Edinburgh University Press.
Durham, W. H. 1991. *Coevolution: Genes, Culture, and Human Diversity*. Stanford, CA: Stanford University Press.
Earle, T. 1989. "The Evolution of Chiefdoms." *Current Anthropology* 30: 84–88.
Edgerton, R. B. 1992. *Sick Societies: Challenging the Myth of Primitive Harmony*. New York: Macmillan.
Eisenstadt, S. N. 1973. *Tradition, Change and Modernity*. New York: Wiley.
———. 1982. "The Axial Age: The Emergence of Transcendental Visions and the Rise of Clerics." *Archives Européennes de Sociologie* 23: 294–314.
———. 2003. *Comparative Civilizations and Multiple Modernities*. 2 vols. Leiden: Brill.
Elliott, J. H. 2006. *Empires of the Atlantic World: Britain and Spain in America 1492–1830*. New Haven, CT: Yale University Press.
Ertman, T. 1997. *Birth of the Leviathan: Building States and Regimes in Medieval and Early Modern Europe*. Cambridge: Cambridge University Press.
Falk, A., and J. J. Heckman. 2009. "Lab Experiments Are a Major Source of Knowledge in the Human Sciences." *Science* 326: 535–538.
Fehr, E., and S. Gächter. 2000. "Cooperation and Punishment." *American Economic Review* 90: 980–994.
Fisher, S. E., and M. Ridley. 2013. "Culture, Genes, and the Human Revolution." *Science* 340: 929–930.
Flannery, K., and J. Marcus. 2012. *The Creation of Inequality: How Our Prehistoric Ancestors Set the Stage for Monarchy, Slavery, and Empire*. Cambridge, MA: Harvard University Press.
Foley, R. A. 1995. *Humans before Humanity: An Evolutionary Perspective*. Oxford: Blackwell.
Frank, S. 1998. *Foundations of Social Evolution*. Princeton, NJ: Princeton University Press.
Friedman, D., and N. Singh. 2004. "Negative Reciprocity: The Coevolution of Memes and Genes." *Evolution and Human Behavior* 25: 155–173.
Gambetta, D. 2009. *Codes of the Underworld: How Criminals Communicate*. Princeton, NJ: Princeton University Press.
Geertz, C. 1975. *The Interpretation of Cultures*. London: Hutchinson.
Gellner, E. 1988. *Plough, Sword and Book: The Structure of Human History*. London: Collins Harvill.
Gerkey, D. 2013. "Cooperation in Context: Public Goods Games and Post-Soviet Collectives in Kamchatka, Russia." *Current Anthropology* 54: 144–176.
Gibbard, A. 1990. "Norms, Discussion, and Ritual: Evolutionary Puzzles." *Ethics* 100: 787–802.
Gintis, H. 2000. "Strong Reciprocity and Human Sociality." *Journal of Theoretical Biology* 206: 169–179.
———. 2009. *The Bounds of Reason: Game Theory and the Unification of the Behavioral Sciences*. Princeton, NJ: Princeton University Press.
Gintis, H., S. Bowles, R. Boyd, and E. Fehr. 2007. "Explaining Altruistic Behaviour in Humans." In *The Oxford Handbook of Evolutionary Psychology*, edited by R.I.M. Dunbar and L. Barrett, 605–619. Oxford: Oxford University Press.
Gintis, H., E. A. Smith, and S. Bowles. 2001. "Costly Signaling and Cooperation." *Journal of Theoretical Biology* 213: 103–111.
Goody, J. 1971. *Technology, Tradition, and the State in Africa*. London: Hutchinson.
Guala, F. 2012. "Reciprocity: Weak or Strong? What Punishment Experiments Do (and Do Not) Demonstrate." *Behavioral and Brain Sciences* 35: 1–59.

Hallpike, C. R. 1986. *The Principles of Social Evolution*. Oxford: Oxford University Press.
Hamilton, W. D. 1964. "The Genetical Evolution of Social Behaviour." I and II. *Journal of Theoretical Biology* 7: 1–52.
———. 1975. "Innate Social Aptitudes of Man: An Approach from Evolutionary Genetics." In *ASA Studies 4: Biosocial Anthropology*, edited by R. Fox, 133–153. London: Malaby Press.
Hardin, G. 1968. "The Tragedy of the Commons." *Science* 162: 1243–1248.
Hayden, B. 1998. "Practical and Prestige Technologies: The Evolution of Material Systems." *Journal of Archaeological Method and Theory* 5: 1–55.
Henrich, J. 2000. "Does Culture Matter in Economic Behavior? Ultimatum Game Bargaining among the Machiguenga of the Peruvian Amazon." *American Economic Review* 90: 973–979.
———. 2004. "Demography and Cultural Evolution: Why Adaptive Cultural Processes Produced Maladaptive Losses in Tasmania." *American Antiquity* 69: 197–214.
Henrich, J., and R. Boyd. 2002. "On Modeling Cognition and Culture: Why Cultural Evolution Does Not Require Replication of Representations." *Journal of Cognition and Culture* 2: 87–112.
———. 2008. "Division of Labour, Economic Specialization, and the Evolution of Social Stratification." *Current Anthropology* 49: 715–724.
Henrich, J., R. Boyd, S. Bowles, C. Camerer, E. Fehr, and H. Gintis, eds. 2004. *Foundations of Human Sociality: Economic Experiments and Ethnographic Evidence from Fifteen Small-Scale Societies*. Oxford: Oxford University Press.
Henrich, J., J. Ensminger, R. McElreath, A. Barr, C. Barrett, A. Bolyanatz, J. Cardenas, G. Camilo, G. Michael, H. Edwins, N. Henrich, C. Lesorogol, F. Marlowe, D. Tracer, and J. Ziker. 2010. "Markets, Religion, Community Size, and the Evolution of Fairness and Punishment." *Science* 327: 1480–1484.
Henrich, J., and R. McElreath. 2003. "The Evolution of Cultural Evolution." *Evolutionary Anthropology* 12: 123–135.
Hinde, R. A., and J. Groebel. 1991. *Cooperation and Prosocial Behaviour*. Cambridge: Cambridge University Press.
Johnson, A. W., and T. Earle. 1987. *The Evolution of Human Societies: From Foraging Group to Agricultural State*. Stanford, CA: Stanford University Press.
Johnson, D.D.P. 2005. "God's Punishment and Public Goods: A Test of the Supernatural Punishment Hypothesis in 186 World Cultures." *Human Nature* 16: 410–446.
Keeley, L. H. 1996. *War before Civilization: The Myth of the Peaceful Savage*. Oxford: Oxford University Press.
Kelly, R. L. 1995. *The Foraging Spectrum: Diversity in Hunter-Gatherer Lifeways*. Washington, DC: Smithsonian Institute.
Kennedy, P. 1987. *The Rise and Fall of the Great Powers: Economic Change and Military Conflict from 1500 to 2000*. New York: Vintage.
Kennett, D. J., and B. Winterhalder, eds. 2006. *Behavioral Ecology and the Transition to Agriculture*. Berkeley: University of California Press.
Killion, T. W. 2013. "Non-agricultural Cultivation and Social Complexity: The Olmec, Their Ancestors, and Mexico's Southern Gulf Coast Lowlands." *Current Anthropology* 54: 569–606.
Knight, A. 1986. *The Mexican Revolution*. Vol. 1, *Porfirians, Liberals & Peasants*. Vol. 2, *Counter Revolution and Reconstruction*. Cambridge: Cambridge University Press.
Knight, J. 1990. *Institutions and Social Conflict*. Cambridge: Cambridge University Press.
Kopytoff, I. 1987. "The Internal African Frontier: The Making of African Political Culture." In *The African Frontier*, edited by I. Kopytoff, 3–86. Bloomington: Indiana University Press.
Kristiansen, K. 1991. "Chiefdoms, States, and Systems of Social Evolution." In *Chiefdoms: Power, Economy, and Ideology*, edited by T. Earle, 16–43. Cambridge: Cambridge University Press.
Laland, K. N., and G. R. Brown. 2002. *Sense and Nonsense: Evolutionary Perspectives on Human Behaviour*. Oxford: Oxford University Press.
Laland, K. N., J. Odling-Smee, and M. W. Feldman. 2000. "Niche Construction, Biological Evolution, and Cultural Change." *Behavioral and Brain Sciences* 23: 131–175.
Leach, E. R. 1961. *Rethinking Anthropology*. London: Athlone Press.
Lee, C. K., and Y. Zhang. 2013. "The Power of Instability: Unraveling Foundations of Bargained Authoritarianism in China." *American Journal of Sociology* 118: 1475–1508.
Lintott, A. 1982. *Violence, Civil Strife and Revolution in the Classical City*. London: Croom Helm.
Lovejoy, P. E. 1983. *Transformations in Slavery: A History of Slavery in Africa*. Cambridge: Cambridge University Press.
Lumsden, C. J., and E. O. Wilson. 1981. *Genes, Mind, and Culture*. Cambridge, MA: Harvard University Press.
Mace, R., C. Holden, and S. Shennan. 2005. *The Evolution of Cultural Diversity: A Phylogenetic Approach*. London: UCL Press.
Mameli, Matteo. 2007. "Evolution and Psychology in Philosophical Perspective." In *The Oxford Handbook of Evolutionary Psychology*, edited by R.I.M. Dunbar and L. Barrett, 21–34. Oxford: Oxford University Press.

Mann, M. 1986. *The Sources of Social Power*. Vol. 1, *A History of Power from the Beginning to A.D. 1760*. Cambridge: Cambridge University Press.
Marlowe, F. W., J. Bergesque, B. Colette, A. Barr, C. Barrett, A. Bolyanatz, J. Cardenas, E. Camilo, J. Ensminger, M. Gurven, E. Gwako, H. Edwins, J. Henrich, N. Henrich, C. Lesorogol, R. McElreath, and D. Tracer. 2008. "More 'Altruistic' Punishment in Larger Societies." *Proceedings of the Royal Society* B 275: 587–590.
Marlowe, F. W., J. Bergesque, B. Colette, C. Barrett, A. Bolyanatz, M. Gurven, and D. Tracer. 2011. "The 'Spiteful' Origins of Human Cooperation." *Proceedings of the Royal Society* B 278: 2159–2164.
Maynard Smith, J. 1982. *Evolution and the Theory of Games*. Cambridge: Cambridge University Press.
McAnny, P. A., and N. Yoffee, eds. 2010. *Questioning Collapse: Human Resilience, Ecological Vulnerability, and the Aftermath of Empire*. Cambridge: Cambridge University Press.
McElreath, R., R. Boyd, and P. J. Richerson. 2003. "Shared Norms and the Evolution of Ethnic Markers." *Current Anthropology* 44: 122–129.
McGrew, W. 2004. *The Cultural Chimpanzee: Reflections on Cultural Primatology*. Cambridge: Cambridge University Press.
McNamara, P. 2008. *The Neuroscience of Religious Experience*. Cambridge: Cambridge University Press.
McNeill, W. H. 1983. *The Pursuit of Power: Technology, Armed Force, and Society since A.D. 1000*. Oxford: Blackwell.
Middleton, J., and D. Tait, eds. 1958. *Tribes without Rulers*. London: Routledge.
Miers, S., and I. Kopytoff, eds. 1977. *Slavery in Africa: Historical and Anthropological Perspectives*. Madison: University of Wisconsin Press.
North, D. C. 1990. *Institutions, Institutional Change and Economic Performance*. Cambridge: Cambridge University Press.
Oliver, B. R., and R. Plomin. 2007. "Twins' Early Development Study (TEDS): A Multivariate Longitudinal Investigation of Language, Cognition and Behavior Problems from Childhood through Adolescence." *Twin Research and Behavior Genetics* 10: 96–105.
Oliver, D. L. 1955. *A Solomon Island Society*. Cambridge, MA: Harvard University Press.
Ostrom, E. 1990. *Governing the Commons: The Evolution of Institutions for Collective Action*. Cambridge: Cambridge University Press.
———. 2005. *Understanding Institutional Diversity*. Princeton, NJ: Princeton University Press.
Ostrom, E., J. Walker, and R. Gardner. 1992. "Covenants, with and without a Sword: Self-Governance Is Possible." *American Political Science Review* 86: 59–87.
Pacciotti, B., and C. Hadley. 2003. "The Ultimatum Game in Southwestern Tanzania: Ethnic Variation and Institutional Scope." *Current Anthropology* 44: 427–432.
Pagel, M. 2012. *Wired for Culture: The Natural Theory of Human Cooperation*. London: Allen Lane.
Patterson, O. 1982. *Slavery and Social Death: A Comparative Study*. Cambridge, MA: Harvard University Press.
Pinker, S. 2002. *The Blank Slate: The Modern Denial of Human Nature*. New York: Penguin Books.
Plomin, R., J. C. De Fries, G. E. McClearn, and M. Rutter. 1997. *Behavioral Genetics*. 3rd ed. New York: W. H. Freeman.
Price, B. J. 1978. "Secondary State Formation: An Explanatory Model." In *Origins of the State: The Anthropology of Political Evolution*, edited by R. Cohen and E. R. Service, 161–186. Philadelphia, PA: Institute for the Study of Human Issues.
Rappaport, R. A. 1999. *Ritual and Religion in the Making of Humanity*. Cambridge: Cambridge University Press.
Richerson, P. J., and R. Boyd. 2005. *Not by Genes Alone: How Culture Transformed Human Evolution*. Chicago: University of Chicago Press.
Rousseau, J. 2006. *Rethinking Social Evolution: The Perspective from Middle Range Societies*. Montreal: McGill-Queen's.
Runciman, W. G. 1982. "Origins of States: The Case of Archaic Greece." *Comparative Studies in Society and History* 24: 351–377.
———. 1989. *A Treatise on Social Theory*. Vol. 2, *Substantive Social Theory*. Cambridge: Cambridge University Press.
———. 2009. *The Theory of Cultural and Social Selection*. Cambridge: Cambridge University Press.
———. 2011. "Empire as a Topic in Comparative Sociology." In *Tributary Empires in Global History*, edited by P. Fibinger Bang and C. A. Baily, 99–107. Basingstoke, UK: Palgrave Macmillan.
Sahlins, M. 1974. *Stone Age Economics*. London: Tavistock.
Sanderson, S. K. 2001. *The Evolution of Human Sociality: A Darwinian Conflict Perspective*. Lanham, MD: Rowman and Littlefield.
Sear, R., D. W. Lanson, and T. E. Dickins. 2007. "Synthesis in the Human Evolutionary Behavioural Sciences." *Journal of Evolutionary Psychology* 5: 3–28.
Segal, N. L. 2012. *Born Together—Reared Apart: The Landmark Minnesota Twin Study*. Cambridge, MA: Harvard University Press.

Segerstråle, U. 2000. *Defenders of the Truth: The Sociobiology Debate.* Oxford: Oxford University Press.
Shennan, S. 2002. *Genes, Memes and Human History: Darwinian Archaeology and Cultural Evolution.* London: Thames & Hudson.
Skocpol, T. 1979. *States and Social Revolutions: A Comparative Analysis of France, Russia, and China.* Cambridge: Cambridge University Press.
Skyrms, B. 1996. *Evolution of the Social Contract.* Cambridge: Cambridge University Press.
———. 2004. *The Stag Hunt and the Evolution of Social Structure.* Cambridge: Cambridge University Press.
Slovik, M. W. 2012. *The Politics of Authoritarian Rule.* Cambridge: Cambridge University Press.
Smout, T. C. 1969. *A History of the Scottish People 1560–1830.* Glasgow: Collins.
Sober, E., and D. S. Wilson. 1998. *Unto Others: The Evolution and Psychology of Unselfish Behavior.* Cambridge, MA: Harvard University Press.
Somit, A., and S. A. Peterson. 1992. *The Dynamics of Evolution: The Punctuated Equilibrium Debate in the Natural and Social Sciences.* Ithaca, NY: Cornell University Press.
Sosis, R., and C. Alcorta. 2003. "Signaling, Solidarity, and the Sacred: The Evolution of Religious Behavior." *Evolutionary Anthropology* 12: 264–274.
Stankiewicz, R. 2000. "The Concept of 'Design Space.'" In *Technological Innovation as an Evolutionary Process,* edited by J. Ziman, 234–247. Cambridge: Cambridge University Press.
Strathern, A. 1971. *The Rope of Moka: Big-Men and Ceremonial Exchange in Mount Hagen, New Guinea.* Cambridge: Cambridge University Press.
Stuart-Fox, M. 1986. "The Unit of Replication in Socio-Cultural Evolution." *Journal of Social and Biological Structures* 1: 67–89.
Tainter, J. A. 1988. *The Collapse of Complex Societies.* Cambridge: Cambridge University Press.
Testart, A. 2013. "Reconstructing Social and Cultural Evolution: The Case of Dowry in the Indo-European Area." *Current Anthropology* 54: 23–50.
Tooby, J., and L. Cosmides. 1992. "The Psychological Foundations of Culture." In *The Adapted Mind: Evolutionary Psychology and the Generation of Culture,* edited by J. H. Barkow, L. Cosmides, and J. Tooby, 19–136. Oxford: Oxford University Press.
Trigger, B. G. 1998. *Sociocultural Evolution: Calculation and Contingency.* Oxford: Blackwell.
Trivers, R. L. 1971. "The Evolution of Reciprocal Altruism." *Quarterly Review of Biology* 46: 35–57.
Turner, J. H., and A. Maryanski. 2008. *On the Origin of Societies by Natural Selection.* Boulder, CO: Paradigm.
von Neumann, J., and O. Morgenstern. 1944. *Theory of Games and Economic Behavior.* Princeton, NJ: Princeton University Press.
Watson, J. L. 1980. "Transactions in People: The Chinese Market in Slaves, Servants, and Heirs." In *Asian and African Systems of Slavery,* edited by J. L. Watson, 223–250. Oxford: Blackwell.
Weingart, P., P. J. Richerson, S. D. Mitchell, and S. Maasen. 1997. *Human by Nature: Between Biology and the Social Sciences.* Mahwah, NJ: Lawrence Erlbaum.
Whitehouse, H. 2003. *Modes of Religiosity: A Cognitive Theory of Religious Transmission.* Walnut Creek, CA: AltaMira Press.
Whiten, A. 2011. "The Scope of Culture in Chimpanzees, Humans and Ancestral Apes." *Philosophical Transactions of the Royal Society B* 366: 997–1007.
Whiten, A., J. Goodall, W. C. McGrew, T. Nishida, V. Reynolds, Y. Sugiyama, C.E.G. Tutin, T. W. Wrangham, and C. Boesch. 2009. "Charting Cultural Variation in Chimpanzees." *Behaviour* 138: 1481–1516.
Whiten, A., R. A. Hinde, C. B. Stringer, and K. N. Laland, eds. 2011. "Culture Evolves." *Philosophical Transactions of the Royal Society B* 366: 935–1187.
Wickham, C. 2005. *Framing the Early Middle Ages: Europe and the Mediterranean 400–800.* Oxford: Oxford University Press.
Wiedemann, T. 1981. *Greek and Roman Slavery.* London: Croom Helm.
Williams, G. C. 1966. *Adaptation and Natural Selection: A Critique of Some Evolutionary Thought.* Princeton, NJ: Princeton University Press.
Wilson, D. S. 2002. *Darwin's Cathedral: Evolution, Religion, and the Nature of Society.* Chicago: University of Chicago Press.
Wilson, E. O. 1998. *Consilience: The Unity of Knowledge.* London: Little, Brown.
Young, H. P. 1998. *Individual Strategy and Social Structure: An Evolutionary Theory of Institutions.* Princeton, NJ: Princeton University Press.

Chapter Twelve

Spencer's Conception of Evolution and Its Application to the Political Development of Societies

Robert L. Carneiro

> After indicating how Spencer first became interested in evolution, the chapter tells how he carefully distinguished its various aspects, culminating in the formulation of his classical definition of the process. This is followed by a discussion of the manifestation of evolution in a number of different fields. The major portion of the chapter is devoted to tracing the course of political evolution, in which Spencer depicts its successive stages, from autonomous villages to states and empires. In doing so he pays particular attention to the role of warfare in this process. Then, turning to more recent times, Spencer describes the tension existing between the military and industrial institutions of societies and how this tension has shaped the modern state.

In the popular mind it was Charles Darwin who introduced the concept of evolution into science. This notion, however, is erroneous. It was Herbert Spencer who did so. Great as Darwin's contribution was, his study of evolution was restricted to the organic world. As Darwin himself said in writing to Spencer about his forthcoming book, *The Origin of Species*, "I treat the subject simply as a naturalist" (Darwin [1890] 1959: I, 497). Spencer, on the other hand, thought of evolution as a master principle, with a far greater reach than merely the animal kingdom. Indeed, he saw evolution as a universal process, operating throughout the cosmos, from the tiniest microorganisms to the largest galaxies. And—as this chapter will attempt to show—he applied evolution to the development of political organization among human societies, from nomadic bands to empires.

Before describing Spencer's treatment of political evolution, though, it seems fitting to see how Spencer first became acquainted with the idea of evolution and how he proceeded to elaborate the concept. As we will see, the conception of evolution has itself evolved, going from inchoate beginnings to the broadly gauged, carefully worked out idea it became at Spencer's hands.

Starting out as a vague notion of transformation, the idea of evolution had existed as far back as classical antiquity. Little, if any, progress was made in expanding the notion during the Middle Ages, an era in which *stability* rather than *change* was the reigning concern. The idea of a Great Chain of Being was the closest that medieval thinkers came to envisioning a connection among living species. And the relationships thus envisioned were logical rather than genealogical.

Even in the seventeenth century, when physical science began to take hold in European thought, it was a science concerned more with statics than with dynamics. And if dynamics was dealt with, it was the dynamics of cyclical recurrences. Newton's universe was a clockwork universe in which the motions of the planets and the stars always brought them back to positions they had previously occupied. Such a view did not readily encompass movement in a discernable and distinct direction and was essentially irreversible. And that, after all, is the hallmark of evolution.

The first formulation of evolution as being transformative, directional change, and to begin tracing its occurrences throughout nature, was the achievement of Herbert Spencer.

It was not until the mid-nineteenth century that Spencer began to see such directional change as manifesting itself in various domains of the natural world. The development of Spencer's ideas along these lines can be traced in detail thanks to the fact that in his writings he left a complete account of it. It began in 1851 when he was asked to review W. B. Carpenter's *Principles of Physiology*. As Spencer explained,

> In the course of such perusal as was needed to give an account of its contents, I came across von Baer's formula expressing the course of development through which every plant and animal passes—the change from homogeneity to heterogeneity.... This phrase of von Baer expressing the law of individual development, awakened my attention to the fact that the law which holds of the ascending stages of each individual organism is also the law which holds of the ascending grades of organisms of all kinds. ([1904] 1924a: I, 384–385)

Seized by the concept of evolution—although he did not yet use the term—Spencer lost no time in advancing it as the process by which animals and plants had come to assume their present forms. The very next year, 1852—a full *seven years* before the appearance of *The Origin of Species*—Spencer published "The Development Hypothesis," an article in which he openly opposed the prevailing biblical account of creation and argued instead that living organisms had arisen through an entirely natural series of events. Moreover, he believed that this development had covered a much longer span of time than the mere 6,000 years allowed for it by the Bible.

Impressed by this article, Darwin wrote to Spencer commenting on its "remarkable skill and force," adding that "your remarks on the general argument of the so-called development theory seem to be admirable" (Darwin [1890] 1959: I, xix). Furthermore, he told Spencer, "I am at present preparing an abstract of a larger work on the changes of species [*The Origin of Species*] but I treat the subject simply as a naturalist, and not from a general point of view" (Darwin [1890] 1959: I, 497).

In "The Development Hypothesis" Spencer left no doubt as to where he stood on the "species question":

> Which, then, is the most rational hypothesis?—that of special creation which has neither a fact to support it nor is even definitely conceivable; or that of modification, which is not only definitely conceivable, but is countenanced by the habitudes of every existing organism? (1852a: 281)

Then in 1855, in his book *The Principles of Psychology*, Spencer reaffirmed his allegiance to the theory of organic evolution. "Life under all its forms," he wrote, "has arisen by a progressive, unbroken evolution ... out of the lowest and simplest beginnings ... and through the immediate instrumentality of ... natural causes" (Spencer [1855] 1896: I, 465n.).

Even earlier—in 1852—Spencer had already formed an idea of the way in which "natural causes" had operated to bring about changes in animal organisms. Indeed, in an article entitled "A Theory of Population Deduced from the General Law of Animal Fertility," Spencer—according to the biologist J. Arthur Thomson—"came within an ace of recognising that the struggle for existence was a factor in organic evolution" (Thomson 1917: 17). In this article Spencer wrote:

> For as those prematurely carried off must, in the average of cases, be those in whom the power of self-preservation is the least, it unavoidably follows, that those left behind to continue the race are those in whom the power of self-preservation is the greatest—are the select of their generation.

And clearly perceiving the long-term consequences of this fact he added:

> So that, whether the dangers to existence be of the kind produced by excess of fertility, or of any other kind, it is clear, that by the ceaseless exercise of the faculties needed to contend with them successfully, there is ensured a constant progress toward a higher degree of skill, intelligence, and self-regulation. (1852b: 500)

In the ensuing years Spencer found evolution manifesting itself not only in the biological realm but among various other classes of phenomena as well. Moreover, at the same time that he was tracing it in wider fields, he was also examining the concept itself, refining it, giving it greater specificity and precision.

Finally in 1862, in his book *First Principles*—the heart of which was devoted to elaborating the concept—Spencer brought forth his classic definition:

> Evolution is a change from an indefinite, incoherent homogeneity to a definite, coherent heterogeneity through continuous differentiations and integrations. (1862: 53)

Although Darwin's name will forever be closely linked to "evolution," it is not generally known that the word itself never appeared in the first five editions of *The Origin of Species*. It is true that the very last word in the book is "evolved," but Darwin did not introduce the noun "evolution" into *The Origin* until the sixth edition of the book, published in 1872. This came a full ten years after Spencer had used the word repeatedly in *First Principles* and taken great pains to work out its definition. And not only did Darwin wait a whole decade before adopting "evolution," when he finally employed the word he used it no more than half a dozen times and with no more precise meaning than "descent with modification." By defining the word in such a limited way Darwin made it clear that he was applying it to nothing beyond those changes undergone by biological organisms.

With Spencer, though, evolution became much more than "descent with modification." It was seen, in fact, as a universal process, operating among phenomena of every kind. Nor was evolution simply *change*, but change in a specific direction, with its characteristics carefully spelled out.

Darwin was well aware of what Spencer had contributed to expanding the horizons of evolution. Writing in the sixth edition of *The Origin of Species* he hailed Spencer as "the great expounder of the principle of Evolution" (Darwin [1859] 1890: 4).

Still, an important distinction remained between the Darwinian and Spencerian conceptions of evolution. It is a fundamental distinction that, to this day, divides scientists into two camps. To most contemporary biologists—as it was to Darwin himself—evolution is simply any change undergone by a plant or animal species. Have the eyes of a species of cave fish degenerated to the point of total blindness? To a biologist, *that* is evolution. To most anthropologists, however, evolution, as it has manifested itself in culture, is change in the Spencerian sense, that is to say, movement in the direction of increasing complexity.

Once Spencer had recognized evolution as a master principle, revealing itself throughout the cosmos, he decided to devote the rest of his life to describing the process in operation, wherever it occurred. So taken, in fact, was Spencer with tracing the course of evolution that in his autobiography he wrote: "Once having been possessed by the conception of Evolution in its comprehensive form, the desire to elaborate it and set it forth was so strong that to have passed life in doing something else would, I think, have been almost intolerable" ([1904] 1924a: II, 460).

Even before he had finished crafting his formal definition of the word, Spencer had begun to deal with examples of evolution in various spheres. In a series of articles written in the mid-1850s he discussed the evolution of such things as manners, fashions, mind, and science itself. Then in 1857—two years before the publication of *The Origin of Species*—in an article in the *Westminster Review* entitled "Progress: Its Law and Cause," Spencer applied evolution systematically to the universe in general, and to human society in particular. "The advance from simple to complex, through a process of differentiations," he wrote, "is seen alike in the earliest changes of the universe to which we can reason our way back, and in the earliest changes which we can inductively establish" (Spencer 1857: 465).

And he went on to enumerate some of the ways in which changes of an evolutionary nature could be discerned in human societies. "It is seen," he said, "in the evolution of Humanity, whether contemplated in the civilized individual, or in the aggregation of races; it is seen in the evolution of Society in respect alike of its political, its religious, and its economical organization" (1857: 465).

We see, then, that by 1857 Spencer viewed the political landscape of mankind as a promising field in which to pursue evolution. Indeed, that society's patterns of development could be studied scientifically with substantial results was something Spencer had foreseen as early as 1851. In his first book, *Social Statics*, he expressed the view that "instead of Civilization being artificial, it is a part of nature; all of a piece with the development of the embryo, or the unfolding of a flower. The modifications mankind have undergone, and are still undergoing, result from a law underlying the whole of organic nature" (Spencer 1851: 65).

Then in 1858 Spencer conceived the grand scheme of surveying the whole of human knowledge—including biology, psychology, sociology, and ethics—from an evolutionary point of view. This project eventually grew into a ten-volume work with the general title of *Synthetic Philosophy*, the completion of which occupied Spencer for almost forty years. To that part of the *Synthetic Philosophy* that he intended to devote to sociology, Spencer had at first allotted only one volume. But by 1860, when he issued a formal prospectus announcing its future publication, *The Principles of Sociology* had been expanded from one volume to three.

The enlarged version of this work was intended to encompass "general facts, structural and functional, as gathered from a survey of Societies and their changes; in other words, the empirical generalizations that are arrived at by comparing different societies, and successive phases of the same society" (Spencer [1904] 1924a: II, 481). And Spencer meant "empirical" quite literally. In the past, social theorists had often been content to *excogitate* just how they thought societies must have attained their present state, with no firm grounding in ethnographic evidence to buttress their speculations. Spencer, however, was determined to acquaint himself with the facts before attempting to weave them into a solid fabric representing the way human societies had actually developed. He was well aware, as he later wrote in his autobiography, that when the time came to start work on *The Principles of Sociology*, "there would be required an immense accumulation of facts so classified and arranged as to facilitate generalization" ([1904] 1924a: II, 171). Accordingly, beginning in 1867, he enlisted the services of three young research assistants who were assigned the task of combing through the ethnographic and historical literature and extracting from it large masses of facts for his later use. Thus by 1874, when Spencer began the actual writing of *The Principles of Sociology*, he had before him a very substantial body of data on which to draw.

In time, Spencer came to see that "this compilation of materials [which] was entered upon solely to facilitate my own work" ([1904] 1924a: II, 261) was potentially of much wider use. As he wrote, having "the essential phenomena presented by each society, the fact dawned upon me that the materials as prepared were of too much value to let them lie idle after having been used by myself only" (quoted in Duncan 1908: I, 186–187). He therefore had the vast amount of data gathered by his research assistants published in eight large folio volumes that appeared between 1873 and 1881 under the title *Descriptive Sociology*. The ethnographic and historical materials included in these volumes were not presented as unorganized, undigested masses of facts but were carefully arranged into categories that Spencer himself had worked out beforehand.

Reviewing the first volume of *Descriptive Sociology*, which was devoted to the English, E. B. Tylor wrote that it provided "a sufficient answer to all disbelievers in the possibility of a science of history. Where the chronicle of individual lives often perplexes and mystifies the scholar, the generalization of social principles from the chronicler's materials shows an order to human affairs where cause and effect take their inevitable course, as in Physics or Biology" (1873: 546).

Descriptive Sociology stands today, deep in the dust of a few major libraries, all but unknown even to social scientists. Yet with its publication, along with *The Principles of Sociology* that was to follow, Spencer may rightfully lay claim to having founded inductive, systematic, comparative sociology.

Armed with this treasure trove of ethnographic and historical facts, Spencer was well provided for the task that lay before him—namely, synthesizing and drawing out of the accumulated evidence wide-ranging generalizations about the development of human society.

Of the three volumes that *The Principles of Sociology* came to comprise, the sections dealing with political organization and its evolution—the subject matter of the present chapter—occur largely in the first two volumes. Looking from a broad perspective at the structure of societies, Spencer distinguished two major types of institutions that he labeled *operative* and *regulative*. Operative institutions were those concerned with the material requirements of society, including such things as subsistence, manufacture, distribution, and exchange. Regulative institutions, on the other hand, were concerned with directing and controlling the behavior of the members of a society so that it would remain a functionally well adjusted and viable whole.

These two institutions—operative and regulative—Spencer noted, were to some extent inversely related. "If for directing social activities in greater detail, extra staffs of officials are appointed the simultaneous results are an increase in the aggregate of those who form the regulating part and a corresponding decrease in the aggregate of those who form the part regulated" (Spencer 1967: 69).

Before discussing the operation of these institutions, though, Spencer had to make clear just what he conceived a society to be. "The mere gathering of individuals into a group," he wrote, "does not constitute them a society. A society, in a sociological sense, is formed only when, besides juxtaposition there is cooperation." Thus, when individuals "pass from a state of perfect independence to the state of mutual dependence ... as fast as they do this they become united into a society rightly so-called" (1967: 63). Then, as soon as a society could be said to exist (except possibly among the very simplest ones), some form of political organization came into being. And about the kind of structure thus formed, Spencer noted: "Political organization is to be understood as that part of social organization which constantly carries on directive and restraining functions for public ends" (1967: 65).

As societies grow larger and more numerous, they increase not only in *mass* but also in *structure*. This must occur if a society is not to break apart but to remain an integrated and functioning whole. The general way in which societies grew as political entities Spencer described as follows: "Social evolution begins with small simple aggregates, ... progresses by the clustering of these into larger aggregates, and ... after being consolidated, such clusters are united with others like themselves into still larger aggregates" (1967: 48). This manner of growth he labeled *compounding* and *recompounding*.

Political evolution, then, proceeded essentially by aggregating and integrating smaller political units into progressively larger ones. The culmination of this process—where it had proceeded to its full extent—was the formation of political units of very large size, such as the Roman Empire in the Old World and the Inca Empire in the New World.

By successive compoundings, then, political entities that at one level constituted autonomous units—that is, *wholes*—became, at the next higher level, *parts* of a greater whole. Moreover, the process by which smaller political entities became larger ones had to proceed in just this fashion. "The stages of compounding and recompounding," said Spencer, "have to be passed through in succession. No tribe becomes a nation by simple [internal] growth, and no great society is formed by the direct union of the smallest societies" (1967: 52).

The dynamic process of political aggregation, Spencer went on to say, was largely the result of conquest warfare. War was the mechanism par excellence by which societies were able to surmount the local autonomies that had at first characterized them. "By force alone," he wrote, "were small nomadic hordes welded into large tribes; by force alone were large tribes welded into small nations; by force alone have small nations been welded into large nations" (Spencer [1873] 1924b: 176).

In the struggle between societies, the stronger ones subjugated and incorporated the weaker ones, and in this manner were created polities of increasingly larger size and structural complexity. So important did Spencer consider conflict to be in this regard that he repeatedly returned to it: "Everywhere wars between societies originate governmental structures, and are causes of all such improvements in those structures as increase the efficiency of corporate action against environing societies" (1967: 33).

But however achieved, aggregation into larger political units alone was not enough. The aggregated parts had also to be fused together into a coherent whole. In brief compass Spencer described the integrative process that societies went through in advancing to the next structural level: "When a compound society has been consolidated by the cooperation of its component groups in war under a single head—when it has simultaneously differentiated somewhat its social ranks and industries ... the compound society [thus formed] becomes practically a single one" (1967: 52).

Throughout history this process—conquest warfare followed by integration of the conquered units—had marked the course of political development. It had seen autonomous bands and villages, at the lowest level of organization, proceed, step by step, to the great states we see today. Spencer summed up this process as follows: "At later stages ... [there] arise still larger aggregates having still more complex structures. In this order has social evolution gone on, and only in this order does it appear to be possible" (1967: 53).

The building of progressively larger political units lent itself to graphic representation and Spencer displayed it in tabular form. He labeled the four levels of political structure to be distinguished as *simple, compound, doubly compound,* and *trebly compound* and presented examples of actual societies typifying each of these stages (1967: 50–51). The Todas were cited as representing *simple* societies, the Chibcha as representing *compound* societies, the Spartans as exemplifying *doubly compound* societies, and the Assyrian empire as representing *trebly compound* societies. In all, more than a hundred societies were apportioned into one or another stage of Spencer's fourfold typology of evolving political structures (1967: 50–53).

One can readily equate Spencer's four levels with categories used by modern-day anthropologists in labeling societies at various stages of political development. Those that Spencer called "simple" are today often designated "autonomous villages." His "compound societies" are easily equatable with "chiefdoms." "Doubly compound" societies are generally regarded as "states," while his "trebly compound" societies are more or less equivalent to "empires."

It is worth noting that the now familiar category of chiefdom—equatable, as we said, to Spencer's "compound society"—was not formally introduced into anthropology until 1955, when it was proposed by Kalervo Oberg (1955) as a *type* of multi-village sociopolitical unit headed by a strong paramount chief. Then in 1862 Elman Service elevated the chiefdom from a *type* to a *stage*, highlighting the fact—implied but not overtly stated by Oberg—that the chiefdom was clearly a category with evolutionary implications, that is, one that could be regarded as the immediate precursor of the state (see Carneiro 1981).

The late entry into cultural anthropology of such an important evolutionary stage as the chiefdom bears witness to the fact that for decades the discipline languished in antievolutionary doldrums. During this period nothing of any consequence along evolutionary lines was even attempted. Robert Lowie's book *The Origin of the State* (1927), for example, whose very title suggests that its author might well have made use of Spencer's stages of sociopolitical evolution, never even took account of it.

Having made the distinctions just described, Spencer was ready to categorize societies into contrasting types of another kind. In addition to his evolutionary typology of political structures, he also proposed classifying societies on an entirely different basis. "We pass now," he wrote, "to the classification [of societies] based on unlikenesses between the kinds of social activity which predominate and on the resulting unlikenesses of organization. The two social types thus essentially contrasted are the *militant* and the *industrial*" (Spencer 1967: 55; italics mine).

Since at one time or another even the simplest societies found themselves facing hostile neighbors and having to prepare to defend themselves, a militant element (even if usually quiescent) existed in all human groups. As Spencer put it, "All societies, simple and compound, are occasionally or habitually in antagonism with other societies and, as we have seen, tend to evolve structures for carrying on offensive or defensive actions" (1967: 53).

Those societies frequently at war Spencer referred to as *militant*, while those relatively peaceful and predominantly concerned with the production and distribution of goods he classified as *industrial*. The dividing line between them, though, was often difficult to discern. "Much less definitive," said Spencer, "is the division to be made among societies according as one or other of their great systems of organs is supreme," and thus "the ratios between these [two categories] admit of all gradations" (1967: 62; see also p. 53).

Still, when the two types of societies have "evolved to their extreme forms [they] are diametrically opposed and the contrasts between their traits are among the most important with which sociology has to deal" (1967: 62).

About the role of warfare in intersocietal relations, Spencer, as we have seen, had much to say. Small, simple societies tended to be peaceful, but in the course of time even they generally became more militant. Indeed, this was often a major step in their evolution. After citing a few examples of peaceful societies, such as the Todas, Spencer remarked that "few, if any, cases occur in which societies of this type have evolved into larger societies without passing into the militant type, for, as we have seen, the consolidation of simple aggregates into a compound aggregate habitually results from war, defensive or offensive, which, if continued, evolves a centralized authority with its coercive institutions" (1967: 59).

Spencer emphasized military success as the principal avenue by which war leaders ascended to become the political leaders of their societies as well, observing that "among the uncivilized [peoples] there is a marked tendency for the military chief to become also the political head." And in societies successful in conquest warfare, political headship by the military leader generally became fixed. Then, moving up the evolutionary ladder to "semi-civilized societies the conquering commander and the despotic king are the same and they remain the same in civilized societies down to late times" (1967: 54). The Zulu and the Ashanti were cited as examples of the latter type of society.

Once the militant element became pronounced in the political structure of a society, it placed an indelible stamp on the rest of its institutions. Eventually the point might be reached in a militant society "in which the claims of the unit are nothing and the claims of the aggregate everything. Absolute subjection to authority is the supreme virtue and resistance to it a crime" (1967: 58).

But while the general rule was that the militant sector grew as societies increased in size, it was not invariably so. Sometimes the industrial sector was the part that most notably enlarged. And as an example of this, Spencer cited ancient Greece: "In Athens, where industry was regarded with comparative respect, ... there grew up an industrial organization which distinguished the Athenian society from adjacent societies while it was also distinguished from them by those democratic institutions that simultaneously developed" (1967: 60).

Athens, though, was more the exception than the rule. More commonly, "where the political and military heads have ... themselves become the heads of the industrial organization, the traits distinctive of ... [the industrial organization] are prevented from showing themselves" (1967: 60). In such instances the influence of the militant element clearly predominated over the industrial. And its influence was not only profound but far-reaching and enduring.

Since as they grew larger and more numerous societies tended increasingly to impinge on one another, they began to develop more effective mechanisms to cope with external threats. "Throughout the society as a whole there spreads a ... form of organization ... for the purpose of maintaining the militant body and the government which directs it," and as a result "there are established over citizens agencies which force them to labor more or less largely for public ends instead of private ends" (1967: 64–65).

Furthermore, as these effects ramified throughout the society "simultaneously, there develops a further organization, still akin in its fundamental principle, which restrains individual actions in such wise that social safety shall not be endangered by the disorder consequent on unchecked pursuit of personal ends." In this way, "conscious pursuit of public ends and the correlative organization, consciously established, exercises coercion" over the citizenry (1967: 65).

However, in those relatively few instances in which the industrial type of society was able to enlarge its sphere relative to that of the militant, a direct reflection of it could be seen in the behavior of its citizens. "In place of the doctrine that the duty of obedience to the governing agent is unqualified, there arises the doctrine that the will of the citizen is supreme and the governing agent exists merely to carry out their will. Thus subordinated in position, the regulating power is also restricted in range. Instead of having an authority extending over actions of all kinds, it is shut out from large classes of actions" (1967: 61).

Here, then, we begin to see the basis of Spencer's dislike of polities in which the freedom of the individual is curtailed, being firmly subordinated to the welfare of the state. This attitude, which Spencer only hinted at in *The Principles of Sociology*, was given full voice a few years later in his book *The Man versus the State* (1884). To illustrate the distinction between the two philosophies of government, in the latter volume Spencer drew on the history of his own country. He did so by contrasting the attitude toward the English monarchy held by the two leading political parties, the Whigs and the Tories. "The Whigs," said Spencer, "'regarded the monarchy as a civil institution, established by the nation for the benefit of all its members'; while for the Tories 'the monarch was the delegate of heaven'" ([1884] 1950: 2).

However, the Liberals of Spencer's day—successors to the Whigs—operating ostensibly in the name of liberalism, introduced into the government of England the very conditions they had traditionally opposed. The Liberals, according to Spencer, had lost sight of their original aims. "Liberalism, getting more and more into power, has grown more and more coercive in its legislation." Indeed, "liberalism has to an increasing extent adopted the policy of dictating the actions of citizens, and, by consequence, diminishing the range throughout which their actions remain free" ([1884] 1950: 5).

Having gained control of Parliament, "the laws made by Liberals are ... greatly increasing the compulsions and restraints exercised over citizens" ([1884] 1950: 21), the result being that a political reversal had occurred. Whereas at one time "the definition [of a Whig] was—'one who advocates greater freedom from restraint, especially in political institutions,'" nowadays "in so far as it has been extending the system of compulsion, what is now called Liberalism is a new form of Toryism" ([1884] 1950: 20).

Contributing significantly to the willingness of the citizens of modern societies to subordinate their own desires to the supposed benefit of the state, Spencer saw an anomaly at work. Present-day societies, while largely industrial in character, still retained major elements carried over from an earlier militant type. As a consequence, "the restriction of government power ... appropriate to the industrial type of society" does not become fully expressed because of "the semi-militant, semi-industrial type [of organization] which now characterizes advanced nations" ([1884] 1950: 131).

To explain the existing situation, Spencer again called on the surviving influence of war on contemporary societies. The subservience of individuals to the state "is necessitated by the maintenance of fitness for war. This involves continuance of such confidence in the ruling agency, and such subordination to it, as may enable it to wield all the forces of the society on occasions of attack or defence; and there must survive a political theory justifying the faith and the obedience" ([1884] 1950: 134). (How strikingly modern this all sounds!)

Still, "in one of these compound communities where the warlike activity is now not considerable"—and here he cited the case of Samoa—a "decline in the rigidity of political control has gone along with some evolution of the industrial type" (Spencer 1967: 60). Then, invoking this inverse relationship between militant and industrial institutions beyond the case of tiny Samoa, Spencer noted that "the regions [of the world] whence changes toward greater political liberty have come are [also] the leading industrial regions" (1967: 61).

Nevertheless, speaking more broadly, Spencer once again pointed to the effects of war in this regard. "The circumstances which render war less frequent," he wrote, "arise but slowly, and since the modifications of nature caused by the transition from a life predominantly militant to a life predominantly industrial can therefore go on only little by little, [hence] it happens that the old sentiments and ideas give place to new ones, by small degrees only" ([1884] 1950: 133).

Ultimately, however, more than just altered social conditions were required for great changes to take place. Early in the pages of *The Study of Sociology*, Spencer enunciated the general proposition that the character of an aggregate is determined by the character of the units composing it ([1873] 1891: 48; [1873] 1924b: 45, 47, 111). He later reiterated this principle and applied it to human societies in particular. Stating that since "the structures and actions throughout a society are determined by the properties of its units," it follows that "the society cannot be substantially and permanently changed without its units [that is, the human beings composing it] being substantially and permanently changed" ([1873] 1961: 365).

In *The Man versus the State*, Spencer reaffirmed this proposition and elaborated it further: "The welfare of a society and the justice of its arrangements are at bottom dependent on the characters of its members"; thus "improvement in neither can take place without improvement in character" of the individuals who constitute it ([1884] 1950: 52). Not much improvement in current institutions could therefore be expected since he believed "the existing type of industrial organization, like the existing type of political organization, is about as good as existing human nature allows" ([1873] 1924b: 229).

Here Spencer seemed to be talking about Western society specifically. Not all societies—and therefore not all individuals in a society—necessarily fell under this stricture, since Spencer recognized marked differences among them.

Evidence for this belief, said Spencer, was to be found in the wide range of societies existing in the world, since "comparing societies of all orders, those which differ widely in their structures are found to differ widely in the natures of their members" ([1873] 1961: 375). From this and similar statements it is clear that Spencer believed that the various groups of mankind were not all equally endowed with those qualities required for them to make major advances in their level of culture.

But such differences in aptitude as existed among the races were by no means unalterable. Human nature was not fixed—as so often asserted—but plastic. The fact that wide variations in intellectual endowment could be found among disparate human groups showed that people—the constituent units of societies—*had* changed over time. It is perhaps too much to say that Spencer believed in the *perfectibility* of man, but he certainly believed in his *improvability*.

While human nature could indeed change in response to altered conditions of life, such changes, as already noted, occurred only slowly. Moreover, the ineluctable fact had to be faced, said Spencer, that the material that such molding conditions had to work with—the human psyche—was decidedly refractory. And as Spencer bluntly stated, "There is no political alchemy by which you can get golden conduct out of leaden instincts" ([1884] 1950: 52).

Yet these "leaden instincts" *could* change. Over time, people as well as their institutions had undergone modifications. The very fact that some human groups, starting from the same dead level of primitiveness, had actually attained a high level of culture demonstrated this.

Spencer had some words to say about the process by which such changes had taken place: "In the course of centuries and thousands of years . . . the members of [various human populations] . . . spreading to different habitats, fall under different sets of conditions . . . [and] we have no alternative but to admit such divergences [in the natures of individuals] as were consequent on such causes" ([1873] 1924b: 308). Indeed, Spencer was ready to assert that the varying conditions encountered by different populations as they moved over the earth's surface could account for even relatively minor differences, such as those between Hindus and Englishmen, and between Dutchmen and Greeks. These ethnic groups "have acquired undeniable contrasts of nature, physical and psychological, which can be ascribed to nothing but the continuous effects of circumstances, material, moral [and] social" ([1873] 1924b: 308).

Looking at the matter more broadly, Spencer remarked that the "phenomenon of social evolution has . . . to be explained with due reference to the conditions each society is exposed to—the conditions furnished by its locality and by its relations to neighboring societies" ([1873] 1924b: 48). The grand conclusion to be reached was that if the various surrounding "conditions are maintained, human nature will slowly adapt to them" ([1873] 1924b: 318).

But in addition to changes in the character of a society's members brought about by varying external conditions, there were also changes resulting from interactions within the society itself. As Spencer noted, over the course of social evolution "there goes on a reciprocal action and reaction between each people and its institutions," changes in one bringing about changes in the other ([1873] 1961: 375). Indeed, these reciprocal interactions between conditions, institutions, and individuals were a conspicuous feature of social evolution. They were the very means by which change occurred, each element modifying the other over time. Speaking more specifically of how individuals were changed by these interactions, Spencer said: "If by altered circumstances [including changes in institutions] . . . some social structures are rendered inactive and dwindle, while others are brought into greater activity and grow, the natures of citizens are modified into congruity with them" ([1873] 1924b: 375).

Spencer also took account of the other side of the coin, pointing out that the "modes of life change the characters of citizens, . . . their changed characters presently cause responsive changes in their institutions" ([1873] 1961: 375). The result of this interaction among the two was the creation of "an adapted class of institutions" (Spencer [1873] 1924b: 395), each suited to a different phase of evolution. Still, as societies evolved, there were bound to be discordances among their components. The various parts continually rubbed against each other, "each slowly modifying the other through successive generations" (Spencer [1873] 1891: 337).

Inevitably, as a result of this recurring friction, the rough edges of the parts of a society were worn down and smoothed over, being brought into greater concordance as a consequence. Some form of accommodation was therefore established among a society's various elements. This could be expected to occur because "ever the tendency is toward congruity between beliefs and requirements" (Spencer [1901] 1979: 157).

Readjustments among the various parts of a society, said Spencer, necessarily took place since "for a society to hold together the institutions that are needed and the conceptions that are generally current, must be in tolerable harmony" ([1873] 1961: 356). And until this harmony was established, forces continued to operate, prompting its various parts to achieve some form of it. Throughout history, Spencer noted, this process could be seen at work, for there "inevitably arise" the need for "perpetual re-adjustment to circumstances," while these circumstances were themselves also "perpetually changing" ([1873] 1961: 361).

As a result of such ever-recurring readjustments, every society could be thought of as an amalgam of the old and the new. Structures newly arisen were always challenging older structures that in turn kept attempting to ward off the changes. This struggle between the old and the new could always be seen, with the new elements ultimately—if slowly—tending to win out over the old. "Ideas and institutions proper to a past social state, but incongruous with the new social state that has grown out of it, surviv[e] into this new social state they have made possible ... [,] disappearing only as the new social state establishes its own ideas and institutions" ([1873] 1961: 361). In the course of this readjustment, temporary arrangements could be expected to arise, only to be eventually superseded. This was but the normal course of social evolution since, as Spencer observed, "there must be transitional stages during which incongruous organizations co-exist: the first remaining indispensable until the second have grown up to its work" ([1873] 1961: 362).

This trajectory, Spencer maintained, was a natural progression, and he argued that it should be allowed to take its course. Events unfolded as they will, and there was no sense trying to hurry them along. Indeed, "the process of social evolution is in its general character so far predetermined, that its successive stages cannot be ante-dated," that is, brought into being before their time. "Hence," he concluded, "no teaching or policy can advance it beyond a certain normal rate" ([1873] 1961: 365, 366).

But if it could not be accelerated, the process could nonetheless be retarded. As Spencer put it, while the course of events "cannot be artificially bettered[,] an immensity of mischief may be done in the way of disturbing and distorting and repressing [it], by policies carried out in pursuance of erroneous conceptions" ([1873] 1961: 366). Spencer was thus a firm believer in "letting social progress go on unhindered" ([1873] 1961: 366), with no attempt being made to interfere with it. Here, then, we see Spencer justifying the doctrine of laissez faire, with which his name is so often associated.

Given the slow nature of its progress, one could not expect social evolution to be marked by great and sudden saltations. In this regard, human societies were no different from other phenomena that changed over time. "If we contemplate the order of nature," said Spencer, "we see that everywhere vast results are brought about by accumulations of minute actions" ([1873] 1961: 366–367). Therefore, "there is no way from the lower forms of social life to the higher but one passing through small successive modifications" ([1873] 1961: 366).

Finally, aware that his strongly deterministic portrayal of social evolution might engender in a would-be reformer an enervating quietism, he confronted the issue thusly: "From the doctrines set forth in this work, some have drawn the corollary that effort in furtherance of progress is superfluous. 'If,' they argue, 'the evolution of a society conforms [to] general laws ... if the changes which, in the slow course of things brings it about" are all but inevitable, "what need is there of endeavours to aid it?'" ([1873] 1961: 374).

There followed three pages of closely reasoned arguments on the matter, concluding with this encapsulation of his views:

> It is only by fulfilling their individual wills ... that citizens produce these aggregate results which exhibit uniformities apparently independent of individual wills.... No such social results could be produced did they not fulfil their wills. ([1873] 1961: 376)

The foregoing passages, drawing extensively from his writings, have brought us face to face with two different Herbert Spencers: one, the social scientist; the other, the political philosopher. And in his recounting of the great events of political evolution, both men are in evidence. In describing the political development of society, from tiny villages to huge empires, and in highlighting the causes and stages of this transformation, we have witnessed Spencer the hard-eyed social scientist. But in decrying the increased intrusion of government into people's lives we encountered Spencer the political philosopher, giving vent to his personal dislikes. It was this Spencer who was ready to call socialism "the coming slavery" ([1884] 1950: 22).

But even here the social scientist shows through. Regardless of how uncongenial Spencer regarded current political trends, he found no realistic alternative to them. There was no wringing of hands, no call to action, no fervent plea that "if only we mount an effort." No, Spencer the social scientist did not allow his predilections to becloud his realistic vision. What he perceived to be approaching irresistibly he did not regard as mere happenstance but as the outcome of specific determinants. And, as he declared elsewhere, conditions and not intentions determine. Thus, in the end, it seems fair to say that in comparing the two Spencers, the social scientist ultimately trumped the political philosopher.

References

Carneiro, R. L. 1981. "The Chiefdom: Precursor of the State." In *The Transition to Statehood in the New World*, edited by G. D. Jones and R. R. Kautz, 37–79. Cambridge: Cambridge University Press.
Darwin, C. (1859) 1890. *The Origin of Species*. 6th ed. London: John Murray.
———. (1890) 1959. "Letter to Herbert Spencer Dated November 25, 1858." In *Life and Letters of Charles Darwin*, edited by Sir Francis Darwin. 2 vols. New York: Basic Books.
Duncan, D. 1908. *Life and Letters of Herbert Spencer*. 2 vols. New York: D. Appleton and Company.
Lowie, R. H. 1927. *The Origin of the State*. New York: Liveright.
Oberg, K. 1955. "Types of Social Structures among the Lowland Tribes of South and Central America." *American Anthropologist* 57: 472–487.
Service, E. R. 1862. *Primitive Social Organization*. New York: Random House.
Spencer, H. 1851. *Social Statics*. London: John Chapman.
———. 1852a. "The Development Hypothesis." *The Leader* 3 (104): 280–281.
———. 1852b. "A Theory of Population Deduced from the General Law of Animal Fertility." *The Westminster Review* 1: 468–501.
———. (1855) 1896. *The Principles of Psychology*. 2 vols. New York: D. Appleton and Company.
———. 1857. "Progress: Its Law and Cause." *Westminster Review* 11: 445–485.
———. 1862. *First Principles*. London: Williams and Norgate.
———. 1873. *The Study of Sociology*. New York: D. Appleton and Company.
———. (1873) 1891. *The Study of Sociology*. New York: D. Appleton and Company.
———. (1873) 1924b. *The Study of Sociology*. New York: D. Appleton and Company.
———. (1873) 1961. *The Study of Sociology*. Ann Arbor: University of Michigan Press.
———. 1876–1896. *The Principles of Sociology*. 3 vols. New York: D. Appleton and Company.
———. (1884) 1950. *The Man versus the State*. London: Watts & Co.
———. (1901) 1979. *The Data of Ethics*. New York: P. F. Collier's Son.
———. (1904) 1924a. *An Autobiography*. 2 vols. London: Watts & Co.
———. 1967. *The Evolution of Society: Selections from Herbert Spencer's Principles of Sociology*, edited by R. L. Carneiro. Chicago: University of Chicago Press.
Thomson, J. A. 1917. "Darwin's Predecessors." In *Evolution in Modern Thought*, edited by E. Haeckel, J. A. Thomson, and A. Weissman, 1–22. New York: Boni & Liveright.
Tylor, E. B. 1873. "Spencer's *Descriptive Sociology*." *Nature* 8: 544–547.

Chapter Thirteen
Darwinian Conflict Theory
A Unified Evolutionary Research Program
Stephen K. Sanderson

> At the turn of the last century, Darwinian approaches to human behavior were popular in social science. That human behavior had a biological foundation was widely accepted and not particularly controversial. But in the 1920s and 1930s a reaction against biological explanations set in, and a kind of social and cultural determinism arose; it remains dominant today in one guise or another. And yet in the 1970s and 1980s a number of social scientists, frustrated with the lack of progress in their field, began to reconsider human biology and turned once again to Darwinism to provide theoretical foundations for a science of society. The new Darwinism—known variously by the names sociobiology, evolutionary psychology, and human behavioral ecology—has led to enormous progress, but in and of itself leaves many social phenomena unexplained. In this chapter I bring other approaches—in particular, sociological conflict theory, rational choice theory, cultural materialism, and social evolutionism—into contact with the new Darwinism and create a synthesis that I call Darwinian conflict theory. Though called a theory for purposes of simplification, Darwinian conflict theory is in actuality a large-scale Lakatosian research program. A crude version of this program was developed some years ago, but the version offered here is much more fully worked out. It contains 51 axioms, 52 postulates, 19 theories, and 354 propositions. The theories and propositions apply to reproductive behavior, parental investment, economic subsistence and exchange, dietary choice, incest avoidance, human sexuality, mate choice, kinship and marriage, gender differentiation and inequality, status and resource competition, geopolitics, aggression and violence, ethnic attachment, and religious beliefs and rituals. I conclude the chapter by indicating the kinds of evidence that would falsify Darwinian conflict theory.

Introduction

Mature sciences consist of research programs, or sets of general axioms and postulates and more specific theories and propositions (Lakatos 1970). The axioms and postulates serve as guides to the formulation of the theories and propositions, which must be not only testable but, in the philosophy of science of Karl Popper (1959), falsifiable. In the social sciences at least, at the core of theories and propositions are explanations, although they may also consist of empirical generalizations. It is these theories and propositions that are subjected to direct tests.

Individual theories and propositions that survive empirical tests reflect favorably on the research program itself. However, Imre Lakatos stresses that it is always the case that some of a research program's theories and propositions will not survive these tests. They may be decisively refuted. But this does not refute the research program so long as the number of falsifications is not too large and alternative theories and propositions can be formulated. Research programs are always subject to emendations as empirical research advances. For example, a cardinal principle in evolutionary biology for the past century has been the emphatic rejection of Lamarckian inheritance of acquired characteristics. This was thought to be impossible. However, it is now theorized, with supporting evidence, that environmental perturbations can affect the expression of genes and that the changes can be transmitted genetically. A new concept, epigenetics, has been introduced (West-Eberhard 2003; Jablonka and Lamb 2005). If the advocates of epigenetics turn out to be correct, then a fundamental postulate of evolutionary biology will have been overturned and replaced by a new postulate, but most of evolutionary biology will still stand. This is one way in which research programs progress.

Research programs in sociology and the social sciences more generally are usually focused on the particular phenomena of subfields, although in principle they can be discipline-wide. Thus in sociology we have the rational choice program of religion developed by Rodney Stark and colleagues (Stark 1996, 1999, 2007; Stark and Bainbridge 1987; Stark and Finke 2000) and the state-centered research program of revolutions (Tilly 1978; Skocpol 1979; Collins 1995; Goldstone 1991; Wickham-Crowley 1992; Goodwin 2001). But the aim of this chapter is much more ambitious. It is to develop a discipline-wide research program and to do so by means of a *synthesis* of several existing programs.

Synthesis involves selecting elements from different research traditions and recombining and fusing them into a novel research tradition that is similar to its parents, yet notably distinct. It involves, in other words, taking portions of traditions t_1, t_2, and t_3 and uniting them into a new tradition, T. In the ideal form of synthesis, the new research program contains axioms, postulates, theories, and propositions all its own; t_1, t_2, and t_3 are abandoned, and T becomes the new foundation for research.

This type of synthesis is exceptionally difficult to achieve. A more easily realized type of synthesis is a *grafting* synthesis (Laudan 1977). Here one selects elements of research programs thought to be compatible and brings them together. It might be claimed that their theories and propositions do not represent different things but simply different aspects of the same thing. A sociological research program might have as a key principle the notion that humans are especially conflict-prone animals and yet fail to offer any rationale for why humans are conflict-prone. This makes the program incomplete and thus insufficient on its own. A remedy is to import elements of another research program that are thought capable of grounding the principle of conflict-proneness—of explaining why there is conflict-proneness in the first place. Or, a research tradition that emphasizes conflict-proneness may have a rationale for conflict-proneness, but the rationale is regarded by those outside the tradition as incorrect, if not altogether misguided. One then strips away that rationale and replaces it with the rationale of a different tradition.

In doing any kind of synthesis, one always has to pick and choose. Different research programs cannot simply be glued together in toto, because they always contain inconsistent and incompatible elements. One has to select consistent, compatible, or complementary features of existing programs and discard those elements that do not logically fit together. One would also be guided by the objective of retaining what has proved to be empirically successful in a program and casting aside what has proved empirically false or at least dubious.

The synthetic research program developed here is a grafting synthesis. I call it *Darwinian conflict theory* (DCT). An early formulation of this program was carried out in 2001, but it was much too crude in that it remained at the level of axioms and postulates (Sanderson 2001). Here I use a revised and extended version of these axioms and postulates to formulate a series of theories and propositions regarding the most salient dimensions of human social life. I offer 51 axioms, 52 postulates, 19 theories, and 354 propositions.

The most important criteria for evaluating research programs and their components are (1) testability, (2) empirical success, (3) parsimony, (4) generality, and (5) productivity (Sanderson 2012; cf. Black 1995). Propositions generated by research programs must be capable of being tested against observations and must be formulated in such a way that they can be falsified. Other things equal, the best theories are those that have been most rigorously tested and that have survived these tests relatively unscathed. Either there are no falsifying observations, or any such observations are few in number (anomalies are a virtual constant in science). Research programs should be parsimonious in that their core principles can be simply and efficiently stated. They should also be highly general, which is to say they apply to the largest number and diversity of phenomena. Finally, they should be productive in the sense that new propositions and empirical predictions can be derived from them.

I contend that the research program offered here meets these criteria with reasonable success. Its theories and propositions can all be falsified. Indeed, they have all been tested, some of them extensively. Many of these have survived falsifying tests quite well. Others require much more extensive testing and thus are highly provisional.

Although DCT contains many theories and propositions, its parsimony lies in the simplicity and straightforwardness of its axioms and postulates. Because these components of DCT apply to an extremely large part of the social world, it has an exceptionally high level of generality.

The Background Research Programs

The background research programs that are part of the DCT synthesis are five in number:

1. Sociobiology
2. Rational choice theory
3. Sociological conflict theory, especially in its more Weberian form
4. Cultural materialism
5. Social evolutionism

What are the principal elements of each that go into the synthesis?

Sociobiology

Sociobiology is a derivative of Darwinian evolutionary biology. It is closely related to two other Darwinian approaches, evolutionary psychology and human behavioral ecology. Its most basic postulates are:

- Humans are organisms whose brains have evolved by natural and sexual selection.
- The brain contains domain-specific modules that represent evolutionary adaptations.
- These evolutionary adaptations, which evolved in the ancestral environment of small hunter-gatherer societies prior to 10,000 years ago, direct behavior with the aims of maximizing survival and reproductive success.

- Evolutionary adaptations interact with a socioecological context, or total set of ecological, demographic, technological, economic, social, political, religious, cultural, and so on, circumstances to produce behavioral outcomes.
- Evolutionary adaptations are the ultimate foundation for the structure of societies, which evolve as social adaptations.

Sociobiology provides the foundational principles for DCT. A proper research program requires a metaphysic, by which I mean here a set of "first principles" beyond which it is not necessary to go. This makes DCT "reductionist" but in the best sense of the term: good science is by its very nature reductionist. However, this reductionism is tempered by the other research programs that make up the synthesis. (For a much fuller discussion of sociobiology, see Sanderson 2012: 157–181.)

RATIONAL CHOICE THEORY

Rational choice theory's basic principles are (Friedman and Hechter 1988):

- Social behavior is the result of individual actors who act purposively to maximize benefits and minimize costs with respect to certain preferences or goals.
- People's intentional actions are subject to constraints in the form of opportunity costs, or costs associated with not pursuing certain courses of action, and institutional constraints, which act as positive or negative sanctions on any course of action.
- Actors possess limited information concerning what choices will best realize their preferences, and thus their assessment of the best means to realize their preferences will sometimes fail.
- Individuals act rationally in accordance with their own subjective sense of what is in their interests.
- Choices made by individuals concern the means to achieve certain ends, not the ends themselves.
- Societies are the aggregated result of the individual choices and decisions of its constituent members.

One limitation of rational choice theory is that many features of human behavior do not involve conscious calculation at all, and thus no real "choice" in the technical sense of the term. Much behavior is driven by unconscious motives over which individuals have no knowledge or control. A second difficulty with rational choice theory is its inability to explain the nature and origin of human preferences. Rational choice theorists simply bracket preferences out and focus entirely on the means to ends, not the ends themselves. This is a serious lacuna.

A solution to both problems is to introduce sociobiology and its relatives. Sociobiology and rational choice theory are alike in that both are methodologically individualist approaches that assume individual actors pursuing their interests. But sociobiology can take rational choice principles further by grounding them in evolutionary principles and thus providing one solution to the problem of preferences (Hirshleifer 1977; Richerson and Boyd 1992; Nielsen 1994). As Hirshleifer (1977: 19) has said, "The biological approach to preferences . . . postulates that all such motives or drives or tastes represent proximate aspects of a single underlying goal—fitness. Preferences are governed by the all-encompassing *drive for reproductive survival*." Sociobiology also assumes that much human behavior is driven by unconscious motivation and thus helps to overcome the other limitation of rational choice theory mentioned above.

What, then, is rational choice theory's distinctive contribution to the synthesis? Does it add anything not already there? Yes. It helps us understand many human choices, and even institutional practices, that cannot be predicted from Darwinian principles alone. For example, most people are heterosexuals and prefer heterosexual sex to any other kind of sex. But what will they do if such sex is unavailable? Masturbation most obviously comes to mind, but over time this is a rather poor substitute since humans are highly social and like human contact, including sexual contact. The next choice would be some sort of homosexual activity, which we know is relatively common in situations where men are confined together and women are absent (prisons, ships at sea, etc.). Here we see that individual actors are trying to achieve certain preferences or goals within the context of environmental constraints. Sociobiology alone does not predict such situational homosexuality. (For a fuller discussion of rational choice theory, see Sanderson 2012: 94–110.)

Conflict Theory

In its most general form, conflict theory's key principles are (Collins 1974, 2009; Sanderson 2012: 32–74):

- The essence of social life is people competing for resources that are scarce.
- Economic resources and social power are the most important, but not the only, resources that people seek.
- Because of the competition for scarce resources, individuals and groups frequently come into conflict over the distribution of these resources.
- This conflict commonly leads to the formation of dominant and subordinate groups; conflict is both intrasocietal and intersocietal.
- On the intrasocietal level, dominant groups tend to gain priority over subordinate groups in structuring society to favor their interests.
- On the intersocietal level, societies seek to realize their interests through dominating and controlling other societies.

It is common to distinguish between Marxian and Weberian versions of conflict theory. Their main differences are:

- Methodological holism (Marx—e.g., individuals are embodiments of class relations and class interests) vs. methodological individualism (Weber—e.g., the actions of states are the actions of individuals)
- Class conflict as the fundamental form of conflict that determines other forms of conflict (Marx—e.g., states serve the interests of dominant classes) vs. no form of conflict is more fundamental than any other form (Weber—e.g., states have their own interests separate from and often in conflict with dominant classes)
- Social conflict is rooted in private property ownership and can be resolved through collectivization of the means of production (Marx) vs. social conflict is integral to social life and inevitable (Weber)
- The source of self-interest: it arises from class membership based on property ownership (Marx) vs. is a natural human condition expressing itself in all dimensions of social life (Weber)

There are other differences, but these are the most fundamental for our purposes (Collins 1974, 2009; Sanderson 2012).

Sociobiology may be considered a type of conflict theory and, in fact, the deepest form of conflict theory. Sociobiology and Marxian conflict theory are theoretical traditions that seem, on the surface at least, utterly incompatible. After all, Marxists are usually extremely critical of sociobiological arguments, on both theoretical and political grounds. But there is much more of a connection than is initially apparent. Jerome Barkow has said that "a sociobiological theory of society . . . is, necessarily, a conflict theory" (1989: 118). Marx himself read *The Origin of Species* in 1860 and in early 1861 said to Engels in a letter that "Darwin's book is very important and serves me as a natural-scientific basis for the class struggle in history" (quoted in Taylor 1989: 409). Indeed, Wilhelm Liebknecht, an important German socialist leader who visited Marx frequently, indicated that "when Darwin drew the consequences of his investigations and presented them to the public, we spoke for months of nothing else but Darwin and the revolutionizing power of his scientific conquests" (quoted in Feuer 1978: 109). Both Marx and Engels were very unhappy with Darwin's reliance on Malthus's concept of the struggle for existence, but nonetheless the "class struggle came to be regarded as the form which the struggle for existence took in class societies; *the materialistic conception of history was derived as a limiting case of the biological struggle as it obtained for the conditions of the human species*" (Feuer 1978: 110; emphasis added). It is most unfortunate that the extraordinary implications of this last idea have never been properly developed. It is one of the main tasks of DCT to draw out these implications and state them formally.

Weberian conflict theory fits even better in terms of the differences between the Marxian and Weberian versions outlined above. Randall Collins recognizes this to some extent when he says that "Darwin is in the background for all of the later nineteenth-century conflict theory" (1974: 148) and that "conflict theory is Machiavelli without the Prince, Marx without Hegel, Darwin without Spencer, Weber without idealism, Freud without Victorianism" (1974: 150). In his early book *Conflict Sociology*, Collins gives prominent attention to ethology, a forerunner of sociobiology. He says that we need to remember that man is an animal, which then takes us back to Darwin (Collins 1975: 91). Unfortunately, Collins abandoned this line of thinking in all of his later work. A golden opportunity was missed. He tells us that humans are highly conflict-prone organisms but cannot tell us why they are conflict prone. The conflict-prone nature of humans is an unexplained given, an assertion that goes completely untheorized. In my view Collins's assertion is correct, but he leaves unanswered the question why it is correct.

Collins is sensitive to the necessity of establishing microfoundations, but his microfoundations are inadequate to sustain any type of conflict theory. These foundations are located in what Collins calls interaction ritual theory (IRT), which he derives from Durkheim and Erving Goffman. Durkheim did not develop this explicitly; Collins sees it as implicit in *The Elementary Forms of the Religious Life*. Goffman developed it explicitly, largely from ethology, which he studied as a graduate student.[1] Collins uses IRT to develop some interesting insights, but it also leads him into dubious assertions, such as claiming that people want material possessions only for their status value. He even feels the need to raise the question of why people eat; the answer is apparently not to survive but to be able to continue to participate in interaction rituals.

In my view a much more useful part of Collins's (2004) IRT is his concept of *emotional energy* (EE). EE is a feeling of exhilaration gained from successful interaction rituals; its downside comes from unsuccessful rituals and is tantamount to a kind of depression. EE is a concept that, sufficiently tweaked, can fit very nicely inside a Darwinian paradigm. It is in essence a kind of psychological kick or payoff individuals get when they are successfully achieving their goals. Status-conferring rituals lead to EE, but status-losing rituals lead to its opposite. The obvious next step in this line of thinking is to see that gaining status has this payoff effect to keep individuals striving for it; the desire to experience EE is the proximate cause of status-seeking, whose ultimate cause is evolutionary.

Without demonstrating any familiarity with Collins's work, Richard Alexander shows how the EE concept can be reformulated in Darwinian terms:

> Happiness and its anticipation are thus proximate mechanisms that lead us to perform and repeat acts that in the environments of history, at least, would have led to greater reproductive success. This is a central hypothesis in evolutionary biology. Paralleling it in importance is the hypothesis that control of resources is the most appropriate route to reproductive success. . . . Similarly, I presume that status is typically a vehicle toward resource control and an outcome of it. If these ideas are correct, then humans should always experience pleasure when they gain in status or increase their control of resources (unless they do so at large expense to close relatives or spouses), and they should experience some converse feeling when they lose status or resource control (except, sometimes, when they transfer it to relatives or spouses). (1987: 26–27)

There is one important difference between EE as Collins conceives it and as it is conceived within DCT. EE for Collins results not just from status attainment but even more from the intensity of social interaction. Interaction rituals are, after all, *interaction* rituals. But interaction rituals, I would contend, will be most likely to produce EE when individuals have central membership roles in groups. This is the link to status striving.

DCT draws more on the Weberian form of conflict theory, although it sees Marx's emphasis on material forces as the most crucial causal conditions as superior to Weber's more eclectic position on this issue (e.g., ideas shape history as much as material conditions). However, Marx's materialism is now outdated and in many ways inadequate and has been substantially improved upon by the cultural materialism of Marvin Harris.

CULTURAL MATERIALISM

Harris's (1968, 1979) cultural materialism is an anthropological approach that has drawn extensively on Marxian historical materialism, cultural ecology, and social evolutionism. A crucial part of Harris's analysis is his formulation of what he calls the *universal pattern*, or the basic components of all societies. Societies are trichotomized into an infrastructure, a structure, and a superstructure. The *infrastructure* consists principally of technology, ecosystems, demography, and techno-environmental relationships. It is subdivided into a *mode of production* and a *mode of reproduction*. The mode of production consists of those things that go into the process of producing the means of human survival. It includes subsistence technology and the basic features of the natural environment. The mode of reproduction consists of those things relating to the production of human life itself. It includes demographic behavior (rates of population growth, population density, age and sex ratios, etc.) and the technology of birth and population control. The *structure* consists of political economy and domestic economy. Political economy involves stratification systems, forms of political organization, and war. Domestic economy includes patterns of marriage, family life, kinship, gender roles, and age roles. The *superstructure* is composed of such things as ideology, art, music, literature, rituals, sports and games, and science.

These components are linked by a causal principle that Harris calls the Principle of Infrastructural Determinism. This holds that *the flow of causation in social life is primarily from the infrastructure to the structure, and then from the structure to the superstructure*. This is understood probabilistically, and allowance is made for feedback from superstructure to structure to infrastructure. But not only does the infrastructure largely determine the structure and superstructure in a synchronic sense; from a diachronic perspective, changes tend to occur first within infrastructures and these changes generate reverberating changes in structures and superstructures. The infrastructure is primary because it consists of the means whereby humans produce the basic conditions of human existence and reproduce human life itself. Structures and superstructures are therefore adaptations to the infrastructural conditions that societies lay down first.

Harris's earlier work was heavily bogged down by a functionalist conception of societies (1968, 1974), but he later switched to rational choice's cost-benefit assumptions (1977, 1979)—from explaining cultural patterns in terms of their adaptive value for societies to explaining them in terms of their adaptive value for individuals. "Just as a species does not 'struggle to survive' as a collective entity, but survives or not as a consequence of the adaptive changes of individual organisms, so too do sociocultural systems survive or not as a consequence of the adaptive changes in the thought and activities of individual men and women who respond opportunistically to cost-benefit options" (1979: 61). This gives a clear link to rational choice theory, and to sociobiology as well despite Harris's strong criticism of that perspective.

Harris's Principle of Infrastructural Determinism is a very useful principle, but it is insufficiently grounded. As Richard Alexander has pointed out, the principles of cultural materialism make sense only *in light of* sociobiological principles (1987: 26–27):

> Harris's analysis takes economic or "productive" ends as ultimate rather than as means to the end of reproductive success. Such analyses are like those which take pleasure and happiness as ultimate ends. They cannot explain why the proximate mechanisms of pleasure and happiness (Harris's "bio-psychological benefits") operate as they do, or even why they exist.... Harris implies that reproductive success, representing "remote and hypothetical interests," is somehow an *alternative* explanation to more proximate "bio-psychological benefits" as "the most certain and powerful interests served by infrastructure." He sees the "struggle to maintain and enhance differential politico-economic power and wealth" as *opposed* to "the struggle to achieve reproductive success." In the sense of comprehensive explanation, however, the relationship between such proximate and ultimate factors is not adversarial. Rather, neither can be explained without the other.... I cannot imagine how cultural materialist explanations of human behavior and institutions can ever make real or complete sense except in light of a continuous history of natural selection of genetic alternatives.

Moreover, Harris was on the cusp of recognizing such a thing himself. Consider, for example, this assertion: "True, sociobiological models based on reproductive success and inclusive fitness can yield predictions about sociocultural differences that enjoy a degree of empirical validity.... But the reason for this predictability is that most of the factors which might promote reproductive success do so through the intermediation of bio-psychological benefits that enhance the economic, political, and sexual power and well-being of individuals and groups of individuals" (Harris 1979: 139). This illustrates almost perfectly the postulate that evolutionary mental adaptations interact with socio-ecological context to produce behavioral outcomes. Cultural materialism's proximate causes are rooted in sociobiology's ultimate causes. People seek economic resources and power because these are the principal means of achieving reproductive success.

Unfortunately, many of Harris's specific theories have now been cast into doubt, if not falsified. These are his theories of war, male domination, the potlatch, the incest taboo, fertility levels, and status seeking. (See Sanderson [2007a: 205–212] for explications and critiques of these theories.) In all cases a Darwinian approach can offer better explanations of these phenomena.

Social Evolutionism

To a large extent, social evolutionism is not an autonomous theoretical approach but a component of other approaches. There are numerous types of theories of social evolution that are not only different but often contradictory (Sanderson 1990, 2007b). Some theories of social evolution have been functionalist and idealist (e.g., Parsonian evolutionism), whereas others have been materialist and employed, at least implicitly, rational choice principles (e.g., Harris, Sanderson). The version of evolutionism endorsed here is of the latter type (for details see Sanderson 1994a, 1995).

Social evolutionism's distinctive contribution is its emphasis on societies as dynamic entities. By looking at how societies change, it is much easier to reveal how and why certain social arrangements may be adaptive. This connects it to Darwinian evolutionism in the sense that change is constant and new forms arise out of old ones as adaptations to new circumstances.

Darwinian Conflict Theory: Axioms

And now to DCT itself. I begin with its axioms and then pass on to postulates, theories, and propositions.

Webster's Encyclopedic Unabridged Dictionary offers several definitions of an axiom: (1) a self-evident truth that requires no proof, (2) a universally accepted principle or rule, (3) a proposition that is assumed without proof for the sake of studying the consequences that follow from it. I use the term here primarily in the third sense, although some of the axioms qualify under the first and second definitions.

I. General

1. Like all other species, humans are organisms that have been built by millions of years of biological evolution.
2. Human bodies and brains are products of *natural selection*. Natural selection is selection for survival in specific environments.
3. Human bodies and brains are also products of *sexual selection*. Sexual selection is selection for the ability to attract mates rather than for survival.
4. The human brain is the locus of human nature.

II. Evolution of the Brain's Architecture

1. The brain evolved to solve the basic problems of survival and reproduction.
2. The brain evolved in the *ancestral environment* of small communities organized around an economy of hunting and gathering.

3. The architecture of the brain consists of *evolutionary adaptations* to the conditions of life in the ancestral environment.
4. These evolutionary adaptations direct behavior.
5. Most evolutionary adaptations are *facultative*. They direct behavior in conjunction with individuals' assessments of environmental context.
6. The ultimate goal of human behavior is to achieve individual *fitness* relative to other individuals. Fitness is *differential reproductive success*.
7. Novel environments, especially modern environments, may deflect behaviors from maximizing reproductive success even though behavior is being directed by the same domain-specific psychological adaptations.
8. Evolutionary adaptations do not require conscious recognition by individuals. The adaptations that direct behavior are usually below the threshold of conscious awareness.
9. The evolutionary adaptations of the brain are *domain-specific* mechanisms, or specialized modules, that are designed to solve specific problems. The brain is not a general all-purpose mechanism.
10. The brain consists of domain-specific adaptive mechanisms because (a) the adaptive problems confronted by our ancestors in the ancestral environment were very specific, and specialized adaptations are much better than general adaptations in solving specific adaptive problems;[2] (b) a great deal of successful behavior is dependent on highly variable environmental conditions requiring behavioral flexibility, and this flexibility requires highly specialized brain mechanisms.[3]

III. Adaptive Arrangements

1. The architecture of the brain consists of evolved *biological* adaptations.
2. Social life consists of evolved *social* adaptations.
3. Many, probably most, of the organizational and institutional features of human social life are the adaptive consequences of people struggling to satisfy their interests. But these social arrangements are deeply impregnated by adaptations at the biological level and thus not autonomous.
4. It is individuals who are the *targets* of adaptations; group adaptations are aggregated individual adaptations.
5. Group adaptations may exist as the result of *intersocietal selection*. But societies are still aggregations of individuals pursuing their interests.

IV. Human Interests

1. Humans are engaged in a struggle for survival and reproduction with their fellow humans that is inevitable and unceasing.
2. Human social life is the complex product of this ceaseless struggle for survival and reproduction.
3. The core of social life is individuals pursuing their interests. In the struggle for survival and reproduction, humans give priority to their own interests over those of others.
4. Humans' most important interests and concerns are reproductive, economic, and political. Political life is primarily a struggle to acquire and defend economic resources, and economic life is primarily a matter of using resources to promote reproductive success.

V. Socioecological Context

1. The brain's architecture interacts with a *socioecological context*, which is the total set of environmental circumstances (natural and social) within which people engage each other.
2. Socioecological context, itself biologically impregnated, enables and constrains the expression of the brain's evolutionary adaptations.
3. To optimize reproductive success, humans must adjust their behavior to socioecological context.
4. The socioecological context is composed of three basic elements: (a) the *ecostructure*, or the basic natural phenomena and social forms essential to economic production and biological reproduction, i.e., the ecological, demographic, technological, and economic structures of a society; (b) the *structure*, or basic social arrangements and institutions of a society apart from the economic; (c) the *superstructure*, or principal beliefs, values, and norms as these are expressed in religion, art, literature, myth, legend, philosophy, art, and music.
5. Although all elements of the socioecological context are of causal importance, they are not of equal importance.
6. The most important causal forces are located in the ecostructure, then in the structure, and last in the superstructure.

VI. Self and Others

1. The pursuit of individual interests leads to cooperative, competitive, and conflictive social arrangements.
2. Many cooperative forms of behavior exist at the level of social groups or entire societies. Cooperative social relations exist because they are the relations that will best promote each individual's self-interests, not because they promote the well-being of the group or society as a whole. Natural selection of cooperative social relations occurs at the level of the individual, not the group or society.
3. Cooperative forms of interaction are found most extensively among individuals who share reproductive interests, i.e., among kin and especially close kin.
4. Outside of kin relations, cooperative relations are most likely to be found among individuals who depend heavily on each other for the realization of their basic interests.
5. When competitive or conflictive behavior will more satisfactorily promote individual interests, cooperative relations will decline in favor of competition and conflict.
6. Competition and conflict under certain socioecological arrangements lead to the formation of socially dominant and socially subordinate groups.
7. Members of dominant groups benefit disproportionately from their social position, and therefore are highly motivated to structure society so that their superior social position can be preserved or enhanced.
8. Social life is therefore disproportionately influenced by the interests and actions of the members of dominant groups.

VII. Culture Acquisition

1. The ecostructures, structures, and superstructures that individuals create can, for purposes of simplification only, be called *culture*.[4]

2. Culture is learned behavior but is biologically impregnated.
3. Culture is not an organic whole or a "thing apart." It is an aggregation of individual beliefs and practices that are the same or similar.
4. Some culture is transmitted by senior to junior generations by direct instruction. This is *transmitted* culture (Tooby and Cosmides 1992).
5. Some culture is acquired by junior generations through imitation. This is *evoked* culture (Tooby and Cosmides 1992).
6. Juniors are strongly inclined to imitate what the majority of both seniors and older juniors do. This is *frequency-dependent imitation* (Boyd and Richerson 1985).
7. Juniors are strongly inclined to imitate seniors and older juniors of high status. This is *status imitation* (Boyd and Richerson 1985).
8. Transmitted culture is more difficult to acquire than evoked culture, which is why it must be taught.
9. Evoked culture is easier to acquire, which is why it can be left to imitation.
10. Humans are creatures of habit and, ceteris paribus, are strongly inclined to resist changes in their society and culture.
11. Imitation will decline in favor of innovation when cultural beliefs and practices decline in their level of adaptiveness.
12. Imitation will decline in favor of innovation when improved opportunities for the pursuit of basic human aims emerge.
13. Some cultural beliefs and practices develop in ways inconsistent with or contradictory to human nature. These practices are unstable and will eventually disintegrate or disappear.

Darwinian Conflict Theory: Postulates, Theories, and Propositions

The definition of a postulate (*Webster's Unabridged*) is essentially the same as that of an axiom. However, I define a postulate here as a fundamental principle that is less general and abstract than an axiom and that is attached to a specific substantive content. Postulates express known or assumed facts. Theories are bundles of related propositions, and propositions are statements of relationships between variables.

The principal postulates, theories, and propositions of DCT follow. After each proposition I use asterisks to indicate the extent to which that proposition has been successfully *corroborated*. Popper uses this term to indicate a theory that has been extensively tested and so far has not been falsified. This term replaces the term *verified*, which implies proved beyond all doubt, an impossibility for Popper. A single asterisk (*) indicates limited corroboration, two asterisks (**) substantial corroboration, and three asterisks (***) a high level of corroboration. References to the relevant empirical literature supporting the propositions are provided in parentheses. In many instances the references are to secondary summaries of the empirical literature, in which case the reader may wish to consult the additional references contained in the summaries.

A. Reproductive Strategies Theory

Postulate. All animals have evolved species-specific reproductive strategies designed to maximize reproductive success.

Postulate. In order to maximize their reproductive success, people adjust their reproductive behavior to socioecological constraints.

Postulate. Reproductive strategies involve trade-offs between the quantity and the quality of offspring.

1. In making reproductive decisions, females assess socioecological context for the level of dependability of male providers.* (Sanderson 2001: 166–168; Ellis 2004; Ellis et al. 2003)
2. Where male dependability is assessed to be high, both menarche and reproduction begin later.* (Sanderson 2001: 166–168; Ellis 2004; Ellis et al. 2003; Chisholm et al. 2005)
3. Where male dependability is assessed to be low, menarche and reproduction begin earlier.* (Sanderson 2001: 166–168; Ellis 2004; Ellis et al. 2003; Chisholm et al. 2005)
4. Fertility behavior is adjusted to levels of infant and child survival.** (Sanderson 2001: 169–175)
5. When infant and child survival levels are low, fertility is high for purposes of replacing offspring lost.** (Sanderson 2001: 169–175)
6. When infant and child survival levels are high, fertility is low because there is little or no need to replace lost children.* (Sanderson 2001: 169–175)
7. Fertility behavior is adjusted to the economic resources available to support offspring.** (Sanderson 2001: 169–175)
8. Fertility is inversely related to the level of female empowerment.* (Sanderson 2001: 170–171; Sanderson and Dubrow 2000)
9. In modern industrial societies, people emphasize the quality of offspring over their quantity.** (Wiley and Carlin 1999; Kaplan and Lancaster 2000; Cleland 2001)
10. Modern industrial societies are characterized by low-low fertility, i.e., fertility below replacement level.*** (Frejka and Ross 2001; Chesnais 2001; Allen 2006; CIA World Factbook 2010)
11. Low-low fertility is a function of the high economic costs of children.** (Wiley and Carlin 1999; Kaplan and Lancaster 2000; Cleland 2001)
12. Low-low fertility is a function of high levels of female empowerment and female labor force participation.** (Hakim 2003)
13. Low-low fertility is a function of the degree of pursuit of creature comforts.* (Chesnais 2001)

B. Parental Investment Theory

Postulate. Humans adjust their investment in offspring so as to maximize their and their offspring's reproductive success.

Postulate. There is a trade-off between the sexes in parental care and mating. The sex that invests more in parental care will invest less in mating, and vice versa.

Postulate. Females invest more in parental care, males more in mating.

1. Women have a natural inclination to mother that exceeds the natural inclination of men to father.*** (Sanderson 2014: 188–192)
2. Women overwhelmingly monopolize the care of infants and young children in all societies.*** (Sanderson 2014: 188–192)
3. Most women need to mother and feel unfulfilled when circumstances prevent them from being able to mother.*** (Hrdy 1999; Sanderson 2014: 191–192)

4. The quality of maternal care is contingent upon the circumstances for successful rearing of an infant.*** (Hrdy 1999; Sanderson 2014: 189–191)
5. In premodern societies, infanticide is more likely when and where the conditions for rearing are poor and the likelihood of infant and child survival are low. Poor rearing conditions include insufficient economic resources, unhealthy or deformed offspring, mothers' lack of social support, and children born too close together.*** (Hrdy 1999; Sanderson 2014: 206–207)
6. Infanticide varies inversely with the extent of mother-infant bonding.** (Sanderson 2014: 205, 207)
7. Natural offspring receive better parental care than step-offspring.** (Daly and Wilson 1988, 1998; Sanderson 2014: 191)
8. Abuse and neglect are more frequently suffered by step-offspring than natural offspring.** (Daly and Wilson 1988, 1998; Sanderson 2014: 191)
9. Infanticide is sex-selective.*** (Sanderson 2014: 207–209)
10. Infanticide is directed more frequently toward the sex with poorer marital and reproductive prospects.** (Sanderson 2014: 207–209)
11. In nonindustrial societies, mothers of high social status will bear more sons, mothers of low status more daughters.** (Sanderson 2014: 200–202)
12. In industrial societies, the social status of mothers is unrelated to the birth of sons versus daughters.** (Sanderson 2014: 203–204)
13. When the marital and reproductive prospects of sons exceed those of daughters, parents will invest more in sons.** (Sanderson 2014: 201–203)
14. When the marital and reproductive prospects of daughters exceed those of sons, parents will invest more in daughters.** (Sanderson 2014: 202–203)
15. In hypergynous societies, daughters of lower-status families have better marital and reproductive prospects than sons.** (Sanderson 2014: 208–209) *Def.*: Hypergynous societies are those in which women systematically marry into higher-status families.
16. In hypergynous societies, sons of higher-status families have better marital and reproductive prospects than daughters.** (Sanderson 2014: 208–209)

C. Economic Subsistence Theory

Postulate. Humans adopt the subsistence strategy that provides the best chances for survival, well-being, and reproductive success within the context of the subsistence strategies known and available at the time.

Postulate. Humans have evolved to maximize efficiency. Other things being equal, they prefer to carry out activities by minimizing the amount of time and energy they devote to these activities, in particular activities considered burdensome and onerous.

1. Modes of economic subsistence are functions of population density and environmental quality.** (Sanderson 1995, 1999)
2. Foraging—hunting and gathering—is the primordial human economic adaptation.*** (Sanderson 2014: 41–46)
3. Most foraging societies exist at subsistence level.** (Sanderson 2014: 46–49)
4. Foraging economies can be sustained only at very low population densities, unless resources are unusually abundant.*** (Sanderson 2001: 264–265)
5. Foragers adopt strategies of resource collection that will optimize calories produced and minimize labor time and energy, except when males seek to acquire

resources that are harder to obtain and that impress women as potential mates, and/or when protein is preferred over plant food.** (Sanderson 2014: 83–87)
6. The ratio of meat to plant foods in the diet increases as latitude increases.*** (Sanderson 2014: 44)
7. Food-storing foragers have larger populations and greater social complexity than non-food-storers.*** (Sanderson 2014: 45–46)
8. Foragers often resist converting to cultivation because cultivation carries greater risks and uncertainties and is often more labor-intensive.* (Sanderson 2014: 52)
9. Foragers will switch to cultivation when increasing population pressure leads to declining caloric returns relative to the amount of time and energy invested.* (Sanderson 2014: 52–53)
10. Agriculture arose worldwide beginning ten millennia ago because of increased population pressures and declining living standards, and also because warmer and wetter climates made cultivation possible.** (Sanderson 2014: 49–53)
11. Cultivation will be intensified in direct proportion to increasing population densities and environmental degradation.*** (Sanderson 2014: 58–59)
12. Pastoralism replaces cultivation in very dry environments.*** (Sanderson 2014: 59–60)

D. Economic Exchange Theory

Postulate. Humans in all societies calculate the benefits and costs of economic actions within the limitations of their knowledge and the constraints of their socioecology.

Postulate. Most individual economic action is self-interested.

Postulate. Humans follow those courses of economic action that maximize benefits and minimize costs.

Postulate. Humans are highly sensitive to incentives for economic gain.

Postulate. People have a natural sense of reciprocity. They seek to exchange like for like.

1. Economic exchange will tend to be mutual and balanced when one party lacks the resources or power to put the other party at a disadvantage.*** (Sanderson 2001: 268–272)
2. Economic exploitation is directly proportional to the possession of superior resources and power by one of the parties.*** (Sanderson 2001: 274–276)
3. The level of development of exchange relations is dependent on the size and complexity of societies.*** (Sanderson 1995)
4. Throughout social evolution, exchange relations have expanded, from the local to the regional to the supraregional to the global.*** (Sanderson 1995)
5. Capitalism is based on the natural human inclination for exchange, and therefore on the incentives of the parties to exchange for gain.*** (Hirshleifer 1977; Berger 1986; Sanderson 2014: 68–69) *Def.*: Capitalism is the production and sale of commodities in a market for the realization of maximum profit.
6. Capitalism is the product of the long-term expansion of exchange relations.** (Sanderson 1994b, 1995)
7. Capitalism develops more easily in societies with greater access to maritime trade.*** (Sanderson 1995)
8. Capitalism develops more easily in societies with decentralized political control.** (Sanderson 1995)

9. Socialism undermines the incentives of parties to exchange for gain.*** (Berger 1986; Kornai 1992)
10. Socialism is incompatible with the natural human inclination for exchange.*** (Berger 1986; Kornai 1992)
11. Socialist economies are unstable.*** (Sanderson 2010; Sanderson and Alderson 2005)
12. Because socialist economies are unstable, they will revert to capitalist economies over time.*** (Sanderson and Alderson 2005)

E. Dietary Choice Theory

Postulate. People make food choices by evaluating the balance of nutritional and caloric benefits and costs of potential food sources.

1. The universal desire for meat is an evolutionary adaptation because animal proteins are more efficient sources of amino acids and other nutrients than plant foods.*** (Harris 1987; Hamilton 1987; Rozin 1987; Lieberman 1987; Sanderson 2014: 81–83)
2. People therefore value animal proteins more than plant foods.*** (Harris 1987; Hamilton 1987; Rozin 1987)
3. People therefore seek a high representation of animal proteins in their diets.*** (Harris 1987; Hamilton 1987; Rozin 1987)
4. Preferred sources of animal protein are large herbivorous animals because they yield a greater energy return per unit of time and effort than small animals.*** (Murdock 1967; Abrams 1987)
5. In foraging societies, people give priority to hunting large herbivorous animals.*** (Sanderson 2014: 83–84)
6. In societies with animal domestication and stock breeding, people depend primarily on large herbivorous animals.*** (Murdock 1967; Abrams 1987)
7. Carnivorous animals will be low-ranked sources of protein because they are much less efficient converters of food sources to flesh than herbivorous species.*** (Harris 1985; Abrams 1987)
8. Carnivorous animals may be eaten when other sources of animal protein are scarce.** (Harris 1985)
9. In modern environments where food is widely available, people may make choices based on evolved adaptations but that lead to suboptimal levels of health and nutrition.*** (Hamilton 1987)
10. Insects have been widely eaten in societies throughout the world and throughout history.*** (Abrams 1987)
11. Insects will be eaten more frequently in societies lacking ample supplies of animal protein and where large swarming insects are common.** (Harris 1985)
12. Most food taboos are placed on meat. Plants and fruits are the subject of few taboos.** (Fessler and Navarrete 2003)
13. Some food taboos exist to protect animals with critical nonfood functions or to prohibit animals that are ecologically and economically costly.** (Harris 1987; Sanderson 2014: 87–92)
14. Tastes and distastes, including disgust reactions, are learned during a critical period of the first two years of life.* (Cashdan 1994; Rozin et al. 1986; Pinker 1997)

15. Disgust is most often associated with animal foods because they are much more likely to contain pathogens than nonanimal foods.** (Fessler and Navarrete 2003)
16. Avoiding foods with high pathogen potential is evolutionarily adaptive.*** (Fessler and Navarrete 2003)
17. People highly esteem sweet foods because of the importance of sweet foods (especially fruits) in the ancestral environment.*** (Harris 1987; Hamilton 1987; Rozin 1987)
18. The desire for sweet foods is an evolutionary adaptation.*** (Harris 1987; Hamilton 1987; Rozin 1987)
19. Dairying economies and genes for adult lactose absorption coevolved in human history.*** (Durham 1991; Sanderson 2014: 92–100)

F. Incest Avoidance Theory

Postulate. Humans rarely mate with close kin. Incest avoidance is the norm in all societies.

Postulate. Incestuous mating is genetically maladaptive and reduces reproductive success.

Postulate. Incest avoidance is an evolved strategy to minimize inbreeding depression, i.e., the production of unhealthy and defective offspring.

1. Incest avoidance is a function of the extent to which children of the opposite sex are reared together in the early years of life.** (Westermarck 1922; Sanderson 2014: 109–115)
2. Children separated at birth and reunited later in life often experience sexual and romantic attraction.** (Sanderson 2001: 218–219)
3. Incest avoidance is often supplemented by strong incest taboos.** (Sanderson 2014: 114–115)
4. Incest taboos above and beyond Westermarck effects result from the recognition of the deleterious effects of close inbreeding.* (Durham 1991)
5. Exogamous marriage represents extended incest avoidance and incest taboos.** (Sanderson 2001: 238–239) *Def.*: Exogamy is the practice of prohibiting marriage within a lineage or clan.
6. Sexual bonding varies inversely with familial bonding.** (Sanderson 2014: 113–114) *Defs*: Sexual bonding = attachment for sexual intercourse. Familial bonding = attachment for caretaking.
7. Incest is most likely to occur between kin who have failed to develop sufficient familial bonds and who experience family dysfunction.** (Sanderson 2014: 114)

G. Mate Choice Theory

Postulate. Human mate choice is the product of sexual selection.

Postulate. Men and women have evolved adaptations for sexual attraction that represent the mating strategies that yield the highest levels of reproductive success.

Postulate. The reproductive potential of males greatly exceeds that of females.

1. Males seek mates who exhibit strong signs of reproductive value.*** (Sanderson 2014: 126–137)
2. Males seek younger females because their reproductive value is greater than that of older females.*** (Sanderson 2014: 129–131)

3. Males value facial attractiveness more than females.*** (Sanderson 2014: 127–129)
4. Faces whose features are average are judged more attractive.*** (Sanderson 2014: 127)
5. Symmetrical faces are judged more attractive.*** (Sanderson 2014: 127–129)
6. Facial attractiveness as judged by averageness and symmetry is a fitness indicator, i.e., an indicator of genetic quality and reproductive value.** (Sanderson 2014: 128)
7. Males prefer females with low waist-to-hip ratios because their reproductive value is greater than that of females with high waist-to-hip ratios.*** (Sanderson 2014: 131–137)
8. Females value status and resources more than males.*** (Sanderson 2014: 137–139)
9. Females prefer as mates males with more status and resources than other males.*** (Sanderson 2014: 137–139)
10. Males with higher status and more resources acquire more and better mates and have more sex with more partners.*** (Sanderson 2014: 141–144)
11. Males with higher status and more resources leave more offspring under conditions of premodern contraception.*** (Sanderson 2014: 141–144)
12. Females with higher levels of facial and sexual attractiveness leave more offspring.** (Sanderson 2014: 128–129)
13. Both sexes value sexual fidelity because infidelity potentially compromises their reproductive interests.*** (Sanderson 2014: 123–125)
14. Males show particular concern with female sexual infidelity, whereas females show more concern for male emotional infidelity.** (Sanderson 2014: 123–125)
15. Female sexual infidelity compromises the reproductive interests of males because females may then cuckold males. A male who is cuckolded commits resources to offspring who are not his own.*** (Sanderson 2014: 123–125)
16. Male emotional infidelity compromises female reproductive interests because males may then abandon their mates for new mates and withdraw resources from the original mates and their offspring.** (Sanderson 2014: 123–125)
17. Both sexes have evolved strategies to detect infidelity.*** (Sanderson 2014: 123–125)
18. Sexual and emotional jealousy are the first line of defense against suspected or actual infidelity.*** (Sanderson 2014: 123–125)
19. Males' additional lines of defense against infidelity include mate guarding by means of claustration and veiling and threatened or actual violence toward mates.*** (Sanderson 2014: 123–125)

H. Sexual Choice Theory

Postulate. Humans are highly sexed, and sex is a major preoccupation of humans everywhere.

1. Most sex is heterosexual, and heterosexuality is the norm in all societies.*** (Uncontested)
2. Heterosexuality is the norm in all societies because it is the only form of sexuality that can promote reproductive success.*** (Uncontested)
3. The male sex drive is stronger and more urgent than the female sex drive.*** (Symons 1979)

4. Copulation is a service provided primarily by women to men in all societies.*** (Symons 1979)
5. Prostitution is primarily a female service to men. Therefore, most prostitutes are women.*** (Posner 1992)
6. Males are more interested than females in multiple mates and sexual variety because such interest promotes male reproductive success more than female reproductive success.*** (Sanderson 2014: 121–122)
7. Males are more interested than females in casual sex because such interest promotes male reproductive success more than female reproductive success.*** (Sanderson 2014: 119–120)
8. Males are more interested in viewing naked female bodies than women are in viewing naked male bodies.*** (Sanderson 2014: 122–123)
9. The male desire to view naked female bodies is an evolutionary adaptation because it increases the probability of sexual intercourse, and by extension reproductive success.*** (Sanderson 2014: 122–123)
10. Pornography exists in all societies and is consumed overwhelmingly by men.*** (Sanderson 2014: 122–123)
11. In societies with high female empowerment, women will display more unrestricted sexual behavior than in societies with low female empowerment.* (Sanderson 2014: 121)
12. A homosexual *orientation*—preferential homosexuality—is rare in human societies because it is nonreproductive.*** (Sanderson 2014: 146)
13. Preferential homosexuality develops when a fetus is exposed to an excess of hormones of the opposite sex during a critical period of neurological development.** (Sanderson 2014: 147–148, 151–152)
14. Many preferential homosexuals exhibit gender atypical behavior in childhood.*** (Sanderson 2014: 149–151)
15. Homosexual *behavior* on the part of preferential heterosexuals—situational homosexuality—is common throughout the world.*** (Sanderson 2014: 144–146)
16. Situational homosexuality will be practiced to the extent that members of the opposite sex are limited or unavailable.** (Sanderson 2014: 145–146)
17. The relative frequency of different sexual practices is determined by the balance of private costs and private benefits of each practice.** (Posner 1992)
18. Masturbation occurs more frequently among middle-class than among lower-class youths because middle-class youths begin to have intercourse at a later age.** (Posner 1992)
19. Petting to orgasm and early marriage are found more frequently in highly religious societies because these societies discourage premarital intercourse.** (Posner 1992)
20. Intolerance of homosexuality makes it more costly, which increases the desire to conceal it. Therefore, the more intolerant a society is of homosexuality, the greater the proportion of homosexuals who marry.** (Posner 1992)
21. The lowest quality of sexual services among prostitutes is provided by streetwalkers and the highest quality by call girls. This is because the search costs for streetwalkers are low and the search costs for call girls are much higher.** (Posner 1992) *Def.*: Search costs are the amount of time and energy expended in finding a sexual partner.
22. Bestiality is more common in rural than in urban areas because the search costs for animals are much lower in rural areas.** (Posner 1992)

23. Urban areas will contain a higher percentage of homosexuals than rural areas because the search costs for homosexual mates are lower in the former.** (Posner 1992)
24. In societies in which there is a high ratio of men to available women, opportunistic homosexuality and prostitution will be more frequent than in societies with an approximately equal ratio of men to available women.** (Posner 1992)
25. As women have more job opportunities in a society, prostitution will occur less frequently.** (Posner 1992)
26. Most rapists are young men.*** (Sanderson 2001: 191–193)
27. Most rape victims are women near their peak fertility.** (Sanderson 2001: 191–193)
28. Rape is a strategy employed by socially marginalized men to mate when conventional mating is difficult or impossible.** (Thornhill and Palmer 2000; Sanderson 2001: 191–193)
29. Rape varies directly with the level of economic inequality.** (Sanderson 2001: 191–193)
30. Rape is more common when the risks of detection and punishment are low.** (Sanderson 2001: 191–193)
31. Rape is common in war because the risk of punishment (but not detection) is low.** (Sanderson 2001: 191–193)
32. Rape is a social violation because it is harmful to a woman's reproductive interests and those of her male kin.*** (Thornhill and Palmer 2000)

I. Marital Choice Theory

Postulate. Marriage exists in all societies.

Postulate. Marriage is a reproductive contract that evolved for the successful rearing of children.

1. Most human societies permit or encourage polygyny, or the marriage of one male to two or more females.*** (Murdock 1967)
2. Most males in most known societies prefer polygyny to monogamy.** (Sanderson 2014: 172–173)
3. Males prefer polygyny because of their desire for multiple copulations and sexual variety.** (Sanderson 2014: 172–173)
4. The number of wives a man has is directly proportional to his status and resources.*** (Sanderson 2014: 171)
5. The greater the prevalence of polygyny, the greater the degree of reproductive inequality among men.*** (Betzig 1986, 2005, 2012)
6. In highly polygynous societies, many men will be monogamous or experience lifelong celibacy.*** (Betzig 1986, 2005, 2012)
7. Although polygyny exists because men want it, women may prefer polygyny over monogamy if the former permits marriage to a man with high status and resources and the latter does not.** (Sanderson 2014: 172–173)
8. Monogamy will displace polygyny when (a) resources are so scarce that no man can support more than one wife (ecologically imposed monogamy), or (b) when companionate marriage is the principal marital arrangement (socially imposed monogamy, or monogamy imposed by law or custom).* (Sanderson 2014: 173–175)

9. All modern industrial societies have socially imposed monogamy because they all have companionate marriage.* (Sanderson 2014: 173–175)
10. Polyandry—the marriage of one woman to two or more men—is rare because it is highly incompatible with male sexual strategies.*** (Sanderson 2014: 175)
11. In the unusual societies in which it is found, polyandry may nevertheless promote reproductive success over several generations.* (Durham 1991)
12. In both nonindustrial and industrial societies, marital dissolution is a positive function of infidelity, especially on the part of the wife.** (Betzig 1989)
13. In nonindustrial societies, marital dissolution is a positive function of infertility.** (Betzig 1989)
14. In both nonindustrial and industrial societies, marital dissolution is a positive function of cruelty or maltreatment, especially on the part of the husband.** (Betzig 1989)
15. In industrial societies, the probability of divorce is a negative function of a couple's number of dependent children.* (Betzig 1989)
16. In nonindustrial societies, to acquire wives the groom's kin group is usually expected to compensate the bride's kin group.*** (Murdock 1967)
17. In societies with limited resources, bride service is one mode of compensation of the bride's kin group.*** (Murdock 1967) Def.: Bride service is work provided by the groom to the bride's kin group.
18. In societies with limited resources, compensation may take the form of the direct exchange of women between lineages or clans.*** (Sanderson 2001: 237–241)
19. In societies with greater resources, the groom's kin group often pays bridewealth to the bride's kin group.*** (Sanderson 2001: 235) Def.: Bridewealth consists of a society's highly valued goods, for example, cattle among cattle pastoralists.
20. Bridewealth payments are a positive function of the perceived reproductive value of the bride.** (Sanderson 2001: 235)
21. Bridewealth payments are a positive function of the degree of polygyny in a society.** (Sanderson 2001: 235)
22. Dowry is most common in highly stratified agrarian societies with socially imposed monogamy.* (Sanderson 2001: 236) Def.: Dowry is a sum of valuables taken by a bride into a marriage.
23. Dowry is a marital strategy in which a family seeks to secure the best husbands for their daughters (i.e., husbands with high status and ample resources).** (Sanderson 2014: 208–209)
24. The greater the level of male power in a society, the larger the age gap between husbands and wives.** (Sanderson 2014: 130)
25. In polygynous societies, as men grow older the age gap between them and their secondary wives increases.** (Sanderson 2014: 129)
26. Capitalist industrialization favors a shift to companionate marriage.** (Coontz 2005)
27. As companionate marriage increases in prevalence, the expectations for marital happiness increase.** (Coontz 2005)
28. As the expectations for marital happiness increase, marital unhappiness increases.* (Coontz 2005)
29. As marital unhappiness increases, the probability of divorce increases.* (Coontz 2005)

J. Kin Selection Theory

Postulate. People organize themselves by genealogical descent in all societies.

Postulate. Humans strongly favor kin over nonkin and close kin over distant kin because such favoritism is a principal means of maximizing reproductive success.

1. In small-scale foraging societies that are highly mobile, nuclear families prevail.*** (Pasternak, Ember, and Ember 1997)
2. In horticultural societies with permanent settlements, people are aggregated into large kin groups (lineages and clans).*** (Pasternak, Ember, and Ember 1997)
3. Lineages and clans are usually exogamous.*** (Murdock 1967)
4. In agrarian societies, where most people are peasant farmers, people live in extended groups, either joint or stem families.*** (Sanderson 2014: 162–163) *Defs.*: Joint family = three generations living under a common roof, pooling resources, and normally headed by the eldest male. Stem family = a married couple, their unmarried minor children, and one married son and his wife and dependent children.
5. Kin relations are the most important social relations in all nonindustrial societies.*** (Sanderson 2014: 162)
6. Kin relations decline in importance in industrial societies but are still pervasive.*** (Sanderson 2014: 163–164)
7. Because males have greater reproductive potential than females, patrilineal descent is the most common form of descent.* (Sanderson 2014: 168) *Def.*: Patrilineal descent is descent through the father's line. Inheritance passes from fathers to sons.
8. In societies where certainty of paternity is low, matrilineal descent is an alternative means of achieving reproductive success.* (Sanderson 2014: 168–170) *Def.*: Matrilineal descent is descent through the mother's line. Inheritance passes from mothers' brothers to maternal nephews.
9. In matrilineal societies, maternal uncle–maternal nephew ties take priority over father-son ties. In patrilineal societies the opposite is true.*** (Sanderson 2001: 222–223)
10. Bilateral descent is found when the reproductive prospects of sons and daughters are approximately equal. (Empirical prediction) *Def.*: Bilateral descent is descent through both fathers and mothers. Inheritance passes from fathers and mothers to sons and daughters.
11. Most patrilineal societies are organized into patrilocal households.*** (Sanderson 2001: 222, 224–225) *Def.*: Patrilocal households involve residence with the husband's father's group.
12. Most matrilineal societies are organized into matrilocal or avunculocal households.*** (Sanderson 2001: 222–223) *Defs.*: Matrilocal households involve residence with the wife's mother's group. Avunculocal households involve residence with the husband's mother's brother.
13. Husband-wife ties are weaker in matrilineal than in patrilineal societies.*** (Fox 1983)
14. Neolocal households are found where nuclear families predominate.*** (Sanderson 2001: 222)

K. Gender Differentiation Theory

Postulate. Humans, like most animal species, are differentiated by sex.

Postulate. Human sexual differentiation is the underlying biological foundation of gender differentiation.

Postulate. Human sexual differentiation interacts with socioecological context to produce gender arrangements and gender-specific behavior.

1. Males are on average more aggressive than females.*** (Sanderson 2014: 216–217)
2. Males are on average more competitive than females.*** (Sanderson 2014: 217–218)
3. Males are on average more risk-prone, females more risk-averse.*** (Sanderson 2014: 218, 220)
4. Males everywhere monopolize warfare.*** (Sanderson 2014: 217)
5. Males everywhere monopolize political leadership.*** (Sanderson 2014: 218–219)
6. Females everywhere monopolize parenting.*** (Sanderson 2014: 219–220)
7. Males and females exhibit different cognitive skills.** (Sanderson 2014: 220–222)
8. Males on average have superior spatial skills, especially for three-dimensional object rotation.** (Sanderson 2014: 220–222)
9. Superior male spatial skills evolved as adaptations facilitating male hunting success.* (Sanderson 2014: 220–222)
10. *Alternative hypothesis*: Superior male spatial skills evolved as adaptations facilitating the male search for mates over wide territories.* (Sanderson 2014: 220–222)
11. Females on average have superior verbal skills.** (Sanderson 2014: 220–222)
12. Females on average have superior skills for object location memory.** (Sanderson 2014: 220–222)
13. Superior object location memory evolved to facilitate female gathering success.** (Sanderson 2014: 221)
14. Gender differentiation is found in all societies.*** (Sanderson 2014: 215)
15. Both sexes have a strong sense of gender identity.*** (Sanderson 2014: 222–224)
16. Gender identity is under the strong influence of sex hormones, especially prenatal hormones.*** (Sanderson 2014: 222–223, 225)
17. In foraging societies, women specialize in plant collection because it is more compatible with child care than hunting.** (Sanderson 2014: 44–45)
18. In foraging societies, men specialize in hunting because of their greater physical strength, better spatial skills, and lesser participation in child care.** (Sanderson 2014: 44–45)
19. In horticultural societies the principal cultivators are usually women.*** (Sanderson 2014: 54)
20. In agrarian societies that use the plow, the principal cultivators are men.*** (Sanderson 2014: 55)
21. In agrarian societies without the plow, women contribute more to cultivation than in agrarian societies with the plow.* (Blumberg 1984, 2009)
22. Men prefer occupations that involve building things, working outdoors, and solving abstract problems.** (Sanderson 2014: 230–232)
23. Women prefer occupations that involve working with people and providing nurturance.** (Sanderson 2014: 230–232)
24. In modern societies, women are overrepresented in occupations that are people-oriented and have a strong nurturant component.*** (Sanderson 2014: 233–234)

25. In modern societies, men are overrepresented in occupations that involve abstract problem-solving.*** (Sanderson 2014: 233–234)
26. In modern societies, men are more likely than women to choose occupations that involve risk and danger.*** (Sanderson 2014: 232–235)
27. Because of their greater upper-body strength, men are more likely to choose occupations that are physically demanding.*** (Sanderson 2014: 232–235)
28. The representation of the sexes in modern occupations is a direct function of their expressed occupational interests.** (Sanderson 2014: 235–237)

L. Gender Inequality Theory

Postulate. Males and females compete for positional advantage.

1. A sex's control over resources is the principal determinant of its degree of positional advantage. The most important of these resources are economic and political.** (Sanderson 2001: 206–212)
2. Women's status is a positive function of their contribution to economic subsistence.** (Blumberg 1984; Sanderson 2001: 206–212)
3. Women's status is higher in horticultural than in agrarian societies without the plow.* (Blumberg 1984; Sanderson 2001: 208)
4. Women's status is lowest in agrarian societies with the plow.** (Blumberg 1984; Sanderson 2001: 208–209)
5. Women's status has improved in modern industrial societies because of their increasing economic contribution.** (Sanderson 2014: 228–229)
6. Women's status has improved in modern industrial societies because of modern technological inventions reducing the amount of time needed for domestic work.** (Sanderson 2014: 228–229)
7. Women's status has improved in modern industrial societies because of innovations in contraceptive technology giving women increasing control over reproduction.** (Tiger 1999)
8. Women's status is higher in matrilineal societies than in patrilineal societies.** (Sanderson 2001: 208)
9. Because men are more competitive than women, they are overrepresented in a society's high-status positions.** (Sanderson 2014: 217–218)
10. In modern societies, many women choose occupations that are highly compatible with child care.*** (Phipps, Burton, and Lethbridge 2001; Browne 2002; O'Neill 2003)
11. Occupations compatible with child care tend to pay less and have fewer opportunities for promotion.*** (Phipps, Burton, and Lethbridge 2001; Browne 2002; O'Neill 2003)
12. Therefore, women tend to be overrepresented in lower-status, lower-paying jobs.*** (Phipps, Burton, and Lethbridge 2001; Browne 2002; O'Neill 2003)

M. Status Competition Theory

Postulate. Status seeking is an evolutionary adaptation that promotes the acquisition of economic resources and mates.

Postulate. Status seeking as an evolutionary adaptation is also valued for its own sake.

Postulate. Status seeking has biochemical foundations in the hormone testosterone and the neurotransmitter serotonin.

Postulate. The acquisition of status promoted reproductive success in the ancestral environment and may continue to do so in modern environments.

Postulate. People living in modern novel environments engage in status competition regardless of its consequences for reproductive success.

1. People compete for status in all of the groups and institutions of all societies.*** (Sanderson 2014: 245–247)
2. Status equality is not natural to humans. To exist, threats to equality must be continually policed.** (Sanderson 2014: 247–248)
3. People acquire *emotional energy* (EE) from status achievement.** (Collins 2004) *Defs.*: Positive EE = confidence, high self-regard, enthusiasm, exhilaration. Negative EE = lack of confidence, low self-regard, disinterest, depression.
4. When people rise in status, their positive EE increases.** (Collins 2004)
5. When people fall in status, their negative EE increases.** (Collins 2004)
6. Status is enhanced through the accumulation of resources.*** (Sanderson 2014: 252–254, 256–259; Veblen [1899] 2007)
7. Status is enhanced by the conspicuous display of resources.*** (Sanderson 2014: 252–254, 256–259; Veblen [1899] 2007)
8. Under some circumstances, status is enhanced by giving resources away.*** (Sanderson 2014: 249–251, 256–259; Bliege Bird and Smith 2005)
9. Status seeking through resource giving signals a person's special ability to produce resources.** (Sanderson 2014: 249–251, 256–259; Bliege Bird and Smith 2005)
10. Status seeking through resource giving may also signal the possession of an extremely large fund of remaining resources.** (Sanderson 2014: 250, 256)
11. The desire for status is infinitely expandable. One can never have enough status.** (Veblen [1899] 2007; Dowling 1979; Hammond 1999)
12. In societies with sharp status differentiation, rituals of deference and demeanor tend to accompany interactions among individuals of higher and lower status.*** (Collins 2009)
13. In societies with sharp status differentiation, high status positions are often accompanied by elaborate dress and other paraphernalia.*** (Collins 2009)
14. Agrarian societies achieved the highest levels of status differentiation in human history.*** (Collins 2009)
15. Status differentiation is accompanied by order-giving and order-taking.*** (Collins 2009)
16. In highly status differentiated societies, people signify high status by the possession of cultural capital.*** (Bourdieu 1984). *Def.*: Cultural capital consists of refinements in the areas of art, music, literature, language, poise, wit, and overall cultural knowledge.
17. Status differentiation has been partially reversed in the transition to modern societies.** (Collins 2009)
18. The reversal of status differentiation is a direct function of the widespread diffusion of wealth throughout a population.** (Lenski 1966)
19. The reversal of status differentiation is signified by the elimination or diminution of titles, paraphernalia of rank, and rituals of deference and demeanor.** (Collins 2009)

N. Wealth Accumulation Theory

Postulate. Humans naturally compete to attain resources because the possession of resources promoted reproductive success in the ancestral environment.

Postulate. In most instances the possession of resources promotes reproductive success in modern environments.

Postulate. In modern environments resource possession is valued for its own sake irrespective of its consequences for reproductive success.

1. Competition for resources normally leads to resource inequality.*** (Sanderson 2014: 245–260)
2. Resource equality can only be maintained if resource competition is constantly policed and leveling mechanisms regularly employed.** (Sanderson 2014: 247–248)
3. Resource equality can only be maintained in societies of very small scale.*** (Sanderson 2014: 245–260)
4. Resource equality can only be maintained in societies living at or near subsistence level.*** (Sanderson 2014: 245–260)
5. When societies exceed subsistence level, resource competition intensifies and resource inequality becomes more likely.*** (Sanderson 2014: 245–260)
6. People are unequally endowed to compete in status and resource competition (e.g., some are bigger, more intelligent, more aggressive or ambitious, more clever, or more deceitful).*** (Lenski 1966)
7. The greater the amount of resources produced beyond subsistence level, the greater the intensity of resource competition and therefore the greater the extent of resource inequality.*** (Lenski 1966)
8. Because most hunter-gatherer societies exist at subsistence level, they lack resource inequality.*** (Testart 1982, 1988)
9. Hunter-gatherer societies with resource abundance and the ability to store food have resource inequality.*** (Testart 1982, 1988)
10. Small-scale horticultural societies produce small economic surpluses. Resource inequality is therefore limited, although status competition may be highly developed.*** (Lenski 1966)
11. Advanced horticultural societies with large economic surpluses have resource inequality in the form of class distinctions based on wealth and status.*** (Sanderson 2014: 252–253; Lenski 1966)
12. Agrarian societies with very large economic surpluses have great resource inequality and extreme wealth gaps between nobles and peasants.*** (Sanderson 2014: 253–254; Lenski 1966)
13. Wealth is more evenly distributed throughout the population in modern industrial societies than in stratified preindustrial societies.*** (Lenski 1966)
14. A more egalitarian distribution of wealth is a function of the shift to market-dominated economies and radical changes in the occupational structure.*** (Lenski 1966)

O. Geopolitical Theory

Postulate. The struggle for power is universal.

Postulate. People naturally compete for power because it confers status and resources, which promoted reproductive success in ancestral environments.

Postulate. Power can also be pleasurable and rewarding in itself.

Postulate. Although people seek to attain and hold power, they dislike being subjected to it.

1. The struggle for power can be suppressed only if it is sufficiently policed.*** (Sanderson 2014: 269–271)
2. The struggle for power can only be sufficiently policed in small-scale societies with extensive face-to-face interaction.*** (Sanderson 2014: 269–271)
3. The struggle for power is limited to the extent that societies possess few resources to control.*** (Sanderson 2014: 269–271)
4. As a society's resources expand, the struggle for power intensifies.*** (Sanderson 2014: 271–281)
5. The struggle for power is greater when the resources to be controlled are of high value.*** (Sanderson 2014: 271–281)
6. In small-scale societies, most justice is private.*** (Sanderson 2014: 270–271)
7. As societies evolve in size and scale, public justice gradually replaces private justice.*** (Sanderson 2014: 270–271)
8. The form of political organization is a function of the degree of population pressure.*** (Carneiro 1970)
9. The form of political organization is a function of the mode of subsistence technology and the level of economic surplus.*** (Lenski 1966; Sanderson 1995, 1999)
10. The form of political organization is a function of the degree of environmental circumscription.** (Carneiro 1970) *Def.*: Environmental circumscription = barriers to exit from an environment due to large bodies of water, areas of inhospitable land, or mountain ranges.
11. The form of political organization is a function of a society's type of economy and the level of its development.** (Sanderson 1995; Collins 2009)
12. The form of political organization is a function of a society's relations with neighboring societies.** (Collins 2009)
13. The form of political organization is a function of a society's degree of external threat.** (Collins 2009)
14. Small-scale societies based on foraging or simple horticulture lack formal positions of power and authority. There are no leaders with binding authority to enforce decisions.*** (Sanderson 2014: 269–271)
15. Where horticulture is more intensive and productive, autonomous villages tend to be brought under centralized control of chiefs who have formal authority and command obedience and deference.** (Carneiro 1981; Sanderson 2014: 271–274)
16. The acquisition and maintenance of a high degree of authority within chiefdoms requires a military apparatus to check rebellion.** (Sanderson 2014: 273–274)
17. Chiefdoms evolve into states when political leaders establish an administration capable of holding a monopoly of force over a defined territory.*** (Sanderson 2014: 274)
18. States control the means of violence through armies and militias.*** (Sanderson 2014: 274)
19. States can usually form only in societies using advanced horticultural or agrarian techniques of subsistence capable of producing large economic surpluses.*** (Sanderson 2014: 274–278)

20. Complex chiefdoms and premodern states use conquest as the principal means of obtaining wealth and other resources (land, slaves, etc.).*** (Sanderson 2014: 278–281; Gat 2006; Snooks 1997)
21. States seek to advance their level of military technology in order to increase the killing power of military forces and weapons and thus the likelihood of successful political conquest.*** (Collins 2009)
22. Most states have centralized bureaucratic leadership.*** (Sanderson 2014: 280)
23. Decentralized feudal states form when an economy is too rudimentary for centralized administration and when the presence of the horse permits a warrior aristocracy mounted on horseback.** (Gat 2006; Sanderson 2014: 279–280)
24. Feudal states are rife with internecine conflict.*** (Sanderson 2014: 279–280)
25. People who are granted or who attain formal authority tend to abuse it. They oppress those subject to it in order to maintain or enhance their power and the resources that accompany it.*** (Sanderson 2014: 267–269)
26. In societies with leaders who have formal authority, people have a natural tendency to obey them.*** (Sanderson 2014: 266–267; Salter 1995: 15–16, 89–95; Somit and Peterson 2005)
27. People are more likely to obey authority if they consider it legitimate.*** (Weber [1923] 1978)
28. Obedience to authority is an evolutionary adaptation because obedient state subjects throughout history were more likely to survive and leave offspring than disobedient subjects. (Untested prediction)
29. The more oppressive the state (up to a point), the greater the likelihood of obedience. (Untested prediction)
30. When the power exercised over them becomes too oppressive, people will rebel against it.*** (Sanderson 2010)
31. In most societies, people subject to power lack the resources necessary to successfully challenge power holders.*** (Sanderson 2010)
32. Revolt against power-holders is common, successful rebellion uncommon.*** (Sanderson 2010)
33. Most attempted revolutions fail because revolutionaries lack sufficient resources to overthrow states with powerful military force.*** (Sanderson 2010)
34. Revolutionaries can succeed only if they are militarily strong, are highly mobilized, and are attempting to overthrow politically and militarily vulnerable states.*** (Sanderson 2010)
35. The ever-present desire for power means that people are not naturally predisposed toward democratic government.*** (Somit and Peterson 2005)
36. Democracy is rare in human history.*** (Somit and Peterson 2005)
37. Democratic government can only arise when the large mass of the population possesses resources necessary for the extraction of democratic concessions from ruling elites. Such resources have only existed in modern capitalist economies.** (Sanderson 2001: 315–318; Sanderson and Alderson 2005: 134–139)
38. Therefore, democratic governments are found only in modern capitalist societies.** (Sanderson and Alderson 2005: 134–139)
39. Democratic government is precarious and unstable because of the natural struggle for power.*** (Somit and Peterson 2005)

P. Human Aggression Theory

Postulate. Aggression is the threat or use of violence against conspecifics. The threshold for human violence is low.

Postulate. Violence is both interpersonal and intergroup.

Postulate. Violence is easily elicited.

1. Interpersonal violence (violent assault, rape, homicide) is common and frequent in societies lacking centralized authority and laws.*** (Sanderson 2014: 298–302; Wrangham and Peterson 1996; Wrangham, Wilson, and Muller 2006)
2. In every society, most interpersonal violence occurs between and among young males.*** (Sanderson 2014: 289–290)
3. In small-scale societies, the level of interpersonal violence is a direct function of the level of competition for women as mates.** (Sanderson 2014: 291–296)
4. In modern societies, the level of interpersonal violence is a function of the degree of economic inequality.** (Blau and Blau 1982; Daly, Wilson, and Vasdev 2001; Sanderson 2014: 291–292)
5. In modern societies, interpersonal violence is most likely among economically marginalized men who are competing for status and access to mates.** (Daly and Wilson 1988)
6. Interpersonal violence in all societies is a function of the degree to which men experience threats to their status and honor.** (Daly and Wilson 1988)
7. Only a small proportion of homicides are directed toward genetic relatives.*** (Daly and Wilson 1988)
8. State-organized societies pacify large populations. They limit interpersonal violence through law. (Uncontested)
9. Violence of husbands toward wives is directly proportional to male suspicions of female infidelity or to actual knowledge of infidelity.*** (Sanderson 2014: 293–294)
10. Violence of husbands toward wives is a positive function of wives' reproductive value.** (Daly and Wilson 1988; Wilson and Daly 1993)
11. Violence of husbands toward wives is a positive function of the age gap between them.** (Daly and Wilson 1988; Wilson and Daly 1993)
12. Violence of husbands toward wives is a positive function of the likelihood or actual occurrence of wives' abandonment of their mates.** (Daly and Wilson 1988; Wilson and Daly 1993; Buss 2005)
13. Interpersonal violence has declined dramatically with societal modernization.*** (Pinker 2011)
14. War in small-scale societies is common and frequent.*** (Keeley 1996; LeBlanc 2003; Sanderson 2014: 298–302)
15. War deaths in small-scale societies are numerous, and war is one of the leading causes of male deaths.*** (Keeley 1996; LeBlanc 2003; Sanderson 2014: 298–302)
16. The level of war in small-scale societies is a positive function of the degree of resource competition and the need to eliminate competitors.** (Sanderson 2014: 303–304)
17. Women are the most important resource inducing small-scale war.** (Sanderson 2014: 304–305)
18. The desire for revenge is a major cause of war in small-scale societies.*** (Chagnon 2013)

19. Chiefdoms and states are conquest societies.*** (Sanderson 2014: 305–310)
20. Large-scale war among chiefdoms and states is a positive function of the need for more land to support denser populations.*** (Carneiro 1970, 1990; Sanderson 1995)
21. Large-scale war among chiefdoms and states is a positive function of the desire of ruling elites for more wealth, power, and status.*** (Sanderson 2014: 305–310; Gat 2006)
22. Competition for women remains a motive, even if only a secondary motive, for war in large-scale societies.* (Gat 2006)
23. War in modern societies is a positive function of ethnic conflict (civil war) and nationalism (interstate war).*** (Gat 2006)
24. Modern democratic societies infrequently fight each other in major wars.** (Pinker 2011)
25. Modern capitalist societies infrequently fight each other in major wars.** (Pinker 2011; Mousseau, Hegre, and O'Neal 2003; Gartzke 2007; Gartzke and Hewitt 2010)
26. Modern capitalist societies infrequently fight each other in major wars because war is no longer the principal means of acquiring wealth in market-based economies.** (Mousseau, Hegre, and O'Neal 2003; Gartzke 2007; Gartzke and Hewitt 2010)

Q. Ethnic Attachment Theory

Postulate. Humans have natural (primordial) ethnic attachments, which may be based on language, culture, physical appearance, or any combination thereof.

Postulate. Because members of the same ethny share more genes in common with each other than with members of other ethnies, ethnic attachments represent extended kin selection and thus promote reproductive success.

Postulate. Ethnic attachments evolved when humans lived in tribes in the ancestral environment.

Postulate. Strong ethnic attachments are evolved adaptations that promoted the survival of one's tribe, and thus one's co-ethnics, in intertribal conflict in ancestral environments.

Postulate. Evolutionary adaptations for strong ethnic attachments persist into modernity.

Postulate. Modern ethnic groups are large-scale tribes.

1. Ethnic attachments frequently lead to the denigration of out-groups. (Uncontested)
2. The degree of denigration of out-groups is a positive function of their linguistic, cultural, or physical differences from the in-group.** (Smith 1981; van den Berghe 1981)
3. Denigration of out-groups will be greater when two or more differences (ethnic markers) exist simultaneously.** (Smith 1981; van den Berghe 1981)
4. Denigration of out-groups will be greater when out-groups exhibit different levels of economic achievement and success (either more or less).** (Smith 1981; van den Berghe 1981)
5. Race differences arose as humans migrated out of Africa and occupied other regions with very different environmental challenges to survival and reproduction.*** (Sanderson 2014: 321–324)
6. Race and ethnicity overlap. Ethnies differ biologically as well as culturally.** (Sanderson 2014: 330–332; Cavalli-Sforza, Menozzi, and Piazza 1994)

7. Racism is a positive function of the physical differences between groups and achievement levels of the respective groups.** (van den Berghe 1967, 1981)
8. Racism is ancient and has existed in many societies.** (Sarich and Miele 2004; Sanderson 2014: 324–326)
9. Ethnic heterogeneity is a positive function of the degree of migration and political conquest.*** (Smith 1986)
10. The greater the degree of ethnic heterogeneity within a state, the greater the level of conflict.*** (Vanhanen 2012)
11. The greater the degree of competition of ethnic groups for resources, the greater the level of conflict.*** (Vanhanen 2012)
12. The more an ethny monopolizes political and economic resources, the greater the level of hostility directed toward it by other ethnies.*** (Vanhanen 2012)
13. Violent ethnic conflict is most likely when two or more ethnies compete for control of a state.* (Wimmer, Cederman, and Min 2009)
14. Increasing worldwide immigration will lead to an increase in the amount and intensity of ethnic conflict. (Empirical prediction)

R. Religious Choice Theory

Postulate. Humans have a natural religious sense that is an evolved adaptation.

Postulate. Religion provides people with rewards that are otherwise unavailable.

Postulate. In nonindustrial societies, most religious beliefs and practices are directed toward this-worldly rewards.

Postulate. In modern industrial societies, most religious beliefs and practices are motivated primarily by the search for other-worldly rewards, or rewards otherwise unavailable in social life.

1. As an evolutionary adaptation, religion promotes health.** (Sanderson 2008b)
2. As an evolutionary adaptation, religion promotes reproductive success.** (Sanderson 2008b)
3. The primordial religious practitioners are shamans.** (Sanderson 2014: 341–342) *Def.*: Shamans are religious practitioners who use trance states for healing and curing and for locating game animals.
4. Some nonindustrial societies have a high god.*** (Swanson 1960; Murdock 1967; Sanderson and Roberts 2008) *Def.*: A high god is a society's only god and is thought to have created the universe and be the source of many natural and supernatural events.
5. Some high gods are active and are worshiped.*** (Swanson 1960; Murdock 1967; Sanderson and Roberts 2008)
6. Some high gods are remote and unconcerned with human affairs.*** (Swanson 1960; Murdock 1967; Sanderson and Roberts 2008)
7. Some high gods are concerned with human morality.*** (Swanson 1960; Murdock 1967; Sanderson and Roberts 2008)
8. Some high gods are unconcerned with human morality.*** (Swanson 1960; Murdock 1967; Sanderson and Roberts 2008)
9. In religious evolution, high gods have become more common, more active, and more concerned with human morality.*** (Sanderson and Roberts 2008)

10. Most religions have no full-time religious practitioners or formal doctrines.*** (Wallace 1966)
11. Ecclesiastical religions arose with the development of civilization and writing.** (Sanderson and Roberts 2008) *Def.*: Ecclesiastical religions are those with priesthoods (often full-time) and official doctrines (often written) and in which priests interpret doctrines for laypersons.
12. Ecclesiastical religions may be polytheistic or monotheistic.*** (Wallace 1966; Sanderson and Roberts 2008)
13. Polytheistic religions with numerous specialized gods are characteristic of nonindustrial states.*** (Stark 2007)
14. Rulers in nonindustrial states look to specialized gods for assistance in the attainment of various worldly goals, such as success in war.*** (Stark 2007)
15. State rulers engage in exchange relationships with specialized gods by means of regular sacrifices of food, especially slaughtered animals.*** (Stark and Bainbridge 1987; Stark 2007)
16. Throughout human history, polytheistic religions have been gradually supplanted by world transcendent religions.*** (Stark 2007)
17. Some world transcendent religions are devoted to the worship of a single omnipresent, omniscient, and omnipotent god.*** (Stark 2007)
18. Some world transcendent religions are polytheistic.*** (Stark 2007)
19. World transcendent religions impose much greater demands on their followers than polytheistic religions.*** (Stark 2007; Norenzayan 2013)
20. World transcendent religions evolved to meet people's changing religious needs.* (Sanderson 2008a)
21. The most important of these needs was release from worldly suffering.* (Sanderson 2008a)
22. The desire for release from suffering was a response to increasing ontological insecurity.* (Sanderson 2008a)
23. Increasing ontological insecurity was the result of the disruptive effects of the increasing intensity and killing power of war.* (Sanderson 2008a)
24. Increasing ontological insecurity was the result of the disruptive effects of large-scale urbanization.* (Sanderson 2008a)
25. Nonindustrial societies contain few atheists.** (Barrett 2004)
26. Secularization is a positive function of high levels of ontological security.** (Norris and Inglehart 2011)
27. Secularization is a positive function of high levels of scientific and educational development.** (Norris and Inglehart 2011)

Falsifying Darwinian Conflict Theory

Popper (1959) has said that a scientific theory must declare, ideally in advance, what it empirically forbids. If what is empirically forbidden is observed to occur, then the occurrence counts as a falsifying test. However, this falsifying test does not necessarily overturn, by itself, the theory or proposition in question. Other tests may be required.

Below is a list of empirical observations forbidden by DCT. To the extent that these forbidden phenomena are observed to occur, DCT is falsified. So far none of these forbidden phenomena have ever been observed. (The list is partial and mainly illustrative.)

A comprehensive list would be a practical impossibility within the space limitations of this chapter.)

1. Foraging societies living at extremely high population densities.
2. Societies in which women hunt and men gather.
3. Agrarian societies in which women plow and men perform domestic work.
4. Societies in which people prefer to maximize the amount of time and energy devoted to economic subsistence.
5. Societies in which individuals are indifferent to the costs and benefits of their economic behavior.
6. Societies in which plant foods are more highly valued than animal proteins.
7. Societies with large-scale dog and cat slaughtering industries.
8. Societies in which men prefer as mates older women judged to be unattractive.
9. Societies in which incestuous mating is widespread throughout the population.
10. Societies in which women show more interest than men in casual sex and sexual variety.
11. Societies in which pornography is consumed primarily by women.
12. Societies in which neither sex expresses sexual jealousy.
13. Societies in which most prostitutes are men.
14. Societies in which men are indifferent to cuckoldry.
15. Societies in which most rapes are committed by high-status men.
16. Societies in which there are as many preferential homosexuals as heterosexuals.
17. Societies in which women prefer as mates men of low status and few resources.
18. Societies in which men seek as mates women of higher status and women seek men who are younger than they are.
19. Societies without marriage.
20. Agrarian societies in which companionate marriage is the norm.
21. Societies in which people consistently favor nonkin over kin and distant kin over close kin.
22. Societies practicing polygyny in which the polygynists are low-status men.
23. Industrial societies organized in patrilineal clans.
24. Foraging societies practicing dowry.
25. Industrial societies with bridewealth payments.
26. Small-scale societies in which half the population chooses to remain childless.
27. Societies in which men perform most of the parental care.
28. Societies in which women invest more in mating than in parental care.
29. Step-offspring consistently receiving better care than natural offspring.
30. Societies without sexual differentiation.
31. Societies in which the sexes have no sense of gender identity.
32. Societies in which women have superior spatial skills and men superior verbal skills.
33. Industrial societies in which occupations with a strong nurturant component are held primarily by men.
34. Societies in which veiling and claustration are directed toward men rather than women.
35. Societies in which women compete more vigorously than men for high-status positions.
36. Societies in which the achievement of high status is accompanied by a decline in emotional energy.

37. Societies in which people of high status take orders from those of low status.
38. Societies of large size and great complexity that have no status distinctions or wealth inequalities.
39. Agrarian societies with constitutional democracies.
40. Societies in which revolts and revolutions are always successful.
41. Societies in which people enjoy being dominated.
42. Societies in which most killing occurs between kin.
43. Societies in which most warriors are women.
44. Agrarian states that do not fight wars.
45. Societies in which most homicides are committed by older women against other older women.
46. Societies lacking a sense of ethnic identification.
47. Societies with high levels of ethnic heterogeneity in which there is no ethnic conflict.
48. Societies without religious beliefs and practices.
49. Hunter-gatherers practicing ecclesiastical religions and modern industrialists practicing shamanic religions.
50. Nonindustrial societies with many atheists.
51. Trajectories of social evolution in which large-scale and complex societies give way to smaller and simpler ones.
52. Trajectories of social evolution in which inequalities decrease rather than increase over time.

Conclusion

DCT is a work in progress. It is unfinished and, indeed, can never be finished. Many more theories and propositions can be added to those that already exist, and new domains of application will arise, which will require theories and propositions of their own. Moreover, some theories and propositions will prove untenable as the result of falsifying tests. They will have to be discarded and replaced with alternatives. Logical and other errors will need to be corrected. But this is the very nature of science. There are always errors of reasoning, anomalies, falsifying tests, new phenomena to be discovered, and new predictions to be made. In the near future revised and updated versions of DCT will need to be produced. Eventually it will disappear and its corroborated propositions will be incorporated into an improved research program. Most of the changes, I suspect, are likely to come from the rapidly expanding fields of neuroscience and cognitive science.

Notes

1. The influence of ethology on Goffman is little recognized (if recognized at all) by sociologists. Frank Salter (1995), himself an ethologist, has identified a number of Goffman's ideas that connect with ethology.
2. Thornhill and Palmer (2000). The evolutionary psychologists Tooby and Cosmides (1989, 1992) point out that the brain could not have evolved as a domain-general organ because such an organ would be too clumsy to have had much adaptive import. "Many adaptive problems that humans routinely solve," Tooby and Cosmides say, "are simply not solvable by any known general problem-solving strategy, as demonstrated by formal solvability analyses on language acquisition" (1992: 111). They add that "domain-general, content-independent mechanisms are inefficient, handicapped, or inert compared to systems that also include specialized techniques for solving particular families of adaptive problems. A specialized mechanism can make use of the enduring relationships present in the problem-domain or in the related features of the world by reflecting

these content-specific relationships in its problem-solving structure. Such mechanisms will be far more efficient than general-purpose mechanisms, which must expend time, energy, and risk learning these relationships through [an inefficient process of trial and error]" (1992: 111).

Special-purpose mental designs are also implied by our knowledge of how nonpsychological adaptations are designed. The human body is nothing at all like a general-purpose system, but rather is an extremely complex system consisting of many highly specialized cells, tissues, and organs that do very specific things.

3. Thornhill and Palmer (2000: 18) quote Donald Symons (1987) on this point: "Extreme behavioral plasticity implies extreme mental complexity and stability; that is, an elaborate human nature. Behavioral plasticity for its own sake would be worse than useless, random variation suicide. During the course of evolutionary history the more plastic hominid behavior became the more complex the neural machinery must have become to channel this plasticity into adaptive action."

4. I do not like the term *culture* because it has been given many, often inconsistent and contradictory, meanings. I have sought to replace it with a more suitable term but have so far been unsuccessful. The closest I have come is the term *socioecological context*, which has a similar meaning. (This term is not my own invention. I picked it up somewhere along the way but have forgotten where I originally obtained it. I might have gotten it from Richard Sosis and Candace Alcorta, or from the evolutionary ecologist Eric Alden Smith.)

References

Abrams, H. L. 1987. "The Preference for Animal Protein and Fat: A Cross-Cultural Survey." In *Food and Evolution: Toward a Theory of Human Food Habits*, edited by M. Harris and E. B. Ross, 207–223. Philadelphia, PA: Temple University Press.
Alexander, R. D. 1987. *The Biology of Moral Systems*. New York: Aldine de Gruyter.
Allen, J. L. 2006. *Student Atlas of World Politics*. 7th ed. New York: McGraw-Hill.
Barkow, J. H. 1989. *Darwin, Sex, and Status*. Toronto: University of Toronto Press.
Barrett, J. L. 2004. *Why Would Anyone Believe in God?* Walnut Creek, CA: AltaMira Press.
Berger, P. L. 1986. *The Capitalist Revolution: Fifty Propositions about Prosperity, Equality, and Liberty*. New York: Basic Books.
Betzig, L. L. 1986. *Despotism and Differential Reproduction*. New York: Aldine de Gruyter.
———. 1989. "Causes of Conjugal Dissolution: A Cross-Cultural Study." *Current Anthropology* 30: 654–676.
———. 2005. "Politics as Sex: The Old Testament Case." *Evolutionary Psychology* 3: 326–346.
———. 2012. "Means, Variances, and Ranges in Reproductive Success: Comparative Evidence." *Evolution and Human Behavior* 33: 309–317.
Black, D. 1995. "The Epistemology of Pure Sociology." *Law and Social Inquiry* 20: 829–870.
Blau, J. R., and P. M. Blau. 1982. "The Cost of Inequality: Metropolitan Structure and Violent Crime." *American Sociological Review* 47: 114–129.
Bliege Bird, R., and E. A. Smith. 2005. "Signaling Theory, Strategic Interaction, and Symbolic Capital." *Current Anthropology* 46: 221–248.
Blumberg, R. L. 1984. "A General Theory of Gender Stratification." In *Sociological Theory 1984*, edited by Randall Collins, 23–101. San Francisco: Jossey-Bass.
———. 2009. "Mothers of Invention? The Myth-Breaking History and Planetary Promise of Women's Key Roles in Subsistence Technology." In *Techno-Well: Impact of Technology on Psychological Well-Being*, edited by Yair Amichai-Hamburger, 227–259. Cambridge: Cambridge University Press.
Bourdieu, P. 1984. *Distinction: A Social Critique of the Judgement of Taste*. Translated by Richard Nice. Cambridge, MA: Harvard University Press.
Boyd, R., and P. J. Richerson. 1985. *Culture and the Evolutionary Process*. Chicago: University of Chicago Press.
Browne, K. R. 2002. *Biology at Work: Rethinking Sexual Equality*. New Brunswick, NJ: Rutgers University Press.
Buss, D. M. 2005. *The Murderer Next Door: Why the Mind Is Designed to Kill*. New York: Penguin Press.
Carneiro, R. L. 1970. "A Theory of the Origin of the State." *Science* 169: 733–738.
———. 1981. "The Chiefdom: Precursor of the State." In *The Transition to Statehood in the New World*, edited by G. D. Jones and R. R. Kautz, 37–79. New York: Cambridge University Press.
———. 1990. "Chiefdom-Level Warfare as Exemplified in Fiji and the Cauca Valley." In *The Anthropology of War*, edited by J. Haas, 190–211. New York: Cambridge University Press.
Cashdan, E. A. 1994. "A Sensitive Period for Learning about Food." *Human Nature* 5: 279–291.

Cavalli-Sforza, L. L., P. Menozzi, and A. Piazza. 1994. *The History and Geography of Human Genes*. Princeton, NJ: Princeton University Press.
Chagnon, N. A. 2013. *Noble Savages: My Life among Two Dangerous Tribes—the Yanomamö and the Anthropologists*. New York: Simon & Schuster.
Chesnais, J. 2001. "Comment: A March Toward Population Recession." *Population and Development Review* 27 (Supplement): 255–259.
Chisholm, J. S., J. A. Quinlivan, R. W. Peterson, and D. A. Coall. 2005. "Early Stress Predicts Age at Menarche and First Birth, Adult Attachment, and Expected Lifespan." *Human Nature* 16: 233–265.
CIA World Factbook. 2010. Washington, DC: Central Intelligence Agency.
Cleland, J. 2001. "The Effects of Improved Survival on Fertility: A Reassessment." *Population and Development Review* 27 (Supplement): 60–92.
Collins, R. 1974. "Reassessments of Sociological History: The Empirical Validity of the Conflict Tradition." *Theory and Society* 1: 147–178.
———. 1975. *Conflict Sociology: Toward an Explanatory Science*. New York: Academic Press.
———. 1995. "Prediction in Macrosociology: The Case of the Soviet Collapse." *American Journal of Sociology* 100: 1552–1593.
———. 2004. *Interaction Ritual Chains*. Princeton, NJ: Princeton University Press.
———. 2009. *Conflict Sociology: A Sociological Classic Updated*. Abridged and updated by S. K. Sanderson. Boulder, CO: Paradigm Publishers.
Coontz, S. 2005. *Marriage, a History: How Love Conquered Marriage*. New York: Penguin Books.
Daly, M., and M. Wilson. 1988. *Homicide*. New York: Aldine de Gruyter.
———. 1998. *The Truth about Cinderella: A Darwinian View of Parental Love*. New Haven, CT: Yale University Press.
Daly, M., M. Wilson, and S. Vasdev. 2001. "Income Inequality and Homicide Rates in Canada and the United States." *Canadian Journal of Criminology* 43: 219–236.
Dowling, J. H. 1979. "The Goodfellows vs. the Dalton Gang: The Assumptions of Economic Anthropology." *Journal of Anthropological Research* 35: 292–307.
Durham, W. H. 1991. *Coevolution: Genes, Culture, and Human Diversity*. Stanford, CA: Stanford University Press.
Ellis, B. J. 2004. "Timing of Pubertal Maturation in Girls: An Integrated Life History Approach." *Psychological Bulletin* 130: 920–958.
Ellis, B. J., J. E. Bates, K. A. Dodge, D. M. Fergusson, L. J. Horwood, G. S. Pettit, and L. Woodward. 2003. "Does Father Absence Place Daughters at Special Risk for Early Sexual Activity and Teenage Pregnancy?" *Child Development* 74: 801–821.
Fessler, D.M.T., and C. D. Navarrete. 2003. "Meat Is Good to Taboo: Dietary Proscriptions as a Product of the Interaction of Psychological Mechanisms and Social Processes." *Journal of Cognition and Culture* 3: 1–40.
Feuer, L. S. 1978. "Marx and Engels as Sociobiologists." *Survey* 23 (4): 109–136.
Fox, R. 1983. *Kinship and Marriage*. New York: Cambridge University Press.
Frejka, T., and J. Ross. 2001. "Paths to Sub-replacement Fertility: The Empirical Evidence." *Population and Development Review* 27 (Supplement): 213–254.
Friedman, D., and M. Hechter. 1988. "The Contribution of Rational Choice Theory to Macrosociological Research." *Sociological Theory* 6: 201–218.
Gartzke, E. 2007. "The Capitalist Peace." *American Journal of Political Science* 51: 166–191.
Gartzke, E., and J. J. Hewitt. 2010. "International Crises and the Capitalist Peace." *International Interactions* 36: 115–145.
Gat, A. 2006. *War in Human Civilization*. Oxford: Oxford University Press.
Goldstone, J. A. 1991. *Revolution and Rebellion in the Early Modern World*. Berkeley: University of California Press.
Goodwin, J. 2001. *No Other Way Out: States and Revolutionary Movements, 1945–1991*. New York: Cambridge University Press.
Hakim, C. 2003. "A New Approach to Explaining Fertility Patterns: Preference Theory." *Population and Development Review* 29: 349–374.
Hamilton, W. J. III. 1987. "Omnivorous Primate Diets and Human Overconsumption of Meat." In *Food and Evolution: Toward a Theory of Human Food Habits*, edited by M. Harris and E. B. Ross, 117–132. Philadelphia, PA: Temple University Press.
Hammond, M. 1999. "Arouser Depreciation and the Expansion of Social Inequality." *Social Perspectives on Emotion* 5: 339–358.
Harris, M. 1968. *The Rise of Anthropological Theory*. New York: Crowell.
———. 1974. *Cows, Pigs, Wars, and Witches: The Riddles of Culture*. New York: Random House.
———. 1977. *Cannibals and Kings: The Origins of Cultures*. New York: Random House.
———. 1979. *Cultural Materialism: The Struggle for a Science of Culture*. New York: Random House.
———. 1985. *Good to Eat: Riddles of Food and Culture*. New York: Simon & Schuster.

———. 1987. "Foodways: Historical Overview and Theoretical Prolegomenon." In *Food and Evolution: Toward a Theory of Human Food Habits*, edited by M. Harris and E. B. Ross, 57–90. Philadelphia, PA: Temple University Press.

Hirshleifer, J. 1977. "Economics from a Biological Viewpoint." *Journal of Law and Economics* 20: 1–52.

Hrdy, S. B. 1999. *Mother Nature: A History of Mothers, Infants, and Natural Selection*. New York: Pantheon.

Jablonka, E., and M. J. Lamb. 2005. *Evolution in Four Dimensions: Genetic, Epigenetic, Behavioral, and Symbolic Variation in the History of Life*. Cambridge, MA: MIT Press.

Kaplan, H. S., and J. B. Lancaster. 2000. "The Evolutionary Economics and Psychology of the Demographic Transition to Low Fertility." In *Adaptation and Human Behavior: An Anthropological Perspective*, edited by L. Cronk, N. Chagnon, and W. Irons, 283–322. New York: Aldine de Gruyter.

Keeley, L. H. 1996. *War before Civilization: The Myth of the Peaceful Savage*. New York: Oxford University Press.

Kornai, J. 1992. *The Socialist System: The Political Economy of Communism*. Princeton, NJ: Princeton University Press.

Lakatos, I. 1970. "Falsification and the Methodology of Scientific Research Programmes." In *Criticism and the Growth of Knowledge*, edited by I. Lakatos and A. Musgrave, 91–196. Cambridge, UK: Cambridge University Press.

Laudan, L. 1977. *Progress and Its Problems: Towards a Theory of Scientific Growth*. Berkeley: University of California Press.

LeBlanc, S. A. 2003. *Constant Battles: Why We Fight*. New York: St. Martin's Press.

Lenski, G. E. 1966. *Power and Privilege: A Theory of Social Stratification*. New York: McGraw-Hill.

Lieberman, L. S. 1987. "Biocultural Consequences of Animals versus Plants as Sources of Fats, Proteins, and Other Nutrients." In *Food and Evolution: Toward a Theory of Human Food Habits*, edited by M. Harris and E. B. Ross, 225–260. Philadelphia, PA: Temple University Press.

Mousseau, M., H. Hegre, and J. R. O'Neal. 2003. "How the Wealth of Nations Conditions the Liberal Peace." *European Journal of International Relations* 9: 277–314.

Murdock, G. P. 1967. *Ethnographic Atlas*. Pittsburgh, PA: University of Pittsburgh Press.

Nielsen, F. 1994. "Sociobiology and Sociology." *Annual Review of Sociology* 20: 267–303.

Norenzayan, A. 2013. *Big Gods: How Religion Transformed Cooperation and Conflict*. Princeton, NJ: Princeton University Press.

Norris, P., and R. Inglehart. 2011. *Sacred and Secular: Religion and Politics Worldwide*. 2nd ed. New York: Cambridge University Press.

O'Neill, J. 2003. "The Gender Gap in Wages, Circa 2000." *American Economic Review* 93: 309–314.

Pasternak, B., C. R. Ember, and M. Ember. 1997. *Sex, Gender, and Kinship: A Cross-Cultural Perspective*. Upper Saddle River, NJ: Prentice Hall.

Phipps, S., P. Burton, and L. Lethbridge. 2001. "In and out of the Labor Market: Long-Term Income Consequences of Child-Related Interruptions to Women's Paid Work." *Canadian Journal of Economics* 34: 411–429.

Pinker, S. 1997. *How the Mind Works*. New York: Norton.

———. 2011. *The Better Angels of Our Nature: Why Violence Has Declined*. New York: Viking.

Popper, K. 1959. *The Logic of Scientific Discovery*. New York: Basic Books. (Original German edition *Logik der Forschung* 1935.)

Posner, R. A. 1992. *Sex and Reason*. Cambridge, MA: Harvard University Press.

Richerson, P. J., and R. Boyd. 1992. "Cultural Inheritance and Evolutionary Ecology." In *Evolutionary Ecology and Human Behavior*, edited by E. A. Smith and B. Winterhalder, 61–92. New York: Aldine de Gruyter.

Rozin, P., L. Hammer, H. Oster, T. Horowitz, and V. Marmora. 1986. "The Child's Conception of Food: Differentiation of Categories of Rejected Substances in the 16 Months to 5 Year Age Range." *Appetite* 7: 141–151.

Rozin, P. 1987. "Psychobiological Perspectives on Food Preferences and Avoidances." In *Food and Evolution: Toward a Theory of Human Food Habits*, edited by M. Harris and E. B. Ross, 181–205. Philadelphia, PA: Temple University Press.

Salter, F. K. 1995. *Emotions in Command: A Naturalistic Study of Institutional Dominance*. Oxford: Oxford University Press.

Sanderson, S. K. 1990. *Social Evolutionism: A Critical History*. Oxford: Blackwell.

———. 1994a. "Evolutionary Materialism: A Theoretical Strategy for the Study of Social Evolution." *Sociological Perspectives* 37: 47–73.

———. 1994b. "The Transition from Feudalism to Capitalism: The Theoretical Significance of the Japanese Case." *Review (Fernand Braudel Center)* 17: 15–55.

———. 1995. *Social Transformations: A General Theory of Historical Development*. Oxford: Blackwell.

———. 1999. *Macrosociology: An Introduction to Human Societies*. 4th ed. New York: Addison Wesley Longman.

———. 2001. *The Evolution of Human Sociality: A Darwinian Conflict Perspective*. Lanham, MD: Rowman & Littlefield.

———. 2007a. "Marvin Harris, Meet Charles Darwin: A Critical Evaluation and Theoretical Extension of Cultural Materialism." In *Studying Societies and Cultures: Marvin Harris's Cultural Materialism and Its Legacy*, edited by L. A. Kuznar and S. K. Sanderson, 194–228. Boulder, CO: Paradigm Publishers.
———. 2007b. *Evolutionism and Its Critics: Deconstructing and Reconstructing an Evolutionary Theory of Human Society*. Boulder, CO: Paradigm Publishers.
———. 2008a. "Religious Attachment Theory and the Biosocial Evolution of the Major World Religions." In *The Evolution of Religion: Studies, Theories, and Critiques*, edited by J. Bulbulia, R. Sosis, E. Harris, R. Genet, C. Genet, and K. Wyman, 67–72. Santa Margarita, CA: Collins Foundation Press.
———. 2008b. "Adaptation, Evolution, and Religion." *Religion* 38: 141–156.
———. 2010. *Revolutions: A Worldwide Introduction to Social and Political Contention*. 2nd ed. Boulder, CO: Paradigm Publishers.
———. 2012. *Rethinking Sociological Theory: Introducing and Exploring a Scientific Theoretical Sociology*. Boulder, CO: Paradigm Publishers.
———. 2014. *Human Nature and the Evolution of Society*. Boulder, CO: Westview Press.
Sanderson, S. K., and A. S. Alderson. 2005. *World Societies: The Evolution of Human Social Life*. New York: Pearson Allyn & Bacon.
Sanderson, S. K., and J. Dubrow. 2000. "Fertility Decline in the Modern World and in the Original Demographic Transition: Testing Three Theories with Cross-National Data." *Population and Environment* 21: 511–537.
Sanderson, S. K., and W. W. Roberts. 2008. "The Evolutionary Forms of the Religious Life: A Cross-Cultural, Quantitative Study." *American Anthropologist* 110: 454–466.
Sarich, V., and F. Miele. 2004. *Race: The Reality of Human Differences*. Boulder, CO: Westview Press.
Skocpol, T. 1979. *States and Social Revolutions*. New York: Cambridge University Press.
Smith, A. D. 1981. *The Ethnic Revival in the Modern World*. Cambridge, UK: Cambridge University Press.
———. 1986. *The Ethnic Origins of Nations*. Oxford: Basil Blackwell.
Snooks, G. D. 1997. *The Ephemeral Civilization: Exploding the Myth of Social Evolution*. London: Routledge.
Somit, A., and S. A. Peterson. 2005. *The Failure of Democratic Nation-Building: Ideology Meets Evolution*. New York: Palgrave Macmillan.
Stark, R. 1996. *The Rise of Christianity: A Sociologist Reconsiders History*. Princeton, NJ: Princeton University Press.
———. 1999. "Micro Foundations of Religion: A Revised Theory." *Sociological Theory* 17: 264–289.
———. 2007. *Discovering God: The Origins of the Great Religions and the Evolution of Belief*. New York: HarperOne.
Stark, R., and W. S. Bainbridge. 1987. *A Theory of Religion*. New Brunswick, NJ: Rutgers University Press.
Stark, R., and R. Finke. 2000. *Acts of Faith: Explaining the Human Side of Religion*. Berkeley: University of California Press.
Swanson, G. E. 1960. *The Birth of the Gods: The Origin of Primitive Beliefs*. Ann Arbor: University of Michigan Press.
Symons, D. 1979. *The Evolution of Human Sexuality*. New York: Oxford University Press.
———. 1987. "If We're All Darwinians, What's the Fuss About"? In *Sociobiology and Psychology: Ideas, Issues, and Applications*, edited by C. Crawford, M. F. Smith, and D. L. Krebs, 121–146. Mahwah, NJ: Lawrence Erlbaum.
Taylor, A. 1989. "The Significance of Darwinian Theory for Marx and Engels." *Philosophy of the Social Sciences* 19: 409–423.
Testart, A. 1982. "The Significance of Food Storage among Hunter-Gatherers: Residence Patterns, Population Densities, and Social Inequalities." *Current Anthropology* 23: 523–537.
———. 1988. "Some Major Problems in the Social Anthropology of Hunter-Gatherers." *Current Anthropology* 29: 1–32.
Thornhill, R., and C. T. Palmer. 2000. *A Natural History of Rape: Biological Bases of Sexual Coercion*. Cambridge, MA: MIT Press.
Tiger, L. 1999. *The Decline of Males*. New York: St. Martin's Press.
Tilly, C. 1978. *From Mobilization to Revolution*. New York: McGraw-Hill.
Tooby, J., and L. Cosmides. 1989. "Evolutionary Psychology and the Generation of Culture, Part I. Theoretical Considerations." *Ethology and Sociobiology* 10: 29–49.
———. 1992. "The Psychological Foundations of Culture." In *The Adapted Mind: Evolutionary Psychology and the Generation of Culture*, edited by J. H. Barkow, L. Cosmides, and J. Tooby, 19–136. New York: Oxford University Press.
van den Berghe, P. L. 1967. *Race and Racism: A Comparative Perspective*. New York: Wiley.
———. 1981. *The Ethnic Phenomenon*. New York: Elsevier.
Vanhanen, T. 2012. *Ethnic Conflicts: Their Biological Roots in Ethnic Nepotism*. Ulster, Northern Ireland: Ulster Institute for Social Research.
Veblen, T. (1899) 2007. *The Theory of the Leisure Class*. New York: Oxford University Press.
Wallace, A.F.C. 1966. *Religion: An Anthropological View*. New York: Random House.

Weber, M. (1923) 1978. *Economy and Society*. 2 vols., edited by G. Roth and C. Wittich. Berkeley: University of California Press.
West-Eberhard, M. J. 2003. *Developmental Plasticity and Evolution*. New York: Oxford University Press.
Westermarck, E. 1922. *The History of Human Marriage*. Vol. II. 5th ed. London: Macmillan.
Wickham-Crowley, T. P. 1992. *Guerrillas and Revolution in Latin America: A Comparative Study of Insurgents and Regimes since 1956*. Princeton, NJ: Princeton University Press.
Wiley, A. S., and L. C. Carlin. 1999. "Demographic Contexts and the Adaptive Role of Mother-Infant Attachment." *Human Nature* 10: 135–161.
Wilson, M., and M. Daly. 1993. "An Evolutionary Psychological Perspective on Male Sexual Proprietariness and Violence against Wives." *Violence and Victims* 8: 271–294.
Wimmer, A., L. Cederman, and B. Min. 2009. "Ethnic Politics and Armed Conflict: A Configurational Analysis of a New Global Data Set." *American Sociological Review* 74: 316–337.
Wrangham, R. W., and D. Peterson. 1996. *Demonic Males: Apes and the Origins of Human Violence*. Boston: Houghton Mifflin.
Wrangham, R. W., M. L. Wilson, and M. N. Muller. 2006. "Comparative Rates of Violence in Chimpanzees and Humans." *Primates* 47: 14–26.

Chapter Fourteen
The Sociocultural Evolution of World-Systems
Christopher Chase-Dunn

> This chapter discusses the differences between biological and sociocultural evolution and provides an overview of the comparative evolutionary world-systems perspective. Research on the growth/decline phases and scale changes in the sizes of cities and empires provides support for the hypothesis of semiperipheral development, and this implies that interpolity relations are an important component of the emergence of sociocultural complexity. The chapter also discusses the contemporary world situation in historical context, focusing on five emergent crises in the twenty-first century.

In order to perceive major transformations in the logic of social change, it is useful to adopt an anthropological framework that compares small-scale human polities and settlements with larger and more complex systems. The rejection of functionalism in social science was accompanied by the rising popularity of a focus on agency and the uniqueness of historical outcomes that made it difficult to perceive the long-run structural continuities and transformations that constitute human sociocultural evolution. The evolutionary structural-functionalism of Talcott Parsons (1966, 1971) was abstract and implied that the Harvard Faculty Club, like earlier English redoubts at Oxford and Cambridge, was the highest form of human civilization. The United States, with its relatively autonomous educational, economic, political, and religious institutions, was the most institutionally differentiated modern society, and this fits Parsons's definition of evolution as increasing differentiation and autonomy of institutional domains. An entire generation of critics rejected this as just another instance of the use of evolutionary theory to prop up the claims of superiority by the powerful, as it had done for the British Empire in the nineteenth century.

But the idea of evolution can be applied without any assumptions about superiority or progress. The scientific study of patterned change and of the emergence of complexity, differentiation, and hierarchy within and between human societies does not require, and is better off without, assumptions about either progress or regress. It is not necessary to assume that complexity or hierarchies are superior to simplicity or equality in order to study these patterns and their causes.

Functionalism, too, need not be thrown out once it is cleansed of nonscientific assumptions. Selection mechanisms and processes need to be explicitly identified (e.g., Turner 2010). The observation that powerful elites often act to increase their rewards and to maintain their privileges beyond what is useful for society as a whole should not preclude us from recognizing that some institutionalized inequalities may be functional for nonelites as well as for elites. Complex and differentiated polities require integration and leadership in order to meet both internal and external challenges. The combination of the functional and conflict theories of stratification leads to the supposition that there is an optimal level of inequality for allowing polities to coordinate their activities and to meet challenges and that inequality beyond that optimal level is probably due to the action of elites who are using their advantages to exploit and dominate nonelites.[1]

Sociocultural versus Biological Evolution

Much confusion has been generated by the failure to clearly distinguish between sociocultural and biological evolution. Sociocultural evolution and biological evolution are different processes, though they share some similar characteristics. Failure to recognize the important differences has often led to theoretical reductionism in which social science is subsumed as a sub-branch of biology and human behavior is seen as mainly determined by genetic inheritance. But the assumption that human behavior is entirely culturally regulated has also been used as an excuse for ignoring advances in neuroscience and genetics. While natural biological evolution is based on the inheritance of genetic material, sociocultural evolution is based on the development of cultural inventions. Both genes and cultural codes are information storage devices by which the outcomes of earlier processes are passed on to future generations. Sociocultural evolution did not exist before the emergence of language. Animals that do not have the biological ability to manipulate complex symbols and to communicate them do not experience the processes of sociocultural evolution. The human animal is uniquely equipped to evolve socioculturally because of the relatively large unpreprogrammed cortex of the human brain and the combinatorial capability of a brain that has syntactic structures built into it (Bergesen 2004). This unusual piece of biological equipment makes possible the learning of complex linguistic codes and their flexible recombination.

In computers, RAM is "random access memory" that can contain changeable data and programs, whereas ROM is "read-only memory" that is permanently programmed when the machine is built. This distinction can be used as an analogy for describing the difference between humans and other animals. Humans have relatively more RAM and so their behavior is less hardwired, more flexible, and programmable by learning and language.

Ants and termites live in large and complex societies, but their behavior in these is largely instinctive and their communications systems are crude. Their social structures are hardwired, and the architecture of their settlements is rigidly bound by their instinctive behaviors of habitat construction. Some animal social structures can vary over relatively short periods of time in response to changing environmental conditions. Thus Argentine ants that have migrated into North America change their territorial strategy to allow individuals to migrate from community to community in a situation in which they are expanding their territory because they have a competitive advantage over other ants and there is little competition between their own colonies.

Edward Wilson (1975) points to what he calls "behavioral scaling," in which both insects and vertebrates change their social behaviors in response to relatively short-term changes in their environments. For insects he argues that the genetic programs are somewhat flexible, allowing for different expressions that depend on environmental circumstances. For vertebrates, especially ones with bigger brains, learning allows for even more flexibility. This kind of flexibility creates opportunities for innovation and the development of complex social structures in the absence of culture. Thus did ants, 30 million years ago, develop a complex division of labor, fungus farming, and imperialism in which the queen of one colony kills the queen of another colony and fools the workers of the invaded colony into raising the offspring of the invaders. This was social evolution without culture made possible by natural selection and the superorganic intelligence that can emerge when large numbers of simple nervous systems collaborate.

Humans learn the cultural software that enables them to build large and complex societies, but the plans are coded in language and symbolic maps that may be modified without having to wait for the evolution of new instinctive behaviors. Language itself has an instinctive basis, and this is why speakers of all natural languages share a somewhat similar grammatical structure. But this biological ability makes possible the great variation that we see in meaning systems and sociocultural institutions, speeding up the process of sociocultural evolution.

When early humans developed stone tools they did not need to genetically select for carnivorous teeth in order to become hunters. Thus, cultural evolution allowed humans to occupy new niches and to adapt in new ways without waiting for biological evolution. It has long been assumed that the advent of sociocultural evolution slowed down the rate of the biological evolution of human genes (e.g., Turner and Maryanski 2008), but there is recent evidence that some aspects of the human genome may have changed rapidly under the influence of sociocultural evolution (e.g., Cochran and Harpending 2009).[2]

So one big difference between biological and sociocultural evolution is in the rate of change. Biological change in large species takes a long time, while sociocultural evolution is much faster and is accelerating. Biological evolution occurs slowly because it is dependent on mating and reproduction and on those few unusual genetic mutations that are adaptive. Sociocultural evolution is accomplished by means of cultural inventions, and these can more easily spread from group to group than can genes. Human societies can "mate" and exchange cultural codes, whereas complex species cannot naturally exchange genetic information. Of course, advantageous genetic mutations can spread within a species, and there may have been important interactions between biological and sociocultural evolution in the last ten millennia. But these are still rather different processes.

There are other rather large and important differences between biological and sociocultural evolution: in biological evolution the source of innovations is mainly the random process of genetic mutation, while in sociocultural evolution innovations occur both accidentally and intentionally as people try to solve problems. This is not to say that sociocultural evolution is entirely rational or even intentional, because many social changes occur as the unintended consequences of the actions of many individuals and groups. But the important point here is that, compared with genetic mutation, social innovation contains an important element of intentionality.

Another difference between biological and sociocultural evolution is in the relationship between simpler and more complex forms. In biological evolution simple one-celled forms of life coevolve and thrive along with more complex multicelled organisms. Viruses and bacteria are doing just fine. In sociocultural evolution the situation is somewhat different. Larger and more complex polities tend to destroy or radically alter the cultures of small-scale polities. States and empires conquer and subjugate stateless peoples (e.g., hunter-gatherer bands and horticultural villagers) by killing off their members and/or assimilating survivors into the states. The plight of indigenous Americans since their incorporation into the Europe-centered world-system is an obvious example. Anthropologists have termed this the "law of cultural dominance." It is not a natural law in the sense that it is impossible for more powerful cultures to allow less powerful ones to survive. That said, there has been a good degree of coevolution as indigenous peoples have learned to cope with subordination in complex and hierarchical societies. Indigenes have recovered demographically and are reconstituting their cultures. They are also increasingly voicing critiques of the modern world-system and proposing alternative futures that are intended to help resolve some of the crises that modernity has produced (Fenelon 2014).

Despite these contrasts, sociocultural evolution is not completely different from biological evolution: both rely on information storage (genes and language) to pass the experiences of one generation on to another; both are mechanisms whereby individuals and groups adapt to changing environments or exploit new environments; and in both, more adaptive changes drive out less adaptive characteristics through competition. And there is one more similarity. In both biological and sociocultural evolution, more complex systems develop out of simpler systems by capturing and controlling free energy (Christian 2004) (see Table 14.1).

So sociocultural and biological evolution are rather different processes, and it is important to understand this distinction because the word "evolution" is often used in ways that cause confusion. Many of the claims of sociobiology and evolutionary psychology about "human nature" are exaggerations of the extent to which human actions are instinctive and based on biological evolution. While there is undoubtedly an important biological basis of human behavior, the idea of human nature is itself a culturally constructed notion that has obvious powerful effects in legitimating some social institutions and delegitimating others. Recognition of the fact that human behavior is less instinctive than the behavior of other animals does not require denial of the biological bases of human actions. There are clearly constraints, as well as possibilities, that emanate from our bodies and our brains. Sociocultural evolution has radically reconstructed the possibilities, and we are now entering a new age of recombinant DNA in which human decisions are radically altering the biological makeup of plants, animals, and ourselves. This is the culturalization of biology.

THE COMPARATIVE EVOLUTIONARY WORLD-SYSTEMS PERSPECTIVE

Hall and Chase-Dunn (2006; see also Chase-Dunn and Lerro 2014) have modified the concepts developed by the scholars of the modern world-system to construct a theoretical

Table 14.1 Similarities and differences between sociocultural and biological evolution

Similarities	
Information transfer across generations	
Adaptation to environments	
Competition drives out less adapted forms	
More complex forms emerge out of simpler forms by capturing free energy	

Differences	
Biological evolution	Sociocultural evolution
Genetic inheritance	Cultural inheritance
Change through genetic mutation	Change through cultural inventions
Propagation of innovations by means of mating	Propagation of innovations by diffusion of information
Slower rate of change	Faster rate of change
Coevolution of simple and complex	Complex drives out simple

perspective for comparing the modern system with earlier, smaller regional world-systems. The main idea is that sociocultural evolution can be explained only if polities[3] are seen to have been in *important interaction with each other* since the Paleolithic Age. World-systems are defined as being composed of those human settlements[4] and polities within a region that are importantly interacting with one another (Hall and Chase-Dunn 2006; Chase-Dunn and Lerro 2014). When communication and transportation technologies were less developed, world-systems were small. The main unit of analysis in this research is the world-system, understood as a set of interaction networks containing multiple polities. Thus, world-systems are politically multicentric, though they differ in the extent to which power is concentrated among a set of core polities or in a hegemonic core state. We use the criterion of political-military interaction—the so-called Political/Military Network (PMN)—to bound regional world-systems.[5] This is an interaction network of polities that are making war and allying with one another. This is what international relations scholars call an "international system."

Many, but not all, world-systems are organized as core/periphery hierarchies in which some polities exploit and dominate the populations of other polities. Semiperipherality is a relational concept that designates an intermediate position within such a core/periphery hierarchy.

Hall and Chase-Dunn (2006) propose a general model of the continuing causes of the evolution of technology and hierarchy within polities and in linked systems of polities (world-systems). This is called the iteration model, and it is driven by population pressures interacting with environmental degradation and interpolity conflict (see Figure 14.1). This iteration model depicts basic causal forces that were operating in the Stone Age and that continue to operate in the contemporary global system (see also Chase-Dunn and Lerro 2014: Chapter 2).

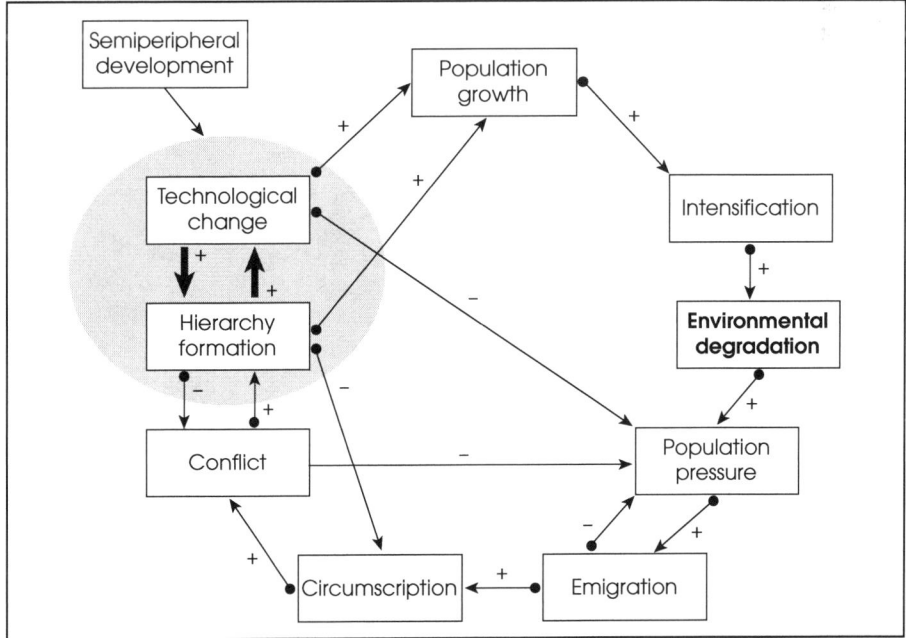

Figure 14.1 The iteration model of sociocultural evolution of world-systems

The lower part of this model as shown in Figure 14.1 is brought to mind by Edward Wilson's descriptions of aggression and warfare among animals. It turns out that the levels of aggression and warfare (and cannibalism) vary with population density and the availability of food. Within-species aggression spaces animals out, and cannibalism and warfare reduce numbers. In other words, part of the demographic regulator is within-species conflict. Most species demonstrate more hierarchy, more aggression, and more territoriality (and more cannibalism and other "abnormal" behaviors) under conditions of high population density relative to the availability of resources. Something similar also works in interspecies relations when there is competition for the same resources. In the comparative human world-systems theory this is what we call the "nasty bottom" of the iteration model.

Population pressure leads to emigration unless the land is already occupied. If the land is full (circumscription), this causes higher levels of within-polity and between-polity conflict (Carneiro 1970). This reduces population pressure by killing users of scarce resources. It is like flour beetles in a jar. Over the long run there is an oscillation about an equilibrium between the population size and the amount of food. Some human world-systems get stuck in the nasty bottom. Patrick Kirch (1991) shows this cycle as revealed in archaeological evidence for the Marquesas Islands. But some human systems break out of the nasty bottom by developing new technologies that allow more resources to be produced in a given area (diversified foraging, gardening, agriculture, industry) or by erecting a new hierarchy that regulates access to scarce resources (chiefdoms, states). Fletcher et al. (2011) have developed a simulation model for how the demographic regulator works in small-scale human systems.

Animal and human patterns overlap considerably, at least at the level of the nasty bottom. It does not require complex symbolic systems to run a simple demographic regulator of this kind. There is no transformation of systemic logics here. These are the continuous realities of demography and resources that continue to be important determinants of the reproduction of both biological and human cultural systems. But human cultural systems also sometimes go through transformations of developmental logic in which some of the rules of the game qualitatively change.

The most important idea that comes out of the comparative evolutionary world-systems perspective is that transformational changes in institutions, social structures, and developmental logics are brought about mainly by the actions of individuals and organizations within polities that are semiperipheral relative to the other polities in the same system. This is known as the hypothesis of *semiperipheral development*.

As regional world-systems became spatially larger and the polities within them grew and became more internally hierarchical, interpolity relations also became more hierarchical because new means of extracting resources from distant peoples were invented. Thus did core/periphery hierarchies emerge. Semiperipherality is the position of some of the polities in a core/periphery hierarchy. Some (but not all) of the polities that are located in semiperipheral positions became the agents that formed larger chiefdoms, states, and empires by means of conquest (semiperipheral marcher polities), and some specialized trading states in between the interstices of the tributary empires promoted production for exchange in the regions in which they operated. So both the spatial and the demographic scale of political organization and the spatial scale of trade networks were expanded by semiperipheral polities, eventually leading to the global system in which we now live.

Upsweeps of Polity and Settlement Size: Semiperipheral Development?

Recent research on changes in the scale of polities and settlements shows support for the hypothesis of semiperipheral development.[6] These studies use both quantitative estimates of the population sizes of the largest settlements in world regions and estimates of the territorial sizes of the largest polities to study the location and timing of changes in the scale of human institutions. Upsweeps in size were defined as instances in which the largest city or empire in a world region reached a peak size that was at least one-third higher than the average of the three previous peak sizes. These instances constitute the events in which the long-term evolutionary trend toward larger polities and settlements occurred. Studying five world regional PMNs (Mesopotamia, Egypt, South Asia, East Asia, and the expanding Central PMN) revealed the existence of eighteen urban upsweeps and twenty-two polity upsweeps over the time periods during which quantitative estimates of city and polity sizes were available for these world regions (Inoue et al. 2012; Inoue et al. 2015). We also found that ten of the eighteen urban upsweeps were produced by semiperipheral development. The finding that semiperipheral development was an important aspect of more than half of the urban upsweeps is strong support for the claim that it is necessary to study whole world-systems in order to explain sociocultural evolution. And ten of the twenty-two polity upsweeps were due to the actions of a semiperipheral marcher state (Ahmed et al. 2013). This means not only that the theory of semiperipheral development does not explain everything about the events in which polity sizes significantly increase in geographical scale, but also that the semiperipheral development hypothesis cannot be ignored in any explanation of the long-term trend in the rise of polity size.

The modern world-system came into being when a formerly peripheral and then semiperipheral region (Europe) developed an internal core of capitalist states that were eventually able to dominate the polities of all the other regions of the Earth. This Europe-centered system was the first one in which capitalism became the predominant mode of accumulation, though semiperipheral capitalist city-states had existed since the Bronze Age in the spaces between the tributary empires. The Europe-centered system expanded in a series of waves of colonization and incorporation (Bergesen and Schoenberg 1980; see Figure 14.2). Commodification in Europe expanded, evolved, and deepened in waves since the thirteenth century, which is why historians disagree about when capitalism became the predominant mode. Since the fifteenth century the modern system has seen four periods of hegemony in which leadership in the development of capitalism was taken to new levels. The first such period was led by a coalition between Genoese finance capitalists and the Portuguese crown (Wallerstein [1974] 2011; Arrighi 1994). After that the hegemons have been single nation-states: the Dutch in the seventeenth century, the British in the nineteenth century, and the United States in the twentieth century (Wallerstein 1984). Europe itself, and all four of the modern hegemons, were former semiperipheral polities that first rose to core status and then to hegemony.

In between these periods of hegemony were periods of hegemonic rivalry in which several contenders strove for global power. The core of the modern world-system has remained multicentric, meaning that a number of sovereign states ally and compete with one another. Earlier regional world-systems sometimes experienced a period of core-wide empire in which a single empire became so large that there were no serious contenders for predominance. This did not happen in the modern world-system until the United States became the single superpower following the demise of the Soviet Union in 1989.

The sequence of hegemonies can be understood as the evolution of global governance in the modern system. The interstate system, as institutionalized at the Treaty of Westphalia in 1644, is still a fundamental institutional structure of the contemporary world political system. The system of theoretically sovereign states was expanded to include the peripheral regions in two large waves of decolonization (see Figure 14.2), eventually resulting in a situation in which the whole modern system became composed of sovereign national states. East Asia was incorporated into this system in the nineteenth century,

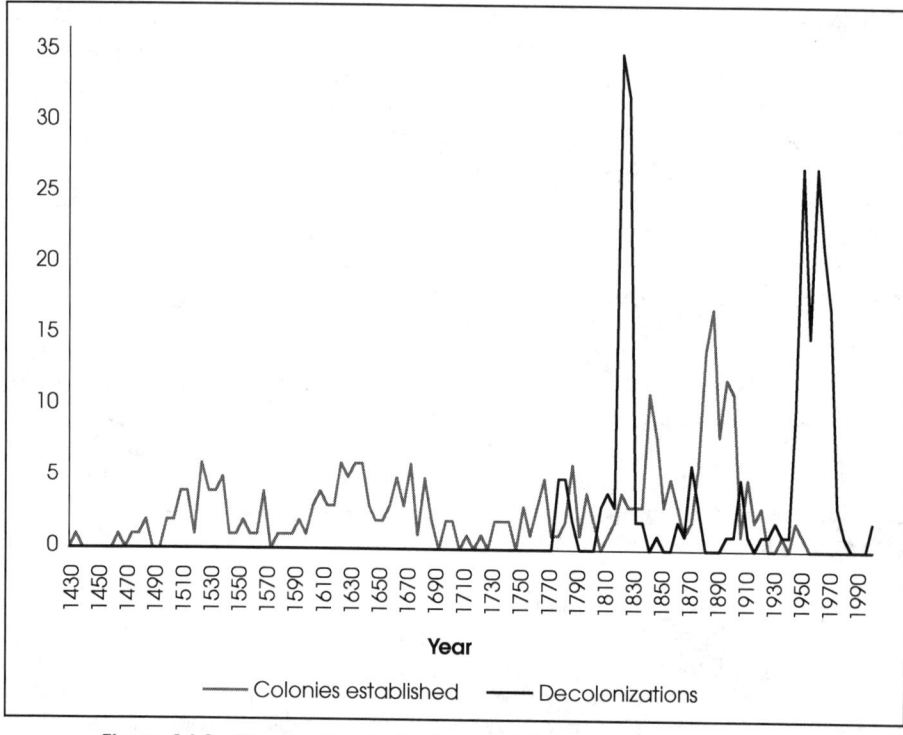

Figure 14.2 Waves of colonization and decolonization since 1400, number of colonies established and number of decolonizations

Source: Henige (1970).

though aspects of the earlier East Asian tribute-trade state system were not completely obliterated by that incorporation (Hamashita 2003).

Each of the modern hegemonies was larger as a proportion of the whole system than the earlier ones had been. And each further developed the institutions of economic and political-military power by which it provided world order such that capitalism increasingly deepened and intensified its penetration of all the areas of the Earth. And after the Napoleonic Wars, in which Britain finally defeated its main competitor, France, global political institutions began to emerge over the tops of the international system of national states. The first proto-world-government was the Concert of Europe, a fragile flower that wilted when its main proponents, Britain and the Austro-Hungarian Empire, disagreed about how to handle the world revolution of 1848. The Concert was followed by the League of Nations and then by the United Nations and the Bretton Woods international financial institutions (the World Bank, the International Monetary Fund, and eventually the World Trade Organization).

The political globalization evident in the trajectory of global governance evolved because the great powers and the largest firms were in heavy contention with one another for geopolitical power and for economic resources, but also because resistance emerged within the polities of the core and in the regions of the noncore. The series of hegemonies, waves of colonial expansion and decolonization, and the emergence of a proto-world-state occurred as the global elites tried to compete with one another and to contain resistance from below. I have already mentioned the waves of decolonization. Other important forces of resistance were slave revolts, the labor movement, the extension of citizenship to men of no property, the women's movement, and other associated rebellions and social movements.

These movements affected the evolution of global governance in part because the rebellions often clustered together in time, forming what have been called "world revolutions" (Arrighi, Hopkins, and Wallerstein 1989; Wallerstein 2004). World revolutions are defined as *a set of local rebellions that take place simultaneously or in a similar time period in regions dominated by core powers*. The rebels may or may not be aware of one another, but the great powers know them because they are trying to maintain order in the system as a whole. The Protestant Reformation in Europe was an early instance that played a huge role in the rise of the Dutch hegemony. The French Revolution of 1789 was linked in time with the American and Haitian revolts. The 1848 rebellion in Europe was both synchronous with the Taiping Rebellion in China and linked with it by the diffusion of ideas, as it was also linked with the emergent Christian Sects in the United States. The year 1917 was the year of the Bolsheviks in Russia, but the same decade also saw the Chinese Nationalist revolt, the Mexican Revolution, the Arab Revolt, and the General Strike in Seattle led by the Industrial Workers of the World in the United States. The year 1968 was a revolt of students in the United States, Europe, Latin America, and Red Guards in China. The year 1989 was mainly in the Soviet Union and Eastern Europe, but important lessons about the value of civil rights beyond justification for capitalist democracy were learned by an emergent global civil society.

We are still in the midst of the current world revolution of 20xx (Chase-Dunn and Niemeyer 2009). The big idea here is that the evolution of capitalism and of global governance is importantly *a response to resistance and rebellions from below*. This has been true in the past and is likely to continue to be true in the future. Boswell and Chase-Dunn (2000) contend that capitalism and socialism have dialectically interacted with one another in a positive feedback loop similar to a spiral. Labor and socialist movements were obviously a reaction to capitalist industrialization, but also the US hegemony and the post–World War II global institutions were importantly spurred on by the World Revolution of 1917 and the waves of decolonization.

WAVES OF GLOBALIZATION AND DEGLOBALIZATION

The comparative evolutionary world-systems perspective also studies waves of spatial integration of interaction networks based on trade and warfare. It is noted that there have been oscillations of expanding and contracting interaction networks since the Stone Age, along with a long-term upward trend toward the greater spatial scale and intensity of interaction networks. Research on international trade since the nineteenth century shows this pattern of expansion, contraction (deglobalization), and an upward trend (Chase-Dunn, Kawano, and Brewer 2000; see Figure 14.3).

Figure 14.3 shows a great nineteenth-century wave of trade globalization (the ratio of international trade to the overall size of the world economy), followed by a short wave between 1900 and 1945, and then a rise from a trough of deglobalization to the current high level. The financial crisis of 2008 caused a reduction in the level of global economic integration, but that decline was reversed by 2012 when the level of trade globalization reached its highest peak since 1820.

TIME HORIZONS

So what does the comparative and evolutionary world-systems perspective tell us about continuities and transformations of systemic logic? Are recent developments just another

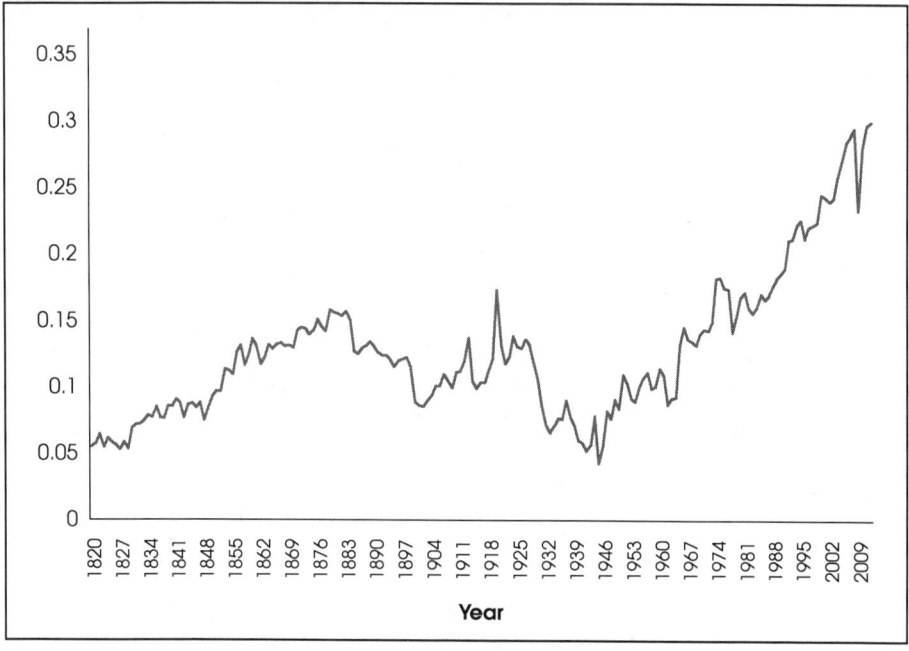

Figure 14.3 Trade globalization, 1820–2012 imports/GDP
Sources: Chase-Dunn, Kawano, and Brewer (2000); World Bank (2014).

bout of financial expansion and collapse and hegemonic decline? Or do they constitute or portend a deep structural crisis in the capitalist mode of accumulation? What do recent events signify about the evolution of capitalism and its possible transformation into a different mode of accumulation?

50,000 Years

From the perspective of the last 50,000 years, the big news is demographic and ecological. After slowly expanding for millennia, with cyclical ups and downs in particular regions, the human population went into a steep upward surge in the last four centuries. Humans have been degrading the environment locally and regionally since they began the intensive use of natural resources. But in the last two hundred years of industrial production, ecological degradation by means of resource depletion and pollution has become global in scope, with global warming as the biggest consequence. A demographic transition to an equilibrium population size began in the industrialized core countries in the nineteenth century and has spread unevenly to the noncore in the twentieth century. Public health measures have lowered the mortality rate, and the education and employment of women outside the home are lowering the fertility rate. But the total number of humans is likely to keep increasing for several more decades. In the year 2000 there were about 6 billion humans on Earth. By the time the population stops climbing, it will be 8, 10, or 12 billion.

This population big bang was made possible by industrialization and the vastly expanded use of nonrenewable fossil fuels. Fossil fuels are captured ancient sunlight that took millions of years to accrete as plants and forests grew, died, and were compressed into oil and coal. The arrival of peak oil production is near, and energy prices will almost surely rise again after a long fall. The recent financial meltdown is related to these long-run changes in the sense that it was brought on partly by sectors of the global elite trying to protect their privileges and wealth by seeking greater control over natural resources and by overexpanding the financial sector. But nonelites are also implicated. The housing expansion, suburbanization, and larger houses with fewer people in them have been important mechanisms, especially in the United States, for incorporating some of the nonelites into the hegemonic globalization project of corporate capitalism. The culture of consumerism has become strongly ensconced both for those who actually have expanded consumption and for those who hope to increase their consumption to the levels of the core.

5,000 Years

The main significance of the 5,000-year time horizon is to point us to the rise and decline of modes of accumulation. The story here is that small-scale human polities were integrated primarily by normative structures institutionalized as kinship relations—the so-called *kinship-based modes of accumulation*. The family was the economy and the polity, and the family was organized as a moral order of obligations that allowed social labor to be mobilized and coordinated, and that regulated distribution. Kin-based accumulation was based on shared languages and meaning systems, consensus-building through oral communication, and institutionalized reciprocity in sharing and exchange. As kin-based polities got larger, they increasingly fought with one another, and some of the polities that developed institutionalized inequalities had advantages over some of those that did not. Kinship itself became hierarchical within chiefdoms, taking the form of ranked lineages or conical clans. Social movements using religious discourses have been important forces of social change for millennia. Kin-based societies often responded to population pressures on resources by "hiving off"—a subgroup would emigrate, usually after formulating grievances in terms of violations of the moral order. Migrations were mainly responses to local resource stress caused by population growth and competition for resources. When new unoccupied or only lightly occupied but resource-rich lands were reachable, the humans moved on, eventually populating all the continents except Antarctica. Once the land was filled up, a situation of "circumscription" raised the level of conflict within and between polities, producing a demographic regulator (Fletcher et al. 2011). In these circumstances technological and organization innovations were stimulated, and successful new strategies were strongly selected by interpolity competition, leading to the emergence of complexity, hierarchy, and new logics of social reproduction.

Around 5,000 years ago the first early states and cities emerged in Mesopotamia over the tops of the kin-based institutions. This was the beginning of the tributary modes of accumulation in which state power (legitimate coercion) became the main organizer of the economy, the mobilizer of labor, and the accumulator of wealth and power. Similar innovations occurred largely independently in Egypt, the Yellow (Huang-Ho) River valley, the Indus River valley, and later in Mesoamerica and the Andes. The tributary modes of production evolved as states and empires became larger and as the techniques of imperialism, allowing the exploitation of distant resources, were improved. This was mainly the work of semiperipheral marcher states (Ahmed et al. 2013). Aspects of the tributary modes (taxation, tribute-gathering, accumulation by dispossession) are still with us, but they have been largely subsumed and made subservient to the logic of capitalist accumulation. Crises and countermovements were often involved in the wars and conquests that brought about social change and evolution of the tributary modes.

A tributary mode became predominant in the Mesopotamian world-system in the early Bronze Age (around 3000 BCE). The East Asian regional world-system was still predominantly tributary in the nineteenth century CE. That is nearly a 5,000-year run. The kin-based mode lasted even longer. All human groups were organized around different versions of the kin-based modes in the Paleolithic, and indeed since human culture first emerged with language. If we date the beginning of the end of the kin-based modes at the coming to predominance of the tributary mode in Mesopotamia (3000 BCE), this first qualitative change in the basic logic of social reproduction took more than 100,000 years.

500 Years

This brings us to the capitalist mode, here defined as based on the accumulation of profits returning to commodity production rather than taxation or tribute. As I have already said, early forms of capitalism emerged in the Bronze Age in the form of small semiperipheral states that specialized in trade and the production of commodities. But it was not until the fifteenth century that this form of accumulation became predominant in a regional world-system (Europe and its colonies). Capitalism was born in the semiperiphery, but in Europe it moved to the core, and the forereachers that further evolved capitalism were former semiperipheral polities that rose to hegemony. Economic crises and world revolutions have been important elements in the evolution of capitalism and global governance institutions for centuries.

Thus, in comparison with the earlier modes, capitalism is yet young. It has been around for millennia, but it has been predominant in a world-system for less than a millennium. On the other hand, many have observed that social change in general has speeded up. The rise of tribute-taking based on institutionalized coercion took more than 100,000 years. Capitalism itself speeds up social change because it revolutionizes technology so quickly that other institutions are brought along, and people have become adjusted to more rapid reconfigurations of culture and institutions. So it is plausible that the contradictions of capitalism may lead it to reach its limits much faster than the kin-based and tributary modes did.

Five Linked Crises in the Contemporary World-System

Many contend that the capitalist world-system is now in crisis. This section outlines the implications of the comparative evolutionary world-systems perspective for an analysis of the contemporary crisis and for possible futures in the twenty-first century. The main idea is that the waves of global integration have been driven by system-wide class and national struggles in which the elites of core states contend with one another and the most successful are those that can effectively deal with the resistance from below. This has produced a spiral of capitalism and socialism that has been connected with the rise and fall of hegemons (Boswell and Chase-Dunn 2000).

The sequence of hegemonies (the Dutch in the seventeenth century, the British in the nineteenth century, and the United States in the twentieth century) constitutes the most important structural feature of the evolution of global governance and political globalization. This is most obviously seen in the increasing size of each of the hegemons relative to the size of the system as a whole. This rise and fall and cyclical upward sequence occurred in the context of successive world revolutions (the Protestant Reformation, 1789, 1848, 1917, 1968, 1989, 2011) in which local rebellions have increasingly clustered in time and become more and more linked with one another. Wallerstein's (2004) discussion of world revolutions notes that the demands put forth in a world revolution do not usually become institutionalized until a consolidating revolt has occurred, or until the next world revolution. Thus, the revolutionaries appear to have lost in the failure of their most radical demands, but enlightened conservatives who are trying to manage hegemony end up incorporating the reforms that were earlier radical demands into the current world order in order to cool out resistance from below.

The world-system scholars have seen the hegemony of the United States as declining since the 1970s, and now many others share this view. An important part of the current crisis is a crisis of US hegemony. The economic hegemony of the United States has been declining in stairsteps since the height of its global power in 1945 (Chase-Dunn et al. 2011). Now the questions are about the rate of decline and what kind of system of authority will replace American hegemony.

The world revolution of 20xx is proceeding apace. It is a messy affair, as all earlier world revolutions have been. It began in 1994 with the Zapatista revolt, warmed up with the global justice movement and the antiwar movement, and really got rolling with the Arab Spring, the anti-austerity movements, and popular rebellions in Brazil, Thailand, and Ukraine (Chase-Dunn and Niemeyer 2009; Mason 2013). It is both similar to and different from earlier world revolutions. And the constellation of social movements that constitute the New Global Left needs to be compared with earlier incarnations of the Global Left in earlier world revolutions.

There are five linked crises occurring simultaneously in the contemporary world-system:

1. A crisis of hegemony and global governance
2. A crisis of inequality and democracy
3. A crisis in the relationship between humans and the natural environment
4. A crisis in the global capitalist system
5. A crisis in the New Global Left

Global Governance

Hegemonic declines of the past have been followed by periods of rivalry and world war among contenders for regional and global power. But the US economic size is so great, and its military power is so preponderant, that a pre–World War I situation of contending militarized challengers is not going to emerge very soon. This is a good thing. The long-term trend toward large-scale political integration and centralization will eventually result in the emergence of a world state, but this is an unlikely development for the next few decades. What is emerging is a multipolar interstate system in which the United States shares power with the existing core states and emerging powers from the semiperiphery (China, India, Brazil, and Russia). This geopolitical structure will also involve multiple and overlapping sovereignties that include the United Nations, international financial institutions (the World Bank, the International Monetary Fund, the World Trade Organization), regional interstate entities, and international nongovernmental organizations. It is not likely that such a complicated world polity will be able to resolve conflicts within and between national societies peacefully, or to deal with global ecological and economic challenges. As the discussion below suggests, this emerging multicentric world polity has not been effective at resolving major conflicts, and in fact efforts to respond to crises in one area (e.g., finance) have exacerbated other crises (e.g., social and political). This is why I speak of a crisis of global governance.

Inequality and Democracy

Huge inequalities between the Global North and the Global South emerged in the nineteenth century and have not increased or been reduced much since then (Bornschier

2010). Some national societies, including the United States, have experienced big increases in within-country inequality since the 1970s. As the world is increasingly integrated by communications technology, people in the Global South have become aware of (and desirous of) the level of living attained by people in the Global North. Also, the contested idea of democracy has spread to nearly all the peoples of the Earth. The result is a crisis of development in a context in which the biosphere is already heavily depleted by the huge consumption and pollution by the Global North. Peter Taylor (1996) called this "Global Impasse." If the people of the Global South eat as many eggs and drive as many cars as the people of the Global North, the biosphere will fry. This is a problem.

Democracy is also a problem at several levels. There is little democracy at the global level (see, e.g., Markoff 2013). The commander-in-chief of the only global military apparatus (782 US military bases all over the world) is elected solely by the voters of the United States. At the UN, the important decisions are made by the powers that won World War II (the Security Council). The president of the World Bank is always from the United States. The managing director of the International Monetary Fund is always from Europe. At the national level, the Global South has seen a wave of regimes that have been elected by majorities of citizens. In some of these, especially in Latin America, reformist and even anti-systemic leaders have managed to occupy the national leadership. But in many of the countries of the Global South, democracy is just polyarchy in which elites manipulate elections in order to maintain their class power (Robinson 1996). The same may be said of many democracies in the core. The growing rule of money in politics in the United States has increasingly made the electoral process a direct extension of the power of the rich. Low-quality democracy has provoked movements for direct democracy in which the voices of average citizens can be heard (Gitlin 2012; Graeber 2013).

The Biosphere

Anthropogenic global warming and pollution are obvious looming crises that are exacerbated by the unwillingness of the powers that be to make serious efforts at reaching solutions. The engagement in more environmentally risky and costly extraction processes—including fracking as well as offshore drilling and tar sands—in order to make money on rising energy prices is making matters much worse. Nuclear power accidents have led to a German declaration of a nuclear-free future, but in Japan the political will behind this idea has declined. The historically high consumption, energy use, and pollution by the Global North is an obstacle to reform in the Global South, especially in China and India, where prodigious levels of greenhouse gas emissions have been reached. This has produced a huge collective action problem with regard to global environmental policies (Roberts and Parks 2007; Bond 2012).

The Global Capitalist System

In comparison with the earlier modes of accumulation, capitalism is yet young. It has been around since the Bronze Age in the form of semiperipheral capitalist city-states that specialized in trade, but it has been predominant in a world-system only since the rise of Europe in the sixteenth century CE. The rise of tribute-taking based on institutionalized coercion occurred in the Early Bronze Age, about 5,000 years ago. The tributary mode of accumulation was the predominant mode until the rise of capitalism in Europe. Thus, capitalism as a fully developed and predominant logic of social change is a fairly recent development.

But the rate of social change has speeded up. Capitalism itself speeds up social change because it provides stronger incentives to revolutionize technology. Rapid technological change speeds up change in all institutions and in culture, and people become adjusted to more rapid reconfigurations of culture and institutions. So it is plausible that, even though capitalism is young, its contradictions could lead it to reach its limits much faster than the kin-based and tributary modes did.

But is it capitalism (a logic of social reproduction based on profit-making) that is currently in crisis? Or is it the current developmental ideology that became predominant in the 1970s—neoliberalism? Or is it the systemic cycle of capitalist accumulation that was associated with the US hegemony? Or is it finance capitalism, which rose to predominance in the core along with neoliberalism? Or is it all the above?

Immanuel Wallerstein (2004) contends that capitalism itself is in crisis because it is reaching certain limits caused by its basic contradictions. The three long-term upward trends (which he calls asymptotes) that capitalism cannot manage are:

1. The long-term rise of real wages
2. The long-term costs of material inputs
3. Rising taxes

All three upward trends cause the average rate of profit to fall. Capitalists devise strategies for combating these trends (automation, capital flight, job blackmail, attacks on the welfare state and unions, financialization), but they cannot really stop them in the long run. Deindustrialization in one place leads to industrialization and the emergence of labor movements somewhere else (Silver 2003). The falling rate of profit means that capitalism as a logic of accumulation will face an irreconcilable structural crisis during the next fifty years and that some other system will emerge. Wallerstein calls the next five decades "The Age of Transition."

Giovanni Arrighi's (1994, 2006) evolutionary account of "systemic cycles of accumulation" is explicitly evolutionary, but rather than positing "stages of capitalism" and looking for each country to go through them (as most of the older Marxists did), he posits somewhat overlapping global cycles of accumulation in which the logic of capitalism widens and deepens and finance capital and state power controlled by capital take on new forms and increasingly penetrate the whole system.

Arrighi (2006) analyzes both the similarities and the differences between the current period of US hegemonic decline and the decades at the end of the nineteenth century and the early twentieth century when British hegemony was declining. Taking a cue from Andre Gunder Frank (1998), Arrighi saw the rise of China as portending a new systemic cycle of accumulation in which "market society" will eventually come to replace rapacious finance capital as the leading institutional form in the next phase of world history. Arrighi (2006) did not discuss the end of capitalism and the emergence of another basic logic of social reproduction and accumulation.

As Arrighi has pointed out, the ascendance of finance capital is driven by the decline of the profit rate in trade and production as those with centrality in the world economy try to devise new ways to squeeze profit out of the system. The financial crisis of 2008 was not really a total collapse, and the balloon of financial "securities" has been reflated. Also the global capitalist class has resisted calls for a green global new deal to save capitalism (Saleh 2012) and has "doubled-down" on austerity, thereby increasing the pressures that lead to rebellion. Neoliberalism may be in crisis, but its proponents and its militarized version, neoconservatism, are still kicking. The banks are trying to take over education in the North and the South in order to expand profit-making opportunities in privatized schools and student loans. At the global level, Dick Cheney is still ascendant, and George Soros and the green new deal are still in the wings.

The New Global Left

The New Global Left is getting very strong, but it is still in formation despite the intensification of the world revolution of 20xx. Big divides remain between the old and new social movements over goals, strategy, and tactics. The horizontalists are still in the ascendance, and normal electoral politics and taking state power are proscribed by a growing segment of progressive and left activists. A global united front that combines labor with horizontalists is possible but may not happen until global Robocop and twenty-first-century fascism get stronger (Mason 2013; Robinson 2013).

These five crises are obviously linked to one another as both causes and effects, and so those who see them as a single interrelated bundle are not wrong.

Both a new stage of capitalism and a qualitative systemic transformation are possible within the next three decades, but a new stage of capitalism is more likely. This could take the form of "market society," as implied by Arrighi—a kinder, gentler form of capitalism in which the rule of finance capital and the military industrial complex are countered by technocrats and civil society, or a related green global Keynesianism that takes responsibility for employing workers who then have the means to purchase the commodities that capital produces. These kinder, gentler forms of capitalism are not rocket science, though they would need to be scaled up to work at the global level. Symbolically this would be a shift from Dick Cheney to George Soros, the enlightened conservative.

If US hegemonic decline is slow, as it has been up to the present, and if financial and ecological crises are spread out in time and conflicts among ethnic groups and nations are also spread out in time and space, then the enlightened conservatives will have their chance to build a new world order that is still capitalist but meets the current challenges, at least partially. Making this happen would still require a revolutionary shove from a powerful united front of antisystemic movements allied with progressive regimes of the Global South. But if the perfect storm of calamities should all come together in the same period, the transnational social movements and progressive national regimes in the Global South may have the chance to radically change the mode of accumulation to a form of global socialism.[7]

Acknowledgments

Thanks to E. N. Anderson, Albert J. Bergesen, Hiroko Inoue, and Thomas D. Hall for helpful comments on an earlier draft of this chapter.

Notes

1. Turchin and Nefedov (2009) emphasize that elite overexpansion is an important part of the demographic secular cycle within polities. Elite overexpansion regularly occurs beyond the carrying capacity of the environment and the system of production.
2. Cochrane and Harpending (2009) usefully summarize the evidence from the HAPMAP study that implies that biological change among humans has speeded up over the past 10,000 years, but then they go on to speculate as to how this might account for uneven development and inequalities among contemporary groups with little evidence to support these speculations.

3. We use the term "polity" to generally denote a spatially bounded realm of sovereign authority such as a band, tribe, chiefdom, state, or empire. We designate polities as subsystems of world-systems because they are easier to bound spatially than are societies.
4. Settlement is a general term that includes camps, hamlets, villages, towns, cities, and the great megacity urban regions that compose the contemporary global urban system.
5. Chase-Dunn and Hall (1997) note that important interaction networks often have different spatial scales. Trade networks, especially those involving prestige goods, usually are much larger than interpolity interaction networks (PMNs) in which polities are allying and fighting. In this study we use the political/military interaction network because this is easier to empirically determine. But we acknowledge that regions that are distant from one another may be importantly interacting by means of trade well before they come into direct military/political contact with one another (see also Chase-Dunn and Jorgenson 2003).
6. The project that has carried out this research is the Polities and Settlements Research Working Group at the Institute of Research on World-Systems at the University of California-Riverside. The project website is http://irows.ucr.edu/research/citemp/citemp.html.
7. For a detailed discussion of the possibility of a perfect storm and analyses of how and why the Global South may be better able to survive a perfect storm, see Kuecker (2007) and Kuecker and Hall (2011).

References

Ahmed, J., A. Álvarez, E. N. Anderson, E. Basmajian, D. Blum, H. Inoue, J. Christian, A. Khan, K. Lawrence, A. Owen, A. Roberts, P. Suppatkul, and C. Chase-Dunn. 2013. "Comparing World-Systems: Semiperipheral Development and Empire Upsweeps since the Bronze Age." Paper presented at the annual meeting of the American Sociological Association, New York, August.
Arrighi, G. 1994. *The Long Twentieth Century*. London: Verso.
———. 2006. *Adam Smith in Beijing*. London: Verso.
Arrighi, G., T. K. Hopkins, and I. Wallerstein. 1989. *Antisystemic Movements*. London: Verso.
Bergesen, A. J. 2004. "Chomsky versus Mead." *Sociological Theory* 22 (3): 357–370.
Bergesen, A. J., and R. Schoenberg. 1980. "Long Waves of Colonial Expansion and Contraction 1415–1969." In *Studies of the Modern World-System*, edited by A. Bergesen, 231–278. New York: Academic Press.
Bond, P. 2012. *The Politics of Climate Justice: Paralysis Above, Movement Below*. Durban, South Africa: University of Kwa-zulu Natal Press.
Bornschier, V. 2010. "On the Evolution of Inequality in the World System." In *Inequality beyond Globalization: Economic Changes, Social Transformations, and the Dynamics of Inequality*, edited by Christian Suter. Berlin: World Society Studies.
Boswell, T., and C. Chase-Dunn. 2000. *The Spiral of Capitalism and Socialism: Toward Global Democracy*. Boulder, CO: Lynne Rienner.
Carneiro, R. L. 1970. "A Theory of the Origin of the State." *Science* 169 (August): 733–738.
Chase-Dunn, C., and T. D. Hall. 1997. *Rise and Demise: Comparing World-Systems*. Boulder, CO: Westview.
Chase-Dunn, C., and A. K. Jorgenson. 2003. "Regions and Interaction Networks: An Institutional Materialist Perspective." *International Journal of Comparative Sociology* 44 (1): 433–450.
Chase-Dunn, C., Y. Kawano, and B. Brewer. 2000. "Trade Globalization since 1795: Waves of Integration in the World-System." *American Sociological Review* 65 (1): 77–95.
Chase-Dunn, C., R. Kwon, K. Lawrence, and H. Inoue. 2011. "Last of the Hegemons: U.S. Decline and Global Governance." *International Review of Modern Sociology* 37 (1): 1–29.
Chase-Dunn, C., and B. Lerro. 2014. *Social Change: Globalization from the Stone Age to the Present*. Boulder, CO: Paradigm Publishers.
Chase-Dunn, C., and R. E. Niemeyer. 2009. "The World Revolution of 20xx." In *Transnational Political Spaces*, edited by A. Mathias, G. Bluhm, H. Helmig, A. Leutzsch, and J. Walter, 35–57. Frankfurt/New York: Campus Verlag.
Christian, D. 2004. *Maps of Time*. Berkeley: University of California Press.
Cochran, G., and H. Harpending. 2009. *The 10,000 Year Explosion: How Civilization Accelerated Human Evolution*. New York: Basic Books.
Fenelon, J. 2014. "Indigenous Alternatives to the Global Crises of the Modern World System." In *Overcoming Global Inequalities*, edited by I. Wallerstein, C. Chase-Dunn, and C. Suter. Boulder, CO: Paradigm Publishers.

Fletcher, J. B., J. Apkarian, R. A. Hanneman, I. Hiroko, K. Lawrence, and C. Chase-Dunn. 2011. "Demographic Regulators in Small-Scale World-Systems." *Structure and Dynamics* 5 (1). http://escholarship.org/uc/item/6kb1k3zk.

Frank, A. G. 1998. *Reorient: Global Economy in the Asian Age*. Berkeley: University of California Press.

Gitlin, T. 2012. *Occupy Nation*. New York: HarperCollins.

Graeber, D. 2013. *The Democracy Project: A History, a Crisis, a Movement*. New York: Spiegel and Grau (Random House).

Hall, T. D., and C. Chase-Dunn. 2006. "Global Social Change in the Long Run." In *Global Social Change*, edited by C. Chase-Dunn and S. Babones, 33–58. Baltimore: Johns Hopkins University Press.

Hamashita, T. 2003. "Tribute and Treaties: Maritime Asia and Treaty Port Networks in the Era of Negotiations, 1800–1900." In *The Resurgence of East Asia*, edited by G. Arrighi, T. Hamashita, and M. Selden, 17–50. London: Routledge.

Henige, D. P. 1970. *Colonial Governors from the Fifteenth Century to the Present*. Madison: University of Wisconsin Press.

Inoue, H., A. Álvarez, E. N. Anderson, A. Owen, R. Álvarez, K. Lawrence, and C. Chase-Dunn. 2015. "Urban Scale Shifts since the Bronze Age: Upsweeps, Collapses and Semiperipheral Development." *Social Science History* 39: 2.

Inoue, H., A. Álvarez, K. Lawrence, A. Roberts, E. N. Anderson, and C. Chase-Dunn. 2012. "Polity Scale Shifts in World-Systems since the Bronze Age: A Comparative Inventory of Upsweeps and Collapses." *International Journal of Comparative Sociology* 53 (3): 210–229. http://cos.sagepub.com/content/early/2012/10/04/0020715212462380.

Kirch, P. 1991. "Chiefship and Competitive Involution: The Marquesas Islands of Eastern Polynesia." In *Chiefdoms: Power, Economy and Ideology*, edited by T. Earle, 119–145. Cambridge: Cambridge University Press.

Kuecker, G. D. 2007. "The Perfect Storm: Catastrophic Collapse in the 21st Century." *International Journal of Environmental, Cultural, Economic and Social Sustainability* 3 (5): 1–10.

Kuecker, G. D., and T. D. Hall. 2011. "Facing Catastrophic Systemic Collapse: Ideas from Recent Discussions of Resilience, Community, and World-Systems Analysis." *Nature and Culture* 6: 18–40.

Markoff, J. 2013. "Democracy's Past Transformations, Present Challenges and Future Prospects." *International Journal of Sociology* 43 (2): 13–40.

Mason, P. 2013. *Why It's Still Kicking Off Everywhere: The New Global Revolution*. London: Verso.

Parsons, T. 1966. *Societies: Evolutionary and Comparative Perspectives*. Englewood Cliffs, NJ: Prentice-Hall.

———. 1971. *The System of Modern Societies*. Englewood Cliffs, NJ: Prentice-Hall.

Roberts, T., and B. C. Parks. 2007. *A Climate of Injustice: Global Inequality, North-South Politics and Climate Policy*. Cambridge, MA: MIT Press.

Robinson, W. I. 1996. *Promoting Polyarchy: Globalization, US Intervention, and Hegemony*. Cambridge: Cambridge University Press.

———. 2013. "Policing the Global Crisis." Paper presented at the PEWS miniconference, "Power and Justice in the Contemporary World-Economy," New York City, August 9.

Saleh, A. 2012. "Green Economy or Green Utopia?: Rio+20 and the Reproductive Labor Class." *Journal of World-Systems Research* 18 (2): 141–145.

Silver, B. J. 2003. *Forces of Labor: Workers Movements and Globalization since 1870*. Cambridge: Cambridge University Press.

Taylor, P. 1996. *The Way the Modern World Works: Global Hegemony to Global Impasse*. New York: Wiley.

Turchin, P., and S. A. Nefedov. 2009. *Secular Cycles*. Princeton, NJ: Princeton University Press.

Turner, J. H. 2010. *Principles of Sociology*. Vol. 1, *Macrodynamics*. New York: Springer Verlag.

Turner, J. H., and A. Maryanski. 2008. *On the Origins of Human Societies by Means of Natural Selection*. Boulder, CO: Paradigm Publishers.

Wallerstein, I. (1974) 2011. *The Modern World-System*. Vol. 1. Berkeley: University of California Press.

———. 1984. "The Three Instances of Hegemony in the History of the Capitalist World-Economy." In *Current Issues and Research in Macrosociology*, International Studies in Sociology and Social Anthropology, Vol. 37, edited by G. Lenski, 100–108. Leiden, Netherlands: E. J. Brill.

———. 2004. *World Systems Analysis: An Introduction*. Durham, NC: Duke University Press.

Wilson, E. O. 1975. *Sociobiology*. Cambridge, MA: Harvard University Press.

World Bank. 2014. *World Development Indicators*. Washington, DC: World Bank.

Chapter Fifteen

The Evolution of the Human Brain

David D. Franks

> The most complex systems that we know of are the human brain and the galaxies of stars in the universe. This chapter describes general characteristics of this brain's development beginning with our first ape ancestor's ascendance from an arboreal lifestyle to a bipedal one on the ground about 6 million years ago. The discussion of the human brain moves through the first bipedal Australopithecines and identifies the many advantages that this allowed. The many facets of tool making starting with *Homo habilis* are described as well as the advantages of fire and cooked meat. Following Ramachandran's work we move from the demands of arboreal life and the abstractions thereof to the development of language. Factors making us a thoroughly social animal are described.

This is a story of an organ that is astonishingly complex, comparable perhaps only to the stars and planets that compose the universe. The organ is, of course, the human brain. Gerald Edelman, a Nobel Prize winner, in *Wider than the Sky* (2004) gives us some insight into this complexity. He tells us that the neocortex, which makes up 76 percent of the human brain, contains 30 billion neurons and 1 million billion connections. If one were to count these connections at the rate of one each second, it would take 32 million years to complete the task.

It should not be surprising, therefore, that the story of the evolutionary development of the human brain is one that began millions and millions of years ago. As Émile Durkheim wisely said, "Nothing comes out of nothing," so the first issue here is, when did this start? Most experts agree that a recognizably human brain originated about 6 million years ago when our ancestors broke from life in the trees to begin a life on the ground.

In this chapter I describe some general characteristics of the course that this evolution took. I review some methods for dating fossils because the content of what we know is only as good as our measures of it. Attention is given to selected human brain parts as contrasted with those of apes. The body of the chapter is a description of our hominin ancestors in terms of the characteristics of their brains along with a description of when these ancestors appeared, when they became extinct, and some notes on their lifestyle that are relevant for their brains. The chapter concludes with attention to the subject of human language and its origins millions of years ago in the brains of our arboreal ancestors.

The story of the evolution of the human brain is a challenging one—challenging for those archeologists who study it largely through fossil remains, and even more challenging for all those hominins who preceded *Homo sapiens* and who laid the groundwork for possessing this human brain as we know it today. The first difficulty comes from the fact that the only evidence about the brain must be inferred from fossils of skulls. Then there is the problem of dating these fossils, which involves using techniques developed by physical sciences, especially geology and organic chemistry. The second difficulty refers to the dangers our ancestors faced from their environment, both physical and animal. Compared with those creatures that saw them as food, they were neither fast nor big nor strong. One can reasonably ask how they survived to set the stage for contemporary human beings. The answer lies not only in the limited stone tools that they could hold in their hands, but more importantly in their ability to interact socially. Especially significant was the social cooperation that such interaction allowed.

Once our ancestors left the trees to walk upright on the ground, they needed larger or at least more complex brains to accomplish this bipedalism. Watson and Black (2008) have located six different brain parts necessary for the balance needed to walk upright. They are the cerebellum, pons, basal ganglia, cerebral cortex, vestibular system, and brain stem. The involvement of so many brain parts in balance suggests that walking upright is of critical importance to the evolutionary development of the hominin brain.

Dating Fossil Finds

The age of a fossil can be estimated by at least ten different methods. The first is relative dating, which simply places a fossil in chronological order according to its horizontal location of higher or lower in a stratum of rocks. Relative dating gives only a relative age, not a numerical age. For example, as the Colorado River cut through the layers of rock of the Grand Canyon it left visible layers of rock in horizontal patterns with the oldest layer at the bottom and youngest at the top. Using what is called stratigraphy, geologists can work out the relative ages of these strata and, by inference, also the age of fossils that are found within the strata. There are eight more specific age-dating methods that use the measurement of one or another of radioactive elements of the fossil that break down at a known rate over time. The amount of radioactive material surviving in the sample gives an estimate of its age. Radioactive carbon is the most common element measured, but potassium and uranium also are used.

What Is Distinctive about the *Homo sapiens* Brain?

Turner (2000: 90–91) describes differences in the relative sizes of brain components in apes and humans. Perhaps most important is the neocortex, which in *Homo sapiens* is three times the size of that of apes. Turner notes there are also more asymmetries in the *Homo sapiens* brain probably because of the distinct separate functions of its hemispheres even though they complement each other. Generally, the right side of the brain is seen as dealing with patterns like the ability to differentiate faces, while the left side deals with speech. The ability to speak is enabled by the Broca's area, which is associated with production of speech, while the Wernicke's area allows for the comprehension of speech. Much of the increase in the size of the human brain is due to the increase in the frontal lobe (Turner 2000: 90–91).

The prefrontal lobe is another area that is significantly developed in the human brain. The human prefrontal cortex is much larger than that of any other primate. This area is critical to cognition as well as to planning, emotional responses, and the decision-making processes these emotions make possible (Damasio 1994). There is also a significant difference in the size of the limbic system of the human brain as compared with other primates;

this larger limbic system allows for more complexity in the way of emotional output in humans compared with apes and their emotional responses.

The septum palladium separates the brain's lateral ventricles. It is attached to the corpus callosum and is where *Homo sapiens* process good feelings as well as rage and sexual gratification. There is a similar brain structure in the great apes, and this suggests that the corpus callosum was present early in our evolutionary line before *Homo sapiens* and its kin separated from the line that became modern apes. Functionally, the amygdala and the hippocampus work together to create memory. Both work in concert "when emotion meets memory" (Philips 2004). The amygdala enables emotionally charged memories (LeDoux 1996). The hippocampus is involved in the storage of two types of explicit declarative memories: semantic memories, which are recalled as facts and knowledge, and episodic memories, which store personal experience. The greater size of these areas in *Homo sapiens* suggests an enhanced role for memory in human brain function as compared with the apes.

The final brain comparisons involve the transition cortices. Functionally the association cortices act first. They compose a big part of the neocortex and are involved in integrating sensory inputs. These generate an image that is temporarily stored in buffers. The transitional cortices then pool the images and send them to the hippocampus, which creates a representation that is sent to the transition cortexes for intermediate storage as a memory (see Turner 2000: 105). In humans the transitional cortex is almost twice as large as in apes, again suggesting that memory plays a more important role for humans.

Notes on the Brains of Our Ancestors

Any tracing of the origins of the human brain must begin with the evolution of the primate neocortex. This area is not only a hallmark of human evolution but also one of the most distinctive traits of primates in general and of *Homo sapiens* in particular (Maryanski 2013: 258). In the course of primate evolution three factors helped to shape the neocortex:

1. The sensory legacy of early anthropoids and the shift to visual dominance
2. The great hominoid die-off that came later, which left only *Homo sapiens* as the survivor
3. A shift to forelimb dominance

The hominid shift to bipedalism in an open-country habitat further modified brain development and affected vision requirements. Although brain tissue does not last, casts of cranial fossil cavities are available that accurately represent the diverse pressures of the brain on the bones of the head; these cranial cavities allow interpretations to be made of brain structures that exist in them. Amazingly, the hominid neocortex is essentially like that of monkeys except for the convoluted surface of the hominin brain that allows it to fit into the brain cavity. This greatly enlarged brain surface provides for a significantly larger and more complex brain area.

The reader should also be aware that, according to some paleontologists, the fossil record should reveal a gradual evolution from ape to linguistic *Homo sapiens*; however, none of them found evidence that this was the case. Instead of finding a progression of one species leading to another, the fossil records show that species that were often seen as following each other actually existed concurrently with each other. Australopithecines did not change into *Homo habilis*, who then progressed to *Homo erectus*, who then became

Homo sapiens. Instead, fossils of *Homo erectus* have been found that were 1.8 million to 200,000 years old, and *Homo habilis* lived in the same time frame.

It may be helpful at this point to review some of the known hominins that preceded *Home sapiens* in time and examine their characteristics. According to Walker (1980), small Australopithecines in East Africa coexisted first with *Homo habilis* and then with *Homo erectus*. Louis Leakey (1971) found fossils from all three species close together in Tanzania. More recently, Meyers and Arsuaga (2013) found ancient hominin DNA in a Spanish fossil dating back about 400,000 years. It had been thought to belong to an ancestor of Neanderthal's labeled Denisovans. New dating methods were used to extract DNA from the femur that was found in a cave that the Spanish referred to as "the pit of bone." Meyers and Arsuaga have extracted twenty-eight nearly complete skeletons of humans from this site.

The reader should be cautioned that new discoveries as to fossil finds and dating techniques occur regularly. This area is a dynamic one in which a new discovery at any time may change our understanding of these creatures dramatically. Our current state of knowledge may be challenged and change tomorrow. The dates and descriptions represent the general view as it stands now.

Australopithecus

Humans and apes split from their last common ancestor 7 million years ago when one branch of great apes left the forest for the savannas; one branch of this line eventually developed into hominins, while others died out over time (Maryanski 2013: 28). The brain size of Australopithecines remained essentially the same during the entire time they existed, a period of 1.5 million years. During that time *Homo erectus* appeared and the two species coexisted. *Homo erectus* differed from the *Australopithecus afarensis* known as Lucy, who became extinct around 2.9 million years ago; the differences can be seen in the more vertical slope of her face, reduced brow ridges, and narrower cheekbones. The more rounded cranium endocasts show a significant increase in frontal and parietal lobes.

There were a number of varieties of Australopithecines over a period of several million years, all in Africa. *Au. afarensis* endured for about 3 million years until global cooling most likely extinguished them. They have been placed as a possible ancestor to the earliest humans because of their humanlike teeth and skull features. Other species of Australopithecines include *Au. ramidus* and *Au. amensis* appearing around 4 million years ago, with *Au. afarensis* coming on the African scene around 3 million years ago. *Au. gahi* and *Au. boisei* also appeared about 3 million years ago. Finally, *Au. sediba* appeared about 2 million years ago.

The earliest of the Australopithecines is called *Au. ramidus*, which means "root" in the local South African language where their fossils were first found. They were small at a little under three feet and weighed only about 110 pounds. Their appearance was about 4.4 million years ago, and they became extinct perhaps 1.4 million years ago. Their brains were about the size of a grapefruit, about 420 cc, a third of the size of ours. This is as close as we have come in finding our oldest ancestor. *Au. ramidus* may be the last common ancestor of chimpanzees and humans. Some even call them the "missing link," but this is misguided. They are ignoring something important about evolution; it happens gradually. There was no species that all of a sudden began to walk on the ground. As always there was intragroup variation with some brave individuals trying out a new behavior or technique and finding it useful while others did not. The expanded distance one could cover by walking would be hard to ignore, especially when an individual could climb back up to the protection of the trees when needed. Green and Alemseged (2012) have examined the shoulder joints of the famous Lucy fossil, who was an Australopithecine species referred to as *Au. africanus*. They think she spent half her life in the trees and the other half on the ground.

The old view was that Australopithecines represented a separate evolutionary experiment that came to a dead end. Some more contemporary scholars contend that one of them, *Au. sediba* of the species line of *Au. ramidus*, was the ancient forerunner of *Homo sapiens*. The preservation of fossil finds of *Au. sediba* is exceptional and allows a detailed picture of its unusual gait. The shoulders were shrugged and the long arms did not swing; the feet turned inward with each step. According to Wong (2013) the totality of evidence does not support *Au. sediba*'s status as a direct forerunner of *Homo sapiens*. *Au. sediba*, known from a female fossil, is dated as 2 million years old, which puts her deep enough in time to be an ancestor of *Homo erectus*. She combines a fascinating mix of features, some very old and some more modern. Most importantly, although her brain was only slightly larger than that of a chimpanzee's, she had an advanced reorganization in her prefrontal lobe. It is important that we do not become so fixed on brain size or quantity that we overlook quality or organization.

Australopithecines were forced to become high-end scavengers when they relocated from the dwindling forests to the savannas. But scavenging in the open spaces could not replace a fruit-enriched forest diet. Australopithecines solved this problem by cracking the bones of dead animals and eating the marrow (Suwa et al. 2009). Australopithecines deserve more credit than is usually given them. Being our first bipedal ancestors, they took small bipedal steps for apes and, as it turned out, a giant leap for mankind.

Bipedalism as developed by Australopithecines is of considerable importance to the evolutionary development of the hominin brain, although this has not always been recognized. Walking upright had tremendous advantages in addition to the greater distance it allowed one to cover. It freed the hands for carrying tools and infants over long distances, and it allowed a view over the grasslands of the savanna; thus, one could watch for the animals that stalked the Australopithecines as well as for those creatures he might catch for food.

Most paleontologists once thought our large brains and tool-making abilities were the pivotal early evolutionary innovation that distinguished hominids from apes. But these features actually came much later and were the result of bipedal ability. Molecular biologists, comparing the DNA of modern humans, chimpanzees, and gorillas, estimate that the decisive separation of apes and hominins occurred 7 million to 5 million years ago.

Recently Anton, Potts, and Aiello (2014) suggested an alternative approach to the idea that one event, like the development of the dry savannas, created the conditions that eventually led to *Homo sapiens*. They argue that the conventional idea that the group of human traits that came together in the genus *Homo* did not develop together but that such traits like tall and large bodies and slow development of children developed piecemeal instead of at the same time. What forced our physical lineage was variation in climate change that made us able to adapt to numerous such changes.

Homo habilis

Homo habilis was our oldest tool-making ancestor living in Africa and Asia in the late and early Pleistocene around 2.3 million to 1.4 million years ago. Nine different sources give numbers that vary from 2.4 million to 2 million years ago for their first appearance and place their extinction about 1.6 million to 1.4 million years ago. During this period, the brain of *Homo habilis* expanded from just under 550 cc to an average of 900 cc. In his early days, his brain capacity was only 100 cc more than that of an Australopithecine, but the later specimens show significant growth. The arms of *Homo habilis* were almost as long as his legs. He still was not very tall—only four feet on average.

Homo habilis lasted for about 1 million years during global climate cooling. He was the first hominid to make stone tools. He is placed as an ancestor to Archaic *Homo sapiens* because of his humanlike teeth and skull features. He ate his food raw because he had no control over fire. This meant that *Homo habilis* lacked the nourishment that cooked food would have provided.

He may have coexisted with Australopithecines and *Homo erectus* for 500,000 years and was the earliest known species to have shown novel differences from chimpanzees and Australopithecines. It is for this reason that he is classified as a hominin species. His place in evolution in relation to *Homo sapiens*, however, is far from clear.

Homo erectus

Some of the *Homo erectus* brains were encased in a skull, which was new from an evolutionary perspective in that it had a larger prefrontal lobe; his brain capacity ranged from 509 to 810 cc compared with our present 1,200–1,600 cc. This species was the earliest of the hominids to use fire in a controlled and purposeful way. Before this, *Homo habilis* knew of fire only when it was caused by lightning or volcanic eruption. Using it to cook food apparently did not occur to him. Much of the brain growth experienced by *Homo erectus*, however, could have been due to the use of fire and consumption of cooked foods. Multiple fossil sites in Europe and the Middle East contain *Homo erectus* fossils with the remains of fire. Consumption of cooked foods shrank the digestive tract, which in turn allowed more energy to be expended on a growing brain.

Cranial capacity increased with *Homo erectus*, whose fossil remains indicate an appearance on the African scene about 1.75 million years ago. *Homo erectus* was not a hunter but a high-end scavenger like his predecessors, who ate the meat of animals killed by other animals. This practice encouraged the development of communication with others of his own species because there was competition from other animals just as hungry as he who had to be held at bay by large numbers of his kind. Turner and Maryanski (2012) hypothesize that a 900 cc brain like that of the later members of *Homo erectus* would be able to have an identity. If so, this would mean they would also have the capacity for self-control and other talents, increasing social cohesion and cooperative acts. *Homo erectus* was certainly fit as they migrated all over the globe. They walked out of mid-Africa into southern Africa as well as to Spain, Italy, Russia, China, and even into Indonesia.

Archaic Homo sapiens

The term "Archaic *Homo sapiens*" refers to various finds of fossil skulls that have characteristics both of *Homo erectus* and of modern humans. Unfortunately there is little consensus on proper taxonomy of hominin fossils that follow *Homo erectus*. As a result they have been assigned to the catchall label of Archaic *Homo sapiens*. Their brain size was larger than that of *Homo erectus* but smaller than that of modern humans. The skull was also more rounded. Many had large brow ridges and were more robust than us. They also had receding chins and foreheads.

Their stone tools were generally similar to those of *Homo erectus* but some showed innovative advances that demonstrated technological intelligence. Their evolutionary line is a mystery. It may be that our true ancestors were a tiny gene pool of perhaps as few as some hundreds or as many as 10,000 individuals most often referred to as "advanced *Homo erectus*," "Archaic *Homo sapiens*," or "*Homo heidelbergensis*" (Maryanski 2013: 281).

Homo sapiens

Homo sapiens appeared 200,000 to 150,000 years ago, again in eastern Africa, the birthplace of primates. Turner and Maryanski (2012) point out that their neuroanatomical character was a mix of characteristics of all mammals and those that involve the fitness of primates in the arboreal habitat. According to Ramachandran (2011) and also Maryanski (2013), this mix involved a shift from a priority given to olfactory senses to a priority of those senses involved in sight. Smell has advantages that we may not appreciate. It is not dependent on light, and odors can travel long distances, especially if there is a wind. Every animal species has its own smell, and within each species, every individual has a specific odor. Turner and Maryanski (2012) join Ramachandran in stressing the importance of visual dominance among primates living in trees with their ability to judge the texture, distance, strength, and elasticity of branches. Keen eyesight and good depth perception can prevent deathly falls in vertical environments. Distinguishing among colors is also important. Selection favored eyes that were spread apart, making a world of three dimensions with straight-ahead vision. This visually acquired world gave rise to different capabilities that were far removed from trees and contributed to the development of human language.

An Amazing Story

Not too many of us would think that Australopithecines' arboreal life created the brain structures needed for the development of language millions of years later. Ramachandran (2011) starts his story about abstraction and language by using the term "exaptation" for a brain structure that evolved for one purpose and later became the basis for something else. Turner and Maryanski also key on the same idea, but use the term "spandrels."

Whatever the word used, Ramachandran (2011: 78) starts his narrative with something apparently far removed from anything having to do with language, namely, synesthesia (i.e., seeing numbers and even days of the week in colors). He then takes us into the very heart of language—the ability to abstract and talk in terms of metaphors. Speaking of metaphors, for sociologists the notion that we talk in terms of metaphors is "old hat" (Lakoff and Johnson 1980). We talk without awareness of metaphors about "slick" and "dense" people or, as Ramachandran (2011: 79) says, "sharp cheese or a loud shirt." He begins by verifying that synesthesia is a valid concept since some had argued that synesthetes were just remembering childhood experiences, presumably of remembering an experience of seeing numbers as colors although they no longer did so. In working with synesthetes, he noticed that the strength of a color depended not only on the number but also on exactly where in the visual field it appeared (Ramachandran 2011: 307). With the subject looking straight ahead, numbers presented off to the side seemed less visibly colored than those that were centrally located. This was true even though the peripheral numbers were larger so as to be equally visible. Ramachandran notes that when one recognizes a face it becomes recognized anywhere. To him, the fact that evoked colors look different in different regions argues strongly against memory associations and for the validity of synesthesia as a real contemporaneous experience.

He notes that in lower mammals the inferior parietal lobe is very small; it is larger in primates and becomes much larger in the great apes. Humans, however, are unique in that a major part of this lobule splits into the angular gyrus and the supramarginal gyrus. This suggested to Ramachandran (2011: 178) that something important was developing in terms of evolution. He thinks that this change allowed for the abstraction necessary for language and the "dissolution of barriers to create modality free representation" (131).

One intriguing example of modality-free representation is the bouba-kiki test. In this test the subject is shown two shapes: one is rounded and looks like a splat of paint, while the other is sharp edged like a jagged piece of broken glass. When people are asked which is called bouba and which is called kiki, they invariably choose bouba for the rounded shape and kiki for the jagged one. This holds true regardless of culture and language. This effect suggests an inherent translation between visualization, sound, and activity in the Broca's area of the brain, which has to do with the production of speech. Ramachandran (2011) points out that this surely involves mirror neurons.

These neurons fire when we perform a certain action like picking up a pencil and when we see someone else do the same thing. The inferior parietal lobule, which is rich in mirror neurons, is well suited for this role. In the case of the bouba-kiki test, the ability to see the commonalities in the dimensions of sound, visualization, and lip movements simultaneously is the essence of abstraction. Understanding what is common between a soft sound (bouba) and a rounded shape or between a sharp sound (kiki) and a sharp-edged shape is the basis of abstraction. This kind of abstraction allows for the development of language where sounds take on arbitrary and ascribed meanings.

If language is essentially built on abstraction, which has no physical form, one can legitimately ask how we can know when language began by using fossil evidence. We do have at least a hint of what is necessary for language in fossil form. The hyoid bone is a small, horseshoe-shaped bone that is distinctive because, instead of being attached to other bones, it is suspended from a muscle of the neck. This allows it to support the tongue and larynx and their muscles. Without this structure we could not make the various and complex sounds that are necessary for speech. According to Greenspan and Shanker (2004: 186) it was speech that made us human, not bigger brains or the ability to walk on our two legs.

The Cro-Magnons

Cro-Magnon humans were named after the cave in which their fossil remains were discovered in France. From a taxonomic standpoint they have no precise species name because they are not different enough from us to warrant one; they are referred to as early modern humans, or EMH. They are dated as living 40,000 to 10,000 years ago and were somewhat stockier than contemporary *Homo sapiens*; they were able to survive throughout the ice ages. The period in which they lived witnessed an amazing outburst of the development of skills and abilities. Noam Chomsky referred to this as the "big bang period," and others use the term "great leap forward." This period can be contrasted with the time of earlier hominins when change came about so slowly and primitive tools were unchanged for millions of years. If we look at the millions of years when Australopithecines, *Homo habilis*, and *Homo erectus* walked on earth and compare their time with the 40,000 years since Cro-Magnons came on the scene, the pace of change is almost blindingly fast. Perhaps change requires a certain critical mass, and once this is achieved, the process accelerates on its own.

Cro-Magnon humans lived in larger and larger groups, which meant they had to develop more social skills and communicative skills than the smaller groups of Neanderthals. Cro-Magnon also cared for their sick and elderly, but it was not limited to high-status leaders as apparently was true of Neanderthals. Cro-Magnon people developed bows and arrows for hunting. Their targets included such large animals as the wooly mammoths, which provided them with hides to keep their bodies warm as well as to insulate their dwellings. They sewed the mammoth hides together using bone needles. They cooked their food over fire and made their own animal traps. A clear indication of their sophistication is found in their extensive cave art created between 13,000 and 25,000 years ago. These caves were found far from their homes, which suggests that they may have had a sacred function (see Fagan 1996).

Although all these capacities of the human brain brought opportunity and power to our ancestors, it must be recognized that this advancement came at a significant cost. Most obvious is the large head of the *Homo sapiens* infant, which makes birth difficult and, until very recently, dangerous to both mother and child. The human infant must be born prematurely as compared with other species, unprepared for life outside the womb and very vulnerable. This makes enormous demands on the individual mother as well as the group as a whole. The prolonged development of the brain requires long periods of nurturing and socialization. The brain is also costly to the individual body. It consumes 20 percent of the body's energy, 20 percent of its calories, 25 percent of its electrochemical energy, and 15 percent of its oxygen. In addition to these demands, a serious side effect of this complexity is that the human brain is so prone to mental disorder (Franks 2010: 3).

Conclusion

To say that the story told here has been a long one is the essence of an understatement. We started with primate forms that appeared 6 million years ago, and dealt with numbers of years and dates that, while cognitively understandable, are beyond our human capacity to emotionally realize. *Homo habilis* made the same stone tools for a million years and seemingly took them for granted without conceiving of the need for modifications. But about 40,000 years ago (just 4 percent of 1,000,000 years) things changed dramatically and the status quo lost its grip.

The early Australopithecines who navigated high branches without falling to their deaths bequeathed to us a lasting inheritance. The brain capacities used for arboreal lifestyles, like visualization, supported the development of abstractions needed for human language. Once our ancestors could form an abstract image of their environment, they had the beginnings of the abstract framework for language.

The evolutionary advantages of bipedalism are important for much more than walking and the advantages thereof. Walking upright is important because it decisively adds to the complexity of our brains. This complexity involves six circuits of the brain needed to support balance, which is a prerequisite for bipedalism.

Modern DNA demonstrates decidedly that interbreeding took place between Neanderthals and early modern humans who coexisted for several thousand or more years. Rather than being quickly overrun by *Homo sapiens*, their disappearance was staggered, which suggests that local population extinctions led to their disappearance.

Another development of the human is the shift in the pace of change in evolution and development that occurred about 40,000 years ago and is referred to as "The Great Leap Forward" by Jared Diamond (1992). This refers to an abrupt increase in human capacities shortly after Neanderthals became extinct at the hands of *Homo sapiens* in the form of Cro-Magnon man. The essence of the great leap forward is *innovation*, but this depends on the circular process of having a critical mass of items at hand. Cro-Magnon's tools represented this innovation well. They included needles with eyes for sewing; composite tools like hammers, fishhooks, ropes, and spears; and even homes made of the ribs of mammoths and covered with hides.

The last, and obviously critical, point about the human brain is that its very nature is social. This has been alluded to but deserves more emphasis. The old and uninformed contention that humans have no distinct nature and that our natures are determined solely by the cultures in which we live flies in the face of what we now know about the human brain. We do have a nature and it is a social one. The human brain, that organ that most characterizes us, is social in its functions from the day we are born until the day we die (Gazzaniga 1985; Franks 2010; Turner 2013; Lieberman 2013; along with many others).

I conclude by saying that our very plastic brains are still changing. The "leap forward" has become a constant. A baby coming into our world twenty years from now will face a very different world from today's. Our brains, and thus our very senses and knowledge, will continue to change.

References

Anton, S., R. Potts, and L. Aiello. 2014. "Evolution of Early *Homo*: An Integrated Biological Perspective." *Science* 345 (6192): 1236828.
Damasio, A. 1994. *Descartes' Error: Emotion, Reason, and the Human Brain*. New York: Avon.
Diamond, J. 1992. *The Third Chimpanzee: The Evolution and Future of the Human Animal*. New York: Harper Perennial.
Edelman, G. M. 2004. *Wider than the Sky: The Phenomenal Gift of Consciousness*. New Haven, CT: Yale University Press.
Fagan, B. M. 1996. *The Oxford Companion to Archaeology*. New York: Oxford University Press.
Franks, D. D. 2010. *Neurosociology: The Nexus between Neurosociology and Social Psychology*. New York: Springer Press.
Gazzaniga, M. S. 1985. *The Social Brain: Discovering the Networks of the Mind*. New York: Basic Books.
Green, D., and Z. Alemseged. 2012. "*Australopithecus afarensis* Scapular Ontogeny, Function, and the Role of Climbing in Human Evolution." *Science* 338 (6106): 514–517.
Greenspan, S., and S. Shanker. 2004. *The First Idea: How Symbols, Language and Intelligence Evolved from Our Primate Ancestors to Modern Humans*. Cambridge, MA: Da Capo Press.
Lakoff, G., and M. Johnson. 1980. *Metaphors We Live By*. Chicago and London: University of Chicago Press.
Leakey, M. D., R. J. Clarke, and L.S.B. Leakey. 1971. "New Hominid Skull from Bed I, Olduvai Gorge, Tanzania." *Nature* 232 (5309): 308–312.
Leakey, R.E.F., and A. Walker. 1980. "On the Status of *Australopithecus afarensis*." *Science* 207 (4435): 1103.
LeDoux, J. E. 1996. *The Emotional Brain*. New York: Simon and Schuster.
Lieberman, M. 2013. *Social: Why Our Brains Are Wired to Connect*. New York: Crown Publishers.
Maryanski, A. 2013. "The Secret of the Hominid Mind." In *The Handbook of Neurosociology*, edited by D. Franks and J. H. Turner, 257–288. New York: Springer Press.
Meyer, M., Q. Fu, A. Aximu-Petri, I. Glocke, B. Nickel, J.-L. Arsuaga, I. Martínez, A. Gracia, J. M. Bermúdez de Castro, E. Carbonell, and S. Pääbo. 2014. "A Mitochondrial Genome Sequence of a Hominin from Sima de los Huesos." *Nature* 505: 403–406.
Ramachandran, V. S. 2011. *The Tell-Tale Brain: A Neuroscientist's Quest for What Makes Us Human*. New York: W. W. Norton & Company.
Suwa, G., R. T. Kono, S. W. Simpson, B. Asfaw, C. O. Lovejoy, and T. D. White. 2009. "Paleobiological Implications of the *Ardipithecus ramidus* Dentition." *Science* 326 (5949): 69, 94–99.
Turner, J. H. 2000. *On the Origins of Human Emotions: A Sociological Inquiry into the Evolution of Human Affect*. Stanford, CA: Stanford University Press.
———. 2013. "Neurosociology and Interpersonal Behavior: The Basic Challenge for Neurosociology." In D. D. Franks and J. H. Turner, eds., *The Handbook of Neurosociology*, 119–137. New York: Springer Press.
Turner, J. H., and A. Maryanski. 2012. "The Biology and Neurology of Group Processes." *Advances in Group Processes* 29: 1–37.
Watson, M. A., and F. O. Black. 2008. *The Human Balance System: A Complex Coordination of Central and Peripheral Systems*. Portland, OR: Vestibular Disorders Association.
Wong, K. 2013. "Is *Australopithecus sediba* the Most Important Human Ancestor Discovery Ever?" *Scientific American* (blog), April 24. http://blogs.scientificamerican.com/observations/2013/04/24/is-australopithecus-sediba-the-most-important-human-ancestor-discovery-ever/.

Chapter Sixteen
The Human Behavioral Ecology of Foragers

Robert L. Kelly

> This chapter reviews the use of human behavioral ecology (HBE) in the social sciences. Like evolutionary ecology in biology, HBE combines previous ecological and evolutionary approaches. It is used most commonly in the archaeological and ethnological study of hunting and gathering societies but is not limited to that form of human society. This chapter reviews contributions of the paradigm to the study of foraging, mobility, technology, food sharing, territoriality, group size, reproductive ecology, division of labor, and social and political organization.

This chapter reviews the application of the paradigm of HBE in the study of hunter-gatherers, or foragers. Although researchers have studied several forms of human society from the perspective of HBE, it has been most prevalent in the study of foragers. Some critics argue that HBE is applied primarily to foragers because the Western world conceives of such people as "closer to nature." Perhaps, but it may also be a product of how it was introduced to anthropology.

HBE is the third paradigm in the social sciences that is aimed at understanding the relationship between humans and their environments. The first was the culture area approach, popular in the early twentieth century (e.g., Wissler 1926), followed by cultural ecology, best known through the work of Julian Steward (1955). Neither of these approaches benefitted from a full understanding of ecology, a field whose modern form arose in the 1920s. The great insight of ecology, one that today seems banal, was recognition that the natural world is interconnected, that one aspect of the natural world does not change without linked change in another area. Ecology was not complete, therefore, until the rise of systems theory (or cybernetics) in the 1950s and 1960s (e.g., Bertalanffy 1968). Studies informed by systems theory, however, focused on ecosystem function, not on explanation. Recognizing that the explanation of ecosystems required a historical perspective, researchers united ecology with evolutionary principles, a field known as evolutionary ecology (Hutchinson 1965; MacArthur 1972; MacArthur and Pianka 1966; Orians 1969; Pianka 1978). Anthropologists Eric Smith and Bruce Winterhalder were introduced to this field during graduate studies at Cornell University (where cultural ecologist Brooke Thomas and evolutionary ecologist Stephen Emlen taught). Both Smith and Winterhalder researched hunter-gatherers, and so evolutionary ecology was introduced to anthropology through the study of foraging societies, and it has been a strong paradigm there for the past thirty years.

BASIC PRINCIPLES

Evolutionary ecology was concerned with understanding the evolutionary basis of animal behavior and biology (collectively termed "adaptive design") in an ecological context. HBE is less concerned with biology and more concerned with understanding how different human behaviors are adaptive within a particular environmental and social context. Two hallmarks of HBE are the use of mathematical and graphical models to predict variation in behavior under different environmental circumstances, and the use of empirical, ethnographic data to test predictions. Researchers working within this paradigm have made important long-term field studies of foragers such as the African Hadza, Aka, Efe, and Bofi; Madagascar's Mikea; the Canadian Inujjuamiut and Cree; the South American Ache, Pumé, Tsimane, and Hiwi; Australia's Meriam and Martu; and Indonesia's Lamalera. Archaeologists, perhaps even more than ethnographers, have applied the paradigm to the study of prehistoric hunter-gatherers (Broughton and Cannon 2010). In its early days, HBE was concerned with foraging behavior because of the obvious link between food and reproductive fitness. In the last thirty years, however, the subjects have expanded to mobility, sharing, technology, reproduction, and social and political organization.

HBE seeks to understand how natural selection has shaped human behavior, and it sees variation in behavior, within and among groups, as the subject rather than "noise" that needs to be explained away. As an evolutionary paradigm, HBE assumes that human behavior to some extent reflects a history of natural selection.

Natural selection changes the frequency of *genotypes* in a population but operates directly on *phenotypes*—the properties of organisms that are produced by the interaction of the genotype with its environment. A phenotype is judged to be more or less adaptive depending on whether it contributes more or less genetic material than other phenotypes to succeeding generations.

For humans, phenotypes include cultural behaviors, and this begs the question of the link between behavioral and genetic variation. A "strong sociobiological thesis" argues for a close link between genetic and behavioral variation. If a behavior is genetically controlled, and if that behavior endows its bearers with greater reproductive success, then it is easy to see how that behavior could become more prevalent in a population. The problem in applying this principle to humans, of course, is that cultural behaviors are not genetically determined.

Therefore, HBE adheres to a "weak sociobiological thesis," which recognizes that there are no genes for behaviors such as hunting or matrilineal descent, but assumes that behaviors that are linked to fitness in a particular natural and social environment that are heritable (through culture) and whose *average* net effect maximizes individual reproductive or inclusive fitness should tend to become prevalent in a population (Cronk 1991).

HBE employs two assumptions: methodological individualism and optimization. Selection operates on variability and favors individuals whose behavior enhances the opportunity to increase fitness. Thus, individual choices rather than cultural norms are the focus. However, HBE recognizes that an individual's goals come from biological and cultural information—cultural norms. The drive to "succeed" entails not only biological directives (to reproduce) but cultural norms as well (e.g., bring home as much meat as possible, spend time with offspring, acquire prestige or wealth). Goals must be defined, but HBE does not assume that the goals of all members of a society will be identical. HBE requires only that individuals be capable of storing knowledge and of understanding (or at least thinking that they understand) the relationship between their actions and goals.

The optimization assumption, for hunter-gatherers, is that foraging efficiency is a proxy measure of reproductive fitness (see Alvard and Gillespie 2004; Smith 2004) and that while there are different specific *reasons* to maximize foraging efficiency, one or more will characterize any environment (Smith 1983: 626). But don't be fooled by the term "optimal." This is merely an assumption that permits the construction of models—for example, what would a forager do if foraging were all that mattered. No one actually expects "optimal" foraging, because there are always conflicting demands: foraging, child care, technology, social obligations, and so on. All choices, therefore, entail an *opportunity cost*, because devoting time to one activity means not devoting time to another. Foraging longer means more food but less time with offspring; collecting berries means less time searching for game.

Since organisms can be pulled in different directions to achieve different goals, choices are inevitably compromises. Recognizing this, some analysts prefer game theoretic approaches (see Smith and Winterhalder 1992) that describe *evolutionarily stable strategies*, mixes of behavioral variants of which none is perfectly "optimal." In addition, since evolution differentially transmits existing information from generation to generation, natural selection produces only the strategy that achieves goals better than other existing ones, and not necessarily the "best" one.

So far, this all sounds plausible for animals, where the link between food and reproduction is obvious. But what about humans, whose behavior is largely driven by culturally defined standards? Although we can find societies where individuals consciously strive to maximize foraging efficiency or prestige, we do not find societies that consciously value "reproductive fitness." Behavioral ecologists argue that individuals who meet culturally defined standards of success should manifest a behavioral variant that achieves greater fitness than other variants. Is this true, or is HBE using evolutionary theory as mere analogy? What about culture?

Many anthropologists reject HBE, asking just how subconscious can a drive for reproductive fitness be and yet still direct behavioral choices? And how do we explain cultural behaviors that seem to go against reproductive fitness, such as vows of chastity or poverty, abortion, or infanticide?

HBE claims that the biological *capacity* for culture must have arisen through a process of natural selection. Individuals who were cultural beings, at some point in the past, became more prevalent in a population at the expense of those hominins who were not cultural. For some this means that cultural behavior is an extension of biological adaptation and operates for similar purposes. Indeed, humans pass on information between generations about kinship, subsistence, religion, morals, aesthetics, and so on. Since cultures change through time, information is obviously lost and gained (brought in through diffusion, independent invention, or "errors" in the enculturative process). This means that culture is analogous to genetics, and so we might assume that it operates according to some principles of inheritance (Bettinger 1991; Boyd and Richerson 1985).

But culture is not a simple extension of biology, and once hominins became cultural the rules of the evolutionary game changed. Recall that evolution is the differential persistence of information—some of that information is genetic, but for humans, much of it is cultural. Cultural information is passed on through enculturation rather than reproduction. We receive our genes from our biological parents, but we acquire our culture from many people. For humans, changes in genotypic frequencies rarely, and perhaps never, have a direct effect on cultural change.

Many anthropologists argue that diversity in human behavior is the manifestation of various cultural values that can only be understood within particular cultural and historical contexts. However, in any given culture at any given time, each individual represents slight variations of cultural norms, and culture change is change in the frequency of these variants. How do behavioral variants within a society change in frequency over time? What determines whether new behaviors or ideas are accepted or rejected, whether an existing behavior becomes more or less prevalent? If the capacity for culture is biological, is there a link between cultural behaviors and biology even if those behaviors are not genetically controlled?

These are not questions that should be answered before inquiry, but are, in fact, the subject of inquiry. Theoretical models (e.g., Boyd and Richerson 1985) show that the cultural transmission of information can produce results contrary to models based solely on biological imperatives. For example, in many past societies wealthy families had the most offspring since more wealth means more food, medical care, housing (and, in some cases, multiple wives), and more offspring raised to adulthood. But in developed nations such as the United States, Japan, and western Europe, this pattern has reversed in the last half-century: wealthy countries have the lowest birthrates. This reflects cultural perceptions among the wealthy as to what is needed to raise children to adulthood (e.g., private schools, expensive extracurricular activities); it is also linked to cultural ideas of gender and work that may be linked to the perceived need to increase family income with two wage-earners. As a result, and despite their resources, wealthy families see offspring as expensive and consequently have few—and so culture affects reproductive fitness. One implication of this observation is that we need more research on how changes in adult activities affect enculturation, the process whereby children learn their culture.

In the remainder of this chapter, we consider those areas of life in foraging societies where HBE has been applied: foraging, mobility, technology, demography, food sharing, territoriality, and social and political organization. The beauty of HBE is that in all these cases, the simple models used can accommodate the many specific variables of human life and lead to predictions for realms of behavior not initially covered by the models; it is a remarkably productive paradigm.

Foraging Behavior

The earliest models from evolutionary ecology to be applied to human societies were optimal-foraging models (Winterhalder and Smith 1981). The most prevalent of these is the Diet-Breadth Model (DBM), which predicts whether a forager will seek a broad or focused set of food resources (Bettinger 2009; Bird and O'Connell 2006; Hill and Hawkes 1983; Smith 1983, 1991). Another is the Patch Choice model, which similarly asks whether a forager uses a broad or narrow range of foraging locality types. We will focus on the DBM.

Optimal-foraging models include a goal, a currency, a set of constraints, and a set of options. The goal is normally maximization of foraging efficiency (food gathered per unit time); the currency is usually calories; constraints include such things as the maximum amount of time that can be spent foraging and competing activities (e.g., caring for children); and the options are the potential food resources.

The DBM uses *search* and *handling costs* to predict which food resources will be taken while foraging (Figure 16.1). Search cost is the time it takes to find a given food resource, and handling cost is how long it takes to harvest and process the food item. Search cost is largely a product of a resource's abundance. Handling cost goes into calculating a resource's *post-encounter return rate* (or, the *return rate*, expressed in kcal/hr). Return rates are based on ethnographic field data or experimental research with reconstructed technologies (e.g., Simms 1987). For example, let's say that a forager expects to encounter a field of ricegrass containing an average of 1,000 kg of seeds for every three hours of searching. The search cost is therefore 3 hrs/1,000 kg = .003 hr/kg—less than a minute per kilogram. Simms (1987: 119) harvested and processed ricegrass using aboriginal technology; after 41 minutes he had 98 grams of edible food, for a handling cost of .68 hr/.098 kg = 6.97 hr/kg. While it takes less than a minute to find a kilogram of ricegrass seeds, it takes seven hours to harvest and process it. Ricegrass contains 2.74 kcal/gram, so its post-encounter return rate is 2.74 × 98 g/41 min = 6.55 kcal/min or 393 kcal/hr.

Post-encounter return rates are crucial because *the DBM assumes that resources are added to the diet in order of their post-encounter return rates*. This is because when a forager encounters a resource, he or she must decide whether to harvest it or search for something better. The decision to harvest a particular resource depends on whether the post-encounter return rate of the resource just encountered is more or less than the return from continuing to search for and harvest higher-ranked resources. In fact, a central tenet of the DBM is that *the decision to include a resource depends on the abundance of higher-ranked resources*.

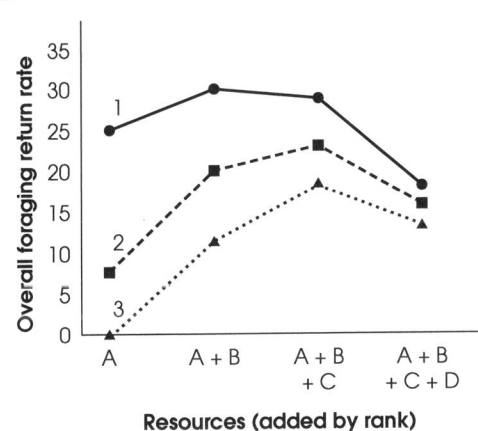

(1) With resources A and B abundant, resource C is not included in the diet.
(2) When resources A and B are rare, resource C is included.
(3) Though most abundant, resource D is never in the diet, even when A is extinct.

Note that the highest overall foraging return rate declines as the diet expands from one of resources A and B; to one composed of A, B, and C; to one composed of only B and C.

Resource	Search time (min)	Hand. time (min)	Kcal/unit resource	Return rate (kcal/min)	In the time it takes to forage unit of resource A (kcal/min)	Overall foraging return rate
A	30 (120)	10	1,000	100	1 (1)	for A: 25.0 (7.7)
B	20 (30)	20	800	40	1 (4)	for A + B: 30.0 (20.0)
C	20	30	800	26	1 (6)	for A + B + C: 28.9 (23.1)
D	10	40	400	10	3 (12)	for A + B + C + D: 18.1 (15.9)

Note: Values in parentheses represent lower abundance of resources A and B (line 2 in graph).

Figure 16.1 A graphic representation of how a hypothetical diet changes with decreases in high-ranked resources

The data needed for the model, however, are complex and difficult to collect from ethnographic studies; and experimentally derived rates can be suspect because the researcher is never as good a forager as "real" hunter-gatherers. Return rates depend on whether resources are taken communally (e.g., rabbit drives) or processed in bulk (seeds, some insects); on the technology (e.g., fishing with nets vs. a hook and line, using dogs); on seasonal changes in food composition (e.g., fat content); on environmental conditions (e.g., soil conditions if digging tubers); on a person's age and skill; and on cultural ideas of what constitutes food. Rather than create complications, however, these variables permit testing of the model in ethnographic cases, for example, how guns (by reducing handling time) change resource selection. The DBM approximates the decision-making process that a forager makes, and it has successfully predicted hunter-gatherer diet in a number of instances (see Kelly 2013).

An important aspect of optimal foraging models is Eric Charnov's (1976) *marginal value theorem* (MVT; Figure 16.2). The original intent of this theorem was to predict when an animal should leave one foraging patch for another. The MVT models common sense: a forager enters a patch, starts collecting berries, and experiences a high return rate. As the patch is depleted, berries become harder to find, and the overall foraging return rate declines. If the forager remains long enough, searching for the last berry, he or she will have to eat the berries already gathered—and the return rate will become negative. The MVT seeks the rule to use in order to know when to leave the patch for another.

Moving takes time, time that could be devoted to picking berries in the current patch. Charnov found that to maximize the foraging return rate, *foragers will move out of a resource patch when the marginal return rate in that patch reaches the average rate for all*

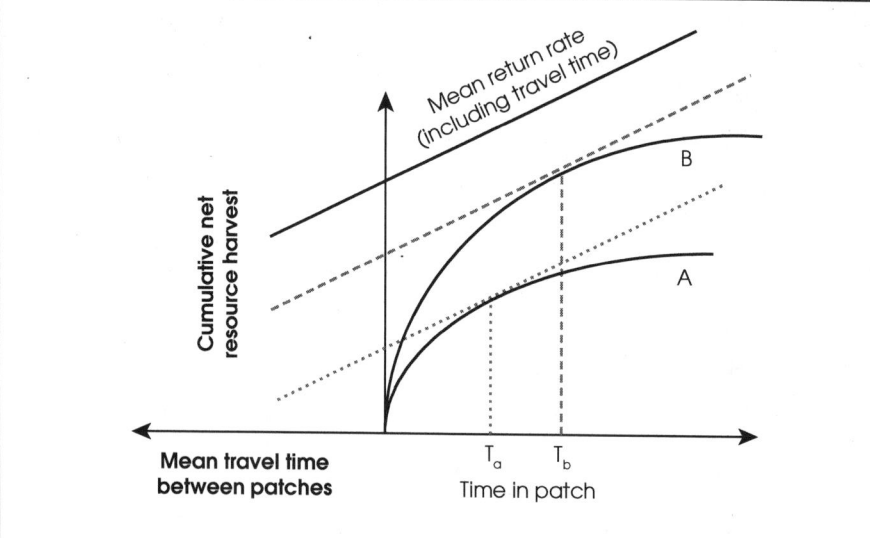

The mean return rate is the average net return rate for the environment *including* travel time between patches. The two curves (A and B) show the change in returns for two foraging patches over time; B is more productive than A. The marginal value theorem predicts that a forager should spend less time in A than in B but in either case would leave long before a patch is completely depleted of food.

Figure 16.2 Graphic representation of the marginal value theorem

potential resource patches, with travel time included. (The marginal return rate at any point along a curve is the slope of a line tangent to the curve at that point.) From this, we can demonstrate that although foragers will remain longer in some patches than in others, *they would always leave before resource exhaustion occurs.* This apparently simple observation has many other applications.

For example, the animal foragers for whom foraging models were initially developed tend to be feed-as-you-go, but humans are *central place foragers*—they harvest food in the field and then return to camp with it. To do so, humans process the food partially—butcher an animal to some degree, or remove pinyon pine seeds from their cones. But time spent processing is time not spent harvesting. The MVT helps because the question "how much should we process a resource in the field?" is similar to "how long should we forage in this patch?" And again, it has to do with distance: process the resource until the return rate, taking travel time to camp into consideration, is equivalent for the unprocessed and processed resource (e.g., Zeanah 2002).

Mobility

Most hunter-gatherers are nomadic, moving in response to the availability of food. We can anticipate how frequently they move with the MVT. As foragers deplete a camp's immediate area, they must travel farther. As they do, they devote more time and energy to walking, and less to foraging. At some point those foragers will decide it is worthwhile to forgo food collection and invest time in moving camp to a new location. Ethnographic data suggest that the maximum daily foraging radius from camp is about 10 km (beyond this, foragers will remain away from camp at night). As expected from the MVT, foragers often move after exploiting food within a <5 km radius. Many variables affect this relationship and the specific outcome: distance to the next camp, the terrain's difficulty, the time it takes to manufacture housing, and travel technology.

This perspective on mobility sheds a different light on sedentism—the lack of camp mobility. And this matters because sedentary communities are associated with non-egalitarian sociopolitical organization (see below). Why stop moving? One might assume that the year-round availability of food within a reasonable foraging radius is a *necessary* condition for hunter-gatherers to become sedentary and remain hunter-gatherers rather than become agriculturalists. But is it a sufficient condition? The MVT predicts that even if a location could be occupied for a year, it would be abandoned long before as a function of diminishing returns. In fact, the MVT suggests that *the only reason hunter-gatherers would not move is if there is no place to move to.* And the most likely impediment would be high population density and groups inhabiting every habitable place on the landscape. Such a situation could encourage sedentism since the alternative would require the cost of physically displacing another group.

This implies that sedentary villages are associated with control of a resource extraction point and that sedentism has a domino effect: when one group becomes sedentary, it increases the cost of moving for everyone else. As in the game of musical chairs, other groups will grab their own places on the landscape—and through a particular historical process. The ideal-free distribution (Figure 16.3) points out that once the returns from the best area have declined to the point where they are equal to the highest rate from a neighboring, less productive area, some people will move to that less productive area. This predicts that in a region undergoing population pressure, over time specific locales will be occupied by sedentary groups in their rank order of foraging returns; some archaeological case studies support this (Kennett 2005).

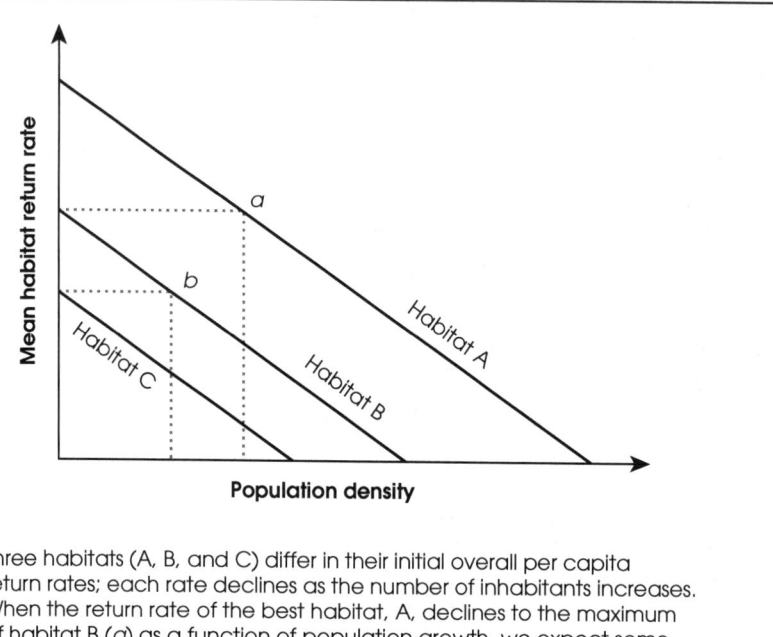

Three habitats (A, B, and C) differ in their initial overall per capita return rates; each rate declines as the number of inhabitants increases. When the return rate of the best habitat, A, declines to the maximum of habitat B (*a*) as a function of population growth, we expect some people to abandon A and move to the unoccupied B. Likewise, as habitat B fills with people, at a per capita return rate equal to *b* some will move to habitat C.

Figure 16.3 Ideal-free distribution

TECHNOLOGY

Although many foragers have few material possessions, and simple ones at that, there are those with an enormous amount of material goods, including some complex tools. There is, in fact, a tight statistical relationship between complex gear, mobility, and risk (Read 2008): as foragers become less mobile and/or as their environment becomes more risky, their gear becomes more complex and specialized. Complex gear is presumably very good at its job, but it also requires time for its manufacture. So the question is, under what conditions is it worth investing time in *making* complex, efficient gear rather than in *using* less complex, less efficient gear?

To answer this question we again turn to the MVT (Bettinger, Winterhalder, and McElreath 2006). The basic form of any technology can be constructed rather quickly and will increase the return over that of foraging with no technology—imagine fishing with your bare hands versus using a simple sharpened stick. Incremental improvements to that sharpened stick will increase the rate of return, but at some point additional improvements will have increasingly smaller effect. In the model (Figure 16.4), the right-hand x-axis is time invested in manufacture, the y-axis is the resulting return, and the left-hand x-axis is the period of time the tool will be used. In this case, the marginal return rate is *relative to manufacturing time*.

This model predicts that a more elaborate, "expensive" technology will replace a simpler technology when the two technologies share a marginal return rate. The marginal return

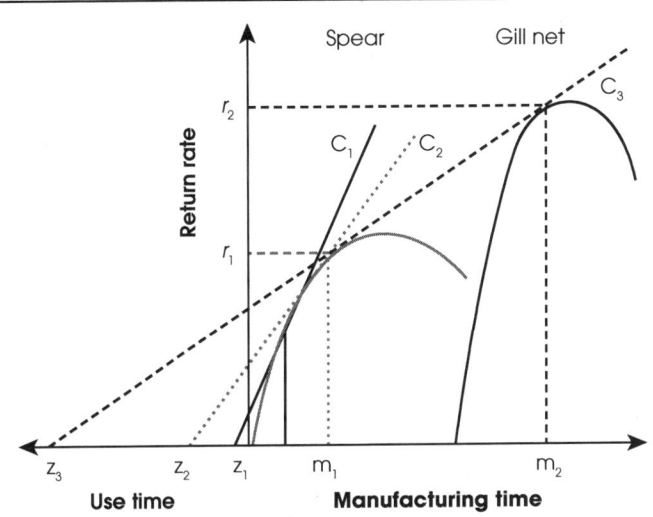

Figure 16.4 A model of technological change, showing a hypothetical relationship between spear and gill net fishing return rates

Source: Based on Bettinger, Winterhalder, and McElreath (2006).

The two curves depict changes in the return rates from spear and gill net fishing with embellishments within each technology type. The right-hand x-axis is time devoted to making and improving each technology; a gill net provides a higher return rate than a simple spear but requires more time to manufacture (m_1 versus m_2). The left-hand x-axis reflects increasing use times of the technology, from z_1 to z_3. Lines C_1 through C_3 are declining marginal return rates that include manufacturing time (just as the marginal value theorem includes travel time between patches). As the use time of the spear increases (in this example, as fish become more important to diet), the left-hand x-axis intercept shifts from z_1 to z_2 to z_3, and the benefit of technological improvements to the spear declines relative to their return. At some point in this process (line C_3) the marginal return rates of the low- and high-investment technologies are equal and, with its higher return rate, it makes sense to invest time in the more expensive technology.

rate decreases as the simpler technology is embellished. At some point, the two curves will share a tangent; when they do, they share a marginal return rate and the model predicts technological change. Increasing embellishments presumably reflects increasing use of a technology; so as a technology is used more, for example, as a population relies more and more on fishing, embellishments eventually drive a population to leapfrog to an entirely new, more complex technology.

It's common sense, but the model leads to several insights: when technology changes, it is expected to change (1) quickly, because the decision to invest in a new technology is normally of the either-or type; (2) pervasively across a population as the benefits and specifications of a new technology become known; and (3) usually irreversibly, because it alters knowledge of the net return that is possible with a new technology, and maintenance/construction becomes embedded in other activities and downtime. Finally, the model suggests that no more than two variants of a technology should exist in a population because it is highly unlikely that the return functions of three technologies would share a single tangent; but two technologies always will and so they might be in use jointly as populations or individuals undergoing similar processes (e.g., change in the food base) experience the pressure to switch at different times.

Food Sharing

Widespread food sharing is often considered a primary characteristic of foragers. And it is for some, but not all. Those who do share often do so after much dunning, and they keep a mental ledger. Sharing does not reflect warm-heartedness as much as it reflects a complex system of debt construction and repayment, and avoidance of the social cost of stinginess. HBE has come up with several ways to account for sharing.

Kin Selection

From an evolutionary point of view, we expect foragers to provide resources to individuals in relation to how closely related they are to them biologically. Following W. Hamilton (1964), the value of the food to the giver, C, should be less than the benefit, B, to the receiver times the fraction of relatedness, r: $Br > C$. For siblings and offspring $r = .5$, for biological cousins $r = .125$, and so on. The other values (B and C) are in fitness terms and are not easily measured. Still, one expectation is that foragers should keep most of their food within their own household. This is true (Kaplan and Hill 1985; Gurven 2004), and it's no surprise that parents share food with their children.

Reciprocal Altruism

The most obvious form of food sharing among foragers is that of meat from large game, and there are three reasons why:

1. Meat is nutritious, and humans have an evolved preference for the taste of fat.
2. Large game enters camp as a package of food that a hunter cannot use all at once (more on this below).
3. Large game is not easily acquired; even the best hunter has off days.

Computer simulations that account for daily variance in returns and the degree of synchronicity in those returns show that a forager increases his (and his family's) average meat intake if he shares high-return-rate but non-synchronous foods—large game—with other hunters and their families, who then return the favor in the future (Winterhalder 1986a). However, ethnographic data also show that some men contribute more meat than others, and good hunters may receive other benefits, such as extramarital affairs (Hawkes 1992), more attention to the hunter's offspring, or assistance when a productive hunter is ill or injured (Allen-Arave, Gurven, and Hill 2008; Gurven et al. 2000).

Tolerated Theft (or Tolerated Scrounging)

Sharing in foraging societies often takes the form of "demand-sharing," where sharing follows badgering rather than reminders of past generosity (Blurton Jones 1987). Tolerated theft predicts food sharing when the cost of defending a resource exceeds the benefit of keeping it. This happens anytime a forager brings in an amount of food that cannot be used immediately, and that is always true of large game. From the sated hunter's perspective, the *immediate* value of leftover meat is not worth fighting over; but it is from the perspective of one who is hungry. Sharing meat avoids the potential cost of fighting over a resource that has little immediate value to its owner. This doesn't mean that foragers fight over food; in fact, they don't. And even small foods that we would not predict would be shared are shared if someone asks. There is a social cost to being stingy, and that cost may be higher than *any* food brought into *any* foraging camp. This actually opens the door for some to game the system and intentionally target shareable foods, a fact that leads us to a final explanation of sharing.

Costly Signaling

Costly signaling hypothesizes that selection has produced the proclivity for the signaling of attributes (genetic or otherwise) through "costly" displays (Zahavi 1997). This is usually thought of in terms of male behavior and sexual selection. Darwin, for example, used this to explain "wasteful" biological elements such as the peacock's tail. With an extravagant and metabolically expensive appendage, the peacock says to potential mates: "I can invest a lot of energy in my tail and yet it does me no harm. I am physiologically stronger than other males. Pick me." Costly signaling moves this idea to the realm of behavior.

For costly signaling to work, a behavior must be costly (this is the *handicap principle*), and it must be honest. Hunting accomplishes this by bringing in a large amount of tasty, nutrient-dense food at one time (Hawkes and Bliege Bird 2002: 58). Some researchers see costly signaling as the primary driver behind men's hunting; men share meat to garner some (reproductive) advantage, for example, more mates, early marriage, wives who are the best foragers, or alliances with other good hunters. (Costly signaling could also explain other "conspicuous consumption" behaviors, e.g., monumental architecture, body modification at coming-of-age ceremonies, expensive public rituals, or eating inefficiently gathered foods such as truffles or caviar).

All of these explain some aspects of sharing, some operating more at one point in a person's life than at another. Young men's hunting may be more explained by costly signaling; older men's hunting by kin selection and reciprocal altruism. Tolerated theft explains some, but more to preserve someone's social standing (and future cooperation) than to alleviate a potential fight.

Territoriality

The economic-defensibility model (EDM) focuses on the cost and benefit of defending resources (Dyson-Hudson and Smith 1978). Similar to tolerated theft, it argues that territoriality occurs when the cost of defending a resource is less than the benefit derived from it. If a resource is not very dense and its occurrence in time and space is unpredictable, then the cost of defending it could be so high as to offset any gains from its exclusive use. Where resources are dense and predictable, they are worth the effort of defense and exclusive use (Figure 16.5). This model accounts for some of the variability we see among foragers' territorial behavior (e.g., Eerkens 2009).

Dense, predictable resources can be defended at low cost, because only a small area must be defended. But with population growth, demand will increase and at some point defense will require increased investment, in *perimeter defense* (building walls, patrolling borders, attacking trespassers, and making retaliatory or preemptive raids). When a population reaches carrying capacity, the benefit of trying to take a resource becomes worth the potential cost and, consequently, so too does defending a resource. What happens, though, where resources are neither dense nor predictable?

Perimeter defense is rare among foragers; more commonly, they acquire *permission to use* land that "belongs" to another group, and that permission is virtually ensured.

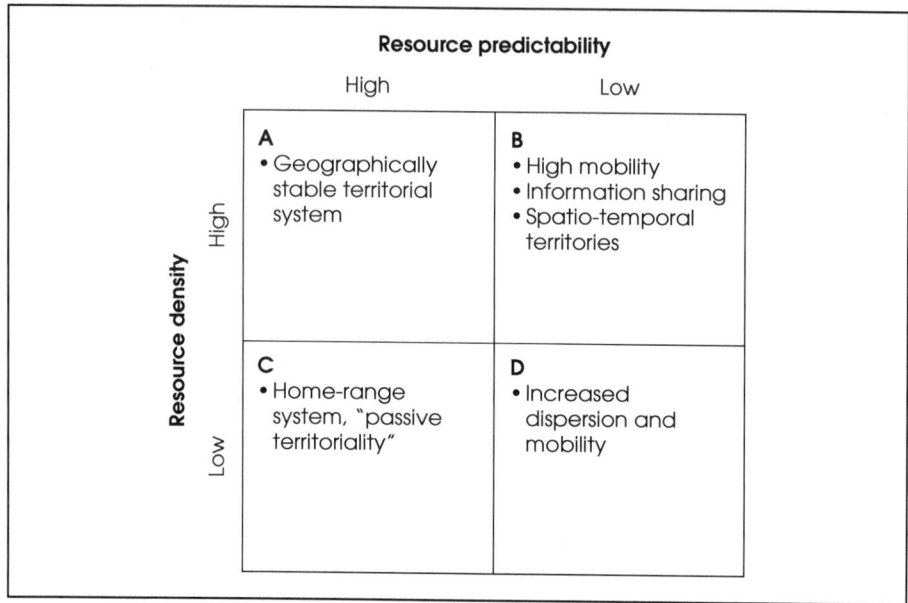

Figure 16.5 The economic defensibility model
Source: Redrawn from Dyson-Hudson and Smith (1978).
Reproduced by permission of the American Anthropological Association from
American Anthropologist 80, no. 1 (March 1978): 26, figure 1.
Not for sale or further reproduction.

Resources are not there for the taking, but they may be there for the asking. The giving of permission is the giving of a gift—and is similar to sharing. And as with sharing, there are costs and benefits to allowing others in: the visitors may reduce the host's foraging efficiency, but they also must reciprocate in the future. Cashdan (1983) argued that the benefits outweigh the costs when resources are scarce and (consequently) territories are large, making them difficult to patrol, and when food productivity is variable across the landscape, meaning that the tables may be turned in a future year. Under these conditions, foragers ensure access to the resources of another group by maintaining social access to that group, and they can do this through myriad social conventions (see Kelly 2013). Trespass is possible but is a poor decision because trespassers may not have sufficient knowledge of a region to make use of it, and if trespassers are detected (through their tracks, smoke from fires, etc.) they risk retaliation and future exclusion.

We can model the conditions for perimeter versus social boundary defense by modifying Winterhalder's (1986a) model of food sharing. Here we use variance in a residential group's return rate over time and the degree of correlation in returns of different groups. High variance means that in some years a group has plenty of food and in other years experiences disaster; low variance means that the group always collects about the same amount of food. High correlation means that when one group is doing well, the other is also doing well, and when one group is doing poorly, so is the other; low correlation means that when one group is doing poorly, another is doing well. Figure 16.6 shows the outcome of this perspective on territoriality.

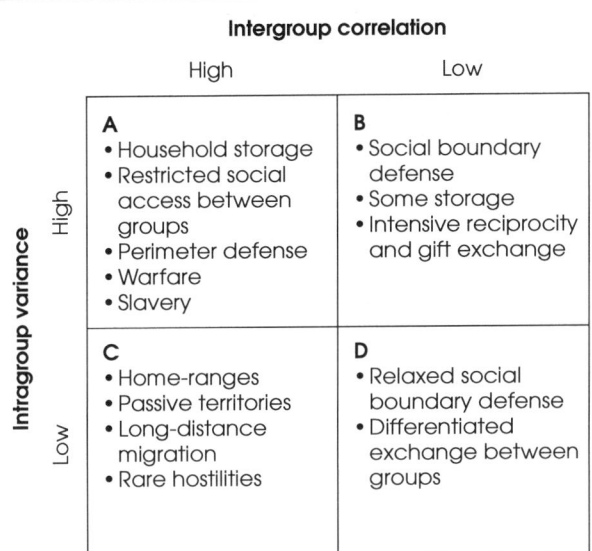

Figure 16.6 The Winterhalder model of sharing relations between individual foragers translated into relations between groups of foragers

The model defines four sets of relationships between groups defined by different combinations of intergroup correlations in return rates and intragroup variance in return rates.

A. High intragroup variance with high intergroup correlation; we expect social access to be restricted, perimeter defense, and household storage; possibly warfare since neighbors cannot help one another in poor times.

B. Social boundary defense, since periods of poor harvest are not correlated, neighbors can assist, and will need assistance in the future. Storage may occur, but more energy may be invested in social storage through reciprocal exchanges.

C. "Home ranges." Since intragroup variance is low, the need to call on neighbors for assistance will be infrequent; we could expect "passive" territories (i.e., groups remain on "their" land because there is no need to move elsewhere).

D. In this case there will be infrequent need for a group to call on its neighbors, but we could expect to see relaxed social-boundary defense maintained through reciprocity. At high population levels, ranges become more restricted, and we could expect to see differentiated exchanges (e.g., meat for carbohydrates) between less mobile populations.

GROUP SIZE

Nomadic foraging societies live in small groups of eighteen to thirty persons (Marlowe 2005; Binford 2001; Hill et al. 2011). But foragers periodically gather into larger groups, for winter camps, communal fishing, and so on. M. Hamilton et al. (2007) found that these various groups tend to increase by a regular factor of four: families consist of 4 or 5 people; a residential group of about 14–17; social aggregations, for example, at winter camps, of 50–60; periodic aggregations of 150–180; and entire "ethnic" populations of

730–950. They argue that these groupings reflect a subliminal consensus about how to most efficiently move food, information, and mates among foragers. For example, consisting of about twenty-five persons, residential group size balances the desire to minimize variance in food intake (through sharing) with the desire to minimize the rate of food depletion (which reduces the frequency of movements; Winterhalder 1986b), maximizes group size without the need for a decision-making hierarchy (Johnson 1982), and maintains reproductive viability (Wobst 1974).

Of these, daily foraging needs are perhaps the most immediate factor in determining group size. Smith (1991) pointed out that per capita foraging return rates can increase with group size—up to a point, after which additional group members do not increase work efficiency but, by taking a share, reduce the per capita return rate (Figure 16.7). This

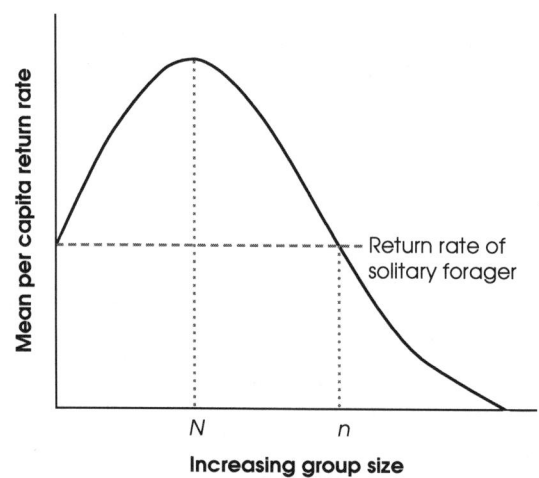

N is the optimal size, where per capita return rate is highest; n is the group size at which the group per capita return rate is equivalent to that of foraging alone. The per capita return rate is:

$$R = \sum_{1}^{n} \frac{(E_a - E_e)}{tn}$$

where:

R = mean per capita return rate
n = total number of foragers for the foraging trip
E_a = total usable energy acquired on trip
E_e = total energy expended on trip
t = total time of trip

If R_x is the group's per capita return rate at size x, current members of the party should allow others to join as long as $R_{x+1} > R_x$. Prospective joiners should try to join the group as long as $R_{x+1} > R_1$. Once group size = N there will be a conflict of interest between group members and prospective joiners.

Figure 16.7 Relationship between foraging-group size and per capita return rate
Source: Redrawn and used with permission from Smith (1991).

sets up conflict once the optimal group size is reached, since some members will still wish to join if their return rate will improve over what they would achieve by foraging alone. Using data on Inujjuamiut hunting parties, Smith (1991) found that groups were slightly larger than the model anticipated, and suggested that this reflected a compromise between a goal of maximizing foraging efficiency and minimizing the risk of social discord.

This may explain why M. Hamilton's study found that residential groups are frequently larger than expected by the 4× factor of increase. It's possible that the optimal co-residing foraging group size for nomadic foragers in many different environments is rather small—fifteen people or so—but that long-term social needs and the avoidance of retaliation results in slightly larger residential groupings. Crucial to studies of group size, territoriality, sharing—everything, in fact—is population growth. A few decades ago researchers assumed that foragers consciously kept their populations in check through contraception, abortion, postpartum taboos on intercourse, and infanticide. Space does not permit a full discussion of these topics (see Kelly 2013), so suffice it to say that there is no evidence these methods work, or that infanticide, outside of some Arctic societies, has a significant impact on population growth. Although hunter-gatherers have long spacing between births (three to four years; Marlowe 2010), there is no evidence that this is intentional, but is instead a product of women's reproductive ecology.

Reproductive Ecology

Nutrition, activity levels, and breastfeeding all work synergistically to affect a woman's *energy storage, balance,* and *flux,* which affect fecundity. *Energy storage* refers to how much energy a woman has stored on her body, *energy balance* to whether a woman is expending more or less energy than she is consuming, and *energy flux* to the rate at which energy is coming in and going out. Leaving aside the physiological details, a woman's body "knows" when it can or cannot afford to become pregnant (see Ellison 2001).

Numerous factors affect a woman's energy storage, balance, and flux, and no single factor matters more than others. Some, such as diet, breastfeeding, and the physical exertion of foraging, are obvious constraints. Others are less so. One of these is juvenile foraging. How much foraging children do affects fertility by influencing a mother's energetic state (by not carrying children), her foraging efficiency, and her perception of the "cost" of children. One variable that factors into the cost of child foraging is the danger involved, which is affected by the difficulty of landscape learning and predators (Blurton Jones, Hawkes, and O'Connell 1996; Marlowe 2005), as well as by skill and strength (Henry, Morelli, and Tronick 2005). There is a growing literature on child foraging (e.g., Tucker and Young 2005; Marlowe 2005; Bird and Bliege Bird 2005). A second factor is child care. Where women can expect help from other women, older children, or fathers, their perceived cost of children declines and they might be more inclined to have another or to allow the next infant to live (Kramer 2005; Hewlett 1991; Daly and Wilson 1988).

Fertility is just one side of the coin; on the other side is mortality, and especially important are infant and juvenile mortality. Pre-adult mortality is high (40 to 50 percent) in preindustrial societies (Hewlett 1991). Violence accounts for some deaths (children are more likely to die of homicide if their father is absent), but accidents and, especially, disease are the primary agents, especially infectious, parasitic, and diarrhea-inducing diseases (Headland 1989; Hill and Hurtado 1996; Hill, Hurtado, and Walker 2007).

Finally, lethal violence—homicide and warfare—can also reduce population growth rates. However, the rates of both seem to vary with population pressure and consequently the cost-benefit ratio of fighting—as population pressure on food resources increases, so too does the incidence of warfare and homicide (Kelly 2013). Warfare, organized battles between two groups, is more prevalent among sedentary than among nomadic hunter-gatherers. While there is violence among nomadic foragers, this tends to be of the sort that occurs in egalitarian societies where tensions may eventually erupt into passionate fisticuffs and occasionally lethal violence.

Division of Labor

A strong empirical and universal pattern among foragers is that men hunt large game and women gather plant foods and small game. This has been a "political" issue, and rightfully so: hunting requires skill and patience, not extraordinary strength or intelligence. But since foraging children breastfeed until they are several years old (due to the lack of weaning foods), children remain with their mothers. Children reduce a woman's efficiency when foraging for sessile plant foods (Hurtado et al. 1992; Marlowe 2010: 214), and they would greatly reduce a woman's hunting efficiency. Women do not hunt, simply because, with children, hunting large game would produce a lower return rate than plant-food collection. Women undertake child-compatible hunting (e.g., communal net hunting) when that activity provides higher returns than other foraging opportunities (Bliege Bird 2007). The importance of this observation is that men are the ones who "own" the highly desirable and sharable resource of large game.

Social Organization

There has been relatively little HBE work into elements of social organization such as kinship, descent, postmarital residence, and marriage (with the exception of polygyny). However, if we look at these elements as manifestations of strategies of social alignment, they can be related to the group size model discussed above. For example, long-distance large-game hunting or warfare removes men from their families for long periods of time and places them at risk. This seems to result in matrilocal postmarital residence as part of a woman's reproductive strategy to ensure that she has kin nearby to assist in child rearing. Rules of residence are related to a number of variables, but all revolve around individuals finding ways to join one group or another. For men, the primary factors may be foraging or warfare, whereas for women it may be assistance in child rearing.

Our group-size model may also account for the development of large corporate groups with a strong unilineal bias as opposed to small groups with bilateral kinship. Unilineal descent provides a justification for large, sometimes very large corporate groups. We might expect such groups to form where control of a resource is possible and perhaps necessary because of increased demand brought on by population pressure. By appealing to some sort of kinship connection, petitioners justify their claim that they should be allowed "in" to the group. Social organization therefore might reflect the outcome of group formation processes, the costs and benefits of joining a group versus keeping others out (Alvard 2003).

Marriage can also be viewed in the same fashion, because marriage creates linkages between corporate groups. Most attention given to marriage has focused on polygyny, using Orians's (1969) polygyny threshold model. This model argues that polygyny forms when females stand to gain greater reproductive fitness benefits (as measured by food, other critical resources, or political access to such resources) as a second or third mate to one male than by mating with a currently single, but resource-poor, male. This model becomes more complicated in human societies, to say the least, because of cultural rules, but also because, as Collier (1988) points out, marriage is often about the relations between men—wife-givers and wife-takers. In bridewealth societies, for example, wife-givers enter into a marriage to acquire labor, while wife-takers gain prestige. These different agendas result in inequality among men, and between men and women. By creating alliances, marriages create cooperative groups that can be understood through the group-size model.

Political Organization

Hunter-gatherers are known for their egalitarian political organization, which is marked primarily by autonomy, more or less individual control over their lives. But some foragers are distinctly nonegalitarian, and the historical shift that brings this change about is complex. It seems to occur only where foragers are sedentary or nearly so, where a key resource-extraction locality can be controlled through territorial behavior, and where population pressure is high. In this context, selection works against egalitarianism in favor of nonegalitarian behaviors.

The *patron-client model* (Smith and Choi 2007) describes the political outcome of sedentary foragers. We can give only an outline of the entire process here (see Kelly 2013). Imagine a group of sedentary foragers living in a region of high population pressure who are situated on a productive resource that fluctuates little from year to year. Given our sharing argument (above), this group has little incentive to share with other, less fortunate groups in the region because the sedentary foragers do not anticipate needing assistance. However, the less fortunate foragers have every reason to try (especially in bad years) to gain access to what the well-positioned group has. They are a constant threat, and one village might buy off another. Recalling the group-size argument, members beyond the "optimal" number might be admitted, through marriage or kinship connections, but at a price: secondary status, which ideologically justifies a reduced share even when contributing actual work. At that moment, nonegalitarian society forms.

This can happen especially where the per capita return rate increases with a larger group size (see also Henrich and Boyd 2008 on the benefits of specialization). Leaders arise in such situations if they take on the cost of ejecting the free-riders who can invade large groups and the cost of coordinating efforts to avoid inefficiency (Hooper, Kaplan, and Boone 2010; Smith and Choi 2007). Their importance is relative to the difference between foraging alone and as part of a group, to the size of the optimal group (I. Hamilton 2000), and to the extent that a resource-extraction locale is defensible.

In return, the leader takes a slightly larger cut of the foraging returns. Hard-working group members benefit because their efforts are not supporting goldbrickers, and yet they do not have to pay the social cost of "being stingy." In economies of scale, foragers benefit in the long term by turning over some of their autonomy to a leader and reducing their maximum possible return rate.

Assuming a leader skims, Boone (2000) shows that the group's average per capita utility curve and the utility curve of the leader are similar to that of Figure 16.7, but that the utility curve of the leader predicts a slightly larger group size. It is to a group leader's advantage to keep members in the group, even when it is not necessarily to the other members' maximum benefit. Culture assists the process, for a leader does not have to maintain a position through brute force, but through the force of ideology, belief systems that "explain" inequality. Any reader of Marx will be familiar with how these systems operate.

This ideology can entail warfare, costly displays, and "generosity." Warfare acquires more resources for loyal followers and preempts attacks. In large groups, a smaller percentage of people are needed for warfare, and thus some can avoid defense's direct cost, free-riding on the efforts of others. Costly displays, such as expensive public feasts, demonstrate a leader's power to would-be adversaries by being an honest signal of the numerical strength of a population and the capacity of a leader to mobilize that strength. Finally, generosity (sometimes through the spoils of war) can buy off the competition and solidify the patron-client relationship. Through a process similar to tolerated theft, additional increments of wealth have less value with increasing amounts of overall wealth (Figure 16.8; Boone 1992). The same increase in wealth holds different potential benefits. Currently wealthy individuals can buy off less wealthy ones because an increase of X amount for them is simply not worth as much as it is to the less wealthy. At high levels of wealth, the social benefits of generosity are worth more than the resource itself. Through this process, inequality tends to propagate itself until some process, well described by Marx, literally overthrows the situation.

Conclusion

Interaction with the physical and social environment is an inescapable fact of human life—for foragers as for anyone else. While no research paradigm contains all the answers, HBE offers a productive research strategy for understanding the mechanism linking environment and society. It offers a perspective and methodology that help us understand how a forager or, in fact, any human makes decisions. And it does so with a firm grounding in evolutionary theory. Behavioral ecology begins with the assumption that people's behavior is aimed at maximizing reproductive success. This is a provisional assumption; culture can alter the process, changing what is meant by "maximize."

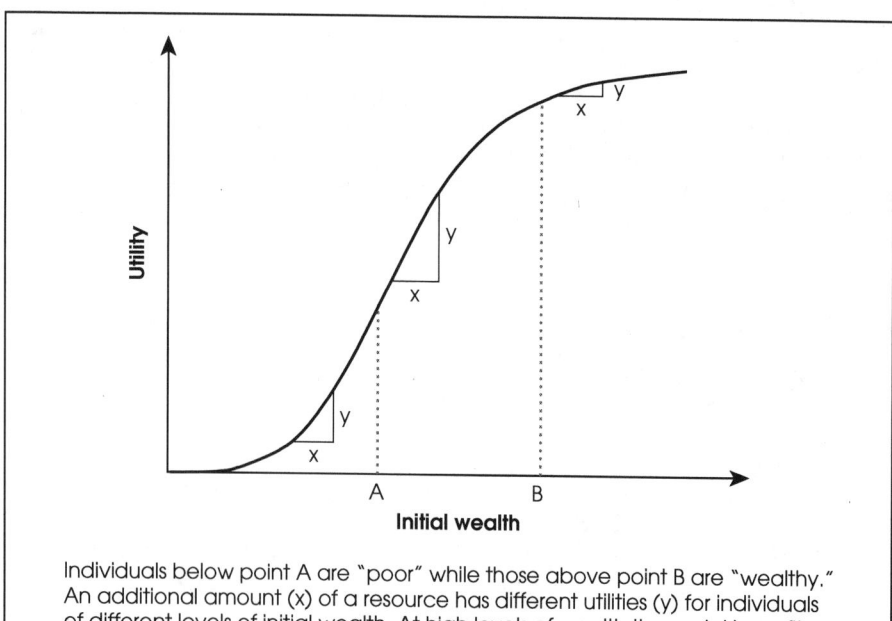

Individuals below point A are "poor" while those above point B are "wealthy." An additional amount (x) of a resource has different utilities (y) for individuals of different levels of initial wealth. At high levels of wealth the social benefits of generosity may be worth more than the resource itself.

Figure 16.8 One potential utility function describing the relationship between the utility of resources and amounts of that resource

Source: Redrawn from Boone (1992). Used with permission from Smith and Winterhalder (1992).

I have focused on foragers in this chapter because that is my specialty, but also to make a point. Foragers play an especially important role in evolutionary research paradigms, because, as the argument goes, our capacities were created in the Pleistocene, when all humans lived by hunting and gathering. Many researchers, especially those outside anthropology, assume that in looking at living foragers they are looking back into the past. This is a dangerous supposition. Living foragers do live under circumstances that are closer to those of our most ancient ancestors than to those of, say, the average university professor. But living foragers are also affected by their social context, which today includes World Bank–sponsored projects, terrorist movements, government-sponsored resettlement programs, tourism, and market craft production. HBE does not assume and does not have to assume that living foragers are pristine relics of the Paleolithic. Living foragers, even those who use guns or snowmobiles or who work at wage labor, provide us with hypotheses and tests of models; but when we look at the modern Hadza, Ache, Efe, or Ju/'hoansi, we are not looking back in time. Too many researchers today make this mistake. Likewise, too many researchers make claims about how foraging lifeways created the human mind (e.g., male-female differences in spatial abilities) when they in fact know little about those lifeways. Hopefully, this chapter can help correct that problem.

References

Allen-Arave, W., M. Gurven, and K. Hill. 2008. "Reciprocal Altruism, Rather than Kin Selection, Maintains Nepotistic Food Transfer on an Ache Reservation." *Evolution and Human Behavior* 29: 305–318.

Alvard, M. S. 2003. "Kinship, Lineage, and an Evolutionary Perspective on Cooperative Hunting Groups in Indonesia." *Human Nature* 14: 129–163.

Alvard, M. S., and A. Gillespie. 2004. "Good Lamalera Whale Hunters Accrue Reproductive Benefits." *Research in Economic Anthropology* 23: 223–245.

Bertalanffy, L. von. 1968. *General System Theory: Foundations, Development, Applications.* New York: George Braziller.

Bettinger, R. 1991. *Hunter-Gatherers: Archaeological and Evolutionary Theory.* New York: Plenum.

———. 2009. *Hunter-Gatherer Foraging: Five Simple Models.* Clinton Corners, NY: Percheron Press.

Bettinger, R. L., B. Winterhalder, and R. McElreath. 2006. "A Simple Model of Technological Intensification." *Journal of Archaeological Science* 33: 538–545.

Binford, L. 2001. *Constructing Frames of Reference.* Berkeley: University of California Press.

Bird, D. W., and R. Bliege Bird. 2005. "Martu Children's Hunting Strategies in the Western Desert, Australia." In *Hunter-Gatherer Childhoods*, edited by B. Hewlett and M. Lamb, 129–146. New York: Aldine de Gruyter.

Bird, D., and J. F. O'Connell. 2006. "Behavioral Ecology and Archaeology." *Journal of Archaeological Research* 14: 143–188.

Bliege Bird, R. 2007. "Fishing and the Sexual Division of Labor among the Meriam." *American Anthropologist* 109: 442–451.

Blurton Jones, N. 1987. "Bushman Birth Spacing: Direct Tests of Some Simple Predictions." *Ethology and Sociobiology* 8: 183–203.

Blurton Jones, N., K. Hawkes, and J. O'Connell. 1996. "The Global Process and Local Ecology: How Should We Explain the Differences between the Hadza and !Kung?" In *Cultural Diversity among Twentieth-Century Foragers: An African Perspective*, edited by S. Kent, 159–187. Cambridge: Cambridge University Press.

Boone, J. 1992. "Competition, Conflict, and Development of Social Hierarchies." In *Evolutionary Ecology and Human Behavior*, edited by E. Smith and B. Winterhalder, 301–337. New York: Aldine de Gruyter.

———. 2000. "Status Signaling, Social Power, and Lineage Survival." In *Hierarchies in Action: Cui Bono?* edited by M. W. Diehl, 84–110. Center for Archaeological Investigations, Occasional Paper 27. Carbondale: Southern Illinois University.

Boyd, R., and P. Richerson. 1985. *Culture and the Evolutionary Process.* Chicago: University of Chicago Press.

Broughton, J. M., and M. D. Cannon, eds. 2010. *Evolutionary Ecology and Archaeology.* Salt Lake City: University of Utah Press.

Cashdan, E. 1983. "Territoriality among Human Foragers: Ecological Models and an Application to Four Bushman Groups." *Current Anthropology* 24: 47–66.

Charnov, E. L. 1976. "Optimal Foraging, the Marginal Value Theorem." *Theoretical Population Biology* 9: 129–136.
Collier, J. 1988. *Marriage and Inequality in Three Classless Societies.* Stanford, CA: Stanford University Press.
Cronk, L. 1991. "Human Behavioral Ecology." *Annual Review of Anthropology* 20: 25–53.
Daly, M., and M. Wilson. 1988. *Homicide.* New York: Aldine.
Dyson-Hudson, R., and E. A. Smith. 1978. "Human Territoriality: An Ecological Reassessment." *American Anthropologist* 80: 21–41.
Eerkens, J. W. 2009. "Privatization of Resources and the Evolution of Prehistoric Leadership Strategies." In *The Evolution of Leadership,* edited by K. Vaughn, J. Eerkens, and J. Kantner, 73–94. Santa Fe, NM: School of Advanced Research Press.
Ellison, P. 2001. *On Fertile Ground: A Natural History of Human Reproduction.* Cambridge, MA: Harvard University Press.
Gurven, M. 2004. "To Give and to Give Not: The Behavioral Ecology of Human Food Transfers." *Behavioral and Brain Sciences* 27: 543–583.
Gurven, M., W. Allen-Arave, K. Hill, and M. Hurtado. 2000. "'It's a Wonderful Life': Signaling Generosity among the Ache of Paraguay." *Evolution and Human Behavior* 21: 263–282.
Hamilton, I. M. 2000. "Recruiters and Joiners: Using Optimal Skew Theory to Predict Group Size and the Division of Resources within Groups of Social Foragers." *American Naturalist* 155: 684–695.
Hamilton, M. J., B. T. Milne, R. S. Walker, O. Burger, and J. H. Brown. 2007. "The Complex Structure of Hunter-Gatherer Social Networks." *Proceedings of the Royal Society B* 274: 2195–2202.
Hamilton, W. D. 1964. "The Genetical Evolution of Social Behavior." *Journal of Theoretical Biology* 7: 1–52.
Hawkes, K. 1992. "Sharing and Collective Action." In *Evolutionary Ecology and Human Behavior,* edited by E. Smith and B. Winterhalder, 269–300. New York: Aldine de Gruyter.
Hawkes, K., and R. Bliege Bird. 2002. "Showing Off, Handicap Signaling and the Evolution of Men's Work." *Evolutionary Anthropology* 11: 58–67.
Headland, T. N. 1989. "Population Decline in a Philippine Negrito Hunter-Gatherer Society." *American Journal of Human Biology* 1: 59–72.
Henrich, J., and R. Boyd. 2008. "Division of Labor, Economic Specialization, and the Evolution of Social Stratification." *Current Anthropology* 49: 715–724.
Henry, P. I., G. A. Morelli, and E. Z. Tronick. 2005. "Child Caretakers among Efe Foragers of the Ituri Forest." In *Hunter-Gatherer Childhoods: Evolutionary, Developmental and Cultural Perspectives,* edited by B. S. Hewlett and M. E. Lamb, 191–213. New York: Aldine de Gruyter.
Hewlett, B. 1991. "Demography and Childcare in Preindustrial Societies." *Journal of Anthropological Research* 47: 1–37.
Hill, K., and K. Hawkes. 1983. "Neotropical Hunting among the Ache of Eastern Paraguay." In *Adaptive Responses of Native Amazonians,* edited by R. Hames and W. Vickers, 139–188. New York: Academic Press.
Hill, K., and A. M. Hurtado. 1996. *Ache Life History: The Ecology and Demography of a Foraging People.* New York: Aldine de Gruyter.
Hill, K., A. M. Hurtado, and R. S. Walker. 2007. "High Adult Mortality among Hiwi Hunter-Gatherers: Implications for Human Evolution." *Journal of Human Evolution* 52: 443–454.
Hill, K. R., R. S. Walker, M. Božicević, J. Eder, T. Headland, B. Hewlett, A. M. Hurtado, F. Marlowe, P. Wiessner, and B. Wood. 2011. "Co-Residence Patterns in Hunter-Gatherer Societies Show Unique Human Social Structure." *Science* 331: 1286–1289.
Hooper, P., H. S. Kaplan, and J. L. Boone. 2010. "A Theory of Leadership in Human Cooperative Groups." *Journal of Theoretical Biology* 265: 633–646.
Hurtado, A. M., K. Hill, H. Kaplan, and I. Hurtado. 1992. "Trade-Offs between Female Food Acquisition and Child Care among Hiwi and Ache Foragers." *Human Nature* 3: 185–216.
Hutchinson, G. E. 1965. *The Ecological Theater and the Evolutionary Play.* New Haven, CT: Yale University Press.
Johnson, G. 1982. "Organizational Structure and Scalar Stress." In *Theory and Explanation in Archaeology,* edited by C. Renfrew, M. Rowlands, and B. Segraves, 389–421. New York: Academic Press.
Kaplan, H., and K. Hill. 1985. "Hunting Ability and Reproductive Success among Male Ache Foragers: Preliminary Results." *Current Anthropology* 26: 131–133.
Kelly, R. L. 2013. *The Lifeways of Hunter-Gatherers.* Cambridge: Cambridge University Press.
Kennett, D. 2005. *The Island Chumash: Behavioral Ecology of a Maritime Society.* Berkeley: University of California Press.
Kramer, K. L. 2005. *Maya Children: Helpers at the Farm.* Cambridge, MA: Harvard University Press.
MacArthur, R. H. 1972. *Geographical Ecology: Patterns in the Distribution of Species.* New York: Harper and Row.
MacArthur, R., and E. Pianka. 1966. "On Optimal Use of a Patchy Environment." *American Naturalist* 100: 603–609.
Marlowe, F. 2005. "Hunter-Gatherers and Human Evolution." *Evolutionary Anthropology* 14: 54–67.

———. 2010. *The Hadza: Hunter-Gatherers of Tanzania*. Berkeley: University of California Press.
Orians, G. H. 1969. "On the Evolution of Mating Systems in Birds and Mammals." *American Naturalist* 103: 589–603.
Pianka, E. 1978. *Evolutionary Ecology*. 2nd ed. New York: Harper and Row.
Read, D. 2008. "An Interaction Model for Resource Implement Complexity Based on Risk and Number of Annual Moves." *American Antiquity* 73: 599–625.
Simms, S. 1987. *Behavioral Ecology and Hunter-Gatherer Foraging: An Example from the Great Basin*. British Archaeological Reports, International Series 381. Oxford.
Smith, E. A. 1983. "Anthropological Applications of Optimal Foraging Theory: A Critical Review." *Current Anthropology* 24: 625–651.
———. 1991. *Inujjuamiut Foraging Strategies*. Hawthorne, NY: Aldine de Gruyter.
———. 2004. "Why Do Good Hunters Have Higher Reproductive Success?" *Human Nature* 15: 343–364.
Smith, E. A., and J.-Y. Choi. 2007. "The Emergence of Inequality in Small-Scale Societies: Simple Scenarios and Agent-Based Simulations." In *The Model-Based Archaeology of Socionatural Systems*, edited by T. Kohler and S. van der Leeuw, 105–119. Santa Fe, NM: School of Advanced Research Press.
Smith, E. A., and B. Winterhalder, eds. 1992. *Evolutionary Ecology and Human Behavior*. Hawthorne, NY: Aldine de Gruyter.
Steward, J. H. 1955. *Theory of Culture Change*. Urbana: University of Illinois Press.
Tucker, B., and A. G. Young. 2005. "Growing Up Mikea: Children's Time Allocation and Tuber Foraging in Southwestern Madagascar." In *Hunter-Gatherer Childhoods*, edited by B. S. Hewlett and M. E. Lamb, 147–171. New York: Aldine de Gruyter.
Winterhalder, B. 1986a. "Diet Choice, Risk, and Food Sharing in a Stochastic Environment." *Journal of Anthropological Archaeology* 5: 369–392.
———. 1986b. "Optimal Foraging: Simulation Studies of Diet Choice in a Stochastic Environment." *Journal of Ethnobiology* 6: 205–223.
Winterhalder, B., and E. A. Smith, eds. 1981. *Hunter-Gatherer Foraging Strategies: Ethnographic and Archaeological Analyses*. Chicago: University of Chicago Press.
Wissler, C. 1926. *The Relation of Nature to Man in Aboriginal America*. New York: Oxford University Press.
Wobst, H. M. 1974. "Boundary Conditions for Paleolithic Social Systems: A Simulation Approach." *American Antiquity* 39: 147–178.
Zahavi, A. 1997. *The Handicap Principle: A Missing Piece of Darwin's Puzzle*. Oxford: Oxford University Press.
Zeanah, D. 2002. "Central Place Foraging and Prehistoric Pinyon Utilization in the Great Basin." In *Beyond Foraging and Collecting: Evolutionary Change in Hunter-Gatherer Settlement Systems*, edited by B. Fitzhugh and J. Habu, 231–256. New York: Kluwer Academic/Plenum Press.

CHAPTER SEVENTEEN
EVOLVING COMMUNITIES
EVOLUTIONARY ANALYSIS IN CLASSICAL AND NEOCLASSICAL HUMAN ECOLOGY

Michael D. Irwin

> Evolutionary analysis in human ecology incorporated theoretical traditions in sociology with perspectives developed in biology. Specifically, early human ecology blended elements of natural selection and the web of life, from Darwin to holistic paradigms emerging in early community ecology, and to systemic macro-level approaches in sociology. This synthesis sometimes used biological concepts as a heuristic to apply sociological concepts to the study of human communities. When using a bioecological heuristic, human ecologists treated human communities as an organic whole and focused on emergent macro-level processes. This was in the tradition of Spencer and Durkheim, but also drew on early bioecologists' treatment of the web of life as an emergent property. On the other hand, early human ecologists often applied patterns observed in biotic communities directly to human communities, treating both human and biotic communities as shaped by general ecological processes. When engaging in this general ecology, human ecologists incorporated micro-level processes, especially individual competition drawn from Darwinian thought. However, they also incorporated the role of culture as a macro-level feature of human communities. Both lines of thought, the metaphorical and the actual general ecology, run through classical human ecology. Evolutionary analysis in early human ecology might best be thought of as an uneasy marriage between biological and social approaches. This changed in the neoclassical reformation of human ecology. Micro-level processes were excised, as was the role of culture in constraining competition. At the same time, neoclassical human ecologists distanced themselves from early bioecological approaches and developed their theory as a distinctly sociological approach. In the process, human ecology's emphasis shifted from evolutionary analysis to the analysis of growth and expansion of social systems.

Human ecology represents one of the earliest efforts to bridge biological and social concepts into a coherent empirical approach to the study of society (Turner and Maryanski 2008: 1; Wortmann 2013: 70; Gross 2004). The approach developed by Park, Burgess, McKenzie, and others (Park and Burgess [1921] 2011; McKenzie 1968) clearly draws its perspective from biological ecologists of the late nineteenth and early twentieth centuries. Through them, human ecologists incorporated Darwinian concepts, including competition, as a basis for biological changes, and the "web of life" as an organizing perspective for understanding ecological communities. Both concepts were considered to shape the character of communities. Of equal importance, human ecologists worked with extant theory in sociology, drawing ideas from Spencer, Comte, Durkheim, Malthus, and Simmel, especially where these theorists dealt with social context, interdependence, and collective action (Abbott 1997). In their 1921 book *Introduction to the Science of Sociology*, Park and Burgess define collective action as the sine qua non of sociology: "While it is true that society has this double aspect, the individual and the collective, it is the assumption of this volume that the touchstone of society, the thing that distinguishes a mere collection of individuals from a society is not like-mindedness, but corporate action.... This existence of a common end is perhaps all that can be legitimately included in the conception 'organic' as applied to society" ([1921] 2011: 1209–1214). Their view on the organic nature of human societies drew especially on the works of Spencer and Durkheim (Schnore 1958) and likewise dealt with the problems of explaining the relationship of individual action to large social forces. This micro/macro issue also had its parallel in biological ecology.

COMMUNITY ECOLOGY IN THE EARLY TWENTIETH CENTURY

In order to disentangle human ecology's biological influences, we need to (1) understand the limited role that natural selection played in early bioecological theory and (2) understand the integration of sociological theory in these early biological formulations. Early works on biotic communities used a very different paradigm than the strongly Darwinian bioecology that emerged after World War II. Orthodox theory of postwar bioecology posits that the basic processes shaping an ecosystem are found at the individual level and involve processes of natural selection. "Natural selection is the most basic ecological process because it appears to be the only mechanism directly responsible for goal-directed behavior on the part of biological organisms. In the past, ecologists have often carelessly attributed goal-seeking behavior to various levels of organization in what might now be characterized as 'fallacies of misplaced teleology'" (Richerson 1977: 3). Current ecology places purposeful action at the micro level. Teleological causes (purposeful goals) are found in the reproductive goals of individual organisms. Competition for reproduction results in natural selection, which drives change at the micro level (among individuals) as well as the macro level (within biotic communities). "Within the context of a creative process like natural selection, it is meaningful to speak of teleological causation in the sense that natural selection results in adapted organisms whose structure and behavior are directed toward maximizing their contribution to the gene pool of the next generation" (Richerson 1977: 3). This process is entirely consistent with a Darwinian explanation of change.

The source of change and adaptation is found in individual competition. The ecosystem is considered a product of population adaptation driven by individual fitness. Although macro-level teleological causes are not rejected, they are simply not preferred over natural selection models (Dunbar 1972). Where natural selection failed to explain the emergence of macro-level processes, teleological behavior at higher levels was required (Richerson 1977: 6). "To demonstrate that the community is a unit of adaptation, we would have to show that communities with unique attributes of organization or function (community adaptations) compete with and replace each other as units" (Ricklefs 1980: 591). Ricklefs finds no convincing evidence of this in the bioecological literature. Others concurred. While community-level selection was possible, it was believed to be a rare event (Lewontin 1970: 15). As a result, natural selection models replaced an older view that viewed the biotic community as the unit of adaption. Biotic communities came to be regarded as loosely coupled systems where most species are relatively independent of one another (Ricklefs 1980: 599). The character of the ecological community is conceived to be a consequence of individual goal-seeking actions in interaction with the environment, thus placing teleology squarely at the micro level. Community-level processes are not a cause of change. The implication is that "the structure and function of a community reflect local ecological conditions more closely than evolutionary history" (Ricklefs 1980: 602).

Conversely, early bioecologists believed that biotic communities were adaptive units and that goal-seeking behavior could exist at the community level. This misplaced teleology, however careless in theoretical hindsight, represents the state of bioecological theory at the time human ecologists were looking to biology for insight. At this time, Darwin had not entirely eclipsed Lamarckian approaches, and biology had not yet firmly linked evolution to the processes of selection and retention of individual traits (Spencer 1893a, 1893b, 1893c; Haines 1988). Community structure in the biotic world looked like a viable mechanism shaping populations, and the treatment of these communities as organic wholes seemed to be a strong approach in understanding biotic ecosystems (Hodgson 2005; Haines 1985).

The biological ecology of their time viewed mutual association and specialization among species as characteristic of all constituent populations within an ecosystem, especially as different species acted on local habitat. The process of invasion of new species, impact on habitat, and resultant adjustment (succession) were assumed to strongly link species to each other and to the environment as a reactive unit. Shifts in these links were thought to reverberate across the biotic community and impact constituent populations. Thus, biotic communities were thought to adapt, as a unit, to environmental conditions. A macro to micro causality was considered likely. As Richerson summarizes, "Allee, et al. (1949: 698) in the authoritative textbook of a generation ago, explicitly linked the reality of ecosystems to the existence of superorganismic units, implying that higher levels of organization have the same highly integrated character as ordinary individuals, presumably including the capacity to be selected as wholes" (Richerson 1977: 9).

Human Ecology Meets Biological Ecology

It is clear that these macro-level causes proposed in bioecology were appealing as an approach that would inform the study of human social organization, to the Chicago School in the 1920s. An ecological approach, introduced in the late nineteenth century, was invigorating biological circles beginning with Ernst Haeckel's (1866) extension of Darwin's idea of the web of life to the interaction among species. These ideas were picked up by naturalists showing that plant and animal communities developed unit characteristics over time (Warming 1895), space (Cowles 1899), and between species (Wheeler 1910) that justified their treatment as a holistic entity characterized by cohesion rather than competition (Thomson 1910; Geddes and Thomson 1911). These early bioecologists acknowledged the role competition plays in selecting and shaping these biotic communities; however, they often placed more emphasis on Darwin's discussion of the interrelationship of life. The web of life concept emphasized cooperative arrangements in these communities. It was a concept readily transferable to human social arrangements. Indeed, notions of cooperative arrangements and the unit character of communities were concepts that biologists drew from social theory.

Treating human communities and systems as an organic whole, as superorganisms, with intrinsic goal-oriented behavior was a perspective widely accepted in nineteenth-century sociology. It was present in the works of Comte and Durkheim. More importantly, it was central to Spencer's sociological approach (Turner 1981; Haines 1988). At this time, Spencer's (1864, 1886) *Principles of Biology* was arguably as influential in biology as Darwin. Further, several of the most influential bioecologists drew as much from Spencer as from Darwin. These included Clements (1916), Thomson (1906), and Wheeler (1910), all widely cited by early human ecologists. As Gross notes, the boundaries between biology and sociology had not yet solidified into disciplinary barriers: "Around the turn of the twentieth century, sociological ideas became influential in the newly emerging field of ecology" (2004: 588). This exchange included bioecologist Frederic E. Clements's adoption of the sociological concept of community as an interdependent social unit, as a metaphor for plant ecosystems (Gross 2004: 589). Wheeler argued that the social organization of ants might modify or supersede selection for specific genetic traits. "Fixed or instinctive behavior has its counterpart in inherited morphological structure as does modifiable, or plastic behavior in well-known ontogenetic and functional changes" (Wheeler 1910: 522). Thomson likewise forayed into the limitations of natural selection, proposing that social selection—processes that work on modification of social organization—had taken the place of natural selection in human populations (1910: 228). Bioecology of the early twentieth century viewed Darwinian natural selection with caution, readily borrowed ideas from sociology, and generated concepts that were clearly more compatible with social theory than with a Darwinian perspective in biology.

These exchanges of ideas between biology and sociology were sometimes metaphorical but were also taken as direct applications. As a result, in the early twentieth century a common core of ideas about communities permeated both disciplines. Darwinian natural selection was considered one force shaping ecological communities, but not the only force. The Darwinian concept of the web of life was viewed as a force underlying emergent properties of biological communities, in much the same manner as proposed by Durkheim and Spencer. This also raised the possibility of system-wide goal-seeking behaviors justifying a teleological causality for ecosystem change that had even stronger counterparts in human systems. All the core sociological concepts proposed by the emerging academic discipline—culture, tradition, mores and folkways, divisions of labor, joint action, common interests and common good—provided ready mechanisms linking micro-level individual action to macro-level purposive behavior (Sumner 1906; Ward 1906; Giddings 1896; Spencer 1874–1896). It was in this environment that human ecology developed.

Early human ecology blended these systemic traditions in sociology with the emerging holistic perspectives of bioecology. Early human ecology shared an empirical focus on material aspects of community with the bioecologists. Like bioecology, human ecology attempted to describe organizational character, structure, and growth of various sociological conceptions of community. Yet their studies also concentrated on primary sociological concerns about the moral, political, and occupational elements of community and society. Using the rubric of an ecosystem perspective they were able to incorporate an eclectic variety of relevant concepts. With such cross-fertilization it is not surprising that sociologists would be drawn to bioecology. The Chicago School sociologists were certainly aware of this work and its drift into sociology through Albion Small from the earliest days of the department (Abbott 1997: 1160–1161; Gross 2004: 583; Gross 1999: 17). By the time Park arrived in Chicago in 1914 these ideas were pervasive, and certainly Park would become aware of them with Clements's return to Chicago in 1921 (Gaziano 1996: 880). This early bioecological approach, in broad terms, tended to take a perspective that was similar to those social theories that were of contemporary interest. In general, bioecology then and now tends to focus on macro-level organization of communities and to de-emphasize individual-level processes, although for postwar ecologists this is purely a matter of subdisciplinary perspective rather than of theory.

> Ecologists are usually not directly interested in the processes of natural selection operating on variable individuals within populations, but rather in the distribution and abundance of populations themselves and their interactions. Ecologists are thus primarily concerned with the phenomena of higher levels of organization ranging upward to ecosystems and the whole biosphere, and they tend to ignore individual variation and the evolution of populations. (Richerson 1977: 4)

Perhaps even more than now, bioecology of the late nineteenth and early twentieth centuries highlighted organizational morphology and macro-level processes found in contemporary sociological approaches, especially those of Durkheim, Spencer, and Comte (Rindos 1985). Embracing this approach also allowed sociologists to acknowledge the role of Darwinian individual selection while focusing on higher-level organization, through a division of labor much like that found in the biology divisions of its day. While evolutionary processes were examined in population genetics, through natural selection, and population ecology looked at these selection processes in relation to the environment, it was "community ecology, which treated the structural and functional aspects of large-scale assemblages of populations" (Richerson 1977: 20).

Classical Human Ecology's Application of Bioecology

For Park, incorporating this macrosocial approach to community into sociology must also have had practical appeal. It kept sociology's distinct disciplinary content and allowed sociologists to keep at arm's length the reductionist contenders in psychology. It helped differentiate sociology from an earlier generation of social history and social philosophy. At this time Park was casting about for a clearer definition of a scientific sociology that would build on existing sociological precepts. In his 1921 essay Park reflected on the progress of sociology, asserting that sociology had moved from a philosophy of history characterized by Comte and Spencer through a period of self-definition of substance and content. The emerging phase, to Park, was one of empirical research that would establish sociology as a science in its own right to a science of society (Park 1921: 169). In ecology, Park would find a perspective that was compatible with major sociological themes but pointed sociology toward research on social processes. The Chicago School human ecologists melded work in history and economics with social survey approaches to community study. The community ecology provided a framework to organize this approach.

> On the other hand, the conception of social relations and society on which this account of succession is based is that suggested by J. Arthur Thompson's description of "the web of life" as "a system of inter-related lives." ... It is this concept of a symbiotic society based on physiological correlation rather than culture which has been adopted and elaborated in writings of the plant and animal ecologists.... In certain places and under certain conditions this interdependence of the species, to which Darwin's expression "the web of life" refers, assumes a relatively permanent, structural character. (Park 1936b: 175)

Clearly, early human ecology synthesized specific elements of biological and social theories. What is not always as clear is the degree to which these ideas were direct applications for observations borrowed from the bioecological literature, or the degree to which human ecologists were using biological concepts as metaphors from which to build a new sociological approach (Gaziano 1996; Faught 1986; Maines, Bridger, and Ulmer 1996). This synthesis also obscured the processes underlying their approach. Various theorists have identified links to biological evolutionism, especially Darwinian approaches. Others have situated human ecology firmly in line with sociological evolutionary approaches, most notably Spencer, but also Durkheim, and many of the sociohistorical themes of the late nineteenth and early twentieth centuries (Gras 1922; Teggart 1925; Weber [1899] 1967). These latter conceptions of social evolution are better characterized as developmental progression rather than an analogy to species progression, at least as proposed by Darwin (Katovich 1987: 373). Even when the root ideas should be easily disentangled, for instance, in parsing biological from sociological concepts, it is not always clear whether Park and McKenzie were directly applying general ecological principles from the biological world, simply borrowing bioecological perspective as metaphor, or whether they were repackaging sociological principles within a general ecological perspective. Indeed, it is not unlikely that any particular concept was used in all three senses at various points in the development of human ecological theory.

Early human ecology used holistic notions, discussed material limitations, and focused on interdependence, competition, mutualism, system equilibrium, and so on. These dimensions certainly had their counterparts in biology. However, many of the concepts also had distinctly sociological roots. Much of what the early human ecologists did was to transform these sociological traditions into a systematic paradigm structured on insights from biological ecology. Later, neoclassical human ecology retained most of the assumptions underlying this paradigm, without the need to tie it to biological theory (Hawley 1950; Duncan 1961; Gibbs and Martin 1959). As a result, central concepts can be traced to several intellectual traditions and probably reflect a certain theoretical ambiguity on the part of individual theorists within human ecology. A certain amount of shifting theoretical influence was to be expected as human ecologists developed their perspective. It was, after all, an approach that was as strongly empirical as it was theoretical.

It is this holistic, unit character of communities composed of the web of life that Park, Burgess, McKenzie, and others find of primary appeal and, indeed, remains the subsequent raison d'être for human ecology throughout the twentieth century (Park 1936a). They treat both society and biotic communities as a material whole, based on interdependencies. Indeed, this was the premise of Park's 1925 presidential address to the American Sociological Society and is the specific commonality that he draws between plant communities in bioecology and sociology (Park 1926: 1). However, in the same address, Park walks through reasons that bioecological communities are substantially different from human communities. Where bioecology relies on a purely spatial notion of community, human ecology is focused on the central problems of sociology, the borders and boundaries of group processes.

> Ecology, in so far as it seeks to describe the actual distribution of plants and animals over the earth's surface, is in some very real sense a geographical science. Human ecology, as the sociologists would like to use the term, is, however, not identical with geography, nor even with human geography. It is not man, but the community; not man's relation to the earth which he inhabits, but his relations to other men, that concerns us most. (Park 1926: 1)

Park goes on to situate the interests of human ecology as found in the interdependencies among individuals as moderated by space. He links these issues directly to sociological thought, drawing from Cooley's interactional framework through Durkheim's treatment of social morphology, rather than to natural selection.

These and other statements have led interpreters to regard early human ecology's use of biological concepts as primarily metaphorical rather than the direct attribution of biological concepts to human communities. For instance, Maines, Bridger, and Ulmer (1996) see Park's use of biological concepts as representing a type of constitutive rhetoric, tying the emerging field of human ecology to an established, scientific approach to the study of society. However, the authors also acknowledge the use of these concepts for analytic application to human systems:

> He used the term "biotic" in two ways: as a metaphor from which he drew the concepts of succession, invasion, and natural areas for purposes of describing population and institutional configurations across space, and as natural resources, which he regarded as dialectically related to social institutions, especially economic ones. It is in this second sense that the cultural and biotic were regarded as fused, a point he worked out later in terms of the dialectics of competition and communication. (Maines, Bridger, and Ulmer 1996: 536)

The dual use of biological concepts is also discussed by Catton. Noting that Park and Burgess, like Hawley, embrace the science of both biology and sociology, he argues that the biological perspective was used to organize sociological ideas rather than biological ones. "Consider the fact that Park and Burgess used materials from Clements and other ecologists in their textbook and called it *Introduction to the Science of Sociology*. . . . The ecological materials were meant to help introduce students to sociological subject matter and sociological thoughtways" (Catton 1994: 85). Catton regards the parallels between biotic and social communities drawn by early human ecologists as a heuristic device as much as a direct application of bioecology to human systems. This point is made even more strongly by Gaziano (1996). Speaking of Park's (1926) early foray into a human ecological perspective on interdependence, Gaziano notes, "Instead of extending biological concepts to the study of humans qua natural organisms, early human ecologists selectively appropriated ideas from one context and applied them in an innovative fashion to a different order of phenomena: the processes of social organization and change. In other words, sociologists used biological concepts as tropes" (1996: 875). This is certainly seen in McKenzie's comparison of invasion and succession in urban areas.

> The structural growth of community takes place in successional sequence not unlike the successional stages in the development of the plant formation. Certain specialized forms of utilities and uses do not appear in the human community until a certain stage of development has been attained, just as the beech or pine forest is preceded by successional dominance of other plant species. And just as in plant communities successions are the products of invasion, so also in the human community the formations, segregations, and associations that appear constitute the outcome of a series of invasions. (McKenzie [1925] 2012: 1224–1228)

Here, McKenzie draws parallels between Clements's (1916) discussion of plant invasion and success, highlighting concepts such as dominance and successional stages. However, McKenzie goes on to discuss the major causes of this apparently biological pattern. All are distinctly social: changes in transportation; changes in architectural fashion, real estate, or aging of infrastructure; industrial transformation; and changes in income distribution. McKenzie uses the classification of invasion and succession developed in bioecology to discuss patterns of change in human communities, but the causes of change are distinctly social. There is no attempt to find a correspondence with plant communities. While acknowledging human communities are shaped by material environmental conditions, McKenzie notes that human systems are proactive in their relationship: "In a word, the human community differs from the plant community in the two dominant characteristics of mobility and purpose" ([1925] 2012: 1073–1084). Despite superficial resemblance to biotic communities, the process shaping human communities "has its inception in the traits of human nature and the needs of human beings" (1088).

McKenzie here and elsewhere seems content to use these biological concepts as an organizing heuristic from which to discuss what he saw as more central human ecological concepts. His student and intellectual confidant, Amos Hawley, discusses this, noting, "He never disclosed the extent or nature of his commitment to a natural history or evolutionary theory of change. There is some reason to believe that he was content to use it simply as a convenient means of ordering a series of events for purposes of exposition. Of greater importance to him was his concept of the process of expansion" (Hawley 1968: xviii). Hawley would return McKenzie's interest in social system expansion with the same ambivalence toward bioecology as he ascribes to McKenzie. Certainly McKenzie, like Hawley, exhibited much more concern with the distinctly social processes involved in change and expansion of human systems (McKenzie [1927] 1968a, [1927] 1968b). Park's work, on the other hand, remained much closer to bioecological thought. At times, bioecology provided a convenient heuristic for discussion of sociological processes. At other times, Park considered competition and selection to be empirical processes impacting both biotic and human communities.

In his 1926 work on the concept of position, Park is certainly employing the metaphor of the biotic community (as discussed by Warming [Warming and Vahl 1909]), stressing that sociology necessarily requires a departure from that biological concept. Yet in later work, Park identifies tangible processes in human communities that are also found in biotic communities: "The same biotic interdependence of individuals and species, which has been observed and studied in plant and animal communities, seems to exist likewise on the human level, except for the fact that in human society competition and the struggle for existence are limited by custom, convention, and law" (1936b: 175). Here the parallels between biotic and human communities are not merely rhetorical. Park is at once proposing a Darwinian notion of competition that operates in plant, animal, and human communities and noting that in human communities this competition is constrained by aspects of society (Faught 1986: 364; Wortmann 2013: 72–73). Park perceives this to be in line with existing biological theory. "In view of modern biological theory and discussion, two modes of adaptation should be distinguished: (a) adaptation through variation [hereditary]; (b) adaptation through modification [acquired]" (Park and Burgess [1921] 2011: 12249–12250).

In this, Park and his contemporaries were drawing from those aspects of natural selection, à la Darwin, as used by bioecologists to explain the emergence of interspecies influence. "Economic competition, as one meets it in human society, is the struggle for existence, as Darwin conceived it, modified and limited by custom and convention. In other respects, it is not different from competition as it exists in plant and animal communities" (Park 1936b: 177). It is a direct mapping of biologic natural selection in biological communities to human communities in which community structure is arrived at through competition and selection among individuals. For Park, competition and selection drive change in both human and biotic communities (Faught 1986: 364). However, where biotic communities move toward equilibrium purely through a symbiotic interdependence that balances competitive processes, in human systems competition is also controlled by culture, norms. There are both biotic and cultural forces at work. Park argues that macro-level forces (culture) in human society systematically minimize competition: "As the equilibrium we call society becomes relatively fixed in social structure, competition is increasingly diminished. Nevertheless, competition persists in human society and continues to manifest itself, as does the sexual instinct, in manifold indirect and insidious ways" (1936b: 177). Competition may reemerge when the social order is disrupted. "Under these circumstances, forces and tendencies formerly held in check are released, and a period of intense activity and rapid change ensues which then continues until the cycle is completed and a new biotic and social equilibrium is achieved" (1936b: 177). While biotic communities cycle through invasion and succession due to competition among organisms, these patterns (invasion and succession) occur in human communities only when community-level constraint breaks down. The proximate cause of change in human communities is found at the macro level. In biotic communities it is entirely a micro-level phenomenon.

Park goes on to discuss how the resolution of competition gives way to order. "Society, in the more inclusive sense in which ecologists have defined it, may be said to exist wherever competition has established some sort of order or war has established some sort of peace. It is the area within which an intrinsic and functional social order has succeeded one that was extrinsic and mechanical" (Park 1936b: 177). In this, social selection culture preempts competition, and the community order is achieved through cooperative arrangements (Gross 2004: 591). Here Park is also drawing from the early bioecological notions that used sociological metaphors for plant and animal communities, which placed a premium on higher-order system properties. "Before Darwin, students of plant and animal life saw in nature, not disorder, but order; not selection, but design. The difference between the older and the newer interpretation is not so much a difference of fact as of point of view" (Park and Burgess [1921] 2011: 9597–9601). This order represents a state of adjustment that entirely exists at the macro level (Park and Burgess [1921] 2011: 12307–12309). The resultant social structure for a community is perpetuated through cooperative arrangements. That is, competitive processes, such as survival of the fittest, give way to a social order based on functional cooperation. In this Park is not merely asserting a modification unique to human systems. He is certainly drawing on an older bioecology as practiced by Clements (1916) and Allee (1938) that had "earlier stressed the 'principle of cooperation' as a mechanism that coordinates natural selection in the generation of both ecological and social communities" (Richerson 1977: 9).

These are notions drawn from Spencer, an intellectual heritage not lost on Park. As Gross states, "Park repeatedly stated that ecology, since it was to be understood as a new term for the older 'economy of nature,' is to be perceived as a sociological perspective used in the biosciences" (2004: 591). From his perspective, Park is simply using a long-standing sociological concept on lend to biology—competition is contained by cultural and structural processes at the community level. Like modern bioecologists, Park also shifted ecological study from evolutionary processes that shape the social system to the way that environmental relationships form the structure and function of the human community. Thus, the role of competition, whether in its biotic or social characterizations, was used by ecologists more to explain the community social structure and the processes by which these communities were formed than to explain long-term patterns of evolutionary change.

If early human ecology exhibits a certain paradigmatic ambiguity, this is to be understood as reflecting a working out of concepts that is to be expected in a developing perspective. It is also indicative of a paradigm that gave equal weight to theory and empirical investigation. Ever an empirical approach, human ecologists were also testing methods and approaches developed in bioecology in the study of human communities and organization (Abbott 1997). Biological concepts were treated as metaphor but were also treated as empirical avenues to be investigated. Thus, many of the empirical designs imported from bioecology—evaluation of the spatial distribution of populations, examining group invasion, succession, and so on—were launched without strong notions of their sociological underpinnings. This amalgamation created a distinct sociology, separate from biological theory and modifying its intellectual antecedents in sociology. However, the patchwork of biological and sociological processes also came with its share of contradictions and internal inconsistencies. By the 1940s human ecology, as it was developed by the classical human ecologists, experienced a barrage of critiques both within and without the perspective.

THE MIDCENTURY REFORMULATION OF HUMAN ECOLOGY

By World War II human ecology had developed a generalized ecological approach with an analytic method inspired by biological ecology but with theory and substance drawn from sociology. The former stressed a holistic notion of interdependent communities, while the latter, drawing from Spencer and Durkheim, stressed a structural and macrosocial approach. Although loosely aligned with Darwinian concepts of individual competition and adaptation, at the same time human ecology integrated Durkheimian and Spencerian orientations toward group adaptation. These contradictions between the biological and sociological dimensions of human ecology were evident and damaging (Saunders 1986: 53), requiring a reformulation of human ecological tenets.

At the same time, bioecology had experienced a sea change in adopting the Darwinian paradigm as the essential explanation of biological change and evolution (Haines 1985: 65). Competition and natural selection were being viewed as a necessary and sufficient explanation of such processes. Purely Darwinian explanations of ecological communities had come to replace the processes by which community structure is formed. Emphasis on communities as units of selection gave way to close examination of the micro-level processes of selection and retention of traits in populations. In short, many of the root bioecological processes that had originally shaped human ecologists' perspectives had been superseded.

Hawley's 1944 article provides a pivotal point of view in this transition. It is a critique of human ecology's lack of theoretical cohesion and of the content of human ecological research. More important is Hawley's rejection of the theoretical centrality of completion in human ecological theory. By excising competition, he eliminates natural selection as an important ecological process. This separates human ecology from the postwar movement toward natural selection that was coming to predominate biological ecology. Hawley describes the field as intellectually chaotic, owing largely to "(1) the failure to maintain a close working relationship between human ecology and general or bioecology; (2) an undue preoccupation with the concept of competition; and (3) the persistence in definitions of the subject of a misplaced emphasis on spatial relations" (1944: 399). At first pass, points one and two seem to be contradictory statements, since general ecology was emphasizing the role of competition (and de-emphasizing the importance of interspecies cooperation). However, Hawley is not proposing that human ecology hew closer to bioecology, rather that bioecology draw more from sociological insights in human ecology.

> That ecology is basically a social science has long been clear to most serious students of the subject. It is apparent, moreover, in almost every aspect of the discipline: in

the root of the term ecology; in the historical details of the subject's development; in the large place given to sociological concepts such as community, society, niche, commensalism, symbiosis, dominance, succession, etc.; and in the manner in which problems for investigation are stated. (Hawley 1944: 399–400)

Hawley is asserting the primacy of a sociological approach in this aspect of the biological realm. Similarly, Hawley distances human ecology from a more Darwinian approach by rejecting competition as the driving force in shaping human ecosystems: "Certainly competition is not the pivotal conception of ecology; in fact, it is possible to describe the subject without even an allusion to competition" (1944: 400).

Hawley argues that Darwin's concept of competition as a struggle for existence among individuals might be better treated as a metaphor of ecosystem dynamics than as the central process shaping ecosystems. Here Hawley views adaptation as the underlying dimension shaping ecosystems. Competition is addressed in human ecology, of course, but more as a variable of interest that is better treated analytically than as a postulate of the ecosystem process. For Hawley, and for subsequent ecologists, the importance of individual competition for resources is less important than the ways that social organization structures itself to maximize specific environments: "Ecology, in other words, is a study of the morphology of collective life in both its static and its dynamic aspects. It attempts to determine the nature of community structure in general, the types of communities that appear in different habitats, and the specific sequence of change in community development" (1944: 403). Thus, a strictly Darwinian notion of change and evolution, built from individual competition and selection, is replaced with a population-level approach focusing on ecosystem adaptation. For this reason, Hawley sees both bioecology and human ecology as essentially population sciences. Human ecology, however, brings sociological concepts of community to bear in understanding the organization of population.

> And out of the adaptive strivings of aggregated individuals there develops, consciously or unconsciously, an organization of interdependencies which constitutes the population a coherent functional entity. The human community, in other words, is basically an adaptive mechanism; it is the means whereby a population utilizes and maintains itself in its habitat. Human ecology, then, may be defined more fully as the study of the development and the form of communal structure as it occurs in varying environmental contexts. (Hawley 1944: 404)

It is the emergent character of community that organizes adaptation of a population. Hawley draws on Spencerian and Durkheimian traditions of macro-level influences on individual behavior and suggests that these traditions may be fruitful in helping bioecologists approach ecosystem organization. He also rejects the Darwinian premise that was coming to predominate biological ecology—that the source of ecosystem change is found in the struggle for existence among individuals.

Thus while Hawley situates the theoretical disorganization of classical human ecology as resulting from equivocal interactions with bioecology scholarship, he is not advocating integrating a Darwinian approach into the study of human communities. On the other hand, Hawley does seem to be advocating the point of view proposed by early bioecologists. "It was recognized early by ecologists that differentiated organisms which influence each other achieve collective adaptation to the conditions of their shared habitat, forming thereby a more or less self-sufficient and localized web of life" (Catton 1994: 80). It is this commonality that Hawley stresses in his call for more cross-fertilization across the ecologies (1944: 404–405).

There is no evidence this ever occurred, which might account for Hawley's (1981, 1986, 1992) further de-emphasis of the interaction between the two disciplines in later works. Certainly beginning with Amos Hawley's 1950 work, human ecologists would turn away from the many specific biological antecedents while striking out to build a theoretical approach distinct from early social theory and breaking with bioecology (Hawley 1950; Schnore 1958). The relationship between bioecology and human ecology is reduced to broad and abstract commonalities. "In a sense human ecology had its origin when a particular biological question was asked of man: How does this species survive? That this question gave rise to a field of sociological interest is mainly due to the answer given: Man survives by collective organization in the exploitation of natural resources. The question, while biological in origin, was answered in terms that are central to sociology; namely, collective organization" (Gibbs and Martin 1959: 30). Once the central focus of human ecology was firmly established as the study of social organization, subsequent ecologists felt free to jettison any further biological connection.

> From Park to Hawley borrowed concepts have dominated theory without contributing to its advancement. Some of these concepts, "competition" being a prime example, have never had their empirical referents clearly established in the human sphere and consequently have produced only purely verbal explanations. Other concepts, such as invasion and succession, far from providing adequate explanations, have only served to further the almost exclusive concern with spatial distribution. In either case, plant and animal concepts, taken as a whole, have a most questionable relevance for human ecology since they do not get at the fundamental attributes of sustenance organization in human populations. (Gibbs and Martin 1959: 34–35)

Cumulative Change: Evolutionary Growth versus Expansion in Neoclassical Human Ecology

Hawley's 1950 work, *Human Ecology: A Theory of Community Structure*, marks the shift from classical to neoclassical human ecology. A number of criticisms had been leveled at the classical human ecological approach. These have been well detailed elsewhere (Saunders 1986; Berry and Kasarda 1977). Criticisms ranged from empirical challenges (Davie 1937) to questionable statistical inferences (Robinson 1950) to general theoretical critiques against its materialist approach (Alihan 1938; Firey 1945). Hawley's 1950 reformulation is largely accepted as a successful answer to these critiques and represents a theoretical and substantive break with early human ecology. "The consequences of Hawley's work in the 1940s and 1950s were twofold. First, it created an agenda for ecological study that advocated systems theory and quantitative measurement.... Second, it almost completely silenced any dialogue with Park's ideas" (Maines, Bridger, and Ulmer 1996: 528).

More than any of the other issues challenging Park's view, Hawley recognized that the most difficult of these attacks were those that challenged Park's formulation of the balance between Darwinian competition at the micro level and macro cultural forces containing these processes. "With the work of Hawley and Duncan, however the emphasis on competition as a basic process in human organization has been replaced by an emphasis on interdependence, while the assertions about the natural basis of ecological processes have become blurred as a result of the attempt to dispense with the biotic-cultural dichotomy" (Saunders 1986: 80).

Hawley himself covers some of the differences between his neoclassical conception and these other ecologies. He sees the ecological concept of succession as analogous to his concept of the internal growth phase. However, Hawley is critical of the original formulation of succession (as used by Clements and Park) and more inclined to a definition made purely in terms of movement toward equilibrium with the environment—a conception closer to modern bioecology than to early ecology (Hawley 1986: 53). "An ecosystem, other things being constant, contains its own limits to growth and those limiting conditions come into operation independent of the composition of the biophysical environment" (Hawley 1986: 54). Here Hawley emphasizes different elements determining equilibrium from classical human ecology. Hawley stresses the structural elements of the ecosystem that limit growth. Hawley instead relies on the notion of "key function" to explain the unit character of the ecological community. In every system of relationships among specialized functions, the connection of a system to the environment is mediated by a limited number of functions.

Functions that mediate between community organization and environmental resources play a critical role in shaping the ecosystem. To the extent that all functions are dependent on a single function there is system closure—that is, the system is dependent on and shaped by that function. Unit cohesion of a community is derived from the interdependencies among these functions. When a key function directly controls environmental access, it shapes the conditions for all subsequent activities. This is seen in production hierarchies within a community that in turn shapes the organization and distribution of metropolitan areas. It is also seen in intercommunity relationships, shaping the organization and distribution of regions, nations, and global interconnections. Key functional activities set the resource conditions for subsequent functions. Thus, the productivity of the key function determines the rates of system growth and also constitutes the limiting condition to system growth. Interdependent, symbiotic linkages to the key function tightly link all elements of the human ecosystem. Because of this, the neoclassical ecological community grows or declines, dies or thrives, as a unit. Growth and evolution are purely a macro-level phenomenon.

This perspective clearly contrasts with Park's emphasis on the moderating effects of culture on individual competition. "There is this difference, however, between a symbiotic and cultural society: namely, that the restraint in the case of symbiotic society (as for example in the plant community) is physical and external. In the case of cultural, i.e., human, society the restraints upon the individual are, so to speak, internal and moral, i.e., based on some sort of consensus" (Park 1936b: 176). Hawley's approach to growth and evolution in ecosystems retains the notions of material interdependence found in the classical human ecological approach. However, the relationship between macro-level cultural constraints and micro-level individual competition is no longer the source of ecosystem change. This was a critical element of Park's approach to ecosystem change. This latter formulation, balancing culture and competition, was the teleological mechanism that allowed Park to use the ecological community as the unit of adaptation and evolution. By jettisoning this element Hawley addresses one of the major theoretical criticisms of the 1940s, that there was an intrinsic disjuncture between individual goal-seeking behavior underlying Darwinian competition at the micro level and macro-level cultural forces containing these processes (Saunders 1986: 66–71).

Additionally, eliminating the role of macro-level culture refocused human ecology on tangible macro-level relationships proposed earlier by McKenzie—the material ecological factors and processes that create the unit character of human communities (McKenzie [1926] 1968: 21–24). Here Hawley abandons Park's teleological mechanism linking individual behavior to macro processes and substitutes a purely structural mechanism, symbiotic interdependence. This perspective draws more from Durkheim than bioecology.

Certainly, this Durkheimian approach is much more influential in neoclassical ecological thought than it ever was in classical approaches (Schnore 1958; Saunders 1986: 82). This had the further effect of divorcing human ecological conceptions entirely from Darwinian processes that are predominant in modern bioecological theory. Although biotic parallels would continue to be used as metaphor and as a heuristic, human ecology was free to develop its own notions of ecosystem change and unit adaptation.

> A further question arises in connection with selection. In the biological model the biophysical environment is regarded as the selective agent. But that not only denies any power of selectivity in the organism, it confuses two possible selecting agents. If we detach the biotic element from the physical element, we find we have separated a dynamic from a passive component. The biotic element, even at the simple organizational level, is usually, if not invariably, organized as a network of relations among species, that is, an ecosystem. (Hawley 1986: 56)

The human ecological community is the unit of adaptation; however, it is an active unit engaging in purposive selection from the environment. Differential selection from the environment—changes in key functional activity—shapes the rest of the ecological community. "In a relatively closed system, the key function is the principle [sic], if not the only, gateway through which environmental influences may enter. The unit in the role is in a position to exercise discretionary power over what may be selected" (Hawley 1986: 61). Strong linkages from the key function create unit character for macro-level system adaptation. In neoclassical ecology, the purposive actions of organizations filling a key functional niche provide the teleological mechanism that directs adaptation. The ecosystem acts as the selecting agent. The environment plays a passive role. This stands in contrast to bioecologists' arguments that it is the environment that is the agent of selection. In population ecology interactions between the environment and populations create adaptation within the ecological community. In community ecology the environment shapes the adaptation of the whole ecosystem (Ricklefs 1980: 602; Dunbar 1972; Lewontin 1970). In either case it is the environment that is the primary cause of selection and adaptation.

In neoclassical ecology it is the ecological community that is the agent of selection. Community structure shapes the nature of adaptation to the environment. Perhaps because of his formulation of the ecosystem as an active unit, evolution, at least in a Darwinian sense, becomes a de-emphasized mode of change in this approach. Hawley has few references to evolution as a central problem in human ecology in his 1950 redefinition of the theory. In his American Sociological Association presidential address, Hawley comes to the conclusion that "it appears that the course of history has progressively reduced the utility of an evolution model in the explanation of cumulative change" (1978: 794). Even where Hawley incorporates evolutionary language into his view of change, the nature of evolution more recalls Park's formulation of disequilibrium (sans culture and competition). Hawley views ecosystem change as encompassing three phases: adaptation, growth, and evolution. As Hawley describes these phases: "(1) adaptation to environment proceeds through the formation of a system of interdependences among the members of a population; (2) system development continues, ceteris paribus, to the maximum size and complexity afforded by the existing facilities for transportation and communication; and (3) system development is resumed with the introduction of new information which increases the capacity for movement of materials, people, and messages and continues until that capacity is fully utilized" (1984: 905). In essence, evolution is simply a new phase of growth that occurs when the ecosystem has opportunity for reorganization. In this sense evolutionary change is simply different developmental stages of system growth and expansion. This is a phenomenon where Darwinian insights are of little use. Neither, it seems, are the earlier social evolutionary approaches. In assessing developmental or evolutionary processes, Hawley argues that "the sweeping homogeneity-to-heterogeneity of Spenser (1921), the equally general mechanical-to-organic solidarity of Simpson (1933), or the more elaborate classificatory schemes of anthropological evolutions (e.g. Goldschmidt 1959) are of no help" (1992: 7).

The neoclassical approach then abandons both direct organicist analogies of an earlier Spencerian theory of change. Neither do Darwinian evolutionary processes play any significant role. Competition and natural selection are in no sense a cause of the human ecological community. Neoclassical human ecology becomes a paradigm primarily concerned with the analysis of macro-level adaptation to the environment through social and economic activities in the key function. While a century of synthesis of biology and sociology shaped this perspective, in the end, this synthesis created a distinct sociology, separate from biological theory and breaking from its intellectual antecedents in sociology. By the end of the twentieth century, the evolutionary approach in human ecology required evaluation in its own right, rather than by the degree to which it continued or modified Darwinian or Spencerian mechanisms.

References

Abbott, A. 1997. "Of Time and Space: The Contemporary Relevance of the Chicago School." *Social Forces* 75 (4): 1149–1182.
Alihan, M. A. 1938. *Social Ecology: A Critical Analysis*. New York: Columbia University Press.
Allee, W. C. 1938. *The Social Life of Animals*. New York: Norton.
Allee, W. C., A. E. Emerson, T. Park, O. Park, and K. P. Schmidt. 1949. *Principles of Animal Ecology*. Philadelphia: Saunders.
Berry, B.J.L., and J. D. Kasarda. 1977. *Contemporary Urban Ecology*. New York: Macmillan.
Catton, W. R., Jr. 1994. "Foundations of Human Ecology." *Sociological Perspectives* 37 (1): 75–95.
Clements, F. E. 1916. *Plant Succession: An Analysis of the Development of Vegetation*. Washington, DC: Carnegie Institute of Washington.
Cowles, H. C. 1899. "The Ecological Relations of the Vegetation on the Sand Dunes of Lake Michigan. Part I. Geographical Relations of the Dune Floras." *Botanical Gazette* 27 (2): 95–117.
Davie, M. R. 1937. "The Pattern of Urban Growth." In *Studies in the Science of Society*, edited by G. P. Murdock, 131–161. New Haven, CT: Yale University Press.
Dunbar, M. J. 1972. "The Ecosystem as Unit of Natural Selection." *Transactions Connecticut Academy of Arts & Sciences* 44: 113–130.
Duncan, O. D. 1961. "From Social System to Ecosystem." *Sociological Inquiry* 31: 140–149.
Faught, J. 1986. "The Concept of Competition in Robert Park's Sociology." *Sociological Quarterly* 27 (3): 359–371.
Firey, W. 1945. "Sentiment and Symbolism as Ecological Variables." *American Sociological Review* 10 (2): 140–148.
Gaziano, E. 1996. "Ecological Metaphors as Scientific Boundary Work: Innovation and Authority in Interwar Sociology and Biology." *American Journal of Sociology* 101 (4): 874–907.
Geddes, P., and J. A. Thomson. 1911. *Evolution*. New York: Henry Holt and Company.
Gibbs, J. P., and W. T. Martin. 1959. "Toward a Theoretical System of Human Ecology." *Pacific Sociological Review* 2 (1): 29–36.
Giddings, F. H. 1896. *The Principles of Sociology*. New York: MacMillan.
Gras, N.S.B. 1922. *An Introduction to Economic History*. New York: Harper & Brothers Publishers.
Gross, M. 1999. "Early Environmental Sociology: American Classics and Their Reflections on Nature." *Humboldt Journal of Social Relations* 25 (1): 1–29.
———. 2004. "Human Geography and Ecological Sociology: The Unfolding of a Human Ecology, 1890 to 1930—and Beyond." *Social Science History* 28 (4): 575–605.
Haeckel, E. 1866. *Generelle Morphologie der Organismen : allgemeine Grundzüge der organischen Formen-Wissenschaft, mechanisch begründet durch die von C. Darwin reformirte Decendenz-Theorie*. Berlin: G. Reimer.

Haines, V. A. 1985. "Organicist to Relational Human Ecology." *Sociological Theory* 3 (1): 65–74.
———. 1988. "Is Spencer's Theory an Evolutionary Theory?" *American Journal of Sociology* 93 (5): 1200–1223.
Hawley, A. H. 1944. "Ecology and Human Ecology." *Social Forces* 22 (4): 398–405.
———. 1950. *Human Ecology: A Theory of Community Structure*. New York: Ronald Press Company.
———. 1968. "Introduction." In *Roderick D. McKenzie on Human Ecology: Selected Writings*, edited by A. H. Hawley, vi–xxii. Chicago: University of Chicago Press.
———. 1978. "Cumulative Change in Theory and in History." *American Sociological Review* 3 (6): 787–796.
———. 1981. "Human Ecology: Persistence and Change." *American Behavioral Scientist* 24 (3): 423–444.
———. 1984. "Human Ecological and Marxian Theories." *American Journal of Sociology* 89 (4): 904–917.
———. 1986. *Human Ecology: A Theoretical Essay*. Chicago: University of Chicago Press.
———. 1992. "The Logic of Macrosociology." *Annual Review of Sociology* 18: 1–17.
Hodgson, G. M. 2005. "Generalizing Darwinism to Social Evolution: Some Early Attempts." *Journal of Economic Issues* 39 (4): 899–914.
Katovich, M. A. 1987. "Durkheim's Macrofoundations of Time: An Assessment and Critique." *Sociological Quarterly* 28 (3): 367–385.
Lewontin, R. C. 1970. "The Units of Selection." *Annual Review of Ecology and Systematics* 1: 1–18.
Maines, D. R., J. C. Bridger, and J. T. Ulmer. 1996. "Mythic Facts and Park's Pragmatism: On Predecessor-Selection and Theorizing in Human Ecology." *Sociological Quarterly* 37 (3): 521–549.
McKenzie, R. D. (1925) 2012. "The Ecological Approach to the Study of the Human Community." In *The City: Suggestions for the Investigation of Behavior in the Urban Environment*, edited by R. E. Park and E. W. Burgess, chap. 3. Kindle edition.
———. (1926) 1968. "The Scope of Human Ecology." In *Roderick D. McKenzie on Human Ecology: Selected Writings*, edited by A. H. Hawley, 19–32. Chicago: University of Chicago Press.
———. (1927) 1968a. "The Concept of Dominance and World-Organization." In *Roderick D. McKenzie on Human Ecology: Selected Writings*, edited by A. H. Hawley, 205–219. Chicago: University of Chicago Press.
———. (1927) 1968b. "Spatial Distance and Community Organization Pattern." In *Roderick D. McKenzie on Human Ecology: Selected Writings*, edited by A. H. Hawley, 94–101. Chicago: University of Chicago Press.
———. 1968. *Roderick D. McKenzie on Human Ecology: Selected Writings*. Chicago: University of Chicago Press.
Park, R. E. 1921. "Sociology and the Social Sciences: The Group Concept and Social Research." *American Journal of Sociology* 27 (2): 169–183.
———. 1926. "The Concept of Position in Sociology." *Papers and Proceedings of the American Sociological Society* 20: 1–14. Retrieved December 30, 2013. http://www.brocku.ca/MeadProject/Park/Park_1926a.html.
———. 1936a. "Human Ecology." *American Journal of Sociology* 42 (1): 1–15.
———. 1936b. "Succession, an Ecological Concept." *American Sociological Review* 1 (2): 171–179.
Park, R. E., and E. W. Burgess. (1921) 2011. *Introduction to the Science of Sociology*. Chicago: University of Chicago Press. Kindle edition.
Richerson, P. J. 1977. "Ecology and Human Ecology: A Comparison of Theories in the Biological and Social Sciences." *American Ethnologist* 4 (1): 1–26.
Ricklefs, R. D. 1980. *Ecology*. 2nd ed. Chicago: Chiron Press.
Rindos, D. 1985. "Darwinian Selection, Symbolic Variation, and the Evolution of Culture." *Current Anthropology* 26 (1): 65–88.
Robinson, W. S. 1950. "Ecological Correlations and the Behavior of Individuals." *American Sociological Review* 15: 351–357.
Saunders, P. 1986. *Social Theory and the Urban Question*. 2nd ed. London: Hutchinson Education.
Schnore, L. 1958. "Social Morphology and Human Ecology." *American Journal of Sociology* 63 (6): 620–634.
Spencer, H. 1864. *The Principles of Biology I*. London: Williams and Norgate.
———. 1874–1896. *Principles of Sociology*. 3 vols. New York: D. Appleton and Company.
———. 1886. *The Principles of Biology II*. New York: D. Appleton and Company.
———. 1893a. "The Inadequacy of Natural Selection I." *Popular Science Monthly* 42 (April): 799–812.
———. 1893b. "The Inadequacy of Natural Selection II." *Popular Science Monthly* 43 (May): 21–28.
———. 1893c. "The Inadequacy of Natural Selection III." *Popular Science Monthly* 43 (June): 162–172.
Sumner, W. G. 1906. *Folkways: A Study of the Sociological Importance of Usages, Manners, Customs, Mores, and Morals*. Boston: Ginn & Co.
Teggart, F. J. 1925. *The Theory of History*. New Haven, CT: Yale University Press.
Thomson, J. A. 1906. *Herbert Spencer*. London: J. M. Dent & Co.
———. 1910. *Darwinism and Human Life: The South African Lectures for 1909*. New York: Henry Holt and Company.
Turner, J. H. 1981. "The Forgotten Theoretical Giant: Herbert Spencer's Models and Principles." *Revue européenne des sciences sociales* 19 (59): 79–98.

Turner, J. H., and A. Maryanski. 2008. "Explaining Socio-Cultural: The Limitations of Evolutionary Theory." *Sociologica* 3: 1–23.

Ward, L. F. 1906. *Applied Sociology: A Treatise on the Conscious Improvement of Society by Society*. Boston: Ginn & Co.

Warming, E. 1895. *Plantesamfund—Grundtræk af den økologiske Plantegeografi*. Forlag, Kjøbenhavn: P.G. Philipsens.

Warming, E., and M. Vahl. 1909. *Oecology of Plants—An Introduction to the Study of Plant-Communities*. Oxford: Clarendon Press.

Weber, A. F. (1899) 1967. *The Growth of Cities in the 19th Century*. Cornell Paperbacks Edition. Ithaca, NY: Cornell University Press.

Wheeler, W. M. 1910. *Ants: Their Structure, Development and Behavior*. New York: Columbia University Press.

Wortmann, H. 2013. "Re-reading Robert E. Park on Social Evolution: An Early Darwinian Conception of Society." *Biological Theory* 7 (1): 69–79.

Chapter Eighteen

Organizational Ecology

Darwinian and Non-Darwinian Dynamics

Jonathan H. Turner

This chapter reviews the basic model of organizational ecology as it has developed over the last thirty years in sociology and other social science disciplines. The adoption of ideas from bioecology for understanding the processes of organizational foundings, niche density, competition, selection, and organizational mortality among populations of organizations altered the analysis of organizations and demonstrated the utility of bringing biology into sociology and the other social sciences. There are, however, limitations to this borrowing of ideas because sociocultural phenomena display properties and dynamics that are much different from those conceptualized within the Darwinian framework. The limitations to use of biological ideas are summarized and used to suggest a reorientation of organizational ecology that draws from both bioecology and mainstream macro sociology.

Organizational ecology emerged in the late 1970s as an explicit adaptation of ideas from bioecology to the study of populations of organizations. The seminal article by Michael T. Hannan and John Freeman (1977) not only added yet another domain of social reality to Darwinian analysis in the social sciences; this approach also dramatically changed how organizations are studied. Hannan and Freeman had been students of Amos Hawley, who carried the urban ecology approach of Chicago School ecological analysis of urban areas and ecological processes more generally into the second half of the twentieth century (e.g., Hawley 1950, 1973, 1978, 1984, 1992); thus, it is not surprising that his students would find a new domain to explain in ecological terms. For Hannan and Freeman (1977, 1984, 1989), as well as for the many who followed their lead (e.g., Astley and Fombrun 1987; Baum, Dobrev, and Bar-Yam 2006; Carroll 1984a, 1984b, 1988, 1997; Dobrev, Kim, and Carroll 2003; Hannan and Carroll 1992), organizations can be conceptualized as occupying a resource niche, with those organizations operating within a particular resource niche constituting a distinct *population of organizations*. Once this shift from the analysis of a single organization to populations of organizations was made, Darwinian ideas could be used to explain the emergence, growth, and decline of organizations. The key variables that explain the life and death of organizations in a resource niche are those typical of other forms of ecological analysis.

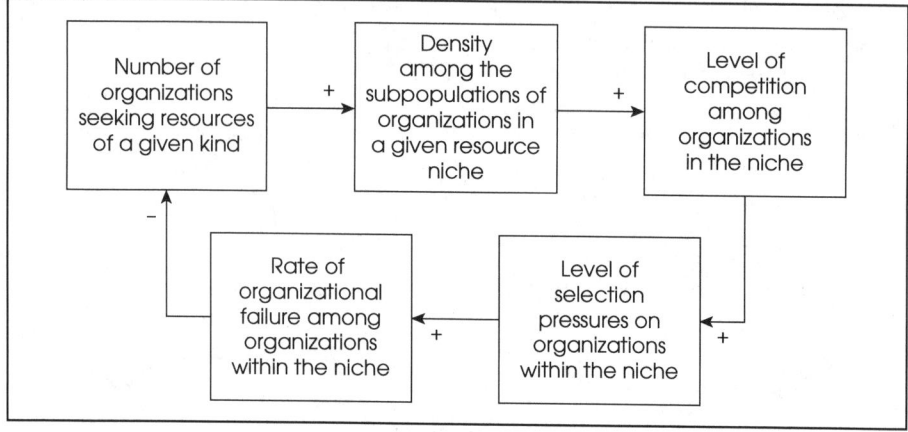

Figure 18.1 The basic Darwinian dynamic in organizational ecology

Basic Dynamics in Organizational Ecology

Resource Niches, Niche Density, Competition, and Selection

The variable forces of resource niches, niche density, competition, and selection are conceptualized in Figure 18.1. A niche is conceptualized as a location of particular types of resources that organizations need to sustain themselves. The number of organizations in a population and the total level of resources available affect the density of organizations in a niche. Low density reduces competition, whereas high density increases competition for resources in a niche. As competition increases, selection pressures increase and begin to sort out those organizations that are most fit from those that are not as fit. Thus, as it was originally formulated, the theory emphasized those processes that increase the number of organizations in a niche, with increases in the number of organizations determining density, selection, and mortality of organizations. One consistent finding from early organizational ecology is that once one organization is successful in securing resources in a niche, other organizations will also be founded and enter this niche; and once this process is set into motion, organizational founding will continue to increase to a point beyond the carrying power of a niche, eventually causing the failure of less fit organizations in a niche. As rates of organizational failure increase, they often decline to a point below the carrying capacity of a niche. This overshoot of the carrying capacity of a niche eventually leads to an uptick in organizational founding and hence an increase in the number of organizations in a niche. This second wave of organizational founding, however, is typically much less than the original proliferation of organizations.

As is the case with urban ecology, competition in a resource niche is institutionalized in sociocultural systems by the expansion of markets (Turner 1995, 2013). The greater the scale, scope, and dynamism of markets, the more these markets will encourage organizations to enter niches where other organizations are enjoying success, institutionalize the competition that ensues from increasing density in a niche, and mark the death of organizations through bankruptcies, mergers, or takeovers by more fit organizations.

Organizational Founding, Legitimacy, and Growth

Despite periodic declines, dynamic markets will always have sustained periods of growth and differentiation, thereby increasing the number of resource niches of material and non-material resources available to organizations. In contrast, the lack of markets or their lack of dynamism limits the number of resource niches and hence the number and diversity of organizational units seeking resources. The first organizations to enter a niche can often enjoy success because of low density and competition for resources in this new niche. The success of these early founders, however, increases the legitimacy of their activities, and as legitimacy increases, ever-more organizations will begin to enter the niche. Legitimacy is an important dynamic in organizational ecology because, as legitimacy increases, uncertainty about prospects of entering a niche is reduced and, moreover, other actors become willing to sponsor organizational founding (through bank loans, sale of stock in equities markets, or governmental approval/subsidies). As these new entrants to a niche enjoy success and survive, legitimacy spreads, eventually causing rates of founding that exceed the carrying capacity of the niche.

When new organizations enter an existing niche, the legitimacy of the organizations already in the niche often leads these new organizations to copy the basic culture and structural templates of successful organizations. This cloning of the culture and structure of existing organizations can create inertial tendencies among organizations that make it difficult for them to change their structure and culture as density and competition increase, with the result that they become vulnerable to selection pressures and potential mortality. Yet, sociocultural systems are not locked into their phenotypes as much as biological organizations, but these inertial tendencies give selection something to select on (Hannan and Freeman 1977; Hannan, Pólos, and Carroll 2007; Dobrev, Kim, and Carroll 2003; Kelly and Amburgey 1991). Organizations often try to restructure themselves to be more competitive, often moving to a new niche or focusing on only a small part of the larger niche in order to remain viable. Yet, these efforts at change can come too late to prevent the death spiral of an organization. For example, Walmart is a basic clone of K-mart, which is a reinvention of the traditional department store into the big-box discount format and organizational template. However, Walmart is simply more efficient than K-mart and has initiated what will probably be a death spiral for K-mart and its parent company, Sears, the last of the old-time department stores. These two types of stores are simply not able to compete with Walmart and various players, such as Target, in this general merchandising niche. Indeed, the list of department store deaths over the last half century is quite long because these stores simply could not restructure themselves because of inertial tendencies solidified and institutionalized by their earlier success in this niche.

Thus, the inertial tendencies of organizations that originally found success in a niche can lead new players in a niche to use the same basic template but more efficiently, with the result that they outcompete early founders. Such has been the case for Walmart in its competition with K-mart and many other big-box discounters in general merchandising that have died off over the past five decades. At other times, organizations try to shift niches to where there is less competition. For example, Penney's department store, which was once very much like Sears and other large department stores, dropped most of its hard goods—appliances, tools, and the like—to focus on soft goods, mostly clothing at a somewhat higher scale than Sears, Woolworth's, and Wards (the "big three" of early department stores in the United States). It enjoyed success for several decades by specializing more than its competition, only to be outdone by new general merchandising by competitors such as Kohl's and Target; indeed, Penney's may also go the way that Sears appears headed—to organizational extinction. What Penney's sought to do is to pursue a strategy of subniche specialization, carving out a more secure subniche for itself until legitimacy kicks in and other organizations begin to enter the same specialized subniche. For example, the rise and fall of clothing stores geared to the "teenage market" has followed this trend, with such stores enjoying initial success, only to be outcompeted by new players adopting the same basic organizational template but in a new and "fresh" format (only to have the same thing done to them by another wave of competitors).

There is also an opposite strategy. Appliance stores emerged in large numbers in the late 1950s in the United States and were often able to outcompete traditional department stores that also carried household appliances (often rebranded in their name). Their focus gave them advantages over larger department stores that had to carry a large overhead and, hence, could not be as flexible as this new type of store. Yet, the mortality rate of these stores is increasing because new players from the larger warehouse sector of various markets have entered this niche. For example, big-box stores like Best Buy or home improvement stores like Lowe's and Home Depot now carry appliances with far less overhead because a large network of big-box stores already exists and allows for volume (discounted) purchasing from manufacturers and because the big-box stores attract a steady volume of "foot traffic" that can be easily lured over to an appliance section.

These kinds of strategies can be pursued in almost all resource niches, but they are more likely in niches where fluctuations in the availability of resources are large, as Hannan and Freeman (1977) originally argued, by the nature of the niche. Some niches have high rates of variability in the levels of resources that they sustain. When resources in niches are highly variable, this often puts larger organizations at a disadvantage compared to smaller, more specialized "subniche players" primarily because the larger organization has to sustain a large overhead in the face of decreasing demand, compared with the smaller player with lower overhead and, thus, the capacity to shift its mix of products. However, Hannan and Freeman originally argued that the *extent* of variation, especially the duration and magnitude of downward shifts in the resources available, shifts the competitive advantage back to larger organizations that often have the capital to ride out variations as well as the greater product mix that can generate resources even as some resources in the niche decline. These hypotheses have not been consistently confirmed, but they give an indication of how fine-tuned ecological analysis of organizations can become. And because this kind of analysis has implications for business success, it is not surprising that most organizational ecologists are now housed in American business schools attached to universities rather than in sociology departments.

Figure 18.2 adds these processes to the model presented in Figure 18.1. The result is a rather robust ecological model that is, at one and the same time, highly theoretical and practical in real-world applications and practice. In many ways, it is a model for capitalist economic development because market dynamics are at the center of the theory. Markets institutionalize competition and hence have large effects on the fitness of organizational phenotypes and their underlying cultural coding. But, markets do more; they also *generate* resource niches. As early sociologists clearly recognized (Spencer [1874–1896] 1898; Simmel [1907] 1990; Durkheim [1893] 1933), markets cause sociocultural differentiation by their ability to link preferences of actors to organizations that can meet those preferences, and each mode of market differentiation potentially becomes a resource niche for organizations seeking profits, members, clients, or adherents.

AGE DEPENDENCE: THE LIABILITIES OF NEWNESS, ADOLESCENCE, AND AGING

Research in organizational ecology has also focused on aging and mortality of organizations in resource niches (e.g., Aldrich and Ruef 2006; Baum and Oliver 1991; Carroll 1983, 1997; Bruderl and Schussler 1990; Freeman, Carroll, and Hannan 1983; Hannan and Freeman 1988). When organizations enter a niche, the risk of failure is high, and only increases if the niche is already densely populated. When organizations create or

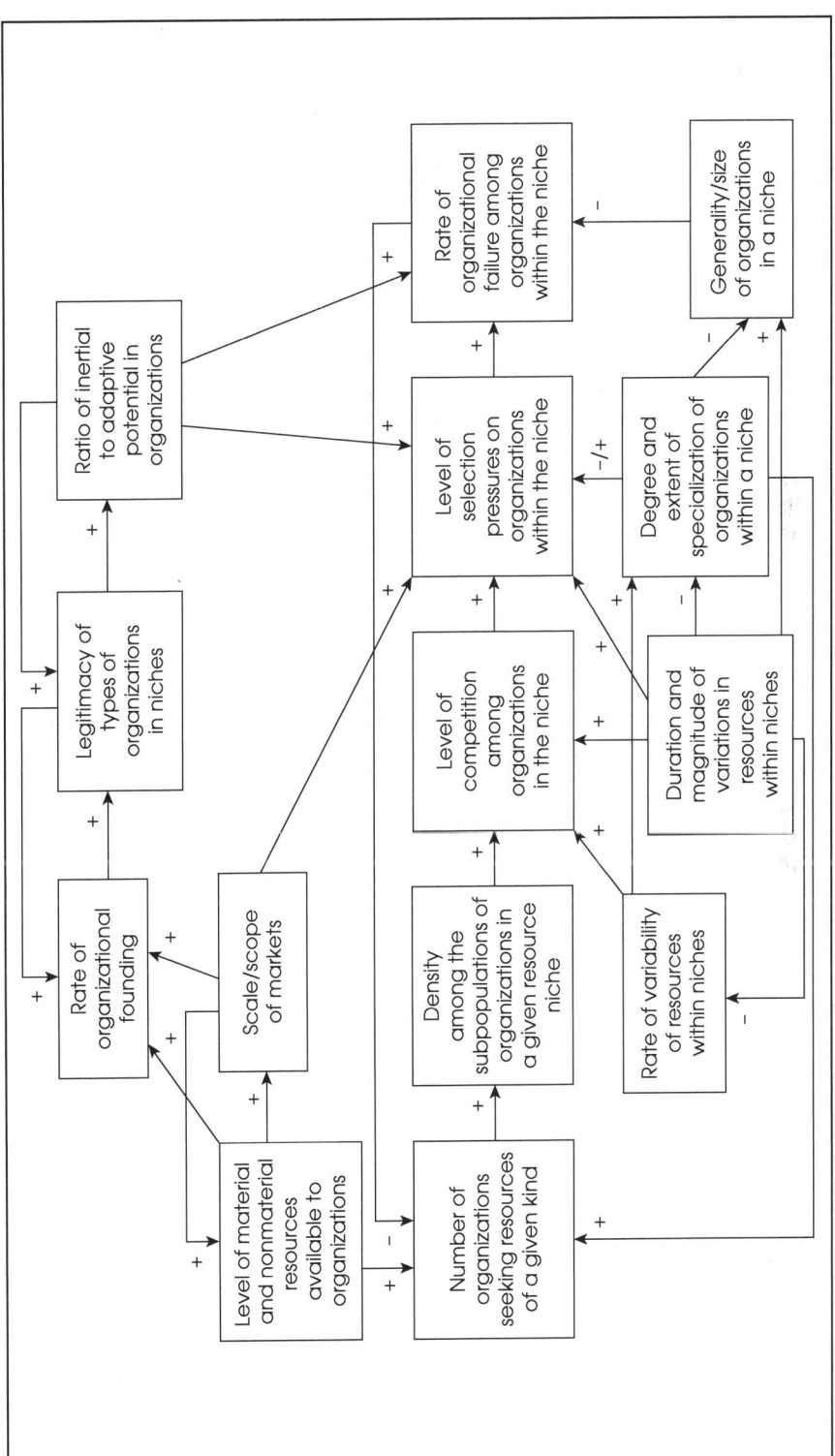

Figure 18.2 The elaborated Darwinian dynamic in organizational ecology

Source: Turner (2013).

enter a previously unexplored niche, there are still risks because there is uncertainty over whether there are resources, per se, and/or an organization's capacity to secure what resources there are. If an organization can be early to the niche and then succeed, this success begins the process of legitimation—as noted earlier. As more organizations enter the niche, often copying a variant of the sociocultural template of early organizations in the niche, legitimacy increases, but so does density, competition, and selection. And if the carrying capacity of the niche is exceeded, then the increasing rate of mortality erodes some of this legitimacy, especially if the resources in a niche also decline.

There are different kinds of legitimation, including (Hannan 2005): (1) regulatory legitimacy bestowed by governmental bodies as they establish rules, laws, regulations, associations, and even professional bodies for organizations in a given type of niche; (2) normative legitimacy by the values, ideologies, and normative systems in the institutional environments of organizations in niches; (3) referential legitimacy, in which the success of at least one organization in a niche justifies the same strategy to new organizations, particularly the standards, norms, practices, and technologies of the organization or organizations that originally founded the niche; (4) certification legitimacy, whereby organizations entering niches are required to display capacities (through licenses and markers of expertise) to operate in a given niche; (5) niche overlaps legitimacy, whereby organizations are given legitimacy by virtue of the success in several, often overlapping niches, with the presumption that access to multiple niches decreases risks of mortality; and, as is emphasized below, (6) segmentation legitimacy, whereby the copying of existing organizational templates by new entrants to a niche bestows confidence in, and legitimacy to, these older players and new entrants to a niche.

When first entering a vacant niche, an organization will be protected from the ravages of density, competition, and selection—at least to the extent that there are resources to be mined in a niche (Freeman, Carroll, and Hannan 1983). But, initial resources may become depleted, with the result that the organization cannot sustain itself. Moreover, to the degree that a niche gains legitimacy, other organizations will enter the niche and begin to increase shares of resources once secured by initial players in the niche. And, even if resources increase in the niche, the result may be a loss of the initial players' shares of resources from the success of competing organizations.

Older organizations risk failure as a consequence of (1) internal inefficiencies, technologies, infrastructures, and distribution systems becoming institutionalized, (2) cultures that do not match up well with a niche, and (3) structural rigidities or inertial tendencies that become increasingly difficult to change. Newer competitors inevitably bring somewhat different structures, cultures, and strategies to a niche, especially a niche where there are already established players. The result can often be harmful to older organizations that reveal inertial tendencies, which are the equivalent of a phenotype in organisms that makes them less fit than the phenotypes of new species or variants of the species in a niche. The outcome is that organizational failures increase, as has been evident in many niches in the history of industrial societies, such as automobile manufacturing (Hannan et al. 1998; Dobrev, Kim, and Carroll 2003), newspapers (Carroll and Delacroix 1982; Carroll and Hannan 1989, 2000), hospitals (Ruef and Scott 1998), savings and loans (Rao and Nielsen 1992), banking (Han 1998), labor unions (Hannan and Freeman 1985, 1988), credit unions (Barron 1995), breweries (Carroll and Wade 1991), life insurance (Ranger-Moore 1997), and other niches in which older organizations simply could not respond to the challenges posed by newer players, especially as the level of resources declined, per se, or as entrance of new organizations increased niche density and increased competition and selection for resources.

Governance structures of organizations can have large effects on risks of mortality of an organization (Oertel and Walgenbach 2010). When organizations lose partners in a niche, risks of mortality increase, although these risks will not be as great for large as opposed to small organizations, nor will risks be as great if an organization that loses partners is already at the adolescent phase in a niche. Incorporation also decreases risks of mortality because it allows for use of the legal system to ride out downturns in niches (e.g., structured bankruptcies). Conversely, risks of mortality decrease as an organization takes on more partners in a niche, thereby forming a confederation of organizations. Smaller organizations entering a niche where density among larger organizations prevails are often at great risk of failure, despite their flexibility and even their new strategies, because they face organizations that can often ride out decreases in resources or engage in practices that erode the capacities of smaller players to secure sufficient resources to survive over the longer term (e.g., price wars, selling at short-term losses to drive out new competitors, or hostile takeover of competitors in equities markets). Even if there are no disproportionately larger organizations in a niche, a density of equal-sized organizations increases the liabilities for any new organization entering a niche; this liability of density increases when there is high homogeneity of products produced or marketed by organizations in a niche. Thus, strategic adaptations become an important force in whether organizations can sustain themselves in dense niches over time (Baum, Dobrev, and Bar-Yam 2006; Delacroix and Swaminathan 1991).

BLAU-SPACE AND THE ECOLOGY OF ORGANIZATIONS

As is evident, a disproportionate amount of theorizing and research on populations of organizations is on profit-seeking organizations in competitive markets within the economy of capitalist societies. Emphasis is on securing monetary resources (profits) from the sale of products and services. But there are many other kinds of niches in complex societies; one of the most important types of niches is generated by diversity in the demographic characteristics of individuals in complex, differentiated societies. Peter Blau conceptualized these as "parameters" marking differences, and J. Miller McPherson and colleagues have focused on organizations that recruit particular types of members defined by parameters (McPherson 1981, 1983a, 1983b; McPherson, Popielarz, and Drobnic 1992; McPherson and Ranger-Moore 1991; McPherson and Rotolo 1996). His work on service clubs in communities documents that the principal resource is membership (and, of course, the dues attached to membership) in an environment that he termed Blau-space, in deference to Blau's (1977, 1994) conceptions of macrostructures as built from the distributions of members of diverse social categories. Traditional service clubs such as the Optimists, Lions, Shriners, Masons, Kiwanis, and the like seek particular types of individuals as members, and the greater the diversity of Blau-space, the greater the number of niches for exploitation (in this case, recruiting members). The same dynamics can play out with many other types of organizations that seek members as a key resource, as is the case with a political party or a social movement organization; they all seek recruits in Blau-space, above and beyond whatever financial resources they may also need to secure.

In Figure 18.3, I have illustrated McPherson's model, which begins with the size of a population and the diversity of resources in Blau-space. McPherson studied service organizations at a time when they were having great trouble recruiting their normal social categories of members in Blau-space: middle-class men in government and businesses within a given community. Historically, incumbents in these categories in Blau-space lost interest in belonging to service clubs in the 1960s and 1970s, thereby shrinking the

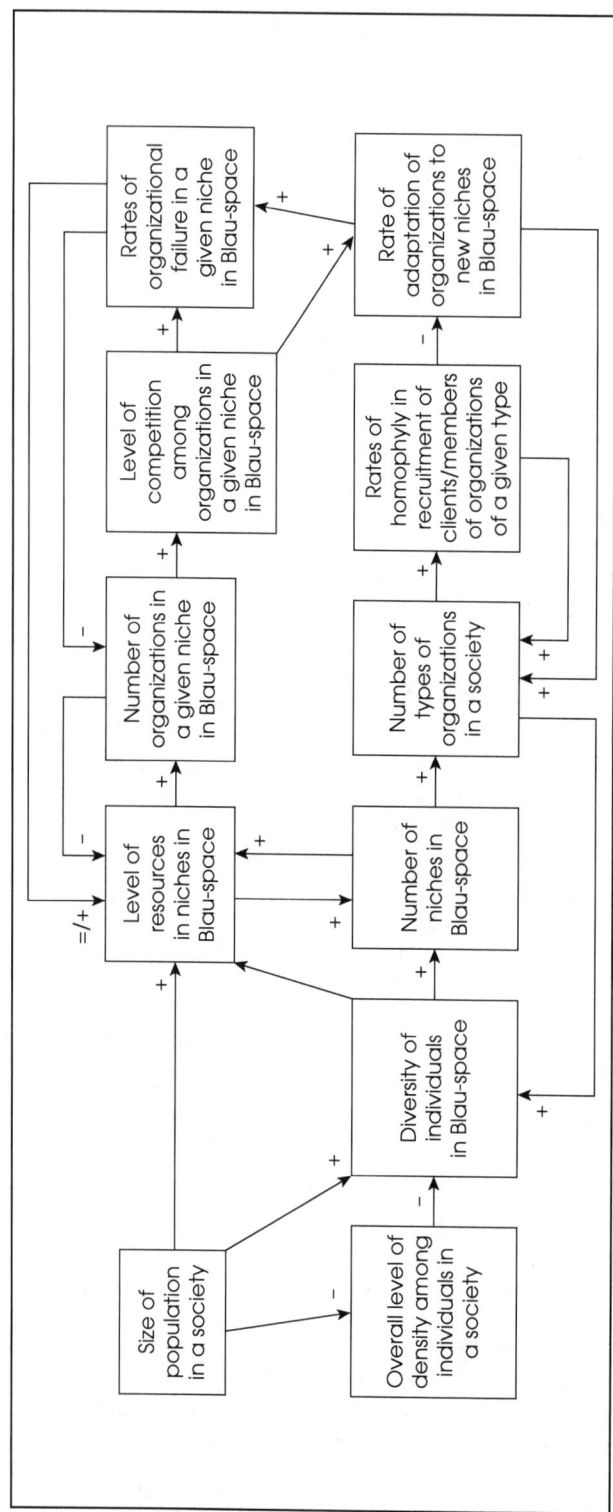

Figure 18.3 McPherson's ecological model of organizational ecology in Blau-space

resources available in their traditional niche and forcing the clubs to seek members from different places in Blau-space: women and select members of the working class and trades. The organizations had, in essence, moved to a new niche where individuals were more willing to join (as status markers) those service clubs. Other types of organizations have had to do much the same thing. For instance, many charities have had to shift their causes and, in the process, their appeals to new portions of Blau-space. The March of Dimes, for example, lost its purpose with the vaccines for polio and, thus, had to shift its mission; in doing so, it changed not only its strategies but also the niches in which it sought contributions. Thus, organizational ecology is not limited to the analysis of profit-seeking economic organizations, because the nature of resources can vary enormously from profits and memberships in nonprofit organizations. Moreover, virtually any organization—church, school, governmental agency, charity, political party, dating service, and so on—can be conceptualized as seeking resources in identifiable niches in Blau-space under conditions of varying density, competition, and selection.

Population size and growth will inevitably increase the diversity of characteristics of individuals in Blau-space. And for many organizations, each parameter marking diversity can represent a potential resource for recruiting members or, in the economic realm, customers. Population size also reduces the density of networks among individuals because it becomes increasingly impossible for all members of a society to be connected to each other. With lowered density, individuals and the corporate units organizing their activities can develop unique characteristics, depending on the environmental niches where they seek resources. The result is lower levels of density in network ties among individuals in larger societies, which, in turn, will also tend to increase the diversity of individuals in Blau-space across a given society.

With an increasing number of niches in Blau-space, the level of differentiation of organizations will increase, to the extent that they seek members from diverse categories in Blau-space. Initially, the differentiation of Blau-space may reduce competition among organizations in any one niche, but over time, as organizations are successful in one niche, rates of founding will increase, thereby increasing organizational density within a given niche in Blau-space, which, in turn, increases competition and selection. However, as organizations compete for resources in Blau-space, they will often differentiate themselves from others in this space as a strategy for recruiting members. This organizational differentiation will often lead to the creation of new niches as differentiated organizations begin to recruit specific types of members in Blau-space. As this process unfolds, the level of homophyly increases as organizations become typified by similar types of members (by age, class origins, ethnicity, religious affiliation, gender, etc.), thereby differentiating organizations further while, at the same time, creating an identifiable niche in Blau-space.

Still, as density, competition, and selection increase within a niche in Blau-space (say, for example, for members or customers of a particular age or gender), it may become increasingly difficult for organizations to sustain the needed memberships or customer base. The result is pressure for increases in the rate of adaptation in which some organizations move to new niches in Blau-space, where density and competition are less. It may be easier for organizations to overcome inertial tendencies when they are outside economic markets and, instead, are recruiting memberships. For example, service clubs rather easily shifted to new niches in Blau-space within communities, and even more rigid structures like the US military services were able to shift to new niches in Blau-space to maintain their forces in the era of an all-volunteer military in the United States. The organization does not have to change its culture or structure to the same degree as an organization in cutthroat competition with other organizations in a market for goods or services;

instead, it only has to accommodate new categories of recruits, while pursuing the same organizational goals using much the same culture and structure.

Implications of Organizational Ecology for Analyzing Macrostructures in Societies

The Building Blocks of Macrostructures and Culture

Societies are ultimately constructed from institutional domains (e.g., economy, polity, law, kinship, religion, education, science) and stratification systems (social classes and inequalities among members of distinctive social categories in Blau-space). Institutions are built from corporate units, especially groups embedded in organizations that are located in communities, whereas stratification typically reveals inequalities in the distribution of resources within institutional domains to members of diverse categoric units, or locations in Blau-space, thereby creating, for instance, a class, ethnic, or gender basis for society-wide stratification. Institutional domains generate resource niches for corporate units, and as these organizations distribute resources unequally across their respective divisions of labor, they cause the formation of categoric units in the stratification systems, thus increasing niches in Blau-space (Turner 2010).

Thus, organizations within institutional domains differentiate in order to address the adaptive problems of a population, and this very differentiation creates diverse resource niches across domains and, often, within domains as well. These niches are composed of both corporate units (and the individuals in them) seeking particular resources and categoric units marking differences among individuals in Blau-space. As societies grow, they differentiate institutional domains and the corporate units in these domains, and as corporate units distribute resources unequally, they cause ever more differentiation in Blau-space built around inequalities. As both Herbert Spencer and Emile Durkheim recognized, these dynamics of differentiation are both a cause and a consequence of institutional dynamics as they evolve in response to population growth.

Population growth thus causes differentiation of institutional domains and the corporate units in these domains, and differentiation of corporate units in domains causes differentiation of individuals in Blau-space and differentiation of categoric units associated with stratification. Once this process is under way, differentiation generates new resource niches and places powerful selection pressures on actors to find mechanisms for integrating this increased differentiation. One of the first sets of mechanisms to evolve is polity and law as regulatory forces that can coordinate differentiated individuals and corporate units. Another mechanism is the creation of markets that connect actors in exchange relations of dependence and interdependence. Once markets evolve, three of the conditions for ecological analysis are in place—that is, differentiated resource niches, social units seeking these resources, and markets institutionalizing competition among these social units.

Inhering in the building blocks of societies and macrostructures, then, are ecological dynamics, and so it should not be surprising that early sociological theorists were drawn to an ecological analysis of societies. But their analysis was decidedly macro in focus, whereas the subsequent development of ecological theorizing in sociology in the twentieth century to the present has clearly been meso level in focus on the ecology of communities and organizations. In recent years, however, there have been several efforts to move ecological analysis back to the more macro level (e.g., Hawley 1984, 1992; Lenski 2005; Turner 1994a, 1994b, 1995, 2010). The key to this conceptual shift is understanding the integrative forces that regulate and control differentiation and the ecological dynamics inhering in such differentiation (as it opens up new resource niches).

Another Type of Non-Darwinian Selection

Herbert Spencer ([1874–1896] 1898) and other functional theorists implicitly argued for another kind of selection pressure on societies: what I have come to term *Spencerian selection*. In sociocultural systems, individual and corporate actors have capacities for agency that enable them, at times, to reconstruct social phenotypes under selection pressures—in a decidedly Lamarckian manner. With the more Darwinian urban and organizational ecology, such agency is often seen as an adaptive response or strategy to overcome inertial tendencies in sociocultural systems that find themselves suddenly having to deal with niche density, intense competition for resources, and high levels of selection pressure. However, perhaps a more prevalent type of selection is under conditions of low density or *no* density of corporate units to resolve pressing adaptive problems. Indeed, most sociocultural evolution of societies has involved borrowing organizational templates, discovering new templates by trial and error, or inventing new types of social units and cultural systems in response to adaptive problems where no viable social phenotypes had been available. Selection is thus a pressure on a population to find a solution or face the disintegrative consequences that come with the death of a society or its conquest by a more fit society.

Many organizational and urban forms of social organization had to be invented *before* they could be selected on, and so, as the scale and complexity of human societies have developed, selection has often been more Spencerian than Darwinian. Individuals and corporate actors have been under pressure to find solutions by inventing new kinds of sociocultural phenotypes; they could not stand around waiting for the sociocultural equivalent of random variations or mutations because they had to act now or face the disintegrative consequences. Only after new sociocultural formations proved adaptive in an environment and began to increase in number and consume resources did the selection shift from Spencerian to Darwinian.

Thus, we need to expand the notion of selection beyond Darwinian natural selection on individual phenotypes as they cause a shift in the distribution of genes regulating these phenotypes. Selection in sociocultural systems has been anything but random; rather, it has been highly instrumental and conscious as actors in social systems have sought to build new kinds of structures and cultures to increase the capacity of a population to survive in its environment. Urban communities and complex organizations were not random variations in phenotypes that could be selected on; rather, they were inventions of individuals organized into corporate units under intense pressure to find solutions to sustain an ever-growing population. They were the product of Spencerian selection, but once in place, they were subject to Darwinian selection dynamics as outlined by urban and organizational ecology. There are, then, multiple types of selection that must be taken into account when social scientists engage in the analysis of multiple levels of selection.

Multilevel Selection Processes and Macrostructural Survival

Unlike organisms, superorganisms, to use Spencer's label for the organization of organisms, involve multiple types of selection operating at multiple levels of social reality. Just as the bodily phenotype of an organism can be conceptualized as a "survivor machine"—to use the colorful wording of sociobiology—so too can each type of social unit be viewed as a survivor machine. What are the basic types of social units? From the micro level to the macro level, these units are encounters, groups, organizations, communities, institutional domains, societies, and even intersocietal systems. These levels of structure are often embedded in each other, but at the same time we must not lose sight that they operate in resource environments (if only the environment imposed by the structure in which they are embedded). Figure 18.4 emphasizes this embedding of smaller inside larger sociocultural formations.

The corporate units embedded in more inclusive corporate units are also the building blocks of institutional domains, and these are, I would argue, the outcome of Spencerian more than Darwinian selection. Populations have been under pressure to differentiate new institutional domains and then integrate them in some manner to meet adaptive problems arising in their external environments (e.g., bioecological, physical, and sociocultural) and in their internal environments (by virtue of growing complexity of societies as they evolve). Spencerian selection has, therefore, caused (1) the development of the institutional domains of societies and the corporate unit structures that make up these domains and (2) the development of structural and cultural mechanisms for integrating these differentiated corporate units within and between domains.

As these corporate units evolved, however, successful adaptations led to segmentation of more like-units; and as segmentation ensued, more Darwinian dynamics supplemented Spencerian selection. As their numbers grew, niche density increased, and thus so did

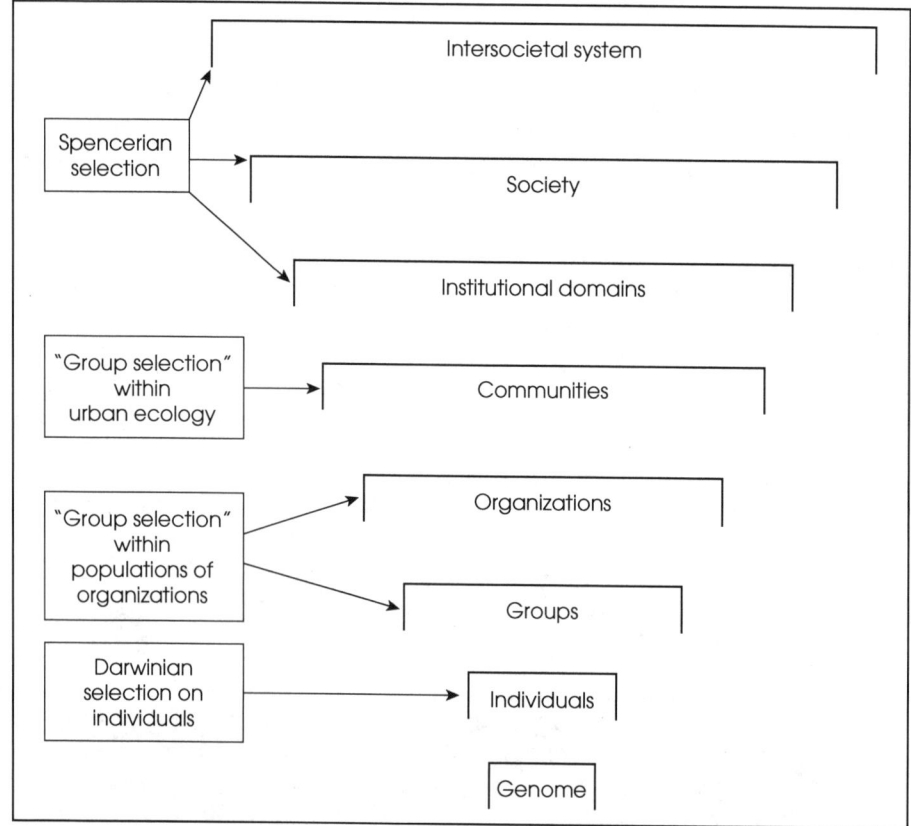

Figure 18.4 Layers of embedding of generic sociocultural formations and the changing nature of selection processes operating

competition and selection, as was outlined in Figure 18.1. The more corporate units have been embedded in each other, the less intense will be these Darwinian processes because the environments (and hence the resources needed for these units to operate) are provided by the structure and integrative mechanisms of the environment generated by the more inclusive structure. For example, groups embedded in the organization may still compete for resources but they do so within the authority structure of the more inclusive organization; and while organizations often compete with each other, as is evident by the dynamics specified by organizational ecology, this competition is constrained by the modes of integration of all corporate units within a domain and between organizations in different institutional domains. Organizations will be guided by the ideology of a domain, by its generalized symbolic media (whether money, love, learning, knowledge, health, authority, etc.), and by the networks often mediated by markets and centers of political power and law. So, the competition is often highly regulated by culture, social structural arrangements, power, and law. Thus, the niches in which organizations must often compete are integrated internally and externally by the use of power and laws attached to polity as autonomous institutional domains, with the result that the competition does not lead to mortality. Perhaps only in capitalist economies, where the ideology of the free market dominates, do we see something like real Darwinian competition. But even here, polity and law can intervene to reduce the competition or to protect those organizations that might go extinct—as was recently evident in the automobile manufacturer bailout in the United States. As a general rule, I suspect, the more the securing of resources by organizations within and across institutional domains is mediated by open and free markets, the more Darwinian will competition become among corporate units, although even here there will be "rules of the competition" coupled with "referees" from polity and law to prevent harmful competition. The converse point is also worth making: the more organizations exist in an environment tightly regulated by centralized centers of administrative power that is able and willing to use coercion, the less will Darwinian processes operate, and the more integration by domination (Weber [1922] 1968) is likely to prevail.

Thus, organizational ecology examines a limiting case: the operation of organizations within market modes of integration. Still, even in systems of top-down domination, there is always some competition for resources, but, as is often the case, mortality is forestalled by the infusion of resources from centers of power, or the competition is highly regulated by centers of power to the point of making organizational "death" less likely.

These considerations, I think, open up new avenues for organizational ecology. The environment of organizations needs to be reconceptualized in several ways. First, organizations seek resources in niches, but these niches are often created, structured, and controlled by the larger organizational units within which corporate units compete for resources. Second, the existence of state-based polity and law imposes limits on competition and also creates a new resource niche for organizations seeking resources. Third, the mechanisms by which organizations within and between institutional domains are integrated have large effects on the degree and nature of competition for resources. Societies integrated by markets loosely regulated by a democratic and decentralized system of power and law will reveal more Darwinian dynamics and higher rates of organizational mortality, whereas a society integrated by domination and tight controls will evidence fewer Darwinian dynamics and perhaps more Spencerian processes initiated by centers of power. And, the more embedded corporate units are inside of each other and then inside discrete and differentiated institutional domains, the more structural and cultural constraints will be imposed on competition for resources in niches within the more inclusive unit. These forces have been underemphasized by not only organizational ecology but also the "new institutionalism" (see Abertyn and Turner 2011), which does not fully appreciate the degree to which the environments of organizations are constrained by the modes of integration among and between corporate units within institutional domains. These varying configurations of mechanisms in societal integration affect not only the resources available to any given organization but also the strategies that each organization can legitimately employ in seeking these resources.

These critiques of the existing literatures represent to me opportunities to expand the ecological analysis of organizations by bringing in macro-level structures—institutions, stratification, societies, and intersocietal systems—as forces that impose constraints on the kinds of niches that are available to organizations and the strategies they are allowed to pursue to secure these resources. I would suggest that a new kind of organizational ecology can *begin* with the analysis of macrostructure and modes or mechanisms of societal-level integration, with an eye to understanding how these macro-level mechanisms of integration affect the distribution of resource niches and the operative dynamics of selection in these meso-level resource niches (see Turner 2010: 115–143 for one typology of such mechanisms).

Conclusion

Organizational ecology demonstrates how ideas from bioecology can be incorporated into the analysis of social phenomena. By reconceptualizing organizations *as populations*, the effects of population growth, density, competition, and selection from Darwinian theory can shed new light on the dynamics of organizations, one of the main building blocks of human societies. The model works best in the analysis of economic actors in capitalist systems where free markets institutionalize competition and selection, but the model can be extended to other types of organizations seeking a wide variety of resources in diverse niches.

Yet, like any wholesale adoption of ideas from biology, there are limits to how far these Darwinian dynamics can be taken in the analysis of sociocultural phenomena. Darwinian analysis will need to be supplemented by the recognition that much evolution in the sociocultural universe is driven by Spencerian selection, in which actors respond to adaptive problems in the absence of any fitness-enhancing variants in sociocultural phenotypes. Instead, variants will need to be invented and imposed to enhance fitness. Related to this point is the fact that selection works at different levels of social organization. Current ecological models in sociology tend to theorize at the meso level of social organization, but the social universe is layered at several different levels, with micro phenomena typically embedded in meso structures like organizations, and with meso-level sociocultural formations being the building blocks of macrostructures while, at the same time, being embedded and constrained by the structure and culture of institutional domains, societies, and systems of societies.

Another necessary consideration is how selection pressures have led to the use of a variety of mechanisms for integrating differentiated corporate units in societies. The particular configuration of integrative mechanisms will have large effects on the nature of the organizational units, the nature of the resource niches in which they seek resources, and the nature of structural and cultural constraints on the dynamics of competition and selection. Attention to these constraining effects of macrostructures emphasizes that, when applied to the social universe, evolutionary analysis must recognize that there are at least two types of selection—Darwinian and Spencerian—operating at multiple levels. Finally, in the social universe, Lamarckian dynamics operate as much as Darwinian processes.

References

Abertyn, S., and J. H. Turner. 2011. "The Old Institutionalism Meets the New Institutionalism." *Sociological Perspectives* 54: 283–306.
Aldrich, H. E., and M. Ruef. 2006. *Organizations Evolving*. London: Sage Publications.
Astley, W. G., and C. J. Fombrun. 1987. "Organizational Communities: An Ecological Perspective." *Research in the Sociology of Organizations* 5: 163–185.
Barron, D. N. 1995. "Credit Unions." In *Organizations in Industry*, edited by G. Carroll and M. T. Hannan, 137–161. New York: Oxford University Press.
Baum, J. A. C., S. D. Dobrev, and Y. Bar-Yam. 2006. *Ecology and Strategy*. Amsterdam: Elsevier.
Baum, J. A. C., and C. Oliver. 1991. "Institutional Linkages and Organizational Mortality." *Administrative Science Quarterly* 36: 187–218.
Blau, P. M. 1977. *Inequality and Heterogeneity: A Primitive Theory of Social Structure*. New York: Free Press.
———. 1994. *Structural Context of Opportunities*. Chicago: University of Chicago Press.
Bruderl, J., and R. Schussler. 1990. "Organizational Mortality: The Liability of Newness and Adolescence." *Administrative Science Quarterly* 35: 530–547.
Carroll, G. R. 1983. "A Stochastic Model of Organizational Mortality: Review and Reanalysis." *Social Science Research* 12: 303–329.
———. 1984a. "Dynamics of Publisher Succession in the Newspaper Industry." *Administrative Science Quarterly* 29: 93–113.
———. 1984b. "Organizational Ecology." *Annual Review of Sociology* 10: 71–93.
———, ed. 1988. *Ecological Models of Organizations*. Cambridge, MA: Ballinger.
———. 1997. "Long-Term Evolutionary Change in Organizational Populations: Theory, Models, and Empirical Findings in Industrial Demography." *Industrial and Corporate Change* 6: 119–143.
Carroll, G. R., and J. Delacroix. 1982. "Organizational Mortality in the Newspaper Industries of Argentina and Ireland: An Ecological Approach." *Administrative Science Quarterly* 27: 169–198.
Carroll, G. R., and M. T. Hannan. 1989. "Density Dependence in the Evolution of Populations of Newspaper Organizations." *American Sociological Review* 54: 524–541.
———. 2000. *The Demography of Corporations and Industries*. Princeton, NJ: Princeton University Press.
Carroll, G. R., and J. Wade. 1991. "Density Dependence in the Organizational Evolution of the American Brewing Industry across Different Levels of Analysis." *Social Science Research* 20: 271–302.
Delacroix, J., and A. Swaminathan. 1991. "Cosmetic, Speculative, and Adaptive Organizational Change in the Wine Industry." *Administrative Science Quarterly* 36: 631–661.
Dobrev, S. D., T. Y. Kim, and G. R. Carroll. 2003. "Shifting Gears, Shifting Niches: Organizational Inertia and Change in the Evolution of the U.S. Automobile Industry, 1885–1981." *Organizational Science* 22: 264–282.
Durkheim, É. (1893) 1933. *The Division of Labor in Society*. Glencoe, IL: Free Press.
Freeman, J., G. R. Carroll, and M. T. Hannan. 1983. "The Liability of Newness: Age Dependence in Organizational Death Rates." *American Sociological Review* 48: 692–710.
Han, J. 1998. "The Evolution of Japanese Banking Industry: An Ecological Analysis." PhD diss., Stanford University.
Hannan, M. T. 2005. "Ecologies of Organizations: Diversity and Identity." *Journal of Economic Perspectives* 19: 51–70.
Hannan, M. T., and G. R. Carroll. 1992. *Dynamics of Organizational Populations: Density, Legitimation, and Competition*. New York: Oxford University Press.
Hannan, M. T., G. R. Carroll, S. D. Dobrev, and J. Han. 1998. "Organizational Mortality in European and American Automobile Industries. Part I: Revisiting the Effects of Age and Size." *European Sociological Review* 14: 279–302.
Hannan, M. T., and J. Freeman. 1977. "The Population Ecology of Organizations." *American Journal of Sociology* 82: 929–964.
———. 1984. "Structural Inertia and Organizational Change." *American Sociological Review* 49: 149–164.
———. 1985. "The Ecology of Organizational Founding: American Labor Unions 1836–1985." *American Journal of Sociology* 92: 910–943.
———. 1988. "The Ecology of Organizational Mortality: American Labor Unions." *American Journal of Sociology* 94: 25–52.
———. 1989. *Organizational Ecology*. Cambridge, MA: Harvard University Press.
Hannan, M. T., L. Pólos, and G. R. Carroll. 2007. *Logics of Organization Theory: Audiences, Codes, and Ecologies*. Princeton, NJ: Princeton University Press.
Hawley, A. H. 1950. *Human Ecology: A Theory of Community Structure*. New York: Ronald.
———. 1973. "Ecology and Population." *Science* 179 (March): 1196–1201.
———. 1978. "Cumulative Change in Theory and History." *American Sociological Review* 43: 787–797.

———. 1984. *Human Ecology: A Theoretical Essay.* Chicago: University of Chicago Press.
———. 1992. "The Logic of Macrosociology." *Annual Review of Sociology* 18: 1–14.
Kelly, D., and T. Amburgey. 1991. "Organizational Inertia and Momentum: A Dynamic Model of Strategic Change." *Academy of Management Journal* 34: 591–612.
Lenski, G. 2005. *Ecological-Evolutionary Theory.* Boulder, CO: Paradigm Press.
McPherson, J. M. 1981. "A Dynamic Model of Voluntary Affiliation." *Social Forces* 59: 705–728.
———. 1983a. "An Ecology of Affiliation." *American Sociological Review* 48: 519–532.
———. 1983b. "The Size of Voluntary Organizations." *Social Forces* 61: 1044–1064.
McPherson, J. M., P. A. Popielarz, and S. Drobnic. 1992. "Social Networks and Organizational Dynamics." *American Sociological Review* 57: 153–170.
McPherson, J. M., and J. Ranger-Moore. 1991. "Evolution on a Dancing Landscape: Organizations and Networks in Dynamic Blau-Space." *Social Forces* 70: 19–42.
McPherson, J. M., and T. Rotolo. 1996. "Testing a Dynamic Model of Social Composition: Diversity and Change in Voluntary Groups." *American Sociological Review* 61: 179–202.
Oertel, S., and P. Walgenbach. 2010. "How the Organizational Ecology Approach Can Enrich Business Research on Small and Medium-Sized Enterprises." *Organizational Ecology* 10: 250–269.
Ranger-Moore, J. 1997. "Bigger May Be Better, but Is Older Wiser?: Organizational Age and Size in the New York Life Insurance Industry." *American Sociological Review* 62: 903–920.
Rao, H., and E. H. Nielsen. 1992. "An Ecology of Agency Arrangements: Mortality of Savings and Loan Associations." *Administrative Science Quarterly* 37: 448–470.
Ruef, M., and W. R. Scott. 1998. "A Multidimensional Model of Organizational Legitimacy: Hospital Survival in Changing Institutional Environments." *Administrative Science Quarterly* 43: 877–904.
Simmel, G. (1907) 1990. *The Philosophy of Money.* Translated by T. Bottomore and D. Frisby. Boston: Routledge.
Spencer, H. (1874–1896) 1898. *The Principles of Sociology.* 3 vols. New York: Appleton Century.
Turner, J. H. 1994a. "The Assembling of Human Populations: Toward a Synthesis of Ecological and Geopolitical Theories." *Advances in Human Ecology* 3: 65–91.
———. 1994b. "The Ecology of Macrostructure." *Advances in Human Ecology* 3: 113–137.
———. 1995. *Macrodynamics: Toward Theory on the Organization of Human Populations.* New Brunswick, NJ: Rutgers University Press.
———. 2010. *Theoretical Principles of Sociology.* Vol. 1, *Macrodynamics.* New York: Springer.
———. 2013. "Ecological Theories." In *Contemporary Sociological Theory,* 133–158. Newbury Park, CA: Sage Publications.
Weber, M. (1922) 1968. *Economy and Society.* Berkeley: University of California Press.

Four
Sex, Gender, and Mating

Chapter Nineteen
Marry In or Die Out
Optimal Inbreeding and the Meaning of Mediogamy
Robin Fox

> This chapter is a rethinking of the analysis of exogamy and endogamy with a new approach to the adaptive benefits of the latter. Bateson's principle of optimal inbreeding in plants and animals leads to the definition of mediogamy (close-cousin marriage) as the human equivalent. Incest avoidance is examined as the driver of human exogamy and as a form of dispersion subject to general laws of fragmentation and dispersion. The basic forms of exogamic marriage, the human phenomenon of endogamy through parallel cousin marriage, and dispersion in animals and humans and its relationship to the preservation of the optimal number (after Malthus) are examined. The possibility that a mechanism other than resource optimization is responsible for population segmentation and dispersion across species, namely, optimization of fertility by consanguineous mating, is examined. Data from four taxa (mammals, birds, fish, and insects) and from human birth records suggest that the same underlying mechanisms are present from single-celled organisms to humans governing population fluctuations and fragmentation that has to do with preserving levels of fertility through optimal inbreeding and losing them through dilution of consanguinity. This challenges the Malthusian resource-based paradigm and makes mediogamy the optimal strategy in human mating systems. The consequences of its decline for fertility levels in current populations are examined.

"Of course we marry cousins. What would you have us do, marry strangers?"
                                                            Groom at a Baghdad wedding

Introduction: Exogamy and Outbreeding

The defining issue at the heart of traditional anthropology—and for that matter, of sociology—in the nineteenth century was *exogamy*: literally "marriage out." John F. McLennan coined the term, contrasting it with *endogamy*, "marriage in." But all the early scholars (Spencer, Tylor, Durkheim, Morgan, Westermarck, Frazer, Freud, et al.) saw at once that there were difficulties with the idea: for a start, the definitions of the terms had to be relative: "marriage out of, or into . . . what?" Thus, marriage with cousins was marriage out of the immediate family, but still could or could not be marriage out of the descent group or kindred depending on its definition. As we shall see, the most elementary form of cousin-marriage exchange results in an intermarrying of two lines of descent that are each exogamous but produce a closed endogamic marriage unit.

The other difficulty came with the search for the most primitive element of human society in the incest taboo, which, the argument went, was the driver of exogamy. Again, this idea had its own relativity problems depending on where the boundaries of inbreeding were set. What counted as "incest"? There is no rule of nature on this; we have to do the defining. Moreover, there was a constant confusion because the term *exogamy* refers specifically to *marriage* out (of whatever), not simply to outbreeding. If *exogamy* was to be the original great human invention, then there had to be *gamy* before there was *exo*. Marriage had to be invented before we could decide who had to marry out of what, and, of course, marriage is a human invention: a set of legal formulations, a contract in effect. It requires language in which to couch the rules (as do taboos). So exogamy cannot just be about the negative avoidance of inbreeding (however defined); it has to be about positive rules of contractual exchange: the central point of the masterwork of Claude Lévi-Strauss (1949). Many scholars, however, continued to use *exogamy* and *incest taboo* as synonyms, a confusion I felt it necessary to address as late as 1967 (*Kinship and Marriage*, chap. 2) with the stunningly obvious: "Incest is about sex; exogamy is about marriage."

Biologists who were addressing the issue of *assortative mating* in animals and plants did not have this problem. They could talk solely in terms of inbreeding and outbreeding because, of course, nonhuman organisms do not by definition have "marriage." It was Patrick Bateson who, I think as early as 1978, first introduced the idea of "optimal outbreeding," and it is interesting to hear why he preferred this to the perhaps more correct "optimal inbreeding":

> Since the notion that inbreeding is "bad" is so deeply ingrained in many people's minds, it seems wiser to preserve "optimal out-breeding" which represents the more congenial departure from conventional thought. Nonetheless, the important issue is optimal *balance* and a terminological argument that distracted from this point would be unproductive. (Bateson 1983: 274, his emphasis)

Fair enough. But I think there is good reason to reconsider that *optimal inbreeding* is a concept that requires some more positive thought since it reverses the obsession we have had (certainly that I have had) with the *avoidance of inbreeding* and looks for the *adaptive advantages of inbreeding* that accrue to all sexually reproducing species, including in the case of humans the added twist of exogamy: an advantage that produces the *optimal balance* between inbreeding and outbreeding that Bateson saw as the heart of the matter.

Incest and Exogamy

First we must recapitulate the arguments about the "incest taboo," which for so long was held to be the necessary precursor and driver of exogamy. The latter was often referred to by anthropologists as an "extension" of the taboo. Taboos on sexual relationships between close kin, between members of the immediate family, were long thought to be a purely human invention. Animals, it was maintained, had no such inhibitions and mated incestuously. Thus, the taboos on such animalistic behavior were thought to be the very foundation of human society; they were the ultimate drumbeat of humanity, by which, in the immortal words of Lévi-Strauss, Culture said "No!" to Nature. Despite taking this momentous step, humans were thought to carry over into their humanness the even deeper drumbeat of their animal desires.

The move from Nature to Culture represented by the imposition of the taboos was seen as precarious and counter to natural motives, which were ineradicable. In consequence, the taboos had to be stern and enforced by constant vigilance. In this traditional view, we all wanted to make love to our nearest kin, but once the momentous leap into Culture had been taken, it would have been disastrous to go back into the maelstrom of animalistic incest. Our societies were built on the presumption of mating outside the family—it was the very definition of humanity itself—and so stern taboos, laws, and punishments were needed to keep incest at bay, stern taboos that were often "extended" well beyond the family itself.

This was a plausible view since societies did almost universally ban sex and marriage within the immediate family, and punishments for breaches of this rule were often severe, including torture and death. In their mythologies, primitive tribes and ancient societies often portrayed incest, and the results of it were usually disastrous. There were exceptions to the rule, but they were almost always royal exceptions: royal persons, as gods on earth, were allowed behavior that was not allowed to ordinary mortals. On the whole, then, it was agreed, there was a "grisly horror" of incest (Freud) that universally afflicted people and led them to impose and enforce the taboos, often extending them beyond the family to members of the clan variously defined. Why, the question went, would we have such strong taboos if we did not have the strong desire in the first place?

Both popular opinion and the collective voice of the behavioral sciences echoed this orthodoxy. But there was always an undercurrent of skepticism. Why, the objectors asked in turn, do we seem, by and large, *not* to want to have sex with our closest relations? This would be the commonsense observation. Incest happens, but in proportion to non-incest, it does not happen very often. And most of this avoidance of incest does not seem to result from fear of punishment; there seems to be a genuine aversion to incest. This aversion seems to vary according to the relationship: strongest between mother and son, weakest between father and daughter, variable between brother and sister. But it is there, and it usually breaks down only in unappetizing circumstances.

The orthodox view says that left to our own devices we would immediately resort to incest and so we have to be reined in by strong taboos and sanctions. To the question why should we not follow the desire to its logical conclusion, the orthodox had a string of often-contradictory answers. There would be a confusion of relationships, there would be bad genetic results, there would be conflict in the family, there would be too much attachment in the family, social bonds outside the family would not form, and so on. The skeptical view says that, on the contrary, left to our own devices we would probably mostly avoid incest spontaneously. The orthodox view asks if this is so, why is there the universal strong taboo?

The skeptic answers that we often taboo things to which we are averse, not because we secretly want to do them, but because we disapprove of people doing things that are generally obnoxious to us. We strongly taboo murder, not because we are all given to implacable murderous impulses, but because we are averse to it, so that even if only a few people do it, it offends us. We do, however, understand the temptation to do it; we have all perhaps felt it momentarily. So the subject fascinates us and permeates our legends and stories from the beginning. Sex and violence, incest and murder persist in our imaginative attempts to interpret ourselves to ourselves.

This has been one of the most interesting debates in the science of man (as we used to call it), and it is no secret that I have come down heavily on the side of the skeptics. I faced the united front of the great ones—Freud, Frazer, Lévi-Strauss, and all their successors—in supporting the views of Edward Westermarck, who basically said that close relationships in childhood led to the development of spontaneous aversion to sex in adulthood. Familiarity did not only breed contempt; it did not breed at all.

What led me to this were two observations. The first was the empirical observation that, in all the societies I looked at, this spontaneous aversion did seem to develop in varying degrees. It developed almost universally where children were reared together and allowed free physical interaction with each other: a situation that would have characterized the long period of our hominid development. The second was that the orthodox view might be totally wrong about what happened in "nature" since this view was not based on observations of nature but on suppositions about it.

Again, in looking at animal behavior under natural conditions—indeed, at the behavior of all sexually reproducing organisms—outbreeding seemed to be the rule, and incest was rare, happening only in creatures that lived in unvarying conditions where the equivalent of cloning would be an advantage. This "natural outbreeding" was especially true in our primate relatives and so by implication in our ancestors during the long haul through the savannas and the ice of the Paleolithic period: the environment of our evolutionary adaptedness; a constantly changing environment in which genetic variation would be a decided advantage.

If the avoidance of close-familial inbreeding was the rule rather than the exception, the human incest taboo was, I argued, not Culture saying "No!" to Nature, but rather saying "OK!" It was an amplification of the natural rather than an opposition to it. But how did this aversion come about? Was it instinctive? Were we born with such a natural aversion? This seemed impossible because we would not necessarily know who our relatives were. In any mammalian species a son knows its mother, and that seems to be the most universally avoided relationship. But it is a wise mammalian child that knows its own father, except in the relatively rare species that mate for life. And brothers and sisters vary a lot in how they relate to each other. An anti-incest instinct does not seem probable. Trivers and Burt, for example, in *Genes in Conflict* (2006), show that maternal and paternal genes *within the same organism* may be at odds about the desirability of different types of inbreeding (with cousins). But in all mammals there seems to be mechanisms that effect a dispersal of the members of the family so that the likelihood of their mating is reduced. Selection doesn't need 100 percent to work, and it can implant a learning device as well as an instinct, and this has the adaptive advantage of flexibility, of varying responses to varying environments. It is a mechanism that can go wrong; it depends on the conditions of learning being met. This is the clue.

Dispersion and Incest Avoidance

Why should this be? Is not the list of possible disasters proposed by the orthodox enough to explain why we avoid it? Not really. We have to go back to an even deeper drumbeat of life to get to the phenomenon of *dispersion* in animal and human life. We have to look to the origins of life as the emergence of self-replicating matter, and then to the crucial revolution that produced sex to replace cloning.

The origin of this sexual reproduction is still a mystery, but whatever the reason, this new form of reproduction won out over its rival (which is still around) by virtue of its ability to produce instant *genetic variability* for natural selection to work on. Close inbreeding results in a loss of such variability, it is argued, hence mechanisms evolved to avoid it. At the same time, if breeding becomes too random, then any beneficial genes will be dissipated rather than concentrated and preserved. It is this reduction of variation that seems to be at the heart of sexual strategies, not the bad genetic effects of close inbreeding. In small bands these effects would usually be bred out, and even scattered bouts of outbreeding would reestablish a healthy stock. We shall look into this with cousin marriage later.

So Nature aims for a middle ground: organisms breed out to avoid losing variability, but not so far out that they dissipate genetic advantages. In human terms this means that the immediate family is taboo, but that *marriage with close cousins* should be preferred, extending effectively to third and fourth cousins as we shall see later. This is exactly what we find in human history until the dramatic growth and disruption of human populations upset the natural balance of the traditional society. Cousins would have been the most likely marriage partners in most traditional societies. There is evidence that people tend to choose mates who are genetically similar (Bateson 1983); cousins are ready-made candidates. These two institutions, avoidance of familial incest and marriage of cousins, are at the heart of our humanity.

What are the human mechanisms that ensure the right result, from Nature's point of view, of resisting familial inbreeding while finding the genetically ideal mate? First, incest avoidance: universally the suckled young male does not seem to want to mate with his mother, and in traditional society this would have been difficult anyway since she would usually be past breeding age when he became mature. The "suckling complex," which itself has a strong hormonal link with sexuality through the hormone *oxytocin*, seems to take care of the mother. Brothers and sisters are usually raised together, and this is what led Westermarck to think they develop an aversion they are not necessarily born with. In cases where they are allowed to play intimately together, before the age of six, they do seem to become actively averse to sex with each other at puberty.

This is well established now, with numerous documented examples. I called it (in "Sibling Incest" in 1962) "the Westermarck effect" to distinguish it from another pattern I called "the Freud effect." Here is my original "law" (which of course is a hypothesis):

> The intensity of heterosexual attraction between co-socialized children after puberty is inversely proportionate to the intensity of physical interaction between them before puberty.

Left to their own devices (at least until age six) it appears the little siblings would act according to Nature's script. We are still not sure what mechanism is involved in this "critical period"—whether it is aversive conditioning, negative imprinting, a cognitive function, or pheromonal (see note 2)—but it happens when the brain is maximally malleable, and it gets fixed. It is important to note that the aversion they would develop was intended to be transient; it was meant to divert the siblings from each other briefly at puberty, long enough for them to mate elsewhere. But if, for example, they were kept around each other in relative isolation with no other sexual outlets, then the sexual imperative might well overcome the aversion.

In the cases that have been closely studied, varying from the Israeli Kibbutzim and the Taiwanese to the Trobriand Islanders and the Western Apache, there was a continuum (Fox [1980] 1983). At one end were the freely romping siblings frolicking together; at the other end—the Freud end—were siblings reared together but not allowed physical contact. There were gradations between these two extremes, but at the Westermarck end the result seemed to be complete aversion, while at the Freud end it was the reverse. Despite the close rearing, the Freud-effect siblings were as sexual strangers to each other at puberty and needed strong taboos and punishments to keep desire in check.

It is a sad parody of human good intentions that incestuous desire in siblings can result from a quite conscious attempt to prevent it. With the Freud effect, Culture saying "No!" to Nature had the paradoxical outcome of *promoting* strong incestuous desires. This is what Freud observed in his own Vienna, and he generalized his observations to mankind at large. For him the first line of human defense against the incestuous wishes was "repression": the desire was pushed into the subconscious and denied. It was dammed up, but the dam was always ready to burst.

The result in either case (Westermarck or Freud) was the same—no incest with siblings. The result was just achieved by different means: aversion and spontaneous avoidance on the one hand, and repression plus strong taboos on the other. In either case the siblings would not be inclined to practice incest, but attitudes toward its occurrence would vary from relative indifference to superstitious horror and all stations in between. The common denominator would be unease about the prospect of incest coupled with a fascination at the possibility of it: something we find throughout the literary treatment of incest (Fox 2011).

Kindred and Affinity

There is a tendency to invoke "the incest taboo" as though it were a homogeneous phenomenon. But the three possibilities are quite different. With fathers and daughters there is less of a barrier; a daughter is a young fertile female after all, and it does happen. This is fundamentally a power relationship—or has been in all traditional societies—and the most open to potential abuse. There is less opportunity for the spontaneous generation of avoidance here. But here we must look beyond the negative banning of sex and into the positive advantages of mating outside the family. This is the other side of the incest coin, and the positive social advantages of this familial exogamy have been at the center of anthropological discussions; the possible biological costs of marrying too far out have had less, if any, attention.

In the pre-language condition of our primate ancestors, when members of a group left to mate elsewhere, they lost all contact with the home group. Among nonhuman primates it is the norm that either the males of a band or the females leave at puberty and mate elsewhere, so that was established. What our hominid ancestors seemed to add to the mix was continuing contact. I tried to put this in the formula:

> While all primates have kin, only humans have in-laws.

A father in early human society had an interest in using his daughters and sisters (all the females he controlled) to forge alliances with other males in different groups: bands or clans. With the advent of hunting and language, all this was made possible, and the first human societies were formed. For a sophisticated extension of this idea, see Bernard Chapais, *Primeval Kinship* (2008).

The catch here is that incest avoidance and taboo were not the result of the social advantages of marrying out, as most thinkers argued. The avoidance was there to start with, but avoidance alone resulted only in our running away from familial relatives and bumping into others (as it were). We must then add to this negative impulse the positive advantages of continuing relationships between bands and clans. This gave the older males (the fathers) a stake in the mating fate of their daughters—of all the females of the band.

So fathers, and all the males, had to develop central nervous systems, based on the enlarging neocortex of the brain, that had the capacity to inhibit their immediate desires, let them practice long-term strategies, and, with the advent of language and naming, allow them to live according to rules of kinship and marriage. For this is what we are now talking about. Avoidance and mating are physical and behavioral responses; marriage is about *rules*. Injunctions about whom you could and could not marry, and what your obligations were to in-laws, were the earliest truly human rules: the rules of what the Anglican prayer book calls "Kindred and Affinity." If there is one basic universal of human society, it is not the incest taboo but something we could perhaps phrase thus:

> Human groups universally define categories of kin and establish rules about eligibility for marriage.

This is what so struck the early searchers after the "origins of exogamy" and rightly so. It introduced something that was definitely new in the world: not the avoidance of incest (that was there anyway) but the enduring relationship between natal kin separated by marriage but linked by kinship, by descent from a common ancestor. The prototype of this is the brother-sister relationship. Lévi-Strauss spoke of an "atom of kinship," and this metaphor catches the spirit of it. The atom as I see it is in fact an atom of kinship *and* marriage: marriage is one of its primitive terms. If we start with the basic group of brothers and sisters, to reach human status (after the advent of tools, hunting, language, and the sexual division of labor), we must add their spouses, as in Figure 19.1.

If the brother and sister cannot marry and breed, their children can, and in most preindustrial societies they were encouraged or enjoined to do so. If the children of the brother and sister marry, we have the basic first-cousin marriage pattern. If it is continued into subsequent generations, it becomes the "double cross-cousin marriage" rule that characterizes the most elementary systems of kinship and marriage, where a man marries a woman who is both his father's sister's daughter and his mother's brother's daughter, as in Figure 19.2. Thus in future generations "brother's wife" and "sister's husband" will themselves be brother and sister.

This is as simple a system of systematic exchange between groups as can be manufactured: the most rudimentary form of *exogamy*. It is best thought of as "sister exchange" (but it could be "daughter exchange"), and this is often how it is phrased: I give you my sister, you give me yours, and the succeeding generations will do the same thing. But what this basically human move does is to set up a tension between the two bonds crucial to the human enterprise: that between the brother and sister on the one hand, and between the brother and his wife on the other—something this simple primeval system beautifully illustrates. There is always a measure of conflict in these dual allegiances, in which a man must play the roles of brother and son, balanced against those of husband and father; a woman must play the roles of sister and daughter, balanced against those of wife and mother.

For the moment it is enough to grasp that while these two descent groups in the diagram are indeed locked together in marriage, there is the potential to include an infinite number of other groups. If group A, a lineage or clan, can exchange sisters/daughters in this way with group B, it can do so with groups C, D, E ... *n*.

Cousin marriage was then the widespread human solution to what in animals Bateson called—or would have liked to have called—"optimal inbreeding." It was the answer to

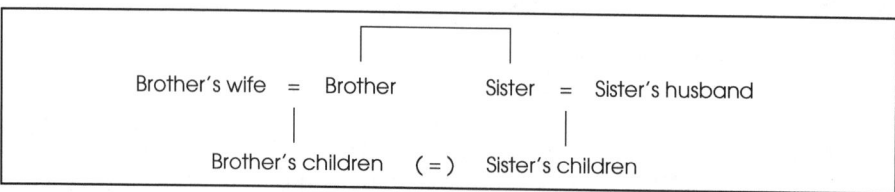

Figure 19.1 The kinship atom

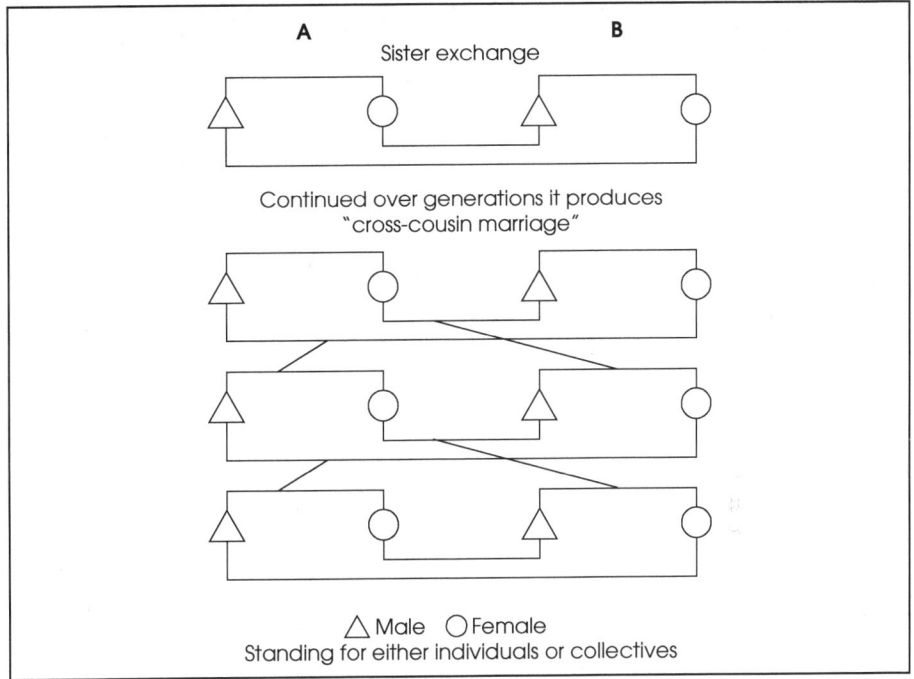

Figure 19.2 Sister exchange and double cross-cousin marriage

the challenge of avoiding the inbreeding load while maximizing inbreeding benefits. In fantasy and sometimes in fact, as with the royal rulers and nobility of Egypt, Persia, Hawaii, the Incas of Peru, and the Calusa Indians of Florida, we refuse the challenge and keep marriage in the nuclear family. But this is rare. More common is the systematic marriage with cousins, most commonly the children of brother and sister (as in Figure 19.2) but sometimes, as with the Arab and other Muslim peoples, with the children of brothers. Let us pause on this for a moment since it raises some interesting issues and has not played the part in the discussion of exogamy and endogamy that it might have done, since the discussion has been about how basic to humanity is the former, while large areas of the globe practice a version of the latter.

COUSINS AND STRANGERS

So having looked at the ubiquitous and elementary double cross-cousin marriage in Figure 19.2, which as we saw is consequentially both exogamic and endogamic, let us look at the purposefully endogamic form, which keeps marriage within the patrilineal group (clan, lineage, or tribe) and the paternal extended family (Murphy and Kasdan 1959).

I received a call from Iraq in 2003 from a *New York Times* reporter, John Tierney, who was baffled by what he had discovered in his Baghdad hotel. Each week there was a lavish wedding in the hotel dining room and ballroom. It all looked very Western, until he discovered that the bride and groom were inevitably cousins, and more than that they were mostly paternal parallel first cousins: the children of two brothers; and if they were not that close, then the bride was usually from the same patrilineal clan/tribe as the groom. Figures showed that some 51 percent of Iraqi marriages fell into this category. When questioned about this, the young people told the reporter, "Of course we marry cousins. What would you have us do, marry strangers? We cannot trust strangers" (Tierney 2003).

One Iraqi informant explained to a colleague of mine that you must marry a cousin—best of all a *bint 'ami*, a daughter of your father's brother—because only members of your own lineage could be trusted to deliver a virgin. Strangers would cheat you on this. Your paternal uncles, you knew, would watch their daughters closely; anyone else's daughter was suspect. (France has recently been embroiled in a controversy over whether failure to disclose loss of virginity is a cause for annulment in Muslim marriages there.) Such a system of close-cousin marriage, the commonest form of preferred marriage in Arab and other Muslim societies, literally keeps the marriage in the family. This goes to the heart of the matter. These groups are inward looking and suspicious of strangers. It is the "mafia solution" to life: never go against the family. Trust is only possible, ultimately, between close relatives, and preferably those of the paternal clan.

It is hard to diagram systematic marriage with the father's brother's daughter (abbreviated FBD for convenience), it being understood that a woman marries her father's brother's son (FBS). Figure 19.3 attempts this. The man we have arbitrarily denoted our EGO (or reference point) can be seen to marry his FBD, and EGO's son in turn marries EGO's brother's daughter. But whom does EGO's brother (B) marry? The answer is that structurally he is the same as EGO and he too would marry a daughter of their common father's brother.

This form of marriage probably originated in the desert-nomad stage of Semitic society when the patrilineal and patrilocal bands (descent through males, residence with the husband and husband's father) of Arab Bedouin wandered isolated in the desert, and when all other bands were potential enemies. They married within their own band, their own clan, their own tribe. Even among the settled Bedouin this was maintained since it kept

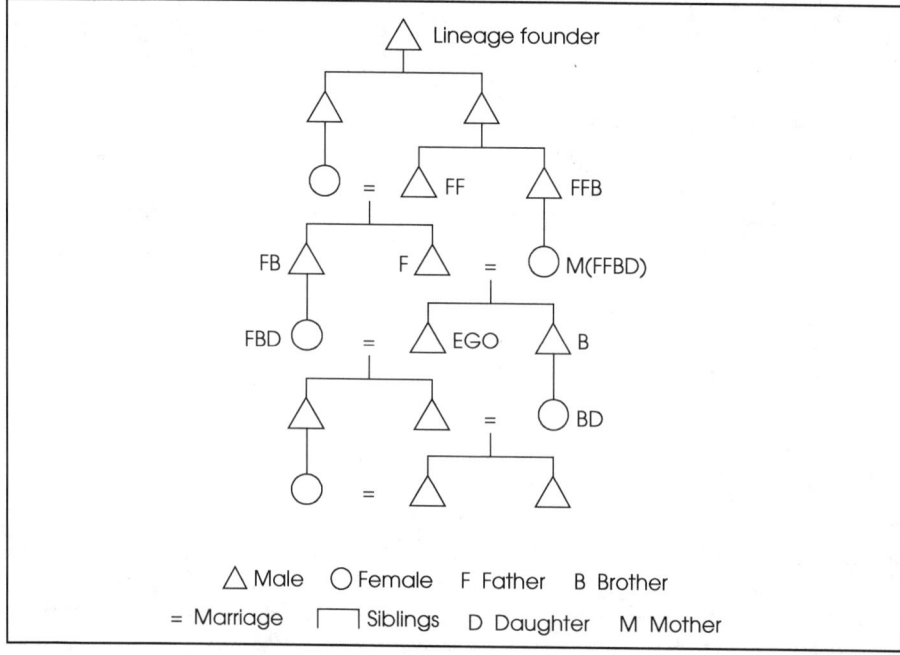

Figure 19.3 **Father's brother's daughter (FBD) marriage**

wealth and property inside the lineage. Outside were the untrustworthy and certainly unmarriageable strangers.

Thus again the social benefits of a form of marriage can be understood without resort to biology, but biological questions are raised. The marriage of brothers' children seems contrary to the Westermarck effect. Would not these paternal cousins have been reared together in the same camp or compound and would not this dampen their ardor for each other? The answer seems to be that they would most probably have been raised in the same village or compound, sometimes in the same house. Research by Alex Walter, in Westermarck's own field site of Morocco, shows that there does indeed seem to be a dampening effect on sexual attraction between the young people, but that the parents welcome this (Walter and Buyske 2003). Marriage is not about sexual attraction, they hold. If the couple's familiarity leads to weak sexual passion, all the better; they can more readily concentrate on the real business of marriage. Also, it seems that childhood association works more negatively on girls than on boys. This may be because the "costs of inbreeding" are far higher for girls than boys, so their predisposition to avoid related males sexually may be more sensitive and intense.

This "marriage in" is then classic *endogamy*, the strongest contrast with the more usual *exogamy*, or "marriage out" of the kinship group. Which cousin you choose matters in this contrast. Cross cousins, the children of opposite-sex siblings—of your father's sister (FZ) and mother's brother (MB)—when chosen as marriage partners, lead you to marry out of your clan or lineage, whether patrilineal or matrilineal, and this is the more usual form. For reasons much debated, marriage with the mother's brother's daughter (MBD) is more common than that with the father's sister's daughter (FZD). Parallel cousins, the children of same-sex siblings, go the opposite way, and like the Arab example above, the marriage of the children of brothers must lead to marriage *within* the kin group. It can, as we saw in the introduction, be a distinction without a difference in that two groups can practice double cross-cousin marriage with each other, thus being perfectly exogamic and still be bound in an endogamic relationship excluding outsiders, as in Figure 19.2.

Through marriage with the son of her father's brother, a woman ensures that her own sons have her father's X chromosome; it is the closest she can get, genetically, to mating with the father or brother. Marriage between the children of sisters is uncommon but does occur (Bittles 2012: table 6.3); any systematic version of it, however, is unknown. The mother's sister is equated with the mother and often called "mother." Her children are like the mother's children (siblings) and treated as such. But the tug of war between kin and in-laws is always there; the mother-in-law joke *is* the oldest in the world.

Animal Dispersion

Let us look deeper into the issue of *dispersion*, since although it is at the root of familial incest avoidance, its adaptive merits go deeper into evolution than those that accrue from the advantages of sexual reproduction. Why should living organisms disperse in the first place? In *The Genius of the Beast*, Howard Bloom (2010), finding his root example of the "evolutionary search engine," describes how bacteria come in two forms: those with stalks (nonmotile) and those with propellers (motile). The stalk bacteria form the basis of colonies and establish themselves. Some of their daughters (they reproduce asexually, of course) are born with stalks and stay where they are, but others are born with those amazing propellers and strike out through the water to form new colonies elsewhere. The push toward dispersion here has solely to do with resources: the bacteria with propellers strike out to find new feeding grounds, and so-called higher organisms are no less driven by this need.

However, as we saw with regard to incest avoidance, once sexual reproduction comes on the scene, they disperse for another essential reason. As Norbert Bischof illustrated in his "Comparative Ethology of Incest Avoidance" in 1975, they disperse to avoid close inbreeding, which they must do to preserve genetic variability, which is what sexual reproduction is all about in the first place. There is considerable dispute (summarized by Trivers in *Social Evolution*, 1985) about why sex replaced cloning as the successful reproductive mechanism, but the details of the dispute do not concern us. What follows from this innovation is what concerns us: the root of the tendency of all these organisms to disperse became, in addition to the search for resources, the conservation of the basic sexual reproductive mode itself. Too-close inbreeding defeats the object of breeding at all, which is the production of genetic variation for natural selection to work on.

Bischof lists the mechanisms that drive sexually reproducing mammals—primates in particular—out of the family breeding group: abduction, repulsion, isolation, emancipation, threat, infantilization, and so on. The net result is not always perfect dispersion, but enough dispersion to ensure that inbreeding is minimized and variability is maximized. Patrick Bateson and his colleagues (1983) showed that birds (quail, for example) mated preferentially with close relatives. This was also true in sexually reproducing plants: dispersal mechanisms force seeds and pollen out of their immediate circle of related plants but land them in a circle of slightly less related plants.[2] This result, it appeared, could be generalized to all sexually reproducing species, plant or animal:

> Breed out, but not too far out.

Sewall Wright (1984) had in the early 1930s already introduced the idea of genetic drift, in which small populations, as a result of dispersion, could be isolated and develop new genetic characteristics, and then spread these characteristics to other populations, thus speeding up the process of evolution: the "Sewall Wright effect." The key here, and the one least debated, is that the relevant populations must first disperse members to form the isolated groups, then further disperse some members to the other groups in order to spread their innovative gene combinations, otherwise the innovating group could just die out and its new adaptations with it. This must have happened numerous times, and those side branches of hominid evolution we see on the evolutionary trees represent such isolated and doomed populations.

Dispersion, then, is vital to evolutionary change both at the primary level of dispersal out of the immediate family and at the secondary level of the dispersal of genes between populations.

Dispersion and Resources: The Ghost of Malthus

Dispersion is rarely a random affair; animals don't just scatter. They not only disperse but do so in regular and predictable ways, as individuals, in families, in flocks, in territories, in migration routes, and so on. That they do so is obvious, but why should there be this form of order rather than a simple free-for-all? Various natural historians, mostly bird watchers like Lack, Howard and Gilbert White, as well as animal watchers like Allee, pondered the problem and saw that it was related to the exploitation of resources. But it was the demographer (and director of the London School of Economics) Sir Alexander Carr-Saunders (1922) who, looking at the Malthusian issue of population control in primitive man, first formulated the theory of the optimum number. There was a theoretical "optimal balance" between population size (species biomass as we would now say) and resources. What was amazing was how closely so-called primitive societies kept themselves to this optimum. If they became unbalanced, classic Malthusian measures were taken to reduce numbers—abortion, infanticide, and abstention being the most common, but emigration was in there too.

Carr-Saunders thought such population limitation was unique to man. The great contribution of V. C. Wynne-Edwards (1962), who acknowledged his debt to Carr-Saunders after initially forgetting it, was to demonstrate how homeostatic population control is common to all social animals down to the protozoa. This is achieved by "conventional competition." As a social scientist myself and a former student of Carr-Saunders's, I remember being astonished when I read Wynne-Edwards's definition of a society as "an organization capable of providing conventional competition." What that drew into the web![3]

Wynne-Edwards might have overemphasized the role of the group in selection, but his careful observations did show that there exist two basic dispersal mechanisms, over and above those communicative and competitive devices that cause dispersion within groups. These he called *irruption* and *emigration* (his Chapter 20). Emigration has two functions: one is the "safety valve" function, which siphons off excess population, and the other is the "pioneering" function, which expands the range of the species and provides for gene exchange. Pioneering, he shows, is a property of expanding populations, especially in uncertain and variable conditions. Under truly erratic conditions, a group will export "pioneers" whenever there is a good season. The underlying principle here is the Malthusian premise:

> Groups cannot grow indefinitely large.

Dispersion is the law of life for all populations, the amount and kind of dispersion being determined, in this view, by the principle of the optimum number. Groups in which individuals with "dispersal traits" that would promote successful emigration had *not* evolved would fail in adverse circumstances. Groups that simply "irrupt" (like lemmings, or at seasonal migration time like wildebeest) are also always at risk; it is the *pioneers* that systematically carry their traits to other areas that succeed: those bacteria with the propellers.

A group of Japanese macaques, observed over many years, was seen to have a hierarchical structure of ranked matrilines. When the group became too large for its territory, it split, with the lower groups in the hierarchy moving off to form their own unit. Over time all the males of group A moved to group B, and vice versa (Fox [1980] 1983: chap. 4). Thus fission and fusion ensured dispersion and genetic diversity; but note that the exchange of males produced an endogamic result uncannily comparable to double-cross-cousin marriage with matrilineal descent in two moieties (symmetrical inverse of Figure 19.2; see note 1). The monkeys were only four kinship terms and one rule away from their human counterpart.

A secondary issue concerns just who emigrates. Is it the successful animals or the marginal failures? It would seem that it might more regularly be the latter since animals that succeed in breeding competition have no motive to leave: it was the lower-ranking macaques that moved. On the other hand, the more successful animals might prosper by leaving in adverse conditions. The "predatory expansion" that we see in humans would always require successful males to lead it, but that is a fairly late development. Even so, another grim regularity seems to be the "rule of tens"—first advanced by Williamson (1996) in his *Biological Invasions*, and can be summarized as follows:

> Not more than ten percent of invasive species are ever established, and only ten percent of these become successful enough to dominate.

Pioneering is always a risky business; the failure rate is massive. As Carr-Saunders saw, primitive human groups can consciously regulate their numbers, but they are not free to buck the basic principle. Their conscious manipulation of it, however, is obviously a highly advantageous trait in itself. The remarkable progress of emigration out of Africa by our *Homo erectus* ancestors has been studied with this in mind. Before 1.8 million years ago, the dispersal rates of hominids matched those of the great apes; with *Homo erectus*, things changed. Sophisticated modern analyses of the diffusion coefficient (D) in mammals, using such variables as the size of the area invaded (z), the time over which the invasion occurs (t), and the intrinsic natural rate of increase of the species (r), produce the formula:

$$D^{1/2} = z/(t)(2r^{1/2})$$

Comparing this coefficient for macaques, *Homo erectus*, and ancient hyaenids, Anton, Facroel, and Yahdi (2001) find that it is much higher in the hominids than in the monkeys, but the hominids are comparable to the hunting and scavenging carnivores, if a bit slower. These acute analysts use this and other data to suggest why there was a virtual explosion of dispersion out of Africa, our larger-brained, tool-using, meat-eating ancestor following the also-dispersing herds of bovids as far as Southeast Asia and China and Europe. But what impresses me is that the hominids were bound by the rules of dispersal. They did not, with their increased brain size, and physical and cultural capacities, just disperse as they pleased or in patterns they made up from scratch. When groups became too large for the carrying capacity of the area they were in, the "pioneers" struck out, in predictable ways, for pastures new. At a predictable rate they colonized the available world.

Human Dispersion

With fully formed *Homo sapiens*, we find the same thing happening, although possessing those deliberate interferences and decisions Carr-Saunders (following Malthus) noted. Groups constantly split up, and under predictable conditions they irrupt or emigrate. If the area is large enough to support them, they will simply split and divide there, dispersing within the area. In doing this they have an advantage over dispersing animals in that they can maintain relationships with the mother group and with each other by symbolic means. Among the Australian Aborigines, we can see how rules of preferential marriage bind dispersed groups together, and how totemic relationships of clanship do the same thing. Thus, dispersed groups remain members of the same clan and marry members of related clans and moieties through such mechanisms as "sister exchange" (Figure 19.2).

Napoleon Chagnon (1968), in *Yanomamö: The Fierce People*, demonstrates just such a structure for this tribe in the Amazon basin, the upper limit of local population being about 150 individuals (and their kinship structure followed the rules of Figure 19.2). The upper level of such integration in foraging conditions still seems to peak at about 2,500 for a tribe and perhaps 5,000 for the so-called linguistic tribe—those speaking the same language. Indeed, at this stage of social evolution, one of the prime functions of language (over and above sheer communication) was to define and maintain such group membership.

But as inevitable as dialect drift was segmentation: the constant push to produce local units that were near kin, usually within the second- or third-cousin range at most. If we want a "law," perhaps it could be (other things being equal, of course):

> The probability that any human group will fragment increases in proportion to the decrease in the average coefficient of relationship among its members.

Corollary: The groups produced by the fragmentation will have a higher average coefficient of relationship than the parent group.

In human terms, the less closely that the members of a group become related to each other over time, the more likely they are to split up. If the average degree of relationship falls below, say, $r = 0.0021$ (the relationship between fourth cousins), then a split is likely to occur, with more closely related people making up the smaller groups. This is the natural tendency; it cannot always be observed in modern conditions (where other things are not equal since free movement is often impossible) with predictable consequences. The more unrelated we become, the more we have to deal with "strangers" and all the threats and complexities that this involves, as the Iraqis reminded us. These are also likely to be "genetic strangers," something that has its own consequences and that we shall explore.

Robin Dunbar (1992, 1993, 1998), in an elegant series of studies featuring precise correlations and the testing of alternative hypotheses, found a constant relationship between group size and the evolution of the neocortex in primates. The large size of the human neocortex poses a problem: it seems to be vastly in excess of what is needed. Dunbar's solution is that it evolved to deal with increasing group size, as did language itself. And what is the ideal group size that it deals with? The answer seems to be that the close personal group averages 12 individuals and the manageable interactive group has an upper limit of 150 individuals: I suspect a lineage of 5+ generations of descent.

This "rule of 150," exemplified in Chagnon's (1968, 1979) Amazonian Indians, matches our rule of fission: groups much above that size will begin to dilute their coefficient of relationship and tend to split. Chagnon found this happened when a group reached about 300. With the advent of language, however, a mechanism arises for extending some recognition, as we have seen, to those who speak the same tongue, peaking at about 5,000. The ideal human cooperative group, the tribe, probably falls somewhere in between. Antony Jay (2014) puts the outer limit at somewhere between four hundred and seven hundred people, this being the largest group that you can reach with an unaided human voice in the open air. The Greeks used carefully spaced heralds to relay speeches to the outer edges of larger groups. The manageable interactive group hovers on the 150 mark, as exemplified by Hutterite group fission, divisions of regular armies, and the number of academics in a discipline's subspecializations.

The same fission will occur as groups get larger and more prosperous. Marshall Sahlins (1961) has seen the segmentary lineage, that perfect model of human group fission, as an instrument of "predatory expansion." Usually acknowledging an eponymous human or divine ancestor (or a totemic counterpart), the lineage splits and divides in succeeding generations. Thus, when an overpopulated group irrupts and either moves into unpopulated areas or takes over an area from another population, it can both move and split into manageable local groups and still keep an overall identity, by the process of lineage segmentation. The Bantu moving into the whole of sub-Saharan Africa, the Arabs moving across North Africa, and the Han Chinese moving into the southeastern provinces all display this dual tendency. The groups would constantly split into small units of kin, but they would share the same name and ancestors and, indeed, could often trace relationships back more than twenty generations, like the Somalis. (The various forms of lineage segmentation are described in my *Kinship and Marriage*, Chapter 8.)

As cultural determinists will be quick to point out, the rules of dispersion differ from culture to culture. Thus exactly who is counted as close kin, and when and how the splits will occur, will be determined by local cultural rules. But there are overpowering similarities. The predatory expansion model, common among pastoralists, is almost exclusively patrilineal (descent through males) and polygynous; matrilineal segmentation would not work in these conditions, and monogamy would be less efficient. Horticulturalists, slowly expanding across empty territories in North America, could be matrilineal and monogamous. There are these constraints that overrule cultural determinism while recognizing the importance of cultural categories, which are themselves, of course, adaptive features of evolved human consciousness (Fox 1979). But what is most impressive is the *constant tendency to segment* itself. Cultural rules merely serve this tendency; they do not initiate it.

So we find a dual impetus driving us both to avoid mating with our closest kin (incest avoidance) and to disperse and break up into kin-related groups if we start mating with too-distant kin. I have tried to relate this to an ecological stress on group resources and the maintenance of the "optimum number"—with the addition of Dunbar's cognitive limits on effective group size and not forgetting the need to have an effective group size that can evolve reciprocal altruism (Trivers 2002). But what about Bateson's "optimal out-breeding" where we started? These mechanisms all come down to the preservation of close-cousin marriage of one sort or another, and is that not in itself a contradiction if such marriages are inherently dangerous themselves? We seem in evolution to be treading a genetically fine line and we should consider this.

Kissing Cousins: Optimal Balance

Charles Darwin and Emma Wedgwood were first cousins. She was his mother's brother's daughter (MBD). They had ten children, of whom three died (not uncommon in the nineteenth century). The survivors went on to distinguished careers and successful marriages. This kind of first-cousin marriage was almost commonplace in nineteenth-century England, where dense webs of kinship and affinity united upper-middle-class business and professional families. Adam Kuper has recently written an excellent account of them in *Incest and Influence: The Private Life of Bourgeois England* (2009). In the United States, anthropologist Lewis Henry Morgan married a first cousin, as did European Albert Einstein. It was not only the intellectual bourgeoisie. Princess Victoria married her first cousin Albert, and European monarchies and aristocracies were connected to each other in networks of cousin alliances.

In Victoria's case, this did have some bad results despite the remarkable fertility of her own marriage in that the recessive allele for hemophilia, which was passed through females and manifested in males, was perpetuated through her descendants. The young Tsarevich Alexei is the best-known example, although the Bolsheviks saw to it that he did not live to die of the disease. This is often cited by opponents of cousin marriage, but people with hemophilia in the family generally would know about it and would do well to be screened along with any intended spouse, cousin or not, since screening is available now; it wasn't then.

George Darwin, Charles's eldest son and a fine mathematician, did the first known surveys of the supposed deleterious results of (first) cousin marriage and, despite sharing his father's concern about his own marriage, found them to be exaggerated and even found a lower incidence of insanity in cousin marriages. He was also the first person to find that close-cousin marriages were more fertile than others, but that this was offset by a slightly higher infant mortality rate (Darwin 1875). No studies since have shown close-cousin marriages to be more than slightly more risky than the marriages of unrelated people; they pose about the same risk as a woman having children after forty. Nevertheless, the idea persists that such marriages always lead to defective and diseased offspring, and thirty US states forbid first-cousin marriage to this day (Bittles 2012). The stereotype of the inbred idiot fostered by such films as *Deliverance* is still predominant.

As an anthropologist I am forced to face the fact that for the vast majority of our existence as a species, close-cousin marriage must have been the norm, if for no other reason than that most of the time there was no one but cousins to marry. Indeed, I have spent much of my professional life analyzing the complexities of systems of marriage that not only allowed but *insisted on* cousin marriage by rule. Not only was it not forbidden, it was prescribed, often with a particular degree of detail. You were enjoined, for example, to marry your double cross cousin under "sister exchange" as we saw, or to marry your mother's brother's daughter but not your father's sister's daughter, or required to marry a mother's father's sister's daughter's daughter, and forbidden to marry a father's father's sister's daughter's daughter, and so on.

The details don't matter for our present purposes. What matters is that in small-scale societies with low mobility, spouses were drawn from a pool of close relatives. Marriage relationships, once set up, were perpetuated over the generations by the rules of cousin marriage. Even in nomadic societies like the ancestors of the Semitic people, marriage with a close cousin was prescribed. The ideal marriage was between the children of two brothers, and this remains the norm in Arab and Muslim societies today, as we have seen, while Jewish law, based on Leviticus, allows such marriages as well as those between paternal uncle and niece.

Students always ask: "Why, then, did our ancestors not all die out as the result of genetic inbreeding?" Good question. The answer is, on the one hand, that those supposed bad effects are dangerous only if there is bad stock to begin with. On the contrary, if the genetic stock is good, then close inbreeding would perpetuate it. Think of thoroughbred horses. My anthropologist daughter Kate Fox has a sideline in breeding Arabian horses whose owners prefer "line breeding," which in fact is cousin breeding, with choice foals showing the most "crosses" to a common illustrious ancestor. "I doubt there are any Arabian horses alive that are not related to each other," Kate tells me. (Florida cracker horse breeders have a proverb that says: "Inbreeding is line breeding that goes badly; line breeding is inbreeding that goes well.") On the other hand, it has been shown that even if genetic diversity is slightly lowered by inbreeding, small periodic doses of outbreeding rapidly restore it. In Ireland, orphan children from the cities would be put up for adoption in isolated villages and the western islands for just such reasons (Fox 1978). Also, if there are truly deleterious homozygotic recessive alleles, then those carrying them would mostly die out and the bad genes with them. The problem, as we saw earlier, would be a largely self-correcting purge in most cases. Exceptions would be cases such as the persistence of the gene for sickle-cell anemia, which carries resistance to malaria and so persists despite its ill effects.

Whatever way you look at it, we today are the products of millennia of cousin marriages, so there must have been something right about them, as with teenage pregnancies. The vast majority of our ancestors were the products of cousin marriages and early pregnancies. Indeed, if most of your ancestors had not married among themselves, you personally would have had more ancestors in the time of Christ than there were people then. Until the population mobility that was a consequence of the geographical discoveries—and even in most places for long after—kissing cousins were the norm.

To summarize the argument at risk of repetition: what we have discovered in our investigation so far is that when we look at mating in general for sexually reproducing species—across the board from plants to mammals—we find the same thing. There is a tendency (except in desperate circumstances) to avoid mating with primary relatives (mother, father, brother, sister, son, daughter), that is, to avoid the closest inbreeding but not to dissipate the genes with too much outbreeding. Beneficial genetic traits have to be consolidated. Genetic diversity on which natural selection can work is thus preserved, but the successful strains are not weakened. Breed out, but not too far out, seems to be the rule of thumb.

We already have the terms *endogamy* for marriage-in and *exogamy* for marriage-out, so perhaps we could call the human marriage of close cousins *mediogamy* if we wish to coin a term. Thus, for humans, mediogamy is in fact an ideal solution: it achieves Bateson's elusive "optimal balance," even his "optimal inbreeding." Kate Fox has suggested to me that it should be "optimogamy"—which it is, but this is not a necessary relationship. We need both terms: mediogamy *is* optimogamy.

Mediogamy and Fertility

We have already seen that the split up of groups at a certain level will help to maintain the "optimum number" in a population; indeed, to the Malthusian mind, this seemed to be what "dispersion" was all about. But some cousins may be more optimal than others.

Recall the "law" (which was in fact a hypothesis) regarding the likelihood of fragmentation in human groups. I will restate it here since it is crucial to the next step of the argument:

> The probability that any human group will fragment increases in proportion to the decrease in the average coefficient of relationship among its members.

This was just a theoretical expectation and was based on dispersion necessary for the conservation of resources, that is, on the preservation of the optimum number. But could it be that there is some decided advantage other than the ecological to such a splitting process that would help to explain it? Could this be that the advantage lies not only with *relative optimum resources* but also with *relative optimum fertility*?

A correspondent of mine, M. L. Herbert, called my attention to studies from Iceland and Denmark (Figure 19.4) published in *Science* (Helgason et al. 2008; see also Labouriau and Amorim 2008), which demonstrated with accurate numbers a very solid fact: *there was a significant positive association between consanguinity and fertility.*

These studies by Helgason and his associates confirmed George Darwin's findings but with far more exact figures. The data from Iceland, where complete records of birth and marriage have been kept for over 165 years, and where the authors could trace accurate and multiple relationship over ten generations, show a simple direct correlation between consanguinity and fertility. The graph in Figure 19.4 is frustratingly hard to read without a full explanation of the axes, but the trend and its import are clear. I will try to stay within their scheme and adapt slightly for clarity (I added the numbers on the horizontal axis, for example).

Figure 19.4 represents children of consanguineous couples. In order of fertility (in their reading the average number of children per marriage) we get second cousin or closer at the top (2), third cousin or closer coming next (3), a falling off of fertility at fourth cousin or closer (4), and then an increasing decline. After sixth cousin or closer (6), the rate of fertility rapidly drops below the average for the population, which puts it below replacement in a population with marginal fertility or holds it there in a population where fertility has already fallen below replacement. If the analysis is continued into the next generation, the highest rate of fertility is in the third- to fourth-cousin range, after which there is the same sharp drop-off.

Now we get to our argument's most interesting connection: remember that fourth cousin ($r = 0.0021$) was where I placed the outer limit for the growth of the natural group, after which it strains to split up and create smaller groups with a higher degree

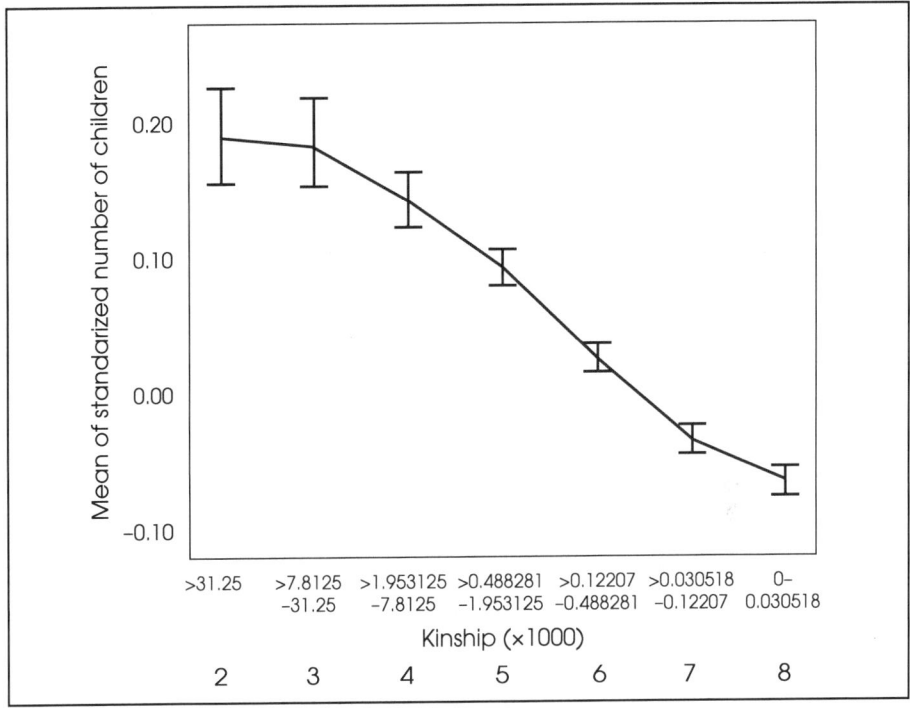

Figure 19.4 Kinship and fertility of human couples in Iceland, 1888–1965
Source: Helgason et al. (2008).

of relationship. What the Icelandic material shows is that this is precisely the point at which the fertility of the group would start its most rapid decline if the group continued to grow. Groups that split up, in other words, and went back to close-cousin marriage would ultimately outbreed those that stayed too large and did not split. It is as if they were anticipating the drastic drop in fertility if the group grew larger and less closely related. These results lead to what may be a more general law that links these findings on consanguinity to my theory of group fission. Let us try it and follow its logic:

> The average fertility of a breeding group is directly proportionate to the average degree of relationship in the group.

We have just seen proof of this in that the *lower* the degree of relationship, the lower the fertility, but the logic of this generalization requires that intrafamilial mating be the most fertile, whatever other disadvantages it may have. Since it happens so infrequently because of incest avoidance, we do not have much to go on by way of comparative statistics. In some species such as tree lice, which live in unvarying circumstances and for which it is advantageous *not* to vary genetically, incestuous mating combines with extremely high fertility (Hamilton 1967). In well-recorded human instances there seems to be no problem with fertility per se in such mating, although it is perhaps offset by higher infant mortality.

The Ptolomies and their sibling-mating Roman imitators in colonial Egypt were certainly fertile enough (Hopkins 1980). Their dynasty lasted 275 years over thirteen generations, and there were further offspring many of whom disappear from recorded history after the children of Cleopatra VII (not by her husband-brothers but by Mark

Anthony and Julius Caesar: a decided and fatal swing toward outbreeding). Figure 19.5 is a simplified genealogy showing, for clarity, the main line of succession of the Ptolomies but by no means all the members. This probable superiority in sheer fertility of incestuous unions would, in evolving populations, be offset in the long run and in general by the loss of genetic variability and the increase in genetic load (inbreeding depression)—not good for organisms in rapidly changing environments where new niche adaptation is crucial. The extended Icelandic data suggest a peak of reproductive success somewhere in the third- and fourth-cousin range.

Even so, we must note that many species have populated large islands and whole continents from the offspring of one immigrating pregnant female. De Queiroz (2014), in his charming *The Monkey's Voyage*, shows, for example, how three of the four families of mammals in South America—monkeys, caviomorphs, and sigmodontines, totaling 673 species—each came from a single female point of origin, or from a very few immigrant females. All the Vervet monkeys on the island of St. Kitts (West Indies)—some 56,000—are descended from one pair brought on a slave ship in the seventeenth century. In the early generations this must have meant incestuous mating (as all human creation legends

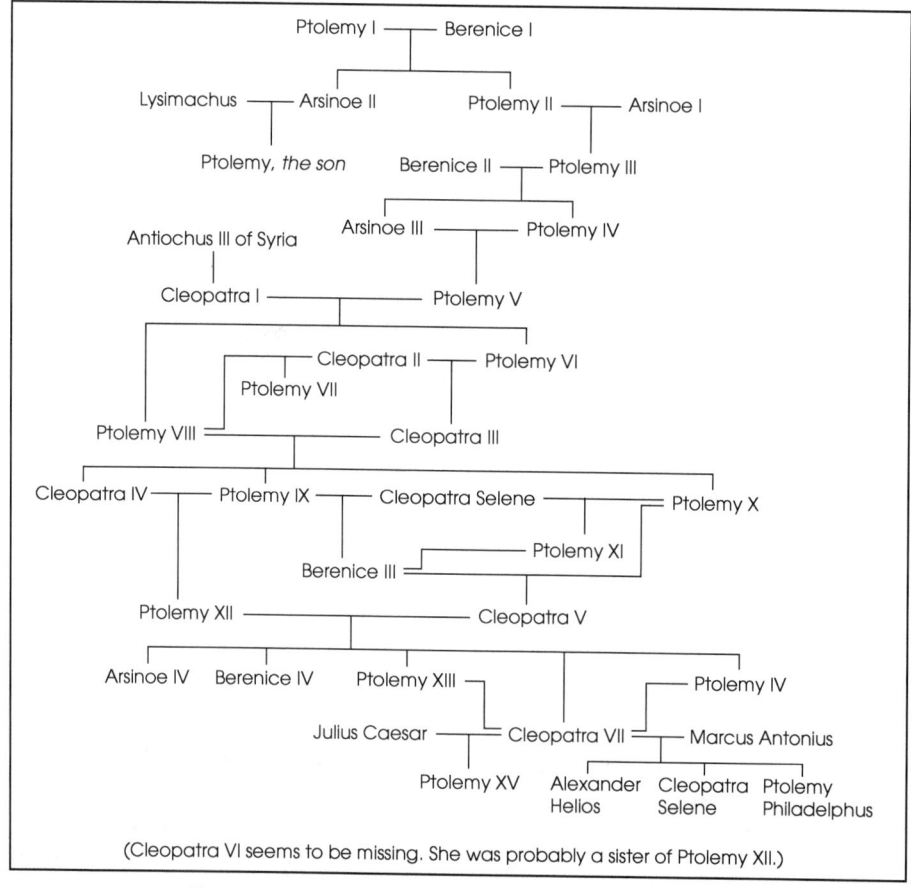

Figure 19.5 Simplified genealogy of the Ptolomies

Source: Wikipedia, s.v. "Ptolemaic Kingdom," last modified October 2, 2014, http://en.wikipedia.org/wiki/Ptolemaic_Kingdom.

are forced to admit). Demographic circumstances (as with the lone gravid female) must often have meant that the only available partners were family members and the choice was between mating with them or going extinct.

The only viable strategy, then, would have been to go with the fertility and take the genetic losses, hoping to come out with a win (Dyke and MacClure 1973). And we must remember that in the current argument the dependent variable is the simple numerical one of *fertility*. Surviving offspring don't have to be perfect or even healthy; they only have to be good enough to produce more surviving offspring when survival is the issue. Clearly this has often worked in evolution, and the surviving offspring have settled down to optimal inbreeding.

To summarize: if breeding groups grow larger and mating takes place with increasingly less closely related people, then their fertility will decline even to the point of extinction. Their route to survival is to split into smaller breeding isolates with higher degrees of fertility and so keep their population numbers above replacement level. The relevant commandment would be the opposite of Sir Edward Tylor's famous "Marry out or die out!" It would in fact be:

Marry IN or die out![4]

Recall that I originally simply asserted, following the Malthusian logic, that groups would split to avoid the overexploitation of resources; but Herbert's data suggest a deeper level of causation. In a brilliant experiment he did with a colleague on fast-breeding fruit flies (Herbert and Lewis 2013), where for two years the food level was kept constant and ample, and space was plentiful, the rapidly breeding flies quickly reached a point where their population collapsed (Figure 19.6). This mirrors those sudden surges and collapses in population we get among rabbits, jungle rats, and mice, for example (Fox et al. 2007). They initially prosper to the point of massive overpopulation, at which point they crash

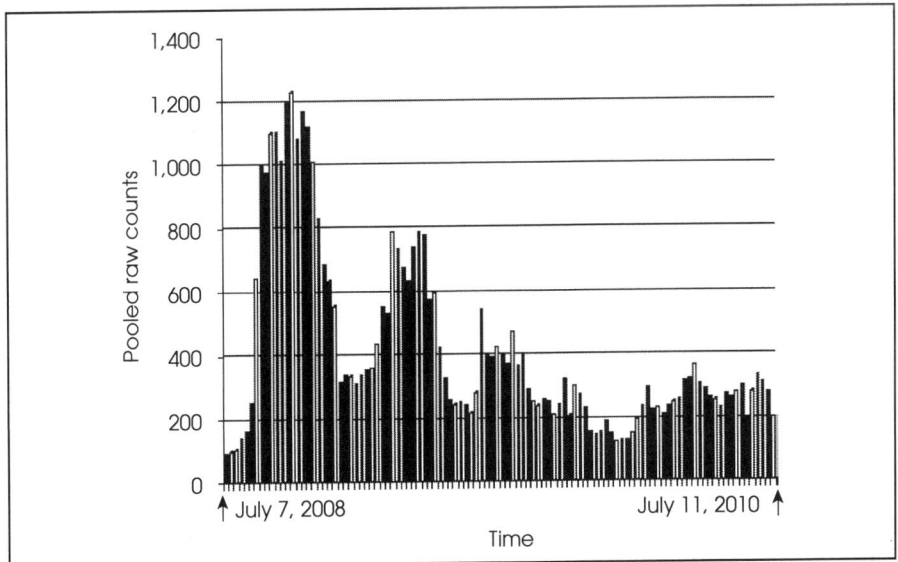

Figure 19.6 Fruit fly population rise and fall over two years
Source: Herbert and Lewis (2013).

and fade out, along a curve of declination with a couple of small recoveries and then a flop. But note that this is a variant of the curve in Figure 19.4. The constant is that *as the population increases, the average degree of relationship declines and the growth rate drops.*

These sudden population upsurges (even as we shall see, our own human surge) seem self-correcting. Why? Perhaps we now have an answer and one that goes beyond the resource-dominated theories of the ecologists and may go further to the root of the collapse of civilizations than the equally resource-dominated theories of Jared Diamond (2005), for example. In fact, the whole Malthusian paradigm may be in question. Our answer may also be a rival for the theory that lower levels of fertility are the result of "rational choice," where the higher costs of children in more developed societies, together with a declining infant mortality rate, lead to a voluntary and conscious lowering of family size. There is no question that choice and resources have their effect, but there is reason to believe that we have overemphasized them at the expense of the more fundamental biological mechanism explored here. In Sweden, for example, the choice to limit family size has been shown to increase the socioeconomic position of immediate descendants but to have catastrophic consequences for long-term reproductive success (Goodman, Koupil, and Lawson 2012). In terms of fitness it is a losing strategy.

Figure 19.7 shows typical curves taken from the comparisons of more than 1,400 species of mammals, birds, fish, and insects from the Global Population Dynamics Database. It plots population growth rate (*pgr*) against population size (*N*) (Sibly et al. 2005). Here is what the authors say:

> We found that the rates of population growth are high at low population densities, but contrary to previous descriptions, decline rapidly with increasing population size and then flatten out, for all four taxa.

The curve is always to the left, sometimes with more than one peak. One obvious curve (not shown here) is linear with a direct relationship between decline in growth rate and size of population. But also typical are the two shown here, the more common "concave" result with an initial surge followed by steady decline as with the fruit flies, and an "n" curve where an initial peak levels and then is followed by a rapid dropoff, as with the Icelandic cousins. But the end result is always the same: "boom and bust" as with the fruit flies and the Icelanders, neither of whom were lacking in space or resources. As the

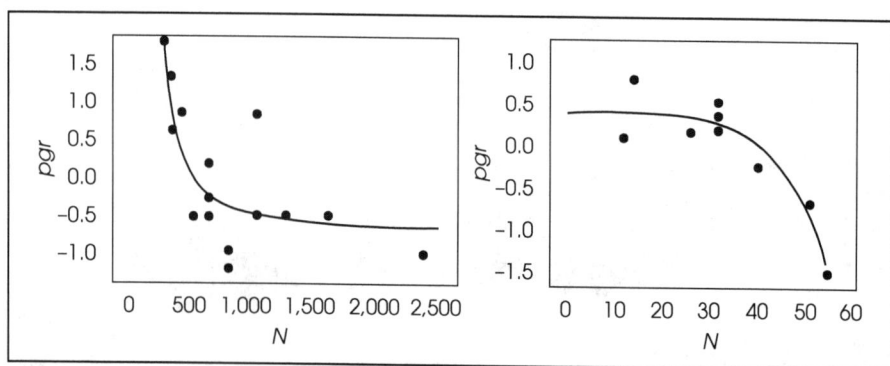

Figure 19.7 Curves of the relationship between fertility (*pgr*) and population growth (*N*) in 1,400 species

Source: Sibly et al. (2005).

population grows, fertility falls, even if the population is well supplied—indeed, *because* adequate resources initially encourage the unsustainable population growth. The question then becomes: is it the overtaxing of resources—the failure of the carrying capacity—that causes the sudden drop?

It is even interesting to ask, as do Herbert and Lewis, if Jared Diamond's data from the population collapse of the Anasazi civilization in the American Southwest, which matches similar and seemingly devastating collapses elsewhere (the Mayan, for example), could not be seen in the same light as the fruit flies and other species. Figure 19.8 is Diamond's (2002) graph of the population of the Long House Valley in northeast Arizona from 800 to 1300 AD showing the population rise and collapse, which fairly mirrors the Anasazi collapse in general.

The time course of the population was followed by counting the number of habitations that were occupied each year according to radiocarbon dating of the remains of their fires (actual population); the other line represents the population modeled on tree ring growth, which was assumed to predict rainfall (modeled population). The number of occupied dwellings tracked closely with tree ring width, and Diamond quite reasonably suggested that rainfall determined the carrying capacity of the valley, so the collapse resulted from drought.

Herbert and Lewis adopt an alternative view, namely, that the farmers were cultivating the trees in order to meet their needs. If this is so, then the population changes may not be drought conditioned but due to a mechanism similar to the one seen in the fruit flies and other species. Early on, the population is low. Eventually it rises exponentially, falls, rises again, and then falls close to zero. The time course from takeoff to the last dwelling falling vacant is about 300 years or roughly 150 years per cycle. If we assume that these modern humans start having children at about 18 and stop at about 40, that would mean a 30+ year generation time or five generations per cycle. So although the profile of the curve is different from that of the flies, the basic cycle time is similar: roughly the time cycle needed to produce fourth and fifth cousins.

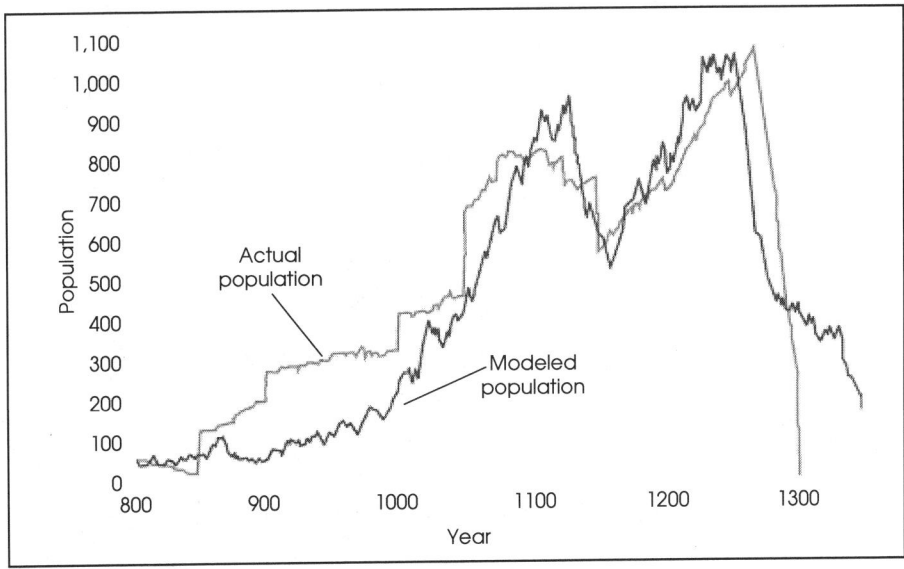

Figure 19.8 Long House Valley population, 800–1300 AD
Source: Diamond (2002).

The match is not perfect. In the Long House Valley experience, the second peak is higher than the first and does not appear to last as long. The peaks of the insect data are toward the left, and the peaks of the mammalian data are, if anything, toward the right. Still, the time course is close enough to encourage us to think that the 5+ generation pattern is widespread in nature and will be found in other species. In either case, regardless of the timing of the peak and decline, there is a constant pattern of peak and inevitable decline. The net result for such rapidly expanding populations, whatever their history, seems to be close to zero.

Diamond's interpretation as it stands leaves him with an interesting problem. He points out that "the Anasazi completely abandoned the valley by 1300, at a time when the model predicts that it could have supported a substantial population" (Diamond 2002: 567). It looks as though the resources could still have supported 200–500 people for another fifty years, but in fact there were none. Thus, there is a gap in the Malthusian resource-based interpretation that might be at least partially filled by a fertility-based approach. The possibilities are tantalizing and open to testing.

Sperm, Bacteria, Kinship, and Generations

The consequences of this congruence of data and theory require some more thought; for example, why are the closer-cousin marriages more fertile? Is this a pre-zygotic or post-zygotic effect? It matters for several practical reasons largely technical and has to do with the control of insect populations. But it is relevant to the human case. We have known, for example, for some time that sperm do not swim placidly to the ova but engage in lethal "sperm warfare" (Birkhead and Pizzari 2002; Eberhard 2009), with only a few sperm making for the eggs and the rest fighting, killing, and blocking any rival sperm, including those that might have survived from other copulations. (The films on this in humans are spectacular, for example, Desmond Morris 1994.)

It has been shown in deer mice (Fisher and Hoekstra 2010) that while male deer mice do not fight over mating advantages, their sperm do. After several males have mated with a female, the sperm form "flying wedges" that together outswim and outblock rival bodies of sperm to reach the ripened ova (Figure 19.9). The sperm that are so bonded and so successful are those of *related males*. The paper suggests that the closer the relation, the

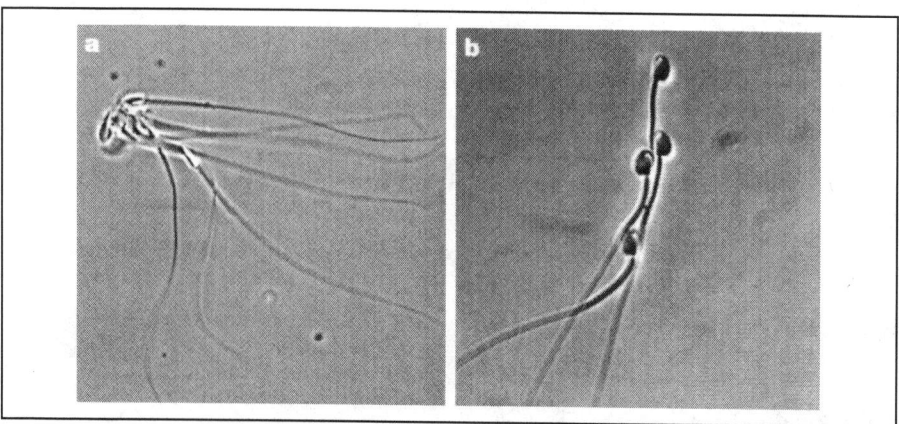

Figure 19.9   Related sperm combine to compete in deer mice ovarian tract
Source: Fisher and Hoekstra (2010).

closer the bond: *bonded fraternal sperm* are the usual winners of the race to the eggs. Given the dazzling complexity of this "post-copulatory sexual selection," with its remarkable division of labor among sperm and the herding and management abilities of ova (what is charmingly called "cryptic female choice"), it is perhaps not too far a leap to assume that the bonded and related sperm can recognize their related ova, or that the ova can recognize them in turn. Given the complexity of what does happen, this would be a likely outcome.

It goes even deeper: as Wynne-Edwards saw, it goes down at least to the protozoa, but it goes even deeper than that. Sperm cells come on the scene with the advent of sexual reproduction, but before that in evolution we have those single-celled bacteria that Howard Bloom described with their stalks or propellers, reproducing asexually by mitosis: cloning. It is known that myxobacteria (which live in soil) have a lively social life (Shimkets 1990). But recent extraordinary research (Pathak et al. 2013) has shown that they have as remarkable a competitive life, and one as governed by kinship, as the evolutionarily more recent sperm. Many of the elements of our story are already there. Let Pathak and his colleagues explain:

> How individual cells recognize each other to cooperate and assemble functional tissues is a fundamental question in biology. Although multicellularity is a trait that is typically associated with eukaryotes, certain groups of bacteria also exhibit complex multicellular behaviors, which are perhaps best exemplified by the myxobacteria. For example, in response to starvation myxobacteria will assemble fruiting bodies, wherein thousands of cells function as a coherent unit in development and cell differentiation.

Now he comes to the guts of it (emphasis mine):

> Here we describe a mechanism where myxobacteria *distinguish sibling and cohort cells from other myxobacteria isolates*. We show that molecular recognition is mediated by a cell surface receptor called TraA. Cell-cell specificity involves *mutual recognition by partnering cells* and is mediated by proposed homotypic TraA interactions. The specificity for recognition is determined by variable sequences found within TraA alleles. Thus, simply swapping TraA alleles between isolates predictably *changes partner recognition*. TraA-TraA recognition in turn leads to the fusion and exchange of outer membrane (OM) components between cells. We suggest that OM exchange allows the cells to communicate and become homogenous with respect to their OM proteome. We further suggest these interactions build a cohesive cell population.
>
> Swapping TraA alleles also reprogrammed social interactions among strains, including the *regulation of motility* and *conferred immunity from inter-strain killing*. We suggest that TraA helps guide the transition of single cells into a coherent bacterial community. . . . In evolutionary terms, TraA functions as a rare greenbeard gene that recognizes others that bear the same allele to confer beneficial treatment.

A "greenbeard gene" is a gene that allows one organism to cooperate with another even if they are not genetically closely related, and is a whole other fascinating story (Haig 1997). Here are individual cells produced from one mother cell by simple division, trying for various reasons to combine into multicellular organisms. They are in essence looking for their sisters, and they will know them by the TraA allele that they carry. But then more amazingly, if they do not have enough siblings, they will transfer TraA to unrelated cells producing instant functional relatives to help build their "cohesive cell population" and win out in competition with other strains.

Like the combative sperm, different strains of unrelated bacterial cells try to kill each other. By transferring TraA the bacteria can grant immunity to strangers and recruit them essentially as pseudo kin. Then they can cooperate in "the regulation of motility"—in causing "irruptions" of kindred bacteria that will swarm off with their propellers to find pastures new. Astonishing. But the features of kin recognition, the bonding of close kin, the manipulation of kinship, and conflict between kinship groups are all there in the most primitive organisms on earth. They were not a consequence of the evolution of sexual reproduction, and although that momentous shift did have a totally transforming result, it was built on mechanisms already present and active.

Figure 19.10 is my adaptation from Pathak et al. (2013) in their summation of the findings. The bacterium at the left (A) binds to a strain sibling (A) and also transfers TraA to an unrelated cell (B). Two other nonstrain cells (C and D) are refused and could end up dead. The two successfully bonded cells exchange outer-membrane material and go on to develop a multicellular reproductive group and to improved evolutionary fitness.

This matters to our argument since kin recognition and cooperation on the one hand, and discriminatory behavior and competition on the other, lie deep in the very origins of life. They are present in plants, which recognize siblings, avoid mating with them, and discriminate in their favor (Dudley and File 2007; File, Murphy, and Dudley 2012). This is important enough, but also because we need to know whether we are dealing with genetic or epigenetic phenomena (or both) in order to assess the role of environmental influences on human fertility: possibly the effect of methylation on sperm cells increasing the likelihood of infertility, as found in mice (Anway et al. 2005). Other researchers have found that these effects were not seen in *inbred* strains of mice: fragmentary but intriguing (Kaiser 2014).

For humans it is often suggested that cousin marriages prevail in the lowest income groups, that these do not use contraception, and that this explains their higher fertility.

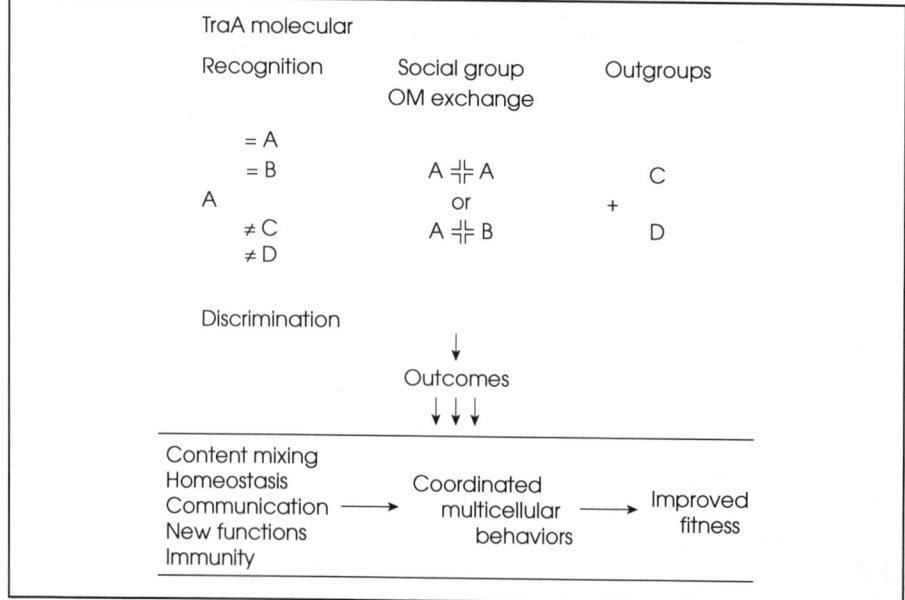

Figure 19.10 TraA mediated cell-cell interactions and myxobacteria social behavior
Source: Adapted from Pathak et al. (2013).

But the data from Iceland alone refute this. Iceland has the most homogeneous population in Europe and one of the least unequal and most healthy in the world. The data on consanguinity and fertility there do not support the decisive influence of class and economic differences.

Alan Bittles (2012), in his encyclopedic *Consanguinity in Context*, goes into this issue in detail for India, for example. He shows that the different rates of cousin marriage fall into a north-south divide: the Hindus in north India average 2.9 percent versus 20.6 percent among their Dravidian coreligionists in the south and west (who in turn match that of Muslims in India of 23.6 percent—my calculation from his figures). This has to do with religion and tradition, not socioeconomic status. In some cases, moreover, the "orthodox" cousin marriage (and among the Dravidians, uncle-niece marriage) is more common among the higher socioeconomic groups, as it was in Victorian England. More strikingly, the consanguineous south shows a much greater normality of sex ratios than the heavily male-biased north, reflecting a higher status and greater equality of women (fewer female infanticides) where cousin marriages are more common.

Bittles also shows that there is a correlation between consanguineous unions and early date of marriage, and also with a longer reproductive span, and that these could help account for some, if not all, of the superiority of the unions regarding fertility: a superiority not affected by a slightly higher infant mortality rate, as George Darwin saw. Note also that the Icelandic material shows a drop with the grandchildren of first cousins but a rise to a maximum with those of third and fourth cousins. Obviously a confluence of factors combines to bring about the superior fertility of close-cousin marriage up to and including conscious human intention.

One reason that distant or non-consanguineous marriages are less fertile than those with close cousins is that the more distantly related we get, the closer we are to speciation or at least subspeciation. Herbert argues that selection is a race and thus speciation is a race such that the more rapidly speciating form has a head start in selection every time a new niche shows up. In the normal course of evolution, about 2,000 generations seems to be the limit beyond which the genes of two relatives-by-descent simply do not "recognize" each other. If the population is 1,000, then indeed the genes will eventually fail to recognize each other because it will take them roughly some 1,999 generations on average (assuming there is no change in gene frequency) to get back together. What we are looking at is perhaps the result of a faster-acting epigenetic mechanism that limits local populations and forestalls the greater catastrophe.

Depending on the turnover of generations for hominids, 2,000 would then represent about 60,000 years of evolutionary time: long enough for some genetic effects but certainly long enough for epigenetic consequences. This would mean that breeding groups that did not split up or limit their size well before ten generations were risking decline and possible extinction. Any study of human group segmentation would show that kinship groups keep well within that limit: the fourth or fifth cousin dropoff point means that groups should segment at least every 120–150 or so years, or earlier. If we do not segment and if we consistently end up marrying relative "genetic strangers," then we push closer to the point where fertility crashes below replacement as a result of what Helgason and his colleagues (2008: 813) neatly call "the breakdown of co-adapted gene complexes."

The 5+ generation rule holds. For a start, this represents the absolute outer limits of complete genealogical memory for unwritten pedigrees. Preliterate societies that respect genealogical depth can remember individual lines of descent for twenty or more generations (Somali, Maori), but how many of us can, without documentary aid, hold in memory all the descendants of our sixty-four great-great-great-great grandparents? Skilled oral genealogists on Tory Island observe a five to seven generation limit (Fox 1978). It is what human systems of kinship categories are about—they subsume numerous individual relatives under relatively few collective kinship terms: Morgan's "classificatory systems" (Fox 2011: chap. 11). This categorization has enabled us, among other things, to keep track of eligible and ineligible marriage partners, as we saw earlier (Fox 1979).

Conclusion: Beyond Malthus

Malthus was right: groups cannot grow indefinitely large; they cannot without dangerous consequences outgrow their optimum number based on available resources. But there are other restrictions: they cannot exceed their cognitive limits of mutual recognition, nor their capacity to produce reciprocal altruism. They cannot be totally inbred, lest they lose the advantages of genetic diversity. But above all, in the course of evolution:

> Groups cannot outgrow their limits of consanguinity.

If they grow too large, they risk not only resource depletion but a population crash through a sharp decline in fertility. In either case they face possible extinction. The solution—which is in fact the driving force of evolution down to the bacteria—has been to split up into smaller groups with higher levels of relatedness and to disperse over wider areas, thus preserving both resources and fertility and spreading innovative genes from one small breeding experiment to another.

In human history until very recent evolutionary times, this has involved Bateson's "optimal inbreeding": the continuation of the avoidance of close-familial breeding, combined with controlled breeding among related kin. In truly human society with language and rules this has meant the pursuit of organized *mediogamy*: marriage with close cousins. The concept of mediogamy resolves the original anthropological conundrum of the relativism of exogamy and endogamy: it is both, and it is the same. In order not to die out, we must both marry out and marry in at the same time.

Perhaps the most extraordinary example of this principle of biosocial engineering being recognized and formalized into human social rules is the kinship group known as the Ayllu of the ancient Incas of Peru. Michael Moseley's (2001) charming cranial illustration (Figure 19.11) shows how this worked. The descendants of a common (and always mummified) male ancestor (or ancestors) would split into two named patrilineal moieties, which would exchange wives (i.e., marry cousins of the opposite moiety, as in Figure 19.2 earlier). This pattern would persist over about 5+ generations, splitting into submoieties (suyu) and lineages, at which point the two moieties would split again into two smaller Ayllu, each with two intermarrying moieties, and so on.

The relationship of descent was continued and symbolized in the mummified male ancestors, and marriage continued to be endogamic with close cousins within the Ayllu, yet exogamic to the moiety. The beauty of the Ayllu is that the moieties were not fixed through time (as were A and B in Figure 19.2), but were constantly re-created by repeated fission over 5+ generation cycles as schematized in Figure 19.12. A is the founding ancestor(s), B and C are the first intermarrying moieties, and the numbered letters are the subsequent moieties.

This splitting process would of course happen de facto with those groups like the Australians and the Yanomamö practicing double cross-cousin marriage as in Figure 19.2. But in theory they cycled on forever.[5]

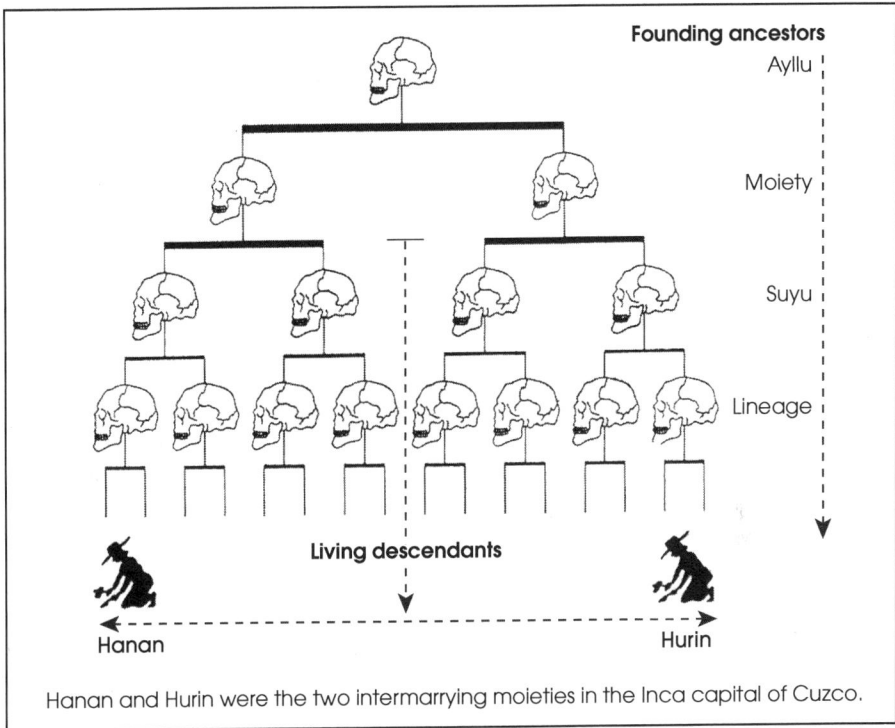

Hanan and Hurin were the two intermarrying moieties in the Inca capital of Cuzco.

Figure 19.11   Idealized Ayllu kinship charter

```
                    A

           B     =      C

      B1 = B2         C1 = C2

  B3↓ = B4↓ B5↓ = B6↓   C3↓ = C4↓ C5↓ = C6↓
```

Figure 19.12   Schematic illustration of moiety fission in the Ayllu

The Ayllu is an example of the classical patrilineal segmentation model, but with the crucial addition of the constant re-creation of intermarrying exogamic moieties. Cousin marriage was practiced in many segmentary systems, usually with either the MBD or the FZD, often with hierarchical implications. Lindholm (1986), for example, has brilliantly demonstrated the close link between Turkish and Arabic sociopolitical systems and their contrasting matrilateral (hierarchical) and patrilineal-parallel (egalitarian) cousin marriage practices. But there was not in any such systems this rule-governed re-creation of smaller inbreeding groups that we find with the Inca. The Ayllu then becomes a de jure realization, in formal human rules, rituals, and symbols, of the ideal evolutionary process.

Close-cousin marriages, far from being "abnormal," are more likely to be one of those entirely normal drumbeats of tribal wisdom that we would do well to heed as we try to push, perhaps unsustainably, beyond it. For example, the further our modern populations have moved away from close-cousin marriage—in Europe initially at the insistence of the Catholic and Orthodox Churches, which banned such previously popular unions—the lower our fertility has dropped.

To be clear, it was dropping in the medieval period, but after the Reformation, which saw a lifting of the ban in Protestant countries, there was a rise that continued until relatively recently. Many other factors, like the widespread cultivation of the potato, for example, were involved in this rise and in the various crashes when it failed (Salaman 1949). But it was also affected by the adoption of the Napoleonic Code in Catholic parts of Europe like Italy, where partible inheritance led to an upsurge in cousin marriage among the peasantry, followed by a rapid population increase in the nineteenth century (Cavalli-Sforza, Moroni, and Zei 2004; Stone, Lurquin, and Cavalli-Sforza 2007). (I wonder what might have happened in Ireland if the potato crop had *not* failed. Would there have been a massive correction anyway?) Currently, however, fertility is declining alarmingly, and in several European countries it has already fallen below replacement levels for the indigenous populations. Governments, like that of Germany, are taking desperate measures to subsidize larger native families. Meanwhile, the difference is being increasingly made up by the higher fertility of cousin-marrying Muslim immigrants from North Africa and Asia. The most popular infant boy's name in Europe in 2013 was Mohammed.

In those "underdeveloped" parts of the world where cousin marriage persists, population has risen and better medical care means more of the children of these fertile consanguine unions survive (and live much longer). The effects of globalization could begin to be felt in these bastions, however, and we are already seeing a decline in general fertility even here, as rates of non-consanguineous marriage increase. I will end with a graph (Figure 19.13) based on UN data showing the progress of fertility rates over the past sixty-five years for the whole world. Fertility rates are dropping everywhere, and life expectancy

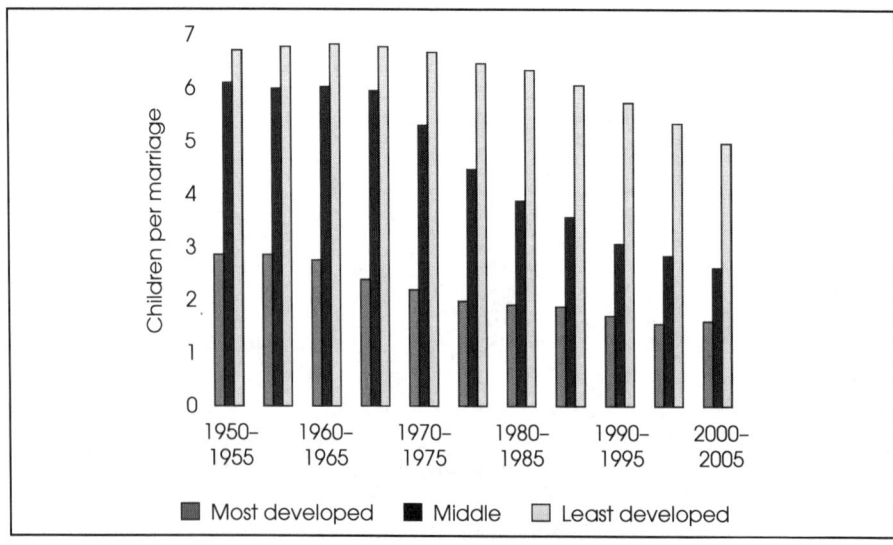

Figure 19.13 Declining world fertility

Source: M. L. Herbert from *U.N. Demographic Yearbooks.*

is dramatically increasing. World population may well outstrip world resources, but not, as envisioned by the population pundits, through a superfluity of babies; rather, it will involve a superfluity of elders with not enough new babies that they can turn into productive workers to support them in their later years. It is already happening, and the fewer cousins we marry the worse it is likely to get.

In an ideal world we would all marry close cousins when young and die at sixty-five.

Acknowledgments

The first part of this chapter draws heavily on my previous material, especially from *The Tribal Imagination*. But in rethinking the whole issue of the benefits of exogamy, I obviously owe an immense debt of gratitude in the second half to Dr. M. Linton Herbert, a practicing radiologist and experimental entomologist who sees well beyond the narrow disciplinary concerns of insect population control to the basic issues lying behind the whole of organic evolution. (See his website at http://www.nobabies.com.) His work has enabled me to make the theoretical link between human mediogamy and general evolutionary processes. The link argument, however, is mine, and any omissions or errors in it are mine also. Suffice it to say that without his original work and ideas and constant help, I could not have made it at all. Alan Bittles read the manuscript and made numerous critical and useful suggestions. I am very grateful for his help. The caveat holds: any remaining errors in fact or logic are mine alone.

Figure 19.11 is from Moseley (2001). It was drawn by Tracey Wellman and is reproduced by permission of the publishers, Thames & Hudson Ltd.

Notes

1. Figure 19.2 shows two intermarrying patrilineal groups: lineage clans or moieties. Structurally, the same result would be produced by intermarrying matrilineal groups (descent through females). The following diagram (from Fox 1993 part 2:4) shows how the one is the structural inverse of the other. Patrilineal is much more common, and this model leads into the subsequent discussion of the contrasting patrilineal parallel cousin marriage. But the point should be noted. Across much of native North America, for example, the matrilineal model was followed. (See Fox 1967, 1993 part 2:4.) There is a strong case, however, for the original hominid group being patrilineal or at least male philopatric (Chapais 2008). The argument on incest avoidance in this chapter only goes far enough to make the chapter's ultimate special point. For excellent recent discussions on all the issues involved, see Chapais (2008) and especially Turner and Maryanski (2005).

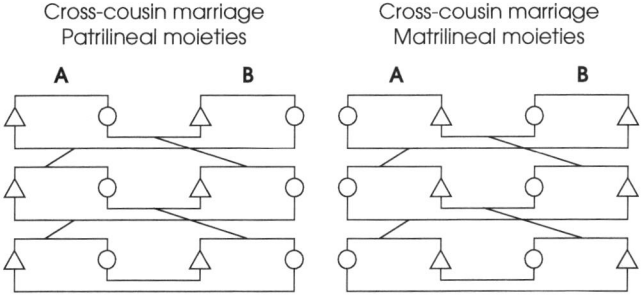

2. Technically, what appears to be aimed at for purposes of strong immune system development is a certain degree of homozygosity in major histocompatibility genes (MHC), which we now know were a Neanderthal contribution to the modern human genome (e.g., Pääbo 2014). How do individuals recognize these genes in others? The indefatigable stickleback has provided incontrovertible evidence of such preferential mating where recognition was present (Kalbe et al. 2009). Some animal and human studies suggest that pheromone factors are involved in mating and that, certainly, sisters recognize fraternal pheromones and prefer others—but not of too different a scent, with "positive aversion" from females for the scent of fathers and brothers, with paternal scent inhibiting the onset of puberty in females (Bittles 2012: 95–97).
3. Wynne-Edwards is in current disfavor because the dominant section of the human behavior and evolution movement, devoted as it is to the principle of individual selection, considers his notions of "group selection" heretical in evolutionary biology. He definitely vacillates between what we might call "group selection" and "the selection of groups"—we still seem to be confused by this, and William Hamilton, to the satisfaction of most biologists, elegantly disproved Wynne-Edwards's theory of group selection accounting for sterile castes in insects. But if we look at the selection of groups, then we can see (as Darwin saw) that individual selection within a group can throw up social behaviors that produce a form of social organization that will be superior to that of other groups in that it promotes greater fitness in its members. (I explored this in the essay "Self Interest and Social Concern" in *Conjectures and Confrontations* [Fox 1997].) There will thus be positive feedback between social organization and individual fitness, and such a group will expand at the expense of groups of conspecifics not so well endowed. The group properties could well be, for example, cooperation and communication, or even morality and religion, promoting more efficient conventional competition (or "ritualized aggression" as Lorenz and the ethologists put it) thus leading to a preservation of the optimum number.

    Framed in this way, there is nothing about traits evolving for the sake of the group or anything such. A growing body of theorists organized and led by David Sloan Wilson, and including Edward O. Wilson (the synthesizer of sociobiology), is beginning to see the differential selection of groups as central to the process of evolution. They call this multi-level selection (MLS) and basically argue that different kinds of selection—individual and group—operate at different levels and that both have to be taken into account to understand, for example, the structure of insect societies (Wilson and Wilson 2007, 2008; Wilson and Sober 1994). It is a sturdy paradigm that does not offend against the canons of individual fitness maximizing at all. But as a "middle-ground" theory it is not attractive to sectarians and has suffered howls of outrage from the kin-selection faithful.
4. To be fair, Tylor's (1889) exact words were "marrying out or being killed out."
5. See Chagnon (1968: 130) for a diagram of village fission that mirrors the Ayllu but without the mummified record and ritual. Also, he demonstrates that when a Yanomamö group fissions the most-related members stay together and the least-related members move. In our scheme that would give the most-related group a decided fertility advantage. This could perhaps be tested with Chagnon's data.

References

Anton, S. C., A. Facroel, and Z. Yahdi. 2001. "Plio-Pleistocene Homo: Patterns and Determinants of Dispersal." In *Humanity from African Naissance to Coming Millennia*, edited by P. V. Tobias, M. A. Raath, J. Moggi-Cecchi, and G. A. Doyle. Firenze: Firenze University Press/Witwatersrand University Press.

Anway, M. D., A. S. Cupp, M. Uzumcu, and M. K. Skinner. 2005. "Epigenetic Transgenerational Actions of Endocrine Disruptors and Male Fertility." *Science* 308 (5727): 1466–1469.

Bateson, P.P.G. 1978. "Sexual Imprinting and Optimal Outbreeding." *Nature* 273: 659–660.

———, ed. 1983. *Mate Choice*. Cambridge: Cambridge University Press.

Birkhead, T. R., and T. Pizzari. 2002. "Evolution of Sex: Postcopulatory Sexual Selection." *Nature Reviews Genetics* 3: 262–273.

Bischof, N. 1975. "Comparative Ethology of Incest Avoidance." In *Biosocial Anthropology* (ASA Studies), edited by R. Fox. London: Malaby Press; New York: Humanities Press.

Bittles, A. 2012. *Consanguinity in Context*. Cambridge: Cambridge University Press.

Bloom, H. K. 2010. *The Genius of the Beast: A Radical Re-Vision of Capitalism*. New York: Prometheus Books.

Carr-Saunders, A. M. 1922. *The Population Problem: A Study in Human Evolution.* Oxford: Oxford University Press.

Cavalli-Sforza, L. L., A. Moroni, and G. Zei. 2004. *Consanguinity, Inbreeding and Genetic Drift in Italy.* Princeton, NJ: Princeton University Press.

Chagnon, N. 1968. *Yanomamö: The Fierce People.* New York: Holt Rinehart and Winston.

———. 1979. "Male Competition, Favoring Close Kin, and Village Fissioning among the Yanomamö Indians." In *Evolutionary Biology and Human Social Behavior: An Anthropological Perspective,* edited by N. A. Chagnon and W. J. Irons. North Scituate, MA: Duxbury Press.

Chapais, B. 2008. *Primeval Kinship: How Pair-Bonding Gave Birth to Human Society.* Cambridge, MA: Harvard University Press.

Darwin, G. H. 1875. "Marriages between First Cousins in England and Wales and Their Effects." *Journal of the Statistical Society* 38: 153–184.

De Queiroz, A. 2014. *The Monkey's Voyage: How Improbable Journeys Shaped the History of Life.* New York: Basic Books.

Diamond, J. M. 2002. "Life with the Artificial Anasazi." *Nature* 419: 567–569.

———. 2005. *Collapse: How Societies Choose to Fail or Succeed.* New York: Viking Penguin.

Dudley, S. A., and A. L. File. 2007. "Kin Recognition in an Annual Plant." *Biology Letters* 3: 435–438.

Dunbar, R. 1992. "Neo-cortex Size as a Constraint on Group Size in Primates." *Journal of Human Evolution* 20: 469–493.

———. 1993. "Co-evolution of Neo-cortical size, Group Size and Language in Humans." *Behavioral and Brain Sciences* 16 (4): 681–735.

———. 1998. *Grooming, Gossip and the Evolution of Language.* Cambridge, MA: Harvard University Press.

Dyke, B., and J. W. MacClure, eds. 1973. *Computer Simulation in Human Population Studies.* New York: Academic Press.

Eberhard, W. G. 2009. "Postcopulatory Sexual Selection: Darwin's Omission and Its Consequences." *Proceedings of the National Academy of Sciences* 106 (supplement 1): 10025–10032.

File, A. L., G. P. Murphy, and S. A. Dudley. 2012. "Fitness Consequences of Plants Growing with Siblings: Reconciling Kin Selection, Niche Partitioning and Competitive Ability." *Proceedings of the Royal Society B* 279: 209–218.

Fisher, H. S., and H. E. Hoekstra. 2010. "Competition Drives Cooperation among Closely-Related Sperm of Deer Mice." *Nature* 463: 801–803.

Fox, J. G., M. Davisson, F. Quimby, S. W. Barthold, C. E. Newcomer, and A. Smith, eds. 2007. *The Mouse in Biomedical Research (Second Edition) Vol. 1: History, Wild Mice and Genetics.* Waltham, MA: Elsevier/Academic Press.

Fox, R. 1962. "Sibling Incest." *British Journal of Sociology* 13: 128–150.

———. 1967. *Kinship and Marriage: An Anthropological Perspective.* Harmondsworth: Penguin. (2nd ed. Cambridge: Cambridge University Press, 1983)

———. 1978. *The Tory Islanders: A People of the Celtic Fringe.* Cambridge: Cambridge University Press. (2nd ed. Notre Dame, IN: Notre Dame University Press, 1983)

———. 1979. "Kinship Categories as Natural Categories." In *Evolutionary Biology and Human Social Behavior: An Anthropological Perspective,* edited by N. A. Chagnon and W. J. Irons. North Scituate, MA: Duxbury Press. (Reprinted in R. Fox, *The Search for Society.* New Brunswick, NJ: Rutgers University Press, 1989)

———. (1980) 1983. *The Red Lamp of Incest: A Study in the Origins of Mind and Society.* Notre Dame, IN: Notre Dame University Press.

———. 1993. *Reproduction and Succession: Studies in Anthropology, Law, and Society.* New Brunswick, NJ: Transaction Publishers.

———. 1997. *Conjectures and Confrontations: Science, Evolution, Social Concern.* New Brunswick, NJ: Transaction Publishers.

———. 2011. *The Tribal Imagination: Civilization and the Savage Mind.* Cambridge, MA: Harvard University Press.

Goodman, A., I. Koupil, and D. W. Lawson. 2012. "Low Fertility Increases Descendant Socioeconomic Position but Reduces Long-Term Fitness in a Modern Post-Industrial Society." *Proceedings of the Royal Society B* 279: 4342–4351.

Haig, D. 1997. "The Social Gene." In *Behavioural Ecology: An Evolutionary Approach,* edited by J. R. Krebs and N. B. Davies, 284–304. 4th ed. Cambridge, UK: Wiley-Blackwell.

Hamilton, W. D. 1967. "Extraordinary Sex Ratios." *Science* 156: 477–488.

Helgason, A., S. Palsson, D. F. Guobjartsson, P. Krisjansson, and K. Stefanson. 2008. "An Association between Kinship and Fertility of Human Couples." *Science* 319: 813–816.

Herbert, M. L., and M. G. Lewis. 2013. "Fluctuations of Fertility in a Real Insect Population and a Virtual Population." *Journal of African Entomology* 21 (1): 119–126.

Hopkins, K. 1980. "Brother-Sister Marriage in Roman Egypt." *Comparative Studies in Society and History* 22: 303–354.

Jay, A. 2014. "Understanding Laughter." In *The Character of Human Institutions: Robin Fox and the Rise of Biosocial Science*, edited by M. Egan. New Brunswick, NJ: Transaction.

Kaiser, J. 2014. "The Epigenetics Heretic." *Science* 343: 361–363.

Kalbe, M., C. Eizaguirre, I. Dankert, T. Reusch, R. Sommerfeld, K. Wegner, and M. Milinski. 2009. "Lifetime Reproductive Success Is Maximized with Optimal Major Histocompatibility Complex Diversity." *Proceedings of the Royal Society B, Biological Sciences* 276: 925–934.

Kuper, Adam. 2009. *Incest and Influence: The Private Life of Bourgeois England*. Cambridge, MA: Harvard University Press.

Labouriau, R., and A. Amorim. 2008. "Comment On: An Association between Kinship and Fertility of Human Couples." *Science* 332 (908): 1634.

Lévi-Strauss, C. 1949. *Les structures élémentaires de la parenté*. Paris: Presses Universitaires de France.

Lindholm, C. 1986. "Kinship Structure and Political Authority: The Middle East and Central Asia." *Comparative Studies in Society and History* 28 (2): 344–355.

Morris, D. 1994. *The Human Animal: Program 4: The Biology of Love*. Bristol: BBC.

Moseley, M. 2001. *The Incas and Their Ancestors: The Archaeology of Peru*. 2nd ed. London and New York: Thames and Hudson.

Murphy, R. F., and L. Kasdan. 1959. "The Structure of Parallel Cousin Marriage." *American Anthropologist* 61: 1, 17–29.

Pääbo, S. 2014. *Neanderthal Man: In Search of Lost Genomes*. New York: Basic Books.

Pathak, D. T., X. Wei, A. Dey, and D. Wall. 2013. "Molecular Recognition by a Polymorphic Cell Surface Receptor Governs Cooperative Behaviors in Bacteria." *PLoS Genet.* 9 (11): e1003891. doi:10.1371/journal.pgen.1003891.

Sahlins, M. D. 1961. "The Segmentary Lineage: An Organization of Predatory Expansion." *American Anthropologist* 63: 322–345.

Salaman, R. 1949. *The History and Social Influence of the Potato*. Cambridge: Cambridge University Press.

Shimkets, L. J. 1990. "The Social and Developmental Biology of the Myxobacteria." *Microbiological Review* 54 (4): 473–501.

Sibly, R. M., D. Barker, M. C. Denham, J. Hone, and M. Pagel. 2005. "On the Regulation of Populations of Mammals, Birds, Fish, and Insects." *Science* 309: 608–609.

Stone, L., P. F. Lurquin, and L. L. Cavalli-Sforza. 2007. *Genes, Culture and Human Evolution*. Oxford: Blackwell.

Tierney, J. 2003. "Iraqi Family Ties Complicate American Efforts for Change." *New York Times*, September 28.

Trivers, R. 1985. *Social Evolution*. Menlo Park, CA: Benjamin/Cummings Publishing.

———. 2002. *Natural Selection and Social Theory*. Oxford: Oxford University Press.

Trivers, R., and A. Burt. 2006. *Genes in Conflict: The Biology of Selfish Genetic Elements*. Cambridge, MA: Harvard University Press.

Turner, J. H., and A. Maryanski. 2005. *Incest: Origins of the Taboo*. Boulder, CO: Paradigm Publishers.

Tylor, E. B. 1889. "On a Method of Investigating the Development of Institutions." *Journal of the Royal Anthropological Institute* 18: 245–269.

Walter, A., and S. Buyske. 2003. "The Westermarck Effect and Early Childhood Co-socialization: Sex Differences in Inbreeding Avoidance." *British Journal of Developmental Psychology* 21: 353–365.

Williamson, M. 1996. *Biological Invasions*. New York: Chapman Hall.

Wilson, D. S., and E. Sober. 1994. "Reintroducing Group Selection to the Human Behavioral Sciences." *Behavioral and Brain Science* 14: 585–654.

Wilson, D. S., and E. O. Wilson. 2007. "Re-thinking the Theoretical Foundation of Sociobiology." *Quarterly Review of Biology* 82: 327–348.

———. 2008. "Evolution 'for the Good of the Group.'" *American Scientist* 96: 380–389.

Wright, S. 1984. *Evolution and the Genetics of Populations*. 4 vols. Chicago: University of Chicago Press.

Wynne-Edwards, V. C. 1962. *Animal Dispersion in Relation to Social Behavior*. Edinburgh and London: Oliver and Boyd.

Chapter Twenty

On the Origins of Gender Inequality

Joan Huber

> The forager groups who represent 99 percent of human time on earth were relatively egalitarian, but 10,000 years ago the invention of the hoe and then the plow entailed a food surplus that led to warfare and a system of social stratification based on birth. The non-fit of reproduction with warfare let men monopolize both war and politics and consigned women to secondary status, but the reproductive constraints were poorly understood until the 1990s. Infants had been suckled at intervals of about fifteen minutes by day (less often at night) for two years, and at a lesser rate for at least two more until the invention of a safe substitute for human milk in the 1880s. The pattern evolved because frequent suckling precluded ovulation; the contraceptive effect maximized survival. If a forager mother gave birth before her older child could join the daily food search, the older one starved. A forager mother thus carried her youngest child everywhere and slept with it at night, for her low-fat milk sated its hunger only briefly. In the 1950s, demographers were still unaware of the contraceptive effect of prolonged lactation, but by the 1990s they agreed that prolonged breastfeeding was universal before the demographic transition. The invention of a safe alternative to human milk induced huge behavioral changes. Biggest and least recognized was the decrease to nearly zero in the number of three- to five-year-olds whose primary food was breast milk. Augmenting the fertility decline, the revolution in child feeding enabled women in modern economies to increase the range of their public activities by a substantial margin.

Introduction: Tools, Food, and Social Power

As humans must eat often or die, hunger is the chief determinant of social relationships (Goody 1976), and the tools used to produce food in a given ecological setting explain the distribution of power (Lenski 1970). A century of research in anthropology suggests that the Pleistocene foragers (who represent 99 percent of human time on earth) were more egalitarian than were the humans in all subsequent societies (Boehm 1999). After the use of tools to produce food led to social stratification based primarily on birth, the pace of social change rose. About 10,000 years ago, the hoe entailed permanent settlements, which attracted marauders, but 4,000 years ago the plow produced a much larger surplus that tempted rulers to seize as much as possible (Pryor 1985). Elites topped pyramidal social structures; peasants, serfs, and slaves were at the base (Lenski 1970).

Three universals prevailed in the cultures anthropologists studied: ideologies favoring men, male monopoly of political office, and female exclusion from prestige spheres (Quinn

1977: 183). As the non-fit of warfare and reproduction enabled men to monopolize war and politics (Collins et al. 1993), women were far more subordinated than were other primate females (Smuts 1985). Like all female apes, women had a cycle of pregnancy and lactation that was nearly continuous during all of their most vigorous years. The pattern evolved because it prevented ovulation (Howell 1979; Vallegia and Ellison 2003). When a woman gave birth before her older child could join the daily food search, the older child starved. Infants had been suckled at intervals of about fifteen minutes by day (less often at night) for two years and at a lesser rate for at least another two years (Xie 1990).

Yet if all women were absent from politics in plow societies, so were most men until the early modern period when inventions like the printing press enabled ordinary people to learn what was going on and to protest it. Women's claims for a voice first arose among the few who could read. Later, economic power migrated from elites to huge government and business entities that needed clerical workers. Such organizations inherently foster gender neutrality because their most basic need is for profits or votes (Jackson 1998). The demand for women workers that spurred women's career changes in the twentieth century was in fact an unplanned outcome of the increasing demand for educated workers (Oppenheimer 1973).

But why was the supply of women workers elastic enough to meet that demand? Where did mothers find the time to work away from home? Some reasons are well known: improved household tools and contraceptives. A third reason is barely recognized even today: a profound revolution in child feeding. By the 1950s, infant formula began to replace human milk in the West (Stuart-Macadam 1995). The use of the bottle induced huge behavioral changes beginning with the decline in the number of women who breastfed at all. By far the biggest (and least noticed) change was the decrease to nearly zero in the number of three- to five-year-olds whose primary food had been human milk (Stuart-Macadam 1998: 58). Also unnoticed is the decrease in the number of daily feeds whether by bottle or breast. Early in the 1900s, American infants were fed whenever they fussed. Now the clock determines the timing (Lawrence and Lawrence 1999). A pattern that marked our species from its beginnings vanished in a century. An explanation of how it came to be so must be based on research in evolutionary biology and anthropology (Hrdy 2011; Huber 2007).

Evolutionary Origins of Human Reproduction

In the mammal line, the evolutionary successes (many species, vigorous radiation) are rats, bats, and antelopes (Gould 1996: 63). Primates, small and unsuccessful mammals (Rowell 1972: 20), appeared 70 million years ago (MYA), attained a heyday 50 to 60 MYA, and then did little until our subspecies (*Homo sapiens sapiens*) produced food and peopled the earth (Lancaster 1975). With the greatest range in social organization of any vertebrate order, primates may be multi-male, monogamous, polyandrous, promiscuous, harem-like, or solitary (Janson 1992: 95). Long after the other great apes split off from our line, chimpanzees split off about 5 MYA; they and bonobos, our two equally closest relatives, split from each other 2 MYA (de Waal 2001: 2). In the hominid line, our species is the only one not yet extinct. Anatomically modern humans emerged in East and South Africa about 150,000 years ago (Turner and Maryanski 2005: 84).

In the 1960s and 1970s the savanna baboon became the model of the human ancestor (Altmann 1998). Emphasizing only the male, some accounts now read like cautionary tales lest women get uppity, yet the absence of women in the models generated a backlash. In the 1980s, research suggested that the infants most likely to survive were those born to the best gatherers and tool users; bipedalism enabled humans to carry food and offspring long distances (Tanner 1981: 268). Hunting large animals, a high-risk activity, likely became common only when supported by gathering (Zihlman 1978). Meat eating (like plant growth) varies with latitude: at the equator, 10 percent of the diet is meat; in the Arctic, 90 percent (Testart 1988).

A theory of human evolution must recognize that humans organize much larger societies than do other primates, whose low levels of sociality lead to weak ties (Maryanski and Turner 1992). It must also explain male bonding, as with chimpanzees; female bonding, as with bonobos; and the nuclear family, whose ties we share with neither species. Human social order revolves around reproductive units that do not exist in other primates (de Waal 2001: 6).

Natural selection is based on the tendency of living organisms to produce more offspring than can survive. Survivors tend to be individuals whose variations best suit a local ecology (Gould 1996: 138). For example, skin color evolved to balance the need for ultraviolet radiation (UVR), which affects body chemicals needed to reproduce. At the equator, humans need a very dark skin to block out too much UVR; at extreme latitudes, a very light skin to admit enough UVR (Jablonski 2006: 80). Human behavior is also affected by cultural change. New technologies can alter optimal responses to problems almost overnight. For example, Henry Ford paid workers five dollars a day so that they could buy the cars that gave teenagers a home away from home while rubber research to improve the ride led to a better condom. A series of remarkable inventions led to a churning of couple relationships that blurred the reciprocities that have long defined family life (Seltzer and Bianchi 2013).

All change, whether biological or cultural, involves trading costs. For example, some tubes in our aquatic ancestors that collected urine from the kidneys were hijacked 350 MYA to carry eggs and sperm to the watery world outside; sex can thus be linked with waste elimination (Potts and Short 1999: 133). Language appeared when humans lived on the same continent; children learn sounds in the same order, p-m-a first (Ruhlen 1994: 122). But the repositioning of larynx, tongue, and pharynx that permits speech also lets food fall into the larynx and cut off air. We are the only mammals who can choke while eating. No free lunch.

Two outcomes of natural selection, bipedal locomotion about 5 MYA and a bigger brain about 2 MYA, ensured that women carry their child everywhere during the child's most vigorous years. About 5 MYA when climate change reduced the carrying capacity of their niche, our ancestors left the trees, which induced changes in behavior, anatomy, and physiology (Trevathan 1987). Bipedalism required pelvic change lest walkers place their legs too far apart (like trying to walk fast in snowshoes). The male pelvis adjusted more easily than did the female one, which had to permit passage of the infant head during birth, a process that became even harder after the doubling in brain size that began 2 MYA. The prime mover for a bigger brain was likely a need for the social skills needed for life in the larger groups that better defended against predators (Falk 1997: 129). The cost of larger groups is that more persons compete for food. Some primates handle competitive tensions by mutual grooming, but complex human groups soon outgrew the capacity of grooming to preserve social order. Members of large groups would be scratching backs all day (Potts and Short 1999: 187). Language may have been the social glue that replaced grooming (Dunbar 1996: 79). Speech lets more people interact at the same time.

The pelvic changes needed for bipedalism coupled with the bigger brain that made birth more difficult for mother and infant made solitary birthing dangerous. Chimps and bonobos go off alone to give birth because the ratio of infant head to maternal pelvis is like that of yolk to white in a boiled egg—plenty of room. In humans, the infant head fills the pelvic cavity with only tiny slivers of space to spare. Human mothers and infants became more likely to survive the birth process with the help of an experienced woman. Even so, for most of human history, one birth in twenty ended in maternal death. In natural settings and in human populations lacking modern health care, women do not tend to outlive men. The female longevity advantage is of recent origin and occurs only in societies with modern medical resources. At about age eighty-five, male and female mortality rates converge (Crews 2003: 136, 107).

The contemporary strategy for birth emerged after the brain doubled in size. About 2 MYA, the hominid brain reached the biggest size that could be born to a mammal otherwise adapted to deliver an infant whose brain is half its adult size at birth (Trevathan 1987: 223). A bigger brain would preclude safe delivery. But natural selection neither enlarged the birth canal nor increased the total size of the adult female (as with gorillas). Instead, the birth occurred before the infant brain made the head too big for safe passage. At birth, the human brain is only 23 percent of its adult size. It attains 45 percent of adult size at seven months, while the chimpanzee brain is 45 percent of adult size at birth. Human females must invest far more time in child care than do any other female mammals (Lancaster 1985: 20).

Passage through the bony maternal pelvis is the hardest part of the birth process for the infant; its passage through the vagina is the most hazardous for the mother. Unless the flesh is cut to widen the opening, tearing of tissue from vagina to anus is common; unless the laceration is repaired, serious infection can occur (Trevathan 1987: 27). The rearrangement of the birth canal created the worst problem. In four-footed species like monkeys (and the probable human ancestor), the entrance and exit of the birth canal have their greatest breadth front to back; the infant head is also largest front to back. The infant emerges facing the front of its mother's body. She can guide it from the birth canal or it could crawl up to her nipples unassisted. Bipedalism unfortunately twisted the human birth canal in the middle so that the entrance is broadest side to side while the exit is broadest front to back. The widest breadths of entrance and exit are thus perpendicular to one another as are the relevant fetal dimensions: the head is largest front to back, but the infant's rigid shoulders are broadest side to side, not an example of intelligent design. The passage of the infant's broad, rigid shoulders through the mother's bony pelvis requires that the infant's chin be pressed against its throat instead of tilted backward. The coupling of this flexion with the restructured bony birth canal requires the infant to undergo a series of rotations to pass through the birth canal without hindrance. As a result of these rotations, the infant tends to be born facing away from its mother, which hinders her ability to reach down and clear a breathing passageway for it or to remove the cord from around its neck should it interfere with the infant's breathing or continued emergence. In most deliveries, if the mother tries to guide the infant from the birth canal, she risks pulling its head backward and damaging its nerves and muscles. This process transformed birth from a solitary to a social event (Trevathan 1999: 195). The human infant is in effect premature, more helpless, and far more work for the mother.

To the end of her reproductive period, a forager mother carried her youngest child everywhere for three or four years and slept with it at night to boot because her low-fat milk sated its hunger only briefly (Hrdy 1999). She gathered nuts and berries and killed small animals daily, all her children in tow, to teach them how to provide for themselves. By contrast, the offspring of nonhuman primates feed themselves and no one else. A sick or injured one can die of hunger or thirst. Relatives do not respond to its need for food (Lancaster 1991). Between 70 and 90 percent of these infants fail to reach adulthood, owing to malnutrition and diseases that follow weaning (Lancaster and Lancaster 1983).

For nonhuman primates, as for most mammals, the juvenile phase is a selection funnel into which many enter but few emerge (Lancaster 1991). About half the infants born to foragers and horticulturists lived long enough to reproduce.

The long period of feeding juveniles and increasing the strength of adult male-female bonds was involved in the emergence of the human family: an adult female, an adult male, and their offspring. Turner and Maryanski (2005) argue that the origin is likely a result of neurological changes that enabled humans to develop organizational forms that were better knit than the weak ties of other ape adults. When humans could not take to the trees, weak ties threatened survival. Tightly knit groups can better fight off predators. Human adults became more organized. However, the ties between mother and infant remained much the same.

The Physiology of Lactation

The physiology of lactation involves the mammary gland and the composition of the milk. UNICEF estimates that 97 percent of women can give milk (Jolly 1999: 330). According to Lawrence and Lawrence (1999), the mammary gland (medical name of the breast) undergoes three phases of growth: in the uterus, childhood, and the pubertal period. The adult female gland consists of a branching system of excretory ducts embedded in connective tissue. When a female is ten to twelve years old, the tree of ducts rapidly extends in a branching pattern. Alveolar buds form a year or two before the onset of menses. New buds sprout for several years, producing alveolar lobes. Female breasts enlarge to adult size at puberty. A nipple contains fifteen to twenty-five milk ducts, each of which opens into it. At birth, a sequence of events governed by hormonal action prepares the breast for lactation (Lawrence and Lawrence 1999). From forty to seventy-two hours after birth, a woman experiences milk coming in as a feeling of fullness, more quickly if she has borne a child earlier. The volume increases for two weeks, starting at less than 100 ml/day and rising to about 600 ml/day at ninety-six hours. Lactose, sodium chloride, and protein stabilize at twenty-four hours. The lactating glands adjust milk supply to demand. Reduction in the sucking stimulus reduces the hormone prolactin and milk synthesis. Variation in milk secretion is rapidly reflected in anatomic change in the mammary gland. In the absence of stimulation, mammary tissue regresses the first week after birth. Unless frequent suckling or use of a breast pump empties the lactating breast, milk production gradually ceases. The absence of suckling initiates the neuron-hormonal reflex to maintain prolactin secretion, and the ensuing engorgement of the breast causes diminished flow by compressing the blood vessels. Even women who never gave birth or breastfed can be induced to lactate (Lawrence and Lawrence 1999: 633). The process should begin several months before the infant's arrival. Lactation may occur in one to six weeks.

As the study of human milk is recent, scientists know less about its composition than one would expect. The milk of cows, goats, and sheep had long been studied owing to its economic importance; most of the research on human milk appeared after 1970 (Lawrence and Lawrence 1994: 91). Anthropologists rarely gathered detailed data on breastfeeding, which was and is very hard to study in the few populations that exercise no deliberate control over fertility (Panter-Brick 1992: 137). Composition and volume are hard to compare owing to different procedures to weigh and test, inconsistent extraction techniques, and variation in sampling time between feeds (Jelliffe and Jelliffe 1978). As studies rarely separate full and partial breastfeeding, averages tend to hide more than they reveal. Retrospective surveys of mothers who nursed their infants cost little but tend to yield unreliable data (Haaga 1988: 307). Interview data reveal low accord between timed data and the mother's memory of feeds (Vitzthum 1997: 247). Direct observation of suckling requires much time; few studies report such data (Ellison 1995: 316).

A question as simple as the volume of milk at a feeding must deal with several issues. The methods must be accurate, reproducible, noninvasive, and relatively easy to use at home, night or day; additionally, they must not interrupt the suckling. Milk composition constantly changes. The fat content increases toward the end of each feeding and rises from early morning to midday; earlier milk differs from later milk at the same feeding. Composition varies with stage of lactation, time of day, sampling time, and maternal nutrition. Pumped samples vary from those obtained by suckling and the content varies by method of pumping. Many of the earlier interpretations of milk content were in error as they were based on pooled samples from many donors at different times and stages of lactation. Maternal diet is a major concern in studies of milk content. Should it be poor, many of the nutrients in her milk will come from her body rather than her diet. The milk of a malnourished mother has about the same proportions of protein, fat, and carbohydrate as that of a well-nourished one, but a malnourished woman produces less milk.

Human milk evolved to meet the needs of infants who nurse on demand. The human brain at birth is relatively small. The infant's need for milk sugar is great because its brain can grow only if it gets large amounts of lactose (Small 1998: 185). Compared with the milk of other mammals, the mature milk of primates about three weeks after birth is dilute, very low in fat and protein, but high in lactose, all of which affect suckling frequency. Species that nurse less often must have milk with a much higher fat content. A mother rabbit returns only once a day to the concealed spot where she parked her offspring. Human milk is characteristic of a species that suckles its young almost continuously (Micozzi 1995: 357), a fact that was unknown to social scientists until the discovery of natural fertility.

Not long ago demographers thought that Malthus got it right: abstinence was the only certain contraceptive. Medical science saw the claim that breastfeeding prevented pregnancy as an old wives' tale because the biomedical nursing pattern had spaced feeds two to five hours apart, and the minimal suppression of ovarian function led physicians to doubt that lactation and fecundity were related (Vitzthum 1997: 244). Demographers were slow to see the significance of premodern child-spacing patterns, and economists were slower still (Page and Lesthaeghe 1981: ix). As recently as the 1950s, demographers were unaware of the effects of lactation on amenorrhea and infecundity (Hobcraft 1994: 413). Lorimer's (1954) influential UNESCO volume on human fertility discussed no effects, nor did Davis and Blake (1956) note any in a landmark paper listing all intermediate variables that affect fertility (Ellison 1995: 305).

In the 1950s Louis Henry defined natural fertility as the absence of deliberate control; a couple's behavior is neither bound to the number of children born nor modified when the number reaches the maximum a couple wants (Leridon and Menken 1977: 3). Giosa (1955) proposed that a major function of lactation might be its role as a natural birth spacer. In 1961, Henry (1961) suggested that lactation might be the primary determinant of natural fertility, and in the 1970s, data on Kalahari foragers revealed a lifetime average of five births (Howell 1979: 291). An international conference of world health groups later announced that breastfeeding was a safe and effective contraceptive (Ellison 1995: 305). Demographers now agree that natural fertility was nearly universal before the demographic transition that began in Western Europe (Wood 1990; Xie 1990). By the 1990s it was clear that the effects of breastfeeding on fertility vary among individuals and societies depending on the sucking stimulus, maternal diet, and secretion of hormones. Intensity interacts with availability of maternal energy to determine metabolic energy available for reproduction and duration of amenorrhea (Vallegia and Ellison 2003: 97).

Biologically, breastfeeding benefits both infant and mother. Infants receive ideal growth nutrients and maternal antibodies against diseases; mothers return more rapidly to their prepregnancy state and have lower rates of obesity later in life. By the 1990s, researchers noted an important new benefit for mothers: breastfeeding decreases the exposure of reproductive tissues to estrogenic hormones. The decline in frequency and duration of breastfeeding among Western women floods their bodies with hormones during a much larger part of the reproductive period; such women experience an average of 450 menstrual cycles over a lifetime versus 50 cycles for women who breastfeed often over a long period (see citations in Crews and Gerber 1994, p. 159, and Stuart-Macadam 1998, p. 57). Abundant calories and fats increase exposure to gonadal steroids by lowering the age of puberty. Women in modern societies carry a risk of malignancy ten to one hundred times greater than that of foragers. The rates of diseases linked to chronic hormone exposure are rising in both sexes: endometrial, colon, breast, and prostate cancer and coronary heart disease (Micozzi 1995; Whitten 1999: 211). The incidence of cancers likely reflects the profound ecological changes of modernization (Ellison 1999).

The biological and social costs of breastfeeding to the infant were and remain very low. The biological cost to the mother typically involves a breast infection that modern medicine can readily cure. By contrast, the social cost was very high when the cycle of pregnancy and lactation excluded her from all political and economic activities, and a study based on data from the National Longitudinal Survey of Youth indicates that it is still substantial (Rippeyoung and Noonan 2012). Economists long ignored the opportunity cost of maternal time (Butz 1977) though ordinary women seem to sense it. Historically, the costs tend to vary by time and place because "women's work" varies with the technology of food production in a given ecological setting, a topic I discuss after a comment on why we like certain foods.

The Origins of Human Food Preferences

Constraints on human diets are a consequence of the interaction of ecology, technology, and social organization. Not long ago, social scientists (like Malthus) held that human inventions increased the food supply, which then spurred population growth. Then Danish economist Ester Boserup (1965) turned Malthus on his head. It was the increase in population size and subsequent need to feed more people that spurred inventions, not the other way around. Hungry people think of ways to produce more food (Cohen 1984: 1). However, there are costs. Digging stick, hoe, and plow make land more productive only with greater input of human labor. People do not turn the soil, fodder animals, or collect manure unless they must (Netting 1993: 103). Technology is more a holding action than a liberating force (Cohen 1977: 285). In order to show how our ancestors coped with infant diet during the last 200,000 years, I first describe the primate diet that prevailed until hunger led foragers to domesticate plants and animals, and then discuss the effect of subsistence tools in given ecological settings on diets in societies based on hoe, herding, and plow technology.

The ancient primate diet consisted primarily of fruits; humans prefer food with similar nutrient and chemical content. According to Nesse and Williams (1994) and Whitten (1999), fruits are unique plants that evolved as sugary lures to give seeds a free ride in an animal gut to a distant germination site. Given fruits survived the selection process by attracting the animals most likely to disperse the seeds at the best time and place. Seeds are often quite poisonous because eating them too soon thwarts a plant's reproductive strategy. When the seeds are ready for a trip in a warm and moist gut to a good site for germination, all fruits signal the appropriate animal carriers that the flesh is sweet, soft, and succulent. When the bitter and astringent chemicals (like tannins) that are highly concentrated in unripe fruit decline, ripening is heralded by bright colors that make the fruit stand out against leaves. To make subtle judgments about ripeness, nutrient content, and plant defenses (which humans generally perceive as bitter), fruit eaters developed a nuanced sense of color, texture, and taste. Primates regained the color vision that had been lost owing to mammals' nocturnal origin, and became trichromatic, sensitive to those parts of the color spectrum that signal the changes in ripening fruit: yellow-orange, yellow, and blue-green. Most of the other animals are dichromatic. Ripening primate-dispersed fruits take on yellow-orange hues; bird-dispersed fruits assume red, blue, white, and purple colors.

Colonizing the globe and adapting to local ecosystems produced an array of diets, but we humans likely retained a perceptual basis for choosing food much like that of the foods relished by other apes. The short history of plant domestication makes it unlikely that our physiological ability to process food chemicals has diverged much from that of our ancestors. Foragers added seeds, roots, and tubers that they could more easily collect and store than the fruits of tropical hardwoods. Contemporary humans are more adapted to a forager diet than to diets that replaced it as our species spread over the globe. For example, scurvy, marked by swollen gums, livid skin spots, and prostration, arose among peoples who moved north and lost easy access to fresh fruit. It often afflicted British sailors on long voyages. They were cured by adding lime juice to their diet, which led to their being called "Limeys." Fruits rich in vitamin C were so important in the primate diet over such a long period that the biochemical machinery to make the vitamin degenerated in all humans and some apes (Nesse and Williams 1994: 130).

From Foraging to Hoe and Herding

Hunter-gatherers had a level of social equality as high as any ever known (Chafetz 1984). Some inequality is unavoidable as each individual (save identical twins) has unique traits that help or challenge him or her in competing for material resources and social esteem. Warfare was rare among foragers. People were few in number, land was plentiful, and crowding minimal: one person to a square mile. Groups easily avoided one another in the search for food (Johnson and Earle 1987). As women's gathering yielded more calories on average than did men's hunting, the incentives for male control of sexuality were low, and casual sex and frequent divorce were common (Collins et al. 1993: 199). Storage was impossible, so there was no steady surplus of food. Each woman nursed only her own infant, for few women have milk enough for two. A woman carried her youngest child in a sling while she collected food. Foragers usually saw twins as bad luck because it was so hard to carry two. A mother might have to kill one or both (depending on the norms), usually by exposure. In very hard times, parents might have to expose an infant when there were too many mouths to feed.

Foragers had no alternatives to human milk as a food for young children. Foods of older children and adults were too tough and hard to chew and digest for those whose guts and teeth were too immature to process incompletely ripe fruit, nuts, insects, and small animals. After foragers learned to use fire, vegetable tubers and meats were cooked to soften them. Even so, they were hard for young children to digest. A mother's need to breastfeed was unquestioned. It was highly unlikely that another lactating woman would be available to serve as a wet nurse (Trevathan 1987: 32; Hrdy 1999: 402).

Societies based on the hoe or herding gave up on foraging when they could not cope with local resource failure. Searching for new ways to ensure a food supply, erstwhile foragers turned to a semi-sedentary mode based on use of the digging stick or hoe in areas of abundant rainfall. Where rainfall was scant or the terrain too rough to permit crops, they herded sheep, cattle, or goats. The two modes differ considerably, but the underlying technology is much the same, for animals and plants were domesticated at about the same time. The hoe or herding societies that succeeded forager bands increased the food supply, but the direct or indirect costs they incurred affected infant diet. For example, the higher the level of social inequality, the less likely it is that poor people get enough to eat. The efforts to restrict resources marked the beginnings of warfare (Johnson and Earle 1987: 58, 245). Biologists see most aggressive behavior as a response to environmental overcrowding (Wilson 1996: 84). Humans must solve the same ecological problems as other species if they are to produce children who live long enough to reproduce (Low, Clarke, and Lockridge 1992). Population pressure spurred the formation of local groups five to ten times larger than a typical family to act on issues concerning food storage and defense. A chief could organize a region if he could establish control over warfare, large-scale technology, central storage, and external trade. In kin-based tribal groups, kinship structure became an organization of coercion that upheld the property system (Collins et al. 1993: 199). The more often a society engaged in warfare, the more likely was social control to be vested in politico-military elites that excluded women.

A digging stick or metal-tipped hoe produces more food than does foraging, but it also requires more labor. According to Friedl (1975: 59ff), before planting crops in tropical forest or grassland savanna, men clear the land, which is often fallowed for as long as ten years and then cleared again to grow sweet potato, taro, yam, and banana in areas like the Pacific Islands and parts of West Africa or tapioca and cassava in tropical South America. East Africa and parts of North and South America produce cereal crops like millet and maize, and rice is grown in parts of South Asia. Domesticated animals like cattle or pigs become prestige objects in exchange as well as a source of meat and milk. Animals like cows, sheep, and goats provided alternatives to breastfeeding in the event of maternal death, but the new options were illusory because bovid milk has too little sugar to nourish a human infant's rapidly growing brain and too much fat to be digested properly.

Hoe cultures display the diversity of gender roles that became the basis for the relativist view of human behavior and belief held by Franz Boas and his students. Patterns of marriage and kinship tended to follow the division of labor, a crucial factor in the devising of reciprocal duties (Friedl 1975). After men cleared the land, both men and women planted and harvested crops, for a woman could do this while toting a nursling in a sling. Older children tended younger ones. Polygyny (a man has more than one wife at a time) increases productivity, for women did (and do) most of the work. Custom holds that a man can become rich only if he has many wives. A man often paid a bride-price to compensate a father for the loss of his daughter's services. The balance of the sexes was less skewed than might be expected because the death rate was high and women married early, men married late. By contrast, polyandry (a woman has more than one husband at a time) occurs only when food production is so difficult that it takes more than one man to support a woman and her children.

Men monopolized war. All adult males served as part-time warriors (Davie 1929: 30; Wright 1942: 84). Views of the few who studied war before the 1960s were widely accepted (Otterbein 1999: 796). Turney-High (1949) held that primitive war was more athletic contest than military exercise. By contrast, recent studies suggest that war was extremely bloody, and men, women, and children suffered great harm (LeBlanc 1999). War spawns sexual politics that typically involve segregation of men's and women's activities (Collins et al. 1993). As war and politics were inextricably intertwined, an extensive search noted that women were political actors in only a few societies in Africa and North America (Hobhouse, Wheeler, and Ginsberg 1930).

Herding societies appeared where tillage was difficult owing to mountainous terrain, a brief growing season, or low rainfall, as in Central Asia, Arabia, North Africa, parts of sub-Saharan Africa, and Europe (Lenski and Lenski 1978: 235). As many herders drank their animals' milk, many adults became able to digest lactose (milk sugar). Most humans lose that ability after weaning (Cavalli-Sforza 2000: 36). Moving livestock to seasonal pastures to convert grass into human food requires a nomadic lifestyle, but spatial mobility often leads to competition with agrarians over territory and disputes over water and stolen animals. The constant threat of conflict during migration stimulates the growth of centralized political authority, and the open grasslands where herders live pose few barriers to movement and political consolidation. A herding society may be as huge as the Asian empire of Ghenghis Khan, but a herding community may be only a little larger than a forager band, as a small unit can more easily maintain a herd in areas where scanty rainfall limits the food supply. About 3,000 years ago Asian herders acquired a huge advantage over the less mobile agrarians in the waves of conquest after they learned to ride their horses; herders devastated Eurasian agrarian empires for more than 2,500 years. Sexual politics peaked when a military aristocracy rule disarmed peasants (Collins et al. 1993).

Anthropologists ignored women in pastoral societies until after the 1970s (Dyson-Hudson and Dyson-Hudson 1980). Gender stratification is perplexing as many herders also depend on the hoe or plow, tools that oppositely affect women's economic productivity. The collection of cross-cultural data on lactation is especially problematic in a mobile population that does not track chronological age (Wiley and Pike 1998). Most data on infant feeding date from the 1980s. Gray (1999: 167) notes that a typical Turkana mother suckles her infant on demand. Suckling lasted less than 2.5 minutes at 10- to 15-minute intervals by day. At night the infant slept at its mother's nipple. Mothers did not usually waken when the infant nursed. Only mothers of children nineteen months or older reported being away from the child more than thirty to sixty minutes.

Plow Societies

Plow societies appeared in West Asia about 4,000 years ago. The first plows were made of wood. Techniques to smelt iron invented about 2,000 years later provided an iron blade. As iron is plentiful, plowshares proliferated and food production soared. Because large stores of food make a tempting target, warfare became widespread and has remained so ever since, thus illustrating a general rule of human organization: the larger the food supply, the greater the temptation to control its production and distribution (Lenski 1970). From its West Asian beginnings, plow technology spread to Europe, East Asia, and North Africa, wherever temperature and rainfall permitted the cultivation of grain crops. In sub-Saharan Africa the plow was rare because oxen, the best draft animals, can thrive neither in the humid zones of Central Africa nor in the West African coastal zones owing to the presence of the tse-tse fly, whose reproductive behavior in an extremely complex life cycle enables it to kill or severely weaken both cattle and humans (Shipton 1994: 357).

Domestication of various grains led to a proliferation of more digestible plant foods that needed much less chewing than did the foragers' roots and tubers. From an early age, an infant could swallow a mushy mix of grain and milk or water, but grain did not supply the nutrients of human milk. Moreover, a grain-based diet was highly dangerous for young children. Stored food is a good home for the disease pathogens that thrive in the warm climates of West Asia where the erstwhile foragers first settled. Most of the food adults ate was contaminated, and some of it was badly spoiled. Adults often developed immunity to many disease-producing organisms, but the immature infant gut, especially in the absence of the immune factors supplied by human milk, was highly vulnerable to pathogens that led to diarrhea and often to death from dehydration.

The most obvious effect of the plow was a vast increase in the Eurasian food supply. For the first time, continuous cultivation of a given area became possible by reducing weeds and turning the soil deeply enough to restore fertility. Use of the plow spurred the domestication of draft animals, and confining them in stalls to prevent their wandering off encouraged the collection of manure. Scattering manure over the fields increased food production, which led to the invention of writing, the better to track a much larger surplus. Early on, Moses became famous as a bureaucrat who watched over the pharaoh's granaries in the valley of the Nile.

Eurasian patterns of social stratification assumed the pyramidal form of feudalism: a ruling elite at the top; a slim layer of merchants, artisans, and craft workers; and at the bottom, a vast layer of peasants, serfs, and slaves. Use of the plow devastated the lives of ordinary people. A food surplus in the countryside coupled with the availability of iron weapons tempted elites to extract as much as possible from impoverished peasants (Goody 1976). The flatter and richer the land and the more food it could produce, the worse off were the men and women who did the work, much worse off than their forager ancestors (Lenski 1970).

With higher population density and settled agriculture, men did most of the heavy work involved in food production. Men monopolized the plow because the management of heavy draft animals in much larger fields was incompatible with the frequent suckling of an infant. With oxen a man could plow in a day an area far larger than a woman could till by hoe (Childe 1951: 100). When men monopolize food production, women become economic liabilities, in need of a dowry as a basis of support (Boserup 1970: 35). The less food women produce, the more they are valued only as mothers. Tropical Africa and Eurasia have different strategies of inheritance owing to the effect of the plow on the value of land coupled with women's low level of productivity (Goody 1976: 97). In the African hoe cultures south of the Sahara, land is plentiful and economic differences among families are minor. There is little pressure to provide an heir to an estate (Goody and Tambiah 1973: 22). Marriage has little effect on a daughter's economic position; all women, married or not, grow crops or do craft work.

The most significant effect of the plow on women's status was a result of the fact that its use made land the chief form of wealth. Individual land ownership gave rise to laws and customs that reflected elite men's monopoly on warfare and related politico-economic institutions. Rule and custom (primogeniture, for example) ensured that land could not be subdivided into pieces too small to support a family. The scarcer the land and the more intensively it was used, the greater the tendency to keep it in the nuclear family, the basic unit of human production and reproduction (Goody 1976: 97). Monogamy prevailed lest too many heirs claim a given property. As women served as transmitters of male property, concern with their sexual "purity" became acute. The larger a woman's endowment, the more her sexual behavior was controlled. In Catholic areas, canon law made divorce difficult or impossible. But monogamy constrained men less than it did women. The fact that men's out-of-wedlock children could inherit no property effectively reduced elite men's interest in controlling the behavior of other men.

Several customs attest the steep decline in women's status in Eurasia and North Africa (Huber and Spitze 1983). Women are in a bad fix when ecology and technology encourage ideologies that define a woman only as a mother because the lower the value of her labor, the less the restriction of her normal body functions affects food production. The plow thus tempted elite men to introduce the practice of depriving women of the use of part of their bodies. For example, in Western Europe, an elite husband could lock a chastity belt around his wife's private parts and carry away the key were he to go off on a crusade. In the North African regions of plow use, such as Egypt, Ethiopia, Somalia, the Sudan, parts of Muslim West Africa, and Yemen, the practice of clitoridectomy is common (El Saadawi 1982: 33). Older women perform the operation on prepubertal girls. The purpose is to prevent sexual pleasure by cutting away part or all of the clitoral prepuce and tip, the entire clitoris, or the clitoris labia minora and part of the labia majora, scraping the two sides raw, then sewing them together save for a tiny opening to let urine or (later) menstrual blood drain, all of this without the use of any drugs to reduce pain or sanitary measures to reduce chances of serious infection. The consequences include chronic urinary infection and difficulties in childbirth and coitus. The custom still exists in parts of North Africa and among its migrants elsewhere, including the United States and Western Europe. It now affects about 140 million women worldwide (*Economist* 2012).

In India the practice of suttee among Hindu elites involved burning a widow alive on her husband's funeral pyre. The rationale was that it was her sins in a previous life that had caused her husband to die first (Stein 1978: 255). Some widows willingly climbed onto the pyre. Others did not. If a widow screamed and cried, her husband's male relatives would tie her down. The death of the wife gave control of the estate to the husband's brothers.

In China, foot-binding was widespread in the wheat-growing areas of the north (Levy 1966). Legend has it that the goal of the so-called lotus foot began when an emperor admired a dancer's feet and legs. The degree of maiming depended on the level of work a woman was expected to do. The bindings, first applied when the little girl was about three, were successively tightened. The pain was severe. Because the foot was made to be inches shorter, walking became nearly impossible. The practice was uncommon in the south because there the chief grain was rice, not wheat. Constant wading in the filthy water of the paddies often led to serious infection. The modern version of foot-binding is less painful. The stiletto heel creates a lotus-foot that makes walking difficult and running impossible but at least it can be taken off at night (Wikipedia 2014).

Yet the chastity belt seems mild compared with the effects of clitoridectomy, foot-binding, and suttee. Why were efforts to control women's sexual behavior so much more ferocious in Asia and North Africa than in Western Europe? Goody (1983) explains the relative mildness of the constraints on European women as an unexpected consequence of the measures the Catholic Church took to induce communicants to bequeath to it their wealth. Canon law reduced each person's number of close relatives (compared with Roman times, for example) by abolishing adoption and close-cousin marriage. Child-marriage was also banned and women often had the right to inherit land. The measures worked. About a third of French productive land was in church hands by the end of the seventh century. In German lands, northern France, and Italy, the church owned twice as much land in the ninth as in the eighth century.

Infant Feeding before Modern Medicine

Settlements became permanent when humans learned how to tend plants to produce the food needed to support the activities that mark urban life. The upside of city life is the flourishing of the arts and the life of the mind. The downside is the effect of crowding on the disposal of human wastes; ubiquitous sewage threatened human health across all social classes. It was not so long ago that Queen Victoria's spouse was a victim of the "bad drains" in Buckingham Palace. Yet however hard urban life was for elites, it was much worse for ordinary folk (Cohen 1989). Nomad foragers had been as tall as the affluent today (Eaton, Eaton, and Konner 1999: 313). The suits of armor in contemporary museums suggest that the knights of old were surprisingly short. Peasants shrank even more on a diet that included far too much bread and not nearly enough meat, fruit, and vegetables. As Braudel (1979: 130) put it, the standard diet in early modern Europe was bread, more bread, and gruel. A diet bad for bones was also bad for teeth (Larsen 2000: 231). Nomad foods had required heavy-duty chewing, which increased the size of jaw muscle and bone. Grain-based foods need little chewing (and the sugar content hastens dental decay). With less use, jaw bone and muscle became smaller, while teeth, more under genetic control, stayed about the same size. However, the discrepancy in size between jaw and teeth gives rise to a degree of malocclusion that now provides a good living for orthodontists.

The level of social stratification induced by plow technology especially affected the infants of peasants and slave women. Any infant whose mother died lost the immune protection of maternal milk, but its chances improved markedly when its family was rich enough to hire a wet nurse, a woman paid to suckle a child not her own. When the wet nurse was also suckling her own child, as often happened, the huge drain on her system made it unlikely that she would have enough milk for two over a prolonged period, and her own child might starve (Wood 1994: 17, 204; Stini 1985: 203). Wealthy parents often bought the life of their own child with that of another (Fildes 1986). In Greek and Roman times slave women had often been used as wet nurses. By the medieval period, the practice was popular among upper-class Europeans. The proto-industrial period spread the demand for wet-nursing across a much wider segment of the class structure, according to European scholars' study of church and state archives; as no such sources are available in the new world, the study of wet-nursing in America is rare (Golden 2001: 3). The availability of wage work for women sharply raised the opportunity cost of prolonged suckling though the death rate of the wet nurses' own infants was very high (Fildes 1988: 193). When many wives worked in the burgeoning French silk industry, the parents shipped a majority of Lyonnais infants to nearby villages (Garden 1975: 122), and Parisian parents sent an even higher proportion of infants away. The death rate of these infants reduces optimism about the nature of our kind.

Hand-feeding of a grain-based pap in the event of maternal death or incapability goes back 4,000 years as indicated by the utensils found by archeologists (Fildes 1986: 262). In late medieval Iceland, the only infants who were fed human milk were those whose mothers were too poor to keep a cow (Hastrup 1985). However, Fildes (1986: 264) noted that in a cold climate with high standards of maternal care and cleanliness, the five-year survival rate of hand-fed and breastfed infants may have differed little because the post-weaning death rates were very high whatever the child's age at weaning.

Infant abandonment occurred when food was scarce. Europeans gave up infants in great number to the end of the Middle Ages (Boswell 1988: 428). Foundling hospitals emerged first in Italy, then Spain, Portugal, and France from the 1200s to the 1600s and then in northern and central Europe in the 1700s. In proto-industrial Europe, whenever male wages were low, infant abandonment was associated with women's opportunities for wage work. In 1780, parents gave up perhaps 8,000 of the 30,000 infants born in Paris (Braudel 1979: 491). According to Kertzer (1993), abandonment rose sharply in Italy after the Catholic Church tightened its rules in response to the Reformation. The church banned all sexual relations outside marriage, but women paid the price. Limiting marriage to the formal ceremony undermined the traditional meaning of a man's promise of marriage, which long had sufficed to initiate sexual relations and was taken by the community as an obligation the man assumed to the woman and any child she bore. A rural woman working as an urban live-in servant was the most likely parent. Whether wet-nursed or fed by hand, few of these foundlings survived childhood (Kertzer 1993: 138).

The death rate of infants whose mothers did not suckle them was lowered only by the advent of modern sanitation (safe water and unspoiled food). At the outset of the Industrial Revolution, poor sanitation amid urban squalor had made human milk optimal for infant survival. Nineteenth-century documents report death rates of 80–90 percent for infants who were not breastfed (Preston and Haines 1991). In the rural "third world" (as in eighteenth-century London), 70 percent of infants died before their second birthday (Fildes 1986: 401). However, by 1910, discovery of the germ theory of disease in the 1880s made the bottle almost as safe as the breast in areas with modern sanitation (Huber 1990). It was safe water and food that induced the decline of gastrointestinal diseases, not medical treatment, for there were no therapeutic measures of value until about 1950 (McKeown 1976).

In both traditional and modern economies, breastfed infants suffer fewer ailments than do the bottle-fed, but so far as I have been able to discover, no evidence indicates that bottle-fed and breastfed children in modern settings differ significantly in the ability to live long enough to reproduce. Modern data are difficult to interpret because breast milk is often supplemented by formula and solid food in the infant's first year (Lawrence and Lawrence 1994: 28). Bottle-feeding clearly remains deadly where clean water is rare. For example, when poor women massively entered wage work in Northeast Brazil in the early 1940s, breastfeeding fell from 96 to 40 percent and kept falling despite extremely high infant death rates (Scheper-Hughes 1992: 317). Expansion of women's market opportunities persistently lowers the rate of breastfeeding (Da Vanzo 1988). In "third world" countries (as in industrializing Europe), mothers often seem to behave as if the opportunity cost of breastfeeding is very high, even when the effects of alternative modes of feeding on their infants' lives are both clear and severe.

Thus, late in the nineteenth century a mode of infant feeding that had evolved over millions of years began to erode as a result of discoveries spawned by modern medicine. Preference for bottle-feeding crossed all class and ethnic lines (Wolf 2001). Commercial firms and physicians took over the task of deciding what and when to feed infants. Mothers scheduled fewer feeds per day whether the mode was breast or bottle. Early on, educated mothers often saw breastfeeding as an outdated practice of immigrant women from poor countries. Later, such mothers were more likely to breastfeed than were less educated women. However, all infants, whatever the mother's educational attainment, were fed substantially less often both day and night than were the infants of their species over the past 200,000 years.

When the women's movement reappeared in the early 1970s, the facts about prolonged lactation were not fully understood. Feminist research tended to focus on such areas as the effect of human milk on infant health, breastfeeding ideologies by race and class, and the social construction of the medical control of pregnancy and lactation. Some feminist theorists, convinced that human behavior is solely a cultural construction, still seem unaware that modern technology effectively altered the social consequences of an ancient biological constraint.

THE SOCIAL CONSEQUENCES OF PROLONGED LACTATION

As male domination has been universal in historical time, one might suspect that its origin was an innate male trait that was absent in females. Until recently, many scientific explanations did indeed ascribe the origin of male dominance to innate sex-linked psychological traits. As Udry (2000: 454) said, humans form social structures around gender because the sexes have different bio-influenced behavioral predispositions, and gendered social structure is a universal accommodation to this biological fact. By contrast, evolutionary biologists see human behavior as a result of a continuously interactive mix of genes with a given environment (Gottlieb 1998). As Maynard Smith (1989: 68) observed, human culture cannot be broken into trait clusters that can be counted and analyzed statistically; culture transcends biological constraints, as in cooking and the use of the wheel, tools, and spectacles. Below, after noting the sex differences in human physiology, I focus on the effects of culture on human behavior.

Physiological sex differences in humans are categorical or statistical. A categorical difference affects all or none of a given group. The only categorical differences in humans are those of reproduction: no man can bear a child or (until recently) provide the only food it could digest. Statistical differences occur in quantifiable degrees. Some of them evolved to permit infant birth or nourishment. For example, men's upper body strength is greater than women's owing to the requirements of breastfeeding. Men tend to be larger and stronger than women, though some women are larger and stronger than most men.

Although the male edge in size and strength is often used to explain why women took no part in warfare, Maccoby (1998) and Goldstein (2001) have shown that this view is invalid. Individual variation and overlap would have enabled a nontrivial minority of women to fight. Nor do testosterone levels explain male dominance (Mazur and Booth 1998). The only well-documented case of a female combat unit in a standing army was in West Africa, the 1700s to the 1900s (Goldstein 2001). They fought well but had to be celibate; if pregnant, they were killed (Herskovits 1938: 85).

The most likely origin of women's secondary status is the fact that any species whose females nursed their young on a battlefield would soon be extinct. This fact suggests two questions: When did warfare become common, and why did women's absence from the battlefield bar them from the politics of making and enforcing laws? The answers to both indicate the sweeping effects of culture on human behavior. Anthropologists generally believe that warfare became common after the advent of hoe culture. For most of human time on earth, war was rare; crowding was minimal, one person to a square mile. After population pressure spawned groups five to ten times larger than a typical family to act on issues of food storage and defense, war became more common (Johnson and Earle 1987). When a chief institutionalized control over central storage, technology, external trade, and warfare, he could organize a region. Bronze weapons were used as early as 3000 BCE, iron weapons about 1500 BCE, and horses 1000 BCE. Metal weapons raised the efficiency and cost of war, and tended to restrict arms-bearing to elites (Andreski 1968: 38). The military was a key element in the formation of large-scale political institutions like complex chiefdoms and states (Earle 1997: 105). In Europe, metallurgy enabled politico-military elites to establish huge kingdoms whose eventual collapse led to feudalism (Bloch 1961). Lack of central control opened the door to robber hordes, for the protection and oppression of peasants fell to local landlords whose knights plundered the locals but protected them from the knightly thugs down the road. The European ruling class was a military one to the end of the old order in France (Keegan 1987: 4).

Women's absence from the battlefield precluded their presence in politics, for war and politics were intricately linked until the 1800s, as I soon note. Conquest always involved politics. Winners pacified losers in order to dun them for taxes, as when migrants from the Asian steppes overran Europe during the decline of Roman hegemony (Heather 1996). After conquest, we-they distinctions justified unequal relations between winners and losers. The cycle of pregnancy and lactation alone would have excluded women from the process of pacification, but a masculine military ideology also played a part (Stiehm 1989; Enloe 1993). Collins et al. (1993) describe the tendency of all-male groups to become solidary around a masculine erotic identity. Sexual politics leads to separate male and female spheres, a dual status system, and the gendering of production. All-male groups still tend to harbor a sexually aggressive culture as in competitive athletics, gang violence, fraternity carousing, and military institutions.

Ethnocentrism stems from functional relations that reflect group interests. Long-term relationships of social inequality are marked by one pivotal factor: one group has a vested interest in preserving the distribution of resources that the relationship brings (Jackman 1994). The conflict of gender interests that begins with reproduction tends to spread into daily life. When ascribed statuses like sex and race are used as axes of social organization, the phenotypic markers and social warp and woof they provide makes for effective social control (Hechter 1987: 186). Male control of decision making enabled them to regulate marriage, inheritance, and property rights such that these institutions embody the self-interest of elite males. For nonelite males, service as warriors instills loyalty to comrades because it maximizes chances of survival on the battlefield. To offset the chances of early death, universal conscription was a carrot that offered full rights to all who served; the idea took root that only armed males had rights of full citizenship (Keegan 1996: 233). Military service infused the modern concept of citizenship from its beginnings (Kerber 1998: 236).

In plow regimes, political and military leadership were linked until inventions like that of the printing press in 1450 eventuated in nation-states with the means and will to require universal education. Military success has become a much less effective stepping stone to high office in the Western democracies. Separation of the entry tracks to leadership in war and politics was a result of new forms of governance made possible and (one hopes) inevitable by a rise in literacy that enabled a better-informed public to figure out what political leaders were really up to and, if needed, to raise enough commotion to encourage leaders to head in another direction. Political success is not based on size, strength, and aggressive proclivities. Larger and stronger males do not necessarily dominate shorter and weaker ones, nor do younger men dominate older ones. Political skills depend much more on other attributes. Human dominance derives from talents like competence, nurturance, flattery, and deception (Maccoby and Jacklin 1974: 274).

Conclusion

After the invention of agriculture, a nearly continuous period of pregnancy and lactation led to women's subordination worldwide. The virtual abandonment of the practice of natural fertility made possible by modern medicine after the 1880s has affected a wide variety of behaviors. During the twentieth century, reduced fertility and scheduled infant feeding have enabled many women to enter the public arena. Thus, modern women will likely press for greater social equality. Scientists will likely seek ways to avoid the exposure of human reproductive tissues to estrogenic hormones. And parents will likely try to compensate infants, born in effect three months early, for the loss of constant human contact and a food supply available on demand.

References

Altmann, S. 1998. *Foraging for Survival: Yearling Baboons in Africa*. Chicago: University of Chicago Press.
Andreski, S. 1968. *Military Organization and Society*. Berkeley: University of California Press.

Bloch, M. 1961. *Feudal Society*. Chicago: University of Chicago Press.
Boehm, C. 1999. *Hierarchy in the Forest: The Evolution of Egalitarian Behavior*. Cambridge, MA: Harvard University Press.
Boserup, E. 1965. *The Conditions of Agricultural Growth*. Chicago: Aldine.
———. 1970. *Women's Role in Economic Development*. London: St. Martin's Press.
Boswell, J. 1988. *The Kindness of Strangers*. Harmondsworth, UK: Penguin.
Braudel, F. 1979. *The Structures of Everyday Life*. Edited and translated by S. Reynolds. New York: Harper and Row.
Butz, W. 1977. *Economic Aspects of Breastfeeding*. Santa Monica, CA: Rand.
Cavalli-Sforza, L. L. 2000. *Genes, Peoples, and Languages*. Translated by M. Seielsted. New York: North Point Press.
Chafetz, J. 1984. *Sex and Advantage*. Totowa, NJ: Rowman and Allenheld.
Childe, G. 1951. *Man Makes Himself*. New York: Mentor.
Cohen, M. 1977. *The Food Crisis in Prehistory*. New Haven, CT: Yale University Press.
———. 1984. "Introduction." In *Paleopathology and the Origins of Agriculture*, edited by M. Cohen and G. Armelagos, 1–22. New York: Academic.
———. 1989. *Health and the Rise of Civilization*. New Haven, CT: Yale University Press.
Collins, R., J. Chafetz, R. Blumberg, S. Coltrane, and J. Turner. 1993. "Toward an Integrated Theory of Gender Stratification." *Sociological Perspectives* 36: 185–216.
Crews, D. 2003. *Human Senescence*. New York: Cambridge University Press.
Crews, D., and L. M. Gerber. 1994. "Chronic Degenerative Diseases and Agriculture." In *Biological Anthropology and Agriculture*, edited by D. Crews and R. M. Garruto, 154–181. New York: Oxford University Press.
Da Vanzo, J. 1988. "Infant Mortality and Socioeconomic Development." *Demography* 25: 581–595.
Davie, M. 1929. *The Evolution of War*. New Haven, CT: Yale University Press.
Davis, K., and J. Blake. 1956. "Social Structure and Fertility." *Economic Development and Cultural Change* 4: 211–235.
de Waal, F. 2001. "Bonobos and Human Social Evolution." In *Tree of Origin*, edited by F. de Waal, 1–17. Cambridge, MA: Harvard University Press.
Dunbar, R. 1996. *Gossip, Grooming, and the Evolution of Language*. Cambridge, MA: Harvard University Press.
Dyson-Hudson, R., and N. Dyson-Hudson. 1980. "Nomadic Pastoralists." *Annual Review of Anthropology* 9: 15–61.
Earle, T. 1997. *How Chiefs Come to Power*. Palo Alto, CA: Stanford University Press.
Eaton, B., S. B. Eaton, and M. Konner. 1999. "Paleolithic Nutrition Revisited." In *Evolutionary Medicine*, edited by W. Trevathan, E. O. Smith, and J. McKenna, 313–332. New York: Oxford University Press.
Economist. 2012. "Female Genital Mutilation." July 27–August 2, 52.
El Saadawi, N. 1982. *The Hidden Face of Eve: Women in the Arab World*. Boston: Beacon.
Ellison, P. 1995. "Breastfeeding, Fertility, and Maternal Condition." In *Breastfeeding: Biocultural Perspectives*, edited by P. Stuart-Macadam and K. Dettwyler, 305–345. New York: Aldine de Gruyter.
———. 1999. "Reproductive Ecology and Reproductive Cancers." In *Hormones, Health, and Behavior*, edited by C. Panter-Brick and C. Worthman, 184–209. New York: Cambridge University Press.
Enloe, C. 1993. *The Morning After*. Berkeley: University of California Press.
Falk, D. 1997. "Brain Evolution in Females: An Answer to Mr. Lovejoy." In *Women in Evolution*, edited by L. Hager, 114–136. London: Routledge.
Fildes, V. 1986. *Breasts, Bottles, and Babies*. Edinburgh: Edinburgh University Press.
———. 1988. *Wet Nursing: A History from Antiquity to the Present*. Oxford: Blackwell.
Friedl, E. 1975. *Women and Men: An Anthropologist's View*. New York: Holt, Rinehart and Winston.
Garden, M. 1975. *Lyon et les Lyonnais au XVIII Siecle*. Paris: Flammarion.
Giosa, R. 1955. "Incidence of Pregnancy during Lactation in 500 Cases." *American Journal of Obstetrics and Gynecology* 70: 162–174.
Golden, J. 2001. *A Social History of Wet Nursing in America*. Columbus: Ohio State University Press.
Goldstein, J. 2001. *War and Gender*. New York: Cambridge University Press.
Goody, J. 1976. *Production and Reproduction*. Cambridge: Cambridge University Press.
———. 1983. *The Development of Family and Marriage in Europe*. Cambridge: Cambridge University Press.
Goody, J., and S. Tambiah. 1973. *Bridewealth and Dowry*. Cambridge: Cambridge University Press.
Gottlieb, G. 1998. "Normally Occurring Environmental and Behavioral Influences on Gene Activity: From Central Dogma to Probabilistic Epigenesis." *Psychological Review* 105: 792–802.
Gould, S. J. 1996. *Full House*. New York: Harmony.
Gray, S. 1999. "Infant Care and Feeding." In *Turkana Herders of the Dry Savanna*, edited by M. Little and P. Leslie, 166–186. New York: Oxford University Press.
Haaga, J. 1988. "Reliability of Retrospective Survey Data." *Demography* 25: 307–314.
Hastrup, K. 1985. *Medieval Iceland*. Oxford: Clarendon.
Heather, P. 1996. *The Goths*. Cambridge: Blackwell.

Hechter, M. 1987. *Principles of Group Solidarity*. Berkeley: University of California Press.
Henry, L. 1961. "Some Data on Natural Fertility." *Eugenics Quarterly* 8: 81–91.
Herskovits, M. 1938. *Dahomey II*. New York: Northwestern University Press.
Hobcraft, J. 1994. "Why Can't Demographers and Physiologists Agree?" In *Human Reproductive Ecology*, edited by K. Campbell and J. Wood, 408–415. New York: New York Academy of Science.
Hobhouse, L., G. Wheeler, and M. Ginsberg. 1930. *Material Culture and Social Institutions of the Simpler Peoples*. London: Routledge and Kegan Paul.
Howell, N. 1979. *Demography of the Dobe !Kung*. New York: Academic.
Hrdy, S. B. 1999. *Mother Nature: A History of Mothers, Infants, and Natural Selection*. New York: Pantheon.
———. 2011. *Mothers and Others: The Evolutionary Origins of Mutual Understanding*. Cambridge, MA: Belknap Press of Harvard University Press.
Huber, J. 1990. "Macro-Micro Links in Gender Stratification." *American Sociological Review* 55: 1–10.
———. 2007. *On the Origins of Gender Inequality*. Boulder, CO: Paradigm Publishers.
Huber, J., and G. Spitze. 1983. *Gender Stratification: Children, Housework, and Jobs*. New York: Academic.
Jablonski, N. 2006. *Skin: A Natural History*. Berkeley: University of California Press.
Jackman, M. 1994. *The Velvet Glove*. Berkeley: University of California Press.
Jackson, R. M. 1998. *Destined for Equality*. Cambridge, MA: Harvard University Press.
Janson, C. 1992. "Evolutionary Ecology of Primate Social Structure." In *Evolutionary Ecology and Human Behavior*, edited by E. A. Smith and B. Winterhalder, 95–130. New York: Aldine de Gruyter.
Jelliffe, D., and P. Jelliffe. 1978. "Volume and Composition of Milk in Poorly Nourished Communities." *American Journal of Clinical Nutrition* 31: 492–515.
Johnson, A., and T. Earle. 1987. *The Evolution of Human Societies*. Palo Alto, CA: Stanford University Press.
Jolly, A. 1999. *Lucy's Legacy*. Cambridge, MA: Harvard University Press.
Keegan, J. 1987. *The Mask of Command*. London: Jonathan Cape.
———. 1996. *The Battle for History: Refighting World War II*. New York: Vintage.
Kerber, L. 1998. *No Constitutional Right to Be Ladies*. New York: Hill and Wang.
Kertzer, D. 1993. *Sacrificed for Honor*. Boston: Beacon.
Lancaster, J. 1975. *Primate Behavior and the Emergence of Human Culture*. New York: Holt, Rinehart and Winston.
———. 1985. "Evolutionary Perspectives on Sex Differences in the Higher Primates." In *Gender and the Life Course*, edited by A. Rossi, 3–27. New York: Aldine de Gruyter.
———. 1991. "A Feminist and Evolutionary Biologist Looks at Women." *Yearbook of Physical Anthropology* 34: 1–11.
Lancaster, J., and C. Lancaster. 1983. "Parental Investment: The Hominid Adaptation." In *How Humans Adapt*, edited by D. Ortner, 33–65. Washington, DC: Smithsonian.
Larsen, C. 2000. *Skeletons in Our Closet*. Princeton, NJ: Princeton University Press.
Lawrence, R., and R. Lawrence. 1994. *Breastfeeding*. 4th ed. St. Louis, MO: Mosby.
———. 1999. *Breastfeeding*. 5th ed. St. Louis, MO: Mosby.
LeBlanc, S. 1999. *Prehistoric War in the American Southwest*. Salt Lake City: University of Utah Press.
Lenski, G. 1970. *Human Societies*. New York: McGraw-Hill.
Lenski, G., and J. Lenski. 1978. *Human Societies*. 3rd ed. New York: McGraw-Hill.
Leridon, H., and J. Menken, eds. 1977. *Natural Fertility*. Liege, Belgium: Ordina.
Levy, H. 1966. *Chinese Footbinding*. New York: Walton Rawls.
Lorimer, F., ed. 1954. *Culture and Human Fertility*. Paris: UNESCO.
Low, B., A. Clarke, and K. Lockridge. 1992. "Toward an Ecological Demography." *Population and Development Review* 18: 1–31.
Maccoby, E. 1998. *The Two Sexes*. Cambridge, MA: Belknap Press of Harvard University Press.
Maccoby, E., and C. Jacklin. 1974. *The Psychology of Sex Differences*. Palo Alto, CA: Stanford University Press.
Maryanski, A., and J. Turner. 1992. *The Social Cage: Human Nature and the Evolution of Society*. Palo Alto, CA: Stanford University Press.
Maynard Smith, J. 1989. *Did Darwin Get It Right: Essays on Games, Sex, and Evolution*. New York: Chapman and Hall.
Mazur, A., and A. Booth. 1998. "Testosterone and Dominance in Men." *Behavioral and Brain Sciences* 21: 353–363.
McKeown, T. 1976. *The Role of Medicine*. London: Provincial Hospitals Trust.
Micozzi, M. 1995. "Breast Cancer, Reproductive Biology, and Breastfeeding." In *Breastfeeding: Biocultural Perspectives*, edited by P. Stuart-Macadam and K. Dettwyler, 347–384. New York: Aldine de Gruyter.
Nesse, R., and G. Williams. 1994. *Why We Get Sick*. New York: Vintage.
Netting, R. 1993. *Smallholders, Householders*. Palo Alto, CA: Stanford University Press.
Oppenheimer, V. K. 1973. "Demographic Influence on Female Employment and the Status of Women." *American Journal of Sociology* 78: 946–961.

Otterbein, K. 1999. "A History of Research on Warfare in Anthropology." *American Anthropologist* 101: 794–805.
Page, H., and R. Lesthaeghe. 1981. "Preface." In *Child-Spacing in Tropical Africa*, edited by H. Page and R. Lesthaeghe, ix–x. London: Academic.
Panter-Brick, C. 1992. "Working Mothers in Rural Nepal." In *The Anthropology of Breastfeeding*, edited by V. Maher, 133–150. Oxford: Berg.
Potts, M., and R. Short. 1999. *Ever since Adam and Eve: The Evolution of Human Sexuality*. Cambridge: Cambridge University Press.
Preston, S., and M. Haines. 1991. *Fatal Years*. Princeton, NJ: Princeton University Press.
Pryor, F. 1985. "The Invention of the Plow." *Comparative Studies in History and Society* 27: 727–743.
Quinn, N. 1977. "Anthropological Studies of Women's Status." *Annual Review of Anthropology* 6: 181–225.
Rippeyoung, P., and M. Noonan. 2012. "Is Breastfeeding Truly Cost Free? Income Consequences of Breastfeeding." *American Sociological Review* 77: 244–267.
Rowell, T. 1972. *The Social Behavior of Monkeys*. New York: Penguin.
Ruhlen, M. 1994. *The Origin of Language*. New York: Wiley.
Scheper-Hughes, N. 1992. *Death without Weeping*. Berkeley: University of California Press.
Seltzer, J., and S. Bianchi. 2013. "Demographic Change and Parent-Child Relationships in Adulthood." *Annual Review of Sociology* 39: 275–290.
Shipton, P. 1994. "Land and Culture in Tropical Africa." *Annual Review of Anthropology* 23: 347–377.
Small, M. 1998. *Our Babies, Ourselves*. New York: Doubleday-Anchor.
Smuts, B. 1985. *Sex and Friendship in Baboons*. New York: Aldine de Gruyter.
Stein, D. 1978. "Suttee as a Normative Institution." *SIGNS* 4: 253–268.
Stiehm, J. 1989. *Arms and the Enlisted Woman*. Philadelphia: Temple University Press.
Stini, W. 1985. "Growth Rates and Sexual Dimorphism: An Evolutionary Perspective on Prehistoric Diets." In *The Analysis of Prehistoric Diets*, edited by R. Gilbert and J. Mielke, 191–226. Orlando, FL: Academic.
Stuart-Macadam, P. 1995. "Biocultural Perspectives on Breastfeeding." In *Breastfeeding*, edited by P. Stuart-Macadam and K. Dettwyler, 1–37. New York: Aldine de Gruyter.
———. 1998. "Iron Deficiency Anemia." In *Sex and Gender in Pathological Perspective*, edited by A. Grauer and P. Stuart-Macadam, 45–63. Cambridge: Cambridge University Press.
Tanner, N. M. 1981. *On Becoming Human*. Cambridge: Cambridge University Press.
Testart, A. 1988. "Major Problems in the Social Anthropology of Hunter-Gatherers." *Current Anthropology* 29: 1–31.
Trevathan, W. 1987. *Human Birth: An Evolutionary Perspective*. Hawthorne, NY: Aldine de Gruyter.
———. 1999. "Evolutionary Obstetrics." In *Evolutionary Medicine*, edited by W. Trevathan, E. O. Smith, and J. McKenna, 183–207. New York: Oxford University Press.
Turner, J., and A. Maryanski. 2005. *Incest: Origins of the Taboo*. Boulder, CO: Paradigm Publishers.
Turney-High, H. 1949. *Primitive War*. New York: Columbia University Press.
Udry, R. 2000. "Biological Limits of Gender Construction." *American Sociological Review* 65: 443–457.
Vallegia, C., and P. Ellison. 2003. "Energetics, Fecundity, and Human Life History." In *The Biodemography of Human Reproduction and Fertility*, edited by J. L. Rogers and H.-P. Kohler, 87–103. Boston: Kluwer.
Vitzthum, V. 1997. "Adaptation in Human Reproduction." In *The Evolving Female*, edited by A. Galloway, M. E. Morbeck, and A. Zihlman, 242–258. Princeton, NJ: Princeton University Press.
Whitten, P. 1999. "Diet, Hormones, and Health." In *Hormones, Health, and Behavior*, edited by C. Panter-Brick and C. Worthman, 210–243. Cambridge: Cambridge University Press.
Wikipedia. 2014. "Chinese Footbinding." Last modified September 22.
Wiley, A., and I. Pike. 1998. "An Alternative Way to Assess Early Mortality in Contemporary Populations." *American Journal of Physical Anthropology* 107: 315–330.
Wilson, E. O. 1996. *In Search of Nature*. Washington, DC: Island Press.
Wolf, J. 2001. *Public Health and the Decline of Breastfeeding*. Columbus: Ohio State University Press.
Wood, J. W. 1990. "Fertility in Anthropological Populations." *Annual Review of Anthropology* 19: 211–242.
———. 1994. *Dynamics of Human Reproduction: Biology, Biometry, Demography*. Hawthorne, NY: Aldine de Gruyter.
Wright, Q. 1942. *A Study of War*. Chicago: University of Chicago Press.
Xie, Y. 1990. "What Is Natural Fertility? The Remodeling of a Concept." *Population Index* 56: 656–663.
Zihlman, A. 1978. "Subsistence and Social Organization in Early Hominids." *SIGNS* 4: 4–9.

Chapter Twenty-One

The Evolution of Tenuous Pair Bonding in Humans

A Plausible Pathway and Indicators of Design

Timothy Crippen

> Pair bonding stands as the principal reproductive strategy adopted by humans and, among other things, underlies relationships, such as households, that are central to the human social condition. And yet, as fundamental as the strategy may be, the durability of specific pair bonds often is extraordinarily fragile. The key goals of this chapter are to explore the evolutionary bases of the pair bonding inclination in humans, primarily by contrasting competing hypotheses that focus either on parental collaboration or on male mating effort and mate guarding as crucial selection pressures governing its emergence and persistence; to explore some of the evidence regarding aspects of human anatomy and physiology suggesting that, as organisms, we are "built to bond"; and to consider why, despite the fact that pair bonding is such a crucial and persistent feature of human social life, the pair bond itself is all too often a tenuous social tie.

Introduction

Few, if any, relationships are as central to the human condition as is the pair bond. The benefits of these cooperative relationships between men and women are many. Among other things, they enable the parties to establish households; to produce joint goods; to satisfy deep-seated urges for companionship and sexual release; and to produce and, to some degree, jointly rear offspring. And yet, despite these and other payoffs, such pair bonds are often riddled with tensions and conflicts that may result in their dissolution.

These facts bespeak a curious irony. How can it be that the pair bond, on the one hand, is so central to the organization of human social existence while, on the other, reveals itself to be a relationship that may be ever so fragile and tenuous? Answers to this question, I shall argue, only begin to reveal themselves when the matter is approached in an explicitly evolutionary key. Such an approach has generally been alien to sociological inquiries on topics such as human mating, household relations, and the family. And yet, as I hope to demonstrate, such an approach contributes substantially to our ability to understand these fundamental aspects of human social relations. Thus, my goal in this chapter is to explore the evolutionary bases of the pair bonding inclination in humans, to review some of the evidence pointing to aspects of human anatomy and physiology suggesting that we are "designed" to bond, and to assess, at least briefly, why, despite the fact that pair bonding is a crucial and universal feature of human social life, the pair bond itself is all too often a tenuous social tie.

Some Preliminary Considerations

A focus on patterns of human pair bonding may begin with awareness of a few facts of capital significance. To start, as an animal behavioral strategy, pair bonding is a rather rare phenomenon. Though exhibited with fairly high rates of occurrence in various species of birds, it is estimated that perhaps no more than 3–4 percent of mammalian species feature the trait (see Alexander 1974; Kleiman 1977; Reichard and Boesch 2003). And, as we shall see, this rarity extends to our nearest evolutionary cousins.

Second, even in species where pair bonding is present, the behavioral strategy never reveals itself in the form of strict, unfailingly durable monogamous relations between adult males and females going about the business of satisfying their sustenance needs and rearing joint offspring. Instead, the strategy is considerably more flexible, frequently bound up with instances of cheating and desertion. Extra-pair copulations are not uncommon; nor is it unusual for specific pair bonds to dissolve, only to find the separated individuals establishing unions with new partners.

Third, my focus on pair bonding is intended to direct attention toward a fundamental and persistent quality of the human condition. For this reason, it bears stressing that the discussion is not about patterns of marriage per se. Where marriage practices are institutionalized and, in some cases, legally binding, they vary considerably, and these variations certainly reveal the profoundly cultural aspects of marital institutions. One finds, for instance, all manner of sanctioned "marital relations" across a diverse range of human societies, relations that, among other things, govern the determination of offspring legitimacy and patterns of property inheritance. Monogamous unions, polygynous unions, polyandrous unions, and even same-sex unions may be observed in the ethnographic, historical, and contemporary record. And yet, underlying this vast landscape of surface variations, and even where marriage as a formal institution is absent, we invariably find that "men and women form enduring *pair-bonds*" (Chapais 2008: 160; emphasis in original) and that these unions represent the predominant reproductive strategy adopted by humans across time and space. It is this enduring and recurrent aspect of human mating behavior on which I wish to focus attention. Thus, I shall dispense with a needlessly lengthy discussion of the distinction between pair bonding (the behavioral universal) and marriage practices (the cultural variable).

Fourth, and lastly as a starting point, where pair bonding exists, it is a behavioral strategy deeply rooted in a species' evolutionary development. This historical legacy is no less true for humans than it is for any other species. For this reason, among others, it is wise to be attentive to what Frans de Waal (2005) has so tantalizingly described as "our inner ape." However much we may wistfully think otherwise, we are reasonably large, tailless, though not excessively hairy primates. We are apes. As such, we share a lengthy evolutionary history with gibbons, orangutans, gorillas, and chimpanzees. To be sure, we are in various ways a most unusual ape. Our big brains and associated cultural capacities, for example, are clearly atypical. But, of greater relevance to the discussion at hand is the fact that, in contrast to the other lesser and great apes, humans exhibit crucial differences with respect to species-typical mating strategies.

In assessing the nature of and variations in animal mating behavior, evolutionary biologists in recent decades have focused attention especially on the ecological demands imposed on an organism's ability to optimize its inclusive fitness. These considerations regarding the ecological constraints on male and female reproductive potential yield a suggestive hypothesis regarding the manner in which the sexes deploy themselves throughout their environment; how this deployment is conditioned by the distribution of resources; and how, taken together, these factors affect variations in general mating strategies. The hypothesis forms the bedrock of contemporary socioecology, a growing body of principles and evidence that offers keen insights into the selection pressures governing animal (including human) social behavior (e.g., Clutton-Brock and Harvey 1977; Smith and Winterhalder 1992; Low 2000).

This socioecological hypothesis, consistent with the theory of relative parental investment (Trivers 1972), predicts that females, whose reproductive interests are so keenly tied to the availability of crucial sustenance resources, distribute themselves throughout their environment primarily to optimize foraging efficiency and to minimize predatory threats. Satisfying sustenance needs for themselves and their offspring and avoiding the risk that they and their progeny may be converted into another's meal are viewed as the chief mechanisms governing the spatial distribution of females in a population. By contrast, males distribute themselves primarily in accordance with the availability of their most crucial reproductive resource, namely, the spatial distribution of females.

Without going into great detail, and thus diverting attention from my principal focus, observations of the behavior of gibbons, orangutans, mountain gorillas, and chimpanzees (both common chimpanzees and bonobos) suggest that variations in habitat, resource availability, and sexual selection pressures have given rise to variations in species-typical mating strategies (see Table 21.1). Spatially isolated monogamous pair bonds among the gibbons; territorially solitary female and male orangutans, with the latter striving to monopolize sexual access to several of the former; multi-female harems of silverback male mountain gorillas; and sexually promiscuous multi-male/multi-female groups of common chimpanzees and bonobos are strategies that have been well documented by primatologists.

The cross-specific evidence suggests that we should be equally attentive to the manner in which ecological pressures influence the mating strategies exhibited by men and women. Furthermore, it encourages us to consider the environmental constraints most likely encountered by our human and prehuman ancestors. For it was in these ancestral environments that our species' basic behavioral traits, including our inclination to enter into pair bonds, were forged and fine-tuned.

A Plausible Evolutionary Pathway

The extensive literature on primate socioecology is fascinating and perhaps should be required reading for all serious students of human social behavior. But of more immediate relevance for my purposes is the extent to which these comparative considerations may help us to understand the emergence and persistence of pair bonding as the principal reproductive strategy in humans. More specifically, the fact that we are phylogenetically most closely related to common chimpanzees and bonobos and that we last shared a common ancestor with them some 5 million to 7 million years ago suggests that we emerged from a line of descent in which our ancestors, too, lived in multi-male/multi-female groups that featured a fair degree of promiscuity—the infamous "primitive horde" that so fascinated scholars as diverse as C. Darwin, F. Engels, L. H. Morgan, and S. Freud (see also Turner and Maryanski 2005). And so, one may reasonably ask: How is it that our species' behavior eventually evolved to a point where generalized promiscuity was replaced with generalized pair bonding? How and why, over the course of our ancestral

The Evolution of Tenuous Pair Bonding in Humans

Table 21.1 Select aspects of the socioecology and mating strategies of the lesser and great apes

Species	Geographic location	Habitat and food resources	Spatial distribution	Predominant mating strategy	Sources
Gibbons (several distinct species)	South and Southeast Asia	Upper canopy of rainforests; subsisting on diet of plentiful and widely dispersed fruits and leaves	Wide dispersion of isolated females in keeping with distribution of food resources, attended by single males	Long-lasting pair bonds between adult males and females	Leighton (1986)
Orangutans (*Pongo pygmaeus* and *Pongo abelii*)	Borneo and Sumatra	Midcanopy level of rainforests; subsisting on diet of plentiful and widely dispersed fruits and leaves	Wide dispersion of isolated females (often accompanied by a maturing offspring) in keeping with distribution of food resources; some males striving to maintain a territory incorporating several females; other males roaming widely with no fixed territory	Polygynous territorial males striving to monopolize sexual access to females within their range; roaming males striving for opportunistic matings; females adopting a generally promiscuous strategy	Rodman and Mitani (1986)
Mountain gorillas (*Gorilla beringei beringei*)	Central Africa	Ground dwellers subsisting on diet of plentiful roots, stems, leaves, and fruit	Small groups of unrelated adult females forming the "harem" of a dominant adult male	Polygyny	Schaller (1963); Fossey (1983); Stewart and Harcourt (1986)
Chimpanzees (*Pan troglodyte* and *Pan paniscus*)	East, Central, and West Africa, north of Zaire River (*P. troglodyte*); Central Africa, south of Zaire River (*P. paniscus*)	Ground dwellers subsisting on diet of plentiful but dispersed fruit and vegetation; some meat resources	Variable size groups (approx. 20–120) of related males and unrelated females	Promiscuity (though, in *P. troglodyte*, dominant males strive to monopolize sexual access to estrus female)	de Waal (1982, 2005); Goodall (1986); Nishida and Hiraiwa-Hasegawa (1986); de Waal and Lanting (1997)

heritage, did the human species-typical mating strategy diverge from that pursued by our nearest ape cousins?

The answer to this question has yet to be determined with any degree of certainty. Indeed, the evolutionary bases of human pair bonding are shrouded in some mystery. Although it stands as the principal reproductive strategy evident across all known human societies, the debate about its origin and development remains unsettled. Nevertheless, this debate focuses attention on several crucial issues. Therefore, it is worth reviewing, at least in its main outlines.

Competing Explanations of the Emergence of Human Pair Bonding

Explanations of the evolution of human pair bonding generally may be grouped into two broad classes—those that emphasize pair bonding as a *parenting strategy* and those that view it primarily as a *mating strategy* (my discussion of these competing viewpoints closely follows assessments offered by Hawkes [2004] and Chapais [2008]; interested readers are urged to consult their insightful accounts). In a manner that flows directly from C. Darwin's ([1871] 1981) theory of sexual selection and R. L. Trivers's (1972) more refined theory of relative parental investment (for detailed discussion of these two theoretical principles, see Lopreato and Crippen 1999: 96–99, 112–116), the starting point here is that in its pursuit of reproductive success, an organism invests time, energy, and resources in some combination of mating effort and parenting effort. Among sexually reproducing species, acquiring mating opportunities is obviously fundamental, though it is generally males who invest greater effort in this quest in contrast to females. For the latter, obtaining mating opportunities is rarely a critical difficulty, whereas for the former, attracting prospective female mates and oftentimes competing vigorously against other males for such access pose a much greater hurdle to overcome. By contrast, females typically invest much more in parenting effort. Indeed, for nearly all mammalian species, females monopolize parenting effort via pregnancy, lactation, and nursing, and nurturing offspring until the latter are equipped to venture off on their own. Mammalian males, by contrast, typically invest few, if any, resources in the care and sustenance of their offspring.

Consider the cases of our near evolutionary cousins briefly alluded to above. In nearly all cases, males compete extensively for access to female mates, while females are primarily responsible for the care and provisioning of their offspring. The diverse mating strategies adopted by gibbons, orangutans, mountain gorillas, and chimpanzees appear to derive from a complex of circumstances primarily revolving around the female quest to obtain adequate food resources, protection from predation, and "good genes" from a male mate and around the male quest to obtain mating opportunities and, where necessary, to guard their mates against encroachment by potential male rivals. In short, male mating effort and, where ecologically necessary, mate guarding in the service of enhancing male reproductive success seem to underlie and largely explain the general patterns of monogamy (in gibbons), polygyny (in mountain gorillas and orangutans), and promiscuity (in common chimpanzees and bonobos) briefly noted in Table 21.1.

The Parental Collaboration Hypothesis

Despite this focus on male mating effort as perhaps the chief means by which primatologists strive to grasp variations in mating strategies among their subjects, for many decades analysts of human pair bonding have sought to explain its origins and development primarily in terms of male parenting effort, or as a mechanism of parental collaboration between mated males and females. Dating back at least to E. Westermarck's (1891) famous treatise, *The History of Human Marriage*, K. Hawkes (2004) refers to this approach as the "hunting hypothesis" that implicates a suite of adaptations presumably accounting for the emergence of the human bonding strategy. Simply put, the argument suggests that ancestral women, limited in mobility due to the demands of pregnancy, nursing, and tending to relatively helpless infants and small children, traded exclusive sexual access and the associated prospect of enhanced paternal confidence to ancestral men for food (especially meat) and for protection against predatory threats. The exchange is neatly encapsulated by reference to what H. Fisher (1982) has described as "the sex contract."

Most recently elaborated in some detail by C. O. Lovejoy (1981, 2009; see also Fisher 1982, 1992), the parental collaboration argument focuses primarily on adaptations for bipedalism, increasing brain size, reduction in canine size and expansion of molar size, tool use, and concealed estrus, all of which allegedly underlie the emergence of the pair bonding strategy. On the face of it, arguments such as Lovejoy's make reasonably good sense. Climatic changes in Africa, associated with the reduction in heavy forestation and the expansion of savanna landscapes, have long been linked with the shift toward hominin bipedalism. This shift toward bipedal locomotion appears to have been well under way with the appearance of *Ardipithecus ramidus* some 4.4 million years ago (Lovejoy 2009) and seems to have become essentially fully developed some 3.5 million years ago based on evidence associated with the discovery of *Australipithicus aferensis* (announced in conjunction with the unveiling of the skeletal remains of "Lucy") and of the famous footprints fossilized in ancient volcanic ash discovered at Laetoli (Lovejoy 1981). Changes in dentition—reduced canine size and a shift toward greater molar dominance—presumably resulting from increasing reliance on terrestrial food resources and enhanced food preparation techniques (e.g., grinding and cooking) became evident with the appearance of *Homo erectus* some 2 million years ago. It is here, too, where we begin to observe evidence of the expanding brain size in the hominin line of descent and associated changes in the pelvic structure of ancestral females.

In brief, the parental collaboration thesis suggests that the evolution of human anatomical and behavioral traits between 2 million and 4 million years ago gave rise to circumstances in which female mobility and productivity were to some degree limited by the demands associated with bearing and caring for children who were unusually immature by general mammalian and primate standards. At the same time, bipedal locomotion and innovations in the manufacturing of tools enabled males to secure and transport food (especially meat) resources to females and their offspring. Such male provisioning and protection from predation seemingly was cemented by the emergence of concealed ovulation and continuous sexual receptivity in females. Given such conditions, ancestral males allegedly were inclined to offer food resources to ancestral females in exchange for exclusive sexual access to the latter. This "food for sex" exchange has thus long been viewed as the dynamic underlying the emergence and persistence of patterns of human pair bonding.

TAKING EXCEPTION TO THE PARENTAL COLLABORATION THESIS

As persuasive as the argument appears at first glance, the thesis suggesting that human pair bonding developed as a result of selection pressures favoring male parental care has been seriously challenged. One problem, emphasized by Hawkes (2004: 444), is that the crucial evolutionary steps posited (e.g., the emergence of bipedalism, the expansion of the human brain, and the emergence of tools principally employed by males for big game hunting) were separated by a few million years. The linkages proposed may well have some analytical merit; nevertheless, as B. Chapais (2008: 157) avers, they are "riddled with untested assumptions and high levels of speculation." By contrast, a more parsimonious explanation may be available, as we shall see.

Another objection voiced by Hawkes to the focus on male provisioning as the crucial selection pressure underlying the emergence of pair bonding in humans is her assertion that, among our hunter-gatherer forebears, male hunting activity likely provided only a modest caloric contribution to the forager diet. She notes that "systematic observation of the actual food consumption [among foragers] showed heavy reliance on plants—except at high latitudes where few plant foods are available" (Hawkes 2004: 444). Her remarks on this score—primarily designed to minimize the role of male provisioning to his mate and their joint offspring via *big game* hunting—unfortunately echo what very well may be an exaggerated claim made by various scholars regarding the relative productive roles of men and women generally observed in hunter-gatherer societies. In fact, the significance of meat relative to other fruit, root, and vegetable sources of caloric intake among foragers is highly variable and does depend critically on a variety of ecological factors. Latitudinal position, noted by Hawkes, is obviously one of these factors, but so too are factors such as altitude, general climatic conditions, average rainfall, the nature and distribution of flora and fauna, and so forth. Thus, the claim that foragers *generally* rely more heavily on the foods produced by the gathering activities of females—an assertion that repeatedly crops up in the professional literature and in textbooks—is little more than academic myth, and a very stubborn one at that. One of the best available analyses of a wide survey of some 180 forager societies that survived into recent centuries reveals, by contrast, that in only 23 percent of them do we find that over 50 percent of consumed calories derive from the eating of plant foods typically gathered by women (Ember 1978). In short, Hawkes's general claim regarding the minimal contribution of male hunting activity to overall food consumption among foragers is likely overstated, and it would be of great service to see it deleted from the "received wisdom" in the social sciences.

Though many of Hawkes's criticisms of the parental collaboration thesis regarding the emergence of human pair bonding are very compelling, the source of her tendency to downplay the significance of male provisioning among our distant ancestors is not difficult to trace. She is, after all, the principal architect of the "showing off hypothesis" that strives to explain male investment in *big game* hunting as a mating, in contrast to a parenting, strategy (Hawkes 1991). She argues that big game hunting is a risky enterprise with a high ratio of failure to success. Moreover, when successful, the hunter scores a load of meat that vastly exceeds what he, his mate, and their joint offspring can possibly consume before it spoils. Thus, most of these meat resources are distributed to others in the community and thereby may be construed as a public, in contrast to a private, good. So, where is the payoff to the hunter for the time, risk, and energy expended in big game hunting? The hunter frequently fails, and when he does succeed the caloric dividends do not appear to benefit him and his family any more than they do others in the community, at least according to Hawkes. In view of these considerations, she asserts that what the successful hunter gains is greater status, an enhanced reputation, that may then enable him to acquire a greater number of mates and to enjoy greater reproductive success in relation to men who are not so gifted. In short, she views big game hunting as an activity that primarily serves the mating interests of males and plays little, if any, role in male parental investment.

In his brief review of Hawkes's "showing off hypothesis," Chapais raises some important objections and argues that the weight of evidence "does not appear to support the view that male hunting is *only* a mating effort" (Chapais 2008: 167; emphasis in original). He cites evidence indicating that reciprocal exchanges of meat resources in forager societies are likely more extensive than Hawkes allows, that hunting effort (measured in terms of calories per unit of work time) is perhaps not as risky in contrast to other forms of food acquisition as Hawkes claims to be the case, and that cross-cultural analysis of forager societies reveals that, in nearly all cases, nuclear families of successful male hunters do receive considerably more of these meat resources than do others in the community. In addition to Chapais's list of criticisms, it is worth noting that not all male hunting activity is designed to secure *big game* resources, which constitutes Hawkes's special emphasis in the elaboration of her "showing off hypothesis."

None of these objections should be taken to mean that successful hunters do not receive a prestige dividend for their efforts, nor that such higher prestige may be converted into some degree of additional male reproductive success (i.e., hunting activity in the context of human forager societies may very well be a crucial aspect of male mating effort in a manner consistent with Hawkes's general thesis). Instead, the concerns expressed merely suggest that Hawkes's claim that male hunting effort cannot be construed, *even in part*, as male parenting effort is perhaps somewhat misleading.

Chapais proceeds to list additional facts regarding conditions likely found in the human ancestral environment that are in fact consistent with the parental collaboration hypothesis for the emergence of pair bonding. For example, in contrast to other primates generally and to our near ape cousins especially, the energetic costs of human mothering are quite considerable. The heavier demands on investment owe not so much to the energetic costs associated with pregnancy and lactation but to the enormous costs associated with the lengthy period of continued dependence among human offspring after they have been fully weaned. Citing evidence based on the work of H. Kaplan and his colleagues (2000), Chapais (2008: 164) notes that, among forager peoples, offspring "eat more than they gather until they reach their mid to late teens." The enormous costs of parenting in humans, relative even to our closest evolutionary cousins, certainly suggest that our ancestral mothers would have benefitted greatly from the food provisions and other forms of assistance offered by others. For this reason, at least one component of the parental collaboration hypothesis of human pair bonding is supported: "the costs of maternity are disproportionately high in our species" (Chapais 2008: 165).

Of course, these greater parenting costs did not necessarily have to be borne by our ancestral fathers. As S. B. Hrdy (2009) has emphasized, such care could have been offered by others, especially by other females in small-scale forager bands. An ancestral woman could have depended on her mother, her aunts, her nieces, her older daughters, or other adult female friends, among others, to aid in providing food, care, and comfort to her dependent young. Hrdy's point is well taken. And yet, to suggest that our ancestral mothers may have relied on the alloparental assistance of other females in the band does not necessarily diminish the possible extent to which fathers also may have contributed crucial resources in the form of food, attention, and protection.

Still, even if fathers offered assistance to their female mates and their offspring, this fact alone by no means lends definitive credence to the claim that pair bonding evolved as an adaptive strategy to promote male parental care. In short, one does not have to diminish or disregard the role of paternal (or step-paternal) care among our forager ancestors in order to challenge the thesis that such provisioning provided a crucial selection pressure on the emergence of human pair bonding. Indeed, as we shall see, there are several good reasons to suppose that male provisioning and the associated inclination to enter into pair bonds with females are much more productively viewed as by-products of selection pressures operating on male mating effort. Still, it is wise to keep in mind that male mating and male parenting investments are not necessarily so clearly distinguishable. As Chapais (2008: 167; emphasis added) notes, what the weight of cross-specific and cross-cultural "evidence suggests is *not* that hunting has *nothing* to do with male mating effort . . . but that it may *also* be a parental effort."

What, then, is one to make of the claims that human pair bonding grew out of selection pressures associated with the necessity for paternal provisioning of increasingly dependent offspring? As summarized by Chapais (2008: 168), two key pillars of the argument do appear to have considerable empirical support—(1) comparatively speaking, human children do require considerable parental investment in order to survive to reproductive maturity, and (2) fathers, in environments approximating our species' evolutionary ancestry, may very well contribute to a reduction in these costs for mothers. Despite these concessions, he is not inclined to accept the parental collaboration thesis, and instead directs his attention toward selection pressures more directly associated with male mating effort and mate guarding as the more likely basis for the emergence and persistence of the human pair bonding strategy.

Hypotheses Emphasizing Male Mating Effort and Mate Guarding

As previously noted, our species' phylogenetic history and our close relationship with chimpanzees strongly suggest that our distant hominin ancestors lived in small communities of males and females who mated primarily in a promiscuous manner. In striving to grasp how this condition of generalized promiscuity transformed over time into generalized monogamy (or, more precisely, into generalized pair bonding), Chapais (2008: 171–179) has proposed a thought-provoking "two-step evolutionary sequence." His argument is logically consistent in structure and faithful to the empirical record, at least so far as can be determined on the basis of the current state of archaeological and ethnographic evidence. His general argument may be summarized as follows.

He begins by noting that (1) among primates and other mammals, polygyny is much more widespread than monogamy as a mating strategy; (2) among primates, one does occasionally observe multiharem structures, but nowhere do we find the multimonogamous family structure found in humans; and (3) in the vast majority of known human societies, polygyny is allowed or approved and is practiced by at least a small fraction of adult men. These facts, in Chapais's view, testify to a legacy of intense male competition for sexual access to females and hint at the very likely possibility that, among our distant ancestors, the first step away from the generalized promiscuity so clearly exhibited by our chimpanzee cousins was in the direction of multiharem groups in which a small number of adult males monopolized sexual access to several adult females.

In support of this view, he notes that where we observe "stable breeding bonds in primates and mammals, whether monogamous or polygynous" (Chapais 2008: 172), such relationships are primarily mating as opposed to parenting unions. Even in the few mammalian species where monogamy is practiced, evidence of parental collaboration is scant—direct paternal care is rarely observed. Thus, "the main function of stable breeding bonds in mammals is reproductive. More specifically, enduring breeding bonds exemplify male strategies of mate guarding" (Chapais 2008: 173).

From this starting point, and with specific reference to the socioecology of hamadryas and savanna baboons, Chapais argues that the emergence of hominin multiharem groups may have resulted from selection pressures operating on male mate competition and on the feeding and predation constraints affecting the behavior of females. In brief, where females are able to forage for food in relatively small groups, a single male may be able to offer them defense in exchange for a monopoly of sexual access (as, for example, among mountain gorillas). But, where female foraging groups are larger (for example, as a means of reducing predation risk), a single male is unable to keep other males entirely at bay. In circumstances such as those encountered by our ancestors as they began to occupy savanna in contrast to forest environments, a few males may have been able to defend and monopolize sexual access to some but not all of the females in these increasingly large groups, thus laying the foundations for the emergence of a multiharem community (as, for example, among baboons). In this setting, a relatively small number of polygynous males enter into stable breeding relations with multiple females. The condition arises out of ecological constraints that govern female foraging behavior and from the male quest to monopolize and stand guard over multiple mates. In short, the bonding strategy between an adult male and several females owes considerably to the male motive to guard mates (mating effort) in contrast to the necessity for males to provision their offspring (parenting effort).

Suppose Chapais's reasoning in this regard has merit. How, then, is the next step in the sequence achieved? How to explain the shift from multiharem groups to communities dominated by what he calls multimonogamous families?

In multiharem groups, a few males are able to monopolize access to multiple females primarily because they are able to dominate other males. Those males who are larger, stronger, and more quick-witted are better able to defend their harems in contrast to males who are not so well equipped. Within this context, Chapais then invites us to imagine the emergence of increasing equality of competitive skill among adult males. What if, for example, it was no longer the case that a few males were so easily able to lord it over the many? He asserts that, in such circumstances, it is unlikely that the harem builders would abandon the strategy of establishing stable breeding relations with females and revert to the sort of promiscuous strategy found, for example, among common chimpanzees and bonobos. Instead, faced with more effective competition from other males, such harem-building males would likely still pursue the effort to establish stable breeding relations with females. But, in view of stiffer male competition, they likely would have to be content to hoard the sexual favors of fewer mates. Hence, as competitive abilities among males become more equally distributed, so too do male mating opportunities and associated levels of reproductive success. Generalized polygyny thus slowly gives way to generalized monogamy. The polygynous inclination of males does not vanish, but the ability of a few males to successfully pursue the strategy becomes increasingly constrained by the mating desires and more equal competitive abilities of other males in the group. The polygynous structure of "multiharem groups" thus slowly gives way to the steady emergence of communities increasingly organized around the principle of monogamy. Or, as Chapais (2008: 177) so engagingly describes the outcome: "Monogamy is maximally constrained polygyny."

In considering the specific case of hominin evolution, Chapais emphasizes the crucial role that technological development may have played as the great equalizer in male mate competition. The emergence of tools fashioned from bone, stone, and wood allowed for the possibility that even a previously weak male opponent could be converted into a potentially lethal competitor.

> In such a context it should have become extremely costly for a male to monopolize several females. Only males able to monopolize tools or males forming coalitions could do so. But because all males *can* make tools and form coalitions, generalized polygyny was bound to give way to generalized monogamy. According to this reasoning, monogamy was not the end product of selective pressures favoring dyadic pair-bonding per se. It was the mere byproduct of other elements merging together over evolutionary time, namely, prior polygyny and the rise of technology. (Chapais 2008: 177; emphasis in original)

Chapais's explanation of pair bonding evolving out of male mate guarding strategies is indeed more parsimonious than alternative explanations that have been proposed to date. Additionally, it perhaps better enables us to understand why, where ecologically feasible, the human male polygynous tendency insistently asserts itself in a variety of sociocultural contexts despite the fact that our species' principal reproductive strategy revolves around generally monogamous pair bonding. And, finally, it is consistent with the fact that, in contrast to other mammals, human males do invest considerable resources in their offspring. While the alleged demand for male provisioning may not have served as a crucial selection pressure for the emergence and persistence of the human pair bonding strategy, the hominin pair bond itself may very well have "operated as a *preadaptation* for the evolution of parental collaboration" (Chapais 2008: 179; emphasis in original).

A Brief Concluding Comment on the Controversy

The debate regarding the evolutionary foundations of human pair bonding remains unsettled. Conclusive evidence in support of the arguments focusing on male parenting effort or on male mating effort has yet to be discovered and articulated. Thus, for the moment, one must concur with Chapais (2008: 172), who cautions that attempts to provide a precise answer to the question are, at best, simply informed guesswork. At the moment, we simply do not know, and we may never know, with any degree of confidence how the human pair bonding strategy emerged over the lengthy course of our species' evolution. As matters currently stand, I find myself most persuaded by those explanations that place special emphasis on patterns of male mate competition and mate guarding. And of those explanations, I find Chapais's (2008) analysis to be especially insightful, and one that he continues to elaborate in an intriguing and rather persuasive manner (Chapais 2013).

Despite the lingering mystery regarding the evolutionary bases of human pair bonding, we do know at least two crucial things relevant to the topic. First, we know that, in contrast to mammals generally and to our nearest evolutionary cousins more especially, we are the only mammalian organism that resides in multi-male/multi-female communities organized principally around mated pairs or, as described by Chapais, in communities organized largely in terms of multimonogamous family units. And, second, we know that whatever this strategy's deep evolutionary history may prove to be, we are organisms that enter this world equipped with various anatomical, physiological, and behavioral traits consonant with the pair bonding strategy. Our design features cannot be denied. And, among them, we may state with a fair degree of confidence that we are organisms that are "built to bond," *at least provisionally.*

Built to Bond: Some Relevant Indicators of Design

In support of the claim that humans by nature are inclined to forge pair bonds—however fragile and tenuous these bonds may be—three important dimensions of our species' physio-anatomical apparatus appear to be directly implicated. The first concerns the degree of sexual dimorphism observed in humans and what it may imply with respect to the male inclination to philander or to adopt polygynous mating tactics. The second involves anatomical indicators of sperm competition in our ancestral past and the extent to which these may suggest some degree of promiscuity in the mating habits of females. And the third facet concerns features of human neuroanatomy and neurophysiology that may underlie and to some degree govern our tendency to be attracted to a particular, special partner with whom we eventually may form a deep and abiding commitment, at least for some period of time. I will consider these factors sequentially.

MODEST DIMORPHISM IN HUMANS

Across a wide range of animal species we observe variation in the degree of sexual dimorphism. In some species, few differences between males and females in anatomy and physiology are observable. In still other species, vast differences in average size, weight, strength, and other physical characteristics are apparent. Significantly, there is a strong, positive correlation between the degree of sexual dimorphism and the tendency toward male polygyny. Generally speaking, greater sexual dimorphism may be viewed as an evolutionary legacy of intense competition among males for access to mating opportunities with females in which larger and physically stronger males who are successful in these contests are able to adopt a polygynous mating strategy (see, e.g., Alexander et al. 1979).

In contrast to other mammals, humans are a rather mildly dimorphic species. This fact alone would lead us to expect that human males are disposed to pursue a polygynous strategy of modest proportions. By way of comparison, consider the relevant characteristics among our near ape cousins discussed briefly above. In contrast to humans, mountain gorillas and orangutans are much more dimorphic, chimpanzees and bonobos are somewhat more dimorphic, and gibbons are less so. The respective mating strategies adopted by these species fit the correlation noted above. Male gorillas compete with each other for access to the sexual favors of several females that make up the victor's harem. Male orangutans compete vigorously for control of territories that encompass the foraging ranges of several females with whom they strive to monopolize sexual access. Male common chimpanzees aggressively compete for positions in well-defined status hierarchies in which the highest-ranking males enjoy privileged (albeit not exclusive) sexual access to estrus females who themselves are remarkably promiscuous, a situation that is different only to some degree among bonobos. By contrast, the relatively non-dimorphic gibbons form fairly long-lasting monogamous pair bonds.

Now consider the human case. By various measures—height and weight, body mass index, canine length, and femur length, among others—human males, on average, are about 10–15 percent larger than human females. This difference clearly exceeds what is observed among gibbons, but it is noticeably lower than what is found among bonobos (in which males are roughly 20 percent larger), common chimpanzees (in which males are approximately 30 percent larger), mountain gorillas (in which males are about 50 percent larger), and orangutans (in which males may be nearly twice the size of females). Given this variation in sexual dimorphism and mating strategies among the lesser and great apes, humans would be expected to display a mildly polygynous inclination.

It bears stressing that this predicted mildly polygynous reproductive strategy does not contradict the assertion that, in general, human males pursue the tactic of pair bonding with females. After all, a mildly polygynous tendency merely suggests that, within a specific population, a fairly small fraction of adult males may be expected to have multiple mates, and the number of such multiple mates would be expected to be fairly limited. Moreover, as emphasized by Chapais (2008), these polygynous unions still represent pair bonds (or relatively stable breeding relationships), and the vast majority of males in such a mildly polygynous species would be expected to participate in monogamous pair bonds.

Considerable ethnographic and historical evidence supports these expectations. Polygyny is a widely accepted practice across a diverse array of human societies (Murdock 1967; Geary 1998). And where polygyny is approved and practiced, it is a strategy that is always adopted by only a few males, males who invariably have at least somewhat higher prestige and greater access to material resources. Across human forager societies, for example, it is estimated that perhaps only 5–15 percent of adult males possess multiple wives at any given time (e.g., Shostak 1981; Lee 1984; Hewlett 1988). And these relatively few polygynous males commonly have only two or, at most, three wives. So, in societies that most closely resemble our species' ancestral condition, the male polygynous tendency is exhibited only to a modest degree, and the vast majority of males bond monogamously, if at all, at any given point in time.

Of course, in historically more recent and highly stratified societies, in which resources are more plentiful and distributed much more unequally, it is not uncommon for a very small number of rich and powerful men to monopolize sexual access to large numbers of women (e.g., Betzig 1986). Emperors, kings, and potentates often maintained large harems numbering into the scores, hundreds, or thousands of women. Thus, where ecologically feasible and socially permissible, the human male polygynous tendency has the potential to assert itself with a vengeance. And yet, even in these cases, such powerful and wealthy males typically had one special bond, one official or royal wife, which among other things sanctioned the legitimacy of heirs to the throne. Still, for the vast majority of individuals living in these large, stratified societies, marriages primarily consisted of monogamous unions.

Indicators of Sperm Competition in Humans

The fact of mild size dimorphism in humans almost certainly connects with at least a modest polygynous tendency and the associated inclination of the human male to exhibit what is sometimes called his "incessantly roving eye" and, on occasion, to philander. And yet, it bears stressing that mated females, too, cheat on their partners from time to time. Extra-pair copulation is by no means an exclusive male tactic. The facts of female promiscuity, polyandrous mating, and infidelity to their mates direct attention to the fascinating topic of sperm competition and to the physio-anatomical adaptations in males that arise from it.

Focus on this issue may be traced to the publication of G. A. Parker's (1970) pioneering work, "Sperm Competition and Its Evolutionary Consequences in Insects." Since then, the literature on the topic has grown to vast proportions and has developed along a number of distinct pathways (see, e.g., Birkhead 2010 for an exceptional review). I shall focus attention on those matters most directly relevant to the treatment of some physio-anatomical design features that are likely indicators of human mating tactics.

Still, some brief introductory comments on the topic are in order. By way of beginning, one may think of sperm competition as a form of postcopulatory sexual selection. It may occur whenever females mate with multiple males and when the sperm from multiple donors is simultaneously retained in a female's reproductive tract. Thus, the female reproductive apparatus may be viewed, at least in part, as the terrain on which sperm contributed by multiple donors do battle, as it were, to enhance the likelihood of achieving a successful fertilization.

Evidence regarding the nature of sperm competition has been gathered and analyzed for a variety of insect, amphibian, reptilian, avian, and mammalian species. In view of the great diversity of relevant traits involved in sexual activity across such a wide range of species, one can easily appreciate the considerable extent to which specific anatomical and physiological mechanisms of sperm competition may vary. Indeed, in various species in which females copulate in quick sequence with several mates, males have evolved an impressive array of reproductively relevant traits—some exceedingly clever—designed to block, remove, or otherwise overwhelm the sperm deposited by their competitors (see, e.g., Batten 1992: 106–110). This cross-specific literature is enormous and fascinating in its own right, but in its entirety not directly relevant to my immediate concerns.

More to the point, we may ask how females potentially benefit, in an ultimate evolutionary sense, from pursuing a promiscuous mating strategy. After all, at least at first glance, it does not appear that females have much to gain in terms of their fitness interests by striving for additional mating opportunities. Once her egg or eggs have been fertilized, additional matings do not confer any greater reproductive success. By contrast, the fitness interests of males may be considerably enhanced by striving to fertilize the eggs of multiple females. This fundamental sex difference in the cost/benefit calculus attending the quest for multiple mating opportunities, among other considerations, has long been linked with the portrait of the sexually eager male in contrast to the sexually coy and reserved female. At least to some degree, this basic difference in one of the more obvious dimensions of male and female reproductive interests may help explain why evolutionary biologists long ignored the phenomenon of female promiscuity or treated it merely as an inconvenient aberration (see Birkhead 2010).

In recent years, however, light has been shed on the possible fitness benefits accruing to a promiscuous sexual strategy among females across a range of sexually reproducing species. As summarized by Birkhead and Pizzari (2002: 263), direct benefits may include (1) acquiring additional resources (e.g., exchanging copulations for food), (2) securing an adequate supply of sperm (especially among certain species of insects), (3) obtaining a new and potentially better partner (especially in species featuring pair bonding), and (4) reducing the risk of male harassment directed at themselves or their offspring (by potentially confusing paternity). Additionally, some indirect benefits of female promiscuity may derive from the potential for (1) producing more genetically diverse offspring, (2) producing more attractive offspring, (3) producing more viable offspring, and (4) securing a more genetically compatible partner. In short, a promiscuous mating strategy may better enable females to secure valuable resources and "good genes" from their sexual partners, assets that may very well enhance their inclusive fitness.

With these considerations in mind, to what extent may we observe indicators of a legacy of female promiscuity and attendant sperm competition in humans? The most persuasive evidence along these lines appears to be found in the analysis of relative testis size and the related level of sperm production in human males in contrast to similar physio-anatomical characteristics in closely related species. Among our near ape cousins, males have relatively larger testes in those species (1) that copulate more frequently and (2) in which several males successively copulate with a single female. In short, the more sexually profligate the species as a whole and/or the more promiscuous its female members, males have evolved the trait of relatively larger testes and the associated capacity to produce greater quantities of sperm per ejaculate (Short 1979; Harcourt et al. 1981).

Consider, for example, the contrasting cases of mountain gorillas and common chimpanzees. Male gorillas generally weigh just over four hundred pounds and possess testes that weigh about one ounce. The considerably smaller male chimpanzee (with an average weight of about one hundred pounds) possesses testes that are nearly four times the weight of the gorilla's (about four ounces). Despite the fact that these large male mountain gorillas have several females in their harem, mating opportunities actually are quite infrequent. Female gorillas enter estrus only about every three to four years, and their period of sexual receptivity is relatively short. A few brief matings are generally all that is required to impregnate a female, thereby ending her estrus cycle and brief period of sexual receptivity. In addition, because of the social structure and spatial proximity of the harem, the dominant male generally can be reasonably assured that he enjoys exclusive sexual access to these females. Evolved patterns of social interaction and territorial distribution thus represent effective means of male mate guarding.

By contrast, chimpanzee groups are composed of a number of sexually promiscuous males and females. When a female enters estrus, dominant males strive to limit the mating opportunities of other males, but they do not always succeed. Instead, an estrus female often mates sequentially with several males. Among chimpanzees, therefore, males with larger testes capable of producing prodigious amounts of sperm have a competitive advantage over those males who are less well endowed. The delivery of greater amounts of sperm, in effect, may have the capacity to overwhelm the competition.

In view of this difference in male mate competition, male gorillas do not need large testes in order to further their reproductive interests, whereas it is advantageous for male chimpanzees to be so equipped. In keeping with the principle of resource allocation, energy that is invested in the production of testicular tissue is energy that cannot be employed for other survival and reproductive purposes. Presumably natural selection has forged physio-anatomical traits consistent with these demands. Male chimpanzees have larger testes because conspecific females mate promiscuously. Over the course of the species' evolution, males with larger testes left more descendants than did their less well-endowed competitors. By contrast, in mountain gorillas the selection pressure for larger testes was not so great or was perhaps entirely absent. Female gorillas are less promiscuous than are their chimpanzee "sisters," and dominant males are well positioned to monopolize sexual access to estrus females in their harems. Thus, allocation of energy to produce larger testes offered no reproductive advantage to the ancestors of male gorillas. Over the course of their evolutionary history, males with relatively smaller testes did quite well in terms of securing reproductive success.

What might these considerations tell us about the mating strategies of humans? Adult men on average weigh about 150 to 175 pounds, and they possess testes that weigh between one and two ounces. Thus, relative to overall body weight, their testicles are not as large as those of chimpanzees, but they are relatively larger than what is observed among mountain gorillas. This fact suggests that sexual selection favored men capable of producing amounts of sperm much greater than what is minimally required to impregnate a generally faithful female mate. The implication is that women were and most likely are, if not as promiscuous as female chimpanzees, less than the paragons of virtue as so often portrayed by the prickly proponents of Victorian morality. Men have relatively large testes because, over the course of our species' evolutionary development, their ancestors equipped with this trait left more descendants. They did so, most likely, because ancestral women were inclined to engage in intercourse with males other than those with whom they were pair bonded.

This "strength in numbers" (or "overwhelming the competition") variant of the sperm competition hypothesis—wherein a relatively modest degree of human female promiscuity served as a selection pressure favoring the evolution of modestly large testicles capable of producing modestly large quantities of sperm—strikes me as the most convincing evidence in support of the claim that ancestors to human females adopted, at least to some extent, promiscuous mating tactics.

In addition to this physio-anatomical evidence, the human male's proclivity toward expressions of sexual jealousy and related tactics of mate guarding are consistent with an evolutionary history featuring at least a modest degree of female promiscuity (see, e.g., Buss 1994). A man's emotional angst in response to evidence of or suspicions about his mate's infidelity and his attempts to limit such a threat from arising in the first place are both indicative of some degree of the promiscuous inclinations for women. These and other psychological indicators of sperm competition and the related phenomenon of cryptic female choice in humans have been reviewed and discussed in an informative manner by Shackelford, Pound, and Goetz (2005).

Before moving on to other relevant aspects of anatomical and physiological traits seemingly associated with human mating strategies, at least brief mention should be made of some rather controversial but somewhat well-publicized claims regarding evidence of sperm competition in humans. I refer to the work of R. R. Baker and M. A. Bellis (1995), who studied the phenomenon in a relatively small sample of young adult couples in Great Britain and who claim to have discovered some remarkable evidence consistent with predictions derived from sperm competition theory. For example, they claim to have found evidence of variations in sperm quantity and quality in ejaculates of males in pair bond relationships that closely track with the time spent apart from their female partners. They claim to have unearthed evidence indicating that mated females are more likely to partake of extra-pair copulations when they are at the most fertile stage of their cycle and that, when they do so, they are more likely to experience a copulatory orgasm (which, according to Baker and Bellis, functions to retain more of the male partner's sperm via what they describe as the "upsucking" action of the female cervix during climax). These and other findings reported by Baker and Bellis have met with considerable and, I think, justifiable criticism from other analysts (see, e.g., Birkhead, Moore, and Bedford 1997; Shackelford, Pound, and Goetz 2005). Despite these criticisms challenging various aspects of Baker and Bellis's methodology and interpretations, their work has enjoyed considerable attention in the popular media. Nevertheless, their reported findings should be treated with great caution.

All told, the facts of modest size dimorphism in humans and of the more well-documented aspects of human anatomy and physiology suggestive of a history of sperm competition in the human line of descent—the evidence of relative testis size and sperm production—are consistent with a species in which males and females enter into pair bonds that, at the same time, are vulnerable to some degree of cheating by one and/or the other partner. But, however much the inclination to stray and perhaps even to move on to another partner, the human animal still appears to be designed to focus its sexual and emotional attentions on that "special someone." However much we may struggle to remain faithful to our mates, however much we may be inclined to cheat, however much we may wish to throw caution to the wind and abandon a specific partner in order to establish a possibly more satisfying union, we nevertheless exhibit an incessant urge to form an attachment with another whom we consider to be the "love of our life."

NEUROANATOMICAL AND NEUROPHYSIOLOGICAL INDICATORS

We are organisms motivated by lustful enthusiasm. A member of the opposite sex attracts our attention and stimulates intense sexual desire. We seem designed to fall "head over heels" in love. And some recent research appears to have uncovered at least some of the neuroanatomical machinery that participates in these romantic inclinations. Helen Fisher (2004) and her colleagues selected male and female subjects who were deeply enmeshed in the initial stages of being in love. The subjects were scanned using functional magnetic resonance imaging to determine if specific aspects of their brains "lit up" when presented with images of the objects of their desire. Their findings indicate that aspects of the caudate nucleus and the ventral tegmental area seem to play a crucial role in governing those intense emotional responses that have so captivated the imagination of poets and musicians over the centuries. As Fisher (2004: 69–70) notes, the caudate nucleus appears to be a key brain region involved in the individual's ability to detect and to respond to rewards of different sorts. When, as organisms, we choose to pursue one reward, rather than another, and to adopt specific tactics in order to achieve that reward, the caudate nucleus apparently plays a key role in these processes. Correspondingly, the activity of the ventral tegmental area, so centrally involved in the production and distribution of dopamine, is known to be associated with a sense of focused attention and determination to achieve specific rewards.

The subjects who participated in the study conducted by Fisher and her associates, as noted above, were those who reported being in the very early stages of a romantic involvement (mean duration, seven months). As she further reports (Fisher 2004: 72–73), a separate team of London-based researchers had performed a series of similar experiments with subjects whose romantic relationships were of somewhat greater length (mean duration, 2.3 years). These researchers also found increased activity in the caudate nucleus in their subjects. In addition, they found that lovers in their sample exhibited elevated activity in the anterior cingulate cortex—a region wherein emotion, attention, and memory interact—and in the insular cortex. This evidence prompted Fisher and her colleagues to reexamine their own findings. Not surprisingly, they found that, among their subjects who were involved in longer-lasting relationships, they too exhibited heightened activity in these two regions of the brain.

These findings are intriguing and may be indicative of crucial neuroanatomical and neurophysiological traits that, to some degree, govern human mating behavior. Of course, this sort of research is still in its infancy, and the results must be treated as no more than tentative, as no more than a first approximation for grasping what certainly must be extraordinarily complex neural structures and functions that are involved in expressions of reproductively relevant human behaviors. Nevertheless, in the view of the current state of knowledge, the work of Fisher and her colleagues is impressive, and I suspect that they have identified key neurological features that participate in our tendency to focus intense romantic interest on some certain, special other and to enthusiastically pursue the potential partner.

Indeed, Fisher (2004: xii) claims that the evidence is consistent with the hypothesis suggesting that we enter this world equipped with "three primordial brain networks that evolved to direct mating and reproduction." The first of these networks allegedly participates in initial expressions of lust, the intense desire for sexual gratification that is powerfully conditioned by the action of testosterone and other androgens in both men and women (Fisher 2004: 80–83). The second network, presumably uncovered by Fisher and her colleagues in their research using functional magnetic resonance imaging technology, exerts influence over our feelings of romantic love and is intimately associated with the action of key neurotransmitters such as dopamine, norepinephrine, and serotonin. And the final network is involved in emotional expressions of deep attachment to which attention now may be turned.

We do not merely lust and develop romantic feelings for certain, specific others. We also are capable of forging abiding commitments to them. We are inclined to bond, to form partnerships that may endure over extended periods of time, sometimes even entire adult lifetimes. Intense attraction is a necessary beginning, but pair bonds are not forged until such time as attraction develops into strong emotional attachment (Bowlby 1969). And, on this score, we have some reasonably secure knowledge about the neurophysiology of attachment in species that are relatively closely related to us. Among mammalian females, for example, a key factor seems to be the action of oxytocin. Among other things, its release stimulates that most intense bonding between a mother and her newborn child.

Similarly, it seems to play a role in the process whereby females bond with male mating partners. By contrast, for mammalian males, the key "attachment hormone" appears to be vasopressin. The phenomenon has been especially well studied in the monogamous male prairie vole (*Microtus ochrogaster*) in contrast to its more promiscuous cousin, the male mountain vole (*Microtus montanus*). The former has a far more dense set of vasopressin receptors in the ventral forebrain in contrast to the latter (e.g., Insel and Carter 1995), and one team of researchers appears to have discovered a single gene that substantially governs this pair bonding preference in male prairie voles in contrast to their mountain cousins (Lim et al. 2004). In view of our shared mammalian ancestry, there is every reason to suspect that oxytocin and vasopressin receptors play potentially similar roles in the tendency of human females and males, respectively, to forge intense pair bond relationships.

The tendencies to respond to lustful impulses and eventually to form strong attachments with a member of the opposite sex underlie the human pair bonding strategy. And yet, ironically, these same inclinations also have the potential for providing the acid that may help to dissolve these partnerships as new objects of lust, romantic love, and emotional attachment present themselves. Although we may be designed to enter into pair bond relationships, we also appear to remain alert to other sexual and romantic opportunities. However content we may be, we are nevertheless creatures open to the prospect that a better bargain may be on the horizon. And, not infrequently, the mated individual finds himself or herself intensely attracted to another party. Such attractions may lead to nothing more than the occasional fling, wherein one partner takes advantage of opportunities for extra-pair copulations while maintaining the existing pair bond. But the attraction may go beyond mere dalliance; it may encourage the besotted soul to abandon his or her partner in the hope of establishing an even more rewarding pair bond with the new object of his or her desire. In short, the adaptive characteristics that underlie the human pair bonding inclination are the very same traits that may participate in the potential unraveling of these relationships.

A Few Concluding Remarks

Given the current state of knowledge, we simply do not know how humans came to rely on pair bonding as our principal reproductive strategy. Still, for reasons elaborated above, arguments that emphasize selection pressures operating on male mating effort and mate guarding seem to be the most persuasive, at least for the moment. But whatever pathway led to the reliance on this strategy, there can be little doubt that the shaping influences of that lengthy evolutionary history resulted in the installation of an array of anatomical, physiological, and behavioral traits that, taken together, incline the human organism to enter into pair bond relations, however frail and tenuous these relationships may be in practice.

As noted, there is irony in the fact that the traits that dispose humans to forge pair bonds are those that also underlie opportunistic mating strategies that may lead to the dissolution of specific unions. Just beneath the surface of our generally monogamous inclinations lurk polygynous and polyandrous tendencies of at least modest proportion ever prepared to assert themselves in a manner that may seriously threaten a given pair bond. In part, for this reason, pair bonds are inherently fragile relationships.

But the ironic qualities of pair bonding do not end there. The fragility of the pair bond, the tendency of adult males and females to establish mating relationships only to find that in so many cases these unions dissolve, points to another curious paradox of the human condition. For it is out of these potentially fragile pair bonds that a universal organizational device emerges, one that represents the social structural basis of all known human societies, the household (Murdock 1949). Wherever one looks—at the temporary huts and campsites that form the core organizational element of human forager societies; at the hearth sites that are so central to the structure of social life in horticultural villages; at the widely dispersed rude cottages of peasants and urban dwellings of craftspeople and merchants in agrarian societies; and, yes, even at the tenements, apartments, and houses of folks living in more recently developed industrial societies—one finds that the household stands as the centerpiece of all other societal structures and processes. Thus, the paradox: a fundamental source of societal durability, the household, emerges from a potentially weak and ephemeral behavioral strategy, the pair bond. It may be said, therefore, that the pair bond, in addition to serving as the principal reproductive strategy adopted by humans, can be regarded as the "fragile foundation" of human societal existence.

References

Alexander, R. D. 1974. "The Evolution of Social Behavior." *Annual Review of Ecology and Systematics* 5: 325–383.
Alexander, R. D., J. L. Hoogland, R. D. Howard, K. M. Noonan, and P. W. Sherman. 1979. "Sexual Dimorphism and Breeding Systems in Pinnipeds, Ungulates, Primates, and Humans." In *Evolutionary Biology and Human Behavior: An Anthropological Perspective*, edited by N. A. Chagnon and W. Irons, 402–435. North Scituate, MA: Duxbury Press.
Baker, R. R., and M. A. Bellis. 1995. *Human Sperm Competition: Copulation, Masturbation, and Infidelity*. London: Chapman & Hall.
Batten, M. 1992. *Sexual Strategies*. New York: G. P. Putnam's Sons.
Betzig, L. L. 1986. *Despotism and Differential Reproduction: A Darwinian View of History*. Hawthorne, NY: Aldine.
Birkhead, T. R. 2010. "How Stupid Not to Have Thought of That: Postcopulatory Sexual Selection." *Journal of Zoology* 281: 78–93.
Birkhead, T. R., H.D.M. Moore, and J. M. Bedford. 1997. "Sex, Science, and Sensationalism." *Trends in Ecology and Evolution* 12: 121–122.
Birkhead, T. R., and T. Pizzari. 2002. "Postcopulatory Sexual Selection." *Nature Reviews Genetics* 3: 262–273.
Bowlby, J. 1969. *Attachment and Loss*. Vol. 1, *Attachment*. New York: Basic Books.
Buss, D. M. 1994. *The Evolution of Desire: Strategies of Human Mating*. New York: Basic Books.
Chapais, B. 2008. *Primeval Kinship: How Pair-Bonding Gave Birth to Human Society*. Cambridge, MA: Harvard University Press.
———. 2013. "Monogamy, Strongly Bonded Groups, and the Evolution of Human Social Structure." *Evolutionary Anthropology* 22: 52–65.
Clutton-Brock, T. H., and P. H. Harvey. 1977. "Primate Ecology and Social Organization." *Journal of Zoology* 183: 1–39.
Darwin, C. (1871) 1981. *The Descent of Man and Selection in Relation to Sex*. Princeton, NJ: Princeton University Press.
de Waal, F. 1982. *Chimpanzee Politics*. New York: Harper and Row.
———. 2005. *Our Inner Ape*. New York: Riverhead Books.
de Waal, F., and F. Lanting. 1997. *Bonobo: The Forgotten Ape*. Berkeley: University of California Press.
Ember, C. R. 1978. "Myths about Hunter-Gatherers." *Ethnology* 17: 439–448.
Fisher, H. E. 1982. *The Sex Contract: The Evolution of Human Behavior*. New York: Quill.
———. 1992. *Anatomy of Love: The Natural History of Monogamy, Adultery, and Divorce*. New York: W. W. Norton and Co.
———. 2004. *Why We Love: The Nature and Chemistry of Romantic Love*. New York: Henry Holt Company.
Fossey, D. 1983. *Gorillas in the Mist*. Boston: Houghton Mifflin.
Geary, D. C. 1998. *Male, Female: The Evolution of Human Sex Differences*. Washington, DC: American Psychological Association.
Goodall, J. 1986. *Chimpanzees of Gombe*. Cambridge, MA: Harvard University Press.
Harcourt, A. H., P. H. Harvey, S. G. Larson, and R. V. Short. 1981. "Testis Weight, Body Weight, and Breeding Systems in Primates." *Nature* 293: 55–57.
Hawkes, K. 1991. "Showing Off: Tests of a Hypothesis about Men's Foraging Goals." *Ethology and Sociobiology* 12: 29–54.

———. 2004. "Mating, Parenting, and the Evolution of Human Pair Bonds." In *Kinship and Behavior in Primates*, edited by B. Chapais and C. M. Berman, 443–473. Oxford: Oxford University Press.

Hewlett, B. S. 1988. "Sexual Selection and Paternal Investment among Aka Pygmies." In *Human Reproductive Behaviour*, edited by L. Betzig, M. Borgerhoff Mulder, and P. Turke, 263–275. New York: Cambridge University Press.

Hrdy, S. B. 2009. *Mothers and Others: The Evolutionary Origins of Mutual Understanding*. Cambridge, MA: Harvard University Press.

Insel, T. R., and C. S. Carter. 1995. "The Monogamous Brain: Prairie Voles and the Chemistry of Mammalian Love." *Natural History* 104: 12–14.

Kaplan, H. S., K. R. Hill, J. B. Lancaster, and A. M. Hurtado. 2000. "A Theory of Human Life History Evolution: Diet, Intelligence, and Longevity." *Evolutionary Anthropology* 9: 156–185.

Kleiman, D. G. 1977. "Monogamy in Mammals." *Quarterly Review of Biology* 52: 39–69.

Lee, R. B. 1984. *The Dobe !Kung*. Chicago: Holt, Reinhart and Winston.

Leighton, D. R. 1986. "Gibbons: Territoriality and Monogamy." In *Primate Societies*, edited by B. B. Smuts, D. L. Cheney, R. M. Seyfarth, R. W. Wrangham, and T. T. Struhsaker, 135–145. Chicago: University of Chicago Press.

Lim, M. M., Z. Wang, D. E. Olazábal, X. Ren, E. F. Terwilliger, and L. J. Young. 2004. "Enhanced Partner Preference in a Promiscuous Species by Manipulating the Expression of a Single Gene." *Nature* 429: 754–757.

Lopreato, J., and T. Crippen. 1999. *Crisis in Sociology: The Need for Darwin*. New Brunswick, NJ: Transaction.

Lovejoy, C. O. 1981. "The Origin of Man." *Science* 211: 341–350.

———. 2009. "Reexamining Human Origins in Light of *Ardipithecus ramidus*." *Science* 326: 74e1–74e8. doi: 10.1126/science.1175834.

Low, B. S. 2000. *Why Sex Matters: A Darwinian Look at Human Behavior*. Princeton, NJ: Princeton University Press.

Murdock, G. P. 1949. *Social Structure*. New York: Free Press.

———. 1967. *Ethnographic Atlas*. Pittsburgh, PA: University of Pittsburgh Press.

Nishida, T., and M. Hiraiwa-Hasegawa. 1986. "Chimpanzees and Bonobos: Cooperative Relationships among Males." In *Primate Societies*, edited by B. B. Smuts, D. L. Cheney, R. M. Seyfarth, R. W. Wrangham, and T. T. Struhsaker, 165–177. Chicago: University of Chicago Press.

Parker, G. A. 1970. "Sperm Competition and Its Evolutionary Consequences in Insects." *Biological Reviews* 45: 525–567.

Reichard, U. H., and C. Boesch, eds. 2003. *Monogamy: Mating Strategies and Partnerships in Birds, Humans, and Other Mammals*. Cambridge: Cambridge University Press.

Rodman, P. S., and J. C. Mitani. 1986. "Orangutans: Sexual Dimorphism in a Solitary Species." In *Primate Societies*, edited by B. B. Smuts, D. L. Cheney, R. M. Seyfarth, R. W. Wrangham, and T. T. Struhsaker, 146–154. Chicago: University of Chicago Press.

Schaller, G. B. 1963. *The Mountain Gorilla: Ecology and Behavior*. Chicago: University of Chicago Press.

Shackelford, T. K., N. Pound, and A. T. Goetz. 2005. "Psychological and Physiological Adaptations to Sperm Competition in Humans." *Review of General Psychology* 9: 228–248.

Short, R. V. 1979. "Sexual Selection and Its Component Parts, Somatic and Genital Selection, as Illustrated by Man and the Great Apes." *Advances in the Study of Behavior* 9: 131–158.

Shostak, M. 1981. *Nisa: The Life and Words of a !Kung Woman*. New York: Random House.

Smith, E. A., and B. Winterhalder, eds. 1992. *Evolutionary Ecology and Human Behavior*. New York: Aldine de Gruyter.

Stewart, K. J., and A. H. Harcourt. 1986. "Gorillas: Variation in Female Relationships." In *Primate Societies*, edited by B. B. Smuts, D. L. Cheney, R. M. Seyfarth, R. W. Wrangham, and T. T. Struhsaker, 155–164. Chicago: University of Chicago Press.

Trivers, R. L. 1972. "Parental Investment and Sexual Selection." In *Sexual Selection and the Descent of Man, 1871–1971*, edited by B. H. Campbell, 136–179. Chicago: Aldine.

Turner, J., and A. Maryanski. 2005. *Incest: Origins of the Taboo*. Boulder, CO: Paradigm Publishers.

Westermarck, E. 1891. *The History of Human Marriage*. London: Macmillan.

FIVE

COOPERATION, HIERARCHY, AND SOCIAL CONTROL

Chapter Twenty-Two

The Evolution of Social Control

Christopher Boehm

> Social control is of interest to many disciplines, but its evolutionary provenance is just beginning to receive attention. Here the origin of group sanctioning is described, based on a cladistic analysis, and the role of moralistic group sanctioning of deviants is accounted for prehistorically and in contemporary hunter-gatherers. The database is composed of fifty contemporary foragers chosen to accurately represent humans as they hunted and gathered in the late Pleistocene. It is hypothesized that group punishment acted as a force of natural selection that was social, rather than environmental, and that social selection could have shaped human gene pools in two ways. One was to promote genes associated with altruism and cooperation and to suppress genes that prepared aggressive, predatory behaviors such as bullying, thievery, or cheating on a cooperative system of meat sharing. The other involved the evolution of a conscience as a means of individual self-control, which protected some deviants from being punished socially and thereby losing fitness. Quantitative data demonstrate that recent prehistoric foragers' punishments range from criticism, ostracism, and shaming to group ejection and capital punishment, while the behaviors being outlawed focused on bullying and thieving. These details provide major insights into the natural history of social control over the past 150,000 years.

Introducing Group Sanctions as Social Selection

It can be argued endlessly whether humans are socially unique in the animal kingdom, but there can be no doubt that we are at least distinctive—with our large brains, our abundant capacity for generating language in a cultural context, and our sense of morality. Here I explore the likelihood that some of this distinctiveness is the evolutionary result of unusual biocultural processes that I shall propose as instances of "social selection" (e.g., West-Eberhard 1979).

For humans, social selection involves two special effects that accrue to gene pools when people's welfare is significantly determined by group moral values. First, there is Alexander's (1987) groundbreaking idea that fitness rewards go to those with good social reputations, and second, there is the hypothesis that punishments from the group as a whole, up to and including killing a deviant, can have profound effects on gene pools (Boehm 1997, 2012b, 2013; see also Otterbein 1988).

It is the evolution of social control and its effects on our social predispositions that interest us here, and it will be proposed that such evolution could have proceeded robustly after humans became anatomically and culturally modern (e.g., Klein 1999), possibly as long ago as 150,000 BP.

Ancestral "Sanctions" and What They Led To

The primitive seeds of social control can be found in the ancient behavior of the close ancestor we share with chimpanzees and bonobos (Boehm 1999, 2012a). Chimpanzees regularly act in small male coalitions to contest unwanted alpha power, and once in a while very large coalitions are formed to attack and wound or kill, or at least exile, males whose domination is particularly disliked. Bonobos regularly form small female coalitions that on average render the smaller females politically equal to the larger males, and very rarely they too can form large coalitions that severely attack forceful males whose behavior is strongly resented (Boehm 2012a). Today's hunter-gatherers act as entire groups to kill, ostracize, shame, or otherwise socially pressure deviants, and we can take a least common denominator from these three species' behavior patterns and assert that a nonmoral version of group sanctioning was ancestrally present. It is biology's parsimony principle that allows us to reach such a phylogenetic conclusion (Wrangham 1987; see also Boehm 2012a).

Thus, Ancestral *Pan* formed political coalitions against dominant individuals in ways that at least are quite suggestive of certain more concerted efforts at group social control, as found in human foraging societies; if we wish to construct social models for what early or later humans were doing *before* 150,000 years ago, this ancestral version of "social control" must always be considered as a *minimal* candidate. Because the human brain was already quite large by 500,000 years ago, we may also assume that at that point some kind of protomorality was intensifying social control by introducing something like "moral outrage."

Deviance and social control theory may be applicable in a crude way to what apes do politically, but it was because of morality that humans' sanctioning became ethos based. It also was based on continuous communication about people's behaviors, and in fact very serious costs can be imposed on deviant individuals as humans define and discuss their social problems—and then take group action. Because modern social control can impose such severe costs, this sanctioning type of social selection was likely to have had significant effects on gene pools once we became moral (Boehm 2012b).

In contrast, selection taking place on the basis of varying individual reputations, which are based on the social preferences of group members, is likely to have been a relatively modern development because reputations are built on moralistic gossip, and gossiping requires symbols that apes never use in natural environments. The least speculative statement that can be made about prehistoric gossiping is that in all probability it was fully in effect by the time people became culturally modern, and that, because language was likely to have evolved gradually along with brain size (see Lieberman 2006), some earlier types of gossiping, reputational selection, and judgmental group sanctioning would have existed before 150,000 BP.

The evolutionary effects of human social selection will be far easier to exemplify in the case of group sanctioning than in the case of reputational selection. However, before we turn to group condemnation and punishment as our main topic here, I shall briefly discuss reputational selection as a very likely social agency of natural selection, one that surely has helped to shape our basic nature. I believe that in this area, sociology and anthropology can be combined with biology to especially good effect, and I should mention that "biology" includes studies of evolved brain functions (e.g., Turner 1997).

Alexander's Theory of Reputational Selection

In *The Biology of Moral Systems*, Richard D. Alexander (1987) came up with the notion of indirect reciprocity, which accurately characterizes hunter-gatherer cooperative generosity. Previously, attempts to explain human generosity in terms of genetic altruism were dominated either by theory of kin selection (Hamilton 1964), which genetically speaking is not even "generous" because when you help your close kin you are, in effect, helping your own genes. Next came the theory of reciprocal altruism (Trivers 1971), which holds that if over time I help you and you help me equally, even though the two of us are unrelated this can raise our fitness compared with other individuals who fail to cooperate, or who cooperate less well.

Alexander's insight was that rather than practicing reciprocal altruism, hunter-gatherers have an entirely different way of getting things done cooperatively. If I am in need, first of all my coresident relatives will often be the main ones to help me, which is nicely explained by kin selection. However, a significant part of the help comes from *unrelated* band members, in the form of an extended safety net. Bands are composed mainly of families that are unrelated (see Hill et al. 2011), so this altruistic assistance is not only considerable but difficult to explain in natural selection terms.

What actually takes place is that these nonrelatives will help a fellow band member altruistically, with no specific expectation that he or she will personally help them in return; then, later, if one of them becomes ill or suffers an accident, they will expect whoever is in the band at the time to likewise step in to help them—again with no expectation of an explicit return favor (Boehm 2009). The point is that help is not reciprocated directly as with Trivers's model—rather, it is given contingently (see Gurven 2006) on the assumption that future help will be forthcoming—but it may well come from others.

Such a system invites free-rider exploitation (e.g., Williams 1966) of those who are disposed to be more helpful, which means that the genes of generous individuals are disadvantaged. However, Alexander proposes that the exceptional altruists who do the most helping are more than compensated because they gain social reputations for being exceptionally generous.[1] This means that they have more potency to attract good marriage partners as economic cooperators and breeders, and this leads to significantly better reproductive success—in spite of the altruistic losses. This helps to explain human altruism's being able to evolve as far as it has, to the point that we have had to define it as a genetic paradox (see Wilson 1975).

These reputational effects provide a human instance of social selection (Boehm 2012c), with individuals influencing one another's evolutionary destinies by showing favor in making partner choices (see Nesse 2007). Social selection takes a variety of other forms in the animal kingdom (see West-Eberhard 1979), but humans' reputational selection can be likened to sexual selection as Darwin (1871) originally described it. In sexual selection, however, it is secondary sexual characteristics such as exceptionally attractive coloration in male plumage, instead of superior personal reputations of males or females, that provide the breeding advantages.

Social Selection through Social Control

In *Moral Origins*, I treat the social control of foragers as yet another agency of human social selection (Boehm 2012c) and provide quantitative evidence to suggest that the selection effects could have been robust. The idea was that many types of social deviance are similarly defined by all hunter-gatherer bands, and the deviants are similarly disadvantaged reproductively by their groups—with significant selection effects. If today's foragers can be used as models for our more recent hunting ancestors, then for thousands of generations social deviants have been losing out on useful social contacts when they were ostracized or expelled from the band, while once in a while their fitness was being damaged very seriously by capital punishment.

When hunter-gatherers practice capital punishment, they are most likely to be punishing the aggressive self-aggrandizers who go against the group's strong egalitarian ethos (Boehm 2013). This means that individuals with unusual bullying propensities will, on average, reproduce less robustly, and that, at the gene-pool level, social selection is working against the disposition to bully (Boehm 2012c). The younger the bully is when punished, the more likely he is to pay high reproductive costs.

Social selection also works in favor of personal self-control (Boehm 2008b), and the agency for such control is the conscience (Boehm 2012b). In effect, the conscience is an evolved psychological mechanism that helps people to assess social situations and assists them in following moral rules. These rules are internalized (Gintis 2004; see also Parsons and Shils 1952), and having an effective conscience can be individually adaptive because capital punishment, physical punishment, and extreme social isolation can be avoided. Thus, having a conscience buffers individuals against the effects of strong reciprocity (see Gintis 2000).

Lesser sanctions like ostracism and shaming impose a reproductive toll on deviants because they involve economic damage, through loss of cooperation benefits. For instance, a free-rider known to be a thief or a cunning shirker is likely to be set back in looking for hunting or gathering partners; the same goes for overaggressive, greedy bullies. Together with capital punishment (see Otterbein 1988), this array of sanctions provided a type of social selection (Boehm 1997) that has not been taken into account sufficiently in evolutionary studies. I propose that it could have played a major part in shaping today's behavior genes, and in particular our social nature.

In effect, this extends human deviance and social control theory backward in time for probably 100,000 to 150,000 years, starting with the point when humans became culturally modern (see McBrearty and Brooks 2000). Here, we will examine these various types of sanctioning using a database of fifty appropriate hunter-gatherer societies, which have been carefully chosen to make them maximally similar to the culturally modern foraging societies that existed in the Late Pleistocene. It was the latter who put the finishing touches on our social nature.

Possibilities for Testing Social-Selection Theories

Alexander's reputational-selection theory is not easy to test, because among contemporary mobile hunter-gatherers it is difficult to demonstrate exactly how a person's reputation affects reproductive success. However, criteria used by the Hadza of Northern Tanzania in mate choice indicate that people who will contribute more efficiently or more generously to a marital economy are preferred (Marlowe 2010; see also Boehm 2012b), and this seems likely for forager partnerships elsewhere, as well. In effect, those who are exceptionally productive or exceptionally altruistic not only can marry earlier but are more likely to pair up with another exceptional altruist because of assortative mating (Wilson and Dugatkin 1997), which brings further benefits through reciprocal altruism. Curiously, Trivers's (1971) theory has not been applied very much to marriage, where long-term mutual economic assistance tends to be stable and often well balanced. But in any event these same altruists are more likely to receive adequate assistance when safety nets come into play.

Alexander's emphasis on mating choices also included other types of economic cooperation (see Nesse 2007), such as partnering in hunting or gathering. It seems very likely that band members give preference to generous partners when they cooperate, but there is only one systematic study that documents this. Among the South American Aché, reputations for generosity have been shown to come into play when people suffer illness or accidents and have to rely on unrelated band members for safety-net support. The finding is that those who in the past have given until it hurts are especially favored in this respect (Gurven 2004; Gurven et al. 2000), so altruists are receiving special fitness-enhancing treatment. We need more studies like this.

Fortunately, information about the effects of group social control is far more abundant, for execution or other punishment of major culprits invariably attracts the attention of ethnographers. From their copious observations we can build a statistical picture of the punishment side of social selection in contemporary foragers, and these patterns can be applied in reconstructing the behavior of earlier foragers who lived in the Late Pleistocene. In reconstructing their behavior we will be calling the distinctively mobile and egalitarian contemporary bands that are useful to such reconstruction "Late-Pleistocene appropriate," or LPA.

LPA Hunter-Gatherers

Over three hundred foraging societies have been ethnographically described, and of these about half are appropriate for use as LPA prehistoric models because they have not been seriously "contaminated" by newer patterns like practicing some horticulture, which arrived with the Holocene. Other such practices include domesticating horses, becoming dependent on farmers for grain that is traded for meat, or engaging so intensively with the fur trade that previous patterns are disrupted.

The relatively "pristine" LPA societies under discussion are economically independent and predictably small, they live in mobile bands composed mainly of nonkinsmen, and they are politically egalitarian in spite of the fact that humans seem basically to be a species given to hierarchy (Boehm 1999)—a trend that strongly reasserted itself after the Holocene (see Knauft 1991), perhaps as early as 15,000 years ago. Eventually certain early farmers began to live in dense concentrations, and later still they developed chiefdoms with fairly authoritative leaders—leaders strong enough to step in and stop internal conflicts. Next came kingdoms and early civilizations, which introduced extreme hierarchy and sometimes despotism (see Flannery and Marcus 2012).

From a sample of fifty LPA foraging societies, there follows a summary of their social control practices, all of which contribute to social selection. The sample of LPA forager societies represents all world areas where hunter-gatherers have lived and have been studied in the field since systematic ethnographic accounts by Westerners began several hundred years ago.

Statistics on Social Sanctioning

Three tables outline the types of crime and sanctions that exist, and show their distributions among these five LPA culture areas. I decided to work with such a sizable sample of fifty LPA societies for two reasons. One was simply to keep outliers from having an undue chance effect on the behavioral central tendencies I was trying to identify, since variance among societies is descriptively amplified by ethnographer biases and differences in theoretical approaches, and by differences in ethnographer competency. Thus, a large sample compensates for the fact that the ethnographies being used for analysis themselves are both far from being complete and far from being standardized in their content. Such problems are expectable in our earliest cultural descriptions, which come from culturally sensitive but untrained explorers and missionaries. However, they also arise with modern ethnography. Another reason for using a large sample was simply to generate at least a few rich qualitative examples of social control (e.g., Lee 1979) to help in that aspect of the analysis; such accounts are very rare.

To keep geographic distribution in balance as much as possible, all available LPA societies from North and South America and from Africa and Asia were included because in these areas the number of such societies was quite small. In the Arctic and in Aboriginal Australia the LPA societies are abundant, so in these two areas I sampled foragers with an eye to maximizing geographic distribution within the region, and on the basis of favoring societies with outstanding ethnography.

Why a New Database?

As a matter of methodology, I must quickly point out that some significant differences exist between this dedicated forager database I am building and the widely used, all-purpose Human Relations Area Files (HRAF) system, which has been assisting scholars in their cross-cultural research for over half a century:

1. The HRAF database is devoted to all types of societies, but today only about two dozen of the several hundred highly varied societies in the HRAF cross-cultural sample are LPA foragers (an equal number are foragers who are ineligible for LPA status). My database is based exclusively on pure hunter-gatherers, and at present there are fifty LPA foragers coded; eventually, this number is expected to rise to 150-plus.
2. The HRAF societies have been chosen using random sampling techniques, while with my database the goal is to code all 150-plus LPA societies and thus enable researchers to choose whether to sample the database or use the entire corpus.
3. HRAF's search criteria range across the entire spectrum of human behavior, while at present mine are focused much more narrowly, just on social and political ideology and behavior, excluding kinship.
4. The *Outline of Cultural Materials* (Murdock 1961), which lists the many coding categories on which HRAF searches are based, is moderately detailed. My coding protocol is finely categorized, which greatly increases the initial coding investment but also increases searching efficiency.
5. More generally, the HRAF system is based on systematic sampling of the thousands of ethnographies that exist, and it is dedicated to research based on tests of statistical significance. My database, while it may be useful statistically in showing major effects, is equally oriented to systematically mining very specific types of material for qualitative analysis, and to identifying outliers.

The reason for developing this separate database is that evolutionary approaches have become so prominent in so many fields of human behavioral research, including anthropology, psychology, economics, and political science. Hunter-gatherer ethnography is crucial to investigations and explanations in this area, and also for the further development of evolutionary sociology.

Capital Punishment

In LPA foraging bands, the main reason for a group's killing a band member on the basis of its egalitarian ethos is that he seems driven to achieve power (Boehm 1999)—power to either despoil or brutalize his fellows, or to boss them around (see Boehm and Flack 2010). In almost half of the societies sampled, such men were occasionally killed, rarely by the band acting as a whole but usually by delegating the task to a close kinsman of the deviant. (This avoids the possibility of the executioner's being killed by the deviant's vengeful kindred.)

Table 22.1 shows that the majority of executions were aimed at serious aggressors, including malicious shamans who tried to dominate other band members, but sizable numbers were aimed at sexual deviants, including committers of incest, or at individuals who endangered the entire band by violating serious taboos. Killed much less often were serious deceivers—thieves and cheaters. In this context it is worth noting that after up to 150,000 years of lethal sanctioning, the innately dominant tendencies that stimulated this sanctioning of bullies apparently were still strong enough to occasionally get someone killed.

This was the case even though the genes that prepared undue individual self-assertion were being suppressed over the generations because capital punishment takes such a toll on fitness—particularly when it is experienced earlier in one's adult life career and it directly curtails reproduction. This is a powerful form of social selection, but it would not have eradicated these deviant behaviors, because in certain contexts the same underlying dispositions would have been useful—for example, socially well-controlled dominance tendencies can make one more competitive, as in working to find marriage partners (see Boehm 2012c), or perhaps more assertive in hunting and gaining reputational benefits thereby.

Table 22.1 Capital punishment in fifty LPA foraging societies

Type of deviance	Specific deviances	Societies reporting
Intimidation of group	Intimidation through malicious sorcery	11
	Repeat murder	5
	Action otherwise as tyrant	3
	Psychotic aggression	2
Cunning deviance	Theft	1
	Cheating (meat-sharing context)	1
Sexual transgression	Incest	3
	Adultery	2
	Premarital sex	1
Miscellaneous	Violation of taboo (endangering group)	5
	Betrayal of group to outsiders	2
	"Serious" or "shocking" transgression	2
Deviance unspecified		7
Total societies reporting capital punishment		24

Source: Data are derived from the author's hunter-gatherer database.
Note: There is some overlap between the coding categories.

OTHER SANCTIONING

Capital punishment may in fact be a very strong central tendency among LPA foragers, or over a long time span it may even be universal, but ethnographically it is reported only for just under half of the societies sampled so far.[2] There are also lesser sanctions (Table 22.2) that address the same type of deviance, and in the case of bullying by sorcery, this is universally reported among the fifty LPA societies coded so far as a deviant behavior (see Table 22.3).

Table 22.2 enables us to compare capital punishment with other types of sanctioning. Capital punishment applies to a considerable range of social deviances, but for any one type at most it was reported for fewer than half of the sample of fifty societies. However, if we bring in lesser types of sanctioning (see Table 22.2), some universals do appear, as do other patterns involving strong central tendencies. We may assume that this entire package must have been in place among LPA foragers from about 150,000 BP to the present, so in terms of social selection there were sufficient generations available for the genetic effects of group punishment to impact gene pools.

Let us examine the distribution of all these lesser social sanctions, which range from gossiping behind a deviant's back to subjecting him to shunning or to temporary group ejection. Gossip has been recognized as an *indirect* form of social control (see Black 1984) because people fear reputational damage, and they rein in their behavior accordingly. Gossip also figures in the identification of deviants and especially of stealthy ones like thieves. *Direct* verbal sanctions include criticism, ridicule, and shaming, all involving aggressive verbal attacks, and a great deal of deviance is headed off by such cues. In fact, in their more extreme forms they can be very persuasive—if the entire group is beginning to gang up with anger that could easily lead to stronger punishment unless reform is forthcoming.

What might be called group-internal social distancing (e.g., Bogardus 1959) ranges from casual social avoidance to ostracism to total shunning, or even to temporary expulsion from the group. On the other hand, I have categorized *permanent* group expulsion with capital punishment as an ultimate sanction, because if a seriously deviant forager cannot gain entry to another band, his very survival can be threatened. In addition, there is the belief that supernatural entities will punish certain types of deviants, and do so even if they remain undiscovered by their peers. Such sanctioning is widespread and likely universal among LPA foragers (see Boehm 2008b).

It would appear that in their basics, most of our human mechanisms of active social control were well developed by the Late Pleistocene, with the obvious exception of formal legal codes with specialized policemen and jurists. These required writing and a judicial apparatus set up by a state, and this was not likely to have existed before about 5000 BP.

Today, variables like deviance and social control are well studied, and as demonstrated here they can readily be brought into evolutionary analysis. An additional variable, however, is the evolutionary conscience (Boehm 2008b), which from a social-psychological perspective serves as a valuable interface between the actor and his punitive community. If a person inherits a more effective conscience, one that is better at identifying social dangers and at inhibiting socially untoward impulses, this provides obvious reproductive advantages because all of the punishments discussed above are potentially avoidable if self-assessment and self-control are fully effective.

WHO WERE THE SOCIAL PREDATORS?

Sociologists from Durkheim (1933) forward have studied social control in modern societies, and a few (e.g., Black 2011) have included examples from tribal farmers or foragers in

432 CHRISTOPHER BOEHM

Table 22.2 Methods of social suppression

Moral sanctioning	% of societies	Total societies	Anderson Islanders	W. Greenland Inuit	!Ko	Murngin	Netsilik Inuit	N. Alaska Inuit	Plateau Yumans	Polar Inuit	Tiwi	Yahgan
Area			ASIA	ARC	AFR	AUS	ARC	ARC	NA	ARC	AUS	SA
Number of sources			14	3	8	9	8	3	9	4	11	3
ULTIMATE SANCTIONS												
Entire group kills culprit	60	6	2	3	1	1	6			1		
Group member selected to assassinate culprit	60	6	2	1		2	10		5	3		
Permanently expelled from group	30	3	4		7		5	2				1
LESSER SANCTIONS												
Group Opinion												
Public opinion	100	10	4	1	27	6	37	19	11	31	11	24
Verbal												
Gossip (as private expression of public opinion)	90	9	2	1	4	5	12	9	6	10	1	11
Ridicule	90	9	2	4	4	1	28	4	4	21		3

Direct criticism by group or spokesman	80	8		1	5	2	3	10		3	3	5
Group shaming	60	6	2	3	2		15	5		12		
Other shaming	50	5			1	1	3	1		3		
Social Distancing												
Spatial distancing (move or reorient domicile or camp)	100	10	6	6	25	2	22	5	6	16	2	10
Group ostracism	70	7		3	8		18	8	4	1		6
Social aloofness (reduced speaking)	70	7			5	1	3	1	2	1	1	3
Tendency to avoid culprit	50	5			3		2	1	2			3
Total shunning (total avoidance)	50	5			1		1	1		1		2
Temporary expulsion from group	40	4	1		1		3	2				
Physical Nonlethal												
Nonlethal physical punishment	90	4	7	6	11	2	21	3	13	21		7
Administration of blows	50	5			4		7	1	1	9		

Source: Data are derived from the author's hunter-gatherer database.
Note: There is some overlap between the coding categories.

Table 22.3 Social predators

Type of deviance	% of societies	Total societies	Anderson Islanders	W. Greenland Inuit	!Ko	Murngin	Netsilik Inuit	N. Alaska Inuit	Plateau Yumans	Polar Inuit	Tiwi	Yahgan
Area			ASIA	ARC	AFR	AUS	ARC	ARC	NA	ARC	AUS	SA
Number of sources			14	3	8	9	8	3	9	4	11	3
INTIMIDATORS												
Murder	100	10	13	7	11	25	77	2	11	25	5	38
Sorcery or witchcraft	100	10	4	10	2	25	36	1	7	10	2	4
Beating of someone	80	8			11	16	8	2	10	15	3	12
Bullying	70	7		1	4		1	3	1	1		1
DECEIVERS												
Stealing	100	10	4	1	6	13	26	6	6	13	4	19
Failing to share	80	8	1	2	4	3	9		1	7		4
Lying	60	6	3		3		15		4	19		3
Cheating (general)	50	5		1		3	7			12		1
Failing to cooperate	40	4		1			4	3		2		
Cheating the group (as in meat-sharing)	30	3					1			7		1
Cheating an individual	30	3				2	3			4		

Source: Data are derived from the author's hunter-gatherer database.
Note: There is some overlap between the coding categories.

their analyses. In terms of ethnographic field studies, a number of cultural anthropologists, such as von Fürer-Haimendorf (1967), have done actual ethnographic field studies oriented to social control; another example is Selby's (1974) *Zapotec Deviance*. The chief problem that leads to sanctioning seems to be threats that arise from aggression.

Males account for the great majority of human aggression (Wrangham and Peterson 1996), and in all of the sampled societies, murder, sorcery, and theft, almost all by men, figured ethnographically as prominent or universal forms of deviance. In all fifty societies they were punished—if not always punished capitally. If this unanimity holds up by the time that an additional one hundred-plus LPA societies have been coded and added to the present database of fifty, this will make it possible to suggest that these three deviance types and their punishment probably are *universal* within the LPA category, and also were likely to have been universal or widespread prehistorically.

Other deviant types are reported less predictably, but in more than half of the LPA societies presently coded, beating or otherwise bullying someone was at least rather frequently mentioned, along with cheating, failure to share, and lying. In addition, all nonliterate human cultures condemn very close degrees of incest (Durham 1991), even though decisive group deterrence is not inevitable. The taboo appears to be universal among foragers and tribesmen, but in a few cases sanctioning is merely supernatural.

All of these outlawings make good evolutionary sense if we start with a highly cooperative group that is composed of individually variable adults who are innately prone to compete for resources. To restrain themselves from taking the high social risks that are inherent in certain deviant behaviors, they must rely on a combination of fear of social consequences and *internalized* rules (Parsons and Shils 1952; see also Gintis 2004) that stem from having a conscience. Unless the individual is a psychopath, this has the effect of at least inhibiting such behaviors. When a predilection for social risk-taking combines with some degree of sociopathy, which involves a serious inability to internalize rules and a low degree of empathy for others (Hare 1993), then their weak consciences will be contributing to the elevated social risks they experience, and to the reproductive risks that follow. Otherwise, there would likely be more sociopaths in today's populations.

Of course, it will be those whose innate tendencies combine with learning experiences to make them reckless in breaking the rules of the band who will be labeled as serious "deviants" and will find themselves facing serious sanctions. Table 22.3 tells us exactly who these predators were likely to have been prehistorically, based on contemporary LPA forager data.

Murderers, malicious sorcerers, and thieves lead the list as statistically universal deviants who cannot restrain themselves. At least a majority of these fifty LPA societies also report physical attacks, bullying, failure to share, and lying as instances of social predation, but keep in mind that ethnographic accounts by their nature are highly incomplete. This means that these last four deviances are likely to be much more widespread than indicated, and conceivably could even be universal within the LPA type—if we were able to monitor all world bands for, say, a millennium.

In the LPA field reports, the various types of noncooperative or cheating behavior shown at the bottom of Table 22.3 were substantially less salient ethnographically, and this could be because in such intimate groups, where cheating is so readily detectable, cheating may not be a problem worthy of group action since people can act as individuals and simply avoid cheaters.

It is not difficult to show that these categories of deviance involve threats to group members and sometimes even to the group as a whole. In fact, we must applaud indigenous rationality for focusing so consistently on behaviors that threaten the personal autonomy of others, often threaten group cooperation as well, and are most effectively addressed through collective action.

The Band Context

Ever since people became culturally modern, and until the Holocene began to phase in, humans have been living in a remarkably similar type of basic social organization: the multifamily foraging band. Actually, the *elementary* social group has to have been the nuclear family (with some allowance made for polygamy), for families are the social units of plant food and small game subsistence sharing, and in fact these sociable reproductive units are free to transfer from band to band. When it comes to the challenge of consuming dangerous large game, it is the entire band that cooperates in the kill and has to divide up the carcasses cooperatively for equalized consumption by individual families. Thus, the band is not only a basic unit of social sanctioning but an important unit of cooperative carnivory—as well as being a valued source of social company. Sometimes, it has also served as a cooperative unit of violent intergroup competition (e.g., Bowles 2006).

Carnivory Is Best Made Cooperative

Intermittently acquired medium-sized carcasses like antelope could nourish an entire hunting team only if all the male hunters were being fed adequately, and this required fair sharing practices. Thus, for good practical reasons cooperative carnivory profited from the suppression of several types of deviance discussed above. Had an alpha-male system prevailed, the most dominant bullies would have been gorging themselves while the subordinates were undernourished, and with part of the hunting team having their health impaired the overall frequency of kills would have been diminished for the group. Thus, keeping down alpha dominance, along with suppressing cheating and meat thievery, was nutritionally useful to all group members in the long run, but especially to those who were less powerful (Boehm 2012c).

In this context, in virtually every foraging band today there is the habit of taking the freshly killed carcass and putting it in the hands of a person who is far more neutral than a typically egoistic successful hunter (Boehm 2004). Chosen by custom is a person whose sense of self is not involved with having made the kill, and who can be trusted to uphold the band's sharing practices. This basic cultural countermeasure substantially protects a carcass from bullies, thieves, and cheaters, but obviously not completely. As we have seen in Tables 22.1–22.3, sanctions still have to be used actively against them sometimes.

Group Cooperation More Generally

If hunter-gatherers are known for their collaborative approach to life, part of the reason is that they appreciate cooperation enough to actively support it. Evidence of this is the "Golden Rule" kind of preaching found in every major religion (Campbell 1975), and recently I have demonstrated that such deliberate promotion of altruism and cooperation seems to have been a hunter-gatherer universal, as well (Boehm 2008b).

Usually, humans' evolutionary history as group cooperators has been focused on hunting, and also on safety nets. The hunting involves acquisition and sharing of sizable carcasses like the antelope and zebra that were targeted so extensively in Africa, starting about a quarter of a million years ago (Stiner 2002). The safety nets involve indirect reciprocity, and help is given to group members who suffer things like broken bones, snakebite, or illness. But another context of people working toward common goals is the same social sanctioning that basically has made social cooperation possible. By ensuring that bullies did not forcefully usurp an egalitarian political order and ruin an equalizing system of meat distribution, people improved their chances in life. The potential victims also acted as groups in suppressing thievery, cheating, and undue selfishness on the parts of would-be free riders to improve their chances further.

In matters that affect the entire group, LPA foragers make their group decisions by consensus, and the main decisions they make collectively are where to migrate next as a band in search of more food—and when and how to sanction a deviant. This last is an extremely important form of cooperation, which helps to make other types of cooperation feasible. By its nature, this social sanctioning has to be *highly* cooperative. This is because if a band does not develop an effective consensus in cracking down on a deviant, too often that deviant's kin and other allies will defend him—and instead of curbing the behavior in question, the would-be sanctioners will find themselves embroiled in a dysfunctional conflict.

Social Selection

In spite of their colorful cultural diversity (see Kelly 1995), LPA bands have a number of distinguishing features. They are enduring but socially flexible groups of unrelated families that join forces to cooperate, and as a band moves around, it tends to favor hunting over gathering. It definitely favors large game over small game, and it cooperates not only in this meat quest but in creating safety nets. But more basically it cooperates in social sanctioning, which makes other kinds of cooperation work with reasonable efficiency. Thus, for many millennia social sanctioning has been a critical piece of the cooperative puzzle that is humanity (Boehm 2012c). Not only does our moral approach support cooperation by suppressing free riders, but I emphasize that by its nature social sanctioning itself requires a high degree of cooperation.

This purposeful social approach has worked efficiently for as much as 150,000 years and possibly even more. It has worked in a wide range of environments and adaptations; it works equally well in a tropical forest or out on cold steppes. It works well whether mega prey like giraffes are being hunted, or the targets are medium-sized ungulates like antelope, or they are limited to smallish game like wallaby or kangaroo simply because nothing larger is available. This approach works whether people are living in typical bands of twenty to twenty-five, or if they aggregate temporarily in much larger groups (e.g., Balikci 1970). It works as long as people are basically trying to make their living in mobile bands.

Social control is all pervasive in LPA forager life (Boehm 1997, 2000), and for that matter in the life of all humans (Brown 1991). Before 15,000 BP we all lived in bands that had to cooperate, and that was when our social nature experienced much of its evolution. Even as we were becoming more proficient at social sanctioning, we were developing consciences that made us more tractable. It was with these developments that morality entered human life.

It is curious that for a long time discussion of group sanctions as a critical mechanism of social selection has been so limited, even though human cooperation is discussed so frequently. In fact, this is a crucial selection mechanism that contributes mightily to the human distinctiveness that is so readily acknowledged by scholars from a variety of disciplines. We are not only the sole moral species; we are the only species that actively and consciously solves a variety of social problems in order to make its cooperation more effective, and does so by ganging up to make deviants reform or, if they can't reform, make them pay or eliminate them.

If social sanctioning is a rather remarkable item in the human cultural repertoire, its evolutionary provenance is seldom explored. Here, I have offered a scenario that traces its evolution from a hierarchical ancestral ape's occasional political rebellions to the routinized moral machinations of culturally modern egalitarian bands in the Late Pleistocene and beyond (see Boehm 1999). By that time we may assume the existence of both a conscience and a scary capacity for group moral outrage, along with an array of moral rules, an apparently quite predictable insistence on egalitarianism, and an enduring ideological concern with social harmony and cooperation.

Conclusion

Humans evolved in a forager niche, but we did not evolve to become foragers and nothing else. Many of the more basic findings about egalitarian hunter-gatherers will also apply to hierarchical modern humans who have developed social classes and live under formal law—but who sometimes still deal in self-help types of social control (see Black 1983) that typify acephalous foragers and tribesmen. A modern democracy, while hierarchical, at least borrows a page from LPA foragers as it combines adequate command and control with careful protection for individual autonomy.

Sociology has been slow to embrace evolutionary approaches like those of Fox (1983) and Turner (2000), but in the past decade this seems to have been changing. A main traditional interest has been in Durkheimian social control, and I believe that a better connection with evolutionary theory can not only enhance studies that look to explain the provenance of moral life, but enhance the study of contemporary social sanctioning as well.

Notes

1. A narrower version of reputational selection is inherent in costly signaling models (Zahavi 1995) as they are applied to humans (e.g., Bird, Smith, and Bird 2001).
2. This is because ethnographers seldom happen to be present for an execution and may fail to ask about past ones. Furthermore, as a rarely occurring but impactful behavior, often the most recent capital punishment incident might go back beyond memory. Reporting may also be reduced if people are not willing to trust the ethnographer with such information (e.g., Lee 1979).

References

Alexander, R. D. 1987. *The Biology of Moral Systems*. New York: Aldine de Gruyter.
Balikci, A. 1970. *The Netsilik Eskimo*. Prospect Heights, IL: Waveland Press.
Bird, R. B., E. A. Smith, and D. W. Bird. 2001. "The Hunting Handicap: Costly Signaling in Human Foraging Strategies." *Behavioral Ecology and Sociobiology* 50: 9–19.
Black, D. 1983. "Crime as Social Control." *American Sociological Review* 48: 34–45.
———. 1984. *Toward a General Theory of Social Control*. Orlando, FL: Academic Press.
———. 2011. *Moral Time*. Oxford: Oxford University Press.
Boehm, C. 1993. "Egalitarian Behavior and Reverse Dominance Hierarchy." *Current Anthropology* 34: 227–254.
———. 1997. "Impact of the Human Egalitarian Syndrome on Darwinian Selection Mechanics." *American Naturalist* 150: 100–121.
———. 1999. *Hierarchy in the Forest: The Evolution of Egalitarian Behavior*. Cambridge, MA: Harvard University Press.
———. 2000. "Conflict and the Evolution of Social Control." *Journal of Consciousness Studies, Special Issue on Evolutionary Origins of Morality* 7: 79–101.

———. 2004. "What Makes Humans Economically Distinctive? A Three-Species Evolutionary Comparison and Historical Analysis." *Journal of Bioeconomics* 6: 109–135.

———. 2008a. "A Biocultural Evolutionary Exploration of Supernatural Sanctioning." In *Evolution of Religion: Studies, Theories and Critiques*, edited by J. Bulbulia, R. Sosis, R. Genet, E. Harris, K. Wyman, and C. Genet, 143–152. Santa Margarita, CA: Collins Foundation Press.

———. 2008b. "Purposive Social Selection and the Evolution of Human Altruism." *Cross-Cultural Research* 42: 319–352.

———. 2009. "How the Golden Rule Can Lead to Reproductive Success: A New Selection Basis for Alexander's 'Indirect Reciprocity.'" In *The Golden Rule: Analytical Perspectives*, edited by J. Neusner and B. Chilton, 151–178. Lanham, MD: University Press of America.

———. 2012a. "Ancestral Hierarchy and Conflict." *Science* 336: 844–847.

———. 2012b. "Costs and Benefits in Hunter-Gatherer Punishment." *Behavioral and Brain Sciences* 35: 19–20.

———. 2012c. *Moral Origins: The Evolution of Altruism, Virtue, and Shame*. New York: Basic Books.

———. 2013. "The Biocultural Evolution of Conflict Resolution between Groups." In *War, Peace, and Human Nature*, edited by Douglas Fry, 315–340. Oxford: Oxford University Press.

Boehm, C., and J. Flack. 2010. "The Emergence of Simple and Complex Power Structures through Social Niche Construction." In *The Social Psychology of Power*, edited by A. Guinote, 46–86. New York: Guilford Press.

Bogardus, E. S. 1959. *Social Distance*. Yellow Springs, OH: Antioch Press.

Bowles, S. 2006. "Group Competition, Reproductive Leveling, and the Evolution of Human Altruism." *Science* 314: 1569–1572.

Brown, D. E. 1991. *Human Universals*. New York: McGraw-Hill.

Campbell, D. T. 1975. "On the Conflicts between Biological and Social Evolution and between Psychology and Moral Tradition." *American Psychologist* 30: 1103–1126.

Darwin, C. 1871. *The Descent of Man and Selection in Relation to Sex*. London: John Murray.

Durham, W. H. 1991. *Coevolution: Genes, Culture, and Human Diversity*. Stanford, CA: Stanford University Press.

Durkheim, É. 1933. *The Division of Labor in Society*. New York: Free Press.

Flannery, K. V., and J. Marcus. 2012. *The Creation of Inequality: How Our Prehistoric Ancestors Set the Stage for Monarchy, Slavery, and Empire*. Cambridge, MA: Harvard University Press.

Fox, R. 1983. *The Red Lamp of Incest: An Inquiry into the Origins of Mind and Society*. Notre Dame, IN: University of Notre Dame Press.

Fürer-Haimendorf, C. von. 1967. *Morals and Merit: A Study of Values and Social Controls in South Asian Societies*. Chicago: University of Chicago Press.

Gintis, H. 2000. "Strong Reciprocity in Human Sociality." *Journal of Theoretical Biology* 206 (2): 169–179.

———. 2004. "The Genetic Side of Gene-Culture Coevolution: Internalization of Norms and Prosocial Emotions." *Journal of Economic Behavior and Organization* 53: 57–67.

Gurven, M. 2004. "To Give and to Give Not: The Behavioral Ecology of Human Food Transfers." *Behavioral and Brain Sciences* 27: 543–583.

———. 2006. "The Evolution of Contingent Cooperation." *Current Anthropology* 47: 185–192.

Gurven, M., W. Allen-Arave, K. Hill, and A. M. Hurtado. 2000. "'It's a Wonderful Life': Signaling Generosity among the Ache of Paraguay." *Evolution and Human Behavior* 21: 263–282.

Hamilton, W. D. 1964. "The Genetical Evolution of Social Behavior I, II." *Journal of Theoretical Biology* 7: 1–52.

Hare, R. 1993. *Without Conscience: The Disturbing World of the Psychopaths among Us*. New York: Guilford Press.

Hill, K. R., R. Walker, M. Bozicevic, J. Eder, T. Headland, A. Hewlett, A. M. Hurtado, F. Marlowe, P. Wiessner, and B. Wood. 2011. "Coresidence Patterns in Hunter-Gatherer Societies Show Unique Human Social Structure." *Science* 331: 1286–1289.

Kelly, L. 1995. *The Foraging Spectrum: Diversity in Hunter-Gatherer Lifeways*. Washington, DC: Smithsonian Institution Press.

Klein, R. G. 1999. *The Human Career: Human Biological and Cultural Origins*. Chicago: University of Chicago Press.

Knauft, B. M. 1991. "Violence and Sociality in Human Evolution." *Current Anthropology* 32: 391–428.

Lee, R. B. 1979. *The !Kung San: Men, Women, and Work in a Foraging Society*. Cambridge: Cambridge University Press.

Lieberman, P. 2006. *Toward an Evolutionary Biology of Language*. Cambridge, MA: Harvard University Press.

Marlowe, F. W. 2010. *The Hadza Hunter-Gatherers of Tanzania*. Berkeley: University of California Press.

McBrearty, S., and A. Brooks. 2000. "The Revolution That Wasn't: A New Interpretation of the Origin of Modern Human Behavior." *Journal of Human Evolution* 39: 453–563.

Murdock, G. P. 1961. *Outline of Cultural Materials*. New York: Taplinger Publishing Company.

Nesse, R. M. 2007. "Runaway Social Selection for Displays of Partner Value and Altruism." *Biological Theory* 2: 143–155.

Otterbein, K. F. 1988. "Capital Punishment: A Selection Mechanism. Comment on Robert K. Dentan, on Semai Homicide." *Current Anthropology* 29: 633–636.

Parsons, T., and E. Shils. 1952. *Toward a General Theory of Action*. Cambridge, MA: Harvard University Press.

Selby, H. 1974. *Zapotec Deviance: The Convergence of Folk and Modern Sociology*. Austin: University of Texas Press.

Stiner, M. C. 2002. "Carnivory, Coevolution, and the Geographic Spread of the Genus *Homo*." *Journal of Archaeological Research* 10: 1–63.

Trivers, R. L. 1971. "The Evolution of Reciprocal Altruism." *Quarterly Review of Biology* 46: 35–57.

Turner, J. H. 1997. "The Evolution of Morality." *Critical Review* 11: 211–231.

———. 2000. *On the Origins of Human Emotions: A Sociological Inquiry into the Evolution of Human Affect*. Stanford, CA: Stanford University Press.

West-Eberhard, M. J. 1979. "Sexual Selection, Social Competition, and Evolution." *Proceedings of the American Philosophical Society* 123: 222–234.

Williams, G. C. 1966. *Adaptation and Natural Selection: A Critique of Some Current Evolutionary Thought*. Princeton, NJ: Princeton University Press.

Wilson, D. S., and L. A. Dugatkin. 1997. "Group Selection and Assortative Interactions." *American Naturalist* 149: 336–351.

Wilson, E. O. 1975. *Sociobiology: The New Synthesis*. Cambridge, MA: Harvard University Press.

Wrangham, R. W. 1987. "African Apes: The Significance of African Apes for Reconstructing Social Evolution." In *The Evolution of Human Behavior: Primate Models*, edited by W. G. Kinzey, 51–71. Albany: State University of New York Press.

Wrangham, R. W., and D. Peterson. 1996. *Demonic Males: Apes and the Origins of Human Violence*. New York: Houghton Mifflin.

Zahavi, A. 1995. "Altruism as a Handicap: The Limitations of Kin Selection and Reciprocity." *Journal of Avian Biology* 26: 1–3.

Chapter Twenty-Three
Human Cooperation
Evolutionary Approaches to a Complex Phenomenon
Lee Cronk

> Humans work together to achieve common goals on larger scales and in a wider variety of ways than do members of any other species. In a word, they cooperate. They do so despite many obstacles to cooperation, which come in two main varieties: (1) collective action dilemmas, which arise from conflicts of interest among would-be cooperators, and (2) coordination problems, which arise from a lack of common knowledge about how cooperation can be achieved. Evolutionary scientists have identified a variety of factors that help people solve these problems. These include kinship, a high likelihood of repeated interactions, an ability to distinguish cooperators from noncooperators and preferentially associate with the former, concerns about audiences and resulting reputations, an ability to send and receive signals regarding individuals' levels of commitment to cooperative enterprises, and the importance of dealing with an uncertain future through risk-pooling arrangements. Although we understand a great deal more about the evolution of human cooperation now than we did a half century ago, when this approach was first developing, much work remains to be done. Some current frontiers in the evolutionary analysis of human cooperation include the study of coordination problems, cultural group selection, coalitional psychology, and a greater appreciation of the institutional and organizational contexts in which most human cooperation occurs.

Introduction

Humans cooperate with one another on larger scales and in a wider variety of ways than do members of any other species. This fact is all the more remarkable given that they do so despite the many obstacles to cooperation that exist. Such obstacles come in two broad varieties: conflicts of interest and a lack of common knowledge. Conflicts of interest lead to situations in which a public good is either not provided at all or not provided at a desired level (Olson 1965), and to situations in which a common pool resource is not managed in a way that will sustain it for future use (Hardin 1968). In both cases, the reason is what is known as the "free-rider problem": everyone would like to see the public good provided or the common pool resource maintained, but because everyone has limited resources to put into such efforts, everyone also would prefer to contribute as little as possible to these outcomes. This is also known as a collective action dilemma or a social dilemma. These situations are a result of the fact that both public goods and common pool resources have what is known as "low excludability": it is hard to prevent people from enjoying them, even if they have not contributed to their production or maintenance. In this way, they contrast with private goods, which have high excludability: although theft of private goods certainly does occur, it is relatively easy to prevent people from consuming them without first paying for them. Common pool resources are more problematic than public goods because they also suffer from "high subtractability," that is, one person's consumption of them diminishes the ability of others to also consume them (Ostrom, Gardner, and Walker 1994).

Lack of common knowledge is a problem in situations in which there may be no conflicts of interest—everyone would benefit if cooperation were to take place—but those who would like to cooperate do not all know how to do so. These situations are known as coordination problems or coordination games (Schelling 1960). They are solved through the creation of not only common knowledge about how to cooperate but also common metaknowledge, that is, common knowledge that there is common knowledge (Chwe 2001). For example, if the goal is the safe evacuation of a crowded theater, it helps if everyone knows that this outcome can best be achieved by walking to the nearest exit in a calm and orderly manner. However, even if everyone does know this, such common knowledge will not help achieve the desired outcome if everyone does not also know that his or her fellow theatergoers are also aware of it. Without that common knowledge, everyone may assume that he or she is the only one in the theater who knows the proper procedure, which will lead theatergoers to behave as if they do not know the proper procedure even though they do. The end result may be a rush to the exits that leads to lower numbers of survivors overall (Ullmann-Margalit 1977).

When traditional social scientists have turned their attention to the phenomenon of human cooperation, they have been most concerned with these kinds of obstacles and how they seem to be overcome so infrequently. This attitude was captured succinctly by economist Mancur Olson, who declared that "unless the number of individuals in a group is quite small, or unless there is coercion or some other special device to make individuals act in their common interest, *rational, self-interested individuals will not act to achieve their common or group interests*" (1965: 2; emphasis in original). When evolutionary scientists look at human cooperation, in contrast, they are struck not so much by the difficulties that beset would-be cooperators but rather by the fact that humans cooperate more often, on larger scales, and in a wider variety of ways than do most nonhumans, including our closest primate relatives. Of course, both of these perspectives are perfectly valid—two sides of the same coin, if you will. At the same time that humans cooperate less frequently than would be beneficial in theory, they do cooperate at rates rarely seen among nonhumans. This chapter summarizes some of the major insights that evolutionary scientists have provided to the study of human cooperation and points toward some possible directions for future research on this topic.

Defining Cooperation

Evolutionary scientists often define cooperation in a way that makes it synonymous with altruism. For example, Nowak (2006: 90) defines cooperation as a situation in which "a donor pays a cost and the recipient gets a benefit." Similar definitions have been used by many others (e.g., Henrich and Henrich 2007; Bowles and Gintis 2003; Lehmann et al. 2008). Thus, when evolutionary scientists claim to be explaining something about cooperation, often they are really explaining something about altruism.

Because altruism is already a perfectly good term to use for situations in which one individual does something that is costly to himself or herself in order to provide a benefit to someone else, I instead define cooperation as simply "working together." This much broader definition of the term includes not only situations that may involve altruism but also those that do not, such as coordination problems. This has the additional advantage of being more in keeping with the way the term has traditionally been used in the nonevolutionary social sciences, thus facilitating communication across disciplines (Cronk and Leech 2013).

What Evolutionary Scientists Know about Human Cooperation

The last half century has seen tremendous progress in the evolutionary understanding of cooperation. Here I provide a brief summary of this approach's main findings regarding what things matter most when we try to explain the phenomenon of human cooperation from an evolutionary perspective. Although each of these is significant in isolation, explaining any particular real-world case of human cooperation may require an understanding of more than one of them.

Kinship

Ever since William D. Hamilton's (1964) development of inclusive fitness theory in the early 1960s, kinship has been the starting point for evolutionary analyses of altruistic behavior. This approach is often referred to as kin selection. The idea is simple: because an organism shares some of its genes with its kin, it can ensure the survival of its genes in future generations not only by reproducing directly but also by doing so indirectly, that is, by helping its kin to reproduce. Hamilton theorized that selection may favor a propensity to help kin even if doing so is costly to the donor (i.e., altruistic) if the cost to the donor in terms of reduced future reproduction is less than the benefit to the recipient in terms of enhanced future reproduction, provided that we also remember to discount the benefit to the recipient by the degree of relatedness between the donor and the recipient. This is now known as Hamilton's Rule.

Applications of Hamilton's Rule have shed light on kin-directed helping behaviors in nonhuman species (e.g., Sherman 1977; Reyer 1980) as well as among humans, particularly in small-scale societies (e.g., Hawkes, O'Connell, and Blurton Jones 1989; Nolin 2010) and within families (e.g., Case, Lin, and McLanahan 2000). However, because relatedness diminishes geometrically with each generational or lateral move away from a focal individual, Hamilton's Rule may be of limited use in explaining altruism or cooperation in large-scale societies or among non-kin. Nevertheless, the underlying psychology of kin favoritism that has been favored by kin selection has the potential to be co-opted by people and institutions trying to foster such behaviors. Thus, the use of such kinship-valenced terms as "brother," "sister," "fatherland," and "motherland" are common in political rhetoric and have been shown to increase the persuasiveness of such rhetoric (Salmon 1988). Similarly, religious organizations that require celibacy often use kin terms (e.g., the Roman Catholic use of such terms as "mother," "father," "sister," and "brother"), and organizations that train suicide bombers use kin terms to manipulate and motivate their recruits (Qirko 2004, 2009). In this same spirit, Maasai pastoralists in East Africa establish dyadic helping and risk-pooling relationships that are referred to by their word for umbilical cord (*osotua*), thus evoking the bond between a woman and her fetus (Cronk 2007; Cronk and Wasielewski 2008; Aktipis, Cronk, and de Aguiar 2011).

Repeated Interactions

If two organisms are unrelated to each other, if cooperation is costly in some way, and if interactions among them are unlikely to be repeated in the future, then selection will not favor them engaging in cooperation with one another. However, if those same two organisms are likely to interact in the future, then selection can indeed lead them to engage in costly, cooperative acts. This, in a nutshell, is the main insight to have emerged from the study of reciprocity (Hume 1740; Trivers 1971; Axelrod and Hamilton 1981; Axelrod 1984; Aumann 1981). The importance of repeated interactions was clearly demonstrated by Robert Axelrod's (1984) famous computer tournament involving the Prisoner's Dilemma game. In the Prisoner's Dilemma, two players are given a choice between two options, usually labeled "cooperate" and "defect." If both cooperate, they both get a moderately high payoff. However, if one defects and the other cooperates, the cooperator gets a very low payoff and the defector a very high one. This creates a temptation to defect rather than cooperate. If they both choose to defect, they both get moderately low payoffs. If the game is played for only one round, the best strategy is to defect in order to avoid the very low payoff associated with cooperating when one's partner defects. However, Axelrod's tournament demonstrated that if the game is iterated, then it makes sense for both players to cooperate because doing so allows them to accumulate moderate payoffs round after round. This core finding has since been corroborated, refined, and elaborated upon in dozens of subsequent studies (e.g., Nowak 2006; Aktipis 2004, 2011).

Switching from a one-shot game to an iterated game makes it more like real life. Although interactions with kin may not be as frequent in modern societies as they were among our ancestors, we do interact repeatedly, day after day, with the same unrelated individuals. In short, life is an iterated game. This high likelihood of future interaction has a profound effect on the kinds of cooperative dilemmas we face. Although the Prisoner's Dilemma and many other situations involve conflicts of interest and are therefore collective action dilemmas, if they occur repeatedly then in effect they become coordination problems: it is in everyone's best interests to find a way to cooperate. Consider, for example, subsistence and food-sharing practices in the community of Lamalera on the Indonesian island of Lembata. Lamalerans make a living from the sea, mainly by hunting whales and other large marine animals, which is done cooperatively, and by fishing, which can be done individually. Cooperative hunting is more productive, but before it can occur, the participants in the hunt must overcome a collective action dilemma: Who will receive which parts of the kill? One possible outcome is that this dilemma will never be overcome, in which case Lamalerans would simply fish for their dinners. However, because the situation has occurred for years and will continue to occur in the future, they have instead come up with clear-cut rules that govern what each participant in the hunt will receive if it is successful. Thus, the iterated nature of the situation has turned it from a collective action dilemma into a coordination problem, and the Lamalerans have responded by coming up with a coordination convention that works to foster cooperation (Alvard 2003; Alvard and Nolin 2002).

Assortment

If individuals vary in terms of their willingness or ability to cooperate with others, it helps if cooperative people can find each other and avoid time-consuming and otherwise costly interactions with uncooperative people. In the evolutionary literature on cooperation, this is known as positive assortment. The value of positive assortment of cooperators was dramatically shown by a Prisoner's Dilemma simulation that differed in one important way from previous simulations using that game: the agents were able to move around in virtual space. The strategy that worked best in this simulation was labeled "Walk Away," which summarizes its advantage over other strategies: if you are dissatisfied with the way your current partner is behaving, walk away and try someone else (Aktipis 2004, 2011). In this way, cooperators can find each other, noncooperators suffer from a lack of partners, and cooperation can thrive.

Assortment's importance has led to a great deal of research on cooperative partner choice in the real world. Some of the earliest research on this topic employed an instrument called the Wason Selection Task (Wason 1966), in which subjects are presented with a logical problem of the "if p then q" variety. Research in the 1960s and 1970s established that most people are quite bad at solving such abstract logical problems, but it was also known that people can perform quite well on such tasks when they are presented in more concrete terms. In the 1980s, evolutionary psychologists Leda Cosmides and John Tooby suggested that such improvements in performance on the task reflect evolved cognitive mechanisms that people use when identifying (and presumably then avoiding) people who cheat in social contract situations (Cosmides and Tooby 2005). In such situations, "cheating" is defined as obtaining some benefit without paying the required cost. For example, if there is a norm that if you borrow my car you must fill the gas tank before returning it to me, but you fail to do so, you are a cheater. The key finding is that although people are generally bad at solving the Wason Selection Task when it is presented to them in the abstract "if p then q" form, they suddenly become quite good at solving it when it is presented to them as a tool for identifying cheaters (e.g., people who borrow cars and return them without filling their tanks). The implication is that selection among our ancestors favored the evolution of this kind of social intelligence because it enabled them to engage in positive assortment. More recent studies have demonstrated additional ways in which we identify cooperators, even at very early ages. For example, a study of six- and ten-month-old infants showed that they preferred to play with toys that had been depicted as behaving in helpful ways to other toys over toys that had been depicted as hindering other toys' efforts to achieve their goals (Hamlin, Wynn, and Bloom 2007).

Audiences and Reputations

One way to avoid noncooperators is to pay attention to how they treat others and to their reputations. This bit of everyday wisdom has been systematized in evolutionary theory under the label "indirect reciprocity" (Alexander 1977, 1987). While true reciprocity involves just two parties who exchange favors, indirect reciprocity is all about the audience: Anne does something nice to Ben because Charlie, who may someday be in a position to help Anne, is watching. Given that we have language, Anne may also be concerned about what Charlie might say to others (Darla, for example) about the way she chose to treat Ben.

This basic insight into human interactions has led to a great deal of research on such issues as the impacts of audiences and reputations on cooperative behavior. For example, a series of studies has shown that simply exposing people to images of eyes—even quite stylized ones—can lead them to behave more cooperatively and generously than when such images are not present (e.g., Haley and Fessler 2005; Bateson, Nettle, and Roberts 2006; Burnham and Hare 2007; Rigdon et al. 2009). Other studies, however, have failed to find such an association (e.g., Fehr and Schneider 2010; Lamba and Mace 2010). This discrepancy was recently explained by a study that made a distinction between brief and lengthy exposure to the images of eyes: brief exposure works to increase cooperativeness, long exposure does not. While brief exposure to such images seems to make people concerned at a nonconscious level about the possible presence of an audience, long exposure provides people with an opportunity to consciously realize that there really is no audience, leading some to then behave in more calculated and selfish ways (Sparks and Barclay 2013).

One implication of indirect reciprocity is that cooperative behavior itself can serve as a signal, which means that signaling theory can play a role in explaining the forms that it takes. If observers are skeptical about an individual's cooperativeness, then the individual needs to come up with a way to overcome that skepticism. One way to do this is with a signal that only a truly cooperative individual could produce. Such signals are known as "costly" or "hard-to-fake" signals. One well-documented example of a costly signal of cooperativeness comes from the island of Mer, a part of Australia located in the Torres Strait. A favorite food on Mer is the meat of the green sea turtle, *Chelonia mydas*. There are two ways to catch turtles, one easy and one quite difficult. The easy way is simply to collect them off the beaches when they are nesting. The difficult way is to catch them at sea, which requires a great deal of both skill and strength. Interestingly, while turtle meat that is collected the easy way is typically eaten within households and shared privately, turtle meat obtained the hard way is shared in public ceremonies involving, on average, more than a third of the island's population. Thus, hunting turtles the hard way is an excellent way to burnish one's reputation not only as a skillful hunter but also as a generous person, and the attention turtle hunters receive helps them obtain more mates and children than nonhunters (Bliege Bird, Smith, and Bird 2001).

Commitment

Signaling theory can also help explain how people overcome one of the most basic and pervasive problems facing would-be cooperators: how can they tell that their fellow cooperators are truly committed to the task at hand (Nesse 2001)? Organizations often overcome this problem by requiring people who want to join them to pay some sort of cost that demonstrates their commitment. Recent research has shown that religious groups are particularly successful at obtaining signs of commitment from their members that then lead to higher levels of cooperation among group members (Irons 2001; Sosis and Alcorta 2003). An interesting demonstration of this comes from an analysis of historical data on communes in nineteenth-century America. Such communes were quite numerous, and while some of them were based on secular ideologies, others were very religious. All of them demanded that their members pay various sorts of costs, ranging from minor things like not drinking coffee or alcohol to more serious things like giving up control over one's own sex life. On average, the religious communes lasted longer than the secular ones. Furthermore, while religious communes lasted longer when their leaders added additional costly requirements for membership, the same effect was not found among secular communes, suggesting that there is something special, though still not well understood, about religious signals of commitment (Sosis and Bressler 2003). Subsequent studies of specific religious communities have corroborated and elaborated upon this finding. For example, levels of cooperation in an experimental game were higher among men belonging to religious kibbutzim in Israel than among men belonging to secular kibbutzim (Sosis and Ruffle 2003). Similarly, but in a very different cultural setting, levels of cooperation in an experimental game played by members of an Afro-Brazilian religion called Candomblé correlated with cooperative behaviors outside the game (Soler 2012). Some critics have argued that findings like these may also be explained by a fear of supernatural punishment for failing to cooperate rather than the hypothesized relationship between signals of commitment and cooperation. Because Candomblé is a religion that does not include a doctrine of supernatural punishment, that study clearly demonstrates the merit of signaling theory in explaining the ability of religious rituals to serve as signs of commitment.

UNCERTAINTY, RISK, AND NEED

Uncertainty about the future is one of the most common and enduring features of the environments in which humans live. Will we be able to find food? Will we have enough water to drink? Will there be a drought, flood, or other calamity? Will our property be stolen by others? Humans have found a variety of ways of dealing with the risk created by such uncertainty (Dorfman 2007). Risk retention consists of accepting risk and absorbing any resulting losses. Examples include storing resources in anticipation of future shortages and self-insurance by institutions. Risk avoidance involves reducing one's dependence on high variability outcomes. For example, focusing one's foraging efforts on reliable plant foods and small game rather than on unpredictable returns from big game hunting is a way of avoiding risk. Risk reduction includes efforts to lower the probability of loss or to reduce the size of losses, such as by buying bonds as well as stocks. Finally, risk transfer is the exchange of risk from one individual or group to another. Risk transfer does nothing to reduce the overall amount of risk, but it allows people to exchange the possibility of a catastrophic loss for the certainty of small, manageable losses. In our society, buying an insurance policy is a common way to transfer risk, but humans have been transferring risk for much longer than insurance companies have been around, primarily by risk-pooling, also known as risk sharing (e.g., Barr and Genicot 2008; Fafchamps and Lund 2003). Because risk transfer, including risk-pooling, is the only one of these four strategies to necessarily involve cooperation, understanding it is an essential part of the evolutionary analysis of human cooperation.

Although many evolutionary scientists have considered risk-pooling to simply be a type of reciprocity (e.g., Gurven 2004), it differs considerably from the sort of back-and-forth, account-keeping, tit-for-tat arrangements for which the theory of reciprocity was originally designed. In reciprocity, relationships are maintained by extensions of credit that create debt that is then repaid. If debts are not repaid, such relationships end. The relationship is thus similar to that between a banker and a lender. Risk-pooling does not work like that. Instead, in risk-pooling systems, favors are provided in response to the recipient's need and with an eye toward the establishment of a partnership that the donor may find useful in the future because of its inherent unpredictability. The relationship is less like that between a banker and a lender and more like that between an insurance company and a person who buys a policy. The person who buys the policy pays the premiums not because he or she is hoping to one day suffer a loss and thus be entitled to a payment. Instead, he or she hopes never to suffer such a loss, making all of the premiums a complete waste of money. But the future is unpredictable, so he or she pays the premiums anyway. Similarly, people who participate in risk-pooling arrangements agree to help others who happen to be in need, not because they are hoping that they themselves will someday be in need but rather because they recognize the very real possibility of such an event.

Risk-pooling partnerships have been documented ethnographically in many African pastoralist societies (e.g., Almagor 1978; Gulliver 1955; Dyson-Hudson 1966). This reflects the fact that pastoralists typically live in marginal areas prone to drought. Livestock are also vulnerable to a variety of diseases and theft. Among Maasai and other Maa-speaking pastoralists in Kenya and Tanzania, such partnerships are referred to as "umbilical cord" (*osotua*) relationships. Such relationships are imbued with a deep sense of responsibility and respect. Within osotua relationships, gifts are given only in response to requests that are based on genuine need. In contrast to relationships governed by the principle of balanced reciprocity, such gifts do not create debt and are never referred to as payments (Cronk 2007; Cronk and Wasielewski 2008). Computer simulations of osotua relationships both in dyads (Aktipis, Cronk, and de Aguiar 2011) and in networks (Hao et al., forthcoming) show that they help livestock owners maintain their herds for longer periods despite the volatile ecology of the region.

Risk-pooling is also the logic behind central place food sharing, a practice common among hunting and gathering peoples (Winterhalder 1986; Cashdan 1985; Wiessner 1982). That such sharing is an example of risk-pooling is demonstrated by the fact that unpredictable foods, particularly large game, are typically much more widely shared than foods that come in small, predictable packages, such as small game, honey, and plants (e.g., Hames 1990; Gurven et al. 2000; Kaplan and Hill 1985; Kaplan, Hill, and Hurtado 1990). Among the Hadza of Tanzania, sharing is maintained by a strong normative expectation. According to Woodburn (1998), the individual Hadza hunter "has no choice about whether he shares the animal he kills. It has to be redistributed" (62). Woodburn also points out that back-and-forth exchange "with other Hadza is reprehensible" (54). Sharing is so important among the Hadza that they even use the notion of indebtedness to differentiate themselves from neighboring groups: "'We have no debt,' they say. Only the general right to share is carried forward over time. Specific claims are not" (54; see also Marlowe 2010). Recently, the effects of variance in resource acquisition on sharing patterns were explored through the use of a computer game in a laboratory setting. Participants rarely shared while foraging in low-variance virtual patches, but considerable sharing took place among foragers in high-variance virtual patches (Kaplan et al. 2012). Similarly, a risk-pooling simulation involving virtual herds rather than foraging found that participants commonly used risk-pooling rather than reciprocity strategies, particularly if they had read brief descriptions of real-world risk-pooling practices before playing the game (Gazzillo et al. 2013). Thus, the logic of risk-pooling through sharing seems to come easily even to people who do not themselves have any personal experience with such systems or the environments and subsistence practices that lead to them.

Need is also the starting point for another explanation for why people sometimes share food and other resources known as tolerated theft (Blurton Jones 1984, 1987) or tolerated scrounging (Isaac 1978). In tolerated theft, one shares one's resources in order to avoid the cost of defending them rather than as a sort of insurance policy. The fact that much sharing in hunting and gathering societies is in response to aggressive requests, a pattern labeled by ethnographers as "demand sharing" (Peterson 1993), shows the value of the tolerated theft model as an explanation of some instances of sharing. As suggested by Blurton Jones (1987), tolerated theft may have been a starting point for exchanges that later developed into a way of reducing day-to-day variance in food intake.

Frontiers in the Evolutionary Study of Human Cooperation

Because human cooperation is such a large and diverse phenomenon, there is still much that we do not understand about it. The rest of this chapter briefly describes a few areas of inquiry that have recently received increasing attention from evolutionary scholars.

Coordination Problems

The bulk of the theoretical literature on cooperation has concerned collective action dilemmas, that is, situations in which cooperation is stymied by the problem of free riders. This has led to a comparative neglect of coordination problems. Recently, many evolutionary scientists have begun to advocate a shift of focus in the direction of coordination problems and how they are solved as a crucial aspect of the human success story (e.g., Alvard 2001; Tomasello 2009). This partly reflects a realization that coordination problems are in many ways more fundamental than collective action dilemmas. After all, in order for a collective action dilemma to exist, there already must be some degree of common understanding among the potential participants in the collective action regarding what constitutes participation and what does not (McAdams 2008). If the goal is to bring home a piece of whale meat, as in the Lamaleran example given earlier in this chapter, does one need to actually harpoon the whale, or can one simply bail or pull on one of the boat's oars? Before the collective action dilemma can be overcome, these kinds of common understandings must first be established.

Given the value of solutions to coordination problems, it is not surprising that evolutionary scientists have suggested that humans may possess a variety of both physical and psychological adaptations designed to help us find such solutions. For example, humans are much better than nonhuman primates at following each other's gaze (Wyman and Tomasello 2007), and it has been suggested that this may be made easier by a couple of unusual morphological features of the human eye. First, the sclera or "whites" of our eyes are indeed white, rather than blending in with the iris and surrounding skin, as is the case with most other primates. Second, our eye openings are also unusually elongated horizontally compared with those of most nonhuman primates. Both of these characteristics may make it easier for us to tell what others are looking at and also to signal to others what we are interested in simply by looking at it (Kobayashi and Kohshima 1997, 2001). This shared *attention* may be a step to shared *intention* (Tomasello and Carpenter 2007), which may in turn be a step toward full-blown theory of mind (Premack and Woodruff 1978). Also known as mentalizing, theory of mind is the ability to imagine the mental states of others and to understand that those mental states may differ from one's own. This mind-reading ability is something at which cognitively normal humans excel. Based on studies of its development in children and of people who lack it in adulthood, theory of mind is an ability that evolved due to selection pressure specifically for its usefulness in social coordination rather than simply as a side effect of our high general intelligence (Baron-Cohen 1995; Baron-Cohen et al. 1995; Emery 2000).

Of course, language is the ultimate coordination norm. Without language, human culture and society as we now know it could not exist. If anyone wants a one-word explanation for why humans are so much more successful at cooperation on both small and large scales than most other species, here it is: *language* (Smith 2010). Language's role in social coordination may also be a good starting point for understanding its evolution. Consider, for example, linguist Derek Bickerton's hypothetical scenario for the emergence of language (Bickerton 2009; Bickerton and Szathmáry 2011; see also Cronk 2004a). Bickerton sees the key difference between language and animal signaling systems as displaced reference: while animal signaling systems are largely limited to references to things that are actually present (e.g., alarm calls that refer to predators), language allows us to refer to things that are not present. Bickerton thinks that displaced reference developed as a way of coordinating the cooperative, aggressive scavenging that some paleoanthropologists see as having been a precursor to social hunting (e.g., Blumenschine 1987). Thus, the first instances of displaced reference—and thus the thin edge of the wedge that separated language from its precursor in animal signaling—may have been efforts to recruit others to help scavenge large kills made by other predators.

CULTURAL GROUP SELECTION

Say the term "group selection" in a room full of evolutionary scientists and you are likely to get reactions ranging from delight to abject horror. The reasons for this divide go back to 1962, when evolutionary biologist V. C. Wynne-Edwards proposed that the differential survival and reproduction of entire groups of organisms rather than that of individual organisms may be responsible for many aspects of animal behavior. Wynne-Edwards's claim was quickly challenged by John Maynard Smith (1964, 1976), George Williams (1966), and others on the grounds that unless groups are isolated and experience frequent extinctions, selection at lower levels, such as that of individual organisms and the genes they possess, will usually have a greater impact than selection at the group level on how selection designs organisms. The result was that most subsequent research on animal behavior, including work on humans conducted within that tradition, rejected the group selectionist framework and focused instead on selection at lower levels. Today, most evolutionary scientists accept the idea that selection can work at multiple levels, but differences of opinion remain regarding its relevant strength at various levels. Particularly in the study of human behavior, group selection continues to have its fans and advocates (e.g., Sober and Wilson 1998).

The situation when we study humans is made more complicated by the fact that groups may be defined either in biological terms (e.g., populations of organisms) or in cultural terms (e.g., tribes, religions, and other groups that share some body of knowledge). This distinction is crucial because, despite their similar names, biological group selection and cultural group selection are quite different processes (Richerson and Boyd 1998). They resemble each other only in that they both involve groups. The actual mechanisms involved in the two processes can be quite different. For example, although biological group selection is weakened when individuals move from group to group, cultural group selection can actually be strengthened by such movement, provided that migrants adopt the culture traits of their adopted groups. Because many such culture traits are social coordination norms, it often makes good sense for the individuals involved to conform to them. This kind of "voting with your feet" may sometimes be a major determinant of which groups fail and which succeed.

The between-group cultural differences that make cultural group selection possible may exist for a variety of reasons, but one of the most interesting arises from the fact that coordination problems can often be solved in a variety of ways. In the United States and much of the rest of the world, people drive their cars on the right side of the road, but traffic flows just as well in countries where people drive on the left side. English is a very effective means of communication, but of course so are French, Urdu, Swahili, and so on. Electrical plugs in the United States have flat prongs, while those used in much of Europe have round ones. Because different coordination norms can perform equally well so long as everyone in a particular location knows about and follows them, groups of people can end up with very different coordination norms. McElreath, Boyd, and Richerson (2003) used a computer simulation to explore the power of coordination games to create between-group differences. Players in the game had two options, and they scored the most points when paired with another player who chose the same option. Players were also endowed with marker traits (a zero or a one) and a propensity to prefer interactions with players with whom they shared a marker. Just as a person's language, accent, clothing, religion, and so on can be reliable indicators of the social coordination norms that he or she is most likely to use, over time the marker traits became reliable indicators of who was playing which game (see also Efferson, Lalive, and Fehr 2008).

For a good real-world example of cultural group selection, one need look no further than competition among companies in a market economy (Johnson, Price, and Van Vugt 2013). Even if they provide the same product or service, companies differ from one another, and those differences are clearly cultural (i.e., due to social learning), not genetic. Furthermore, those cultural differences lead to differential success among companies, with some surviving and others failing and shutting their doors. Of course, companies also have characteristics that make them somewhat unusual among the wide variety of culturally defined groups that humans form. First, competition among them is intense, with companies being founded and dying out with great frequency. Second, companies are normally quite discrete from one another, with occasional mergers or acquisitions duly noted as important exceptions to this rule. Third, companies are functionally integrated and have clear corporate structures. In contrast, other culturally different groups might better be thought of simply as categories, that is, people who share some common characteristic but do not interact in an interconnected set of roles or within any sort of corporate structure (Keesing 1975). Consider ethnic "groups," for example. Particularly in nonstate societies, such "groups" are really just categories, that is, people who share a bundle of culture traits (e.g., a common language) but do not necessarily have any sort of functionally integrated corporate structure.

These differences among different kinds of culturally defined groups may lead to different kinds of cultural group selection. Selection among companies (e.g., Arthur 2012), political interest groups (e.g., Baumgartner et al. 2009; Gray and Lowery 1997), organized religions (e.g., Stark 1996), descent groups (Keesing 1975; Cronk and Gerkey 2007; Gerkey and Cronk 2014) or other corporate, functionally integrated groups will largely be on culture traits that influence their ability to achieve their group-level goals, possibly at the expense of their constituent individuals. Let's call this "hard cultural group selection." When cultural group selection occurs among "groups" that are really just categories lacking functional integration, such as those shaped by shared ethnicity (Barth 1969), spirituality (e.g., Fuller 2001), and nationality (Anderson 1991), then no such traits exist. Instead, such groups differ in terms of the extent to which the culture traits that are prevalent within them help their members to survive and reproduce. Let's call this "soft cultural group selection." To understand the distinction between hard and soft cultural group selection, it might help to recall the contrast George C. Williams (1966: 16) drew between a "fleet herd of deer," in which fleetness is a characteristic of the herd, and a "herd of fleet deer," in which fleetness is a characteristic of the individual members of the herd and the fleetness of the herd as a whole a mere side effect. Between these two extremes lies what we might call "firm cultural group selection": selection among groups based on characteristics that provide less functional integration than is seen in corporate groups but more than is seen in categories.

Selection among companies, states, or any other functionally integrated corporate groups will suffice as an example of hard cultural group selection. For an example of soft cultural group selection, consider the possibility that some ethnic groups may succeed and others may fail because some happen to have culture traits that help their bearers survive and reproduce but have nothing to do with the group's ability to work as a unit. I have documented one instance of soft cultural group selection among the Mukogodo of Kenya, who learned to emulate the ethnic identity of a much larger, wealthier, and more successful group, the Maasai, to a point where they have almost totally lost all markers of their previously quite distinct ethnic identity, including not only their language but also their subsistence practices and religion (Cronk 1989, 2002, 2004b). As for "firm cultural group selection," consider selection acting on characteristics that provide some functional integration but not as much as that seen in corporate groups. Again, consider the Maasai. Although Maasai society has never been fully functionally integrated in the manner of a chiefdom or state, they do have other institutions that provide a limited degree of functional integration at local and regional levels. These include a descent system, an age-set system, and the more diffuse osotua risk-pooling system mentioned earlier in this chapter

(Cronk 2007; Cronk and Wasielewski 2008; Aktipis, Cronk, and de Aguiar 2011), all of which may have helped the Maasai succeed in competition with neighboring groups. Firm cultural group selection might be implicated in some episodes of religious conversion, as well. For example, Ensminger (1997) has argued that the spread of Islam in Africa was aided by the fact that it brought with it an innovative system of organizing trade. Finally, although corporate groups and categories are quite different, they may be closely related to one another in a functional sense. "People who manufacture and sell Hondas" is a corporate group, while "people who own Hondas" is a category. They are related in that the ability of the corporate group to attract people to the category determines its success in competition with other corporate groups. Similarly, "clergy and other officials of the United Methodist Church" is a corporate group that is dependent for its success on how many people consider themselves to be in the category "Methodist."

COALITIONAL PSYCHOLOGY

What impact might cultural group selection have on our evolved psychology? To date, most advocates of cultural group selection (e.g., Henrich 2004) have answered this question with a list of the same kinds of characteristics that would be favored by biological group selection: altruism, other-regarding preferences, prosociality, and so on. In some instances of cultural group selection, this must be true. Hard cultural group selection, for example, may involve some sacrifice on the part of the individuals in a group, which could provide selection pressure that rewards individual tendencies toward altruism and other prosocial behaviors. The research described earlier in this chapter on the greater longevity of religious than secular communes and its association with the costs they impose on their members may be a case in point. However, most culturally defined groups have more flexible memberships and fewer barriers to membership than religious communes, and their success often depends less on the costs they impose on their members than on the benefits they provide to them (Clark and Wilson 1961). Given that people can often move from group to group and that such movement can enhance rather than undermine the power of cultural group selection, its main effect on human psychology may have been to enhance our ability to deal with coalitions rather than to make us generally prosocial.

Depending on the type of cultural group selection that is operating, cultural group selection may favor different sorts of characteristics in individuals. When soft cultural group selection acts on categories, it will favor an ability to correctly predict the impact of membership in different categories on one's own success. By itself, this would not necessarily favor prosociality or cooperativeness. Although some categories of people may be more successful than others because they have found ways to be more cooperative, others may have succeeded by finding ways to avoid costly social entanglements. Hard cultural group selection among corporate groups, in contrast, should favor individual characteristics that enable entire groups to function well as integrated wholes. Individuals play specific and important roles in such groups, and group members need to know that everyone involved is committed to playing those roles. This should lead to individuals who become emotionally attached and committed to such groups and who send convincing signals to their fellow group members regarding those attachments and commitments. Paradoxically, selection on individuals to move from less successful to more successful groups would also favor an ability to shift loyalty from one group to another. The perfect person in this scenario would be one who feels and signals an honest commitment to the groups to which he or she belongs but who can also switch loyalties to other groups and then send equally convincing signals of his or her newfound commitments. Obviously, such "perfection" may be difficult to achieve. Our actual coalitional psychology may be a suboptimal mixture of these two abilities, involving considerable anguish and internal conflict in the face of uncertain, conflicting, and shifting loyalties.

Evidence of our flexible coalitional psychology can be found in the existing social psychological literature. For example, it has long been known that people find it surprisingly easy to form attachments even to quite arbitrary and temporary groups. For example, Tajfel, Billig, and Bundy (1971) had people rate paintings by Klee and Kandinsky and then divided them into two groups based ostensibly (but not actually) on their preferences. Subjects who then had to divide a sum of money between members of their own group and the other group gave more to members of their own group. More recently, social psychologists in England focused on the coalitional psychology of football (soccer) fans, in particular fans of Manchester United (Levine et al. 2005). Subjects who had already been identified as fans of Manchester United were given a series of questionnaires to heighten their sense of identification with the team and with their fellow fans. They were then taken across campus for the second part of the study. As they were walking across campus, a confederate playing the role of a jogger fell down and shouted as if in pain. The experimental condition was in which of three shirts the jogger was wearing: a Manchester United shirt, a plain shirt, or a shirt branded with the logo of MU's bitter rival, Liverpool FC. All but one of the subjects who saw a fellow Manchester fan fall down came to his aid, but they helped the runner in the plain shirt only a third of the time, and they helped the Liverpool fan even less often. In a follow-up study, the researchers again recruited Manchester United fans, but this time they gave them questionnaires that primed their sense of being football fans in general rather than Manchester fans in particular. This time, both the Manchester United and the Liverpool FC shirts elicited high rates of helping compared with the plain shirt, thus demonstrating the ease with which people's group identifications can be manipulated.

Because coalitions are flexible, people should be able to pick up cues that are easily changed, such as clothing and jewelry, as well as those that are more fixed, such as accents and physical similarities. To explore this, Kurzban, Tooby, and Cosmides (2001) showed people photographs of members of two rival basketball teams and told them to form impressions of the individuals on the teams. Each picture was paired with a statement that the person had supposedly made about the teams' rivalry. The actual pairing of sentences with photos was randomized across subjects. Subjects were then given a surprise memory test involving matching statements with photos. Because this was a difficult task, they made a lot of errors, and the patterns in the errors reveal that they used statements associated with faces along with other cues, such as the basketball jersey colors, to identify coalitions. One of this study's most interesting findings is that flexible cues such as the statements people make and the clothes they wear swamp the effects of race as a coalitional cue. This makes sense in light of how our ancestors lived. Given that their mobility was limited by how far they could walk, they were very unlikely to have encountered people as physically different from themselves as we routinely do now, and it would make little sense for us to have an evolved tendency to focus on race when determining coalitions. Kurzban, Tooby, and Cosmides's conclusion is that racism may simply be a misfiring of a psychological mechanism designed to pick up on more flexible coalitional cues. The encouraging conclusion of the study is that race's importance as a way to sort people into groups is greatly diminished when it is disconnected from actual coalitions.

INSTITUTIONAL CONTEXTS

Most human cooperation takes place not in a vacuum but rather within existing institutional and organizational structures. The evolutionary approach to human cooperation might be greatly enhanced through greater attention to such structures and how they interact with our evolved psychological propensities. What exactly is meant by the word "institution" has been the subject of much debate, with some scholars focusing on formal organizational structures and others using the term to refer to any "stable, valued, recurring patterns of behavior" (Huntington 1968: 12). Philosopher John Searle (2005) captured what makes institutions special: they have the power to assign people and objects to statuses that allow them to do things that they would not be able to do solely by virtue of their own inherent properties. Thus, paper and round bits of metal are just that—paper and round bits of metal—but money is an institution that facilitates economic cooperation. Similarly, my ability to teach classes and assign grades stems from the fact that I am employed by a university as a professor, not from any personal characteristic of mine. Searle's definition is useful because it captures what is special about both formal organizations and informal norms and conventions.

Although social scientists have devoted an enormous amount of work to the study of human institutions, little has been done on the ways in which such institutions interact with our species' evolved psychology. A recent exception was provided by anthropologist Drew Gerkey (2010, 2013), who examined the relationship between cooperation and institutions among the Koryak, a reindeer-herding and salmon-fishing people who live in the northern part of the Kamchatka peninsula in the far east of Russia. One of Gerkey's main research tools was the public goods game, or PGG. In a PGG, people are divided into small groups, usually of four. The group memberships and actions of the individuals are known only to the experimenter. Everyone is given an initial endowment (in this case, two hundred rubles) and the opportunity to contribute any portion of it, including none at all, to a common pot. The experimenter then doubles the pot and divides it equally among all people in the group. Players go home with whatever they kept from their initial endowments plus whatever they received from the common pot. Because everyone may be tempted to hold back on their donations to the pot for fear that others won't contribute to it, the PGG effectively captures the problem of free riders.

Gerkey's PGGs yielded two interesting findings. First, his participants were the most generous ever recorded among the dozens of PGG studies that have been conducted around the world, with many of them giving all of their endowments to the common pot. The reason appears to have to do with the issue of risk and uncertainty discussed earlier in this chapter. The physical environment in which the Koryak live is a difficult one with an extremely severe climate. As a result, they have become accustomed to helping each other out. One of his interviewees explained the situation this way: "In the North . . . a loner doesn't survive. That's why we support each other. We help each other" (Gerkey 2010: 141). Even participants who expected others to give less still often gave their entire endowment to the common pot. Second, in addition to using standard PGGs, Gerkey also had his participants play games framed with references to two institutions that all Koryak know well: the modern descendant of a Soviet-era collective farm, called a *sovkhoz*, and a post-Soviet collective institution called an *obshchina* that is meant to harken back to traditional cooperative structures. Although those institutions exist to foster cooperation, when the games were framed with references to those institutions, contributions to the common pot actually went down rather than up. The framing seems to have the effect of making the games more real by tying them to institutions that, as the participants well know, do not always work as well to enhance cooperation in the community as their members might like.

Conclusion

Early applications of evolutionary theory to the problem of human cooperation stayed close to the approach's roots in animal behavior studies, focusing on such trans-specific phenomena as kinship, assortment, and the likelihood of future interactions. From there, evolutionary scientists moved on to consider things that are more important or unique to humans, such as audiences, reputation, language, signs of commitment, and risk-pooling. The frontier areas described above follow this basic trajectory. For example, although the presence of culture and thus of group-level differences attributable to culture has been documented in other species (e.g., Rendell and Whitehead 2001; Whiten et al. 1999), it is safe to say that the impact of cultural group selection has been felt most powerfully among humans. As evolutionary scholars focus more of their attention on aspects of human cooperation that do not have good nonhuman analogs, they will need to master not only the evolutionary literature on cooperation but also the large existing literature on the topic generated by social and behavioral sciences.

Acknowledgments

I would like to thank Frank Batiste, Drew Gerkey, Beth L. Leech, Michelle Night Pipe, Montserrat Soler, and Helen Wasielewski for their thoughtful comments on an early draft of this chapter. I would also like to thank my collaborators C. Athena Aktipis, Rolando de Aguiar, Yan Hao, and Dieter Armbruster for their contributions to my understanding of risk-pooling and need-based transfers. This publication was made possible through the support of a grant from the John Templeton Foundation. The opinions expressed in this publication are my own and do not necessarily reflect the views of the John Templeton Foundation. Of course, I retain responsibility for any errors or shortcomings.

References

Aktipis, C. 2004. "Know When to Walk Away: Contingent Movement and the Evolution of Cooperation." *Journal of Theoretical Biology* 231 (2): 249–260.

———. 2011. "Is Cooperation Viable in Mobile Organisms? Simple Walk Away Rule Favors the Evolution of Cooperation in Groups." *Evolution and Human Behavior* 32 (4): 263–276.

Aktipis, C. A., L. Cronk, and R. de Aguiar. 2011. "Risk-Pooling and Herd Survival: An Agent-Based Model of a Maasai Gift-Giving System." *Human Ecology* 39: 131–140.

Alexander, R. D. 1977. "Natural Selection and the Analysis of Human Sociality." In *Changing Scenes in the Natural Sciences*, edited by C. E. Goulden, 283–337. Philadelphia: Philadelphia Academy of Natural Sciences.

———. 1987. *The Biology of Moral Systems*. Hawthorne, NY: Aldine de Gruyter.

Almagor, U. 1978. *Pastoral Partners: Affinity and Bond Partnership among the Dassanetch of South-West Ethiopia*. Manchester, UK: Manchester University Press.

Alvard, M. 2001. "Mutualistic Hunting." In *Meat-Eating and Human Evolution*, edited by C. Stanford and H. Bunn, 261–278. New York: Oxford University Press.

———. 2003. "Kinship, Lineage Identity, and an Evolutionary Perspective on the Structure of Cooperative Big Game Hunting Groups in Indonesia." *Human Nature* 14 (2): 129–163.

Alvard, M., and D. Nolin. 2002. "Rousseau's Whale Hunt? Coordination among Big Game Hunters." *Current Anthropology* 43 (4): 533–559.

Anderson, B. R. 1991. *Imagined Communities: Reflections on the Origin and Spread of Nationalism*. London: Verso.

Arthur, C. 2012. *Digital Wars: Apple, Google, Microsoft and the Battle for the Internet*. London: Kogan Page Publishers.

Aumann, R. J. 1981. "Survey of Repeated Games." In *Essays in Game Theory and Mathematical Economics in Honor of Oskar Morgenstern*, edited by R. J. Aumann, 11–42. Mannheim, Germany: Bibliographisches Institut.

Axelrod, R. 1984. *The Evolution of Cooperation*. New York: Basic Books.

Axelrod, R., and W. D. Hamilton. 1981. "The Evolution of Cooperation." *Science* 211: 1390–1396.
Baron-Cohen, S. 1995. *Mindblindness: An Essay on Autism and Theory of Mind*. Cambridge, MA: MIT Press.
Baron-Cohen, S., R. Campbell, A. Karmiloff-Smith, J. Grant, and J. Walker. 1995. "Are Children with Autism Blind to the Mentalistic Significance of the Eyes?" *British Journal of Developmental Psychology* 13: 379–398.
Barr, A., and G. Genicot. 2008. "Risk Sharing, Commitment, and Information: An Experimental Analysis." *Journal of the European Economic Association* 6 (6): 1151–1185.
Barth, F. 1969. *Ethnic Groups and Boundaries*. Boston: Little Brown and Company.
Bateson, M., D. Nettle, and G. Roberts. 2006. "Cues of Being Watched Enhance Cooperation in a Real-World Setting." *Biology Letters* 2: 412–414.
Baumgartner, F. R., J. M. Berry, M. Hojnacki, D. C. Kimball, and B. L. Leech. 2009. *Lobbying and Policy Change: Who Wins, Who Loses, and Why*. Chicago: University of Chicago Press.
Bickerton, D. 2009. *Adam's Tongue*. New York: Hill and Wang.
Bickerton, D., and E. Szathmáry. 2011. "Confrontational Scavenging as a Possible Source for Language and Cooperation." *BMC Evolutionary Biology* 11: 261.
Bliege Bird, R., E. A. Smith, and D. W. Bird. 2001. "The Hunting Handicap: Costly Signaling in Male Foraging Strategies." *Behavioral Ecology and Sociobiology* 50: 9–19.
Blumenschine, R. A. 1987. "Characteristics of an Early Hominid Scavenging Niche." *Current Anthropology* 28: 383–407.
Blurton Jones, N. G. 1984. "Selfish Origin for Human Food Sharing: Tolerated Theft." *Ethology and Sociobiology* 5: 1–3.
———. 1987. "Tolerated Theft: Suggestions about the Ecology and Evolution of Sharing, Hoarding, and Scrounging." *Social Science Information* 26: 31–54.
Bowles, S., and H. Gintis. 2003. "Origins of Human Cooperation." In *Genetic and Cultural Evolution of Cooperation*, edited by P. Hammerstein, 429–443. Cambridge, MA: MIT Press.
Burnham, T. C., and B. Hare. 2007. "Engineering Human Cooperation: Does Involuntary Neural Activation Increase Public Goods Contributions?" *Human Nature* 18: 88–108.
Case, A., I. Lin, and S. McLanahan. 2000. "How Hungry Is the Selfish Gene?" *Economic Journal* 110: 781–804.
Cashdan, E. A. 1985. "Coping with Risk: Reciprocity among the Basarwa of Northern Botswana." *Man* 20 (3): 454–474.
Chwe, M. S. 2001. *Rational Ritual: Culture, Coordination, and Common Knowledge*. Princeton, NJ: Princeton University Press.
Clark, P. B., and J. Q. Wilson. 1961. "Incentive Systems: A Theory of Organizations." *Administrative Science Quarterly* 6: 129–166.
Cosmides, L., and J. Tooby. 2005. "Neurocognitive Adaptations Designed for Social Exchange." In *The Handbook of Evolutionary Psychology*, edited by D. M. Buss, 584–627. New York: Wiley.
Cronk, L. 1989. "From Hunters to Herders: Subsistence Change as a Reproductive Strategy among the Mukogodo." *Current Anthropology* 30 (2): 224–234.
———. 2002. "From True Dorobo to Mukogodo Maasai: Contested Ethnicity in Kenya." *Ethnology* 41 (1): 27–49.
———. 2004a. "Continuity, Displaced Reference, and Deception." *Behavioral and Brain Sciences* 27 (4): 510–511.
———. 2004b. *From Mukogodo to Maasai: Ethnicity and Cultural Change in Kenya*. Boulder, CO: Westview Press.
———. 2007. "The Influence of Cultural Framing on Play in the Trust Game: A Maasai Example." *Evolution and Human Behavior* 28: 352–358.
Cronk, L., and D. Gerkey. 2007. "Kinship and Descent." In *The Oxford Handbook of Evolutionary Psychology*, edited by R.I.M. Dunbar and L. Barrett, 463–478. Oxford: Oxford University Press.
Cronk, L., and B. L. Leech. 2013. *Meeting at Grand Central: Understanding the Social and Evolutionary Roots of Cooperation*. Princeton, NJ: Princeton University Press.
Cronk, L., and H. Wasielewski. 2008. "An Unfamiliar Social Norm Rapidly Produces Framing Effects in an Economic Game." *Journal of Evolutionary Psychology* 6 (4): 283–308.
Dorfman, M. S. 2007. *Introduction to Risk Management and Insurance*. Upper Saddle River, NJ: Prentice Hall.
Dyson-Hudson, N. 1966. *Karimojong Politics*. Oxford: Clarendon.
Efferson, C., R. Lalive, and E. Fehr. 2008. "The Coevolution of Cultural Groups and Ingroup Favoritism." *Science* 321: 1844–1849.
Emery, N. J. 2000. "The Eyes Have It: The Neuroethology, Function and Evolution of Social Gaze." *Neuroscience and Biobehavioral Reviews* 24: 581–604.
Ensminger, J. 1997. "Transaction Costs and Islam: Explaining Conversion in Africa." *Journal of Institutional and Theoretical Economics* 153: 4–29.
Fafchamps, M., and S. Lund. 2003. "Risk-Sharing Networks in Rural Philippines." *Journal of Development Economics* 71 (2): 261–287.

Fehr, E., and F. Schneider. 2010. "Eyes Are on Us, but Nobody Cares: Are Eye Cues Relevant for Strong Reciprocity?" *Proceedings of the Royal Society B: Biological Sciences* 277: 1315–1323.
Fuller, R. C. 2001. *Spiritual but Not Religious: Understanding Unchurched America*. Oxford: Oxford University Press.
Gazzillo, S., B. Sopher, C. A. Aktipis, and L. Cronk. 2013. "The Origins of Risk Sharing: An Experimental Approach." Working paper, Department of Economics, Rutgers University.
Gerkey, D. 2010. *From State Collectives to Local Commons: Cooperation and Collective Action among Salmon Fishers and Reindeer Herders in Kamchatka, Russia*. PhD diss., anthropology, Rutgers University.
———. 2013. "Cooperation in Context: Public Goods Games and Post-Soviet Collectives in Kamchatka, Russia." *Current Anthropology* 54 (2): 144–176.
Gerkey, D., and L. Cronk. 2014. "What Is a Group? Conceptual Clarity Can Help Integrate Evolutionary and Social Scientific Research on Cooperation." *Behavioral and Brain Sciences* 37 (3): 260–261.
Gray, V., and D. Lowery. 1997. "Life in a Niche: Mortality Anxiety among Organized Interests in the American States." *Political Research Quarterly* 50: 25–47.
Gulliver, P. H. 1955. *The Family Herds: A Study of Two Pastoral Tribes in East Africa, the Jie and Turkana*. London: Routledge & Kegan Paul.
Gurven, M. 2004. "To Give or Not to Give: An Evolutionary Ecology of Human Food Transfers." *Behavioral and Brain Sciences* 27 (4): 543–583.
Gurven, M., W. Allen-Arave, K. Hill, and M. Hurtado. 2000. "'It's a Wonderful Life': Signaling Generosity among the Ache of Paraguay." *Evolution and Human Behavior* 21 (4): 263–282.
Haley, K. J., and D.M.T. Fessler. 2005. "Nobody's Watching? Subtle Cues Affect Generosity in an Anonymous Economic Game." *Evolution and Human Behavior* 26: 245–256.
Hames, R. 1990. "Sharing among the Yanomamo: Part I, The Effects of Risk." In *Risk and Uncertainty in Tribal and Peasant Economies*, edited by E. A. Cashdan, 89–106. Boulder, CO: Westview.
Hamilton, W. D. 1964. "The Genetical Evolution of Social Behaviour I and II." *Journal of Theoretical Biology* 7: 1–52.
Hamlin, J. K., K. Wynn, and P. Bloom. 2007. "Social Evaluation by Preverbal Infants." *Nature* 450: 557–560.
Hao, Y., L. Cronk, C. A. Aktipis, and D. Armbruster. Forthcoming. "Risk Pooling on a Network." *Evolution and Human Behavior*.
Hardin, G. 1968. "The Tragedy of the Commons." *Science* 162: 1243–1248.
Hawkes, K., J. F. O'Connell, and N. G. Blurton Jones. 1989. "Hardworking Hadza Grandmothers." In *Comparative Socioecology: The Behavioural Ecology of Humans and Other Mammals*, edited by V. Standen and R. A. Foley, 341–366. London: Basil Blackwell.
Henrich, J. 2004. "Cultural Group Selection, Coevolutionary Processes, and Large-Scale Cooperation." *Journal of Economic Behavior and Organization* 53: 3–35.
Henrich, N., and J. Henrich. 2007. *Why Humans Cooperate: A Cultural and Evolutionary Explanation*. Oxford: Oxford University Press.
Hume, D. 1740. *A Treatise of Human Nature. Book III: Of Morals*. London: Thomas Longman.
Huntington, S. 1968. *Political Order in Changing Societies*. New Haven, CT: Yale University Press.
Irons, W. 2001. "Religion as a Hard-to-Fake Sign of Commitment." In *Evolution and the Capacity for Commitment*, edited by R. M. Nesse, 292–309. New York: Russell Sage Foundation.
Isaac, G. L. 1978. "Food Sharing and Human Evolution: Archaeological Evidence from the Plio-Pleistocene of East Africa." *Journal of Anthropological Research* 34: 311–325.
Johnson, D.D.P., M. E. Price, and M. Van Vugt. 2013. "Darwin's Invisible Hand: Market Competition, Evolution and the Firm." *Journal of Economic Behavior and Organization* 90: S128–S140.
Kaplan, H., and K. Hill. 1985. "Hunting Ability and Reproductive Success among Male Ache Foragers: Preliminary Results." *Current Anthropology* 26 (1): 131–133.
Kaplan, H., K. Hill, and A. M. Hurtado. 1990. "Risk, Foraging, and Food Sharing among the Ache." In *Risk and Uncertainty in Tribal and Peasant Economies*, edited by E. A. Cashdan, 107–143. Boulder, CO: Westview.
Kaplan, H. S., E. Schniter, V. L. Smith, and B. J. Wilson. 2012. "Risk and the Evolution of Human Exchange." *Proceedings of the Royal Society B: Biological Sciences* 279 (1740): 2930–2935.
Keesing, R. 1975. *Kin Groups and Social Structure*. New York: Holt, Rinehart and Wilson.
Kobayashi, H., and S. Kohshima. 1997. "Unique Morphology of the Human Eye." *Nature* 387: 767–768.
———. 2001. "Unique Morphology of the Human Eye and Its Adaptive Meaning: Comparative Studies on External Morphology of the Primate Eye." *Journal of Human Evolution* 40: 419–435.
Kurzban, R., J. Tooby, and L. Cosmides. 2001. "Can Race Be Erased? Coalitional Computation and Social Categorization." *Proceedings of the National Academy of Science* 98 (26): 15387–15392.
Lamba, S., and R. Mace. 2010. "People Recognize When They Are Really Anonymous in an Economic Game." *Evolution and Human Behavior* 31: 271–278.
Lehmann, L., K. Foster, E. Borenstein, and M. Feldman. 2008. "Social and Individual Learning of Helping in Humans and Other Species." *Trends in Ecology and Evolution* 23: 664–671.

Levine, M., A. Prosser, D. Evans, and S. Reicher. 2005. "Identity and Emergency Intervention: How Social Group Membership and Inclusiveness of Group Boundaries Shape Helping Behavior." *Personality and Social Psychology Bulletin* 31: 443–453.

Marlowe, F. 2010. *The Hadza: Hunter-Gatherers of Tanzania*. Berkeley: University of California Press.

Maynard Smith, J. 1964. "Group Selection and Kin Selection." *Nature* 201: 1145–1147.

———. 1976. "Group Selection." *Quarterly Review of Biology* 51 (2): 277–283.

McAdams, R. H. 2008. "Beyond the Prisoners' Dilemma: Coordination, Game Theory and the Law." John M. Olin Law and Economics Working Paper No. 437 (second series), Public Law and Legal Theory Working Paper No. 241, University of Chicago.

McElreath, R., R. Boyd, and P. J. Richerson. 2003. "Shared Norms and the Evolution of Ethnic Markers." *Current Anthropology* 44: 122–129.

Nesse, R. M., ed. 2001. *Evolution and the Capacity for Commitment*. New York: Russell Sage.

Nolin, D. A. 2010. "Food-Sharing Networks in Lamalera, Indonesia: Reciprocity, Kinship, and Distance." *Human Nature* 21 (3): 243–268.

Nowak, M. A. 2006. *Evolutionary Dynamics*. Cambridge, MA: Harvard University Press.

Olson, M. 1965. *The Logic of Collective Action*. Cambridge, MA: Harvard University Press.

Ostrom, E., R. Gardner, and J. Walker. 1994. *Rules, Games, and Common-Pool Resources*. Ann Arbor: University of Michigan Press.

Peterson, N. 1993. "Demand Sharing: Reciprocity and the Pressure for Generosity among Foragers." *American Anthropologist* 95 (4): 860–874.

Premack, D. G., and G. Woodruff. 1978. "Does the Chimpanzee Have a Theory of Mind?" *Behavioral and Brain Sciences* 1 (4): 515–526.

Qirko, H. N. 2004. "'Fictive Kin' and Suicide Terrorism." *Science* 304 (5667): 50–51.

———. 2009. "Altruism in Suicide Terror Organizations." *Zygon: Journal of Religion and Science* 44 (2): 289–322.

Rendell, L., and H. Whitehead. 2001. "Culture in Whales and Dolphins." *Behavioral and Brain Sciences* 24: 309–382.

Reyer, H. 1980. "Flexible Helper Structure as an Ecological Adaptation in the Pied Kingfisher (*Ceryle rudis rudis* L.)." *Behavioral Ecology and Sociobiology* 6 (3): 219–227.

Richerson, P. J., and R. Boyd. 1998. "The Evolution of Human Ultra-Sociality." In *Ideology, Warfare, and Indoctrinability*, edited by I. Eibl-Eibisfeldt and F. Salter, 107–143. Oxford: Berghahn Books.

Rigdon, M. K., M. Ishii, M. Watabe, and S. Kitayama. 2009. "Minimal Social Cues in the Dictator Game." *Journal of Economic Psychology* 30: 358–367.

Salmon, C. 1988. "The Evocative Nature of Kin Terminology in Political Rhetoric." *Politics and the Life Sciences* 17 (1): 51–57.

Schelling, T. 1960. *The Strategy of Conflict*. Cambridge, MA: Harvard University Press.

Searle, J. R. 2005. "What Is an Institution?" *Journal of Institutional Economics* 1 (1): 1–22.

Sherman, P. W. 1977. "Nepotism and the Evolution of Alarm Calls." *Science* 197: 1246–1253.

Smith, E. A. 2010. "Communication and Collective Action: Language and the Evolution of Human Cooperation." *Evolution and Human Behavior* 31: 231–245.

Sober, E., and D. S. Wilson. 1998. *Unto Others: The Evolution and Psychology of Unselfish Behavior*. Cambridge, MA: Harvard University Press.

Soler, M. 2012. "Costly Signaling, Ritual and Cooperation: Evidence from Candomblé, an Afro-Brazilian Religion." *Evolution and Human Behavior* 33 (4): 346–356.

Sosis, R., and C. Alcorta. 2003. "Signaling, Solidarity, and the Sacred: The Evolution of Religious Behavior." *Evolutionary Anthropology* 12: 264–274.

Sosis, R., and E. Bressler. 2003. "Cooperation and Commune Longevity: A Test of the Costly Signaling Theory of Religion." *Cross-Cultural Research* 37: 211–239.

Sosis, R., and B. Ruffle. 2003. "Religious Ritual and Cooperation: Testing for a Relationship on Israeli Religious and Secular Kibbutzim." *Current Anthropology* 44: 713–722.

Sparks, A., and P. Barclay. 2013. "Eye Images Increase Generosity, but Not for Long: The Limited Effect of a False Cue." *Evolution and Human Behavior* 34 (5): 317–322.

Stark, R. 1996. *The Rise of Christianity*. Princeton, NJ: Princeton University Press.

Tajfel, H., M. G. Billig, and R. P. Bundy. 1971. "Social Categorization and Intergroup Behaviour." *European Journal of Social Psychology* 1 (2): 149–178.

Tomasello, M. 2009. *Why We Cooperate*. Cambridge, MA: MIT Press.

Tomasello, M., and M. Carpenter. 2007. "Shared Intentionality." *Developmental Science* 10 (1): 121–125.

Trivers, R. 1971. "The Evolution of Reciprocal Altruism." *The Quarterly Review of Biology* 46 (1): 35–57.

Ullmann-Margalit, E. 1977. *The Emergence of Norms*. Oxford: Clarendon Press.

Wason, P. C. 1966. "Reasoning." In *New Horizons in Psychology*, edited by B. M. Foss, 135–151. Harmondsworth, UK: Penguin.

Whiten, A., J. Goodall, W. C. McGrew, T. Nishida, V. Reynolds, Y. Sugiyama, C.E.G. Tutin, R. W. Wrangham, and C. Boesch. 1999. "Cultures in Chimpanzees." *Nature* 399: 682–685.

Wiessner, P. 1982. "Risk, Reciprocity and Social Influences on !Kung San Economics." In *Politics and History in Band Societies*, edited by E. Leacock and R. B. Lee, 61–84. Cambridge: Cambridge University Press.

Williams, G. C. 1966. *Adaptation and Natural Selection*. Princeton, NJ: Princeton University Press.

Winterhalder, B. 1986. "Diet Choice, Risk, and Food Sharing in a Stochastic Environment." *Journal of Anthropological Archaeology* 5 (4): 369–392.

Woodburn, J. 1998. "Sharing Is Not a Form of Exchange: An Analysis of Property-Sharing in Immediate Return Hunter-Gatherer Societies." In *Property Relations: Renewing the Anthropological Tradition*, edited by C. M. Hann, 48–63. Cambridge: Cambridge University Press.

Wyman, E., and M. Tomasello. 2007. "The Ontogenetic Origins of Human Cooperation." In *Oxford Handbook of Evolutionary Psychology*, edited by R. Dunbar and L. Barret, 227–236. Oxford: Oxford University Press.

Wynne-Edwards, V. C. 1962. *Animal Dispersion in Relation to Social Behavior*. London: Oliver & Boyd.

Chapter Twenty-Four

When and Why Power Corrupts

An Evolutionary Perspective

Charleen R. Case and Jon K. Maner

> Leaders play a critical role in helping their groups achieve important goals. Sometimes, however, leaders are more interested in their own personal capacity for power than they are in helping their groups succeed. This chapter describes recent evolutionary theories and research aimed at elucidating the situational and motivational factors that influence the behavior of leaders. Drawing from findings observed in nonhuman primates as well as those in humans, the chapter describes how human motivations for elevated social rank are similar to and different from those of our closest extant relatives. The chapter also reviews recent research documenting common situations that occur in both humans and other primates that might set the stage for negative leadership behaviors, as well as specific strategies leaders use to minimize threats to their power. The chapter closes by discussing promising avenues for future research aimed at applying an evolutionary perspective to understand leadership. An evolutionary perspective provides valuable conceptual tools for understanding both the constructive and destructive aspects of leadership behavior.

Leaders play a critical role in group behavior. Leaders help group members coordinate with one another, establish and prioritize their goals, and pursue the goals that are most important to the well-being of the group. In performing those duties, leaders typically experience relatively high degrees of status and power (Anderson, Kraus, et al. 2012; Henrich and Gil-White 2001). Status and power are conferred to leaders under the (often implicit) social contract that they will use that power and status to pursue actions that benefit the group (Boehm 1999; Van Vugt 2006). Although leaders are able to use their elevated positions to help their groups achieve beneficial outcomes, some power-hungry leaders may cause their groups to fail by prioritizing their own personal capacity for power over the goals of their group. That is, some leaders may care more about protecting or enhancing their own power than they do about serving the group.

Such behavior makes abundant sense when one considers that having elevated social rank reflects a fundamental social motivation—one that humans share with many other group-living species. Indeed, an evolutionary perspective is useful for understanding this dark side of leadership. An evolutionary perspective helps elucidate the specific evolved motives that drive people to strive for high social rank, helps identify the strategies that people might use to attain and maintain their rank, and helps illuminate specific factors within the person and the situation that moderate people's behavior within social hierarchies.

Because the success or failure of achieving group goals often hinges on the behavior of leaders, it is important to understand why there are so many apparent failures of leadership. Indeed, understanding the conditions under which leaders are most likely to selfishly prioritize their own goals over the good of the group is a critical goal for research. To that end, examining the psychology of power and status through the lens of evolutionary psychology is exceptionally useful; by explicating the adaptive function of power and status-driven behaviors, social scientists can better predict when certain leaders might wield their power against the interest of those they lead.

This chapter is divided into four main sections. In the first section, we describe evidence for the many benefits associated with possessing status (i.e., elevated social rank) and the power that often comes with it. Drawing from findings observed in nonhuman primates as well as those in humans, we describe how human motivations for elevated social rank are similar to and different from those of our closest extant relatives. In the second section, we describe the tension that sometimes exists between leaders and their followers. Although leaders are tasked with helping their group succeed, there are situational factors that cause some leaders to become more concerned with preserving their power than fostering group goals. In that section, we describe common situations that occur in both humans and other primates that might set the stage for negative leadership behaviors. The third section describes recent research on leaders' selfish use of power as a means to protect their role atop the hierarchy. There, we highlight some of the specific strategies leaders use to minimize threats to their power, focusing on those strategies that might harm group functioning or keep groups from obtaining their goals. In the fourth and final section of this chapter, we discuss promising avenues for future research aimed at applying an evolutionary perspective to understand leadership.

Power and Prestige: Two Benefits of Status

One characteristic that many contemporary human groups share in common with ancestral groups and other primates is that they are organized hierarchically. Within any social hierarchy, some individuals enjoy more status (as defined by their rank in the hierarchy) than others. In humans, high-status individuals typically enjoy some level of prestige (as defined by the level of respect they receive from their group) and power (as defined by their access to and control over resources).

There are many benefits associated with having the prestige and power that come with holding high social rank. Hierarchically arranged groups are characterized by asymmetric control over resources, such that leaders (compared with followers) enjoy relatively greater control over the distribution and use of valued group resources. Consequently, high-ranking individuals, as compared with those of lower rank, tend to experience greater happiness, health, and overall well-being (Keltner, Gruenfeld, and Anderson 2003; Kifer et al. 2013; see also Anderson, Willer, et al. 2012). Furthermore, evolutionary theories posit that having high social rank increases one's reproductive success—across many species, high-ranking group members are better able than subordinate individuals to attain mating partners and to provide essential care to offspring (e.g., Ellis 1995; von Rueden, Gurven, and Kaplan 2011). For example, high-ranking males tend to be more attractive to females and thus have greater access to potential mates than low-ranking males (Sadalla, Kenrick, and Vershure 1987). As another example, high-ranking chimpanzee females tend to have better reproductive success than their subordinate counterparts (Pusey 2012; Pusey and

Schroepfer-Walker 2013). This appears to be due, in part, to the fact that high-ranking females have greater access to quality food sources than those of lower rank (e.g., Murray, Eberly, and Pusey 2006; Pusey et al. 2005; Wittig and Boesch 2003). In short, the social, material, psychological, and genetic benefits to having status are substantial. Thus, individuals of elevated social rank often have greater reproductive fitness, meaning they are likely to have more viable offspring than their lower-ranking counterparts.

Given that individuals at the bottom of their group's hierarchy do not experience the same fitness advantages as those possessing high social rank, humans (like many other primates) of lower rank often are highly motivated to seek and procure positions of status over others. Then, once those positions are achieved, they are vigorously protected (Barkow 1989; Wilson and Daly 1992). Indeed, the desire for high social rank has been likened to other basic social motives, such as the desire for positive relationships (Kenrick et al. 2002).

Disentangling Power, Prestige, and Status

In addition to high social status, leaders are typically endowed with power. Although power and status often go hand in hand, they reflect conceptually and operationally distinct constructs. Consistent with the recent literature, we operationally define status as an individual's rank within a social hierarchy, and we define power as an individual's relative control over group resources (Archer 1988; Keltner, Gruenfeld, and Anderson 2003; Magee and Galinsky 2008). Thus, power is intimately related to the concept of dominance in the nonhuman primate literature. Alpha male chimpanzees, for example, have preferential access to food, desirable spaces, mates, and grooming partners. One essential feature of power is that it affords the capacity to influence others by providing or withholding resources and administering punishments (Keltner, Gruenfeld, and Anderson 2003; Magee and Galinsky 2008). That aspect of power is also observed in nonhuman primates. In dominance hierarchies, higher-ranking individuals use aggression and intimidation to assert their dominance over subordinate group members (Sapolsky 2005). Due to coalitional or exchange relationships, high-ranking primates also sometimes give preferential treatment to some group members over others (e.g., Nishida 1983; Xia et al. 2013).

Although power appears fairly analogous (if not homologous) to nonhuman primate dominance, the prestige element of status may be uncommon (if at all present) in nonhuman primate hierarchies. Therefore, prestige may be an attribute that is unique to human hierarchies. Like power, prestige confers on those who hold it greater access to group resources (Henrich and Gil-White 2001). However, there is a fundamental difference between prestige and power: whereas powerful individuals can influence others through the control they have over group resources, prestigious group members have social influence as a result of being respected by members of the group. That is, the subordinates of prestigious individuals grant deference to them because they are perceived as possessing knowledge and skills deemed valuable to the group (Henrich and Gil-White 2001). Hence, although humans may be unique in that they can acquire positions of high social rank through the freely conferred deference of others, they still share with other primates the capacity for achieving social rank through coercion and manipulation of group resources.

Individual Differences in Status-Seeking Traits

Individuals differ in the extent to which their approach to status and leadership is motivated by a desire for power versus prestige, even though the position often begets the leader both. Exemplifying the link between human power and nonhuman dominance, *dominance* motivation reflects a strategy by which people attain and maintain positions of leadership through coercion and the selfish manipulation of group resources. Leaders with high levels of dominance motivation are concerned with establishing and preserving their own personal capacity for power, regardless of whether that power has been freely granted to them by subordinates (Barkow 1989; Ellis 1995; Fodor 1985; Henrich and Gil-White 2001). In contrast, those who adopt a *prestige*-based approach to leadership typically achieve and maintain leadership positions by displaying desirable traits and abilities that benefit the group, not by dominating others or using power for personal gain (e.g., Chagnon 1992). Indeed, the distinction between dominance and prestige is similar to one made between personalized power (using power for personal gain) and socialized power (using power to benefit other people; e.g., McClelland 1970, 1975; Winter 1973; see also French and Raven 1959). Such distinctions highlight the importance of differentiating prosocial from selfish aspects of leadership, as a leader can use his or her position of high status either to benefit the self or to benefit the group.

Notwithstanding the fundamental differences between dominance and prestige, the two motivations are not mutually exclusive. Whereas some individuals are primarily motivated by either dominance or prestige, many people are motivated by both. That means that even predominantly benevolent leaders may, to some extent, desire power and control over their subordinates. And yet, some leaders are much more preoccupied with solidifying their power than others. Given that many leadership positions afford the capacity for both prestige and dominance, what situational factors might cause some types of leaders to work toward securing their power, even when doing so means behaving in ways that run counter to the group's goals? We take up that question in the next section.

The Essential Tension between Leaders and Followers

There often exists a fundamental conflict between the motivations of leaders and those of followers (Boehm 1999; Van Vugt, Hogan, and Kaiser 2008; see also Van Lange et al. 2007). Because hierarchies typically are malleable and status roles are continually shifting (e.g., Sapolsky 2005; Van Vugt, Hogan, and Kaiser 2008; see also Ellemers, Wilke, and Van Knippenberg 1993), followers sometimes attempt to decrease the power gap between themselves and leaders to avoid exploitation (Boehm 1999). Conversely, leaders sometimes are motivated to maintain or increase the power gap in order to protect their privileged position within the group (e.g., Case and Maner, forthcoming; Maner and Mead 2010; Mead and Maner 2012; McClelland 1975; Tiedens, Unzueta, and Young 2007; Van Vugt, Hogan, and Kaiser 2008). Consider that a CEO might feel threatened by a midlevel manager who is smart and skilled and makes excellent managerial calls, because these things could signal that the midlevel manager might be a better bet for running the company and might challenge the CEO's position atop the corporate hierarchy. Thus, when leaders feel that their position of power is threatened by one or more subordinates, they may behave in ways that minimize the potential threat and protect their power. Therefore, leaders who are motivated to maintain their high social rank despite the needs and goals of their group members should be most likely to selfishly exert their power when environmental cues indicate that their power is tenuous. Such individuals are more likely to be motivated by power than by prestige.

Concerns about Losing Status

Because hierarchies are typically malleable, dominant leaders may chronically fear a loss of their power (Tetlock 2002). Indeed, such is often the case for alpha male chimpanzees and other top-ranking primates. High-ranking male chimpanzees, for example, often display increased levels of psychological stress because they must constantly defend their position (Anestis 2010; Sapolsky 2005). That is one reason alpha male chimpanzees appear so much larger than the other males in their group; their anxiety causes their hair to stand on end as a means to make them appear larger than those who aim to usurp their position as alpha (de Waal 1982).

Above and beyond chronic concerns about losing status, the situational stability of a group's hierarchy may be one cue that increases the extent to which leaders worry that their power might be lost. Indeed, hierarchies vary in the extent to which their malleability is explicit; in some situations, for example, groups are tasked with making decisions about leadership roles (e.g., during political elections) and under those circumstances the potential threat to a leader's power is likely to become especially salient and immediate. Such explicit instabilities within a hierarchy might amplify the extent to which dominant leaders are motivated to enact strategies aimed at safeguarding their power (Tetlock 1981). Indeed, when situations cause dominant leaders to believe that their power can be lost, they often respond by prioritizing the ability to maintain their power, even when doing so undermines the goals of their group (Case and Maner, forthcoming; Maner and Mead 2010; Mead and Maner 2012). In contrast, when leaders are assured that their power is unlikely to be lost, even highly dominant leaders prioritize the good of the group because there is little need to safeguard their power.

Qualities of the Subordinate

Not all subordinates are equally threatening to leaders' power. Dominance-motivated leaders are likely to perceive some subordinates, more than others, as threats to their power. High-ranking nonhuman primates, for example, often behave agonistically toward other high-ranking subordinates who specifically threaten their power (Sapolsky 2005). In fact, those explicit power-protecting behaviors are extremely characteristic of our closest extant relative, the chimpanzee. Alpha male chimpanzees behave in particularly hostile ways toward beta males (de Waal 1982; Nishida 1983; Nishida and Hosaka 1996). Such behaviors are motivated by the fact that a beta, as second in rank, poses the greatest threat to an alpha's position of power.

In humans, highly talented subordinates are similar to beta male chimpanzees: subordinates who possess skills that are valuable to the group may receive respect and deference from other group members that, in turn, can increase the subordinates' status and power. Because those individuals are thus in a particularly strong position to take over the leader's role, they can be threatening to their group's current leader, particularly if the leader is concerned about maintaining his or her position atop the hierarchy (Van Vugt, Hogan, and Kaiser 2008). Thus, human leaders sometimes act agonistically toward talented subordinates, just as alpha chimpanzees act toward betas.

It is worth noting the irony underlying that pattern of behavior: although highly skilled group members are best equipped to help their group succeed and achieve its goals, it is precisely those group members who might receive the ire of their power-hungry leaders. Those talented group members need not demonstrate any desire for increased social rank in the group; merely being an asset to group success is enough to provoke dominant leaders to mistreat valuable group members.

Power-Maintenance Tactics: When Leaders Suppress Subordinates

Powerful leaders employ a variety of strategies in order to prevent group members from usurping their high-ranking position. In nonhuman primates like chimpanzees, high-ranking individuals often perform elaborate displays of their physical prowess toward lower-ranking group members as a means of intimidation (Boehm 1999; de Waal 1982). To do so, they may aggressively drum on buttress roots, swing branches, and throw rocks, all while charging their targets.

Unlike high-ranking nonhuman primates, human leaders typically cannot act in openly hostile ways toward their subordinates. Such open hostility is often perceived as breaking the leader's social contract with the group and, thus, could cause subordinates to band together against the leader. Instead, leaders who wish to suppress a talented subordinate typically rely on other, subtler tactics. Many of these strategies, while indirect, still closely resemble tactics employed by nonhuman primates in the sense that they are aimed at reducing the threat a subordinate poses to one's own status and power. For example, a manager might schedule particular employees to work long days and weekends or might assign certain employees to tedious yet menial projects as a way of subordinating them.

Using controlled laboratory settings, our work has demonstrated that some leaders do, in fact, feel threatened by skilled subordinates and behave in ways designed to suppress them. In many of our studies, participants were assigned to a condition of tenuous leadership (in which changes to the hierarchy were possible and thus their power could be lost), stable leadership (in which the hierarchy was inflexible and no changes to leadership could occur), or an egalitarian control condition (in which participants all had equal authority). Participants in the two leadership positions were also given power: the ability to direct the work of their group members, to evaluate them at the end of the session, and to give or withhold monetary rewards from them based on those evaluations. Participants were also given the opportunity to make important decisions for their group—a task often required of real leaders. With that opportunity, leaders were able to choose between helping their group achieve its goals, on one hand, and maintaining their own powerful position, on the other. Such studies provided a picture of how and when leaders might subordinate their followers as a way of protecting their own position of power and privilege.

DEMOTION AND OSTRACISM

One way powerful leaders might suppress a subordinate is by decreasing the subordinate's influence in the group. This might be done by either decreasing the social rank of the subordinate or, in extreme cases, ostracizing him or her from the group. Indeed, demotion and ostracism often are outcomes of extreme competition for rank in nonhuman primates. If an alpha male chimpanzee succeeds in defending his powerful role from an upstarting beta male, for example, the relatively high-ranking subordinate may fall farther down the hierarchy and might even suffer exclusion from the group (Nishida 1983; Nishida and Hosaka 1996).

Similar demotion and ostracism tactics have been demonstrated in human leaders. In two studies conducted by Maner and Mead (2010), participants were assigned to a leadership role in a group and were told that one of the group members was exceptionally skilled at the task the group would be performing. The optimal strategy for enhancing group performance would have been to embrace that person's skill and to give that person the opportunity to play a sizable and influential role in the task. However, leaders with a strong desire for power did just the opposite. In one study they assigned the skilled subordinate to a role within the group that carried almost no influence at all over the task and assigned less competent people to carry out the task. This prevented the skilled subordinate from demonstrating his or her skill and, as a consequence, gaining status and social rank. In a second study, dominant leaders actually attempted to exclude the skilled subordinate from the task entirely, voting to ostracize him or her from the group.

Ironically, those leaders chose to exclude the most talented group member, while at the same time voting to include a relatively incompetent group member. Although excluding a highly competent subordinate from one's group would not help the group perform well, it would ensure that he or she would not gain social rank and threaten the dominant leader's powerful position. Notably, such behavior was observed only among leaders with a strong desire for dominance, not among those who instead sought prestige. Among leaders who were high in dominance motivation, the desire to protect their power apparently overwhelmed the desire to help the group perform well.

In a real-world setting such as at a corporate office, company leaders often have some control over employee promotions and demotions, and can greatly influence the hiring and firing process. It is possible, then, that some CEOs might sometimes work to suppress particular employees through demoting or firing them. In particular, the above studies by Maner and Mead (2010) suggest that dominant leaders whose power is tenuous are the most likely to employ those strategies. Additionally, employees exhibiting skills valuable to the group may be most likely to be targets of those strategies. Because demotion and firing of leader-threatening but otherwise highly valuable group members would be especially transparent to the rest of the group, dominant leaders might use subtler tactics. Rather than demoting a skilled subordinate, for example, a power-hungry leader might instead promote less talented group members.

Vigilance and Control

An even subtler tactic leaders might employ to suppress subordinates is closely monitoring their behavior. If subordinates behave in ways that might jeopardize the leader's power, such vigilance would allow the leader to immediately step in to prevent subordinates from ascending in rank. Again, this is a strategy employed by some high-ranking nonhuman primates. Alpha male chimpanzees are vigilant of subordinates, particularly those that might attempt to usurp their alpha status. They closely monitor ingroup rivals and intervene when those rivals behave in ways that jeopardize the alpha's position (de Waal 1982; Nishida 1983; Nishida and Hosaka 1996).

One way to heighten vigilance as a means of being able to readily exert control over subordinates is by increasing one's proximity to potentially threatening rivals. Mead and Maner (2012) conducted several laboratory studies investigating whether leaders who felt threatened by a talented group member might attempt to increase their proximity to him or her. In one study, leaders high in dominance motivation chose to work in the same room as the subordinate, even though it was explained to them that working independently and in different rooms would help the group perform better. In two other studies, dominant leaders chose to sit close to a skilled subordinate so that the leader could keep a close eye on what the subordinate was doing. In the first of these studies, dominance-motivated leaders moved their chair closer to where their subordinate was going to be seated. In the second, those leaders chose a group seating arrangement that positioned them closest to the skilled subordinate. Such behaviors were not intended simply to watch and perhaps learn from the skilled subordinate, because leaders were not vigilant of the subordinate when the leader's power was secure. The only participants who closely monitored the skilled subordinate were those leaders who were worried about losing their power within the group and for whom power was tenuous. Thus, dominant leaders sought proximity to skilled subordinates as a way to monitor and reduce the threat they posed to the leader's social rank.

Most physical or interpersonal threats cause individuals to attack or become avoidant (Griskevicius et al. 2009; Öhman and Mineka 2001; Park, Faulkner, and Schaller

2003; Schaller, Park, and Faulkner 2003). However, as described above, powerful leaders sometimes instead seek proximity to those who threaten their social rank. Thus, strategic vigilance toward and control of threatening subordinates seems to be a special case wherein possessing power allows dominant leaders to attain and maintain proximity to the threat. This might be because powerful, high-ranking individuals have not only greater control over resources (Archer 1988; Keltner, Gruenfeld, and Anderson 2003) but the ability to punish or withhold resources from subordinate group members while staying relatively free from direct punishment themselves (Keltner, Gruenfeld, and Anderson 2003; Magee and Galinsky 2008). Those aspects of their powerful role may allow leaders to safely remain in proximity to threatening subordinates in order to remain vigilant for opportunities to exert control over them.

Outside the laboratory, there are many examples of how powerful leaders can monitor and control their subordinates. For example, dominant managers might be particularly likely to stop by the cubicles of their more talented employees to ensure that they are, indeed, doing what the managers have asked of them. Some managers may take that strategy one step further and even micromanage their talented employees as a means of controlling them and preventing them from behaving in ways that might gain them status in the office. Conversely, less skilled subordinates who might benefit from extra managerial supervision may not receive attention from power-driven leaders who are more concerned with maintaining their power than ensuring the success of their company. These examples illustrate how, even in contemporary organizational settings, behavior can be strongly shaped by evolved social motives related to dominance and status—motives that humans share in common with many other group-living species.

COALITION SUPPRESSION

One critical function served by leaders is facilitating cooperation and coordination among group members (Van Vugt 2006). However, despite the fact that leaders are typically expected to promote positive relationships among subordinates, some leaders may instead create divisions among their followers. Although an individual subordinate may pose a threat to a leader's power, that subordinate would be much better equipped to appropriate a leader's position with the support of other group members.

The threat of subordinate coalition formation appears to be what motivates alpha male chimpanzees to engage in a behavior known as *separating intervention* (de Waal 1982; Nishida 1983; Nishida and Hosaka 1996). Although an alpha male can often hold his own against a beta who attempts to claim alpha status, his prospects of maintaining power drop dramatically when the beta male recruits help from the gamma male (the third ranking male). Then, the alpha must combat two males at once. To prevent that from occurring, alpha males thwart instances of beta-gamma bonding: they direct elaborate, threatening displays of their physical strength toward the two males and charge them when they are caught allo-grooming and sometimes even when they are just sitting beside one another. This sends the males fleeing and helps the alpha keep the beta male from forming a strategic alliance with the gamma (de Waal 1982).

Recent research has investigated whether, like alpha male chimpanzees, dominant leaders interested in protecting their power might try to prevent talented subordinates from forming relationships with other group members, even though doing so could ultimately detract from the well-being of the group as a whole (Case and Maner, forthcoming). Indeed, in several experiments, dominant leaders sequestered skilled subordinates and prevented them from bonding with other group members. In one experiment, leaders limited the degree to which a talented subordinate could communicate directly with other group members. In a second experiment, leaders sought to physically isolate a talented subordinate by placing him or her in a room alone, away from other group members. In a third experiment, leaders went beyond simply limiting interaction among subordinates by specifically preventing a talented subordinate from socializing with others on a close, interpersonal level. In a fourth experiment, leaders paired a talented subordinate with a group member who possessed an incompatible personality type, thus decreasing the likelihood that the two subordinates would bond interpersonally. These findings suggest that leaders who feel threatened by skilled group members sometimes seek to isolate those individuals in order to prevent them from forming coalitions and, ultimately, as a means of protecting their own power.

In corporate environments, high-ranking managers concerned with maintaining power may work to divide highly skilled subordinates as a means of preventing them from forming coalitions with other group members. Those dividing strategies might take the form of assigning tasks to skilled subordinates that must be completed individually or even just failing to introduce new group members to them. Because many organized groups must reach their goals through the combined efforts of several group members working together, dominant leaders may disadvantage their group by separating skilled subordinates from their peers. Talented group members often have ideas or skills worth sharing with other group members or may be particularly energizing and motivating team members. Thus, preventing them from interacting closely with other subordinates could possibly do the group a huge disservice.

SUMMARY OF FINDINGS

Leaders can employ a variety of strategies aimed at suppressing subordinates as a means of securing their own high social rank, along with the many benefits that come with that rank. As a means of protecting their own powerful position, leaders might divide subordinates, closely monitor and control them, or even demote and ostracize them. Recent evidence demonstrates that there are several personal and situational factors that make leaders more or less likely to use those self-serving strategies.

First, strategies aimed at suppressing subordinates seem to be observed only among leaders high in dominance motivation, a trait quite characteristic of chimpanzees striving to attain and maintain alpha status. Because leaders high in dominance motivation greatly desire power and control, they tend to use the power they possess to maintain their privileged position atop the social hierarchy. Leaders low in dominance motivation, in contrast, do not generally seek to suppress subordinates. Indeed, leaders unconcerned with having power and control sometimes seek to increase the social contact between talented subordinates and other group members (Case and Maner, forthcoming). Moreover, leaders who seek prestige rather than power tend not to suppress their subordinates; those leaders instead tend to prioritize the goals of the group over their own personal capacity for power (Maner and Mead 2010).

Second, evidence for strategies of subordinate suppression is observed primarily when the leader's power is tenuous and might be lost. Although human and nonhuman primate hierarchies are often malleable (Anestis 2010; Sapolsky 2005), leaders for whom this malleability is salient are most concerned with maintaining their powerful position. In contrast, when leaders are assured that their role is irrevocable, they have no immediate need to actively maintain it. Thus, even highly dominant leaders who feel that their position is stable do not use strategies aimed at suppressing subordinates.

Third, because subordinates possessing valuable skills might receive deference and status from other group members (Henrich and Gil-White 2001), strategies of subordinate suppression were primarily directed toward subordinates who were especially talented. In studies that differentiate between highly skilled and less skilled subordinates, dominant leaders did not work to suppress less talented group members, because they did not present as much of an immediate threat to the leader's power. Because talented group members are especially likely to be able to help the group work toward its goals, leaders who suppress those individuals are working directly against the interest of those they lead in favor of their own selfish goals.

Unanswered Questions and Future Directions

Thus far, this chapter has focused primarily on the strategies leaders use when selfish motivations for power cause them to ignore the goals of their group and even hinder their group's chances of achieving its goals. However, the prevalence of leadership throughout history and across species suggests that leadership provides a stable strategy for effective group functioning and goal attainment (e.g., Van Vugt, Hogan, and Kaiser 2008). What factors, then, promote leadership behavior that is beneficial for the group? Investigating such factors provides several valuable opportunities for further research.

Goal Alignment of Leaders and Followers

One factor that may set the stage for positive leadership behaviors involves the extent to which a leader's goals are aligned with those of his or her group. In many of the studies presented above, leaders were specifically presented with conflicting goals in order to evaluate which they would prioritize. But leaders do not always need to choose between behaviors that enhance their own power and behaviors that help the group achieve its goals. Although leaders sometimes encounter this kind of conflict of interest, there are many situations in which leaders must make decisions for the group that are not in discord with their own personal goals. For example, often a leader's tenure depends on the success of the group. Sometimes the success of a corporation increases the CEO's ability to maintain his or her own position of privilege. In such circumstances, one would expect even selfishly motivated leaders to behave in ways aimed at achieving group success.

Another situation in which even highly dominant leaders might work to foster positive group outcomes is when their group is in competition with another group. Historically, intergroup competition played a key role in the emergence of leadership (Van Vugt 2006), and leadership is one strategy through which groups have been able to combat outgroup threats (Van Vugt and Spisak 2008). Indeed, under conditions of intergroup competition, even dominant leaders often work to help their group achieve its goals and view skilled subordinates as allies to be embraced rather than as threats to be subordinated (Maner and Mead 2010; Mead and Maner 2012). In addition to specific situations like intergroup threat that might cause leaders to act benevolently, some leaders possess certain dispositional characteristics that lead them to act in the interest of their followers.

Status and Prestige

Unlike their primate relatives, humans often gain positions of high influence through the acquisition of respect (Henrich and Gil-White 2001). As previously described, the element of status that focuses on respect differs from power in that it is acquired when a group recognizes that one of its members possesses valuable skills that help the group reach its goals. Those group members then freely confer deference to that talented individual. Prestige-motivated people—those who seek to attain respect, appreciation, and admiration from their group members—are more concerned with gaining and maintaining respect than power. Thus, they should be especially concerned with fostering positive group outcomes and helping their group to succeed as a means of retaining respect.

Closely examining the behavior of leaders who are motivated by prestige and respect (as opposed to dominance and power) provides intriguing opportunities for further investigation. For example, how prestige-motivated individuals work to foster group goals is as of yet not fully explored. There is some preliminary evidence that prestige-focused leaders work to increase cooperation and affiliation among subordinates (Case and Maner, forthcoming). However, few studies have been designed specifically to test how prestige-driven leaders might engage in effective leadership behavior. Because respect is granted to group members who possess talents deemed valuable by the group, prestige-focused leaders may be particularly attentive to what their subordinates think is best for the group. That might lead to positive group outcomes as those leaders work to provide their group with what it desires, but there is also the potential for it to backfire. Leaders who are overly concerned with being liked by their group may pander too much to what their subordinates think they want—not what they need.

Hormones

Hormones play an influential role in determining which individuals are most likely to achieve high status. Specifically, baseline levels of circulating testosterone are correlated with overall status-seeking behavior; high basal levels of that androgen have been found to predict status-seeking behavior in human and nonhuman primates (Anestis 2010; Beehner et al. 2006; Dabbs and Hargrove 1997; Dabbs et al. 1988; Mazur and Booth 1998; Sellers et al. 2007). However, testosterone is also affected by social rank (Anestis 2010; Brockman et al. 1998). In humans, testosterone increases immediately prior to a status competition and changes after a victor is declared; the act of winning a contest against a rival tends to temporarily increase an individual's level of testosterone, whereas losing one decreases it (Booth et al. 1989). An individual's baseline level of testosterone may predict whether he or she will be particularly motivated to attain and maintain a leadership role, with greater testosterone levels predicting greater status-seeking behavior. Furthermore, once an individual attains the role of leader, he or she may experience a significant increase in testosterone. Because testosterone is associated with aggressive and dominant behavior, a leader's level of testosterone may have important implications for how he or she treats subordinate group members.

One interesting question for future research pertains to the distinction between dominance and prestige. Testosterone has been implicated in overall levels of status-striving, but research has not fully differentiated between the hormonal underpinnings of dominance and prestige. We would speculate that testosterone might be more closely linked with dominance than with prestige, given the strong link between testosterone and dominant behavior in nonhuman primates. Nevertheless, this remains an empirical question that future studies would profit from exploring.

Followers

The majority of the work on group behavior and hierarchy has focused on leaders. This makes sense from the standpoint that many of the most influential decisions in society are made by those who have power and status rather than by those who lack power and status. However, the majority of people in contemporary society have been at the bottom of social hierarchies rather than at the top.

Indeed, the number of people at the top versus the bottom of the hierarchy today is likely very different from how our ancestors' groups were structured. Whereas relatively few leaders sit atop steep hierarchies in the modern world, hierarchies of hunter-gatherers were probably relatively flat, meaning that group members had relatively equal levels of power (Boehm 1999). Indeed, in present-day hunter-gatherer groups, upstarts are quickly recognized and suppressed by other group members.

Further research is required to understand how subordinate group members at the bottom of steep, contemporary social hierarchies might work to keep from being exploited by their powerful leaders. It may be especially important for followers in such hierarchies to band together against power-hungry leaders because the power gap between each individual group member and those at the top is so large. Indeed, such banding together of followers is the basis of many workers' unions and special interest groups. To this end, it is possible that group members who are especially low in status are especially cooperative and affiliative to other low-ranking group members. Such prosociality may serve multiple functions. First, it would afford subordinates the ability to establish reciprocal relationships with one another as a means to share the limited resources granted to those without status. Second, it would also allow subordinates to form coalitions with others who share their goal of avoiding exploitation from leaders who may abuse their power.

Conclusion

Groups can provide enormous benefits to their members. Yet, a group's welfare can suffer tremendously when leaders abuse their power. Contemporary groups differ from ancestral groups in part because many contemporary groups are much larger and involve hierarchies that are much steeper. This can set the stage for the abuse of power. The abuse of power can quickly transform groups from being sources of strength and opportunity to sources of threat and exploitation. Thus, it is important to understand when, why, and how leaders abuse their power.

Because the drive for increased social rank is a fundamental motivation that humans share with many other species, adopting an evolutionary perspective when investigating leadership behavior is particularly useful. This perspective helps elucidate the specific motives that drive people to strive for high social rank, helps identify the specific strategies that people might use to attain and maintain their rank, and helps illuminate specific hormonal and motivational factors within the person and factors within the situation that moderate people's behavior within the social hierarchy. There are many adaptive benefits to possessing elevated social rank, and humans can achieve those benefits by acquiring status, as well as the power and prestige that often accompany it.

Because many of the most crucial adaptive problems humans faced throughout evolutionary history were inherently social in nature, we have evolved a multitude of psychological mechanisms dedicated to navigating our complex social world, including aspects of the social world that involve hierarchy. Examining the psychologies of leadership, power, and status through an evolutionary lens affords behavioral scientists the ability to make theoretically based predictions about why, when, and how individuals might work to gain and maintain such positions and why certain leaders may behave in corrupt ways. Once we understand the adaptive mechanisms underlying various forms of leadership behavior, then the field can work to develop policies aimed at promoting positive leadership strategies that benefit the leader and the group he or she serves.

References

Anderson, C., M. W. Kraus, A. D. Galinsky, and D. Keltner. 2012. "The Local-Ladder Effect: Social Status and Subjective Well-Being." *Psychological Science* 23: 764–771.

Anderson, C., R. Willer, G. J. Kilduff, and C. E. Brown. 2012. "The Origins of D: When Do People Prefer Low Status?" *Journal of Personality and Social Psychology* 102: 1077–1088.

Anestis, S. F. 2010. "Hormones and Social Behavior in Primates." *Evolutionary Anthropology: Issues, News, and Reviews* 19: 66–78.

Archer, J. 1988. *The Behavioural Biology of Aggression*. Cambridge: Cambridge University Press.

Barkow, J. 1989. *Darwin, Sex, and Status*. Toronto: University of Toronto Press.

Beehner, J., T. Bergman, D. Cheney, R. Seyfarth, and P. Whitten. 2006. "Testosterone Predicts Future Dominance Rank and Mating Activity among Male Chacma Baboons." *Behavior, Ecology, and Sociobiology* 59: 469–479.

Boehm, C. 1999. *Hierarchy in the Forest*. London: Harvard University Press.

Booth, A., G. Shelley, A. Mazur, G. Tharp, and R. Kittok. 1989. "Testosterone, and Winning and Losing in Human Competition." *Hormones and Behavior* 23: 556–571.

Brockman, D. K., P. L. Whitten, A. F. Richard, and A. Schneider. 1998. "Reproduction in Free-Ranging Male *Propithecus verreauxi*: The Hormonal Correlates of Mating and Aggression." *American Journal of Physical Anthropology* 100: 137–151.

Case, C., and J. K. Maner. Forthcoming. "Divide and Conquer: When and Why Leaders Undermine the Cohesive Fabric of Their Group." *Journal of Personality and Social Psychology*.

Chagnon, N. A. 1992. *Yanomamo*. Fort Worth, TX: Harcourt Brace.

Dabbs, J. M., and M. F. Hargrove. 1997. "Age, Testosterone, and Behavior among Female Prison Inmates." *Psychosomatic Medicine* 59: 477–480.

Dabbs, J. M., R. B. Ruback, R. L. Frady, C. H. Hopper, and D. S. Sgoutas. 1988. "Saliva Testosterone and Criminal Violence among Women." *Personality and Individual Difference* 9: 269–275.

de Waal, F.B.M. 1982. *Chimpanzee Politics: Power and Sex among Apes*. New York: Harper & Row.

Ellemers, N., H. Wilke, and A. Van Knippenberg. 1993. "Effects of the Legitimacy of Low Group or Individual Status on Individual and Collective Status-Enhancement Strategies." *Journal of Personality and Social Psychology* 64: 766–778.

Ellis, L. 1995. "Dominance and Reproductive Success among Nonhuman Animals." *Ethology and Sociobiology* 16: 257–333.

Fodor, E. M. 1985. "The Power Motive, Group Conflict, and Physiological Arousal." *Journal of Personality and Social Psychology* 49: 1408–1415.

French, J.R.P., and B. Raven. 1959. "The Bases of Social Power." In *Studies in Social Power*, edited by D. Cartwright, 150–167. Ann Arbor: University of Michigan Press.

Griskevicius, V., J. M. Tybur, G. M. Gangestad, E. F. Perea, J. R. Shapiro, and D. T. Kenrick. 2009. "Aggress to Impress: Hostility as an Evolved Context-Dependent Strategy." *Journal of Personality and Social Psychology* 96: 980–994.

Henrich, J., and F. J. Gil-White. 2001. "The Evolution of Prestige: Freely Conferred Deference as a Mechanism for Enhancing the Benefits of Cultural Transmission." *Evolution and Human Behavior* 22: 165–196.

Keltner, D., D. H. Gruenfeld, and C. Anderson. 2003. "Power, Approach, and Inhibition." *Psychological Review* 110: 265–284.

Kenrick, D. T., J. K. Maner, J. Butner, D. V. Becker, and M. Schaller. 2002. "Dynamical Evolutionary Psychology: Mapping the Domains of the New Interactionist Paradigm." *Personality and Social Psychology Review* 6: 347–356.

Kifer, Y., D. Heller, W.Q.E. Perunovic, and A. D. Galinsky. 2013. "The Good Life of the Powerful: The Experience of Power and Authenticity Enhances Subjective Well-Being." *Psychological Science* 24: 280–288.

Magee, J., and A. Galinsky. 2008. "Social Hierarchy: The Self-Reinforcing Nature of Power and Status." *Academy of Management Annals* 2: 351–398.

Maner, J. K., and N. L. Mead. 2010. "The Essential Tension between Leadership and Power: When Leaders Sacrifice Group Goals for the Sake of Self-Interest." *Journal of Personality and Social Psychology* 99: 482–497.

Mazur, A., and A. Booth. 1998. "Testosterone and Dominance in Men." *Behavioral and Brain Sciences* 21: 353–397.

McClelland, D. C. 1970. "The Two Faces of Power." *Journal of International Affairs* 24: 29–47.

———. 1975. *Power: The Inner Experience*. Oxford: Irvington.

Mead, N. L., and J. K. Maner. 2012. "On Keeping Your Enemies Close: Powerful Leaders Seek Proximity to Power Threats." *Journal of Personality and Social Psychology* 102: 573–591.

Murray, C. M., L. E. Eberly, and A. E. Pusey. 2006. "Foraging Strategies as a Function of Season and Rank among Wild Female Chimpanzees (*Pan troglodytes*)." *Behavioral Ecology* 17: 1020–1028.

Nishida, T. 1983. "Alpha Status and Agonistic Alliance in Wild Chimpanzees (*Pan troglodytes schweinfurthii*)." *Primates* 24: 318–336.

Nishida, T., and K. Hosaka. 1996. "Coalition Strategies among Adult Male Chimpanzees of the Mahale Mountains, Tanzania." In *Great Ape Societies*, 114–134. Cambridge: Cambridge University Press.

Öhman, A., and S. Mineka. 2001. "Fears, Phobias, and Preparedness: Toward an Evolved Module of Fear and Fear Learning." *Psychological Review* 108: 483–522.

Park, J. H., J. Faulkner, and M. Schaller. 2003. "Evolved Disease-Avoidance Processes and Contemporary Antisocial Behavior: Prejudicial Attitudes and Avoidance of People with Disabilities." *Journal of Nonverbal Behavior* 27: 65–87.

Pusey, A. 2012. "Magnitude and Sources of Variation in Female Reproductive Performance." In *Evolution of Primate Societies*, edited by J. Mitani, J. Call, P. Kappeler, R. Palombit, and J. Silk, 343–366. Chicago: University of Chicago Press.

Pusey, A. E., G. W. Oehlert, J. M. Williams, and J. Goodall. 2005. "Influence of Ecological and Social Factors on Body Mass of Wild Chimpanzees." *International Journal of Primatology* 26: 3–31.

Pusey, A. E., and K. Schroepfer-Walker. 2013. "Female Competition in Chimpanzees." *Philosophical Transactions of the Royal Society of London B* 368: 20130077.

Sadalla, E. K., D. T. Kenrick, and B. Vershure. 1987. "Dominance and Heterosexual Attraction." *Journal of Personality and Social Psychology* 52: 730–738.

Sapolsky, R. M. 2005. "The Influence of Social Hierarchy on Primate Health." *Science* 308: 648–652.

Schaller, M., J. H. Park, and J. Faulkner. 2003. "Prehistoric Dangers and Contemporary Prejudices." *European Review of Social Psychology* 14: 105–137.

Sellers, J. G., M. R. Mehl, R. Matthias, and R. A. Josephs. 2007. "Hormones and Personality: Testosterone as a Marker of Individual Differences." *Journal of Research in Personality* 41: 126–138.

Tetlock, P. E. 1981. "Pre- to Post-Election Shifts in Presidential Rhetoric: Impression Management or Cognitive Adjustment?" *Journal of Personality and Social Psychology* 41: 207–212.

———. 2002. "Social-Functionalist Metaphors for Judgment and Choice: The Politician, Theologian, and Prosecutor." *Psychological Review* 109: 451–472.

Tiedens, L. Z., M. M. Unzueta, and M. J. Young. 2007. "An Unconscious Desire for Hierarchy? The Motivated of Dominance Complementarity in Task Partners." *Journal of Personality and Social Psychology* 93: 402–414.

Van Lange, P.A.M., D. De Cremer, E. Van Dijk, and M. Van Vugt. 2007. "Self-Interest and Beyond: Basic Principles of Social Interaction." In *Social Psychology: Handbook of Basic Principles*, 2nd ed., edited by A. Kruglanski and E. T. Higgins, 540–561. New York: Guilford Press.

Van Vugt, M. 2006. "Evolutionary Origins of Leadership and Followership." *Personality and Social Psychology Review* 10: 354–371.

Van Vugt, M., R. Hogan, and R. Kaiser. 2008. "Leadership, Followership, and Evolution: Some Lessons from the Past." *American Psychologist* 63: 182–196.

Van Vugt, M., and B. R. Spisak. 2008. "Sex Differences in the Emergence of Leadership during Competitions within and between Groups." *Psychological Science* 19: 854–858.

von Rueden, C., M. Gurven, and H. Kaplan. 2011. "Why Do Men Seek Status? Fitness Payoffs to Dominance and Prestige." *Proceedings of the Royal Society B* 278: 2223–2232.

Wilson, M., and M. Daly. 1992. "What about the Evolutionary Psychology of Coerciveness?" *Behavioral & Brain Sciences* 15: 403–404.

Winter, D. G. 1973. *The Power Motive*. New York: Free Press.

Wittig, R. M., and C. Boesch. 2003. "Food Competition and Linear Dominance Hierarchy among Female Chimpanzees of the Tai National Park." *International Journal of Primatology* 24: 847–867.

Xia, D. P., J. H. Li, P. A. Garber, M. D. Matheson, H. H. Sun, and Y. Zhu. 2013. "Grooming Reciprocity in Male Tibetan Macaques." *American Journal of Primatology* 75: 1009–1020.

Chapter Twenty-Five
Biosociology of Dominance and Deference
Allan Mazur

> Allocation and maintenance of rank in status hierarchies of human face-to-face groups are in many ways similar to what is observed in dominance hierarchies of other primates, especially in species close to us, the African apes. This is prima facie evidence that human behaviors of dominance and deference are homologous with those of other primates. Language, exclusive to humans, may be an exception, or, as here, it may be incorporated into a general primate model. The present model emphasizes that all individuals signal that they are (or ought to be) of high or low status in the group. Group members may accept these signs, consensually forming the group's hierarchy. Or one individual might challenge another for higher rank, their disagreement eventually resolved through one or more dominance contests. Among humans, dominance contests are usually nonviolent, even polite, but can nonetheless be decisive. In a dominance contest, each contestant tries (perhaps unconsciously) to "out-stress" the other until one, in effect, concedes the higher rank. Proximate neurohormonal mechanisms underlie rank allocation, including the neurophysiology of stress and the influence of testosterone.

Introduction

The biosocial model of status in face-to-face groups applies to all social primates, taking language-using humans as a special case. Status (or dominance) ranks are allocated among members of a group through direct communication whereby each member signals that it has, or ought to have, high (or low) status, that is, more (or less) power, influence, and valued prerogatives than other members. Every member signifies its rank through physical or vocal demeanor. For example, behavioral signs of dominant status include erect posture, glares, eye contact, strutting, and (in humans) assertive or confident speech, while deferent signs include slouching, eye aversion, and whining or submissive speech.

The status interactions of monkeys are often aggressive, sometimes causing physical damage. In African apes, our evolutionarily closest relatives, status is normally allocated peacefully though with occasional physical attack. Violence is rare among adult humans, who usually determine their relative status politely, often without being conscious of any sorting process. The term *dominance*, as used here, does not connote aggressiveness, rudeness, or unpleasantness, but simply refers to having the higher rank.

Another clarification: The model applies only to status in face-to-face groups, not to formal hierarchies of large organizations or to socioeconomic stratification of large societies. These formal or large-scale hierarchical structures are not found among nonhuman primates. Apparently they were not present among humans until the adoption of agriculture 10 millennia ago, allowing communities to grow so large that members did not know or interact with all others as individuals, a situation that allowed (or encouraged) new hierarchical arrangements to emerge though cultural processes.

Dominance/Status Hierarchies in Face-to-Face Groups

Dominance (or status) hierarchies are a reliable feature of primate societies. To avoid an overly simple picture of these structures, several qualifications are needed. Status rank may be persistently relevant in species with fairly permanent groups, or only occasionally relevant for animals that forage alone. Rankings are usually but not necessarily transitive. The relative status of two individuals may depend, in part, on the proximity of allies. Sometimes the highest-ranking position is shared by a coalition of two or three animals. It is often easier to identify a male ranking than a female ranking. Rankings are usually less clear in the wild than in captive colonies where animals are forced into close contact. Also, some species simply show less overt status behavior than others, and status ranking may become prominent only during the breeding season or in periods of food scarcity. Given these qualifications, it is still clear that there is a general primate pattern of fairly consistent rank ordering with respect to influence, power, and valued prerogatives.

Among humans, face-to-face status (dominance) hierarchies have corollary features long recognized in classical social psychology. Here I briefly enumerate five corollaries that we now know are also found among nonhuman primates, at least those evolutionarily closest to us, and therefore plausibly having an evolved basis. (See Mazur 2005 for an extended treatment.)

1. *An individual's rank depends partly on extrinsic attributes that are not obviously prerequisites for status in the group.* Thus, a person may have high status in the small group simply by virtue of being older, or male, or coming from a wealthy family—features Berger and his colleagues labeled "diffuse status characteristics" (Berger, Cohen, and Zelditch 1972). Sex and age are reliable status determinants in nonhuman primates, too, but it seems inappropriate to consider them extrinsic attributes (as we do in humans) since they are clearly correlated with strength, size, experience, and perhaps relevant hormonal differences. More relevant is the tendency, known in several primate species, for an animal's status to be influenced if not fully determined by the rank of its mother. Broader family connections have similar influence. Troops of Old World monkeys such as baboons, macaques, and vervets are composed of different matrilineal families, each arranged in a stable, linear dominance hierarchy. All females of one matriline outrank all females of another. Female baboons recognize that a reversal in the status of two matrilines affects their own status (Bergman et al. 2003).
2. *Over the long run, group members interact more with others of similar rank ("near-peers") than with members of dissimilar rank.* Among nonhuman primates, interaction usually occurs within age-sex categories (excepting sexual and mother–offspring relations). Since males usually dominate females, and adults dominate juveniles, the effect is to concentrate interaction among near-peers. Within age-sex categories, monkeys and chimpanzees often form coalitions, their decisions to give or withdraw support seemingly calculated to earn enhanced status (de Waal 1989). Tabulations of pair-wise interactions among monkeys and apes show more interaction with near-peers than would be expected by chance (Mazur 1973).

3. *High-ranked members—particularly the leaders—perform service and control functions for other members and for the group as a whole.* Leaders of baboon and macaque troops are in the forefront during inter-troop combat or in defense against a predator. When a dispute breaks out between troop members, the leader may stop it with a threat, and will protect a mother with an infant who is threatened by another animal. High-ranking chimpanzees sometimes adopt a control role, breaking up fights or systematically protecting the weak against the strong (de Waal 2000).
4. *Low-ranked members appear more nervous than high-ranked members; high-ranked members can manipulate the stress experienced by—and thereby the performance of—low-ranked members.* Early accounts of macaque behavior often describe low-ranking members of a stable hierarchy as "nervous, insecure" or "cowering" (e.g., Southwick 1963). In human groups or gangs, the cool confidence of leaders versus the timidity of lowest-ranked members has become a cliché.
5. *Humans and apes usually establish and maintain status rank without physical fights, aggressive threats, or overt gestures of submission.* Displays of dominance must be viewed within the broader context of communication. Lower primates are limited, repetitive, and stereotypic in their displays; higher primates are more flexible, using diverse and novel forms of expression. Apes are capable of violent dominance displays, but these are infrequent. During her pioneering years of studying chimps in the wild, Jane Goodall found her subjects apparently so uncompetitive that she could not at first discern their dominance relationships. "However, when regular observations became possible on the interactions between the various individuals it gradually became evident that the social status of each chimpanzee was fairly well defined in relation to each other individual" (van Lawick-Goodall 1968: 315). Most human adults are rarely, if ever, violent in face-to-face competition for status.

These status corollaries, thought by early social psychologists and sociologists to be uniquely human, are in fact common among primates, especially in those most like us physically. Thus, we have a prima facie case that status-related behaviors evolved along with our physical form, and that they might be explained proximately by neurophysiological mechanisms.

STATUS SIGNS

Every individual primate has certain observable *signs* (or *signals*—I use the terms interchangeably) that suggest his or her social status is (or ought to be) high or low. Those displaying high-status signs are not guaranteed to hold correspondingly high rank in their group's status hierarchy, but if we know an individual's signs we can make a better than random guess about his or her actual status.

Some status signs are limited to a particular species, such as the silver hair on the back of a dominant male gorilla. Others are similar across primate species. For example, large size, physical strength, vigor, good health, being adult (vs. being juvenile), being male, and (among the higher primates) having a high-ranked mother are all signs associated with high status, while their opposites suggest low status. The range and flexibility of status signs are least among the lower primates (prosimians), increase among monkeys, are more so in apes with their protocultures, and are most flexible among humans with full cultures. Wearing expensive and fashionable clothing is a signal of high status among humans. A beautiful wife, desirable to other men, or one with a rich dowry, gives prestige to her husband; a rich or powerful husband or protector elevates a woman's rank.

Among humans, the prestige one holds in the larger society—perhaps as a representative of "legitimate" or "official" authority, or by virtue of occupation, wealth, education, or family lineage—carries over into face-to-face interaction, although it may have no relevance in that context. A surgeon and a plumber, meeting casually outside their professional roles, are likely to rank themselves so that the plumber defers to the surgeon, even though medical skills are irrelevant to the situation. (If the toilet is flooding, the plumber will enjoy a temporarily elevated status.) A famous person, like a visibly wealthy one, can usually dominate an intimate social gathering.

It is useful to divide status signs into two categories: *constant* signals that individuals display persistently whether they want to or not (e.g., size, sex, age), and *controllable* signals that individuals can quickly change by their own (conscious or unconscious) efforts. Among controllable status signals are body postures, facial expressions, direct staring or eye aversion, advancing toward or retreating from another individual, and relaxed and confident demeanor versus nervous fidgeting, growling, grinning, or crying. Among humans, language carries many of these controllable signals either in tone, semantic content, or nonverbal gestures that accompany speech. Items of dress, cosmetics, and accessories also serve humans as controllable status signs.

FACES

Facial appearance and facial gestures are among the most impressive status signs in higher primates, especially among the apes and humans in whom facial musculature is most flexible, subtle, and expressive. Our eyes, brows, and mouth are critical features for quickly altering visible demeanor, and their manipulation can blatantly or subtly change the meaning read into a facial signal. Subjects shown portraits posed with differing eyebrow positions (raised or lowered) or with differing mouth positions (smiling or neutral), and asked to judge which is more dominant (i.e., which is more respected, more likely to tell others what to do, more leader-like), tend to choose portraits with lowered brows and unsmiling mouths (Keating, Mazur, and Segall 1977). The reader may easily see this perceptual difference due to eyebrow position in cartoon faces (Figure 25.1).

Apart from controllable gestures, certain faces simply look more dominant than others, perceptions that are constant across diverse cultures (Keating et al. 1981). Ulrich Mueller and I wondered if the perception of dominance conveyed by yearbook portraits

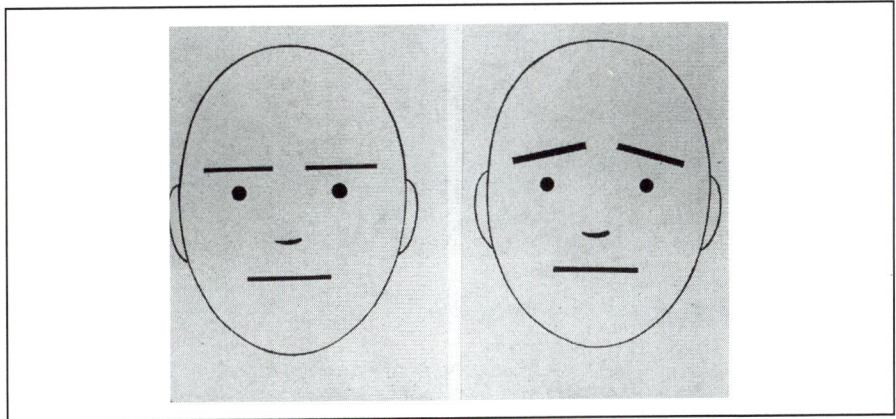

Figure 25.1 Cartoon expressions of dominance and deference

of the West Point Class of 1950 had any effect on their subsequent careers in the United States military (Mueller and Mazur 1996). Judges blind to the purpose of our study were asked to rank cadet portraits on a seven-point scale of dominance-submissiveness (1 = very submissive, 7 = very dominant). Figure 25.2 shows four cadets of varying facial dominance, and formal portraits of the same men after all had achieved the rank of general.

All cadets entered West Point as undifferentiated plebes. The first time they were given ranks was in junior year when nearly half were elevated to corporal, the rest remaining privates. As seniors they were ranked again, with one-quarter of the class named cadet officers and the rest sergeants. At graduation everyone received the rank of second lieutenant. By 1963, nearly everyone remaining on active duty had been promoted to major. During the early 1960s, roughly three-quarters of these men were invited to spend an academic year at the army's Command and General Staff College for additional training. This was a critical branch point because men who did not attend this college were almost certain to advance no higher than lieutenant colonel. Graduation from Staff College is an essential but not sufficient requirement for an invitation to a war college, the second crucial branch point. Less than half of the graduates from Staff College were admitted to a war college to receive training at the level of division command.

Did looks ever affect promotion? At West Point they did. In junior year, cadets with the most dominant-looking faces were twice as likely to make corporal as those with the least dominant-looking faces. In senior year the promotion rate of the most dominant-looking men was five times that of their least dominant-looking classmates.

After West Point the dynamics of rank attainment changed. Facial dominance did not predict promotion to major or lieutenant colonel, or selection to staff or war colleges,

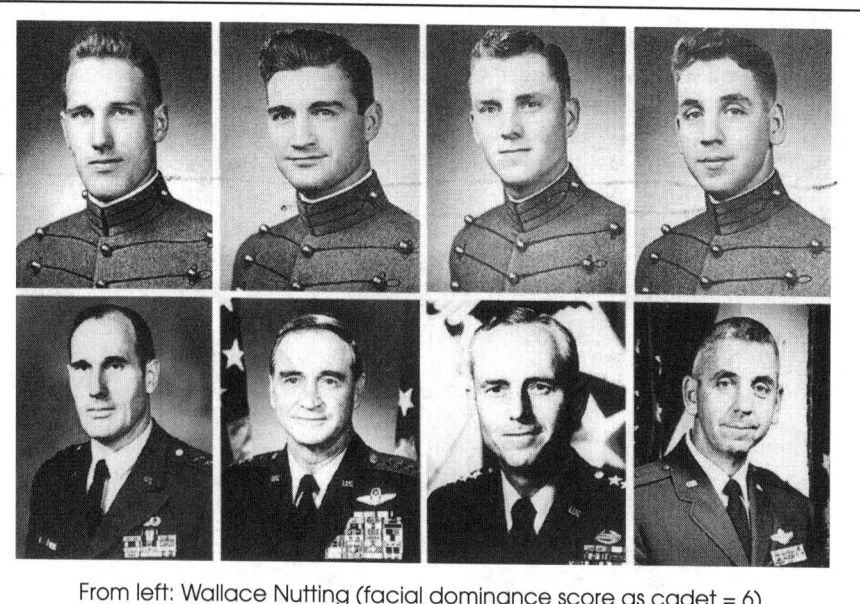

From left: Wallace Nutting (facial dominance score as cadet = 6), Charles Gabriel (5), John Wickham Jr. (4), and Lincoln Faurer (3).

Figure 25.2 Men of varying facial dominance who became high-ranked generals, shown as cadets and in late career

Source: Cadet portraits are from the West Point yearbook The Howitzer 1950; officer portraits are from Pentagon archives.

nor did it predict the rapidity of these advancements. What did count was the rate of advance; some men were on a fast track, racing through successive promotions ahead of their classmates, but these men did not have especially dominant faces. Promotions in midcareer are decided impersonally by boards of officers who do not know the candidates but look at their dossiers.

Colonels who enter a war college make up the pool from which generals are drawn. Nearly everyone who reaches this stage has an excellent record, so personnel files do not differentiate very well. The pool is relatively small, about 108 men for the Class of 1950. At this level in the hierarchy, someone on the promotion board almost certainly knows each candidate personally and would have heard of others by reputation or through advice from mentors and colleagues. Promotions at this stage are similar to the selection of cadet officers back at West Point in the sense that those making the selection know the men as individuals rather than from impersonal records. Therefore, it is not surprising that the criteria for selection to the highest ranks are again highly personal, including whether the man *looks* like a leader. For war college graduates, the number of promotions beyond colonel increased significantly with facial dominance as measured from cadet portraits taken twenty-plus years earlier. Men with dominant faces had an advantage in promotion to general (Mueller and Mazur 1996).

A question that inevitably arises is, what do dominant faces look like? Everyone knows because anyone can sort portraits on that basis, but facial dominance is a gestalt concept, difficult to describe in simple terms. The computer technique of morphing several portraits together, in essence blending them into one "average" face, has provided remarkable insights into our perceptions of others, for example, showing that a morph of many young women's faces is more attractive than most of the individual faces (Perrett 2010). Using the same technique, Robert Ward and Robin Kramer of Bangor University in the United Kingdom produced one morphed portrait from seven of our dominant-looking cadets, and another morphed portrait from seven of our submissive-looking cadets. These are shown side by side in Figure 25.3.

Readers may compare the two morphs, judging which looks more dominant or leader-like, and then find the usual answer at the end of this paragraph. Some researchers suggest that a higher ratio of facial width-to-height (FWTH) accounts for much of the perception of dominant rather than submissive faces (e.g., Carré, McCormick, and Mondloch 2009; Lefevre and Lewis 2013), but in this particular case FWTH, as kindly measured by Justin Carré, is 1.92 for both morphs. (The left morph is reliably judged to look more like a leader.)

Figure 25.3 Each morphed portrait combines seven cadet portraits. Which one looks more like a leader?

Allocating Ranks

Dominance hierarchies, once set, are fairly stable. But when a new group forms, there must be an initial allocation of ranks, and in established groups some individuals occasionally alter their positions. How are these initial rankings, and later changes in rank, determined? The short answer is that ranks are allocated either *cooperatively*, by consensus of those involved, or *competitively*, when there is disagreement over who should be superior.

Primate species vary in the degree to which they allocate ranks competitively. Among the prosimians, as well as baboons and macaques, rank allocation within newly formed groups and changes of rank within established groups are usually accompanied by overt conflict that produces a victor and vanquished. Among apes and humans, rank allocation is often cooperative, and when there is competition it usually stops short of physical attack.

We may explore the decision to compete or cooperate by visualizing two individuals (Ego and Alter) meeting for the first time. If their interaction is very brief or casual, the notion of ranking may never arise. In more extended or serious meetings, each appraises the status signs of the other, forming some idea of his relative standing. If Ego perceives that Alter's status signs exceed his own, he may defer to Alter without any dispute. In a classic study of the American court system, when jury members elected a foreman, they favored men with prestigious occupations, though sex and occupation were irrelevant to the foreman's task (Strodtbeck, James, and Hawkins 1957). Ego, in explaining such concessions, may offer that Alter *belongs* in the higher rank, or that Alter *deserves* it, or that Alter *could easily take it* if Ego resisted, or that Alter may be more *competent* in the duties of high rank.

It is a long-established finding that even when no obvious status signs distinguish participants from each other in a newly formed group, they still tend to stratify cooperatively, often within the first minutes of interaction (e.g., Fisek and Ofshe 1970). This was a surprising finding when first reported because social psychologists did not recognize that barely perceptible status signs, like those emanating from the face or from postural cues, convey ranking information as effectively as blatant markers like sex, race, and occupation.

The signaling capability of an eye glance was demonstrated decades ago with the following experiment devised by Strongman and Champness (1968). Start with three unacquainted subjects. Taking two at a time, there are three possible pairs. Seat each pair of subjects at a table so they are face to face but with a screen blocking their view of each other. Remove the screen and tell subjects to get to know each other. Typically, as the screen is removed, the pair makes eye contact. One person holds the glance longer than the other, and we describe this person as "out-glancing" the other. Repeat the procedure for the other two pairs. A transitive ordering occurs if one person out-glances the other two, one person out-glances one but is out-glanced by another, and one person is out-glanced by two others. Strongman and Champness found a nearly transitive eye-glance hierarchy among ten subjects, matched pair-wide in a round-robin tournament. Eugene Rosa and I found perfect transitivity in a round-robin tournament of six subjects (Rosa and Mazur 1979).

Rosa went further, asking if rank in this momentary eye-glance hierarchy predicts rank in the status hierarchy that emerges when the same subjects are brought together in prolonged discussion. He ran twenty groups, each composed of three unacquainted college students undifferentiated by age, race, sex, or social class; half the groups were male, half female. First, Rosa put each threesome through a pair-wise round-robin to establish the eye-glance hierarchy. Later he brought the three subjects together in a half-hour discussion, measuring each person's status by the amount he or she talked during the discussion. He corroborated this ranking afterward by asking subjects to rate who contributed the most ideas and best guidance to the group. Sixteen of the twenty groups formed a transitive eye-glance hierarchy. In these transitive groups, Rosa found that eye-glance rank significantly predicted status ranking in the following discussion (Rosa and Mazur 1979). Eye glance is only one of many facial gestures that can signal dominance or deference, and these are usually accompanied by parallel signals in speech and body posture, producing an integrated presentation of high or low status.

People do not always accept their status ranking so easily. Ego's decision to comply or compete depends on his motivation to dominate or the stakes that may be on the table. An individual who has experienced a recent rise in stature, perhaps from a victory or by passing through puberty, may be unusually pugnacious and challenge someone with impressive status signs. When Ego is on home territory, or protecting group members or valued possessions, and Alter is an intruder, then Ego is particularly likely to rise to a challenge. Among humans, a substantive disagreement—perhaps over a point of information or ideology—may escalate into a dominance competition so that winning becomes an end in itself, with the original substantive disagreement relegated to secondary importance. If both Ego and Alter decide to compete, their relative ranks are then determined by the outcome of one or more short *dominance contests*.

Dominance Contests

Nonhuman primates often establish and maintain their dominance hierarchies through a series of short face-to-face competitions between members of the group. Usually these are pair-wise contests, but occasionally they involve more than two individuals at once. Some competitions involve fierce combat to determine victor and vanquished. Others are mild, as when one animal is obviously the more powerful or assertive, or the other appears fearful. In such cases, a simple stare by the powerful animal, followed by the fearful animal averting its eyes or yielding something of value (perhaps food or a sitting place), may suffice to determine the winner. Sometimes a single contest is all that is needed to allocate ranks or to verify a preexisting status relationship, but often the outcome is settled only after a series of contests.

A mechanism postulated to operate across this range of competition is the manipulation of discomfort levels during these contests. In this model, a threat or attack is an attempt by one animal to "out-stress" or intimidate the opponent by inducing fear, anxiety, or other discomfort. The animal that out-stresses its adversary is the winner.

At first glance, the model seems inappropriate to humans, who usually form status hierarchies politely. Chimpanzees, bonobos, and gorillas—the primates most like us—are more subtle in their status competition than monkeys or prosimians, and humans continue that trend. The emotional distribution of status occurs less stressfully among us than among nonhuman primates, but stresses are not wholly absent.

The model becomes clearer if we consider a concrete example. The eyes of two strangers, Ego and Alter, meet by chance across a room. Let us say that Ego decides to hold the glance. The chance eye contact now becomes a dominance encounter. Ego's stare makes Alter uncomfortable. Alter may avert his eyes, thus relieving his discomfort while in effect surrendering, or he may stare back, making Ego uncomfortable in return. In the latter case, the stare-down continues with each individual trying to out-stress the other until finally one person succumbs to the discomfort (and to the challenger) by averting his eyes. The matter thus settled, the yielder usually avoids further eye contact, though the winner may occasionally look at the loser as if to verify his victory.

In the biosocial model, Ego's stare is assumed to cause stress in Alter. Alter's eye aversion is assumed to relieve his own felt stress. Typically in stare-downs of this kind, the levels of discomfort are low, and the adversaries may be barely aware of their contest. But in this context, staring is an assertive sign of high status. Eye aversion is a deferent sign associated with low status. In other words, a dominant act (staring) elicits stress in the recipient; a deferent act (eye aversion) relieves stress in the actor. A central assumption of the model is that most dominant and deferent acts work this way, inducing or relieving stress, respectively. These actions are the means through which adversaries wage their dominance contest, aiming "darts" at one another. When the stress becomes too great for one, he switches from dominant to deferent actions, thereby relieving his stress and simultaneously signaling his acceptance of the lower rank. Normally a dominance-seeking person stresses adversaries through means that are polite or at least socially acceptable, and without exceeding the norms of, say, business or sports competition.

Stress

Stress is an organism's subjective-plus-physiological responses to threatening or demanding stimuli. Subjectively, this response is experienced as discomfort, whether as anxiety, fear, anger, annoyance, or depression. Physiologically, it involves a complex response of the neurohormonal system: release of adrenocorticotropin from the anterior pituitary, glucocorticoids (including cortisol, in humans) from the adrenal cortex, epinephrine (adrenaline) from the adrenal medulla, and norepinephrine from the sympathetic nerves of the autonomic nervous system, all of which produce effects on other parts of the body.

This total reaction is often called the "fight-or-flight response" because it admirably prepares the organism to flee or face up to the threat. The central nervous system is aroused; the body provides glucose for quick energy; skeletal muscle increases contractility and loses fatigue; heart output increases; blood is shunted from viscera and the periphery of the body to the heart, lungs, and large muscles; and there is increased ventilation. This is not a wholly stereotyped pattern, its different components coming more or less into play depending on the character of the threat and the previous experience of the organism.

The model assumes that during status contests, Ego's dominant actions are perceived as threatening by Alter and therefore produce a stress response in Alter. That this occurs during violent contests involving overt threats and attacks can hardly be doubted. The occurrence of milder stress responses during more subtle contests, such as stare-downs, is less obvious although well supported by experimental evidence (Mazur et al. 1980).

With stress a central variable in the biosocial model, we can explain some of the corollary features of status hierarchies, described at the beginning of this chapter. In most species, the low-ranked members of a group show more stress symptoms than higher-ranked members during common interaction. Often the low-ranked are described as "nervous, insecure," while those of high rank appear "relaxed, confident." We now see that the processes of rank allocation, especially dominance contests, encourage the upward movement of those group members most able to withstand stress and best equipped to impose stress on others, while those with the most difficulty handling stress, or the least interest in stressing others, move downward. Thus, there is a natural sorting that places individuals who are comfortable with stress near the top of the hierarchy and those who are "nervous" at the bottom.

Top-ranked individuals are well equipped with high-status signs and can easily impose stress on those down the hierarchy, enforcing compliance if it is not freely given. The imposition of stress is not only a powerful sanction on those below; it directly inhibits their performance as well. While the stress response admirably equips the body for the gross actions of fight or flight, it also produces muscle tension and tremor that interfere with finer actions, such as those required for controlled accuracy in sports or weapons competition. By intimidating our opponent in a duel or tennis match, we degrade his or her body's usual level of skill, diminishing the chances of scoring against us. Extreme stress can enervate an organism and, if chronic, cause physical morbidity. It is difficult for one of low rank to act dominantly toward a higher-ranked individual, for such an action is "presumptuous" (in human terms) and therefore may produce more stress on the low-status actor than on his higher-status target.

The stress variable also explains why the leaders rather than the low-ranked members of the group are most likely to face external threats such as predators, strange intruders, or hostile conspecifics. Those who handle stress most comfortably have been sorted into the high ranks, so they, rather than the low-ranked nervous individuals, are least intimidated by external threat and therefore most likely (or willing) to advance against it. In human groups, the individuals who best handle stress are not only prone to become leaders but also, depending on circumstances, may be the thrill seekers and those most willing and able to violate laws or other norms.

CONVERSATION

Theorists have the choice of treating language-using humans as unique, to be explained on our own terms, or of treating conversation as simply one of several alternate modes whereby primates communicate with conspecifics. I have chosen the latter course. The commonalities across the status hierarchies of humans and nonhuman primates seem to me a compelling reason for this choice.

The biosocial model of status works independently of the mode of communication used between Ego and Alter, as long as they can distinguish dominant (high-status) acts from deferent (low-status) ones. To include language as a mode of communicating dominance and deference, we need only specify how actors experience dominance and deferent actions during conversation. One obvious way is through the words that each person speaks, since these may carry lexical meaning indicating that the speaker (or listener) is a high- or low-status person, for example, "I came, I saw, I conquered" versus "I am the dust beneath your feet."

Since conversations also carry meaning in their form and action—apart from the particular string of words—we often recognize the relative status of conversing foreigners even though we do not understand their speech. It is these features of form and action, independent of grammar or lexicon, that are sometimes described as a set of rules usually followed in natural conversation (Mazur 2005). For present purposes, a simpler exposition is sufficient.

Conversation requires turn-taking. Small group researchers and conversational analysts know well that those of high rank generally speak more, and indeed, quantity of speech is often taken as an empirical measure of one's status in the group. Of course, leaders are free to remain silent if they wish, and they may induce lower-ranked members to take and hold the floor by asking them questions or simply by looking silently at them (perhaps with raised eyebrows), thus prodding them to continue talking. High-ranked members have the prerogative to start the conversation, to introduce or terminate particular topics, and to end the conversation. High-ranked members are free to violate the usual rules of turn-taking, for example, by "talking over" someone who has not finished speaking, or by remaining silent when a lower-ranked person tries to give them the floor. It would be stressful for low-ranked members to act this impudently, so they rarely do so unless to purposively challenge another member.

In newly formed groups that are initially undifferentiated by status, one person may move to the fore, setting new topics, pacing the conversation, and allocating speaking turns—all signs of high rank. Others in the group may accept this person as the de facto leader. Or, one or more others may challenge him or her as a usurper, in which case there is a dominance contest with contenders talking over one another, perhaps disagreeing about the topic under discussion, until status allocation is settled—usually politely and fairly quickly—or one contender may exit. In any case, the entire interaction, seen through the lens of the biosocial model, is an exchange of dominant and deferent signs, of stressing others while relieving one's own stress, until statuses are allocated or the group dissolves.

TESTOSTERONE

There are active research programs on the proximate neurophysiological mechanisms underlying dominance and deference in humans (and other primates). Obviously from the foregoing discussion, the physiology of stress is important; it is the subject of my own current research. Here I touch briefly on the hormone testosterone, which for decades has been implicated in the dominance/status processes of primates (Mazur 1976) as well as other mammals and even birds (e.g., Wingfield et al. 1990).

Testosterone is the key hormone involved in dominance and deference interactions among mature males, though evidence is equivocal for females (Mazur and Booth 1998; Carré et al. 2013). The precise mechanisms of action and strength of effects in humans remain uncertain (Batrinos 2012). Ethical and practical constraints have limited experiments on human subjects that compare behavior under testosterone with placebo treatments; however, there is by now considerable correlational research from surveys and observational studies, and some ingenious experiments that depend on variations in endogenous testosterone.

It is clear that the link between testosterone and dominance is reciprocal. Not only does testosterone affect dominance behavior, but changes in dominance behavior or in social status cause changes in testosterone level. By now there have been several reports of testosterone changes in young men in contests as varied as athletic events, laboratory competitions, and elections.

Male testosterone varies in predictable ways both before and after competitive matches. Among athletes, for example, testosterone rises shortly before their matches, as if in anticipation of the competition. This pre-competition boost may promote dominant behavior, increasing the chance of victory. For one or two hours after the match, testosterone of winners is usually high relative to that of losers. These effects appear not only in physically taxing sports but in chess competition, in symbolic changes in social status (graduation from medical school), vicariously in sports fans when their favored team wins or loses a game, and in election partisans when "their" candidate wins or loses an election (reviewed in Mazur 2005; Archer 2006; Stanton et al. 2009). The rise in testosterone following a win is associated with the subject's elated mood. If the mood elevation is lessened because the subjects have won by luck rather than through their own efforts, or because they do not regard the win as important, then the rise in testosterone is lessened or does not occur at all.

In a dominance contest, Ego's decision to compete with Alter, or to defer, depends on his motivation to dominate, which hypothetically depends on his testosterone level (among other factors). A man who has experienced a recent rise in testosterone, perhaps from a prior victory or a symbolic elevation in status, should be unusually assertive and may challenge someone of relatively high status. If both Ego and Alter decide to compete, their subsequent ranks are determined according to who successfully out-stresses whom.

If the winner (say, Ego) experiences rising testosterone as a result of his victory, this should sustain or increase his assertiveness and his display of dominant signs such as erect posture, sauntering or striding gait, and direct eye contact with others. Thus bolstered, Ego may seek out new dominance encounters and is primed to win them. The feedback between high testosterone and dominant demeanor may explain the momentum often associated with strings of triumphs. Success begets a high testosterone response, which begets more dominant behavior, which begets more success. Part of this sequence has been demonstrated by Mehta and Josephs (2006) and Carré, Putnam, and McCormick (2009).

On the other side, Alter, the loser, experiences a drop in testosterone, reducing his assertiveness and increasing his display of deferential signs such as stooped posture, smiling, or eye aversion. Faced with a new dominance encounter, he is now at a psychic and physiological disadvantage. One defeat begets another. Alter is more likely than before to retreat or submit. This may be an adaptive response, saving Alter from further losses and perhaps from additional damage.

Mehta and Josephs (2010) have proposed a promising "dual hormone" hypothesis whereby testosterone and cortisol jointly regulate dominance. They provide evidence that testosterone effects noted above are most likely to occur when a person's cortisol is low. This hypothesis is intuitively appealing, suggesting that the people most likely to act dominantly, to break norms or otherwise scale stressful barriers, are those least bothered by the stressor, thus low in cortisol. For high-cortisol individuals, the barrier is too intimidating to challenge.

Improvements in Research Methods

The biosocial model is useful only insofar as it can be tested empirically and provide worthwhile new hypotheses. Therefore I give primary importance to data collecting. Improvements in methodology over the past few decades have been so striking that I mention them here, hoping to encourage readers toward their own empirical studies.

Until the availability of radioimmunoassay in the 1960s, the measurement of endogenous testosterone was elusive because it is produced by the body in tiny amounts. A normal man has on the order of a hundred-thousandth gram of hormone per liter of blood, women roughly a seventh as much. Early studies relating testosterone and behavior in men, dating from the 1980s, required a nurse to draw blood samples from subjects. By the 1990s it was practical (and relatively inexpensive) to measure *free* testosterone (i.e., testosterone not bound to protein, which is assumed to be the physiologically active portion) and cortisol from saliva samples easily collected in the field. This led to numerous studies of subjects in athletic competitions and other natural settings (e.g., Dabbs 2000).

These studies were all correlational, depending on natural variation of endogenous hormones. Controlled experiments, in which human subjects are given a hormone treatment versus a placebo, were limited to medical settings, constrained by ethical and safety considerations, and barely, if at all, concerned with behavior. Quite recently, as (legal) testosterone preparations have become widely available, and the safety of human subjects ensured, we are beginning to see double-blind experiments by psychologists and behavioral economists testing the effects of testosterone compared with placebo. This research is increasingly practical outside of medical facilities; however, it is not yet fully satisfactory. Hormone exposures are low and brief, and numbers of subjects small, so published reports may reflect false positives, and there are apparent inconsistencies in findings; for example, one group reported that testosterone treatment increases competition in bargaining for money while another group found it decreases competition (Zak et al. 2009; Eisenegger et al. 2010). Further improvements in experimental method should soon reconcile and extend these findings.

The connection between variation in testosterone (whether endogenously or via experimental treatment) and behavior does not occur instantly but over periods of time ranging from several minutes to hours or longer. It is possible through functional magnetic resonance imaging (fMRI) to detect changes of blood flow, with time resolution in seconds, in particular regions of the brain in response to experimental stimuli. Increased blood flow shows which parts of the brain are affected by the experimenter's manipulation. This enables the testing of hypotheses about how testosterone affects dominance/submissiveness by acting on specific regions of the brain or connections between regions (e.g., Terburg and van Honk 2013). Thus, Goetz et al. (2014) showed pictures of threatening faces to subjects lying in an fMRI scanner, and found that those subjects who had previously been treated with testosterone showed more threat-related reactivity of the amygdala and hypothalamus than did subjects whose testosterone had not been artificially raised. These are preliminary findings but promise future dividends.

As appealing as it is to scan the brain in operation, fMRI has severe limitations because it must be done in a medical setting, and subjects must lie still in an encircling and loud machine while numerous brain scans are taken to allow statistically valid signals to emerge from irrelevant noise. Subjects in the scanner cannot participate in real social interaction, instead being asked to react to stimuli presented to them as they remain prone, for example, to angry and neutral faces shown repeatedly on a computer screen.

Another promising avenue of measurement is the tracking of peripheral physiological responses during social interaction. Galvanic skin response (GSR) is the most familiar of these, having a venerable tradition among psychologists interested in emotional reactivity. Unfortunately, as is well known from this long experience, GSR has little specificity, reacting to all kinds of things that are irrelevant to the object of experimentation; I've found it too noisy to be useful in studying dominance contests. Heart rate is another candidate, quickening under severe challenge or other stressors, but it has the opposite problem from GSR, being too stable to detect the slight stresses that occur during polite interaction.

The peripheral measure that seems "just right," neither too noisy nor too stable, is thumb blood volume (TBV). A decrease in TBV is a convenient indicator of stress, showing the shift of blood from the periphery of the body to the heart, lungs, and large muscles, an important feature of the fight-or-flight response. To measure TBV, a sensor is connected to the subject's thumb with a Velcro cuff, so with each pulse beat an electric signal is sent to a recorder. The resulting waveform moves up and down with the beating heart. Rather than measuring the time interval between peaks (pulse *rate*), we measure the height of the waveform, that is, the distance from the top of one beat to the bottom of the next. As blood flows away from the thumb (under stress), the waveform narrows; as blood flows back to the thumb (relaxation), the waveform widens.

In the old days, when I first measured stress during face-to-face interaction, pressure sensors on the thumb sent electrical signals to electromechanical pens that drew waveforms in ink on a paper roll as it was driven across a table. After each run, we took measurements from the paper roll, using a pencil and ruler. TBV was averaged over ten-second intervals, a crude measurement.

We knew that when strangers are put together, they usually rank themselves by status fairly quickly, but we did not know what kinds of stresses occur during these encounters. A methodological problem was the synchronization of physiological waveforms with videotaped social interaction, which may have been off by a few seconds. Therefore we needed a simple (if stilted) interaction, insensitive to imprecisions of timing, and for this a stare-down was suitable.

Two paid naïve subjects, strangers of the same sex, sat across a table from each other, with a screen between them. Sensors were attached to their thumbs, and after a period of acclimation, the screen was removed and, as instructed, they did not look at one another until signaled to do so by the experimenter. On signal they stared at each other for twenty seconds and then were instructed to look away. Subjects in the stare-down condition later reported feelings of discomfort, and their waveforms showed a significantly greater decrease in TBV (i.e., greater stress) than that of subjects in control conditions of no stare or of unreciprocated stare.

A variant of this experiment took advantage of the difference in perceived dominance of a person whose brows are lowered rather than raised (see Figure 25.1). A naïve subject sat across the table from a "subject" who, unknown to the real subject, was an experimental confederate. Depending on a random draw, the confederate engaged in the stare-down with either raised or lowered brows. Subjects' TBV decreased significantly more when the confederate lowered his brows, intensifying his dominant aspect, than when his brows were raised (Mazur et al. 1980).

Admittedly crude experiments, far from the grail of studying stresses during conversation, these were nearly as much as the methods of the time allowed. Alan Booth and David Brinkerhoff of Penn State University pushed the state of the art by showing that mean TBV throughout argumentative conversations about abortion was lower (more stressful) than in control conditions, but that was as far as any of us could go, and the topic became quiescent (Brinkerhoff and Booth 1984).

There is now greatly improved instrumentation—computerized, of course, and reasonably priced—allowing close synchronization of videoed conversations with simultaneously recorded physiology and automated data analysis. The old pressure sensors on the thumb are now plethysmograph transducers that measure blood flow more accurately by optical means. (This can be done wirelessly.) The low-end system I use is sold by Biopac Systems of Goleta, California, and consists of an MP36 acquisition unit, which is the hardware interface between sensors on subjects and the computer. BSL Pro software (versions 3.7.1 of 4.0.1) controls data acquisition and analysis, and closely synchronizes video recording of subjects with physiological recording.

Data can be processed and analyzed directly on the computer screen. Now my only need for pen and ink is to write the check to pay for it all. That done, I am with pleasure returning to the old hole with a better spade. The following section describes preliminary results of this new research, with the hope that others will join in. One warning: As with an adult's first experience with a modern computer game, you cannot jump right in, so expect a period of learning, preferably with the help of an eager graduate student.

STRESS DURING CONVERSATION

Beginning from the plateau reached by Brinkerhoff and Booth three decades ago, I wondered if conversational pairs had to be strangers and argumentative for stress to occur. Recruiting undergraduates as subjects, I asked each respondent to bring a friend with whom to participate. When the pair arrived, instead of seeking topics upon which they disagreed, we picked topics of mutual interest. The ensuing conversations were similar to those run by Brinkerhoff and Booth except now between friends and without argument. Nonetheless, results clearly showed more stress—lower mean TBV—during conversation than in quiet silences that preceded and followed each conversation. This occurred for male pairs, female pairs, mixed-sex pairs—either friends or romantically involved—and one pair apparently high on recreational drugs. Stress was not the simple product of argument between strangers but a feature of conversation per se. (No doubt the strangeness of the experimental setting raised stress levels, but still there was a marked difference between quiet and conversational periods in that setting.)

During playback, researchers can watch the physiological responses in subjects as they are speaking to one another, as if adding a previously unseen dimension to the interaction. Subjects' TBV waveforms fluctuate during their conversations, sometimes widening, sometimes narrowing, sometimes narrowing more, and then widening again. My naïve assumption at the inception of this work was that casual discussions between friends would be physiologically stable, but on the contrary, in "looking under the skin" one sees physiological stress as an integral component of the conversation.

To explore the nature of these stresses under tighter control, I recruited mostly male undergraduates as paid subjects. Each subject formed with me an unequal status dyad, a student talking one-on-one with a newly met professor. Beforehand, the student suggested subjects for discussion. To avoid quick turn-taking, I asked each subject, when he spoke, to talk for at least thirty seconds, and I would do the same. Obviously the strangeness of the setting is a threat to external validity, but subjects played along and seemed reasonably relaxed, producing friendly, informal conversations.

Figure 25.4 shows a waveform measured from one student. (Raw signals are processed through a digital filter that removes anomalous beats and centers the waveform on the abscissa, thus excluding extraneous features.) The waveform begins (at the left) near the end of a distracting video, used to acclimate the subject to the setting (Piferi et al. 2000), and continues through roughly twenty-five minutes of conversation. First the professor speaks, then the student, in alternating turns. The labels above the waveform, "Listening" and "Speaking," refer to the student-subject. These extended periods were not pure listening or speaking, because they were punctuated by interjections or questions from either side, which seemed appropriate in the flow of talk.

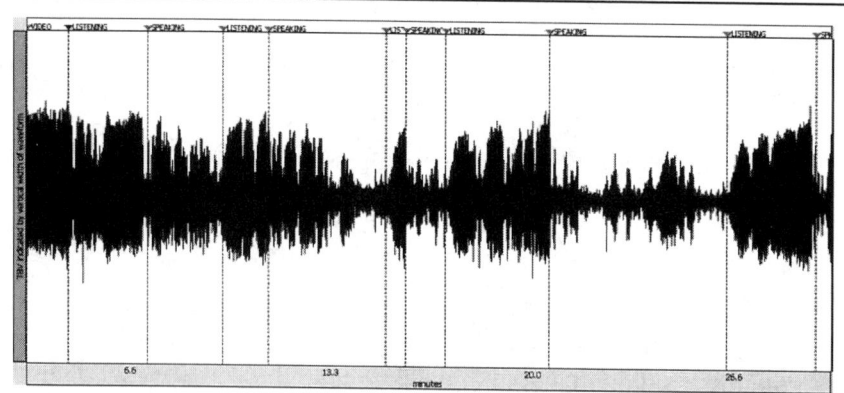

Narrowing of the waveform indicates increasing stress on the student; widening indicates increasing relaxation. Labels across the top tell when the student is listening to the professor and when he is the speaker. The long speaking and listening periods are interrupted by brief interjections or questions, as in the normal flow of conversation.

Figure 25.4 Waveform of a male student during about twenty-five minutes of casual conversation with a previously unknown professor

TBV is indicated by the (vertical) width of the waveform. As expected, the student's waveform is wider (i.e., more relaxed) while he watches the distracting video than during the following conversation. More importantly, there is variation within the conversation. TBV is lower (i.e., the waveform is narrower) when the student is the speaker than when he is the listener. In other words, the student is more relaxed when listening to the professor than when talking to him, possibly explaining why students fall asleep during lectures. That aside, the main point is that it is more stressful to speak than to listen, at least when conversing with someone of higher rank.

These preliminary findings are best viewed as illustrative hypotheses. Running about eighty subjects of both sexes in different formats, I saw considerable individual variation. The general pattern of higher stress while speaking than while listening was not inevitable. (Indeed, two subjects showed the opposite pattern, consistently more relaxed when talking than when listening.)

Presumably, to minimize his or her stress, a student might prefer not to speak at all; however, this is precluded by the conversational demands of the professor. In a group larger than a dyad, where the student could have evaded directives to take the floor, he or she might have said very little. This mirrors the well-known result of small group research that higher-ranked members dominate the floor, while low-ranked members remain submissively quiet, thus avoiding the stress of speaking out.

This research continues, asking, for example, if there is a similar difference between the stresses of speaking and listening when members of the dyad are of similar status. Preliminary results indicate there is, but not as distinct as when rankings are as different as professor and student.

Apart from the first-order effect that conversation is more stressful than silence, and the second-order effect that speaking is more stressful than listening, there are third-order variations in stress *within* a listening or speaking period, clearly seen in Figure 25.4. Their meanings remain to be explored. (Waveforms sometimes expand or contract for no externally visible reason, perhaps reflecting the subject's unspoken thoughts.) My tactic focuses on violations of turn-taking, either speaking over another person before he or she has relinquished the floor, or refusing to speak when given the floor. Both actions act as dominant signals.

Imagine Ego speaking and Alter interrupting. Ego may relinquish the floor, in effect deferring to Alter (a likely outcome if Alter is of higher status), or Ego may continue speaking despite Alter's interruption, asserting his own priority. If both continue speaking (perhaps at higher volume), they are competing for dominance. The situation is like a stare-down, a mutual confrontation until one breaks off.

Exploring one such violation, I wait until the subject finishes a speaking turn. Instead of taking my own turn, I continue to look at him while remaining silent. For example, one student was explaining his activities in a university organization that served city needs, concluding:

> Student: ". . . bridging the gaps here in Syracuse [University] along with the ones in the city—the university and the city—they have to be a little more connected, in my opinion. So, yah."
> [Student signals the end of his turn by looking at the professor, who remains silent. Two seconds pass.]
> Student: "And, um—anything else?"
> [Two more seconds of silence.]
> Student: "I guess, uh."

[Another two seconds pass. Then student resumes speaking.]
Student: "I guess one of my favorite events I did with that organization was..."

Figure 25.5 shows about forty seconds of the subject's waveform surrounding the professor's dominating turn violation. The student ends his speaking turn with "So, yah." His TBV constricts as the professor remains silent. After six seconds, including some hesitant utterances by the student, he resumes continuous speech, and we see his waveform widening.

Conclusion

We are past the naiveté of postwar social science when human behavior was regarded as biologically immaculate, the product entirely of cultural socialization and operant conditioning. There is no scientific doubt today that humans are an evolved species, not only in physical form but to a considerable extent in the underpinnings of our behavioral repertoires. The present challenge for biosocial science is to explicate how evolution is best incorporated into research and theoretical explanations of behavior.

The approach of this chapter is to examine humans in the context of our cousins, the living primates. Focusing on the dominance/status hierarchies of face-to-face groups, we see that many behaviors once considered by social scientists as strictly human phenomena are in fact part of the general primate pattern or appear in those primates most closely related to us, the African apes, giving prima facie grounds that these are evolved tendencies. A stronger (testable) case for homology is made by identifying proximate neurohormonal mechanisms—for status processes the neurophysiology of stress and testosterone—that underlie these behaviors and function similarly among other primates, even within the uniquely human context of conversation.

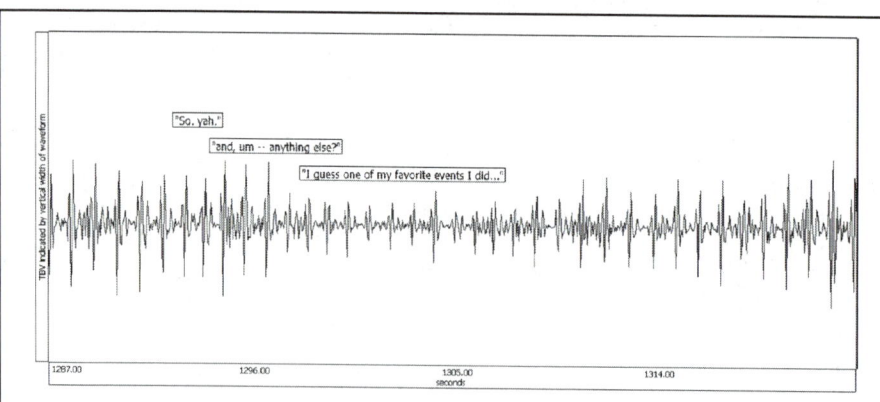

After the student finishes his speaking turn with "So, yah," the professor violates turn-taking by continuing to look at the student silently. Narrowing of the waveform indicates increasing stress on the student. After about six seconds, the student resumes talking.

Figure 25.5 Waveform of a male student during about forty seconds

Acknowledgments

I appreciate the advice of Alan Booth, Justin Carré, Robert Josephs, and Robert Ward.

References

Archer, J. 2006. "Testosterone and Human Aggression." *Neuroscience and Biobehavioral Reviews* 30: 319–345.
Batrinos, M. 2012. "Testosterone and Aggressive Behavior in Man." *International Journal of Endocrinology and Metabolism* 10: 563–568.
Berger, J., B. Cohen, and M. Zelditch. 1972. "Status Characteristics and Social Interaction." *American Sociological Review* 37: 209–219.
Bergman, T., J. Beehner, D. Cheney, and R. Seyfarth. 2003. "Hierarchical Classification by Rank and Kinship in Baboons." *Science* 302: 1234–1236.
Brinkerhoff, D., and A. Booth. 1984. "Gender, Dominance, and Stress." *Journal of Social and Biological Structures* 7: 159–177.
Carré, J., J. Campbell, E. Lozoya, S. Goetz, and K. Welker. 2013. "Changes in Testosterone Mediate the Effect of Winning on Subsequent Aggressive Behavior." *Psychoneuroendocrinology* 38: 2034–2041.
Carré, J., C. McCormick, and C. J. Mondloch. 2009. "Facial Structure Is a Reliable Cue of Aggressive Behaviour." *Psychological Science* 20: 1194–1198.
Carré, J., S. Putnam, and C. McCormick. 2009. "Testosterone Responses to Competition Predict Future Aggressive Behavior at a Cost to Reward in Men." *Psychoneuroendocrinology* 34: 561–570.
Dabbs, J., Jr. 2000. *Heroes, Rogues and Lovers*. New York: McGraw-Hill.
de Waal, F. 1989. *Chimpanzee Politics*. Baltimore: Johns Hopkins University Press.
———. 2000. "Primates: A Natural Heritage of Conflict Resolution." *Science* 289: 586–590.
Eisenegger, C., M. Naef, R. Snozzi, M. Heinrichs, and E. Fehr. 2010. "Prejudice and Truth about the Effect of Testosterone on Human Bargaining Behavior." *Nature* 463: 356–359.
Fisek, M., and R. Ofshe. 1970. "The Process of Status Evolution." *Sociometry* 33: 327–346.
Goetz, S., L. Tang, M. Thomason, M. Diamond, A. Hariri, and J. Carré. 2014. "Testosterone Rapidly Increases Neural Reactivity to Threat in Healthy Men: A Novel Two-Step Pharmacological Challenge Paradigm." *Biological Psychiatry* 76: 324–331.
Keating, C., A. Mazur, and M. Segall. 1977. "Facial Gestures Which Influence the Perception of Status." *Sociometry* 40: 374–378.
Keating, C., A. Mazur, M. Segall, P. Cysneiros, W. Divale, J. Kilbride, S. Komin, R. Leahy, B. Thurman, and R. Wirsing. 1981. "Culture and the Perception of Social Dominance from Facial Expression." *Journal of Personality and Social Psychology* 40: 615–626.
Lefevre, C. E., and G. J. Lewis. 2013. "Perceiving Aggression from Facial Structure." *European Journal of Personality*. doi: 10.1002/per.1942.
Mazur, A. 1973. "A Cross-Species Comparison of Status in Small Established Groups." *American Sociological Review* 38: 513–550.
———. 1976. "Effects of Testosterone on Status in Primate Groups." *Folia Primatologica* 26: 214–226.
———. 2005. *Biosociology of Dominance and Deference*. New York: Rowman & Littlefield.
Mazur, A., and A. Booth. 1998. "Testosterone and Dominance in Men." *Behavioral and Brain Sciences* 21: 353–363.
Mazur, A., E. Rosa, M. Faupel, J. Heller, R. Leen, and B. Thurman. 1980. "Physiological Aspects of Communication via Mutual Gaze." *American Journal of Sociology* 90: 125–150.
Mehta, P. H., and R. A. Josephs. 2006. "Testosterone Change after Losing Predicts the Decision to Compete Again." *Hormones and Behavior* 50: 684–692.
———. 2010. "Testosterone and Cortisol Jointly Regulate Dominance: Evidence for a Dual-Hormone Hypothesis." *Hormones and Behavior* 58: 898–906.
Mueller, U., and A. Mazur. 1996. "Facial Dominance of West Point Cadets as a Predictor of Later Military Rank." *Social Forces* 74: 823–850.
Perrett, D. 2010. *In Your Face: The New Science of Human Attraction*. London: Palgrave Macmillan.
Piferi, R., K. Kline, J. Younger, and K. Lawler. 2000. "An Alternative Approach for Achieving Cardiovascular Baseline." *International Journal of Psychophysiology* 37: 207–217.
Rosa, E., and A. Mazur. 1979. "Incipient Status in Small Groups." *Social Forces* 58: 18–37.
Southwick, C. 1963. *Primate Social Behavior*. Toronto: Van Nostrand.

Stanton, S., J. Beehner, E. Saini, C. Kuhn, and J. Labar. 2009. "Dominance, Politics, and Physiology." *PLoS ONE* 4 (10): e7543.

Strodtbeck, F., R. James, and C. Hawkins. 1957. "Social Status in Jury Deliberations." *American Sociological Review* 22: 713–719.

Strongman, K., and B. Champness. 1968. "Dominance Hierarchies and Conflict in Eye Contact." *Acta Psychologica* 28: 376–386.

Terburg, D., and J. van Honk. 2013. "Approach–Avoidance versus Dominance–Submissiveness." *Emotion Review* 5: 296–302.

van Lawick-Goodall, J. 1968. "A Preliminary Report on Expressive Movements and Communications in the Gombe Stream Chimpanzees." In *Primates: Studies in Adaptation and Variability*, edited by P. Jay, 313–374. New York: Holt, Rinehart and Winston.

Wingfield, J., R. Hegner, A. Dufty Jr., and G. Ball. 1990. "The 'Challenge Hypothesis.'" *American Naturalist* 136: 829–846.

Zak, P. J., R. Kurzban, S. Ahmadi, R. Swerdloff, J. Park, L. Efremidze, K. Redwine, K. Morgan, and W. Matzner. 2009. "Testosterone Administration Decreases Generosity in the Ultimatum Game." *PLoS ONE* 4 (12): e8330. doi: 10.1371/journal.pone.0008330.

Chapter Twenty-Six

Intergroup Threat and Extralegal Police Aggression

An Evolutionary Interpretation

Malcolm D. Holmes

With the emergence of stable social groups among early hominins, natural selection favored the development of mental mechanisms for rapidly identifying and responding to ingroup and outgroup members. One characteristic response to outgroup members who posed potential threats to resources or personal safety would have been defensive aggression. The mental mechanisms underlying the behavior continue to inform social interaction among modern humans, sometimes eliciting aggression that is unnecessary and subject to legal sanction. The disproportionate police use of extralegal aggression in disadvantaged minority neighborhoods clearly illustrates this behavioral pattern. This chapter describes the evolution of emotional and cognitive processes involved in intergroup relations and shows how those archaic mental mechanisms may trigger acts of excessive force, the most serious form of extralegal police aggression, in disadvantaged minority neighborhoods.

Introduction

A crucial development in the evolution of hominins was the emergence of relatively stable social groups. Considerable scholarship across disciplines emphasizes that a relatively weak species confronting a physical habitat that posed significant adaptive problems, including predation avoidance and food acquisition, was unlikely to have survived in the absence of cooperative group relationships (see, e.g., Brewer and Caporael 2006; Moffett 2013; Turner and Maryanski 2012). Although essential for survival, the emergence of cooperative foraging bands created the ancillary problem of intergroup contact, which often proved less cooperative than intragroup relations. Violence between groups may have been commonplace (e.g., Chagnon 1988; Manson and Wrangham 1991). Initiating raids against other groups was a mechanism for securing somatic and reproductive resources that may have enhanced inclusive fitness. This pattern of violence posed an adaptive problem analogous to interspecific predation. Just as the evolution of predator-avoidance strategies reduced the risk of predation, survival demanded the evolution of closely related defensive mechanisms to protect against the threats posed by conspecific outgroup members. While adaptive throughout most of our species' existence, the mental processes that allow rapid identification of and response to potential threats may promote needless intergroup aggression in the complex societies that exist today. This chapter examines that possibility in an evolutionary analysis of extralegal police aggression, particularly the use of excessive physical force, in minority communities.

Maintaining social order necessitates the use of coercive mechanisms of social control against law violators and dissidents who challenge existing social arrangements (Weber [1922] 1968). Complex societies rely on various formal institutions to prevent and punish such rule breaking. The police play an especially prominent role by virtue of holding a monopoly on the legitimate domestic use of force to protect citizens and officers from the dangerous people in their midst (Bittner 1970). When significant social inequalities characterize a society, such as in the United States, policing entails protecting social arrangements that advantage privileged segments of society. Those groups perceived as threats to the status quo, notably racial and ethnic minorities, bear the brunt of coercive strategies of control by the police (Holmes and Smith 2008). Although most police use of force is undertaken lawfully to overcome resistance by suspects, it also may be used extralegally for reasons extraneous to legitimate duties. This unwarranted use of coercive control undermines the legitimacy of the police and fosters tension between them and minority communities. Cities pay out millions of dollars to settle lawsuits alleging police misconduct involving minority citizens and spend millions more on programs to improve police-minority relations.

Given that the police control the legitimate means of coercion, they need not resort to extralegal means to protect themselves when confronted with potential dangers. The dynamics of extralegal force may differ considerably from those involved in the legitimate use of force by the police, which constitutes a fundamental part of the police role (Holmes and Smith 2012). Police departments establish official regulations for using various forms of force (which range from verbal commands and threats to severe physical harm), banning those that violate civil or criminal statutes or that may embarrass the department (Klockars 1996). Prohibited uses of force are best described by the term "extralegal police aggression," as they include behavior that expressly aims to injure another person either physically or psychologically (Holmes and Smith 2012). Research generally demonstrates that minority citizens are disproportionately targets of various forms of extralegal police aggression. Most of the time these actions convey little risk for officers, as the actions are normally employed clandestinely, involve less serious violations, and leave little evidence after the fact. Periodically, however, police use of excessive physical force cannot be easily covered up, and in such cases officers may face severe sanctions, including lengthy prison sentences. Why, then, would the police risk employing excessive physical force?

Several theories have been developed to explain the use of excessive force by the police, but two explanations that focus on social-structural characteristics of communities have received the most consistent empirical support. One hypothesis maintains that police-citizen relations reflect the social divisions, deeply rooted in the social structure, that separate dominant and subordinate racial/ethnic groups and produce intergroup conflict. In this view, the structural characteristics of society underlie the formal and informal organization of police agencies and promote the proclivity of police to target minorities, who may be perceived as criminal threats by the dominant group and the police, for aggressive strategies of control (e.g., Chambliss 2001; Smith and Holmes 2003). Communities with relatively large minority populations, therefore, will have a disproportionate incidence of excessive force (e.g., Holmes 2000; Smith and Holmes 2003, 2014). The other explanation focuses on the ecological organization of cities (e.g., Holmes and Smith 2008, 2012). Spatially segregated minority populations may be seen as special threats by the police who patrol their neighborhoods and, therefore, are more likely to experience excessive force by the police (e.g., Smith and Holmes 2014). Taken together, the intergroup-conflict and group-segregation models suggest police use of excessive force against minority citizens may be elicited by outgroup threats directly perceived by officers.

The generic social-psychological processes underlying defensive responses to outgroup threat offer a promising line of analysis to develop a more comprehensive explanation of excessive force (Holmes and Smith 2008). Highly interrelated mental processes of emotion and cognition would have proven highly adaptive over the course of hominin evolution, as they allow automatic and rapid responses to ingroup and outgroup members that would have increased prospects of survival among members of small foraging bands. The ability to quickly identify, without any form of social interaction, those who could be approached safely and those who potentially posed threats and should be avoided altogether, approached cautiously, or perhaps aggressed against would have conveyed obvious advantages. The archaic neural circuitry that produced these response patterns endures in modern humans and underlies a complex neurological architecture that facilitates threat detection and defensive response in intergroup contexts. Although highly adaptive in small homogeneous societies, this mental system may generate forms of intergroup aggression defined as violations of law in the complex societies of the contemporary world.

In this chapter, I make the case that these evolved social-psychological processes underlie the differential deployment of excessive force by police in urban communities characterized by racial/ethnic diversity and segregation. In certain respects, the nature of intergroup interaction between minority citizens and the police, and especially of the ecological contexts in which a good part of it takes place, approximates conditions confronted by our ancestors throughout hominin evolution. I begin by outlining evolved social-psychological mechanisms of emotion and cognition that facilitate rapid detection of actual and potential threats from outgroup members and may trigger an aggressive response to those threats. I then present the case for understanding extralegal police aggression as involving these processes.

Evolution of Emotional, Cognitive, and Behavioral Responses to Outgroup Threat

Imagine two otherwise similar hominins, one highly attuned to potential threats from members of other social groups and one relatively indifferent to the possibility of such dangers. Under what conditions would natural selection have favored the individual who was alert to the possibility that an unfamiliar outsider might expropriate somatic and reproductive resources, versus the one who was less alert to the possibility of such usurpations? If experience demonstrated that outsiders posed little threat but that intergroup social interaction proffered little benefit (i.e., exchanges of resources), the answer would be that neither individual would possess a clear adaptive advantage. Were outsiders likely to exchange resources and to pose little danger, embracing outgroup members would be the more adaptive alternative. In that circumstance the less suspicious individual would be advantaged. Should, however, outsiders sometimes pose significant threats to one's personal safety or resources, strategies of avoidance or aggression would be more adaptive and the individual attuned to threat would hold an advantage. Clearly these scenarios oversimplify the patterns of intergroup exchange that eventually culminated in complex human societies, but they point to a persistent conundrum of human social interaction. To what degree should our responses to outsiders be infused with caution?

Evidence from the fossil record indicates that in the distant past hominins began living in multilevel foraging societies characterized by a fission-fusion system in which groups split apart and re-formed over time (Grove, Pearce, and Dunbar 2012). The effects of hominin mental processes such as pro-social emotions and ingroup social identity on the social organization of such societies are key issues for evolutionary analysis (e.g., Brewer and Caporael 2006; Moffett 2013; Turner 2000). So too are the dynamics of intergroup relations, although the low density of early hominin populations may have initially limited contact among unfamiliar bands (Brewer 2007). Some early intergroup contact may have involved cooperative exchanges of resources, but contact between members of different groups also could have posed threats to somatic and reproductive resources (Kenrick, Ackerman, and Ledlow 2003). There is considerable evidence of lethal intergroup violence among humans in simple societies (e.g., Chagnon 1988; Manson and Wrangham 1991), as well as among chimpanzees (Manson and Wrangham 1991), suggesting that intergroup violence would have occurred among early hominins. Research on intergroup warfare argues it is an adaptive strategy that enhances inclusive fitness by acquisition of resources and elimination of competitors while minimizing risk by the selection of relatively defenseless targets. Strategies of conspecific threat avoidance would have evolved concomitantly, grounded in predator defense mechanisms that existed among mammals long before the first hominins appeared (Öhman and Mineka 2001). Aggression furnishes a dual-purpose strategy that may have been used offensively to expropriate the resources of others, as well as defensively to thwart such appropriations (Buss and Shackelford 1997). Of course, it is but one tactic of intergroup interaction, which requires a flexible mental system for perceiving and responding to potentially threatening encounters while simultaneously identifying and attending to opportunities for rewarding exchanges (Kenrick, Ackerman, and Ledlow 2003).

Here I focus specifically on threat detection and defensive aggression occurring in intergroup interaction. Preliminarily, the logic of natural selection suggests threat recognition mechanisms that allow rapid identification of ingroup and outgroup members (i.e., those who can be approached safely, and those who must be approached cautiously—if at all) would have considerable utility. Once a potential outgroup threat is identified, an appropriate context-specific response must be elicited, with aggression being one option. The neuroanatomy of humans evolved to address this adaptive problem through a highly complex and interrelated set of emotional and cognitive processes (see, e.g., Phelps 2006).

EMOTIONAL RESPONSE MECHANISMS

The hominin line that eventually led to modern humans (*Homo sapiens*) appeared several million years ago in the emerging ecology of savannas that took hold in Africa as tropical forests retreated in the face of climate change. Long before the appearance of the first hominins, mammals possessed subcortical neural mechanisms of emotional response that provided "solutions" to common adaptive problems (e.g., predation avoidance). The earliest hominins came equipped with comparatively sophisticated brains well organized for emotional responses, but it was the subsequent evolution of the brain that made the highly organized social life essential to survival in open environments possible (Turner 2000). The subcortical limbic structures responsible for emotion were reorganized and elaborated, and these structures were rewired to neocortical and brain-stem systems. These preadaptations paved the way for the emergence of an expanded emotional repertoire, which allowed the forging of social bonds necessary to support stable social structures.

The emotional bonds that linked our hominin ancestors to socially organized life existed long before their brains were capable of rationally calculating the potential benefits and costs of such arrangements (Massey 2002). The full expansion of the prefrontal cortex (responsible for conscious, rational thought) did not take place until *Homo sapiens* emerged about 150,000 years ago; thus, the completely developed cognitive capacities of modern humans make up but a very small part of our species' evolutionary history. Insofar as humans possess rational cognition, it is built on preexisting emotional structures that still profoundly influence thinking (Phelps 2006). Underlying the environmentally sensitive cognitive information-processing system are evolutionarily older brain regions (e.g., the brain stem, hypothalamus, and amygdala), which the genome specifies far more precisely (Damasio 1994). These regions, central to the survival of the organism, cannot be left to chance—they regulate basic life processes, including basic emotional responses.

Ever since the publication of Charles Darwin's (1872) *The Expression of the Emotions in Man and Animals*, considerable scholarly attention has focused on the identification of basic human emotions. Fear and anger are prominent in the emotional arsenal of animals, and scholars have uniformly classified them as primary emotions (Turner 2000). Fear activation takes place in the amygdala, among the most ancient subcortical limbic regions, and it provides an invaluable system of protection against interspecific and intraspecific threats. Fear makes the avoidance of predation and other dangers possible, and modern humans remain highly attuned to threatening stimuli (Öhman and Mineka 2001). Anger also originates in the amygdala and may be tied to fear in defensive aggression (Turner 2000).

If fear plays such a vital part in survival, it would be expected that the amygdala can seize control over other parts of the brain when a human encounters a threatening situation (LeDoux 1996; Öhman and Mineka 2001). That is exactly what the amygdala does. It heavily influences numerous higher-order thought processes when one confronts a potential danger, serving as part of an arousal system that directs information processing to the emotion-producing stimulus. At the same time, it is relatively impenetrable by other neural regions. So long as the threatening stimulus is present, the amygdala will drive the arousal system that maintains hypersensitivity in cortical networks and automatically activate the neural networks that elicit involuntary responses. The initial response may buy time and allow one to take conscious control and consider alternative strategies. Fear may, however, produce behavioral responses to stimuli before cognitive processes can exert any influence on behavior (LeDoux 1996; Öhman and Mineka 2001). A potentially threatening stimulus, such as rustling leaves that may signal the presence of a snake, requires an automatic defensive response, even if it turns out to be unnecessary. A quick-and-dirty subcortical defense system that requires no cognitive input possesses immense survival value.

Either instinctive or learned triggers may elicit these unconscious emotional responses (LeDoux 1996; Öhman and Mineka 2001). Instinctive triggers require no conditioning or higher mental processes for an animal to respond reflexively to a threatening stimulus. These triggers involve environmental threats that remain stable over long expanses of time and may be most effectively responded to without the necessity of learning. Innate stimulus-emotional response relationships may make up a relatively small part of the human behavioral repertoire. Learned triggers no doubt play a much larger role in a species with a highly plastic capacity to acquire information from social environments presenting threats that vary across time and space, but trial-and-error learning can be costly given that it takes time to develop an adaptive response. Fortunately, the rudimentary processes of classical fear conditioning, which are heavily influenced by the amygdala, provide a rapid and efficient means of acquiring, storing, and expressing fear responses (LeDoux 1996; Öhman and Mineka 2001; Phelps 2006). Fear conditioning occurs when a neutral stimulus (e.g., faint sounds) becomes associated with an aversive event (presence of a predator) and elicits an innate response (e.g., freezing). When those sounds are heard again, the response will be activated irrespective of whether a predator is actually present. While "fear conditioning opens up channels of evolutionarily shaped responsivity to *new environmental events*" (LeDoux 1996: 143; emphasis added), prospects for survival would have improved among early hominins with an aversion to relatively invariant threats in their environment. Therefore, humans may come evolutionarily "prepared" to learn fear when confronted with certain naturally occurring threats to survival among our ancestors (Seligman 1971; Öhman and Mineka 2001). Research shows that fear-inducing stimuli that would have confronted early hominins (and earlier mammals), such as snakes and spiders, compared with fear-irrelevant ones, such as flowers, result in fear conditioning that occurs quickly and is not easily extinguished (Öhman and Mineka 2001).

Of particular interest here is the fear of racial outgroups prevalent among modern humans. Insofar as *Homo sapiens* divided into what we commonly think of as "races" in recent evolutionary history, natural selection could not have specifically prepared humans to fear members of other races (Olsson et al. 2005). But a mechanism that enhanced the ability to readily identify small phenotypical variations among conspecifics without simultaneously inviting detection by potentially threatening outsiders (or predators) could have proven highly adaptive. Hominin evolution provided an invaluable device that serves this purpose, a high degree of visual acuity that was dominant over auditory, haptic, and olfactory senses, which would have made interaction among conspecifics highly dependent on vision (Turner and Maryanski 2012). Human social interaction relies heavily on various facial cues (Turner and Maryanski 2012), and the amygdala is particularly attentive to facial indicators of threat (Phelps 2006). For example, an angry face may be a fear-relevant stimulus that humans come prepared to learn (Öhman and Mineka 2001). Were earlier hominins "pre-wired" to fear of outsiders based on subtle phenotypical distinctions among groups, more visible physical differences (such as skin tone) would clearly signify outgroup status and potential threat that may evoke prepared fear conditioning in humans.

A study demonstrating a robust fear-conditioning effect associated with race supports that argument (Olsson et al. 2005). In that study, black and white participants were presented with images of black and white male faces with neutral expressions. Racial outgroup faces constituted the fear-relevant stimulus, ingroup faces the fear-irrelevant stimulus. During the acquisition (fear-conditioning) trials in both experiments, mildly uncomfortable electric shocks were paired with one stimulus category (face), whereas the other was presented without shock. No shocks were administered during the extinction trials. Skin conductance responses were measured to determine the emotional salience of the stimuli during acquisition and extinction trials. Conditioned fear of others was fully extinguished for racial ingroup (fear-irrelevant) stimuli, but not for racial outgroup (fear-relevant) stimuli. In other words, white participants' conditioned responses to black faces were not fully extinguished, and neither were black participants' conditioned responses to white faces. The only social factor that influenced the response pattern was the participants' history of close interracial contact (dating), which attenuated conditioned fear of outgroup members. That finding is consistent with the possibility that fear of evolutionarily significant threats is not automatically and invariably activated in all individuals; rather, it may be selectively sensitized to be triggered when a preexisting anxiety or an aversive context exists (Öhman and Mineka 2001). Insofar as fear conditioning is influenced by patterns of intergroup interaction, the spatial separation of races characteristic of American cities (see Massey 2005) may produce aversive interactional contexts that exacerbate the natural tendency of humans to fear members of dissimilar racial/ethnic groups.

COGNITIVE RESPONSE MECHANISMS

A rapid expansion of the hominin brain began about 2.2 million years ago (Turner and Maryanski 2012). The resulting modern human brain is remarkably complex, so much so that the trillions of synapses within it cannot be specified entirely by one's genetic makeup (Damasio 1994). The evolutionarily modern outer layers of the brain are highly plastic. Those neural regions (contained in the neocortex) record our acquired experiences and responses to them. They produce mental images and willful actions. This complex architecture enables and coordinates conceptualization, transmission, and processing of information, the cognitive systems that were essential to the eventual emergence of complex forms of human social organization (Massey 2005). The genome specifies only a general arrangement of those systems and circuitries, the precise arrangement of which continues to be formed by physical and social environments long after birth (Damasio 1994). Yet, these capabilities remain intricately connected to and influenced by the archaic emotional brain. The remarkably swift expansion of the brain could only have occurred so quickly because natural selection built on existing neuroanatomical structures (Turner and Maryanski 2012). Processes of learning, memory, perception, and information processing in humans involve the interaction of emotional and cognitive neural circuitry (Phelps 2006). For example, the evolution of an expansive neocortex created new ways of learning fear through observational and symbolic learning, but the amygdala influences these processes much as it does fear conditioning. Even rational thinking, the ability to build scenarios and plan lines of action, is infused with and constrained by underlying emotions (Damasio 1994; Tooby and Cosmides 1990). At the same time, the cognitive processing of information made possible by the human neocortex permits far more flexible responses than those triggered only by the more rigid limbic regions that control emotion.

Human social life is often complex and demanding, even in comparatively simple societies (Kurzban and Leary 2001), and requires individuals to attend to both novel and invariant stimuli in the social environment (Macrae and Bodenhausen 2000). Much of everyday life consists of orderly and predictable events, but people must always be prepared to deal with unexpected occurrences. Thus, an adaptive mind needs to be highly flexible and capable of rapidly digesting various types of stimulus events (Johnston and Hawley 1994). Two complementary learning/memory systems (see McClelland, McNaughton, and O'Reilly 1995) endow humans with the balance of "stability and plasticity" essential for navigating the complexities and uncertainties of social life (Macrae and Bodenhausen 2000). One's survival may depend on the capacity to respond speedily and adaptively to novel and unexpected stimuli (Shallice 1988). The fast-learning hippocampal system enables humans to form transient representations of unique events, but barring repeated exposure these episodic memories have little impact on long-term memory. However, stimuli that produce an emotional response and enhance prospects of future survival are less likely to be forgotten (Phelps 2006).

The slow-learning neocortical system contains the generic information that accumulates through repeated exposure to various stimuli. The information encoded in this system resists change and addresses the need for enduring representations of the social world. Ideally these cognitive structures (often termed schemas) are simple, coherent, and relatively stable; they provide a priori organization for interpreting new experiences (Markus and Zajonc 1985). Some cognitive categorizations "tag" information using the physical and social characteristics of people (Taylor 1981). These categorizations minimize within-group differences and maximize between-group differences, thus generating stereotypic attributions about groups. Activation of stereotypes encoded in schemas occurs automatically and inescapably influences the person-perception process (Fiske 1998).

Numerous studies demonstrate that people use cues about race and gender to categorize and respond to others (see Fiske 1998; Macrae and Bodenhausen 2000). Negative racial and ethnic stereotypes become well established in children's memories long before they acquire the ability to critically assess the validity of stereotype content (e.g., Allport 1954; Devine 1989). Stereotypical conceptions of race/ethnicity may acquire cognitive primacy for various reasons (Fiske 1998). An individual's race/ethnicity provides visual cues (physical features and customary attire) that allow ready identification of putative category membership and symbolizes a person's position in the social hierarchy. The more visible a stigmatizing cue, the greater its negative influence on social interaction (Kurzban and Leary 2001). Moreover, race/ethnicity indicates reputed behavioral propensities. People tend to overestimate the strength of the relationship between undesirable behaviors and outgroup membership, anecdotally generalizing the objectionable behavior of certain individuals to all members of a social category (an "illusory" correlation) (Hamilton 1981). For example, whites perceive blacks and Mexican Americans as threats to their personal safety (Cottrell and Neuberg 2005). Studies of both adults (Duncan 1976) and schoolchildren (Sagar and Schofield 1980) show that interpretations of an ambiguous shove or a bump in a hallway depend on the race of the actor. The presence of a black actor may automatically prime (i.e., stimulate) activation of the stereotype that associates blacks with violence. Consistent with that assumption, these studies show that white participants (as well as black ones in the schoolchildren study) perceive a black actor's ambiguously aggressive behavior as more hostile and threatening than the same behavior by a white actor. Acts that seem innocuous when performed by a white person seem threatening when performed by a black person.

When encountering someone new, humans rely on their cognitive schemas of social category membership to guide social interaction (Macrae and Bodenhausen 2000). Once activated, stereotypic categorizations of outgroup members provide expectancies that influence ensuing information processing. Activated categorical representations guide assimilation and integration of subsequently encountered information, producing a greater emphasis on stereotype-consistent information (e.g., Fyock and Stangor 1994; Macrae, Milne, and Bodenhausen 1994; Macrae, Stangor, and Milne 1994). Moreover, in the absence of evidence clearly contradicting stereotype-based expectancies, category activation leads to more stereotypic judgmental and memory effects (e.g., Bodenhausen 1988). Stereotypic categories are, therefore, cognitively functional because their use preserves mental resources by channeling information into preexisting categories and demanding little conscious cognitive effort. Routine social interactions habitually invite quick appraisal and minimal effort.

The activation of a negative racial stereotype does not necessarily produce an adverse response to the target person. Research shows that some conditions elicit rapid, automatic responses, whereas others permit activation of higher-order cognitive processes that give rise to more careful assessments and deliberate reactions (Macrae and Bodenhausen 2000). The controlled component of cognitive function demands conscious effort and provides for flexible responses (Devine 1989). In circumstances permitting more controlled thinking, the disassociation of unconscious (implicit) negative racial stereotypes and conscious, non-prejudiced beliefs may occur. Stereotype activation is equally strong and automatic among both high- and low-prejudice individuals, but the more egalitarian beliefs of the latter may overcome automatic negative responses triggered by the underlying stereotype. Still, "in situations in which controlled processes are precluded or interfered with, automatic processing effects may exert the greatest influence on responses" (Devine 1989: 15).

Time pressure is a key factor in the solicitation of automatic processing effects. This point is demonstrated in an investigation of stereotypic behavioral responses, which used a video-game protocol to study "shooting" decisions for armed and unarmed black and white targets (Correll et al. 2002). One experimental condition imposed time constraints on shooting decisions, which produced errors consistent with the prediction that automatic (unconscious) stereotypic biases influence perceptions of and responses to people of different racial identities. Participants were more likely to shoot black than white unarmed targets, and less likely to shoot white than black armed targets. Other factors also may play a role in generating stereotypic judgments and responses in interpersonal interactions. When lacking motivation or cognitive capacity to think about others, people rely more heavily on their cognitive categorizations (Fiske 1998; Macrae and Bodenhausen 2000). One's cognitive load may be affected by conditions such as complex and competing environmental stimuli, which tax cognitive resources and encourage stereotypic responses in otherwise routine situations lacking novel features (see Macrae and Bodenhausen 2000). Moreover, the social context in which a stereotype target is encountered may influence automatic reactions. For example, whites' reactions to a black target are more negative when the target is depicted on a dilapidated street corner than when depicted inside a church (Wittenbrink, Judd, and Park 2001).

The extensive literature on racial stereotyping suggests that people unconsciously encode the race of every person they encounter, which influences subsequent information processing and activates automatic reactions to the target person. But does race encoding make sense evolutionarily? Recall that "racial" variation appeared quite recently in the evolutionary history of our species. It seems implausible that the specific encoding of race could have resulted from an adaptive cognitive mechanism (Cosmides, Tooby, and Kurzban 2003). Automatic race encoding may be the by product of a cognitive architecture that evolved for another reason. One possible explanation of the robust cognitive race encoding phenomenon is that race "serves as a rough-and-ready coalition cue" (Cosmides, Tooby, and Kurzban 2003: 177). This makes sense given that prepared fear learning of potentially threatening outgroup members based on small phenotypical distinctions would have conveyed an adaptive advantage to early hominins. That mechanism evolved long before the complex cognitive machinery responsible for race encoding, which would have elaborated preexisting emotional apparatuses of ingroup/outgroup response. In short, humans rely on highly interrelated emotional and cognitive mechanisms to automatically encode and respond to phenotypical differences that signify who can be approached safely, and who cannot.

Clearly these processes may bestow significant adaptive advantages, but they also may impose costs. Automatic responses may have operated relatively free of error in the small, homogeneous foraging bands where these adaptations evolved. Ingroup members and members of closely allied groups would have been readily recognizable to one another, while unallied outgroup members would have differed physically and culturally to varying degrees. In that social milieu, the ability to visually detect subtle distinctions among individuals would have facilitated rapid, accurate identification of and adaptive responses to potentially threatening conspecifics. Given that emotional and cognitive mechanisms simplify the social world, inaccurate threat assessments and responses would occur far more frequently in complex societies characterized by exponentially larger populations and far greater physical and cultural diversity, and today humans may incur significant social costs as a result of misperceiving conspecific threats. Yet, mental mechanisms for quickly identifying and responding to potential outgroup threat may still convey significant benefits.

Aggressive Responses to Perceived Threats

The range of possible responses in humans to a conspecific threat is analogous to that seen among other mammals confronting a predator (Blanchard and Blanchard 1988). The initial tendency is to flee. If that is not a viable option, the prey animal may freeze. If the threatening animal continues to approach, defensive aggression may be triggered. Selection of the most appropriate line of action involves a risk assessment based on the strength of the emotion, the nature of the situation, and the animal's internal states (such as previous learning and hormone levels). Whether in response to a predator or a conspecific threat, "structures in the amygdala, hypothalamus, and midbrain [are linked] to the elicitation, modulation, and organization of defensive behavior, including defensive threat and attack" (Blanchard and Blanchard 1988: 51). Although low population density may have frequently made other defensive options more feasible among our hominin ancestors (Brewer 2007), sometimes contact with outgroup members may have carried risks that warranted the potential costs associated with the expression of defensive aggression (Buss and Shackelford 1997). Fear conditioning would have been the primary mental process motivating the response in early hominins, and it remains an underlying basis for aggression in *Homo sapiens* (Öhman and Mineka 2001). Defensive aggression among humans involves additional psychological complexity because of our highly evolved cognitive abilities.

Acts of aggression involve a temporal sequence that determines the relative contribution of emotional and cognitive processes to the behavior. Initially aggressive responses are largely under the control of unconscious mental systems, whereas later actions increasingly come under the control of conscious cognitive processes (Geen 1998). The appearance of a threatening target automatically activates unconscious emotional and cognitive mechanisms that trigger a rudimentary affective response, which, in turn, elicits expressive-motor reactions, memories, and cognitions (Berkowitz 1993). An immediate aggressive response is driven primarily by emotion. Should that response be held in check, the early impulsive stage of emotional aggression is followed by a period during which the aggressive tendency comes under greater cognitive control. However, conscious memories also contain emotional content, and cognitive appraisals (attempts to interpret and make sense of one's emotions) occur only after emotional arousal has already taken place. Thinking about the instigating event that generated one's emotional state may either amplify angry feelings and aggressive tendencies or reduce them. Past fear and anger associated with similar encounters may elicit those emotions again.

Although the opportunity for conscious deliberation does not preclude an aggressive response, the passage of time may amend the motivation for and severity of aggression. As an aggressive response unfolds and begins to entail conscious deliberation, instrumental ends increasingly become involved (Berkowitz 1993). Socially learned provocations and conscious cognitive processes are dominant in purely instrumental (or functional) forms of aggression, which provide a means of avoiding painful experiences or acquiring desirable outcomes (Bandura 1986). Humans interpret stimuli and organize that information into predictive expectations and beliefs. The forms, frequency, situations, and targets of aggression may be learned vicariously by observing others and may then be honed by the modeling and reinforcement of the behavior. Affective learning may also occur vicariously, and people may learn to fear others in the absence of firsthand experience with them. Events that instigate aggressive responses (e.g., verbal and physical challenges), appropriate targets of aggression (e.g., negatively stereotyped racial and ethnic minority group members), and means and justifications for aggression thus acquire meaning socially.

Just as conditioning may unconsciously elicit fear in an environment where danger has been encountered previously, the knowledge that dangers may lurk there sustains conscious awareness of potential threats yet to be experienced, even when their occurrence is empirically improbable, thus eliciting both fear and defensive behavior. When painful outcomes occur irregularly and unpredictably, beliefs about potential dangers and the effectiveness of defensive strategies cannot be altered easily (Bandura 1986). The nonoccurrence of a painful outcome following a defensive act provides evidence that danger was averted and confirms the utility of the behavioral response, which makes it difficult to eliminate an established defensive behavior irrespective of its actual utility or potential cost.

A Social, Emotional, and Cognitive Model of Extralegal Police Aggression

In certain respects, the policing of some minority communities in the United States approximates social conditions of intergroup contact that occurred among early hominins and is, therefore, instructive in regard to how evolved behavioral propensities may persist even when they convey no clear advantage in the contemporary world. The police are charged with "invading" highly segregated and profoundly disadvantaged minority neighborhoods to protect the lives and material resources of unrelated citizens. Yet, they routinely encounter objective and symbolic threats in interactions with some of the citizens whom they must protect, which can trigger defensive behavior, including excessive physical force. Evolved processes of emotion and cognition, activated in the context of disadvantaged minority neighborhoods, may elicit these gratuitous reactions.

Social and Psychological Preconditions to Police Aggression

Much of the conflict between police and minorities in the United States involves African American and Hispanic (particularly Mexican-origin) citizens, who constitute the largest and most threatening outgroups in American society (Holmes 2000; Smith and Holmes 2003; Weitzer and Tuch 2006). Whereas white urban neighborhoods have very low levels of economic and social disadvantage, most African American neighborhoods have very high levels (Peterson and Krivo 2010). The degree of Hispanic neighborhood disadvantage does not match that experienced by blacks, but Hispanics also tend to reside in relatively disadvantaged neighborhoods compared with whites. These disadvantaged urban neighborhoods present a host of challenging circumstances—dilapidated buildings, social isolation, poverty, crime, drugs, weapon availability, violence, and social disorder/incivilities—that may pose objective threats to the police (e.g., Anderson 1999; Massey and Denton 1993; Peterson and Krivo 2010; Phillips 2002; Skogan 1990). Much urban police work takes place in such locales (Bass 2001). Subcultural conflicts of interest between police and minority citizens play out in these neighborhoods and create normative rifts that often place the two groups at odds with one another. Citizens want the police to solve chronic problems of crime and social disorder, while the police seek to dispense quickly with the menial calls that are the staple of their day-to-day work (Van Maanen 1978). Furthermore, the police demand respect for their authority and status, expecting citizens to obey their commands. Yet some minority citizens hold police in contempt, seeing them as representatives of an oppressive white power structure (Anderson 1999; National Association for the Advancement of Colored People and the Criminal Justice Institute at Harvard Law School [NAACP] 1995) and are likely to evade or resist them (Weitzer and Brunson 2009).

The shared perceptions of distrust and threat that exist among police and minorities in disadvantaged neighborhoods may generate group dynamics that reinforce ingroup solidarity and intergroup conflict. These processes may be explained in part by various group-conflict theories (e.g., Campbell 1965). Normative conflicts between police and citizens may elicit various less severe forms of extralegal aggression by the police (Holmes and Smith 2008, 2012), but the inevitable violations of competing norms during police-citizen encounters would be unlikely to instigate unwarranted aggression of a serious nature by either party, as the potential cost of its use would outweigh any possible benefit (see, e.g., Brunson and Miller 2006). While the approach of group-conflict theory offers important insights into distal background tensions that precipitate acts of extralegal police aggression, alone it cannot provide an adequate explanation.

The police and citizens comprise distinctive and highly visible groups (or coalitions), and the highly interrelated emotional and cognitive mechanisms that allow rapid identification of and response to ingroup and outgroup members are more likely to trigger acts of excessive physical force (Holmes and Smith 2008, 2012). Entering areas of concentrated minority disadvantage may routinely activate emotional responses, especially fear, among the police. Their day-to-day work in such areas exposes them to the most difficult social conditions of urban life (e.g., Bayley and Mendelsohn 1968; Crank 1998). For example, they are acutely aware of the high degree of gun violence prevalent in many inner-city neighborhoods. Cities with a high degree of black segregation have a higher incidence of homicides of police compared with less segregated cities (Kent 2010). Police officers may become unconsciously and consciously conditioned to associate such areas, as well as certain types of people, with criminality and danger (e.g., Bayley and Mendelsohn 1968; Meehan and Ponder 2002). Unconscious mechanisms for acquiring, storing, and retrieving emotional memories may generate fear among officers who patrol minority neighborhoods (Holmes and Smith 2008). Conscious apprehension may also arise from emotion-laden memories, a response police officers may learn personally from encounters with threatening citizens, as well as vicariously from other officers' war stories. Thus, anonymous black males in disadvantaged neighborhoods routinely arouse extreme caution, as they are normally perceived as dangerous until proven otherwise (Anderson 1990). Heightened fear of citizens prime the police officer for defensive aggression in the face of perceived threats, whether real or imagined.

Stereotyping of minority citizens may exacerbate emotional responses. The cognitive preeminence of racial/ethnic stereotypes and the conditions that activate their use are particularly evident in encounters involving the police and minorities in impoverished locales. Complex demands and time constraints typify street-level policing in those environments, circumstances that inescapably stress officers' cognitive resources and, therefore, may habitually elicit stereotypic responses in interactions with citizens (Holmes and Smith 2008). There is no strategic advantage in wasting precious time and cognitive resources on the humdrum problems that provide the mainstay of their day-to-day work. Racial/ethnic identity allows swift dispositional inferences useful for predicting likely outcomes of interactions in neighborhoods where omnipresent dangers and challenging social conditions exist. The environment of street-level policing yields fertile ground for stereotypic judgments, ones that may trigger gratuitous acts of aggression. For example, an experimental study of shooting bias using a national sample of police officers found that the participants made video-game shoot/don't shoot decisions more rapidly for stereotype-congruent targets (unarmed whites and armed blacks) and more slowly for stereotype-incongruent targets (armed whites and unarmed blacks) (Correll et al. 2007). This tendency was most pronounced among officers who worked in areas with large populations, high rates of violent crime, and greater concentrations of minorities. Police officers were not more likely to mistakenly "shoot" unarmed blacks, but the video-game format did not entail the fatigue, stress, and real dangers of street-level work. Moreover, the artificial video-game protocol would not have elicited fear, an emotional response that would precede and reinforce stereotypical information processing in the situations officers actually encounter on the street.

Whereas the activation of a stereotype may occur unconsciously and automatically elicit a behavioral response without forethought, suppression of the stereotype and a more controlled response may occur when circumstances permit subsequent deliberation (Devine 1989). However, American society is rife with stereotypes and ideologies that conflate race and criminality, particularly the inherent propensity for violence among African Americans and those of Mexican origin (e.g., Bender 2003; Loury 2003). Police stereotypes of minority citizens parallel those of the larger society and may be continually reinforced by selective personal experience and departmental folklore (e.g., Bolton and Feagin 2004; NAACP 1995; Smith and Alpert 2007). Conditions of disadvantaged minority neighborhoods may reinforce stereotypes that link blacks to violence (e.g., Correll et al. 2007), and everyone encountered in such places may be perceived as a potential threat (Smith 1986). For their part, minority citizens residing in these neighborhoods often stereotype the police as dangerous racists and thugs (e.g., Anderson 1990; Brunson 2007). Continually reinforced by selective personal experience, vicarious accounts, and folklore, stereotypes provide constant reminders of the threats posed by outgroup members, thus amplifying intergroup tensions and the propensity for aggressive behavior by police.

Perceived Threat and Extralegal Police Aggression

Already emotionally and cognitively primed by the challenging conditions of minority communities, police officers may respond with unjustifiable aggression whenever a "dangerous" citizen is encountered. Even those who are not actually dangerous may wear clothes or evince a demeanor that fits a stereotype and signifies threat (Anderson 1999; see also Skolnick 1975). The programming of an officer's emotional and cognitive schemas may immediately stimulate aggression without consideration of possible consequences, and periodically these spontaneous acts may be quite harsh. Officers' predispositions to respond quickly are amplified by formal training and informal socialization that strongly reinforce the necessity of responding rapidly and decisively to perceived danger (Crank 1998). Thinking about the instigating event that generated one's emotional state may amplify fearful and angry feelings and intensify aggressive tendencies.

Instrumental ends increasingly become involved as an aggressive response unfolds (Geen 1998). The social learning that takes place on the street, and perhaps more subtly during some types of formal training (e.g., Fyfe 1996), identifies minorities as threatening people deserving of extralegal aggression, a belief system deeply embedded in police subculture (e.g., Independent Commission on the Los Angeles Police Department 1991; NAACP 1995). When minority citizens are divested of their human qualities through mechanisms such as pejorative stereotyping and racist ideology, self-regulating mechanisms lose their grip (Bandura 1983; Berkowitz 1993), disinhibiting police officers and enhancing prospects of extralegal aggression occurring. Force that is unnecessary and unjustified from a legal standpoint may prove useful for informally handling the difficult challenges posed by day-to-day police work in disadvantaged minority neighborhoods. Police officers may rely on extralegal aggression to reestablish their authority or defend their social status (Hunt 1985; Skolnick and Fyfe 1993). It may also send a deterrent message to the larger minority community. Such conscious acts are generally less severe, serving to impose an extralegal punishment deemed appropriate in police subculture, but not one so harsh as to risk formal legal sanctions (Holmes and Smith 2008, 2012). Severe cases of extralegal police aggression (serious excessive physical force) may be more likely to occur early in the temporal sequence of an aggressive police response to a citizen, before conscious deliberation may temper an officer's response.

Various mediating/moderating factors increase the likelihood of excessive force being used in disadvantaged minority neighborhoods (Holmes and Smith 2012). These include demand characteristics of policing (e.g., the occupational necessity of confronting danger rather than fleeing it), situational characteristics of police-minority interactions (e.g., lack of credible bystanders to corroborate citizens' complaints), and personal beliefs of officers (e.g., adherence to traditional police culture that embraces selective and aggressive law enforcement). One factor thought to reduce the use of excessive force against minority citizens is the presence of minority police officers. Compared with white officers, minority officers may be more sensitive to and less threatened by disadvantaged minority neighborhoods. Yet, the available evidence indicates that the presence of minority officers, whether situationally or in aggregate, does not reduce the deployment of extralegal police aggression (including excessive force) against minority citizens (Brunson and Miller 2006; Cao and Huang 2000; Hickman and Piquero 2009; Pate and Fridell 1993; Smith and Holmes 2003, 2014). Apparently minority officers perceive the impoverished citizens of disadvantaged neighborhoods as threats to their personal well-being and authority much the same as white officers do (Smith and Holmes 2003, 2014).

In short, the part of the theory briefly outlined here maintains the proximate causes of police use of excessive physical force involve ordinary emotional and cognitive processes that, in interaction with the social characteristics of disadvantaged neighborhoods, trigger aggressive responses to minority citizens perceived as threats. This approach predicts that the highest incidence of excessive physical force will be observed in cities with relatively large and highly segregated black and Hispanic populations. To test those hypotheses, my colleague and I examined the incidence of sustained excessive force complaints in US cities with populations of 100,000 or more (Smith and Holmes 2014). The results were generally consistent with theoretical predictions. A particularly striking finding appears for black segregation. As shown in Figure 26.1, a curvilinear relationship between the segregation measure (a set of dummy variables indicating quintiles of segregation) and the incidence of sustained force complaints exists. The graph reveals that the predicted value of sustained complaints (after setting the other predictor variables at their means) increases in cities in the third and fourth quintiles compared with the lower quintiles, but more importantly it demonstrates a dramatic difference between the most segregated cities in comparison with all other quintiles. The predicted value of sustained complaints in the fifth quintile is about thirteen times larger than in the first quintile, and it is nearly four times larger than in the fourth quintile. These highly segregated cities contain severely disadvantaged neighborhoods (see Massey and Denton 1993) that would be expected to trigger archaic mental processes among police officers patrolling them, processes that would have been highly adaptive in our ancestral environs.

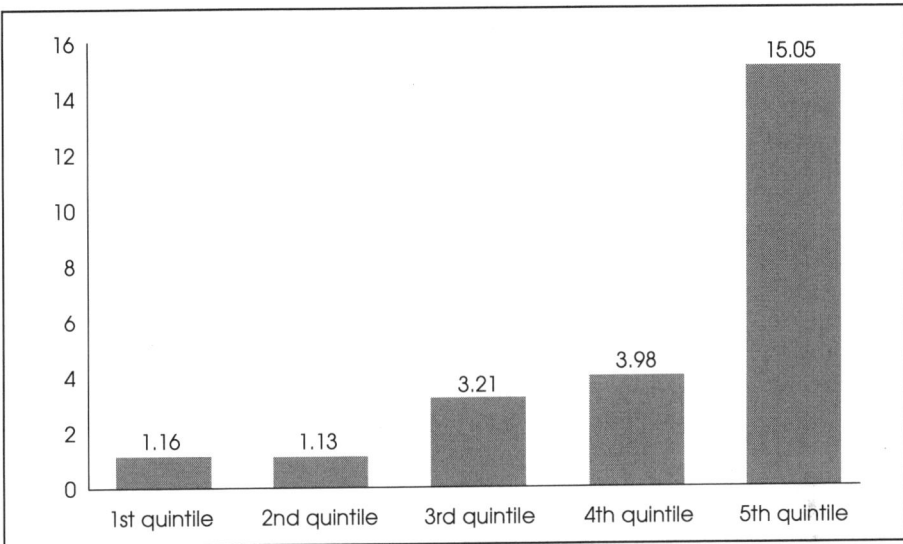

Figure 26.1 Predicted number of sustained citizen complaints by black dissimilarity quintile
Source: Adapted from Smith and Holmes (2014: 95).

Conclusion

This chapter extends the theory of extralegal police aggression partially sketched out above to systematically develop the distal evolutionary underpinnings of the behavior. This perspective maintains that actual conflicts of interest, the central idea of much theory and research on extralegal police aggression, are neither necessary nor sufficient to cause excessive physical force targeting minorities (Holmes and Smith 2008, 2012). Rather, it is the interaction of a social structure deeply divided along race and class lines and proximate social-psychological mechanisms of emotion and cognition activated by perceived threat that is largely responsible for the behavior.

Throughout the evolutionary history of our species, the development of emotional and cognitive mechanisms for identifying and responding to ingroup and outgroup members contributed to the existence of relatively stable foraging societies. Unfettered by the constraints of modern legal codes, individuals behaved in ways that helped ensure their survival, including defensive aggression against outgroup members perceived as threats. While the emotional and cognitive processes involved in such defensive responses evolved in response to the adaptive problems of life in small, local bands, those archaic mechanisms remain deeply embedded in the neuroanatomy of modern humans. The brain fully evolved while our ancestors still lived in simple foraging societies, long before the advent of even the smallest of cities (Massey 2005). Although still conveying numerous advantages in day-to-day social interactions, these mechanisms are less functional in the context of complex societies comprising large populations of diverse origins. Unfortunately, these processes may instigate intergroup conflict that no longer serves an adaptive end. The ongoing tensions between police and minority groups in the United States poignantly illustrate the issue, but these dynamics pertain more generically to many forms of intergroup aggression in contemporary societies (e.g., gang violence).

The insights provided by an evolutionary analysis extend to policy considerations. Given that the police are charged with protecting all citizens equally, the pattern of excessive force described here presents a social problem of considerable consequence. While other dimensions of police-minority tensions exist, the use of excessive force is at the heart of minority citizens' concern about policing in their communities (e.g., NAACP 1995). Various organizational reforms for ameliorating police-minority tensions have been widely touted by police administrators and scholars (Holmes and Smith 2008). In this organizational perspective, the formal and informal characteristics of police departments are thought to determine the street-level behavior of police officers, which may foster police-minority tensions and promote the use of excessive force. Policy recommendations aim to alter the structure or culture of police departments by employing greater bureaucratic control over officers, developing strategies to make officers more professional, and creating greater accountability of officers to the community they serve. Although these organizational policies may produce other laudable outcomes, there is little evidence to suggest that their implementation will reduce the incidence of excessive force (Holmes and Smith 2008; Smith and Holmes 2003, 2014).

The currently fashionable organizational proposals to alleviate the existing pattern of police-minority tensions rely on a popular social psychology that oversimplifies the deeply rooted mental processes underlying intergroup conflict. An implicit assumption of these recommendations, as well as much of social science, is that human behavior is highly malleable and can be modified for the better with relative ease. Research on biological bases of threat response and the social psychology of intergroup relations provides a robust body of evidence that humans come "programmed" to automatically detect and respond defensively to outgroup members perceived as threatening, even when they pose no actual danger. Still, the available evidence suggests that even simple prepared fear responses may be influenced by environmental factors such as close interracial contact (e.g., Olsson et al. 2005). Moreover, automatic activation of racial stereotypes may be conditioned by social context (Wittenbrink, Judd, and Park 2001), and activated stereotypes may be overridden by conscious beliefs (e.g., Devine 1989).

Unfortunately, generating more positive responses to outgroup members requires conditions not commonly seen in police-minority interactions in disadvantaged locales. The ingroup/outgroup dynamics of police-minority relations are characterized by an asymmetrical distribution of resources and power, and they are often played out in social contexts that reinforce fear and racial stereotyping. Selective social control by the police alienates many minority citizens, who may see the police as a mechanism of oppression rather than of protection, whereas the hostility of many minority citizens, along with the conditions of disadvantaged neighborhoods, may intensify the perception of immediate and ongoing threat among the police. In stark contrast to these circumstances, improvements in intergroup relations depend on equal-status contact between groups (e.g., Allport 1954; Fiske 2003), as well as contact that is extended, constructive, and cooperative (Fiske 2003). Clearly, the problem of police-minority tensions will not be resolved easily in the structural milieu of contemporary American society, which includes many disadvantaged minority neighborhoods that trigger the social-psychological processes that have produced defensive aggression throughout hominin existence.

Acknowledgments

The author thanks Christopher Holmes and Richard Machalek for helpful comments on a draft of this chapter.

REFERENCES

Allport, G. W. 1954. *The Nature of Prejudice*. Reading, MA: Addison-Wesley.
Anderson, E. 1990. *Streetwise: Race, Class, and Change in an Urban Community*. Chicago: University of Chicago Press.
———. 1999. *Code of the Street: Decency, Violence, and the Moral Life of the Inner City*. New York: W. W. Norton.
Bandura, A. 1983. "Psychological Mechanisms of Aggression." In *Aggression: Theoretical and Empirical Reviews*, Vol. 1, edited by R. G. Geen and E. I. Donnerstein, 1–40. New York: Academic Press.
———. 1986. *Social Foundations of Thought and Action: A Social Cognitive Theory*. Englewood Cliffs, NJ: Prentice-Hall.
Bass, S. 2001. "Policing Race, Policing Place: Social Control Imperatives and Police Discretionary Decisions." *Social Justice* 28: 156–176.
Bayley, D. H., and H. Mendelsohn. 1968. *Minorities and the Police: Confrontation in America*. New York: Free Press.
Bender, S. W. 2003. *Greasers and Gringos: Latinos, Law, and the American Imagination*. New York: New York University Press.
Berkowitz, L. 1993. *Aggression: Its Causes, Consequence, and Control*. Philadelphia: Temple University Press.
Bittner, E. 1970. *The Functions of Police in Modern Society*. Washington, DC: US Government Printing Office.
Blanchard, D. C., and R. J. Blanchard. 1988. "Ethoexperimental Approaches to the Biology of Emotion." *Annual Review of Psychology* 39: 43–68.
Bodenhausen, G. V. 1988. "Stereotyping Biases in Social Decision Making and Memory: Testing Process Models of Stereotype Use." *Journal of Personality and Social Psychology* 55: 726–737.
Bolton, K. Jr., and J. R. Feagin. 2004. *Black in Blue: African-American Police Officers and Racism*. New York: Routledge.
Brewer, M. B. 2007. "The Importance of Being We: Human Nature and Intergroup Relations." *American Psychologist* 62: 728–738.
Brewer, M. B., and L. R. Caporael. 2006. "An Evolutionary Perspective on Social Identity." In *Evolution and Social Psychology*, edited by M. Schaller, J. Simpson, and D. Kenrick, 143–161. New York: Psychology Press.
Brunson, R. K. 2007. "'Police Don't Like Black People': African-American Young Men's Accumulated Police Experience." *Criminology and Public Policy* 6: 71–102.
Brunson, R. K., and J. Miller. 2006. "Young Black Men and Urban Policing in the United States." *British Journal of Criminology* 46: 613–640.
Buss, D. M., and T. K. Shackelford. 1997. "Human Aggression in Evolutionary Psychological Perspective." *Clinical Psychology Review* 17: 605–619.
Campbell, D. T. 1965. "Ethnocentric and Other Altruistic Motives." In *Nebraska Symposium on Motivation*, edited by D. Levine, 283–311. Lincoln: University of Nebraska Press.
Cao, L., and B. Huang. 2000. "Determinants of Citizen Complaints against Police Abuse of Power." *Journal of Criminal Justice* 28: 203–213.
Chagnon, N. A. 1988. "Life Histories, Blood Revenge, and Warfare in a Tribal Population." *Science* 239: 985–992.
Chambliss, W. J. 2001. *Power, Politics and Crime*. Boulder, CO: Westview Press.
Correll, J., B. Park, C. M. Judd, and B. Wittenbrink. 2002. "The Police Officer's Dilemma: Using Ethnicity to Disambiguate Potentially Threatening Individuals." *Journal of Personality and Social Psychology* 83: 1314–1329.
Correll, J., B. Park, C. M. Judd, B. Wittenbrink, M. S. Sadler, and T. Keesee. 2007. "Across the Thin Blue Line: Police Officers and Racial Bias in the Decision to Shoot." *Journal of Personality and Social Psychology* 92: 1006–1023.
Cosmides, L., J. Tooby, and R. Kurzban. 2003. "Perceptions of Race." *TRENDS in Cognitive Sciences* 7: 173–179.
Cottrell, C. A., and S. L. Neuberg. 2005. "Different Emotional Reactions to Different Groups: A Sociofunctional Threat-Based Approach to 'Prejudice.'" *Journal of Personality and Social Psychology* 88: 770–789.
Crank, J. P. 1998. *Understanding Police Culture*. Cincinnati, OH: Anderson.
Damasio, A. 1994. *Descartes' Error: Emotion, Reason, and the Human Brain*. New York: Penguin.
Darwin, C. 1872. *The Expression of the Emotions in Man and Animals*. London: Watts.
Devine, P. G. 1989. "Stereotypes and Prejudice: Their Automatic and Controlled Components." *Journal of Personality and Social Psychology* 56: 5–18.
Duncan, B. L. 1976. "Differential Social Perception and Attribution of Intergroup Violence: Testing the Lower Limits of Stereotyping of Blacks." *Journal of Personality and Social Psychology* 34: 590–598.
Fiske, S. T. 1998. "Stereotyping, Prejudice, and Discrimination." In *The Handbook of Social Psychology*, 4th ed., Vol. 2, edited by D. T. Gilbert, S. T. Fiske, and G. Lindzey, 357–411. Boston: McGraw-Hill.
———. 2003. *Social Beings: A Core Motives Approach to Social Psychology*. New York: Wiley.
Fyfe, J. J. 1996. "Training to Reduce Police-Civilian Violence." In *Police Violence: Understanding and Controlling Police Abuse of Force*, edited by W. A. Geller and H. Toch, 165–179. New Haven, CT: Yale University Press.

Fyock, J., and C. Stangor. 1994. "The Role of Memory Biases in Stereotype Maintenance." *British Journal of Social Psychology* 33: 331–343.

Geen, R. G. 1998. "Aggression and Antisocial Behavior." In *The Handbook of Social Psychology*, 4th ed., Vol. 2, edited by D. T. Gilbert, S. T. Fiske, and G. Lindzey, 317–356. Boston: McGraw-Hill.

Grove, M., E. Pearce, and R.I.M. Dunbar. 2012. "Fission-Fusion and the Evolution of Hominin Social Systems." *Journal of Human Evolution* 62: 191–200.

Hamilton, D. L. 1981. "Illusory Correlation as a Basis for Stereotyping." In *Cognitive Processes in Stereotyping and Intergroup Behavior*, edited by D. L. Hamilton, 115–144. Hillsdale, NJ: Lawrence Erlbaum and Associates.

Hickman, M. J., and A. R. Piquero. 2009. "Organizational, Administrative, and Environmental Correlates of Complaints about Police Use of Force." *Crime & Delinquency* 55: 3–27.

Holmes, M. D. 2000. "Minority Threat and Police Brutality: Determinants of Civil Rights Criminal Complaints in U.S. Municipalities." *Criminology* 38: 343–367.

Holmes, M. D., and B. W. Smith. 2008. *Race and Police Brutality: Roots of an Urban Dilemma*. Albany: State University of New York Press.

———. 2012. "Intergroup Dynamics of Extra-Legal Police Aggression: An Integrated Theory of Race and Place." *Aggression and Violent Behavior* 17: 344–353.

Hunt, J. 1985. "Police Accounts of Normal Force." *Journal of Contemporary Ethnography* 13: 315–341.

Independent Commission on the Los Angeles Police Department. 1991. "Report of the Independent Commission on the Los Angeles Police Department."

Johnston, W. A., and K. J. Hawley. 1994. "Perceptual Inhibition of Expected Inputs: The Key that Opens Closed Minds." *Psychonomic Bulletin & Review* 1: 56–72.

Kenrick, D., J. Ackerman, and S. Ledlow. 2003. "Evolutionary Social Psychology: Adaptive Predispositions and Human Culture." In *Handbook of Social Psychology*, edited by J. Delamater, 103–122. New York: Kluwer Academic/Plenum.

Kent, S. L. 2010. "Killings of Police in U.S. Cities since 1980: An Examination of Environmental and Political Explanations." *Homicide Studies* 14: 3–23.

Klockars, C. B. 1996. "A Theory of Excessive Force and Its Control." In *Police Violence: Understanding and Controlling Police Abuse of Force*, edited by W. A. Geller and H. Toch, 1–22. New Haven, CT: Yale University Press.

Kurzban, R., and M. R. Leary. 2001. "Evolutionary Origins of Stigma: The Functions of Social Exclusion." *Psychological Bulletin* 127: 187–208.

LeDoux, J. 1996. *The Emotional Brain: The Mysterious Underpinnings of Emotional Life*. New York: Simon and Schuster.

Loury, G. 2003. *The Anatomy of Racial Equality*. Cambridge, MA: Harvard University Press.

Macrae, C. N., and G. V. Bodenhausen. 2000. "Social Cognition: Thinking Categorically about Others." *Annual Review of Psychology* 51: 93–120.

Macrae, C. N., A. B. Milne, and G. V. Bodenhausen. 1994. "Stereotypes as Energy-Saving Devices: A Peek inside the Cognitive Toolbox." *Journal of Personality and Social Psychology* 66: 37–47.

Macrae, C. N., C. Stangor, and A. B. Milne. 1994. "Activating Social Stereotypes: A Functional Analysis." *Journal of Experimental Social Psychology* 30: 370–389.

Manson, J. H., and R. W. Wrangham. 1991. "Intergroup Aggression in Chimpanzees and Humans." *Current Anthropology* 32: 369–390.

Markus, H., and R. B. Zajonc. 1985. "The Cognitive Perspective in Social Psychology." In *The Handbook of Social Psychology*, 3rd ed., Vol. 1, edited by G. Lindzey and E. Aronson, 137–230. New York: Random House.

Massey, D. S. 2002. "A Brief History of Human Society: The Origin and Role of Emotion in Social Life." *American Sociological Review* 67: 1–29.

———. 2005. *Strangers in a Strange Land: Humans in an Urbanizing World*. New York: W. W. Norton.

Massey, D. S., and N. A. Denton. 1993. *American Apartheid: Segregation and the Making of the Underclass*. Cambridge, MA: Harvard University Press.

McClelland, J. L., B. L. McNaughton, and R. C. O'Reilly. 1995. "Why There Are Complementary Learning Systems in the Hippocampus and Neocortex: Insights from the Success and the Failures of Connectionist Models of Learning and Memory." *Psychology Review* 102: 419–457.

Meehan, A. J., and M. C. Ponder. 2002. "Race and Place: The Ecology of Racial Profiling African American Motorists." *Justice Quarterly* 19: 399–430.

Moffett, M. W. 2013. "Human Identity and the Evolution of Human Societies." *Human Nature* 24: 219–267.

National Association for the Advancement of Colored People and the Criminal Justice Institute at Harvard Law School [NAACP]. 1995. *Beyond the Rodney King Story: An Investigation of Police Conduct in Minority Communities*. Boston: Northeastern University Press.

Öhman, A., and S. Mineka. 2001. "Fears, Phobias, and Preparedness: Toward an Evolved Module of Fear and Fear Learning." *Psychological Review* 108: 483–522.

Olsson, A., J. P. Ebert, M. R. Banaji, and E. A. Phelps. 2005. "The Role of Social Groups in the Persistence of Learned Fear." *Science* 309: 785–787.
Pate, A. N., and L. A. Fridell. 1993. *Police Use of Force: Official Reports, Citizen Complaints, and Legal Consequences.* Washington, DC: Police Foundation.
Peterson, R. D., and L. Krivo. 2010. *Divergent Social Worlds: Neighborhood Crime and the Racial-Spatial Divide.* New York: Russell Sage Foundation.
Phelps, E. A. 2006. "Emotion and Cognition: Insights from Studies of the Human Amygdala." *Annual Review of Psychology* 57: 27–53.
Phillips, J. A. 2002. "White, Black, and Latino Homicide Rates: Why the Difference?" *Social Problems* 49: 349–373.
Sagar, H. A., and J. W. Schofield. 1980. "Racial and Behavioral Cues in Black and White Children's Perceptions of Ambiguously Aggressive Acts." *Journal of Personality and Social Psychology* 39: 590–598.
Seligman, M.E.P. 1971. "On the Generality of the Laws of Learning." *Psychological Review* 77: 406–418.
Shallice, T. 1988. *From Neuropsychology to Mental Structure.* New York: Cambridge University Press.
Skogan, W. G. 1990. *Disorder and Decline: Crime and the Spiral of Decay in American Neighborhoods.* New York: Free Press.
Skolnick, J. H. 1975. *Justice without Trial: Law Enforcement in a Democratic Society.* 2nd ed. New York: Wiley.
Skolnick, J. H., and J. J. Fyfe. 1993. *Above the Law: Police and the Excessive Use of Force.* New York: Free Press.
Smith, B. W., and M. D. Holmes. 2003. "Community Accountability, Minority Threat, and Police Brutality: An Examination of Civil Rights Criminal Complaints." *Criminology* 41: 1035–1063.
———. 2014. "Police Use of Excessive Force in Minority Communities: A Test of the Minority Threat, Place, and Community Accountability Hypotheses." *Social Problems* 61: 83–104.
Smith, D. A. 1986. "The Neighborhood Context of Police Behavior." In *Crime and Justice: A Review of Research*, Vol. 8, edited by A. J. Reiss Jr. and M. Tonry, 313–341. Chicago: University of Chicago Press.
Smith, M. R., and G. P. Alpert. 2007. "Explaining Police Bias: A Theory of Social Conditioning and Illusory Correlation." *Criminal Justice and Behavior* 34: 1262–1283.
Taylor, S. E. 1981. "A Categorization Approach to Stereotyping." In *Cognitive Processes in Stereotyping and Intergroup Behavior*, edited by D. L. Hamilton, 83–114. Hillsdale, NJ: Lawrence Erlbaum and Associates.
Tooby, J., and L. Cosmides. 1990. "The Past Explains the Present: Emotional Adaptations and the Structure of Ancestral Environments." *Ethology and Sociobiology* 11: 375–424.
Turner, J. H. 2000. *On the Origins of Human Emotions: A Sociological Inquiry into the Evolution of Human Affect.* Stanford, CA: Stanford University Press.
Turner, J. H., and A. Maryanski. 2012. "The Biology and Neurology of Group Processes." *Advances in Group Processes* 29: 1–37.
Van Maanen, J. 1978. "Kinsmen in Repose: Occupational Perspectives of Patrolmen." In *Policing: A View from the Street*, edited by P. K. Manning and J. Van Maanen, 115–128. Pacific Palisades, CA: Goodyear.
Weber, Max. (1922) 1968. *Economy and Society.* 3 vols. Edited by G. Roth and C. Wittich. New York: Bedminster Press.
Weitzer, R., and R. K. Brunson. 2009. "Strategic Responses to the Police among Inner-City Youth." *Sociological Quarterly* 50: 235–256.
Weitzer, R., and S. A. Tuch. 2006. *Race and Policing in America: Conflict and Reform.* New York: Cambridge University Press.
Wittenbrink, B., C. M. Judd, and B. Park. 2001. "Spontaneous Prejudice in Context: Variability in Automatically Activated Attitudes." *Journal of Personality and Social Psychology* 81: 815–827.

Six
From Primate Legacies to Future Directions

Chapter Twenty-Seven
A Salience Theory of Learning and Behavior and Rights of Apes

Duane M. Rumbaugh

> A career-long research program with primates has led to an enhanced perspective of intelligence and its evolution in relation to elaboration of the brain. Contrary to the pronouncements of learning theorists, reinforcement of behavior does not give us an adequate framework within which to account for intelligence, species differences in their learning, or a valid framework for understanding how comprehensive learning can be. Empirical research and the syntheses of findings across decades have led us to a rational behaviorism, one that brings focus to the salience of concurrent stimuli and events and the strength of responses elicited by stimuli and events that occur rather contiguously in time. The construct of amalgams is introduced as the syntheses of concurrent stimuli and events in relation to the responses and the strengths thereof that are emitted. And it is through the brain's search for "best fits" between amalgams that new behaviors, new solutions to challenges, can be generated. Finally, the issue of animal rights is addressed with emphasis placed on the responsibilities of humans as they harvest resources from planet Earth.

The Limitations of Behaviorism: Explaining Emergents

In B. F. Skinner's famous experiments, he documented that rats easily learn to press a bar in their cage if it results in getting a food pellet. Getting the food pellet was said to *reinforce* the response of bar pressing. If bar pressing produced the delivery of a food pellet only when a light came on in the cage, the rat learned to press when it saw the light and not when it was off. Skinner said that the rat's behavior was therefore under the control of the light. For that reason, he called the light a *discriminative stimulus.* Skinner and other early behaviorists argued that "operant conditioning" of the rat's behavior can be understood solely in terms of the stimuli present and the behaviors that had been rewarded or punished in the past. Ivan Pavlov, Edward Thorndike, John B. Watson, B. F. Skinner, and many others in a long and distinguished history of behaviorism believed that the only true subject matter of psychology was observable behavior. They argued that any behavior could be understood if the animal's past exposure to paired stimuli and the ensuing consequences—that is, its *reinforcement history*—are known. This basic conditioning paradigm, however, has had great difficulty accounting for the more complex forms of behavior that seemed increasingly prevalent in larger-brained animals. The bigger the

---

The content of this chapter shares much in common with the author's book, *With Apes in Mind* (2013).

brain, the harder it was to find explanations for more complex behaviors such as language, music, and mathematics, which intuitively seem to involve higher mental processes such as thinking, predicting, and imagining.

What has been even more difficult to explain with the behaviorist approach is how organisms come up with novel behaviors in the first place. For behaviorists, even novel behaviors were to be accounted for in terms of reinforcement history, but how can this be so? After all, the novel behaviors would have had to occur before they could be reinforced even once. But, by definition, novel behaviors have never occurred before. How are respondent and operant theories to explain the behavior of Kohler's chimpanzees, who piled up boxes in their yard to reach a banana strung high overhead? What reinforcement history can explain this novel problem-solving behavior? And what about Kanzi (Savage-Rumbaugh et al. 1993), the bonobo who has emphatically demonstrated the capacity to acquire language without any direct reinforcement? Indeed, Kanzi learned to use lexigrams just by watching his mother being taught to use her keyboard of lexigrams. She had been reinforced for learning, whereas Kanzi had not. He had simply observed the sessions as he played around in the classroom, and yet he learned while his mother, who had been subject to an intense conditioning effort, did not.

We call such complex and novel behaviors "emergents" in recognition of the fact that they seem to emerge spontaneously and were never learned or taught. *Emergents* encompass insight and creativity but include many other phenomena such as numerical reasoning, counting, mathematics, compositions, and language. Importantly, emergents may also provide for a new capacity, such as an ape's comprehension of the words of human speech, which requires the ability to understand semantic definitions and to decode the syntax of novel sentences of request (Savage-Rumbaugh et al. 1993; Hillix and Rumbaugh 2004). The class of emergent behaviors encompasses all those behaviors we typically describe as creative or original, and these behaviors become increasingly frequent as our attention shifts from monkeys to apes to humans.

The behaviors we seek to describe and explain may be arrayed along a continuum, from basic instincts to the highest forms of creative and abstract thought, as shown in Figure 27.1. The theory that we have developed to encompass all these types of behaviors is called salience theory (Rumbaugh et al. 2007). The theory is eclectic. It includes many components that are parts of preceding theories. The theory does not reject any body of empirical evidence and intends no derision of the giants of our time (see Greenberg and Haraway 1998; Naour 2009; Konner 2010; Kazdin 2013; Domjan 2003; and Tuttle 2014). Earlier theories needed extension, to be interrelated, and in some cases to be reinterpreted. They can be seen as special contributions to a more general and encompassing theory, one

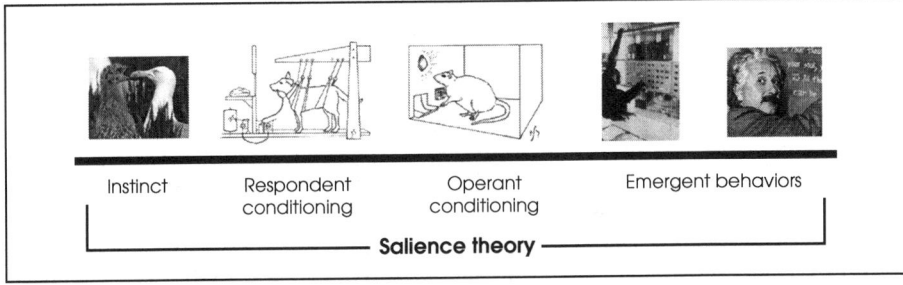

Figure 27.1 Salience theory embraces instinct, respondent and operant conditioning, and emergent behaviors

that also accounts for emergent behaviors—those novel, creative, and surprising behaviors so typical of monkeys and apes, but also found in many species of birds and mammals.

Salience Theory

Outline of the Theory

Salience theory is the result of our attempt to construct a comprehensive theory that embraces behavior, from highly heritable and stereotyped instincts through conditioning and on to the emergence of highly complex cognitive and creative behaviors that are adaptive, despite having no history of systematic training or reinforcement. History has regarded both respondent and operant conditioning as depending on stimulus events that occur at nearly the same time as the responses to be conditioned. Pavlov's famous dogs learned the salivation response when an essentially neutral stimulus, such as a bell, was presented slightly before the delivery of food to the dog's mouth. Skinner's rat learned the bar-press response when bar pressing was accompanied by a food pellet reward. But we hold that trying to explain behavior solely in terms of the events (receiving meat powder or pellets) acting on responses is to take too narrow a view of what is occurring. Rather than limiting emphasis to events acting on responses, salience theory treats organisms as foraging beings that are constantly surveying their perceptual worlds to determine what it offers for sustaining life and providing comfort. As foragers, they are generally assessing and pursuing adaptation to the most salient stimulus events around them.

Organisms learn by paying attention to the regularities and patterns that surround them, and they pay increasing attention to the more salient aspects of their environment, those that are the best predictors of future events. Although a great deal can be learned from a single event, a really skillful forager benefits from a history of various kinds of events. As a sailor I learned to pay critical attention to the luff of the sail on my sailboat *Lionessa*. To non-sailors a slight waffling of the sail where it attaches to the mast is of no consequence, but to sailors it informs them of a shift in the wind and the need to alter their course at least a bit. We learn to pay attention when nature is trying to tell us something.

The brain, especially of the higher primates, is tuned to detect, to remember, and to integrate predictive relationships (Rumbaugh and Washburn 2003). There is no need to reward or reinforce animals to learn everything that is important to them; their brains will, in measure, generate knowledge through observations and by integrating experiences of the past. For the higher primates and humans in particular, it is as natural and effortless as breathing. The most seasoned sailors are likely to survive an extreme and enduring storm at sea as they recall the lessons of their sailing history and apply them creatively. Relevant to our story here are the accounts of pilots who have brought their huge passenger planes to successful landings only by rapidly determining how they could control their multiengine plane by skillfully throttling the engines when no other control was available because hydraulic systems were dead.

Brains are inherently sensitive to things and events that tend to occur either together or sequentially. Brains have become highly proficient in these operations in response to the selective pressures of survival. Brains have evolved to be sensitive to the logical patterns of environments and the experiences associated with them. If an environment has no logical structure, it generates only noise. Brains learn nothing from noise. On the other hand, in environments where there is logic and/or relationships between things and events, brains take in a great deal of information and organize it to achieve "best fits" among both the specifics and principles to be extracted from life experiences. Emergent behaviors and capacities are posited to form and to facilitate adaptation through enhanced efficiencies of behavior and new patterns of behavior.

Emergents (Rumbaugh, Washburn, and Hillix 1996) reflect the natural operations of the brain as being composed of keen pattern-detection and synthesizing systems. The patterns detected include those from classical and instrumental conditioning. In addition, they include observations obtained through the course of everyday life. Whether the patterns to be detected are provided by conventional conditioning paradigms or through observations of daily events, it is their logical structure that provides information for the generation of emergents.

Attending to the predictive relationships in environments enables organisms to garner the resources needed to sustain life, while avoiding pain and risk. Observations of external events, including, notably, the actions of significant others in a social group, provide the basis for a great deal of learning, from birth through maturity. Salience theory encourages study of the variety of experiences that life offers, and searches for the antecedents and the consequences of learned and emergent behaviors, just as does reinforcement theory, but it also provides a model for incorporating instincts and conditioned behaviors into the generation of new *emergent* behaviors and skills.

SALIENCE

The concept of *salience* is central to our theory. The salience of a stimulus is the property of the stimulus that determines whether it captures an organism's attention. At the level of instinctive behavior the salience of an object can be predetermined by the genes. The red dot on a gull's beak is particularly salient to a newly hatched gull. Without any learning it will peck at this red dot, which triggers its mother to provide it food from her gut. Other environmental events are salient to organisms because of their intensity. Animals are naturally startled by lightning, thunder, sharp roars, and screams. These events command attention. Still other stimuli acquire their salience through respondent or operant conditioning. The bell, particularly when it has been paired with meat powder, is a salient stimulus for the dog. The light in the rat's cage becomes a salient stimulus for the rat after being paired with the delivery of the food pellet.

Novel stimuli in particular have the power to command attention. An unfamiliar noise when you are alone in the house at night will rivet your attention immediately. We assume that organisms attend most closely to the most salient events in their perceived worlds, and particularly to those that are the strongest predictors of future events the animal cares about.

AMALGAMS

Salience theory posits that stimuli that reliably occur together somehow combine to form a unit analogous to an *amalgam*, in that they share their saliences and response-eliciting properties interactively, according to their respective strengths. *Amalgams* are posited in our model as the basic units of learning. As the organism attends to objects and events that are reliably associated in time, it learns about them, including whether they are, or might become, significant resources, or risks, related to survival, pain, discomfort, and so on. The brain is viewed as generating an endless flow of amalgams that reflect experience as time flows on.

The brain also organizes the amalgams into natural *templates* that may be understood as the arrangement of multiple experiences into an abstract pattern or file. Brains have become uniquely honed to do so in the interest of a species' survival and fitness. To understand the relationship between amalgams and templates, consider a hypothetical situation. Suppose that you playfully toss a ball to a chimpanzee and, after a few times, it learns to catch it. And maybe you get the chimpanzee to throw it back to you after playing for a while. If you do this often enough, the ape may generalize this behavior into a pattern or routine we can call "playing a game of catch." We can say that a *playing-catch* template may have been created in memory from the combination of several underlying amalgams, *catching a softball, throwing a softball,* and *taking turns.* From acquiring this template it is a natural step to "playing catch" with, say, somebody's hat or other object—a novel behavior never learned before. From this, then, the chimpanzee might on its own throw an apple or a snowball or a tool *at* someone, not to play catch but to hit them because of anger. Here I would say that we have seen an emergent behavior.

Chimpanzees seemingly disdain and fear electric fencing that keeps them from going where they would otherwise freely go. One of our chimpanzees learned in one observation that, if one takes hold of the fiberglass wand that supports the wire, shock can be totally avoided. It learned this skill by watching a technician do that to repair fencing that had been knocked down in a storm. Thereafter, the chimpanzee took hold of the fiberglass wands to pull down any electric fencing that impeded her going wherever she wanted to go. An emergent means of dealing with electric fences had been formed by observation, one in which the fiberglass wands of the fencing became highly salient.

Amalgams and their associated templates are combined in memory to form a matrix of knowledge and experience that enables the performance of familiar tasks in more efficient ways. Salient events trigger associated amalgams and templates and allow the organism to solve novel problems and challenges or otherwise create and invent new solutions. And so, *memory systems store the knowledge thereby derived in a logical set of "files," which allows the natural operations of the brain to formulate creative behavioral patterns and solutions to novel challenges. Metaphorically, their storage might be thought of in terms of chords which, in their interaction with other memory chords, can be synergistic through the natural physics known otherwise to be characteristic of chords (e.g., fundamentals, resonance, harmonics, overtones; Rumbaugh 2002).*

The adaptive complexity of the brain is basic to the formation of amalgams and the processes of defining the best fit among them through their integration into templates. Constructive biases of the neural system determine what is significant enough to create new amalgams and relate them through templates across the vast reaches of time and experience.

Rethinking Reinforcement

We know that what is learned via specific reinforcement of specific responses does not necessarily limit what is learned (Rumbaugh and Washburn 2003). What the subject learns might well be far more complex than, and even qualitatively different from, a particular behavior that had been specifically reinforced. For instance, a rhesus monkey (Figure 27.2) was trained with reinforcement over the course of several months and thousands of training trials to control a joystick with its foot in a complex interactive computer task. Use of a hand was precluded, hence never trained. Only in a later test was the monkey given an opportunity to use either its hand or its foot to do the task. Now, since all reinforced training had been with its foot, use of its hand should have been at most a remote probability. Yet, when given the choice, the monkey promptly used its hand, scoring significantly better than it had ever done with its foot. Clearly, this finding is inconsistent with basic reinforcement theory.

What, then, is the role of reinforcement, which has historically been so central to the analysis of learned behavior? To answer this question and to understand the role of

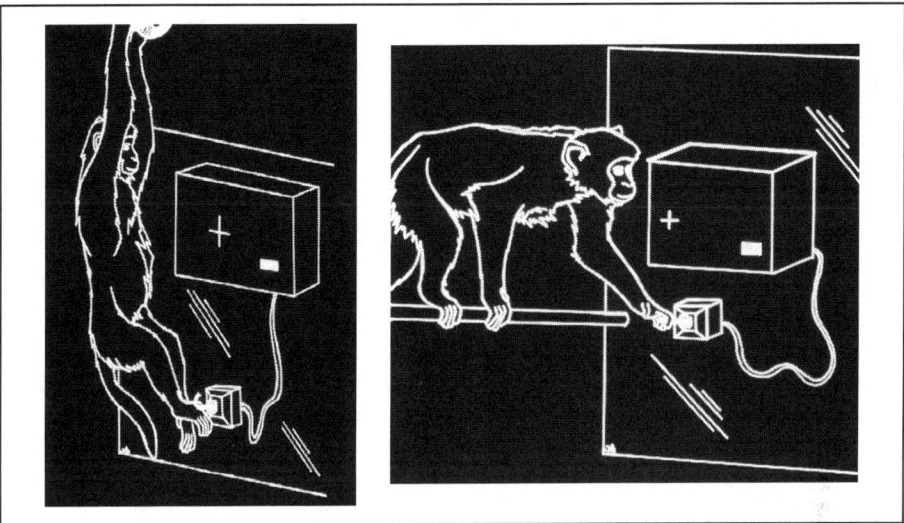

Figure 27.2 A rhesus trained to use his foot uses his hand instead when given a choice

reinforcement in salience theory, we need to go back a bit and see how the term has been applied in the past.

Theorists have used a variety of definitions of reinforcement and of the processes by which reinforcement strengthens a response or behavior. Thorndike (1898) originally suggested that habits are formed through the consequences of satisfiers and annoyers, or through the establishment of bonds between stimuli and responses. More recently, reinforcement has been defined empirically as anything that increases the probability of a response or a behavior. Other definitions of reinforcement have included reduction of biological needs, or differences in the probabilities of two or more responses, with the responses of higher rates reinforcing responses of lower rates. For instance, given a choice, a hungry rat will more likely eat than press a bar. Thus, eating can be a reinforcer for pressing a bar.

Advocates of controlling and modifying behavior testify to the effectiveness of reinforcement and its pragmatic effects. Although we do not deny the seemingly special power of reinforcement in the acquisition and control of behavior, we suggest that it has no special power apart from its salience, its strength as a stimulus, and its response-eliciting properties as it enters amalgam formation interacting with other contiguous stimuli. The same rationale holds both for unconditional stimuli in Pavlovian conditioning and for rewards in instrumental and operant conditioning contexts.

Recall that the effect of reinforcement is said to be on the response per se, not on the organism. But the exclusive emphasis on responses alone cannot yield the comprehensive framework that we seek. For instance, what is the origin of new and creative behaviors (i.e., emergents) that have no training history? These novel behaviors cannot reflect single histories of specific reinforcement because all responses, either elementary or highly complex and novel, must occur at least once *before* reinforcement of them can occur. Emergent behaviors can be so novel, so complex, that even selective shaping of behavior that could lead to them is almost beyond conception. On the other hand, emergents are expected in widely experienced organisms that have had rich and logically structured rearing histories.

520 Duane M. Rumbaugh

Although we have no objection to a limited definition of reinforcement as a term to define an operation within an experimental paradigm, such as the vending of a reward, we advise that the term be dropped because of its intimate bonding with the reinforcement theorists' essentially empty organism approach. From our perspective, *reward* is fully satisfactory as a substitute term for *reinforcer*.

Summary

Viewing the organism as a foraging being, not just a composite of responses, is central to the understanding of our salience theory of learning and behavior. Foraging beings' efforts—even those looking for a pay raise, or for an understanding of an internal combustion engine, or for a general education—suggest an integration of instinct, respondents, operants, and emergents. This integration of experiences both stimulates and contributes to creativity and cognition. Instincts, respondents, operants, and perceived predictive relationships among events are the bases for a rich variety of amalgams.

Accordingly, once processed by the brain to attain the best fit in terms of both natural and acquired templates, amalgams contribute substantively to the development of an organism's knowledge base about its niche and capabilities. That knowledge, in turn, underlies the generation of complex behaviors (i.e., emergents) that enhance efficiency in behavior (see Figure 27.3) and, long-term, the symbolic interactions that service language, mathematics, music, art, and thought.

Although great gaps of knowledge need to be filled by neuroscience and continuing behavioral research, we contend that salience theory advances the consilience of

Figure 27.3 A lowland gorilla strikes a significant emergent gait

psychology, biology, and neuroscience (Kazdin 2013; Konner 2010; Naour 2009; Rumbaugh and Washburn 2003).

Rational Behaviorism: How Apes Led to Our New Theory Based on Salience, Amalgams, and Emergence

Before the foundation of the Language Research Center (LRC), while I still lived in San Diego, California, I witnessed the development of some amazing behaviors in apes, behaviors that we now call *emergents*. Here I will recount my observations of a gibbon, a lesser ape species of which I was particularly fond. My initial curiosity stemmed from seeing them walk bipedally when they came to the ground from their lofty cages at the San Diego Zoo. I thought then that they must be extremely bright and would do well on our learning set tests, but that did not turn out to be the case. Our five gibbon subjects basically failed to acquire learning sets, falling far short of the standards set by the great apes.

But my story here of some fifty years ago is about another gibbon, Gabby (Gabrielle), who learned to use a rope and washcloth in truly innovative ways. She was a hybrid gibbon (*Hylobates lar X moloch*), stunning in her appearance. The San Diego Zoo knew of my special fascination for gibbons and had offered her to me for care and study because at the time (1960s) it did not wish to include hybrids of any species in its collections.

Gabby was about two years old when she came to my house and her home. At the time, I had no gibbon caging, so I designed a cage for her to live in on the cliffside of my home property in El Cajon. There she had a beautiful view of the El Cajon valley and eucalyptus trees that I had planted. The cage was constructed with bars on which she could brachiate in an arm-over-arm style the length of the cage, then swing around to go back to the other end for full stretch and use of her arm and body muscles.

She did very well and seemed happy. My daughter, Joan, took her out on the lawn most days and also gave her bicycle rides. Gabby would sit on the handlebars of the bike and face forward as Joan would go as fast as she could. Gabby's hair streamed back over her head. It was a great sight!

To continue the story, let me emphasize that Gabby had not had toys, nor had she seen anyone of any species use ropes or washcloths. She had no history whatsoever of being trained or conditioned. She was as naïve a gibbon as one might find anywhere. And when she moved to my property, we never encouraged her or rewarded her to perform any specific behaviors. Whatever she did, she learned from her own experiences and explorations. Her skills with the rope were several and, in the purest sense of the word, were *emergent* (see Figure 27.4). The same is true for her use of the washcloth, as described below.

Just how Gabby obtained the rope and washcloth I do not know. Somehow she got them on her own initiative from being in or around my home. With no training whatsoever Gabby flailed the rope around and around, and over the course of several days she learned to drape it over one of the bars. If she failed to do that, the rope was likely to drop through the bottom of her cage. Though it remained within easy reach, she learned to keep it available for ready use.

Gabby also developed innovative, emergent uses for her washcloth. She carried it often in her hand and used it to turn on her water valve for a drink. The valve sometimes squirted when first activated. She used the washcloth to block the valve so she would not get squirted in her face, something that she seemed not to like. Gradually she learned to place the water-soaked cloth at the end of one of her bars so that water dripping from it would pool onto a piece of angle iron that was a structural part of her caging. She frequently

Gabby creatively learned to place the rope over a bar in her cage and then to adjust the ends for equivalent length. Gradually she learned to hold on to both ends of the rope and spin around, and then to swing to and fro on it wildly. She seemed to love doing it.

Gabby also came to weave the rope in and out of the top and sides of the chain link that formed her cage, a fine emergent use of the rope. When she wove it into the top of her cage she frequently held both ends and swung on it.

Figure 27.4 Gabby using her rope in innovative, emergent ways

refilled her little pool of water, and now and then would stop and sip from it. Again, her behaviors are fine examples of emergents. Now, to be clear, Gabby also drank freely from her water valve and also sucked water from her washcloth once it was fully soaked. These she did for her own "taste" of how to drink water. No use of her cloth was necessary to get all the water she wanted.

Gabby's use of tools provides us with remarkable instances of emergents. Gibbons are not given to using tools in any form, yet in captivity she learned how to use a rope and washcloth innovatively—with reason. The rope enhanced her locomotion, and the washcloth provided her with various ways in which to drink water. She had no model for these behaviors and certainly no intentional reinforcement from us. These were Gabby's innovations—her inventions, her emergents.

I think she was so creative in part because of the limited materials with which she had to work. Had the construct of emergents been in my thinking then, I'm certain that a number of experiments would have been conducted. At the time, the behaviors interested us, but not as much as they do now.

Note that initially Gabby seemingly exhausted the attributes of both the rope and washcloth. For instance, early on she would grab just one end of the rope after having draped it over a bar. She generally had a surprised look on her face when leaping off one bar and grabbing for the rope only to find that it slipped off the bar and did not enhance

She did that for her own pleasure and was never trained or rewarded by anyone for doing it. That she seemingly enjoyed the enhanced swinging suggested to me that gibbons, in the wild, brachiating hand-over-hand, probably enjoy learning and practicing new skills. (Note that the washcloth is at the right end of the bar over which she has draped her rope.)

Figure 27.5 By holding both ends of her rope, Gabby is able to swing in a wide, graceful arc

Figure 27.6 A gibbon brachiates from one tree to another
Source: Photo courtesy of Ray Carpenter.

her swinging. It was as though such times were moments of discovery. What must I do to get things to work right? She learned to grasp both ends of the rope so that she could swing with it. Her exploratory interactions with the rope were surely critical for the development of her final emergent behaviors.

Rational Behaviorism

As a result of research over the course of the past sixty years, with the continued help of apes and monkeys such as Gabby and many a sterling colleague, I can now point to a number of findings and developments that help us understand the nature of the changes that occurred across eons of time as the primates evolved from insectivores to prosimians, monkeys, apes, and humans. In 1955, as a newly minted PhD in experimental psychology, I had little doubt that my graduate years at the University of Colorado had imbued my brain with all of the principles and procedures necessary for understanding the behaviors of all life forms, including the primates of the San Diego Zoo. But it was not to be. Most of those principles and procedures would prove to be flawed, if not totally incorrect. Some of the key principles thus imbued included the following:

1. *Learning was learning was learning.* It mattered not whether one studied behavior in rodents, birds, monkeys, apes, or the ubiquitous college sophomore; the principles derived from the study of any one organism generalized to all other life forms. Although diverse animal forms used what they had learned according to their own needs of adaptation, they all learned by the same principles.
2. *Reinforcement of behavior always determined what was learned.* If you knew an animal's past history of reinforcement, you knew all you needed to know to explain its behavior. And it was behavior, observable behavior, that mattered. Learning was nothing less and nothing more than observable changes in behavior. Internal mental processes, if they even existed, were discounted as the proper subject matter of psychology.
3. *Animals didn't think.* To even think that they might think was unscientific and anthropomorphic and not to be tolerated. To the contrary, monkeys and apes, and other mammals and birds as well, are now known to integrate separately acquired bits of information and skills into new innovative patterns of behavior that are necessary to solve new problems.

In summary, animals were thought not to be capable of planning and never to reason or think, never to hold a grudge, not to learn other than by doing, not to learn by observation, and not to be substantially influenced by how they were reared or by the environment within which they matured. They certainly were not thought capable of complex communications, and certainly not symbolic communications.

All of these points have now been replaced in my thinking by a *rational behaviorism* that holds that all experiences and observations, including those based in genetics (i.e., instincts) and those based in conditioning, exploration, observation, and general life experiences in any form that are salient (e.g., grab attention), can be used as constituents of amalgams.

Amalgams capture real life's constituent interactions of stimuli, responses, and events. Constituents that form amalgams are weighted (e.g., carry dominance) in accordance with their saliences (e.g., their strength and attention-captivating properties) and their response-eliciting properties. Amalgams are formed by the brain in real time and then interrelated to form a cumulative knowledge base from which the constituent units of new behaviors can be formed to avoid tiresome ways of doing repetitive tasks and to evoke creative processes that are known so well among humans.

Darwin was on the correct track when he argued for the biological continuity of all species, no matter how diverse (Greenberg and Haraway 1998). But continuity is also the guiding principle for psychology and behavior, including language behavior and, also, personality (Weiss, King, and Murray 2011). Whatever the attributes are of humans and their psychology, root traces can be discerned within the animal kingdom. The study of all forms of life in the animal kingdom teaches us that we humans are not creatures apart from animals, but are, rather, animal forms that are incredibly complex and incredibly creative agents of behavior (Konner 2010).

I should add here that, even at the time of my graduate studies during the mid-twentieth century, there was evidence to the contrary on all of the points just iterated. Notwithstanding, the evidence to the contrary did not take hold, did not get traction, if you will, because of the long-standing beliefs that learning processes were the same across species and that reinforcement was the primary determinant of what was learned. The ability to think was adamantly reserved for humans.

When my colleagues and I came forth with a salience theory of learning and behavior, we postulated that learning takes the form of amalgamations of events and behaviors across time. The amalgams generated in memory by each species reflect the environmental niches to which that species must adapt. What is important to adaptation is learned more readily than things that are not so important. An ape, for example, will likely pay more attention to the paw print, scent, or guttural growl of a leopard than it will to a bird flying overhead. The paw print, the scent, the growl, and the presence of the leopard itself form an amalgam. In this amalgam the leopard itself has the highest salience, the growl and scent somewhat less salience, and the paw print the least, but still powerful, salience.

Each constituent stimulus event and behavior that enters into the formation of an amalgam carries weight or dominates the attributes of that amalgam as a function of its salience and its response-eliciting properties. Thus, the amalgam representing "Danger! Leopard!" is triggered most strongly by the actual presence of the leopard, but to a lesser extent by the growl, scent, and paw print. It is contiguity and temporal patterning among the constituent units that provide the basis for learning, as encapsulated in amalgams.

Then what is a reinforcer? In the case of the "Danger! Leopard!" amalgam the presence of the leopard itself is the initial reinforcer; it is the strongest and the prime response-eliciting stimulus. That reinforcer *dominates* an amalgam more than other stimuli such as the paw print, scent, and growl because of its greater strength and response-eliciting properties.

Amalgams are interrelated and retained in memory, and across time they form a knowledge base to which neural processes refer whenever the environment changes and new problems/challenges are encountered. Thus, there are not "reinforcers" and "other-than-reinforcers" but, rather, streams of stimuli and events that the brain uses selectively to form amalgams into which the strength, the salience, and the response-eliciting properties of each constituent member are weighted in the formation of any/all amalgams.

Consistent with salience theory, organisms tend to interrelate whatever they learn with what they have learned in the past, in order to enhance their competence in new and novel ways. In this way, they are able to comprehend far more than what they have been rewarded to learn in any new task at hand.

LESSONS FROM THE ZOO STUDIES

The most important discovery of the San Diego Zoo studies was that smaller-bodied, smaller-brained primates are more likely to learn as though stimulus-response association is their only mode of acquiring competence. By contrast, larger-bodied, larger-brained primates frequently shift from stimulus-response associative learning to relational learning. Accordingly, they appear to learn overarching principles, as well as the specifics of test procedures.

This finding made possible the development of the Transfer Index (Rumbaugh and Pate 1984a, 1984b) and the definition of a *qualitative* shift in transfer-of-learning skills that results in a shift from predominantly negative transfer to positive transfer, in relationship to the absolute brain size. Thus, the Transfer Index demonstrates how quantitative elaboration of the primate brain leads to qualitative changes in transfer of training. In brief, *quantitative changes* in the elaboration of the primate brain can lead to *qualitative changes* in processes that make for remarkable differences in adaptation via emergent behaviors and capacities.

Other findings from my zoo years are as follows:

1. Infant great apes frequently surpass the learning abilities of adult apes, especially if the adults have not had intellectually challenging contexts as they mature.
2. The more arboreal (i.e., tree-dwelling) primates tend to fixate visually on stimuli of the immediate foreground and may not attend to relevant stimulus cues that are more distal (Rumbaugh, Gill, and Wright 1973). Perhaps this tendency was selected to protect the eyes as the small primates ran through branches and twigs.
3. Where the species has limited learning ability, as in the case of the squirrel monkey, learning each of a series of learning-set problems to a criterion greatly accelerates the formation of learning sets, the learning-how-to-learn phenomenon developed by Harry F. Harlow (1949; also see Rumbaugh 1971, 1997; Rumbaugh and McQueeney 1963; Ternes, Abordo, and Rumbaugh 1965).
4. Unless apes in captivity are reared in enriched environments with challenges, they seemingly become less and less clever as they approach full maturity.
5. Great apes and other primates can be very poor losers when they make errors. They can whine, cry, sulk, balk, and aggress against people and test apparatus. My brief work with killer whales at San Diego Sea World clearly revealed that they, too, have these tendencies when they make errors. (A killer whale, at least initially, earned a Transfer Index equivalent to that of the squirrel monkey.) Clearly, they have incentives for which they work. Failing to get them induces frustration.
6. The diminutive squirrel monkey is not a facile learner. One might conclude that it has little to offer, but consider the following. The squirrel monkey is fundamentally a quadruped. This holds true even for squirrel monkey mothers, who are notably passive in the delivery and care of their newborn (Rumbaugh 1965). The newborn even has to pull its way from the birth canal. Notwithstanding, the female can become an active caregiving mother who will cradle her infant bipedally if/when her infant is compromised by illness or by anything at birth that makes it unable to cling to the fur on her ventrum. I suggest that the roots of the human bipedal posture and gait were likely selected for by the demands of infant care, notably with the enlargement of the infant's head and attendant dependency when born (Rumbaugh 1970).

Yerkes Primate Center Research

In 1969, my research with primates was relocated to the Yerkes Regional Primate Research Center of Emory University, Atlanta. There I continued my comparative studies of learning. Working with the great apes in that facility only confirmed my faith in their innovative abilities and how they were able to combine different experiences to enhance task performance (Rumbaugh, Riesen, and Wright 1972). If taught to do a series of tasks with various materials, they are much more innovative in new situations. Even a one-year-old orangutan, still a baby, can be so innovative as to spontaneously use a rope to retrieve food that is otherwise beyond its reach.

The LANA Project Revisited

An article about Lana appeared in *Time* magazine in 1974 (see Figure 27.7). She was also the first ape to be editorialized in the *New York Times* (1975). Her accomplishments in language were accurately presented. Lana readily learned the functional use of more than one hundred lexigrams (Rumbaugh 1977). She also learned rules of grammar that were programmed into the computer and then, quite innovatively, generated new sentences using her lexigrams, or otherwise used her standard stock sentences to convey her needs and to resolve novel frustrations.

Lana learned to read and write with her lexigrams (see Figure 27.8). If she made an error in formulating one of her stock sentences, she would promptly erase it and thereby avoid doing more work on it to no avail. And if we gave her grammatically correct stems of sentences known to her, she would promptly complete them with about 90 percent accuracy. If the sentence beginnings that we gave her were invalid, she would promptly erase them. Her eraser was the PERIOD key, intended for ending sentences on which she worked; she extended efficient use of it to that of electronic erasure—a good example of an emergent behavior.

Lana spontaneously asked for things whose names she didn't know by using the words that she did know. For example, a cucumber was requested as the "banana which-is

Science: *Lessons for Lana*
Monday, Mar. 04, 1974

According to an old saw, if a chimpanzee is allowed to punch the keys of a typewriter at random for a long enough time, it will eventually peck out Hamlet. Lana, a playful three-year-old female chimpanzee at Emory University's Yerkes Regional Primate Research Center, will never accomplish that feat, but she is already one up on the hypothetical chimp. Under the tutelage of the center's scientists, Lana is rapidly learning how to read and write in a brand-new language called Yerkish...

Figure 27.7   Article in *Time* magazine about Lana's language accomplishments

green," an overly ripe banana as the "banana which-is black," an orange as the "apple/ball which-is orange," a purse as the "box which-is purple," and so on, in dozens of instances.

She also learned to ask for names of things that she did not know, such as a box, and used them subsequently to request that they be given to her. Lana still remembered the meanings of these lexigrams twenty years later even though they had not been used (Beran et al. 2000). Lana's naming of Munsel color chips (Essock, Gill, and Rumbaugh 1977) was very similar to the names that we gave them. Hence her color vision corresponds closely to our own.

Though reared apart from other chimpanzees in a research context, Lana in later years had two infants and was an excellent mother to them (Figure 27.9).

She was so quick that she could catch the M&M before it fell into the food cup. The next dispenser on the right dispensed whatever was in it. We could have a variety of foods in the tray; Lana would visually check to see what was next in line and request it appropriately—*Please machine give piece of banana* (or bread, or whatever). The machine didn't "know" what was next in place and just dispensed whatever was next. But Lana was specific. She exceeded the requirements of the situation again and again.

Figure 27.8 Lana at her keyboard

Figure 27.9 Lana and her second infant Mercury

Despite the broad dissemination of Lana's accomplishments and those of several other apes, contemporary arguments about the language abilities of apes appear to remain remarkably impervious to our findings. Even her ability to master the complexities of cross-modal perception (Rumbaugh 1977) in only twenty-seven trials failed to move scientists off their dime as they continued to believe that only humans have language. (Apes without language required hundreds or thousands of training trials to learn to perceive cross-modally. Without cross-modal competence, many hold that language competence is impossible. Apes were thought to be incompetent for cross-modal tasks, but Lana and others proved the case to the contrary.) I concluded that Lana learned far more about language from scientists than scientists could/would learn from her native vocalizations and communication skills. Had she been a human child, her data would have been accepted as being extremely revealing of language acquisition processes.

The principles learned from Lana worked very well in providing service to a number of language-challenged young adults who then lived at the Georgia Retardation Center (Sevcik, Romski, and Wilkinson 1991; Parkel, White, and Warner 1977). For the first time in their lives, they were able to talk with their loved ones and to obtain specific items that they wanted through use of a keyboard identical to the original one used with Lana. Social communication was far more effective in teaching them than was the basic shaping of and conditioning of motor responses.

Early rearing, early experiences, even from birth, are extremely important to a young ape's development of cognitive and social competence. Nursery-reared apes, especially if socially isolated, are rarely normal in any regard (see Figure 27.10). They are mentally dull, affectively brittle, and parentally awkward or incompetent, and lack even species-normal communication skills. Chimpanzees reared even for only the first two years on their course to maturity at fourteen years will be deficient cognitively and socially. Only their simple learning skills remain uncompromised. Their recovery of functions and competence is fractional at best. A safe generalization is that if something is good for a human child, it's very likely to be good for an infant ape.

Highlights of LRC Research

The LRC's Computerized Test System, initially developed for NASA, has proven to be revolutionary. It is used in dozens of laboratories here and abroad. It showed that chimpanzees can master, solely by observation, the skilled use of a joystick and thereby directional control of a cursor's movement on a monitor. Fortuitously, it proved to be an automation of the Wisconsin General Testing Apparatus (Washburn and Rumbaugh 1992). More importantly, it has allowed for a complete rewrite of the learning principles and abilities of the rhesus monkey and has enhanced comparative psychological inquiry with a wide variety of species—including humans (Washburn and Rumbaugh 1991).

In a computer task that we devised, Lana learned to count out numbers of blocks on a computer screen, but not with precision, up to four. Thus, rather than formally counting, she came to approximate numbers or quantities of items in accord with arabic numerals. In recent years, however, she has counted to seven (Beran and Rumbaugh 2001).

At the LRC we demonstrated that bonobos and a chimpanzee can comprehend some human speech—not just single words but the meanings of novel sentences of request as well. They acquire this capacity through the course of development if reared in a language-structured environment. None of the discrete-trial language-taught apes were capable of understanding human speech and its syntax when tested in controlled conditions.

Through comparative studies of learning and the acquisition of capacities that provided for the emergence of both comprehension (Savage-Rumbaugh et al. 1993) and production

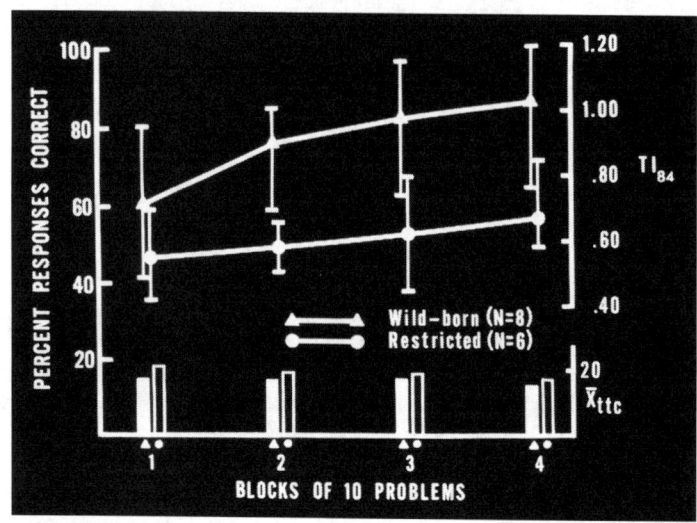

These chimpanzees were in a study initiated by Henry Nissen when the Yerkes Center was still in Orange Park, Florida. Wild-born group-raised chimpanzees were clearly superior to chimpanzees that were reared in very restricted environments during their first two years of infancy. The apes were fourteen years of age when tested with the transfer index (TI). The two groups did not differ in simple learning to a criterion (portrayed in lower pairs of vertical bars), but they were profoundly different in their transfer-of-learning skills. Early rearing clearly had a lasting effect on their cognitive competencies.

Figure 27.10 The effects of early rearing on cognitive competencies
Source: Davenport, Rogers, and Rumbaugh (1973).

of language, we have sustained the founding credo of the LRC: "So That Together We Might Learn of Language."

On the Issues of Rearing and Rights—Animal and Human

What are the consequences and implications of raising an ape as we might raise a human child? If an ape becomes impressively less apelike and more humanlike in its demeanor and manifest competence, should it be given status as a civilized creature with rights to some degree commensurate with our own? How does the capability of an ape to comprehend and use language and numerals challenge our own ideas of what it means to be human? And what is our responsibility to these beings and to their brethren in the wild, in zoos, or in medical research facilities?

These and other important questions can be addressed by focusing on the effects that early rearing can have on both apes and humans. With tongue in cheek, I had tentatively titled this chapter *On Becoming a Nonanimal, but Not Human, Either*. Though the great apes remain biologically apes through and through, particularly when they are young, their demeanor and competencies can become so qualitatively different from those typical for their species that questions come to mind about their rights. Biologically, we all remain loyal to our basic genetic animal endowments. But if apes become more civilized by our own behavioral standards, do they become, to a degree, human?

The ape intellect is so plastic during infancy that its functions can be constructively elaborated to afford new modes of expression that are otherwise foreign to free-living apes (for example, see Figure 27.11). There is also much evidence that their cognitive capacities can be impaired by impoverished rearing, rearing in extreme isolation, and lack of logical stimulation, even for a small fraction of their infant development—just as cognitive capacities can be impaired for humans raised in deprivation.

I believe that it's fair to assert that apes that have been raised, as ours have, in a language-saturated environment become nonanimals in the sense that they no longer typify apes found in the wild or in laboratories or zoos. They do, in fact, lose part of their animal nature, just as we humans lose part of our animal nature through the course of early rearing in civilized cultural settings. If we ask, in scientific terms, "What is human?" we can answer quite comfortably. But if we ask, "What is it *like* to be human? What is the ultimate human and ape potential?" we get into highly equivocal areas. For instance, I don't really know whether you, my readers, are human or not. I'm trusting that you are human, and I'm writing to you as though you are, but for all I know you may all be very clever computer-based systems that have been placed here to learn from this and other books and sources. Nevertheless, I willingly infer and trust that you are indeed human, that you also believe me to be human, and that we will make allowances for one another—even for our shortcomings. In effect, we assume many things. In a peculiar sense, we are anthropomorphizing as we assume that others of our kind perceive and experience things just as we do. In a similar manner, one finds when working with apes reared in the close company of humans that it becomes quite natural to extend to them the same courtesy we extend to our fellow humans—to assume that they understand us and are trying to communicate complex things with us.

We have demonstrated conclusively that many of the apes we worked with learned symbols and used them meaningfully in communication and problem solving, just as we use words. The evidence is overwhelming that there is no essential difference between

Kanzi learned by observing Nick Toth of the Stone Age Institute and from his own experience. He learned because he needed sharp-edged knives to cut rope, leather, and other materials to get access to items that he wanted. He rejected dull-edged stones and made new sharp chips for use as needed. Detailed study of Kanzi's stone tools revealed that they shared much in common with those of our early ancestors (Toth et al. 1993; Schick et al. 1999). Kanzi was honored by the Stone Age Institute for his sterling contributions to the understanding of the origins of stone tool fabrication. He has made and used three kinds of stone tools for different functions. Within limits, he knows what he needs and then makes it.

Figure 27.11 Kanzi has become a skilled flint knapper

what words are to them and what they are to us. This stands in direct contradiction to Cartesian thought, which holds that apes and other animals are naught but senseless beast machines that can neither think nor feel even the worst of apparent pain.

With their graphic symbols, their lexigrams, our apes can do many things better than they could without those symbols:

- They can accomplish cross-modal perception. Shown the picture of an object, they can retrieve it from several other items in a box, using touch alone.
- They can also retrieve the correct object by touch alone when shown only the lexigram representing the object.
- They can announce what they are going to retrieve from an array of objects that they've seen in another room.
- They can, and do, recount what happened yesterday to an otherwise unknowing listener.
- They can remember promises and insist that they be fulfilled.
- They can ask humans who are their friends to retrieve out-of-reach items for them.
- They can remember where they have seen others hide food in the woods outside their cages and then, at a time of their choosing, ask someone to get the item for them.
- They can identify hidden items by name, and at times even state that it is covered with leaves and sticks.
- They can then direct the person to the specific spot to retrieve the item through the orchestrated use of their lexigrams, vocalizations, pointing, and affective behaviors.
- They celebrate when the food is retrieved and given to them.
- They also celebrate when they anticipate that they are, at last, successfully solving a computer task.
- They can learn symbols for hundreds of items and events and locations.
- They can learn to comprehend human speech—not just single words, but the specifics of hundreds of novel requests, understanding embedded phrases with aplomb.
- They can understand human speech, even if it is severely degraded.
- They can and do announce what it is that they are about to do, where they are going, what assistance they want from others, and how they feel.
- They can even ask another to keep a secret.

Now, how can the committed skeptic, if there be one among my readers, account for these behaviors unless they are based on the use of language? These are remarkable accomplishments for young apes and even for young children. They are things that apes generally can't do. Neither apes in the wild nor those in zoos can do these things.

So, at the end of my career, with all fears of not being tenured or promoted in the university behind me, I feel responsible for making it clearer to the world what apes as animals are, on the one hand, and what they can become, on the other, depending on early rearing.

Let me be clear: One should not say that *the* chimpanzee, *the* gorilla, *the* orangutan, or even *the* human can or cannot do certain things. What each can do depends ever so heavily on their conditions of rearing and how their behavior is measured. And, it isn't so much that we teach them or that we reinforce certain responses or certain behaviors. Rather, it is what their brains amalgamate and integrate from the events of their lives.

I believe that much knowledge is generated by the natural and ongoing operations of the primate brain, selected for its sensitivities to predictive relationships between things/events of the environment and its proclivities to search for inherent logical relationships between those things/events. Thus, as we study apes we attain a better understanding of ourselves as primates.

We humans do not exist clearly and cleanly apart from all other forms of life. There is a fraternity of being, of adaptation, that is based on experience, learning, and behavior—one that must be accounted for by a single comprehensive psychology, and one that embraces both ape and human.

Early in the twentieth century, both Wolfgang Koehler and Robert M. Yerkes recognized that apes needed social interactions with others of their kind to be what they are. A lone chimpanzee could not, in fact, be a typical chimpanzee. Henry Nissen's mid-twentieth-century study of chimpanzees reared in impoverished conditions defined the problem very clearly. Asocial rearing, even during only the first two years of life, produced chimpanzees with lifelong handicaps in their social, communicative, and reproductive behaviors. They were also profoundly handicapped in their abilities to transfer learning between similar situations. Animals they were, but not complete chimpanzees. It is probably no overstatement to argue that, if all chimpanzees had such limited competence, their species would die out in one generation.

Even within the infant ape's first two years of life, a substantial degree of structuring of intelligence occurs. The infant ape observes a great deal that is done by his or her mother and other family members. Wild chimpanzees who are reared in natural social conditions grow up to exhibit competence in many ways. They learn how to be chimpanzees, something that their genetics predispose them to learn rapidly, given the chance. Their cognition becomes focused on the ways of chimpanzees in the wild.

We need to better understand our relationship with animals. Apes are what I would call a "transient group of primates." Interestingly, and in support of our thesis, even the late Geoffrey H. Bourne, who was a biomedical researcher and director of the Yerkes Laboratories in the 1960s and 1970s, concluded in his books that although apes aren't human, they aren't animals, either. They are something else. Today, that is our intellectual challenge.

This challenge may well be anathema to science and understandably so. Yet there is a growing sensitivity to the potential of apes for being humanlike, and an increasing recognition that they should no longer be used carte blanche in all kinds of unnecessary and invasive research that is insensitive to their needs, and perhaps rights, as sentient beings.

So, Who Are the Beasts?

Today, we increasingly recognize that animals have some basic rights that should be respected. But the issue is not animal rights so much as it is human rights and human responsibility for nature and planet Earth. We don't really have the right to despoil the oceans, the air, and the montage of ecological systems that have evolved over the course of millions of years. We don't really have the right to ruin all of nature. But we are doing that. We don't really have the right to extinguish wild populations of animals—but we're doing that, too. We certainly don't have any right to decimate the small and irreplaceable natural populations of apes in the world, all of which are rapidly approaching extinction. We don't have the right to kill them en masse and sell their carcasses on the meat tables of the world—but it is being done with increasing frequency.

What, After All, Are Human Rights?

Do human rights really include the right to exploit all resources of planet Earth so that humans can live more comfortably and feed overflowing populations for the short-term future? I don't believe for a moment that any definition of human rights, other than those that are completely selfish and blind to future consequences, could begin to validate such actions. Certainly there are no inalienable rights that validate our ill-advised exploitation of Earth's natural resources. If only we could stop reproducing so prolifically so that we could decrease the vast population increases of today and the future. What better cause than the rights of animals might constrain us from doing so?

Sadly, animals cannot claim and defend their rights. The future of many animal species hinges on how we define and constrain the exercise of our own rights, none of which are other than what we have defined them to be.

I close by proffering that *if... if* animals could define and assert their rights, they might be far more considerate, far more benevolent to all species, even to humans, than we are. Humans continue to selfishly pursue growth in populations, domineering economies, venting our personal frustrations through senseless violence, and continuing to develop ever more devastating methods for war and intimidation.

How shall we go about building a world based on respect for life, respect for the balance of nature, respect for diversity, and a genuine sense of *responsibility* to conserve the beauty and vibrancy inherent in nature? Unless we come to our senses and live by a sense of genuine responsibility for nature and planet Earth, we will consume or pollute it all beyond repair.

Though planet Earth is warming and undergoing radical changes, there is yet sufficient time for us to save a great deal. To do so, we need a philosophy of life and a new psychology, perhaps modeled on the one presented in this book, that will enable us to understand the processes that support the metamorphosis that humans and apes undergo as they mature and become *socialized*. The richness of life is not to be defined basically by profit and growth of the economy. The simple reinforcement of responses doesn't do it. A new approach is necessary if we are to master our destinies and live synergistically with nature on planet Earth and not measure success by short-term goal achievement. We need a psychology that generates a sense of respect and responsibility in all that we do. Time remains for us to do so.

And the Chimpanzee Who Has Guided This Trek?

And now as my trek with apes to "tell it as it is" nears the bottom of the page, with only a few remaining, we can ask, *Where has it taken us?* And, above all, *Who is my best chimpanzee confidant, my consult?* It's Lana. She was and is the grandmother of all of my professional life. She has taken me by the hand and led the way throughout this account.

Her successors, notably Panzee and Panbanisha, have been very, very gratifying. They have taught me a lot. But then so did Albert, the gorilla. He taught me first and foremost that if one does not have a truly trusting relationship with an ape, it will never reveal its "mind." Kanzi (Figure 27.12), a king maker, trusted some but not all. With his closest and most trusted allies, he showed it all.

And now there is Teco, about whom this book conveys nothing—but his mind is to come in the future. Who is Teco? He is Kanzi's son. He will be a head-turner, a teacher, a professor. He was born at the Iowa Primate Learning Sanctuary. Check him out on the web. But of them all, who is my queen? *Lana! Laurels for Lana!* Had she not opened the door to her mind so well, so thoughtfully, so smartly in the LANA Project, there would have been no trek laid out for us to take as we have in this book. Neither would there have been the LRC nor the Iowa Primate Learning Sanctuary.

But the trek is not over. In fact, it will never end. For we now know that the ape can become very much like us—in mind, in class, in learning, in its psychology. Though it will remain a partner apart from our social life, the ape always has us *in mind,* just as we remain mindful of it.

Perhaps it's best that the mystery that surrounds the question as to what the ape really is should stand forever. That we should live so long to have that mystery resolved. Thank you, Lana. We will never forget you. Long life and joy to you in your last days. Remember, Lana, the laurels are first and foremost for you.

Figure 27.12 After a hard day of play and fun, Kanzi walks bipedally as though on his way home

Acknowledgments

The author is grateful to the National Science Foundation for support of research with the San Diego Zoo and San Diego University. The National Institute of Child Health and Human Development (grants HD060563, HD38051, and HD 06016), the National Aeronautics and Space Administration (grant NAG2-438) and Georgia State University supported much of the research here summarized. Preparation of this chapter was supported by NICHD grant 060563. Ken Schweller's assistance also is gratefully acknowledged. The author extends special recognition to E. Sue Savage-Rumbaugh for her extraordinary scholarship with bonobos across several decades. Without her dedication, we would have little knowledge of this remarkable species' social behavior, its remarkable ability to learn and use symbols in communication, and its several points of contrast with other apes.

References

Beran, M. J., J. L. Pate, W. K. Richardson, and D. M. Rumbaugh. 2000. "A Chimpanzee's (*Pan troglodytes*) Long-Term Retention of Lexigrams." *Animal Learning and Behavior* 28: 201–207.
Beran, M. J., and D. M. Rumbaugh. 2001. "'Constructive' Enumeration by Chimpanzees (*Pan troglodytes*) on a Computerized Task." *Animal Cognition* 4: 81–89.
Davenport, R. K., C. M. Rogers, and D. M. Rumbaugh. 1973. "Long-Term Cognitive Deficits in Chimpanzees Associated with Early Impoverished Rearing." *Developmental Psychology* 9: 343–347.
Domjan, M. 2003. *The Principles of Learning and Behavior*. 5th ed. Belmont, CA: Wadsworth/Thomson Learning.
Essock, S. M., T. V. Gill, and D. M. Rumbaugh. 1977. "Language Relevant Object and Color-Naming Tasks." In *Language Learning by a Chimpanzee: The LANA Project*, edited by D. M. Rumbaugh, 193–206. New York: Academic Press.
Greenberg, G., and M. M. Haraway, eds. 1998. *Comparative Psychology: A Handbook*. New York: Garland Publishing.
Harlow, H. F. 1949. "The Formation of Learning Sets." *Psychological Review* 56: 51–65.
Hillix, W. A., and D. M. Rumbaugh. 2004. *Animal Bodies, Human Minds: Ape, Dolphin, and Parrot Language Skills*. New York: Springer Kluwer/Academic Press.
Kazdin, A. E. 2013. *Behavior Modification in Applied Settings*. Long Grove, IL: Waveland Press.

Konner, M. 2010. *The Evolution of Childhood: Relationships, Emotion, Mind.* Cambridge, MA: Belknap Press of Harvard University Press.

Naour, P. 2009. *E. O. Wilson and B. F. Skinner: A Dialogue between Sociobiology and Radical Behaviorism.* New York: Springer.

Parkel D. A., R. Z. White, and H. Warner. 1977. "Implications of the Yerkes Technology for Mentally Retarded Human Subjects." In *Language Learning by a Chimpanzee: The LANA Project*, edited by D. M. Rumbaugh, 274–283. New York: Academic Press.

Rumbaugh, D. M. 1965. "Maternal Care in Relation to Infant Behavior in the Squirrel Monkey." *Psychological Reports* 16: 171–176.

———. 1970. "Learning Skills of Anthropoids." In *Primate Behavior*, Vol. 1, edited by L. A. Rosenblum, 1–70. New York: Academic Press.

———. 1971. "Evidence of Qualitative Differences in Learning among Primates." *Journal of Comparative and Physiological Psychology* 76: 250–255.

———, ed. 1977. *Language Learning by a Chimpanzee: The LANA Project.* New York: Academic Press.

———. 1997. "The Psychology of Harry F. Harlow: A Bridge from Radical to Rational Behaviorism." *Philosophical Psychology* 10: 197–210.

———. 2002. "Emergents and Rational Behaviorism." *Eye on PsiChi* 6: 8–14.

———. 2013. *With Apes in Mind: Emergents, Communication & Competence.* Distributed by Amazon.com.

Rumbaugh, D. M., T. V. Gill, and S. C. Wright. 1973. "Readiness to Attend to Visual Foreground Cues." *Journal of Human Evolution* 2: 181–188.

Rumbaugh, D. M., J. E. King, M. J. Beran, D. A. Washburn, and K. L. Gould. 2007. "A Salience Theory of Learning and Behavior—With Perspectives on Neurobiology and Cognition." *International Journal of Primatology* 28: 973–996.

Rumbaugh, D. M., and J. A. McQueeney. 1963. "Learning-Set Formation and Discrimination Reversal: Learning Problems to Criterion in the Squirrel Monkey." *Journal of Comparative and Physiological Psychology* 7: 435–439.

Rumbaugh, D. M., and J. L. Pate. 1984a. "The Evolution of Primate Cognition: A Comparative Perspective." In *Animal Cognition*, edited by H. L. Roitblat, T. G. Bever, and H. S. Terrace, 569–587. Hillsdale, NJ: Lawrence Erlbaum.

———. 1984b. "Primate Learning by Levels." In *Behavioral Evolution and Integrative Levels*, edited by G. Greenberg and E. Tobach, 197–210. Hillsdale, NJ: Lawrence Erlbaum.

Rumbaugh, D. M., A. H. Riesen, and S. C. Wright. 1972. "Creative Responsiveness Objects: A Report of a Pilot Study with Young Apes." *Folia Primatologica* 17: 397–403.

Rumbaugh, D. M., and D. A. Washburn. 2003. *Intelligence of Apes and Other Rational Beings.* New Haven, CT: Yale University Press.

Rumbaugh, D. M., D. A. Washburn, and W. A. Hillix. 1996. "Respondents, Operants, and Emergents: Toward an Integrated Perspective on Behavior." In *Learning as a Self-Organizing Process*, edited by K. Pribram and J. King, 57–73. Hillsdale, NJ: Lawrence Erlbaum.

Savage-Rumbaugh, E. S., J. Murphy, R. A. Sevcik, S. Williams, K. Brakke, and D. M. Rumbaugh. 1993. "Language Comprehension in Ape and Child." *Monographs of the Society for Research in Child Development* (2 and 3).

Schick, K. D., N. Toth, G. Garufi, E. S. Savage-Rumbaugh, D. M. Rumbaugh, and R. A. Sevcik. 1999. "Continuing Investigations into the Stone Tool-Making and Tool-Using Capabilities of a Bonobo (*Pan paniscus*)." *Journal of Archaeological Science* 26: 821–832.

Sevcik, R. A., M. A. Romski, and K. M. Wilkinson. 1991. "Roles of Graphic Symbols in the Language Acquisition Process for Persons with Severe Cognitive Disabilities." *Augmentative and Alternative Communication* 7: 161–170.

Ternes, J. W., E. J. Abordo, and D. M. Rumbaugh. 1965. "Effect of Criterional Learning-Set Training Where Problem Objects Are Encased in Plexiglas Bins." *Perceptual and Motor Skills* 21: 544–546.

Thorndike, E. L. 1898. "Animal Intelligence: An Experimental Study of the Associative Processes in Animals." *Psychological Monographs: General and Applied* 2(4): 1–109.

Toth N., K. D. Schick, E. S. Savage-Rumbaugh, R. A. Sevcik, and D. M. Rumbaugh. 1993. "Pan the Tool-Maker: Investigations into the Stone Tool-Making and Tool-Using Capabilities of a Bonobo (*Pan paniscus*)." *Journal of Archaeological Science* 20: 81–91.

Tuttle, R. H. 2014. *Apes and Human Evolution.* Cambridge, MA: Harvard University Press.

Washburn, D. A., and D. M. Rumbaugh. 1991. "Ordinal Judgments of Numerical Symbols by Macaques (*Macaca mulatta*)." *Psychological Science* 2: 190–193.

———. 1992. "The Language Research Center's Computerized Test System (LRC-CTS) for Environmental Enrichment and Psychological Assessment." *Contemporary Topics* 31: 11–16.

Weiss, A., J. E. King, and L. Murray. 2011. *Personality and Temperament in Nonhuman Primates.* London: Springer Press.

Chapter Twenty-Eight

Language Use Among Apes

Audio-Visual Archival Documentaries for Ape Language and Cognition

Ken Schweller

> The online resources listed in this chapter document Duane Rumbaugh's career-long work with apes and provide a more detailed look into the experiments and findings underlying his salience theory of learning and behavior. I have chosen to comment specifically on those aspects of Rumbaugh's work that shed light on the evolution of language, as this has always been one of the most difficult unresolved problems for evolutionary biologists. How can it be that nearly all humans effortlessly acquire language, whereas few, if any, animals seem able to acquire even the rudiments? If language is simply learned behavior, why is it so seemingly difficult for our closest relatives, the chimpanzees and bonobos, to acquire it?

The Problem of Language

Darwin himself recognized the challenge that language presented to his theory of evolution, and he struggled to account for it in terms of adaptive imitation and natural selection: "I cannot doubt that language owes its origin to the imitation and modification of various natural sounds, the voices of other animals, and man's own instinctive cries, aided by signs and gestures" (1871: 87). The German linguist Max Muller was one of the first to criticize Darwin's accounts, asserting that language was the "one great barrier between the brute and man" and that "no process of natural selection will ever distil significant words out of the notes of birds and the cries of beasts" ([1861] 1966: 340). The debate that surrounded this topic and the apparent inability to resolve the issue by empirical means caused the Linguistics Society of Paris in 1886 to declare the question irresolvable and to refuse to accept any more treatises on the subject. The problem has persisted to the present day, and so we can ask: how are we to account in evolutionary terms for the seemly unique existence of human language?

Current theories dealing with the origins of language fall along the familiar nature/nurture continuum. On the nurture end of the spectrum lies the purely behaviorist approach that language is learned like any other behavior; on the nature end stands the linguistic theory that language requires a specific brain structure unique to humans and, hence, cannot be acquired by nonhumans. Rumbaugh has critiqued these theories as being insufficient or implausible and has offered instead an explanation of language development based on salience theory, reviewed in Chapter 27.

Chomsky's Arguments for the Uniqueness of Human Language

MIT linguist Noam Chomsky has argued that in acquiring language, children must also acquire a knowledge of the underlying structure of sentences, effectively a set of generative rules that allows them to produce novel grammatical sentences of any length, the so-called "generative" aspect of language. He originally argued that this ability was made possible by a language acquisition device (LAD), a brain structure that predisposes humans to understand language, a template of sorts to be filled in by whatever particular language they were exposed to. No reinforced learning was necessary at all. Chomsky (2010) has since narrowed his claim and accepted that many aspects of language represent general cognitive abilities that may be present in apes or acquired through learning, but he continues to maintain that human language is distinctive in its generative aspect and he claims this ability is based on the fact that humans alone have the ability to think recursively. Recursion, then, is viewed as the final bastion separating humans and all other animals. He further holds that this faculty is only recently evolved in humans and cannot be discovered in apes.

Rumbaugh's Salience Theory

Rumbaugh has argued that neither a purely behavioral approach nor the notion of unique brain structures is sufficient to account for language, which he views as an emergent behavior not unlike mathematics, art, and music. Rumbaugh addressed the shortcomings of the behavioral theories in Chapter 27 and posited instead a salience theory and rational behaviorism. Neither could Rumbaugh accept Chomsky's discontinuity view that humans possess unique brain structures alien to apes and all other animals. In the introduction to his recent book, *With Apes in Mind*, he states that "whatever the attributes are of humans and their psychology root traces can be discerned in the animal kingdom" (Rumbaugh 2013: 207). Since Rumbaugh has already adequately critiqued the behavioral point of view, I will limit my comments to a few examples where his work directly contradicts the uniqueness theories of Chomsky. These critiques address what Chomsky considers to be the central tenets of human language, generativity and recursion, each of which is examined below.

Generativity

Chomsky claims that a hallmark of language is the distinctly human ability to generate an infinite number of novel sentences conforming to an underlying set of grammatical rules. Sue Savage-Rumbaugh's and Duane Rumbaugh's work with both Lana and Kanzi have demonstrated that apes can come to possess this ability in at least a rudimentary form. Whereas the Lana experiments focused on sentence production, later work with the bonobo, Kanzi, concentrated more heavily on comprehension as a measure of language competence. In the video entitled "Kanzi and Novel Sentences," Savage-Rumbaugh demonstrates Kanzi's ability to understand complex requests such as "Can you put the pine needles in the refrigerator?" (see http://www.youtube.com/watch?v=2Dhc2zePJFE). She is wearing a welder's mask so that there is no possibility of accidental cuing. Clearly Kanzi is able to comprehend a great number of these novel sentences conforming to grammatical rules. Note also that because the sentences are novel they could not have been learned through a history of contingent reinforcement.

Recursion

Chomsky holds that the ability to comprehend and produce recursive sentences is uniquely human. But there is evidence that both Kanzi and Lana are capable of dealing with recursive sentence structures. On the comprehension side, consider Savage-Rumbaugh's 1993 monograph *Language Comprehension in Ape and Child*, where Kanzi's comprehension of recursive requests is clear (see p. 100). On the production side, consider one of the sentences Lana produced on her lexigram keyboard:

"Lana want Tim give M&M to Lana"

This is an example of a simple form of recursion, an embedded sentence. The syntactic diagram in Figure 28.1 illustrates that her production conforms to a simple recursive rule:

Sentence → Subject + Verb + Sentence

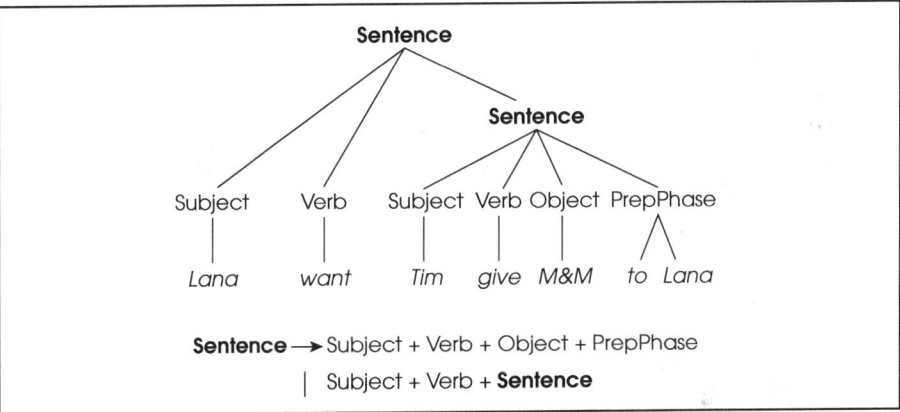

Figure 28.1 Recursive sentence produced by Lana

Additional Internet Resources

The following resources are available on the Internet to further document Rumbaugh's salience theory of learning and behavior and his contention that language is best understood as an emergent much like art, music, and mathematics.

With Apes in Mind

Rumbaugh's primate research over the course of his long career is documented and illustrated in his most recent book, *With Apes in Mind* (2013). The book covers his early work with primates at the San Diego Zoo, the launching of the Learning Research Center in Georgia, the development of the lexigram system, and his work with Lana, other chimpanzees, and bonobos (see http://www.withapesinmind.com).

Apes with Apps

The article "Apes with Apps," by Ken Schweller, appeared in the July 2012 publication of *IEEE Spectrum*. It provides a brief history of early ape language research, the LANA project, and the creation of the lexigram keyboard and documents Kanzi's current use of keyboard technologies (see http://spectrum.ieee.org/computing/software/apes-with-apps/0).

The Amazing Apes

The Amazing Apes, a documentary film of the LANA project, was made at the Yerkes Regional Primate Research Center in Atlanta, Georgia (Burrud 1977). It gives an excellent overview of the experimental setup and shows how easily and eagerly Lana used the lexigram keyboard (see http://www.youtube.com/watch?v=HiWDKXRzSmU).

Lana Keyboard Simulator

An interactive computer program has been written to allow users to experience firsthand what it was like for Lana to operate Rumbaugh's first lexigram keyboard. Lana turned on the machine by grabbing the "Go Bar." She could then enter a sequence of lexigrams and the machine would respond appropriately. In this case her request "Please Machine Make Slide" was rewarded by a slide displaying M&Ms. The program was built by Ken Schweller and may be downloaded from http://www.threelittlecorgis.com/lanaKeyboardsim/ (see Figures 28.2 and 28.3).

Figure 28.2   Lana keyboard simulator

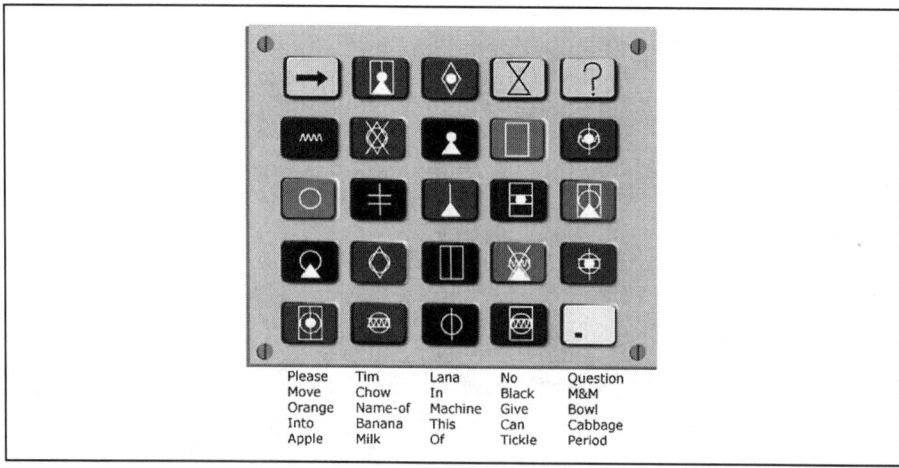

Figure 28.3   A close-up of one of the first panels on which Lana worked

Second Life—*LANA* Lab

A YouTube video shows a simulation of the LANA lab in a virtual multiuser environment (see Figure 28.4). It was developed by Ken Schweller and his psychology students (http://www.youtube.com/watch?v=9-nXIUDbe6g).

Lana Chimpanzee Counts

The video "Lana Chimpanzee Counts," by Duane Rumbaugh, documents Lana's performance on the NuMath program (see Figure 28.5), designed to teach basic counting and enumeration skills (http://threelittlecorgis.com/lanacounts/). An ape's ability to acquire some degree of numerical competency directly supports Chomsky's (2010) admission that the use of recursion, which he claims uniquely characterizes human language, may have evolutionary precursors in our ancestors' counting ability.

Figure 28.4 Online simulation of Lana's lab

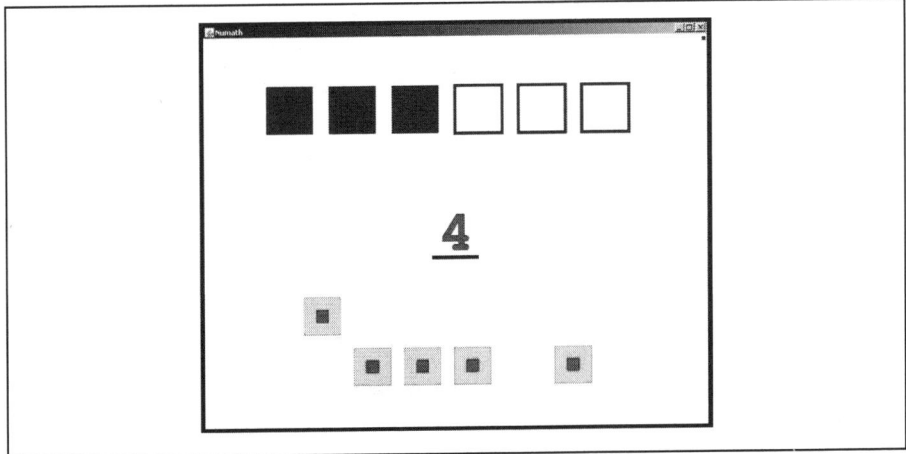

Figure 28.5 NuMath

Sherman and Austin

Documentary footage of Sherman and Austin was taken in the late 1970s as the chimpanzees learned to interpret and use lexigrams in a truly symbolic way (see Figure 28.6). These films demonstrate "the use of imitation, joint regard, mutual gaze, pointing, joint attention, cooperation, sharing, joint intentionality, nonverbal synchronicity linked to symbolic exchanges, and spontaneous creative behaviors entailing all of these capacities" (Savage-Rumbaugh 2014). At the time the films were made these behaviors were not widely believed to be characteristic of apes (http://kanzi.bvu.edu/SandAvideos2.html).

Ape Language: From Conditioned Response to Symbol

A visual supplement for Sue Savage-Rumbaugh's book of the same name. Duane Rumbaugh narrates. These videotapes document many of the early experiments with the chimpanzees Lana, Sherman, and Austin. Skeptical readers may judge for themselves by viewing these tapes whether in fact these apes have acquired and use an abstract symbol system (see http://kanzi.bvu.edu/apelanguage2.html).

Video Documentation

The "Kanzi" archives, put together by Sue Savage-Rumbaugh and Ken Schweller, include additional video, commentary, and PDF files related to pivotal studies in the history of ape language research (see http://kanzi.bvu.edu).

Current Lexigram Keyboards

Figure 28.7 shows an image of the first of three panels in the lexigram system now being used by Kanzi and the other bonobos. To view all three current panels, see http://threelittlecorgis.com/lexigrams.

Figure 28.8 shows a screen from an amusing video of an avatar in a virtual environment using a lexigram keyboard (see http://www.youtube.com/watch?v=so48I8mUNZM).

Figure 28.6 Sherman and Austin

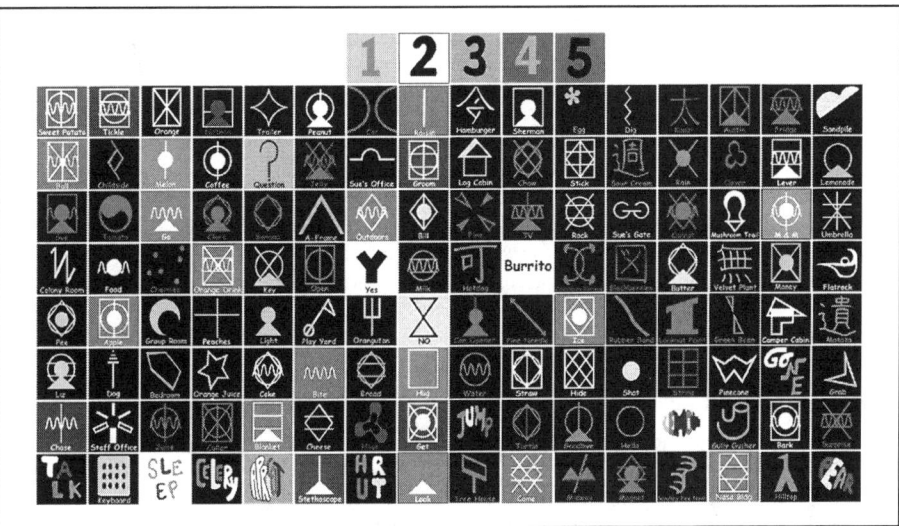

Figure 28.7   Current lexigram keyboard, panel 1

Figure 28.8   Lexigram keyboard in an online virtual environment

LEXIGRAM APP

The full lexigram keyboard used by the bonobos at the Ape Cognition and Conservation Initiative (ACCI) is available as an iPad mobile app. This is the same app that Kanzi and his son, Teco, use. In addition to providing a full keyboard, it allows the researchers to select a small set of lexigrams and present them as a slide show to focus on particular words or to present food, person, and activity choices (created by Ken Schweller, https://itunes.apple.com/us/app/lexigram-slider/id792131885?mt=8).

Latest Keyboards

The lexigram keyboards have undergone continuous development since they were first designed by Rumbaugh and incorporate the latest computer technologies. Kanzi's "Slider Keyboard" (Figure 28.9), codesigned by Schweller and Savage-Rumbaugh, allows creation of new lexigrams "on the fly." When Kanzi expresses interest in a word or concept not presently on the board, a new lexigram can be designed and instantly added to the board along with a synthesized voice (Figure 28.10).

A mobile app uses voice recognition to convert speech to a stream of lexigrams (developed by Schweller and Savage-Rumbaugh).

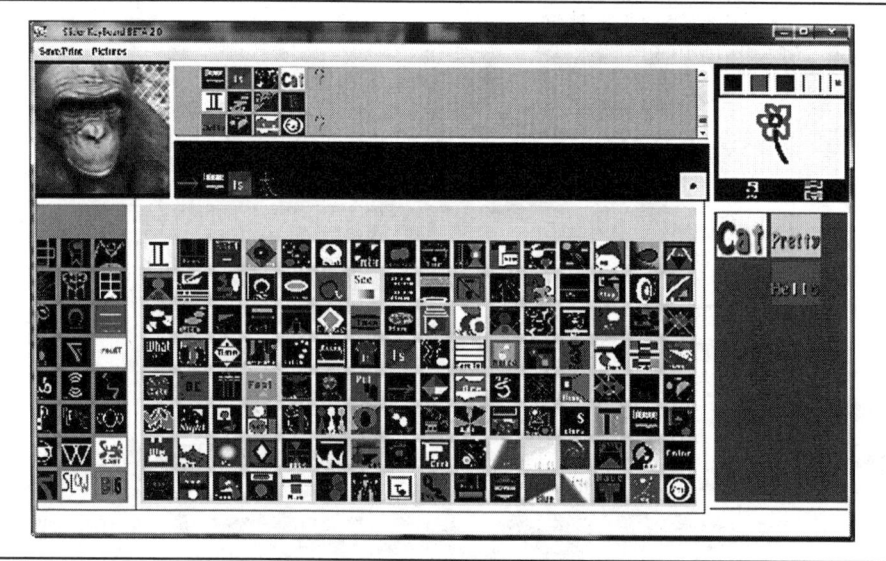

Figure 28.9   New lexigram keyboard

Figure 28.10   Lexigram keyboard for mobile apps

·Figure 28.11 Bonobo facility at the Ape Cognition and Conservation Initiative

Language Research Center

The Language Research Center at Georgia State University continues its long tradition of social, cognitive, and biobehavioral research with apes (http://www2.gsu.edu/~wwwlrc/).

Ape Cognition and Conservation Initiative

The ACCI in Des Moines, Iowa, is home to Kanzi, Teco, and three other bonobos (Figure 28.11). It is dedicated to the conservation and protection of great apes worldwide, as well as responsible and sustainable research aimed at uncovering the evolutionary origins of human language, cognition, and behavior (http://apeinitiative.org).

References

Burrud, B. 1977. *The Amazing Apes* (TV program). Burbank, CA: Bill Burrud Productions.
Chomsky, N. 2010. "Some Simple Evo Devo Theses: How True Might They Be for Language?" In *The Evolution of Human Language*, edited by R. K. Larson, V. Deprez, and H. Yamakido, 45–62. Cambridge: Cambridge University Press.
Darwin, C. 1871. *The Descent of Man, and Selection in Relation to Sex*. 2 vols. London: Murray.
Müller, F. M. (1861) 1996. "The Theoretical Stage, and the Origin of Language." In *Lectures on the Science of Language*, 7–41 (Lecture 9). Reprinted in R. Harris, ed., *The Origin of Language*. Bristol: Thoemmes Press.
Rumbaugh, D. M. 2013. *With Apes in Mind*. CreateSpace Independent Publishing Platform.
Savage-Rumbaugh, E. S. 2014. "Video Documentation." http://kanzi.bvu.edu.
Savage-Rumbaugh, E. S., J. Murphy, R. A. Sevcik, S. Williams, K. Brakke, and D. M. Rumbaugh. 1993. *Language Comprehension in Ape and Child*. Monographs of the Society for Research in Child Development, Nos. 2 & 3.

Chapter Twenty-Nine

Evolutionary Sociology

A Cross-Species Strategy for Discovering Human Nature

Jonathan H. Turner and Alexandra Maryanski

> Sociobiology and evolutionary psychology have made extraordinary claims about how the social universe can be explained in Darwinian terms. These approaches, however, often remain ignorant of, and unreceptive to, sociological theory and research on social processes, with the result that their explanations of the social order always seem both reductionist and rather simplistic. In this chapter, an alternative to these approaches is outlined, an approach we term *evolutionary sociology*. Part of this new evolutionary sociology is highly Darwinian and, like sociobiology and evolutionary psychology, seeks to explain the evolution of biologically driven behavioral propensities. This approach, however, emphasizes the selection pressures on primates as they evolved first in niches within the arboreal habitat and later in niches of the terrestrial habitat of the African savanna. An entirely new kind of explanation is generated using research findings on (1) network structures of present-day primates, (2) cladistic analysis for the social structures and behaviors among the last ancestors to humans and extant apes, (3) preadaptations in primates that could be subject to selection, (4) behavioral propensities of primates and mammals that could also be subject to selection over the last 7 million years, and (5) comparative neuroanatomy on the differences between great-ape brains and human brains, with these differences marking the footprints of natural selection on the hominin ancestors of humans.

The development over the last few decades of evolutionary approaches to studying human behavior has created new opportunities to study what, rather loosely, used to be termed "human nature." By adopting a Darwinian approach in understanding the evolution of humans' hominin ancestors, it is possible to address this question of "human nature" less speculatively. There will, of course, always be some speculation in trying to understand the evolution of humans' hominin ancestors over the last 8 million years. Yet, with the legacy of field research on primates and especially the great apes (chimpanzees, gorillas, and orangutans), and with the development of new analytical tools for making comparisons between humans and extant apes, it is now possible to infer the behavioral propensities of humans' hominin ancestors and the selection pressures working on these ancestors. Thus, a Darwinian approach that is comparative and historical has the potential for generating new understandings of how hardwired behavioral propensities of humans influence the process of social interaction and the construction of patterns of social organization.

In this chapter, we view our version of this cross-species comparative approach as one useful strategy for reviving evolutionary analysis in sociology, which can be labeled the *new evolutionary sociology*. Evolutionary sociology consists of many diverse approaches, including new types of stage models of societal evolution, but our strategy can be viewed as an alternative to sociobiology (e.g., Wilson 1975, 1978) and evolutionary psychology (e.g., Barkow, Cosmides, and Tooby 1992; Cosmides and Tooby 1992; Chapters 7–9 in this volume). This evolutionary sociology involves six basic elements: (1) analysis of the existing data on the behavioral and organizational features of primates and their various patterns of social organization; (2) cladistic analysis of these data to make inferences about the behavioral propensities and patterns of social organization among the last common ancestor of extant apes, particularly the great apes, and humans' hominin ancestors; (3) analysis of the selection pressures under which primates first evolved; (4) analysis of the ecology—habitat and niches—and changes in this ecology that imposed new selection pressures on primates and on humans' hominin ancestors; (5) analysis of the genetically driven behavioral propensities of primates as well as the preadaptations evident in species close to the human line and the likelihood that selection began to work on these propensities as humans' ancestors adapted to new ecological conditions; and (6) comparative neuroanatomy on the brains of great apes and humans in order to uncover how selection rewired the hominin brain after the split with the last common ancestor to humans and great apes. Each of these points of attack is reviewed below.

Behavioral and Organizational Propensities Among Extant Primates

Weak-Tie Apes

Our approach begins with a review of the field data on primate societies (Maryanski 1986). These studies were coded using a simple measure of network tie strength as (1) weak/nonexistent ties, (2) moderate ties, and (3) strong ties. By emphasizing the networks rather than behavior per se, it is possible to get a sense of the strength of ties among age and sex classes in primate societies. We will not fully summarize the data here since they have been published in many places (see Maryanski 1987, 1992, 1993, 1996; Maryanski and Turner 1992; Turner and Maryanski 2005, 2008; Turner 2000). The remarkable findings are that among the great apes, very few strong ties are formed, as is evident in Table 29.1. The reason for this weakness is that among all apes, sexual relations are promiscuous and thus paternity can never be known; moreover, females transfer from their natal community at puberty, never to return, and thereby break the possibility of intergenerational ties among adult females. These females are replaced by immigrating females from different communities, but since they come from disparate origins, they remain virtual strangers to each other even as they sit in proximity and allow their young offspring to play together. The same is true for males, except among chimpanzees, where males stay in their natal community and sustain (1) moderate to strong ties with their mothers, whom they often visit, and (2) moderate to strong "friendship ties" with other males and their brothers. But, except for temporary troops of gorillas, there are no permanent groups among the great apes; rather, they reveal a fusion-fission pattern of brief group formation followed by dispersal, with many individuals wandering about their home ranges alone. At times, however, males will form troops for patrolling the border of their home range to prevent incursions by males from other communities.

The result is that among the great apes, there are not sufficiently strong ties among key age and sex classes to support group structures or dense networks. The only really

Table 29.1 Strength of social ties among extant species of great apes

	Species of ape			
	Gorillas (Gorilla)	Chimpanzees (Pan)	Orangutans (Pongo)	Last common ancestor
Adult-to-Adult Ties				
Male-male	0	0/+	0	0*
Female-female	0	0	0	0*
Male-female	0/+	0	0	0*
Adult-to-Adult Offspring Procreation Ties				
Mother-daughter	0	0	0	0*
Father-daughter	0	0	0	0*
Mother-son	0	+	0	0*
Father-son	0	0	0	0*
Adult-to-Preadolescent Offspring Ties				
Mother-daughter	+	+	+	+*
Father-daughter	0	0	0	0*
Mother-son	+	+	+	+*
Father-son	0	0	0	0*

0 = no or very weak ties; 0/+ = weak to moderate ties; + = strong ties
* denotes a reconstructed social structure—in this case the likely structure of the last common ancestor to humans and extant great apes. As is evident, this structure is most like that of contemporary orangutans.

strong tie is between a mother and her offspring, but this tie disappears when females in all great ape societies leave their natal community forever and when males in gorilla and orangutan societies also leave at puberty, with, as noted above, chimpanzee males being the only offspring among all apes to remain in the natal community. Still, ape males do not live in groups with their mothers or even brothers; rather, they meet and visit, and males can at times form bonds to assert dominance.

This lack of kinship ties and the virtual absence of intergenerational ties, coupled with little propensity to form groups, makes apes comparatively unsocial, forming few strong or enduring ties, while evidencing fleeting and fluid group formations that do not endure. Thus, to the extent that present-day great apes can give us a view of what humans' early ancestors were like, it is clear that these distant ancestors were not strong-tie or group-forming animals. And, while extant great apes have certainly evolved over the last 8 million years, their respective habitats and niches have not changed dramatically, with the result that this weak-tie structure in great ape societies was probably evident among humans' hominin ancestors that split off from the ape line some 7 million to 8 million years ago or, closer to home, when hominins and the ancestors of contemporary chimpanzees (humans' closest ape cousin) split some 3 million to 4 million years ago.

Strong-Tie Monkeys

In contrast to apes, monkeys evidence almost the opposite pattern of tie formation and group structure. Females in monkey societies never leave their natal group and form dense matrilines across generations and among collateral kin. In contrast, males migrate out of their community at puberty and enter the competition for dominance in other groups, with dominant males trying to horde females in a harem pattern of sexual reproduction, although males are rarely fully successful in this reproductive strategy. Males become arrayed in a lineal dominance hierarchy that, when coupled with the dense and enduring network ties among female kin, makes monkeys highly group oriented. They do not have the same sense of a larger community (as large as ten square miles) evident among the great apes; instead, they have a very strong sense of the local group, with virtually all activities and movements being part of coordinated group action.

In sum, then, apes and monkeys evidence very different tie patterns, leading to vastly different societal formations. Monkeys are oriented to groups; apes are not group oriented at all and, instead, recon who belongs in their larger community or home range, which they will defend in temporary patrols of community boundaries. Otherwise, they live alone or form temporary groups that never last very long. Thus, this dramatic difference between apes and monkeys gives us our first clues to an important aspect of human nature: to the extent that humans are evolved apes, this propensity for weak ties is probably still in the genome and represents one behavioral propensity that, today, guides human behavior and organization, even after hominins and humans clearly became more group oriented and more attuned to generational kinship relations.

Cladistic Analysis

Careful coding of behaviors of extant primates can provide clues to what their ancestors were like. Cladistic analysis is an approach in biology that uses present-day data on behaviors and organizational forms of species to reconstruct the behavioral propensities and structures of the ancestral forms of these species. The basic logic is very much like reconstruction of the origins of modern languages: look for what all languages thought to have evolved from a common root language have in common. Similarly, in cladistic analysis, the emphasis is those behaviors, social structures, and phenotypical traits that a set of related species have in common. When diverse but related species reveal common behavioral patterns, it is reasonable to hypothesize that the last common ancestor to these species also possessed these common traits because, otherwise, one would have to hypothesize that these traits miraculously evolved independently of each other. Thus, for the common ancestor of the great apes, we can be reasonably confident that female and male transfer from their natal community was a behavioral propensity of their ancestor. It is also likely that sexual relations between males and females were highly promiscuous, with paternity never known and, thus, with kinship being nonexistent, except for mother nurturance of young offspring (a trait common to virtually all mammals). Furthermore, since groups do not form for any length of time among great apes, the last common ancestor to apes was not group organizing; rather, the only universal social unit was a sense of community or home range. Adult females probably did not form strong ties with one another, because having immigrated from other communities, they would be strangers to one another.

In pursuing these lines of argument, Alexandra Maryanski concluded that the last common ancestor was probably organized like contemporary orangutans, even though orangutans are the most distant genetically from humans among the great apes (they still are very close, sharing as much as 95 percent of their genes with humans, although these are arrayed on twenty-four rather than twenty-three pairs of chromosomes). Orangutans are virtually solitary, live alone, and do not form groups, except for a brief time when males seek sexual partners and for a longer time when mothers nurture their offspring until puberty, at which point offspring leave the mother's community forever. Thus, males live alone and wander the Asian forests, and females do the same, unless they have pre-adolescent children. The last common ancestor of contemporary great apes and humans was, therefore, highly individualistic, mobile, and not disposed to form any permanent relations beyond mother-infant bonds. Even though this ancestor lived millions of years ago, it is unlikely that such a powerful set of bioprogrammers could have been wiped out of the hominin and human genome.

Selection Pressures on Apes and the Ecology That Generated Them

General Selection Pressures in the Arboreal Habitat

When the first rodent-like animal climbed or clawed its way into the arboreal forests of Africa some 63 million years ago, the initial selection pressures revolved around increasing the efficiency and safety of movement to secure food in the more precarious three-dimensional habitat of trees, where one false step could mean death by the pull of gravity. The most fundamental shift driven by selection was the movement toward visual rather than olfactory dominance among the sense modalities of evolving primates. In all mammals and animals in general, one sense modality must be dominant, with the others subordinated to this dominant sense modality in order to avoid sensory conflict. Most mammals are olfactory dominant, with hearing (auditory), touch (haptic), and sight (vision) being subordinated to smell. Smelling one's way around trees is clearly not fitness enhancing, and so natural selection began to rotate the eye sockets forward to the point of overlapping, which, in turn, would produce three-dimensional sight—a much more adaptive trait in the arboreal habitat. As vision became dominant, other sense modalities had to be subordinated to it. Among those, modalities located in the neocortex—that is, auditory along the temporal lobe and haptic in the temporal lobe—were subordinated to vision in the occipital lobe by creating new association cortices around the inferior parietal lobe where the occipital, parietal, and temporal lobes meet. Smell, which is located in subcortical areas of the brain and, thereby, is not directly under neocortical control, was subordinated by dramatic reduction in its power. Humans do not smell very well compared with most other mammals, but even when we do smell a powerful odor, we immediately begin to look for it, as we do for something that feels or sounds unusual and that demands our attention.

We will explore preadaptations later, but a very important one was wired into the primate brain with this shift to visual dominance. The basic capacity for language—evident among all the great apes when subject to training—was put into place in the association cortices around the inferior parietal lobe. This capacity is a preadaptation because it was an outcome of selection pressures that were pushing for visual dominance and, in the process, just happened to install the basic neurological wiring for language.

With this shift to visual dominance came anatomical changes to the basic mammalian body. Flexible and very strong hands, wrists, arms, and legs evolved to facilitate rapid movement through the trees; a more generalized body skeleton evolved so that the body was more flexible as it was guided by hands, arms, and feet that were able to grab hold of branches for movement along the tops of branches, for suspension below branches, and for swinging from branch to branch. These also can be seen as preadaptations for tool use and everything else that humans can do with the very sensitive hands and strong arms, wrists, and shoulder joints. Walking upright also became possible with the more generalized skeleton and flexible legs and hip joints, giving selection something to work on if upright walking eventually had fitness-enhancing value.

SELECTION AND ADAPTATION TO SPECIALIZED NICHES IN THE ARBOREAL HABITAT

Monkeys and apes were not vastly different for many millions of years, except for some life history characteristics (apes on average are bigger than monkeys and take longer to develop in and out of the womb), but around 23 million years ago, monkeys clearly gained an advantage in the arboreal habitat (perhaps through their ability to eat unripe fruit, which is something that present-day apes cannot do), with the result that they began to take over the niches in the verdant portions of trees, where more food, room, and support by thicker branches were available to support larger and more permanent groups (Maryanski and Turner 1992; Turner and Maryanski 2008). Apes were increasingly pushed to the terminal feeding areas of the arboreal habitat, where there was less room, less structural support by thin branches, and less food to support larger groupings. The result is that apes became smarter than monkeys because of their need to remember routes through branches that were more difficult to navigate, and they also developed the capacity to brachiate (or rotate their arms 360 degrees in their shoulder socket) when swinging from branch to branch. Even more significantly, apes developed the very unusual weak-tie and nongroup structures evident in apes today because it was no longer possible to support larger groups so high in the trees where food, support, and room were so much less than in the niches occupied by monkeys. Kin attachments and grouping propensities would work against apes moving to new terminal feeding areas; thus, selection worked to break down sociality, permanent and strong social ties, and group formations as the basic adaptive strategies typical of most mammals. Apes became more individualistic, mobile, and at times, almost loners because of the limitations imposed by the terminal feeding areas of the arboreal habitat.

THE SHRINKING FORESTS AND FORCED ADAPTATIONS TO THE AFRICAN SAVANNA

Around 10 million years ago, the climate became colder and the forests in Africa began to shrink, thereby opening up the vast African savannas. Many species of primates were thrust out onto the savanna. Some lived in the forests bordering the savanna, but many were forced out onto the savanna full-time where what had been fitness enhancing in the trees would be less so on the savanna. Monkeys have had relatively little trouble adapting to open-country savanna conditions filled with predators because, in contrast to apes, they are well organized with larger males (with their large canines) encircling smaller females and offspring as they march across the savanna in almost militaristic style. It is a rare predator that would dare attack such a well-structured phalanx; and so, monkeys have always prospered on the savanna.

In contrast, apes are very poorly suited for the savanna, where selection pressures favor well-organized groups exhibiting strong ties among at least some members (female matrilines provide the structural core of monkey groupings). Aside from not possessing, it appears, any behavioral propensities for forming permanent groups or kin relations between males, females, and their offspring, apes can be highly emotional when aroused, thus attracting predators. They have a reduced sense of smell and hence cannot smell predators as most savanna-dwelling animals can. Apes are also slow; they are built for moving about in trees, using upper-body movements for brachiation rather than all-out speed on land, thereby making it difficult to flee four-legged predators. And so it is not surprising that apes began to go extinct. Selection pressures for cohesive group organization for defending against predators and for collective foraging for food do not guarantee that animals will change in the needed direction.

Selection may have developed several strategies, such as enhancing the modest but very evident propensities of apes to form hierarchies, but without female matrilines, hierarchies alone would not provide enough stability and cohesiveness to groups. Selection did enlarge some apes, such as *Gigantapathecus* (who was eight feet tall), and some of these very large apes were able to survive for a time; but the large amount of food required to feed such a brute and to expel the heat generated by such a large body mass eventually led to their extinction some 1.6 million years ago (where they were in competition with humans' most immediate ancestor, *Homo erectus*). The result was that all apes living on the savanna went extinct, except for the hominin ancestors of humans. How, then, did hominins beat the odds under selection pressures for group organization that a terrestrial habitat filled with predators imposes on a species?

What Did Natural Selection Have to Work On?
Existing Behavioral Propensities and Preadaptations

There is now a rich literature on the behavioral propensities of primates, and particularly the great apes. As noted earlier, since the habitats and even the niches of present-day great apes have probably not changed dramatically, we can reasonably assume that these behavioral propensities were evident among the last common ancestors of apes and humans. They were, therefore, available for selection to work on and enhance, although some of these propensities seem sufficiently developed that they would not need to be enhanced. Of course, when the brain of hominins finally began to grow beyond the range of extant chimpanzees, this change alone could have dramatically increased these behavioral propensities. But, as we will argue in the next section, on comparative neuroanatomy, growth of subcortical areas of the brain and the consequent enhancement of emotional capacities and propensities among hominins occurred long before the dramatic growth of the neocortex with *Homo erectus*, beginning about 2 million years ago. Indeed, the enhancement of hominins' emotional capacities would, we feel, have an even more dramatic effect on existing behavioral propensities than changes in the neocortex. For emotions are much like a turbo charger on behaviors; and so, with the enhancement of hominin emotionality, all other behaviors wired into primate neurology would also be enhanced.

We are focusing on those behavioral propensities and preadaptations that could increase the strength and perhaps length of social bonds that, in turn, would promote social solidarity and group formation. The ecology of the African savanna generated intense selection pressures for animals that can form groups to defend against predators and forage for food; in fact, these pressures were so intense that they led to the mass extinction of all apes, with only humans able to survive today in open-country savanna conditions. Somehow, humans' hominin ancestors beat these odds and kept the hominin clade evolving, and as we will argue, it was through the rewiring of subcortical areas for emotion. As emotional capacities increased, they probably had large effects on the extant behavioral capacities and preadaptations evident among primates, especially apes. Let us begin with preadaptations.

PREADAPTATIONS

Visual Dominance and Language

As noted earlier, in the shift to visual over olfactory dominance, the brain was significantly rewired around the inferior parietal lobe (Geschwind 1965a, 1965b, 1985; Geschwind and Damasio 1984; Maryanski and Turner 1992; Ettlinger 1977; Jarvis and Ettlinger 1977; Passingham 1982: 51–55). A consequence of this shift in sensory dominance was installation of the basic capacity for language in those primates reaching a certain threshold of intelligence. It appears only the great apes exceed this threshold, because only chimpanzees, gorillas, and orangutans among all primates can use signs or pictograms to communicate meanings at about the level of a three-year-old human child (Rumbaugh and Savage-Rumbaugh 1990; Savage-Rumbaugh and Lewin 1994; Savage-Rumbaugh, Sevcik, and Hopkins 1988; Savage-Rumbaugh et al. 1993; Bickerton 2003); non–great apes like gibbons and siamangs as well as all monkeys cannot use symbols to create intended meanings. Since the last common ancestor to contemporary apes and humans also must have had this trait (by the reasoning of cladistic analysis), the capacity for language was available to natural selection, if communicating meanings with phonemes, morphemes, and syntax would increase fitness of hominins by increasing social bonds and solidarity. Since speech in the human measure appears to be a recent trait (Enard 1978; Enard et al. 2002a, 2002b), perhaps unique only to humans, the first language probably was not verbal as much as gestural, communicated through face and body. It is hard to imagine that this incredible capacity for language simply sat there in the hominin phenotype and genome for millions of years and was not touched by natural selection; and as we will argue, this capacity was subject to natural selection to produce the first and primal language of hominins and now humans: the language of emotions.

The Palette of Primary Emotions

Virtually all mammals possess at least the four primary emotions of *assertion-anger*, *aversion-fear*, *disappointment-sadness*, and most importantly, *satisfaction-happiness*. Anger and fear were inherited from reptiles, but the addition of sadness and happiness may be unique to mammals, although intelligent birds also seem to possess these emotional capacities. Social solidarity in the absence of dedicated bioprogrammers for group formation can be generated only by positive emotions, and so if natural selection was to enhance hominin sociality, bonding, and group formation, the power of the three negative emotions had to be mitigated, while the salience and power of the satisfaction-happiness continuum had to be expanded. Most mammals reveal bioprogrammers for herds, packs, pods, troops, and other group formations, and so, even when negative emotional states arise in these groupings, the bioprogrammers keep members together. But, with evolving apes, these bioprogrammers had been lost or at least greatly attenuated, and thus some other force was needed to promote social bonding. Since positive emotional arousal is what gives human groups solidarity, selection obviously hit upon this "solution" at some point during hominin evolution. And, coupled with the preadaptation for language, the emotional capacities of hominins could be greatly expanded to produce subtle and nuanced forms of communication and bonding, as we will outline shortly.

Mother-Infant Bonding

All mammals evidence mother-offspring attachments, sometimes for life but almost always for infancy through juvenile stages of development. A discrete area of the mammalian brain—the anterior cingulate gyrus—is where playfulness, mother-offspring bonds, and the separation cry of infants and often mothers are generated. Thus, this area could be subject to additional selection to increase mother-infant bonds, but the question is, Could natural selection have extended this same propensity for emotional attachments to adult males? There is no clear answer, but if mother-offspring bonds could be enhanced and, then, mother-father relations (or relations with at least another adult male) could be forged, then something like a family could begin to evolve.

Lack of Harem Mating Patterns

Among monkeys, dominance hierarchies generate harem mating patterns where the dominant males seek to horde females as their exclusive sexual partners. Apes reveal less powerful tendencies for dominance, although lead-silverback gorillas often try to control access to females (with not much success since females sneak off to mate with other males). Chimpanzees evidence open promiscuity with no efforts by males to control access to "their" females, and so there was probably a lack of any harem-like behavioral propensities in the last common ancestor to great apes and hominins. Thus, the ability to build up family was not programmed in any direct way among hominins, and so the question is, How was kinship ever to emerge among these ancestors? Part of the answer has to be emotional bonds between males and females, but were these enough to overcome the behavioral propensities for promiscuity? The answer is probably no, since humans remain highly promiscuous. But the lack of a harem pattern allowed for the possibility that a family pattern of male-female bonding could potentially occur, if selection could find an alternative route to overcome promiscuity. As will be evident shortly, and as is noted in Table 29.2, there is a curious anomaly in the subcortical areas of the human brain when compared with an ape brain: the center for sexual pleasure—the septum in all mammals—is twice as big in humans, controlling for body size, as in apes. And since apes are already highly sexed and promiscuous, why would this increase in size ever be necessary? It may be that something more than sexual pleasure was wired into the hominin and then human septum: additional pleasures associated with emotions that we might term "love" or some such label. Pleasure with the relationship outside of sex per se is necessary for monogamous (at least in name) marriage and nuclear kin units built from marriage. Perhaps, coupled with expanding the range of emotions that hominins and then humans could experience and communicate to each other, an enlarged septum allowed for sex and more enduring emotional attachments to evolve—thereby creating what was a very unusual structure for a great ape: the nuclear family. So, the high sexual drives of apes and their general propensity for promiscuity ironically gave natural selection an opening to select on the septum to produce just the opposite: reduced promiscuity and increased commitment to sexual partners with offspring.

Life-History Preadaptations

Apes are very different from monkeys in terms of what are sometimes called "life-history characteristics" (Turner and Maryanski 2008: 34). Apes are not only bigger than monkeys on average (a trait built into their genome); they take longer to develop at all phases of the life cycle (gestation, nursing, infancy, and juvenile), and they live longer and space births further apart than monkeys—and these differences are dramatic. For example, an adult male baboon (a large monkey) will be in a gestation phase for 175 days, nurse for 420 days, and remain an infant for 1.6 years, whereas a chimpanzee male (ape) will remain in the womb for 228 days, nurse for 1,460 days, and be an infant for 3.0 years. This long life history can be viewed as a preadaptation for what was to occur for apes and hominins: increases in brain size, thus allowing more time for the brain to develop in the womb while ensuring that there will be adequate parental care when the ever-larger brain increasingly forced early birth so as to get the larger head of babies through the female's cervix. Longer periods of nursing, infant care, and even juvenile care (7.0 years for chimps and only 4.4 years for baboons) could be selected upon, as could the average spacing of offspring (1.7 years for baboons and 5.6 years for chimpanzees), to allow biologically and neurologically immature apes and hominins to complete what could not be accomplished in the womb. An animal programmed to turn out offspring rapidly and nurse for a limited time could not have a hominin or human baby that is completely helpless at birth and for several years after birth; and so, only animals with longer life-history characteristics programmed into their genome could support larger-brained offspring, and thus, the life-history characteristics of apes can be considered a preadaptation allowing for the brain of hominins to grow. Moreover, prolonged parental care involves kissing (licking) and other expressions of love, which, increases the energy of offspring, perhaps leading energetic offspring to become bored, which, in turn, leads to another important preadaptation for sociality: play (see below). Thus, many of the behaviors associated with high solidarity can be found in parental care (Eibl-Eibesfeldt [1971] 1996), which in the case of apes, ended with offspring transfer from their natural community at puberty to other communities. Still, in the lone case where offspring remain in the regional community—chimpanzee males—their bond with their mother (their father cannot be known because of promiscuity) indicates that they are capable of forming lifelong attachments if they remain in the same community as their caretaker. Thus, once other forces began to keep parents and offspring together in early quasi-kinship systems, the behaviors brought out in play among the young could be adapted to more enduring social relations.

Play

Young mammals almost universally play, which involves a number of rather complex activities (Burghardt 2005): to assume a role (say, as aggressor or pursued), to initiate role-playing, to coordinate switches in roles, to be aggressive without hurting play partners, to know the rules of the game, and other behaviors that must be coordinated. This play is programmed into the genome and is probably wired in the anterior cingulate gyrus. This play is probably very much like training to participate in roles for various forms of groupings among mammals, and although apes do not form permanent groups, play is probably essential to many of the interactive techniques that apes use to communicate and, when necessary, coordinate activities (see next section, on behavioral propensities). For some time, scholars have viewed play as a necessary precursor to behaviors that are more humanlike, such as role-taking, ritual, mimicry, and interpersonal attunement (Huizinga [1949] 1955; Bekoff and Pierce 2009; Bellah 2011). Still others have argued that play and ritual are necessary precursors to the evolution of mind and cultural beliefs (Donald 1991, 2001; Bellah 2011).

Low Levels of Grooming and Reliance on Cognitive Mapping

Robert Dunbar (1996) has argued that language is a kind of "verbal grooming" that arises when groups become too large for grooming to sustain direct physical contact with all group members. Indeed, the growth in brain size was not a cause of larger groups, but instead, larger groupings created selection pressures for larger brains to sustain group solidarity. There are several problems with Dunbar's analysis (Maryanski 1997), and one of them is that apes do not groom as extensively as monkeys. Thus, solidarity is not sustained by grooming, and indeed, apes reveal relatively low levels of solidarity and virtually no group formation propensities. But, part of the argument makes some sense: larger groupings in larger communities would require a larger brain to remember who is part of the community. Thus, one reason that apes' brains are larger than those of monkeys may be because apes form larger regional communities and, thereby, must keep track of who does and who does not belong in the community. The lack of intense grooming among apes would create more selection pressure to enlarge the brain to remember who is, and is not, a member of a regional population. And, it is this larger brain coupled with the preadaptation in the shift to visual dominance that allows great apes to possess the capacity for language, which is clearly a component of culture in the human measure. But the language that Dunbar talks about was not the spoken language of humans but, as we will argue, the language of emotions that evolved much earlier among hominins, millions of years before the hominin brain grew to a significant degree. Still, it is quite possible that once emotions allowed for increased group solidarity within communities, the growth of groups and regional communities would impose new selection pressures on a larger brain to remember who does and does not belong in a community and its subgroups. And, with a larger brain and eventually the capacity for more articulate sounds, something like spoken language could evolve, but we would argue that this occurred very late in hominin evolution. Nonetheless, there had to be preadaptations for this sudden jump in linguistic capacities to occur, and one of these preadaptations was the increasing size of the neocortex in *Homo habilis* (500 cc compared with 375 cc for chimpanzees and hominins like the famous *Australopithecine*, Lucy) and then 900 cc for *Homo erectus*. And as the brain grew and emotion-arousing rituals became the key to group solidarity, it is easy to see how these rituals could lead to cultural representations, especially with larger brains capable of using artificial symbols to construct shared meanings in the form of histories, myths, stories, and other cultural productions made possible by spoken language—all of which would increase group solidarity and, at the same time, allow for larger sociocultural formations.

Behavioral Propensities

Let us now move from preadaptations that could be subject to selection, if they enhanced fitness, to behavioral propensities evident in apes and, in many cases, in mammals more generally. Among apes, a number of behavioral propensities could, if subject to further selection, increase social bonding. In many ways, these behavioral propensities would seem adequate, by themselves, to make hominins more social and group oriented, but the fact that the subcortical areas of the brain were under such intense selection for enhanced emotions suggests that increasing emotions was essential to making these behavior propensities effective for sociality and group formation. What, then, are some of these propensities?

Reading of Face and Eyes

Apes are able to read gestures in the face and eyes of conspecifics (Osgood 1966; Menzel 1971; Stanford 1999; Mitani and Watts 2001; Turner and Maryanski 2008), and, in fact, they will follow gaze and eye movements to determine what another is observing and thinking (Hare, Call, and Tomasello 2001, 2006; Tomasello and Call 1997; Call and Tomasello 2008; Povinelli 2000; Povinelli and Eddy 1997; Itakura 1996; Baizer et al. 2007; Tomasello, Hare, and Fogleman 2001; Okamoto et al. 2002). Since humans do much the same when trying to determine the emotional states of others, this behavioral propensity was probably selected upon as emotional capacities increased during hominin evolution.

Imitation of Facial Gestures Revealing Emotions

The ability of both human and ape infants to imitate orofacial movements of caretakers indicates that they are programmed to learn gestures carrying meanings at a very early age (Emde 1969; Ekman 1984; Sherwood et al. 2004; Tomonaga 1999; Subiaul 2007; Horowitz 2003; Gergely and Csibra 2006). Among human infants, a newborn infant can mimic with facial gestures the four primary emotions emitted by caretakers within weeks of birth. Thus, human infants are programmed to read emotions *years before* they can read and emit vocal gestures, indicating that this developmental sequence probably reflects the evolutionary sequences in which the language of emotions evolved long before speech. This conclusion is supported by more recent discoveries of some of the genes regulating the body systems necessary for finely articulated speech among humans; it appears that these genes have been under selection for only about 200,000 years (Enard et al. 2002a, 2002b). These findings further suggest that a language built around emotions was probably the first language to evolve among hominins and, moreover, that spoken language was piggy-backed onto the more primal language of emotions (rather than the other way around, as is often assumed with body language being an adjunct to speech).

Capacities for Empathy and Role-Taking

The great apes evidence the capacity for empathy by reading the gestures of conspecifics to determine their emotional states and, then, to respond to them appropriately (de Waal 1996, 2009). Thus, the behavioral capacity for what George Herbert Mead (1934) termed "role-taking" is evident among the great apes and, hence, was part of the behavioral repertoire of humans' hominin ancestors (what Mead termed "role-taking" was conceptualized, seventy years later, as "theory of mind" by Premack and Woodruff [1978]). Moreover, this is rather deep role-taking in that hominins, like contemporary apes, possessed the capacity to determine the emotional states that drove the actions of others—or what Alfred Schutz ([1932] 1967) termed "because of" motives. Whether additional selection was needed to enhance this innate capacity is hard to know, but if such was the case, there was an existing ability on which to select and make humans even more empathetic and better role-takers.

Rhythmic Synchronization

The discovery of mirror neurons in monkeys and, later, apes and humans indicates that there is a neurological basis for empathy and, equally important, for the rhythmic synchronization of body and verbal sounds among apes and humans (Rizzolatti et al. 2002). Apes fall into a kind of rhythmic synchronization of bodies when interacting, and as theorists like Randall Collins (2004) have documented, so do humans. In fact, without this rhythmic synchronization, the emission of rituals and arousal of emotions are difficult. Indeed, greeting rituals are what kick-start the synchronization, and, together, rituals and synchronization increase the flow of positive emotions, not only for humans but for apes and, hence, humans' hominin ancestors.

Collective Emotional Effervescence

Field studies indicate that on those occasions when larger numbers of chimpanzees assemble in propinquity to each other, a kind of "carnival" occurs. Bodies fall into synchronization and emotions are aroused in rather uninhibited acts typical of human festivals, such as Mardi Gras. In reporting on Spencer and Gillen's ([1899] 1939) account of Australian aborigines, Émile Durkheim ([1912] 1965) emphasized this "collective effervescence" as the essence of social solidarity (and also as the origin of religion), leading individuals to represent with totems their sense of a power external to them and to the development of beliefs about their collective organization. Thus, the propensity to be emotionally aroused when interacting with others increases solidarity, and, perhaps, this capacity was selected upon to charge up positive emotions that could lead to social bonding and increased group solidarity among hominins and, with the evolution of spoken language, to symbolic representations of this solidarity and the use of rituals to charge up emotions to reaffirm group solidarity.

Reciprocity

Higher primates, including monkeys, possess a sense of reciprocity (Cosmides 1989; de Waal 1989, 1991, 1996; de Waal and Brosnan 2006), as do higher mammals in general (as anyone who has a cat can document when a dead animal is dumped at the door in exchange, presumably, for being fed a daily diet by caretakers). Exchange reciprocity is one of the essential properties of strong social bonds in groups. One form of exchange critical to sustaining longer-term social relations is reciprocal exchange, where resources given at one point in time will, at a later point in time, be reciprocated—thereby strengthening social bonds over time between givers and receivers of resources.

Calculations of Justice

Primates calculate justice and perceived fairness in exchange relations. For example, a capuchin monkey will stop exchanging with a caretaker if another capuchin is seen as getting more rewards for emitting specific behaviors (Brosnan, Schiff, and de Waal 2005; Brosnan and de Waal 2003). Such calculations involve a comparison of the reward payoffs of others and their respective behaviors to get these rewards, which can be seen not only as a behavioral capacity giving exchanges a moral character but also as a precursor to morality itself. A recent study of chimpanzees indicates a step toward a nonverbal sense of morality when a chimpanzee stopped exchanging with a caretaker because a relative was not receiving the same reward as the chimp who stopped exchanging because the caretaker was not being "fair" (Brosnan and de Waal 2003).

Seeing Self as Object

Apes, along with other highly intelligent mammals (Gallup 1970, 1979, 1982) such as dolphins and African elephants, can recognize themselves in a mirror. This neurological capacity suggests that they can see "themselves as objects," to use G. H. Mead's (1934) phrase, "in their environments"; and from this capacity it is a short step to have a sense of identity and evaluate this identity from the perspective of others and, if culture exists, from cultural standards or what Mead termed "the generalized other." Moreover, as Cooley (1902) emphasized in his notion of "the looking glass self," humans experience emotions about themselves in such evaluations of self; and with the enhancement of hominins' emotional capacities, more robust and nuanced views of self could evolve. And the more emotions are tied to self, the more approval and validation of self by others would increase the power of these others and organized groups of individuals and, thereby, operate as a force of group formation with individuals' sense of self dependent on the approval of group members.

Weaker Hierarchies

Monkeys tend to form linear hierarchies of dominance among males, and sometimes among females in matrilines. Such hierarchies impose a limit on the kinds of social structures that can exist in monkey societies. In contrast, apes vary considerably on the strength and linearity of their hierarchies. Gibbons and siamangs, who are distant from the human line and, hence, not great apes, reveal equality between males and females; orangutans do not seem to possess hierarchies, because they are virtually solitary and do not need them; gorillas form hierarchies around lead silverbacks who try to control their foraging groups, with varying degrees of success; and chimpanzees do, at times, compete for dominance and form somewhat loose hierarchies, especially if they find themselves forced to remain in proximity. Yet, hunter-gatherers had very powerful norms of equality, and indeed, early humans appeared to work very hard to avoid letting others dominate over them (Boehm 1993), probably because they realized that dominance created tension and conflict that were dysfunctional for the solidarity of the band. Still, there is some behavioral propensity among humans' closest primate relative to recognize status differences and status hierarchies, and so this weaker propensity for hierarchy was probably evident in the last common ancestor to extant chimpanzees and humans' hominin ancestors. All mammals recognize differences in age and sex categories, and they often recognize differences in conspecifics from other packs, groups, herds, or pods. And so it should not be surprising that hominins probably recognized all of these differences, plus status differences over who was more powerful. But the hierarchies among chimpanzees and probably the last common ancestor were more relaxed and not so linear compared with those among monkeys, where most males were (and still are) rank-ordered; and in fact, hierarchies do not always form or, if they do, they often dissipate. This weaker sense of status is perhaps an important preadaptation because it kept hominins from trying to get better organized *only* through hierarchy, which is built from negative rather than positive emotions and, thus, must be accompanied by strong bioprogrammers for group organization in the face of negative emotions aroused by hierarchy. But it did something else: it made hominins aware of status differences in general and forced them to adjust their respective lines of conduct in terms of relative status—something that humans do constantly (Berger and Zelditch 1985). Thus, role-taking was not just about understanding internal states; it could also be adapted for understanding status in a process of status-taking of not only differences by age and sex but also those status distinctions built around power and perhaps abilities at various tasks. But unlike propensities to create linear dominance hierarchies, those among hominins were looser, perhaps only temporary when group coordination was most needed, and given promiscuity and the lack of the harem system so evident among monkeys, hierarchy did not dominate early forms of group formation among hominins and, later, bands of hunter-gatherers. In fact, it was kept at bay among hunter-gatherers because of its disruptive effects on more individualistic apelike hominins. By being so, any propensities for dominance did not undo what selection was working on in expanding the emotional palette of hominins for forging emotional bonds, as is explored below.

These nine behavioral propensities would seem, at first blush, to be sufficient for increasing social bonds and group solidarity, if subject to selection. But comparative neuroanatomy suggests that they were not, because, otherwise, natural selection would not have so dramatically rewired subcortical areas of the brain and the connections between neocortical areas, especially the prefrontal cortex, and these subcortical areas. Clearly, something more was needed. We will argue that it was a larger, more nuanced palette of emotions that could charge up preadaptations and existing behavioral propensities to make hominins more social and group oriented.

COMPARATIVE NEUROANATOMY

EXPANDING THE EMOTIONAL PALETTE

Since behaviors are, ultimately, driven by the brain, changes in the brain signal alterations in behavioral propensities. If we compare great-ape brains with those of humans, there are two significant differences: (1) the larger size of neocortical and subcortical areas of the human brain and (2) the greater connectivity within neocortical and subcortical areas, as well as between these two basic areas of the brain. The neocortex gets most of the press in sociological accounts of the brain because it is presumed that culture and language are made possible by the larger neocortex, which in humans is three times the average size of the neocortex of great apes, controlling for body size. More significantly, the subcortical areas of the human brain are, on average, twice the size of their counterparts in the great-ape brain.

Table 29.2 compares measurements of key subcortical areas of the brain, along with the gross overall size of the human neocortex relative to that in great apes. The numbers in the text indicate how much greater than the size of a small rodent-like mammal, *Tenrecinae*, various brains structures are for great apes and humans, using 1 as a base for *Tenrecinae*. The measurements of the subcortical structures listed in Table 29.2 were not selected to document increases in human emotions, and so they do not constitute a direct test of our hypothesis. Still, many of the structures measured are important for emotions. For example, the amygdala is the ancient area for fear and anger inherited from reptiles; the hippocampus stores unconscious emotional memories and is responsible for memory formation in general through tagging of cognitions with emotions; the thalamus transfers inputs from sensory modalities to the relevant lobe in the neocortex *and* to subcortical emotion centers; the pituitary gland generates hormones and neuroactive peptides that have large effects on emotional arousal; and the diencephalon in general is where various neurotransmitters are activated and where reuptake of key emotion-generating neurotransmitters is regulated. So, even though the data in Table 29.2 were not collected for our purposes, these measurements are a good proxy for recording the work of natural selection to enhance human emotionality.

It can be hypothesized that the enlargement of subcortical areas of the brain occurred relatively early, if enhancing emotions would promote fitness of hominins that increasingly had to survive in open-country savanna conditions, where group organization would be

Table 29.2 Relative size of brain components of apes and humans, compared with *Tenrecinae*

Brain component	Apes (Pongids)	Humans (Homo)
Neocortex	61.88	196.41
Diencephalon	8.57	14.76
Thalamus		
Hypothalamus		
Amygdala	1.85	4.48
Centromedial	1.06	2.52
Basolateral	2.45	6.02
Septum	2.16	5.48
Hippocampus	2.99	4.87
Transition cortices	2.38	4.43

Sources: Data from Stephan (1983); Stephan and Andy (1969, 1977); Stephan, Baron, and Frahm (1988); Stephan, Frahm, and Baron (1981); and Eccles (1989).

Note: Numbers represent how many times larger than *Tenrecinae* each area of the brain is, with *Tenrecinae* representing a base of 1.

essential. One of the great liabilities of apes on the savanna is that they are highly emotional—especially chimpanzees, compared with gorillas and orangutans. Moreover, they lack control of emotions, and a loud primate on the savanna is soon a dead one. Thus, natural selection may initially have increased the neuronets between the prefrontal cortex, where thought and decision making occur, and subcortical emotion centers of the brain, giving hominins greater power to control loud emotional outbursts.

With the increased neocortical control, the next step was to expand the varieties of primary emotions. Apes already evidence variations on primary emotions, and so adding more variations would not be a dramatic step requiring mutations, which would almost always be harmful to the brain (Fisher 1930). Rather, directional selection on the tails of bell curves describing the distribution of brain structures in terms of size and varieties of emotions made possible could move the genome of hominins rather rapidly, creating the palette of primary emotions delineated in Table 29.3.

If increased emotionality promoted fitness by increasing the strength and variety of emotional connections among hominins, then selection would keep going to expand the emotional repertoire of hominins. The easiest route to this expansion after increasing varieties of low, medium, and intense primary emotions outlined in Table 29.3 would be to combine primary emotions, much as primary colors can be combined to form a very large variety of colors and shades of colors (Plutchik 1980). In Table 29.4, we outline one possible process whereby a greater amount of one primary emotion is mixed, in some unknown neurological way, with a lesser amount of another primary emotion. As can be seen, the palette of emotions is dramatically expanded. This strategy of combining primary emotions also mitigates against a problem with using emotions to forge social bonds and solidarity: three of the four primary emotions are negative and, hence, would not promote social bonding. By combining emotions, some of the negativity of *fear, anger,* and *sadness* can be mitigated and, indeed, can promote more nuanced emotional states that are less disruptive to social bonds. Of course, some very negative and volatile emotions are also produced, emotions such as *vengeance*, which is a mix of anger and happiness at bringing harm to enemies.

The last phase of emotional evolution was, we believe, combining the three negative emotions to produce the two most important emotions of social control: *shame* and *guilt*. Table 29.5 outlines the hypothesized relationship among the three primary negative emotions in producing these important emotions, which, it should be added, chimpanzees do not feel (Boehm 2012). Shame and guilt may be unique to humans, and if so, there must have been intense selection pressures on subcortical areas of the brain, coupled with expansion of the neocortex, to wire the brain to produce these moral emotions. *Shame* is the feeling that one has not met the expectations of others, and it makes people feel small and attacks persons' sense of self. *Guilt* is the feeling that one has violated moral codes. Both emotions are mostly sadness, coupled with varying amounts of anger and fear. Shame is mostly sadness, with a lesser amount of anger and still less of fear; guilt reverses the order of anger and fear. Animals that can experience shame and guilt are motivated to avoid feeling these very painful emotions; thus, individuals engage in self-control to meet expectations and abide by evolving moral codes. With more self-control, negative sanctioning by others—and the inevitable disruption of social bonds produced by such negative sanctioning—is reduced, thereby making social solidarity more likely.

However, because shame and guilt are so painful, another route to avoiding their full impact is to repress them. And, since there are more neuronets between the neocortex and subcortical areas of the brain, this pushing of negative emotions from consciousness (probably into the hippocampus, where emotional memories are stored, and to which

Table 29.3 Variants of primary emotions

Primary emotion	Low intensity	Moderate intensity	High intensity
Satisfaction-Happiness	Content Sanguine Serenity Gratified	Cheerful Buoyant Friendly Amiable Enjoyment	Joy Bliss Rapture Jubilant Gaiety Elation Delight Thrilled Exhilarated
Aversion-Fear	Concern Hesitant Reluctance Shyness	Misgivings Trepidation Anxiety Scared Alarmed Unnerved Panic	Terror Horror High anxiety
Assertion-Anger	Annoyed Agitated Irritated Vexed Perturbed Nettled Rankled Piqued	Displeased Frustrated Belligerent Contentious Hostility Ire Animosity Offended Consternation	Dislike Loathing Disgust Despise Detest Hatred Seething Wrath Furious Inflamed Incensed Outrage
Disappointment-Sadness	Discouraged Downcast Dispirited	Dismayed Disheartened Glum Resigned Gloomy Woeful Pained Dejected	Sorrow Heartsick Despondent Anguished Crestfallen

Sources: Data from Turner (1999a, 1999b).

the neocortex does not have direct access) allows persons to avoid the full brunt of pain. Yet, repressed emotions tend to increase in intensity and to transmute into one of their constituent emotions (Turner 2007). In the case of shame, the second most active emotional state, *anger*, is likely to emerge and be felt and expressed. Indeed, shamed persons often carry *diffuse anger*, which is hardly conducive to social bonds. Similarly, the second emotion in guilt—*fear*—emerges as *diffuse anxiety* among persons who are chronically experiencing and then repressing guilt. Diffuse anxiety is also hardly conducive to forming and sustaining social bonds. Thus, there is an emotional dark side to shame and guilt when they are repressed, although it is likely that repression becomes more widespread

Table 29.4 Combinations of primary emotions

Primary emotion		First-order elaborations
Satisfaction-Happiness		
Satisfaction-happiness + aversion-fear	generate	Wonder, hope, relief, gratitude, pride, reverence
Satisfaction-happiness + assertion-anger	generate	Vengeance, appeased, calmed, soothed, relish, triumphant, bemused
Satisfaction-happiness + disappointment-sadness	generate	Nostalgia, yearning, hope
Aversion-Fear		
Aversion-fear + satisfaction-happiness	generate	Condescension, mollified, rudeness, placated, righteousness
Aversion-fear + assertion-anger	generate	Abhorrence, jealousy, suspiciousness
Aversion-fear + disappointment-sadness	generate	Bitterness, depression, betrayed
Assertion-Anger		
Assertion-anger + satisfaction-happiness	generate	Abhorrence, jealousy, suspiciousness
Assertion-anger + aversion-fear	generate	Bitterness, depression
Assertion-anger + disappointment-sadness	generate	Betrayed
Disappointment-Sadness		
Disappointment-sadness + satisfaction-happiness	generate	Acceptance, moroseness, solace, melancholy
Disappointment-sadness + aversion-fear	generate	Regret, forlornness, remorse, misery
Disappointment-sadness + assertion-anger	generate	Aggrieved, discontent, dissatisfied, unfulfilled, boredom, grief, envy, sullenness

Table 29.5 The structure of shame and guilt

Emotion	Rank-ordering of constituent primary emotions		
	1	2	3
Shame	Disappointment-Sadness (at self)	Assertion-Anger (at self)	Aversion-Fear (at consequences for self)
Guilt	Disappointment-Sadness (at self)	Aversion-Fear (at consequences for self)	Assertion-Anger (at self)

as the scale and complexity of societies increase; and so, in the evolution of hominins in simple human hunter-gatherer bands, repression may have been far less common and thus not as disruptive to the solidarity of the band as it is today, where repression can be chronic among large numbers of individuals in multiple groups within complex societies.

EMOTIONS AND SOCIAL SOLIDARITY

If we consider what is necessary for social bonds and group solidarity today among humans, we can get a better sense of how natural selection was working. For interactions to proceed smoothly, individuals must open the interaction with ritual greetings and then move into talk that becomes rhythmically synchronized with bodies and turn taking in conversations; with rhythmic synchronization, positive emotions are aroused and begin to flow among those interacting. As these emotions increase, it is likely that the interaction will be iterated and with each iteration individuals will begin to develop particularistic culture—memories of past interactions and events unique to the interacting parties. If this particularistic culture becomes valued, individuals will symbolize it in some way—words, phrases, dress, or even totems or emblems—and they will engage in ritual affirmations of these symbols, thereby ramping up the solidarity. During this flow of what Collins (2004) terms *interaction rituals*, other key processes are occurring, including (1) role-taking and other processes revolving around reading gestures to understand each other's internal emotional state and disposition for action, (2) the exchange of resources in accordance with standards of justice and fairness, (3) mutual verification of identities presented by individuals, (4) achieving a sense of mutual trust and inclusion in ongoing activities, (5) developing a sense for the relevant norms and other cultural codes, and (6) making and understanding each other's role and relative status position (Turner 2002, 2010).

Emotions are at the center of all these processes. Without the arousal of emotions, interactions will stall. Thus, it is clear that for interpersonal processes to achieve some degree of collective solidarity, emotions must be aroused through initial rituals and then successively through synchronization of talk and body language, through symbolization and ritual acts toward these symbols, through role-taking, through exchanges that are reciprocal and fair, through mutual verifications of individuals' sense of self and the identities presented during the course of the interaction, through understanding of respective status locations and roles, and so on. All of the things that sociologists consider unique to humans cannot have any power to forge bonds of solidarity without the arousal of positive emotions and perhaps also the sense of threat that comes from experiencing potential shame and guilt.

It is not so far to argue that everything that humans do when interacting and developing commitments to groups is driven by emotions. And so, it was for this reason that without emotions, the preadaptations and behavioral propensities listed earlier were, by themselves, not enough to achieve the group solidarity necessary for survival on the savanna. Even the capacity for empathy, where emotions can be mutually read and interpreted, cannot, alone, generate the necessary solidarity. There must be arousal of emotions and symbolizing of the group as a whole, as happens when chimpanzees engage in carnival or aboriginals experience what Durkheim termed "emotional effervescence" that is then symbolized as an external power emanating from the supernatural.

EMOTIONS AND LANGUAGE

Social scientists often have a view of spoken language as what makes cultural codes moral, but in fact, a sense of morality or of what is right and proper can exist outside spoken language. Primates already have a sense of justice and fairness built into their calculations of resource distributions, and they experience negative emotions when resources are not fairly distributed. None of this sense of justice is spoken, but rather it is felt. Once animals can experience emotions when expectations are not realized, when others do not behave as they should, when rituals are not honored, when reciprocal activities (as quasi roles) are not pursued, and when status differences are not honored, they experience negative emotions and are prepared to sanction others. Culture that controls individuals is built on the already-present capacity among higher mammals, but it needs some extra emotional force.

Yet, Turner (2000) has argued that this emotional force is not just arousal of emotions but also the development of a proto-language, which humans today use when trying to determine each other's emotional state. If we observe any strip of interaction, there is more than just talk; there is also what is often termed "body language," and the latter is indeed a language. It has phonemes, morphemes, and syntax. Studies of emotions often use still pictures to capture emotional states (e.g., Ekman 1984), but this practice distorts the real nature of emotions as flows of emotional phonemes and morphemes, organized by a grammar or syntax. Use of video sequences of interaction, with the sound turned off, can be easily read and interpreted by most persons in a culture. Indeed, watching a foreign movie without subtitles or a domestic movie with the sound turned off is not particularly difficult, because once staging cues about context are understood, it is relatively easy to read the actors' emotions as they unfold over time, and, thereby, follow the plot line of the movie. Social scientists often see this emotional language as a supplement to the vocal tract, but in an evolutionary sense, the production of emotional sentences carrying mutual meanings is the more primary form of language. Indeed, it evolved millions of years before the vocal track of late hominins or humans was transformed to make finely articulated speech possible (Enard et al. 2002a, 2002b).

Spoken language was piggy-backed onto this language of emotions, and it still is the sidekick, not the main player, any time that humans seek to form bonds and create a sense of solidarity. If words are used, they are used to arouse emotions because it is emotions that drive interaction. Words and voice inflections can carry emotions, and we suspect that the language of emotions involved voice inflections without finely articulate speech among hominins because, as noted earlier, the genes regulating many of the lips, tongue, facial muscles, and other body requirements for finely articulated human speech have been under selection for only about 200,000 years—the time frame for the emergence of *Homo sapiens*. Thus, before speech as we know it, hominins survived by the constant expansion of the language of emotions, which is what humans learn first when they are born and which is still the most important language system for forging social bonds.

If culture were only language and articulation of rules, it would be like a dry instruction manual—guidance with no compelling power. For culture to have the power to regulate, it must be tagged with emotions and have emotional impacts on individuals. And so, culture as a product of spoken language perhaps had to wait until the language of emotions was sufficiently developed to provide the emotional energy behind spoken words, organized into complex symbol systems. With a larger palette of nuanced emotional states and wider varieties of emotions to put together into meanings, the inherent complexity of spoken language systems could evolve with an equally complex and nuanced system of emotional tags. Imagine, for example, Shakespeare without the nuanced but fundamental emotional states created by the syntax of emotions that accompanies the words of his plays. Indeed, more than anything else, the words in Shakespeare's plays are designed to activate and highlight the language of emotions.

And so, the preadaptation for language was used, we argue, rather early in hominin evolution. Once a true language began to evolve, it pushed for further selection on hominins' emotional repertoire, culminating in the development of the emotions of social control: shame and guilt. With more emotional valences available, more phonemes and morphemes would be produced, and the syntax stringing these together into systems of meaning could become more complex as role-taking skills increased and, eventually, as spoken language was piggy-backed onto the grammar of emotions. From this perspective, then, emotions are more important than culture in the evolution of humans because they were the key to the survival of humans' hominin ancestors and, moreover, were the force that activated and intensified all other preadaptations and behavioral propensities of the last common ancestor of the hominin line with the lines of the great apes. From this emotional intensification came the complex interpersonal processes that typify all interactions among humans and that are the basis for group solidarity. Finally, spoken language and culture built from meanings contained in texts of arbitrary symbols could only occur on an already extant base of interpersonal mechanisms evident in preadaptations and existing behavioral propensities of apes driven by the language of emotions (Duchin 1990).

Some Further Implications

What if monkeys rather than apes were humans' more immediate cousins, and what if one of the ancestors of present-day monkeys was our last common ancestor to the hominins that became human? It would be necessary, of course, to change the name of the movie franchise extolling our world to be a planet of apes, but more fundamentally humans as we know them would not exist, because monkeys do not have major problems adapting to the African savanna or to other rather extreme habitats, like snow-covered mountain ranges. Humans would, therefore, not be smart enough to make a movie or to communicate with complex symbols. Monkeys are organized by dominance hierarchies and matrilines, and as a result, they do not need greater intelligence, expanded emotions, complicated interpersonal mechanisms, language, or culture to get organized; they are *already organized* in ways that allowed for easy adaptation to the savanna. Natural selection would have left monkeys alone because they were well adapted, and, thus, a smarter monkey capable of action in human terms would not have ever evolved—perhaps for the benefit of other species, including our fellow ape cousins.

Another implication is pursued by Richard Machalek (1992), where he analyzes what it takes to create macro societies. If humans' ancestors were monkeys, we would be monkeys; and we would never have thought of making a movie like *Planet of the Apes*. Monkeys are oriented to the group, not the regional population or any macro-level formation, and certainly not the whole globe. They live their lives out in troops, with females never leaving their troop, and with males coming into a troop from their natal troop to join in the competition for dominance. Monkeys could never create a macro society of even thousands of individuals, to say nothing of millions or billions of people. Rather, they would have produced a world of group-oriented primates.

In contrast, the only stable unit of organization among the great apes is the regional community, which for chimpanzees can be as large as ten square miles. Groups are not permanent, but chimpanzees will defend this larger community formation from incursion by males from other communities, killing them if necessary. Only a weak-tie, individualistic, mobile, and less group-oriented primate could create a macro society because such societies are built around weak ties among strangers who occupy status positions and play roles. True, most of the evolutionary pressure on hominins was to get group oriented, but even with all of this pressure, human groups are very different from monkey groups, on several scores. First, they are not created or sustained by bioprogrammers. They are constructed from interactions that arouse emotions of bonding and commitment, and they *must be constantly nurtured* to be sustained. Second, groups are not wholly inclusive of individuals; they often break up among hunter-gatherers, and as societies become large, individuals begin to have multiple group affiliations eventually culminating in the complexes of group affiliations so ably described by Georg Simmel ([1900] 1955) in the early twentieth century. Indeed, as we have argued (Maryanski and Turner 1992; Turner and Maryanski 2008), modern capitalist societies are far more attuned to our "ape nature" than are the horticultural, pastoral, and agrarian societies that followed hunting and gathering. Modern societies allow for individualism, choice, and mobility; societies following hunting and gathering caged people in systems of kinship and political power. The result, we hypothesized, is that there was always a subtle selection pressure emanating from humans' ape ancestry to escape these cages of horticulture and agrarianism. Over time, these pressures led individuals to invent societies where individuals have more freedom to choose group affiliations, and to drop them if they so choose. A monkey could not do this, but for an ape, this would be a natural behavior.

A macro society among such a large animal as a human is a remarkable achievement. No other large animal has been able to construct such a society—only insects and, we suppose, microorganisms like bacteria, if their swarms can be considered a society. Why should this be so? Part of the answer elaborated upon by Machalek and Martin in Chapter 1 of this volume is that most animals are oriented to kinship and the group, whereas kinship for humans is a tenuous construction (given the promiscuity among apes and, no doubt, early hominins), and groups are also constructions that must be nurtured. Moreover, one cannot build a macro society without connecting groups into larger social formations like complex organizations and then linking organizations together to form institutional domains like economy, polity, law, education, and so on. Humans use power, markets and interdependencies, and culture to integrate groups into organizations, organizations into communities, organizations into institutions, and institutions into societies and intersocietal systems. An evolved ape that looked beyond the group is the only animal that could build up groups into such colossal formations as societies and intersocietal systems composed of millions and billions of big-bodied animals. Moreover, only an individualistic and mobile evolved ape could move about many groups in many organizations on a regular basis and interact, much of the time, with strangers occupying status locations in social structures and playing roles in terms of cultural norms.

For the viability of the planet it may not have been a good thing that we created a planet of 6.8 billion apes and growing, organized into industrial production fueled by market demands and profit motives, but it was only possible because we are *not* evolved monkeys, at least in any immediate sense. Apes separated from monkeys over 20 million years ago when monkeys got the upper hand; a planet overfilled with evolved apes indicates that humans are now more successful, at least for the present, but at a cost to all other primates and, indeed, life forms on earth. Thus, even if we bring evolutionary sociology to the present, we can understand much more about the social universe as it unfolds today by pursuing the strategy that we propose for one branch of evolutionary sociology that can be used by the other social sciences and biology.

Conclusion

One of the unfortunate failings of social science in the twentieth century was the abandonment of evolutionary thinking in the early decades of that century. There were, of course, good reasons for rejecting eugenics and social Darwinism, but as with so much in the intellectual world, the baby was thrown out with the bathwater. It took the emergence of sociobiology (e.g., Wilson 1975, 1978) and, later, evolutionary psychology (e.g., Barkow, Cosmides, and Tooby 1992; Chapters 7–9 in this volume), with all of their flaws of overgeneralization and reductionism, to bring Darwinian theory back into the social sciences from entomology and other biological origins. Stage models of societal evolution also helped bring the idea of evolution—this time of superorganisms, as Herbert Spencer ([1874–1896] 1898) called them—back into sociology and, to a lesser extent, anthropology and political science. With the growing sense of threat from sociobiology as inadequate to explain the complexity of the social world and, then, the emergence of evolutionary sociology in the 1990s, sociologists began to develop their own forms of Darwinian analysis to correct for what were seen as serious flaws in both sociobiology and evolutionary psychology. This revival of evolutionary thinking has gone in many directions, from agent-based modeling to new fields like neurosociology (Franks 2010; Franks and Turner 2013)—all of which fall under the general rubric of evolutionary sociology. For, not all evolutionary sociology is wholly Darwinian, and even those who use portions of biological theory and Darwinian concepts remain skeptical that a simple borrowing of ideas from biology will be adequate to explain the complex dynamics of human sociocultural formations (see Chapter 10 in this volume).

In this chapter, we have outlined one approach to exploring issues that are of interest to sociobiology and evolutionary psychology without making what we see as unwarranted assumptions about maximization of fitness and creation of new modules in the brain. We employ basic ideas from biology and bioecology but adopt them to the vision of sociologists. For us, the big problem was getting weak-tie apelike hominins more organized at the group level so that they could survive the rigors of the African savanna. Groups are not natural social units for apes, and thus, for the first human societies to be organized around two groups—nuclear kinship units and bands—was the outcome of intense selection pressures, working on existing preadaptations and behavioral propensities. Such an analysis not only tells us the nature of humans, as evolved apes; it also informs contemporary analyses of behavior and interaction as they create, sustain, or change sociocultural formations. Sociology has been guilty of viewing too much of social reality as constructed by culture, perhaps as the legacy of the rejection of evolutionary ideas at the beginning of the last century. Sociology can no longer afford to make this mistake because other fields and disciplines have made incursions into sociology, without really having very much knowledge about how societies operate. It is far better for sociologists themselves to explore the interface between biology and evolution of this biology, on the one side, as it affects and is affected by the complex sociocultural formations of human societies. And so, by whatever name we want to give it, evolutionary sociology must grow as a field if the challenge and the mistakes of other disciplines' efforts to enter sociology are to be met head-on.

References

Baizer, J. S., J. F. Baker, K. Haas, and R. Lima. 2007. "Neurochemical Organization of the Nucleus *Paramedinaus Dorsalis* in the Human." *Brain Research* 1176: 45–52.

Barkow, J. H., L. Cosmides, and J. Tooby, eds. 1992. *The Adapted Mind: Evolutionary Psychology and the Generation of Culture*. New York: Oxford University Press.

Bekoff, M., and J. Pierce. 2009. *Wild Justice: The Moral Lives of Animals*. Chicago: University of Chicago Press.

Bellah, R. 2011. *Religion in Human Evolution: From the Paleolithic to the Axial Age*. Cambridge, MA: Harvard University Press.

Berger, J., and M. Zelditch Jr. 1985. *Status, Rewards, and Influence*. San Francisco: Jossey-Bass.
Bickerton, D. 2003. "Symbol and Structure: A Comprehensive Framework for Language Evolution." In *Language Evolution: The States of the Art*, edited by M. S. Christiansen and S. Kirby, 77–93. Oxford: Oxford University Press.
Boehm, C. 1993. "Egalitarian Society and Reverse Dominance Hierarchy." *Current Anthropology* 34: 227–254.
———. 2012. *Moral Origins: The Evolution of Virtue, Altruism, and Shame*. New York: Basic Books.
Brosnan, S. F., and F.B.M. de Waal. 2003. "Fair Refusal by Capuchin Monkeys." *Nature* 128: 40.
Brosnan, S. F., H. C. Schiff, and F.B.M. de Waal. 2005. "Tolerance for Inequity May Increase with Social Closeness in Chimpanzees." *Proceedings of the Royal Society of London* 272: 253–258.
Burghardt, G. 2005. *The Genesis of Animal Play: Testing the Limits*. Cambridge, MA: MIT Press.
Call, J., and M. Tomasello. 2008. "Do Chimpanzees Have a Theory of Mind: 30 Years Later." *Trends in Cognitive Science* 12: 187–192.
Collins, R. 2004. *Interaction Ritual Chains*. Princeton, NJ: Princeton University Press.
Cooley, C. H. 1902. *Human Nature and the Social Order*. New York: Scribners.
Cosmides, L. 1989. "The Logic of Social Exchange: Has Natural Selection Shaped How Humans Reason?" *Cognition* 31: 187–276.
Cosmides, L., and J. Tooby. 1992. "Cognitive Adaptations for Social Exchange." In *The Adapted Mind: Evolutionary Psychology and the Generation of Culture*, edited by J. H. Barkow, L. Cosmides, and J. Tooby. New York: Oxford University Press.
de Waal, F.B.M. 1989. "Food Sharing and Reciprocal Obligations among Chimpanzees." *Journal of Human Evolution* 18: 433–459.
———. 1991. "The Chimpanzee's Sense of Social Regularity and Its Relation to the Human Sense of Justice." *American Behavioral Scientist* 34: 335–349.
———. 1996. *Good Natured: The Origins of Right and Wrong in Humans and Other Animals*. Cambridge, MA: Harvard University Press.
———. 2009. *The Age of Empathy: Nature's Lessons for a Kinder Society*. New York: Three Rivers Press.
de Waal, F.B.M., and S. F. Brosnan. 2006. "Simple and Complex Reciprocity in Primates." In *Cooperation in Primates and Humans: Mechanisms and Evolution*, edited by P. Kappeler and C. P. van Schaik, 85–106. Berlin: Springer-Verlag.
Donald, M. 1991. *Origins of the Modern Mind: Three Stages in the Evolution of Culture and Cognition*. Cambridge, MA: Harvard University Press.
———. 2001. *A Mind So Rare: The Evolution of Human Consciousness*. New York: Norton.
Duchin, L. 1990. "The Evolution of Articulate Speech: Comparative Anatomy of the Oral Cavity in Pan and Homo." *Journal of Human Evolution* 19: 687–697.
Dunbar, R. 1996. *Grooming, Gossip and the Evolution of Language*. London: Faber and Faber.
Durkheim, É. (1912) 1965. *The Elementary Forms of the Religious Life*. New York: Macmillan.
Eccles, J. C. 1989. *Evolution of the Brain: Creation of Self*. London: Routledge.
Eibl-Eibesfeldt, I. (1971) 1996. *Love and Hate: The Natural History of Behavior Patterns*. New York: Aldine.
Ekman, P. 1984. "Expression and the Nature of Emotion." In *Approaches to Emotion*, edited by K. Scherer and P. Edman, 319–343. Hillsdale, NJ: Lawrence Erlbaum.
Emde, R. N. 1969. "Level of Meaning for Infant Emotions: A Biosocial View." In *Development of Cognition, Affect and Social Relations*, edited by W. A. Collins, 1–37. Hillsdale, NJ: Lawrence Erlbaum.
Enard, W. M. 1978. "Myths about Hunter-Gatherers." *Ethnology* 17: 439–448.
Enard, W. M., et al. 2002a. "Intra- and Interspecific Variation in Primate Gene Expression Patterns." *Science* 296: 340–342.
Enard, W. M., et al. 2002b. "Molecular Evolution of TOXP2, A Gene Involved in Speech and Language." *Nature* 418: 869–872.
Ettlinger, G. 1977. "Cross-Modal Equivalence in Non-human Primates." In *Behavioral Primatology*, Vol. 1, edited by A. M. Schriver. Hillsdale, NJ: Erlbaum.
Fisher, R. A. 1930. *The Genetical Theory of Natural Selection*. Oxford: Clarendon.
Franks, D. D. 2010. *Neurosociology: The Nexus between Neuroscience and Social Psychology*. New York: Springer.
Franks, D. D., and J. H. Turner, eds. 2013. *Handbook of Neurosociology*. New York: Springer.
Gallup, G. G., Jr. 1970. "Chimpanzees: Self-Recognition." *Science* 167: 88–87.
———. 1979. *Self-Recognition in Chimpanzees and Man: A Developmental and Comparative Perspective*. New York: Plenum Press.
———. 1982. "Self-Awareness and the Emergence of Mind in Primates." *American Journal of Primatology* 2: 237–248.
Gergely, G., and G. Csibra. 2006. "Sylvia's Recipe: The Role of Imitation and Pedagogy." In *The Transmission of Cultural Knowledge*, edited by N. J. Enfield and S. C. Levinson, 229–255. Oxford: Berg Press.

Geschwind, N. 1965a. "Disconnection Syndromes in Animals and Man, Part I." *Brain* 88: 237–294.
———. 1965b. "Disconnection Syndromes in Animals and Man, Part II." *Brain* 88: 585–644.
———. 1985. "Implications for Evolution, Genetics, and Clinical Syndromes." In *Cerebral Lateralization in Nonhuman Species*, edited by S. Glick. New York: Academic.
Geschwind, N., and A. Damasio. 1984. "The Neural Basis of Language." *Annual Review of Neuroscience* 7: 127–147.
Hare, B., J. Call, and M. Tomasello. 2001. "Do Chimpanzees Know What Conspecifics Know?" *Animal Behavior* 61: 139–159.
———. 2006. "Chimpanzees Deceive a Human Competitor by Hiding." *Cognition* 101: 495–514.
Horowitz, A. C. 2003. "Do Humans Ape? Or Do Apes Human? Imitation and Intention in Humans (*Homo sapiens*) and Other Animals." *Journal of Comparative Psychology* 117: 325–336.
Huizinga, J. (1949) 1955. *Homo Ludens: A Study of the Play-Element in Culture*. Boston: Beacon Press.
Itakura, S. 1996. "An Exploratory Study of Gaze-Monitoring in Non-human Primates." *Japanese Psychological Research* 38: 174–180.
Jarvis, M. J., and G. Ettlinger. 1977. "Cross-Modal Recognition in Chimpanzees and Monkeys." *Neuropsychologia* 15: 499–506.
Machalek, R. 1992. "Why Are Large Societies So Rare?" *Advances in Human Ecology* 1: 33–64.
Maryanski, A. 1986. "African Ape Social Structure: A Comparative Analysis." PhD diss., University of California.
———. 1987. "African Ape Social Structure: Is There Strength in Weak Ties?" *Social Networks* 9: 191–215.
———. 1992. "The Last Ancestor: An Ecological-Network Model on the Origins of Human Sociality." *Advances in Human Ecology* 2: 1–32.
———. 1993. "The Elementary Forms of the First Proto-human Society: An Ecological/Social Network Approach." *Advances in Human Evolution* 2: 215–241.
———. 1996. "African Ape Social Networks: A Blueprint for Reconstructing Early Hominid Social Structure." In *Archaeology of Human Ancestry*, edited by J. Steele and S. Shennan, 229–255. London: Routledge.
———. 1997. "The Origin of Speech and Its Implications for the Optimal Size of Human Groups." *Critical Review* 11(2): 233–249.
Maryanski, A., and J. H. Turner. 1992. *The Social Cage: Human Nature and the Evolution of Society*. Stanford, CA: Stanford University Press.
Mead, G. H. 1934. *Mind, Self, and Society*. Chicago: University of Chicago Press.
Menzel, E. W. 1971. "Communication about the Environment in a Group of Young Chimpanzees." *Folia Primatologica* 15: 220–232.
Mitani, J., and D. Watts. 2001. "Why Do Chimpanzees Hunt and Share Meat?" *Animal Behavior* 61: 1–69.
Okamoto, S., M. Tomonaga, K. Ishii, N. Kawai, M. Tanaka, and T. Matsuzawa. 2002. "An Infant Chimpanzee (*Pan troglodytes*) Follows Human Gaze." *Animal Cognition* 5: 107–114.
Osgood, C. E. 1966. "Dimensionality of the Semantic Space for Communication via Facial Expressions." *Scandinavian Journal of Psychology* 7: 1–30.
Passingham, R. E. 1982. *The Human Primate*. Oxford: Freeman.
Plutchik, R. 1980. *Emotion: A Psychoevolutionary Synthesis*. New York: Harper and Row.
Povinelli, D. J. 2000. *Folk Physics for Apes: The Chimpanzee's Theory of How the World Works*. Oxford: Oxford University Press.
Povinelli, D. J., and T. J. Eddy. 1997. "Specificity of Gaze-Following in Young Chimpanzees." *British Journal of Developmental Psychology* 15: 213–222.
Premack, D., and G. Woodruff. 1978. "Does the Chimpanzee Have a Theory of Mind?" *Behavioral and Brain Sciences* 1: 515–526.
Rizzolatti, G., L. Fadiga, L. Fogassi, and V. Gallese. 2002. "From Mirror Neurons to Imitation: Facts and Speculations." In *The Imitative Mind: Development, Evolution and Brain Bases*, edited by W. Prinz and A. N. Meltzoff, 247–266. Cambridge: Cambridge University Press.
Rumbaugh, D., and E. S. Savage-Rumbaugh. 1990. "Chimpanzees: Competencies for Language and Numbers." In *Comparative Perception*, Vol. 2, edited by W. Stebbins and M. Berkley. New York: Wiley and Sons.
Savage-Rumbaugh, S., and R. Lewin. 1994. *Kanzi: The Ape at the Brink of the Human Mind*. New York: John Wiley and Sons.
Savage-Rumbaugh, S., J. Murphy, J. Sevcik, K. Brakke, S. L. Williams, and D. Rumbaugh. 1993. *Language Comprehension in the Ape and Child*. Monographs of the Society for Research in Child Development 58. Chicago: University of Chicago Press.
Savage-Rumbaugh, S., R. Sevcik, and W. Hopkins. 1988. "Symbolic Cross-Model Transfer in Two Species." *Child Development* 59: 617–625.
Schutz, A. (1932) 1967. *The Phenomenology of the Social World*. Evanston, IL: Northwestern University Press.
Sherwood, C. C., R. L. Holloway, J. M. Erwin, and P. R. Hoff. 2004. "Cortical Orofacial Motor Representation in Old World Monkeys, Great Apes and Humans." *Brain Behavior and Evolution* 63: 82–106.

Simmel, G. (1900) 1955. "The Web of Group Affiliations." In *Conflict and the Web of Group Affiliations*. New York: Free Press.
Spencer, B., and F. J. Gillen. (1899) 1939. *The Native Tribes of Central Australia*. London: Macmillan.
Spencer, H. (1874–1896) 1998. *The Principles of Sociology*. 3 vols. New York: Appleton.
Stanford, C. 1999. "Great Apes and Early Hominids: Reconstructing Ancestral Behavior." In *The Nonhuman Primates*, edited by P. Dolhinow and A. Fuentes. London: Mayfield Publishing.
Stephan, H. 1983. "Evolutionary Trends in Limbic Structures." *Neuroscience and Biobehavioral Review* 7: 367–374.
Stephan, H., and O. J. Andy. 1969. "Quantitative Comparative Neuroanatomy of Primates: An Attempt at Phylogenetic Interpretation." *Annals of the New York Academy of Science* 167: 370–387.
———. 1977. "Quantitative Comparison of the Amygdala in Insectivores and Primates." *Acta Anatomica* 98: 130–153.
Stephan, H., G. Baron, and H. Frahm. 1988. "Comparative Size of Brains and Brain Components." In *Neurosciences*, Vol. 4, edited by H. Steklis and J. Erwin. New York: Alan Liss.
Stephan, H., H. Frahm, and G. Baron. 1981. "New and Revised Data on Volumes of Brain Structures in Insectivores and Primates." *Folia Primatologica* 35: 1–29.
Subiaul, F. 2007. "The Imitation Faculty in Monkeys: Evaluating Its Features, Distribution, and Evolution." *Journal of Anthropological Science* 85: 35–62.
Tomasello, M., and J. Call. 1997. *Primate Cognition*. Oxford: Oxford University Press.
Tomasello, M., B. Hare, and T. Fogleman. 2001. "The Ontogeny of Gaze Following in Chimpanzees, *Pan troglodytes*, and Rhesus Macaques, *Macaca mulatta*." *Animal Behavior* 61: 335–343.
Tomonaga, M. 1999. "Attending to the Others' Attention in Macaques' Joint Attention or Not?" *Primate Research* 15: 425.
Turner, J. H. 1999a. "The Neurology of Emotions: Implications for Sociological Theories of Interpersonal Behavior." In *The Sociology of Emotions*, edited by D. Franks and C. Smith. Greenwich, CT: JAI Press.
———. 1999b. "Toward a General Sociological Theory of Emotions." *Journal for the Theory of Social Behaviour* 29: 133–162.
———. 2000. *On the Origins of Human Emotions: A Sociological Inquiry into the Evolution of Human Affect*. Stanford, CA: Stanford University Press.
———. 2002. *Face to Face: Toward a Sociological Theory of Interpersonal Behavior*. Stanford, CA: Stanford University Press.
———. 2007. *Human Emotions: A Sociological Theory*. Oxford: Routledge.
———. 2010. *Theoretical Principles of Sociology*. Vol. 2, *Microdynamics*. New York: Springer.
Turner, J. H., and A. Maryanski. 2005. *Incest: Origins of the Taboo*. Boulder, CO: Paradigm Publishers.
———. 2008. *On the Origins of Societies by Natural Selection*. Boulder, CO: Paradigm Publishers.
Wilson, E. O. 1975. *Sociobiology: The New Synthesis*. Cambridge, MA: Harvard University Press.
———. 1978. *On Human Nature*. Cambridge, MA: Harvard University Press.

CHAPTER THIRTY
EVOLVED HUMAN SOCIALITY AND LITERATURE
Joseph Carroll

Evolutionary social science has been a cumulative research program for less than fifty years, and evolutionary literary study for only about twenty years (Degler 1991; Pinker 2002; Carroll 2008a). Until the past few years, evolutionary accounts of human behavior have been hampered by imperfect theories of inclusive fitness, human social dynamics, and culture. The standard theory of inclusive fitness restricted concepts of cooperation to kinship and reciprocity (Wilson and Wilson 2007; Pinker 2012). Evolutionary social science, concentrating on basic animal needs and basic forms of social interaction, tacitly restricted culture to trivial differences in the manifestation of adaptive behaviors that had supposedly reached fixity at some indeterminate point in the Pleistocene (Barkow, Cosmides, and Tooby 1992; Hill 2007; Carroll 2012a). Much of the work done in evolutionary literary study has reflected these limitations in theoretical biology and in evolutionary social science, and it has also failed to register the full range of concepts available within sophisticated interpretations of literature (Carroll 2004a: 187–188; Carroll 2010).

Within the past few years, theoretical biology, evolutionary social science, and evolutionary literary study have been correcting basic mistakes, producing new concepts, and reaching a more complete and adequate understanding of human behavior, including cultural and literary behavior. This chapter integrates these new concepts and demonstrates how they can be used to understand specific literary works. Separate sections are devoted to ideas from theoretical biology about the sources of cooperation in all living things, to ideas from the social sciences about human social organization, to ideas from evolutionary aesthetics about the adaptive function of the arts, and to ideas from literary theory about how meaning works in fiction. A section discussing specific literary examples illustrates the way the arts help generate group identity, integrate individuals into groups, and mediate between the needs of individuals and the claims of groups.

THE SOURCES OF COOPERATION: RECENT DEVELOPMENTS IN THEORETICAL BIOLOGY

Until the past few years, theoretical biology was dominated by inclusive fitness theory— the gene's-eye view propounded by theorists such as G. C. Williams, W. D. Hamilton, and Richard Dawkins. That theory took all of biology as its scope, but it had clear applications to human behavior. With respect to humans, the moral implications were articulated in Dawkins's claims that selfish genes make selfish people (Dawkins 1976; Symons 1979; Trivers 1985; Alexander 1987; Carroll 1995: 364–368; D. S. Wilson 1999; Pinker 2012;

Gintis 2014). Adherents of inclusive fitness theory could deal most effectively with egoistic impulses, mate selection, kin relations, dominance hierarchies, and reciprocity. They could not deal effectively with group identity. For almost all individual people, individual identity is bound up in the sense of belonging to one or more social groups. Those groups do not consist only of kin and closely monitored reciprocators. They include tribes, nation-states, religions, political parties, social classes, ideologies, clubs, voluntary organizations, and other such groups. Identity within a group directly influences behavior. The role a person takes within such groups and the fate of the group as a whole radically alter the quality of experience. Being a social outcast or a respected leader, sharing in victory or being defeated in war—such conditions profoundly influence the neuro-affective states of individual minds.

For some three decades, David Sloan Wilson and other theoretical biologists have challenged inclusive fitness theory and have offered updated versions of "group selection" as an alternative. The debate between advocates of inclusive fitness theory and advocates of group selection has often been confused and unproductively repetitive (Nesse 2012; Pinker et al. 2012), but it has at least drawn attention forcefully to group-level phenomena in human behavior. Recent work in game theory and the theory of major transitions in evolution offer a way out of the impasse between inclusive fitness and group selection. Game theorists offer mathematical analyses of large-scale patterns of "cooperation" and "defection" or "selfishness" in social behavior. Theorists of the major transitions study the evolution of hierarchical complexity in biological organization.

Both game theorists and theorists of major transitions identify "cooperation" as a salient principle in their research. Richard Michod, a theorist of major transitions, declares that "the evolution of cooperation is the central problem of social evolution" (2011: 175). Martin Nowak, a game theorist, argues that cooperation should be included along with mutation and selection as a basic principle of evolution. "From cooperation can emerge the constructive side of evolution, from genes to organisms to language and complex social behaviors" (Nowak and Highfield 2011: xviii).

The most important principle that emerges from the work of Nowak and his collaborators is that cooperative individuals can interact selectively with one another. Nowak calls this principle "network reciprocity" and identifies it as one of five main sources of cooperation (Nowak 2006; Nowak, Tarnita, and Antal 2010; Nowak and Highfield 2011). In network reciprocity, "cooperators prevail because they can form clusters, either in physical space, on networks, in phenotype space or in sets. Individuals within such clusters gain a higher payoff than defectors that try to invade them" (Nowak, Tarnita, and Antal 2010: 25). The other four principles, already recognized among theoretical biologists, are kin selection, direct reciprocity (mutual back-scratching), indirect reciprocity (extending reciprocity credit, as it were, to individuals known to be cooperators), and group selection (selection operating on competing social groups).

Adding network reciprocity to the other sources of cooperation overcomes "the free-rider problem." In inclusive fitness theory and in earlier forms of game theory, defection had seemed to eliminate the possibility of cooperative effort extending beyond kinship and direct and indirect reciprocity. It seemed that all cooperative interactions would ultimately succumb to defectors who gain advantages from the cooperators and do not pay the price of cooperation. Selection seemed inevitably to favor defection. Since humans do in reality display large-scale cooperation, the theory of inclusive fitness, defined as kin selection supplemented by direct and indirect reciprocity, could not adequately account for human social behavior (D. S. Wilson 1999; Boehm 2012). Advocates of group selection concede that defection is a winning strategy within a group but argue that groups with more cooperators would succeed against groups with fewer cooperators. That solution requires that groups proliferate and reproduce at rates exceeding reproduction among members of a group—a solution that severely limits the scope of cooperation (D. S. Wilson 1997; Sober and Wilson 1998; Wilson and Wilson 2007; Pinker et al. 2012; E. O. Wilson 2012). Efforts to get around this problem end up defining "groups" in ad hoc ways that render the concept indeterminate (Nowak 2006; Nowak, Tarnita, and Antal 2010; Nowak, Tarnita, and Wilson 2010; Nowak and Highfield 2011).

Major transitions theory integrates the idea of cooperation with the idea of hierarchical organization in biological systems. Within an organism, interactions among genes are shaped by the functional structure of the organism. Each cell contains the genome of the whole organism. Protein coding genes are switched on and off through complex networks of regulatory genes that subordinate individual cells to the systemic needs of the organism. In parallel fashion, within social animals, interactions among the individual organisms are shaped by the functional structure of the social group. Gintis (2014) gets this idea into clear focus: "Just as the genome codes for the patterns of interactions of loci in the genome, so it codes for the characteristic patterns of interactions of loci in two or more carriers; i.e., the genome codes for the social structure of the organisms it creates" (497).

Defection or social cheating is a pervasive feature in human social life. Nonetheless, humans internalize cooperative norms. The norms for specific human social groups vary within limits (Brown 1991, 2000, 2004; Sripada and Stich 2005), but the disposition to internalize norms is part of the evolved genetic heritage of the human race (Boehm 1999; Gintis 2003; Hill 2007; Henrich et al. 2010; Chudek and Henrich 2011; Fukuyama 2011: 339–440; Gintis 2011; Boehm 2012; Buckholtz and Marois 2012; Gintis and van Schaik 2012). People are not merely aggregated individuals; they are dependent parts of a functional social whole.

Boehm (2012) argues that pressure to behave in accordance with group norms was a major selective force in human evolution. He designates that force "social selection." Buckholtz and Marois (2012) identify specifically human cognitive mechanisms produced by social selection—adaptations that bias individuals to internalize group norms and thus to behave in cooperative ways. Chudek and Henrich argue that such adaptations "substantially increase phenotypic assortment and facilitate the spread of self-reinforcing cooperative norms, creating genetic selection for a prosocial psychology" (2011: 219, 220). Phenotypic assortment—the likelihood that similar individuals will interact with one another—structures human populations in such a way that cooperators are more likely to interact with other cooperators. That principle is a specifically human form of what Nowak calls "network reciprocity." By providing an explanation for human social interaction that cannot be reduced to kin selection, direct reciprocity, indirect reciprocity, or group selection, social selection breaks out of the impasse produced by the debate between proponents of kin selection and proponents of group selection.

Humans are not cells in an organism, but neither are they autonomous units interacting competitively with other autonomous units. Describing phases in major transitions in individuality, Simpson (2011) specifies the degree of integration between individuals and social groups in humans. A major transition in individuality consists in the evolution of a new reproductive individual that subsumes smaller individuals. Major transitions include the evolution of replicating molecules, molecules within cells, nucleated cells, multicellular organisms, and social animals. In a major transition, organisms develop means to favor cooperation and punish defection (Michod 2011). Once a major transition is complete, the reproductive capabilities of the components are subsumed within the reproductive capability of an individual at a higher level of hierarchical complexity (Maynard Smith and Szathmáry 1995: 4; Michod 2011). Human social groups represent an approach to a major transition—the creation of a new corporate individual. Simpson identifies three phases in a transition: an aggregate phase, a group phase, and an individual phase:

> All that is required in the aggregate phase is for membership in an aggregate of other organisms to have an effect on fitness.... Groups themselves do not form offspring per se, but they can fragment and form new groups by fission.... [For the evolution of individuals,] it is the partitioning of life history into growth and reproduction that is important. (2011: 209, 210, 216)

By Simpson's (2011: 220) criteria, human social groups fall into the middle category, the group phase. They are intermediately individuated. Human sexual dyads and their offspring cannot thrive outside of social groups. Human families are embedded within kin groups. Even in ancestral environments, kin groups are embedded in social groups that include non-kin (Hill et al. 2011). In post-agricultural environments, non-kin form the bulk of large-scale groups. Human social groups reproduce generationally. Like a species, they continue in existence as distinct reproductive lineages, outliving their generations, and they sometimes also fission or extend themselves in colonies (Morris 1968; Chagnon 1983; Foley and Gamble 2009).

The Evolution of Human Sociality

The Current State of Knowledge

In theoretical biology, the origins of cooperation for all of life are becoming clear. We now also have a clear understanding about the main causal interactions among the factors—anatomy, physiology, technology, diet, provisioning, mating, parenting, power structures, and symbolic representation—that produced a species-typical behavioral repertory adapted to hunting and gathering (Wrangham and Peterson 1996; Hrdy 2005, 2009; Wade 2006; Kaplan, Gurven, and Lancaster 2007; Lancaster and Kaplan 2007; Burkart, Hrdy, and van Schaik 2009; Foley and Gamble 2009; Hill, Barton, and Hurtado 2009; Kaplan, Gurven, and Winking 2009; Kaplan, Hooper, and Gurven 2009; Klein 2009; Wrangham 2009; Burkart and van Schaik 2010; Muehlenbein and Flinn 2011; Gintis and van Schaik 2012). We know that hunters and gatherers display three main forms of cooperation: cooperation among adult males for hunting, war, and defense against predators; cooperation between adult males and females for provisioning each other and their offspring; and cooperation among adult females for care of the young. We know too that humans evolved a unique capacity to combine cooperative effort among adult males with dyadic mating and dual parenting (Geary and Flinn 2001; Flinn, Geary, and Ward 2005; Flinn and Ward 2005).

The next step in building an adequate evolutionary model of human social behavior is to bridge the gap between groups organized for hunting and gathering—bands, clans, and tribes—and the larger, more complex societies that have appeared since the invention of agriculture. Fewer researchers have devoted attention to this range of problems than to the problems of hominid evolution, and the explanations are less fully developed. Nonetheless, a usable basic toolkit for social analysis can be constructed from six concepts: (1) dominance and reverse dominance, (2) leadership, (3) internalizing norms, (4) strong reciprocity or third-party enforcement of norms, (5) institutions for the enforcement of norms, and (6) legitimacy in the exercise of power. Dominance and reverse dominance define a range in the distribution of power in human social groups. Leaders organize and direct social power. The internalization of norms is the chief means through which individual humans form units within cooperative corporate bodies. Strong reciprocity actively enforces behaviors necessary to sustain cooperative activity. Institutions for the enforcement of norms distinguish complex, hierarchically organized societies from loosely aggregated band-level societies. Legitimacy characterizes institutions that function in accordance with the norms internalized by the members of a community.

DOMINANCE AND REVERSE DOMINANCE

Over evolutionary and historical time scales, the broadest and most basic pattern in the development of human social organization consists of a sequence of alternations between dominance and reverse dominance. Dominance is the exercise of controlling force on individual members of a social group. In chimpanzee societies, one adult male, or a small coalition of adult males, dominates all other chimpanzees in a band (Wrangham and Peterson 1996; Boehm 1999; de Waal 2005, 2007). All adult males dominate all adult females; all adults dominate all juveniles. Using violence or the threat of violence, dominant males gain first access to prime foods and also to fertile females. Reverse dominance, a term used interchangeably with "egalitarianism," is a uniquely human form of social organization and is the form prevalent among hunter-gatherer bands. Reverse dominance means that groups of adult males collectively suppress dominance behavior in individual males. Males who assert dominance by bullying or by taking more than their share of food face sanctions extending from shaming to banishment to execution (Boehm 1999, 2012).

In the evolutionary history of prehuman and human social organization, alternations of dominance and reverse dominance have passed through four main stages: (1) chimpanzee-like dominance centered in individual males or small coalitions of males; (2) hunter-gatherer egalitarianism among adult males; (3) the resurgence of personal dominance as an organizing principle of post-agricultural societies; and (4) the resurgence of egalitarianism in liberal democracies. Boehm (1999, 2012) argues that simple chimpanzee-like dominance characterized the behavior of the last common ancestors of hominids and chimpanzees; that hunters and gatherers almost universally practiced reverse dominance; that the hunting and gathering ecology lasted long enough for egalitarianism to be deeply embedded in evolved human social dispositions; and that in human social groups, dispositions for collectively repressing individual dominance have always been held in strong tension with dispositions for individual dominance. Leading theorists of human social evolution have assimilated Boehm's arguments, and those arguments have also had an impact on evolutionary literary studies (Bowles and Gintis 2004, 2011; D. S. Wilson 2007; Wilson and Wilson 2007; Johnson et al. 2008; Bowles 2012; Carroll et al. 2012b; Gintis and van Schaik 2012; Haidt 2012; Richerson and Henrich 2012; van Vugt and Ronay 2014).

Cumulable and defensible resources open up opportunities for renewed assertions of individual dominance. Even in resource-rich pre-agricultural societies with isolable and defensible sources of food, strong males and their followers can sometimes commandeer accumulated resources and use them for coercive subordination (Foley and Gamble 2009; Kaplan, Hooper, and Gurven 2009). Agriculture makes cumulable and defensible resources readily available and thus alters the egalitarian equilibrium of hunter-gatherer social dynamics. "Material wealth allows aspirants to positions of social dominance to control enough allies and resources to offset the capacity of subordinate individuals to disable and kill them" (Gintis and van Schaik 2012: 34). The resurgence of dominance in post-agricultural societies manifests itself in the prevalence of chiefs in tribal societies and in oligarchies, monarchies, aristocracies, and dictatorships. Reverse dominance resurfaced in Greek city-states and in the Roman republic but became a worldwide phenomenon only during the past two centuries (Wrangham and Peterson 1996; Roberts 2003; Fukuyama 2011).

LEADERSHIP

The exercise of power in post-agricultural societies combines the dominance hierarchies of our primate heritage with the willing cooperation that characterizes hunter-gatherer societies (van Vugt and Ronay 2014: 13). In an essay summarizing evolutionary research on leadership, van Vugt and Ronay define leadership "in terms of the coordination of the actions of two or more individuals to accomplish joint goals" (2014: 2). The stipulation "joint goals" distinguishes leadership from raw assertions of dominance designed only to benefit the dominant individual or his kin (2014: 13).

Leadership in hunter-gatherer groups differs from leadership in post-agricultural societies in two main ways: duration and generality. In hunter-gatherer culture, leadership is temporary and specific to some task in which a leader has special expertise—"hunting, making weapons, or preparing a new campsite" (van Vugt and Ronay 2014: 6). Complex modern societies with large populations dedicated to specialized tasks have coordination requirements greater than those in hunter-gatherer bands. To meet those requirements, they create hierarchies in which leaders have power that is more permanent and general than the power delegated to leaders in hunter-gatherer bands.

In post-agricultural societies, hierarchies invested with authority are all pervasive. Liberal democracies have relatively high levels of egalitarianism, but they nonetheless have presidents, prime ministers, cabinets, administrative bureaucracies, and hierarchically organized armies, police forces, and judiciaries. In hierarchically organized societies, the exercise of power varies in duration and generality from dictators for life at one extreme to presidents elected for finite periods at the other. But even presidents hemmed in by voters, legislators, and judiciaries have power more lasting and general than the powers delegated to leaders in hunter-gatherer bands.

Whether temporary or permanent, chosen for specific tasks or invested with general power, leaders achieve legitimacy by eliciting the willing cooperation of individuals and directing them toward common goals in accordance with community norms. Qualities that have been found to be universally valued in leaders help them fulfill those functions: "integrity, persistence, humility, competence, decisiveness, and vision" (van Vugt and Ronay 2014: 6).

INTERNALIZED NORMS, STRONG RECIPROCITY, INSTITUTIONS, AND LEGITIMACY

In both hunter-gatherer groups and complex modern societies, cooperative effort depends on the human ability to internalize norms. That ability manifests itself in strong reciprocity—the willingness to incur costs in order to enforce collective values (Bowles and Gintis 2004, 2011; Buckholtz and Marois 2012). Strong reciprocity gives evidence that individuals care about the systemic logic that sustains a society even when they are not directly harmed by infractions against that logic. Strong reciprocity confirms that the functional structure of a social system has been encoded in the motivational repertoire of individual people within that system.

Analyzing the mechanisms of social learning that contribute to the human ability to internalize norms, Chudek and Henrich single out "prestige and conformity biases" as particularly important (2011: 219). Prestige bias is a disposition for imitating the behavior of high-status individuals. Conformity bias is a disposition for imitating the behavior of a majority. Both learning biases contribute to "phenotypic assortment," the likelihood that "regularly interacting individuals resemble one another" (2011: 219). The two biases are prerequisites for specifically human forms of cooperative social interaction, but they have a darker side. Like all adaptations, they can become isolated and exaggerated, and can produce pathological results. In its pathological extreme, prestige bias produces cults of personality centered on authoritarian leaders like Hitler, Stalin, and Mao (Oakley 2007). Conformity bias can produce mindless adherence to social conventions. As a mechanism for reinforcing group identity, it also contributes to demonizing people who are not members of the group, who do not wear its insignia or speak its dialect.

In hunter-gatherer bands, norms are enforced by face-to-face interaction—a perpetual stream of gossip and social monitoring (Boehm 1999, 2012). In larger, more complex societies, face-to-face interaction and direct collective enforcement of norms are not possible. Societies have to develop institutions that enforce social norms. Buckholtz and Marois argue that the codification of "norms into laws, and the attendant establishment of state-administered systems of criminal justice that are charged with norm compliance" are "one of the most important developments in human culture" (2012: 657). Distinguishing states from tribes, Fukuyama argues that states possess a centralized authority backed by "a monopoly of the legitimate means of coercion, in the form of an army and/or police" (2011: 80).

Internalizing a norm signifies that a person regards socially enforced standards of behavior as just or legitimate. As Fukuyama puts it, "Legitimacy means that the people who make up the society recognize the fundamental justice of the system as a whole and are willing to abide by its rules" (2011: 42). Haidt also distinguishes legitimate authority from pure coercion: "Human authority" is "not just raw power backed by the threat of force. Human authorities take on responsibility for maintaining order and justice" (2012: 143).

What constitutes legitimate authority? Willing cooperation can be distinguished from pure coercion, but norm compliance is never so perfect that societies can dispense with coercive authority. All societies have a structure of power, and in all societies that power is used for the enforcement of norms. Even egalitarian hunter-gatherer bands exercise power in collectively suppressing dominance among individual males. If people are to internalize norms, they must also internalize power structures. The problem, then, is to identify the conditions under which people identify a structure of power as right or just.

In hierarchical societies with dramatic differences in prestige, privilege, and power, internalizing a power structure could hardly develop among less privileged members of the community unless society satisfied the basic needs of animal life: sustenance, shelter, protection from assault, and opportunities for reproduction, including opportunities for the family life that is integral to the human reproductive system (Geary and Flinn 2001; Bjorklund and Pellegrini 2002; Flinn and Ward 2005; Geary 2005a; Bjorklund 2011; Salmon and Shackelford 2011). Distinguishing human communities from chimpanzee communities, Foley and Gamble observe that "the key development is the addition of social structures both below—families and descent groups—and above—shared political systems, segmentary lineage systems and trade networks" (2009: 3277). "Community" in this usage means a loosely organized band. For community members to recognize power as legitimate, the structures above the level of the loosely organized band would need to be synchronized with the structures below that level. That is, political systems would have to accommodate families and descent groups.

Network reciprocity expands community in prosocial ways, but it has not suppressed kinship as a binding force in human life. "Kinship runs like a thread through the course of human evolution, from the beginnings of the last common ancestor through to the present day. The maintenance of kinship through several generations (descent groups) is both a truly unique development and also fundamental to the way in which communities both hold together and ultimately divide" (Foley and Gamble 2009: 3277). Hill et al. dispute the idea that band-level societies are primarily constituted by "close kin," but by their own reckoning, about three-quarters of contemporary hunter-gatherer bands are linked by genealogical or marital ties (2011: 1287).

Providing for basic animal needs, including reproductive needs, would reduce impulses for revolt and would offer a positive inducement for participating in a social system. In itself, though, that inducement would not be sufficient to make people assimilate the functional structure of the group to their individual identities, encoding the organization of the society as a whole into their own motivational structures. Humans are conscious and imaginative. Their beliefs and values are crucial parts of their motivational structures. In order to internalize the functional structure of a group, people would have to feel that they have a social role that is valuable and valued within the larger social body and also that the social body itself has some intrinsic value. That kind of feeling is evident whenever a group displays group pride, for instance, when they salute a flag with reverence or voluntarily contribute to the erection of some building or monument dedicated to their religion or their political culture.

The categories delineated in this section—dominance and reverse dominance, leadership, internalized norms, strong reciprocity, and legitimacy—can be reduced to four components: power, values, individuals, and groups. Dominance and reverse dominance identify different ways in which social power is exercised, either by individuals or by groups. Leaders are individuals who organize and direct the power latent in groups. Internalized norms are shared values that influence individuals. In strong reciprocity, individuals use power to enforce shared values. Legal institutions are contrivances for delegating strong reciprocity to individuals and groups such as the police and the judiciary. Leaders and members of legal institutions achieve legitimacy by exercising power in accordance with the shared values of the social group. The analytic arguments in the chapter thus presuppose that power, values, individuals, and groups are basic components of human social dynamics.

The Social Functions of Literature and the Other Arts

To understand how literature functions socially, specifically social functions need to be located within a broader hypothesis about the adaptive functions of literature and the other arts. Multiple alternative hypotheses have been proposed, but the broadest ideas have converged toward a common point: that literature and the other arts affect cognitive and emotional organization, influence motives, and help regulate behavior (Dissanayake 1992, 2011; Deacon 1997; E. O. Wilson 1998: ch. 10; Panksepp and Panksepp 2000; Salmon and Symons 2004; Carroll 2008a, 2008b, 2012a; Mar and Oatley 2008; Boyd 2009; Dutton 2009; Carroll et al. 2010a, 2012b; Tooby and Cosmides 2010; Easterlin 2012, 2013; Gottschall 2012). Basic human motives are channeled into specific cultural norms that are articulated in imaginative form through myths, legends, rituals, images, songs, and stories. Humans universally regulate their behavior in accordance with beliefs and values that are made vividly present to them in the depictions of art, including fictional narratives, dramatic representations, films, and poetic verses.

The idea that the arts affect cognitive and emotional organization, influence motives, and help regulate behavior subsumes more particular ideas that the arts can provide practically useful information (Scalise Sugiyama 1996, 2001a, 2001b, 2004, 2006), offer game-plan scenarios to rehearse potential adaptive challenges (Pinker 1997), provide means for sexual display (Miller 2000; Dutton 2009), enhance pattern recognition and stimulate creativity (Boyd 2009), and provide a medium for shared social identity (Dissanayake 2000; Boyd 2009). All arguments that the arts have some adaptive function set themselves in contrast to the idea that aesthetic responsiveness is merely a side effect of cognitive powers that evolved to fulfill more practical functions (Pinker 1997, 2007b; Carroll 2012a: ch. 5; Carroll et al. 2012a: 12–13).

The uniquely human need for art derives from unique human powers of cognition. In all animals except humans, narrowly channeled sensory inputs and somatic urges produce a limited range of stereotyped responses. For human minds, in contrast, behavior must adapt to a cognitive field that includes percepts, inferences, causal relations, contingent possibilities, analogies, contrasts, hierarchically organized ideas, hypothetical scenarios, symbolic images, aesthetic structures, evocative depictions, and narrative sequences. High intelligence enables humans to generate plans based on mental representations of complex relationships, engage in collective enterprises requiring shared mental representations, and generate original solutions to the problems of life (Mithen 1996; Potts 1996; E. O. Wilson 1998: ch. 10; Geary 2005b; Tomasello et al. 2005; Tomasello and Carpenter 2007; Burkart, Hrdy, and van Schaik 2009). Humans do not operate automatically, but neither do they operate on the basis of purely rational deliberations about means and ends. They operate through the influence of emotionally charged mental images—images of themselves, the worlds they inhabit, the social groups of which they are a part, and their own roles within those groups. The arts, like religions and ideologies, are emotionally valenced. And indeed, religions and ideologies make use of the arts to convey their messages in emotionally persuasive ways.

Humans inhabit imagined virtual worlds in which demons, witches, gods, and magic have often been as real as predators, prey, fellow humans, and the weather. The desire for spiritual salvation has sometimes spurred humans to ignore hunger and thirst and to suppress the desire for sex and family. Belief in a cause animated by ideals often leads them to sacrifice their lives. Even in rational and skeptical modern environments, humans still need emotionally charged images to shape their sense of purpose and guide their moral judgments. Hence the passion attached to symbols such as national flags, the swastika, the hammer and sickle, and even the donkey and the elephant.

All tribes have myths of origin. Every ethnic group, religious sect, nation, political party, and ideological movement makes itself imaginatively distinct through symbols, historical narratives, monuments, songs, pictorial representations, ceremonies, and aesthetic styles (Brown 1991; Hill, Barton, and Hurtado 2009). Individual humans share in the collective imagination of their social groups, and within those groups, they construct narratives about their own individual lives (McAdams 1985, 1993, 2001, 2006, 2008, 2011; McAdams and Ochberg 1988; McAdams and Bowman 2001; De St. Aubin, McAdams, and Kim 2003). They envision their lives extending into the future, and they look beyond their own individual lives to the continuing life of their descendants and their communities. In contrast to chimpanzees, humans do not live in communities populated solely by the conspecifics with whom they come directly into contact. Their communities include fabled ancestors, generations of the future, and every person, living or dead, who shares beliefs and values that subordinate individuals to some collective body.

Literature and the other arts perform an indispensable and uniquely human function. They help build the imaginative virtual worlds in which people live. They are communicative, public, and shared. They form one of the most important media through which collective, shared consciousness binds people into a community. They help generate group identity, integrate individuals into groups, and mediate between the needs of individuals and the claims of groups. Stories, plays, and poems can affirm the legitimacy of power structures or express protest against those structures. They can help individuals internalize the norms of their culture or resist those norms. Fictional narratives can culminate in a marriage within a beneficent social order, depict shattered lives within a pathological social order, or cast individuals as heroic contenders against social injustice. Even when authors adopt a stance of resistance and protest, they appeal to principles of social justice that they anticipate their readers will share. Whether affirming or denying the legitimacy of a given structure of power, authors give voice to a community defined by shared beliefs and values.

Political structures interact in reciprocally causal ways with changing material and social conditions—ecological, economic, technological, and military—and also with changing cultural conditions, for instance, the rise or decline of religions or ideologies, and the impact of science on worldviews. The imaginative virtual worlds of literary works respond to all such conditions, depicting them, reflecting on them, and judging them, whether to celebrate them, protest against them, or guide them toward some better future. Every individual person constructs his or her own imaginative virtual world (McAdams 1993, 2001, 2008, 2011; McAdams et al. 2004; McAdams, Josselson, and Lieblich 2006; Carroll 2012e), but all such worlds are heavily influenced by the imaginative structures available within a given culture. Literary authors are singularly potent agents in constructing imaginative virtual worlds. They are influenced by the beliefs and values current in their communities but also, in turn, influence those beliefs and values (Carroll et al. 2012a). Great authors have powerful minds capable of independent judgment and original creative construction. They thus help shape the imaginative virtual worlds that define their communities.

How Meaning Works in Fiction

In order to affect beliefs and values, dramatic and narrative fiction must engage readers emotionally and absorb them into an author's imagined world. An author fabricates imaginary people (characters), their environments (settings), and their actions (plots). In depicting a story, the author envisions readers, organizes the story in ways that engage readers' minds, and modulates style and tone in ways that convey the author's attitude toward the characters, settings, and plot. By conveying a sense of his or her own attitude toward the depicted events, the author gives grounds for making intuitive inferences about the author's temperament, outlook, beliefs, and values. A story can be presented only from within the worldview of the author. When readers become absorbed in a story, they also necessarily enter into the author's worldview. Readers are thus simultaneously engaging in two vicarious experiences. They are sharing in the experiences of the characters in the story, and they are sharing in the author's experience of the story being told. Readers have subjective, qualitative sensations that reflect the subjective qualitative sensations of both the characters and the author (Mar and Oatley 2008; Mar et al. 2011; Oatley 2011; Carroll 2012c, 2012d, 2012e, 2013b).

Imagine a reader is sitting on a park bench and has just finished reading William Golding's *Lord of the Flies*, still holding the novel in her lap. A stranger sits down on the bench, looks at the book, and says, "Oh, I've heard of that novel. What's it about?" The reader might say something like this: "It's about a group of English school boys who are being evacuated in the midst of a nuclear war. They are wrecked and stranded on a tropical island, with no adult supervision. At first, they make an effort to behave in a cooperative and responsible way, but some boys split off from the others, become hunters, and revert to savagery. Three of the main characters, Ralph, Piggy, and Simon, try to uphold standards of civilized behavior, but Simon is killed when he stumbles into the midst of a frenzied, savage dance, and Piggy is murdered by one of the hunters. When adults finally appear on the scene, Ralph is being hunted by the savage band and is on the verge of being murdered. It's a very bleak and disturbing book."

A casual summary of this sort intuitively registers much of what makes up the meaning of a fictional story: the literal subject (characters, setting, and plot), chief thematic concerns (a conflict between civilization and savagery), and a tone or mood (disturbing). The beliefs and values of the author are almost automatically channeled into the summary of events. The contrast between savagery and civilization clearly slants evaluation in favor of civilization. The protagonists, identified by name, favor behaving "in a cooperative and responsible way," terms that are laden with positive evaluative content. The boys who form a savage band are "frenzied" and are responsible for "murder," evidently not a good thing. The listener on the bench would naturally assume that sympathy and concern are channeled toward the three boys who try to sustain the values of civilization and that the bad guys, the antagonists, are the boys who "revert to savagery." In this context, the word "revert" signals degeneration, falling back into a lesser state. Hearing that the protagonists are persecuted and that two of them are murdered, the curious stranger will not be surprised to hear the reader say that "it's a very bleak and disturbing book." Moreover, the stranger is likely to register that the negative emotional tone does not refer simply to the unpleasant fact that the protagonists suffer. He would also register that the book suggests something about the vulnerability of civilization—the ease with which savagery emerges spontaneously and overwhelms the good intentions of well-disposed people. Noting that the story takes place in the context of a nuclear war, he would probably surmise that the story about children on a desert island is intended also to say something about adult behavior, exposing atavistic passions that can spiral out of control and create havoc on a monumental scale. All of this—the characters, setting, and events; the attitudes of the implied author; the reader's own responses; and the inferences about thematic implications—is part of the meaning of the story.

Social Themes in Plays, Short Stories, and Novels

Organization of the Literary Examples

This section is designed to give a feeling for how social themes work in plays, short stories, and novels. The examples are organized into the categories delineated in the section titled "The Evolution of Human Sociality." Separate sections are devoted to dominance and reverse dominance, leadership, internalizing norms, strong reciprocity, institutions for enforcing norms, and legitimacy in exercising social power. The examples are from diverse periods with diverse social structures, and the authors have diverse attitudes toward the societies they depict. All these forms of diversity are subsumed within the general social function of the arts: helping generate group identity, integrating individuals into groups, and mediating between the needs of individuals and the claims of groups.

Dominance and Reverse Dominance

Many characters in fiction and drama exemplify pure dominance striving. Instances include the title character in Christopher Marlowe's *Tamburlaine*, the title character in Shakespeare's *Richard III*, Satan in Milton's *Paradise Lost*, the title character in Henry Fielding's *The Life and Death of Jonathan Wild, the Great*, Lady Catherine de Bourgh in Jane Austen's *Pride and Prejudice*, the lawyer Tulkinghorn in Charles Dickens's *Bleak House*,

Mrs. Proudie in Anthony Trollope's *Barchester Towers*, the renegade Ivory agent Kurtz in Joseph Conrad's *The Heart of Darkness*, Sauron in J.R.R. Tolkien's *Lord of the Rings*, the pigs in George Orwell's *Animal Farm*, Jack Merridew, the leader of the savage band of boys in *Lord of the Flies*, and Voldemort in J. K. Rowling's Harry Potter series. In all but a very few depictions, dominance striving is negatively valenced. That is, authors adopt a stance of disapproval and dislike toward the dominant individual, and readers readily acquiesce in the author's feelings. Reading literary depictions activates and reinforces the inherited dispositions for suppressing dominance in individuals.

As Western society has shifted from a feudal system founded on ownership of land to a mercantile and industrial economy driven by entrepreneurial effort, the impulses of reverse dominance have articulated themselves as a hegemonic ideology—the ideology of liberal bourgeois democracy. That is the ideology exemplified by Victorian novels. A quantitative study of hundreds of characters in nineteenth-century British novels finds that the novels stigmatize dominance behavior and valorize self-effacing prosociality (Johnson et al. 2008, 2011; Carroll et al. 2009, 2010b, 2012a, 2012b). Protagonists are typically prosocial and agreeable. They make friends, build coalitions, and help non-kin. Antagonists have a single-minded fixation on attaining dominance—wealth, power, and prestige. They are egoistic isolates, cultivating no social relationships outside relations of dominance. Drawing on Boehm's research on reverse dominance, the authors conclude that these novels perform a social function like that of gossip in a hunter-gatherer community. The egalitarian ethos that binds hunter-gatherers into a cooperative community binds the reading public into a virtual community. Literacy makes it possible for virtual communities to include millions of readers.

Dominance and cooperation are basic components of human social evolution. Consequently, it seems likely that the tendencies at work in Victorian novels would find expression in other periods and other national literatures. Christian ideology, which began in the Middle East 2,000 years ago, exemplifies reverse dominance. At least in theory, Christian doctrine valorizes the poor and meek and stigmatizes the powerful and domineering. Christian forms of egalitarian ideology pervade European literature through the seventeenth century and persist even now in secularized forms. Like Christianity, Marxism and its ideological affiliates are driven by impulses of reverse dominance.

Suppressing dominance in individuals produces environments conducive to willing cooperation. Reverse dominance has thus been a chief engine driving the evolution of affiliative social feelings. Expansive egalitarian affiliation helps generate compassion for weak and vulnerable members of society. A combination of compassion for the weak and resentment against dominant members of a social hierarchy animate many novels depicting the plight of the poor. Salient examples include Benjamin Disraeli's *Sybil, or the Two Nations*; Elizabeth Gaskell's *North and South* and *Mary Barton*; Dickens's *Hard Times* and *Bleak House*; the fairy tales of Oscar Wilde; George Gissing's *The Nether World*; Upton Sinclair's *The Jungle*; and John Steinbeck's *The Grapes of Wrath*. In the United States, slavery produced a distinct racial variant on the impulse to affirm common humanity. In Mark Twain's *Huckleberry Finn*, Jim, a runaway slave, displays love of family, remorse for wrongdoing, gratitude for generosity, and loyalty to his friend Huck. Uncle Tom, the title character in Harriet Beecher Stowe's *Uncle Tom's Cabin*, resists the domination of his slave masters not by outright rebellion but by turning the other cheek, forgiving his enemies, and thus indirectly casting moral opprobrium on a social order grounded in domination.

Among hunter-gatherers, suppressing dominance means suppressing bullying, boasting, and assertiveness (Boehm 1999, 2012). The equivalent in a civil society translates into manners, codes of politeness designed to avoid the appearance of issuing commands and thus displaying dominance (Pinker 2007a: 380–392; Salter 2008). Novels designed to depict social relations among highly cultivated people are sometimes called "novels of manners." Preeminent examples include novels by Fanny Burney, Maria Edgeworth, Jane Austen, Anthony Trollope, Elizabeth Gaskell, George Eliot, Margaret Oliphant, William Dean Howells, Edith Wharton, Henry James, and E. M. Forster. Such novels create dramatic tension by filtering urgent animal passions through the restraints imposed by polite codes of speech. In many such novels, characters behave in cruel and treacherous ways but never raise their voices or use intemperate, violent forms of expression.

Reverse dominance is a defining feature of liberal ideology in modern bourgeois societies. Kurt Vonnegut's story "Harrison Bergeron" offers a futuristic dystopian vision of egalitarianism enforced as public policy. In the society depicted in the story, a Handicapper General devises handicaps that cripple any special talent that might allow individuals to rise above the average. Harrison's father, for example, is highly intelligent. To scatter his thoughts and render his mind mediocre, he is equipped with a mechanism that periodically produces loud, shattering noises inside his head. Harrison himself is a genius and a gifted athlete. He is thus exceptionally laden with handicaps—loud noises to interrupt his thinking, heavy spectacles to render him half blind and give him headaches, three hundred pounds of scrap metal to weigh him down, and disfiguring disguises to make him ugly. Even so, he is considered so dangerous that he is kept in prison. He escapes, has a moment of freedom, and is then gunned down by the Handicapper General.

Reverse dominance in the government of modern democracies drew inspiration from the model of the Roman Republic. Two of Shakespeare's Roman plays, *Coriolanus* and *Julius Caesar*, take the conflict between dominance and reverse dominance as their central theme. Though Shakespeare is writing in English during the Renaissance, his plays capture the spirit of politics in Ancient Rome. Roman government passed through two main phases: (1) a republic governed by a combination of a patrician senatorial class and leaders of the common people and (2) an empire governed autocratically by a single man. *Coriolanus* is set in the republican period and displays the power of a collective egalitarian body to bring down a dominant male. *Julius Caesar* is set at the moment of transition between the republican period and the emergence of authoritarian rule.

In *Coriolanus*, the title character is a patrician Roman general who despises the common people. Though highly successful as a soldier, the scorn he expresses for the plebeians renders him so unpopular that he is forced into exile. Enraged by this treatment, he allies himself with enemies of Rome and leads them to the gates of the city. He is ultimately dissuaded only by the pleas of his own family members within the city. Having abandoned both loyalty to Rome and then loyalty to the enemies of Rome, he is a man without a country. He is killed by his former allies, but his death is less important emotionally than his ultimate isolation. His dominance striving activates reverse dominance in the people of Rome. Caught in this dynamic, stubbornly insisting that his personal superiority gives him a right to dominate, he destroys all the social ties that could give meaning to his life. His passions outrun his judgment. Until it is too late, he fails to register that the claims of family outweigh even the claims of the individual ego, that families are necessarily embedded in a social network, and that no one can make individual dominance a successful long-term strategy in isolation from all social networks. In a hunter-gatherer culture, being expelled from a group because of dominance behavior can amount to a death sentence (Gat 2006; Boehm 2012). That is also the case with Coriolanus.

Rome is a highly militarized society, founded essentially on conquest. In that political environment, the flow of power tends to center at the top of a military hierarchy. Caesar and Caesarism are almost inevitable manifestations of that underlying logic. In *Julius Caesar*, the struggle of Brutus, Cassius, and the other republicans is a spasmodic and ultimately ineffectual effort to suppress dominance in an individual. As Shakespeare presents them, neither Caesar nor the republicans are antagonists. They are media for the working out of a disequilibrium in the relations between political organization and the organization of social power. Hence the peculiarly noble character of the mood that prevails in the play. The speeches of all the main characters, except the Machiavellian manipulations of Marc Antony, resonate with integrity and Stoic fatalism—a quality of tone very different from the tragic anguish of *King Lear* or *Macbeth*, and different also from the chilling atmosphere of cunning cruelty in *Richard III*.

Leadership

In parallel with the actual exercise of power, literary representations of power occupy a range between two polar extremes: leaders envisioned as directing the energies of spontaneously cooperative individuals at one extreme, and tyrants envisioned as exercising pure dominance at the other. The middle ground between the extremes is occupied by varying degrees of willing cooperation and coercive power.

In *Troilus and Cressida*, Shakespeare's play about the Trojan War, the Greek warrior Ulysses articulates an idealized image of the leader as a pure embodiment of the collective will of his people. The Greeks have been stalled for years in their siege of Troy. In a counsel to discuss the situation, Ulysses addresses himself to Agamemnon, the leader of the Greeks:

> *Agamemnon,*
> *Thou great commander, nerve and bone of Greece,*
> *Heart of our numbers, soul and only sprite [spirit].*
> *In whom the tempers and the minds of all*
> *Should be shut up, hear what Ulysses speaks. (Shakespeare 1997:*
>   *1.3.54–58)*

Ulysses follows up this salutation with a speech on hierarchy that is widely regarded as a key to Renaissance ideas about social organization. Ulysses's term for "hierarchy" is "degree":

> *Take but degree away, untune that string,*
> *And, hark, what discord follows! . . .*
> *Force should be right; or rather, right and wrong,*
> *Between whose endless jar justice resides,*
> *Should lose their names, and so should justice too. (1.3.109–118)*

"Justice" is the exercise of power in accordance with publicly accepted standards of right and wrong. In Shakespeare's history plays, there are two chief ways in which leadership can fail: (1) through weakness, failing to incorporate the power latent in the state, or (2) through tyranny, pure dominance devoid of legitimacy.

The two ways leadership can fail might seem mutually exclusive, but Shakespeare's Richard II combines them. Richard alienates the aristocracy by wrongly appropriating the property of Bolingbroke, the future Henry IV. He abuses his power but has not sufficient command over the power of the state to meet the insurrection led by Bolingbroke. Richard is deposed and ultimately executed. He seems less interested in governing than in contemplating the image of himself as king. After being deposed, he wallows in self-pity, stubbornly insists on his "divine right" as an anointed king, but nonetheless articulates an anguished awareness that he is unfit to govern.

Shakespeare's King Lear has a thematic kinship with Richard II. Feeling himself weaken with age, he invests his two oldest daughters with the power and property that appertain to the sovereign, but he still wants to enjoy the prestige and deference accorded a king. Despising the claims of prestige not supported by wealth or power, his daughters mock and humiliate him. One daughter says, "I pray you, father, being weak, seem so" (Shakespeare 1997: 2.4.201). Both Richard II and Lear become narcissistically absorbed in articulating their inner torments. Neither is ever able fully to reconcile himself to a world in which privilege depends on power and is not automatically conferred on a person simply because that person feels he or she has a right to it.

Among Shakespeare's depicted kings, Henry V most fully exemplifies the spirit of leadership. Henry leads his nation to war in France and achieves success in combat. His success depends in good part on his ability to marshal the enthusiastic cooperation of his subordinates. His speech to his troops at the siege of Harfleur exemplifies the way he presents himself as a medium for directing the best energies of his soldiers:

> On, on, you noblest English.
> Whose blood is fet [derived] from fathers of war-proof!
> Fathers that, like so many Alexanders,
> Have in these parts from morn till even fought
> And sheath'd their swords for lack of argument:
> Dishonor not your mothers; now attest
> That those whom you call'd fathers did beget you.
> Be copy now to men of grosser blood,
> And teach them how to war. And you, good yeoman,
> Whose limbs were made in England, show us here
> The mettle of your pasture; let us swear
> That you are worth your breeding; which I doubt not;
> For there is none of you so mean and base,
> That hath not noble lustre in your eyes.
> I see you stand like greyhounds in the slips,
> Straining upon the start. The game's afoot:
> Follow your spirit, and upon this charge
> Cry, "God for Harry, England, and Saint George!" (Shakespeare 1997: 3.1.17–34)

Henry appeals to the pride of birth and lineage in the nobles, evoking the martial valor of generations. Though appealing to the nobles' consciousness of being of finer blood, he also appeals to the pride of the yeomen, lifting them up to a level with the nobles. He attributes their personal worth to the English environment that produced them and then includes England in the final invocation—"for Harry, England, and Saint George." Personal pride and pride in group identity are thus blended into one. Henry motivates both nobles and yeomen through pride rather than fear. Both groups respond to the image of themselves as part of a national culture personified in Saint George. Henry's own role, as he presents it, is the privilege of stimulating and leading men whose valor evokes his genuine admiration. In Henry's rhetoric, hierarchy is only an instrument for the realization of willing cooperation.

In Shakespeare's plays, kings who seek power for the sake of power alone end up isolated and hated. Macbeth offers a particularly poignant example. Richard III is a psychopath who cares only for power. Losing the love and respect of his followers means little or nothing to him. Macbeth, in contrast, is tormented by guilt at having murdered his king and his friend Banquo, and he keenly feels the loss of love and respect among his subjects:

> *I have lived long enough: my way of life*
> *Is fall'n into the sear, the yellow leaf;*
> *And that which should accompany old age,*
> *As honor, love, obedience, troops of friends,*
> *I must not look to have; but, in their stead,*
> *Curses, not loud but deep, mouth-honor, breath,*
> *Which the poor heart would fain deny, and dare not. (Shakespeare 1997:*
>   5.3.22–28)

Receiving love and respect from people one values is a deep psychological need. That need can be reconciled with the exercise of power, but only if a leader acquires legitimate authority by directing collective efforts toward common goals and in accordance with community norms.

Kings personify the body politic. Consequently, in plays about kings, personal domination is synonymous with authoritarian rule. In the twentieth century, the expansion of bureaucracy introduced a new kind of authoritarian rule: the totalitarian state. That is the subject of George Orwell's futuristic dystopian novel *1984*. Though collectivist, the totalitarian state, in Orwell's conception, is motivated by the same atavistic lust for power that animates characters like Tamburlaine, Richard III, and Jack Merridew. That motive is made explicit in a scene of torture and interrogation. The protagonist, Winston Smith, has resisted the state, has been captured, and is being reeducated by O'Brien, a high party functionary. O'Brien asks, "What is our motive? Why should we want power?" Winston wrongly assumes that O'Brien and the party rationalize their motives. He answers, "You are ruling over us for our own good" (Orwell 1949: part 3, ch. 3). O'Brien instantly twists a dial to inflict severe pain. "That was stupid, Winston, stupid!" The correct answer is that the lust for power is an irreducible motive, an intrinsic good:

> "The Party seeks power entirely for its own sake. We are not interested in the good of others; we are interested solely in power. Not wealth or luxury or long life or happiness: only power, pure power.... Power is not a means, it is an end. One does not establish a dictatorship in order to safeguard a revolution; one makes the revolution in order to establish the dictatorship. The object of persecution is persecution. The object of torture is torture. The object of power is power." (Part 3, ch. 3)

O'Brien has reduced all social interaction to relations of power. That conception eliminates willing cooperation to achieve common goals. Winston is helpless to rebut O'Brien, and Orwell offers no authorial reflections countering O'Brien's claims. Nonetheless, Orwell can be confident that his readers will respond with revulsion to O'Brien's vision of a society reduced to sadistic domination and abject subjugation. Emotional responses to the nightmare vision of *1984* draw on the same evolved social dispositions that activate responses to antagonists in Renaissance dramas, Victorian novels, and modern fantasy novels. By activating those responses, Orwell makes the modern totalitarian state emotionally intelligible. Like nightmares that wake us from sleep, and like horror stories about monsters (Clasen 2012b, 2012c), Orwell's novel attunes our minds to danger.

INTERNALIZING NORMS

Most human experience takes place in the space somewhere in between the isolated egoistic self and the fully integrated cell within a social organism. Science fiction sometimes envisions alien species that form superorganisms. Peter Watts's *Blindsight* gradually reveals that soldiers defending an alien planet from human incursion are actually only cells of the planet itself, which is a single living organism. In depictions of humans, the image of individuals as cells within a superorganism is usually restricted to dystopian nightmare visions like those of Yevgeny Zamyatin's futuristic dystopian novel *We*, Orwell's *1984*, and Madeleine L'Engle's science fiction children's novel *A Wrinkle in Time*. In *1984*, O'Brien makes the cell-organism conception explicit:

> "Can you not understand, Winston, that the individual is only a cell? The weariness of the cell is the vigour of the organism.... Every human being is doomed to die, which is the greatest of all failures. But if he can make complete, utter submission, if he can escape from his identity, if he can merge himself in the Party so that he is the Party, then he is all-powerful and immortal." (Orwell 1949: part 3, ch. 3)

The party forms a single social individual, and that individual adopts a stance of sadistic domination toward all other individuals:

> "How does one man assert his power over another, Winston?"
> Winston thought.
> "By making him suffer," he said.
> "Exactly. By making him suffer. Obedience is not enough. Unless he is suffering, how can you be sure that he is obeying your will and not his own? Power is in inflicting pain and humiliation."

Though perfectly integrated within itself, in its relations to others, the party is the institutional equivalent of a psychopath.

Among individual people, psychopaths come closest to occupying the extreme pole of asocial or antisocial egoism (Hare 1999; Baron-Cohen 2005, 2011; Oakley 2007; Widiger and Smith 2008; Raine 2013). As objects of horrified fascination, psychopaths bulk large in literature. Salient instances include Shakespeare's Richard III; Iago in Shakespeare's *Othello*; Daniel Quilp, the malignant dwarf in Dickens's *The Old Curiosity Shop*; the title character in Sheridan Le Fanu's Victorian novel *Uncle Silas*; the title character in Bram Stoker's *Dracula*; Mr. Hyde of Robert Louis Stevenson's *Dr. Jekyll and Mr. Hyde*; the vicious teenage thug Alex in Anthony Burgess's *A Clockwork Orange*; the renegade Blue Duck in Larry McMurtry's *Lonesome Dove*; and Patrick Bateman, the sadistic yuppie serial killer in Bret Easton Ellis's *American Psycho*.

Some few fictional works invite readers to participate vicariously in psychopathic cruelty. The novels of the Marquis de Sade, Burgess's *A Clockwork Orange*, and Ellis's *American Psycho* fall into that category (Carroll 2012c). But psychopathy is never modal in human society or in literature. In all cultures, specific norms emerge from a core of prosociality. Dispositions for promoting prosociality through cultural means have coevolved with human sociality (Bowles and Gintis 2011). Prosociality is not optional as a social norm. It is a necessary precondition for the existence of any human society. Sensationalistic depictions of psychopathic cruelty can offer titillations at the margins of a culture, but a society of psychopaths would be a contradiction in terms.

Since internalizing norms is a crucial part of human nature, plays and novels frequently depict characters gossiping about one another, putting moral pressure on one another, and undergoing the experience of guilt and shame. In romantic comedies, one very common story line involves a protagonist learning a lesson. For instance, in Austen's *Pride and Prejudice*, Fitzwilliam Darcy makes a rude and presumptuous proposal of marriage, is rebuked for not behaving like a gentleman, and takes the lesson to heart. In a grimmer and graver tonal range, characters violate moral norms in ways that lead to prolonged agonies of guilt. Salient instances include Macbeth, Claudius in *Hamlet*, Raskolnikov in Dostoevsky's *Crime and Punishment*, and Jim in Conrad's *Lord Jim*.

The bias for conformity—going along with the crowd, doing as others do—is a mechanism for social learning and for internalizing norms (Chudek and Henrich 2011: 219). Since it operates in tension with independent observation and judgment, it offers a rich field for satire in literary representation. Sinclair Lewis's *Main Street* depicts a narrow-minded, small-town world in which any distinction or individuality results in ostracism. In *Adam Bede*, George Eliot preaches the doctrine of loving "my everyday fellow men" (1968: ch. 17), but in *Middlemarch* her everyday fellow men are for the most part small-minded, conventional people who collectively impede every effort toward higher forms of moral and intellectual life. In Joseph Heller's *Catch-22*, written in the McCarthy era, the sinister Captain Black starts a Glorious Loyalty Oath Crusade. The soldiers are soon so busy signing loyalty oaths, pledging allegiance to the flag, and singing "The Star-Spangled Banner" that they have no time for anything else. The title character in Mark Twain's *Huckleberry Finn* is a boy who runs away from his abusive father and floats on a raft down the Mississippi River with Jim, a runaway slave. Huck suffers torments of conscience for having helped Jim steal himself from his rightful owner. Jim's sincere friendship and gratitude ultimately overcome the urgings of Huck's conscience, and Huck decides he will accept the burden of having committed a mortal sin. "All right, then, I'll go to hell" (Twain 1999: ch. 31). Twain clearly intends readers to understand that Huck's sense of guilt is a reflex of conventional values that conflict with his intuitive humanity.

Prestige bias—imitating individuals with high status—also operates in tension with independent observation and judgment. When prestige bias and conformity bias are combined and driven to an extreme, they produce societies in which an authoritarian leader seconded by secret police enforces thought control. That toxic combination appears in two major dystopian novels, Zamyatin's *We* and Orwell's *1984*. The individuals in *We* are designated "numbers" and have names that are combinations of a single letter and a set of digits. They eat in vast collective dining halls and masticate in synchronized movements of their jaws (Cooke 2002). Their every thought and movement is directed by the Benefactor. In *1984*, Winston's subjugation to the Party reaches its culmination when he submerges himself in the cult of personality centered on Big Brother, modeled on Stalin. At the end of the novel, Winston is sitting in a café, drinking gin, looking up at a poster of Big Brother:

> He gazed up at the enormous face. Forty years it had taken him to learn what kind of smile was hidden beneath the dark moustache. O cruel, needless misunderstanding! O stubborn, self-willed exile from the loving breast! Two gin-scented tears trickled down the sides of his nose. But it was all right, everything was all right, the struggle was finished. He had won the victory over himself. He loved Big Brother. (Orwell 1949: ch. 23)

The cult of personality is in part a reversion to the pure dominance hierarchies that characterize the last common ancestor of humans and chimpanzees (Wrangham and Peterson 1996; Boehm 1999, 2012). In *Lord of the Flies*, the leader of the savage band, Jack, institutes an authoritarian government based on his charismatic personality. When Jack makes a pronouncement, he has two boys stand forth and declare, "The chief has spoken" (Golding 1954: ch. 8). Human dominance differs from chimpanzee dominance in that humans can at least transiently rise above individuality and merge themselves imaginatively into a single social entity. The members of Jack's tribe paint themselves with clay and dance and chant in unison. After killing a pig, they chant, "Kill the pig. Cut her throat. Spill her blood" (ch. 4). Moving together in time is a universal means of unifying individuals into a single social body (McNeill 1995).

Strong Reciprocity

Bowles and Gintis define strong reciprocity as "a predisposition to cooperate and a willingness to punish defectors" (2011: 166). Giving aid to people who display prosocial impulses and punishing antisocial behavior spring from the same adaptive need to form communities. When other members of the aristocracy kill Richard III and Macbeth, they are engaging in the punitive aspect of strong reciprocity. The affiliative aspect of strong reciprocity appears in stories in which characters go out of their way to support prosocial impulses in others.

George Eliot's *Middlemarch* (2000) offers scenes illustrating both punitive strong reciprocity and affiliative strong reciprocity. In a punitive episode, word has gotten out that a wealthy banker and philanthropist, Bulstrode, has engaged in dishonorable acts. He attends a council meeting in which one of the council members, speaking for the whole group, denounces Bulstrode and begins the process that will result in Bulstrode being ostracized. The effect is devastating. Bulstrode's recognition of his public humiliation "rushed through him like the agony of terror which fails to kill, and leaves the ears still open to the returning wave of execration" (2000: ch. 71). A doctor in the town, Lydgate, is mistakenly believed to have been complicit in Bulstrode's wrongdoing. Eliot's female protagonist, Dorothea Brooke, comes to Lydgate and asks him to tell her the full story of his relations with Bulstrode. She promises to spread that story to everyone she knows and thus to clear Lydgate's name. "They would know that I could have no other motive than truth and justice. I would take any pains to clear you.... There is nothing better that I can do in the world" (ch. 76). Knowing that Lydgate has money troubles, and believing in his mission as a medical scientist, she also helps him out financially. Dorothea is represented as having a morally refined character, but her behavior is not implausible. Consider that in our own current world, prizes like the Nobel Prize or the MacArthur Prize are designed to offer public recognition of social contributions and also to give material rewards for those contributions.

Strong reciprocity confirms the force of social norms in the minds of individuals. It gives evidence that individuals have internalized the principles that shape individuals into a collective entity, a social body. The need to coalesce into a social body can go still deeper than that, can become a primary need independent of the principles of justice that inform strong reciprocity. Shirley Ann Jackson's "The Lottery," one of the most frequently anthologized short stories, offers a way into that deeper social dynamic. "The Lottery" is a satiric dystopian horror story set in a small mid-American farming village in the middle of the twentieth century. The townspeople gather for the annual lottery. There is a feeling of general festivity and social goodwill, with an undercurrent of excitement. The whole community participates in the lottery. Each year, one person draws a slip of paper with a black mark on it. The whole community joins together in stoning that person to death. In the episode depicted in the story, the winner of the lottery is a housewife, Tessie Hutchinson. Her husband and children join in the stoning. The frequency with which this story has been anthologized indicates that it exercises an uncommon fascination, but it is also mysterious, puzzling, a little opaque. What does it mean? Students most often default to the assumption that the lottery represents mindless conventionalism, and there is some evidence for that reading. No one in the story can remember precisely what the lottery is for, and its most fervent supporter, Old Man Warner, is clearly a depiction of reactionary conservatism. But the peculiar thing about this convention is that it has no content. Unlike the convention that Huckleberry Finn violates, no one gains anything tangible from the stoning. A slave owner gets the labor of the slave. That has economic value. Maintaining respect for property is a clearly understood moral norm. Stoning an innocent neighbor to death has no evident material payoff. The payoff is only psychological. The punitive action is not designed to enforce any social norm, but it nonetheless fulfills a psychosocial function. By collectively killing a randomly chosen person, the villagers subordinate individuals and families to the community as a whole. The villagers merge ritualistically into a single social body that manifests its unity by destroying an individual cast out from the group.

A similar psychosocial dynamic is at work in the scene depicting Simon's death in *Lord of the Flies*. Frightened by a coming storm and an imaginary Beast supposedly lurking in the jungle, Jack's tribe adapt their pig-killing chant to help ward off their fear. "Kill the beast! Cut his throat! Spill his blood!" (ch. 9). While they are dancing and chanting, Simon comes out of the forest and stumbles into the midst of their group, eager to explain to them that there is no Beast. Caught up in an exalted frenzy, imagining him as the Beast, they stab and beat him to death.

The collective social actions that piled up skulls in Aztec temples, burned or hanged witches up through the seventeenth century, staged public executions as mass entertainment up through the eighteenth century, levied death sentences on party members in the Moscow show trials, and produced acres of human bones in the Cambodian killing fields—all these forms of gratuitous social cruelty suggest that Jackson's story captures something real in human social psychology.

"The Lottery" might reasonably be charged with paranoiac exaggeration. An opposite kind of exaggeration, naïve and sentimental, is at work in the principle of "poetic justice." That term used in reference to plots in novels and plays means that prosocial characters have good outcomes and antisocial characters have bad outcomes. Authors who conform to the convention of poetic justice create plots that give emotional satisfaction to both the positive and punitive impulses at work in strong reciprocity. Christian eschatology, exemplified in Dante's *Divine Comedy*, is a cosmic form of poetic justice. It provides an obvious kind of moral satisfaction, suggesting that human concepts of justice are at work in the deeper causal fabric of the universe. That kind of thinking, in secularized form, prevails heavily in the eighteenth century and is exemplified in Alexander Pope's optimistic pronouncement that *"whatever is, is right"* (1950: epistle 1, stanza 10). In his novel *Candide*, Voltaire, satirizing the optimistic philosophy of Leibnitz, depicts his protagonists suffering a series of catastrophes to which the philosopher Pangloss always responds that everything always turns out for the best in this best of all possible worlds. British novelists of the eighteenth and nineteenth centuries are more discreet than Pangloss, but they nonetheless usually conform to the convention of poetic justice. The hero or heroine, despite making mistakes, is basically good-hearted, prosocial; he or she undergoes trials, glimpses the possibility of disaster, and in the end achieves good fortune. The pattern is suggested in one of the first English novels, Richardson's *Pamela*, which has as a subtitle, "Virtue Rewarded." Until the last twenty years or so of the nineteenth century, virtue was rewarded more often than not, and few antagonists escaped some kind of punishment for their misdeeds, but the retaliation often did not come directly from the hands of the protagonist. Punitive acts were left up to third parties or even inanimate objects. The fate of the villain Rigaud in Dickens's *Little Dorrit* offers a paradigmatic instance. He is crushed to death inside a house that collapses of its own weight.

After about 1880, the strong correlation between prosociality and ultimate good fortune disappears (Carroll et al. 2012b: 132–133). The mood of the later part of the century becomes more bleak, less trusting, less confident that principles of justice permeate the fabric of the universe. Growing skepticism about a beneficent deity and an increasing awareness of the inhuman magnitude of the universe contribute to that shift in mood. Faith in the Christian scheme had been diminishing at least since the seventeenth century. Dryden's philosophical poem *Religio Laici* (1682) gives expression to the doubt engendered by the imaginative impact of world exploration, which revealed whole continents outside the Christian dispensation. A similar expansion was at work in astronomy, eliminating the geocentric and heliocentric cosmos. Early in the nineteenth century, anthropological and ethnographic work on the composition of the Bible had shaken faith in the belief that the Bible is the revealed Word of God, and geology had already begun extending time backward into unimaginable eons, further diminishing the imaginative plausibility of a mythic system centered on human affairs. The publication of *The Origin of Species* in 1859 was in some ways merely a final nail in the coffin for the imaginative plausibility of the Christian myth. Writers such as Hardy and Conrad, who had absorbed the main intellectual currents of the nineteenth century, had to confront a world of harsh realities in which human justice could find a rationale and a satisfaction only within itself, regardless of the good fortunes that might or might not attend prosocial people.

Shakespeare remains so central a figure in English literary history in part because he had already accepted responsibility for that kind of moral universe. The eighteenth century could not bear to read *King Lear* in its original form. The pure and virtuous Cordelia, an embodiment of faithfulness, is hanged. For more than a century, the version of the play that was performed on the stage was a version that had been rewritten to conform to the convention of poetic justice (Carroll 2012b). The good are not always rewarded in Shakespeare, but viciousness is usually punished. Antisocial behavior produces a disequilibrium in society, unleashing strong reciprocity. Richard III, Macbeth, Prince John in *Much Ado about Nothing*, Iago in *Othello*, Claudius in *Hamlet*, and in *King Lear* Edmund, Cornwall, Goneril, and Regan all come to bad ends. For Lady Macbeth, strong reciprocity need not be enforced by external agents. It comes from within. Tormented by guilt for helping her husband murder their king, she commits suicide. That kind of moral support for justice—punishment from without and from within—remains an active force in modern fiction because it conforms to social and psychological reality.

Institutions for Enforcing Norms

Legal institutions are designed to solve basic problems in the formation of complex societies with large populations and hierarchically organized structures of power. They provide specialized expertise and formal procedures for investigating, judging, and punishing infractions against community norms. By transferring punitive authority to the state and offering an approximation to objectivity in the adjudication of disputes, societies forestall the destructive spiral of blood feuds.

Like all contrivances, legal institutions solve some problems but create new ones. Citizens can easily become alienated from complex and impersonal bureaucracies invested with coercive power. They observe that authorities entrusted with the task of inflicting punishment sometimes abuse their powers and that the sadistic desire to inflict punishment can be a motive in itself. They observe that the police and the judiciary incorporate the underlying structure of power in a society and that their policies almost inevitably reflect the interests of the ruling classes. They notice too that the police and the judiciary tend to protect their own agents and perpetuate their own activity. Such observations produce fears and resentments that find expression in satiric and dystopian fiction.

Countervailing feelings are prompted by the unavoidable necessity, in complex societies, for institutionalizing coercive power. At an emotional extreme opposite that of satiric and dystopian fiction, in many novels the police and the judiciary exemplify social justice. A dialogue in Conrad's novel *The Secret Agent* exemplifies the two extremes. Stevie, a retarded boy, "had formed for himself an ideal conception of the metropolitan police as a sort of benevolent institution for the suppression of evil" (1985: ch. 8). His sister corrects him. "Don't you know what the police are for, Stevie? They are there so that them as have nothing shouldn't take anything away from them who have" (ch. 8).

In the bulk of plays and novels, the attitudes that govern depictions of the legal system fall somewhere in between these two extremes. In many novels and plays, the legal system is present simply as a fact of life, like a feature of the landscape, a target neither for moral resentment nor for reverential respect. Like fire or gravity, it sets boundaries and creates consequences for human behavior. Because the law is such a prominent feature of human social life, a great many fictional dramas work themselves out around it. Almost unconsciously, characters regulate their behavior with regard to legal constraints. They also sometimes take refuge in the law, finding safety in it, and not infrequently they come into fatal collision with it. In detective stories, protagonists are engaged in ferreting out guilty secrets. The law in such cases is something like a board in a board game; it defines the parameters of play.

In its simplest version, a paranoiac vision of legal systems reduces police action to state-sanctioned sadism like that envisioned by O'Brien, the party functionary who tortures Winston Smith in *1984*. Images of sadistic police brutality pervade stories of the Holocaust and the Soviet Gulag: Alexander Solzhenitsyn's *One Day in the Life of Ivan Denisovich*, Varlam Shalamov's *Kolyma Tales*, Vasily Grossman's *Everything Flows* and *Life and Fate*, and Tadeusz Borowski's *This Way for the Gas, Ladies and Gentlemen*.

Totalitarianism and global war in the middle of the twentieth century provided an environment in which legal sadism could be plausibly overgeneralized. One such overgeneralization appears in Joseph Heller's *Catch-22*, published in 1955. In a chapter titled "The Eternal City," the protagonist Yossarian, an American bombardier stationed in Italy, walks through Rome at night, witnessing a series of nightmarish scenes of brutality and horror. In one scene, "a single Italian with books" is being attacked by "a slew of civilian policemen with armlocks and clubs" (1961: ch. 39). As he is being hauled away, the man cries out, "Police! Help! Police!":

> Yossarian smiled wryly at the futile and ridiculous cry for aid, then saw with a start that the words were ambiguous, realized with alarm that they were not, perhaps, intended as a call for police but as a heroic warning from the grave by a doomed friend to everyone who was *not* a policeman with a club and a gun and a mob of other policemen with clubs and guns to back him up.

Through Yossarian, Heller tacitly includes America in the scope of this generalization. "Mobs ... mobs of policemen—everything but England was in the hands of mobs, mobs, mobs. Mobs with clubs were in control everywhere" (ch. 39). In the late sixties in America, that view of the police contributed its emotional force to the riots and demonstrations against the war in Vietnam—with the police routinely designated "pigs" and America spelled with a "k" instead of a "c" (Amerika), thus mimicking German spelling and evoking fascist militarism.

The police and the judiciary form a continuum. The police deliver suspects to the judiciary and enforce the judgments of the court. Even in cases that do not involve criminal action, the power of the court can stimulate dystopian horror stories in the minds of writers prone to distrust government. Dickens is one such writer. In *Little Dorrit*, the whole of the government is embodied in the Circumlocution Office, designed purposefully to make sure that nothing ever gets accomplished. That same distrust inspires Dickens's depiction of the Court of Chancery in *Bleak House*. Chancery is the institution entrusted with resolving disputes over wills and inheritance. As Dickens conceives it, Chancery subsists only to make business for lawyers, with ruinous effects on anyone who gets lost in its labyrinths. One of the main characters in *Bleak House* becomes absorbed in a case, Jarndyce and Jarndyce, from which he hopes to gain a fortune. The case has dragged on for many generations. "Innumerable children have been born into the cause; innumerable young people have married into it; innumerable old people have died out of it. Scores of persons have deliriously found themselves made parties in Jarndyce and Jarndyce without knowing how or why" (Dickens 1977: ch. 1). No one understands the case, and it has no hope of ever being resolved legally. It comes to an end only when the whole estate is found to have been consumed in legal costs. The character who has pinned his hopes on the case dies in despair.

Dickens's vision of the judicial system, though based on a real case, has a close kinship with the surrealistic nightmare vision of Franz Kafka's novel *The Trial*. The protagonist in the trial, Josef K., is arrested and summoned to court. He is not informed what the charges against him are, or by what authority he is being tried. He gets a lawyer, but the lawyer's explanations offer no clarification. The lawyer tells him that documents have to be filed, but that no one knows what the documents should contain. That might not matter, since the documents are not usually read, but if the accuser becomes insistent, the court officials say that the documents have to be gone over carefully. By that time, though, the documents have usually been lost. Like Jarndyce and Jarndyce, the process continues interminably, with no end in sight. Someone who knows the court fairly well tells K. that to his knowledge no defendant has ever been acquitted. As in Jarndyce vs. Jarndyce, although there is no legal resolution to the case, there is an end to it. K. is abducted from his room, taken to a quarry, and stabbed to death.

All police have coercive power, but not all societies are equally arbitrary, corrupt, or vicious in the exercise of power. Satires of the law like those of Dickens and Kafka tacitly invoke a standard of justice the law is supposed to embody, and for Dickens, at least, one main motive for satire is to put moral pressure on the judicial system so that it will more adequately embody that standard. Orwell's depiction of the totalitarian state is modeled on Stalinist Russia and has a real historical solidity to it. Yossarian's impression that all societies except England are ruled by mobs with clubs, in contrast, is a glib sort of cynicism that, when challenged, Yossarian is not himself willing to maintain. In the final chapter of *Catch-22*, Yossarian has a conversation with Major Danby, who tells him, "This is not World War One. You must never forget that we're at war with aggressors who would not let either one of us live if they won." Yossarian reluctantly concedes the point.

The necessity of the law is made evident in scenes depicting its absence—for instance, the mob violence depicted in Benjamin Disraeli's *Sybil, or the Two Nations*, Dickens's *Barnaby Rudge*, and Eliot's *Felix Holt*; the sadistic anarchy that reigns in Cormac

McCarthy's *Blood Meridian* (a historical novel) and *The Road* (a post-apocalyptic novel); the ugly passions animating men in the lynchings depicted in William Faulkner's "Dry September," Steinbeck's *Of Mice and Men*, Jean Toomer's "Blood Burning Moon," and Walter Van Tilburg Clark's *The Ox-Bow Incident*; and the horror of any scene in which psychopathic violence becomes even temporarily a dominant social force, as it does in *Richard III*, *King Lear*, Dickens's *Oliver Twist*, Emily Brontë's *Wuthering Heights*, Conrad's *Nostromo*, Larry McMurtry's *Lonesome Dove*, McCarthy's *No Country for Old Men*, and Ellis's *American Psycho*.

In *Lonesome Dove*, two former Texas Rangers hang one of their old comrades, a genial but morally lax man who has inadvertently become associated with a gang of psychopaths. The psychopaths have wantonly murdered innocent people. In a frontier world without active law enforcement, the ex-Rangers enforce a crude and simple code of justice. Hanging their old friend gives them grief, but they have no moral doubt about the necessity of enforcing a simple code of retributive justice. McMurtry does not suggest that he himself has any ironic distance from their view of the matter.

In *Lord of the Flies*, a large seashell, a conch, becomes a symbol of the law. When the boys first assemble, they establish a rule for discussion. Whoever holds the conch has the floor and can speak without interruption. After Jack has lured or coerced most of the boys to join his tribe, they attack Piggy in order to steal his glasses, which can be used for starting a fire. The crisis of the story occurs when Piggy and Ralph go to Jack's fortress to demand the return of the glasses. Piggy carries the conch with him in a futile effort to appeal to law. As Ralph and Jack are fighting, Piggy is "still holding out the talisman, the fragile, shining beauty of the shell" (ch. 10). Jack's sadistic henchman, Roger, above them on a high rock, uses a lever to roll a boulder down on Ralph and Piggy. Ralph ducks, but without his glasses Piggy is too blind to see the danger coming. "The rock struck Piggy a glancing blow from chin to knee; the conch exploded into a thousand white fragments and ceased to exist" (ch. 10). Piggy is knocked off the cliff and his skull smashed open on a rock below. The phrase "the fragile, shining beauty of the shell" is a literal description of the shell and also a metaphoric description of what the shell represents—the fragile beauty of the law. Moments like this clearly establish Golding's own judgment about the moral significance of the conflicts depicted in the story. Jack is driven by a lust for power, and Roger is an instrument of that power. Ralph and Piggy resist the reversion to simple dominance.

Golding's evaluative stance is implicit in his symbolic imagery, his evident sympathy with Piggy and Ralph, and his evident dislike of Jack and Roger. In *Billy Budd, Sailor*, Herman Melville makes the same basic stance explicit in reflective commentary on the story. Billy is a young seaman on board a British warship during the period of conflict with revolutionary France. The spirit of social revolt has seeped over from France into England and has produced two recent naval mutinies. Billy has a frank and open nature and elicits the dislike of an under-officer, who slanderously accuses him of spreading mutiny. Billy has a stutter that chokes his speech when he becomes emotionally aroused. Enraged at the false accusation and unable to defend himself verbally, Billy strikes the under-officer, who dies from the blow. The attack is a capital offense. The captain of the ship, Captain Vere, believes that Billy is innocent of any mutinous intent and that his accuser is a scoundrel. He nonetheless strictly applies the law, and Billy is hanged.

A story of this sort could be written from any number of ideological standpoints, including the generalized distrust and dislike of judicial authority evident in writers like Dickens, Kafka, and Heller. Before recounting the central events of the story, Melville establishes his own unequivocally conservative ideological stance. Describing the mutiny preceding the events of the story, he says that the British common sailors "ran up with huzzas the British colors with the union and cross wiped out; by that cancellation transmuting the flag of founded law and freedom defined, into the enemy's red meteor of unbridled and unbounded revolt" (1986: ch. 3). There can be little doubt that "founded law and freedom" have a positive valence set in polar opposition to the "unbridled and unbounded revolt" of the French Revolution. Reflecting on the transitory nature of the mutinous impulses in the British navy, Melville suggests that the mutiny "may be regarded as analogous to the distempering irruption of contagious fever in a frame constitutionally sound, and which anon throws it off" (ch. 3). The story is told chiefly from the perspective of Captain Vere, whose perspective evidently corresponds closely to Melville's own. Vere is an intellectual, a learned and reflective man. He is of aristocratic lineage, but Melville absolves him of petty self-interest in his resistance to French radicalism. "While other members of that aristocracy to which by birth he belonged were incensed at the innovators mainly because their theories were inimical to the privileged classes, Captain Vere disinterestedly opposed them not alone because they seemed to him insusceptible of embodiment in lasting institutions, but at war with the peace of the world and the true welfare of mankind" (ch. 7). In supporting legally constituted authority, Vere is motivated neither by class interest nor by the desire for personal power. "Though a conscientious disciplinarian, he was no lover of authority for mere authority's sake" (ch. 21). He is motivated by the necessity for maintaining discipline in his fighting force. In a period of mutinous feelings, laxity in enforcing hierarchical subordination could, he fears, lead to anarchic revolt. From Vere's perspective, and from Melville's, the case is "a moral dilemma" working to a "tragic" outcome (ch. 21).

Legitimacy

The legitimacy of a social order would be absolute if the structure of power and the structure of internalized norms in a society were in perfect concord. That is, of course, never the case. Even in biological organisms, cancerous cells defect from the social body. Human societies are much messier, less coherent, than biological organisms. The needs and impulses of individuals usually work in some tension with the demands of society. Individuals are enmeshed in families and kin groups that contain internal conflicts and that also often work in tension with the demands of the larger society (Fukuyama 2011). Individuals and kin groups coalesce into classes, trades, ethnic groups, cities, and geographical regions that have to negotiate conflicting interests. In complex post-agricultural societies, all social power structures constitute temporary equilibria among diverse forces pulling in many different directions simultaneously. Legitimacy, therefore, is always a matter of degree.

Novels of poverty such as *Sybil, Bleak House, North and South, The Jungle,* and *The Grapes of Wrath* raise questions of social legitimacy because they depict societies that fail to provide for the basic physical needs of its members. Questions of legitimacy arise also in novels that depict people deprived of a valued place in society. That kind of problem is most obvious in cases in which racial minorities are reduced to slavery or treated as second-class citizens. Instances include *Uncle Tom's Cabin*, Ralph Ellison's *Invisible Man*, Toni Morrison's *Beloved*, and Thomas Keneally's *The Chant of Jimmie Blacksmith*. The societies depicted in literary dystopias typically eliminate close personal ties, which are necessary for human well-being. In the societies depicted in *We* and in Aldous Huxley's *Brave New World*, families have been eliminated and all sustained intimate relationships are discouraged. As O'Brien puts it in *1984*, "We have cut the links between child and parent, and between man and man, and between man and woman" (Orwell 1949: part 3, ch. 3). Dystopian novels are by definition repudiations of a whole society. Realist novels can also depict societies that, in the view of their authors, fail to provide a worthwhile quality of life. In V. S. Naipaul's *A Bend in the River*, an Indian merchant living in the postcolonial Congo watches his society slide inexorably into a chaos presided over by a lunatic cult of personality. In that kind of environment, as one character observes, "Nothing has any meaning" (1980: ch. 17).

Like authorial attitudes toward legal systems, authorial attitudes toward social legitimacy vary along a continuum, from complete acceptance at one extreme to complete repudiation at another. Jane Austen and Anthony Trollope give little or no evidence of questioning the legitimacy of the social order in which their characters live. Austen's characters inhabit a hermetic social universe in which servants and members of the lower classes are usually invisible. In Trollope's fictive world, social forces typically work in concert, even without conscious collective intent, to resolve conflicts and bring about harmonious results in accordance with the principles of poetic justice. In contrast to Austen and Trollope, Dickens frequently expresses outrage over government corruption and the condition of the poor. He is nonetheless as skeptical as Melville about the anarchic forces let loose in the French Revolution. The protagonists of *A Tale of Two Cities* stand apart from both the arrogant cruelty of the aristocrats and the vindictive cruelty of the revolutionaries. The title character in Eliot's *Felix Holt, the Radical* is a politically conscious proletarian intellectual but only the mildest kind of "radical." He wants voting rights eventually extended to the working class but is more eager to improve their education so that they will be capable of participating responsibly in political life. In the first half of the twentieth century, many American writers gave voice to the discontents of the working class. In his *USA* trilogy, John Dos Passos envisions heroes of the labor movement struggling against the exploitative and personally corrupting forces of capitalism. John Steinbeck's *The Grapes of Wrath* has a similar ideological orientation. Before the Second World War, that kind of orientation made some writers sympathetic to an idealized and sanitized image of Soviet Russia. In consequence, they were hostile to Arthur Koestler's *Darkness at Noon*, which cast an unwelcome light on the brutality and dishonesty of the Soviet state. Leftist ideology remains a strong force in contemporary American intellectual life, especially among academics but also among some literary authors. In *The Corrections*, Jonathan Franzen adopts a Foucauldian perspective concordant with that of academic literary radicals. From that perspective, all government control is exploitative and abusive. Franzen's protagonist spends time in Lithuania during an anarchic meltdown of government. "It warmed his Foucaultian heart, in a way, to live in a land where property ownership and the control of public discourse were so obviously a matter of who had the guns" (2001: 441; Carroll 2013a). This kind of declaration has an evident kinship with Yossarian's claim that "mobs with guns" are in control everywhere. Franzen and Heller both erase distinctions between fascist dictatorships, totalitarian police states, and liberal democracies.

Among literary works that take social legitimacy as their chief theme, Conrad's *Heart of Darkness* has a special prominence. Conrad's embedded narrator, Marlow, tells a story of an adventure that profoundly affected his imagination, still troubles him, and provokes him to meditative effort. The meditation is complex, ironic, elusive, and sometimes contradictory, but it is nonetheless governed by a basic antithesis between savagery and civilization. Because Marlow and Conrad believe in civilization and regard Africa as a site of savagery, Conrad has sometimes been charged with racism and colonialist presumption (Achebe 1977; Said 1993). In reality, no story animated chiefly by racial chauvinism could maintain a central place in the canon of Western literature, much less in the curriculum of modern English departments. Marlow witnesses savagery among the natives in the Congo—that is, he sees tribal life not dissimilar to the tribal life that prevailed in Britain before the Roman conquest. Marlow's narrative, told to other men sitting on a boat on the Thames, opens with that declared equivalency. "'And this also,' said Marlow suddenly, 'has been one of the dark places of the earth'" (2011: ch. 1). Civilization distinguishes itself from tribal life through legal institutions designed for the formal enforcement of community norms (Fukuyama 2011). As Conrad and Marlow see it, the whites in the Belgian Congo create only a hideous parody of civilization. They represent "a rapacious and pitiless folly" disguised with absurd pretenses of law and justice (ch. 2). Marlow has a habituated feeling of living in an atmosphere of civilized norms. In Africa, that feeling is assailed by images of savagery on one side and images of a degenerate parody of civilization on the other. Those dual challenges produce a severe psychological strain that results in a hallucinatory intensity of imaginative observation. Everything he sees on his journey takes on a dreamlike symbolic quality. *Heart of Darkness* has become canonical in part because Marlow effectively communicates the peculiar intensity of the imaginative experience produced by his struggle to sustain his belief in the legitimacy of civilization.

The situation of the story is simple. Out of a spirit of curiosity, Marlow takes employment as captain of a river steamer owned by a Belgian company that trades for ivory in the Congo. Marlow is sent deep into the jungle to bring out an agent who has fallen sick. He discovers that the agent, Kurtz, had succumbed to the temptation of assuming absolute power over a savage band. Kurtz had become leader of a native tribe and had conducted raids on other tribes to steal their ivory. But he had not become just an ordinary brigand. He had set himself up as a god to be worshipped and had presided over "certain midnight dances ending with unspeakable rites" that "were offered up to him—do you understand?—to Mr. Kurtz himself" (2011: ch. 2). Those rites probably involve human sacrifice—heads on poles adorn the entrance to Kurtz's camp. Telling the story to his friends on board a boat in the Thames, Marlow struggles to explain what had gone wrong with Kurtz:

> He had taken a high seat amongst the devils of the land—I mean literally. You can't understand. How could you?—with solid pavement under your feet, surrounded by kind neighbours ready to cheer you or to fall on you, stepping delicately between the butcher and the policeman, in the holy terror of scandal and gallows and lunatic asylums—how can you imagine what particular region of the first ages a man's untrammelled feet may take him into by the way of solitude—utter solitude without a policeman—by the way of silence—utter silence, where no warning voice of a kind neighbour can be heard whispering of public opinion? These little things make all the great difference. When they are gone you must fall back upon your own innate strength, upon your own capacity for faithfulness. ... your power of devotion, not to yourself, but to an obscure, back-breaking business. (ch. 2)

That obscure, back-breaking business is the work of civilization. As a prelude to his tale, Marlow speaks disparagingly of "the conquest of the earth, which mostly means the taking it away from those who have a different complexion or slightly flatter noses than ourselves" (ch. 1). Nonetheless, he declares that colonialism can have a genuine moral rationale. "What redeems it is the idea only. An idea at the back of it; not a sentimental pretence but an idea; and an unselfish belief in the idea—something you can set up, bow down before, and offer a sacrifice to" (ch. 1). The idea is the idea of decency, restraint, constructive work—the effort to create a society in which the structure of power is regulated by internalized norms of justice vested in responsible institutions. In place of that idea, Kurtz sets himself up alone as the object to which men must bow down and offer a sacrifice. That is, Kurtz reverts to pure dominance as a mode of government.

On the relation between internalized norms and strong reciprocity, Marlow makes contradictory claims. He claims that strong reciprocity ("the whispers of public opinion") and the presence of legal institutions (the police and the gallows) "make all the difference." But he also claims that without those external supports one can still appeal to one's "capacity for faithfulness"—that is, to internalized norms. Kurtz succumbs to the temptations of savagery because he is "hollow at the core" (ch. 2). Marlow is not.

Conrad lives at the meditative extremes of moral consciousness, sometimes vibrating firmly and passionately with convictions about civilization and honor, sometimes groping in fog and confusion for what he believes, sometimes standing in terror on the brink of moral emptiness. He is often perplexed, but he does ultimately affirm that civilization is a real thing, not just a pretense; it is the indispensable framework within which people of integrity must organize their activity.

Heart of Darkness and *Lord of the Flies* are radically different in manner and style. *Lord of the Flies* is spare and restrained, sticking closely to objective description. The narrative in *Heart of Darkness* is delivered from a highly particularized, personal perspective, and the language is rhetorical and reflective to a high degree. Despite these differences, the two works resonate at the same ethical wavelengths. They are both thematically centered on a contrast between savagery and civilization. Kurtz and Jack both revert to savagery. Ralph and Marlow both hold on desperately, with difficulty and confusion, to an ideal of civilization. The "fragile shining beauty" of the conch in *Lord of the Flies* is a symbol for what Marlow calls "an unselfish belief in the idea—something you can set up, bow down before, and offer a sacrifice to." What Ralph and Marlow offer a sacrifice to is not just this or that social group, but a social concept—the concept of civilization.

Conclusion

Readers participate in an imagined virtual world created by an author and also, simultaneously, stand outside that world, encompassing it within their own worldview. In this respect, authors and readers are like any other people engaged in a communicative transaction. Professional literary critics and scholars are readers who have specialized training and extensive experience in this particular kind of communicative transaction. They evoke the subjective, qualitative sensations expressed in literary works; analyze the organization of subject, style, and tone that produce those sensations; articulate their own evaluative responses; register the responses of other readers; make comparisons that help define and classify works; and analyze the relation of literary works to their sources: the lives and minds of authors, the material and social conditions in which a work is produced, and cultural traditions that include religious, philosophical, and literary traditions. All of this critical and scholarly activity can take place only within the mind of the critic and scholar—his or her perceptions, emotions, ideas, beliefs, and values.

Emotional and aesthetic responsiveness is heavily dependent on the personality and sensibility of individual readers, but even the most subjective responses are influenced by a reader's ideas—conceptions about human nature, society, and literature itself. The most objective and scholarly aspects of professional literary study abstract away from variations in individual responsiveness and aim at classification and explanation. Classification is like taxonomy in biology. It is descriptive and analytic but presupposes that certain categories form natural kinds that cut nature at its joints. Explanation presupposes that specific literary works are produced by causes such as human communicative psychology, the material and social conditions in which an author writes, cultural traditions, and the temperament and mind of the author. A scholar's ideas about the causal forces producing literature thus fundamentally shape his or her commentary on literary works.

Until the late 1970s, most professional literary study used an eclectic mix of ad hoc terms for the purposes of classification and causal explanation (Carroll 2004b). The largest, most general terms used in literary taxonomy are concepts of "genre." Multiple schemes of genre have been proposed; none has achieved the kind of general acceptance that attends on Linnaeus's taxonomy of plants and animals (Fowler 1982). In the middle of the twentieth century, Northrop Frye argued that "what is at present missing from literary criticism is a co-ordinating principle, a central hypothesis which, like the theory of evolution in biology, will see the phenomena it deals with as parts of a whole" (1951: 96). Frye proposed "myths" and "archetypes" as that central coordinating principle. In *Anatomy of Criticism* (1957), he produced a taxonomy based on myths and archetypes. Though Frye appealed to evolutionary biology as a model for an explanatory system, he did not appeal to biology as a source of causal explanation. Frye was a Christian minister and a Romantic mystic. His archetypes are autonomous spiritual forces emanating from a transcendental center—that is, from God (Carroll 1995: ch. 10). Since the middle of the twentieth century, no further large-scale efforts at taxonomy have been made. Fashioning taxonomies presupposes the existence of natural kinds, and since the late 1970s, most literary theorists have repudiated the idea that nature has an inherent structure that can be objectively ascertained.

The literary theory current now in the academic literary establishment blends Derridean linguistic epistemology, Marxist social theory, Freudian psychology, radical feminist conceptions of gender, and Foucauldian conceptions of social power (Sommers 1994; Carroll 1995, 2004a, 2011; Headlam Wells 2005; Menand 2005; Boyd 2006, 2009; Wells and McFadden 2006; Gottschall 2008a; Culler 2011; Carroll et al. 2012b). In this theoretical amalgam, the source theories are assimilated to an overarching belief that culture alone shapes human minds and motivates human behavior. Like Durkheim, Boas, and other seminal theorists in the social sciences, most literary theorists in the current academic literary establishment explicitly repudiate the idea that evolved and genetically transmitted dispositions significantly constrain culture (Freeman 1983; Fox 1989; Degler 1991; Tooby and Cosmides 1992; Carroll 1995; Pinker 2002).

In contrast to theorists who identify culture as an autonomous causal force, evolutionary literary theorists or "literary Darwinists" argue that culture is constrained and directed by the evolved and adapted characteristics of the human mind (Carroll 1995, 2004a, 2011, 2012b, 2013a; Storey 1996; Cooke and Turner 1999; Easterlin 2000, 2012; Scalise Sugiyama 2001c; Cooke 2002; Gottschall and Wilson 2005; Headlam Wells 2005; Flesch 2007; Martindale, Locher, and Petrov 2007; Nordlund 2007; Saunders 2007, 2009, 2010, 2012; Gottschall 2008b, 2012; Boyd 2009; Boyd, Carroll, and Gottschall 2010; Clasen 2010, 2011, 2012a, 2012b, 2012c; Swirski 2010, 2011; Williams 2010; Carroll et al. 2012b; Gansel and Vanderbeke 2012; Jonsson 2012). Because evolutionary biology and the evolutionary social sciences have greater scientific validity than alternative explanations of psychology and society, scholarship that draws on them for taxonomic and explanatory ideas has the potential for giving a more true and adequate account of fictional works.

The bulk of current academic literary criticism defaults to analyzing social themes in literary depictions. For decades now, literary criticism has concentrated on three categories: gender, class, and race. For the past thirty years or so, many commentaries on these themes have been conducted within the framework of Michel Foucault's ideas about social dynamics. Foucault reduces all social interactions to three roles: exploitative elites who control social discourse, a deluded populace, and alienated intellectuals who reveal the insidious machinations of social power (Carroll 1995: ch. 11, 2013a). In Foucault's own words, "Power is always exercised at the expense of the people" (1977: 211). Consequently, "the intellectual's role" is to engage in "a struggle against power, a struggle aimed at revealing and undermining power where it is most invisible and insidious" (207, 208).

Compared with the concepts that currently prevail in the academic literary establishment, concepts based on human life history theory and gene-culture coevolution identify a broader range of human concerns and offer a more adequate understanding of social dynamics. A minimal set of basic human concerns would include survival, growing up, mating, parenting, family life, life within a social group, conflict between social groups, and the life of the mind (Carroll 2012e). Most human behavior is embedded in a social context, but not all literary works focus chiefly on social themes. Some works concentrate on the relations between dyadic sexual couples or between parents and children. Some depict protagonists defending themselves against natural dangers, struggling with mental illness, trying to come to terms with God, or seeking intellectual or artistic fulfillment. Some works do clearly take social themes as a central concern, but those themes include more than dominance, subjugation, and resistance. Internalized norms, willing cooperation, and identification with a social body fundamentally shape human behavior and the quality of experience. They are, consequently, major themes in literary depictions.

Because literary works are embedded in social contexts, literary scholars draw on the findings of professional historians and also conduct their own historical research. Like literary study, history has lacked any central coordinating principle. Until recently, historians, like literary scholars, either used ad hoc analytic constructs, adopted ideas from contiguous disciplines like economics or sociology, or fabricated their own general systems. A general system like that of Arnold Toynbee has a close parallel with the system of genres fabricated by Northrop Frye (Carroll 1995: 117). Toynbee and Frye were both immensely learned and ingenious, but their systems were embedded in no network of established scientific ideas. They thus failed to establish a paradigm—a conceptual framework within which further research can produce cumulative empirical knowledge integrated with scientific knowledge in other fields.

Until the late nineteenth century, human behavior was the province of intuitive folk psychology, speculative philosophy, and literary depiction. It is now the province of evolutionary social science. Theorists of literature and history can now draw on biological concepts that identify natural kinds in human behavior. In this chapter, for instance, life within a human social group has been situated within the systemically integrated phases of human life history, and it has been analyzed using concepts that derive from research into the evolved basis of human social life: dominance, reverse dominance, leadership, internalized norms, strong reciprocity, legal institutions, and legitimacy. Those concepts have been reduced to four basic elements: individuals, groups, power, and values. The interplay of these elements in literary depictions has been assimilated to the idea that literary works help generate group identity, integrate individuals into groups, and mediate between the needs of individuals and the claims of groups. That concept has been lodged within the broader hypothesis that literature and the other arts affect cognitive and emotional organization, influence motives, and help regulate behavior. That hypothesis about the adaptive function of the arts has been closely associated with an implication from the theory of gene-culture coevolution: that cultural imagination is a crucial functional feature of the specifically human adaptive repertoire. Using evolutionary concepts makes it possible to see social themes in literary works as "parts of a whole" (Frye 1951: 96).

Evolution is itself the central coordinating principle necessary to establish literary theory as a genuine paradigm.

In recent years, historians and evolutionary scientists have begun to integrate evolutionary ideas with research into specific historical periods (D. S. Wilson 2002; Gat 2006; Turchin 2006; Fukuyama 2011; Pinker 2011). These efforts have produced important results but have been limited by the impasse between selfish gene theory and group selection. We can be confident that integrative biocultural historical research will continue, that it will benefit from the recent developments in evolutionary social theory delineated in this chapter, and that future developments in evolutionary social theory will offer new opportunities for analyzing the social dynamics in specific historical societies. Literary scholarship can both draw from this biocultural historical research and contribute to it. Literary works are inspired by the cultural imagination of their times and in turn help shape that cultural imagination (Carroll et al. 2012b; Gottschall 2012). Because cultural imagination interacts causally with material conditions and forms of social organization, literary scholarship should constrain and stimulate historical scholarship. Because material conditions and forms of social organization interact causally with evolved social dispositions, findings about social and cultural dynamics in specific historical periods should constrain and stimulate evolutionary social theory. Working cooperatively toward common goals, evolutionary social theorists, historians, and literary scholars can produce results more satisfactory than could be produced by researchers remaining within the boundaries of their own disciplines. We have only just begun to discover what that kind of collective effort can offer us.

References

Achebe, C. 1977. "An Image of Africa." *Massachusetts Review* 18: 782–794.
Alexander, R. D. 1987. *The Biology of Moral Systems*. Hawthorne, NY: de Gruyter.
Barkow, J. H., L. Cosmides, and J. Tooby. 1992. *The Adapted Mind: Evolutionary Psychology and the Generation of Culture*. New York: Oxford University Press.
Baron-Cohen, S. 2005. "The Empathizing System: A Revision of the 1994 Model of the Mindreading System." In *Origins of the Social Mind: Evolutionary Psychology and Child Development*, edited by B. J. Ellis and D. F. Bjorklund, 468–492. New York: Guilford.
———. 2011. *The Science of Evil: On Empathy and the Origins of Cruelty*. New York: Basic Books.
Bjorklund, D. F. 2011. "You've Come a Long Way, Baby: Evolutionary Developmental Psychology." *Evolutionary Review: Art, Science, Culture* 2: 10–20.
Bjorklund, D. F., and A. D. Pellegrini. 2002. *The Origins of Human Nature: Evolutionary Developmental Psychology*. Washington, DC: American Psychological Association.
Boehm, C. 1999. *Hierarchy in the Forest: The Evolution of Egalitarian Behavior*. Cambridge, MA: Harvard University Press.
———. 2012. *Moral Origins: The Evolution of Virtue, Altruism, and Shame*. New York: Basic Books.
Bowles, S. 2012. "Warriors, Levelers, and the Role of Conflict in Human Social Evolution." *Science* 336: 876–879.
Bowles, S., and H. Gintis. 2004. "The Evolution of Strong Reciprocity: Cooperation in Heterogeneous Populations." *Theoretical Population Biology* 65: 17–28.
———. 2011. *A Cooperative Species: Human Reciprocity and Its Evolution*. Princeton, NJ: Princeton University Press.
Boyd, B. 2006. "Getting It All Wrong: Bioculture Critiques Cultural Critique." *American Scholar* 75: 18–30.
———. 2009. *On the Origin of Stories: Evolution, Cognition, and Fiction*. Cambridge, MA: Harvard University Press.
Boyd, B., J. Carroll, and J. Gottschall, eds. 2010. *Evolution, Literature, and Film: A Reader*. New York: Columbia University Press.
Brown, D. E. 1991. "The Universal People." In *Human Universals*, 130–141. Philadelphia: Temple University Press.
———. 2000. "Human Universals and Their Implications." In *Being Humans: Anthropological Universality and Particularity in Transdisciplinary Perspectives*, edited by N. Roughley, 156–174. Berlin: de Gruyter.
———. 2004. "Human Universals, Human Nature and Human Culture." *Daedalus* 133: 47–54.
Buckholtz, J. W., and R. Marois. 2012. "The Roots of Modern Justice: Cognitive and Neural Foundations of Social Norms and Their Enforcement." *Nature Neuroscience* 15: 655–661.

Burkart, J. M., S. B. Hrdy, and C. P. van Schaik. 2009. "Cooperative Breeding and Human Cognitive Evolution." *Evolutionary Anthropology: Issues, News, and Reviews* 18: 175–186.
Burkart, J. M., and C. P. van Schaik. 2010. "Cognitive Consequences of Cooperative Breeding in Primates?" *Animal Cognition* 13: 1–19.
Carroll, J. 1995. *Evolution and Literary Theory*. Columbia: University of Missouri Press.
———. 2004a. *Literary Darwinism: Evolution, Human Nature, and Literature*. New York: Routledge.
———. 2004b. "'Theory,' Anti-theory, and Empirical Criticism." In *Literary Darwinism: Evolution, Human Nature, and Literature*, 29–40. London: Routledge.
———. 2008a. "An Evolutionary Paradigm for Literary Study." *Style* 42: 103–135.
———. 2008b. "Rejoinder to the Responses." *Style* 42: 308–411.
———. 2010. "Three Scenarios for Literary Darwinism." *New Literary History* 41: 53–67.
———. 2011. *Reading Human Nature: Literary Darwinism in Theory and Practice*. Albany: State University of New York Press.
———. 2012a. "The Adaptive Function of the Arts: Alternative Evolutionary Hypotheses." In *Telling Stories: Literature and Evolution*, edited by C. Gansel and D. Vanderbeke, 50–63. Berlin: de Gruyter.
———. 2012b. "An Evolutionary Approach to *King Lear*." In *Critical Insights: The Family*, edited by J. Knapp, 83–103. Ipswich, MA: EBSCO.
———. 2012c. "The Extremes of Conflict in Literature: Violence, Homicide, and War." In *The Oxford Handbook of Evolutionary Perspectives on Violence, Homicide, and War*, edited by T. K. Shackelford and V. Weekes-Shackelford, 413–434. Oxford: Oxford University Press.
———. 2012d. "Meaning and Effect in Fiction: An Evolutionary Model of Interpretation Illustrated with a Reading of 'Occurrence at Owl Creek Bridge.'" *Style* 26: 297–316.
———. 2012e. "The Truth about Fiction: Biological Reality and Imaginary Lives." *Style* 46: 129–160.
———. 2013a. "Correcting for *The Corrections*: A Darwinian Critique of a Foucauldian Novel." *Style* 47: 87–118.
———. 2013b. "Violence in Literature: An Evolutionary Perspective." In *Evolution of Violence*, edited by T. K. Shackelford and R. D. Hansen, 33–52. New York: Springer.
Carroll, J., J. Gottschall, J. A. Johnson, and D. J. Kruger. 2009. "Human Nature in Nineteenth-Century British Novels: Doing the Math." *Philosophy and Literature* 33: 50–72.
———. 2010a. "Imagining Human Nature." In *Evolution, Literature, and Film: A Reader*, edited by B. Boyd, J. Carroll, and J. Gottschall, 211–218. New York: Columbia University Press.
———. 2010b. "Paleolithic Politics in British Novels of the Longer Nineteenth Century." In *Evolution, Literature, and Film: A Reader*, edited by B. Boyd, J. Carroll, and J. Gottschall, 490–506. New York: Columbia University Press.
———. 2012a. "Graphing Jane Austen: Agonistic Structure in British Novels of the Nineteenth Century." *Scientific Study of Literature* 2: 1–24.
———. 2012b. *Graphing Jane Austen: The Evolutionary Basis of Literary Meaning*. New York: Palgrave Macmillan.
Chagnon, N. A. 1983. *Yanomamö: The Fierce People*. New York: Holt, Rinehart and Winston.
Chudek, M., and J. Henrich. 2011. "Culture-Gene Coevolution, Norm-Psychology and the Emergence of Human Prosociality." *Trends in Cognitive Sciences* 15: 218–226.
Clasen, M. 2010. "The Anatomy of the Zombie: A Bio-psychological Look at the Undead Other." *Otherness: Essays and Studies* 1: 1–23.
———. 2011. "Primal Fear: A Darwinian Perspective on Dan Simmons' *Song of Kali*." *Horror Studies* 2: 89–104.
———. 2012a. "Attention, Predation, Counterintuition: Why Dracula Won't Die." *Style* 43: 396–416.
———. 2012b. *Monsters and Horror Stories: A Biocultural Approach*. Aarhus, Denmark: Aarhus University.
———. 2012c. "Monsters Evolve: A Biocultural Approach to Horror Stories." *Review of General Psychology* 16: 222–229.
Conrad, J. 1985. *The Secret Agent: A Simple Tale*. Edited by M. Seymour-Smith. Harmondsworth, UK: Penguin.
———. 2011. *Heart of Darkness: Complete, Authoritative Text with Biographical, Historical, and Cultural Contexts, Critical History, and Essays from Contemporary Critical Perspectives*. Edited by R. C. Murfin. Boston: Bedford Books of St. Martin's Press.
Cooke, B. 2002. *Human Nature in Utopia: Zamyatin's We*. Evanston, IL: Northwestern University Press.
Cooke, B., and F. Turner. 1999. *Biopoetics: Evolutionary Explorations in the Arts*. Lexington, KY: ICUS.
Culler, J. D. 2011. *Literary Theory: A Very Short Introduction*. Oxford: Oxford University Press.
Dawkins, R. 1976. *The Selfish Gene*. New York: Oxford University Press.
De St. Aubin, E., D. P. McAdams, and T. Kim. 2003. *The Generative Society: Caring for Future Generations*. Washington, DC: American Psychological Association.
de Waal, F. 2005. *Our Inner Ape: A Leading Primatologist Explains Why We Are Who We Are*. New York: Riverhead Books.
———. 2007. *Chimpanzee Politics: Power and Sex among Apes*. Baltimore: Johns Hopkins University Press.

Deacon, T. W. 1997. *The Symbolic Species: The Co-evolution of Language and the Brain*. New York: Norton.
Degler, C. N. 1991. *In Search of Human Nature: The Decline and Revival of Darwinism in American Social Thought*. New York: Oxford University Press.
Dickens, C. 1977. *Bleak House: An Authoritative and Annotated Text, Illustrations, a Note on the Text, Genesis and Composition, Backgrounds, Criticism*. Edited by G. Ford and S. R. Monod. New York: Norton.
Dissanayake, E. 1992. *Homo Aestheticus: Where Art Comes from and Why*. New York: Free Press.
———. 2000. *Art and Intimacy: How the Arts Began*. Seattle: University of Washington Press.
———. 2011. "In the Beginning, Evolution Created Religion and the Arts." *Evolutionary Review: Art, Science, Culture* 2: 64–81.
Dutton, D. 2009. *The Art Instinct: Beauty, Pleasure, and Human Evolution*. New York: Bloomsbury Press.
Easterlin, N. 2000. "Psychoanalysis and 'the Discipline of Love.'" *Philosophy and Literature* 24: 261–279.
———. 2012. *A Biocultural Approach to Literary Theory and Interpretation*. Baltimore: Johns Hopkins University Press.
———. 2013. "The Functions of Literature and the Evolution of Extended Mind." *New Literary History* 44: 661–682.
Eliot, G. 1968. *Adam Bede*. Edited by J. Paterson. Boston: Houghton Mifflin.
———. 2000. *Middlemarch: An Authoritative Text, Backgrounds, Criticism*. Edited by B. G. Hornback. New York: Norton.
Flesch, W. 2007. *Comeuppance: Costly Signaling, Altruistic Punishment, and Other Biological Components of Fiction*. Cambridge, MA: Harvard University Press.
Flinn, M. V., D. C. Geary, and C. V. Ward. 2005. "Ecological Dominance, Social Competition, and Coalitionary Arms Races: Why Humans Evolved Extraordinary Intelligence." *Evolution and Human Behavior* 26: 10–46.
Flinn, M. V., and C. V. Ward. 2005. "Ontogeny and Evolution of the Social Child." In *Origins of the Social Mind: Evolutionary Psychology and Child Development*, edited by B. J. Ellis and D. F. Bjorklund, 19–44. New York: Guilford.
Foley, R., and C. Gamble. 2009. "The Ecology of Social Transitions in Human Evolution." *Philosophical Transactions of the Royal Society B: Biological Sciences* 364: 3267–3279.
Foucault, M. 1977. *Language, Counter-Memory, Practice: Selected Essays and Interviews*. Edited by D. F. Bouchard. Translated by D. F. Bouchard and S. Simon. Ithaca, NY: Cornell University Press.
Fowler, A. 1982. *Kinds of Literature: An Introduction to the Theory of Genres and Modes*. Cambridge, MA: Harvard University Press.
Fox, R. 1989. *The Search for Society: Quest for a Biosocial Science and Morality*. New Brunswick, NJ: Rutgers University Press.
Franzen, J. 2001. *The Corrections*. New York: Farrar, Straus and Giroux.
Freeman, D. 1983. *Margaret Mead and Samoa: The Making and Unmaking of an Anthropological Myth*. Cambridge, MA: Harvard University Press.
Frye, N. 1951. "The Archetypes of Literature." *Kenyon Review* 13: 92–110.
———. 1957. *Anatomy of Criticism: Four Essays*. Princeton, NJ: Princeton University Press.
Fukuyama, F. 2011. *The Origins of Political Order: From Prehuman Times to the French Revolution*. New York: Farrar, Straus and Giroux.
Gansel, C., and D. Vanderbeke. 2012. *Telling Stories: Literature and Evolution*. Berlin: de Gruyter.
Gat, A. 2006. *War in Human Civilization*. Oxford: Oxford University Press.
Geary, D. C. 2005a. "Evolution of Paternal Investment." In *The Handbook of Evolutionary Psychology*, edited by D. M. Buss, 483–505. Hoboken, NJ: Wiley.
———. 2005b. *The Origin of Mind: Evolution of Brain, Cognition, and General Intelligence*. Washington, DC: American Psychological Association.
Geary, D. C., and M. V. Flinn. 2001. "Evolution of Human Parental Behavior and the Human Family." *Parenting: Science and Practice* 1: 5–61.
Gintis, H. 2003. "The Hitchhiker's Guide to Altruism: Gene-Culture Coevolution, and the Internalization of Norms." *Journal of Theoretical Biology* 220: 407–418.
———. 2011. "Gene-Culture Coevolution and the Nature of Human Sociality." *Philosophical Transactions of the Royal Society B: Biological Sciences* 366: 878–888.
———. 2014. "Inclusive Fitness and the Sociobiology of the Genome." *Biology and Philosophy* 29: 477–515.
Gintis, H., and C. P. van Schaik. 2012. "Zoon Politicon: The Evolutionary Roots of Human Sociopolitical Systems." In *Cultural Evolution*, edited by P. J. Richerson and M. H. Christiansen, 25–44. Cambridge, MA: MIT Press.
Golding, W. 1954. *Lord of the Flies: A Novel*. London: Faber and Faber.
Gottschall, J. 2008a. *Literature, Science, and a New Humanities*. New York: Palgrave Macmillan.
———. 2008b. *The Rape of Troy: Evolution, Violence, and the World of Homer*. Cambridge: Cambridge University Press.

———. 2012. *The Storytelling Animal: How Stories Make Us Human*. Boston: Houghton Mifflin Harcourt.
Gottschall, J., and D. S. Wilson. 2005. *The Literary Animal: Evolution and the Nature of Narrative*. Evanston, IL: Northwestern University Press.
Haidt, J. 2012. *The Righteous Mind: Why Good People Are Divided by Politics and Religion*. New York: Pantheon Books.
Hare, R. D. 1999. *Without Conscience: The Disturbing World of the Psychopaths among Us*. New York: Guilford.
Headlam Wells, R. 2005. *Shakespeare's Humanism*. Cambridge: Cambridge University Press.
Heller, J. 1961. *Catch-22*. New York: Simon and Schuster.
Henrich, J., J. Ensminger, R. McElreath, A. Barr, C. Barrett, A. Bolyanatz, J. Camilo Cardenas, M. Gurven, E. Gwako, and N. Henrich. 2010. "Markets, Religion, Community Size, and the Evolution of Fairness and Punishment." *Science* 327: 1480–1484.
Hill, K. 2007. "Evolutionary Biology, Cognitive Adaptations, and Human Culture." In *The Evolution of Mind: Fundamental Questions and Controversies*, edited by S. W. Gangestad and J. A. Simpson, 348–356. New York: Guilford.
Hill, K., M. Barton, and A. M. Hurtado. 2009. "The Emergence of Human Uniqueness: Characters Underlying Behavioral Modernity." *Evolutionary Anthropology: Issues, News, and Reviews* 18: 187–200.
Hill, K. R., R. S. Walker, M. Bozicevic, J. Eder, T. Headland, B. Hewlett, A. M. Hurtado, F. Marlowe, P. Wiessner, and B. Wood. 2011. "Co-residence Patterns in Hunter-Gatherer Societies Show Unique Human Social Structure." *Science* 331: 1286–1289.
Hrdy, S. B. 2005. "On Why It Takes a Village: Cooperative Breeders, Infant Vocalization and the Evolution of Language." In *Evolutionary Perspectives on Human Development*, edited by R. L. Burgess and K. MacDonald, 167–188. Thousand Oaks, CA: Sage.
———. 2009. *Mothers and Others: The Evolutionary Origins of Mutual Understanding*. Cambridge, MA: Harvard University Press.
Johnson, J. A., J. Carroll, J. Gottschall, and D. J. Kruger. 2008. "Hierarchy in the Library: Egalitarian Dynamics in Victorian Novels." *Evolutionary Psychology* 6: 715–738.
———. 2011. "Portrayal of Personality in Victorian Novels Reflects Modern Research Findings but Amplifies the Significance of Agreeableness." *Journal of Research in Personality* 45: 50–58.
Jonsson, E. 2012. "'Man Is the Measure': Forster's Evolutionary Conundrum." *Style* 46: 161–176.
Kaplan, H. S., M. Gurven, and J. B. Lancaster. 2007. "Brain Evolution and the Human Adaptive Complex: An Ecological and Social Theory." In *The Evolution of Mind: Fundamental Questions and Controversies*, edited by S. W. Gangestad and J. A. Simpson, 269–279. New York: Guilford.
Kaplan, H., M. Gurven, and J. Winking. 2009. "An Evolutionary Theory of Human Life Span: Embodied Capital and the Human Adaptive Complex." In *Handbook of Theories of Aging*, edited by V. L. Bengston, D. Gans, N. M. Pulney, and M. Silverstein, 39–60. New York: Springer.
Kaplan, H. S., P. L. Hooper, and M. Gurven. 2009. "The Evolutionary and Ecological Roots of Human Social Organization." *Philosophical Transactions of the Royal Society B: Biological Sciences* 364: 3289–3299.
Klein, R. G. 2009. *The Human Career: Human Biological and Cultural Origins*. Chicago: University of Chicago Press.
Lancaster, J. B., and H. S. Kaplan. 2007. "Chimpanzee and Human Intelligence: Life History, Diet, and the Mind." In *The Evolution of Mind: Fundamental Questions and Controversies*, edited by S. W. Gangestad and J. A. Simpson, 111–118. New York: Guilford.
Mar, R. A., and K. Oatley. 2008. "The Function of Fiction Is the Abstraction and Simulation of Social Experience." *Perspectives on Psychological Science* 3: 173–192.
Mar, R. A., K. Oatley, M. Djikic, and J. Mullin. 2011. "Emotion and Narrative Fiction: Interactive Influences before, during, and after Reading." *Cognition & Emotion* 25: 818–833.
Martindale, C., P. Locher, and V. M. Petrov. 2007. *Evolutionary and Neurocognitive Approaches to Aesthetics, Creativity, and the Arts*. Amityville, NY: Baywood.
Maynard Smith, J., and E. Szathmáry. 1995. *The Major Transitions in Evolution*. Oxford: W.H. Freeman Spektrum.
McAdams, D. P. 1985. *Power, Intimacy, and the Life Story: Personological Inquiries into Identity*. Homewood, IL: Dorsey Press.
———. 1993. *The Stories We Live By: Personal Myths and the Making of the Self*. New York: William Morrow.
———. 2001. "The Psychology of Life Stories." *Review of General Psychology* 5: 100–122.
———. 2006. *The Redemptive Self: Stories Americans Live By*. Oxford: Oxford University Press.
———. 2008. "Personal Narratives and the Life Story." In *Handbook of Personality: Theory and Research*, edited by O. P. John, R. W. Robins, and L. A. Pervin, 242–262. New York: Guilford.
———. 2011. "Life Narratives." In *Handbook of Life-Span Development*, edited by K. L. Fingerman, C. A. Berg, J. Smith, and T. C. Antonucci, 509–610. New York: Springer.
McAdams, D. P., N. A. Anyidoho, C. Brown, Y. T. Huang, B. Kaplan, and M. A. Machado. 2004. "Traits and Stories: Links between Dispositional and Narrative Features of Personality." *Journal of Personality* 72: 761–784.

McAdams, D. P., and P. J. Bowman. 2001. "Narrating Life's Turning Points: Redemption and Contamination." In *Turns in the Road: Narrative Studies of Lives in Transition*, edited by D. P. McAdams, R. Josselson, and A. Lieblich, 3–34. Washington, DC: American Psychological Association.

McAdams, D. P., R. Josselson, and A. Lieblich. 2006. *Identity and Story: Creating Self in Narrative*. Washington, DC: American Psychological Association.

McAdams, D. P., and R. L. Ochberg. 1988. *Psychobiography and Life Narratives*. Durham, NC: Duke University Press.

McNeill, W. H. 1995. *Keeping Together in Time: Dance and Drill in Human History*. Cambridge, MA: Harvard University Press.

Melville, H. 1986. *Billy Budd, Sailor and Other Stories*. Edited by F. Busch. New York: Penguin.

Menand, L. 2005. "Dangers Within and Without." In *Profession 2005*, edited by R. G. Feal, 10–17. New York: Modern Language Association of America.

Michod, R. E. 2011. "Evolutionary Transitions in Individuality: Multicellularity and Sex." In *Major Transitions in Evolution Revisited*, edited by B. Calcott and K. Sterelny, 169–198. Cambridge, MA: MIT Press.

Miller, G. F. 2000. *The Mating Mind: How Sexual Choice Shaped the Evolution of Human Nature*. New York: Doubleday.

Mithen, S. 1996. *The Prehistory of the Mind: A Search for the Origins of Art, Religion, and Science*. London: Thames and Hudson.

Morris, J. 1968. *Pax Britannica: The Climax of an Empire*. New York: Harcourt.

Muehlenbein, M. P., and M. V. Flinn. 2011. "Patterns and Processes of Human Life History Evolution." In *Mechanisms of Life History Evolution: The Genetics and Physiology of Life History Traits and Trade-Offs*, edited by T. Flatt and A. Heyland, 153–168. Oxford: Oxford University Press.

Naipaul, V. S. 1980. *A Bend in the River*. New York: Vintage.

Nesse, R. M. 2012. "Cooperation Has Many Explanations, but Social Selection Has Been Neglected (Response to Pinker's 'The False Allure of Group Selection')." *Edge.org* 20.

Nordlund, M. 2007. *Shakespeare and the Nature of Love: Literature, Culture, Evolution*. Evanston, IL: Northwestern University Press.

Nowak, M. A. 2006. "Five Rules for the Evolution of Cooperation." *Science* 314: 1560–1563.

Nowak, M. A., and R. Highfield. 2011. *Supercooperators: Altruism, Evolution, and Why We Need Each Other to Succeed*. New York: Free Press.

Nowak, M. A., C. E. Tarnita, and T. Antal. 2010. "Evolutionary Dynamics in Structured Populations." *Philosophical Transactions of the Royal Society B: Biological Sciences* 365: 19–30.

Nowak, M. A., C. E. Tarnita, and E. O. Wilson. 2010. "The Evolution of Eusociality." *Nature* 466: 1057–1062.

Oakley, B. A. 2007. *Evil Genes: Why Rome Fell, Hitler Rose, Enron Failed and My Sister Stole My Mother's Boyfriend*. Amherst, NY: Prometheus Books.

Oatley, K. 2011. *Such Stuff as Dreams: The Psychology of Fiction*. Chichester, UK: Wiley-Blackwell.

Orwell, G. 1949. *Nineteen Eighty-Four*. New York: Harcourt.

Panksepp, J., and J. B. Panksepp. 2000. "The Seven Sins of Evolutionary Psychology." *Evolution and Cognition* 6: 108–131.

Pinker, S. 1997. *How the Mind Works*. New York: Norton.

———. 2002. *The Blank Slate: The Modern Denial of Human Nature*. New York: Viking.

———. 2007a. *The Stuff of Thought: Language as a Window into Human Nature*. New York: Viking.

———. 2007b. "Toward a Consilient Study of Literature." *Philosophy and Literature* 31: 162–178.

———. 2011. *The Better Angels of Our Nature: Why Violence Has Declined*. New York: Viking.

———. 2012. "The False Allure of Group Selection." *Edge.org*.

Pinker, S., S. Brand, D. Everett, D. C. Queller, D. C. Dennett, H. Gintis, H. Whitehouse, R. McKay, P. J. Richerson, J. A. Coyne, M. Hochberg, R. Boyd, S. Mathew, M. Drasnow, A. Delton, N. Baumard, J. Haidt, D. S. Wilson, M. E. Price, J. Henrich, R. M. Nesse, R. Dawkins, H. Cronin, and J. Tooby. 2012. "The False Allure of Group Selection [a Target Article with Multiple Respondents]." *Edge.org* 20.

Pope, A. 1950. *An Essay on Man*. Edited by M. Mack. London: Methuen.

Potts, R. 1996. *Humanity's Descent: The Consequences of Ecological Instability*. New York: Morrow.

Raine, A. 2013. *The Anatomy of Violence: The Biological Roots of Crime*. New York: Random House.

Richerson, P., and J. Henrich. 2012. "Tribal Social Instincts and the Cultural Evolution of Institutions to Solve Collective Action Problems." *Cliodynamics: The Journal of Theoretical and Mathematical History* 3.

Roberts, J. M. 2003. *The New History of the World*. Oxford: Oxford University Press.

Said, E. W. 1993. *Culture and Imperialism*. New York: Knopf.

Salmon, C., and T. K. Shackelford. 2011. *The Oxford Handbook of Evolutionary Family Psychology*. New York: Oxford University Press.

Salmon, C., and D. Symons. 2004. "Slash Fiction and Human Mating Psychology." *Journal of Sex Research* 41: 94–100.

Salter, F. K. 2008. *Emotions in Command: Biology, Bureaucracy, and Cultural Evolution.* New Brunswick, NJ: Transaction Publishers.

Saunders, J. P. 2007. "Male Reproductive Strategies in Sherwood Anderson's 'The Untold Lie.'" *Philosophy and Literature* 31: 311–322.

———. 2009. *Reading Edith Wharton through a Darwinian Lens: Evolutionary Biological Issues in Her Fiction.* Jefferson, NC: McFarland.

———. 2010. "Paternal Confidence in Hurston's 'The Gilded Six-Bits.'" In *Evolution, Literature, and Film: A Reader,* edited by B. Boyd, J. Carroll, and J. Gottschall, 392–408. New York: Columbia University Press.

———. 2012. "Female Mate-Guarding in Lawrence's 'Wintry Peacock': An Evolutionary Perspective." *College Literature* 39 (4): 69–83.

Scalise Sugiyama, M. 1996. "On the Origins of Narrative." *Human Nature* 7: 403–425.

———. 2001a. "Food, Foragers, and Folklore: The Role of Narrative in Human Subsistence." *Evolution and Human Behavior* 22: 221–240.

———. 2001b. "Narrative Theory and Function: Why Evolution Matters." *Philosophy and Literature* 25: 233–250.

———. 2001c. "New Science, Old Myth: An Evolutionary Critique of the Oedipal Paradigm." *Mosaic* 34: 121–136.

———. 2004. "Predation, Narration, and Adaptation: 'Little Red Riding Hood' Revisited." *Interdisciplinary Literary Studies* 5: 110–129.

———. 2006. "Lions and Tigers and Bears: Predators as a Folklore Universal." In *Anthropology and Social History: Heuristics in the Study of Literature,* edited by H.-E. Friedrich, F. Jannidis, U. Klein, K. Mellmann, S. Metzger, and M. Willems, 319–331. Paderborn, Germany: Mentis.

Shakespeare, W. 1997. *The Riverside Shakespeare.* Edited by G. B. Evans and J.J.M. Tobin. Boston: Houghton Mifflin.

Simpson, C. 2011. "How Many Levels Are There? How Insights from Evolutionary Transitions in Individuality Help Measure the Hierarchical Complexity of Life." In *The Major Transitions in Evolution Revisited,* edited by B. Calcott and K. Sterelny, 199–225. Cambridge, MA: MIT Press.

Sober, E., and D. S. Wilson. 1998. *Unto Others: The Evolution and Psychology of Unselfish Behavior.* Cambridge, MA: Harvard University Press.

Sommers, C. H. 1994. *Who Stole Feminism? How Women Have Betrayed Women.* New York: Simon and Schuster.

Sripada, C. S., and S. Stich. 2005. "A Framework for the Psychology of Norms." In *The Innate Mind: Culture and Cognition,* edited by P. Carruthers, S. Laurence, and S. Stich, 280–301. Oxford: Oxford University Press.

Storey, R. F. 1996. *Mimesis and the Human Animal: On the Biogenetic Foundations of Literary Representation.* Evanston, IL: Northwestern University Press.

Swirski, P. 2010. "When Biological Evolution and Social Revolution Clash: Skinner's Behaviorist Utopia." *Evolutionary Review: Art, Science, Culture* 1: 18–23.

———. 2011. *American Utopia and Social Engineering in Literature, Social Thought, and Political History.* New York: Routledge.

Symons, D. 1979. *The Evolution of Human Sexuality.* New York: Oxford University Press.

Tomasello, M., and M. Carpenter. 2007. "Shared Intentionality." *Developmental Science* 10: 121–125.

Tomasello, M., M. Carpenter, J. Call, T. Behne, and H. Moll. 2005. "Understanding and Sharing Intentions: The Origins of Cultural Cognition." *Behavioral and Brain Sciences* 28: 675–691.

Tooby, J., and L. Cosmides. 1992. "The Psychological Foundations of Culture." In *The Adapted Mind: Evolutionary Psychology and the Generation of Culture,* edited by J. H. Barkow, L. Cosmides, and J. Tooby, 19–136. New York: Oxford University Press.

———. 2010. "Does Beauty Build Adapted Minds? Toward an Evolutionary Theory of Aesthetics, Fiction, and the Arts." In *Evolution, Literature, and Film: A Reader,* edited by B. Boyd, J. Carroll, and J. Gottschall, 174–183. New York: Columbia University Press.

Trivers, R. 1985. *Social Evolution.* Menlo Park, CA: Benjamin/Cummings.

Turchin, P. 2006. *War and Peace and War: The Life Cycles of Imperial Nations.* New York: Pi Press.

Twain, M. 1999. *Adventures of Huckleberry Finn: An Authoritative Text, Contexts and Sources, Criticism.* Edited by T. Cooley. New York: Norton.

van Vugt, M., and R. Ronay. 2014. "The Evolutionary Psychology of Leadership: Theory, Review, and Roadmap." *Organizational Psychology Review* 4: 1–22.

Wade, N. 2006. *Before the Dawn: Recovering the Lost History of Our Ancestors.* New York: Penguin.

Wells, R. H., and J. McFadden. 2006. *Human Nature: Fact and Fiction.* London: Continuum.

Widiger, T. A., and G. T. Smith. 2008. "Personality and Psychopathology." In *Handbook of Personality: Theory and Research,* edited by O. P. John, R. W. Robins, and L. A. Pervin, 743–769. New York: Guilford.

Williams, T. O. 2010. "Challenging Evolutionary Metaphors of Survival: Morris's *News from Nowhere.*" *Evolutionary Review: Art, Science, Culture* 1: 39–41.

Wilson, D. S. 1997. "Altruism and Organism: Disentangling the Themes of Multilevel Selection Theory." *American Naturalist* 150: S122–S134.

———. 1999. "A Critique of R. D. Alexander's Views on Group Selection." *Biology and Philosophy* 14: 431–449.

———. 2002. *Darwin's Cathedral: Evolution, Religion, and the Nature of Society*. Chicago: University of Chicago Press.

———. 2007. *Evolution for Everyone: How Darwin's Theory Can Change the Way We Think about Our Lives*. New York: Delacorte.

Wilson, D. S., and E. O. Wilson. 2007. "Rethinking the Theoretical Foundations of Sociobiology." *Quarterly Review of Biology* 82: 327–348.

Wilson, E. O. 1998. *Consilience: The Unity of Knowledge*. New York: Knopf.

———. 2012. *The Social Conquest of Earth*. New York: Liveright.

Wrangham, R. W. 2009. *Catching Fire: How Cooking Made Us Human*. New York: Basic Books.

Wrangham, R. W., and D. Peterson. 1996. *Demonic Males: Apes and the Origins of Human Violence*. Boston: Houghton Mifflin.

Chapter Thirty-One

Contrast Effects in Social Evolution and Schumpeter's Creative Destruction

Michael Hammond

> Our evolutionary heritage of contrast sensitivity leaves humans with internal reward release rules for positive emotions and physical pleasures that are very responsive to social creations offering high-contrast familiarity and serial novelty. Joseph Schumpeter's model of capitalist creative destruction and its impact on more static traditional cultures is examined in terms of changes in the use of these reward rules as social structures offering serial novelty are substituted for classic structures rooted in fixed high contrasts. One factor in the inequality compression and decompression of capitalist economies from the Great Depression until the present might also be found in the shifting impact of these rules as this historic substitution proceeds.

Joseph Schumpeter's famous description of capitalism as a "perennial gale of creative destruction" is part of a wider model of economic and social change in which "steel frame" precapitalist cultures based on rigid structures and low rates of innovation are replaced by the emergence of capitalist cultures based on serial novelty in all aspects of production and consumption. At the core of his model is the idea that there are two deep structures of rewards that drive individuals to pursue two different general strategies of action, one rooted in the appeal of stable recurring arousers and one based on the appeal of multiple innovations. However, as an economist, Schumpeter only sketches these two alternatives and does not inquire deeply into the origin of such reward dynamics. These strategies are recast in terms of internal reward release rules for high-contrast familiarity and for serial novelty. Both are rooted in our evolutionary heritage, but humans are able to play with these rules in a number of different ways and to create some special social structures triggering additional rewards. This play is often deadly serious, but it is important to use terms like "play" and "create" in order to stress that these outcomes are not themselves permanently put in place by our evolutionary past. From this perspective, it would appear that the impact of Schumpeter's perennial gale is even more radical than he envisioned. The compression of income inequality with Roosevelt's New Deal and World War II is a sign for Schumpeter that capitalism is beginning to wind down. The reversal of that compression in so many capitalist countries today seems to indicate something very different about the dynamics of serial novelty in creative destruction.

Creative Destruction

The economist Joseph Schumpeter is most widely known for his 1942 analysis of the emergence of capitalism as a "perennial gale of creative destruction" that never can be stationary in providing "the new consumers' goods, the new methods of production or transportation, the new markets, the new forms of industrial organization that capitalist enterprise creates" ([1942] 1976: 82–83, 87). For Schumpeter, capitalism is fueled by the unique historical mixture of elevated inequality and serial innovation. The twin engines of creativity and power drive the entrepreneur, the combiner who forges technologies and other aspects of the production process together in new ways, and who unequally but deservedly reaps the profits of these combinations. From his perspective, the economic turbulence and inequality that are part of such creative destruction are a small price to pay in return for the cornucopia of economic expansion resulting from incessant innovation offering heretofore unseen variety and novelty on a mass scale to the consumer. Capitalism could provide more of what many had before in lesser quantities, and more of what only the rich had earlier in history. In one of his pithy summaries, he notes that "Queen Elizabeth owned silk stockings. The capitalist achievement does not typically consist in providing more silk stockings for queens but in bringing them within the reach of factory girls in return for steadily decreasing amounts of effort" (1976: 67). The same is true for a host of other goods and services that previously were only for the rich, including financial services such as mortgages and credit. Since there are far more factory girls than queens, it is such incessant changes in economic productivity on a mass scale that set capitalism apart from previous economic systems.

Surges in productivity have to be matched by surges in consumption. Schumpeter sees clearly that needs have to be expanded or even created in order to provide markets for the new productivity. "Want and effective demand are not the same thing. If they were, the poorest nations would be the ones to display the most vigorous demand," which is clearly not the historical case (1976: 114). Basic needs do not drive a capitalist economy, and no other system creates as many acquired needs as capitalism. Indeed, individuals must be taught to "want new things" (Schumpeter 1934b: 65). The creation of these needs also requires new financial engines such as the installment buying and extended consumer credit of the 1920s to help fuel serial innovation.

The emergence of creative destruction is part of an even wider leap in economic evolution, the movement to predominantly dynamic rather than static cultures. Before capitalism, statics are "the general rule throughout the history of mankind" (Schumpeter [1911] 2003: 111). No human culture is entirely static over the long run; but with the dominance of statics, there is little long-term change, or when real change occurs, it is only in response to external pressures that, once met, settle into another generally static pattern. Thus, for most of history, people are wed to the old and change only when forced to adapt to some outside force that then leads to a new traditionalism. In terms of general reward packages, the first and by far the most common in history is one in which novelty is only occasional, and stimuli with a high degree of repetitiveness over the long term are the most rewarding existential anchors. Individual security is normally found by embedding in a set of these predominantly unchanging traditional structures.

Schumpeter asserts that capitalism is different. Rather than being driven by exogenous factors, capitalism is a process of endogenous change propelled by forces "from within, incessantly destroying the old one, incessantly creating a new one" (1976: 31, 83). There is a restlessness never seen before on such a grand scale. Capitalism is change that feeds upon itself, casting aside whatever stands in the way of further change. New products create new needs and new consumers, and thereby set the stage for new producers to begin the cycle over. This leap to a more dynamic system is rooted in a second set of general reward packages in which novelty is serial and eventually comes to mark every aspect of the culture.

Schumpeter believes that individuals in a predominantly static culture or a capitalist dynamic culture are not necessarily more or less happy or more or less better off on some absolute scale (1976: 129). There is no such definitive existential measure. Interests driven by a high degree of repeatability can have the same energy as novelty-driven needs; and these reward packages, as well as the social creations fueled by these rewards, can be substituted for each other. Indeed, Schumpeter's vision of social evolution is essentially a substitution narrative in which different reward packages come to dominate the social world.

In Schumpeter's model, all large-scale cultures are marked by elevated inequality. There are two key tipping points in the social evolution of that inequality. Using dating very common in the 1940s, he notes that after about 50,000 years in "primitive" hunting and gathering cultures similar to our context of origin, organized farming emerges around 6000 BC, along with new forms of political domination (1976: 121, 139). With farming comes a crucial increase in social scale in terms of population and technology. The expanded social scale leads to the classic pyramidal and static inequality structures of political and economic concentration in a small elite whose primary goal becomes recreating itself as long as possible. However, competition among these elevated inequality societies leads to the gradual accumulation of a wide variety of technologies, and this sets the stage for a second tipping point with a challenge to these traditional elites by the new capitalist elites as cultures move from a primarily static to a more dynamic mode.

Schumpeter notes that much of early capitalism begins as part of inter-state competition between elites who are still predominantly noncapitalist, but at some point, the tables are turned (1976: 133–136). Expanding mass production and consumption attack a host of preindustrial micro and macro status distinctions. Traditional inequality generally stands in the way of these economic innovations. The peasant, the village, and the craft guild all provide status anchors that imitate the fixed and pyramidal status distinctions of the emperor or the king, and by extension, of god or the gods. This is the "steel frame" (1976: 135–136) of the precapitalist feudal structure, a frame that is similar in form from top to bottom and is marked by a strong web of high contrast and fixed status distinctions at all levels. This framework has to be swept aside by the serial novelty of creative destruction, but it cannot be replaced by a similar construction offering just a new set of fixed status distinctions throughout the culture. Any such fixed distinctions would interfere with the incessant stream of new goods and services that is a necessary part of capitalist economic change. For example, according to Schumpeter, feminism is one part of the anti-ascriptive push of an increasingly dynamic world. Feminism is "an essentially capitalist phenomenon" (1976: 127) in which a fixed elevated ascriptive status distinction that individuals from all levels of society have clung to in the past has to give way to challenges by those seeking a different place in the new production and consumption system. The same is true for many other high-contrast ascriptive status distinctions that individuals have embraced in the past. These too must be at least significantly eroded and perhaps even destroyed by the capitalist storm.

This creative destruction does not mean the end of elevated inequality for a small percentage of the population. Instead, the entrepreneur embraces inflated inequality, but this time cast in a more dynamic rather than static form. For Schumpeter, pecuniary success in promoters' profits is the most important source of large fortunes, but this wealth is only part of the motivational package driving the entrepreneur. There is also the will to compete, the pleasure in social power, and the satisfaction in doing great things (1934b: 92–94). All of these motives are not unique to capitalism (1976: 123), any more than elevated inequality is unique to capitalism; but they are different in impact because they are not primarily directed to the hope of building permanent pyramids of inequality. Compared with the history of precapitalist inflated inequality, entrepreneurs rarely succeed in setting up long-term dynasties. Instead, their innovation package is more or less quickly replaced by another, which in turn is itself replaced. This is one reason why Schumpeter is not overly concerned about monopolies in the capitalist system. They are temporary at best, until they too are swept away by a new storm of innovation (1976: 93, 99).

All this elevated inequality is crucial to the high rate of innovation by entrepreneurs. That is one reason why Schumpeter is distressed by the compression of economic inequality with Roosevelt and the New Deal. The "modern taxation of incomes and inheritance" expresses "an anti-capitalist attitude" and is "possibly the forerunner of complete elimination of the typically capitalist income brackets" (1976: 192). This trend is magnified by the heavy taxation of upper incomes and the state intervention economic policies typical of wartime in capitalist countries. Furthermore, Schumpeter believes that "social legislation for the benefit of the masses is not simply something which has been forced upon capitalist society" (1976: 127), but instead such a basic safety net is an integral part of the new dynamic world. However, as with taxation, he asserts that Roosevelt's New Deal goes too far in this kind of social legislation; and in general, such extreme types of government policy "are in the long run incompatible" with capitalism (1976: 64).

For Schumpeter, cycles are the key to capitalism. Most importantly, there is a "prosperity phase" (1976: 70) producing "an avalanche of consumers' goods" (1976: 68). The long-term impact of these surges is cumulative, such that the size of the avalanche grows over time. According to Schumpeter, in the last sixty years before the Great Depression, relative economic expansion shows an average rate of increase of about 2 percent per year (1976: 64–65). Over so many decades, the compounding inherent in this relative gain eventually results in a major cumulative gain in absolute terms. Thus, the decade before 1929 represents the greatest material avalanche the United States has ever seen in such a few years. However, as an inevitable part of economic cycles, the prosperity phase is necessarily followed by a period of economic turmoil and more unemployment as adjustments are made to the preceding gale of creative destruction. These periods are painful, but necessary, and set the stage for another period of recovery and then surging prosperity, to be followed by another pull back.

In general, Schumpeter is quite sanguine about recessions and depressions because in his view economic progress and turmoil always go hand in hand. In 1934, he writes that economic depressions are "not simply evils, which we might attempt to suppress, but forms of something which has to be done, namely, adjustment to change" (1934a: 16). However, in the economic and political depths of 1942, Schumpeter sees the Great Depression as something more profound. In the face of the great collapse of 1929–1932 and the painfully slow recovery, many political leaders and intellectuals have lost faith; and for more and more people, it is time to turn to something else that offers more security and less of a cyclical whipsaw existence. Schumpeter does not believe that this severe depression is the crisis point that will lead to breakdown of the capitalist system (1976: 111), but at some time in the future, these kinds of cycles are most likely going to trigger a truly radical change.

All of these developments are part of another social evolutionary sequence, because, according to Schumpeter, "there is inherent in the capitalist system a tendency toward self destruction" such that the "capitalist process not only destroys its own institutional framework but it also creates the conditions for another" (1976: 162). Like Marx, Schumpeter believes that capitalism is its own grave digger, but this self-destruction is not rooted in a falling rate of profit or a law of increasing misery. Instead, the very success of capitalism paradoxically sets the stage for its downfall. Having overcome general material scarcity for the first time in history, capitalism becomes a victim of its own success. The material affluence it makes possible on a mass scale also creates dissatisfaction with these achievements (1976: 145–146). There is a new kind of social unrest that comes with the capitalist combination of "secular improvement that is taken for granted" coupled with the "individual insecurity" that inevitably accompanies the frantic pace of change in capitalism (1976: 145). At some point, there emerge "a distribution of political power and a socio-psychological attitude" hostile to capitalism (1976: 112). People are less and less willing to accept the ups and downs of the capitalist roller coaster, and the appeal of more stable systems grows, even if these alternatives are not as ruthlessly innovative. This is one reason why the comparably greater social security of socialism is the ultimate end of the capitalist leap into history.

Furthermore, Schumpeter notes that something deeply moral and hence deeply appealing is missing in capitalism. "The stock exchange is a poor substitute for the Holy Grail" (1976: 137). This moral scarcity explains in part why secular religions like prophetic Marxism were so appealing after the victory of capitalism over feudalism, and why it is generally easier for socialism to claim the higher moral plane. Eventually, this paucity of a higher morality will also weigh on the long-term possibilities of creative destruction. Faced with all these developments, entrepreneurs will see that their time has come and gone, and the world will move off in another direction. Thus, for Schumpeter, capitalism is a great leap in our history, and yet it cannot avoid an eventual crippling of its core principles, just as so many other civilizations have come to an end "before they had time to fill to the full the measure of their promise" (1976: 130).

The Evolutionary Background

Schumpeter's favorite style of analysis is dramatic exaggeration, hence the steel frame of rigid strength and durability, and the perennial gale of impermanence and renewal. But strikingly, these two archetypes point to two of the most effective strategies for triggering additional reward release from the human body. These preconscious triggers for positive emotions and physical pleasures are rooted in our biological evolution. Both can provide additional rewards on a mass scale, and not just for the occasional individual or small group (Hammond 2013). One bonus window emerges early and is predominant throughout most of our history. The second is the new pugnacious kid on the block, which is one of the reasons Schumpeter finds it so very appealing. Both have their origins in contrast effects.

Individuals of any species cannot respond to all stimuli equally. Stimuli must be ranked in one way or another, and responded to appropriately. One of the most common ranking systems is in terms of contrast sensitivity. Different stimuli are perceived to have different contrast values, and this leads to different responses. In regard to attractive stimuli, neuroscientists have demonstrated this quality in regard to human food preferences, attachment, status, novelty, and a host of other activities (Aron et al. 2005; Berridge et al. 2010; Bunzeck et al. 2012; Chiao et al. 2009; Fisher et al. 2002; Ly et al. 2011; Montague and Berns 2002; Zink et al. 2008). The general rule is that different contrast values trigger different degrees of reward release per presentation, and those differences in reward release shape the number of repetitions that continue to trigger at least some rewards. The higher the contrast value of an attractive stimulus, the greater the reward spike per presentation, and the greater the number of repetitions that still produce some rewards. These rewards can have elements of neurochemistry, emotion, and physical pleasure in many different combinations, but the same basic release pattern applies across the spectrum of rewards (Hammond 2013). Given our general behavioral flexibility and our outstanding cognitive skills, humans have the capacity to take advantage of preconscious contrast sensitivity in order to trigger additional reward release.

Familiar arousers are the most common category of stimuli. The reward release rule for familiarity is that higher-contrast values can release more rewards per presentation, and also can trigger more rewarding repetitions, than lesser contrasts. That is, there is a double bonus for high-contrast familiarity. High contrasts can gather higher reward spikes and can slow the repetition suppression of rewards. As we shall see below, these responses leave a window of opportunity to further exploit rewards. This double bonus also means that individuals will pay extra costs in terms of time, effort, and risk in order to reap these rewards. However, these costs generally cannot be much greater than the rewards they bring in. Otherwise, individuals will look elsewhere for a better cost–benefit ratio. Social creations that can spread and even offset some of those costs while offering high-contrast and high-repetition arousers are going to be very appealing throughout a population.

Novelty presents another window for exploiting contrast sensitivity with a double reward bonus. In the short term, attractive novel arousers have a contrast impact producing more rewards per presentation than familiar stimuli in the same value category (Bunzeck and Duzel 2006; Bunzeck et al. 2012; Kakade and Dayan 2002). In turn, this bonus makes additional repetitions more attractive until familiarity sets in, and novelty rewards decrease and then disappear. Furthermore, in a halo effect, mixing novel arousers with more familiar ones reduces the repetition suppression rates for those familiar stimuli (Bunzeck et al. 2012), and it would be most interesting to see if there is a similar halo effect when familiar high-contrast arousers are mixed with lesser-contrast stimuli. The evolutionary origin of these novelty reward responses is tied to their occasional but important role in our early history. Once again, as we shall see below, these responses leave a window of opportunity to extract additional rewards.

The downside of using novelty to trigger additional rewards is that any specific set of rewards is sooner or later self-extinguishing as repetitions pile up over time. However, since the decline of one set of novelty rewards sets the stage for a new round of rewards, there is a possibility to overcome this problem by the use of serial novelty in which there is a string of novel arousers stretched out over time in order to provide a long-term amplified reward total. With sufficient serial novelty, the reward totals can equal packages of high-contrast familiar arousers. Once again, these extra rewards mean that individuals will be willing to pay some extra costs in order to access such reward packages; and once again, social creations that can offset or otherwise limit some of these costs are going to be very popular. It is only late in our history that serial novelty can be offered on a mass scale, but when that possibility finally emerges, there is a radical change.

In terms of these reward rules, long-term high-contrast serial novelty would be the most effective reward trigger of all. However, so far in our history, this option has been available for only a few individuals or small groups. No culture has yet found a vehicle to provide such arouser packages consistently to most or to all of a population, and it is this mass scale that is under consideration here. Instead, as we shall see below, what have emerged on a mass basis are social creations with serial novelty having occasional high contrasts but on average a lesser average contrast value and fewer repetitions than social creations with the consistent high contrasts and high repetitions of some special familiar arousers. The potential reward release totals of these two packages are quite similar.

In summary, for familiar arousers, the consistent high-contrast window is going to be most effective in piling up additional rewards. For novel arousers, serial novelty is going to be the most effective. This provides two alternatives. First, stress long-term high contrasts and high repetition in playing with our reward release rules. Second, stress long-term serial novelty with some high contrasts but on average with lesser contrasts and fewer repetitions. Of course, these two platforms can also be mixed and matched in different proportions. Historically, many cultures have offered a predominance of high-contrast familiar arousers, with only occasional novelty and rarely, if at all, with serial novelty. Contemporary capitalist cultures offer less regular high-contrast distinctions on a mass basis, but do offer far more serial novelty. This often means a contest between high-contrast familiarity and serial novelty as platforms for triggering the bonus reward release we all find so attractive. This contest can sometimes be almost friendly, but very often it is more or less antagonistic.

High-Contrast Familiarity and Religion

Different interests have different potentials for making use of one or another of these platforms to extend an interest and reward harvesting across a wide swath of the population. Once again, it is important to note that such playing with our reward release rules is often deadly serious, but using a term like "play" emphasizes that these outcomes are not a permanent part of our evolutionary heritage. Historically, the first basic interest to be extended on a mass scale is our attachment interest, and the clear preference in this extension is for the familiar high-contrast package (Hammond 2013).

Attachment is wired preconsciously to provide strong ties with a high repetition tolerance to a small range of individuals, and weaker ties with a lower repetition tolerance to a larger range of individuals. With a high repetition tolerance, even small contrasts can produce a very strong reward total. For instance, with infatuation, such small contrasts can take on special value with high rewards for very many repetitions over a limited period of time (Aron et al. 2005). High-contrast values are nice, but they are not necessary for strong ties. Instead, it is a high repetition tolerance that is the key to long-term high reward totals for this limited number of very special personal bonds. These ties are not fixed imprints. As with most all evolved aspects of our species, there is significant behavioral flexibility in this regard. There are also rewards available for a larger number of less strong ties with a lower repetition tolerance and hence a lower reward total.

The space for these additional ties opens up a window for triggering additional arousal release by exploiting contrast sensitivity. If some super high contrast ties could be found, then these high contrasts could trigger some high reward spikes and also increase the attractiveness of further repetitions. That is, such a creation could both produce an increase in repetition tolerance and bring in reward totals similar to those of strong personal ties. What could provide such high contrasts, particularly in our context of origin with very small populations and limited technological resources? In such circumstances, with individuals having regular interaction with most all other individuals on a daily basis, the limited variety of natural differences in real human beings is unlikely to possess such high-contrast qualities. However, imaginary beings with elevated contrast values will do just fine; and using our wonderful cognitive skills, this is precisely what humans create again and again in their religions.

These special beings may be imaginary in origin, but they are real in their physiological impact on reward release; therefore, they feel real to those who believe in them. Indeed, this is what some neuroscience research on religion and rewards indicates in looking at the overlap with religious arousers and personal tie arousers in terms of stimulus impact on certain areas of the brain, clearly showing that one part of the deep appeal of religion is found in the attachment interest (Kirkpatrick and Granquist 2008; McNamara 2009; Newberg, d'Aquili, and Rause 2001). Being imaginary, these special beings are also available on a mass scale. Virtually every member of a population has the opportunity to embrace them. Similarly, being imaginary, they are also available on a consistent long-term basis. Of course, in order to access these additional arousers, individuals must be willing to pay some extra costs in terms of time and effort. The key is to keep the costs in line with the benefits that come from playing with our reward release rules in this manner. Creating and maintaining such extraordinary beings on an individual basis is possible, but not probable. The costs are just too monumental. However, a collective construction can support those beings more easily without such a massive cost to any specific individual; and the social creation of religion has proven to be the most time-tested platform for providing individuals with the means to control costs while providing regular access to these very special arousers.

Of course, the deep appeal of these creations would most often be more for high-contrast familiarity than for novelty. After all, why are so many of these religious beings so appealing? One reason is that they do not have to die, so they can be there year after year and decade after decade, consistently providing existential anchors. From their permanent elevated positions, they regularly can have powers over parts of the world where humans so often appear to be powerless. Occasional novelty in religion might have some attractive qualities, but in total, there would be only a limited appeal in comparison with the rewards from such eternal consistency and familiarity. Similarly, the even greater impermanence of serial novelty is not going to be attractive to most believers most of the time, and this is especially true at the micro social scale of our early history. As a result, in Schumpeter's terms, such cultures deeply embracing these high-contrast social creations are going to be more static than dynamic.

The Elevation of Inequality

Our status interest is the second interest that historically is amplified by these bonus windows. Although not as advanced as the study of the inner workings of attachment, status is a research area that neuroscientists are beginning to study more and more (Chiao et al. 2009; Izuma, Saito, and Sadato 2008; Ly et al. 2011; Martinez et al. 2010; Saxe and Haushofer 2008; Zink et al. 2008). Here the basic reward wiring is somewhat different than attachment, but the outcome is much the same because there is another window for exploiting the reward release potential of contrast sensitivity. And once again, the first social creations to use this reward window intensely are more static than dynamic.

A status interest is almost by definition contrast sensitive; but of course, among species, there are many ways to frame this contrast sensitivity (Hammond 2012, 2013). For instance, in both experimental and natural settings for nonhuman primates like the chimpanzee, long-term elevated status distinctions appear even when there are only a small number of individuals. For this to regularly occur, there must be preconscious wiring with rewards for a high degree of repetition in terms of status interaction with any single individual. With even small natural differences among individuals, this high repetition tolerance can bring high reward totals from using these personal differences in the pursuit of status. Furthermore, contrast sensitivity will favor higher-contrast status arousers with more reward spikes and more repeatability. Status interactions between specific individuals can occur again and again, and reward harvesting continues for the dominant individuals. Thus, even with very small populations, there can be a major status expansion for a few members.

The historical evidence from anthropology and paleoanthropology suggests that the human case is different. There are status distinctions in all populations who live in the micro social scale of our context of origin as hunters and gatherers; but if the same basic rules for status reward release exist in humans as in some other primates such as the chimpanzee, human populations should all have the same elevated status inequality of these other primates. Instead, human micro populations exhibit occasional short-term elevated status spikes, but rarely are individuals successful in making these distinctions permanent. Any such attempts to produce inflated inequality are generally met with successful resistance over the long term (Boehm 1999). Human status reward rules could be one key factor in this pattern. The evidence suggests that humans do not have the same repetition tolerance for status interaction with any single individual that some other primate species have. Given a more limited repetition tolerance, even if some individuals try to use high contrasts to increase rewards over time, there is not at this social scale enough variety of individuals consistently available to trigger the elevated reward totals necessary to compensate for the high costs of creating and defending high-status positions over the long term.

However, in these same cultures, status spiking occurs in a number of occasional and temporary situations, and this is unlike the case in many other primate species without an elevated status pattern. These spikes appear in circumstances in which the variety of status arousers is increased, in terms of either circumstantial variety or numerical variety. For instance, there are periodic gatherings when normally dispersed populations come together for one reason or another, such as raiding or warfare, information and mate exchanges, religious rituals, and so on (Henrich 2010; Johnson and Earle 2000; Powell, Shennan, and Thomas 2010). Such temporary assemblies create special opportunities for status differentiation fueled by the additional variety of circumstances and individuals. The high contrast between these special situations and normal daily life would be one source of additional rewards, and this high contrast would also promote more rewarding repetitions. The extra variety of individuals available for reinforcing more elevated distinctions would be another source of extra rewards. The regular expansion of social differentiation in these special situations seems to indicate the existence of status reward rules with this behavioral scaling. However, these special conditions are not sustainable. Over time, these groups break up and return to a smaller base and more repetitive behavior patterns, thereby dampening most opportunities to continue reaping the extra status rewards of the special situations. Of course, this behavioral flexibility in scaling status reward release always has some messy qualities because it leaves open the possibility that some individuals might make inappropriate responses to different conditions. Nonetheless, metaphorically speaking, natural selection is interested in what works and not necessarily in what is the cleanest or most elegant, and it is clear that this flexibility is generally useful in our early history.

With the exodus from our context of origin, larger population concentrations become a permanent part of the social landscape, and the status arouser variety available only occasionally in earlier history now is the normal situation. The result is a reversal of fortune as the very rules that limit the growth of inequality in our context of origin now become the fuel for a regular expansion of status distinctions. With expanded variety, there is less repetition of any specific arouser, and hence more rewards. This means that individuals will also bear more costs in the pursuit of those additional rewards. Furthermore, in order to take even more advantage of such expanded variety, some individuals can seek out long-term high-contrast status distinctions that offer both higher reward spikes on average and more repetitions. These inflated distinctions can offer even greater reward totals, and this means that individuals will bear even more costs in their pursuit. However, there normally are not natural differences among individuals great enough to sustain such elevated contrast values. Instead, there must be a magnification of natural differences among individuals, or like religion, a creation of high contrasts by simply fabricating inflated differences. In addition, some individuals can seek out a highly disproportionate share of key social and economic resources to embody these high contrasts and to promote the harvesting of additional reward release for other interests. Such accumulations are very costly to the society as a whole, and only an elite few can be maintained within a population.

Is there a vehicle to facilitate mass access to such additional reward release through the status inflation of whole groups throughout a population? One problem in such a mass expansion is that there are even fewer natural differences between groups of individuals than there are among individuals, such that high-contrast natural differences are not going to be available for reward triggers in the pursuit of elevated distinctions. Where, then, to find such distinctions? The solution to this problem is once again, just as with religion, to use our cognitive skills to create elevated distinctions having little or no reality outside of a belief in them. One path is to use small or moderate natural performance differences between groups (such as differences in gender and physical strength), inflate these differences, and then attribute to them a host of other high-contrast distinctions. Another path is to take nonperformance differences like skin color and attribute to such superficial differences all kinds of other high-contrast distinctions. Or simply fabricate differences between groups based on culture or whatever, and ascribe to these fabrications a host of other distinctions. Next, make these inflated attributions permanent so they can consistently offer high-contrast familiarity, and use these attributions to try to exclude others from any fair competition for access to even the small social resources that a group might control. These fixed elevated distinctions can lead to additional reward release, and just as in the case of religion, they will feel real. Of course, being completely or largely imaginary, these high-contrast arousers can be made regularly available throughout a population. Similarly, as with religion, creating and maintaining such distinctions is monumentally costly for a specific individual, but a collective construction can offer a better deal. Thus, the exodus produces a permanent mass reward window that earlier had only been open on an occasional and temporary basis.

There are significant costs associated with these social status creations. Inflated inequality produces many categories of winners and losers, and the negative consequences of being in the loser category also escalate. The fact that so many individuals have borne so much of these costs for so long demonstrates just how addictive can be the additional reward release coming from mass elevated inequality. Naturally, the best way to reinforce these emerging distinctions is to deny their historicity and to make them in principle eternal and permanent divisions, such as by declaring them the work of the gods. Once again, throughout much of our history, it is in Schumpeter's terms the static construction that is preferable in triggering these additional rewards; and it is no wonder that powerful statics like religion and ascriptive inequality so often become entangled with one another and work together to handicap resistance to such status inflation over the long run.

Given the massive costs that such a pyramidal pattern creates for so many individuals, resistance to elite domination does not disappear; but cooperation and coordination by groups opposing this domination are severely handicapped, if not paralyzed, by the predominance of inflated ascriptive distinctions throughout the population. Generally, resistance either fails outright or, when successful in the short term, is transformed over time into another version of the very structures it originally opposed. Specific elites and constellations of mass ascriptive inequality rise and fall as these pyramidal social constructions topple and reemerge again and again, but the general pattern remains the same. It is high-contrast familiarity in inflated status distinctions that spreads through a population and dominates despite its enormous social costs. Novelty in status rewards occurs only occasionally and only for a small part of the population. This is even truer for serial novelty. And after all, how could any such novelty compete on a broad basis with the emergent and ever-present post-exodus reward surge of fixed social creations like elevated ascription?

Just as in the case of the emergence of religion, the expansion of reward release in such mass status inflations is not infinite. Indeed, it is hard to see the natural selection logic in infinite needs (Hammond 2012). This would be the case for both basic interests and any expansion windows that are directly or indirectly a part of human biological evolution. In regard to status, there are some important rewards to be reaped by making more regular use of a reward release pattern that is used more occasionally in our context of origin; but these extra rewards are limited, and hence any interest rooted in such rewards will be limited rather than endlessly expansive. As social scale grows, status pyramids become more elevated and elaborate; but this does not mean that the status interest itself is expanding or that more and more rewards can be harvested by any specific individual on that pyramid. Instead, as scale grows, if there is a continuing commitment to a pyramidal pattern of status differentiation, groups must divide and subdivide in order to provide a growing range of variety and contrasts necessary to simply continue to take full long-term advantage of our status reward rules. Such stacking is a form of variety and contrast creation in the face of expanding social scale. It keeps the extra rewards flowing, but it does not necessarily increase that flow for any specific individual. As noted earlier, given the great costs to the society as a whole for any position at the top of a pyramid, only a few individuals can take full advantage of stacking and embody these distinctions with significant accumulations of economic and political power. Most have to make do with whatever status distinctions they can access, such as elevated ascription protecting even small amounts of a social resource. This mass trade-off opens a window for a great substitution when a new reward-triggering opportunity begins to emerge.

The Second Exodus and the Great Substitution

The basis of this new opportunity to play with our reward release rules comes from the gradual accumulation of technology over millennia. Eventually, this accumulation reaches a take-off point where continuing competition among still predominantly agrarian elite systems could begin to propel technology forward at a greater and greater rate until it could fully emerge as a key part of the scaffolding for a new social system. Why is technology so important in terms of our reward release rules? First, with its mass production capacities, it can compete on a mass basis with the reward release power of high-contrast and high-repetition social creations like ascriptive inequality. Second, it can compete while offering many individuals a better cost–benefit ratio in terms of the time, effort, and risk involved in the pursuit of these amplified rewards. This makes technology a very tempting vehicle to put to use in substituting one reward release package for another.

With technology's productivity surge, contrast sensitivity can be tapped to offer additional reward release by reducing repetition through increased variety and novelty in goods and services for a host of interests. This productivity offers regularly rewarding additions that are available only occasionally and temporarily earlier in history, and it can often make this offer without a parallel increase in costs. With technology's boost, novelty can be transformed from an occasional to a serial part of the lives of many individuals. Technology does not have to rely as much on high contrasts, and hence to have potentially high costs, for additional reward release. It can stress more short-term additions, but in a manner that can add up over time to a grand total equal to the alternative classic additions. Generating such extensive variety and novelty on one's own is once again possible, but highly improbable, and it is collective constructions like serially innovative mass production technologies that are most appealing. Altogether, technology's full emergence justifies being labeled as the second exodus (Hammond 2012).

Of course, technology is not sufficient by itself in offering up such an alternative platform for additional reward release. It is necessary, but it must also be linked to innovations in social organization, finance, and a host of other parts in the new dynamic civilization. That is one reason why the entrepreneur, the combiner, is so attractive to Schumpeter. Entrepreneurs have to make adaptations not just with technology, but in all aspects of the productive process if they are to succeed in the gale of serial innovations. That is also why Schumpeter focuses so much of his analysis on multiple innovations in multiple areas of the entire culture as the world moves from a predominance of static social structures and social lives embracing high-contrast familiarity to a more dynamic mode in which serial novelty becomes more and more preeminent through the process of creative destruction.

Familiar ways of doing things mean that once something is learned, it can be returned to again and again. Familiarity also means that the costs are generally known for accessing these arousers. As long as the rewards keep coming from such return visits and the costs are also familiar, it is often not easy to get individuals to look elsewhere for such rewards. Lessening repetition by increasing the distinct variety of attractive arousers is fine in itself, but there is always a potential cost problem lurking in this alternative. How to increase variety without incurring too many additional costs that make less appealing any additional rewards reaped from additional variety? This is an especially important question in the face of the declining marginal utility that normally accompanies the addition of variety for most all of our interests. For instance, if individuals have some familiar foods that are attractive and readily available, they may be interested in some additional variety, but only if the costs are limited to access those additions. Each addition is likely to provide a lower marginal reward gain than the earlier additions. If the costs of accessing these food additions remain the same as with the first foods, then with rewards declining, the cost–benefit ratio for each addition is likely to be less appealing and eventually to discourage continued interest. However, if technological and social innovations allow access to all the additional foods without an equivalent cost increase, or even at a lesser cost, then the cost–benefit ratio shifts dramatically. In the capitalist era, the productivity of multiple innovations has had the impact of controlling costs for such increased variety and thereby making this new reward release platform more enticing.

The cost–benefit problem is even more acute in regard to novel arousers. After all, novelty rewards are self-extinguishing. Novelty can be very appealing in terms of both increasing reward spike averages and making short-term repetitions more desirable; but if the costs are not known, are very difficult to assess, or even continue after the rewards are gone, then novelty becomes less appealing. Serial novelty can be even more difficult in this regard, because individuals now must assess costs and benefits over a longer time span in which novel arouser is followed by novel arouser. However, once again, if technological and social innovations limit some or all of these potential costs, then serial novelty is that much more attractive. In fact, extensive variety and serial novelty in goods and services for a host of interests are extremely difficult to provide on a mass scale without such innovations. If this was not the case, then our earlier history should be marked by low technology culture after culture adding variety and novelty to their reward packages on a regular and long-term basis. The actual historical record shows the opposite. Without vast technological aids to control costs, adding much variety and novelty as reward releasers on a mass basis is almost impossible.

Of course, even major technological innovations are no guarantee that such additional variety and novelty will become available across a population. For instance, many important technological changes are associated with the exodus from our context of origin, but most of these are soon overwhelmed by population growth. Population surges with the new technologies that make possible horticultural and agricultural societies, and the resultant changes in per capita income, are not all that great. This leaves little opportunity to provide a significant increase in the variety of arousers available to a wide range of individuals. For example, in regard to a food interest, neuroscientists have demonstrated that many primates and all humans have elaborate reward architecture for responding to different foods (Berridge et al. 2010; Rolls et al. 1986). If the technological changes of the exodus could make available heightened variety and novelty in food availability, then many rewards would be available; but much the opposite actually occurs historically. More people are sustained, but with less food variety, and often with less food quantity and quality. Of course, with a series of technological innovations, there would be a point where such food provisioning is possible on a mass basis; but long before that occurs, there emerge elevated inequality structures with little interest in such developments.

The focus of these pyramidal structures is to limit further changes and to resist possibilities that might alter the status quo. The result is that only an elite is able to take full advantage of the post-exodus changes in food production in order to have a quantity and variety of food that could also provide bonus rewards from something like serial novelty. This same pattern occurs in regard to interest after interest for which increased variety and serial novelty could have been alternative sources of reward release. New technologies are resisted outright or severely dampened in their impact by the demands to keep the powerful elite status quo going. In the face of such innovation dampening, it is no wonder that the possibilities of using technologies on a mass scale as an alternative reward release source only appear late in our history. Similarly, after the exodus, there are occasional cases of serial novelty where an individual or small group rises from obscurity to fame and fortune. However, these surges are few and far between; when they are successful, they most often become over time another form of static inequality.

Even in generally static cultures, Schumpeter (1976: 133–136) notes that technological innovations continue, particularly in regard to areas of competition between these pyramidal structures such as in military matters, but at a very slow rate on an occasional basis. However, after millennia of a gradual accumulation of technologies, there eventually emerges a point where a new alternative mass source of bonus rewards would be available. Once again, it is important to stress that this reward release option only appears late in our history. To compete with the reward release power of classic high-contrast and high-repetition social creations like religion and ascriptive inequality, wave after wave of technological innovation would be required, and even to begin this competition requires a vast amount of time. Such a sea change also requires a new elite to emerge as its champion, and for Schumpeter, this new elite is the capitalist class. What sets them apart from previous elites is not inequality itself, but rather the commitment of this new high-inequality group to a process of creative destruction.

In Schumpeter's world, an occasional innovation is no longer enough. Innovation must follow innovation as this new dynamic culture gradually takes hold, starting slowly but then gaining momentum. Any specific innovation is unlikely to match the very high-contrast values of classic social creations. Mass production can only make widely available the occasional radical addition, and most often, the new offerings have a lesser contrast value. However, there can be a great many of these non-high-contrast additions. Such serial innovation can offer occasional high contrast and a cornucopia of lesser-contrast variety and novelty that has the same potential reward total for a host of basic and acquired interests that classic fixed high contrasts provide. Thus, over the long run, it can compete with and serve as a substitute for earlier social creations offering another path to additional reward release.

Inflated ascription and the mass production of an expanding range of goods and services are not as compatible with one another in comparison with combining high-contrast packages like religion and ascription. A religion-backed high-contrast ascription is based on trying to exclude whole groups as much as possible from access to key social resources, be it in terms of marriage partners, economic resources, political positions, or whatever. Without such exclusions, the contrast value of the status distinction decreases, and so does the reward release. However, as Schumpeter notes, a mass production economy requires mass consumption, and this in turn requires that many are not excluded from access to the increased range of goods and services being produced. Mass production must be directed more to inclusion rather than exclusion. If such production is a small part of the total production of an economy, then high-contrast ascription can still thrive, but as this production spreads, mass elevated ascription must more or less gradually give way as more individuals seek alternative vehicles for harvesting rewards. Ascription does not have to disappear completely, but at least it will have to take on a lighter imprint.

The potential for social organization and political cooperation in nonelites grows as these mass inflated ascriptive distinctions erode; and this has a major impact on long-term resistance to traditional elites and to the emerging capitalist elite. Of course, in the face of the continuing deep appeal of high-contrast arousers, it is not surprising that the new capitalist elite try to use their special positions in a mass production economy to continue to maximize inflated inequality and the many different rewards tied to it. However, once again, such positions are very costly to the economy as a whole, and only a limited number can be sustained even in a very rich society. Many more will substitute alternative reward packages, and many will have to embrace a more moderate inequality in adopting this substitution.

The New Deal

In predominantly static preindustrial cultures, much of the strength of classic elites comes from the fact that so many individuals across the population try to imitate more or less successfully the elite use of high-contrast differentiation. As noted earlier, the widespread embrace of this high-contrast platform severely handicaps successful long-term resistance to such elites. However, the emerging mass production economy cannot rely as heavily on this imitation. Mass production requires mass consumption, and both require an erosion of elevated mass ascription. The long-term success of the new capitalist elite greatly depends on their new role in promoting an economic machine providing a greater and greater variety and novelty in goods and services; and they face growing political and organizational pressure from nonelites seeking a share of this mass production sufficient to fuel a mass reward substitution. The new elite cannot ignore these substitution dynamics;

and as the gradual shift from a mostly static to an increasingly dynamic economy gains momentum over time, the new deal between capitalists and consumers becomes more and more important and takes different forms in different circumstances.

There are basically three long-term tools to meet these substitution demands. First, there is economic growth producing a larger pie per capita over time. This means that there are simply more goods and services to go around. Second, there is economic redistribution. This means dividing up the pie differently such that, for instance, even if the total distribution remains significantly unequal, some who earlier got a smaller share now get more. Third, there is the possibility of using debt to access additional goods and services. Debt can occur at both the micro individual level and the collective macro level. A mass consumption culture is incredibly demanding on all these tools as the great substitution spreads across a population, and each of these tools can be problematical as they struggle to deliver year after year and decade after decade the goods and services to fuel alternative reward-triggering packages. There are going to be many tipping points in any such developments, just as there are with classic high-contrast bonus packages from earlier history.

The decade after World War I in the United States is an example of one such point. In this decade, the implicit deal between capitalists and consumers took the form of a promise that when the productive powers of the new technologies demonstrated so fully in the tragedy of World War I were turned to peaceful ends, there would be a new age emerging in a truly mass consumer culture. So great is this potential that it could even support an income inequality surge at the very top. In fact, this decade is marked by a vast expansion in delivering mass goods and services, as well as a sharp jump in economic inequality. Never had so much been promised, and never had so much been delivered, at least for a short time. However, this combination turns out to be unsustainable, and the end result is a massive crash. This is a gigantic failure in terms of the new deal that capitalism was supposed to offer after World War I; and in the United States, the failure leads to Roosevelt's own New Deal.

The collapse of the post–World War I deal between capitalists and consumers triggers a radical change; and after World War II, something approaching this promised consumer cornucopia actually does begin to appear. Regular economic growth plus the progressive distribution of that growth due to the income inequality compression rooted in the Great Depression and World War II produce an explosion in goods and services that the world has never seen before. Indeed, it appears that the very inequality compression policies that Schumpeter so opposed help to create the general economic prosperity he so believed in. However, beginning in the 1970s and 1980s, this second deal begins to run into headwinds, and economic inequality begins growing again. But even when hit further by the collapse of many risky innovations in financial services and the Great Recession, there seems to be little in the way of widespread momentum for another radical new deal. This is all the more surprising given the reaction to economic turmoil earlier in the last century. Does this mean that there no longer must be as much additional economic growth or inequality compression in order to have a sufficient level of mass consumption for many to continue to reap a satisfactory package of reward release and therefore not embrace another radical social experiment?

As with our other interests, there is no reason to assume that an acquired taste for something like technology-driven variety and serial novelty is inherently and endlessly expansive. As noted earlier, such infinite needs do not make much sense in terms of natural selection. There are some important rewards to be reaped by making more regular use of a reward release pattern that is used more occasionally in our context of origin; but these extra rewards are limited, and hence an acquired interest rooted in such rewards will be limited rather than forever expansive. There may be occasional individuals who exhibit the extreme version of this new interest in an almost pathological form, but not populations as a whole over the long run. When one set of reward releasers is replacing another, it may appear as if the new needs are infinite, but this should not be the case once the substitution is mostly in place. Thus, if technology-driven acquired interests are infinite, then once they had spread throughout the population, there would be ceaseless pressure for high growth and extensive redistribution, because nothing else could meet such expanding demands. However, if such interests are not infinite, then a shift could occur as the substitution of reward platforms becomes more complete. It is this second alternative that appears to better describe the situation today.

If these technology-supported needs are not infinite, there will be a point at which the general economic pie becomes big enough on a per capita basis, and has so much variety and novelty built into it, that the individual share of that pie for many who are not rich would still be large enough to provide a wide range of variety and novelty in goods and services with sufficient reward release to basically satisfy most individuals. These circumstances could produce a great deal of risk aversion in which many are not predisposed to embrace the kind of radical change that is attractive when the economic pie is smaller and there seems to be more to gain and less to lose. For many, further surges in economic growth would be nice, but not absolutely necessary. These individuals could even be fearful of adding more fuel to the ongoing fire of incessant change by supporting another Roosevelt-like New Deal to spur more expansive growth rates, or to significantly redistribute shares of the economic pie much more equitably. Such caution would not indicate just a comfortable complacency, but rather a loss aversion strategy that appears to be the safest course in an ever-changing and unpredictable world of serial novelty. On the other hand, if these new needs are infinite, then any such slowdown would be unacceptable even for a short period of time. Surging economic growth would not just be nice but absolutely necessary on a mass scale; and anything that seems to stand in the way of such growth would be in danger. However, such a crises mentality does not seem to be the general case today.

At this juncture, in another reversal of fortune, an opening would occur for a few seeking even more extraordinary economic gains with the high-contrast values that have been attractive so often in our history. Much or even most all of that further growth could be absorbed by this small economic elite, again without leading to the type of collective action for inequality compression that appeared earlier when the economic pie was much smaller. The elite could seek to increase their relative share of the pie by taking back some of the relative losses that had occurred in the decades just before and after World War II. Economic inequality could then grow away from the levels of postwar income inequality compression. Different countries decompress to different degrees depending on a host of local circumstances. For countries that did not have this compression, inequality could continue at higher levels than those of the compression level of that postwar period.

All of this seems to be the pattern in the United States from the 1980s onward. A less extreme version of the same pattern also seems to be appearing in Canada and in more and more high per capita income European nations that earlier exhibited the same income inequality compression as the United States (Piketty 2014). Indeed, even when the creative destruction of globalization and many disastrous innovations in financial services led to the difficulties and distress of the Great Recession, the push for radical change worldwide has been limited at best. There has been a great deal of talk, but little concrete action that would significantly alter this pattern. Proposals to patch up the basic safety net or tinker with income tax rates seem to have widespread sympathy, but such actions are not going to alter very much of this expanded inequality. There are, of course, many factors in these developments, but perhaps lurking behind them all are the long-term effects of the substitution of technology-inflated high-variety and novelty arousers for the classic arouser packages that marked our earlier history. With sufficiently expanded economies, a basic safety net, and a wide spread of reward substitution, there is the possibility that very elevated inequality can coexist over the long term with high variety and novelty mass consumption, thereby combining both of the most powerful reward release triggers rooted in our evolutionary heritage.

This dynamic might also apply to the impact of changing economic growth rates. One of the striking developments of post–World War II capitalism is that year-to-year growth rates are higher on average than the 2 percent per year average that Schumpeter highlighted for the previous half century before 1928. These higher growth rates are crucial to the sheer size of the avalanche of goods and services that facilitate the great substitution of reward platforms on such a widespread basis during these decades. At first glance, this success would seem to imply that if these elevated growth rates are not available, there would be an immediate and widespread political backlash and movements for heavy state intervention to try to restore those higher growth rates. However, as with inequality decompression, such a radical response does not seem to be the general case. Once again, many seem to be hesitant to risk the inflation or other kinds of economic destabilization that might accompany any attempt by the state to gear up growth rates to previous highs. This too would suggest that for many individuals a deep shift has occurred in terms of changing reward release patterns and, with a sufficiently large general economic pie, that higher inequality and lower growth rates could coexist over some period of time.

This coexistence does not imply that there are not widespread problems of one kind or another. The dynamic culture form that Schumpeter envisions is one of continual, grinding change requiring constant adjustment and adaptation at all levels of the society. The spread of serial novelty will not alter just consumption patterns but also the nature and appeal of jobs producing these goods and services, as well as the educational preparation for those jobs. Different individuals and groups are going to be more or less able or willing to make such relentless changes. As Schumpeter notes in analyzing predominantly static and dynamic cultures, there is no absolute measure of whether one or the other is ultimately better in existential terms (1976: 129); and without such a basic metric, there are always going to be controversies and conflicts within and between such different reward platforms. Furthermore, in terms of our evolutionary origins, neither of the great post-exodus reward-triggering structures of high-contrast familiarity or serial novelty represents "true" human nature. Both bonus packages play with our ancient reward release rules in post-exodus conditions very different than our context of origin in which those rules were forged by natural selection. As a result, both have problematical elements built into them.

On the one hand, if there is nothing inherently natural about static elevated inequality, there will always be conflict and struggles of one kind or another in creating and maintaining any specific social creation embracing such inequality. The collapse of one pyramid will set the stage for the rise of another, and this will go on century after century. As an elite fights within itself, or with other elites, or with nonelites, many will suffer grievously and die early in a dynamic that can never reach a definitive conclusion. On the other hand, if there is nothing natural about long-term serial novelty, there will always be a host of difficulties based on the self-extinguishing qualities of the reward bonuses offered by such novelty. Many will feel as though they are running harder and harder just to keep up with the erosion of rewards not based on classic high-contrast familiarity. In such a race, creative destruction will often appear as a glass half full and half empty at any time, making it difficult for many to judge exactly where they stand, thereby producing insecurity and even fear. As creative destruction goes global, there will be even more unpredictable elements that can have a negative effect on any temporary success in one country or one part of the world with reward harvesting using this new platform. Furthermore, since so little persists in these new reward packages, there are bound to be some who look nostalgically for an alternative to the restlessness in such a self-extinguishing pattern; and this quest will bring them into conflict, and sometimes violent conflict, with others who no longer embrace a belief in a more fixed package of reward release.

Schumpeter passed away in 1950, well before the impact of post–World War II capitalism was fully evident. He saw the potential for another avalanche of production, but he also feared it would be once again blunted by political intervention into the normal cycle of capitalist expansion and contraction (1976: 386, 398). It is clear that he was wrong about the soon-to-be decline of capitalism and its perennial gale of development. Capitalism managed to survive the income inequality compression of the New Deal and post–World War II planning policies that Schumpeter opposed, and not only to thrive within many traditionally capitalist cultures but also to spread around the world. However, from the 1980s onward, the income compression that many of us had hoped would be the standard for the new capitalism began to erode and to resemble more and more pre-compression levels of inequality, without triggering a radical push back like the New Deal. This shift seems to affirm Schumpeter's belief that elevated inequality in capitalism can be accepted or at least tolerated as long as the system is productive enough in its ups and downs to continue to provide over time a basic safety net for the poor and an unmatchable cornucopia of variety and novelty in goods and services to a wide swath of the population. Of course, it remains to be seen whether the current combination of elevated inequality and mass consumption is a true tipping point, or just another swing along the way with a new era of inequality compression soon to appear as the majority seek to gain back some of their own recent losses.

Similarly, the widespread acceptance of a slowdown in economic growth over the last years might indicate that Schumpeter also had been right in his long-term analysis of the relative growth rate of capitalism and the impact of such a rate on the long-term prospects of capitalism. As noted earlier, he put that average growth rate at about 2 percent per year over the long run in the half century before the Great Depression (1976: 64–65). The cumulative impact of this 2 percent is significant over such an extended period and produces a growing avalanche of goods and services, such that within the small circle of capitalist countries in the world at the time, there are few successful anti-capitalist political movements during this period. There is an even higher relative growth rate in the decades after World War II in many capitalist countries, but it is not clear if such a higher rate is necessary over the longer term. If he were alive today, Schumpeter might argue that the Great Recession and the limited political impact of such economic turmoil in terms of fueling a mass anti-capitalist movement indicate that cumulative growth has reached a point where it is possible once again to have a lower average growth rate than appeared during the initial postwar decades, and not to immediately face a major political crisis demanding radical action by the state. This too would indicate a deeper change in reward release dynamics as the cumulative impact of high technology variety and serial novelty spreads throughout a population.

It is also clear that Schumpeter was wrong about the emerging appeal of socialism in capitalist countries, or even its continuing appeal in socialist countries. Despite the roller-coaster nature of economic change in capitalism, many individuals continue to believe that it is superior over the long run at providing a wide range of both variety and novelty across the population. Many socialists came to believe the same thing as their own social system was unable for one reason or another to fully embrace serial innovation across all sectors of the society. Perhaps this too is just a temporary setback, and at some time in the future, Schumpeter's prediction will come true as the turmoil of capitalism fades in favor of one or another form of socialism. However, at least for now, it seems that Schumpeter vastly underrated just how addictive capitalist creative destruction would become around the world.

Conclusion

Joseph Schumpeter's creative destruction is part of a larger model of economic change based on the transformation of precapitalist static cultures into a more dynamic form. Schumpeter's vision of these developments is reanalyzed in terms of different patterns of reward release rooted in our biological evolution. Two reward release platforms of high-contrast familiarity and serial novelty highlight the deep motivational structure of Schumpeter's model. Serial novelty in a wide variety of goods and services can provide on a mass scale the same additional reward release that high-contrast familiarity in inflated inequality did earlier in our history. However, with new technologies supporting such novelty, the costs for many individuals are not as great as they were for such inequality. This sets the stage for the substitution of a new mass reward platform. As this substitution proceeds, there are a number of possible impacts on social and economic inequality.

References

Aron, A., H. Fisher, D. Mashek, G. Strong, H. Li, and L. Brown. 2005. "Reward, Motivation, and Emotion Systems Associated with Early-Stage Intense Romantic Love." *Journal of Neurophysiology* 94: 327–337.
Berridge, K., C. Y. Ho, J. M. Richard, and A. G. Feliceantonio. 2010. "The Tempted Brain Eats: Pleasure and Desire Circuits in Obesity and Eating Disorders." *Brain Research* 1350: 43–64.
Boehm, C. 1999. *Hierarchy in the Forest: The Evolution of Egalitarian Behavior*. Cambridge, MA: Harvard University Press.
Bunzeck, N., C. Doeller, R. Dolan, and E. Duzel. 2012. "Contextual Interaction between Novelty and Reward Processing within the Mesolimbic System." *Human Brain Mapping* 33 (6): 1309–1324.
Bunzeck, N., and E. Duzel. 2006. "Absolute Coding of Stimulus Novelty in the Human Substantia Nigra/VTA." *Neuron* 51 (3): 369–379.
Chiao, J., T. Harada, E. Oby, Z. Li, T. Parrish, and D. Bridge. 2009. "Neural Representations of Social Status Hierarchy in Human Inferior Parietal Cortex." *Neuropsychologia* 47: 354–363.
Fisher, H., A. Aron, D. Mashek, H. Li, and L. Brown. 2002. "Defining the Brain Systems of Lust, Romantic Attraction, and Attachment." *Archives of Sexual Behavior* 31 (5): 413–419.
Hammond, M. 2012. "Back to the Future: The Partial Reversal in Social Evolution Theories." Paper presented at the Annual Meeting of the American Sociological Association, Denver, CO.
———. 2013. "The Neurosociology of Reward Release, Repetition, and Social Emergence." In *Handbook of Neurosociology*, edited by D. Franks and J. Turner, 311–329. New York: Springer.
Henrich, J. 2010. "The Evolution of Innovation-Enhancing Institutions." In *Innovations in Cultural Systems: Contributions from Evolutionary Anthropology*, edited by M. J. O'Brien and S. Shennan, 99–120. Cambridge, MA: MIT Press.
Izuma, K., D. Saito, and N. Sadato. 2008. "Processing of Social and Monetary Rewards in the Human Striatum." *Neuron* 58 (2): 284–294.
Johnson, A. W., and T. Earle. 2000. *The Evolution of Human Societies*. Stanford, CA: Stanford University Press.
Kakade, S. M., and P. Dayan. 2002. "Dopamine: Generalization and Bonuses." *Neural Networks* 15: 549–559.
Kirkpatrick, L., and P. Granquist. 2008. "Attachment and Religious Representations of Behavior." In *Handbook of Attachment*, edited by J. Cassidy and P. Shaver, 906–933. New York: Guilford Press.

Ly, M., M. Haynes, J. Barter, D. Weinberger, and C. Zink. 2011. "Subjective Socioeconomic Status Predicts Human Ventral Striatal Responses to Social Status Information." *Current Biology* 21 (9): 794–797.

Martinez, D. O., R. Narendran, M. Slifstein, F. Liu, D. Kumar, A. Broft, R. Van Heertum, and H. Kleber. 2010. "Dopamine Type 2/3 Receptor Availability in the Striatum and Social Status in Human Volunteers." *Biological Psychiatry* 67 (3): 275–278.

McNamara, P. 2009. *The Neuroscience of Religious Experience*. Cambridge: Cambridge University Press.

Montague, R., and G. Berns. 2002. "Neural Economics and the Biological Substrates of Valuation." *Neuron* 36 (2): 265–284.

Newberg, A., E. d'Aquili, and V. Rause. 2001. *Why God Won't Go Away: Brain Science and the Biology of Belief*. New York: Ballantine Books.

Piketty, T. 2014. *Capital in the Twenty-First Century*. Cambridge, MA: Harvard University Press.

Powell, A., S. Shennan, and M. Thomas. 2010. "Demography and Variation in the Accumulation of Culturally Inherited Skills." In *Innovations in Cultural Systems*, edited by M. J. O'Brien and S. Shennan, 137–160. Cambridge, MA: MIT Press.

Rolls, E., E. Murzi, S. Yaxley, S. Thrope, and S. Simpson. 1986. "Sensory Specific Satiety: Food-Specific Reduction in Responsiveness of Ventral Forebrain Neurons after Feeding in the Monkey." *Brain Research* 368: 79–86.

Saxe, R., and J. Haushofer. 2008. "For Love or Money: A Common Neural Currency for Social and Monetary Reward." *Neuron* 58 (2): 164–165.

Schumpeter, J. (1911) 2003. "The Theory of Economic Development." In *Joseph Alois Schumpeter*, edited by J. Backhaus, 61–116. Boston: Kluwer.

———. 1934a. "Depressions." In *Economics of the Recovery Program*, edited by D. Brown, E. Chamberlin, and S. Harris, 3–22. New York: McGraw Hill.

———. 1934b. *The Theory of Economic Development: An Inquiry into Profits, Capital, Interest, and the Business Cycle*. Cambridge, MA: Harvard University Press.

———. (1942) 1976. *Capitalism, Socialism, and Democracy*. London: George Allen and Unwin.

Zink, C., Y. Tong, Q. Chen, D. Bassett, J. Stein, and A. Mayer-Lindenberg. 2008. "Know Your Place: Neural Processing of Social Hierarchy in Humans." *Neuron* 58 (2): 273–283.

INDEX

Accumulation, rise and decline of modes of, 276, 277–278. *See also* capitalism
Acquired behavior, 51
Adaptation(s): as axiom of Darwinian conflict theory, 237; competing, 55–56n4; and criticism of evolutionary studies of human behavior, 160–161; defined, 55n2, 138; emergence of, 39; environmental change and, 40–41; human affairs functions as, 32–35; human affairs functions as Darwinian, 35–36; hypothesized, in Darwinian population biology, 44; instantiation and manifestation of, 6–12; mental, 16–18, 25–26; and midcentury reformulation of human ecology, 326; religious sense as, 258; strategies as units of, 47
Adapted mind: emergence of notion, 5; prepared learning, 5–6. *See also* Adapted social mind; Evolved mental adaptations; Evolved psychological mechanism(s); Mental adaptations; Psychological adaptations
Adapted social mind: further study of, 25; modular mind hypothesis, 7–9; overview, 6–7; theories regarding, 25–26; Turner's conception of, 9–12. *See also* Adapted mind; Evolved mental adaptations; Evolved psychological mechanism(s); Mental adaptations; Psychological adaptations
Adaptive mutation, 69
Adaptive problems: defined, 138; and domain-specific adaptive mechanisms, 237, 261n2; and emergence of stable social groups, 493; emotional response mechanisms for, 496; in environment of evolutionary adaptedness, 140–142; inability to meet all, 26; and maladaptive behavior, 144; in Spencerian selection, 107, 343, 344, 346
Adding: as kind of variation, 59, 60; variation through, 60–64
Affiliative strong reciprocity, 590
Affinity, exogamy and, 355–357
Age and aging: as attribute determining status rank, 14, 475; of organizations in resource niches, 336–339
Agency: and defining evolution in sociocultural systems, 96; sociocultural evolution and focus on, 267; and Spencerian selection, 343
Aggregate phase in transition, 575
Aggression: as chief problem leading to sanctioning, 435; defensive, 502, 504; evolution of aggressive responses to outgroup threats, 502–503; human aggression theory, 256–257; intergroup, in simple societies, 496; moralistic, 11–12, 26; and racial stereotyping, 500; as response to overcrowding, 391; testosterone levels and, 18–19; and warfare among animals, 272. *See also* Extralegal police aggression; Violence
Agricultural Revolution, 143
Agriculture: in economic subsistence theory, 242; effect of, on natural selection, 145; and emergence of new hierarchical arrangements, 475, 576; evolutionary sociology and evolution of, 203–204. *See also* Post-agricultural societies
Aiello, L., 289
Albert (gorilla), 534
Alda, Alan, 18
Alexander, Richard D.: on emotional energy concept, 234; on principles of cultural materialism, 235; theory of reputational selection, 424, 426, 427–428
Almond, D., 130
Altruism: and defining cooperation, 442–443; and dual inheritance theory, 198–199; and group selection in biology and sociology, 78; kinship and, 443; and limits of biological theory in social sciences, 98–99; reciprocal, 426, 427; reputational selection theory and, 428
Amalgams: in rational behaviorism, 524–525; in salience theory, 517–518, 520
The Amazing Apes, 540
Amygdala: and cognitive response mechanisms to outgroup threats, 498, 499; and defensive behavior, 502; function of, 287, 497, 560
Anasazi, 371–372
Anastomizing processes, 70, 71
Androgen: and gender behavior, 15; status-seeking and, 470
Anger: and combination of primary emotions, 563(table); as primary emotion, 497, 553; repressed shame turns to, 562; and social bonding, 561; and variants of primary emotions, 562(table)
Animal rights, 530–535
Animals: root traces of human psychology in, 525; thinking in, 524, 525, 531–532
Anterior cingulate cortex, 418
Anterior cingulate gyrus, 553–554, 555
Anton, S., 289, 362
Ants: social systems of, 24; sociocultural evolution of, 268–269
Ape Cognition and Conservation Initiative (ACCI), 543, 545
Ape Language: From Conditioned Response to Symbol (Savage-Rumbaugh), 542
Apes: adaptation to savanna, 551–552; adaptation to specialized niches in arboreal habitat, 551; behavioral propensities in hominins and, 10–11, 180, 546, 549; communication with, 531–532; comparative neuroanatomy between humans and, 559–566; competence with recursive sentence structures, 538–539; comprehension of novel sentences, 538; development of cognitive and social competence in young, 529–530; and existing behavioral propensities and preadaptations in early hominins, 552–559; failure-induced frustration in, 526; history of evolution, 181–182; humanness and rights of, 530–534; humans as, 403; implications of cladistic analysis for evolution of human brain, 184–188; importance of first years

of, 529–530, 533; innovation in, 527; investment in mating versus parenting effort, 406; language capacity, 178; learning of infant, 526; as means of understanding evolution of human brain, 180; organization among, 566–567; resources for salience theory and, 539–545; selection pressures on, 550–552; sexual dimorphism of, 413; sociality of, 10–11, 182–183; socioecology and mating strategies of, 405(fig.); status rank among, 471, 475, 476; testis size and sperm competition among, 415–416; weak-tie, 547–548. *See also* Primates
"Apes with Apps" (Schweller), 539
Appliance stores, 336
Arboreal habitat: and forced adaptation to savanna, 551–552; and history of primate evolution, 181–182, 184; selection pressures in, 550–551
Archaic *Homo sapiens*, 290
Arms races, 39–41, 43, 44, 56n4, 56n10, 204
Arrighi, Giovanni, 281
Arts, social functions of, 579–582. *See also* Literary scholarship; Literary works
Ascription, 619, 622
Assertion-anger: and combination of primary emotions, 563(table); as primary emotion possessed by mammals, 553; and variants of primary emotions, 562(table)
Assortative mating, 351, 427
Assortment, positive, 444–445
Atheism, 173
Athens, Greece, and Spencerian selection, 222
Atom of kinship, 356
Attachment: emotional, 554; ethnic attachment theory, 257–258; to groups, 452–453; high-contrast familiarity and religion and, 615–616; neurophysiology of, 418–419; and sexual versus familial bonding, 244. *See also* Network tie strength; Pair bonding; Social bonding
Audience, and reputation in cooperation, 445–446
Austen, Jane, 589, 597
Austin (chimpanzee), 542
Australopithecine afarensis, 288, 407
Australopithecine ramidus, 288
Australopithecine sediba, 289
Australopithecines/Australopithecus, 288–289, 293, 556
Authority: in geopolitical theory, 254, 255; legitimate, 578. *See also* Leaders; Leadership
Automobile industry, American, 104–105
Autonomous villages: in geopolitical theory, 254; in Spencer's political evolution, 221
Aversion-fear: and combination of primary emotions, 563(table); as primary emotion possessed by mammals, 553; and variants of primary emotions, 562(table)
Axelrod, Robert, 444
Axioms: of Darwinian conflict theory, 230, 236–239; in research programs, 228
Ayllu, 376, 377

Baker, R. R., 417
Band, as unit of social sanctioning and cooperative carnivory, 436
Barkow, Jerome, 233
Barr, A. B., 18
Barthold, J. A., 128
Bateson, Patrick, 351, 360
Beach, S.R.H., 18
Beatty, John, 40
"Because of" motives, 557
Begley, Sharon, 168
Behavior genetics, and evolutionary sociology, 195–196
Behavioral biology, Tinbergen's four questions, 49–51
Behavioral ecology: attacked by Gould, 162; and genetic determinism, 164; social parasitism in, 25; and sociobiology, 3, 13, 196. *See also* Human behavioral ecology (HBE)

Behavioral plasticity, 262n3
Behavioral propensities: and concept of tabula rasa, 5; emotion and, 564, 566; and evolution in sociocultural systems, 98–100; hardwired, in apes and hominins, 10–11, 180, 546, 549; hardwired, in monkeys, 184; subject to selection in apes and hominins, 552–559. *See also* Preadaptations
Behavioral scaling, 268–269
Behaviorism: limitations of, 514–515; rational, 524–525. *See also* Salience theory
Bellis, M. A., 417
A Bend in the River (Naipaul), 597
Berger, J., 475
Berger, P. L., 4
Betzig, L., 123
Bias: behavioral, 182; confirmation, 173; conflict with formed, 172–173; conformity, 577–578, 589; political, 195, 207; prestige, 577–578, 589; selection, 35
Biased learning, 5–6, 167, 577–578
Bible, 592
Bickerton, Derek, 449
Big bang period, 292, 293
Big game hunting, 304–305, 408–409, 436, 444, 447
Bilateral descent, 249
Billig, M. G., 453
Billy Budd, Sailor (Melville), 595–596
Bioecological communities, differences between human communities and, 321
Bioecology: classic human ecology's application of, 320–325; and community ecology in early twentieth century, 317–318; and development of human ecology, 318–320; and midcentury reformulation of human ecology, 325–326
Biological evolution: defined by Darwin, 178; group selection in, 80; major transitions in, 48–49; modes of innovation in, 65; programmed and reinforced behavior in, 68; social evolution and, 52, 88, 89; versus sociocultural evolution, 268–270; variation in human affairs versus, 40
Biological group selection, 450, 452
Biological sciences: Darwinian, 53; social sciences as, 31, 32–36
Biological selection, 51. *See also* Biological group selection
Biophobia, 23, 137
Biosocial model of status, 471–472, 481–482, 483, 485
Biosphere, crisis of, 280. *See also* Environment, exploitation of
Biotic communities, 317–318, 321–324
Bipedalism: advantages of, 293; brain parts necessary for, 286; and demands of infant care, 526; effects of, 289; and evolutionary origins of human reproduction, 385–386; hominid shift to, 287, 288–289; and parental collaboration hypothesis, 407; and selection pressures on apes, 551
Bird, R. B., 129
Birkhead, T. R., 415
Bischof, Norbert, 360
Bittles, Alan, 375
Blau, Peter, 339
Blau-space, 339–342
Bleak House (Dickens), 594
Blindsight (Watt), 588
Bloom, Howard, 359
Blute, M., 63, 80
Body language, 557, 564, 565
Boehm, C., 574, 576
Bonobos: birth, 385; comprehension of human speech, 529–530; dimorphism in, 413; group sanctioning among, 425; mating behavior, 404, 413; novel behavior, 515; social control among, 425; status competition among, 481
Bookstein, F. L., 129
Booth, Alan, 487
Boserup, Ester, 389

INDEX 631

Bottle-feeding, 15, 384, 396
Bouba-kiki test, 292
Bouchard, F., 61
Bourke, A.F.G., 61, 64, 83, 84, 88
Bourne, Geoffrey H., 533
Bowles, S., 590
Boyd, R., 198, 450
Brain: and behavioral propensities in early hominins, 552; and composition of human milk, 388; Darwinian conflict theory and evolution of, 236–237; distinctive aspects of *Homo sapiens*, 286–287; energy use, 293; evolution of, as domain-general organ, 261n2; evolution of, in response to outgroup threats, 496–502; evolution of human, 179, 185–188, 285–286; and evolutionary origins of human reproduction, 385–386; exempt from evolution under SSSM, 137; of human ancestors, 287–293; hypotheses on evolution of, 161–162; implications of cladistic analysis for evolution of, 184–188; and learning from experience, 516–517; and limitations to evolutionary psychology, 177–178; mutations in, 178–179; perception of, in evolutionary psychology, 142; relative size of components in apes and humans, compared to *Tenrecinae*, 560(table); and Savanna Principle, 143–144; selection pressures on apes and evolution of, 550; social bonding and size of, 555–556. *See also* Neuroanatomy
Bridewealth and brideservice, in marital choice theory, 248
Bridger, J. C., 322, 327
Brinkerhoff, David, 487
Broca's area, 179, 187, 286, 292
Brooks, David, 164
Brown, Jerram, 159
Buckholtz, J. W., 574, 578
Bundy, R. P., 453
Burgess, E. W., 317
Burt, A., 353
Buss, David M., 139

C. elegans, hierarchical "fate map" of, 61–62
Caldwell, John, 125
Cameron, E. Z., 130
Cancer, 48, 62, 389
Candide (Voltaire), 591
Candomblé, 446–447
Capital punishment, among hunter-gatherers, 427, 430–431
Capitalism: crises in contemporary world-system, 278–282; and economic exchange theory, 242; in Europe-centered world-system, 273; evolution of, 275, 276–278; in human aggression theory, 257; Schumpeter's views on, 610, 612–613. *See also* Creative destruction
Caregiving, and serial reciprocity in early Christianity, 20–23
Carnivory, cooperative, 304–305, 436, 444, 448
Carr-Saunders, Alexander, 360–361
Cashdan, E., 306
Catch-22 (Heller), 593–594
Categoric units: in Blau-space, 342; change in, due to selection pressures, 77; creation of social-class, 102; as meso-level social unit, 84, 101
Catholic Church, 394
Catton, W. R., Jr., 322
Caudate nucleus, 417–418
Cell-cell specificity, 373
Certification legitimacy, 338
Chagnon, Napoleon, 362, 363
Champness, B., 480
Chapais, B., 408–409, 410–411, 412
Charities, 341
Charnov, Eric, 300–301
Chase-Dunn, C., 271–272, 283n5
Chastity belt, 394
Cheating, in cooperation, 445
Cheating detection mechanism, 8, 9, 11, 26

Chicago School, 318, 319, 320
Chiefdoms: in human aggression theory, 257; in Spencer's political evolution, 221
Child care: in foraging societies, 250; human investment in, 386; in modern societies, 251; and reproductive ecology, 309
Child foraging, 309
Childbirth, 57n12, 293, 385–386. *See also* Fertility; Mortality
Children: abandonment of infants, 395–396; acquisition of language, 538; among foragers, 390, 391; bipedalism and care of, 526; diet of plow-society, 392–393; division of labor in foraging societies, 310; evolution of ape and hominin, 554–555; and female choice theory of marriage institution, 153; gender inequality and feeding of, 384; incest avoidance among siblings, 354–355; in industrialized societies, 125, 298; infant feeding before modern medicine, 394–396; infant feeding in herding societies, 392; Trivers-Willard effect, 130–131
Chimpanzees: birth, 385; brain size at birth, 386; common ancestry with, 10, 180, 196; comprehension of human speech, 529–530; dominance among, 576; dominance in humans versus, 590; fear over status-loss among, 463–464; group sanctioning among, 425; hierarchies among, 182, 558–559; importance of first years of, 529–530, 533; LANA Project, 527–530; mating behavior, 404, 405(table), 406, 413, 554; network ties in, 547, 548(table); organization among, 566; and organization of amalgams into templates, 517–518; power-maintenance tactics among, 464–465, 466, 467; social control among, 425; sociality of, 182–183; status competition among, 481; status and reproductive success among, 461–462; symbol use in, 553; testis size and sperm competition among, 416
China: Arrighi on rise of, 281; correlation between male status and offspring in, 124(table); foot-binding in, 34–35, 394; global warming and, 280; market practices in, 208; reproductive success of elite women in, 123; revolutions in, 275
Chomsky, Noam, 538 539, 541
Christianity: eschatology as form of poetic justice, 591; reverse dominance exemplified by, 583; serial reciprocity in early, 22–23. *See also* Catholic Church
Chudek, M., 574, 578–579
Cladistic analysis, 180, 183, 184–188, 549–550
Clarke, E., 61
Class. *See* Socioeconomic status
Classification, of literary works, 599–600. *See also* Taxonomies of social sciences
Clements, Frederic E., 319
Clitoridectomy, 394
Cloning, 353, 360, 373
Coalitional psychology, 452–453
Coalition suppression, as power-maintenance tactic, 467–468
Coase, Ronald, 36
Coevolution. *See* Dual inheritance
Cognitive mapping, 555–556
Cognitive organization, affected by literature and arts, 579–580
Cognitive response mechanisms, evolution of, to outgroup threats, 499–502, 507
Cohen, B., 475
Cohen, L. E., 25
Collective action, 317
Collective action dilemmas, 441–442, 444, 448–449
Collective emotional effervescence, 557–558
Collins, Francis, 172
Collins, Randall, 233–234, 398, 557
Colonization, 273, 274(fig.), 597–599
Color: vision in chimpanzees, 528; vision and fruit, 390
Commitment, in cooperation, 446–447

Common descent, theory of, 60, 66, 69
Common knowledge, lack of, as obstacle to cooperation, 441, 442
Common pool resources, excludability from, 441–442
Communes, signs of commitment in, 446, 452
Community ecology: and classic human ecology's application of bioecology, 320; in early twentieth century, 317–318
Community-service organizations, competition among, 97
Comparative evolutionary world-systems perspective, 270–272, 275–282
Competing adaptations, 55–56n4
Competition: and altruistic tendencies, 78; and classic human ecology's application of bioecology, 323–324; in comparative evolutionary world-systems perspective, 272; conflict theory and, 232–234; and corporate unit death, 97; between corporate units, 87; as criterion for Darwinian selection, 86; cultural group selection and, among companies in market economy, 450–451; and defining evolution in sociocultural systems, 96–97; and differentiation in Blau-space, 341; and dispersion, 361; dominance contests, 481–483; of embedded corporate units, 345; emergence of, 39, 76; and ethnic attachment theory, 258; evolution of societies through market, 93; in geopolitical theory, 253–254; in human aggression theory, 257; intergroup, and emergence of leadership, 469; and language of *Homo erectus*, 290; and midcentury reformulation of human ecology, 325, 326; moderating effects of culture on, 328; and multiharem groups, 411; and natural selection in bioecology, 317, 318; in neoclassical human ecology, 327; in organizational ecology, 334, 335–336, 346; polygyny and, 148; sperm, 372–374, 414–417; for status rank, 251–252, 476, 480; and suppression of subordinates, 464–469; and technology accumulation, 619; testosterone and, 484; in urban ecology, 93; wealth accumulation theory, 253
Competitive altruism, 199
Compound societies, 220, 221
Computerized Test System of LRC, 529
Concert of Europe, 274
Conflict theory, principal elements of, 232–234. *See also* Darwinian conflict theory
Conflicts of interest: and extralegal police aggression, 503, 507; as obstacle to cooperation, 441
Conformity bias, and internalization of norms, 577–578, 589
Conrad, Joseph: *Heart of Darkness*, 597–599; *The Secret Agent*, 593
Consanguinity, correlation between fertility and, 366–367, 375, 376, 378
Conscience, as agency for self-control, 427, 431, 435
Constant status signals, 477
Constructive-type pathway of evolutionary innovation, 64–65
Consumerism, 277
Consumption: mass, 611, 622, 623, 625, 626; and Schumpeter's creative destruction, 610
Continuity: between corporate units, 87–88; as criterion for Darwinian selection, 86–87; as guiding principle for psychology and behavior, 525
Contrast sensitivity: evolutionary background, 613–615; high-contrast familiarity and religion, 615–616; and new deal, 622–627; overview, 609–613; status and, 616–619; and technology accumulation, 619–620
Control, as power-maintenance tactic, 466–467
Controllability, female, 13–14
Controllable status signals, 477
Convergent evolution, 70, 195, 203, 205
Conversation: as mode of communicating dominance and deference, 483–484; preliminary results on research regarding stress in, 487–490

Cooked foods, 290
Cooley, C. H., 558
Cooperation: as axiom of Darwinian conflict theory, 238; and classic human ecology's application of bioecology, 324; and coalitional psychology, 452–453; coalition suppression and power maintenance, 467–468; commitment in, 446–447; coordination problems, 448–449; defining, 442–443; and dual inheritance theory, 198–199; evolutionary scientists' knowledge regarding, 443–448, 575; evolutionary study of, 448–454, 455; group sanctioning and, 436–438; group selection and, 78, 79, 449–452; in hunter-gatherer societies, 83; impact of audiences and reputations on, 445–446; in institutional contexts, 453–454; and intergroup contact, 493; kinship and, 443; and limits of biological theory in social sciences, 98–99; obstacles to, 441–442; positive assortment in, 444–445; in rank allocation, 480; and recent developments in theoretical biology, 572–577; and repeated interactions, 444; reputational selection theory and, 428; among subordinates, 471; and suppression of dominance, 583; and survival of human ancestors, 286; uncertainty, risk, and need in, 447–448
Cooperative carnivory, 304–305, 436, 444, 448
Coordination games, 442, 450
Coordination norms, 449, 450
Coordination problems, 442, 444, 448–449, 450
Coriolanus (Shakespeare), 584
Corporate groups: and categories, 452; development of large, in foraging societies, 310; selection among, 451, 452
Corporate units: and biological theory in social sciences, 102; as building blocks of institutional domains at macro level of social organization, 101, 344; Darwinian selection of, 85–88; death of, 97; defined, 89n1; differentiation of, 342; embedded, 344–345; as evolutionary individuals, 88–89; evolution of, 94–95; fitness of, 85; formation of, 77–78, 84, 88; "generations" for, 104; innovation and, 97; institutions built from, 342; integrative mechanisms for differentiated, 346; logic of evolutionary transitions applied to, 84; as meso-level social unit, 101; reproduction of, 84–85
Corpus callosum, 287
The Corrections (Franzen), 597
Cortisol, 482, 485
Cosmides, Leda: coalition psychological study of, 453; concept of adapted mind, 8–9, 25–26; and criticism of evolutionary studies of human behavior, 161, 162; on evolution of brain as domain-general organ, 261n2; and Standard Social Science Model, 5; and Wason Selection Task, 445
Costly signaling, 305, 311–312, 445
Cousin-marriage exchange: in Arabic and Muslim societies, 357–359; and atom of kinship, 356; conclusions, 376–379; as historical norm, 364–366; and optimal outbreeding, 364; preferred for dispersion, 354; results of, 351; as solution to optimal inbreeding, 356–357. *See also* Cross-cousin marriage; Double cross-cousin marriage; Mediogamy
Creative destruction: and contrast sensitivity, 613–615; elevation of inequality, 616–619; high-contrast familiarity and religion, 615–616; and New Deal, 622–627; overview, 609–613; and second exodus, 619–622
Crime: property, 25; sexual selection theory and, 17–18; violent, 148
Crippen, T., 79–80
Crises, in contemporary world-system, 278–282
Criticism, as verbal sanction, 431
Cro-Magnons, 292–293
Cross-cousin marriage: patrilineal and matrilineal moieties, 379n1; as social glue of Yanomamö, 117–118. *See also* Cousin-marriage exchange; Double cross-cousin marriage

Cross-modal perception, 529, 532
Cuckoldry, 139, 140, 144–145, 245
Cultural anthropology: biological views of social behavior in, 114–118; evolutionary stages in, 221; paradigm shift in social sciences and growth of Darwinian social science, 118–120
Cultural capital, 252
Cultural dominance, law of, 269
Cultural evolution: approach to Darwinian, as carried by strategies, 44–49; Darwinian, not confined to humans, 50; problems facing Darwinian, 53–54; strengths of Darwinian, 54–55; as subcategory of Darwinian evolution, 49; variation, 67–68
Cultural group selection, 450–452, 455
Cultural materialism, principal elements of, 234–236
Cultural replicators, 42–43
Cultural selection: in biological domain, 50; and dual inheritance, 197–200; memes as smallest units of Darwinian, 44–49; operation of Darwinian processes in, 51, 80; Runciman on, 51–52, 80; transition to social selection, 201–205
"Cultural variant," 198
Culture: acquisition as axiom of Darwinian conflict theory, 238–239; building blocks of, 342–343; dispersion and, 363–364; effects of, on human behavior, 397–398; emotion and language and, 565, 566; evoked, 239; in evolutionary literary theory, 600; and human behavioral ecology, 297–298; incest taboo as result of, 351–352; learning by, 68; moderating effects on competition, 328; of new organizations in existing niche, 335–336; and organization failure, 338; social behavior attributed to, 4–5, 167, 170–171, 385; sociocultural evolution without, 268–269; as system, 95–96; transmitted, 239
Culturgen, 57n13
Culturology, 116–117
Cybernetics, 295
Cycles, economic, 612

Dalerum, F., 130
Damasio, A., 178
Danchin, É., 67
Darkness at Noon (Koestler), 597
Darwin, Charles: on evolution of emotions, 11, 12; and group selection debate, 78; on language, 537; limitations of theory of evolution, 215; marriage of, 364; on origin of man, 2; on "Principle of Divergence," 69–70; Spencer and, 216, 217–218; theory of common descent, 66
Darwin, George, 364, 366
Darwinian conflict theory: axioms of, 236–239; conclusions, 261; and conflict theory, 232–234; and cultural materialism, 234–236; dietary choice theory, 243–244; economic exchange theory, 242–243; economic subsistence theory, 241–242; ethnic attachment theory, 257–258; falsifying, 259–261; gender differentiation theory, 250–251; gender inequality theory, 251; geopolitical theory, 253–255; human aggression theory, 256–257; incest avoidance theory, 244; kin selection theory, 249; marital choice theory, 247–248; mate choice theory, 244–245; overview, 228–230; parental investment theory, 240–241; postulates, theories, and propositions of, 239–259; and rational choice theory, 231–232; religious choice theory, 258–259; reproductive strategies theory, 239–240; sexual choice theory, 245–247; and social evolutionism, 236; and sociobiology, 230–231; status competition theory, 251–252; wealth accumulation theory, 253
Darwinian selection: criteria for, 85, 86–87; death of corporate units in, 107; and evolution in sociocultural systems, 96; levels of, operating in human affairs, 51–52
Dawkins, Richard, 79, 95, 165, 172, 572

De Queiroz, A., 368
Debt: reciprocity and, 21, 23, 447, 448; as tool to meet substitution demands, 623
Decision theory, Kanazawa on failed predictions of, 16–17
Decolonization, 274
De-Darwinization, 48–49, 57n14, 61, 72n1
Defection, 8, 11, 26, 201, 573–574
Defensive aggression, 502, 504
Deference: conversation as mode of communicating, 483–484; eye glance and, 481–482; female, toward males, 14; testosterone and, 484–485
Deglobalization, 275–282
Demand sharing, 304–305, 448
Democracies: in geopolitical theory, 255; war between, 39–40, 56n9, 257
Democracy, crisis of inequality and, 279–280
Demotion, as power-maintenance tactic, 465–466
Denigration of out-groups, and ethnic attachment theory, 257
Department stores, death of, 335–336
Depressions, economic, 612
Descriptive Sociology (Spencer), 219
"The Development Hypothesis" (Spencer), 216
Deviants: cooperative carnivory and, 436; sanctions for, 431, 435; and social control as social selection, 426–427; social predators, 434(table)
Diamond, Jared, 371–372
Dickens, Charles, 594, 597
Dickins, T. E., 67
Diencephalon, 560
Dietary choice theory, 243–244
Diet-Breadth Model (DBM), 298–301
Diffuse anger, 562
Diffuse anxiety, 562
Diffuse status characteristics, 475
Dimorphism, sexual, in humans, 413–414
Directed learning, 5–6
Disadvantaged neighborhoods. *See* Extralegal police aggression
Disappointment-sadness: combination of primary emotions, 563(table); as primary emotion possessed by mammals, 553; and variants of primary emotions, 562(table)
Discriminative stimuli, 514
Dispersion: in animals, 359–362; of great apes, 547; human, 362–364; incest avoidance and, 353–355; and mediogamy and fertility, 366
Displaced reference, 449
Divergence, Darwin on, 69–70
Division of labor: and evolutionary transitions in individuality, 83; in hoe societies, 391; human behavioral ecology applied to, 310; in hunter-gatherer societies, 46; and parental collaboration hypothesis, 408–409; and reproduction of corporate unit, 84–85; reproductive, and emergence and pervasiveness of patriarchy, 14–15; specialization in, 76, 93
The Division of Labor in Society (Durkheim), 93
Divorce, in marital choice theory, 248
Dobzhansky, T., 64
Domain-specific adaptive mechanisms, 237
Domazet-Lošo, T., 66, 67
Domestication, piebald trait and, 56–57n11
Dominance: behavioral signs of, 471; conversation as mode of communicating, 483–484; in facial expression, 477–479; future research on prestige and, 470; and harem mating patterns among monkeys and apes, 554; law of cultural, 269; in literature, 582–585, 590; and network tie strength in monkeys, 549; power and, 462; power maintenance and, 466, 467; reverse, 575–577, 582–585; status-seeking and, 462–463; suppression of, 583–584; testosterone and, 19–20, 484–485; as tool for social

analysis, 575–577; and turn-taking in conversation, 489–490. *See also* Hierarchy; Leaders; Leadership; Rank and ranking; Status
Dominance contests, 19–20, 481–482, 484–485
Dominance hierarchies: defined, 462; in face-to-face groups, 475–485; in monkeys, 549, 554, 566
Dominance motivation, 462–463, 466, 468
Double cross-cousin marriage, 356, 357(fig.), 359, 361, 376
Doubly compound societies, 221
Dowry, in marital choice theory, 248
Dramaturgical school of sociological theory, 4
Drift, in human affairs, 32–33
"Dual hormone" hypothesis, 485
Dual inheritance: and cultural selection, 197–200; and evolutionary sociology and evolution of agriculture, 204
Dunbar, Robert, 555–556
Dunbar, Robin, 363
Duplication, evolution by, 60
Durkheim, Émile: applies natural selection to human societies, 76, 93; on collective emotional effervescence, 557; and emergence of sociology, 116–117; and interaction ritual theory, 233
Durkheimian selection, 87, 88, 107, 108
Durkheim's dictum, 116, 117

Eastern societies, macrosociological agenda and institutions of, 208
Ecclesiastical religions, 259, 261
Ecological degradation, 276–277
Ecology, 295. *See also* Community ecology; Human ecology
Economic cycles, 612
Economic-defensibility model, 305
Economic exchange theory, 242–243
Economic growth, 623, 625, 626
Economic redistribution, 623, 624
Economic subsistence theory, 241–242
Economics: evolutionary theory of economic change, 31–33; and limits on intentional design and rational choice, 36–38. *See also* Creative destruction; Markets
Ecostructure, 238
Edelman, Gerald, 285
Edlund, L., 130
Educational attainment: link between reproductive success and, 126, 127, 129; Trivers-Willard effect, 130–131
EEA (environment of evolutionary adaptedness). *See* Environment of evolutionary adaptedness (EEA)
Egalitarianism: in liberal democracies, 576, 577; in political organization of foraging societies, 311. *See also* Reverse dominance
Eisenstadt, S. N., 208
Eliot, George: *Felix Holt, the Radical*, 597; *Middlemarch*, 589, 590
Embryological development: induction in, 72n3; mosaic development, 62; regulative development, 62; von Baer's laws, 66–67
Emergents: defined, 515; in Gabby the gibbon, 521–524; origin of, 519; pattern detection and, 516–517. *See also* Innovation; Salience theory
Emigration: as dispersal method, 361–362; population pressure leading to, 272
Emotional effervescence, 557–558, 564
Emotional energy, 233–234, 252, 260
Emotional organization, affected by literature and arts, 579–580
Emotional response mechanisms, evolution of, to outgroup threats, 496–498, 507
Emotion(s): and behavioral propensities in early hominins, 552; collective emotional effervescence, 557–558; and comparative neuroanatomy between apes and humans, 559–566; and defensive aggression, 502; emergence of,

83; and evolution of human brain, 186, 187; expansion of, 559–564; and extralegal police aggression, 504–505; and formation of social ties, 26; in great apes, 185; and imitation of facial gestures, 556–557; language and, 564–566; moral, 12, 561; moralistic aggression and, 11–12; as preadaptation in early hominins, 553; and reading of face and eyes, 556; repressed, 561–564; scholarly attention focused on, 497; and seeing self as object, 558; serial reciprocity in early Christianity and evolved social, 21, 22, 23; social bonding and language of, 556; social solidarity and, 564; study of sociology of, 12; and Turner's conception of adapted social mind, 10, 11
Empathy: capacity for, as preadaptation in early hominins, 557; and evolution of human brain, 186; in great apes, 185; serial reciprocity in early Christianity and, 22
Empires: and evolution of statehood, 206; and hypothesis of semiperipheral development, 273; in sociocultural evolution, 269; in Spencer's political evolution, 221
Endoduplication, 60
Endogamy: and animal dispersion, 359–362; conclusions, 376–379; cousin-marriage exchange, 357–359, 364–366; and human dispersion, 362–364; kindred and affinity, 355–357; mediogamy and fertility, 366–372; relativity problems of, 350–351
Energy balance, 309
Energy flux, 309
Energy storage, 309
Ensminger, J., 452
Environment, exploitation of, 276–277, 280, 533–534
Environment of evolutionary adaptedness (EEA): in adapted mind notion, 5; and criticism of evolutionary studies of human behavior, 161–163; defined, 143; evolved psychological mechanisms and, 140–142; and prepared learning, 6; and public choice theory, 17
Environmental circumscription, 254
Environmentalism. *See* Standard Social Science Model (SSSM)
Environments: adaptations and, 40–41; dangers of human ancestors', 286; human behavior as product of, 137, 163–164, 196, 237; inheritance of environmentally induced phenotypic changes, 67; interaction between phenotypes and, 65, 68; reconceptualization of organizations', 345; speed of evolution and, 146
Epidemics, and serial reciprocity in early Christianity, 20–23
Epigenetics, 18, 229
Episodic memories, 287, 499
Ethnic attachment theory, 257–258
Ethnocentrism, 398
Ethology, 233; influence of, on Goffman, 261n1
Europe: Concert of Europe, 274; early-medieval and early-modern and evolution of statehood, 206; and evolution of modern world-system, 273
Evo-devo, 51, 63, 64–65, 68–69, 72
Evoked behavior, 51
Evoked culture, 239
Evolution: defined by Spencer and Darwin, 217–218; history of idea, 215–216; reticulate, 69–71. *See also* Biological evolution; Convergent evolution; Cultural evolution
Evolution and Human Behavior (academic journal), 119
Evolutionary anthropology, 119, 158
Evolutionary contingency thesis, 40–41
Evolutionary ecology, 295–296
Evolutionary growth, in neoclassical human ecology, 327–330
Evolutionary macrosociology, 207–209
Evolutionary nets, 69–71
Evolutionary psychology: alternative view on, 98; basic theoretical structure of, 139–142; cooperative behaviors explained by, 99; criticism of, 157–159, 170; as danger to integrity of social sciences, 94; emergence of, 136; and evolutionary sociology, 196–197, 547; and limits

INDEX 635

of biological theory in social sciences, 109; and neo-Darwinian evolutionary theory, 4; overview, 137–139; principles of, 142–143; relevance in modern populations, 122, 130; relevance to social sciences, 146–153; Savanna Principle, 143–146. *See also* Evolutionary psychology, limitations to

Evolutionary psychology, limitations to: changes in neuroanatomy, 179–180; conclusions, 188; elementary considerations, 178–179; history of primate evolution, 181–184; implications of cladistic analysis for evolution of human brain, 184–188; overview, 177–178

Evolutionary sociology: basic elements, 547; behavioral and organizational propensities among extant primates, 547–549; cladistic analysis, 549–550; and comparative neuroanatomy between apes and humans, 559–566; conclusions, 567–568; cultural selection and dual inheritance, 197–200; emergence of, 2; evolution of statehood, 205–206; and evolutionary game theory, 200–201; evolutionary macrosociology, 207–209; in evolutionary study of human behavior, 158; and existing behavioral propensities and preadaptations in hominins, 552–559; further implications of, 566–567; and limits of evolutionary psychology, 188; overview, 194–195, 546–547; and selection pressures on apes, 550–552; and sociobiology, 195–197; transition from cultural to social selection, 201–205

Evolutionary structural-functionalism, 267

Evolutionary studies of human behavior (EHB), criticism of: course of action regarding, 172–173; genetic determinism charge, 163–165; inferiority of evolutionary hypotheses compared with proximate ones, 166–167; justification of immoral behavior and unjust political systems, 168; "no time machine" argument, 161–163; overview, 157–158; panadaptationist charge, 160–161; persistence of, 168–172; rebuttals to, 169(table); reductionism charge, 165–166; researchers as unscientific, 158–160

Evolutionary transitions in individuality, 77, 81–85, 88

"Evolved actors," 13

Evolved mental adaptations, 16–18, 25–26. *See also* Adapted mind; Adapted social mind; Mental adaptations; Psychological adaptations

Evolved psychological mechanism(s): conscience as, 427; and maladaptive behavior, 144–145; producing desire to maximize welfare of children, 151–153; and Savanna Principle, 143; suicide bombing and, 150; in theoretical structure of evolutionary psychology, 138–140, 141(fig.)

Exaptations, 50, 64–65, 291

Exchange reciprocity, 558

Excludability, from public goods and pool resources, 441–442

Exogamy: and animal dispersion, 359–362; conclusions, 376–379; and cousin-marriage exchange, 364–366; dispersion and incest avoidance, 353–355; and human dispersion, 362–364; and incest avoidance theory, 244; incest taboo and, 351–353; kindred and affinity, 355–357; mediogamy and fertility, 366–372; relativity problems of, 350–351

Experience, learning from, 516–518

Exploitation: economic, in economic exchange theory, 242; emergence of, in human affairs, 39; of environment, 276–277, 280, 533–534; social, 25

Expulsion, permanent, as ultimate sanction, 431

External validity, 53

Extralegal police aggression: conclusions, 506–508; overview, 493–494; perceived threat and, 505–506; social and psychological preconditions to, 503–505; theories regarding, 494–495

Eye glance, 480–482. *See also* Gaze

Eye(s): gaze and morphological features of, 449; reading, 556. *See also* Eye glance; Gaze; Vision; Visual dominance

Face monitoring, 184, 556

Face-to-face groups: biosocial model of status in, 471–472; improvements in research methods on status among, 485–490; status hierarchies in, 475–485

Facial appearance and gestures: imitation of, 556–557; as status signs, 477–481

Facroel, A., 362

"Failed" states, 206

Fairness: calculation of, as preadaptation in early hominins, 558; language and, 564–565

Familiarity: in creative destruction, 620; reward release rule for, 614

Family connections, as attribute determining status rank, 475

Father's brother's daughter (FBD) marriage, 358–359

Fats, preference for, as evolved psychological mechanism, 138, 140, 144

Fear: and combination of primary emotions, 563(table); conditioning, 497–498, 499, 502–503; and extralegal police aggression, 504; as primary emotion possessed by mammals, 553; of racial outgroups, 498; repressed guilt turns to, 562; and social bonding, 561; as survival mechanism, 497; and variants of primary emotions, 562(table)

Felix Holt, the Radical (Eliot), 597

Female choice theory of marriage institution, 151–153

Female controllability, 13–14

Female infanticide, 123

Feminism, Schumpeter on, 611

Fertility: of close-cousin marriages, 364; decline in world, 378; income and, 124; lactation and, 384, 388; male versus female, 125–126; mediogamy and, 366–372, 375; in modern societies, 125–129; and molecular recognition, 372–374; mortality and, 123; and population growth, 376, 378; and reproductive ecology, 309; in reproductive strategies theory, 240. *See also* Reproduction

Feudal states, in geopolitical theory, 255

Feudalism, 393, 397, 611

Fiction, meaning in, 581–582

Fidelity: and female controllability, 13–14; in mate choice theory, 245. *See also* Infidelity

Fidelity of heredity, as criterion for Darwinian selection, 86

Fieder, M., 126, 129

Fight-or-flight response, 481–482

Fildes, V., 395

Fire, *Homo erectus*'s use of, 290

Firm cultural group selection, 451–452

First-cousin marriage pattern, 356

First-order logistical loads, 76–77, 84

First Principles (Spencer), 217

Fisher, Helen, 407, 417–418

Fisher, R. A.: and emergence of sociobiology, 3; on group selection, 78; model of sex ratio, 53, 55, 57n12

Fitness: assessing, in sociocultural systems, 95, 106; as axiom of Darwinian conflict theory, 237; capital punishment and, 430; of corporate units, 85, 87; as criterion for Darwinian selection, 85–86; differences in, due to intrinsic characters of individuals, 86; in Durkheimian selection, 107; and evolutionary transitions in individuality, 82–83; in human behavioral ecology, 296, 297; increased emotionality promoted by, 560–561; of individuals of elevated social rank, 462; mutation and, 178–179; and social reputation, 424; and socioeconomic status in preindustrial societies, 123; in Spencerian selection, 107–108, 346. *See also* Inclusive fitness; Reproductive fitness

FMRI (functional magnetic resonance imaging), 486

Foley, R., 578–579

Followers: future research, 470–471; tension between leaders and, 463–464. *See also* Subordinates

Food: dietary choice theory, 243–244; in foraging societies as regards parental collaboration hypothesis, 408–409; gender inequality and, 383–384; of *Homo habilis* and *Homo erectus*, 290; of infants before modern medicine, 394–396; origins of human food preferences, 389–390; production and gender inequality in herding societies, 393; war and supply of, 392. *See also* Food sharing
Food sharing: cooperation and, 444; human behavioral ecology applied to, 303–305; risk-pooling and, 448; social control and, 436; turtle meat on island of Mer, 446
Foot binding, 33, 34–35, 394
Foraging behavior, human behavioral ecology applied to, 298–301
Foraging societies: in economic subsistence theory, 241–242; and evolution of responses to outgroup threats, 495–496; and gender differentiation theory, 250; gender equality and transition to herding societies, 390–392; gender inequality in, 383–384; human behavioral ecology applied to social organization of, 310–311; infant care in, 386–387; intergroup relations among, 496; living, 313; and parental collaboration hypothesis, 408–409; polygyny in, 413–414; systems of reciprocity and exchange in, 8. *See also* Human behavioral ecology (HBE); Hunting-gathering societies
Formal sociology, 24, 25
Formula, infant, 15, 384, 396
Fortes, Meyer, 117
Fossil fuels, 276
Fossils: conclusions regarding brain evolution, 287–288; dating, 286
Foucault, Michel, 600–601
Fox, Kate, 365, 366
Fox News, 173
Frank, R. H., 11–12
Franzen, Jonathan, *The Corrections*, 597
Free rider problem, 441
Free riding: and network reciprocity, 573; and public choice theory, 17; and public goods game, 454; reputational selection theory and, 426. *See also* Parasitism
Freeman, Derek, 171
Freeman, John, 333, 336
Frequency-dependent imitation, 200, 239
"Freud effect," 354–355
Friedl, E., 391
Fruits, 389–390
Frye, Northrup, 600, 601
Fukuyama, F., 578
Functional magnetic resonance imaging (fMRI), 486
Functionalism, 25, 33–34, 267
Functions: as adaptations, 32–35; as Darwinian adaptations, 35–36; defined, 55n2; in human ecology, 328–329; identifying, 49–50; of redundant copies of genes, 60; sequence of events resulting in emergence of, 50

Gabby (gibbon), 521–524
Galvanic skin response (GSR), 486
Gambetta, Diego, 148
Gamble, C., 578–579
Game theory: as alternative to inclusive fitness theory and group selection, 573; and evolutionary sociology, 200–201; and human behavioral ecology, 297; Kanazawa on failed predictions of, 16–17; notion of strategy, 33–34
Gametes, 82
Gaze, 449, 486–487. *See also* Eye glance
Gaziano, E., 322
Gender, in literary criticism, 600–601
Gender differentiation theory, 250–251
Gender inequality: evolutionary origins of human reproduction, 384–387; evolutionary perspectives on, 13–16; and infant feeding before modern medicine, 394–396; and origins of human food preferences, 389–390; and physiology of lactation, 387–389; in plow societies, 392–394; and social consequences of prolonged lactation, 396–398; tools, food, and social power and, 383–384; and transition from foraging to herding societies, 390–392
Gender inequality theory, 251
Gene-culture coevolution, 198
Gene duplication, 60
General intelligence (IQ), and evolved mental adaptation, 16, 17
General Motors, 104
Generativity, 538
Generosity, and political organization of foraging societies, 311–312
Genes: as biological replicators, 42–43; in constructive-type pathway of evolutionary innovation, 64–65; and cultural transmission, 68; in inductive-type pathway of evolutionary innovation, 64–65; link between behavior and, 296; memes and, 198; regularity of composition of, 56n10
Genetic determinism, as criticism of evolutionary studies of human behavior, 163–165
Genetic drift, 360
Genetic inbreeding, 365
Genetic strangers, 363, 375
Genre, in literary taxonomy, 600
Geopolitical theory, 253–255
Gerkey, Drew, 454
Geschwind, N., 178
Gestalt switch, 33–34, 45
Gibbons: emergents in Gabby, 521–524; hierarchies among, 558; mating behavior of, 404, 405(table), 406, 413; social bonding in, 182
Gibbs, J. P., 327
Gigantapathecus, 552
Gintis, H., 574, 576, 590
Giosa, R., 388
Global capitalist system, crisis in, 280–282
Global governance: crisis of, 279; evolution of, 274–275, 278
"Global Impasse," 280
Global Innovation Index, 69
Globalization, 274, 275–282, 378
Godfrey-Smith, P., 48, 61, 72n1, 85–87
Gods, high, 258
Goetz, S., 486
Goffman, Erving, 233, 261n1
Golding, William, *Lord of the Flies*, 581–582, 590, 591, 595, 599
Goodman, A., 128, 129
Gorillas: Albert, 534; emergent gait in, 520(fig.); hierarchies among, 182, 558; mating behavior of, 183, 404, 405(table), 406, 413, 554; network ties in, 547–548; status competition among, 481; status signs in, 476; symbol use in, 553; testis size and sperm competition among, 415–416
Gossip: as indirect form of social control, 431; prehistoric, 425
Gottlieb, Anthony, 159, 166
Gould, Stephen Jay, 50, 158–161, 166, 167, 170, 171
Grafting synthesis, 229–230
Grains, domestication of, 392–393
Gratitude, 12, 21, 22, 23
Great Chain of Being, 64, 68, 215
Great Depression, 612, 623
Great leap forward, 292, 293
Great Recession, 623, 624, 626
Greenbeard gene, 373
Greenspan, S., 292
Grooming, 555–556
Gross, M., 319, 324
Group-conflict theory, 504

Group identity, 452–453, 573, 578
Group-internal social distancing, 431, 433(table)
Group phase in transition, 575
Group sanctioning: aggression leading to, 435; among Late-Pleistocene appropriate hunter-gatherers, 431; band as unit of, 436; cooperation and, 436–437; methods of, 432–433(table); as social selection, 424–425, 437–438; statistics on, 424–425
Group selection: as alternative to inclusive fitness theory, 573; cooperation and, 449–452, 455, 573; cultural selection and, 197–198; and limits of biological theory in social sciences, 106; and network reciprocity, 574; Wynne-Edwards's notion of, 380n3
Group selection debate, 77, 78–81
Group size: human behavioral ecology applied to, 307–309; and political organization of foraging societies, 311; relationship between evolution of neocortex and, 363; size-complexity hypothesis, 83; and social organization of foraging societies, 310. *See also* Population growth; Population size
Group solidarity. *See* Social bonding
GSR (galvanic skin response), 486
Guilt, 23, 187, 561–562, 563(table), 589

Hadza, 448
Hagen, E. H., 162
Haidt, J., 578
Haldane, J.B.S., 78
Hall, Brian K., 65
Hall, T. D., 271–272, 283n5
Hamilton, M., 307–308, 309
Hamilton, W. D., 3, 142, 304, 380n3, 443
Hamilton's Rule, 443
Handicap principle, 305
Handling costs, in Diet-Breadth Model, 298–299
Hangingfly, 164–165
Hannan, Michael T., 333, 336
Happiness: and combination of primary emotions, 563(table); as primary emotion possessed by mammals, 553; and variants of primary emotions, 562(table)
Hard cultural group selection, 451, 452
Hard-to-fake signals. *See* Costly signaling
Harem mating patterns, 182–183, 405(table), 410–411, 415–416, 554
Harris, Marvin, 114, 234–236
"Harrison Bergeron" (Vonnegut), 584
Hawkes, K., 406–407, 408
Hawley, Amos, 323, 325–330, 333
Hayek, Friedrich, 36
Health systems, as unit of selection, 103–104
Heart of Darkness (Conrad), 597–599
Hegemony/hegemonies: crisis of global governance and, 279; decline of US, 281, 282; periods of, 273–275; sequence of, in evolution of globalization, 278–279
Helgason, A., 366
Hellberg, J., 17
Heller, Joseph, *Catch-22*, 593–594
Hemophilia, 364
Henrich, J., 574, 578–579
Henry, Louis, 388
Henry V (Shakespeare), 586
Herbert, M. L., 371, 375
Herding societies, transition from foraging to, 390–392
Heredity: of corporate units, 87; fidelity of, as criterion for Darwinian selection, 86. *See also* Inheritance
Heritability: of fitness, 85–86; sociobiological study of, 195–196
Heterosexuality, in sexual choice theory, 245
Hierarchy: biological, 81; communication of rank in, 471; corollary features of status, 482–483; in face-to-face groups, 475–485; and fear over status loss, 463–464;

future research on followers in, 470–471; and harem mating patterns among monkeys, 554; among humans and primates, 461–463; in hunter-gatherer versus post-agricultural societies, 577; in major transitions theory, 574; and power-maintenance, 464–469; as preadaptation in early hominins, 558–559; and selection pressures on apes, 552. *See also* Leaders; Leadership; Power; Rank and ranking; Status
High-contrast familiarity, 615–616, 619, 625, 627
High gods, 258
Hippocampus, 287, 461–462, 499, 560
Hirshleifer, J., 231
History of evolution, 215–216
Hoe cultures, 390–392, 397
Hominids: dispersion of, 362; evolution of brain, 287, 289, 290, 386
Hominins: aggressive responses to perceived threats in, 502; behavioral propensities and preadaptations in, 10–11, 180, 546–547, 549, 552–559; cognitive response mechanisms in, 499, 501; emotional response mechanisms in, 496–497, 498; emotions and language in, 654–656; emotions and social solidarity among, 564; evolution of, 566–567; evolution of brain, 285–290, 292, 297, 407; evolution of responses to outgroup threats, 495–496; expansion of emotions in, 559–564; and limitations to evolutionary psychology, 177–188; mating behavior in, 410–412; social ties in, 26
Homo erectus: coexistence with Australopithecines, 288; emigration out of Africa, 362; evolution of brain, 290, 556; and parental collaboration hypothesis, 407
Homo habilis, 289–290, 293, 556
Homo sapiens, 286–287, 291
Homosexuality, 232, 246, 247
Honor cultures, 19–20
Hopcroft, R., 13–14, 126, 130
Horgan, John, 163–164
Horizontal cultural transmission, 68
Horizontal gene transfer, 70–71
Hormones: androgen, 15, 470; avenues for future research on status and, 470; cortisol, 482, 485; oxytocin, 354, 418–419; studies on, 485; testosterone, 18–19, 470, 484–486; vasopressin, 419
Household, 420
HRAF (Human Area Relations Files) system, 429
Hrdy, S. B., 409
Huber, J., 14–15
Huber, S., 126, 129
Huckleberry Finn (Twain), 589
Hull, David, 71
Human affairs: functions of, as adaptations, 32–35; functions of, as Darwinian adaptations, 35–36; limits of intentional design and rational choice in, 36–38; no-memes objection to Darwinism about, 42–44; operation of Darwinian processes in, 44–49; problems facing Darwinian approach to, 53–54; regularities in, as local equilibria, 38–42; strengths of Darwinian approach to, 54–55
Human aggression theory, 256–257
Human Area Relations Files (HRAF) system, 429
Human behavioral ecology (HBE): applied to division of labor, 310; applied to food sharing, 303–305; applied to foraging behavior, 298–301; applied to group size, 307–309; applied to mobility, 301–302; applied to political organization, 311–312; applied to reproductive ecology, 309–310; applied to social organization, 310–311; applied to technology, 302–303; applied to territoriality, 305–307; basic principles, 296–297; conclusions, 312–313; overview, 295. *See also* Behavioral ecology
Human ecology: application of bioecology in classic, 320–325; and community ecology in early twentieth century, 317–318; development of, 318–320; evolutionary growth

versus expansion in neoclassical, 327–330; midcentury reformulation of, 325–327; overview, 316–317. *See also* Human behavioral ecology (HBE)
Human Ecology: A Theory of Community Structure (Hawley), 327
Human exceptionalism, 137, 142, 171–172
Human intentionality, 36–38, 56n8
Human interests, as axiom of Darwinian conflict theory, 237
Human nature: as culturally constructed notion, 269; in evolutionary psychology, 142; as social, 293–294; sociobiology and inquiries into, 3–4; Spencer and evolution of, 224–225; in Standard Social Science Model, 137
Human Nature—An Interdisciplinary and Biosocial Perspective (academic journal), 119
Human rights, 533–534
Huneman, P., 61
Hunting, big game, 304–305, 408–409, 436, 444, 447
Hunting-gathering societies: capital punishment among, 427, 430–431; cooperative behaviors in, 83, 436–437; and Darwinian cultural evolution as carried by strategies, 45–46; databases on, 429; exercise of power in, 578; hierarchies among, 559; leadership in, 577; norm enforcement in, 578; reputational selection theory and, 426; resource equality in, 253; reverse dominance in, 576; social control in, 426–427, 428; social predators in, 431–436; social selection in, 437–438; statistics on social sanctioning in, 424–425; suppression of dominance in, 583–584; systems of reciprocity and exchange in, 8. *See also* Foraging societies; Human behavioral ecology (HBE)
Hybridization, 70–71
Hypergynous societies, 241
Hypothalamus, 486, 497, 502
Hypothesis of semiperipheral development, 272–275
Hypothesized adaptations, 44

Iceland, study on consanguinity and fertility in, 366–367, 375
Ideal-free distribution, 301, 302(fig.)
Images: brain's reaction to, according to Savanna Principle, 143–144, 149; recognition of mirror, 185
Imposed behavior, 51–52
Inbreeding. *See* Mediogamy; Optimal inbreeding
Incest avoidance: development of, 353; dispersion and, 353–355, 360; exogamy and, 355; and incest taboo, 352
Incest avoidance theory, 244
Incest taboo: exogamy and, 351–353; father-daughter, 355; relativity problems of, 351; sanctioning of, 435
Inclusive fitness: and cultural materialism, 235; in individual and group selection models, 81; intergroup warfare as adaptive strategy enhancing, 493, 496; in theoretical biology, 572–573
Income: link between reproductive success and, 126–128; reproduction and, 123–125. *See also* Wealth
India: consanguinity and fertility in, 375; global warming and, 280; reproductive success of elite women in, 123; suttee practice in, 394
Indirect reciprocity, 426, 436–437, 445–446, 573
Individual phase in transition, 575
Individual selection, and group selection debate, 52, 79, 80–81, 380n3
Individualism: in human behavioral ecology, 296; methodological, in Weberian conflict theory, 232
Individuality: evolutionary transitions in, 77, 81–83, 88, 89n2; human society and evolutionary transitions in, 83–85
Induction, in embryological development, 72n3
Inductive-type pathway of evolutionary innovation, 64–65
Industrial societies: fertility in, 125–126; in gender inequality theory, 251; in kin selection theory, 249; and maladaptive behavior, 144; in marital choice theory, 248; in parental investment theory, 241; in religious choice theory, 258; in reproductive strategies theory, 240; Spencerian evolution and political development of, 221–224; in wealth accumulation theory, 253. *See also* Industrialization
Industrialization: and ecological degradation, 276–277; reverse dominance and, 583; trait desirability and, 146. *See also* Industrial societies
Inequality: crisis of, 279–280; elevated, 625, 626; and New Deal, 623; in Schumpeter's creative destruction, 610, 611–612; status and elevation of, 616–619
Inequality compression, 623, 624, 626
Infant formula, 15, 384, 396
Infanticide: female, 123; among foragers, 390; in parental investment theory, 241; as population growth control, 309
Infants. *See* Children
Infidelity: and jealousy in romantic relationships, 138, 144; in mate choice theory, 245; and sperm competition, 414–416; and violence in human aggression theory, 256
Infrastructural Determinism, Principle of, 235
Infrastructure, in cultural materialism, 234–235
Inheritance: defining, in sociocultural systems, 94–95; theories of, 67. *See also* Heredity
Innovation: in apes, 527; of corporate units, 97; in Schumpeter's creative destruction, 610, 611, 612; technology and, 620–622. *See also* Emergents; Learning; Salience theory
Insects: consanguinity and fertility among, 367; dietary choice theory, 243; explained by evolutionary theory in biology, 98; sociocultural evolution of, 268–269; sterile worker castes in, 78
Instinctive triggers, 497
Institutional differentiation, 108
Institutions: construction of, 342; cooperation and, 453–454; emergence of economic, 36–38; for enforcement of norms, 576, 577–579, 592–596; evolution of, for collective action, 201; functionalism and, 33; human-contrived, 38; and link between socioeconomic status and reproductive success, 129–130; operative and regulative, 219; preventing rule breaking in complex societies, 494; remodeling and redesign of, 35; revolution and, 207–208; Runciman on selection of, 52; as sets of coordinated strategies, 34, 44–45; and transition from cultural to social selection, 202–204
Insular cortex, 418
Intentionality, human, 36–38, 56n8
Interaction principle, 20
Interaction ritual theory (IRT), 233–234
Interaction rituals, 233–234, 564
Interpolity relations, 272
Intersocietal selection, 80
Interstate system, 273, 279
Intrasocietal selection, 80, 237
Intrinsic characters, 86–87
Introgressive evolution, 69–71
IQ (general intelligence), and evolved mental adaptation, 16, 17
Irons, Bill, 119–120
Irruption, 361, 362, 374
Islam, 148–150
Isomorphs, 109
Iteration model of sociocultural evolution of world-systems, 271–272

Jablonka, E., 67
Jackson, Shirley Ann, "The Lottery," 590–591
Jay, Antony, 363
Jealousy, sexual, 138–139, 140, 144–145
Joint family, in kin selection theory, 249

Jones, J. H., 128, 129
Josephs, R., 485
Judicial system, in literature, 594
Julius Caesar (Shakespeare), 584–585
Justice: calculation of, as preadaptation in early hominins, 558; in geopolitical theory, 254; and internalization of norms, 578; language and, 564–565; in literary works, 581, 585, 590, 592, 595; poetic, 591–592

Kafka, Franz, *The Trial*, 594
Kanazawa, S., 16–17, 151
Kanzi (bonobo), 515, 531, 534, 538–539, 542, 544
Kaptijn, R., 126–127
Kertzer, D., 395
Key function, in human ecology, 328–329
Keynes, John Maynard, 40
Kin recognition, among cells, 372–375
Kin selection: cooperation and, 79–80, 443, 573; and ethnic attachment theory, 257; and food sharing, 304; and network reciprocity, 574; social structure and culture explained by propensities for, 98
Kin selection theory, 249, 426
King Lear (Shakespeare), 586
Kinship: atom of, 356; cooperation and, 443; emergence of, among hominins, 554; exogamy and, 355–357; in hoe societies, 391; and macro societies, 567; mathematically precise definition of, 118–119; in micro realm of social world, 101; and network reciprocity, 578–579; and social organization of foraging societies, 310; and social solidarity, 117; transition from cultural to social selection traced in evolution of, 203; views on, in anthropology, 115–116; views on, in cultural anthropology, 116
Kinship-based modes of accumulation, 277–278
Kirch, Patrick, 272
K-mart, 335
Koehler, Wolfgang, 533
Koestler, Arthur, *Darkness at Noon*, 597
Koran, 148, 149
Koryak, 454
Koupil, I., 128, 129
Kramer, Robin, 479
Kupiec, J., 61
Kurzban, R., 453

Labor. *See* Division of labor
Lactation, 14–15, 384, 387–390, 392, 395–398. *See also* Milk
Laissez faire, 226
Lakatos, Imre, 229
Lamalera community, 444
Lamarckian inheritance and evolution, 67–68, 94, 95
Lamb, M. J., 67
Lana (chimpanzee), 527–530, 534–535, 538–541
"Lana Chimpanzee Counts" (Rumbaugh), 541
Lana keyboard simulator, 540
LANA lab, 541
LANA Project, 527–530, 534, 539, 540
Land, as form of wealth, 393
Language acquisition, 164–165, 167, 184
Language instinct, 5–6
Language Research Center (LRC), 529–530, 545
Language(s): capacity for, as preadaptation, 550, 553; Chomsky's arguments for uniqueness of, 538–539; and communication with apes, 530, 531–532; controllable status signals in, 477; as coordination norm, 449; and definition and maintenance of group membership, 362, 363; and emotion in hominins, 654–656; and evolution of human brain, 187, 291–292, 293; evolution of speaking and eating anatomy, 385; great apes' capacity for, as by-product of previous selection, 178, 179; of *Homo erectus*, 290; kin-based accumulation based on, 277; and LANA Project, 527–530; merging of, 71; as mode of communicating dominance and deference, 483–484; problem of, 537; salience theory and, 538–545; as social glue, 385; and sociocultural evolution, 268, 269; as "verbal grooming," 555
Lappegård, T., 127, 128
Lateral cultural transmission, 195
Law of cultural dominance, 269
Law enforcement, 576, 577–579, 592–596. *See also* Extralegal police aggression; Regulative institutions
Lawson, D. W., 129
Leaders: and abuse of power, 471; avenues for future research on, 469–471; evolutionary study of, 460–461; of foraging societies, 311–312; goal alignment of followers and, 469; power-maintenance tactics of, 464–469; role of, in conversation, 483–484; service and control functions of, 476; status-seeking traits of, 462–463; tension between followers and, 463–464. *See also* Authority; Dominance; Leadership; Power; Status
Leadership: in literature, 585–588; as tool for social analysis, 575–576, 577. *See also* Authority; Dominance; Leaders; Power; Status
Leakey, Louis, 288
Learned triggers, 497
Learning: amalgams as basic units of, 517, 520; through biological and cultural means, 68; and emergents in Gabby the gibbon, 521–524; flawed conclusions regarding, 524, 525; of infant great apes, 526; of Kanzi, 531; and novel behavior, 515; and organization of amalgams into templates, 517–518; in primates, 526; through reinforcement, 518; relevance to human social behavior, 5–6; in salience theory, 516, 525
Learning bias, 5–6, 167, 577–578
Learning-how-to-learn phenomenon, 526
Legal systems, 105, 576, 577–579, 592–596
Legitimacy: certification, 338; in exercise of power, 576, 577–579, 596–599; in organizational ecology, 334–336, 338
Leimar, O., 65
Lenski, G., 80
Lévi-Strauss, Claude, 351, 356
Lewis, M. G., 371
Lewontin, Richard, 85, 158–159
Lexigram keyboards, 540, 542–544
Liberalism: reverse dominance as defining feature of, 584; Spencer on, 223
Liebknecht, Wilhelm, 233
Life-history preadaptations, 554–555
Limbic system, 286–287, 497, 499
Limits of biological theory in social sciences: conclusions, 108–110; defining evolution in sociocultural systems, 94–98; evolving dimensions of sociocultural systems, 98–103; identifying units of selection in sociocultural evolution, 103–106; nature of selection in social and biotic universes, 106–108; overview, 92–94
Lindholm, C., 377
Line breeding, 365
Lineage segmentation, 363–364, 375, 376
Literacy, gender inequality and, 384
Literary scholarship, 599–602
Literary works: dominance and reverse dominance in, 582–585; institutions for enforcement of norms in, 592–596; internalization of norms in, 588–590; leadership in, 585–588; legitimacy in exercise of power in, 596–599; social functions of, 579–582; strong reciprocity in, 590–592
Little Dorrit (Dickens), 594
LM/IS graphs, 40
Local equilibria: competing adaptations in, 55–56n4; regularities in human affairs as, 32, 38–42, 44; strategies and, 46–47; unraveled by arms race, 54

640 INDEX

Lonesome Dove (McMurtry), 595
Lopreato, J., 13, 79
Lord of the Flies (Golding), 581–582, 590, 591, 595, 599
Lorimer, F., 388
"The Lottery" (Jackson), 590–591
Lovejoy, C. O., 407
Luckmann, T., 4

Maasai, 447–448, 451–452
Macbeth (Shakespeare), 587, 592
Machalek, R., 18, 24, 25, 80
Macroeconomics, 40
Macro-level processes: in bioecology, 320; competition minimized through, 324; in early twentieth-century community ecology, 317, 318; and midcentury reformulation of human ecology, 326
Macro realm of social world, 84, 100–102
Macro social sciences: defined, 146; evolutionary psychology's relevance to, 147, 153
Macro societies: evolution of, 24; evolution of hominins and, 566–567
Macrosociology, evolutionary, 207–209
Macrostructures, organizational ecology and analysis of, 342–346
Maines, D. R., 322, 327
Major additions, 61–64
Major transitions, 47–49, 60–64; in individuality, 77, 81–85, 89n2; phases in, 575; and recent developments in theoretical biology, 573, 574–575
Maladaptive behavior, 144–145
Male crime: polygyny and, 148; sexual selection theory and, 17–18
Mammary glands, 387
Maner, J. K., 465–466
March of Dimes, 341
Marginal value theorem (MVT), 300–301, 302
Marital choice theory, 247–248
Marital dissolution, 248
Market competition: and creation of resource niches, 97; evolution of societies through, 93
Market society, 282
Markets: and communist societies, 208; creation of, in macrostructures, 342; cultural group selection and, 450–451; dynamic, in organizational ecology, 334–335; and evolutionary game theory, 201; as generators of resource niches, 336; institutionalization of competition through expansion of, 334; and limits on intentional design and rational choice, 36, 37–38; and structure and regulation of selfish activity, 100
Marois, R., 574, 578
Marriage: Arab cousin-marriage exchange, 357–359; in hoe societies, 391; in human aggression theory, 256; marital choice theory, 247–248; versus pair bonding, 403; and relevance of evolutionary psychology to social sciences, 150–153; rules of, 355–356; and social organization of foraging societies, 310–311. *See also* Cousin-marriage exchange; Endogamy; Exogamy; Polygyny
Martin, D. O., 130
Martin, M. W., 18
Martin, W. T., 327
Martyrs, promises for Muslim, 148–149
Marx, Karl, on *The Origin of the Species*, 233
Marxian conflict theory, 232–233
Maryanski, Alexandra: concept of adapted mind, 9, 10, 25–26; on *Homo sapiens*, 291; on organization of primate common ancestor, 549–550; on origin of family, 387; studies on primates, 182–184; use of cladistic analysis, 24
Mass consumption, 611, 622, 623, 625, 626
Mass production, 611, 619, 620, 622
Mate choice theory, 244–245

Mate guarding, 13–14, 145, 245, 406, 410–412, 416–417, 419
Mate preference characteristics, 13–14, 131, 150–151, 162–163
Maternal effect hypothesis, 67
Matrilineal descent, 117, 249
Matrilocal households, 249
Maynard Smith, John, 48, 60–61, 63, 81, 82, 200, 397
Mazur, A., 18, 19–20
McElreath, R., 450
McKenzie, R. D., 321, 322–323
McLennan, John, 114–115, 350
McMurtry, Larry, *Lonesome Dove*, 595
McPherson, J. Miller, 339
Mead, George Herbert, 557, 558
Mead, Margaret, 170–171
Mead, N. L., 465–466
Meaning, in fiction, 581–582
Meat: dietary choice theory, 243; and parental collaboration hypothesis, 408–409; sharing, 304–305, 436, 444, 448
Mediogamy, 366–372, 375, 376–378. *See also* Cousin-marriage exchange
Mehta, P., 485
Melville, Herman, *Billy Budd, Sailor*, 595–596
Memes: in cultural selection, 198; in Darwinian cultural selection, 44–49; defined, 57n13; and defining evolution in sociocultural systems, 95–96; no-memes objection to Darwinism about human affairs, 42–44; "technomemes," 204
Memory: brain parts dealing with, 287; and cognitive response mechanisms, 499; object location, of women, 146, 250
Men: crime and, 17–18, 148; and division of labor in foraging societies, 310; and EHB hypothesis regarding indiscriminate sex, 159–160; in gender differentiation theory, 250–251; in gender inequality theory, 251; in human aggression theory, 256; individual preferences guiding reproductive behavior, 131; investment in mating versus parenting effort, 406; link between socioeconomic status and reproductive success among, 123, 124(table), 126–129; male versus female fertility, 125–126; in mate choice theory, 244–245; mate preferences and selection, 150–151; ovulation's effect on behavior, 162–163; reproduction and spatial distribution of, 404; in reproductive strategies theory, 240; in sexual choice theory, 245–246; sexual jealousy as evolved psychological mechanism, 138–139, 140, 144–145. *See also* Gender inequality; Pair bonding
Mental adaptations: expression of, in contemporary societies, 16–18; further study of, 25; theories regarding, 25–26. *See also* Adapted mind; Adapted social mind; Evolved mental adaptations; Evolved psychological mechanism(s); Psychological adaptations
Mer, costly signaling on island of, 446
Merger: Hull on, 71; of social units, 96
Meso realm of social world, 84, 100–102, 105
Mesoudi, A., 68
Metal weapons, 397
Metaphors, 291
Michod, R. E., 62–63, 72n1, 82, 85, 573
Micro realm of social world, 84, 100–102
Micro social sciences, 146, 153
Microevolution, 65
Microfoundations, 36, 147, 233
Micro-level processes, in early twentieth-century community ecology, 317, 318
Middlemarch (Eliot), 589, 590
Militant societies, 221–224
Milk: ability to digest lactose, 392; benefits of human, 389; composition and volume of human, 387–388; human versus bovid, 391; production of human, 387. *See also* Lactation

INDEX 641

Mind, theory of, 449, 557
Minnesota Study, 196
Minority communities, extralegal police aggression in, 494, 503–508
Minority police officers, 506
Mirror, self-recognition in, 558
Mirror neurons, 185, 292, 557
Mitosis, 373
Mobility: human behavioral ecology applied to, 301–302; technology and, 302
Modern Synthesis, 3, 94, 98
Modernization, theory of, 208–209
Modular mind hypothesis, 7–9
Modularity: and evolution of human brain, 185–188; and limitations to evolutionary psychology, 177–178, 179; variation through, 60
Molecular recognition, 372–375
Money, emergence of, 36, 37
Monkeys: adaptation of, to savanna, 551; adaptation to specialized niches in arboreal habitat, 551; behavioral propensities in, 184; birth in, 386; harem mating patterns among, 554; hierarchies among, 558; history of primate evolution, 181–182, 183, 184; as hypothetical nearest cousin to humans, 566–567; life-history characteristics of, 554–555; reinforcement learning in, 518; on St. Kitts, 368–369; status interactions among, 474; status rank among, 475; status signs in, 476; strong-tie, 548–549; thinking and learning in, 524, 526, 530
Monogamy: in herding societies, 393; in marital choice theory, 247–248; transformation from promiscuity to, 410. *See also* Pair bonding
Moody, M., 21
Moral emotions, 12, 561
Moralistic aggression, 11–12, 26
Morality: and calculations of justice, 558; and evolution of human brain, 187; language and, 564–565; in religious choice theory, 258; religious versus evolutionary arguments regarding, 172; and social control, 425, 437
Morgan, Lewis H., 203
Mortality: female versus male, 386; fertility and, 123; in organizational ecology, 334, 335, 345; of organizations in resource niches, 336–339; and reproductive ecology of foraging societies, 309
Mosaic development, 62
Moseley, Michael, 376
Mother-infant bonding, 182, 241, 550, 553–554
Mukogodo, 451
Müller, G. B., 67
Muller, Max, 537
Multicellularity: among bacteria groups, 373; and evolutionary transitions in individuality, 82; fitness and, 82–83; reproduction and, 48–49; social group formation, 61
Multiharem groups, 410–411
Multi-level selection, 79, 80, 343–346, 380n3
Mutation: adaptive, 69; evolution by punctuation equilibrium versus, 207; fitness and, 178–179; as mode of variation, 59; in Modern Synthesis of evolutionary thinking, 94
Mutualism, 39
Myrskylä, M., 128
Myxobacteria, 373–374

Naipaul, V. S., *A Bend in the River*, 597
Nasty bottom of iteration model, 272
Natural selection: adaptation for social ties through, 26; adapted mind as product of, 5, 7, 8, 12; applied to human societies, 76; as axiom of Darwinian conflict theory, 236; in basic theoretical structure of evolutionary psychology, 141(fig.); in bioecological theory, 317–318, 319, 323, 325; and common descent, 69–70;

of cooperative social relations, 238; of corporate units, 85–88; cultural selection and, 197–198; defined, 236; emotions and social solidarity and, 564; and evolution of brain and behavioral propensities, 180, 184–185, 187; evolution influenced by factors other than, 161; and evolution of kinship systems, 203; evolutionary contingency thesis and, 41; in evolutionary psychology and evolutionary sociology, 158; and foundation of psychology, 2; in human behavioral ecology, 296, 297; language and, 537; locally invariant regularities produced by, 56–57n11; modifies existing biological structures, 178; and no-memes objection to Darwinism about human affairs, 42, 43; and offspring production, 385; and outgroup threats, 495, 496; and regularities as local equilibria, 40–41; replicator/vehicle summary of, 89n5; reputational selection as likely social agency of, 425–426; requirements of, 145; selection pressures on apes in evolutionary sociology, 550–552; and sexual reproduction, 159–160, 353; versus sexual selection, 138, 153n1; sociocultural selection and, 201–202. *See also* Group selection
Naturalistic fallacy, 168
Nelson, R., 52–53
Neoclassical human ecology, 321, 327–330
Neocortex: and behavioral propensities in early hominins, 552; cladistic analysis for evolution of human brain, 186–187; and cognitive response mechanisms to outgroup threats, 499; evolution of primate, 287; evolutionary psychology and evolution of, 177, 179–180; and expansion of emotional palette, 559–561; group size and evolution of, 363; guilt and shame and, 561–562; in *Homo sapiens* and apes, 286; linguistic capacity and increased size of, 556; and move from olfactory to visual dominance, 550; neurons and connections in, 285
Nesse, R., 389
Nets, evolutionary, 69–71
Nettle, D., 126
Network reciprocity, 573, 574, 578–579
Network tie strength: among apes, 182–183, 551; and behavioral propensities in early hominins, 552; among extant primates, 547–549, 566–567; high-contrast familiarity and religion and, 615. *See also* Attachment; Pair bonding; Social bonding
Neuroanatomy: changes in, 179–180; evolution of, in response to outgroup threats, 496–502; and evolution of pair bonding, 417–419; evolutionary sociology and comparative, of apes and humans, 559–566; human social behaviors built on primate, 178; mutations in, 178–179
Neuronets, 10, 177–178, 180, 186, 187, 561
Neurosociology, 24, 188
New Deal, 612, 623, 626
New evolutionary sociology, 547
New Global Left, 282
Niche density: and corporate unit death, 97; and organization failure, 339; in organizational ecology, 334; and population size in Blau-space, 341; and Spencerian selection, 343
Nielsen, F., 79
1984 (Orwell), 587–588, 589
Nissen, Henry, 533
Nongenetic inheritance, 67–68
Nonreciprocity: evolved cognitive algorithm for detecting, 8–9; moralistic aggression and, 11–12; as threat to humans and their ancestors, 26
Norm of reaction, 5–6, 20
Normative legitimacy, 338
Norm(s): emergence of, 83; institutions for enforcement of, 576, 577, 592–596; internalization of, 574, 576, 577–579, 588–590, 599; of reciprocity, 7; strategies constituting, 49; strong reciprocity and, 590–591

Novel behaviors, 515, 519. *See also* Emergents; Innovation
Novel stimuli, salience of, 517
Novels of manners, 584
Novelty: cost-benefit problem and, 620–621; expansion of, 623–624; reward release rule for, 614–615; serial, 609, 614–615, 619, 620–621, 625, 627; and technology accumulation, 619–620
Nowak, Martin, 442, 573
NP-hard problems (nondeterministic polynomial-time hard problems), 37
Nuclear power, 280
NuMath program, 541
Numerical competency, of apes, 541
Nursing offspring. *See* Lactation; Milk

Oberg, Kalervo, 221
Object, seeing self as, 558
Oblique cultural transmission, 68, 195
Observation, learning through, 515, 516–518
Obshchina, 454
Occipital lobe, 179, 550
Ohno, Susumu, 60
Okasha, S., 62, 63, 81, 85
Olfactory dominance, 550, 553. *See also* Smell, sense of
Olson, Mancur, 442
Ontological insecurity, in religious choice theory, 259
Operant conditioning, 514, 516, 517
Operative institutions, 219
Ophidiophobia, 6
Opportunistic homosexuality, 247
Optimal-foraging models, 298–301
Optimal inbreeding, 351, 356–357, 366, 369, 376
Optimal outbreeding, 351, 364
Optimum number principle, 360–361, 364, 366
Orangutans: emergents in, 527; hierarchies among, 558; mating behaviors of, 404, 405(table), 406, 413; network ties in, 182, 183–184, 185, 548(table), 549–550; symbol use in, 553
Organizational ecology: age dependence in, 336–339; basic Darwinian dynamic in, 334(fig.); Blau-space and, 339–342; Darwinian ideas institutionalized in, 93, 102; elaborated Darwinian dynamic in, 337(fig.); emergence of, 333; implications of, for analyzing macrostructures in societies, 342–346; limitations of, 97; organizational founding, legitimacy, and growth in, 334–336; overview, 346; resource niches, niche density, competition, and selection in, 334
Organizational founding, 334–336
Organizations: evolution of, 102; functionalism and, 33; human-contrived, 38; and macro societies, 567; remodeling and redesign of, 35; as sets of coordinated strategies, 34, 44–45
The Origin of the Species (Darwin), 217, 233
Origins of life, as variations, 68–69
Orwell, George, *1984*, 587–588, 589
Osotua relationships, 443, 447–448
Ostracism: as power-maintenance tactic, 465–466; reproductive toll of, 427
Ostrom, Elizabeth, 201
Outgroup threats: evolution of cognitive responses to, 499–502; evolution of defense mechanisms protecting against, 493–494; evolution of emotional responses to, 496–498; evolution of responses to, 495–503, 508; extralegal police aggression elicited by, 494–495
Ovulation: prevented by lactation, 384, 388; sexual attraction and, 162–163
Oxen, 392
Oxytocin, 354, 418–419

Pair bonding: conclusions, 419–420; emergence of, 406; indicators of design, 412–419; neuroanatomical and neurophysiological indicators, 417–419; overview, 402–403; parental collaboration hypothesis, 406–410; plausible evolutionary pathway toward, 404–412; preliminary considerations, 403–404. *See also* Monogamy
Palmer, Craig, 161, 168
Paradigm Darwinian populations, 86–88
Paradigm Durkheimian populations, 87
Parasitism, 7, 25, 39. *See also* Free riding
Parental collaboration hypothesis, 406–410
Parental investment theory, 240–241
Parietal lobe: in *Australopithecus*, 288; in humans versus lower mammals and apes, 291; inferior, and bouba-kiki test, 292; and language of emotions, 187; and move from olfactory to visual dominance, 550, 553; and preadaptation for language, 178, 179, 186
Park, R. E., 317, 319, 320, 321–322, 323–324, 327
Parsons, Talcott, 267
Passions within reason, 11–12
Patch Choice model, 298
Paternity uncertainty: in apes, 183, 547; and gender inequality, 13–14; and matrilineal descent in kin selection theory, 249; sexual jealousy and, 139, 144
Pathak, D. T., 373
Patriarchy, emergence and pervasiveness of, 14–15. *See also* Gender inequality
Patrilineal descent, 117, 249
Patrilocal households, 249
Patron-client model, 311
Penney's department store, 335
Perimeter defense, 305–306, 307(table)
Permanent group expulsion, as ultimate sanction, 431
Phenotypes: and behavioral propensities, 100; in constructive-type pathway of evolutionary innovation, 64–65; as criteria for Darwinian selection, 85; in inductive-type pathway of evolutionary innovation, 64–65; inheritance of environmentally induced phenotypic changes, 67; interaction between environments and, 65, 68; in natural selection, 296; sociocultural, 104, 105–106, 107, 335, 343
Phenotypic assortment, 574, 578–579
Phobias, 6
Phylotypic stage, 66
Piebald, 56–57n11
Pigliucci, M., 67
Pinker, Steven, 158, 172
Pioneering, 361, 362
Pituitary gland, 560
Pizzari, H.D.M., 415
Plagues, and serial reciprocity in early Christianity, 20–23
Plasticity alleles, 18
Play: and incest aversion, 354; as preadaptation in early hominins, 555
Plow societies, 384, 392–394, 398
Poetic justice, 591–592
Police aggression, in literature, 593–594. *See also* Extralegal police aggression
Political aggregation, 220–221, 224
Political evolution, Spencer and, 219–224, 227
Political organization: defined by Spencer, 220; and geopolitical theory, 254
Political/Military Network (PMN), 271, 273, 283n5
Politics, gender inequality and, 383–384, 397–398
Polity size: and hypothesis of semiperipheral development, 272–273; in sociocultural evolution, 269
Polity/polities: hierarchy within, 271–272; kin-based, 277; and reduction of competition among corporate units, 345
Pollet, T. V., 126
Pollution, 276, 280. *See also* Environment, exploitation of
Polt, Richard, 166
Polyandry, 248, 391
Polygamy, 45, 154n2

INDEX 643

Polygyny: correlation between sexual dimorphism and, 413; defined, 153–154n2; determinants of marriage institution, 152(fig.); in hoe societies, 391; in marital choice theory, 247–248; as primate mating strategy, 410; and reproductive motives of suicide bombing, 148, 149, 150, 151
Polygyny threshold model, 310–311
Polytheistic religions, 259
Pool resources, excludability from, 441–442
Popper, K., 239, 259
Population biology, Darwinian, 44
Population density: aggression and, 391; aggression and warfare vary by, 272; in organizational ecology, 346
Population genetics, 71
Population growth: differentiation of institutional domains caused by, 342; and diversity in Blau-space, 341; effects of, 76–77, 84, 88, 277; and evolution of statehood, 205; fertility and, 369–372, 376, 378; of foraging societies, 309–310; industrialization and, 276; in organizational ecology, 346; and Spencerian selection, 107–108; technology and, 621. *See also* Group size
Population size: and food production, 389; and hypothesis of semiperipheral development, 272–273; optimum number principle, 360–361. *See also* Group size
Pornography, 149
Positive assortment, 444–445
Post-agricultural societies: leadership in, 576–577; legitimacy in, 596
Post-encounter return rates, in Diet-Breadth Model, 299–300
Postulates: in Darwinian conflict theory, 230, 239–259; in research programs, 228; of sociobiology, 230–231
Potts, R., 289
Power: abuse of, 471; avenues for future research on, 469–471; as benefit of status, 461–463; defined, 462; and enforcement of norms, 578; evolutionary study of, 460–461; Foucault on exercise of, 601; institutionalization of coercive, 593; legitimacy in exercise of, 576, 577–579, 596–599; literary representations of, 585–588; maintenance tactics, 464–469; struggle for, in geopolitical theory, 253–255; and tension between leaders and followers, 463–464. *See also* Dominance; Hierarchy; Leaders; Leadership; Rank and ranking; Status
Preadaptations: capacity for language as, 550; of early hominins, 553–556; in inductive-type pathway of evolutionary innovations, 64–65; in notion of adapted mind, 5; selection operates on, 178, 185. *See also* Behavioral propensities
Preferential homosexuality, 246
Prefrontal cortex, 184, 186, 286, 496–497, 559, 561
Prefrontal lobe, 286, 289, 290
Preindustrial societies: desirable traits in, 146; socioeconomic status and fitness in, 123
Prepared learning, 5–6
Prestige: avenues for future research on status and, 469–470; as benefit of status, 461–463; in face-to-face interaction, 477; future research on dominance and, 470; and suppression of subordinates, 468. *See also* Status
Prestige bias, 577–578, 589
Pride and Prejudice (Austen), 589
Primary emotions, 553, 561, 562(table), 563(table)
Primates: behavioral and organizational propensities among extant, 547–549; and changes in neuroanatomy, 179–180; cladistic analysis of extant, 549–550; diet of ancient, 389–390; and evolutionary origins of human reproduction, 384–385; evolutionary pathway toward pair bonding in, 404; and existing behavioral propensities and preadaptations in early hominins, 552–559; failure-induced frustration in, 526; hierarchy among, 461–463; history of evolution, 181–184; human social behaviors built on neuroanatomy of, 178, 179; infant care among, 386–387; learning in, 526; mating strategies among, 410; milk of, 388; rank allocation in, 480; social ties among, 10–11; status competition among, 481; status signs in, 476–477. *See also* Apes
"Principle of Divergence," 69–70
Principle of Infrastructural Determinism, 235
The Principles of Sociology (Spencer), 218–223
Prisoner's Dilemma, 17, 201, 444–445
Private goods, excludability from, 442
"Problem of order," 198, 201
Production: effects of population growth on, 76–77; mass, 611, 619, 620, 622; and Schumpeter's creative destruction, 610, 611; and technology accumulation, 619–620; tributary modes of, 277
Promiscuity. *See* Sexual promiscuity
Property crime: as attributable to processes of social organization and interaction, 25; sexual selection theory and, 17–18
Propositions: in Darwinian conflict theory, 230, 239–259; in research programs, 228–229
Prosociality: coalitional psychology and, 452; among followers, 471; internalization of norms and, 588; poetic justice and, 591–592; strong reciprocity and, 590
Prostitution, in sexual choice theory, 246, 247
Proteins, dietary choice theory, 243
Proximity, as power-maintenance tactic, 466–467
Psychological adaptations, 138–139. *See also* Adapted mind; Adapted social mind; Evolved psychological mechanism(s); Mental adaptations
Psychology, natural selection and foundation of, 2
Psychopaths, 588–589, 595
Ptolomies, 367–368
Public choice theory, 17
Public goods, excludability from, 441–442
Public goods game (PGG), 454
Punctuated equilibrium, 207
Punishment: and dual inheritance theory, 199; and evolutionary game theory, 200–201
Punitive strong reciprocity, 590–592

Queller, D. C., 81

Race: in determining coalitions, 453; encoding, 501; and ethnic attachment theory, 257, 258; and extralegal police aggression, 494, 503–508; fear-conditioning effect associated with, 498; in literary criticism, 600–601; and novels of social legitimacy, 596, 597–598
Racial stereotyping, 500–501, 504–505, 508
Rahman, Q., 67
Ramachandran, V. S., 291–292
Rank and ranking: allocation of, 480–481, 482; behavior and, 476; dependent on extrinsic attributes, 475; effect of facial appearance on, 477–479; establishment and maintenance of, among humans and apes, 476; interaction among, 475; in primate hierarchies, 475; service and control functions based on, 476; stress tolerance and, 483. *See also* Dominance; Hierarchy; Leaders; Leadership; Power; Status
Rape, 161, 168, 247
Rational behaviorism, 524–525
Rational choice: and evolutionary game theory, 200; fertility and, 370; limits of, in human affairs, 36–38; principal elements of, 231–232; and Principle of Infrastructural Determinism, 235
Rational expectations model, 40
Reaction, norm of, 5–6, 20
Rearranging, as kind of variation, 59, 60
Rebellions, in geopolitical theory, 255
Reby, D., 130
Recessions, economic, 612, 623, 624, 626
Reciprocal altruism, 426, 427
Reciprocity: capacity for, as preadaptation in early hominins, 558; cooperative behaviors as result of, 79–80; direct,

573; and evolution of human brain, 186; and food sharing, 304; among great apes, 185; indirect, 426, 436–437, 445–446, 573; and limits of biological theory in social sciences, 98–99; and modular mind hypothesis, 7–9; moralistic aggression and, 11–12; network, 573, 574, 578–579; versus risk-pooling, 447; serial, 20–23; strong, 199, 576, 577–579, 590–592
Recognition, among cells, 372–375
Recursion, 538–539, 541
Reductionism: as criticism of evolutionary studies of human behavior, 165–166; Darwinian conflict theory and, 231; and distinguishing between biological and sociocultural evolution, 268; of sociobiology and evolutionary psychology, 109
Referential legitimacy, 338
Regularities: of gene composition, 56n10; as local equilibria, 38–42; locally invariant, produced by natural selection, 56–57n11
Regulative development, 62
Regulative institutions, 219. *See also* Law enforcement
Regulatory legitimacy, 338
Rehage, J. S., 65
Reinforcement: definitions of, 518–519; flawed conclusions regarding, 524, 525; in salience theory, 514–515
Relative dating, 286
Religion: arts and, 580; divide between atheism and, 173; ecclesiastical, 259; and elevation of inequality in creative destruction, 618; evolution of altruistic cooperation and, 199; high-contrast familiarity and, 615–616; human exceptionalism reinforced by, 171–172; in micro realm of social world, 101; secular, 613; world transcendent, 259. *See also* Christianity
Religious choice theory, 258–259
Religious communes, signs of commitment in, 446, 452
Replication and replicators: in biology and human affairs, 42; and evolutionary transitions in individuality, 82; major transitions and, 47–49
Replicator-vehicle approach, 89n5
Reproduction: of corporate unit, 84–85; and costly signaling, 305; and cultural materialism, 235–236; of deviants, 427; dispersion and sexual, 360; income and, 123–125; link between socioeconomic status and, 123, 124(table), 126–130; major transitions and, 47–49; mate choice theory, 244–245; neuroanatomy related to, 417–419; origin of sexual, 353–354; origins of human, 384–387; parental investment theory, 240–241; of strategies, 47; strategies of apes, 405(fig.). *See also* Fertility; Pair bonding
Reproductive ecology, human behavioral ecology applied to, 309–310
Reproductive fitness: behavioral ecologists' theories on evolution and, 196; culture's effect on, 298; foraging efficiency as proxy measure of, 297; and human behavioral ecology, 296, 297; maximized through social natural selection, 202; of mutant beliefs and norms, 204; polygyny and, 310; selection for, 48; social rank and, 462. *See also* Reproductive success
Reproductive strategies theory, 239–240
Reproductive success: cultural materialism and, 235–236; economic subsistence theory and, 241; emergence of pair bonding and, 406; ethnic attachment theory and, 257; and evolution of brain, 237; evolutionary sociology and, 139; geopolitical theory and, 254; human behavioral ecology and, 296, 312; incest avoidance theory and, 244; income and, 128; income and female, 128; and kin selection theory, 249; of leaders, 461–462; and maladaptive behaviors, 144–145; and marital choice theory, 248; and mate choice theory, 244; as motivation for suicide bombing, 148–150; optimal number of children maximizing, 129; and parental investment theory, 240; polygyny and, 411; promiscuity and, 159–160; reciprocity

and, 8; and relevance of evolutionary psychology to modern populations, 131; and religious choice theory, 258; reproductive strategies theory and, 239; resource control and, 234; and sexual choice theory, 245–246; sexual selection and, 138; status and, 123, 126–127, 129, 131, 145, 252, 408–409, 461–462; status and female, 125–126, 129–130; Trivers-Willard effect, 130–131; variation in, among Yanomamö men, 117–118; and wealth accumulation theory, 253. *See also* Reproductive fitness
Reputation, in cooperation, 445–446
Reputational selection, 424, 425–426
Research programs: criteria for evaluating, 230; and empirical tests, 228–229; synthesis in, 229–230
Resource control, status and, 461, 462
Resource defense, 305–306
Resource defensibility model, 306(fig.)
Resource equality, in wealth accumulation theory, 253
Resource exploitation, dispersion and, 360–362
Resource giving, status seeking through, 252
Resource niches: aging and morality of organizations in, 336–339; generated by differentiation, 342; generated by institutional domains, 342; in organizational ecology, 333, 334–336
Respondent conditioning, 516
Retaliation, 11–12. *See also* Vengeance
Reticulate evolution, 69–71
Return rates: in Diet-Breadth Model, 298–301; group size and, 308–309; of hunting versus gathering, 310; and political organization, 311; as relative to tool manufacturing time, 302–303; of sharing large game, 304
Reverse dominance: in literature, 582–585; as tool for social analysis, 575–577. *See also* Egalitarianism
Reverse engineering, 12
Revolution: in evolutionary macrosociology, 207–208; in geopolitical theory, 255; world revolutions, 275, 278–279
Reward packages, and Schumpeter's creative destruction, 610–611, 614, 621, 622, 626
Reward release: and contrast sensitivity, 613–614; and elevation of inequality, 616–619; high-contrast familiarity and religion, 615–616; and New Deal, 623–626
Reward release rules: in creative destruction, 609; for familiarity, 614; for novelty, 614–615; technology and, 619–622
Rhythmic synchronization, 557, 564
Richard II (Shakespeare), 585–586
Richerson, P. J., 198, 317, 318, 320, 450
Ricklefs, R. D., 317
Ridicule, as direct verbal sanction, 431
Risk alleles, 18
Risk avoidance, 447
Risk-pooling, 447–448
Risk reduction, 447
Risk retention, 447
Risk transfer, 447
Robertson, B. A., 65
Roles: evolution of slavery and, 205; institutional, 202–203
Role-taking: capacity for, as preadaptation in early hominins, 557, 559; emotions and social solidarity and, 564
Rome, 584–585
Ronay, R., 577
Rønsen, M., 127, 128
Rosa, E., 480–481
"Routine," as unit of selection, 52–53
Routine activities theory, 25
Rumbaugh, Duane, 538–539, 541. *See also* Salience theory
Runciman, W. G., 51–52; on group selection, 80

Sadness: and combination of primary emotions, 563(table); as primary emotion possessed by mammals, 553; and social bonding, 561; and variants of primary emotions, 562(table)

Sahlins, Marshall, 115, 363
Salience theory: amalgams in, 517–518; animal rights and, 530–534; and concept of salience, 517; and emergents in Gabby the gibbon, 521–524; as explanation of emergents, 515; and LANA Project, 527–530; lessons from San Diego Zoo studies, 526; outline of, 516–517, 538–539; and rational behaviorism, 524–525; resources for, 539–545; role of reinforcement in, 518–519; summary of, 520
Salter, Frank, 261n1
San Diego Zoo studies, 526, 539
Sanctioning. *See* Group sanctioning
Sanderson, S. K., 79
Sanitation, advent of modern, 396
Satisfaction-happiness: and combination of primary emotions, 563(table); as primary emotion possessed by mammals, 553; and variants of primary emotions, 562(table)
Savage-Rumbaugh, Sue, 538, 539, 542, 544
Savanna: emotion and survival in, 560–561; fitness of apes for, 184; forced adaptation to, 551–552; monkeys' adaptedness to, 566; survival of human ancestors on, 182, 184
Savanna-IQ Interaction Hypothesis, 16–17
Savanna Principle, 16, 143–146, 148–149
Schemas, 499–500, 505
Schneider, David, 114
Schumpeter, Joseph. *See* Creative destruction
Schutz, Alfred, 557
Schwander, T., 65
Schweller, Ken, 539, 541, 542, 544
Scrounging, 304–305, 448
Scurvy, 390
Search costs: in Diet-Breadth Model, 298–299; in sexual choice theory, 246–247
Searle, John, 454
Second exodus, 619–622
Second-order logistical loads, 77, 84
The Secret Agent (Conrad), 593
Secularization, 259
"Secularization" thesis, 199
Sedentism, 301, 311
Segmentary lineage, 363–364, 376
Segmentation legitimacy, 338
Selection: biological, 51; Darwinian, 51–52, 85, 86–87, 96, 107; and differentiation in Blau-space, 341; Durkheimian, 87, 88, 107, 108; intersocietal, 80, 237; multi-level, 343–346, 380n3; in organizational ecology, 334, 346; reputational, 424, 425–426; societal, 77, 80; sociocultural, 201–202; Spencerian, 87, 107–108, 342, 344, 346. *See also* Cultural selection; Group selection; Kin selection; Natural selection; Sexual selection; Social selection
Selection bias, 35
Self, seeing, as object, 558
Self-control: and avoidance of shame and guilt, 561; conscience as agency for, 427, 431, 435
Self-esteem, female, 14
Semantic memories, 287
Semiperipheral development, hypothesis of, 272–275
Semiperipherality, 271, 272
Sensitivity alleles, 18
Separating intervention, 467
Septum, 554
Septum palladium, 287
Serial novelty, 609, 614–615, 619, 620–621, 625, 627
Serial reciprocity, in early Christianity, 20–23
Service, Elman, 115, 221
Service clubs, Blau-space and, 339–341
Sewall Wright effect, 360
Sex, as attribute determining status rank, 475
Sex ratio, 53, 55, 57n12
Sexual choice theory, 245–247

Sexual dimorphism, in humans, 413–414
Sexual jealousy: and evolutionary history of female promiscuity, 416–417; as evolved psychological mechanism, 138–139, 140, 144–145
Sexual maturity, speed of evolution based on, 145
Sexual promiscuity: evolutionary psychological approach to studying, 159–160; and harem mating preadaptation, 554; and male mating effort, 410, 411; in primate evolution, 183, 404; in sexual choice theory, 246; and species-typical mating strategies, 404, 405(table); and sperm competition, 412, 414, 415, 416–417
Sexual reproduction: dispersion and, 360; origin of, 353–354
Sexual selection: in basic theoretical structure of evolutionary psychology, 141(fig.); in Darwinian conflict theory, 236; defined, 138, 236; evolution of psychological mechanisms through, 139; reputational selection theory and, 426; requirements of, 145; as separate from natural selection, 153n1; sperm competition as form of, 414
Sexual selection theory, 17–18
Shakespeare, William: dominance and reverse dominance in works of, 584–585; leadership and power in works of, 585–587; poetic justice in works of, 592
Shamans, 258
Shame and shaming, 187, 427, 431, 561–562, 563(table), 589
Shanker, S., 292
Sharing, in foraging societies, 8. *See also* Food sharing
Sherman (chimpanzee), 542
Showing off hypothesis, 408–409
Sih, A., 65
Simons, R. L., 18
Simple societies, 221, 222, 496
Simpson, C., 574, 575
Single cell organisms, combined into single multicellular organism, 48
Sister exchange, 356, 357(fig.), 362
Situational homosexuality, 232, 246
Size-complexity hypothesis, 83, 84, 88
Skin color, evolution of, 385
Skinner, B. F., 514
Slater, Dan, 157–158, 159, 160–161, 162, 168, 170, 171
Slavery, 203, 204–205
Smell, sense of: in apes, 550, 552; in *Homo sapiens*, 291. *See also* Olfactory dominance
Smith, Eric, 295
Snakes, fear of, 6
Social bonding: and emotion in hominins, 561–564; among extant primates, 547–549; and hominin behavioral propensities and preadaptations, 552–559; among humans versus monkeys, 566–567. *See also* Attachment; Network tie strength; Pair bonding
Social change, rate of, 278, 281
Social control: of apes and human ancestors, 425–426; capital punishment in Late-Pleistocene appropriate foraging societies, 430–431; and cooperation in hunter-gatherer societies, 436–437; emotions of, 561–562; food sharing and, 436; group sanctioning as social selection, 437–438; in Late-Pleistocene appropriate hunter-gatherers, 428; origin of group sanctioning, 424–425; reputational selection theory, 426; sanctioning in Late-Pleistocene appropriate foraging societies, 431; social predators and, 431–436; social selection through, 426–427; statistics on social sanctioning, 424–425; and testing social-selection theories, 427–428
Social dilemma, 441–442
Social distancing, group-internal, 431, 433(table)
Social evolution: and classic human ecology's application of bioecology, 321; defined by Spencer, 220; principal elements of, 236; Schumpeter's vision of, 611; Spencer on, 224–226. *See also* Creative destruction
Social exploitation, 25

Social facts, 24, 116
Social glue, 117–118, 385. *See also* Social solidarity
Social group formation, 61
Social legitimacy, 576, 577–579, 596–599
Social parasitism, 7, 25, 39. *See also* Free riding
Social predators, 431–436
Social reality, levels of, 84, 100–103, 105
Social sciences: abandonment of evolutionary thinking in, 567–568; as biological sciences, 31, 32–36; future of, 51–55; rejection of functionalism in, 267; Spencer applies evolution to, 218–227. *See also* Limits of biological theory in social sciences
Social selection: capital punishment as, 430; group sanctioning as, 424–425, 437–438; and recent developments in theoretical biology, 574; reputational selection theory and, 426; Runciman on, 51–52; testing theories of, 427–428; Thomson on, 319; through social control, 426–427; transition of cultural selection to, 201–205
Social solidarity, 117, 552, 553, 557, 561, 564. *See also* Social glue
Social units: agency of, 96; basic types of, 343–344; evolution of, 95; in levels of social reality, 101
Socialism: capitalism and, 275, 626–627; and creative destruction, 613; and economic exchange theory, 243; Spencer on, 227
Sociality: cross-species analysis of, 24; evolution of human, 575–579; and evolution of human brain, 186; formation of, 26; in herding societies, 393; human, as product of natural selection, 196; of humans and apes, 10–11; of monkeys and apes, 181–184; structured around gender, 397
Socialization, human behavior as product of, 137, 163–164
Societal selection: Runciman on, 80; theories of, 77
Society/societies: classification of, 207; construction of, 102, 342; in cultural materialism, 234; defined by Spencer, 220; Spencer applies evolution to, 218–227; Spencer's classification of, 221–224
Sociobiology: adapted mind notion derived from, 5; alternative view on, 98; criticism of, 5, 158–159, 170; and cross-species analysis, 24; as danger to integrity of social sciences, 94; defined, 3; early supporters of, 119–120; emergence of, 2–3; evolutionary sociology as alternative to, 547; in evolutionary study of human behavior, 158; impact of, 3–4; initial reactions to, 18; and interaction between biological and sociocultural factors in social behavior, 20; and limits of biological theory in social sciences, 109; principal elements of, 230–231; and Principle of Infrastructural Determinism, 235; rational choice theory and, 231; relevance in modern populations, 122–131; subdisciplines of, 195–197; theoretical explanation of gender inequality, 13–16; as type of conflict theory, 233
Sociobiology: The New Synthesis (Wilson), 2, 3, 4, 118
Sociocultural evolution of world-systems: versus biological evolution, 268–270; comparative evolutionary world-systems perspective, 270–272; globalization and deglobalization, 275–282; hypothesis of semiperipheral development, 272–275; iteration model of, 271–272; overview, 267–268
Sociocultural factors: interaction between, and biological factors in social behavior, 18–23; social behavior attributed to, 167, 171
Sociocultural selection, 201–202
Socioecological context, as axiom of Darwinian conflict theory, 238
Socioeconomic status: fertility of women in modern societies, 125–129; link between reproductive success and, 126–130; in literary criticism, 600–601; and reproductive success in preindustrial societies, 123, 124(table); Trivers-Willard effect, 130–131
Sociological analysis: application of evolutionary thinking to, 3–4, 13–23; cladistic analysis, 24

Sociology: and classic human ecology's application of bioecology, 320; collective action and, 317; Durkheim and establishment of, 116–117; formal, 24, 25; human ecology's analytic method inspired by, 325; neurosociology, 24, 188; relevance of biology to, 197; Spencer and, 219–220. *See also* Evolutionary sociology
Sociopathy, 435
Soft cultural group selection, 451, 452
Somatic cells, 43, 72n2, 82–83
Soviet Union, 96
Sovkhoz, 454
Spandrels, 178, 185, 291
Specialization, resulting from competition, 76, 93
Speciation, 65, 70, 93, 97, 107, 375
Speed of evolution: based on sexual maturity, 145; biological versus sociocultural, 269; and environment, 146; of human ancestors, 292, 293
Spencer, Herbert: defines evolution, 217–218; early interest and concept of evolution, 215–217; lays foundations of psychology and sociology, 2; and manifestation of evolution in varying fields, 217, 218–219; notion of "survival of the fittest," 92–93; and political evolution, 220–224, 227; and social evolution, 224–226; superorganisms in sociological approach of, 319; views on evolution, 215
Spencerian selection, 87, 107–108, 342, 344, 346
Sperm competition, 372–374, 414–417
Splitting, Hull on, 71
Spontaneous order, 36–38
Squirrel monkey, 526
Standard Social Science Model (SSSM), 5, 6, 8, 9, 15, 136–137, 196
Stark, R., 20–22
States and statehood: emergence of, 277; evolution of, 205–206; in geopolitical theory, 254–255; in human aggression theory, 257; in sociocultural evolution, 269; in Spencer's political evolution, 221; subservience to, 223
Status: avenues for future research on, 469–471; biosocial model of, 471–472; defined, 462; and elevation of inequality in creative destruction, 616–619; and emotional energy, 233–234; evolutionary study of, 460–461; female, attainment, 14; in gender inequality theory, 251; hierarchies in face-to-face groups, 475–485; imitation, 239; improvements in research methods on, 485–490; and male polygynous tendency, 414; in mate choice theory, 245; and mate preferences and selection, 150–151; power and prestige as benefits of, 461–463; and power-maintenance, 463–469; sources of, 126. *See also* Dominance; Hierarchy; Leaders; Leadership; Power; Prestige; Rank and ranking; Socioeconomic status
Status competition theory, 251–252
Status differentiation, 252
Status signs, 476–477, 480–481
Status spiking, 617
Stearns, S. C., 83–84
Stem family, 249
Stereotyping, 499–501, 504–505, 508
Sterile worker insects, 78
Stets, J. E., 12, 22, 23
Still, M., 17–18, 151
Strategies: adoption of, in Darwinian approach to human affairs, 44–49; ambiguity of term, 45; functionalism and, 33–34; making distinctions between, 51; routines as, in evolutionary theory of economic change, 52; Runciman on selection of, 52
Stratification systems, 15, 77, 101(table), 102, 103, 342
Stress: in conversation, 483–484, 487–490; in dominance contests, 481–482; measuring, 486; in status hierarchies, 482–483; triggered through gaze, 486–487
Strong reciprocity: and dual inheritance theory, 199; in literature, 590–592, 599; as tool for social analysis, 576, 577–579

Strong ties: among apes, 182–183; among extant primates, 547–549
Strongman, K., 480
Structure: in cultural materialism, 234; as element of socioecological context, 238; of new organizations in existing niche, 335–336; and organization failure, 338, 339; and Principle of Infrastructural Determinism, 235
Subcortex: evolution of, in response to outgroup threats, 496, 497; evolutionary psychology and, 177, 186–187; and expansion of emotional palette, 559–561; and move from olfactory to visual dominance, 550
Subordinates: banding together of, 471; prestige granted by, 462; suppression of, 464–469; as threats to status, 464. *See also* Followers
Substituting, variation through, 59, 60–61
Subtractability, of common pool resources, 442
Subtracting, variation through, 59, 60
Succession, in neoclassical human ecology, 327–328
Suicide bombing, and relevance of evolutionary psychology to social sciences, 148–150
Superorganisms: and defining evolution in sociocultural systems, 98, 99–100; evolution of, 106, 108, 109; multilevel selection processes of, 343–344; in science fiction, 588; treatment of human communities and systems as, 318–319; as unit of selection, 103
Superstructure: in cultural materialism, 234; and culture acquisition, 238; as element of socioecological context, 238; and Principle of Infrastructural Determinism, 235
Survivor machines: evolution of, 99, 106; and evolution in sociocultural systems, 96, 98; and layering of social reality, 100; in micro realm of social world, 101; social units as, 343; sociocultural embedding as, 105–106; as unit of selection, 103–104
Suspicion, 12
Suttee, 394
Sweets, preference for, as evolved psychological mechanism, 138, 140, 144, 244
Symbiosis, 70–71
Symons, Donald, 262n3
Sympathy: as moral emotion, 12; serial reciprocity in early Christianity and, 22
Synesthesia, 291
Synthesis, in research programs, 229–230
Synthetic Philosophy (Spencer), 218
Systems theory, 295, 327
Szathmáry, E., 48, 60–61, 63, 81, 82

Taboos: food, 243; incest, 244, 351–353, 355, 435
Tabula rasa, 4–12, 24, 26, 137
Tajfel, H., 453
Taste preferences, as evolved psychological mechanism, 138, 140, 144
Tautz, D., 66, 67
Taxonomies of social sciences: as biological, 32–36; division of, 51; in evolutionary sociology, 207
Taylor, Peter, 280
TBV (thumb blood volume), 486–487, 489
Technology: accumulation of, 619–622; and food production, 389; human behavioral ecology applied to, 302–303; and male mate competition, 411. *See also* Tools
Technology-driven acquired interests, 623–624
"Techno-memes," 204
Teco (bonobo), 534
Teleological causation, 317, 319
Television, brain's reaction to, according to Savanna Principle, 143–144, 149
Templates, amalgams and, 517–518
Temporal lobe, 179, 187, 550
Termites, sociocultural evolution of, 268
Territoriality, human behavioral ecology applied to, 305–307
Testis size, sperm competition and, 415–416

Testosterone: in dominance and deference interactions, 484–485; measurement of, 485; social behavior and, 18–19; status-seeking and, 470; studies on, 485–486
Thalamus, function of, 560
Theft, tolerated, 304–305, 448
Theoretical biology: and evolution of human sociality, 575–579; recent developments in, 572–577
Theory of common descent, 60, 66, 69
Theory of mind, 449, 557
"A Theory of Population Deduced from the General Law of Animal Fertility" (Spencer), 217
Thinking, in animals, 524, 531–532
Thomson, J. Arthur, 217, 319
Thorndike, Edward, 518–519
Thornhill, Randy, 161, 168
Thumb blood volume (TBV), 486–487, 489
Tierney, John, 357–358
Time pressure, in generating stereotypic behavioral responses, 501
Tinbergen, Niko, 44, 49–51
Tolerated theft, 304–305, 448
Tooby, John: coalition psychological study of, 453; concept of adapted mind, 8–9, 25–26; and criticism of evolutionary studies of human behavior, 161, 162; on evolution of brain as domain-general organ, 261n2; and Standard Social Science Model, 5; and Wason Selection Task, 445
Tools: of Archaic *Homo sapiens*, 290; of Cro-Magnons, 292, 293; and emergents in Gabby the gibbon, 521–524; and food production, 389; gender inequality and, 383–384; made by Kanzi the bonobo, 531. *See also* Technology
Totalitarianism and totalitarian state, 587–588, 593–594
Toynbee, Arnold, 601
TraA cell surface receptor, 373
Trade globalization, 275–282
Trade networks, 272, 283n5
Trading costs of change, 385
"Tragedy of the commons," 201
Transfer Index, 526
Transition cortices, 287
Transmitted culture, 239
Trebly compound societies, 221
Tree of life, 69–71
The Trial (Kafka), 594
Tributary modes of accumulation and production, 277, 280
Trivers, Robert: on desirability of inbreeding, 353; and emergence of sociobiology, 3; moralistic aggression, 11–12, 26; theory of reputational selection, 427
Trivers-Willard effect, 130–131
Troilus and Cressida (Shakespeare), 585
Trollope, Anthony, 597
Turner, J. H.: concept of adapted mind, 9–11, 25–26; on emotion and serial reciprocity, 22, 23; on group selection, 80; on *Homo sapiens*, 291; on moral emotions, 12; on origin of family, 387; theory of selection in society, 76
Turney-High, H., 391
Turn-taking, in conversation, 483, 489–490
Turtle hunting, 446
Twain, Mark, *Huckleberry Finn*, 589
Twins' Early Development Study, 196
Tylor, E. B., 219

Udry, J. R., 15, 397
Ulmer, J. T., 322, 327
Umbilical cord relationships, 443, 447–448
Unconditional altruism, 198
Unexpected events, speedy and adaptive responses to, 499
Unilineal descent, 310
United States: and crisis of democracy, 280; decline of, 279, 281, 282
Universal pattern, 234

Urban ecology, 93, 333, 334
Urban life, effects of, 394–396. *See also* Extralegal police aggression

Van den Berghe, Pierre, 142
Van Schaik, C. P., 576
Van Valen, L., 65
Van Vugt, M., 577
Variation: abundance of, as criterion for Darwinian selection, 86; basic kinds of, 59–60; behavioral and genetic, 296; as blind, 55n3; and competition in organizational ecology, 336; conclusions on, 71–72; of corporate units, 87; in creative destruction, 620–621; dispersion and, 360; evo-devo, 64–65; expansion of, 623–624; introgressive evolution, 69–71; major additions, 61–64; major transitions, 60–64; modularity, 60; nongenetic inheritance and cultural evolution, 67–68; origin of life, 68–69; rates of, 69; and sexual reproduction, 353–354; in Spencerian selection, 107–108; von Baer's laws, 66–67
Vasopressin, 419
Vengeance, 561. *See also* Retaliation
Ventral tegmental area, 417, 418
Vertical cultural transmission, 68
Victoria, Queen, 364
Victorian novels, dominance and prosociality in, 583
Vigilance, as power-maintenance tactic, 466–467
Vining, D. R., Jr., 122, 123
Violence: in competition for status, 476; human aggression theory, 256–257; intergroup, 493, 496; racial stereotyping and, 505; and reproductive ecology of foraging societies, 309–310. *See also* Aggression
Violent crime: polygyny and, 148; sexual selection theory and, 17–18
Virgins, promised to Muslim martyrs in afterlife, 148–149
Vision: of arboreal primates, 526, 550–551; of chimpanzees, 528; and detection of threatening outgroup members, 498; fruit color and, 390; importance of, 291. *See also* Eye glance; Eye(s); Gaze; Visual dominance; Visual gestures
Visual dominance, 178, 184, 291, 550–551, 553, 556
Visual gestures, 184
Vitamin C, 390
Voltaire, *Candide*, 591
Von Baer, Karl Ernst, 66
Von Baer's laws, 66–67, 216
Vonnegut, Kurt, "Harrison Bergeron," 584
Vrba, S., 50

Walking upright. *See* Bipedalism
Wallerstein, Immanuel, 278, 281
Walmart, 335
Walter, Alex, 359
War and warfare: and aggression among animals, 272; as common following advent of hoe culture, 397; between democracies, 39–40, 56n9, 257; and evolution of altruism, 199; evolution of societies through, 92–93, 96; food supply and, 392; among foragers, 390; gender inequality and, 383–384, 397–398; among herding societies, 391; in human aggression theory, 256–257; influence on contemporary societies, 223–224; intergroup, as adaptive strategy enhancing inclusive fitness, 496; and militant societies, 221; political aggregation as result of, 220; and political organization of foraging societies, 311; and reproductive ecology of foraging societies, 309–310; restricted resources and, 391; role in intersocietal relations, 222; women as participants in, 397
Ward, Robert, 479
Wason Selection Task, 8, 445
Watt, Peter, *Blindsight*, 588
We (Zamyatin), 589

Weak ties: development of, among apes, 551; among extant primates, 547–548
Wealth: land as form of, 393; offspring and, 298; and political organization of foraging societies, 312. *See also* Income
Wealth accumulation theory, 253
Weapons, metal, 397
Web of life, 317, 318, 319, 320
Weberian conflict theory, 232, 233, 234
Wedgwood, Emma, 364
Wernicke's area, 179, 187, 286
West Point cadets, study on facial appearance and rank in, 477–479
Westermarck, Edward, 352–353, 354
Westermarck effect, 354, 359
Wet-nursing, 395
Wheeler, W. M., 319
White, Leslie, 116–117
Whitten, P., 389
Williams, George C., 3, 78–79, 161, 389, 451
Williamson, M., 361
Wilson, David Sloan, 79, 380n3, 573
Wilson, Edward O.: on behavioral scaling, 268; and criticism of evolutionary studies of human behavior, 168–169; on group selection, 380n3; on human nature and intelligence, 16; on ophidiophobia, 6; *Sociobiology: The New Synthesis*, 2, 3, 4, 118
Wimsatt, William C., 66
Winter, S., 52–53
Winterhalder, Bruce, 295, 306–307
With Apes in Mind (Rumbaugh), 539
Women: control over sexual behavior of, 393–394; and division of labor in foraging societies, 310; and EHB hypothesis regarding indiscriminate sex, 159–160; fertility in modern societies, 125–126; in gender differentiation theory, 250–251; in gender inequality theory, 251; in human aggression theory, 256; individual preferences guiding reproductive behavior, 131; investment in mating versus parenting effort, 406; link between socioeconomic status and reproductive success among, 123, 128, 129–130; in mate choice theory, 245; mate preferences and selection, 150–151; ovulation and attractiveness, 162–163; and parental investment theory, 240–241; and physiology of lactation, 387–389; promiscuous sexual strategy among, 415–417; reproduction and spatial distribution of, 404; and reproductive ecology, 309; in reproductive strategies theory, 240; in sexual choice theory, 246; and sociobiology in modern populations, 122; status attainment of, 14. *See also* Gender inequality; Pair bonding
Woodburn, J., 448
World revolutions, 275, 278–279
World-systems. *See* Comparative evolutionary world-systems perspective; Sociocultural evolution of world-systems
World transcendent religions, 259
Worldviews, conflicts with formed, 172–173
Wright, Robert, 172
Wright, Sewall, 116, 117, 360
Wynne-Edwards, V. C., 78, 361, 380n3, 449–450

Yahdi, Z., 362
Yanomamö: double cross-cousin marriage, 376; family size, 117–118, 362, 363; implications of study of, 119; kinship, descent, and social solidarity among, 117
Yanomamö: The Fierce People (Chagnon), 115, 118
Yerkes, Robert M., 533
Yerkes Regional Primate Research Center, 527, 540

Zamyatin, Yevgeny, *We*, 589
Zelditch, M., 475
Zoological perspective in social science, 118
Zootype, 66

About the Contributors

John Alcock is an emeritus regents' professor at Arizona State University. He is the author of *Animal Behavior: An Evolutionary Approach,* now in its tenth edition (2013). He has also authored a number of other books, including *The Triumph of Sociobiology* (2003) and *The Evolution of Insect Mating Systems* (with Randy Thornhill, 1983), which covers his research into the reproductive behavior of insects.

Marion Blute is a professor emeritus in the Department of Sociology at the University of Toronto. Professor Blute's research interest is theory, particularly evolutionary epistemology, generalized Darwinism, and multi-process selection theory. The basic principle is that all knowledge acquiring and utilizing processes are selection processes. These include (gene-based) biological evolution by natural selection, (neural-based) individual learning by reinforcement and punishment, and (social learning or meme-based) sociocultural evolution by sociocultural selection. She is also interested in how these processes interact, including gene-culture coevolution. Her monograph *Darwinian Sociocultural Evolution: Solutions to Dilemmas in Cultural and Social Theory* was published by Cambridge University Press in 2010.

Christopher Boehm is director of the Goodall Research Center and professor of biological sciences and anthropology at the University of Southern California. He has done field work with Navajos, Montenegrin Serbs, and wild chimpanzees, and he is the recipient of a Simon Guggenheim Fellowship, a fellowship at the School for Advanced Research in Santa Fe, and the Stirling Prize in Psychological Anthropology. His research interests include egalitarianism and the origins of morals, and he is developing a hunter-gatherer database dedicated to evolutionary research.

Robert L. Carneiro received degrees in political science and anthropology from the University of Michigan. In 1957, after teaching briefly at the University of Wisconsin, he began working for the American Museum of Natural History, where he was curator of South American Ethnology until his retirement in 2010. He has served as a visiting professor at several universities, including Pennsylvania State University and the University of Victoria. His ethnographic field work has been among the Kuikuru of central Brazil, the Amahuaca of eastern Peru, and the Yanomamö of southern Venezuela. He has written five books, including *Evolutionism in Cultural Anthropology* (2003). Besides South American ethnology he has made a special study of cultural evolution, especially political evolution.

Joseph Carroll is Curators' Professor in the English department at the University of Missouri–St. Louis. In addition to monographs on Matthew Arnold and Wallace Stevens, he is the author of *Evolution and Literary Theory* (1995), *Literary Darwinism: Evolution, Human Nature, and Literature* (2004), and *Reading Human Nature: Literary Darwinism in*

Theory and Practice (2011); he is the lead author of *Graphing Jane Austen: The Evolutionary Basis of Literary Meaning* (2012). He has produced an edition of Darwin's *Origin of Species* (2003) and is a coeditor of *Evolution, Literature, and Film: A Reader* (2010) and *Darwin's Bridge: Uniting the Sciences and the Humanities* (forthcoming).

Charleen R. Case is a graduate student of social psychology at Florida State University and a pre-doctoral researcher at the Kellogg School of Management at Northwestern University. She received her BA in psychology and anthropology from Miami University in 2010 and her MS in social psychology from Florida State University in 2013. Her research explores hormonal and cognitive processes that underlie the attainment and maintenance of social relationships, with an emphasis on social processes within group hierarchies and coalitions.

Napoleon A. Chagnon grew up in Michigan and attended the University of Michigan, where he earned all of his degrees in anthropology (BA 1961, MA 1963, and PhD 1966). He initially taught at the University of Michigan in the Department of Anthropology (1961–1966) but held a joint appointment as a research associate in the Department of Human Genetics (1966–1971). He moved to the Pennsylvania State University in 1972 and from there to Northwestern University in 1980. He spent a sabbatical in 1980 at King's College, Cambridge University, and participated in the third and final year of a sociobiology research project based at King's College. In 1984 he moved to the University of California at Santa Barbara and retired there in 1999. On his election to the National Academy of Sciences in 2012 he was offered an appointment in the Anthropology Department as a distinguished research scientist and was also appointed as an adjunct research scientist in the Institute of Social Research at the University of Michigan, his alma mater. He is putting the voluminous data he collected on the Yanomamö Indians of southern Venezuela over the course of some thirty years and twenty-five field trips into an archive that will be distributed and curated by ICPSR, a subdivision of Michigan's Institute of Social Research.

Christopher Chase-Dunn is a distinguished professor of sociology and director of the Institute for Research on World-Systems at the University of California-Riverside. His recent research focuses on the causes of empire expansion and urban growth (and decline) in the Afroeurasian world-system over the last 5,000 years. His studies of structural globalization and global state formation in the modern world-system have been supported by the National Science Foundation.

Timothy Crippen is a professor of sociology at the University of Mary Washington. He has specialized expertise in the evolution of various aspects of human social behavior and in sociological theory. He is coauthor of *Crisis in Sociology: The Need for Darwin* (2001). His work has been published in *Social Forces*, *Human Nature*, and *Sociological Perspectives*, among other academic journals, and he has contributed chapters to various edited scholarly volumes.

Lee Cronk is a professor in the Department of Anthropology at Rutgers University in New Brunswick, New Jersey. His most recent book, coauthored by Beth L. Leech, is *Meeting at Grand Central: Understanding the Social and Evolutionary Roots of Cooperation* (2013). Together with C. Athena Aktipis, he is codirector of the Human Generosity Project, a multidisciplinary effort to improve our understanding of human cooperation, with a particular focus on generosity.

Matthew B. Dunn is an evolutionary sociologist, who is interested in using evolutionary theory as a tool for understanding the dynamics of social structure. He is also interested in the developing field of evolutionary social psychology. Matthew received his MA in sociology from the University of California at Riverside. His master's thesis used sociobiology and identity theory to explain human cooperation.

Robin Fox is a university professor of social theory at Rutgers, where he founded the Department of Anthropology in 1967. Born in England in 1934, he was educated at the London School of Economics and at Harvard, with post-doctoral work at the Stanford University School of Medicine. He did fieldwork among the Pueblo Indians of New Mexico and Arizona and with the Gaelic-speaking Irish of Tory Island, receiving a D.Sc. from the University of Ulster for this work. He also worked with primate groups in Bermuda and the Caribbean. He taught at the universities of Exeter and London in the UK before joining Rutgers. From 1970 to 1982, he and his colleague Lionel Tiger served as codirectors of research for the H. F. Guggenheim Foundation, where they fostered the science of social behavior now known as sociobiology. They wrote *The Imperial Animal* (1970), which introduced evolutionary and ethological thinking to the social sciences. He has been a visiting professor at Oxford, Cambridge, Paris, California (San Diego), and Los Andes (Colombia) and has written or edited nineteen books, the best known of which is probably *Kinship and Marriage* (1967), which in all its editions and translations has been one of the most widely used anthropology texts in the world. His latest book is *The Tribal Imagination: Civilization and the Savage Mind* (2011). In 2013 he was elected to the National Academy of Sciences, and in 2014 a festschrift for him was edited by Michael Egan: *The Character of Human Institutions: Robin Fox and the Rise of Biosocial Science*.

David D. Franks is a professor emeritus at Virginia Commonwealth University. He is perhaps best known for his work in establishing neurosociology as a legitimate sociological field. His recent publications include *The Nexus between Neuroscience and Social Psychology* (2010), "Critique and Refinements of the Neurosociology of Mirror Neurons" in *Biosociology and Neurosociology* (with Jeff Davis, 2012), *The Handbook of Neurosociology* (with Jonathan Turner, 2013), and "The Neurosociology of Emotion" in *The Handbook of Emotion* (2014).

Michael Hammond is a retired professor of sociology at the University of Toronto. He is currently writing a book on the many contrast effects in human social evolution.

Malcolm D. Holmes is a professor of sociology at the University of Wyoming. Racial/ethnic disparities in criminal justice outcomes have been a long-standing focus of his research. His recent work primarily analyzes the social-psychological dynamics and social-structural contexts associated with the use of excessive force by the police. Currently he is engaged in an aggregate-level analysis of homicides by police involving minority victims in large American cities.

Rosemary L. Hopcroft is a professor in the Department of Sociology at the University of North Carolina at Charlotte. Her research interests are in applications of evolutionary theory to sociological issues. Her forthcoming book is *Evolution and Gender: Why It Matters for Contemporary Life* (Paradigm Publishers).

Fifteen years as a full-time housewife and mother sensitized **Joan Huber** to the social consequences of biomarkers like gender and race that create huge groups of second-class citizens. Retiring as provost at Ohio State in 1994 gave her time to learn enough biology to assess the effect of lactation on women's political status after the invention of agriculture. *On the Origins of Gender Inequality*, a biosocial explanation of the gendering of political dominance during the last 10,000 years, was published in 2007.

Michael D. Irwin is an associate professor and chair of the Department of Sociology at Duquesne University. His research focuses on the role of space and place in shaping social networks and communities and in creating social inequalities. His articles on spatial processes have been published in *American Sociological Review*, *Social Forces*, *Rural Sociology*, and elsewhere.

Satoshi Kanazawa is an evolutionary psychologist and intelligence researcher, Reader in Management at the London School of Economics and Political Science, and associate editor of the American Psychological Association journal *Evolutionary Behavioral Sciences*. He has written over one hundred peer-reviewed scientific articles and book chapters in all of the social sciences (psychology, sociology, political science, economics, and anthropology) as well as in biology, medicine, epidemiology, demography, and criminology. His article "Why Liberals and Atheists Are More Intelligent," published in the March 2010 issue of *Social Psychology Quarterly*, was widely reported in the media throughout the world, with a combined viewership of 400 million people worldwide (estimated by Meltware News). He is the author of *The Intelligence Paradox: Why the Intelligent Choice Isn't Always the Smart One* (2012) and coauthor of *Why Beautiful People Have More Daughters* (with Alan S. Miller, 2007).

Robert L. Kelly has studied the archaeology, ethnology, and ethnoarchaeology of hunter-gatherers since 1973 in the western United States and Madagascar. He has authored over one hundred articles, books, and reviews, including *The Lifeways of Hunter-Gatherers* (2013) and the textbooks *Archaeology* (2012) and *Archaeology: Down to Earth* (with David Hurst Thomas, 2013). He is a past president of the Society for American Archaeology and has been a professor of anthropology at the University of Wyoming since 1997. He currently researches hunter-gatherer demography and climate change in Wyoming.

Shane J. Macfarlan is an assistant professor of cultural anthropology in the Department of Anthropology at the University of Utah. His research interests include the evolutionary ecology of human cooperation, social cohesion, and natural resource management in Latin America and the Caribbean. He has conducted research in rural communities of the Commonwealth of Dominica and Baja California Sur, Mexico, since 2005.

Richard Machalek is a professor of sociology at the University of Wyoming. He has conducted evolutionary analyses on topics such as expropriative crime, megasociality among humans and eusocial insects, emergent properties of nonhuman societies, social parasitism, and religious altruism.

Jon K. Maner is a professor of management and organizations at the Kellogg School of Management, Northwestern University. His research investigates motivated social processes from evolutionary and social psychological perspectives and covers topics in domains including power, leadership, and group processes. Professor Maner is the recipient of the 2007 Sage Young Scholar Award and the 2013 APA Distinguished Scientific Award for Early Career Contribution to Psychology. He currently serves as an associate editor of the *Journal of Personality and Social Psychology*. He received his BA (1995) and MA (1997) from the University of Virginia and his PhD (2003) from Arizona State University.

Michael W. Martin is a professor and chair of sociology at Adams State University. His research areas have included social exchange, status generalization, and, most recently, evolutionary sociology.

Alexandra Maryanski is a professor of sociology at the University of California at Riverside. She has devoted her career to analyzing what primate behavior and social structure can do to inform sociological analysis of human societies. She is the author of a number of books and many dozens of articles using data on primates to understand the nature of humans and the effects of this nature on patterns of human social organization. Her most important books are *The Social Cage: Human Nature and the Evolution of Society* (with J. H. Turner, 1992), *Functionalism* (1979, with J. H. Turner), *Incest: The Origins of the Taboo* (with J. H. Turner, 2005), and *On the Origins of Societies by Natural Selection* (with J. H. Turner, 2008). Her forthcoming book of Émile Durkheim's analysis of religion seeks to bring data from primates to test Durkheim's hypotheses about the origins of societies.

Allan Mazur, an engineer and a sociologist, is a professor of public affairs in the Maxwell School of Syracuse University. He is the author or coauthor of nearly two hundred scholarly articles and eight books, among them *Biosociology of Dominance and Deference* (2005) and *Implausible Beliefs in the Bible, Astrology, and UFOs* (2008). Professor Mazur is a fellow of the American Association for the Advancement of Science.

Alex Rosenberg (PhD 1971, Johns Hopkins) joined the Duke faculty in 2000. He is the R. Taylor Cole Professor of Philosophy (with secondary appointments in the biology and political science departments). Rosenberg has been a visiting professor and fellow at the Center for the Philosophy of Science, University of Minnesota, as well as the University of California, Santa Cruz, and Oxford University and a visiting fellow of the Philosophy Department at the Research School of Social Science, of the Australian National University. He has held fellowships from the National Science Foundation, the American Council of Learned Societies, and the John Simon Guggenheim Foundation. In 1993 Rosenberg received the Lakatos Award in the philosophy of science. In 2006–2007 he held a fellowship at the National Humanities Center. He was also the Phi Beta Kappa-Romanell Lecturer for 2006–2007. Rosenberg has written twelve books on the philosophy of social science (especially economics), the philosphy of biology, the philosphy of science more generally, and problems of causation.

Duane Rumbaugh is regents' professor emeritus of psychology and founding director of the Language Research Center, Georgia State University. His comparative studies of the nature of learning, numerical cognition, and language in relation to brain evolution and development date back to 1958, when he conducted research with the great apes at the San Diego Zoo. He developed the salience theory of learning and behavior and is author or editor of more than a dozen books and of several hundred articles. He led the development of the computerized symbol keyboard used to study the language potential of apes and of young language-challenged persons. That keyboard served as a model to stimulate many other keyboards by others. He also led the Language Research Center's Computerized Test System (LRC-CTS) that fortuitously automated the Wisconsin

General Testing Apparatus. It is used in laboratories in the United States and abroad and has served to significantly upgrade the cognitive abilities of many primates, including rhesus. He is a long-term colleague of David A. Washburn, director of the LRC, and William A. Hillix, professor emeritus of San Diego State University. Along the course of his career he has authored educational films, one of which, "Survey of the Primates," is still in demand after fifty years. His main interests have been in comparative learning, cognition, and language skills.

W. G. Runciman has been a Fellow of Trinity College, Cambridge, since 1971, researching on comparative and historical sociology.

Stephen K. Sanderson is currently a visiting professor at the University of California, Riverside, where he specializes in comparative-historical sociology, sociological theory, and evolution and human behavior. He is the author or editor of fourteen books in twenty editions and has published several dozen articles in professional journals, edited collections, and handbooks. His most recent books are *Rethinking Sociological Theory: Introducing and Explaining a Scientific Theoretical Sociology* (2012), *Human Nature and the Evolution of Society* (2014), and *Modern Societies: A Comparative Perspective* (2015). He is currently finishing a book on the evolutionary origins of the world religions.

Ken Schweller is an emeritus professor of computer science and psychology at Buena Vista University in Storm Lake, Iowa. He is currently head programmer at the Ape Cognition and Conservation Initiative in Des Moines, Iowa, where he develops computer programs and mobile apps to provide the bonobo residents with cognitive stimulation and enrichment opportunities.

Jonathan H. Turner is distinguished professor of sociology, University of California at Riverside, and university professor, University of California. He is primarily a general theorist who has, in recent years, become interested in bringing biological ideas into sociology. He is the author of forty books and several hundred articles, but much of his recent work has focused on using evolutionary theory, primatology, cladistic analysis, neurology, emotions, and sociological theory in an effort to integrate biology and sociology.